REFERENCE                                    BAT

HV
7921          Encyclopedia of law
.E53             enforcement.
2005
V. 1


$295.00

# *Encyclopedia of*
# LAW ENFORCEMENT

# *Encyclopedia of*
# LAW ENFORCEMENT

## Volume 1
### State and Local

# Larry E. Sullivan ★ *Editor-in-Chief*
*John Jay College of Criminal Justice, New York, NY*

## Marie Simonetti Rosen ★ *Editor*
*John Jay College of Criminal Justice, New York, NY*


A SAGE Reference Publication

**SAGE Publications**
Thousand Oaks ▪ London ▪ New Delhi

*For information:*

Sage Publications, Inc.
2455 Teller Road
Thousand Oaks, California 91320
E-mail: order@sagepub.com

Sage Publications Ltd.
1 Oliver's Yard
55 City Road
London EC1Y 1SP
United Kingdom

Sage Publications India Pvt. Ltd.
B-42, Panchsheel Enclave
Post Box 4109
New Delhi 110 017  India

Printed in the United States of America

*Library of Congress Cataloging-in-Publication Data*

Encyclopedia of law enforcement / Larry E. Sullivan, general editor.
    p. cm.
A Sage Reference Publication.
Includes bibliographical references and index.
ISBN 0-7619-2649-6 (cloth)
    1. Law enforcement—Encyclopedias. 2. Criminal justice, Administration of—Encyclopedias.
I. Sullivan, Larry E.
HV7921.E53 2005
363.2′0973′03—dc22

                                        2004021803

This book is printed on acid-free paper.

04  05  06  07  10  9  8  7  6  5  4  3  2  1

| | |
|---|---|
| *Acquisitions Editor:* | Jerry Westby |
| *Associate Editor:* | Benjamin Penner |
| *Editorial Assistant:* | Vonessa Vondera |
| *Production Editor:* | Denise Santoyo |
| *Developmental Editor:* | Yvette Pollastrini |
| *Systems Coordinator:* | Leticia Gutierrez |
| *Copy Editor:* | Liann Lech |
| *Typesetter:* | C&M Digitals (P) Ltd. |
| *Indexer:* | Pamela VanHuss |
| *Cover Designer:* | Michelle Lee Kenny |

# Contents

ENCYCLOPEDIA OF LAW ENFORCEMENT,
VOLUME I: STATE AND LOCAL

# List of Entries

# Reader's Guide

## AGENCIES/ASSOCIATIONS/ORGANIZATIONS

Academy of Criminal Justice
    Sciences
Airborne Law Enforcement
    Association
American Society of Criminology
Burns Detective Agency
Child Welfare
Commission on the Accreditation of
    Law Enforcement Agencies
Crime Stoppers
Federal Law Enforcement Officers
    Association
Fraternal Organizations
Hispanic American Police Command
    Officers Association
International Association of
    Campus Law Enforcement
    Administrators
International Association of
    Chiefs of Police
International Association of Women
    Police
Mothers Against Drunk Driving
National Association of Women Law
    Enforcement Executives
National Black Police Officers
    Association
National Native American Law
    Enforcement Association
National Organization of Black Law
    Enforcement Executives
National Rifle Association
National Sheriffs' Association

Police Executive Research Forum
Police Foundation
U.S. Police Canine Association, Inc.

## CIVILIAN/PRIVATE INVOLVEMENT

*America's Most Wanted*
Bondsman or Bail Agent
Bounty Hunters
Burns Detective Agency
Citizen's Arrest
Citizen Police Academies
Crime Stoppers
Militias
Pinkerton National Detective Agency
Police Explorers
Private Policing
Vigilantes
Volunteers
Wackenhut Corporation
Wells Fargo

## COMMUNICATIONS

Calls for Service
Communications Interoperability
Computer-Aided Dispatch
Dispatch
Interagency Cooperation . . . or Not
Information Technologies
National Law Enforcement
    Telecommunications Systems
Response Time

## CRIME STATISTICS

Clearance Rates
Crime Statistics
Crime Statistics and Analysis
Homicide Trends in the
    United States
National Crime Victimization
    Survey
National Incident-Based Reporting
    System (NIBRS)
Uniform Crime Reports

## CULTURE/MEDIA

*America's Most Wanted*
Law Enforcement Television
    Network
Law Enforcement Memorials
National Law Enforcement
    Memorial Fund
News Media and Police
Perp Walk
Police Fiction
Police Museums
Public Perceptions/Attitudes
    Toward Police
Television (Cop Shows)

## DRUG ENFORCEMENT

Asset Forfeiture, State
Comprehensive Drug Abuse
    Prevention and Control Act

Child Molestation
Child Pornography
Cold Case Investigations
Computer Crime
Crime Scene Investigation
Domestic Violence Enforcement
Drunk Driving Enforcement
Gangs Investigation
Homicide Investigation
Identity Theft and Identity
    Crimes
Missing Persons Investigations
Office of Criminal Investigations
Organized Crime Control
Serial Murder Investigation
Sex Crimes Investigation
Vidocq Society

## INVESTIGATIVE COMMISSIONS

Christopher Commission, The
Crown Heights Report
Knapp Commission, The
McCone Commission, The
Mollen Commission, The
National Advisory Commission
    on Civil Disorders (Kerner
    Commission)
National Commission on Law
    Observance and Enforcement
    (Wickersham Commission)
President's Commission on Law
    Enforcement and the
    Administration of Justice
Rampart Investigation, The

## LAW AND JUSTICE

Crimes, Federal Jurisdiction
Death Penalty, Federally Eligible
    Crimes
Identity Fraud Complaint Center
International Criminal Justice
    Mechanisms
Parole Officers
Peace Officers
Probation Officers
Prosecutors
Repeat Offenders
Restorative Justice
Theories of Policing

## LEGISLATION/LEGAL ISSUES

Antiterrorism and Effective Death
    Penalty Act
Brady Handgun Violence
    Prevention Act
Campus Safety and Security Acts
Children's Online Privacy
    Protection Act
Church Arson Prevention Act
Comprehensive Drug Abuse
    Prevention and Control Act
Consent Decrees
Freedom of Information Act
Fugitive Felon Act
Gun Control
Gun Control Act
Harrison Act
Hate Crime Statutes
Hate Crimes, Law Enforcement
    Response to
Hate Crimes Statistics Act
Immigrants (Policy Toward)
Mann Act
Marijuana Tax Act
Megan's Law: Community
    Notification of Registered
    Sex Offenders
Motor Vehicle Theft Act
Narcotics Control Act
Omnibus Crime Control and
    Safe Streets Act
Posse Comitatus Act
Privacy Act
Prohibition Law Enforcement
Pure Food, Drink, and
    Drug Act
Racketeer Influenced and Corrupt
    Organizations Act
Sex Offender Civil Commitment
USA PATRIOT Act
Violence Against Women Act
Violent Crime Control & Law
    Enforcement Act (1994)
Volstead Act

## MILITARY

Intelligence and Security Command,
    Department of the Army,
    Department of Defense
Militarization of American Police
Military Police, Department of the
    Army, Department of Defense

Military Policing
National Guard
Naval Criminal Investigative
    Service
U.S. Air Force Office of Special
    Investigations
U.S. Air Force Security Police
U.S. Criminal Investigation
    Command, Department of the
    Army, Department of Defense

## MINORITY ISSUES

Affirmative Action in Policing
Cultural Competency/Sensitivity
    Training
Depolicing
Gays in Policing
Hate Crimes
Hate Crimes, Law Enforcement
    Response to
Immigrant Law Enforcement
Immigrants (Policy Toward)
International Association of
    Women Police
National Association of Women Law
    Enforcement Executives
National Native American Law
    Enforcement Association
National Organization of Black Law
    Enforcement Executives
Profiling, Racial
Race Relations
Tribal Policing
Women in Federal Agency Law
    Enforcement
Women in Federal Law Enforcement
Women in Policing, State
    and Local

## PERSONNEL ISSUES

Affirmative Action in Policing
Assaults on the Police
Body Armor
Cultural Competency/Sensitivity
    Training
Drug Testing of Employees
Drug Testing of Police
Early Warning Systems
Education of Police
Evaluation of Officers

# List of Contributors

Acker, James R.
*State University of New York–Albany*

Agatino, Daniel
*Munmouth University*

Almeida, Bryant Daniel
*New York County District
   Attorney's Office*

Alpert, Geoffrey P.
*University of South Carolina*

Amendola, Karen L.
*Police Foundation*

Bailey, Frankie Y.
*State University of New York–Albany*

Bartlett, Dennis Alan
*NABIC*

Belcher, Ellen H.
*John Jay College*

Blumstein, Alfred
*Carnegie Mellon University*

Bracey, Dorothy H.
*John Jay College*

Braga, Anthony A.
*Harvard University*

Brooks, Marvie
*John Jay College*

Brotherton, David
*John Jay College*

Burke, Tod W.
*Radford University*

Byrne, Dara N.
*John Jay College*

Canavan, Francis P.
*Pact Training LLC*

Capeci, Jerry
*The New York Sun*

Carrel, Barbara Goldman
*John Jay College*

Carter, David L.
*Michigan University*

Chermak, Steven
*Indiana University*

Clear, Todd R.
*City University of
   New York*

Clowers, Marcia
*John Jay College*

Cohen, John D.
*PS Comm LLC*

Cole, Simon A.
*University of California–Irvine*

Collica, Kimberly
*Monroe College*

Collins, Judith M.
*Michigan State University*

Curro, Isabelle L.
*John Jay College*

Curtis, Ric
*John Jay College*

De Forest, Peter
*John Jay College*

DeMaio, Enrico
*St. John's University*

Diamond, Drew
*Police Executive Research Forum*

Dine, Kim C.
*Frederick, Maryland Police Dept.*

Donovan, Pamela
*Bloomsberg University*

D'Ovidio, Rob
*Drexel University*

Doyle, James R.
*Guidance Software*

Drylie, James J.
*West Orange, New Jersey, Police
   Department*

Dulin, Adam
*Sam Houston State University*

Dunham, Janice K.
*John Jay College*

Edge, Christine Ivie
*Georgia Southern University*

Egger, Steven A.
*University of Houston–Clear Lake*

Feinberg, Lotte E.
*John Jay College*

Forst, Brian
*American University*

Fridell, Lorie
*Police Executive Research Form*

Frost, Natasha A.
*State University of*
*  New York–Westbury*

Fyfe, James J.
*John Jay College*

Geberth, Vernon J.
*P.H.I. Investigative Consultants, Inc*

Giblin, Matthew J.
*York College of Pennsylvania*

Gibson, Camille
*Prairie View A&M University*

Goldstock, Ronald
*New York University*

Gormley, Paula
*John Jay College*

Grant, Heath B.
*John Jay College*

Green, Nicole R.
*John Jay College*

Greenberg, Martin Alan
*State University of New York–Ulster*

Greene, Dana
*John Jay College*

Gross, Gretchen
*John Jay College*

Jeff Gruenewald
*Indiana University*

Haberfeld, Maria (Maki)
*John Jay College*

Hadfield, Karyn
*John Jay College*

Hecht, Michelle R.
*Indiana University*

Heffernan, William C.
*John Jay College*

Hemmens, Craig
*Boise State University*

Henry, Vincent E.
*Pace University*

Herman, Susan
*National Center for Victims of Crime*

Holden, Richard N.
*Central Missouri State University*

Holland, Kim
*University of Arkansas–Little Rock*

Horan, James J.
*John Jay College*

Horne, Peter
*Mercer County Community College*

Hummer, Don
*University of Massachusetts–Lowell*

Hurban, Holly
*John Jay College*

Ijames, Steve
*Springfield, Missouri, Police*
*  Department*

Jacobson, Michael
*John Jay College*

Jones-Brown, Delores D.
*John Jay College*

Jordan, Casey
*Western Connecticut State University*

Kaminski, Robert J.
*University of South Carolina*

Karmen, Andrew
*John Jay College*

Kelling, George
*Rutgers University*

Kenney, Dennis
*John Jay College*

Kessler, Rachel A.
*John Jay College*

King, Joseph F.
*John Jay College*

Kiriakova, Maria
*John Jay College*

Kleinig, John
*John Jay College*

Klinger, David A.
*University of Missouri–St. Louis*

Klockars, Carl B. (deceased)
*University of Delaware*

Kobilinsky, Lawrence
*John Jay College*

Kraska, Peter B.
*Eastern Kentucky University*

Lab, Steven P.
*Bowling Green State University*

Latzer, Barry
*John Jay College*

LeBeau, James L.
*Southern Illinois*
*  University–Carbondale*

Levine, James P.
*John Jay College*

Linn, Edith
*Kean State University*

Louden, Robert
*John Jay College*

Lovely, Richard W.
*John Jay College*

Lyman, Michael D.
*Columbia College of Missouri*

Mac Donald, Heather
*Manhattan Institute*

Magers, Jeffrey S.
*Stephen Austin State University*

Maghan, Jess
*Forum for Comparative
    Correction*

Manatu, Norma
*John Jay College*

Mandery, Evan J.
*John Jay College*

Manning, Peter K.
*Northeastern University*

Mastrofski, Stephen D.
*George Mason University*

Maxwell, Christopher D.
*Michigan State University*

Mayo, Lou
*Police Association for College
    Education*

McAndrew, John Brendan
*John Jay College*

McCarthy, William F.
*State University of New
    York–Corning*

McDonald, Phyllis P.
*Johns Hopkins University*

McKee, Adam J.
*University of Arkansas at
    Monticello*

McNickle, R. G. "Nick"
*New York Sports Clubs*

Moore, Mark H.
*Harvard University*

Morrow, Tyrone Russell
*Fairfax County Police Department*

Murphy, Rick
*Project SafeCom*

Natarajan, Mangai
*John Jay College*

Newbold, Katherine
*XG Consultants Group Inc.*

O'Rourke, Hugh E.
*Westchester Community College*

Ortiz, Christopher W.
*Vera Institute of Justice*

Pascarella, Joe
*Queens College, City University
    of New York*

Pate, Anthony
*COSMOS Corp.*

Penrod, Stephen
*John Jay College*

Phillips, Nickie
*John Jay College*

Pilant Grossman, Lois
*Wings Publishing Company*

Pisani, Angelo
*St. John's University*

Rodriguez, Dennis
*Tampa Police Department*

Rojek, Jeff
*St. Louis University*

Rowland, John
*St. John's University*

Saunders, Jessica
*John Jay College*

Sawers, Deborah L.
*John Jay College*

Schafer, Joseph A.
*Southern Illinois University–Carbondale*

Schulz, Dorothy Moses
*John Jay College*

Scott, Michael S.
*University of Wisconsin*

Scrivner, Ellen
*Chicago Police Department*

Segal, Lydia
*John Jay College*

Sexton, Ellen
*John Jay College*

Shkutzko-Penola, Diane T.
*John Jay College*

Silverman, Eli B.
*John Jay College*

Skogan, Wesley G.
*Northwestern University*

Smith, Margaret Leland
*John Jay College*

Sonner, Andrew
*Court of Special Appeals of
    Maryland*

St. George, Joyce
*Pact Training LLC*

Stahl, William J.
*John Jay College*

Stein, Abby
*John Jay College*

Sullivan, Elena E.
*Emory University*

Sullivan, John P.
*Los Angeles Sheriff's Department*

Sullivan, Larry E.
*John Jay College*

Sullivan, Mara
*St. John's University*

Taylor, David B.
*Niagara University*

Taylor, Ralph B.
*Temple University*

Ternes, Anne
*Office of the New York State
    Inspector General*

Terry, Karen J.
*John Jay College*

Van Raalte, Ronald C.
*Law Enforcement Memorial
    Association Inc.*

Volpe, Maria R.
*John Jay College*

Walker, Anders
*John Jay College*

Walker, Jeffrey T.
*University of
    Arkansas–Little Rock*

Wallenstein, Martin
*John Jay College*

Walsh, Jeff
*John Jay College*

Ward, Richard H.
*Sam Houston State University*

Weisheit, Ralph A.
*Illinois State University*

Wells, William M.
*Southern Illinois
    University–Carbondale*

Williams, Lisa A.
*John Jay College*

Wylie-Marques, Kathryn
*John Jay College*

# Introduction

Security is now and has always been the primary function of government. All societies require some form of law enforcement capability to function effectively. Throughout history, governments of all types have relied on either public police agencies or informal means to effect conformity to social norms, standards, and laws. Given how essential law enforcement is to society, it is surprising how little we really know about how it actually functions. The job of law enforcement is always complex and sometimes dangerous. Police function under much public scrutiny, yet the complexities of what police do and why they do it rarely come to our attention. Readers of this encyclopedia will be introduced to the vagaries and nuances of the field, because it is critical to have a more informed citizenry so that when issues concerning public safety come to our attention, as they do on an almost daily basis, we can judge the situation fairly and wisely.

We cannot strictly equate policing with law enforcement in general, but what we do know on the subject is primarily based on policing in large urban settings. So far, few reference works have been published on law enforcement in the federal, state, local, rural, or private sectors. Our knowledge of international and comparative law enforcement is almost nonexistent, and policing in Western democracies can be qualitatively different from policing in emerging countries or other areas using different legal systems. In many countries, law enforcement—indeed, government itself—is almost entirely lacking. In worst-case scenarios, police are used primarily as a force of terror to keep dictators in power. Regimes fall and rise daily, and people find themselves in lawless and violent states. In the early 21st century alone, we can think of such states as Afghanistan, Iraq, Somalia, and Haiti, to name only a few, that find themselves without effective policing powers.

Although there is a plethora of studies on crime and punishment, law enforcement as a field of serious research in academic and scholarly circles is only in its second generation. When we study the courts and sentencing, prisons and jails, and other areas of the criminal justice system, we frequently overlook the fact that the first point of entry into the system is through police and law enforcement agencies. My work in the field of crime and punishment has driven this fact home with a sense of urgency. Approximately 800,000 men and women work in law enforcement in the United States alone, and they are held to higher standards than the rest of us, are often criticized, and function under intense public scrutiny. Ironically, they are the most visible of public servants, and yet, individually, they often work in near obscurity. But their daily actions allow us to live our lives, work, play, and come and go. They are "the thin blue line"—the buffer between us and the forces of disorder.

Our understanding of the important issues in law enforcement has little general literature on which to draw. Currently available reference works on policing are narrowly focused and sorely out of date. Not only are there few general works on U.S. law enforcement in all its many facets, but the student and general reader will find very little on current international policing. Policing has changed dramatically over the past century, but our general understanding of it comes primarily from the news media and police television shows and movies. The public seems to gain much of its knowledge of policing from popular television shows such as *Law and Order* and the *CSI: Crime Scene Investigation* series. What we see on television is simplistic and conflates within its 42-minute hour a year's worth of police work. Those of us in the academic field of criminal justice research see an urgent need for providing students and the general interested public balanced information on what law enforcement does, with all of its ramifications. Because democracy can remain strong only with an informed public, our goal is to provide the necessary information for an understanding of these institutions dedicated to our safety and security. To this end, we have gathered a distinguished roster of authors, representing many years of knowledge and practice in the field, who draw on the latest research and methods to delineate, describe, and analyze all areas of law enforcement.

The criminal justice field is burgeoning and is one of the fastest growing disciplines in colleges and universities throughout the United States. The *Encyclopedia of Law Enforcement* provides a comprehensive, critical, and descriptive examination of all facets of law enforcement on the state and local, federal and national, and international stages. This work is a unique reference source that provides readers with informed discussions on the practice and theory of policing in a historical and contemporary framework. Each volume treats subjects that are particular to the area of state and local, federal and national, and international policing. Many of the themes and issues of policing cut across disciplinary borders, however, and a number of entries provide comparative information that places the subject in context. The *Encyclopedia of Law Enforcement* is the first attempt to present a comprehensive view of policing and law enforcement worldwide.

It is fitting and appropriate that we present this information in an encyclopedia, traditionally and historically the gateway to the world of knowledge, a gateway that leads to further studies for those who want to pursue this fascinating and important field. The encyclopedia is the most comprehensive, durable, and utilitarian way in which to present a large body of synthesized information to the general public. Encyclopedias trace their beginnings back to *Naturalis Historia* of Pliny the Elder (23–79 A.D.), in which he collected much of the knowledge of his time in numerous volumes. They became standard and necessary reference tools during the Enlightenment with Denis Diderot's *Encyclopédie* in 1772 and the first edition of the monumental *Encyclopedia Britannica* in 1771. These seminal compendia attempted to present an entire body of knowledge to its readers. The modern encyclopedias broke new ground in the transmission of ideas, and over the centuries, they have been updated and improved. Some editions have become classics in themselves, such as the 11th edition of the *Encyclopedia Britannica*.

Specialty encyclopedias are more a phenomenon of the modern age. The field of criminal justice has matured in the past generation, and its monographs and journals present a large body of specialized research from which to draw. The subspecialty of law enforcement, however, has not received the focused treatment of a comprehensive reference work until now. The study of policing and law enforcement has come a long way since the first attempts at police professionalism at the turn of the 20th century. At that time, we also saw the initial professional publications in policing by way of such partisan, anecdotal police histories as Augustine E. Costello's *Our Police Protectors* (1885) on New York and John J. Flinn's *History of the Chicago Police* in 1887. In no way can we call these works scholarly, although they did give us a glimpse into the activities of the local police departments. It was only with the age of general crime commissions, beginning in the 1930s and culminating in the President's Commission on Law Enforcement and the Administration of Justice in 1967, that we saw the development of a large body of data on police activities. And it was also in the 1960s that the first College of

Police Science was founded at the City University of New York (1964), which became the John Jay College of Criminal Justice in 1966, the foremost college of its kind in the world. Within the decade, journals devoted to the scholarly study of the police were founded, and thus, this academic subspecialty of criminal justice was on the road to professional respectability. In the past 40 years, the field of law enforcement has grown and evolved rapidly.

Law enforcement (or lack thereof) is a complex social and political process that affects everyone. Explanations of its role in society are basic to our understanding of the proper maintenance of social order. Older reference works on policing were limited given the few available sources on which they drew. But a large enough body of scholarly work now exists that a reference work such as this encyclopedia can provide coverage of most U.S. law enforcement concepts, strategies, practices, agencies, and types, as well as the comparative study of world law enforcement systems. Police and law enforcement officers do a variety of things in a day and need to draw on a body of knowledge that includes law, sociology, criminology, social work, and other disciplines. This encyclopedia attempts to answer all the questions on what an officer or an agency, here and abroad, does, but also attempts to explain the reasons for an officer's proper and improper actions. In numerous articles, we also show the development of policing, its functions, the impact of technology and modern culture on law enforcement, and the impact that court decisions have on every facet of the field. Law enforcement worldwide was profoundly affected by the terrorist attacks on New York and Washington on September 11, 2001, and many of the field's methods, concepts, principles, and strategies have changed because of the ubiquity of terrorism. Most of the relevant articles in this encyclopedia reflect these changes. As a reference work, it will be essential reading for anyone interested in the field of law enforcement.

The *Encyclopedia of Law Enforcement* offers the professional, the student, and the lay user information unavailable in any other single resource. Its aim is to bring interdisciplinary treatment to the myriad topics that touch on all facets of law enforcement.

To this end, the editors have assembled more than 300 specialists in the field—academics and practitioners alike—to provide the most current treatment on more than 550 topics. These entries range from simple descriptive essays on federal law enforcement agencies to the most sophisticated analysis of contemporary theories of policing. The broadening of the field of law enforcement affected the process of selection of topics. Some selections were driven by theoretical interests, whereas others were practical and more specific. Our goal is to survey the entire field of law enforcement and to be as comprehensive as possible. For ease of use, we have divided the volumes into three areas of law enforcement: state and local, federal and national, and international. Each volume contains a master index. The longest entries cover key issues in law enforcement, large federal agencies, and major countries of the world. Many of the short entries are descriptive, especially when covering a small federal agency police force, or for a smaller country that provides little information on its law enforcement bureaucracy or that has an insignificant law enforcement presence. Some countries, especially those in social and political flux, have been omitted owing to the dearth of information and/or the almost total lack of a police force. Other entries are analytical and cover the most up-to-date theories and philosophies of law enforcement. The main focus of each entry is on currency, although some historical background is usually covered by the author. A glance at the tables of contents gives a good idea of the many perspectives from which a reader can view a given topic. For instance, a brief look at the essay on police accountability leads the reader to investigate the whole panoply of law enforcement, including police impact on constitutional rights, use of force, civilian oversight, theories of policing, and other areas. Given the interrelatedness of these topics, most authors, when possible, treat their subjects using cross-disciplinary or comparative methods. Some authors give a practical viewpoint of law enforcement, whereas others use empirical research and discuss theories and concepts. In general, the encyclopedia combines the disciplines of criminology, sociology, history, law, and political science to elucidate the most contemporary and up-to-date view of law enforcement as it is practiced and studied in the world today. An encyclopedia of this kind would be incomplete without such comparative and/or cross-disciplinary coverage. As it now stands, it is the most invaluable tool for all who work in or are interested in the field because it brings together in one work the most recent research and practice of law enforcement.

Some of the subjects are controversial, but we have requested that authors cover alternative views evenhandedly and fairly. We did not include any biographical entries, which can be found in the myriad biographical sources available today. But in order to present the most comprehensive coverage possible, important personages are included in the subject entries. All relevant legal cases affecting law enforcement are cited in the text and in the bibliographies. The discussion of legal cases is especially useful for the generalist not trained in the law, and we have attempted to explain these court cases and laws succinctly and concisely. Bibliographies to guide the reader to documentation on the subject and further research are included after each entry. The bibliographies include relevant books, journal articles, scholarly monographs, dissertations, legal cases, newspapers, and Web sites. (A comprehensive reading list is presented at the end of each volume as well). The Reader's Guide classifies the articles into 24 general subject headings for ease of use. For instance, under Terrorism, we have grouped such subjects from Chemical and Biological Terrorism on both the local and national levels to an essay on foreign terrorist groups. Policing Strategies will guide the reader from the Broken Windows strategy to Zero Tolerance. Entries are organized alphabetically and are extensively cross referenced. The international volume, in addition to presenting all available information on policing in most of the countries of the world, also includes analytical essays on such subjects as Community Policing, Police and Terrorism, History of Policing, and Women in Policing.

It has been a great pleasure working with Sage Publications on this project. I would especially like to thank Rolf Janke, Publisher of Sage Reference; Jerry Westby, Executive Editor; and Benjamin Penner, Associate Editor, for all of their wise counsel in bringing this publication to fruition. I owe a deep debt of gratitude to the administrators, faculty, students, and staff of the John Jay College of Criminal Justice, whose support made this work possible. I could not have worked with three better editors: Marie Simonetti Rosen was responsible for Volume 1, Dorothy Moses Schulz for Volume 2, and M. R. Haberfeld for Volume 3. I also want to thank the members of our editorial board for their valuable assistance during all stages of the project. I owe special thanks to our project manager, Nickie Phillips, for her excellent handling of the numerous technical details that a project of this magnitude entails. None of this could have been done without the assistance of the outstanding librarians of the Lloyd Sealy Library of the John Jay College of Criminal Justice. To them, I owe a deep and lasting debt of gratitude.

*Larry E. Sullivan, Editor-in-Chief*

# About the Editors

**Larry E. Sullivan** is Chief Librarian and Associate Dean at the John Jay College of Criminal Justice and Professor of Criminal Justice in the doctoral program at the Graduate School and University Center of the City University of New York. He holds an M.A. and Ph.D. in history from The Johns Hopkins University, an M.S.L.S from the Catholic University in Washington, D.C., and a B.A. from De Paul University in Chicago. He was also a Fulbright Scholar at the University of Poitiers in France where he studied medieval history and literature. Prior to his appointment at John Jay in 1995, he was the Chief of the Rare Book and Special Collections Division at the Library of Congress where he had responsibility for the nation's rare book collection. Previous appointments include Professor and Chief Librarian at Lehman College of the City University of New York, Librarian of the New-York Historical Society, and Head Librarian of the Maryland Historical Society. He first became involved in the criminal justice system when he worked at the Maryland Penitentiary in Baltimore in the late 1970s. That experience prompted him to begin collecting literature written by felons and to write the book *The Prison Reform Movement: Forlorn Hope* (1990 and 2002). A specially bound copy of this book representing the Eighth Amendment was featured at the exhibition of artist Richard Minsky's "The Bill of Rights" series at a number of art galleries in 2002 and 2003. Sullivan's private collection of convict literature has been on public exhibition at the Grolier Club in New York and at the John Jay College of Criminal Justice. He based his book, *Bandits and Bibles: Convict Literature in Nineteenth Century America* (2003), on these prison writings. He is the author, co-author, or editor of over fifty books and articles in the fields of American and European history, penology, criminal justice, art history, and other subjects, including the above books and *Pioneers, Passionate Ladies, and Private Eyes: Dime Novels, Series, Books and Paperbacks* (1996; with Lydia C. Schurman) and the *New-York Historical Society: A Bicentennial History* (2004). Besides many publications in journals, he has written entries in numerous reference publications over the years, including the *Worldmark Encyclopedia of the States, Collier's Encyclopedia, Encyclopedia of New York State, Encyclopedia of the Prison, International Dictionary of Library Histories, Dictionary of Library Biography, Encyclopedia of Library History, Dictionary of Literary Biography,* and the *Dictionary of the Middle Ages.* He serves or has served on a number of editorial boards, including the *Encyclopedia of Crime and Punishment,* the *Handbook of Transnational Crime and Justice,* and the journal *Book History.* Sullivan has delivered papers at meetings of the American Historical Association, the Modern Language Association, the American Society of Criminology, the Academy of Criminal Justice Sciences, the Society for the History of Authorship, Reading and Publishing, and the American Library Association, among others. He has consulted on the development of criminal justice libraries and on rare book and manuscript xxiv

collections. At John Jay College, in addition to directing the largest and best criminal justice library in the world, he teaches graduate- and doctoral-level courses in Advanced Criminology, Punishment and Responsibility, and the Philosophical and Theoretical Bases of Contemporary Corrections. Work in progress includes the book *Crime, Criminals, and Criminal Law in the Middle Ages.*

**Maria (Maki) R. Haberfeld** is Associate Professor of Police Science, and Chair of the Department of Law, Police Science, and Criminal Justice Administration at the John Jay College of Criminal Justice in New York City. She was born in Poland and immigrated to Israel as a teenager. She holds two bachelor's degrees, two master's degrees, and a Ph.D. in criminal justice. During her army service in the Israel Defense Force, in which she earned the rank of sergeant, she was assigned to a special counter-terrorist unit that was created to prevent terrorist attacks in Israel. Prior to coming to John Jay, she served in the Israel National Police, in which she earned the rank of lieutenant. She has also worked for the U.S. Drug Enforcement Administration, in the New York Field Office, as a special consultant.

Haberfeld has taught at Yeshiva University and New Jersey City University. Her research interests and publications are in the areas of private and public law enforcement, specifically training, police integrity, and comparative policing (her research involves police departments in the United States, Eastern and Western Europe, and Israel). She has also done some research in the area of white-collar crime, specifically organizational and individual corruption during the Communist era in Eastern Europe. For 3 years (from 1997 to 2000), she was a member of a research team, sponsored by the National Institute of Justice, studying police integrity in three major police departments in the United States. Between 1999 and 2002, she was also a principal investigator on a research project in Poland, sponsored by the National Institute of Justice, where she studied the Polish National Police and its transformation to community-oriented policing. She has received additional grants from the PSC-CUNY Research Foundation to continue her research in

Poland, with particular focus on the balancing act between the public perceptions of the new police reform and rampant accusations of police corruption and lack of integrity.

Haberfeld has recently published a book on police training, *Critical Issues in Police Training* (2002); presented numerous papers on training-related issues during professional gatherings and conferences; and written a number of articles on police training, specifically on police leadership, integrity, and stress. In addition, she has been involved in active training of police officers on issues related to multiculturalism, sensitivity, and leadership, as well as provided technical assistance to a number of police departments in rewriting procedural manuals. She is a member of a number of professional police associations, such as the International Association of Chiefs of Police, International Police Association, and American Society of Law Enforcement Trainers. From 2001 to 2003, she was involved in developing, coordinating, and teaching a special training program for the NYPD. She has developed a graduate course titled "Counter-Terrorism Policies for Law Enforcement," which she teaches at John Jay to the ranking officers of the NYPD. Her most recent involvement in Eastern Europe includes redesigning the basic academy curriculum of the Czech National Police, with the emphasis on integrity-related training.

**Marie Simonetti Rosen** is the publisher of *Law Enforcement News,* a publication of John Jay College of Criminal Justice, the City University of New York. As publisher of one of the nation's leading publications in policing, she has chronicled the trends and developments that have shaped and transformed law enforcement in America during the last three decades. A well-known expert in policing, she is often cited in the mainstream press.

In the publication's 30-year history, it has reported on the evolution of such developments as problem-oriented policing, community policing, and the influence of "Broken Windows" and Compstat in the nation's law enforcement agencies. Under Rosen's leadership, *Law Enforcement News* has followed the increased use of science and technology in the criminal justice system and has reported extensively on crime rates, use of force, pursuits, police integrity and oversight, standards and training, and minority relations. It regularly covers both state and federal court decisions and legislation that affect criminal justice policy and practice.

*Law Enforcement News* has influenced a generation of police leadership. The newspaper's articles are frequently reprinted in college and professional texts. The publication's reporting has been a factor in the development of legislation and public policy in such areas as health and safety issues, bias-related crime, higher education for police, psychological screening of police recruits, and the police response to the mentally ill. The paper has earned major national awards for its coverage of policing on tribal reservations and the impact of the September 11, 2001, terrorist attacks on law enforcement practitioners.

Her annual analysis of policing that appears in the publication's Year-in-Review issue is widely cited and appears in the Appendix to Volumes 1 and 2. Rosen received her B.A. from the City University of New York.

**Dorothy Moses Schulz** is Professor at John Jay College of Criminal Justice at the City University of New York, where she teaches courses in criminal justice, police history, police administration, and women in policing. Schulz joined the faculty of John Jay College in 1993 after a career in policing. She was the first woman captain with the Metro-North Commuter Railroad Police Department and its predecessor, the Conrail Police Department. She was one of the first women to hold a supervisory rank in any rail or transit police agency, and among her assignments was serving as the commanding officer of New York City's Grand Central Terminal, the midtown Manhattan landmark through which about three quarters of a million people pass daily. Previously she had been director of police operations for the New York City Human Resources Administration. Before beginning her career in policing, she was a reporter and copy editor for a number of municipal newspapers and a freelance editor for a variety of magazines and book publishers. Immediately before joining the John Jay College faculty, she was the director of security at the Fashion Institute of Technology at the State University of New York in New York City.

A well-known expert on historical and current issues involving women in policing, she is the author of *From Social Worker to Crimefighter: Women in United States Policing* (1995), which traces the more than 100-year history of women in policing. The book describes how the fluctuating fortunes of feminism helped early policewomen but how in the 1960s women were forced to reject their historical roles when they sought a wider presence in law enforcement. Her new book, *Breaking the Brass Ceiling: Women Police Chiefs and Their Paths to the Top* (2004), highlights the women—police chiefs and sheriffs—who have made it to the very top rank of law enforcement. Based on historical research, questionnaire data, and interviews, the book describes the careers of pioneering and present women police chiefs and sheriffs, who make up about 1% of law enforcement chief executive officers.

A frequent speaker at police and academic meetings, Schulz received a B.A. in journalism from New York University, an M.A. in criminal justice from John Jay College, and a Ph.D. in American studies from New York University. She has addressed conferences of the International Association of Women Police (IAWP), the Women in Federal Law Enforcement (WIFLE), the National Center for Women & Policing (NCW&P), the Senior Women Officers of Great Britain, and the Multi-Agency Women's Law Enforcement Conference sponsored by the U.S. Border Patrol in El Paso, Texas, as well as at the Federal Law Enforcement Training Center in Glynco, Georgia, and the Canadian Police College in Ottawa, Ontario. In 2003 and 2004, she assisted the New York City Police Museum on exhibits documenting the history of women in the department.

Schulz has also retained her involvement with rail and transit policing. From 1994 to 1997 she was the principal investigator on the Transit Cooperative Research Program's *Guidelines for the Effective Use of Uniformed Transit Police and Security Personnel*, the largest transit policing grant funded in the United States, and she has overseen a number of Federal Transit Administration triennial audits of urban transit system police departments. She is completing research for a book on the history of railroad policing in America.

In 1998, she was a visiting scholar at the British Police Staff College/National Police Training,

Bramshill, Hampshire, England, and she has received research grants from the St. Louis Mercantile Library at the University of Missouri, St. Louis; the Newberry Library, Chicago; the Minnesota Historical Society, St. Paul; the City University of New York, University Committee on Research; the International Association of Chiefs of Police, and the National Association of Female Law Enforcement Executives.

Schulz has delivered papers at meetings of the American Society of Criminology, the Academy of Criminal Justice Sciences, and the American Historical Association and has published in a number of police and historical journals. She was a coeditor of police topics for *Crime and the Justice System in America: An Encyclopedia* and has contributed articles to other reference publications, including the *Encyclopedia of Crime and Punishment*, the *Encyclopedia of Homelessness*, the *Encyclopedia of New York State*, and the *Encyclopedia of Women and Crime*.

# ACCOUNTABILITY

The development of accountability in American law enforcement is intertwined with the evolution of individual rights, personal freedoms, and internal and external drives for police professionalism. *Webster's* defines accountability as "subject to the obligation to report, explain, or justify actions." Throughout much of history, outside of the United States, police have been accountable to the heads of nation-states whether the authority figure was a king (Hammarabi); a monarch (King John of England); or a dictator (Napoleon, Stalin, Hitler). Even in the United States, a progressive democracy in world terms, police have answered to local politicians, judges, and legislators, and have not always been concerned with individual rights or ethical operations. The idea that police should be accountable to the citizens they served did not appear in history until the 1980s and 1990s in the United States. In the meantime, police agencies have progressed through several iterations of accountability.

1. *Movement Toward Standardization and Professionalism.* During the 1920s and 1930s, the police were controlled by local—and, often, lesser—politicians largely through the hiring and firing process. Politicians influenced almost every aspect of law enforcement, from employment and promotion, to appointment of the police chief, to arrest practices and services—all of which were driven by political needs. During these years, corruption generally permeated local government and was expressed as payoffs for not enforcing laws on drinking, gambling, and prostitution. As a result, a movement to incorporate civil service hiring regulations, which had been available at the federal level since 1893 but largely ignored, became the first step toward some form of police accountability. Simultaneously, the police themselves, through the efforts of progressive chiefs such as August Vollmer and William Parker, began to articulate rules, policies, and procedures; develop training; and institute other administrative functions to professionalize policing. Although these new institutional practices provided police executives with a means to standardize the behavior of individual officers, constitutional rights and issues of legality were considered totally academic until the 1960s.

2. *Police Accountability to Protect Constitutional Rights.* The concept of natural law and natural rights was developed initially by Hugo Grotius (16th-century Holland) and John Locke (17th-century England) and was inculcated into the American Declaration of Independence and the U.S. Constitution. It provided broad rights to U.S. citizens and some control over the police and judiciary, such as

habeas corpus, the right to remain silent, and the right to an attorney. Nonetheless, law enforcement remained generally allied with the judiciary and legislature in such a way that when charges were brought against a criminal defendant, that defendant was unofficially presumed guilty. Ultimately, the antiestablishment movement directed citizens to focus on the role of police in the protection of individual rights and freedoms. During the 1960s and 1970s, citizens began to demand accountability of individuals managing government, schools, and other institutions, and questioned their untested competency to govern. This movement had a direct impact on law enforcement starting in 1966 with the Supreme Court decision requiring a Miranda Warning, which was an effort to remind arrestees that they did not have to speak when taken into custody by police. Other Supreme Court decisions continued to support the movement to reform the police. The civil rights movement gained momentum during this same period. The outcry and turmoil of the 1960s and 1970s forced police to interact with the community, not as a dictator of the laws preserving the status quo for the "haves," but as a servant of all the people, to protect them within their communities as they went about the business of pursuing their own definition of life, liberty, and happiness. Community control of the police began to surface in the form of neighborhood and municipal civilian oversight boards, and community policing.

3. *Police Fiscal Accountability.* In the 1970s, many states and municipalities experienced severe budget restrictions, ultimately leading to the concept of "Management by Objectives" (MBO). Municipal agency objectives, including those of the police, were tied to budget lines. Some objectives were "outcome" objectives specifying impact, such as a reduction in burglaries by 2%. Most were "output" objectives, such as an increase in burglary arrests or an increase in percentage of stolen property recovered. Output objectives are simply measures of productivity and not indicative of whether or not the police have had an impact on a problem or issue. Whereas an objective may be to increase the percentage of stolen property *recovered,* there is no relationship to the amount of property *stolen;* therefore,

this did not constitute a measure of effectiveness. A second flaw in the MBO system, rendering it largely ineffective, was the typical review of results of objectives. Results were most often reviewed at the end of the fiscal year in preparation for the next budget cycle, with no consequences for having failed to achieve an objective; new objectives would be set and the cycle repeated.

4. *Accountability for Police Behavior.* Some modern theorists maintain that the police had no accountability until the 1990s. However, the form of accountability exercised by the police was control of the behavior of individual police officers by the police department itself and not accountability for crime reduction and other outcomes. Rules, policies, and procedures pertained primarily to the behavior of individual officers, such as requirements for a high-speed chase; requirements for secondary employment; and the imposition of punishment if the officer became involved in a traffic accident while intoxicated, if he or she tested positive for illegal substances, or when an officer was insubordinate to a superior. Internal Affairs units, established to enforce the rules and regulations, were notoriously secretive and closed about their investigations. An officer under investigation had few rights to fair and equal treatment. However, these units did provide police executives with a means to strictly control the behavior of their personnel on and off the job, if they so chose.

5. *Accountability and Community Policing.* The decade of the 1980s was a time of articulating, developing, and implementing community policing. Officers received training in methods of organizing neighborhoods; conducting meetings with citizens; seeking neighborhood input on problems; and, for some, solving problems using neighborhood resources. Chiefs and commanders had the capacity to determine whether or not an officer was exercising his or her responsibilities with an assigned neighborhood, but unless the jurisdiction at large was inflamed about an issue or concerned about a problem, little other accountability was evident. The expectations for results were usually community satisfaction with the police rather than

improved public safety in a neighborhood. So, although a modicum of accountability existed (e.g., for procedures and activities), practices to review results were not in place.

6. *Department Accountability for Crime Reduction.* In 1985, the crack epidemic spread rapidly across the United States, resulting in police everywhere scrambling for new techniques, greater productivity, and creative strategy development to eradicate drug trafficking and violence. Officer accountability for individual behavior was still very much an issue, especially with greater numbers of civilian review boards coming into their own. Corruption scandals gained the attention of citizens and political leaders, with extensive investigations and levying of punishments. Little attention was paid to the outcomes of police action. Measures of effectiveness for illegal substances were the amount of drugs taken off the street, or the number of arrests of dealers and users. The overall impact of police activities was simply not addressed because it would entail knowledge of the amount of drugs available and/or the size of the population of traffickers—data considered impossible to obtain for comparative purposes. In the 1990s, a conceptual movement swept the country as the result of work being conducted for the government of the District of Columbia and the federal government. David Osborne promulgated the notion that rather than monitoring the number of rats the public works unit captured, the number of restaurant health violations detected by public health, and the number of citizen complaints received by the public relations unit, far more could be achieved if the three respective units worked together to find methods to eradicate the rat population entirely. In other words, focus on the outcome of work rather than levels of productivity. In policing, a similar event occurred when a new commissioner in New York City dared to set a goal of crime reduction. He publicly declared that he and his department would reduce crime significantly. Law enforcement agencies, in many respects, had had a free ride. Prior to the 1970s, crime was generally cyclical and/ or sporadic and ignored by political leaders. Furthermore, during the 1970s, criminal justice researchers concluded, on the basis of very little research, that police activities did not, and could not,

have an impact on crime levels, because other factors in society caused crime. Therefore, the police were a power vacuum in the cauldron of city life. The New York City Transit Police demonstrated the folly of the supposition that police could not affect crime levels by achieving substantial crime reduction on the subways. Most criminal justice theorists considered the subway experience an aberration. However, when the same police management team accomplished similar results for all of New York City, police chiefs in other parts of the country began to experiment with the new methods of managing police operations. Criminal justice researchers remained skeptical. Nonetheless, although chiefs accepted responsibility for crime reduction themselves, they accomplished it by holding patrol commanders accountable for reducing crime and related problems in their assigned geographic areas. Simultaneously, all other specialized units were held accountable to support patrol. This was a new and remarkably different form of accountability for police agencies. The police shifted their focus from productivity and officer behavior to crime reduction and public safety. These same methods of managing for results, often called Compstat, were soon adopted by whole cities. Some set outcome objectives and then, echoing their experience with MBO, checked on progress at the end of the year. Others, however, understood the importance of continuous monitoring and assistance in strategy development and achieved significant results using this process.

7. *Accountability Through Performance Evaluation.* Performance evaluation in law enforcement has been in existence since the 1930s but has rarely been effective. Too often, performance evaluation is tied to salary increases, which prohibits supervisors from rendering objective ratings. Most police receive ratings of above average or outstanding; few, if any, are considered average or unsatisfactory. Some departments have experimented with performance evaluation using behavior anchors and periodic review of progress. There is an expectation that behavior anchors force a focus on work outcomes rather than outputs, and constitute a measure of effectiveness. Most often, however, these

systems are so work intensive that they are either abandoned after a period of time or regarded as a pro forma exercise, with everyone still receiving high ratings. Performance evaluation still needs extensive development if it is to contribute to accountability and effectiveness.

8. *Conclusions.* Techniques to identify citizens' concerns for police performance, measure and monitor police progress in addressing citizens' issues, and report back to the citizenry are being developed and field-tested. Some police departments are using computerized early-warning systems that, among other things, keep track of citizen complaints, which are considered part of an officer's periodic performance evaluations. Accountability in the modern police agency includes ensuring professional behavior of police officers; efficient use of resources; comprehensive strategy development to ensure public safety and crime-free neighborhoods; and, most importantly, protecting individual rights and freedoms by reporting to its citizens. This is a large order that only the most technically competent will achieve. Nonetheless, it is a goal well worth striving for, because history clearly shows that the quality of a democracy is dependent upon the accountability of its police.

*Phyllis P. McDonald*

*See also* Civilian Complaint Review Boards, Complaints Against Police, Compstat, Consent Decrees, Early Warning Systems, Performance Evaluation of Police Departments, Police Management

### For Further Reading

Bratton, W. J. (1998). *Turnaround: How America's top cop reversed the crime epidemic.* New York: Random House.

Haberfeld, M. R. (2002). *Critical issues in police training.* Upper Saddle River, NJ: Prentice Hall.

McDonald, M. G. (2003). *Judicial changes that have impacted police operations.* Unpublished manuscript.

McDonald, P. P. (2002). *Managing police operations: Implementing the New York crime control model.* Belmont, CA: Wadsworth.

Murphy, P., & Plate, T. (1977). *Commissioner: A view from the top of American law enforcement.* New York: Simon & Schuster.

Osborn, D., & Gaebler, T. (1993). *Re-inventing government: How the entrepreneurial spirit is transforming the public sector.* New York: Plume.

# ∾ AFFIRMATIVE ACTION IN POLICING

Throughout the past 150 years, the police and many of the communities they serve have struggled with a history of tension and conflict, often fueled by allegations that officers target and harass racial minorities while failing to root out racist attitudes and practices within their own ranks. Recent high-profile cases such as the beating of Rodney King in Los Angeles and the assault on Abner Louima in New York have served only to heighten concerns.

Internally, it remains true that most American law enforcement agencies do not accurately reflect the communities that they serve. The Bureau of Justice Statistics estimated that as of 1997, only 6% of all full-time sworn police department employees were women, 12% were African American, 8% were Hispanic, and 2% were from other ethnic backgrounds. Comparatively, women comprise 46.5% of the U.S. population. African Americans or Black Americans comprise more than 12% of the population, and individuals of Hispanic or Latino origin represent more than 12% of the population. Americans who identify as members of other ethnic groups comprise just under 10% of the population according to the Census Bureau. A 10-year comparison of police departments shows that from 1990 to 2000, the percentage of Hispanic officers rose from 9% to 14%, black officers rose from 18% to 20%, and women increased from 12% to 16%.

There are numerous reasons why police agencies may benefit from hiring officers who are members of groups that are underrepresented in the department. Evidence suggests that members of certain groups have unique skills that can enhance police services. For example, some studies contend that women are less likely to use excessive force, or that language barriers within the community can be broken by hiring members of newly arrived immigrant groups, according to the National Crime Prevention Council. There are also legal reasons why police agencies may choose to embrace diversity. The Equal Employment Opportunity Act of 1972 prohibits bias in hiring based on race, color, religion, sex, or national origin. Furthermore, the Act allows individuals to sue employers who are engaging in discriminatory behavior. Prior to 1972, employment discrimination was already illegal, but this law provided individuals with an avenue to challenge unfair practices. The new legislation also pushed law enforcement agencies to reevaluate their own recruitment, hiring, and evaluation procedures. Legal challenges could be both financially and psychologically costly to police agencies and communities, and enhancing diversity served as a potential deterrent to future legal challenges.

Although all of these factors are important, for many police observers, the primary incentive for hiring diverse officers is the added effectiveness that some attribute to the maintenance of a police department that reflects the community. This is so, they argue, because the police must rely on community members to report crimes, provide information, and support the maintenance of public safety. Because a key element of partnership building is establishing trust among the participants, the failure to maintain positive relations with diverse communities and the limitation of diversity of culture or thought can only be harmful to the organization's mission. The importance of this need becomes more obvious in light of the most recent national census showing that between 1990 and 2000, the total population of the United States increased by 13.2%, and whereas the majority white population—representing 75.1% of the total—increased by 5.9% during this period, the minority African American and Hispanic communities increased by more than 15% and 50%, respectively. If these Census Bureau predictions prove to be accurate, within the space of a few generations, no single racial or ethnic group will hold a clear majority in the United States. Instead, the country will be made up of a collection of significant "minorities," namely black, white, and Hispanic. Unless steps are taken to ensure that police departments across the country better represent and serve the needs of all of these communities, continuing demographic changes will likely leave the police dangerously out of touch, and furthermore make policing by consent—an essential part of a free and democratic society—increasingly difficult.

In the absence of a coordinated national strategy, state and local police departments have largely been left to develop their own solutions to the problems of attracting greater numbers of minority applicants. Police departments across the country have tried to expand recruitment efforts to focus on minority members of the community and have, often under the auspices of civil service commissions, retooled entry-level examinations. To date, however, these efforts have yielded mixed results. For example, despite the fact that the numbers of African American and Hispanic officers have been rising steadily since the 1960s, according to recent figures from the Bureau of Justice Statistics, both groups together still comprise less than 20% of the total number of officers in service. There is also continuing evidence to suggest that minority officers still do not receive the same promotional opportunities as white officers. Although it is true that considerable variations exist across different police departments—in Chicago and Detroit, for example, black officers are far more likely to hold supervisory positions than in New York or Philadelphia—only some of this disparity can be explained by reference to differences in local demographics. Some departments have tried to deal with this disparity by using various methods of promoting officers from civil service lists. These solutions have sometimes been challenged by white officers as reverse discrimination, and courts have occasionally ruled in their favor. What is clear is that race continues to play a part in determining what opportunities are available to minorities within the police.

Although it would be unfair to single out the police as the only employment area still grappling with diversity and affirmative action issues, in recent years, numerous police agencies have been required by the federal courts to develop affirmative action programs to hire more minority group members and women. In these cases, the courts have found that some selection criteria, especially physical requirements and entry-level testing, were discriminatory when not clearly related to job performance. Some experts, such as Robert Sheehan and Gary Cordner (1995) believe that carefully selecting personnel on the basis of affirmative action can significantly strengthen police staff.

*Dennis Kenney*

### For Further Reading

Grieco, E. M., & Cassidy, R. C. (2001). *Census 2000: Overview of race and Hispanic origin.* Washington, DC: U.S. Census Bureau.

Lonsway, K. (2000). *Hiring & retaining more women: The advantages to law enforcement agencies.* Available: http://www.womenandpolicing.org

National Crime Prevention Council. (1995). *Lengthening the stride: Employing peace officers from newly arrived ethnic groups.* Washington, DC: Author.

Roberg, R., Kuykendall, J., & Novak, K. (2002). *Police management.* Los Angeles: Roxbury.

Sheehan, R., & Cordner, G. (1995). *Police administration.* Cincinnati, OH: Anderson.

Sullivan, P. (1987). Attitude structures of different ethnic and age groups concerning police. *Journal of Criminal Law and Criminology, 78,* 177–196.

## ଓଚ AIRPORT SECURITY

Despite the federalization of aviation security personnel, particularly in the aftermath of the September 11, 2001, terrorist attacks on New York City and Washington, DC, daily aviation activities and oversight remain with the states. Providing police and security at large airports is a task that often involves a stew of jurisdictions with various mandates. Numerous federal and local law enforcement and security organizations are represented in large airports, with no uniform regulations or procedures across the country when it comes to providing policing services. In some localities, such as Logan Airport in Boston, the Massachusetts state police force has jurisdiction, whereas airports in New York City's metropolitan area use a specialized law enforcement agency called the Port Authority Police. Some cities, like Los Angeles, use police departments that are dedicated to providing service specifically for the airport. Police service for small airports is usually provided by local sheriffs or state law enforcement agencies.

Passenger services and screening are provided by the airport carriers under some degree of federal oversight. Because airports are points where international borders are crossed, federal immigration and customs agencies have had a longstanding presence in most of the country's largest airports. There have even been times when the National Guard has been deployed to provide security. What was already a complex policing situation became all the more so after September 11, 2001, when Islamic extremists hijacked three commercial jetliners and turned them into guided missiles to strike the World Trade Center in New York City, and the Pentagon. A fourth plane, probably headed for the nation's capital, crashed in Pennsylvania. The hijackers exploited a number of vulnerabilities in the country's security system, but prominent among them was the weakness in airport security. It was the only time in America's history, at least so far, when air traffic over the entire United States was stopped.

The terrorist attack prompted a top-to-bottom examination of police services and security for the nation's airports. There have been numerous commissions, congressional studies, and reviews since the attack that continue even now. Many of the federal jurisdictions that handled matters involving airports have been restructured and placed under the newly created Department of Homeland Security.

On both the local and federal level, lawmakers quickly found that they had to enact law and policy that dealt with objects not previously considered dangerous weapons. At the time, box cutters, like those used by the attackers, were, in fact, objects that were legally allowed on a plane. Many states, such as California and Idaho, tightened laws regarding dangerous weapons in airports and on planes.

One of the first areas of scrutiny was airport screening. For the most part, the airports contracted private security firms to provide this service. It was found, however, that screeners did a poor job. They were badly trained and poorly paid, and they were hired without sufficient background checks. To correct this shortcoming, screeners became federalized under the Transportation Security Administration, although there was considerable concern that the federal government could not efficiently handle taking the responsibility for hiring, training, and effectively supervising approximately 55,000 employees. Airport security directors, many of whom came from local policing, were appointed to the country's largest airports. For the most part, they are responsible for aviation security, including passenger screening, baggage and cargo, perimeters, ticket counters, lobbies, and gates. But even with the federalization that occurred, the country is trying to find ways to handle this labor-intensive function. For example, a pilot program, currently in progress by the Transportation Security Administration, has allowed some airports to go back to employing privately contracted security screeners. Citing staffing demand problems, some 25% of the nation's commercial airports no longer want to use government employees for screening passengers and baggage.

Screening of cargo and baggage for explosives and other dangerous substances continues to be problematic, with increasing use of canines and personnel. At least one airport uses highly sensitive scanning equipment for this purpose. A number of airports are using in-line screening systems, where baggage moves on a conveyor belt directly from check-in to screening machines.

Background checks are now required for almost all airport employees, particularly those working as security guards. More emphasis has been put on criminal histories and the immigration status of potential applicants. Such checks are conducted by state law enforcement agencies as well as by the Federal Bureau of Investigation.

Far more controversial, however, has been checking the backgrounds of passengers. At this time, those who enter U.S. airports from a number of foreign countries must be fingerprinted and photographed—a program that may be expanded. Critics of the nation's efforts point to emphasis on international flights, while downplaying the risk of domestic flights. Checking passenger names, along with other information located in an assortment of databases, remains a problem, with issues of privacy clashing with issues of safety.

Although 3 years have passed since the terrorist attacks of September 11th, law enforcement in airports continues to be a mixed bag of local, state, federal, and private personnel. There are few venues where so many areas of law enforcement are concentrated. Although airport security has improved since the attacks, experts maintain that we have a long way to go in the areas of prevention and preparedness in the event of a terrorist attack. For example, newscasts are full of stories of undetected weapons either carried by passengers or planted by officials testing the security system.

*Marvie Brooks*

***See also*** Specialized Law Enforcement Agencies

## For Further Reading

Chan, C. (2004). *Aviation legislation: 2003 state legislative summary*. Available: http://www.ncsl.org/programs/esnr/03aviationleg.htm

International Association of Chiefs of Police. (2002). *2002 state legislative report*. Retrieved April 1, 2004, from http://www.theiacp.org/leg_policy/Legupdate/2002/2002 statereport.pdf

International Association of Chiefs of Police. (2003). *2003 state legislative report*. Retrieved April 1, 2004, from http://www.theiacp.org/documents/pdfs/WhatsNew/2003%20State%%20Report.pdf

Morris, R. (2002). *Aviation security state legislation in 2002: Transportation review*. Retrieved April 1, 2004, from http://www.ncsl.org/programs/esnr/aviationrev02.htm

Transportation Security Administration. (2004, April 22). *TSA releases performance report on contract screeners at five U.S. airports*. Retrieved May 12, 2004, from http://www.tsa.gov/public/display?content=090005198009d340

## ✷ AMERICA'S MOST WANTED

*America's Most Wanted* (*AMW*) is a top-rated "reality" crime TV show inaugurated on Fox Broadcasting on July 27, 1981, that doubles as entertainment and public service. Generally, cases that have stumped law enforcement authorities, typically those involving fugitives and missing children, are presented each week on the Fox network and its affiliates. The show's popularity is due both to its voyeuristic and sensationalist format, and its appeal for public assistance by urging viewers to help solve the crimes and to catch alleged criminals by calling in tips to a toll-free number.

Seen by more than 13 million American households a week, the show has been a tremendous success, not only with the public but with law enforcement officials as well, who credit it with helping them apprehend more than 750 criminals to date—many on the most-wanted list. Perhaps *AMW*'s biggest high-profile coup was the recovery of 15-year-old Elizabeth Smart, who had been abducted from her home in Salt Lake City, Utah, on June 5, 2002. After an *AMW* segment aired several times in early 2003 profiling her alleged abductor, Brian David Mitchell, two couples simultaneously spotted Mitchell walking near Salt Lake with two women dressed in long robes and veils on March 12, 2003. They immediately called 911, stunned police arrested Mitchell, and Elizabeth became the 36th child to be recovered successfully in the 16-year history of *AMW*. The continuing popularity of *AMW* is due in no small part to follow-up reports of captures and recoveries on both the show and its Web site (www.americasmostwanted.com), which provide closure to cases and reinforce viewer perception that *AMW* works and that they, too, might be lucky and catch one of its "Most Wanted." So great has been the show's popularity that when Fox tried to cancel *AMW* in the fall of 1996 because of weak ratings, the station was deluged with hundreds of thousand of letters of protest from fans, law enforcement, and government officials. It was subsequently reinstated in an expanded 1-hour format, which includes a greater emphasis on sensationalistic reenactments of crimes.

*AMW* is hosted by John Walsh, an actor with strong credibility stemming from a personal tragedy in 1981 in which his 6-year-old son, Adam, was abducted from a department store and killed. A nationally acclaimed and recognizable advocate of missing and exploited children, Walsh presents the "facts" of each crime case with the authoritative, get-tough-on-crime manner of a law enforcement officer. Dressed in a black leather jacket with his hair slicked back, legs astride, and arms crossed, Walsh exhorts viewers between *AMW* segments to catch "the bad guys." Live footage of actual people involved in the cases, as well as reenacted segments performed by actors, are interspersed with Walsh's reporting of events and lurid promotional trailers.

Reenacted segments are often highly dramatic—introduced with pathos-laden language and filmed with sinister music, lighting, and other sensational effects geared at eliciting viewer fear and loathing. Actual testimony of crime victims and their families, witnesses, law enforcement officials and experts, as well as apprehended criminals, contribute to the show's semblance of "reality."

Before *America's Most Wanted*, law enforcement agencies' primary means of finding missing children, fugitives, and criminals was the post office or sheriff's "Wanted" notice. In the 1930s, radio crime dramas such as "True Detective Mysteries" dealt with actual police cases—describing a wanted criminal at the end of each program. Traditionally, movies have dealt with tabloid-like murders involving real crimes, using documentary-look techniques and sensationalist elements that are the precursors of *AMW*. TV picked up on the moviegoer's fascination with reality-based crime stories by producing a long line of police crime dramas that began with *Dragnet* (quickly followed by *Highway Patrol* and *The Untouchables*). However, the most direct precursor of *America's Most Wanted* was a show called *Crime Stoppers* in the mid-1970s. It consisted of a brief dramatization of a recent crime and an appeal to the public to help solve it. Police departments routinely elicit the help of the public through their local news media, and in the aftermath of the September 11, 2001, terrorist attacks, a number of areas have established special phone numbers to report suspicious activity.

*America's Most Wanted* is seen by supporters and many law enforcement officials as giving citizens an active role in safeguarding themselves and the public. In a letter urging Fox to reinstate *AMW* in 1996, the FBI stated that the show had empowered millions of Americans to combat crime safely and constructively. Fox entertainment president Peter Roth wrote at the time that people told the station that the program made them feel safer. However, media critic Grey Cavender believes that the show has actually made people feel more fearful. According to Cavender, *AMW* contributes to society's sense of danger by depicting horrible crimes in which helpless, innocent people (like the viewer) are victimized by seemingly ubiquitous and random violence (Cavender & Fishman, 1998). Viewer fear and victimization finds an antidote in the show's hype of the power of policing and surveillance to safeguard the public. Cavender believes that the self-congratulatory tone of the show's host, law enforcement personnel, and even captured criminals (who laud the show's crime-fighting powers) contribute to public support for opportunistic crime control policies. What this suggests is that reality-crime TV shows like *America's Most Wanted* blur the line between news and entertainment, creating viewer desire for sensationalized news stories which can feed public fears.

*Kathryn Wylie-Marques*

**See also** Crime Stoppers, Television Cop Shows

## For Further Reading

Cavender, G., & Fishman, M. (Eds.). (1998). *Entertaining crime: Television reality programs.* New York: Aldine de Gruyter.

Walsh, J. (1997). *Tears of rage: From grieving father to crusader for justice.* New York: Pocket.

Walsh, J. (2001). *Public enemies: The host of* America's Most Wanted *targets the nation's most notorious criminals.* New York: Pocket.

## ❧ ARREST

Arrest, the portal to the criminal justice system, occurs when a legal authority deprives a person of liberty in order to force him or her to answer a criminal charge. Most arrests are made by police officers, but peace officers, such as probation or court officers, also make arrests pursuant to their official duties. Under circumscribed conditions, private individuals may make arrests, although this is discouraged by professional law enforcement.

The processing of an arrest can vary in length from under an hour to more than a day, depending on police and prosecutorial procedures, case complexity, witness availability, and other contingencies. The formal recording of an arrest, known as *booking,* consists of noting an arrest time, basic identifying information about the arrestee, and the charges. Usually, this is followed by photographing and fingerprinting the suspect. If interrogated, the suspect must first be informed of his or her constitutional rights regarding counsel and self-incrimination. An affidavit describing the offense(s) is then prepared for presentation at the first court appearance, known as an *arraignment.* Defendants are usually arraigned (formally charged and asked to enter an initial guilty/not guilty plea) within 48 hours of arrest.

Juvenile arrest processing differs significantly from that of adults. Police may take youth into custody for *status offenses* (acts deemed unacceptable for minors, such as drinking or truancy) as well as for crimes. Depending on such factors as the seriousness of the behavior, the child's history, and the cooperation of parents or other caretakers, police officials may release the child to a caretaker without formalizing the arrest or proceeding to a court hearing. Conversely, if circumstances warrant, the youth may remain in custody and then be brought directly to juvenile court. Many jurisdictions also have laws and procedures wherein the most serious juvenile offenders are arraigned in adult court.

Arrest-making at all government levels is regulated by the Fourth Amendment's prohibition against unreasonable seizures and requirement that arrest warrants be issued based only on probable cause. In practice, courts and state statutes have allowed law enforcement agents with probable cause to proceed *without* a warrant in about 95% of arrests. If the offense in a warrantless arrest is minor, agents must establish probable cause through their *presence*—a term interpreted as either seeing the offense or perceiving it through other senses, as when feeling a weapon, hearing a cry for help, or smelling marijuana. Offenses classified as misdemeanors may or may not require the agent's presence, depending on local statutes and procedures, but felony arrests *do not* require the officer's presence.

Acting on an arrest warrant, an official need not physically possess the warrant when making the arrest, but must promptly bring the arrestee before the court of issuance. Jurisdictions differ as to the circumstances requiring an arrest warrant, but in the 1980 case of *Payton v. New York,* the Supreme Court declared that any arrest at a private residence without suspect consent or emergency circumstances always requires a warrant.

That same year, the Supreme Court also sought to distinguish an arrest from the many situations in which police detain persons for questioning on less than probable cause. It held in *United States v. Mendenhall* (1980) that an arrest occurred "only if, in view of all the circumstances surrounding the incident, a reasonable person would have believed that he is not free to leave." At such time, Miranda protections are applicable.

This "free-to-leave" standard has been applied in subsequent court cases, but it has not clarified the moment when an individual is *officially* under arrest. This varies greatly among agencies. A Police Foundation study found that 16% of police departments record an arrest at the point when any restraint is used on a suspect; 11% record an arrest when the suspect is brought to the station house, and the majority document the arrest at a subsequent time.

These discrepant definitions of arrest are but one source of uncertainty in the *arrest rates* (arrests per 100,000 population) and *arrest clearances* (number of offenses solved by an arrest and referral for prosecution) compiled in the FBI's Uniform Crime Reports (UCR). Some of the 9,000+ police agencies that report in the UCR follow its guidelines very loosely. Furthermore, departments may manipulate data in their favor by misclassifying crimes, labeling them as unfounded, or clearing an excess number of offenses through a single arrest. Finally, citizens report only about 36% of crimes, and this varies greatly with the type of crime.

Nevertheless, police agencies and criminologists continue to rely on the UCR as a gauge of arrest productivity and effectiveness. These data show that in the year 2001, there were 9,324,953 arrests reported by local, county, and state police officers, or about 4,841 arrests per 100,000 population (almost 5%). The arrest rate over the past decade (1991–2000), like the crime rate, has dropped substantially for all eight of the UCR's Index Crimes (murder, forcible rape, aggravated assault, robbery, burglary, arson, larceny, and auto theft). Clearance rates for index crimes over this period were 20.5% overall, with those involving actual or threatened violence cleared at a higher rate, 47.5%, and those involving property cleared at a rate of 16.7%.

The UCR also calculates total arrests by approximating arrest figures in jurisdictions not reporting. In 2001, there were 13,699,254 estimated arrests, a 2.1% decrease from the previous year. About 2.2 million of these, or 16.4%, were for index crimes. The single largest arrest category was drug-related offenses, generating 1.6 million arrests, or 11.7% of the total, followed closely by drunk driving, for which there were 1.4 million arrests.

On average, patrol officers make under two arrests per month, mostly for quality-of-life and public order offenses. Officers often decline arrests, even when legally justified. This discretion is influenced by many factors, such as offense seriousness; suspect demeanor; victim cooperation; and the race, class, and gender of both suspect and victim. An officer's desire to earn overtime or to avoid lengthy, arduous arrest processing may also weigh in the decision.

Arrest-making is also affected by a police agency's enforcement policies. For instance, in the 1980s, many departments instituted mandatory arrest for drunk driving and domestic violence. Cities such as New York, which, in 1993, adopted a vigorous strategy toward quality-of-life violations, encourage a high volume of arrests in lieu of summonses. Research suggests that such crackdowns do deter repeat criminal behavior, particularly among first-time offenders, although they do not necessarily produce a generalized or long-term effect on crime rates.

*Edith Linn*

***See also*** Citizen Arrests, Discretion, Domestic Violence Enforcement, Drunk Driving Enforcement, Fingerprints, Interrogation, Juvenile Crime/Programs/Units, Miranda Warning, Stop and Frisk, Uniform Crime Reports

## For Further Reading

Federal Bureau of Investigation. (2002). *Crime in the United States, 2001.* Washington, DC: Government Printing Office.

Maguire, K., & Pastore, A.L. (Eds.). (1997). *Sourcebook of criminal justice statistics 1996.* Washington, DC: Bureau of Justice Statistics.

Payton v. New York, 445 U.S. 573 (1980).

Sherman, L. W., & Glick, B. D. (1984). *The quality of police arrest statistics.* Washington, DC: The Police Foundation.

United States v. Mendenhall, 446 U.S. 544 (1980).

Walker, S., & Katz, C. M. (2002). *The police in America.* New York: McGraw-Hill.

# 〜 ARSON INVESTIGATION

## BACKGROUND

Humankind has no doubt been destroying property and life with fire since it was first discovered. Historically, setting fire to your enemy's property has been a common form of retribution. Determining the cause of such a fire is an art that dates back to at least 300 B.C.E., where Roman law decreed that the "Quarstionarius"—the Roman equivalent of today's state fire investigator—determines the cause of all fires.

During the 1800s, the predominant image of the arsonist shifted to that of the pyromaniac, or one who could not fight off the compulsion to start fires. Today, we recognize that arson has a variety of motives, such as revenge, profit, vandalism, fraud, excitement/thrill seeking, hero/vanity, concealment of another crime, and terrorism.

The events of September 11, 2001, mark one of the deadliest and most costly arsons the world has ever seen. Islamic terrorists initiated three explosions and resulting fires in the two World Trade Center towers in New York City and in the Pentagon in Virginia by hijacking and flying three commercial airliners into them. The direct costs of these fires are staggering: more than 3,000 lives lost, thousands more injured, and billions of dollars in property damage. The indirect costs are incalculable. Arson has the distinction, when measured on a cost-per-incident basis, of being the most costly of all crimes.

## PROBLEMS ASSOCIATED WITH ARSON INVESTIGATION

By their very nature, fires are destructive, which often makes it difficult to find evidence of the cause of the fire. Prior to initiating a criminal arson investigation, a determination must be made that the fire was indeed arson (the intentional damaging of a building by fire) and not accidental or caused by nature (e.g., lightning). This usually requires a separate scientific inquiry called the fire investigation.

In some jurisdictions, arson investigators are trained in fire investigation; however, the more common method relegates this task to fire service personnel. Unfortunately, fire investigation, for the purpose of preventing future fires, is generally not as interesting to firefighters, who are more interested in suppression. Fire investigation, for the purpose of arson detection, was also shunned by the fire service because it was viewed as a law enforcement responsibility.

On the other hand, much of the law enforcement community viewed this function as the exclusive province of fire department personnel because of the general belief that one could not acquire the skills necessary to conduct a fire investigation without years of experience fighting fires. These problems are compounded by the volunteer nature of the fire service in many areas of the country. In such organizations, funds for fire investigation and training are scarce to nonexistent.

Another problem that has plagued arson investigations is that they are sometimes begun based on a false determination of arson. This is usually the result of a lack of scientific understanding of fire behavior and the misinterpretation of arson evidence. Unfortunately, fire/arson investigators were, in the not-too-distant past, forming opinions without a sound body of scientific knowledge.

Despite such an early beginning, the field has been slow to evolve from an art to a scientific inquiry. However, with the advent of fire research, many beliefs commonly accepted in the past have now been superseded.

As a result, many observations of fire damage formerly believed to be proof positive of a particular cause may now have more than one explanation. Ironically, it may be said, then, that our increased knowledge of fire has made determining the cause of fire more difficult, rather than easier.

## ARSON INVESTIGATION AS A FIELD OF STUDY

For many years, the study of fire/arson investigation was largely ignored. During the 1960s and early 1970s, the United States began to experience a dramatic increase in incendiary fire conduct. Many areas within our cities were being compared to the aftermath of World War II. Consequently, many textbooks, handbooks, and other manuals began to appear. Only a few of the texts were perceived as authoritative sources, and peer-reviewed professional and scholarly journals dedicated to the subject of fire and arson investigation did not exist.

One peer-reviewed journal, the *Journal of Forensic Science* (a publication of the American Academy of Forensic Science), has published only a few articles on fire investigation. Most of the texts were written by field investigators (with backgrounds in the fire service or law enforcement), forensic scientists, or engineers. A handful were authored by noteworthy public and private organizations such as the Federal Emergency Management Agency's National Fire Academy, the National Fire Protection Association, International Fire Service Training Association, the Center for Fire Research of the National Bureau of Standards (now known as the National Institute for Testing and Standards), the Investigations Institute of the National Association of Fire Investigators, and the Institute of Fire Engineers.

Also, many newsletters and periodicals have come and gone, but the *Fire and Arson Investigator,* which is the official publication for the International Association of Arson Investigators, has been consistently published since 1949. Perhaps the greatest problem with the literature is that much of it is not supported by science. Nevertheless, this is the body of knowledge as it existed and on which most investigators relied to learn their trade.

One of the most significant events in the transition from an art to a science has been the publication by the National Fire Protection Association of *NFPA 921: Guide for Fire and Explosion Investigations.* The authors advocate relating fire investigation to the scientific method and have questioned a number of long-standing rules of thumb and theories that were used in making cause determinations by incorporating new knowledge of fire behavior gained through research (primarily conducted by the Center for Fire Research).

## PRESENT-DAY ARSON INVESTIGATIONS

Despite the progress in our knowledge and training, arson continues to be one of the most difficult crimes to solve. Many problems remain: Evidence is destroyed by the fire; the crime scene, unlike with any other crime, is difficult to impossible to protect as a result of firefighting operations; it is generally a crime of stealth; for the most part, it remains a bifurcated investigation with the cause determination made by fire service personnel; investigators are not required to become certified; and the increased knowledge recently gained by fire research ironically has made the task of determining the cause of fires more difficult. In addition, investigators are often under pressure by their agencies to determine the cause even if they cannot substantiate it.

*Angelo Pisani*

### For Further Reading

Cote, A., & Bugbee, P. (1988). *Principles of fire protection.* Quincy, MA: National Fire Protection Association.

DeHaan, J. D. (1991). *Kirk's fire investigation.* Englewood Cliffs, NJ: Prentice Hall.

National Fire Protection Association. (2001). *NFPA 921: Guide to fire and explosion investigations.* Quincy, MA: Author.

## ꧁ ART THEFT INVESTIGATION

From time to time, the mass media become preoccupied with a sensational case of art theft, and to the general public, it might seem that such crimes are rare and difficult to commit. However, according to data collected by international law enforcement and insurance agencies, losses from art theft amount to billions of dollars annually. Private collections and churches are targeted more often than public museums; 50% of stolen objects are paintings and sculptures. The most frequent mode of art theft is burglary and robbery. It can be considered white-collar, blue-collar, or violent crime, planned or spontaneous. The annual percentage of successful art theft recovery is in the low teens, and many investigations extend for years. Art theft investigation shares detective techniques with narcotics cases, including going undercover to penetrate international markets, protecting low-level buyers in order to get to the major dealers, and using informants.

However, cases of art theft never allow for the evidence to be destroyed.

Art and antiques theft has a long history but has become epidemic since the mid-20th century, when prices at the public art auctions hit the $1 million mark, drawing the attention of the underworld to exploit this market. Illicit trade in cultural objects is one of the top global crimes fought by police, along with money laundering, drug smuggling, illegal arms trafficking, and terrorism. Recent investigations demonstrate a shift in motivation for art theft. Fewer objects are stolen to satisfy somebody's passion for art; rather, they are increasingly used as a means of extortion, initial collateral for narcotic networks or laundering the profits of crime, a medium of exchange between criminals, or a way to obtain political favors from the government.

With the globalization and openness of borders between countries, the smuggling of cultural objects is easier, but investigating this often invisible crime is more complex. Professional art squads are a rarity in national police forces; art thefts are routinely underreported; and many art objects in private collections as well as cultural institutions are not properly secured, insured, or documented. In addition, the laws of many countries are inadequate in protecting the owners of stolen art. In the past decade, private collectors, museums, art dealers, insurance companies, and law enforcers have collaborated in creating an environment that is less attractive to art thieves and forgers. Since 1990, it has become standard practice to check the Art Loss Register, the largest private computerized database of stolen and missing art from around the world, to verify the legitimacy, or "good title," of a work before it is acquired, sold, or insured. In 1993, the Getty Information Institute developed the Object ID, which is the international documentation standard for the description of stolen or illegally exported cultural property and art. The standard has been translated into a dozen languages and increases the compatibility of many databases of lost art used by police, customs officials, museums, and insurance companies worldwide. The standard has also helped these agencies to exchange information more seamlessly. New

security technologies have emerged for marking art objects for identification, including the use of chemical codes, electronic tagging, bar codes, microphotography, and laser fingerprinting.

As a rule, art theft investigation is conducted by local detectives, although some European countries, specifically Italy and France, who have the highest rates of art theft, have created specialized forces dedicated to this area of investigation. Italy was the first to organize an art squad, called Carabinieri for the Protection of Cultural Patrimony (Comando Carabinieri Tutela Patrimonio Artistico), with 80 members in 1969. Their officers receive specialized training, including a 3-month course in art history. France created a similar but smaller force with 40 officers in 1975 called the Central Office for the Fight Against Traffic in Cultural Goods (Office Central de lutte contre le traffic des biens culturels). The Art and Antiques squad in England's New Scotland Yard was formed in 1968. It was merged with the Flying Squad in 1995 because of the increasing link between art theft, drug smuggling, and terrorist networks. For the same reason, the U.S. Customs Art Fraud Investigation Center, set up in 2000 to track and seize stolen art, was subsumed into the newly formed U.S. Department of Homeland Security in 2002.

The FBI maintains the National Stolen Art File, although this institution does not have a specialized art theft unit. FBI agents in the Violent Crimes and Major Offenders sections handle cases involving interstate or international art theft for which the federal government has investigative jurisdiction.

In the United States, New York and Los Angeles are major centers for art and antiques trade. The first American art theft detail was attached to the Safe, Loft, and Truck Squad of the New York City Police Department. In 1971, four detectives volunteered to take a 6-week training course in art history, but only one detective remained on the force. The one-man art theft squad was later renamed the Art and Identification Unit and was dissolved in 1990. Today, the Los Angeles Police Department Art Theft Detail is the only law enforcement unit in the country dedicated to fighting art crimes full-time. The two-detective squad was formed in 1983 and has recovered nearly $50 million in stolen artworks since 1993.

International and, in many cases, multidisciplinary cooperation among law enforcement agencies is imperative in tracing and recovering stolen works of art. The International Criminal Police Organization (Interpol) has disseminated information pertaining to cultural property among its 177 member countries since 1947. There are 55 state liaison offices of Interpol in the United States that process art loss and theft cases of substantial commercial or cultural value, as well as those that were stolen under particularly serious circumstances. In Europe, a multicountry police force, Europol, has been coordinating the European Union's law enforcement efforts against organized crime, including art theft, through its centralized communication network since 2002.

The first attempts to sell stolen art over the Internet were prosecuted by the New York State Police Computer Crime Unit in 1999, when animation images worth $100,000 were auctioned on the eBay Web site. The Cyber Crimes Center of the United States' newly renamed Immigration and Customs Enforcement Bureau investigates the trafficking of art and cultural objects over the Internet.

A number of international legal instruments have been developed for safeguarding the world's cultural heritage: Hague Convention for the Protection of Cultural Property in the Event of Armed Conflict (1954), UNESCO Convention on the Means of Prohibiting and Preventing the Illicit Import, Export and Transfer of Ownership of Cultural Property (1970), and UNIDROIT (International Institute for the Unification of Private Laws) Convention on Stolen or Illegally Exported Cultural Objects (1995). The United States became a party to the UNESCO treaty in 1983, although it still has not ratified the UNIDROIT convention. In accordance with the UNESCO Convention, the U.S. Department of State accepts requests from other countries for import restrictions on archaeological or ethnological artifacts, the pillage of which places their national cultural heritage in jeopardy. The president appoints an 11-member Cultural Property Advisory Committee to review these requests and make recommendations to his office on the appropriate action to take.

*Maria Kiriakova*

## For Further Reading

Adams, L. (1974). *Art cop Robert Volpe: Art crime detective.* New York: Dodd, Mead.

Palmer, N. (Ed.). (1998). *The recovery of stolen art: A collection of essays.* London: Kluwer.

Spiel, R. E., Jr. (2000). *Art theft and forgery investigation: The complete field manual.* Springfield, IL: Charles C Thomas.

## ✂ ASSAULTS ON THE POLICE

Policing is dangerous business. Law enforcement officers are victims of nonfatal assaults more often than workers in any other occupation, and they are murdered at rates second only to taxicab drivers/chauffeurs. FBI records indicate that during the decade ending in 2001, an average of more than 130 police officers died each year in the line of duty, and this figure does not include the 72 officers who perished from the terrorist attack on September 11, 2001. Almost half of the officers who died in recent years lost their lives at the hands of criminals who attacked them. FBI figures for this time frame also show that more than 19,000 other officers were injured in assaults perpetrated by citizens each year, and that just under 41,000 other officers were victims of attacks in which they suffered no injuries.

As dramatic as these figures are, historical data indicate that violence directed at the police has actually decreased in recent years. According to data kept by the National Law Enforcement Officers Memorial Fund, the two periods of greatest risk for fatal assaults were the years of Prohibition and the early 1970s; the 1920s and early 1930s saw an average of about 120 officers killed feloniously each year, whereas about 150 officers were murdered each year in the early 1970s. Between these two peaks, fatal assaults on officers dropped considerably, reaching a low point during World War II, then fluctuating until the early 1960s, when the numbers began to rise at a precipitous rate, topping out at more than 160 officers murdered in 1973.

The number of officers murdered dropped quite markedly during the rest of the 1970s and through the 1980s, as did nonfatal attacks on officers. This general downward trend in the number of officers killed and assaulted continued into the 1990s, with FBI data indicating there were more than 15,000 fewer assaults on officers (55,971 vs. 71,794) and 24 fewer officers murdered (42 vs. 66) in 1999 as compared to 1990. It is important to note that this trend was not continuous throughout the decade, however, but rather was marked by several peaks and valleys. Moreover, the downward trend observed in the 1990s did not continue into the current decade, as the number of officers assaulted in 2001 was more than 1,500 higher than 1999, and the number of officers murdered jumped by 28 (exclusive of the September 11th attacks).

Although there has been considerable variability in the number of officers killed and assaulted over the years, other aspects of attacks on officers have been remarkably consistent. Regarding fatal attacks, for example, the vast majority of officers slain in each of the past 15 years died from gunshots—more than four out of five. And FBI figures indicate that about 75% of officers murdered by firearms each year were shot with handguns. Some experts maintain that these numbers would be higher if it were not for the increasing use of body armor. Clearly, firearms, and handguns in particular, pose the greatest fatal threat to police officers year in and year out.

In terms of nonfatal assaults, firearms have played a substantially different role over the years. Guns were used in just under 4% of the 60,000 or so assaults that occurred each year in the decade ending in 2001. Suspects used knives in about 2% of the attacks, some other sort of weapon approximately 12% of the time, and were unarmed in the remaining 82% of the assaults reported to the FBI.

Attacks on officers are not evenly distributed around the clock. The most dangerous time for officers was between midnight and 2 a.m., when 16% of the assaults that took place in the decade ending in 2001 occurred. Other notably risky blocks of time included the hours between 10 p.m. and midnight (15%), 8 p.m. to 10 p.m. (14%), and 6 p.m. to 8 p.m. (11%). The safest times for officers were 6 a.m. to 8 a.m., and 8 a.m. to 10 a.m., when 2% and 3% of assaults occurred, respectively.

There are also notable differences in assaults based on where officers work when attacked. In 2001, for example, officers who worked for big-city police departments (those serving populations of 250,000 or more) had an almost 1 in 5 chance of being attacked, as 17.9 of every 100 officers were assaulted. These officers were only slightly more likely to be assaulted than were their peers working in cities with populations of 100,000 to 249,999, who were attacked at a rate of 17.7 per 100 officers. As the size of the jurisdictions for which officers work decreases from that point, the risk of assault drops notably, so that police working in small towns (those with populations of fewer than 10,000) were attacked at a rate of 7.4 per 100 officers. Finally, law enforcement personnel who serve rural counties are least likely to be assaulted, at a rate of just 5.3 per 100 officers.

The level of danger officers face also varies across regions of the nation; more officers are killed in the South than in any other place. According to FBI statistics for the years 1992–2001, for example, nearly half (47.5%) of the almost 600 officers murdered during that decade worked for southern police agencies (22.5% were slain in the West, 18.9% in the Midwest, and 11.1% in the Northeast). It is important to note that the disproportionate number of officers killed in the South holds even when one factors in population size and the number of police officers employed.

Although officers are liable to be attacked at any time and in any place, the data clearly show that some times and places are more dangerous for the police. What is unclear is what the future holds for the rate at which officers are killed and assaulted. The peak years of fatal violence during Prohibition and the early 1970s were times of considerable social upheaval, for example, and we may be heading that way again. The police are on the front lines of the current domestic threat posed by foreign terror and are thus likely to find themselves increasingly in harm's way. In the current century, then, police work may well be more dangerous than it has been for quite some time.

*Robert J. Kaminski and David A. Klinger*

**See also** Body Armor, Use of Force

## For Further Reading

Federal Bureau of Investigation. (various years). *Law enforcement officers killed and assaulted.* Washington, DC: Author.

Kaminski, R. J., Jefferis, E. S., & Chanhatasilpa, C. (2000). A spatial analysis of American police killed in the line of duty. In R. L. Turnbull, H. E. Hendrix, & B. D. Dent (Eds.), *Atlas of crime: Mapping the criminal landscape* (pp. 212–220). Phoenix, AZ: Oryx.

http://www.nleomf.org

# ❧ ASSET FORFEITURE, STATE

Each state and territory in the United States has its own forfeiture statute. Hundreds of statutes exist that are linked to a variety of state crimes, including drug offenses. Generally, state statutes apply language and procedures modeled after the provisions of federal forfeiture laws. As with federal forfeiture, state statutes define the conduct giving rise to forfeiture and a state officer's authority to seize property. Similarly, many state statutes provide for judicial, administrative, and summary forfeiture.

Most states provide for judicial *in rem* or *in personam* proceedings, which are applied to civil and criminal forfeitures, respectively. Civil forfeitures proceed as *in rem* actions. *In rem* is a legal proceeding against an asset in which the state forfeits all right, title, and interest in that asset. Criminal forfeitures are *in personam* proceedings against the asset's owner for the purpose of obligating that owner to forfeit the owner's interest in the property to the government.

Administrative forfeiture applies to specified property valued below a statutory threshold. Administrative forfeitures are also *in rem* actions that provide authority to a seizing agency to forfeit a property without judicial involvement. In administrative

forfeitures, the state needs only to provide notice of the seizure to potential innocent claimants. If no one files a claim within a specified time, the property is forfeited, through default, without invoking a judicial proceeding against the property. On the other hand, if a claimant files a claim to the property, the case proceeds judicially and a judge determines whether the asset will be forfeited.

Forfeiture at both the state and federal levels occurs under two theoretical precepts. The first, facilitation theory, allows for the forfeiture of property involved in the manufacture, delivery, and sale of controlled substances. It can include automobiles, boats, or airplanes used to transport drugs, as well as real estate used to store drugs or as the location where drugs are trafficked. Under proceeds theory, property that represents the profit of certain unlawful activities can be seized by the government. This theory is most applicable for money laundering and other financial crimes, such as racketeering and fraud. Property that is subject to forfeiture under this legal theory includes bank accounts, financial instruments (e.g., stocks), real estate, jewelry, cash, electronic equipment, vehicles, and so on.

Some assets are illegal altogether. Examples include Schedule I and Schedule II drugs. In such cases, the state may seize the property under summary forfeiture proceedings. The state need not provide notice of the seizure to potential claimants because no legal possessory interest exists for the property.

Many small law enforcement agencies do not have forfeiture programs because of a lack of startup funds and other resources (e.g., storage facilities, appraisers, real property managers, financial investigation expertise). Other jurisdictions maintain minimal forfeiture activity. For such jurisdictions, federal agencies can provide the catalyst for asset forfeiture proceedings.

In 1982, to encourage states that had not yet passed laws regarding forfeiting the profits of drug trafficking, the Drug Enforcement Administration developed a Model Forfeiture of Drug Profits Act that suggested that states allocate revenue generated through seizure and forfeiture to drug enforcement.

However, even though all states were seizing illicit substances during routine narcotics operations, few were following the federal example of seizing drug profits. For these state and local agencies, Congress provided an equitable sharing provision in the Comprehensive Crime Control Act of 1984. This provision allowed federal agencies to divide the proceeds derived from civil forfeitures with all participating law enforcement agencies. The provision was further designed to encourage future cooperation between state and local agencies and the federal agencies that processed the forfeitures. Equitable sharing results when the federal agency agrees to process a seizure under federal forfeiture laws and remits proceeds back to the participating state or local agency.

Today, state and local agencies can participate with agencies in either the Department of Justice or Department of Treasury, through joint investigations, that lead to the forfeiture of property to be shared. State and local agencies may provide intelligence or directly participate in the investigation leading to the seizure. The amount shared with the state and local agencies depends upon the degree of state and local investigatory participation.

Before 1990, properties valued at more than $100,000 had to be forfeited judicially. This forfeiture requirement changed in August 1990 when President George H.W. Bush signed a law authorizing the administrative forfeiture of hauling conveyances and financial instruments without regard to value, as well as property other than real estate, up to a value of $500,000. All real estate must be forfeited judicially, regardless of value.

State and local law enforcement agencies can receive equitable sharing revenues through one other means. These agencies may request that a federal agency "adopt" the property that the state or local agency has already seized through its own efforts. Such adoptions are authorized when the behavior giving rise to the seizure is in violation of a federal law and the federal law provides for forfeiture. The proceeds derived, either from the direct forfeiture (as in currency) or forfeiture and sale of the forfeited asset (as in real estate, vehicles, jewelry, etc.), are then equitably shared with the state and local agencies.

In these cases, the federal agencies that adopt seizures are entitled to 20% of the proceeds for administrative fees.

As in state forfeitures, the adopting federal agency may forfeit the property through one of two means. The first is through the administrative forfeiture process. In order to forfeit an asset administratively, the federal investigative agency is required to advertise the forfeiture for a specified amount of time in order to provide potential claimants the opportunity to respond to the seizure. The adopting agency also makes the final decision regarding whether or not an asset is forfeited.

On the other hand, as mentioned previously, judicial forfeiture is required for any property valued in excess of $500,000, real estate, and when an innocent owner claim has been filed. Unless a claim is filed, monetary instruments and hauling conveyances may be forfeited administratively, regardless of value.

The equitable sharing or adoption process begins with the state or local agency's submission of a formal written request to the field office of the pertinent federal agency. According to federal guidelines, property that is equitably shared should be used for training, purchasing equipment, and providing community policing efforts that result in further seizures. However, asset forfeiture is not without its critics.

In recent years, several states, such as Colorado, Utah, New Mexico, and Washington, have restricted, at one time or another, law enforcement's ability to seize assets under state forfeiture law. Those who support restricting asset forfeiture believe that it adds an uncomfortable profit incentive for police and that it amounts to double jeopardy. In some localities, legislation has been enacted that allows police to seize assets under civil forfeiture only when a conviction is first gained, or narrows the range of property subject to seizure, such as that which is intrinsically harmful to the public (e.g., child pornography or illicit drugs). Other laws enacted affect how forfeited proceeds are appropriated, which in turn may affect the adoptive seizures. In Utah, for example, law enforcement agencies must turn over forfeited funds to the state treasury, which ultimately diverts the proceeds to state schools. When asset funds went down as a result of this restriction, so did the amount of resources dedicated to antidrug police activities. Legislation was then introduced that would once again allow police agencies to keep forfeiture funds.

*Paula Gormley*

*See also* Drug Enforcement

*For Further Reading*

Ashbaugh, R. L. (2000, August). *State and local equitable sharing program: Memorandum audit report* (Office of the Inspector General Report No. 00-18). Available: http://www.usdoj.gov/oig/au0018

Executive Office for Asset Forfeiture. (1994). *Guide to equitable sharing of federally forfeited property for state and local law enforcement agencies.* Washington, DC: U.S. Department of Justice.

Hartman, V. E. (2001). Implementing an asset forfeiture program. *FBI Law Enforcement Bulletin, 70*(1), 1–7.

Render unto seizure: Colorado cops get short shrift in forfeiture debate. (2002, June 30). *Law Enforcement News, 28*(580), pp. 1, 10.

Williams, H. E. (2001). *Asset forfeiture: A law enforcement perspective.* Springfield, IL: Charles C Thomas.

# ✺ AUXILIARY/ RESERVE/PART-TIME POLICE

The establishment of full-time police forces has not abated the need for supplemental personnel. Most local and state police agencies in America recruit and train civilian employees. In addition, since the end of World War I, the use of unpaid volunteers in sworn or nonsworn capacities has become standard practice in many police departments. The titles of such volunteers have varied over the 20th century, but by the second half of the century, there emerged two distinctive categories for unpaid or low-paid volunteers: *auxiliary* and *reserve.* The titles *reserve deputy sheriff, reserve posse member,* and *reserve officer* are more common throughout the western and southern regions of the United States, whereas the designation *auxiliary police officer* appears to be in common usage in the eastern regions, especially the Northeast. Irrespective of the specific title in use, there are units in every state. However, three states lead the nation with respect to the total number of such volunteer police officers: Ohio, Florida, and California. Over the years, training for these volunteers has vastly improved, and complete background investigations are conducted for candidates. For example, all new California reserve police officers are required to attend a basic police academy, as mandated by the California State Commission on Peace Officer Standards and Training (POST). The training requirement is the same academy program required of all regular full-time officers.

Part-time police officers are typically employed in small departments to supplement the work of regular full-time police officers in order to limit expenditures. In addition, there may be a special need for such personnel during special events or a long tourist season. An hourly salary is paid, but there are few other benefits. In some agencies, prior service as a reserve police officer may be required for this assignment. This is required mainly for financial reasons because reserves will have attended a basic police officer academy and have had time to develop a record for dependability and honesty. Significantly, the part-time police officer candidate will have paid for his or her own training.

The recruitment of large numbers of auxiliary police was led by federal and state civilian defense initiatives during World War II and the Korean War, when the shortage of males at the homefront helped to deplete the ranks of the regular police. For several decades following World War II, auxiliaries generally received less training than reserves and were given assignments that involve "observation and reporting." This has been the case in New York City since 1951. On the other hand, reserves have been provided more extensive training and are given a wider range of duties that may include working crime scenes and assisting with drug and traffic accident investigations. Unlike some auxiliary police units, reserves are typically armed. Furthermore, in agencies that meet Commission on Accreditation for Law Enforcement Agencies

(CALEA) standards, sworn volunteer police officers must receive the same training as regular police officers.

In 1973, the first recommended standards for reserve officers appeared in the *Report on Police* presented by the National Advisory Commission on Criminal Justice Standards and Goals. The Commission recommended that every state immediately establish minimum standards for reserve officer training and selection. In particular, it urged that reserve training programs meet or exceed state standards that regulate the training of regular, part-time, or reserve officers. Significantly, standards for auxiliaries were omitted. But the fact remains that in some jurisdictions, auxiliary police officers may still be used in the same manner as reserves. Presently, however, progress appears to be in the direction of both auxiliaries and reserves achieving sworn status and training parity with regular police, thus making the two titles equivalent. An example of this trend has occurred in Virginia. The Virginia State Code 15.2–1731 provides for the use of auxiliary officers. The City of Williamsburg has declared that the term *auxiliary* is synonymous with *reserve* for compliance with CALEA stanzards. The use of these terms is often seen in many localities where the names changed back and forth over time.

One of the earliest and largest reserve police programs was established in February 1918 when 600 commissioned officers of the "Citizens Home Defense League of the City of New York" voted to change its name to "Police Reserves of the City of New York." At the height of the reserves' activities, there were 14,000 members. Old photographs depict units wearing olive drab-colored uniforms and campaign hats in the style of army soldiers of that era. There were machine gun, rifle, motor boat, women's, and aviation units and divisions. Numerous auxiliary/reserve units were developed during World War II and the cold war that followed.

The duties of these individuals vary from place to place. For example, several Southern California law enforcement agencies have also developed successful technical reserve programs in order to tap the technical expertise of citizens. The Los Angeles County Sheriff's Department uses technical reserves in its Motion Picture Unit. In 1993, the unit was composed of more than 100 members from the community's television and film industries. The unit has produced training films and has filmed special events. Because of the nature of this work, such volunteers are not sworn officers and do not carry firearms. The West Des Moines Police Reserve Unit performs general support for the police department, and it offers participants an excellent opportunity to learn about policing. The reserves conduct surveillance, serve as a second officer in a two-officer patrol unit, assist with criminal investigations, and provide additional help at community events. In River Grove, Illinois, 11 part-time and 30 auxiliary officers help patrol the community, transport prisoners, and fill in on holidays and during village festivals and parades. They use their own funds to purchase equipment and must attend extensive training sessions. Hundreds of such organizations exist, many of which maintain Web sites.

As a result of the September 11, 2001, attacks, President Bush called upon Americans in 2002 to get directly involved in homeland defense by volunteering to help with local first-responder organizations, such as fire, police, and rescue units. At the time, he established a new Citizen Corps to encourage participation. This renewed attention may have come just in time for many of the nation's auxiliary and police reserve programs. For example, in 1995, there were nearly 10,000 reserve officers in California, but by 2000, that number had dropped to about 6,500. According to Frank Decker, a law enforcement consultant for the California POST, "People don't have as much time as they used to. You have both husband and wife working and trying to take care of the family."

*Martin Alan Greenberg*

*See also* Volunteers

### For Further Reading

Brown, W. F., Jr. (1993). Technical reserve program: Community volunteers in action. *FBI Law Enforcement Bulletin, 62*(3), 10–11.

Greenberg, M. A. (1984). *Auxiliary police: The citizen's approach to public safety.* Westport, CT: Greenwood.

Greenberg, M. A. (2001). *The evolution of volunteer police in America.* Unpublished doctoral dissertation, City University of New York.

Kirchner, R. W. (1992). Looking for a challenge? Try being a cop. *Medical Economics, 69*(9), 197–201.

Parrilla, L. (2002, December 12). Ranks of reserves dwindle. *Ventura County Star,* p. A1.

Sobieraj, S. (2002, January 31). Bush asks Americans to volunteer. *The Daily Gazette,* p. A4.

Weinblatt, R. (2001). Reserves aid rural counties. *Law and Order, 49*(1), 30–32.

# B

## ✑ BALLISTICS

Ballistics is the area of forensic science that deals with the study of firearms, ammunition, and bullet trajectory (flight path). Firearms include handguns (revolvers or semiautomatics), rifles, and shotguns. Much of ballistics involves what happens when a weapon is fired. Pulling the trigger of a firearm causes its firing pin to strike the primer that is located at the base of the cartridge. The ignition of the primer detonates gunpowder within the cartridge, resulting in its conversion into a gas. The rapid increase in pressure within the cartridge causes the bullet to simultaneously expand and be propelled through the barrel of the gun.

The barrel of a firearm is manufactured with helical grooves carved into its inner surface. As a result, most of the barrel contains *lands* and *grooves*. Lands refer to the high points of the inner surface between adjacent grooves. The spiraled grooves cause the bullet to rotate laterally as it is propelled through the barrel. The imparted spin of the bullet helps provide stability and prevent wobbling or tumbling as it traverses through the air with minimal loss of velocity and without changing direction along its trajectory. Twist refers to the length of the barrel per revolution. Twist can be left- or right-handed, and the barrel may be tooled with different numbers of grooves. The caliber of a gun and its

ammunition refers to the internal diameter of the barrel. It is usually expressed in fractions of an inch (e.g., 0.38-caliber) or in millimeters (e.g., 9 mm). At times, the examiner may not be able to characterize a bullet that has become severely deformed as a result of having struck a hard object. Instead, the bullet can be weighed. The number of grains can be used to determine its caliber (1.0 grain = 1/7000 of a pound). All of the above factors are called *class* characteristics and are used to describe the barrel and bullets fired from a firearm. A barrel with six right-handed grooves would create a bullet with six striations with a right-handed twist.

It should be no surprise that a bullet in flight does not travel in a straight line. The bullet must obey the laws of physics. In addition to the forces propelling the bullet forward, the force of gravity simultaneously pulls the bullet downward. The bullet's velocity (measured in feet per second, or feet/sec) is affected by a number of factors, including the frictional forces caused by the air. Some bullets, because of their shape and design, are more aerodynamic and will have less drag than a blunt-nosed or irregularly shaped bullet. A bullet's velocity depends in part on the amount of drag present. A bullet that has a larger mass and is more aerodynamically designed will travel faster than one with smaller mass and/or an irregular shape. Wind can also have an effect on a bullet's trajectory by causing the bullet to drift. The *ballistic coefficient* is a number that reflects a bullet's length, diameter, and shape and indicates its ability to overcome air resistance. A ballistic coefficient of 1.0 indicates that this bullet will retain its velocity and energy, and exhibit a relatively flat trajectory, which is an ideal characteristic when the target is at a relatively far distance. Most bullets have coefficients between 0.7 and 1.0. The shape of the bullet can affect not only its maximum speed, but also its penetrating power and degree of destruction of the target.

Muzzle velocity is the velocity of the bullet in feet/sec measured at 15" from the muzzle. The kinetic energy of a bullet in flight is the amount of work done by this bullet over a given distance and is expressed in foot-pounds in the English system. It is calculated as the mass of the projectile in grains times the square of the velocity (feet/sec)$^2$ divided by 450,400. *Magnum* refers to a cartridge that produces higher energy than what is expected for its bore size.

The firearms examiner is often asked to determine if a bullet was fired from a particular weapon or if two bullets match in their microscopic characteristics and therefore were fired from the same gun. As the bullet is propelled through the barrel in an expanded state, markings are created on the lead or its copper jacket as its surface is pressed against the spiraled grooves within the barrel. These *striations* are created as a direct result of the bullet moving across the lands and grooves of the barrel. Microscopic imperfections (nicks, scratches, and scrapes) in the barrel created by machining of the steel barrel in the process of forming the grooves will also result in unique impressions on the surface of the bullet. These striations are considered to be *individualizing* characteristics. In fact, two guns manufactured consecutively on an assembly line can be differentiated from one another by the minute imperfections present in the grooves.

The firearms examiner can learn a great deal from observation of the cartridge casing. Pulling the trigger of a gun or rifle causes the firing pin to hit the primer at the base of the shell casing, leaving an impression on either the rim or the center of the base depending on the type of firearm and ammunition (rimfire or centerfire). The firing pin impression—breechface

marks formed when the casing is propelled backward, striking the breechface of the gun—extraction, ejection, and chamber marks are all helpful in matching bullets and in identifying a particular firearm. These markings on the bullet and shell casing can help to determine if a particular gun was used to fire this ammunition. Bullets and shell casings can be compared using a compound comparison microscope. The examiner can reach one of three possible conclusions: identification (two bullets match, two shell casings match, a bullet or shell casing matches the weapon); exclusion (nonmatch); or undetermined.

Handgun and rifle ammunition is referred to as a cartridge or a round and consists of four parts: the casing, primer, powder, and projectile or bullet. The bullet can be molded lead alone or lead combined with a metal jacket. Bullets can be manufactured in the form of *full metal jacket* (jacketed lead does not expand and penetrates more easily and deeply than simple lead); *jacketed hollow point* (exposed lead at the tip of the bullet will expand down to the depth of the cavity and can mushroom or break up like shrapnel); *semijacketed hollow point* (has more exposed lead than the latter); *full metal cone* (lead core is enclosed in a copper jacket that has a cone shape and a flat point); *soft point* (exposed lead that expands when target is struck); *wadcutter* (solid lead with flat nose, used for target shooting); *lead semiwadcutter* (solid lead with semipointed nose and sharp shoulder); and *round-nosed lead* (solid lead with rounded face).

Bullets designed for rifles may have a full metal jacket (heavy copper jacket—little or no expansion, good penetration); or a full metal jacket with a boat tail (designed with a tapered base to reduce drag). The bullets may be hollow point with a boat tail (HPBT—hollow point with aerodynamic design), or soft point (exposed lead tip—expands upon hitting target). AP ammunition refers to armor-piercing rounds.

Shotgun ammunition includes shot, buckshot, and slugs. Shot particles come in sizes ranging from 0.22 inches (5.59 mm) to 0.08 inches (2.03 mm). Buckshot particles range in diameter from 0.36 inches (9.14 mm—No. 000) to 0.24 inches (6.10 mm—No. 4). They are also designated by numbers in a range including No. 000, 00, 0, 1, 2, 3, and 4 (largest to smallest). Slugs can be either rifled or nonrifled.

The firearms examiner may be asked to determine if a particular person fired a gun, the location from which the gun was fired, or the distance between muzzle and target. Analysis of the pattern of gunshot residue (GSR) on the target can sometimes help establish the distance. GSR pattern analysis is especially helpful when the muzzle of the gun was less than 18 inches from the target. The shorter the distance, the denser the distribution of particles within the pattern and the smaller the overall size of the pattern. When the distance exceeds 2 feet, there may be no GSR on the target, or there may be so little that a pattern cannot be discerned.

Gunshot residue (GSR) can be found on anything in the vicinity of a gun when it has been fired, especially the muzzle and ejection port. GSR is produced primarily from the primer components of most cartridges. The most common technique for collection of GSR from clothing or skin is the tape lift method. The particles of GSR can be analyzed using scanning electron microscopy to examine size (0.5–200 microns) and morphology (usually spherical), and an elemental detection method such as energy dispersive X-ray microanalysis (EDX). GSR particles contain relatively large amounts of barium, antimony, and lead and may also contain aluminum and copper. Because GSR can be found in a pattern, it is important not only to identify the characteristic particles, but also to determine the distribution that they form. The pattern is influenced by firearm characteristics such as barrel length, caliber, and type of ammunition.

Black gunpowder, which is unstable, has been replaced by smokeless powder as the preferred propellant. The former leaves a great deal of residue in the gun barrel, unlike the latter. Single-base smokeless gun powder contains nitrocellulose and up to 23 organic compounds, most of which contain nitrate or nitrogen. Double-base powder contains nitrocellulose and nitroglycerine. Triple-base powder contains nitroguanidine in addition to nitrocellulose and nitroglycerine. Although methods exist to determine the presence of nitrates in a questioned GSR sample, interpretation is made more difficult by the ubiquity of nitrates in the environment. The Walker test, developed in the 1940s, chemically detects the presence of nitrites. The modified Griess test detects nitrites and can also be used to determine distance from muzzle to target by examining the pattern of nitrite on the item. In this test, a photographic paper is exposed to a hypo solution so that it is no longer sensitive to light. It is then treated with a mixture of sulfanilic acid in distilled water and alphanaphthol in methanol. The treated photographic paper is now placed adjacent to an item of clothing (or other substrate) suspected of bearing the GSR. The back of the item is then steam ironed with a dilute acetic acid solution in the iron rather than water. The vaporized acetic acid penetrates the item and causes a reaction between the nitrite on the item and the chemicals on the photographic paper, resulting in the appearance of orange specks on the paper. Sodium rhodizonate can be used to test for the presence of lead on the item. The item is sprayed with a solution of sodium rhodizonate prepared in distilled water. The item appears yellow to orange in color. After a buffer solution is sprayed on the item, the background color disappears, and any lead turns bright pink. The area is now treated with dilute hydrochloric acid, HCl, and the pink color becomes blue, confirming the presence of lead.

A procedure has been developed to determine if an individual has held a gun in his or her hand. Pyridyldiphenyl triazine can be sprayed on the palm of the hand to reveal impressions made by metallic parts of the weapon. The pattern appears as magenta-colored marks on the palm.

Once the bullet hits its target, it can either ricochet or penetrate. When the target is human, the pathologist determines the entry and exit wound, if it exists; the distance the victim was from the muzzle (contact, intermediate [up to 2 feet], or distant); the course of the bullet; and damage produced from the point of entry to the point of exit (or its location in situ). Visually, one may see soot or stippling (small specks of gunshot residue) and bullet wipe at the entrance site. Bullet wipe appears as a ring containing substances such as lead, carbon, dirt, and lubricants that are transferred from the bullet as it penetrates the target. To verify the muzzle-to-target distance, the same gun should be test fired at targets placed at varying distances. GSR patterns can then be compared.

Bullets and cartridge casings found at crime scenes involving shootings with either handguns or rifles are now computerized and added to a federal database operated by the FBI and the Bureau of Alcohol, Tobacco and Firearms (ATF). This database is known as the National Integrated Ballistics Information Network (NIBIN). NIBIN combines the FBI's Drugfire database with the ATF's Integrated Ballistics Information System (IBIS) database, both of which were introduced in 1993. Currently, hundreds of thousands of digitized images of bullets and shell casings are currently in this database and accessible to ballistics labs throughout the United States. This national database is especially useful when crimes are committed in different jurisdictions or across state lines. If the computer indicates a hit, individual examiners can review the findings and draw their own conclusions. The examiner can also use firearm reference software that can provide many characteristics (manufacturer, make, model name, caliber, ammunition capacity, etc.), including images of more than 2,000 firearms.

*Lawrence Kobilinsky*

*See also* Forensic Science, Weapons

### For Further Reading

Heramb, R. B., & McCord, B. R. (2002). The manufacture of smokeless powders and their forensic analysis: A brief review. *Forensic Science Communications, 4*(2). Available: http://www.fbi.gov/hq/lab/fsc/current/mccord.htm

Leifer, A., Avissar, Y., Berger, S., Wax, H., Donchin, Y., & Almog, J. (2001). Detection of firearm imprints on the hands of suspects: Effectiveness of PDT reaction. *Journal of Forensic Science 46*(6), 1442–1446.

http://members.aye.net/~bspen/ballistics.html

http://www.eskimo.com/~jbm/ballistics/cdkd.html

http://www.firearmsid.com/A_distanceExams.htm

## ◎◎ BODY ARMOR

Deputy Sheriff Isaac Smith, the first law enforcement officer to lose his life in the line of duty, was fatally shot in 1792. Yet it was not until April 2, 1931, that one of the first demonstrations of ballistic wear for the personal protection of law enforcement personnel was documented by Washington, D.C.'s *Evening Star.* Unfortunately, most ballistic-resistant designs of the time were neither effective nor practical for everyday police use.

Due to the dramatic rise in officer fatalities from handguns during the 1960s, the National Institute of Law Enforcement and Criminal Justice, predecessor of the National Institute of Justice (NIJ), instituted a program to create lightweight body armor for police personnel. In the 1970s, government researchers Lester Shubin and Nicholas Montanarelli tested DuPont's new Kevlar® plastic fabric (invented to replace steel belting in radial tires) for its ballistic resistance potential. Kevlar® proved successful in repelling bullets and quickly became incorporated into an Army prototype developed in 1973.

Fabricated from seven layers of fabric, the Kevlar® vest was designed to protect police officers against bullet penetration and blunt trauma injuries incurred from their most common threats, the .38 special and .22 long rifle. In 1975, the vest succeeded in an extensive field test to assess its effectiveness and wearability by not interfering with professional duties, physical movement, or personal comfort. Moreover, it saved 18 officers' lives and ensured a 95% chance of survival if shot with a .38 caliber bullet at 800 feet/sec velocity.

Today, there are two major categories of body armor: ballistic-resistant and stab- (or puncture-) resistant. Stab-resistant armor is often worn by members of the corrections community to meet the unique knife threats these officers face on a daily basis. Ballistic-resistant armor is further divided into two main groups. Concealable soft body armor, worn routinely as undergarments by law enforcement officers in the line of duty, is designed for protection against handgun bullets. Nonconcealable or tactical body armor is generally a hard armor outer garment worn by Special Weapons and Tactics teams for protection against rifle and pistol bullets. Although models differ in fabric, design, features, construction, and assembly, ballistic-resistant garments are generally constructed from multiple layers of protective fabric in order to absorb and disperse the energy from a bullet's impact over the entire area of a vest to prevent penetration and reduce the harmful effects of blunt trauma.

Ballistic-resistant body armor is commonly referred to as "bulletproof." However, neither concealable nor nonconcealable armor is designed to offer full protection against every caliber bullet at all velocities and ranges. Moreover, because most armor designs are vestlike in nature, much of an officer's body remains vulnerable to attack. Fortuitously, ballistic armor has also demonstrated nonballistic benefits in preventing serious, and potentially fatal, injury from automobile accidents and physical assault, and some protection against knives.

The NIJ's *Ballistic Resistance of Personal Body Armor* serves as the national standard for police professionals and industry manufacturers. It is accepted worldwide for establishing minimum performance requirements for personal body armor. Originated by the Office of Law Enforcement Standards of the National Institute of Standards and Technology, and produced as part of the Law Enforcement and Corrections Standards and Testing Program, these standards are based on the laboratory testing and performance evaluation of representative samples supplied by manufacturers.

After four revisions over 28 years, the current NIJ Standard-0110.04 for ballistic armor was published in September 2000. It delineates seven performance levels demonstrated to protect against clearly outlined degrees of ballistic threat based on bullet composition, shape, caliber, mass, angle of incidence, and impact velocity. Although these standards are voluntary, most police units require officers to wear NIJ-compliant armor. The National Law Enforcement and Corrections Technology Center (NLECTC) administers a compliance testing program for personal ballistic products through independent, NIJ-accredited laboratories. Comprehensive listings of compliant models are available online through the NLECTC's Justice Technology Information Network.

Because of the complexity involved in selecting police protective wear, NIJ's *Selection and Application Guide to Personal Body Armor* assists state and local agencies in matching departmental threat levels to NIJ protection levels. The *Selection Guide* includes discussions of climate, sidearms and ammunition, and style and personal fit in order to encourage the routine, full-time use of armor by all on-duty law enforcement officers. Generalized care and maintenance information is incorporated along with a strong appeal for the institutionalized practice of routine inspection of all departmental armor. This point is fittingly illustrated by the replacement of 1,000 defective vests in 2003 issued to the NYPD because one officer noticed that his vest lost resiliency when wrinkled. Departmental and independent laboratory tests confirmed that the vests were defective.

The FBI estimates that protected officers are 14 times more likely than nonprotected officers to survive a firearms assault. Although the statistics are convincing, the everyday wear rate for on-duty officers is estimated to be as low as 42% and as high as 72%. Moreover, no mandatory vest policy exists across state or local lines, and many agencies neither supply nor finance protective armor for their officers. In 2000, only 77% of local departments supplied vests to their officers, only 56% required all field officers to wear protective armor, and only 6% allocated a cash allowance toward the individual purchase of police vests.

The federal government shares the goal of saving officers' lives by promoting the use of personal body armor. The Bulletproof Vest Partnership Grant Acts of 1998 and 2000 allow state, local, and tribal law enforcement agencies to purchase NIJ-approved armor for half the manufacturers' price. Federal surplus NIJ-compliant armor is donated to state and local officers through the James Guelff and Chris McCurley Body Armor Act of 2002. A growing threat to the police community exists in the criminal use of ballistic protection. At least 28 states currently possess statutes against the use of armor during the commission of a crime. The federal government, through the Guelff and McCurley Body Armor Act of 2002, provides legislative assistance through enhanced sentencing and criminalizing both the use of armor by violent felons and armor trafficking across state lines.

*Barbara Goldman Carrel*

**See also** Assaults on Police, Ballistics

*For Further Reading*

Bureau of Justice Statistics. (2003). *Local police departments 2000.* Washington, DC: Author.

*National body armor survey.* (1991). New York: City University of New York, John Jay College of Criminal Justice and Strategic Polling Corporation.

National Institute of Justice. (2002a). *Ballistic resistance of personal body armor.* Washington, DC: Author.

National Institute of Justice. (2002b). *Stab resistance of personal body armor.* Washington, DC: Author.

National Law Enforcement and Corrections Technology Center. (2001). *Selection and application guide to personal body armor.* Rockville, MD: Author.

Westrick, A. J. (1998). Surviving "fatal" encounters: An analysis of violence involving police officers wearing body armor, their situational definitions, interactional experience and symptoms of post-traumatic stress disorder (Doctoral dissertation, Wayne State University, 1998). *Dissertation Abstracts International,* 9915750.

## ᏇᎦ BOMBS AND BOMB SQUADS

The history and development of bomb disposal squads in the United States are scarred by injury, death, and lawsuits. In fact, change or advancement has usually been the unfortunate by-product of a major injury or death. Currently, approximately 440 of these specialized units exist in the United States (approximately 405 police department units and 35 fire department units) that are responsible for the detection and rendering safe of Improvised Explosive Devices (IEDs), hazardous materials, and weapons of mass destruction. In total, approximately 2,300 certified bomb technicians in the United States have graduated the elite Hazardous Devices School (HDS) at the Redstone Arsenal, Huntsville, Alabama, which has been administrated by the Federal Bureau of Investigation since 1971. Approximately 125 women have successfully completed the HDS training, and approximately 42 females are active certified bomb technicians in the United States. The majority of these bomb technicians perform other full-time police or fire duties and are on-call for these specialized calls. These technicians must maintain proficiency with the use of x-ray equipment and interpretation, robot manipulation (217 bomb squads have robots), bomb suit

use, water cannons or disrupters deployment, explosive detection canine development and use, and a variety of other detection and disruption tools. Current intelligence information updates regarding terrorist methods and devices are essential for the successful deployment of a bomb squad response team. The New York City Police Department Bomb Squad, which is the oldest and largest bomb squad in the United States, celebrated its 100th anniversary in 2003 and is currently staffed with approximately 42 full-time bomb technicians.

Prior to 1971, responsibility for handling IEDs, except in a few major metropolitan areas, was given to the United States Armed Forces Explosive Ordnance Disposal (EOD) units. Based on the increase of radical and terrorist bombings in the 1960s and 1970s, the federal government—in the form of the Law Enforcement Assistance Administration—and public safety agencies—in the form of the International Association of Chiefs of Police—entered into agreements to respond to this urgent situation. The International Association of Bomb Technicians and Investigators was founded in 1973 with a charter mandate to maintain and enhance the professionalism of bomb technicians and bomb crime scene investigators.

Selection and training of U.S. bomb technicians has evolved from an informal process of trial and error at several municipal police agencies to a rigorous, professional, and national selection, training, and certification program under the aegis of the Federal Bureau of Investigation. Instruction subjects include chemistry, electricity, electronics, explosives, and terrorist methods and operations. Graduates from HDS must survive a battery of physical tests, written exams, and hands-on clinical "real" problems, rendering safe IEDs both remotely and with hand-entry techniques. These requirements, curriculum, and standards establish and define these bomb technicians as a truly professional group that possesses both a unique argot and a specialized professional practice.

The improvised explosive device or bomb is the threat object that bomb response teams most often confront. The most common IED in the United States is a pipe bomb. Available data indicate that between 1973 and 1998, 43,776 actual and attempted bombing incidents were reported in the United States. The single highest reporting year was 1994, with 3,163 incidents. Between 1980 and 1999, there were 272 terrorist incidents, plus 55 suspected terrorist incidents and 130 terrorism incidents that were prevented. Between 1981 and 2001, there were 2,939 U.S. citizen casualties resulting from international terrorism. What makes the IED so dangerous is that it is unpredictable. As opposed to military ordinance, which are manufactured to meet government standards and for which detailed information regarding descriptions and methods for disarming is published in government texts, IEDs are fabricated by unknown bombmakers whose knowledge and skills can range from poor to excellent or novice to expert. The IEDs may not even perform in the manner the designer intended. This makes the rendering safe of these devices by the bomb disposal teams very dangerous and requires investigative and assessment skills to design a response plan that provides maximum safety for both the general public and the bomb technicians. Usually before the bomb technician attempts a render-safe procedure, the area near the IED is evacuated to a minimum of 1,000 feet. If the bomb squad arrives after a bomb has exploded, they are usually tasked with the postblast crime scene investigation. This requires specially designed techniques for searching for evidence at a bombing scene. Bomb technicians practice procedures attempting to find the parts that remain after an IED has functioned.

*William F. McCarthy*

**See also** Emergency Services Units

## For Further Reading

Gadson, L., Michael, M., & Walsh, N. (2003). *FBI Bomb Data Center: 1999 bombing incidents general information bulletin 99-1*. Quantico, VA: Federal Bureau of Investigation.

Jernigan, D., & LaBrusciano, M. (1994). Bomb squads: Developing mutual aid agreements. *FBI Law Enforcement Bulletin, 63*(10), 18–21.

Klein, H., & Vorst, M. (2001). *Containment devices for small terrorist bombs for law enforcement* (Final report). Washington, DC: National Institute of Justice.

Strandberg, K. (1998). Bomb squads. *Law Enforcement Technology, 25*(6), 42–44.

## ❧ BONDSMAN OR BAIL AGENT

Bail is the means by which the U.S. criminal justice system permits the release of a defendant from custody while ensuring his appearance at all required court proceedings. Bail (from the French *bailler,* to deliver) is the legacy of Anglo-Saxon jurisprudence wherein defendants were delivered to their sureties, who gave security for their appearance. Current practice allows a number of kinds of bail, the most common of which are the following:

1. Deposit bail, usually 10% of the face amount of the bond, deposited with the court, returnable to the defendant upon making required appearances.

2. Own recognizance release, wherein the defendant is released on his or her promise to appear, but liable for the full amount of the bail should he or she default in appearing.

3. Financially secured release through a commercial surety, called a bondsman or bail agent. (The commercial bond approach is by far the most effective, as demonstrated in a Bureau of Statistics study that compared commercial bonding with all other pretrial release methods in getting defendants to court.)

This entry focuses on the third method of bail and the role of the bail agent. Bail bonds initially were put up by people who pledged their own property as security for the bond. They became known as "property bondsmen." This genre still exists in a limited fashion in a few southern states, but it is becoming a thing of the past because most states prefer the uniformity of regulation and collection certainties where corporate sureties are employed. Hence, the following information will focus on the bail agent, who is a professional retail bond writer and who generally operates as an independent contractor using a surety company's credentials in posting his or her client's appearance bond.

When a person is arrested on probable cause of having committed a criminal offense, he or she is incarcerated and booked into a detention facility. Bail is determined by a preset bail schedule or by a magistrate prior to arraignment. A bail agent is contacted, and he or she arranges to post the defendant's bail, whereupon the defendant is released. The bail agent charges the defendant a premium (usually 10% of the bond) for assuming the risk of the defendant's not appearing. If the defendant fails to appear, the court declares the bond forfeited and the bail agent, usually after getting an opportunity to recover the absconded defendant, has to pay the forfeiture, which constitutes the full amount of the bond. (In addition, most jurisdictions permit revocation, which allows the agent to return the defendant to custody before the court date in order for the agent to avoid liability. This may require the agent to return the premium to the defendant.)

Bail is a straightforward procedure, but can be complicated by a number of factors. Bail is both a criminal and civil matter. The bond is an integral part of a criminal case, but attempts to collect breaches of the bond's conditions are strictly civil in nature. Furthermore, significant statutory variation, involving bail forfeiture, exoneration, remission, and fugitive recovery, vary from state to state, within political subdivisions of states, and between federal and state criminal justice systems. In addition, there are a myriad of differences in local court rules, practices, forms, and procedures. Many states regulate commercial bail through their departments of insurance. A bail insurance company must qualify for admission in each state under the same standards as any other insurance company. Some states even require a company to maintain funds on deposit with the insurance department as a hedge against forfeitures. Other states leave administration of bail to local sheriffs, courts, judges, or bail bond boards.

Most states regard bail as a form of insurance. Hence, bail agents are licensed and regulated like any other insurance producer, subject to certain basic qualifications and prelicensing and continuing education requirements. Most states also require bail agents to be appointed by an admitted bail insurance company. In addition, some states require that the bail agent be certified by a bail insurance company with a "qualified power of attorney," the purpose of which is to confer limited authority on the agent to execute bonds (usually for a specified amount).

The relationship between the bail agent and the surety, that is, the bail insurance company, is of a contractual nature wherein the surety allows the agent to use, for a fee, the surety's financial standing and credit as security on bonds. In addition, the contract also specifies that the agent is an independent contractor whose customers and risks are his or her own. The bonds he or she writes are his or her own and not those of the surety. Furthermore, the bail agent is bound to hold the surety harmless for any loss, costs, or damages on bonds written.

If the defendant fails to appear, thus violating the bail bond's primary condition, the bond is declared forfeited. The specific procedure whereby the bond is forfeited and judgment entered against the bail agent varies widely from jurisdiction to jurisdiction. Many jurisdictions allow the agent time to apprehend and surrender the defendant before the forfeiture judgment has to be paid. Courts can also set aside forfeiture judgments if there is good cause why the defendant did not appear.

A bail agent is exonerated from liability on a bail bond when it has been revoked or its conditions have been met. In most cases, this takes place when the defendant makes all required court appearances, is convicted or acquitted, pleads guilty or nolo, or the charges are dropped.

Bail agents perform an extraordinarily valuable public service to law enforcement and accused people alike. The Bail Clause of the Eighth Amendment to the Constitution embodies the long-standing Anglo-American tradition of favoring pretrial release of accused people. This frees up crowded jail space and permits defendants to participate more fully in their own defense. Bail agents, backed by the financial resources of surety insurance companies, make possible the pretrial release of in excess of 2 million defendants annually, at no expense to taxpayers, by providing assurances to the state that the people charged with crimes will appear as scheduled to answer charges.

*Dennis Alan Bartlett*

***See also*** Bounty Hunters

*For Further Reading*

Blackstone, W. (1979). *Commentaries on the laws of England* (Vol. 3). Chicago: University of Chicago Press.

U.S. Bureau of Justice Statistics. (1994, November). *Pretrial release of felony defendants, 1992* (NCJ–148818). Washington, DC: Author.

Watson, J. W., & Labe, L. J. (2001). Bail bonds. In American Bar Association (Ed.), *The law of miscellaneous and commercial surety bonds* (pp. 127–142). Chicago: American Bar Association.

http://www.americanbailcoalition.com

# ⁊ BOUNTY HUNTER

A person arrested on probable cause of having committed a crime is entitled to bail (except for a capital crime) under the Eighth Amendment. If the person charged, called a principal, is released from jail through the services of a bail agent, he or she is released from detention but is not "free"; only the conditions of confinement have changed. The principal has paid the bail agent a premium for posting the bond and assuming the risk of his or her not appearing in court. The purpose of the bond is to ensure that the principal appears in court to answer the charges pending and, in the interim, to allow the principal to resume the semblance of as normal a life as possible and help in the preparation of his or her defense. In terms of the obligation to appear, the principal is in the custody of a bail agent, who has promised the court that the principal will appear, or the bail agent will have to forfeit the amount of the bond. Hence, the bail agent has a financial incentive to see that his or her charge appears in court at the proper time.

If the principal fails to make the court appearance, unless there are mitigating circumstances, he or she is declared a fugitive, a warrant is issued for his or her arrest, and the bond is forfeited. In most jurisdictions, the bail agent has an interval (called a "time certain period" that varies widely from state to state, for example, as much as 10 days to 10 years) within which to return the absconded principal to court before being required to pay the forfeiture.

Most bail agents operate established places of business that hinder their dropping all other business in order to pursue an absconder. Therefore, the bail agent appoints and contracts with a person qualified to pursue and arrest the absconded principal. The Supreme Court has long upheld the right of the bail agent or his or her appointee to apprehend the principal.

> [The bail agent or bounty hunter] Whenever they choose to do so may seize him [the fugitive] and deliver him up in their discharge; and if that cannot be done at once, they may imprison him until it can be done. They may pursue him into another State; may arrest him on the Sabbath; and, if necessary, may break and enter his house for that purpose. The seizure is not made by virtue of new process. None is needed. It is likened to the rearrest by the sheriff of an escaping prisoner. (*Taylor v. Taintor,* 1872)

Furthermore, the courts have made clear that this authority can be delegated.

> I see nothing, on general principles, against allowing this power to be exercised by an agent or deputy; and no case is to be found where the right has been denied. . . . The law recognizes the act of an authorized agent as equal to that of the principal [the bail agent]. (*Nicolls v. Ingersoll,* 1810)

The person who pursues the fugitive on behalf of the bail agent is called a bounty hunter or bail recovery agent. Some states require that bounty hunters be licensed, but others do not. Some states prohibit bounty hunters. Statutes regulating a bail fugitive recovery vary widely throughout the United States (see www.americanbailcoalition.com and go to the Compendium of Bounty Hunter Laws).

For the most part, bounty hunters work for bail agents under contract on a case-by-case basis, getting paid a percentage of the amount of the bond, but only if they recover the absconder. Many defendants miss a court date because of neglect or fright. Most of these voluntarily return to court after nothing more than a reminder. A large percentage of missing absconders will be found at their homes or jobs. Some will be found at the homes of friends. Others, facing the consequences of a serious crime, will try to run away to avoid settling up with the criminal justice system. This is a difficult and expensive choice because it is almost impossible to disappear without a trace in modern American society.

Invariably, because the absconder finds it difficult to change his or her lifestyle, or to sever ties with family, friends, and material possessions, he or she will leave a trail that ultimately leads back to him or her. In order to apprehend the fugitive, the bounty hunter must first find him or her, a process called skip tracing. Essentially, bounty hunting is an intellectual exercise. With the exception of the apprehension, most of the bounty hunter's effort is detective work dedicated to tracking down the missing principal. The bounty hunter's most useful tools are simple household appliances such as the telephone and an Internet-linked computer. Furthermore, a number of databases are easily accessible, such as motor vehicle, traffic ticket, postal, property, court, and police records, as well as fugitive files. After locating the runaway, the bounty hunter must take the fugitive into custody. This is the most dangerous part of the bounty-hunting process, even though, in most cases, no resistance is offered. The next step is to take the fugitive back to jail. Once the fugitive is back in police custody, the bond is exonerated and the bail agent is free from the liability under the bond. In spite of media sensationalism about bounty hunter abuses, the reality is that there are very few instances of ill treatment at the hands of bounty hunters.

Bounty hunters are a part of the bail bond system and perform an extraordinarily valuable public service to law enforcement. Bounty hunters are credited with recovering approximately 35,000 fugitives annually. Without their efforts, these fugitives would either remain at large, or significant state and local police resources would need to be diverted from other law enforcement activities to secure their capture. In short, the system works well, returning many fugitives to custody at no cost to the government.

*Dennis Alan Bartlett*

**See also** Bail Agents

Burton, B. (1984). *Bounty hunter.* Boulder, CO: Paladin.
Burton, B. (1990). *Bail enforcer: The advanced bounty hunter.* Boulder, CO: Paladin.
Nicolls v. Ingersoll, 7 Johns. 145, 154 (N.Y. 1810).
Taylor v. Taintor, 83 U.S. (16 Wall.) 366, 21 L. Ed. 287 (1872).
http://www.americanbailcoalition.com
http://www.bounty-hunter.net/home.htm

# "BROKEN WINDOWS" OR INCIVILITIES THESIS

The term *incivilities thesis* refers to a family of closely related, exploratory, problem-solving techniques about the roles played by misdemeanors, uncivil and rowdy behaviors, some delinquent acts, and lack of property and facilities maintenance in urban communities (Taylor, 1999, 2001). Over the past quarter century, theorists and policymakers have enlarged the scope and nature of these roles. During this period of theoretical elaboration, advocates of this perspective have suggested relevant outcomes affected include individual and community fear levels, and changes therein; community crime rates, and changes in those rates; and whether neighborhoods remain stable or enter or accelerate a period of decline.

This entry describes this theoretical growth process in brief; outlines shifting reasons behind its popularity; summarizes some criticisms made of these ideas; points to some ongoing areas of conceptual confusion; and highlights relevant, empirical supporting evidence.

## ORIGINS AND DEVELOPMENT

The seed sprouted in the mid-1970s. Urban civil disorders of the 1960s had raised concerns about citizens' safety and law enforcement in major cities, concerns reflected in the Kerner Commission report (1968), and giving rise to the Crime Control Act and the Law Enforcement Assistance Administration, a precursor of the current National Institute of Justice. Results were coming in from the first series of national victimization surveys. These interviews also asked about fear of crime.

The surveys showed that the number of those fearful of crime far outstripped the number of crime victims. Those reporting higher fear levels lived in cities. When broken down demographically by gender and some simple age categories, researchers learned that those most fearful (elderly women) were least likely to be victimized, whereas those least fearful (young males) were most likely to be victimized.

James Q. Wilson, a political scientist and policy scholar, suggested in 1975 that people were afraid of disorder, not just crime. He argued that disorders, which were much more ubiquitous than crime, were what caused high fear levels. Thus, the kernel of the thesis emerged.

Other researchers over the next 5 years elaborated the idea. "Fear of crime" was more than "fear" of "crime" (Garofalo & Laub, 1978). It was not just that urban residents in some areas were surrounded with disorder; such conditions implied that public officials or agencies could not or would not bother to fix things (Hunter, 1978).

Initial discussions of disorder included both physical features of the neighborhood and features of street life. The list of relevant features is potentially quite lengthy and, as will be noted later, dependent upon who is making the list. Nonetheless, relevant physical features typically included abandoned houses; vacant lots, especially if they were weedy and/or trash-filled; abandoned, burned-out, or stripped cars; shuttered stores; properties or yards inadequately maintained; houses in poor structural condition; litter; graffiti; and streets, sidewalks, or streetlights in need of repair. Later, following the "crack invasion" of the mid to late 1980s, discarded crack vials or syringes were added to the list. Also added after the crack invasion were relevant behaviors by groups of rowdy and lewd unsupervised teens, "hey honey" hassles, public drinking or drunkenness, public drug sales or drug use, and neighbors fighting or arguing on the streets. With increased homelessness in the 1980s, problems such as public urination, panhandling, or just the presence of the homeless appeared on the list.

In 1982, James Q. Wilson teamed with noted police researcher George Kelling to produce the next iteration of the thesis: the "broken windows" hypothesis. They social-psychologized the thesis, made it longitudinal, and focused on seemingly banal and trivial physical features of locale. Most importantly, they also offered the police a role in disrupting disorder's disastrous consequences (Wilson & Kelling, 1982).

The dynamic they suggested went as follows. Unattended signs of physical disrepair, such as the proverbial broken window, encouraged local teens and preteens to further acts of mischief. (This notion has some support from a well-known field demonstration—not really an experiment—from the late 1960s.) Emboldened local miscreants will scare away the "eyes on the street," the street "regulars" such as stay-at-home moms or senior citizens who hang out and keep an eye on the street (Jacobs, 1968). Once the "eyes" retreat, the local miscreants are further emboldened, and, perhaps more importantly, potential offenders from outside the area see what has happened and now move into the locale, setting off a serious wave of street crimes such as purse snatches and stickups.

Foot-patrolling officers, the authors suggested, could and should play a role in short-circuiting this spiral of decline. They could do so by engaging in order-maintenance policing, also called problem-oriented policing, problem-solving policing, or community policing. Officers would take care of these matters before they became a trend and before they resulted in more serious criminal elements moving into the area. So, officers might badger a lazy landlord to fix his or her property, roust rowdy teens from corners, push panhandlers away from busy transit stops, or contact a city agency to get a trash-filled lot cleaned out and fenced or an abandoned car towed.

To their credit, and often overlooked, Wilson and Kelling addressed two particularly thorny issues in their initial exposition: where and whose. In which neighborhood or street block should such a strategy be employed? They thought such initiatives were applied most effectively in "teetering" neighborhoods—those places where a slide into decline seems to have started or appears about to start. Left unaddressed, unless you presume that police or some other city agencies know where these locales are exactly, is the question of how to identify such locales, and feed this information on a regular basis to police patrol planners.

On the question of whose order is to be maintained, and whose disorder is to be suppressed, the authors recognized that these orders might vary from neighborhood to neighborhood. So, what police might be encouraged to aggressively patrol against in one neighborhood, those same officers might tolerate in the community next door. The authors worried about such discrepancies. They also admitted that officers would need to contact different key actors in a neighborhood and learn about causes of concern that might differ. What a corner store owner sees as a problem might not be a problem for other residents on a block. Although the authors failed to resolve these concerns, they thoughtfully surfaced them.

The next version arrived in capsule form in 1986, and in elaborated form in 1990. Skogan completely ecologized the thesis (Skogan, 1986, 1990). Whereas Wilson and Kelling concentrated on the street block level, essentially small-group dynamics, Skogan suggested that the processes enveloped entire communities in urban locations. He devoted additional attention to the process of neighborhood decline, suggesting that disorders could make independent contributions to neighborhood decline. He further specified relevant indicators of decline, such as businesses less willing to move in, stable residents more willing to move out, and declines in house market values. He reanalyzed cross-sectional data from several cities to support his points.

The last elaboration arrived in 1996, wherein Kelling and Coles blamed the move away from order-maintenance policing to changes taking place in the 1960s and 1970s in the courts (Kelling & Coles, 1996). They argued that around that time, given growing concerns about civil rights violations and excessive uses of police force, courts became increasingly skeptical about slapping serious sentences or fines on such minor offenders. According to the authors, the courts became increasingly concerned that such discretionary police responses were motivated by concerns other than order maintenance. At the same time, officers grew increasingly wary of civil suits in such cases. Left unmentioned in their discussion are the roles played by prison and jail overcrowding in driving such changes in sentencing practices.

## WHY SO ATTRACTIVE?

The incivilities thesis is really a coat of many colors. It has gained admirers and advocates in different epochs for different reasons. In the late 1970s and early 1980s, police were stymied about what to do about crime. Many cities were witnessing sharply increasing crime rates at this time, and, following the famous Kansas City patrol experiment, many police seriously questioned the value of patrolling. At the same time, policymakers were recognizing that fear of crime was a substantial social problem in its own right. The incivilities thesis suggested something police could do that might help with both crime and fear.

In the early and mid-1980s, strategies such as foot patrolling and clusters of strategies labeled community policing or problem-oriented policing gained in popularity. The incivilities thesis gave police officers something to look out for and intervene about when they were on foot. It provided the community policing officers topics of discussion at community meetings. It legitimized responding to residents' concerns when those concerns were not crimes per se, because those concerns were conceptually linked to later serious crimes or more widespread flight, which, it was presumed, would emerge were these problems left unchecked.

By the late 1980s and the early 1990s, in many cities, community policing initiatives continued. But the new wave of innovation came from William Bratton's successful war in New York City on squeegee kids, turnstile jumpers in the subway, and unsavory street characters in general. The era of zero-tolerance policing was emerging. Police were turning—or returning, some would argue—to aggressively policing disorderly street behavior and misdemeanors. These strategies seemed successful (Bratton, 1998; Silverman, 1999). In New York City, crime was dropping. (Less often mentioned, it also was dropping in other major cities not highlighting such strategies.) Misdemeanor arrests of turnstile jumpers in subways often turned up large numbers of people wanted on warrants. Residents and visitors felt less hassled on the street. By the mid-1990s, many other cities were seeking to emulate Bratton's model.

Again, the incivilities thesis provided the payoff logic. Yes, it was plausible that with this more aggressive policing style, there were likely to be more instances of biased policing. African Americans on the street were perhaps more likely to be hassled by police than whites. (Anderson, 2001, argues that the evidence proves otherwise.) Yes, it seemed plausible that instances of excessive use of force by police might increase. But the incivilities theorists argued that the police should not be deterred. Such short-term risks were outweighed by the longer term benefits of more stable communities, increased street life, and lower fear of crime.

In addition to these period-specific sources of attractiveness mentioned here to explain the continuing, if shifting, popularity of the "broken windows" thesis, others have suggested two additional sources of popularity (Lehrer, 2002). The thesis returns policing to one of its origins: fighting disorder, first enshrined as a concern in Sir Robert Peel's principles of policing. Additionally, it makes policing a helping or service profession.

## CONCEPTUAL CONCERNS

Two major conceptual concerns emerge regarding the thesis (Taylor, 2001, pp. 93–125). First, are the dynamics specified by the thesis accurate? More specifically, do incivilities play the roles attributed to them on street blocks or in neighborhoods? How long does it take for these causal processes to cycle in the face of either increasing or decreasing incivilities? In the case of urban residential contexts, we know from empirical and conceptual work on human territorial functioning that an ongoing dialectic is always playing out between street regulars and those viewed as deviant, whether those deviants are backsliding homeowners, rowdy renters, or truculent teens on the corner (Taylor, 1987, 1988). The same dynamics, albeit with a different intensity, play out in suburban settings as well (Gans, 1967). But what we do not know is how

closely linked in time those variations in physical and social disorder are to psychological, emotional, and behavioral outcomes. Except for a couple of studies (see below), we have little longitudinal examination of these temporal dynamics. The appropriate levels of analyses, according to the thesis itself, are street blocks and neighborhoods. Studies of whole cities or whole police departments are theoretically misaligned.

The second concern is sociopolitical, focusing on the social construction of "disorder" and the dichotomizing of the orderly versus the disorderly (Harcourt, 1998, 2001). There are two threads here. The first is that definitions of order and disorder, or who is orderly and who is disorderly, depend on who does the defining. The "meaning" of public urination, for example, depends on where and when and who. This point was initially acknowledged by Wilson and Kelling, and they admitted being troubled by potentially different yardsticks in different neighborhoods. The contextually dependent nature of disorder definitions emerges also from the symbolic interactionist component of human territorial functioning in residential contexts (Taylor, 1987, 1988).

The related thread is that this dichotomizing process in effect produces the same villains that the zero-tolerance policing strategies seek to eliminate. It unrealistically creates a gaping gulf between the law abiders and the law breakers. More plausibly, the gulf is perhaps a narrow stream, easily traversed. In American fiction, even that stalwart 1920s symbol of middle-class conformity, Sinclair Lewis's George F. Babbitt, took to carousing with hard-drinking flappers and procuring Prohibition-era whiskey for his party.

## EMPIRICAL SUPPORT

Central to the arguments here, when we look at the theory and not the surrounding polemics, is the idea that incivilities make an independent contribution over time to changes in an individual, on a street block, or in a neighborhood. Which level of analysis you care about depends on whether you are examining, respectively, the early, middle, or later versions of the thesis.

At one point in time, individuals—usually urban residents—who see more surrounding disorder in their locale also usually report higher levels of concern for their safety and weaker attachment to locale (Taylor, 2001, pp. 220–223). Over time, we also see an individual-level contribution of perceived incivilities to changes in reactions to crime and local sentiment. Residents who, at Time 1, saw their respective blocks as more problem-ridden compared to their neighbors' were more likely over the following year to become less satisfied with the block, to feel more vulnerable, and to worry more about crime (Robinson, Lawton, Taylor, & Perkins, in press). So, the thesis finds confirmation from individual-level cross-sectional and longitudinal work.

Street block analyses find cross-sectional and lagged connections to fear and to concerns about crime-related problems (Perkins, Meeks, & Taylor, 1992; Perkins & Taylor, 1996; Perkins, Wandersman, Rich, & Taylor, 1993). But more rigorous analyses attempting to isolate an independent ecological impact of incivilities to changes in reactions to crime and local commitment show no lagged effects of incivilities on reactions to crime and local commitment (Robinson et al., in press). But this last study does show these outcomes shifting as perceived group-level incivilities themselves shift over a year time frame. So, we can say that perceived incivilities changes on a block accompany perceived changes in block satisfaction and perceived risk, but it is not clear that the incivilities *cause* such changes.

A small handful of studies do point toward the short-term crime-reducing benefits of broken windows-reduction programs at the address or site level (Green, 1995, 1996; Mazerolle, Kadleck, & Roehl, 1997). Whether such benefits persist over a lengthy period of time remains unknown.

At the neighborhood level, over an extended period of time, we find that initial incivilities contribute to later changes in some serious crimes and to some aspects of neighborhood decline (Taylor, 2001, pp. 179–200). But the contributions are neither as sizable as anticipated nor as consistent across outcomes or incivilities indicators as expected. More powerfully predictive of neighborhood futures were fundamentals of neighborhood fabric, such as status and stability.

## IMPLICATIONS FOR LOCAL LAW ENFORCEMENT

It is hoped that problem-oriented policing and a recognition of the importance of police–citizen partnerships are here to stay. In some ways, these themes represent a return to the earliest orientations of policing.

If these themes remain relatively permanent parts of modern policing, whether in urban, suburban, or rural locations, police strategists should have at their disposal a wide array of methods that will improve neighborhood life. The work to date on the broken windows thesis suggests that these planners would be wise to use fully all the strategies and tactics available to them, and not rely solely or largely on reducing incivilities to prevent crime or to preserve neighborhoods or stabilize shaky ones.

*Ralph B. Taylor*

***See also*** Community Policing, Police Discretion, Problem-Oriented Policing, Quality of Life, Theories of Policing, Zero Tolerance

## *For Further Reading*

Anderson, B. C. (2001, July/August). The illusion of order [Book review]. *Commentary, 112,* 69–70.

Bratton, W. (1998). *Turnaround.* New York: Random House.

DuBow, F., McCabe, F., & Kaplan, G. (1979). *Reactions to crime: A critical review of the literature.* Washington, DC: U.S. Government Printing Office.

Gans, H. J. (1967). *The Levittowners.* New York: Pantheon.

Garofalo, J., & Laub, J. (1978). The fear of crime: Broadening our perspective. *Victimology, 3,* 242–253.

Green, L. (1995). Cleaning up drug hot spots in Oakland, California: The displacement and diffusion effects. *Justice Quarterly, 12,* 737–754.

Green, L. (1996). *Policing places with drug problems.* Thousand Oaks, CA: Sage.

Greene, J. R., & Taylor, R. B. (1988). Community-based policing and foot patrol: Issues of theory and evaluation. In J. R. Greene & S. D. Mastrofski (Eds.), *Community policing: Rhetoric or reality?* (pp. 195–224). New York: Praeger.

Harcourt, B. E. (1998). Reflecting on the subject: A critique of the social influence conception of deterrence, the broken windows theory, and order-maintenance policing New York style. *Michigan Law Review, 97,* 291–389.

Harcourt, B. E. (2001). *Illusion of order: The false promise of broken windows policing.* Cambridge, MA: Harvard University Press.

Hunter, A. (1978). *Symbols of incivility.* Paper presented at the annual meeting of the American Society of Criminology, Dallas, Texas.

Jacobs, J. (1968). Community on the city streets. In E. D. Baltzell (Ed.), *The search for community in modern America* (pp. 74–93). New York: Harper & Row.

Kelling, G., & Coles, S. (1996). *Fixing broken windows: Restoring order and reducing crime in American cities.* New York: Free Press.

Kerner, O. (1968). *Report of the National Advisory Commission on Civil Disorders.* New York: Bantam.

Lehrer, E. (2002, Summer). Broken windows reconsidered. *Public Interest, 148,* 146–151.

Lewis, S. (1922). *Babbitt.* New York: Harcourt Brace.

Mazerolle, L. G., Kadleck, C., & Roehl, J. (1997). Controlling drug and disorder problems: The role of place managers. *Criminology, 36*(2), 371–404.

Perkins, D., & Taylor, R. B. (1996). Ecological assessments of disorder: Their relationship to fear of crime and theoretical implications. *American Journal of Community Psychology, 24,* 63–107.

Perkins, D. D., Meeks, J. W., & Taylor, R. B. (1992). The physical environment of street blocks and resident perceptions of crime and disorder: Implications for theory and measurement. *Journal of Environmental Psychology, 12,* 21–34.

Perkins, D. D., Wandersman, A., Rich, R., & Taylor, R. B. (1993). Physical environment of street crime: Defensible space, territoriality and incivilities. *Journal of Environmental Psychology, 13,* 29–49.

Robinson, J., Lawton, B., Taylor, R. B., & Perkins, D. P. (in press). Multilevel longitudinal impacts of incivilities: Fear of crime, expected safety, and block satisfaction. *Journal of Quantitative Criminology.*

Rosen, M. (1999, May 15–31). If it's broken, fix it! An interview with Professor George Kelling. *Law Enforcement News, 25,* 511–512.

Silverman, E. (1999). *NYPD battles crime: Innovative strategies in policing.* Boston: Northeastern University Press.

Skogan, W. (1986). Fear of crime and neighborhood change. In A. J. Reiss, Jr., & M. Tonry (Eds.), *Communities and crime* (Vol. 8, pp. 203–230). Chicago: University of Chicago Press.

Skogan, W. (1990). *Disorder and decline: Crime and the spiral of decay in American cities.* New York: Free Press.

Taylor, R. B. (1987). Toward an environmental psychology of disorder. In D. Stokols & I. Altman (Eds.), *Handbook of environmental psychology* (pp. 951–986). New York: Wiley.

Taylor, R. B. (1988). *Human territorial functioning.* Cambridge, UK: Cambridge University Press.

Taylor, R. B. (1999). The incivilities thesis: Theory, measurement and policy. In R. L. Langworthy (Ed.), *Measuring what matters* (pp. 65–88). Washington, DC: National Institute of Justice/Office of Community Oriented Policing Services.

Taylor, R. B. (2001). *Breaking away from broken windows: Evidence from Baltimore neighborhoods and the nationwide fight against crime, grime, fear and decline.* New York: Westview.

Wilson, J. Q. (1975). *Thinking about crime.* New York: Basic Books.

Wilson, J. Q., & Kelling, G. (1982, March). Broken windows. *Atlantic Monthly, 211,* 29–38.

## ✍ CALLS FOR SERVICE

The number 9-1-1 has been designated by the Federal Communications Commission (FCC) as the three-digit "Universal Emergency (telephone) Number" for public use throughout the United States to request emergency assistance. This nationwide telephone number is intended to give the public direct access to a public safety call center, commonly referred to in the emergency communications industry as a Public Safety Answering Point (PSAP). A PSAP, typically managed by a local or county government, is staffed by call-takers (people who answer the call) and dispatchers (people who assign the call to the appropriate personnel—police, fire, and/or emergency medical services). The 9-1-1 systems are commonly funded through a user fee that is assessed to subscribers of commercial, residential, and cellular telephone service as a portion of their monthly telephone bill.

In 1967, during the administration of President Lyndon Johnson, The Commission on Law Enforcement and Administration of Justice recommended the concept of a single number for reporting police emergencies. The first 9-1-1 call was placed in Halleyville, Alabama, in 1968. As of October 2002, 99% of the population and 96% of the geographic United States have access to 9-1-1, and an estimated 200 million calls are placed over municipal and county 9-1-1 systems each year. It is estimated that there are more than 7,500 PSAPs in the United States.

There are three types of 9-1-1 systems:

**Basic 9-1-1** is a communication system in which the call is delivered to a PSAP without any type of caller identification information.

**Automatic Number Identification (ANI) Enhanced 9-1-1** is a system in which the call is delivered to the PSAP in such a way that the call-taker is able to see the caller's telephone number on a special screen.

**Enhanced 9-1-1 (E 9-1-1)** is a system in which the call is delivered to the PSAP in such a way that the call-taker is able to see the caller's telephone number and address on a special screen.

### CELLULAR 9-1-1

When the technology supporting E 9-1-1 systems was originally designed, it did not take into account the complexities of cellular telephone technology. As use of cell phones increased, so did the number of calls placed to 9-1-1 centers. Originally, cell phone calls placed to 9-1-1 did not include information regarding the identification and location of the caller. Of primary concern was ensuring that law enforcement and rescue workers had the ability to locate cell phones used to dial 9-1-1. In an effort to address this critical public safety problem, the FCC issued a "First Report and Order" on June 12, 1996, calling for all wireless carriers to implement 9-1-1 and E 9-1-1. The nation's wireless carriers were ordered to have the technology in place so that public safety personnel answering 9-1-1 calls would be able to identify the location of a caller within 50 feet. Although progress has been made in this area, it is not yet in place throughout the country.

## THE IMPACT OF 9-1-1 ON COMMUNITY-ORIENTED POLICING

Clearly, the designation of 9-1-1 as the nation's universal emergency number has simplified the public's ability to get emergency help when needed. However, the use of 9-1-1 also has had a significant impact on policing methods and even the culture of policing in America. Throughout the 1970s and 1980s, police departments operated in an environment where effectiveness was often measured by the number of calls received by the local 9-1-1 system or how fast emergency service vehicles arrived on scene following a call to 9-1-1. The public learned quickly that no matter what the nature of the problem—emergency, nonemergency, public safety, or public services—calls to 9-1-1 were answered quickly and usually resulted in on-site police response.

By the late 1980s, 9-1-1 evolved into the preferred method used by the public to report all types of problems and requests, not just emergencies. The public's reliance (and, in some cases, overreliance) on 9-1-1 affected the way police departments operated in a number of ways. Police organizations became much more reactive in orientation because as calls to 9-1-1 increased, police officers found that their work day focused almost exclusively on responding to call after call. Although police officers were still assigned specific beat areas, it was not uncommon for them to be sent to calls outside those areas. The priority was placed on how many calls an officer handled and how quickly the officer cleared a call.

A key component of President Bill Clinton's anticrime policy was the establishment of the Office of Community Oriented Policing Services (COPS) within the Department of Justice. COPS provided funding for 100,000 new police officers to help undermanned police departments around the country and to encourage the adoption of new, community-oriented policing strategies that had shown great promise in communities such as San Diego. Since its inception, the COPS office has provided more than $6 billion in grants to state and local agencies for technology and resulted in 109,139 new police officers working with community members.

The national focus on community-oriented policing resulted in many police departments replacing the highly reactive, 9-1-1-driven policing strategies of the 1970s and 1980s with proactive, information-driven, community-centric, crime prevention activities. Instead of driving around randomly in cars and responding to emergency calls, police are now on foot and on bicycles—visible fixtures in neighborhoods. They work with community leaders to identify conditions that breed disorder; they share information about potential problems; and they forge common strategies for preventing crime, not simply catching criminals after the fact.

## 3-1-1—ACCESS TO NONEMERGENCY POLICE AND GOVERNMENT SERVICES

In 1997, the FCC assigned the telephone number 3-1-1 for nationwide nonemergency police services and for access to other nonemergency government services. Baltimore, Maryland, was the first city to implement 3-1-1 for police nonemergency service. The FCC found that this assignment would serve the public interest by making it easier for individuals to obtain service from state and local governments, while also reducing the number of nonemergency calls that clog 9-1-1 systems.

The number 3-1-1 has been identified as a critical part of the nation's homeland security efforts. In its December 2001 report, "A National Action Plan for Safety and Security in America's Cities," the United States Conference of Mayors recommended that

since 9-1-1 systems in many cities would be quickly overwhelmed in the event of a weapons of mass destruction incident, existing 9-1-1 systems need to be upgraded and 3-1-1 systems, or equivalent systems that can handle incoming calls from the public and provide up-to-date information or instructions, should be put in place. (Morial, 2001, p. 11)

Since 1997, more than 28 jurisdictions began using or installing 3-1-1 systems. Most of these jurisdictions recognize that 3-1-1 serves as an effective way for the public to access information and request nonemergency services from local government. Many local leaders identify 3-1-1 as a key part of their efforts to improve service delivery:

- Baltimore, Maryland: Baltimore has expanded its 3-1-1 system to provide public access to all city agencies for nonemergency services and inquiries. In its first year of operation, Baltimore's 3-1-1 CitiStat program achieved an overall savings of $13.2 million. The savings was primarily in overtime reduction ($6 million). The other key benefits were increased revenue, reduced absenteeism, and termination of extraneous expenditures.

- Rochester, New York: Less than a year after it implemented a 3-1-1 police nonemergency system, the Rochester Police Department used its 3-1-1 call-takers to disseminate information about the September 11, 2001, terrorist attacks. The public also used 3-1-1 to report suspicious materials or activity and inquire about the safety of particular locations. Call-takers helped alleviate public fear by dispelling unfounded rumors and providing an avenue for the public to connect with local law enforcement, provide tips to police, and obtain accurate information regarding ongoing events.

- Austin, Texas: The launching of the Austin Police Department's 3-1-1 system on September 17, 2001, preceded the early stages of the anthrax scare. A successful public education campaign immediately diverted calls from the 9-1-1 systems to 3-1-1 (averting a shutdown), and the 3-1-1 system processed more calls than the 9-1-1 system by the end of October. In Austin, all incoming 3-1-1 call information is entered into a CAD/RMS system, which is also captured by the 3-1-1 statistical reporting software. This information is then provided to the chief of police and the city manager via daily e-mail and helps generate a daily bulletin of calls requiring a response, which is provided to all city staff and personnel.

## DIFFERENTIAL POLICE RESPONSE

Differential police response (DPR) is a method of handling calls for service in which calls are screened, triaged, and classified prior to a police officer being dispatched. The basic concept is that not all calls for assistance require the dispatch of a police unit, and, in some cases, calls for service can be handled more effectively by taking a report over the telephone, transferring the call to officers equipped with wireless telephones, directing the caller to another government or nongovernment entity, and/or scheduling a future appointment with a representative of the police department.

The DPR concept was developed in recognition of the fact that not all calls for assistance are of the same priority; police response should be based on the seriousness of the call. Most calls do not require an immediate response by the police. Departments that have used DPR methodology have reported sizable increases in patrol time available for crime prevention, directed patrol, and other functions. As part of their DPR efforts, some departments allow nonviolent, less serious crime reports to be taken over the telephone, by Internet, or by U.S. mail.

The overall objectives of DPR methodology focus on effective response to emergencies, effective problem solving, and effective management of the call receipt and response processes. Specific objectives are the following:

- Provide rapid, quality emergency response to reported public safety threats
- Separate emergency call processing (9-1-1) from nonemergency call processing (3-1-1 and seven-digit), with the latter being housed in a citywide call center serving all city agencies
- Provide sufficient personnel for public safety threat response so that officers and citizens will feel protected
- Maximize the utilization of personnel and improve the management of the call center process for emergency and nonemergency calls
- Create an information management capability that makes past and present incident information available on a real-time basis to call-takers and incident or problem responders

## REVERSE 9-1-1 CALLING

A community notification system, commonly referred to as reverse 9-1-1, allows police agencies to broadcast a prerecorded message to a group of homes and businesses within specific neighborhoods or even locations throughout an entire region. It is a way to rapidly broadcast crime prevention alerts; evacuation and safe return notifications; and geographically based information about all types of public safety-related situations (prison escapes, bomb threats, specific crime problems, arson investigation, sexual predators, natural disasters, terrorism alerts, etc.).

*John D. Cohen*

*See also* Computer Aided Dispatch, Dispatch

### For Further Reading

Chapman, R., Baker, S., Bezdikian, V., Cammarata, P., Cohen, D., Leach, N., Schapiro, A., Scheider, M., Varano, R., & Boba, R. (2002). *Local law enforcement responds to terrorism: Lessons in prevention and preparedness.* Washington, DC: U.S. Department of Justice, Office of Community Oriented Policing Services.

Morial, M. H. (2001). *A national action plan for safety and security in America's cities.* Washington, DC: United States Conference of Mayors.

*9-1-1 fast facts.* Retrieved from http://www.nena.org/911_facts/911fastfacts.htm

Ozanich, B. (1996). *E 9-1-1 data base guide.* Coshocton, OH: National Emergency Number Association.

Schlanger, E. (2002, June). *Baltimore CitiStat presentation.* Paper presented at the Columbus, Ohio 3-1-1 Summit, Columbus, OH.

http://www.nena.org

## ⊗ CAMPUS POLICING

In response to the homicide of a Lehigh University student in 1986, and as a direct result of tireless campaigning by that victim's family, the U.S. Congress passed the Crime Awareness and Campus Security Act of 1990. The bill mandated institutions of higher education to make both annual crime statistics as well as a comprehensive plan for student safety available to campus constituents upon request. This groundbreaking legislation (along with a number of other bills passed in the years since), coupled with steadily increasing campus crime rates, has led to vast expansions of existing crime prevention programs as well as the implementation of new and innovative responses to incidences of violence by both campus public safety departments and administrators at U.S. colleges and universities. For example, Michigan State University instituted a community policing program in the late 1980s in an effort to reduce increasing rates of property and interpersonal crimes, and the University of Illinois at Chicago in 1991 developed a cooperative initiative with the Chicago Police Department's 12th Precinct to reduce auto theft rates for parts of the city surrounding the UIC campus.

The University of Maryland took a more direct approach in the early 1980s in response to increases in violent crime. The campus increased its number of sworn, armed officers 40%, it implemented checkpoints at campus entrances during evening hours, and fortified the dormitories with heavy-duty security devices (such as stronger locks and shatter-proof door glass). These examples lead one to believe that the range and scope of university efforts to address criminal issues are virtually limitless. Indeed, every school has its own unique crime problems that it must address, and the demands placed upon campus police departments can be extreme.

In efforts to ensure the safety of their constituents and spare themselves the potential liability for lax responses to campus criminality, most large colleges and universities have adopted aggressive, proactive strategies to prevent crimes from ever occurring. The issues of potential liability and civil litigation are main reasons for the proliferation of new innovations in campus security. Furthermore, colleges and universities now have the responsibility to alert students about potential risks of on-campus criminality, as well as to provide adequate protection services as advertised. If the school does not live up to its end of this bargain, courts have had no problems assessing monetary penalties against these schools on behalf of crime victims and their families.

Many of these programs or policies are adaptations of strategies used by municipal departments, such as community- or problem-oriented policing. Other schools prefer innovations used by private and industrial security contractors that focus on environment and physical design to reduce the opportunity for offenders to successfully commit an offense. While many of these crime prevention techniques are easily adapted to any given campus, each school must assess and respond to its most pressing security needs. Without doubt, a cooperative, as opposed to an adversarial, relationship between the campus law enforcement body and the constituents of the school must be in place before any program is initiated. A significant part of any needs assessment policy making must include follow-up evaluation of program effectiveness and feasibility.

The reality is that campus crime affects the bottom line for many colleges and universities. Prospective students and parents of those students now have easier access to campus crime statistics since the passage of the Campus Crime and Security Act of 1990. Decisions about which school the student chooses to attend are based, at least partially, upon whether a significant risk of victimization on campus or in the surrounding community exists. Higher-than-average crime figures and/or a prevailing climate of fear among the constituents of a campus could have grave implications for the recruiting process. At a time when the competition for top students is particularly high, an institution certainly does not want a nonacademic factor such as disproportionately high crime rates to possibly influence the student's decision to matriculate. Furthermore, postsecondary institutions must remain cognizant of the successful civil suits initiated by students and parents against universities for crimes that, conceivably, could have been prevented, or for which the campus response to a given crime was ineffective or insufficient.

## DILEMMA OF POLICING THE UNIVERSITY CAMPUS

Earlier reports of campus crime indicated that many law enforcement officers at large universities believed criminal activity, especially crimes of violence, to be the work of persons not associated with the institutions. However, more current research into the area of on-campus violence and victimization indicates that those individuals committing violent crimes tend to be legitimate members of the campus environment, and usually are fellow students. These crimes of violence on campus that involve students as constituents and victims are often impulsive in nature, the result of an argument or disagreement, and most often occur at night or on weekends, when resident students are not in classes, but in or near campus housing units. Such instances of interpersonal violence also frequently involve the use of alcohol by the perpetrator, the victim, or both.

It has been suggested that something about the collegiate experience and/or the campus environment is providing license for otherwise law-abiding young people to commit acts of deviance that they would not otherwise perpetrate, and indeed would perhaps frown upon in a larger societal context. This presents a dual problem for the heads of campus policing departments, who are faced with rising instances of interpersonal violence at their institutions and the knowledge that their own students are perhaps the source of this upswing. Given this information, it is not difficult to understand why campus leaders are somewhat reluctant to divulge campus crime information to prospective students and other interested parties, and why proponents of the Crime Awareness and Campus Security Act had little objection from lawmakers in getting the legislation passed.

Nine out of 10 public institutions of higher learning use sworn officers, as compared to less than half of private institutions. There are more than 11,000 full-time sworn officers in 4-year colleges and universities with 2,500 or more students. Most of these officers are armed. These police agencies also employ 10,000 civilians. Campus police are a recognized section of the International Association of Chiefs of Police.

*Don Hummer*

### For Further Reading

Beeler, K. J., Bellandese, S. D., & Wiggins, C. A. (1991). *Campus safety: A survey of administrative perceptions and strategies.* Washington, DC: National Association of Student Personnel Administrators.

Benson, B. L. (1993). Community policing works at Michigan State University. *Journal of Security Administration, 16*(1), 43–52.

Crime Awareness and Campus Security Act of 1990, 20 U.S.C. 1092 (1990).

Fisher, B. S., Sloan, J. J., Cullen, F. T., & Lu, C. (1997). The on-campus victimization patterns of students: Implications for crime prevention by students in post-secondary institutions. In S. P. Lab (Ed.), *Crime prevention at a crossroads.* Cincinnati, OH: Anderson.

Frost, G. A. (1993). Law enforcement responds to campus crime. *Journal of Security Administration, 16*(1), 21–29.

Griffaton, M. C. (1993). Forewarned is forearmed: The Crime Awareness and Campus Security Act. *Case Western Law Review, 43,* 525–590.

Johnson, R. P. (1994). Implementing community policing in a university environment. *Campus Law Enforcement Journal, 24*(3), 17–21, 34–35.

Pagon, M. (1995). Policing the university community: Police discretion and officer–student relations. *Campus Law Enforcement Journal, 25*(1), 3–8, 35.

Phillips, P. W. (1993). Campus law enforcement as community policing and problem-oriented policing. *Campus Law Enforcement Journal, 23*(6), 19–22.

Pollard, J. W., & Whitaker, L. C. (1991). Cures for campus violence, if we want them. In L. C. Whitaker & J. W. Pollard (Eds.), *Campus violence: Kinds, causes, and cures.* New York: Haworth.

Sloan, J. J., Fisher, B. S., & Cullen, F. T. (1997). Assessing the Student Right-to-Know and Campus Security Act of 1990: An analysis of the victim reporting practices of college and university students. *Crime & Delinquency, 43*(2), 148–168.

# ✑ CANINE (K-9) UNITS

Canine units, little more than a handful of patrol officers and their dogs a century ago, have become a versatile and indispensable part of law enforcement at the local, state, and federal level. Today, thousands of trained canine units operate in every state, doing work that demands the instincts and highly developed eyes, ears, and nose of the dog and the special skills of its handler. Canine units control crowds; seek out missing children, fugitives, hidden drugs, explosives, cadavers, concealed weapons, and evidence; and are found everywhere, from the nation's airports, prisons, subways, hospitals, and piers to its national parks and schools.

The use of dogs in policing in the United States began in 1907, when the first patrol dog programs were inaugurated in South Orange, New Jersey, and New York City. Until 1952, there were only 14 canine units involving trained police dogs and their handlers clustered in the industrialized Northeast and the Upper Midwest. The longest running of these early programs, located in the affluent Parkville section of Brooklyn, lasted 44 years. Lauded for significantly reducing the burglaries and crime that had plagued the area at night, the Parkville canine program ended in 1951 with the advent of radio-equipped patrol cars. Starting around the mid-1950s, police dog programs grew rapidly across the country. By the beginning of the 1990s, almost 3,000 programs had been implemented, of which 2,000 were still in operation. Today, more than 7,000 canine units are housed in law enforcement agencies across the country.

Many police departments have one or more canine units because they have proven efficient and cost-effective in reducing crime. At the request of their local police departments, community civic associations generally fund the units. Although the types of dogs used for police work depend on their function, the most all-purpose or generalist dog used by the majority of both specialized and nonspecialized canine units is an intact male or spayed female German Shepherd. The dog is obtained when it is between 18 months and 4 years old from special breeders (and sometimes from the local animal shelter) and then trained by a special canine trainer who works with both the dog and its handler. Because the dog is trained to respond to only one handler, the selection of the handler is extremely important. These are generally seasoned officers who are disciplined, determined, mature, intelligent, reliable, and patient, and who genuinely like dogs. The handler must be willing to take on the considerable task of establishing and maintaining a close relationship with the dog he or she has opted to partner. The handler receives special compensation for caring for the dog at his or her home, as well as a car to transport it in, but he or she generally spends many uncompensated hours in ongoing training of the dog. There is a saying, "There are no dog mistakes, only handler mistakes." The dog is only as effective as its handler. The handler must be able to make quick assessments of the crime situation and split-second tactical judgments on how best to deploy the dog. The effectiveness of canine units is a factor of the quality of the dog's training, the ability and skill of the handler, and decisions made by superiors about how the unit should be deployed. Because handler and dog are both responsible for protecting each other's lives, they become inseparable and develop a deep and lasting relationship. There are many reported cases where the death of a dog in the line of duty is as personally devastating to the handler as if he or she had lost a family member. Often, the department and community are deeply affected as well and will hold a funeral for the fallen animal.

The generalist canine unit that is the staple of many state and local police departments is often cross-trained to perform a variety of tasks because it is more economical than having special tactical dogs. The patrol dog serves as its handler's partner and protector during their daily 8-hour shift. Together, they respond to the usual patrol emergencies: control fights; pursue and apprehend felony offenders; track fugitives or lost individuals; and search both outdoors and in buildings to locate, apprehend, and arrest hidden or resistant individuals. The dog finds, entraps, holds, and guards the fugitive for its handler, and serves as a powerful psychological deterrent to criminals and unruly crowds. Using its exceptional sense of smell, the dog helps its handler locate evidence, drugs, and bombs. In addition to combating crime, the dog performs an important community relations function— visiting schools and community events to build trust between the police and citizens.

In the face of public outcry over police use of deadly force, many law enforcement professionals view canine units as an effective means of reducing the possibility that police officers will need to resort to deadly force. In 1990, San Diego police officers shot 22 suspects wielding nontraditional weapons, such as baseball bats, trowels, and knives, and 12 of these suspects died. The public anger over "excessive use of police force" persuaded the San Diego Police Department (SDPD) to expand the number and scope of its canine units, from building and area searches, and finding evidence, narcotics, or explosives, to include alternatives to deadly force. A subsequent study by the SDPD showed that the decrease in suspects shot by officers, as well as officer injuries, was proportional to the increased deployment of canine units. Many incidents were found to have been resolved just by the presence of a police dog without either the dog biting the suspect or the officer having to resort to deadly force. However, because of the controversial "find and bite" policy, where a dog is released by its handler to chase and then secure a suspect with its teeth, some police officers and injured claimants have argued that the police dog is deadly force. Officer Van Bogardus, a retired Los Angeles Police Department canine handler, believes that a dog bite is deadly force and that too many police departments have a policy of "find and bite" where "find and hold" (in which the dog merely corners the suspect by baring its teeth and barking) would suffice. Bogardus has come up with a basic criterion for when a dog should be allowed to bite an assailant: to protect the dog, the handler, or other officers only if the handler has probable cause to believe that such force is reasonable and necessary to prevent death or serious bodily injury to him- or herself or another person. Police departments with canine units have faced greater liability from dog bites, and there is currently a debate over the "find and bite" policy.

The flip side of the use of police dogs as alternatives to deadly force is the problematic deployment of canine units in crowd control. The value of dogs as effective instruments of crowd control had never been disputed until the civil rights era. During the Birmingham riots, when national media showed crowd control canines viciously attacking black demonstrators, it vividly called to mind the dogs that were used to track fugitive slaves. A huge public outcry over the use of dogs in civil rights demonstrations, Vietnam protests, and urban riots of the 1960s jeopardized the existence of canine units all across America. Some units were discontinued, and the furor led to serious revision of the rules of police dog use and improved training. According to case law, the police dog is an instrument of force, comparable to a police baton, which is subject to the rules that apply to police use of force. Substantial force inflicting serious injury may be reasonable and necessary according to the circumstances confronting officers.

Specialized or "tactical" canine units generally focus on one specific area, such as tracking, drug and bomb detection, or crowd control. Because tactical canines must be superior dogs to the general patrol dog and require more extensive training, tactical canine units are more expensive. Some police agencies have purchased and trained dogs solely for tracking fugitives and missing persons. Canine tracking and retrieval powers have proven invaluable to police work tracking humans. The dog's acute sense of smell, which can be 200 times more powerful than a human's, has never been surpassed by technical means. Although the bloodhound has the best sense of smell, other dogs are more often used for tracking—especially German Shepherds, which have 200 million to 220 million smelling cells in their nose compared to the 124 million to 147 million for the next best breed, border collies. One of the most famous uses of tracking dogs was the capture of James Earl Ray, the assassin of Dr. Martin Luther King, Jr., who had escaped into the woods from a state penitentiary in Tennessee. Using two bloodhounds, trackers found Ray hidden under a pile of leaves miles from the prison. Cadaver dogs are another type of specialized canine. Tracker dogs are frequently owned and trained by nonprofit associations, private citizens, and even police officers because they are expensive to own and maintain and may not be needed often. Unlike the generalist dog, who will respond only to its handler, tracker dogs will work with anyone and are made available through nonprofit associations such as The United States Police Canine Association, which provides training and certification, and sets performance standards for search-and-rescue dogs and their handlers.

As drug smuggling and the threat of terrorism have grown, specialized canine units have become an invaluable component of the nation's law enforcement arsenal. The U.S. Customs Service is the preeminent user of narcotics detection canine units at ports of entry to the United States, where dogs have been instrumental in locating billions of dollars in hidden drugs. Narcotics canine units are also used today for drug detection on public school campuses. However, the biggest growth in specialized canine units has been in response to terrorist bomb threats. In 1971, the U.S. Capitol Police began using bomb-sniffing German Shepherds when an antiwar terrorist blew up a Capitol bathroom. After President Clinton signed The Anti-Terrorism Act in response to the explosion of TWA Flight 800 and the Atlanta Centennial Park bombing, 50 bomb-sniffing dogs were introduced into the nation's largest airports. Since the September 11, 2001, terrorist attacks, when canine units from across the country participated in the search for bodies, the use of canine units to sniff out terrorist bombs has mushroomed. Bomb-sniffing dogs are being used by airlines, cruise ship lines, and nuclear power plants, as well as at bridges, tunnels, national monuments, and anywhere else there is the threat of terrorism. Since September 11, 2001, the demand is greater than the supply. The U.S. government alone wants to more than double its pack by adding 10,000 more sniffer dogs. The shortage is so acute that it has driven up prices for preferred breeds. Because of their superior sense of smell, German Shepherds were fetching $20,000 in 2003, and dogs that would sell for $2,500 in normal times were going for as much as $13,000. Although dogs generally are not used to detect viral and poisonous substances because their systems are similar to humans, "Sgt. Speckles" and 12 of his canine cohorts, who were trained to detect minute trace elements, died from anthrax inhalation when they were enlisted to sniff for traces in the U.S. Capitol post office.

*Kathryn Wylie-Marques*

### For Further Reading

Chapman, S. G. (1990). *Police dogs in North America.* Springfield, IL: Charles C Thomas.

Hawley, D. L. (1997, February). K-9 bite liability is a growing concern. *Police*, p. 16.

Lilly, R. J., & Puckett, M. B. (1997). Social control and dogs: A sociohistorical analysis. *Crime & Delinquency, 43*(2), 123–147.

Resch, R. C. (1997, February). K-9s in law enforcement: They're worth the effort. *Police*, p. 5.

Savage, D. (1996, February 29). Necessary weapon, or excessive force? *Los Angeles Times*, p. A-1.

# ∽ CHAIN OF CUSTODY

Chain of custody is a concept in the study and application of law that applies to the proper handling of evidence within a criminal proceeding. It refers to the ability to positively guarantee the identity, integrity, and chronological history of evidence from the point of acquisition through to examination and testimony. The sensitive nature of evidence, as used in a court of law to convict a person or persons of a crime, requires strict custodial procedures to be followed in a precise and careful manner to avoid later allegations of tampering or misconduct. These custodial procedures are carefully logged, documented, and attested via signature by every identifiable person at every stage of custody, thus creating a probable chain of custody that can be traced back to the point of acquisition. Thus, the chain of custody becomes a legal, chronological, written record of those individuals who have had custody of the evidence from the point of its initial acquisition until its final disposition.

The chain of custody begins when evidence is collected and is maintained until the evidence is disposed of. In a proper chain of custody, an identifiable person must always have documented physical custody of a piece of evidence. This documentation ensures continuous accountability, which is important because if not properly maintained, it may render evidence inadmissible in a court of law.

According to N.J. Practice, Criminal Procedure by Honorable Leonard Arnold, J.S.C. (West Publishing), Volume 32, Chapter 21, Section 1034, a party seeking to introduce an item of physical evidence must prove that the item was taken from a particular person or place that makes the item relevant as evidence in the trial. Such proof is provided by testimony identifying the item as having been taken from that person or place, and by evidence tracing custody of the item from the time it was taken until it is offered in evidence. This latter evidence is necessary to avoid any claim of substitution or tampering (*State v. Johnson,* 1966).

The very first link in the chain of custody is the investigator, officer, or detective who takes custody of the evidence at the scene of the crime or search warrant, and who then carefully documents its position, collection, and handling. Custody of the evidence is then signed over to an evidence clerk for storage in a secure place. All investigators, officers, or detectives who recover physical evidence must turn that evidence over to the evidence clerk, who is then legally responsible for the evidence from that time forward until trial.

In cases where evidence must be submitted to a laboratory for examination, the evidence is signed out by an investigator or other person empowered by the prosecutor, thereby becoming the new custodian. This transaction is logged by the evidence clerk, and signed by the person taking custody of the evidence. It is then promptly delivered directly to the laboratory, where custody changes hands again. Documentation must be obtained at every step of the way, carefully logging times; dates; case numbers; the nature of the evidence; and, more importantly, the names of the custodians. At all times, documentation must be signed by both parties involved in the exchange in order to maintain a proper chain of custody and maintain the integrity of the evidence.

The identification of evidence and chain of evidence rules require that the proponent of the evidence show that the evidence has not been tampered with, and that there has not been any irregularity that altered its probative value (*State v. Roszkowski,* 1974).

When the laboratory has completed its analysis of the evidence, the investigator or person empowered by the prosecutor must again acquire custody of the evidence, using the same procedure of documentation, and then return the evidence to the evidence clerk. Once again, identification of the evidence and documentation is exchanged by all parties involved. This transaction—and every succeeding transaction including the collection of the evidence, examination, analysis, and its appearance in court—is completely documented.

These documented procedures allow all of the physical evidence to be introduced into trial by calling the various investigators who recovered and marked each item of physical evidence, the custodians, and the laboratory specialists who examined the evidence. Testimony covers not only the acquisition, examination, and results of analysis of every piece of evidence, but also the method of reception, storage, and chain of custody.

*Bryant Daniel Almeida*

### For Further Reading

Casey, E. (2002). *Handbook of computer crime investigation.* San Diego, CA: Academic Press.

Genge, N. E. (2002). *The forensic casebook: The science of crime scene investigation.* New York: Random House.

Park, R. C., & Waltz, J. R. (1999). *Cases and materials on evidence* (9th ed.). New York: Foundation Press.

State v. Johnson, 90 N.J. Super. 105, 216 A.2d 397 (App.Div.1965), aff'd 46 N.J. 289, 216 A.2d 392 (1966).

State v. Roszkowski, 129 N.J. Super. 315, 323 A2d 531 (App.Div. 1974).

## &#8658; CHAPLAINS

The law enforcement chaplain is an experienced, ordained person of faith, endorsed by a recognized religious body, who is appointed as a support position to the police department in matters of faith. The position of law enforcement chaplain was created to assist police departments by offering spiritual guidance and counseling to law enforcement personnel and their families.

Chaplains have been associated with the military for centuries. Their services and heroic actions have often been noted in historical records of significant battles. There is, however, no known record of the first appointed law enforcement chaplain in the United States. Evidence points to the implementation of the chaplaincy in the late 19th century.

The law enforcement chaplain believes that religion is a powerful consolation to the stresses and strains of a position frequently under pressure and in danger. The chaplain claims to bear witness to the love and power of God to law enforcement officers, their families, other members of their department, and the people they serve. They provide services to all of their charges, regardless of race, sex, or creed.

Chaplaincy differs from being a pastor in that it is primarily a ministry of presence. The role of the chaplain is to serve, not to preach. According

to International Conference of Police Chaplains past-president (2001–2003) Dan Nota, a chaplain who advocates a particular religious perspective while working with a public agency would probably suffer legal problems with the city, as well as the local chapter of the American Civil Liberties Union.

The chaplain functions as an assistant to the Chief of Police. The chaplain is authorized to visit the district precincts and officers of the agency. Chaplains have access to all buildings and scenes where the presence of law enforcement officers indicates the need for a chaplain's services. The chaplain does not interfere with an officer in the performance of duty.

The law enforcement chaplain has similar duties among most police departments. The chaplain attempts to bring a spiritual, or religious, component to the agency and its community. He or she offers assistance when an officer or his or her family is injured, ill, or killed and when an officer or his or her family experiences such domestic problems as debt or substance abuse. The chaplain gives pastoral care and counseling by visiting the sick or injured officers and department personnel in homes and hospitals. The chaplain also assists victims and makes death notifications. He or she may serve as part of a department's Crisis Response Team and assist at suicide incidents. The chaplain also serves as liaison with other clergy in the community and provides for the spiritual needs of the incarcerated. When requested, chaplains will attend and participate in funerals of active or retired members of their departments. In addition, the chaplain often leads prayers and invocations at events, and he or she can make referrals in cases beyond his or her ability to assist or when specialized attention is needed. Finally, the chaplain is expected to respond to all major disasters such as bombings, building collapses, explosions, multiple fire alarms, unusual industrial accidents, and so on.

According to the International Conference of Police Chaplains (ICPC), the law enforcement chaplain should meet several qualifications. He or she should be an ordained or licensed clergy person and evidence a religious compassion, understanding, and love for others. The chaplain should be certified, have at least 5 years of experience, and be endorsed for this vocation by a recognized religious body. He or she should demonstrate a broad range of experience, be emotionally stable, and be flexible in time and manner. The chaplain must be free of a criminal record and of offenses involving moral corruption. The chaplain is on a 24-hour call of duty determined by the supervisor. He or she should have a significant interest in law enforcement chaplaincy as evidenced by training, experience, and inclination.

The ICPC exemplifies the standards and responsibilities of the law enforcement chaplain. The Conference consists of chaplains from all over the world who are dedicated to their vocation. Every member of the organization is pledged to the values and morals stipulated by the ICPC's code. The Conference also provides training sessions throughout the United States and one national seminar per year.

The chaplain's primary responsibility is to assist the law enforcement officer with counseling or moral support. Most important, the chaplain must know that he or she must be with the officer in time of need, whenever and wherever that may be.

*Elena E. Sullivan*

*For Further Reading*

http://www.icpc4cops.org

## ᘒ CHEMICAL AND BIOLOGICAL TERRORISM, LOCAL RESPONSE TO

Chemical and biological weapons are rarely used by terrorists, yet they have captured the public imagination. These weapons have the potential to kill many thousands of people, but are far more difficult to acquire, control, and use effectively than conventional weapons. Chemical and biological weapons, although often classed together, have very different characteristics and require quite different responses. A chemical attack on civilians can be considered in many ways similar to a hazardous materials incident, whereas a biological weapons attack would be more like a disease epidemic. Both, of course, would have the added complication of requiring a criminal investigation and could spread considerable fear through the community.

The first responders on the scene of a chemical weapons attack would be local responders. Despite the multiple federal response teams trained to deal with the aftermath of a terrorist attack, the brunt of response will be borne by local units. Law enforcement officers, often the first responders to arrive, have been nicknamed "blue canaries"; just as canaries were used in mines to indicate the presence of bad air, collapsing police officers may indicate the presence of noxious chemicals. But even without protective equipment, officers arriving at the scene of a chemical weapons release would not necessarily be physically affected. Depending on environmental conditions and the nature of the agent, the chemicals may have dissipated or inactivated fairly quickly. If trained appropriately, 9-1-1 operators may be able to warn responders of the presence of chemical hazards. Hazardous materials units (HazMat) or the fire service, either of which routinely assesses chemical hazards, would command the scene. Law enforcement responsibilities would include establishing perimeter control, maintaining an exclusion zone or multiple zones into which only appropriately protected responders would be allowed to enter, and generally securing the area. Other duties would include evidence collection from the crime scene, crowd control, and recording contact information from victims and witnesses. Following a large event, maintaining security at hospitals may be necessary. Police officers might be required to organize an orderly neighborhood evacuation, or alternatively, persuade people to remain indoors.

For large-scale events, the National Guard would be asked to assist law enforcement. The National Guard is normally under the authority of the state, but in extreme circumstances might be put under federal command.

Successful response to and investigation of a bioterrorism attack would necessitate close cooperation between the law enforcement and public health communities. Medical professionals would be the first to see indications of a biological terrorist attack, but may not recognize the initial cases as nonnatural disease occurrences. Unusual symptoms or lab findings, disease clusters, or increases in cases of flu-like diseases outside the normal influenza season would be cause for concern. However, a disease new to the United States would not necessarily have been introduced by a bioterrorist—HIV, the West Nile virus, SARS, and the Hanta virus arrived without the aid of terrorists.

In 1996, a criminal investigation was initiated after public health authorities notified the police that an outbreak of gastroenteritis among medical center staff was caused by an unusual bacterium, a strain of *Shigella dysenteriae* rare in the United States, but stocked by a laboratory at the center. A staff member had grown the bacterium at work and used it to contaminate her colleagues' breakfasts. In Oregon in 1984, an extensive epidemiological investigation was carried out by public health officials of two mass outbreaks of salmonellosis affecting more than 700 people. A year later, a member of a local cult confessed to having deliberately poured *Salmonella* cultures into salad bars in local restaurants. Members of the Bhagwan Shree Rajneesh commune had grown and disseminated the bacteria in a bizarre attempt to influence the outcome of local elections. Two people were convicted of violating the federal antitampering act. In both of these cases, the public health community was the first to become aware of a health problem necessitating a criminal investigation.

Law enforcement and public health investigations differ. Law enforcement investigations attempt to gather evidence that will withstand legal scrutiny in court. Public health investigators seek sufficient information to identify the cause of a disease outbreak, with the aim of halting it and preventing future outbreaks. Evidence collected in the course of a legitimate public health investigation may be used in a criminal investigation, but only if a proper chain of custody has been maintained.

Public health officials are granted certain enforcement powers under a body of law known as "police powers." If goods are a danger to public health, officials may destroy them with minimal due process and no compensation to the owner.

Quarantine or other limitations of liberty may be imposed on individuals who threaten public health. They may take enforcement actions without prior court hearings, and they may search and seize without probable-cause warrants.

State governments have the primary legal authority and responsibility for public health. Many public health laws were written in response to historic epidemics and are considered by health law experts to be outdated and in need of reform. It is unknown how effectively they could be used to counter a large-scale bioterrorist attack. During the early years of the AIDS epidemic, out of concern for individual rights, some states passed legislation restricting public health police powers. If a massive bioterrorism attack ever took place, quarantine, forcible treatment and/or vaccination, and other actions severely infringing on individual rights might be mandated, but would doubtless be appealed in the courts. Regardless of the legality of the public health authorities' orders, they would be ineffective without adequate enforcement. During the first TOPOFF exercise (a weapons of mass destruction response exercise involving *top* federal and local *officials*, held in 2000), law enforcement and National Guard representatives indicated that they would be unable to force people to stay within their homes. Law enforcement authorities have voiced concern about the level of force that might be required to enforce unpopular restrictions, including perimeter maintenance and quarantine, and have expressed doubts about whether officers would be willing to use unusual levels of force in such a situation.

Conflicts of opinion may develop between law enforcement and public health authorities regarding choosing between potentially protecting the population and collecting evidence to support criminal investigations. Careful joint planning of bioterrorism responses before an event takes place can identify and resolve potential conflicts.

The overwhelming majority of suspected biochemical weapons events are hoaxes. The challenge for local responders is to develop a standard response routine that is both appropriate for dealing with a hoax without overreacting, and capable of confronting a genuine attack appropriately and safely.

*Ellen Sexton*

*See also* Counterterrorism, Emergency Services Units, National Guard

## For Further Reading

Bolz, F., Dudonis, K., & Schulz, D. (2002). *The counterterrorism handbook: Tactics, procedures and techniques.* Boca Raton, FL: CRC.

Burke, R. (2000). *Counter-terrorism for emergency responders.* New York: Lewis.

McBride, D. (Ed.). (2003). *Bioterrorism: The history of a crisis in American society.* New York: Routledge.

Richards, E. (2002, October). Collaboration between public health and law enforcement: The constitutional challenge. *Emerging Infectious Diseases, 8*(10), 1157–1159.

# ✂ CHILD ABDUCTION INVESTIGATIONS

Parental abductions make up the majority of child abductions in the United States. More than 350,000 family abductions occur in the United States each year. Statistics from the U.S. Department of Justice also show that an estimated 58,200 children were abducted by non-family members in 1999. About 6% of these cases make up the most serious cases where the child is murdered, ransomed, or taken with the intent to keep. In more than 50% of child abductions where the child is not taken by a family member, the child is taken from the street, a car, or a park. In many of these cases, the child is killed or seriously injured a short time after being kidnapped. Initial missing child reports are typically made more than 2 hours after the incident, and among abducted children who are murdered, three fourths of the killings occur within the first 3 hours after the abduction. In order to assist in finding these non-family-abducted children as quickly as possible, the AMBER Alert was created.

The AMBER Alert, which stands for *America's Missing: Broadcast Emergency Response,* was created in 1996 as a response to the kidnapping and murder of a 9-year-old girl, Amber Hagerman, by a stranger in Arlington, Texas. The goal of the AMBER Plan is to involve the entire community in assisting in the safe return of abducted children. The AMBER Plan is a voluntary partnership between law enforcement agencies, media, and others to distribute an urgent bulletin in the most serious child abduction cases. Once law enforcement has confirmed a missing child report, an AMBER Alert is sent to various media outlets such as radio stations, television stations, cable companies, the Internet, and electronic highway billboards. Broadcasters interrupt programming using the Emergency Alert System (EAS) to air a description of the missing child, the suspected abductor, and details of the abduction. The alert also provides information about how members of the public who have information relating to the abductions may contact the police or other appropriate law enforcement agencies. This system is the same concept that is used during severe weather emergencies or other emergencies that threaten life or property. Because the EAS is typically used to notify the public about severe weather and other emergencies, as well as for civil and national emergencies, overuse of the system is possible. In order to prevent overuse, the following criteria must be met to activate the EAS for an AMBER Alert:

- Although there is variation among states, generally a child must be 15 years of age or younger, or with a proven mental or physical disability.
- Law enforcement must confirm the child has been abducted.
- Law enforcement must believe that the circumstances surrounding the abduction indicate that the child is in danger of serious bodily harm or death.
- There must be enough descriptive information about the child, abductor, and/or suspect's vehicle to believe an immediate broadcast alert will help.

The AMBER Alerts are used only for the most serious child abduction cases, where law enforcement believes the child is in real danger. The alerts are not used for runaways or most parental abductions.

The alerts are currently used in 41 states, and their use has proved to be effective. At least 60 children have been recovered throughout the United

States because of the aid of the AMBER Alert program. For example, a 10-year-old girl was found in Klamath Falls, Oregon, just hours after she was reported missing by police in Redmond with the state's first AMBER Alert. Although the AMBER Alert is very helpful, it also has pitfalls, such as false reports of abductions and computer and technological problems.

Currently, much is being done to enhance the AMBER Alert. SBC Communications and the California Trucking Association have created programs to distribute the alerts. BellSouth bolstered AMBER Alert programs across its nine-state region through a communication system that notifies 15,000 BellSouth field technicians in support of search efforts in child abduction cases. Furthermore, America Online has allowed customers to receive alerts via e-mail, mobile phones, and pagers since November 2002. Finally, U.S. President George W. Bush signed legislation to establish a national AMBER Alert system on April 30, 2003. This child protection bill encourages states to establish AMBER Alert systems to quickly post information about child abductions. The law has provisions to bolster the child abduction alert system and to stiffen penalties for sex crimes against children. In addition, the bill mandates a national coordinator for the system at the Justice Department and also makes federal grants available to states that have implemented such systems.

*Mara Sullivan*

**See also** Child Molestation, Child Welfare Agencies, Missing Persons

*For Further Reading*

*Amber Alert success.* (2003, March). *Law & Order, 51*(3), 6.

Amber Alert sweeps the nation. (2002, December 15/31). *Law Enforcement News, 28*(589–590), p. 6.

*BellSouth announces partnership with AMBER Alert programs to support search efforts in child abduction cases across Southeast.* (2003). Retrieved July 15, 2003, from http://web.lexis-nexis.com/universe/document?_m=0d640bf2e1150

Child-snatchings are news, but a problem? (2002, December 15/31). *Law Enforcement News, 28*(589–590), p. 6.

Federal Communications Commission. (2003). *The AMBER plan.* Retrieved July 15, 2003, from http://www.fcc.gov/cgb/consumerfacts/AMBERPlan.html

New York State Division of Criminal Justice Services. (2002). *Missing and Exploited Children Clearinghouse: The AMBER Alert plan.* Retrieved July 15, 2003, from http://criminaljustice.state.ny.us/missing/aware/amber.htm

## ✇ CHILD MOLESTATION

Child molestation is commonly defined as inappropriate sexual conduct with a child by an adult or someone substantially older than the child. In 2001, there were more than 85,000 substantiated cases of child sexual abuse reported to law enforcement agencies and Child Protective Services (CPS). Moreover, according to research conducted by the U.S. Department of Justice (Snyder, 2000), 34% of all sexual assaults reported to law enforcement involve children younger than 12, and more than 14% involve children younger than 6 years of age. These findings include only the number of cases that are reported to authorities, not how many cases will ultimately be prosecuted nor the number of cases that actually occur. Difficulties associated with prosecuting child molestation cases often occur in the reporting and investigation of these types of offenses.

In addition to the general problem of sexual crimes being underreported, the retraction of reports is of significant concern to investigators and prosecutors. Although false accusations do occur, it is not the norm. Recanted reports are more likely the result of manipulation by the perpetrator, family pressures, or the child's own psychological conflicts. Manipulation by the offender and the victim's apprehension are also the cause of delayed reporting. Children often do not become comfortable discussing their abuse until adulthood. This was the court's reasoning in the recent landmark case, *Stogner v. Superior Court* (2001). The California legislature revised its laws governing the prosecution of sexual abuse cases by eliminating the statute of limitations. This decision will have a monumental effect on the prosecution of child sexual abuse cases if upheld by the U.S. Supreme Court.

In an effort to combat reporting problems, legislatures have imposed mandatory reporting laws. All states now have statutes that require individuals or agencies to disclose known or suspected sexual abuse cases to CPS agencies. These mandatory reporters typically include school officials, child care providers, health care workers, mental health workers, and law enforcement officers. Collaboration among all agencies and institutions that work with victims of child molestation helps assist in the investigation and prosecution of these cases, while limiting the possibility of revictimizing the child. To further assist in this process, some states have established Special Victims Units. The officers who work in these specialized units are highly trained in investigating sexual offenses and interviewing victims, minimizing the possibility that errors will be made that could compromise the case. Although precautions are taken, some investigative problems are still common, including difficulties in interviewing children and collecting physical evidence.

The police are rarely the first individuals to interview the child about the molestation. Any previous recounting of the abuse, as well as any preliminary interviews conducted by other agencies, is imperative information to law enforcement because the child's recollection may be influenced by these discussions. Inappropriate questioning or coaxing by untrained interviewers can contaminate later interviews. The use of judgmental, leading, and/or suggestive questioning may lead to evidence found unreliable in court, as found in *New Jersey v. Michaels* (1994). This type of questioning is a common mistake, given the problems associated with eliciting information about sexual abuse, and can be eliminated with proper training and supervision.

Interviewing children is a difficult task and, if at all possible, should be conducted without a parent or caretaker in the room. It is often difficult for the child to be completely forthcoming because of a fear of disappointing the parent. Another concern to consider is the child's ability to comprehend questioning and articulate accurately what occurred. This difficulty may be due to his or her developmental age, apprehensiveness stemming from guilt and shame, and confusion about what behavior(s) constitute sexual abuse. Some sexually abusive behaviors will seem normal to children, and that can impair their ability to distinguish between what is and is not appropriate. Furthermore, children often have mixed emotions about discussing the abuse because in the vast majority of cases, the accused is someone that the child knows or loves. They may also fear reprisal or disapproval from parents and friends. Finally, they may be fearful because of threats and manipulation by the perpetrator, and extremely reluctant to disclose information. Patience and building rapport with the child can assist in reducing most of the problems associated with interviewing.

In cases where the abuse is recent, it is important that the child undergo a medical exam to collect physical evidence and provide any necessary medical care. Law enforcement should maintain a close collaborative relationship with the hospital personnel who collect the physical evidence. There are a growing number of hospitals and clinics that now have specialized forensic examiners (Sexual Assault Nurse Examiners) to collect evidence and work with pediatric populations. However, in many cases, there will be no physical evidence that the child was molested, or the findings will be inconclusive because of the nature of the abuse, such as that often found in cases of fondling and masturbation. In these cases, it may be the word of the child against the accused individual. Lack of evidence is also prevalent in any case that comes to the attention of investigators weeks, months, or even years after the offense(s) have occurred.

*Lisa A. Williams*

**See also** Child Welfare, Special Victims Unit

### For Further Reading

Goldstein, S. (1999). *The sexual exploitation of children: A practical guide to assessment, investigation, and intervention* (2nd ed.). Boca Raton, FL: CRC.

New Jersey v. Michaels, 136 N.J. 299 (1994).

Snyder, H. N. (2000). *Sexual assault of young children as reported to law enforcement: Victim, incident, and offender characteristics* (NCJ 182990). Washington, DC: National Center for Juvenile Justice.

Snyder, H. N., & Sickmund, M. (1999, September). *Juvenile offenders and victims: 1999 national report.* Washington, DC: National Center for Juvenile Justice.

Stogner v. Superior Court, 93 Cal. App. 4th 1229 (2001).

U.S. Department of Health and Human Services, Administration on Children, Youth and Families. (2003). *Child maltreatment 2001.* Washington, DC: U.S. Government Printing Office.

Wood, J., & Garven, S. (2000). How sexual abuse interviews go astray: Implications for prosecutors, police, and child protection services. *Child Maltreatment, 5*(2), 109–118.

# ෨෬ CHILD PORNOGRAPHY

## WHAT IS CHILD PORNOGRAPHY?

Child pornography is broadly defined as the visual depiction of sexually explicit conduct involving a minor child. Child pornography can appear in a variety of visual media forms, such as photography film, pictures, magazines, videotapes, movie films, compact discs, zip disks, read-only memory (CD-ROM), and digital video technology (DVD). Child pornography can be transmitted through hand-to-hand contact, mail, computer bulletin board systems, USENET newsgroups, Internet Relay Chat channels, electronic mail, Internet clubs, and a surfeit of frequently changing Web sites.

The precise definition of child pornography remains unclear, and lawmakers have had to depend on subjective community standards when developing policies banning such materials. Federal laws prohibiting child pornography expanded the definitions of child pornography in the past decade to protect both male and female children under 18 years of age. The requirement that pornography must be manufactured for commercial distribution to be prohibited by law was removed. It is now illegal to produce, distribute, advertise, or knowingly possess even one piece of child pornography. All 50 states have their own statutes prohibiting child pornography, and the definitions and penalties vary by state. There are also many international laws prohibiting child pornography, and these vary greatly by country.

New technological advances have made it possible to create visual depictions that appear to be minors engaged in sexually explicit conduct that are virtually indistinguishable from actual photographs of real children. The Child Pornography Prevention Act of 1996 tried to include these images in the definition of child pornography, but the Supreme Court struck down the legislation and found this to be a violation of the First Amendment. In the United States, virtual child pornography must be determined to be obscene under the same standards as other forms of pornography in order to be regulated.

## WHO IS INVOLVED IN CHILD PORNOGRAPHY?

Some collectors molest children and keep the pornography to create a permanent record for arousal and gratification. Others use pornography to lower children's inhibitions, validate and confirm the child sex offender's belief systems, blackmail victims, and/or sell it for profit or trade. However, not all collectors of child pornography molest children, and not all children pictured in child pornography have been sexually abused. Some collectors never molest children but use the pornography for sexual arousal. Other collectors are actively involved in sharing, trading, and selling pornography, whereas others have no involvement with the child pornography underground.

The majority of child pornography is believed to be homemade. It is produced at home and distributed by trading or selling it in the underground market. Commercial child pornography consists of professionally produced and printed depictions with paid models and production staff. Commercial producers rely greatly on the homemade child pornographers for new material, and many homemade images become public through commercial producers. The main difference is the intention to profit.

The children involved in pornography fall into three broad categories:

> Older children who are already involved in prostitution and become involved in commercial pornography or are photographed or filmed by their customers
>
> Younger children, usually prepubescent, who are coerced or manipulated into posing for pornographic videotapes or photographs, often in conjunction with actual molestation
>
> Children of any age who are molested by acquaintances or family members and are photographed or videotaped

The children depicted in pornography can suffer from physical and psychological trauma. They face a potential lifetime of revictimization because of the continued use and distribution of videos, pictures, or computer images. Children need appropriate follow-up care and counseling for their symptoms, including guilt, shame, embarrassment, and inappropriate sexual responses.

## USEFUL TECHNIQUES WHEN INVESTIGATING CHILD PORNOGRAPHY

Child pornography is truly a hidden crime. There are a multitude of problems in uncovering and investigating these cases. Many victimized children will not volunteer their involvement in child pornography often from fear or shame and/or their relationship with the child pornographer. Investigators are reluctant to ask children involved in other sexual abuse cases if pictures or videos were taken. Another difficulty is the fact that many cases not only originate outside local jurisdictions, but some even cross international borders, which complicates the investigative process even further. Often, these other countries do not have sufficient laws to prevent the production, distribution, or possession of child pornography.

Investigators must understand their own state laws and be familiar with federal statutes and the opportunities for dual prosecution. Sometimes, state law is more restrictive than the federal law, and in other states, federal charges will carry greater penalties. In general, the following rules apply: Local police and sheriff's agencies have jurisdiction over local offenses; some states have specialized investigation bureaus for when child pornography investigations span beyond city and county limits; the Federal Bureau of Investigation has jurisdiction when child pornography is transported across state lines; the Postal Service investigates child pornography disseminated through the mail system; and the U.S. Customs Service deals with the importation of child pornography from foreign markets. Many cases involve more than one jurisdiction, and therefore, multidisciplinary, multijurisdictional teams are essential to a coordinated, informed response.

Production, dissemination, and possession patterns of child pornography have increased and changed radically with the accessibility created by the Internet and other technologies. These emerging patterns of child pornography possession have required a change in investigative techniques requiring officers to constantly stay abreast of the current trends. Investigators usually receive specialized training in the use of computers for child pornography cases. Investigators must also be well versed in the legal considerations for obtaining search warrants, proper handling of computer equipment and stored communications, and the use of privileged and confidential communications in these types of cases.

The increase in prosecution and conviction of offenders in model programs around the country suggests that the most effective means of identifying, investigating, and prosecuting child sexual exploitation cases is to adopt a multijurisdictional and multidisciplinary approach. By enabling the law enforcement, child welfare, and service provider communities to combine expertise, manpower, and other institutional resources on these complex cases, investigations can be more thorough, prosecutions more numerous, and services more complete.

*Jessica Saunders and Lisa A. Williams*

### For Further Reading

Arnaldo, C. A. (Ed.). (2001). *Child abuse on the Internet: Ending the silence.* New York: Berghahn.

Goldstein, S. L. (1999). *The sexual exploitation of children: A practical guide to assessment, investigation, and intervention* (2nd ed.). Boca Raton, FL: CRC.

Klain, E. J., Davies, H. J., & Hicks, M. A. (2001). *Child pornography and the criminal justice response.* Washington, DC: American Bar Association Center on Children and the Law.

## ❧ CHILD WELFARE

Child abuse and neglect are very serious issues faced by our country. In a current survey, half of all Americans think that child abuse and neglect are the most important public health issues—more important than other issues such as drug and alcohol abuse, heart disease, and HIV/AIDS. Over the past decade, the percentage of reported child maltreatment has risen consistently. Between the years of 1985 and 1995, there was a 49% increase in reported child maltreatment. However, many cases of child abuse and neglect go unreported. Three million referrals to Child Protective Services agencies were made in the year 2000 concerning the welfare of approximately 5 million children. Nationally, 61.7% were screened in, and 38.3% were screened out. Screened-in referrals were those that received investigations to determine if the allegations of maltreatment could be substantiated, and screened-out referrals were referred to other service agencies. Approximately 32% of the investigations found that the child was either maltreated or at risk of maltreatment.

There are many different definitions of child maltreatment. As defined by the federal Child Abuse Prevention and Treatment Act, a child is a person who has not attained the lesser of the age of 18, or, except in cases of sexual abuse, the age specified by the child protection law of the state in which the child resides. Child abuse and neglect is any recent act or failure to act on the part of a parent or caretaker that results in death, serious physical harm, sexual abuse, or exploitation, or an act or failure to act that presents an imminent risk of serious harm. Sexual abuse is the employment, use, persuasion, inducement, enticement, or coercion of any child to engage in, or assist any other person to engage in, any sexually explicit conduct or simulation of such conduct for the purpose of producing a visual depiction of such conduct. In addition, sexual abuse is also the rape, statutory rape, molestation, prostitution, or other forms of sexual exploitation of children, or incest with children. If any of the aforementioned acts are committed, it is a crime.

All states have legislation regarding the treatment of child abuse and neglect. The general purpose of the legislation is to protect children from harm, and the laws express this goal. Child welfare laws differ in every state, but certain ones are generally enforced in most states, albeit differently. For example, the first step in enforcing the laws that

protect children in most states is the reporting procedure. There are mandated reporters, such as police, psychologists, teachers, and other professionals. Agencies such as hospitals, schools, day care centers, mental health agencies, and social service agencies report a majority of suspected child abuse. More than half of the referrals that were screened in were made by professionals, law enforcement officers, social service workers, and physicians. Other members of the community, including family members, made the remaining screened-in reports. Even though the majority of reporters are not law enforcement officers, these officers do have many responsibilities that include enforcing the law, focusing on accused perpetrators, making arrests, and protecting children from future harm.

Once the child abuse or neglect is reported, the agency usually responsible for investigating child abuse cases is either Child Protective Services or the Department of Social Services. Because the suspected child abuse is reported to an outside agency, the primary responsibility for investigations and decisions regarding these investigations lies with the specific agency. In addition, these agencies are expected to reduce as well as prevent child abuse and neglect. Child welfare agencies are also responsible for safety assessment, risk assessment, and ongoing assessment at case closure. The agencies are to determine what the client's needs are and to decide what services will best address those needs.

Even though most states use child welfare agencies to follow up on reported child abuse and neglect, some states have different methods. For example, in five counties in Florida, the sheriff's office has taken over the investigations from the state's Department of Children and Families. Governor Jeb Bush implemented this change in order to break the Department of Children and Families bureaucracy into smaller, community-based agencies.

Courts also play a role in enforcing child welfare laws. Even though they do not have as critical a role as child welfare agencies, they play an important part in determining whether children will be taken from their homes, the time children remain in foster care, and where they will live permanently. Courts also play a crucial role in setting and monitoring child safety, system accountability, timeliness, and coordination of system resources. In 2000, court actions were initiated for 15.3% of the victims of child abuse or neglect.

Recently, there have been many problems regarding child welfare. There are many communication problems between the agencies and individuals charged with protecting children, as well as between law enforcement officers and child welfare agencies. Another problem is that there are not enough child welfare workers for the number of cases assigned. The average number of investigations per investigation/assessment worker was 73 per year. Therefore, child welfare workers get assigned many more cases than they are able to handle. In addition, only slightly more than half of the child victims received postinvestigation services. These failures of the child welfare system are apparent in one case of child abuse and neglect in Newark, New Jersey. Two young boys, who were starving and filthy, were found in a basement, along with the decomposed body of their brother. Even though there were multiple reports of suspected abuse, the state agencies charged with protecting children had closed the case a year before. Many reports of child abuse and neglect go uninvestigated in some of New Jersey's impoverished neighborhoods. The majority of children in foster care in New Jersey are not followed up on according to federal guidelines. Furthermore, caseworkers do not conduct interviews with community members, who might be able to help remove children from abusive households.

*Mara Sullivan*

## For Further Reading

Brooks, C. M., Perry, N. W., Starr, S. D., & Teply, L. L. (1994). Child abuse and neglect reporting laws: Understanding interests, understanding policy. *Behavioral Sciences and the Law, 12,* 49–64.

Flango, V. (2001, April). Measuring progress in improving court processing of child abuse and neglect cases. *Family Court Review.* Retrieved February 1, 2003, from http://web.lexis-nexis.com/universe

Meier, E. (2000, July/August). Current legislative issues related to children. *Pediatric Nursing, 26.* Retrieved February 1, 2003, from http://web12.epnet.com/delivery

Portwood, S., Grady, M. T., & Dutton, S. (2000, February). Enhancing law enforcement identification and investigation of child maltreatment. *Child Abuse & Neglect, 24,* 195–207.

U.S. Department of Health and Human Services. (1993). *The third national incidence study of child abuse and neglect.* Washington, DC: National Clearinghouse on Child Abuse and Neglect Information.

Willis, C. L., & Wells, R. H. (1988). The police and child abuse: An analysis of police decisions to report illegal behavior. *Criminology, 26,* 695–714.

## ∞ CHRISTOPHER COMMISSION, THE

The Christopher Commission was a special, independent investigative body created on April 1, 1991, by Los Angeles Mayor Tom Bradley to examine the structure and operations of the Los Angeles Police Department (LAPD) with the assistance of the Los Angeles District Attorney's Office. The Commission's mission was to recommend reform to eliminate the excessive use of force by law enforcement, specifically by the LAPD. Its creation was a response to the George Holliday videotape of 27 California law enforcement officers, 23 of whom were from the LAPD, who were present at the savage beating of 25-year-old African American motorist Rodney King on Sunday morning, March 3, 1991. The videotape was the subject of numerous press reports both in the United States and throughout the world. The beating involved 56 baton strikes, plus numerous kicks to King's head and body by four LAPD officers—Sergeant Koon and officers Briseno, Powell, and Wind. King sustained numerous injuries, including a broken right ankle; broken cheekbone; and, according to his lawyers, 11 skull fractures, kidney damage, brain damage, and broken teeth. The videotape's existence is also significant because Paul King, the brother of Rodney King, had failed in his attempts to file an official complaint against the law enforcement officers involved. Among other things, the Commission discovered that such difficulties in filing an excessive-use-of-force complaint against officers were commonplace.

The Christopher Commission was eventually merged with another commission that had been created by then-LAPD Chief Darryl Gates. The Commission members were Warren Christopher, former Deputy Attorney General (Chairperson); John Arguelles, retired state Supreme Court Justice (Vice Chairperson); Roy Anderson of the Lockheed Corporation and the board of trustees for Stanford University; Leo F. Estrada, an associate professor at the University of California, Los Angeles (UCLA); Mickey Kantor, a law partner at Manatt, Phelps and Phillips; Andrea Sheridan Ordin, a former U.S. Attorney; John Slaughter, president of Occidental College; Dr. Robert Tranquada, Dean, University of Southern California School of Medicine; Willie Barnes, former Commissioner of Corporations of California; and Richard Mosk, former international judge and staff member of the Warren Commission. Also, three senior advisors were assigned to the Christopher Commission: Jesse Brewer, a retired officer from the LAPD with 38 years of service; James Q. Wilson, a widely published UCLA professor on crime and urban issues; and Patrick Murphy, former police commissioner of both New York City and Detroit. The Commission also had a staff of more than 60 lawyers and three accounting and data analysis firms.

The Commission heard testimony from 50 expert witnesses and more than 150 members of the community in five public hearings in different parts of Los Angeles. More than 500 LAPD officers were interviewed, and about 650 responded to a survey. The Commission also examined LAPD complaint reports, the paperwork of 83 civil damage lawsuits, and communication transcripts from patrol car mobile digital terminals (MDTs). The investigation lasted more than 3 months. The final report was 297 pages long. Its primary findings focused on use-of-force policies and practices, complaint procedures, applicant screening and recruitment, training, management and supervision, and organizational structure.

Although LAPD policy required officers to use the minimum force necessary to gain control of volatile situations, the Commission found that where such use-of-force policies existed, they were often not followed and received little attention from police management. Poor supervision was a key finding of the Commission. For example, 63 LAPD officers each had 20 or more misuse-of-force allegations filed against them between 1987 and March 1991. For the most part, these officers had received positive performance evaluations. The Commission also found evidence of biased attitudes and conduct unsuited for police work. Much of this evidence came from a review of 182 days of MDT transcripts of police communication from 1989 to 1991 that revealed hundreds of improper messages, including many officers speaking in jest of beating suspects of color.

The Commission's recommendations included changes throughout the LAPD's command structure that were intended to encourage positive attitudes among officers and increase accountability by incorporating direct responsibility to civilian representatives. It found flaws with an organizational structure in which a Police Commission was responsible for making departmental policy even though the head of the Police Commission was an active LAPD officer and, as such, accountable to the Chief of Police. The Christopher Commission thought it unlikely that such a person could defend an agenda that was contrary to that of the police chief.

The Commission determined that the applicant screening of officers was inadequate. Although psychological examinations were administered, there was little attention given to an applicant's prior behavior, which, according to criminologists, is the best predictor of future conduct. They also concluded that police work itself shapes attitudes and behaviors. Thus, training and trainers merited greater attention. At the time, LAPD officer training involved 6 months in the police academy (which included 8 hours of diversity training), 1 year on the job under the supervision of field training officers (FTOs), and periodic training thereafter. The Commission recommended more diversity training, stricter criteria for officers to serve as FTOs, and more rotation of supervising officers. It also recommended more training in the use of verbal skills to deescalate dangerous situations.

Additionally, many officers with excessive force complaints were often paired with each other or assigned to work in settings where suspects were particularly vulnerable to abuse—such as jail duty. The Commission recommended against such practices and also recommended that complaints be considered in promotion decisions.

A major recommendation was to substantially change the way complaints against officers were taken and investigated. From 1986 to 1990, there were 2,152 complaints, of which only 42 were sustained. Many individuals had been overtly or subtly discouraged from filing complaints. In predominantly Hispanic communities, there were often no Spanish speakers made available for the purpose of taking complaints. Problems were found with the resources allocated and the process used for investigating complaints. Further hampering the process, officers were often allowed to do an unrecorded investigative preinterview before an interview of record. To remedy this situation, the Commission recommended the creation of an Office of Inspector General under the Police Commission to investigate and oversee the disciplinary process in serious complaints. The Christopher Commission also recommended greater independence for the Police Commission, greater compensation for its members, and service for a maximum of 5 years.

Less than 10 years later, the LAPD would find itself in the midst of another scandal involving cops assigned to antigang activities who engaged in corrupt and brutal behavior. The Rampart Investigation, as it was called, eventually led to the imposition of a federal consent decree. Many police observers maintain that failure to fully implement the recommendations of the Christopher Commission led to this later scandal.

*Camille Gibson*

*See also* Knapp Commission, McCone Commission, Mollen Commission, Rampart Division Investigation, Use of Force

### For Further Reading

Bobb, M. J., Epstein, M. H., Miller, N. H., & Abascal, M. A. (1996). *Five years later: A report to the Los Angeles Police Commission on the Los Angeles Police Department's implementation of Independent Commission recommendations.* Los Angeles: Special Counsel, Los Angeles Police Commission.

Christopher Commission Report. (1991). *Report of the Independent Commission on the Los Angeles Police Department.* Los Angeles: Independent Commission on the Los Angeles Police Department.

Commission on Accreditation for Law Enforcement Agencies. (1999). *Standards for law enforcement agencies* (4th ed.). Fairfax, VA: Author.

Langan, P., Greenfeld, L., Smith, S., Durose, M., & Levin, D. (2001). *Contacts between police and the public: Findings from the 1999 national survey.* Washington, DC: U.S. Department of Justice.

Lasley, J., & Hooper, M. (1998). On racism and the LAPD: Was the Christopher Commission wrong? *Social Science Quarterly, 79*(2), 378–389.

Los Angeles Board of Police Commissioners. (1996). *In the course of change: The Los Angeles Police Department five years after the Christopher Commission.* Los Angeles: Los Angeles Police Department.

## ∞ CITIZEN POLICE ACADEMIES

Citizen police academies (CPAs) are intended to provide community residents with insights into the nature of police work. These programs are designed to serve a community relations function by educating citizens about the structure and operation of their local police department. Citizens are exposed to the various problems faced by the police in their community in the hope that CPA graduates will become more sympathetic to the difficulties of modern police work. Ideally, graduates will act as advocates for their local police, multiplying such a program's benefits.

The idea driving CPA programs is that educating a small number of citizens on how local police agencies and officers operate will improve broader community support. This idea was first applied in 1977 in the Devon and Cornwall Constabulary in the United Kingdom. The Constabulary designed a 10-week "Police Night School" that select citizens were invited to attend. This school met one night a week, with different police personnel volunteering to teach various topics to the citizen-students. The curriculum was designed to provide attendees with a general understanding of British policing, as well as the challenges faced by local constables. The night school was well received by both constables and citizens, and similar programs were implemented in other British constabularies.

In 1985, the Orlando, Florida, Police Department implemented America's first CPA program. The structure and content of the curriculum used in Orlando was based upon the British model. The program also offered attendees the opportunity to observe an officer during a "ride along" and to receive basic training in the use of police firearms. In the following years, CPA programs were adopted by a number of agencies across the United States. Most of these programs continued to emulate the initial British model (a 10- to 12-week program meeting once a week for 3 hours), although agencies modified aspects of the curriculum to better reflect community issues. Most CPA programs are designed to educate the general public, but a small proportion have curricula designed to meet the needs and interests of senior citizens, youth, or business owners.

Research has estimated that about one third of medium and large police agencies operate some type of CPA. In one of the few studies to systematically examine the structure of CPA programs across the country, Vic Bumphus, Larry Gaines, and Curt Blakely (1999) found the average CPA was an 11-week program meeting once a week for 3 hours. These scholars found that the most common topics covered in CPAs were criminal law, patrol operations, investigations, crime prevention, use of force, community policing, narcotics enforcement, homicide investigation, community services, and a "ride along." There is, however, variation in the content of CPA curricula. These researchers noted that some programs are used more as a public relations tool than as a mode of educating the public on the challenges of police work. They suggest that programs in the former category focus more attention on dynamic and exciting aspects of police work, such as firearms training, tactical demonstrations, and arrest procedures, and deemphasize community services, crime prevention, and investigations.

Although one or two officers may coordinate CPA programs and oversee each session, most programs make use of a range of instructors to provide different aspects of the curriculum. Police officers working in crime prevention and on community policing assignments may discuss the philosophies and programs employed by the sponsoring agency. Prosecutors or judges may present information on how arrestees are handled by local judicial systems. Investigative personnel may lecture on the nature of local crime problems and the techniques used in undercover operations. Civilian or sworn personnel responsible for collecting and processing forensic evidence may discuss how crime scenes are handled.

Most of the agencies sponsoring CPAs advertise their programs in local media outlets in an effort to attract attendees. Agencies vary in the criteria they use to select program participants. Some agencies subject program applicants to a basic criminal history check and exclude those who have been convicted of committing a crime. This approach is rational if agencies are concerned that the program may provide the local "criminal element" with an education on police procedures and tactics. Viewed alternatively, however, excluding those convicted of a crime may mean that agencies exclude the very citizens who might benefit the most from participating in a CPA program.

Most attendees begin their CPA experience with a positive image of the sponsoring agency and its officers (Schafer & Bonello, 2001). Although this allows for a harmonious academy experience for both instructors and attendees, it may mean that CPAs "miss the mark" in their efforts to improve community relations with some segments of the population. The very people who may benefit the most from a CPA experience (members of marginalized groups within a community) may be least likely to participate. Agencies should question whether the time and money invested in CPA programs are worthwhile given the types of attendees they attract. Is it enough to educate those who are already supportive of the police and to make their positive attitudes even more positive, or would agencies be better served if they tried to improve the perceptions and understandings of citizens who have historically distrusted the police?

The variation in academy curricula illustrates that there is no agreement on the appropriate goals of CPA programs. Some agencies use CPAs to educate citizens, foster support for the agency, and increase citizen volunteerism in support of community programs. Other agencies use CPAs as a tool to generate improved community relations and to highlight the more glamorous image of the police as tough crime fighters. Analogously, many agencies may "preach to the choir" by educating citizens who already trust and support the local police, rather than using CPA programs to improve relations that have historically been strained. No one approach is inherently right. Despite their popularity with both the police and citizens, the effectiveness of CPA programs has not been established. and their impact on police–community relations remains unclear.

*Joseph A. Schafer*

## For Further Reading

Bumphus, V. W., Gaines, L. K., & Blakely, C. R. (1999). Citizen police academies: Observing goals, objectives, and recent trends. *American Journal of Criminal Justice, 24*(1), 67–79.

Greenberg, M. A. (1991). Citizen police academies. *FBI Law Enforcement Bulletin, 60*(8), 10–13.

Schafer, J. A., & Bonello, E. M. (2001). The citizen police academy: Measuring outcomes. *Police Quarterly, 4,* 434–448.

## ∾ CITIZEN'S ARREST

The role of the private person in matters of criminal pursuit and arrest has its formal roots in medieval England with the Statutes of Winchester in 1285. Without an officially organized police force, ordinary citizens were obligated to either initiate an arrest themselves upon witnessing a crime, or immediately join a communal hue and cry to pursue and capture a suspected criminal. Because of the advent of professional law enforcement and rising criminality in emerging densely populated urban centers in the 17th and 18th centuries, citizen-initiated arrests and captures were discouraged, and therefore diminished in number. Although 18th-century English common law officially made an arrest by a private person as legitimate as that of a peace officer's, precise regulations for citizen's arrest further limited its scope and application.

English common law rules on citizen's arrest were later absorbed into Anglo-American law and codified in arrests by private persons or arrests without warrant at the state level. In the United States, the law enforcement community has historically applauded citizen participation in crime prevention. However, the preferred role for a private citizen has been confined to merely providing information or assisting in arrests only when called upon by a government agent in the dual hopes of restraining vigilante justice and reinforcing police professionalism. By the 19th century, most states had formulated citizen's arrest laws restricting a private individual's scope of arrest and attaching damages to wrongful arrests in order to discourage the abuse of its power, in particular, and its practice, in general.

At present, there are indeed cases of ordinary citizens exercising their legal right to arrest. However, the laws of citizen's arrest are most often employed by public officials—federal agents (customs inspectors or drug enforcement agents) or state law enforcement personnel performing arrests outside their jurisdictional authority—or private police personnel, such as security guards or private investigators without license to arrest. Ordinary citizens performing arrests are most likely to be store owners or employees detaining suspected shoplifters, or private citizens carrying out arrest orders from government agents.

In the United States, the authority to perform a citizen's arrest still rests on common law and is regulated by state legislation and judicial interpretation presented through state case law. Although specifics in the application of these laws may vary from state to state, the majority of states' laws are statutorily similar. In general, a private person has the same right to arrest as a peace officer. Moreover, a citizen's arrest is as legally valid and binding as an arrest made by an officer. The arrest must be made promptly or within a reasonable amount of time, using no more force than is necessary and reasonable. Following an arrest, the arrestor is obligated by law to bring the person arrested before a magistrate or peace officer without delay, or within a reasonable amount of time. Unlike a law enforcement agent, however, an ordinary citizen performs an arrest at his or her own peril and is therefore subject to criminal responsibility (false imprisonment or kidnapping) and/or civil liability (false arrest or slander) if statutory requirements for the arrest are not evidenced.

According to common law, and in most state jurisdictions, a private person may make an arrest without a warrant when a felony or misdemeanor constituting a breach of the peace is committed *in his or her presence*. However, in some jurisdictions, such as California and the District of Columbia, a citizen's arrest may be performed for any misdemeanor committed in one's presence, not just a breach of the peace (5 Am. Jur. 2d *Arrest* § 57). In some states, such as New York and Georgia, an arrest may also be made if a felony is merely attempted in one's presence and the apprehension of the suspect may actually prevent the perpetration of the crime (6A C.J.S. *Arrest* § 13). Finally, as per common law and in most states, a private person may lawfully make an arrest without warrant for a felony *not committed in his or her presence* if a felony has actually been committed and one has probable or reasonable cause to believe that the suspect has actually committed the crime.

Although a private person making a citizen's arrest is acting on behalf of the sovereignty, legally, he or she is not acting as an agent of the state. Thus, arrests made by private individuals are not subject to Fourth Amendment challenges (6A C.J.S. *Arrest* § 12). As long as a citizen's arrest is lawful and is not induced or supported by any government official, a search subsequent to arrest is deemed reasonable and evidence is admissible in court (Bassiouni, 1977, p. 66). State search-and-seizure laws do, however, vary with regard to private police forces (security guards) making citizens' arrests. Moreover, some authorities maintain that a state's constitutional right to privacy safeguards against searches conducted by private individuals (79 C.J.S. *Searches and Seizures* § 43).

Citizen's arrest laws do not cover shoplifting in that these laws generally pertain to misdemeanors that amount to a breach of peace that are committed in the presence of an arrestor. Shoplifting is not a breach of the peace, nor is it customarily committed in the presence of others. Therefore, most states have enacted separate shoplifting statutes that allow merchants, or their employees or agents, the authority to stop, question, search, and detain a person suspected of shoplifting in a reasonable manner for a reasonable period of time until the arrival of a law enforcement agent. This "shoplifting detention authority," however, is granted to merchants, their agents, and peace officers, not private citizens.

*Barbara Goldman Carrel*

***See also*** Arrest, Search and Seizure

### For Further Reading

Bassiouni, M. C. (1977). *Citizen's arrest: The law of arrest, search and seizure for private citizens and private police.* Springfield, IL: Charles C Thomas.

The law of citizen's arrest. (1965). *Columbia Law Review, 65,* 502–513.

## ✆ CIVIL LIABILITY

Law enforcement officials are subject to civil liability for intentional actions on their part to deprive citizens of constitutional rights. This liability derives primarily from the Ku Klux Klan Act of 1871, enacted as a response to the systematic injustices leveled against blacks in the aftermath of the Civil War. Although written with a narrow constituency in mind, the Act is cast in broad terms, providing a remedy against "any person" who, under color of state law, deprives any person of "any rights, privileges or immunities secured by the Constitution." The Act is codified as 42 U.S.C. §1983.

During the 1960s and 1970s, the U.S. Supreme Court began widening the coverage of Section 1983 to match its expansive language. In *Monroe v. Pape* (1961), the Court held that Section 1983 provides a remedy for any constitutional violation committed under color of state law. Prior to that decision, the Court had left unresolved the question of whether the phrase "under color of state law" includes actions taken by public officials in the course of their duties, but not mandated by the law of the state. In 1971, the Court went a step further, ruling in *Bivens v. Six Unknown Named Agents of Federal Bureau of*

*Narcotics* that a private right of action existed for violations of constitutional rights by federal officials, analogous to that of Section 1983. These decisions significantly increased the limits of personal liability for state and federal officers.

At the same time, the Court developed a scheme to protect individual public officials from Section 1983 and *Bivens* liability. Common law had long recognized certain immunities for public officials. Judges, legislators, prosecutors, the president, and other members of the executive branch are all absolutely immune from liability for actions taken within the scope of their discretionary authority. In 1967, the Court began a process of extending a qualified immunity to law enforcement officers and other government officials for actions taken during the execution of their official duties.

In *Pierson v. Ray*, the Court established a good-faith defense for public officials. The *Pierson* Court held that police officers who had arrested several black ministers in a "whites only" area of a train station were immune from damages so long as they "reasonably believed in good faith that the arrest was constitutional." The *Pierson* standard contained both an objective component (reasonable belief) and a subjective component (good faith).

In *Harlow v. Fitzgerald* (1982), the Supreme Court abandoned the subjective prong of the test, thus broadening the scope of protection afforded officers. The new test shielded government officials from civil liability as long as their conduct did not "violate clearly established statutory or constitutional rights of which a reasonable person would have known." Under *Harlow*, if the right violated by an official is found to be not clearly established at the time of the official's action, the official is shielded from liability even if a court determines that a violation of constitutional rights occurred and even if the official knew that his conduct violated the plaintiff's rights.

Qualified immunity is thus a broad protection. Even if an officer believes him- or herself to be violating a citizen's constitutional rights—and even if he or she is right in this belief—he or she is nevertheless protected from liability as long as that violated right has not been clearly established.

According to *Anderson v. Creighton* (1987), a right is clearly established if the "contours of the right are sufficiently clear that a reasonable official would understand that what he is doing violates the right." Again, an especially knowledgeable officer who intentionally violates someone's rights may nevertheless be exempt if an officer of average knowledge would not have been aware of the right. Subjective intent is irrelevant to the determination of immunity. Moreover, qualified immunity is a protection from suit, not just a shield from liability. Unless a plaintiff can show that the right he or she alleges to have been violated was clearly established, his or her claim will be dismissed.

The doctrine of qualified immunity encompasses two policy choices. First, it reflects a decision that public officials should not be held strictly liable for knowledge of the law. For ordinary citizens, ignorance of the law is not a defense. Second, it reflects a judgment that officers should be held to what essentially amounts to gross negligence standard of care.

One justification for this departure from common practices is the fear that, absent these protections, officers will be inhibited from performing their duties. Given the uncertainty that often surrounds the parameters of constitutional principles, officers may be unclear whether their potential conduct violates the law. Given the possibility of Section 1983 liability, officers may be fearful of subjecting themselves to liability. Qualified immunity helps to prevent paralysis in the face of uncertainty in the law.

At the same time, as some scholars have noted, qualified immunity may undesirably extend nearly blanket protection to public officials, a problem sometimes referred to as moral hazard. Insurance companies enforce deductibles to prevent against the risk of moral hazard—without a theft deductible, a driver might have no incentive to lock his or her car. The deductible ensures that the incentives of the driver and the insurance company are consistent.

One aspect of the moral hazard of qualified immunity doctrine is that under the existing standard, officers have no incentive to educate themselves as to the law because an officer's state of mind is irrelevant. A second problem is that the Court has set the bar for "clearly defined" principles so high, that few rights will be protected under Section 1983. A third problem is that constitutional rights will not continue to evolve: In cases where qualified immunity is claimed, if a court determines that the principle alleged to have been violated is not clearly established, then the matter is dismissed without a determination of whether the defendant's rights actually were violated. Few precedents are established, making it harder still to bring future claims. A fourth problem is that victims go uncompensated, and, although state agencies can insure themselves against the cost of potential lawsuits, it is difficult, if not impossible, for an ordinary citizen to insure him- or herself against violations of his or her civil liberties.

As a consequence of these considerations, some observers have proposed bifurcating the qualified immunity standard; that is, establishing separate standards for higher- and lower-level public officials. There are some compelling reasons to protect higher-level public officials from suit: The behavior of elected officials is checked to some extent by the political process, and the costs of having elected officials involved in lawsuits are particularly high. These concerns are not present for lower-level officials. Without question, some costs attach to having police officers present in court to testify in legal proceedings, but these costs are categorically different from having, say, the Secretary of State spend his or her days giving depositions.

Nevertheless, the Supreme Court rejected an argument for a bifurcated qualified immunity standard in *Anderson v. Creighton*. Writing for the majority, Justice Scalia held that a split standard would create unnecessary confusion. Thus, the status quo remains: State and federal officials are subject to liability for violations of constitutional rights under Section 1983 and *Bivens*. They are entitled to immunity, however, unless the plaintiff can show that the right alleged to have been violated was clearly established.

*Evan J. Mandery*

## For Further Reading

Anderson v. Creighton, 483 U.S. 635 (1987).
Bivens v. Six Unknown Named Agents of Federal Bureau of Narcotics, 403 U.S. 388 (1971).
Harlow v. Fitzgerald, 457 U.S. 800 (1982).
Monroe v. Pape, 365 U.S. 167 (1961).
Pierson v. Ray, 386 U.S. 547 (1967).

# ✑ CIVIL RIGHTS VIOLATIONS BY POLICE

The Department of Justice (DOJ) investigates civil rights violations committed by police officers as well as violations that suggest patterns and practices of misconduct within law enforcement agencies. The Criminal Section of the DOJ Civil Rights Division prosecutes officers under 18 U.S.C. § 242, which pertains to color of law violations. Color of law violations include excessive use of force, unexplained shootings, sexual abuses, dangerous restraint techniques, unlawful searches and seizures, false arrests, and filing false reports while acting in an official capacity. Two examples of color of law violations are the 1992 indictments of four Los Angeles Police Department (LAPD) officers for the 1991 beating of Rodney King and the 2000 indictment of Jacksonville Deputy Sheriff Karl T. Waldon for the false arrest, robbery, and killing of local businessman Sami Safar. The Special Litigation Section indicts police agencies under 42 U.S.C. § 14141 wherever an investigation provides evidence of an existing pattern or practice of misconduct by its employees. Known as The Police Misconduct Statute, 42 U.S.C. § 14141 has been used in DOJ lawsuits against police departments in Pittsburgh, Pennsylvania; Steubenville, Ohio; and New Jersey, among others. Police departments in Washington, DC, and Highland Park, Illinois, have resolved pending lawsuits by signing the Memoranda of Understanding, which allows the DOJ to monitor each department's compliance with reform measures over at least a 5-year period.

One of the DOJ's most publicized convictions for criminal civil rights violations involved the 1991 videotaped beating of Rodney King by four LAPD officers. Although the officers were acquitted by a local jury in 1991, the Criminal Section and the U.S. Attorney's Office in Los Angeles conducted an investigation that led to the 1992 federal indictment on two color of law violations. Three of the officers were indicted for excessive use of force, and the fourth, their supervising sergeant, was indicted for failure to stop the others from using such methods. In 1993, two of the officers, Sergeant Stacey Koon and Officer Laurence Powell, were convicted. This federal conviction eventually led to a review of the LAPD's practices.

In 2000, the Criminal Section and the U.S. Attorney's Office for the Middle District of Florida indicted Jacksonville Deputy Sheriff Karl T. Waldon, three former officers, and three civilian co-conspirators for committing murder, robberies, thefts, and drug offenses. In 1998, Waldon arrested a Jacksonville businessman, Sami Safar, on a false pretext, drove him to a remote location, strangled him, and stole the $50,000 bank withdrawal Safar recently made (Office of the United States Attorney, 2003). Waldon was eventually convicted on 14 counts, including color of law violations and obstruction of justice.

The Police Misconduct Statute allows the Special Litigation Section to direct action against police departments for failure to discipline, train, or monitor the officers' actions. This statute was developed as a response to the beating of Rodney King and The Christopher Commission's report that condemned the LAPD for ineffective investigations of civilian complaints and officer supervision. In 1996, the pattern or practice principle was applied to investigations of police departments in Pittsburgh, Pennsylvania, and Steubenville, Ohio. The investigation claimed that police officers in both cities made false arrests, conducted illegal searches and seizures, and used excessive force while making arrests or while individuals were in custody. Officers were also heard using racial slurs when dealing with African Americans. The departments were criticized for improper management, failure to investigate civilian complaints, failure to discipline officers charged with misconduct, and failure to provide adequate training and supervision. Both cities entered into consent decrees that included provisions such as better use-of-force training and policies, stronger reporting mechanisms, development of early warning systems to officers at risk of color of law violations, improved disciplinary procedures, and a compliance monitoring system (Livingston, 1999).

In April 1999, the New Jersey Attorney General's office published a report that New Jersey state troopers were using racial profiling as a basis for traffic stops and searches. The review was prompted by public outcry and attention from incidents such as the 1998 shooting of three unarmed black and Latino men traveling to basketball trials on the New Jersey interstate highway. The DOJ filed a lawsuit against New Jersey state police from evidence of discriminatory practices and inadequate punishment of officers. According to the Civil Rights Division's Activities and Programs Brochure (2002), the police department entered into a 5-year consent decree that included reforms such as requiring state troopers to refrain from using race or ethnicity when selecting motorists for traffic stops; documenting the race, ethnic origin, and gender of all drivers stopped; and providing the reason for the stop. The decree also developed the Management Awareness Program, which requires supervisors to use and review computerized information on traffic stops and misconduct investigations as an early warning system to identify discriminatory behaviors.

The Special Litigation Section also uses the Memoranda of Understanding to resolve investigations with law enforcement agencies without entering into a lawsuit. The Memoranda of Understanding authorizes the Section to monitor an agency's measure of compliance or progress with reforms in a consent decree. In 2001, the Metropolitan Police Department in Washington, DC, signed a Memoranda of Understanding after the Section investigated allegations of excessive force. Also in 2001, the Highland Park, Illinois, police department signed the Memoranda in order to resolve an investigation into racial profiling allegations. In 2002, the City of Cincinnati, prompted by riots and public outcry from the unexplained police shootings of several African American civilians, signed a collaborative agreement with the DOJ to reform excessive-force practices.

*Dara N. Byrne*

**See also** Complaints Against Police, Use of Force

## For Further Reading

*Civil Rights Division's Activities and Programs Brochure.* (2002). United States Department of Justice. Retrieved

October 31, 2003, from http://www.usdoj.gov/crt/activity .html

Deprivation of Rights Under Color of Law, 18 U.S.C. § 242.

Livingston, D. (1999). Police reform and the Department of Justice: An essay on accountability. *Buffalo Criminal Law Review*, 2(2), 817–859.

Office of the United States Attorney Middle District of Florida. (2003). Press release. Retrieved October 31, 2003, from http://www.usdoj.gov/usao/flm/pr/012703waldon.pdf

Violent Crime Control and Law Enforcement Act, 42 U.S.C. § 14141 (1994).

## ✎ CIVILIAN COMPLAINT REVIEW BOARDS

Civilian complaint review boards, also referred to as citizen oversight of police, operate in diverse ways. These boards include citizens in the process of handling complaints against individual police officers and monitoring police organizations. A general goal is to enhance police accountability by ensuring that officers use appropriate levels of force, officers treat individuals without bias, police organizations support policies and procedures that facilitate professionalism, and procedures exist for the fair receipt and investigation of complaints against the police. Dramatic incidents of police misconduct focus attention on the mechanisms that exist or do not exist to prevent and respond to such conduct. Citizen involvement in oversight of police is viewed by advocates as one potentially valuable part of a system that can prevent misconduct; it is not seen as a panacea for preventing police misconduct. Traditionally opposed by police practitioners, citizen oversight is also viewed with skepticism and is believed to produce harmful results.

Two general mechanisms exist to hold police accountable. Internal mechanisms are those within police organizations and include formal policies, direct supervision, leadership, and internal affairs units. External mechanisms are outside of police organizations and seek to ensure that police are accountable to the public for their conduct. Court decisions in the United States serve this function by compelling police to change their practices. These include landmark decisions such as *Mapp v. Ohio* and *Miranda v. Arizona*, and lesser-known civil decisions

that hold municipalities liable for police conduct, such as *Thurman v. City of Torrington, CT*. Other external mechanisms include law enforcement accreditation bodies, the media, "watchdog groups," and civilian complaint review boards. Civilian complaint oversight mechanisms exist in many nations around the world, including Australia, Canada, and the United States.

## GROWTH OF CITIZEN OVERSIGHT

Citizen involvement in oversight of police grew significantly in the last two decades of the 20th century. In 2001, more than 100 different citizen oversight bodies existed in the United States, up from the 13 that existed in 1980. Rather than exhibiting steady growth, this trend is characterized by failures, setbacks, and successes across several decades. Interest in the idea of involving citizens in police oversight appeared in the 1920s and, over time, has tended to grow out of high-profile conflicts between communities and police, many involving minority communities. A handful of cities in the United States experimented with citizen involvement during the 1950s. One of the first important citizen oversight agencies appeared in Philadelphia in 1958. Despite important failures of citizen review during the 1960s, the trend persists today. Interest in citizen review boards during the past 30 years has coincided with more widespread concern about public accountability and citizen involvement in government. In general, citizen oversight is part of a system of checks on police power.

An important reason for the creation of civilian review boards is the recognition that internal oversight mechanisms, including rules and procedures, police supervision, and police handling of citizen complaints, can and do fail in important ways. Several high-profile cases and many seemingly mundane occurrences illustrate that the failures of police to control misconduct are not isolated anecdotes. A significant result of these failures is the erosion of public confidence in the ability of the police to ensure internal accountability. The growth of citizen oversight has also coincided with increased openness of at least some police organizations, greater awareness and concern about the extent of police misconduct, and the spread of community policing.

The "code of silence" in policing is believed to be a significant impediment to quality investigations into police misconduct. The code of silence is the idea that police officers are not cooperative during investigations of fellow officers. External oversight procedures are believed to help overcome this problem. Evidence suggests that concerns about the code of silence are valid. Following investigations of police conduct in New York and Los Angeles, the Mollen and Christopher Commissions concluded that the code of silence is a significant impediment to thorough investigations of police conduct. A 2000 report on the results of a national survey of police officers in the United States shows that the code of silence remains an important part of policing. Whereas more than 70% of responding officers indicated that the code of silence is not an essential part of the trust required for good policing, more than 50% of respondents indicated that officers do not always report serious abuses of authority by fellow officers.

Numerous commissions that have studied serious instances of civil unrest and police–community conflicts concluded that complaints against the police should be subjected to external review procedures. In 1931, the Wickersham Commission recommended the creation of independent bodies that would aid citizens with complaints against police, the 1968 Kerner Commission report advised that there be some body external to municipal agencies that would review citizen complaints, and a 1981 U.S. Civil Rights Commission report recommended that citizen complaint processes undergo external review. Today, the International Association of Chiefs of Police endorses citizen involvement in complaint procedures. These recommendations imply that external review could reduce the chances and severity of police misconduct and could also improve police–community relations.

## DIVERSITY OF FORMS

Citizen review agencies have been characterized as falling into one of five categories that vary in terms of their structure and function. Nevertheless, some agencies blend elements of different types. The first type of organization receives and investigates citizen complaints; the second type reviews police investigations into complaints; the third receives appeals of police investigations and dispositions and may make recommendations to the police; the fourth type primarily serves a monitoring role; and the fifth type consists of nonsworn police employees who are involved in the complaint process.

Civilian complaint review boards serve two primary functions: independent handling of complaints against police and monitoring of police organizations. The independent nature of civilian review boards is a defining feature because it is believed to enhance the fairness of the complaint process by reducing the influence police have and to make the complaint process more open to the public. The independent nature of civilian review boards is believed to overcome the limitations of internal oversight processes, such as the code of silence; make police organizations more open to public examination; increase complainant satisfaction; improve police–community relations; and reduce community concerns about high-profile abuses of power. Opponents, however, contend that independent civilian review will be ineffective and could possibly lead to problems for the following reasons: Outsiders cannot fully appreciate police decisions; civilians are not qualified to effectively review and investigate police actions; effective oversight procedures already exist; the process will be unfair to officers; and officers may begin to second-guess their actions, thus compromising effective policing.

The independence of citizen oversight procedures is complex because it refers to several aspects of oversight. The independence of review procedures can vary in terms of structure, operation, and perception. Civilian review boards can be constructed so that they are apart from police organizations and commonly include citizens who are not employed by a police organization. The actual structure of these boards does not necessarily mean they will operate independently. For instance, some boards may be dependent on police-led investigations into complaints, whereas others have authority to investigate complaints and subpoena witnesses. Finally, civilian review boards can be perceived as more or less independent of police. Perceived independence becomes significant when the legitimacy of complaint procedures is in doubt, and a goal is to enhance police–community relationships. Studies of citizen review procedures show significant variability on these dimensions.

Whereas the independent review function focuses attention on the individual actions of police officers, the monitoring function is more concerned with the police organization. The monitoring role is significant because it has the potential to examine broader issues and produce meaningful changes within police organizations. The potential of the monitoring function makes sense given that characteristics of police organizations, such as culture, can greatly affect misconduct. Citizen review boards that serve a monitoring role review police policies and make recommendations, oversee the complaint process, engage in community outreach, and solicit information from citizens about their experiences with police. External oversight procedures in San Jose, California; Boise, Idaho; San Diego, California; Los Angeles County; and Portland, Oregon engage in monitoring activities.

## EFFECTIVENESS

Prominent failures of civilian oversight bodies, such as those in Philadelphia; New Orleans; Washington, DC; and New York have been cited to suggest that these mechanisms are ineffective. However, very little empirical evidence exists on the effectiveness of citizen oversight. Experts agree that assessing the effectiveness of citizen oversight procedures is a difficult task. In order to understand the successes and failures of citizen review, it is first necessary to identify evaluative criteria. The outcomes commonly identified as being appropriate are increased public confidence in police, greater fairness and completeness in complaint investigations, reduced police misconduct, ensured discipline for misconduct, police adherence to policies and procedures, and improved public satisfaction with the complaint process.

One common standard used to evaluate citizen oversight is the rate of sustained complaints. Low sustain rates by citizen review boards are sometimes viewed as evidence of ineffectiveness. The use of sustain rates is problematic because there is no established standard for comparison, and sustain rates capture only one function of review bodies. In addition, the nature of citizen oversight bodies might bring to light more mundane complaints, such as rudeness, that are difficult to sustain and might increase the total number of complaints, reducing the chance for high sustain rates. Another way to think about assessing the effectiveness of citizen review is to consider the arguments that support and oppose citizen involvement in oversight. These concerns, such as the ability of citizens to conduct fair and thorough investigations and whether citizen review affects the quality of police behavior, have not been sufficiently tested.

Cases of failure and success point to some common factors that seem to be important determinants of effective citizen oversight. First, effectiveness might depend on how well the agencies work together. This can be especially important if the citizen oversight body depends on the police organization for important information. Second, the structure of the review agency may not provide the opportunity for meaningful oversight. Oversight agencies that are largely dependent on police and lack meaningful power are likely to fail. Third, citizen oversight agencies established by a local ordinance, rather than Memoranda of Understanding or mayoral executive order, tend to have the power and authority that increase the chances of having an impact. Fourth, a citizen review body is likely to be successful if it works with a police organization that is committed to learning and improving. Fifth, a review body requires a minimum level of staffing, funding, and leadership in order to increase the chances of success. Experts contend that citizen oversight agencies are likely to succeed if they perceive their role as being broad and engage in a wide variety of activities, including monitoring tasks such as policy review.

*William M. Wells and Joseph A. Schafer*

*See also* Civil Rights Violations by Police, Community Relations, Complaints Against Police, Corruption/ Integrity, Early Warning Systems, Internal Affairs, Police Brutality, Police Code of Silence, Police Misconduct, Race Relations, Use of Force

*For Further Reading*

Finn, P. (2001). *Citizen review of police: Approaches and implementation.* Washington, DC: U.S. Department of Justice.

Goldsmith, A. J. (Ed.). (1991). *Complaints against the police: The trend to external review.* Oxford, UK: Clarendon.

Kappeler, V. E., Sluder, R. D., & Alpert, G. P. (1998). *Forces of deviance* (2nd ed.). Prospect Heights, IL: Waveland.

Walker, S. (2001). *Police accountability: The role of citizen oversight.* Belmont, CA: Wadsworth.

Walker, S. (2003, February). *Best practices in police accountability* [Online]. Available: www.policeaccountability.org

Weisburd, D., Greenspan, R., Hamilton, E. E., Williams, H., & Bryant, K. A. (2000). *Police attitudes toward abuse of authority: Findings from a national survey.* Washington, DC: U.S. Department of Justice.

# ෨෨  CLEARANCE RATES

*Clearance rates* are the percentage of reported or discovered crimes that are solved by the police. Cases are considered solved when arrests are made, even though they may not result in a conviction. *Exceptional clearances* are instances when police believe they have identified the perpetrator but are unable to make an arrest, as is the case when the perpetrator commits suicide or flees the country, or when the victim will not cooperate. Clearances also can occur when someone arrested for a particular offense then confesses to other crimes or is implicated in their commission.

Clearance rates vary enormously from crime to crime. Thus, data from the Uniform Crime Reports assembled by the Federal Bureau of Investigation (FBI) show the following nationwide clearance rates in the year 2000 (FBI, 2001):

| | |
|---|---|
| Murder | 63.1% |
| Forcible rape | 46.9% |
| Robbery | 25.7% |
| Aggravated assault | 56.9% |
| Burglary | 13.4% |
| Larceny-theft | 18.2% |
| Motor vehicle theft | 14.1% |
| Arson | 20.5% |

## USES OF CLEARANCE RATES

Clearance rates are useful for several purposes. First, they provide an indication of the risk of committing crimes; that is, it is much easier to get away with committing some crimes than others. The knowledge that police are relatively successful solving certain kinds of offenses can function as a deterrent to those contemplating such actions. Where clearance rates are low, as in the case of auto theft, the message goes out that citizens need to be particularly vigilant and take self-protective measures, such as using steering wheel clubs and alarm systems.

Second, clearance rates are a measure of police productivity—how well the police are doing their job and whether, over time, their performance is improving or declining. Examining the clearance rates of different cities or police precincts within cities is a means of judging the effectiveness of law enforcement in a comparative context. It is especially useful in evaluating special units assigned to particular categories of crimes, such as sex crime units.

Thus, clearance rates are a means of holding police departments and divisions accountable. Reward and punishment of police administrators can be based in part on the objective standard of success in catching criminals rather than intuitions about the quality of their work. Deploying and redeploying of police officers to various locales and responsibilities can also be done more rationally when shortcomings are measured accurately. Clearance rates used in such fashion are part of a standard strategy used by the leadership of modern police departments entailing the use of quantitative data as a management tool (Silverman, 1999).

## PROBLEMS WITH CLEARANCE RATES

There are a number of drawbacks in relying on clearance rates, which suggest that they should be interpreted cautiously. First is the issue of accuracy: There is significant potential for error in both the numerator and the denominator of the rate. As to the number of crimes solved (the top of the fraction), the police decision to make an arrest does not mean they have found the right person. Because of mistakes by eyewitnesses, flawed analysis of physical evidence, stereotyping of offenders, and a host of other factors, police sometimes get things wrong. The fact that a significant number of people charged either have their cases dismissed or are acquitted by juries bears this out. It is important to note that exculpation of the charged individual by one means or another does not eliminate the case from the cleared case file and thereby reduce the clearance rate.

Clearance of cases is especially suspect when police and prosecutors get the accused to confess to previously unsolved cases. Because police have a great incentive to boost their clearance rates, they will sometimes encourage such multiple confessions as part of a plea bargain: Criminals who say they committed *more* crimes ironically may wind up getting *lesser* sentences. Thus, a classic study of policing done by criminologist Jerome Skolnick (1966) revealed that one burglar admitted committing 400 separate offenses. It seems probable that at least some of these burglaries were done by others, and it seems especially improbable that a career criminal who committed crime routinely could remember and differentiate that many instances of misconduct. The phenomenon of falsified confession came to public attention during a 2004 investigation of clearance rates in Broward County, Florida, which showed (among other things) that one offender, in fact, had been in jail when 6 of the 21 crimes to which he confessed were committed (O'boye, 2004).

The denominator of the clearance rate fraction is also problematic. Many crimes are never reported to the police, particularly those that are relatively minor. Participants in fights often do not report assaults against them out of embarrassment; those who have property stolen often do not call police because they are skeptical that anything will be done; victims of domestic violence often fail to report out of fear of retaliation. Thus, clearance rates are artificially inflated because the number of crimes reported is far less than the true number that really happened. What is most paradoxical is that really good police departments may wind up looking worse (i.e., having lower clearance rates) because the confidence that citizens have in them prompts them to report a far greater percentage of crimes than would be reported to slipshod departments that the citizenry does not trust.

Another problem with the denominator is that some crimes come to the attention of the police only when they engage in proactive law enforcement. Drug sales are a good example: Unless police pose as desirous buyers (i.e., "buy and bust" operations), drug sales rarely come to their attention; the same is true of prostitution. The clearance rate in such victimless crimes looks very high, when in fact, the vast majority of offenses are unrecorded and very few are ever solved.

Not only are clearance rates fraught with the potential for error, but there is controversy about how they are used (Levine, Musheno, & Palumbo, 1986). Because the rates are used to evaluate police performance, reliance on them may heighten the importance of the law enforcement function of police at the expense of order maintenance, problem solving, and social service. Their use may pressure agencies to promote arrests when another course of action, such as informal intervention, may well be more beneficial socially, as in the case of a brawl among juveniles, where sparing participants a criminal record might be desirable. Police may also be encouraged to make shoddy arrests that will never stand up in court, to bolster the image of effectiveness; quantity of arrests rather than quality is stressed.

## CONCLUSION

Clearance rates are an important indicator of the success of one aspect of police responsibility—apprehending criminals. However, as is true of any empirically based performance indicator, they cannot be accepted at face value; they are only an approximation of reality because exactitude is impossible. Moreover, because the police role in society is so complex and multifaceted, care must always be taken to use clearance rates together with measures of how well police perform their other duties and how positively they are perceived by the public.

Achieving high clearance rates is a means to the end of having a safe, orderly, and just society, not an end in itself.

*James P. Levine*

## For Further Reading

Federal Bureau of Investigation. (2001). *Crime in the United States, 2000*. Washington, DC: U.S. Government Printing Office.

Levine, J., Musheno, M., & Palumbo, D. (1986). *Criminal justice in America: Law in action*. New York: Wiley.

O'boye, S. (2004, April 2). Broward sheriff's office begins review of "cleared" cases. *South Florida Sun-Sentinel*. Available: http://forum.parklandvote.com/viewtopic.php?t=88

Silverman, E. (1999). *NYPD battles crime: Innovative strategies in policing*. Boston: Northeastern University Press.

Skolnick, J. (1966). *Justice without trial*. New York: Wiley.

## ☙ COLD CASE INVESTIGATIONS

Most homicide investigators consider the first 72 hours the most crucial for developing the leads necessary to solve a case. An investigation that lacks viable leads, cooperative witnesses, or physical evidence may be stalled indefinitely. With passing time, these unsolved cases become "cold." Departmental budget constraints, personnel changes, and the soaring homicide rate have all contributed to the growing number of unsolved cases. Specialized cold case squads have become a popular option for many police departments and prosecutors' offices overwhelmed by large numbers of unsolved cases. Reallocation of resources, focused on the review of these cold files, and advancements in computer technology and DNA analysis have made the resolution of some cold cases possible.

The homicide rate progressively increased in the United States every year from 1960 through the mid-1990s; the greatest escalation occurred between the mid-1980s and early 1990s. Overburdened detectives, forced to handle multiple ongoing investigations while still responding to new crime scenes, could not conduct the necessary investigative follow-up.

Budget restraints and the retirement and transfer of personnel also contributed to the increased caseload for detectives, as well as the reliance on less experienced officers to work new or ongoing cases. Crime labs and medical examiners' offices also felt the burden of this growing caseload, and a backlog of evidence analyses led to delayed reporting to the homicide investigators.

The cases most likely to become cold are gang- and drug-related deaths; deaths of immigrants, transients, and the homeless; and cases where the victim is unidentified. Traditionally, one of the most important investigative tactics is uncovering the relationship between killer and victim to establish a motive. However, many of these unsolved cases either involved minor arguments, often drug- or gang-related, that escalated to violence, or resulted from seemingly random attacks in which the killer had no known previous relationship with the victim. Traditional investigative approaches, focused on uncovering motive, proved ineffective in solving these seemingly motiveless homicides; it was increasingly difficult to establish the relationship between victim and perpetrator. Particularly in gang- and drug-related crimes, killers and witnesses themselves were killed or incarcerated for other crimes before they could be identified and interviewed. Other witnesses had questionable credibility or were unwilling to come forward with evidence. As a result, while the homicide rate increased, the homicide *clearance* rate across the nation dropped sharply.

Cold case squads were created specifically to alleviate the backlog of unsolved cases. Most were formed when the murder rate began to decline in the late 1990s, when departments could reallocate resources to begin investigating cold files. The staffing and setup of a cold case investigative unit varies based on municipality and departmental resources. A squad can be a single full-time investigator, or multiple investigators working either part- or full-time; some squads enlist retired homicide detectives on a volunteer basis. Squads can become established departments or act as ad hoc squads assigned to high-profile cases. The squads are often housed within a police agency, but can also be established in prosecutors' offices. Often, officers working cold cases are not assigned shift rotations and do not respond to fresh homicide crime scenes. In some cases, the absence of an established squad does not dissuade many tireless officers, motivated by particular cases that haunt them, from continuing to work on cold cases. Many squads use outside resources and expertise, including collaborating with the U.S. Marshals Service and the FBI. In some jurisdictions, such as Washington, DC, FBI agents are actually assigned to the cold case squad. The U.S. attorney for Washington, DC, also assigns a full-time prosecutor who handles only the cases generated by the cold case squad.

Most of the cases referred to the squad are at least a year old and are prioritized according to the likelihood of solvability. Although most investigators agree that the first 48 to 72 hours are critical to solving a homicide case, cold case investigators acknowledge that the passage of time can prove a benefit. With time, relationships change and former allies become adversaries; once-reluctant witnesses come forward. Some witnesses develop their own trouble with the criminal justice system and provide information on cold cases in exchange for favorable consideration. Offenders may boast of their crimes to others. Programs such as Crime Stoppers, which offer cash rewards for information, are now available and encourage anonymous informants to come forward with new leads. Frequently, a witness in one cold case will have information about a second case involving the same subject or occurring in the same neighborhood.

Advancements in DNA analysis, fingerprint technology, and more sophisticated computer networks have greatly aided cold case investigations. One example, the Combined DNA Index System (CODIS), is network software developed to link local, state, and national forensic DNA laboratories. DNA profiles are collected from crime scene evidence, convicted offenders, and unidentified remains or profiles from relatives of missing persons. CODIS allows crime scene evidence to be compared with offender databases for a potential match. Even if a specific suspect is not identified, different crimes may be linked to each other, sometimes uncovering

a serial pattern. A cold case in one jurisdiction may be linked to an ongoing or cold case in another, and the information sharing between the two may keep both respective investigations alive, potentially moving them forward.

Even with these technological advancements and the decrease in the homicide rate, many law enforcement agencies continue to struggle with budgetary and personnel concerns. Recognizing this financial and personnel burden, the Vidocq Society, an exclusive, crime-solving, nonprofit organization, was founded in 1990. The Society, made up of forensic experts, investigators, and private citizens, meets monthly in Philadelphia, Pennsylvania, to collectively dissect a single case and its evidence to refocus a cold case investigation. All work is done in close collaboration with law enforcement and is undertaken by the Society at no cost to the victims' families or law enforcement.

*Karyn Hadfield*

***See also*** Clearance Rates, Homicide Investigation, Vidocq Society

### For Further Reading

National Institute of Justice. (2002). *NIJ special report: Using DNA to solve cold cases*. Washington, DC: Author.

Regini, C. L. (1997). The cold case concept. *FBI Law Enforcement Bulletin, 66*, 1–6.

Turner, R., & Kosa, R. (2003). *Cold case squads: Leaving no stone unturned* (BJA Bulletin). Washington, DC: Bureau of Justice Assistance.

## ❧ COMMUNICATIONS INTEROPERABILITY

### OVERVIEW

The ability of public safety personnel to communicate in a timely, reliable, and secure manner via radio has always been a critical requirement for the mission operations of public safety and disaster response personnel at the local, state, federal, and tribal levels. Compounding that requirement, recent acts of domestic terrorism, civil disturbance, youth violence, and natural disasters requiring multiagency and multijurisdictional public safety response have dramatically underscored the need for public safety officials to better communicate in order to coordinate their efforts at the scene of an incident—not just within agencies, but across jurisdictional and functional lines. This communications capacity, essential to the protection of lives and property, is known as interoperability.

Interoperability is formally defined as communications links that permit persons from two or more different agencies to interact with one another and to exchange information according to a prescribed method in order to achieve predictable results. In simple terms, it is the ability of public safety officials to communicate across different wireless systems on demand and in real time.

## CURRENT ENVIRONMENT AND BACKGROUND

Although significant progress has been made in advancing public safety communications interoperability nationwide since the 1990s—particularly in the wake of the events of September 11, 2001, which elevated the issue to a national priority—most states and local jurisdictions, and the federal government, continue to face significant challenges to achieving seamless wireless communications.

Specific barriers to achieving interoperability include aging infrastructure, lack of interjurisdictional cooperation, funding constraints, insufficient spectrum and spectrum inefficiency, disparate technologies due to a lack of standards, and security issues.

### Aging Infrastructure

Much of the nation's public safety wireless infrastructure is antiquated—with most systems more than 15 years old, and many 20 to 25 years old. The maximum optimal life cycle for much of this equipment is 8 years, meaning public safety agencies rely on wireless networks that are two or three generations behind technologically. Furthermore, many wireless networks were developed incrementally over the years, in part because of funding constraints,

and their expansion often lags behind demographic shifts or other development changes. The net effect of these conditions is less-than-optimal network design, poor coverage, and dead spots within and between jurisdictions.

### Lack of Coordination and Partnerships

The lack of coordination and partnerships among government leaders and public safety officials in planning for and implementing public safety land mobile radio (LMR) systems has created a challenge that is, in many cases, as significant as the technological barriers to interoperability. In fact, findings from an analysis of fire and emergency medical services communications interoperability indicate a significant need for coordinated approaches, relationship building, and information sharing—all critical to solving key interoperability issues such as spectrum sharing, funding, standards development, and systems security.

Several important issues have emerged as challenges to successful coordination and partnership activities. These issues include "turf issues" associated with the management and control of radio systems, the lack of a shared priority for interoperability, and limited sharing of interoperability solutions within the public safety community.

Jurisdictional boundaries often create artificial barriers that hinder cooperation and collaboration in situations in which achieving interoperability is necessary. One such barrier relates to the management and control of wireless systems. Historically, individual communications managers and technical radio specialists were solely responsible for providing communications for their respective agencies, resulting in the development of stand-alone systems that served the mission of a single agency or jurisdiction at the expense of cost efficiencies and interoperability. In addition, the importance of, and need for, interoperability is not sufficiently understood by decision makers or the organizations that influence those decision makers. Finally, information sharing and best practices regarding interoperability are not established or available at all levels of government. Improving communications interoperability requires a willingness to collaborate, despite jurisdictional boundaries or political barriers.

### Funding Constraints

The interoperability problem is further exacerbated by funding shortfalls, which limit or eliminate equipment and network upgrades. Frequently, covering basic maintenance costs is a challenge—obtaining funds for a major upgrade, or for a complete system replacement, is nearly impossible. Federal agencies and state governments have not had sufficient funding to build out their respective networks, let alone ensure interoperability. In some cases, funding shortfalls result in officials dropping or ignoring requirements for interoperability among interacting public safety networks.

Funding challenges persist in large part because elected officials and budget directors are not provided with sufficient information to justify interoperability investments. Without such investments, public safety agencies will be ill-equipped to handle current and future public safety communication requirements, and public safety missions will be compromised.

### Insufficient Spectrum and Spectrum Inefficiencies

Public safety communicators, already hampered by congestion and interference resulting from insufficient radio spectrum, are facing increased need and competition for this finite resource. In the public safety community, growing requirements for transmission of data, images, and video are increasing spectrum needs. Meanwhile, well-resourced commercial entities are vying for the same spectrum to enable new applications for wireless technology.

Because it has been so difficult for public safety to acquire spectrum, public safety agencies have been required to use their existing spectrum more efficiently. Many members of the public safety community have sought the creation of more rational national policy to accommodate spectrum needs.

The National Telecommunications and Information Administration narrowband mandate requires all federal agencies operating LMR wireless systems to be more efficient with their spectrum resources

by using or migrating toward narrow channel widths. The Federal Communications Commission also has modified spectrum management rules and regulations to encourage efficient spectrum use—making it possible, for example, for local, state, and federal agencies to share spectrum.

## DISPARATE TECHNOLOGIES DUE TO LACK OF STANDARDS

Frequently, public safety personnel from different jurisdictions cannot talk to each other because their radios and other communication equipment come from competing manufacturers that use proprietary, incompatible technology. In the absence of rigorous standards, vendors have delayed development of fully standards-compliant equipment across all public safety frequency bands. The result has been incompatible equipment; insufficient marketplace competition; and, for the public safety community, persistent high costs.

### Security Issues

Further complicating the interoperability challenge is the need to ensure the security of advanced communications systems. Experts are working with the public safety community and industry to define security guidelines, standards, and procedures for public safety communications. Public safety agencies must incorporate security measures into their existing systems to the greatest extent possible.

In some cases, interoperability between federal and state/local (nonfederal) agencies has been limited by the use of encryption measures designed to enhance security. Due to the sensitive nature of federal law enforcement communications, many federal agencies communicate only over encrypted radio channels and adhere to the Advanced Encryption Standard developed by the National Institute of Standards and Technology. Conversely, most nonfederal agencies do not require encrypted communications, although some nonfederal public safety organizations use encryption for various tactical operations, such as narcotics investigations. Because of the lack of encryption capabilities among nonfederal agencies, federal agencies often refrain from patching their frequencies through locally controlled audio switches and across local systems. As a result, the standard for ensuring security can actually limit the application of federal-to-nonfederal interoperability solutions.

All of these challenges put mission effectiveness and force protection at risk at a time when the nation's federal law enforcement and public safety personnel, police officers, firefighters, and emergency medical services personnel are being thrust into the forefront of homeland security response. Improving the current state of affairs requires these issues to be addressed in a coordinated manner.

## IDENTIFYING AND IMPLEMENTING INTEROPERABILITY SOLUTIONS

A number of government-led organizations are working to overcome these challenges and identify and implement solutions for achieving interoperability on a national scale. These include the Public Safety Wireless Network Program, the Wireless Public Safety Interoperable Communications Program, and the Federal Law Enforcement Wireless Users Group, among others.

These organizations and many others work to research, identify, and develop interoperability solutions via a number of activities, including promoting partnerships among public safety agencies, conducting case studies in several regions of the nation, initiating pilot projects to test and refine interoperability solutions, addressing spectrum policy and funding issues important to public safety, and investigating issues associated with system security and standards and technology development.

Interoperability solutions vary widely, depending on such factors as an agency's mission, geographic location, and existing capabilities. They range from short-term, rapidly deployable solutions, to complex, permanent solutions. A variety of solutions have been successfully implemented, tested, and demonstrated by first responders and are used on a daily basis.

Some examples of proven technical solutions to first-response interoperability challenges include the following:

- Audio matrix switches implemented in the Washington, DC, metropolitan area. These switches receive audio output from one wireless system and convert it to output suitable for one or more other systems—making it possible for agencies using different wireless technologies to communicate with one another. Four of these switches are implemented at strategic locations within the Washington metropolitan area. They have similar designs, so they are easily repeatable at each location.
- A console interface implemented in the Salt Lake City area during the 2002 Winter Olympics. Interoperability is achieved by establishing an audio connection between dispatch consoles. The console interface can use existing infrastructure and equipment because it works regardless of frequency band, modulation, or system configuration.
- An Incident Commanders Radio Interface (ICRI) solution that is crossband and cross-system capable. This solution provides reliable radio links among under- and above-ground emergency response teams working in and around the Washington, DC-area Metrorail tunnels. The ICRI unit consists of interconnected standard radio interface ports, an extended distance or remote radio interface port, and a telephone port.
- Shared talk groups and a console-to-console patch between 800 megahertz (MHz) trunked systems in El Paso, Texas, and Las Cruces, New Mexico, enable all of the agencies that have access to either city's system to interoperate between one another without the use of leased telephone circuits. The solution provides a redundant, direct frequency link between systems from different manufacturers with proprietary protocols.

Other interoperability solutions that have been implemented include console patching via microwave links, directional antennas, and leased telephone circuits; transportable audio switches; and consolidation of different agencies' antennas at a single radio tower site.

## THE FUTURE OF INTEROPERABILITY

Through the efforts of national organizations, and several programs and activities fostering interoperability solutions at the state and local levels, public safety wireless interoperability is improving.

In April 2003, the National Interoperability Scorecard, a state-by-state assessment of public safety wireless communications interoperability, was released. The scorecard shows that the nation's efforts to improve wireless interoperability are succeeding. Overall, the nation's interoperability score improved 41%, from 40.82 on a scale of 100 in 2001, when the first measurement of interoperability was released, to 57.65 in 2003.

The 2003 National Interoperability Scorecard measured interoperability with respect to six key issue areas: shared systems development, coordination and partnerships, funding, spectrum, standards and technology, and security. The most significant improvements reported in the new assessment were in the areas of security, standards and technology, and coordination and partnerships. Insufficient funding for wireless interoperability initiatives remains a significant challenge.

*Rick Murphy*

### For Further Reading

Arnold, A. (2002). *Final activities report for the National Communications Interoperability Assessment Project.* Washington, DC: U.S. Department of Justice.

Community Research Associates. (2004). *Developing multi-agency interoperability communications systems: User's handbook.* Washington, DC: U.S. Department of Justice.

Smith, B., & Tolman, T. (2000, April). Public safety and the interoperability challenge. *National Institute of Justice Journal.* Washington, DC: National Institute of Justice.

## ✑ COMMUNITY POLICING

Community policing may be the most important development in policing in the past quarter century. Across the country, police chiefs report that they are moving toward this new model of policing, which supplements traditional crime fighting with problem-solving and prevention-oriented approaches that emphasize the role of the public in helping set police priorities. What police departments are doing when they do community policing varies a great deal. Agencies point to a long list of projects as evidence that they are involved. These range from bike and foot patrols to drug awareness programs in schools, home security inspections, storefront offices, and citizen advisory committees. In some places, community policing is in the hands of special neighborhood officers, whereas in other places, it involves the transformation of the entire police department. In some cities, residents participate in aggressive neighborhood watch patrols as part of their city's program, although in many more places, public involvement is limited to being asked to call 9-1-1 quickly when they see something suspicious. Agencies have mounted sophisticated public relations campaigns to sell their programs, and they compete hotly for national awards for innovation. Assistant chiefs get promoted, and chiefs move to more visibly prominent cities because they are said to have made a success out of community policing.

So, what is community policing? Although it is often described by the things that police officers do (including the examples just mentioned), community policing is actually a strategic rather than programmatic innovation. Its advocates characterize it as transforming the "professional" model of policing that has been dominant since the end of World War II, shifting in a fundamental way to one that is proactive, prevention oriented, and community sensitive. It seems to mean different things to different people because the range and complexity of programs with which it is associated are large and continually evolving. At root, however, community policing is not defined by a list of particular tactics. In its fullest expression, community policing affects the structure and culture of police departments, not just their activities. Police departments embracing community policing tend to adopt at least three new, interrelated organizational stances: They involve the community, they decentralize, and they adopt a problem-solving orientation. In turn, these changes reverberate back, reshaping the mission and methods of policing.

### Community Involvement

Community policing is defined in part by efforts to develop partnerships with groups and individual community members. These are intended to help the police to better listen to the community, enhance constructive information sharing, build trust with the public, and involve them in setting public safety priorities. Police need to reorganize in order to provide opportunities for citizens to come into contact with them under circumstances that encourage these exchanges. To this end, departments hold community meetings and form advisory committees, establish storefront offices, survey the public, and create informational Web sites. In some places, police share information with residents through educational programs or by enrolling them in citizen-police academies that give them in-depth knowledge of law enforcement. This is one reason why community policing is an organizational strategy but not a set of specific programs—how it looks in practice should vary considerably from place to place, in response to local circumstances.

Civic engagement usually extends to involving the public in some way in efforts to enhance community safety. Community policing promises to strengthen the capacity of communities to fight and prevent crime on their own. The idea that the police and the public are "co-producers" of safety, and that they cannot claim a monopoly over fighting crime, predates the current rhetoric of community policing. In fact, the community crime prevention movement of the 1970s was an important precursor to community policing. It promoted the idea that crime was not solely the responsibility of the police. The police were quick to endorse the claim that they could not solve crime problems without community support and assistance, for it helped share the blame for crime rates that were rising at the time. Now police find that they are expected to lead this effort. They are being called upon to take the lead in mobilizing individuals and organizations around crime prevention. These efforts include neighborhood watch, citizen patrols, and education programs stressing household target-hardening and the rapid reporting of crime. Residents are asked to assist the police by reporting crimes promptly when they occur and cooperating as witnesses. Even where these ideas are well established, moving them to center stage as part of a larger strategic plan showcases the commitment of the police to resident involvement.

Another important set of partnerships involves relationships with other organizations that have direct responsibility for the quality of neighborhood life. This includes the schools and agencies responsible for health, housing, trash pickup, graffiti cleanups, and the like. Effective community policing requires responsiveness to citizen input concerning the needs of the community. It takes seriously the public's definition of its own problems, and this inevitably includes issues that lie outside the traditional competence of the police. Officers can learn at a public meeting that loose garbage and rats in an alley are big issues for residents, but some other agency is going to have to deliver the solution to that problem.

### Decentralization

Decentralization is an organizational strategy that is closely linked to the implementation of community policing. Decentralization strategies can be twofold. More responsibility for identifying and responding to chronic crime and disorder problems can be delegated to mid-level district commanders. Departments have had to experiment with how to structure and manage real decentralization that gives mid-level managers real responsibility, and how to hold them accountable for measures of their success. Here, community policing intersects with another movement in policing, one toward a culture of systematic performance measurement and managerial accountability. At the same time, more responsibility for identifying and responding to community problems may be delegated to individual patrol officers and their sergeants, who are, in turn, encouraged to take the initiative in finding ways to deal with a broad range of problems specific to the communities they serve. Dual decentralization is adopted not only so that police can become more proactive and more preventive, but also so that they can respond efficiently to problems of different magnitude and complexity. Under the professional model, marching orders for the police have traditionally come from two sources: calls from the public concerning individual problems, and citywide initiatives or programs originating at police headquarters or even City Hall. They are not organized to respond to the groups and community institutions that make up "civil society." Decentralization, paired with a commitment to consultation and engagement with local communities, allows the police to respond to local problems that are important to particular communities.

Structurally, community policing leads departments to assign officers to fixed geographical areas and to keep them there during the course of their day. This is known as adopting a "turf orientation." Decentralization is intended to encourage communication between officers and neighborhood residents, and to build an awareness of local problems among working officers. Line officers are expected to work more autonomously at investigating situations, resolving problems, and educating the public. They are being asked to discover and set their own goals, and sometimes to manage their work schedule. This is also the level at which collaborative projects involving both police and residents can emerge. Usually, community policing departments attempt to devolve authority and responsibility further down the organizational hierarchy, to facilitate decision making that responds rapidly and effectively to local conditions. The goal is to encourage the local development of local solutions to locally defined problems, whenever possible. In this, the police are not independent of the rest of society, for large organizations in both the public and private sectors have learned that decentralization can create flexibility in decision making at the customer contact level. Often, there are also moves to flatten the structure of the organization by compressing the rank structure, and to shed layers of bureaucracy within the police organization to speed communication and decision making.

## Problem Orientation

Community policing also involves a shift from reliance on reactive patrol and investigations toward a problem-solving orientation. Problem-oriented policing is an analytic method for developing crime-reduction strategies. It stresses the importance of discovering the situations that produce calls for police assistance, identifying the causes that lie behind them, and designing tactics to deal with these causes. This involves training officers in methods of identifying and analyzing problems. As a strategy, problem solving represents a departure from the traditional approach to policing, which too often was reduced to driving fast to crime scenes in order to fill out paper reports of what happened. Rather than just responding sequentially to individual events, problem solving calls for recognizing patterns of incidents that help identify their causes and how to deal with them.

Problem-solving policing can proceed without a commitment to community policing. A key difference between problem-solving and community policing is that the latter stresses civic engagement in identifying and prioritizing a broad range of neighborhood problems, whereas the former frequently focuses on patterns of traditionally defined crimes that are identified using police data systems. Problem-oriented policing sometimes involves communities as a means to address particular issues, but more often it is conducted solely by specialized units within the police department. On the other hand, community policing involves communities as an end in itself. Problem-oriented community policing also recognizes that the solutions to chronic problems may involve other agencies and be fundamentally "nonpolice" in character; in traditional departments, this would be cause for ignoring them. Because community involvement tends to expand the definition of police responsibilities to include a broad range of neighborhood problems, this requires, in turn, that police form partnerships with other public and private agencies that can join them in responding to residents' priorities.

## New Mandates and Methods

Important features of community policing flow from decentralization, community involvement, and adoption of a problem-solving orientation. These almost inevitably lead to an expansion of the police mandate. Controlling serious crime by enforcing the criminal law remains the primary job of the police. But instead of seeing the police exclusively in these terms, and viewing activities that depart from direct efforts to deter crime and bring offenders to account as a distraction from their fundamental mission, advocates of community policing argue that the police have additional functions to perform and different ways to conduct their traditional business.

They argue that the crime control and security-enhancing effectiveness of the police might actually be strengthened by recognizing the importance of different police functions rather than focusing solely on reducing crime by threatening and making arrests.

Better listening to the community can produce different policing priorities. Officers involved in neighborhood policing quickly learn that many residents are deeply concerned about problems that previously did not come to police attention. The public often focuses on threatening and fear-provoking conditions rather than discrete and legally defined incidents. Often, they are concerned about casual social disorder and the physical decay of their community rather than traditionally defined "serious crimes," but the police are organized to respond to the latter. Community residents are unsure that they could (or even should) rely on the police to help them deal with these problems. Thus, these concerns do not generate complaints or calls for service, and as a result, the police know surprisingly little about them. The routines of traditional police work ensure that officers will interact mostly with citizens who are in distress because they have just been victimized, or with suspects and troublemakers. Accordingly, community policing requires that departments develop new channels for learning about neighborhood problems. And when they learn about them, they have to have systems in place to respond effectively.

New thinking about the ends of policing also includes the idea that police should provide "quality service" to the taxpayers who employ them. Traditionally, quality service meant fast, courteous response to calls for service. Now, for example, it has grown to encompass the role of police in providing information, practical advice, and counseling, and referring callers to public and private agencies that are able to assist them further with their problems. Attention to the "bedside manner" of the police was first driven by the movement for better care for crime victims, but developing a customer orientation is now a touchstone of public sector organizations of all kinds. Police have also gotten into the "fear reduction" business. Reducing fear is now being seen as important in its own right,

but promoting the reclamation of public spaces and the exercise of effective informal social control, as well as fostering public cooperation in crime reporting by getting people to step forward as witnesses, can also enhance the crime control effectiveness of the police.

Community policing also has driven new interest in crime prevention, altering the means of policing as well as the mission. Under the professional model, crime prevention was deterrence based. To threaten arrest, police organized themselves to patrol the streets looking for crimes (random and directed patrol), respond to emergency crime calls from witnesses and victims (rapid response to 9-1-1 calls), and find guilty offenders (criminal investigation). But concerned residents do not want the crime that drives these efforts to happen in the first place, and their instinct is to press for true prevention. Police-sponsored prevention projects are in place throughout the country. Problem solving has brought crime prevention theories to the table, leading police to tackle the routine activities of victims and the crucial roles played by "place managers," such as landlords or shopkeepers, and not just offenders. An emphasis on target hardening has gotten them involved in conducting home security surveys and teaching self-defense classes. But when communities talk about prevention, they mostly talk about their children and ways of intervening earlier with youths who seem on a trajectory toward serious offending. Much of the work preventing the development of criminal careers lies with agencies besides the police, such as family courts, child protection agencies, parents, peer networks, and schools. To their efforts, the police add involvement in athletic and after-school programs, D.A.R.E. presentations in schools, special efforts to reduce violence in families, and initiatives that focus attention on keeping youths out of gangs.

## UNANSWERED QUESTIONS

One unanswered question about community policing is whether it can survive the withdrawal of federal financial support and attention. Under the 1994 Violent Crime and Law Enforcement Act, the federal government spent billions of dollars to support community policing. Federal agencies sponsored demonstration projects designed to spur innovation and promote the effectiveness of community policing. Another federal bureau promoted it in a series of national conferences and publications. The largest agency funded tens of thousands of new positions for police officers. The Act specified that one of the roles of these new officers should be "to foster problem solving and interaction with communities by police officers." Innovations such as community policing highlight the importance of training for officers, and the Act also funded the creation of regional community policing centers around the country. By 1999, 88% of all new recruits and 85% of serving officers worked in departments that were providing some community policing training. Many police departments also applied for technology support grants under the Act. The goal of this program was to release sworn officers from office jobs and increase their efficiency in the field by employing information technology and hiring civilian technical staff to support it.

The issue is whether police departments will continue to expand and staff their community policing components. Federal financial support for community policing certainly will be on the wane. Now, crime is down, and federal largess toward local law enforcement is being redirected to post-September 11th concerns. Even where commitment to community policing is strong, maintaining an effective program can be difficult in the face of competing demands for resources. Community policing continues to ask officers to think and act in new and unaccustomed ways, and many of its presumed benefits do not show up in police information systems. Community policing will need continued community support.

The second question is whether community policing can live up to its promises. Like many new programs, its adoption in many instances preceded careful evaluation of its consequences. The effectiveness of community policing has been the subject of some research, ranging from its impact on crime to how openly it is embraced by the officers charged with carrying it out. There has not been enough research to definitively address the effectiveness

question. It is clear that implementing a serious community policing program is risky and hard, and departments can fail at it. Surveys and ethnographic studies find that officer buy-in is both critical and difficult to achieve, and that problem solving does not come naturally to many police officers. Ironically, research also finds that community support for community policing cannot be assumed. Residents have to be motivated to get involved, and to keep them involved requires evidence of accomplishment. Cities also have a history of not following through very well on promises made in poor and disenfranchised communities, and residents there have to be convinced that "this time, it is for real."

*Wesley G. Skogan*

***See Also*** Theories of Policing

## For Further Reading

Alpert, G., & Piquero, A. (2000). *Community policing: Contemporary readings* (2nd ed.). Prospect Heights, IL: Waveland.

Kelling, G., & Coles, C. (1996). *Fixing broken windows: Restoring order and reducing crime in our communities.* New York: Touchstone.

Skogan, W., & Hartnett, S. (1997). *Community policing, Chicago style.* New York: Oxford University Press.

Skolnick, J., & Bayley, D. (1986). *The new blue line: Police innovations in six American cities.* New York: Free Press.

Skolnick, J., & Bayley, D. (1988). *Community policing: Issues and practice around the world.* Washington, DC: National Institute of Justice.

Trojanowicz, R., & Bucqueroux, B. (1990). *Community policing: A contemporary perspective.* Cincinnati, OH: Anderson.

Zhao, J. (1996). *Why police organizations change: A study of community-oriented policing.* Washington, DC: PERF.

## ✌ COMMUNITY RELATIONS

Historically, the relationship between police and community has been problematic. Friction between police and community may be attributable to various issues. The values and goals inherent to traditional policing, such as a considerable emphasis on crime fighting, conceivably work against improving relations with the community. Additionally, the discretion afforded police enables them to make a variety of decisions that can have a significant positive or negative impact on citizens' lives. Focused on crime control and equipped with broad discretion, police officers have often been scrutinized for alleged mistreatment of community members. Incidents involving excessive force and invasions of privacy increased the rift between police departments and their communities. In response to criticisms, policing in the United States underwent several eras of reform. In the midst of efforts to make improvements, police departments in the United States continued to seek community affirmation despite allegations of corruption. By the mid-1980s, American policing began to embrace the notion of community policing. Community policing focuses on collaboration between police and communities to resolve neighborhood crime and disorder. Certain mechanisms, including citizen police academies, emerged to prompt greater cohesion between police departments and the communities they serve.

The values and goals associated with traditional policing, coupled with the broad discretion exercised by officers, complicate the relationship between police and community. Traditionally, the occupational subculture of policing upholds the separation of police from the public. Assumed critical to effective policing, social distance between officer and citizen emerges as a prominent theme in police training. The "us versus them" mentality facilitates the role of officer as crimefighter in the war on crime. Despite this perceived opposition, police actually rely on the public for needed information and mobilization of police responses.

Concern for legitimacy in American policing provided the catalyst for police reform beginning in the 1920s. During this era of change, police sought to overcome allegations of selective law enforcement. Measures undertaken from the 1920s through the 1960s strove to make the police legally accountable. To establish the police as a legitimate organization, departments adopted a military style of organization and administration. Development of increased police technology, such as the use of

police dispatch, and emphasis on police uniformity initiated the divide between police and community. The 1950s and 1960s evoked militant reactions from police officers attempting to deal with the challenges to authority posed by civil rights activists and antiwar protestors. Police response at the 1968 Democratic National Convention in Chicago rendered the police institutionally unaccountable. By the late 1960s, the National Advisory Commission on Civil Disorders cited poor or aggressive police behavior as the cause of the majority of urban riots.

Heated criticism of police practices prompted further police reform beginning in the 1970s. During this time, police departments began to experiment with ways to increase cohesion between police and the public. By the 1980s, community policing practices developed. Community policing stresses greater interaction between police and their communities with regard to collaborative problem solving. In community policing, police and citizens work together in addressing persistent neighborhood crime and disorder. Police focus expands to include attention to public safety, crime, fear of crime, and community quality of life. Communities are recognized as participants in the shaping of police objectives and interventions. The goal of community building, reflected in victim assistance and increased rapport with minority community members, changes the focus of law enforcement by engaging the community in identifying crime and crime-related situations.

The primary goal of community policing, to strengthen the partnership between the police and their communities, is actualized in a variety of ways. One strategy is the development of citizen police academies (CPAs). Striving to enrich the understanding between police and citizens, CPAs educate citizens about police operations, policies, and procedures. CPAs also encourage dialogue between officers and citizens. In addition to receiving information regarding police department operations, CPA participants become more supportive of police work and develop a heightened awareness and appreciation of police efforts. CPA participants gain an understanding of what the police do as well as why they do what they do. By creating a group of community members that is simultaneously knowledgeable about police procedures and able to influence public opinion toward the police, CPAs encourage improved relations between the police and the public. Furthermore, interaction between officers and CPA participants generates a clearer understanding of citizens' concerns and their perceptions of the police. With the use of such instruments as the CPAs, modern police forces clearly understand the importance of improving their relations with the communities they serve.

*Christine Ivie Edge*

*See also* Citizen Police Academies, Community Policing, Complaints Against Police, Corruption/Integrity

### For Further Reading

Bittner, E. (1974). Florence Nightingale in pursuit of Willie Sutton: A theory of the police. In H. Jacob (Ed.), *The potential for reform of criminal justice.* New York: Russell Sage.

Chevigny, P. (2002). Conflict of rights and keeping order. *Criminology & Public Policy, 2*(1), 155–160.

Cohn, E. (1996). The citizen police academy: A recipe for improving police-community relations. *Journal of Criminal Justice, 24*(3), 265–271.

Greene, J. (2000). Community policing in America: Changing the nature, structure, and function of the police. In National Institute of Justice (Ed.), *Criminal justice 2000* (Vol. 3). Washington, DC: U.S. Department of Justice.

Lipsky, M. (1980). *Street-level bureaucracy: Dilemmas of the individual in public services.* New York: Russell Sage.

## ∞ COMPLAINTS AGAINST POLICE

The unique role of the police is shaped by many factors, the most critical of which is the authority to use force. According to Egon Bittner (1975), this one distinguishing feature is at the core of the police role in society. By virtue of the powers that police officers have to restrict movement and take away liberties, the relationship between the police and the community is often a tenuous one. Based upon the nature of the interactions between citizens and the police, it is inevitable that a certain proportion will result in complaints against police.

The most common sources of complaints against police involve rude or discourteous behaviors, such as a condescending tone or inappropriate language. More serious forms include racial profiling, the improper use of force or excessive force, illegal searches, unjustified frisking, and other violations of civil rights. The sanctions associated with substantiated claims range from warnings or reprimands to more formal discipline, such as suspension or termination. Police officers also face the chance that they may be subjected to a civil suit filed by wronged parties.

Limited research has found that the majority of citizen complaints regarding the use of excessive force are filed against younger, inexperienced, male officers who are working in high-crime neighborhoods and, thus, making a higher number of arrests for index crimes. However, there is no conclusive evidence that complaints are merely a function of job specialization, such as patrol or narcotics. Although there are also no clear indications that possessing a college degree or maintaining residency requirements for officers results in fewer complaints, male police officers appear disproportionately in these reports. The gendered nature of complaints was most pronounced in the well-known Christopher Commission Report in the early 1990s. Of the 132 Los Angeles Police Department officers who were determined to be the worst offenders in terms of citizen complaints, use of force, and police shootings, not a single officer in this group was female. This is despite the fact that female officers at the time made up 13% of the police force.

In responding to citizen complaints, administrators are often in precarious situations. If they do not support their officers, they risk demoralizing the department and losing the respect of the rank and file. Such demoralization, especially in the aftermath of a particularly newsworthy case, has sometimes caused officers to back off of situations where normally, they might intervene. Conversely, if police agencies do not seem responsive to citizens, they could severely damage the department's relationship with the community it serves.

Most police departments use multiple methods to ensure police officer accountability. Internal mechanisms include the proper recruitment, selection, and training of officers; a strong administrative leadership structure; and internal investigations (often referred to today as the Office of Professional Standards). External means include print and television media, the potential for civil redress, and independent citizen complaint review boards. In addition, more citizens have taken to using video cameras as a means of documenting police behavior. The proliferation of video technology has increased the probability that incidents in question will be caught on tape, providing an additional form of oversight. In larger departments, police themselves have video cameras mounted to the dashboards of their police cars. Although initially resistant to this technology, officers now realize its value, because many complaint cases come down to the citizen's word against the officer's. In many cases, the video evidence can protect an officer from a false accusation and provide proof to clear the officer of any wrongdoing.

Complaints against police are best viewed as barometers of change in a department rather than an absolute measure of police performance in that community. In other words, a dramatic spike in complaints could provide a red flag about an emerging problem with a particular unit in the department. However, at any given time, there is no absolute measure of police treatment of citizens, because there are a number of reasons why citizens do not report all incidents of police misconduct. Although some may feel offended, they do not consider it significant enough to file a formal complaint. Others expect that the police will do very little to investigate a complaint against a fellow officer. The fact that most departments still require a person to go directly to the police department to file a complaint is inconvenient for most and intimidating for others. Some citizens might fear that there could be repercussions if they report police misconduct. A small number of police departments around the country are now attempting to simplify and improve the process by allowing citizens to file complaints electronically and by doing a more thorough job of investigating them. Both of these efforts could have the unintended consequences of artificially increasing the number of complaints filed each year.

In Bittner's original essay, he also stated that the police use of force is rarely examined. Although that might have been true in the early 1970s, it is not the case today. Police departments today pay very close attention to the complaints that they receive. The costly investment that is made to put police officers on the street can be wasted if they have problem officers in their ranks. Monitoring the complaints allows supervisors to develop new forms of training that address interpersonal communication and cultural diversity and sensitivity. Police departments also develop thoughtful and targeted community relations programs. One program with the potential to reduce complaints is a citizen police academy that aims to educate citizens about the nature and process of police work. In many instances, citizens misinterpret standard police behavior and conclude that they are being personally targeted. For example, the presence of a backup unit for routine officer safety can be interpreted by motorists that the police perceive them as dangerous. An emerging initiative focuses on addressing citizens' complaints through a mediation process. Currently, only about a dozen such programs are in operation around the country. However, they have the potential to foster greater understanding and mutual respect, while at the same time giving a voice to both the community members and the police.

Successful crime prevention necessitates a strong working partnership between law enforcement agencies and the citizens they serve. When that relationship is damaged, it undermines confidence and trust in the police; reduces the quality of life for residents; and, ultimately, endangers the community. Therefore, it is imperative that police departments carefully review all complaints against the police and identify mutually beneficial short- and long-term solutions to improve the partnership with the community.

*David B. Taylor*

***See also*** Accountability, Christopher Commission, Citizen Police Academies, Civilian Complaint Review Boards, Early Warning Systems, Use of Force, Video in Patrol Cars

## For Further Reading

Bittner, E. (1975). *The functions of the police in modern society: A review of background factors, current practices, and possible role models*. New York: Jason Aronson.

Brandl, S. G., Stroshine, M. S., & Frank, J. (2001). Who are the complaint-prone officers? An examination of the relationship between police officers' attributes, arrest activity, assignment, and citizens' complaints about excessive force. *Journal of Criminal Justice, 29,* 521-529.

Christopher Commission. (1991). *Report of the Independent Commission on the Los Angeles Police Department.* Los Angeles: Author.

Walker, S., Archbold, C., & Herbst, L. (2002). *Mediating citizen complaints against police officers: A guide for police and community leaders.* Washington, DC: Office of Community Oriented Policing Services.

## ✑ COMPSTAT

The crime analysis and management approach known as Compstat is widely heralded, frequently imitated, and even described as one of policing's most innovative and far-reaching developments in the past 75 years. Yet Compstat's origins, essential operations, and dynamics are widely misunderstood, leading to many mistaken beliefs.

### ORIGINS

In early 1994, the New York City Police Department (NYPD) started to redesign its entire organizational structure and managerial operations. Upon taking office in January 1994, the new commissioner, William Bratton, and his top aides recognized that in order to establish new, exacting standards of operational performance, the department required data to be gathered and analyzed in a timely manner to ensure effective crime-reduction strategies.

Yet when Commissioner Bratton called for a weekly, one-on-one, current events briefing with a representative from each of the NYPD's eight bureaus during the early months of his administration, a disturbing reality surfaced: The NYPD did not know its current crime statistics because there was a reporting time lag of 3 to 6 months. This news was met with incredulity, especially when some headquarters offices maintained that current data could not be routinely generated.

Two precincts were then pressed to generate crime activity statistics on a weekly basis. During the second week of February 1994, all precincts provided a hand count of the seven major crimes for the first 6 weeks of 1993 compared to the same period in 1994. The Patrol Bureau's staff computerized this crime activity and assembled it into a document referred to as the Compstat book. (The name Compstat arose from "Compare Stats," a computer file name, and not, as is commonly thought, from an abbreviated version of "computer statistics.") The first Compstat book included current data on a year-to-date basis for crime complaints and arrests for every major felony category, as well as gun arrests, compiled on citywide, patrol borough, and precinct levels. When it was discovered that some of the arrest statistics were inaccurate, precinct commanders were made accountable for all errors, thereby elevating the level of responsibility from a clerical task to an administrative obligation. (This is in contrast to the previous practice whereby precinct commanders did not view crime reduction as their foremost responsibility and were essentially on their own in combating crime.)

A key to the development of Compstat was the staff's continuous enhancement and refinement of precinct activity and crime data. The Compstat book became more accurate as arrests were downloaded directly from the NYPD's On-Line Booking System. Early versions detailed weekly changes in rates of reported crime and made comparisons among precincts. The third Compstat book noted the top 10 precincts in regard to crime increases and decreases (weekly and monthly) by percentage. Similar ratings were given on a monthly and a yearly basis by percentage and absolute number. Later versions provided 16 pages of rankings by all commands for week, month, and year, categorized by all major crimes—murder, rape, robbery, felony assault, burglary, grand larceny, and grand larceny auto. Arrests by precinct were presented for the seven major crimes. These figures were viewed as an indicator of patrol effectiveness. Rankings spurred analysis of precinct activities, crime trends, and results and drove commanders to better performance. The March 1994 data would prove crucial to Compstat's evolution from a book of vital crime statistics to an arena in which, depending on the results of their crime strategies, commanding officers (COs) would be rewarded or punished.

## LAUNCHING THE PROCESS

Compstat meetings grew out of a need for a mechanism to improve precinct COs' crime-fighting accountability and performance. In April 1994, top officials were searching for ways to sharpen the NYPD's crime-fighting focus. At that time, boroughs held monthly field robbery meetings in which precinct COs and robbery and anticrime sergeants met with the borough staffs (to whom they reported) to discuss robbery trends. Robbery was considered a bellwether crime, but there was no forum for analysis and coordinated action. Each unit, such as transit, patrol, and housing, had its own way of attacking and recording burglaries. Discussions concentrated primarily on the number of robberies in various commands, not on patterns. Top-level executives requested that the Brooklyn North patrol borough hold its monthly robbery meeting at headquarters—One Police Plaza. At the outset, precinct commanders and others were nervous because they did not know what to expect from the top brass. After the Brooklyn borough CO's overview of special conditions, several precinct COs were called to the front of the room. Their presentations, although suitable for public community council meetings, lacked in-depth analyses of complex crime problems. The meeting was abruptly terminated, but shortly thereafter, monthly meetings at headquarters for each borough became required. By April 1994, the NYPD leadership decided to use the headquarters meetings to link the newly released drug and gun strategies with the Compstat books. The meetings, held Wednesday and Friday mornings, became mandatory. They began promptly at 7:00 a.m., when there would be few distractions. High-ranking department officers could not delegate this assignment, even though their work days generally began at 10 a.m.

## MAPPING CRIME

Intensified crime fighting was not contingent just on habitual strategy meetings, crime analysis, and timely and accurate information. Data also had to be portrayed clearly and in a format that could be acted upon quickly. The key was to provide department-wide access to crime location details. Traditionally, some precincts had sporadically maintained simple pin maps to record where robberies occurred. But the maps had low priority, civilians did the plotting, and many precinct commanders rarely used the information when deciding where to deploy their anticrime units. Because the department did not mandate map use, the assumption was that the maps were not that important.

The Compstat staff pinmapped all robberies, shootings, grand larcenies, and murders within a high-crime precinct, and this information was used by headquarters to redeploy antinarcotics and gun teams to high-profile hot spots. All precincts were ordered to maintain pin maps, cover them with acetate overlays for each of the major index crimes and bring them into Compstat meetings. Pin mapping was now part of the furniture.

As computer capabilities improved at headquarters and at precincts, pin maps were replaced by overlay maps created by crime-mapping computer software. The new maps, showing crime activity in the city, were displayed on large video screens. The computer-made maps included narcotics complaints; time, day of week, and location of crime events; as well as information regarding police deployment and arrest activity. Later, Compstat recorded and mapped the times and places of precinct shootings and their relationship to drug-dealing sites. A powerful software tool, MapInfo 94, was used that employed attention-grabbing colors and shapes. When projected on the war room's large overhead screen and small individual screens, the overlays of colors superimposed on street locations were impressive. For the first time, crime and arrest data that were previously floating in the vast NYPD universe were brought together through the convergence of Compstat books and crime strategy meetings. The result was information that formed patterns and allowed the tracking of homicides with drug complaints, with gun arrests, and with desk appearance tickets that dealt with quality-of-life arrests. Crime data became easy to read and digest.

## QUALITATIVE INFORMATION

As the Compstat meetings evolved, the top level sought not only more quantitative information about crime complaints, arrests, patterns, and trends, but also qualitative information about precinct and community conditions and their relationship to effective crime fighting.

In late 1994, the Compstat staff developed commander profiles for every precinct. The commander profiles provided information about appointment date and years in rank, education and specialized training, more recent performance evaluations, and previous command positions. Since 1994, the profiles have expanded to include community demographics, crime statistics, summons activity, available resources, average response time for the delivery of services, domestic violence incidents, unfounded radio runs, and officers' absences. These last two items are believed to be an important indicator of commander morale. Later, "integrity monitoring" was added in order to convey the importance of citizen complaints and charges of brutality and misconduct. Subsequently, profiles have been developed for detective squad commanders, robbery unit supervisors, borough commanding officers, narcotics supervisors, housing bureau supervisors, and transit bureau supervisors.

From the very beginning, commander profiles have been instrumental in enhancing accountability. Now regularly distributed at all Compstat meetings, profiles open the door for the top brass to regularly match a face with performance. These supervisory profiles help the upper echelon evaluate and compare supervisors when making promotion and transfer decisions. The material is also increasingly geared to specific unit operations. For example, investigative profiles for detectives and members of narcotics units furnish information about arrest activities, caseloads and clearances, the number and ranks of assigned personnel, their absence rate, and the number of perpetrator debriefings and search warrants executed. Narcotics supervisors' profiles also specify registered confidential informants; long-term buy operations; and narcotics activity intelligence reports received, investigated, and closed.

The quest for qualitative information continues. Beginning in 1996, photos of precinct areas—taken when crime activity peaks—have been displayed at some Compstat meetings. For example, photos

might show precinct conditions during hours when panhandlers are prohibited from loitering near ATM machines. If photos reveal deteriorating conditions, such as drug activity or loitering, the times of the day when the photos were taken are compared with the times when narcotics and patrol officers work and arrest violators. Immediate attention is riveted on the problem (in this case, how officers' schedules differ from crime patterns), and remedies are planned.

## THE DIMENSIONS OF COMPSTAT

The value of Compstat lies in its diversity. What started out as an informational need to know crime stats has developed into formal meetings (known as Compstat meetings) whereby *all* levels of the department participate to identify precinct and city-wide crime trends, deploy resources, and assess crime control strategies. The story of Compstat is the story of a multifunctional vessel expanding beyond the goal of command accountability. It is a now a vehicle for planning, evaluation, and coordination.

Compstat's major dimensions take place on three vital levels. Pyramid-like, the top level, informational sources and analyses, is most visible to the observer. One must be fairly close to the process to view the second layer of management and planning. Finally, the bottom layer, organizational learning, which constitutes the structural base of the other two layers, is the least visible and the layer that tends to generate change. These three levels can be summarized by the 25 Cs of Compstat.

### Top Level–Information Sources and Analyses–7 Cs

This first layer, informational sources and analyses, may be likened to the tip of this iceberg structure. It is the most visible aspect of Compstat meetings.

1. *Crime Trends, Patterns, and Clusters.* For the first time, all key members are focused on crime conditions at a meeting devoted primarily to fighting crime.

2. *Crime Analyses.* How well is it being done, by whom, and how frequently?

3. *Cross-Reference Tool.* How is deployment stacking up against crime patterns? Where are the narcotics and other arrests being made, compared to shootings and citizen narcotics complaints?

4. *Characteristics of Precincts.* Spotting emerging trends—gangs, locations, special problems.

5. *Community Involvement.* How involved is the community? What are citizens' complaints?

6. *Criminology.* Precinct commanders and staff are area criminologists. There are repeatedly questions about victims, patterns, and deployment. In many respects, Compstat *is* criminology in practice.

7. *Coordinative Mechanism Within the Criminal Justice System.* Members of other criminal justice agencies regularly attend these meetings, and issues of joint concern and operational tactics periodically arise. Compstat is one device to partially overcome separations in the criminal justice system.

## Middle Level—Management Evaluation and Planning Tool—8 Cs

This middle level is less visible to the casual observer because it is partially submerged below the surface.

1. *Commanding Officer's Authority and Accountability.* This is a central tool to clinch devolution of crime management to the local level. At the same time, Compstat has served as a means for assessing performance and evaluating personnel. For the first time, COs and high-ranking headquarters chiefs have regular encounters. This facilitates familiarity with performance as opposed to previous name recognition only.

2. *Crime Strategies.* Crime strategies are featured, evaluated, assessed, and refined at Compstat meetings. They can include city-wide, selective strategies, and technological advances.

3. *Concrete Results, Not Just Activities.* This philosophy is the product of a management and leadership style that now says that success does not come from making the fewest mistakes.

It comes from getting results. You do not get results without action. Compstat provides both the data and the setting for comparing results with activities, means with ends, arrests with crime reduction, quality-of-life summons with index crime, and deployment strategies with crime results.

4. *Communications and Decision Making.* A department of various generalist and specialist units requires constant attention to communications and shared decision making. Integration of organizational parts is a perennial issue. The focus is on who owns this problem and who is working on this problem.

5. *Connective Linkage Within the Organization.* Compstat has spread. Each borough has at least twice-monthly Compstat meetings. Precinct Compstat meetings are used by precinct commanders for coordinative, strategic, and preparatory purposes.

6. *Circulation of Messages.* Compstat has not replaced the grapevine but has become one of its major transmission vines. There is no quicker way to disseminate a message on organizational priorities and interests than to raise it at a Compstat meeting. Each borough also has a crime strategist who attends all headquarters Compstat meetings and reports back to his or her respective borough.

7. *Compstat College.* The Police Academy instituted a program in which commanding officers share with other commanding officers and others their experiences with a particular crime strategy with which they have good results. The idea is that senior people can learn from others with similar responsibilities.

8. *Creation of New Information Avenues.* This is just one example of Compstat growing institutional offshoots. Various departmental units now include a column in their official informational sheets (often called Compstat Corner) to inform their members of items that have arisen at Compstat meetings and pertain to their responsibilities. Each borough has a Pattern Identification Module that serves as its crime-fighting intelligence center. Each issues "Alerts" to crime trends and or patterns.

## *Bottom Level–Organizational Learning–10 Cs*

This layer represents the least visible but the deepest and perhaps most profound aspects of Compstat.

1. *Constant Experimentation.* Much of the NYPD Compstat and other activities fall under the heading of what organizational theorists call double loop learning. This contrasts with single loop learning, the predominant mode of most organizations, which occurs when the detection and correction of error enables the organization to continue with its present policies or achieve its present objectives. Double loop learning, on the other hand, is rarer and more fundamental because it involves questioning basic operating assumptions, entertaining different approaches, and experimenting with various arrangements. The NYPD, for example, has experimented with competing organizational and managerial arrangements devoted to different major antidrug efforts. This experimentation and change is reflected in many Compstat efforts.

2. *CPR—Courtesy, Professionalism, Respect.* One way that this is being conveyed and monitored is in Compstat recordings of complaints against police officers. Precinct commanders are now being held accountable, in Compstat data and meetings, for civilian complaints—an outgrowth of Compstat's focus on accountability.

3. *Critical Thinking.* In terms of assessing game plans and their effectiveness, Compstat meetings reflect this in numerous ways—this emerges in what may be labeled the 10 Ds.

   – Discovering difficulties and obstacles
   – Defending positions; debunking the past and discarding current practices
   – Demand for ownership or responsibility
   – Diagnoses of problems
   – Designing alternative strategies
   – Deployment of resources
   – Delegation and coordination of responsibilities and devolution of authority
   – Dissemination of information
   – Defining solutions
   – Delivering solutions

4. *Change Agent.* As the police scholar Herman Goldstein has observed, organizational change is multidimensional. Compstat has played an integral role in the change process. Compstat has been continually interlaced with and has often spearheaded other key change processes, including reorganization.

5. *Coterie of Dedicated Staff.* The fact that Compstat is a departmental unit is far more well known inside than outside the NYPD. This dedicated and imaginative Compstat office prepares for and analyzes meetings and data and develops new Compstat informational components and issues.

6. *Creative Problem Solving.* Compstat is the platform where new problem-solving approaches are often presented, reviewed, analyzed, reexamined, and circulated. Many of these problems are first developed at the precinct level.

7. *Continuity and Consistency.* Compstat is the central mechanism for consistent follow-up and constant monitoring. Compstat's regularity ensures that organizational strategies are systematically pursued. At the core of Compstat is constant monitoring. From its inception, Compstat meetings have been held regularly with very few exceptions. High-level participants from headquarters and the boroughs rarely miss meetings, further sustaining Compstat's continuity and consistency. Events, incidents, and discussions raised at one Compstat meeting are recorded, remembered, and revisited by these participants at subsequent meetings.

8. *Control.* Compstat and other departmental innovations have thrust responsibility and accountability down to the borough and precinct levels. Authority is still exercised at the top, but it is now a more informed control based on results, not just activities.

9. *Central Nervous System.* Compstat serves as a barometer of organizational well-being. If things go wrong, if information is not being shared, it will emerge at some point at a meeting. The flow of a meeting can be interrupted when it becomes apparent that previous department decisions (e.g., the distribution of equipment from headquarters units to the field) have not been followed through.

10. *Center Stage in the Department and Elsewhere.* Whether or not a patrol officer has attended a Compstat meeting, he or she has an opinion about Compstat. Compstat meetings have a street-level

reputation as the stage on which precinct commanders are grilled on crime reduction efforts. This view reinforces the patrol officer's desire to combat crime. Precinct commanders occasionally bring precinct officers who have performed heroic feats and are applauded for their accomplishments. The fact that Compstat has been noted at least twice on the television show "NYPD Blue" illustrates how its reputation has permeated through some of popular culture.

In 1996, Compstat was awarded the prestigious Innovations in American Government Award from the Ford Foundation and the John F. Kennedy School of Government at Harvard University. Compstat has been adopted by numerous law enforcement agencies around the globe. The NYPD has sponsored several 3-day Compstat conferences, each time attracting more than 400 attendees, including representatives from more than 75 police departments in the United States and other countries. Hundreds of law enforcement officials from around the world regularly visit Compstat meetings—a further testimony to Compstat's credibility and adaptability. In 2004, the Innovations in American Government Award was given to the city of Baltimore for applying the Compstat process city-wide.

*Eli B. Silverman*

***See also*** Crime Statistics and Analysis, Quality-of-Life Enforcement, Theories of Policing

## For Further Reading

Bratton, W. (1998). *Turnaround: How America's top cop reversed the crime epidemic.* New York: Random House.

Henry, V. (2002). *The Compstat paradigm: Management accountability in policing, business, and the public sector.* Flushing, NY: Looseleaf.

Maple, J. (1999). *The crime fighter: Putting the bad guys out of business.* New York: Doubleday.

McDonald, P. (2002). *Managing police operations: Implementing the New York crime control model: Compstat.* Belmont, CA: Wadsworth.

O'Connell, P. (2001). *Using performance data for accountability: The New York City Police Department's CompStat model of police management.* Arlington, VA: Pricewaterhouse-Coopers.

Silverman, E. B. (1999). *NYPD battles crime: Innovative strategies in policing.* Boston: Northeastern University Press.

Silverman, E. B., & O'Connell, P. (1999). Organizational change and decision making in the New York City Police Department. *International Journal of Public Administration, 22*(2), 217–259.

## ❧ COMPUTER AIDED DISPATCH

### WHAT IS COMPUTER AIDED DISPATCH?

Computer aided dispatch (CAD) is a computer management system designed to aid law enforcement by allowing instant communication between the police dispatcher and field officers. With CAD, the dispatcher is better able to provide the officer valuable information necessary to enhance officer safety, increase response time, and improve service to the community.

### HOW IT WORKS

Depending upon the CAD system (there are many variations available), the emergency operator receives a call from a citizen (usually via the emergency telephone number system, such as 9-1-1). As the information is provided and coded into the computer, the operator forwards the data to the police dispatcher. The data immediately flash on the dispatcher's computer screen. The CAD system will give the dispatcher the caller's location and telephone number (caller ID). CAD will also color code the call on the computer screen to aid in the prioritizing of the dispatched call. For instance, a robbery-in-progress call may be coded "red" to notify the dispatcher that the call received is of high priority and should be dispatched to the field units immediately. The dispatcher will then forward this information to the officer.

### Prior to CAD

Before computer automation in law enforcement, communication between the police dispatcher and the police officer was quite cumbersome. Because 9-1-1 systems did not exist, the citizen called the police department directly and was transferred to a police operator. The operator hand-recorded on a color-coded index card (the color represented the priority level of the call) the name, address, and phone number of the caller; the nature of the problem; and so on. This information was then forwarded to the police dispatcher (who was often in another room) via a conveyer belt, or an open window if the rooms were adjoined. The dispatcher checked his or her log to determine which officer was available to receive the call and then recorded on the card the time the call was dispatched, the arrival time of the officer, and the departure time (when the officer cleared the call). The dispatcher was responsible for knowing the location of the officers and their status at all times. If an officer wished further information regarding a complaint, the officer had to contact the dispatcher repeatedly, sometimes requiring the dispatcher to call the complainant and/or another police agency member. For instance, the dispatcher may have had to contact the Warrant Department to ascertain if an outstanding warrant on an individual existed.

### Benefits of CAD

Unlike the old hand system, CAD allows immediate communication between the police dispatcher and the police officer at the touch of a button. The CAD system provides detailed information addressing the answers to questions that are most useful for the dispatcher and responding officers. Who is the closest officer to the scene? Is the officer available to respond to the call? What is the best route to respond to the call, including recent road construction, one-way streets, and so on, as well as the nearest cross street? (The system must be constantly updated for this information to be accurate and to better increase response time.) What are the dangers near or at the location? For instance, have gunshots been fired? Is the location known for heavy drug trafficking? Are there toxic chemicals in the area? Have officers responded to that location previously? What was the status of previous calls to that location? Is there a personal history on the individuals involved? Did the officer note any particular dangers or warnings for future responding officers (e.g., suspect has a history of mental illness)?

CAD records the time the call was received, time of dispatch, and so on. The CAD system may also note floor plans to buildings, which may prove particularly useful if an officer is responding to a burglary-in-progress call or a hostage situation. Some CAD systems have incorporated automated transponders within patrol vehicles to allow the dispatcher to track patrol units. This is beneficial if the dispatcher wishes to note the exact location of the officer in the event of an emergency (officer needs assistance) or to better allocate personnel to a scene.

## MOBILE DIGITAL TERMINALS

Many police agencies have enhanced their CAD system by linking the computer system directly to police vehicles via minicomputers called mobile data terminals (MDTs). A benefit to this system is that dispatching can be conducted electronically, similar to e-mailing the officer. The information that is electronically dispatched is revealed on the computer screen in the officer's patrol vehicle (or in some cases, cellular telephones). The officer can retrieve the message and transmit messages via a keyboard located in the patrol vehicle. MDTs create a direct interface between important computer information and the patrol unit. The officer can directly enter the information he or she wishes into the MDT (e.g., to conduct a driver's license check or to run a vehicle license plate) to receive an immediate response, without the services of the dispatcher or interfering with radio communication. With MDT, information can be stored on the computer for easy and convenient reference. The stored information can also be shared with other local and federal law enforcement agencies in a matter of moments.

CAD is designed to aid in the communication process between the police dispatcher and the officer. CAD provides immediate information to the dispatcher and officer, allowing potential risks to be identified (hot spots). It also enables officers to respond more quickly, provides for more effective communication within and between law enforcement agencies, and works as a management tool to better serve the public.

*Tod W. Burke*

*See also* Dispatch

*For Further Reading*

Dempsey, J. S. (1999). *An introduction to policing* (2nd ed.). Belmont, CA: Wadsworth.

Swanson, C. R., Territo, L., & Taylor, R. W. (1993). *Police administration: Structures, processes, and behavior* (3rd ed.). New York: Macmillan.

## ✍ COMPUTER CRIME

Definitions of computer crime have evolved to reflect the increased use of computers in society. Early definitions describing computer crime as a type of white-collar crime reflect the limited availability and use of computers prior to the development of the personal computer (PC). Criminal activity connected to early computers generally involved economic and large-scale financial frauds related to an offender's employment responsibilities or attempts to access protected information. In the United States, the investigation of these early computer crimes fell, primarily, under the jurisdiction of the military investigative services or federal law enforcement agencies such as the Federal Bureau of Investigation and Secret Service.

The development of the PC and the commercialization of the Internet transformed the computer from a tool used by skilled employees within government agencies and large corporations to a tool used by the public-at-large. The widespread adoption of computers in the home, office, and classroom, and the ensuing proliferation of business and consumer software applications, increased both the opportunities to commit a computer crime and the types of illegal activities that could be committed using a computer. In 1993, Barry Hurewitz and Allen Lo offered a broad definition of computer crime that covers the numerous illegal acts that one can currently commit with a computer. They define computer crime as "any act involving a computer that may be prosecuted under criminal law" (Hurewitz & Lo, 1993, p. 496). Computer crime can be further explained by examining the potential relationships between computers and criminal activity. Computers can be targets and instruments of crime. Computers also can be incidental to crime, but may contain evidence of criminal activity

that has occurred outside of cyberspace. When targeting computers, offenders access them without authorization, or they damage hardware, software, or data. Commonly referred to as hacking, or cracking, by the popular media, targeting computers for criminal purposes is nothing more than a modern-day form of trespass or vandalism. Access to targeted computers is often gained by exceeding one's authorized computer privileges, by coercing naïve computer users into providing their passwords, or by using software tools that exploit known vulnerabilities in hardware and software. Software and data may be damaged through the use of rogue codes (e.g., viruses, worms, and Trojan horses) or by simply altering or deleting the targeted files. Motives for targeting computers include civil disobedience, profit, peer recognition, revenge, curiosity, terrorism, and the intellectual challenge of bypassing security software.

A computer may also be used as an instrument to commit a traditional crime in a high-tech manner. Criminals who use computers enjoy the same benefits as law-abiding citizens do. Namely, computers enable interaction without physical proximity and increase our capacity to process information. Consequently, computers and related technologies have the potential to simplify many traditional crimes. For example, producers of child pornography have replaced expensive cameras and complicated editing equipment with home computers, digital cameras, and point-and-click graphics software.

The Internet, as compared to face-to-face exchanges and postal mail, provides child pornographers with a faster and more anonymous means to distribute pictures and videos.

E-mail, chat rooms, instant messengers, newsgroups, online message boards, and Web sites have been used by stalkers to send harassing and threatening messages. For example, Allan Munn was convicted of aggravated harassment by the Criminal Court of the City of New York for posting a message to an Internet newsgroup that threatened to kill Lieutenant Steven Biegel of the New York City Police Department (*New York v. Munn,* 1999). The facelessness of cyberspace allows offenders to send threatening messages under the guise of a fictitious screen name or pseudonym.

Computer technologies can also be used as instruments for theft and fraud. Home computers, recordable CD and DVD drives, and the Internet facilitate, for example, the unlawful duplication and distribution of copyrighted material (e.g., music, movies, and software). With a PC, an aspiring counterfeiter no longer needs to apprentice under a master forger. Easy-to-use desktop publishing software and affordable, high-quality color printers have made the forging of official documents (e.g., passports and driver's licenses) and financial instruments (e.g., checks and currency) a crime that requires little skill. Additionally, the detached nature of cyberspace provides cover to thieves who wish to fraudulently purchase goods from online merchants using stolen credit cards.

The Internet also has the potential to simplify both stock manipulation schemes and advance-fee frauds. The global reach of the Internet increases the number of suitable targets for criminal victimization. For example, fictitious claims about a particular stock posted to online financial bulletin boards have the potential to reach millions of investors for a fraction of the cost that would be incurred when using postal mail to disseminate the same information to the same number of investors.

Besides being targets and instruments of crime, computers may contain evidence of crimes that have occurred in the physical world. Here, evidence of illegal activity is left on a hard drive or other storage media (e.g., floppy disk, zip disk, or flash memory card). Spreadsheet, word processor, and database files may contain, for example, client lists of drug dealers and prostitutes, part inventories from chop shops, and betting records from illegal gambling operations. Additionally, Denning and Baugh (1997) tell how terrorist organizations have used computers to help plan and coordinate attacks. A computer belonging to the terrorist group responsible for the bombing of the World Trade Center in 1993 contained files that detailed plans to attack U.S. interests in the Far East.

The movement of crime from the physical world into the virtual world has rendered most traditional forensic techniques useless in the fight against computer crime. Evidence of traditional crimes, or crimes occurring in the physical world, exists primarily in the form of tangible goods. Evidence of computer-related crime is primarily made up of digital data, or electronic impulses and magnetic fields, and is, conversely, intangible. The intangible nature of digital data has resulted in the development of forensic techniques specific to the field of computer science that enable investigators to reconstruct, recover, and analyze digital information related to a criminal act.

*James R. Doyle and Rob D'Ovidio*

***See also*** Evidence, Identity Theft

## For Further Reading

Charney, S. (1994). Computer crime: Law enforcement's shift from a corporeal environment to the intangible, electronic world of cyberspace. *Federal Bar News and Journal, 41*(7), 489–494.

Denning, D. E., & Baugh, W. (1997). *Encryption and evolving technologies: Tools of organized crime and terrorism.* Washington, DC: U.S. Working Group on Organized Crime, National Strategy Information Center.

D'Ovidio, R., & Doyle, J. R. (2003). Cyberstalking: Understanding the investigative hurdles. *FBI Law Enforcement Bulletin, 72*(3), 10–17.

Grabosky, P., Smith, R. G., & Dempsey, G. (2001). *Electronic theft: Unlawful acquisition in cyberspace.* Cambridge, UK: Cambridge University Press.

Hurewitz, B. J., & Lo, A. M. (1993). Computer-related crimes. *American Criminal Law Review, 30,* 495–521.

New York v. Munn, 688 N.Y., S.2d 384 (1999).

Parker, D. B. (1976). *Crime by computer.* New York: Scribner.

# ⁊ CONFESSIONS

Confession is the highest drama. In every Hollywood crime story, fabled cops ply their trade and bad guys seal their fate in the interrogation room, where ruthless, third-degree tactics unlock the guilty suspect's compulsion to confess. In such stories, the moment of confession is fully climactic. *Sign on the dotted line, pal. Case closed.*

In the real world, too, an individual's admission of guilt may be tantamount to conviction. Notwithstanding empirical evidence that casts doubt on the validity of confession evidence, and the legal questions that surround self-incrimination, a suspect's declaration of guilt carries almost unequaled weight with police, the courts, and the public.

Because confessions are potentially so damaging to criminal defendants, both federal and state courts have codified criteria for entering confessional statements into evidence. The admissibility of confession evidence is determined by its adherence to a set of fairly succinct legal guidelines. Explicitly excluded from the courtroom are statements obtained through brute force or under extreme duress, coerced by threat and intimidation, or manipulated with promises of immunity or leniency. Also proscribed are statements made in ignorance or in contravention of Miranda protections.

## LEGAL HISTORY

Despite Blackstone's warning in the mid-18th century that confessions were not to be trusted, in the history of American jurisprudence, the acknowledgment of guilt by a defendant has traditionally been sufficient to win a conviction, even absent corroborating evidence.

Although the legal standard throughout the 19th century implied that confessions should be "voluntary," no particular set of guidelines existed that defined the circumstances under which a confession would be considered coerced. Indeed, a series of lower and appellate court decisions well into the 20th century suggested that even confessions elicited under great duress could be entered into evidence. In an extreme example, the Mississippi Supreme Court affirmed a lower court ruling that the confessions of three defendants were admissible although the men had been hanged, whipped, and tortured prior to *voluntarily* admitting their crimes (*Brown v. Mississippi,* 1936). Because the Fifth Amendment protection against self-incrimination did not extend to the states, the Supreme Court had to rely on the due process clause of the Fourteenth Amendment to exclude the guilty admissions of the three men.

Beginning in the 1940s, the Supreme Court began to give the lower courts some guidance on the construction of voluntariness tests that could take into account the "totality of the circumstances" under which a confession was elicited. The Court, in a variety of cases, outlined the factors governing admissibility. These considerations included defendant characteristics such as age, IQ, or mental state, and interrogation methods (e.g., the threat of violence, sleep deprivation, ignoring a suspect's request for counsel, etc.).

In rulings handed down over the next two decades, the Supreme Court mandated greater restrictions on the interrogatory process, prohibiting most police questioning prior to a court appearance, where, presumably, the judge would advise the defendant of his or her rights regarding self-incrimination. However, because these rulings involved the rights of federal defendants, the proviso did not apply to interrogations by state police.

The first attempt to nationalize interrogation guidelines came with the landmark ruling in *Escobedo v. Illinois* in 1964, which guaranteed the right to counsel during police questioning. However, narrow interpretations by the state courts of the ruling's applicability meant that it was of little practical use to most suspects, particularly indigent suspects who had no lawyer. Ernest Miranda, accused of a rape in Arizona, was one such subject. The Arizona Supreme Court upheld the admission of confession evidence in Miranda's case, saying that the facts did not closely enough resemble the facts in *Escobedo* to necessitate suppression.

In 1966, the Supreme Court's decision in *Miranda v. Arizona* expanded and extended protections to defendants in state cases by instituting a "warning and waiver" requirement in place of the Court's earlier voluntariness test. The Court held that all confessions elicited during police custody were inherently compelled unless the accused was fully apprised of the right to remain silent and to have counsel present during questioning. Therefore, statements obtained without the knowing and voluntary waiver of these rights could be suppressed.

A tremendous political backlash greeted the *Miranda* decision, with conservatives insisting that the new Court ruling advantaged criminals while handcuffing the police. To remedy what they saw as too sweeping a reform, Congress passed the Omnibus Crime Control and Safe Streets Act of 1968, in which Section 3501 rejected *Miranda*'s presumption of coercion and discarded the rule that automatically excluded confessions given in the absence of Miranda warnings. Over the next 32 years, the Department of Justice alternately enforced or ignored Section 3501's dictates, depending upon which political party happened to be in power. Players on each side of the controversy sought a judicial solution, namely that either *Miranda* or Section 3501 would be deemed unconstitutional.

Not until the year 2000, when the Court ruled Section 3501 unconstitutional because of its attempt to override *Miranda,* was the federal statute formally invalidated. The Miranda warnings and waivers system was left intact. Advocates for the accused, however, claim that the police still find ample ways in which to circumvent *Miranda*'s protections.

## INTERROGATION TECHNIQUES

Since the days of the famed third degree, law enforcement has drastically changed the tenor—if not the intent—of criminal interrogation procedures. Responding to a feared drop in conviction rates precipitated by a variety of Supreme Court decisions to suppress confession evidence deemed coerced, police have devised increasingly subtle ways of getting suspects to confess to crimes.

Texts on the subject recommend that the interrogation room be located in an isolated corner of the police station. The room should be relatively bare and sterile: a table and a couple of chairs, a one-way mirror, and no place to hide or rest. The interrogating officers begin with the premise of the suspect's guilt. They may offer sympathy, supply justifications for the crime, and imply leniency in exchange for a guilty admission (minimization techniques), or they may exaggerate the seriousness of the crime and present the suspect with false evidence or the supposed confession of a confederate (maximization techniques). Officers keep the detainee focused on recounting the facts of the crime (some of which may be fed to the suspect, consciously or unconsciously,

through the questioner's own words) toward the end of obtaining a signed confession.

Although the courts have regularly rejected confessions elicited through overt intimidation or blatant pledges of leniency, typically they have not excluded confessions obtained through subtler kinds of pressure. Trickery and deceit are still effective—and legally acceptable—methods of educing self-incriminating statements from recalcitrant subjects.

## FALSE CONFESSIONS

Confession evidence is very persuasive. But even if it is voluntarily submitted, is it authentic? High-profile crimes can elicit hundreds of unsolicited confessions from totally innocent crime aficionados hungering for a taste of the spotlight. Suspects may confess to crimes they did not commit in order to protect a loved one, because they want to be punished or to get attention, or simply because of an overwhelming need to comply with an authority figure. Under intense pressure, or in the case of vulnerable subjects, innocent individuals may even come to believe in their own guilt, internalizing the message of their interrogators.

Laboratory tests have demonstrated how easy it is to get people to sign a confession and how potentially damaging that signed statement might be in a court of law. Under even moderate stress (the appearance of a confederate who claims to have witnessed the subject committing some misdeed), totally innocent people will confabulate details that implicate them in fictional offenses and sign statements professing their guilt. Mock juries, even when told to disregard self-incriminating statements, weigh confessions heavily, underscoring how very prejudicial a defendant's admission of guilt can be.

Experts on the psychology of confessions state that there are three key questions surrounding confession evidence. First, are the protections against coercion afforded by the Supreme Court sufficiently reflected in the interrogatory practices of law enforcement? Second, are even subtle forms of police pressure likely to invite an unacceptably high rate of false confession? Third, are juries disproportionately swayed by confession evidence, even when the weight of contradictory evidence points elsewhere? Given the sparseness of empirical investigations in this area, the verdict is still out on all three counts. Only an expansion of scientific knowledge regarding the validity, the voluntariness, and the impact of confession evidence can inform, and potentially reform, the way that confessions are elicited and used. Because four out of five criminal suspects currently waive their Miranda rights, it is an area in sore need of investigation.

In an effort to prevent false confessions, a small number of jurisdictions have adopted a policy of videotaping interrogations—a practice commonplace in Great Britain. In 2003, Illinois became the third state after Alaska and Minnesota to require taping. The police departments that so far have adopted this practice tend to be small. Large departments, where criminal case volume is significantly higher, have been reluctant to institute such a policy. To bolster the practice, in February 2004, the American Bar Association unanimously accepted a resolution that urges law enforcement agencies to videotape interrogations of criminal suspects.

*Abby Stein*

## For Further Reading

Brown v. Mississippi, 297 U.S. 278 (1936).

Escobedo v. Illinois, 378 U.S. 478 (1964).

Inbau, F. E., Reid, J. E., & Buckley, J. P. (1986). *Criminal interrogation and confessions* (3rd ed.). Baltimore: Williams and Wilkins.

Kassin, S. M. (1997). The psychology of confession evidence. *American Psychologist, 52*(3), 221–233.

Miranda v. Arizona, 384 U.S. 467 (1966).

Thomas, G. C. (2000). The end of the road for Miranda v. Arizona? On the history and future of rules for police interrogation. *American Criminal Law Review, 37*(1), 1–40.

U.S. v. Dickerson, 166 F. 3rd 667 (4th Circuit, 1999).

## ᴓᴕ CONSENT DECREES

A consent decree is an enforceable agreement reached between two parties involved in a lawsuit. The agreement is binding and serves to settle the dispute at issue and all subsequent claims. Both parties are involved in the negotiation of the specific provisions contained within the decree, but ultimately, the final document is approved by an officer of the court. Upon judicial review and approval of the decree, both parties become subject to the court and rely upon it for any clarification and enforcement purposes. Upon satisfactory compliance, the respondent can appeal to the court for the dissolution of the consent decree. If the respondent fails to satisfy his or her part of the consent decree, the other party can appeal to the court for the reinstatement of the original lawsuit and the continuation of the trial. In addition, the offending party can be held in contempt of court for failing to follow the decree's stipulations.

## BACKGROUND

Consent decrees are not new to the arena of jurisprudence. They have been widely used to settle disputes arising between private corporations and local governments. In the past, these instruments have been used to settle cases involving pollution claims, health care issues, educational issues, child welfare issues, and unfair hiring claims. In addition to their use in these areas, consent decrees have been widely used throughout the criminal justice system.

Consent decrees have a long history of use within the correctional system. Litigation stemming from the treatment of prisoners and poor living conditions inside of jails and prisons has historically been settled through the use of consent decrees. For example, in 1978, jails in Suffolk County, Massachusetts, became the subject of civil suits brought on behalf of inmates claiming that the jails far exceeded the maximum number of allowable inmates. In 1979, the case was settled through the use of a consent decree in which Suffolk County agreed to build new jail facilities. Other decrees have been used to settle litigation concerning the mistreatment of prisoners. In 1972, the Rhode Island prison system became the subject of a consent decree that mandated several procedural changes to the disciplinary practices in the state prison system. By the end of the 1970s and early 1980s, consent decrees had become common in many state correctional systems. In addition to their ubiquity, the focus of many of these decrees began to expand. For example, the 1979 Duran Consent Decree, involving New Mexico state prisons, sought to revamp and redefine the majority of the operational procedures in the state prison system.

Consent decrees have also been used as settlement instruments in police departments. During the 1970s, many police departments were sued over unfair and unequal hiring and promotional practices. This line of litigation was in response to discriminatory actions by police agencies against minorities and females seeking employment or advancement within many of the country's largest police departments. As a result, many of these suits were settled through consent decrees. Decrees seeking to rectify unfair hiring practices were negotiated in many jurisdictions, including Milwaukee, New Jersey, San Francisco, and Los Angeles. Many of these decrees established hiring standards and set various quota systems as a remedy. For example, the 1975 Milwaukee decree mandated that 40% of the candidates admitted into the police academy must be minority and 20% must be female. In Los Angeles, the 1979 Blake decree established similar guidelines, mandating specific hiring percentages for several minority categories and females. Other decrees varied in their remedies, opting to establish an alternate method of relief. For example, a decree reached in Youngstown, Ohio, established a quasi-affirmative action system. The decree stipulated that the department generate two lists of candidates from their promotional exam, one made up of minority officers and the other of Caucasian officers. The decree further mandated that equal numbers of candidates be promoted from each list.

In later years, litigation concerning unfair hiring practices began to focus around civil service examinations given to candidates for police employment. Many of these examinations were criticized as being biased against minorities. As a result, in the late 1980s and early 1990s, several police departments were sued by the Department of Justice and subsequently entered into consent decrees mandating the creation of fair entrance examinations. In 1990, the Department of Justice sued the Philadelphia Police Department over unfair hiring practices stemming from their civil service examination. The result of that litigation was a consent decree mandating the creation of a new entrance exam. Later that year, the Nassau County, New York, Police Department entered into a similar decree that also mandated the creation of a new entrance exam. Specifically, the decree stipulated that the exam must be shown not to have an adverse impact on minorities and females.

In 1994, consent decrees took on a much more important and expanded role in police agencies. Beginning that year, the federal government passed legislation that allowed for litigation and subsequent use of consent decrees as a vehicle to advance police accountability and reform. This meant that consent decrees could now be used to address such issues as racial profiling, police brutality, and excessive use of force. Prior to 1994, this was unheard of in policing. Consent decrees were solely used as a remedy for unfair hiring or promotional practices.

The main reason for the absence of consent decrees in the area of police reform was that the federal government had no statutory vehicle to intervene in local police practices. This all changed with the passing of the Violent Crime Control and Law Enforcement Act of 1994. Specifically, Section 14141 of this Act made it illegal for any "governmental authority . . . to engage in a pattern or practice of conduct by law enforcement officers . . . that deprives persons of rights, privileges, or immunities secured or protected by the constitution or laws of the United States" (42 U.S.C. Section 14141). In addition to outlining prohibitive behavior, this section also enumerated retributive action. The second half of Section 14141 empowered the attorney general to seek civil action to "obtain appropriate equitable and declaratory relief to eliminate the pattern or practice" (42 U.S.C. Section 14141).

Prior to this Act, the only other major piece of legislation that held local police agencies accountable to the Constitution was 42 U.S.C. Section 1983. Section 1983 actions allowed individuals to seek federal redress against state and local police agencies, but this Act did not provide a statutory basis for the government to initiate civil action. Therefore, the federal government was precluded from taking action against local police agencies under Section 1983. Section 14141 filled this void, allowing the government to initiate a claim. In fact, the second half of the section specifically empowered the attorney general to enter into a civil action "for or in the name of the United States" against any governmental authority violating Part 1 of the section (42 U.S.C. Section 14141). Armed with this piece of legislation, the Department of Justice, through its Special Litigation Section, began to officially investigate local police agencies in 1996. By 1997, it had brought its first civil action against Steubenville, Ohio. This was immediately followed by action against the City of Pittsburgh, Pennsylvania.

As it turned out, this relatively innocuous section of the Violent Crime Control and Law Enforcement Act of 1994 had far-reaching implications for the management and accountability of law enforcement agencies nationwide. Section 14141, with its prohibitions and prescriptive relief, formally ushered in the era of the use of police consent decrees as reform instruments within police departments.

## PATTERN AND PRACTICE INVESTIGATIONS

Since the signing of the Violent Crime Control and Law Enforcement Act, there have been 14 "pattern and practice" investigations carried out by the Department of Justice. Diverse agencies from a wide cross-section of the country have found themselves subject to the scrutiny of pattern and practice investigations. These investigations have been carried out in many major urban police departments, such as Los Angeles, Detroit, and New York City. But allegations of police misconduct are not limited to these large agencies. Smaller police departments, such as the one in Steubenville, Ohio, have also found themselves the subject of Department of Justice investigations. As of 2003, a total of six federal pattern and practice investigations have been completed and brought to suit in federal district courts. In five of the jurisdictions—Steubenville,

Ohio; Pittsburgh, Pennsylvania; New Jersey; Los Angeles; and Detroit—the litigation resulted in the establishment of consent decrees. In another jurisdiction, Columbus, Ohio, the civil suit was dropped in lieu of the city's agreement to enter into a memorandum of agreement with the Department of Justice.

Even though these were diverse jurisdictions differing in size, region, and philosophies, many of the issues involved were similar. Allegations of excessive use of force, differential enforcement, racial and gender bias, false arrest, and brutality were all cited in differing combinations as reasons for the initial investigations. In Steubenville, Ohio, the police force was alleged to have participated in incidents involving false arrests, excessive force, filing of false charges, and improper search and seizure practices. The Pittsburgh Bureau of Police was alleged to have allowed a pattern of excessive force to flourish within its ranks. In addition, allegations of racial and gender bias, improper complaint investigation, and improper search and seizure practices plagued the department. The Los Angeles Police Department (LAPD) had similar allegations lodged against it. In addition, a major scandal within the LAPD's Rampart Division helped to solidify the perception that the LAPD was a police force in need of reform. New Jersey state troopers were alleged to have racially profiled African American and Hispanic motorists, singling them out for enforcement and disproportionate searches. Finally, the allegations against the Detroit Police Department led to the creation of two separate consent decrees. The first one concerned use of force and deficiencies found in the department's use-of-force policy in addition to other policies. The second decree concerned the handling of prisoners in the custody of the department.

## CONSENT DECREES

With similar allegations lodged against these jurisdictions, it is not surprising that the remedies and reforms outlined in the consent decrees in these jurisdictions are also very similar. The decrees that exist now follow the same formula in outlining reforms. All of the decrees mandate changes to the policies and practices surrounding training, management, complaint investigation, use of force, and traffic stop data collection. In addition, they all mandate the use of automated personnel data collection and analysis systems commonly referred to as early warning systems. All of these reforms are slated by the decrees to occur within a 5-year life span beginning with the signing of the decree. In total, the decrees have between 75 and 100 mandated reforms that must be carried out.

The first area covered by a majority of the decrees is training. The decrees mandate both in-service and academy training for all officers in cultural diversity, ethics, and integrity. In addition, most of the decrees mandate leadership training for all departmental personnel in supervisory positions. Finally, the decrees mandate increased training under the department's use-of-force curriculum and in verbal deescalation skills. The next major area covered is use of force. The decrees mandate that the departments establish a comprehensive use-of-force policy and create a use-of-force report if they do not have one in existence. Each incident that generates a report is to be reviewed by supervisory officers, and the data contained within it is to be entered into the early warning system. The next major area that the decrees cover is complaint investigation. In many of the decrees, the complaint intake process is slated to be revamped. The decrees require that the complaint filing process be opened up to allow for the intake and investigation of anonymous, third-party, fax, mail, and telephone complaints. It is further stipulated in many of the decrees that all complaints be investigated to the fullest extent possible and in a reasonably timely manner.

The most widely cited provision in all of the current consent decrees is the creation and use of an automated early warning system. These systems have been heralded for their ability to bolster accountability in police agencies by tracking personnel data and alerting potential problematic officers. In order to enhance these systems, the consent decrees require the collection of traffic stop data; use-of-force data; complaint data; civil claims;

search data; arrest data; and personnel data, such as sick time, suspensions, vehicular accidents, and commendations. These data must be collected for each officer, and the system must have the ability to report on an individual-officer basis, precinct basis, shift basis, and department-wide basis.

The last major provision contained in all of the current consent decrees concerns the establishment of an independent monitor. All of the decrees require that the police agency or municipality appoint an independent monitor to ensure that all of the stipulations contained within the decree are being carried out in a timely manner. Ultimately, the monitor is considered to be an officer of the court with responsibility to the court. The crux of the monitor's duty is to measure compliance with the decree and create quarterly reports for the court summarizing the level of compliance. Depending upon the individual's ability and involvement, the monitor can play a crucial role. For example, researchers in Pittsburgh found that their monitor facilitated their compliance by producing a time line and assisting in the clarification of the mandated reforms.

## CONSENT DECREES AS POLICE REFORM INSTRUMENTS

It is hard to completely grasp the ability of consent decrees to create effective reform in police agencies because of their relatively short time in existence. The literature surrounding consent decrees in other areas shows that both successes and failures abound. Many times, the central issues contained in some of the consent decrees did not address the original problem at hand. In others, there was a disconnect between what the court mandated and what was actually carried out. In still others, there was a clear lack of enforcement and evaluation.

Can consent decrees provide a vehicle for substantial reform within police agencies? At the present time, there appears to be no real answer to this question, but a preliminary look into the operations of some of the agencies with consent decrees shows their potential to create reform. Of the six existing consent decrees, only the Pittsburgh decree has reached completion. After 5 years of operation under the consent decree, the Pittsburgh Bureau of Police demonstrated that the department was committed to reform and that it had made accountability a priority. To call it a total success, though, would be misleading. In September 2002, the Western District Court of Pennsylvania decided to bifurcate the consent decree, thereby removing the Pittsburgh Bureau of Police from under its control but continuing to monitor the Office of Municipal Investigations (the independent complaint investigation body in Pittsburgh). In its decision, the court ruled that the Bureau of Police had substantially complied with the provisions of the consent decree for a period of 2 years as required by the decree for removal. The court decided to keep the consent decree in effect for all of the provisions pertaining to the Office of Municipal Investigations (OMI). The reason for this was that OMI had failed to clear a tremendous backlog and was therefore out of compliance with numerous provisions of the decree. But when the focus is shifted solely to the operations and practices of the Bureau of Police, the decree can be considered a major success. It has been shown that the Bureau of Police made substantial strides toward complete compliance. By the end of the decree, the Pittsburgh Bureau of Police emerged as a national leader in personnel evaluation and monitoring, traffic stop data collection, and incident reporting policies.

Similar successes are being achieved in the New Jersey State Police. According to the monitors' fourth report, "[They] have made significant strides to bring the organization into compliance with the requirements of [the] decree" (Lite, Greenberg, DePalma, Rivas, & Public Management Resources, 2001). Specifically, they are in initial compliance with 91 of the 96 tasks listed in the decree. Difficulties have also been encountered. In the monitors' seventh report (Lite, Greenberg, DePalma, Rivas, & Public Management Resources, 2003), it was noted that officers' field performance was still not in compliance, as evidenced by instances of problematic searches.

Even with these successes, it is clear that problems and unintended consequences can surface. The effect of a consent decree on individual officer and departmental morale is problematic at best. In addition, the stigma associated with federal intervention can cause the citizenry to completely lose faith in its police, exacerbating an already tenuous situation. Finally, the tremendous costs associated with complying with the consent decree (e.g., purchasing computer systems, paying a monitor's salary) can jeopardize spending on other governmental services, such as bus service and education. The effect of consent decrees on these issues remains unclear, but it is obvious that they have one.

What is clear is that federal litigation and consent decrees have the potential to bring substantial reform to police departments. The events of the past few years have shown that consent decrees are emerging as a new form of police accountability, but the true barometer for the success of consent decrees remains to be tested. The ultimate goal of any form of police accountability must be the creation and preservation of lasting reform. It has been demonstrated that the few police departments operating under federal consent decrees have created substantial reform, but what occurs when the decree ends? Can the reforms and advancements made under the decree become acculturated into the operational philosophy of the department? The test of time will reveal these answers, but based upon the current examples, it appears that consent decrees have the potential to emerge as a powerful new method to create police reform and advance accountability.

*Christopher W. Ortiz*

***See also*** Accountability, Early Warning Systems

## For Further Reading

Davis, R., Ortiz, C., Henderson, N., Miller, J., & Massie, M. K. (2002). *Turning necessity into virtue: Pittsburgh's experience with a federal consent decree.* New York: Vera Institute of Justice.

Del Carmen, R., & Smith, M. (1997). Police, civil liability, and the law. In R. Dunham & G. Alpert (Eds.), *Critical issues in policing: Contemporary readings* (3rd ed.). Prospect Heights, IL: Waveland.

42 U.S.C. Section 14141.

Ginger, J. (1997). *Pittsburgh monitor's first quarterly report.* Pittsburgh, PA: Author.

Gottfredson, L. (1996). Racially gerrymandering the content of police tests to satisfy the U.S. Justice Department: A case study. *Psychology, Public Policy, and Law, 2*(3/4), 418–446.

Lite, Greenberg, DePalma, Rivas, and Public Management Resources. (2001). New Jersey monitors' fourth quarterly report (2001). Available: www.state.nj.us/lps/monitors_report_4.pdf

Lite, Greenberg, DePalma, Rivas, and Public Management Resources. (2003). New Jersey monitors' seventh quarterly report (2003). Available: http://www.njpublicsafety.com/monitors_report_7.pdf

Livingston, D. (1999). Police reform and the Department of Justice: An essay on accountability. *Buffalo Criminal Law Review, 2*(2), 143–168.

# CORONER AND MEDICAL EXAMINER SYSTEMS

A short time before the Norman Conquest, the Office of the Coroner was established in England. The coroners at that time were appointed by the king, and their duty was to represent and protect the interests of the Crown. Specifically, the coroner's function was to ensure the passage of the decedent's property to the legal recipient. As time passed, the Office assumed additional duties, and the coroners were empowered to select a jury to hear evidence in cases of unnatural deaths. These proceedings, called an inquest, were needed to decide the nature and circumstances of a death, and also to try to determine why a person died. If sufficient evidence was presented at an inquest to charge a person with the crime of felonious homicide, the sheriff would apprehend the responsible individual. The coroner would then seize the property of the accused and turn it over to the Crown. When an individual committed suicide, the coroner would also confiscate the property for the Crown. So, from its inception, the role of the coroner was to investigate the nature of deaths and to be responsible for the disposition of the decedent's physical possessions.

In England, the coroner system gradually changed over time, and many important duties were stripped from the Office. Today, the role of the coroner is to hold inquests only for deaths of a suspicious nature. The basic duties of the coroner system were introduced into America by the early English settlers. Thus, all of the duties of present-day coroners in the United States and Canada have a basis in medieval English law.

The Office of the Coroner in the United States is generally filled by an individual elected by the general voting population. The term of office is usually 4 years, with some variation at the local level. The qualifications for the position are quite straightforward, with minimum requirements being the attainment of a certain age and an eligible voting resident of the election district. However, many locations have recently enacted more stringent legislation that increases the basic educational background required and in some instances, a license to practice medicine or a doctorate in a forensically related area is required.

The basic duties of an elected coroner are to investigate deaths that occur within his or her jurisdiction; determine the cause and circumstances that led to the expiration; present the findings, if necessary, to the local prosecutor's office; and protect the property of the decedent. All properties are the responsibility of the coroner, and the Office must ensure that the disposition of said property is in concert and agreement with all existing law.

Different local governments have decided that the coroner system is not efficient for the duties it must perform. Specifically, the difficulty arises because in many situations, the coroner is not a licensed physician and thus is not able to certify the cause of death nor perform postmortem examinations. Secondarily, with the advances in medicine, a specialty has developed: the forensic pathologist. To accommodate the needs of large metropolitan jurisdictions, the medical examiner system has been created. This system shares some responsibilities with the coroner system, such as determination of the cause of death of an individual under investigation, but the medical examiner does not have the added task of protecting the property of the dead person.

A medical examiner is usually appointed by the local government entity to serve for a defined period of time that varies from location to location. The individual who occupies this position is generally a board-certified forensic pathologist, which means that the person has fulfilled the requirements to be a licensed physician, gone further to complete training in pathology, and then completed a highly specialized residency program in forensic pathology. At the conclusion of this training, the individual must demonstrate knowledge and proficiency in the specialty by successfully completing an examination and other requirements for board certification—a long and dedicated path of education for a person to pursue.

In the United States, there is a mixture of the two systems. Some states have just the coroner system, others have medical examiners, and a few have both types and hybrids of each. In the early 1990s, the U.S. Department of Health and Human Services compiled a listing of the various systems operating in the United States and its territories. The list below gives the type of system that the individual states use for death investigation.

## State Death Investigation System by Type

1) Medical examiner systems (total 22 states/jurisdictions)
   a) State medical examiners
      i) Alaska
      ii) Connecticut
      iii) Delaware
      iv) District of Columbia
      v) Iowa
      vi) Maine
      vii) Maryland
      viii) Massachusetts
      ix) New Hampshire
      x) New Jersey
      xi) New Mexico
      xii) Oklahoma
      xiii) Oregon
      xiv) Rhode Island
      xv) Tennessee
      xvi) Utah
      xvii) Vermont
      xviii) Virginia
      xix) West Virginia
   b) District medical examiner (1 state)
      i) Florida
   c) County medical examiner (2 states)
      i) Arizona
      ii) Michigan

2) Mixed medical examiner and coroner systems (total 18 states)
   a) State medical examiner and county coroner/medical examiners (9 states)
      i) Alabama
      ii) Arkansas
      iii) Georgia
      iv) Kentucky
      v) Mississippi
      vi) Montana
      vii) North Carolina
   b) County medical examiner/coroner (11 states)
      i) California
      ii) Hawaii
      iii) Illinois
      iv) Minnesota
      v) Missouri
      vi) New York
      vii) Ohio
      viii) Pennsylvania
      ix) Texas
      x) Washington
      xi) Wisconsin

3) Coroner systems (total 11 states)
   a) District coroners (2 states)
      i) Kansas
      ii) Nevada
   b) County coroners (9 states)
      i) Colorado
      ii) Idaho
      iii) Indiana
      iv) Louisiana
      v) Nebraska
      vi) North Dakota
      vii) South Carolina
      viii) South Dakota
      ix) Wyoming

## Territory Death Investigation by Type

i) Medical Examiner System (3 areas)
   (a) Territorial medical examiner
      1. Guam
      2. Puerto Rico
      3. U.S. Virgin Islands

ii) Coroner system (1 area)
   (b) Territorial coroner
      1. American Samoa

Canada has a mixture of both medical examiner and coroner systems in its different provinces.

The principal difference between both systems is determined by tradition and the type of role each plays in the medical-legal death investigation. In most instances, the coroner is generally a layperson with no formal training in medicine and so has difficulty determining the cause of death. In these instances, the coroner is responsible for the decedent and takes charge of the body; then, in consultation with an appointed coroner's physician, they ascertain the medical reasons for the death. If an autopsy is required to establish or confirm the cause of death, a forensic pathologist is used to perform the postmortem examination. When all of the information from the death scene has been collected—including physical evidence, medications, past medical history, testimony of attending physicians, and past criminal justice history—the pathologist is able to embark on the dissection. The autopsy itself consists of three phases; the first is the gross anatomical examination. The pathologist examines the overall physical condition of the body, noting any abnormalities that may be present. Then, via the classic Y-shaped incision, the pathologist removes the breast cover and exposes both the thoracic and abdominal organs. Each organ is examined in detail, with sectioning when necessary, to obtain a thorough understanding of the status of each. Sections are taken at this point for microscopic examination (histology) at a later time. Once the main trunk has been studied, the skull cap is removed and an examination of the brain and other systems of the head is done. Again, samples are taken for histological study. While performing the autopsy, physiological samples (i.e., blood, stomach contents, vitreous humor, etc.) are taken and preserved for toxicological analysis in the laboratory. After completion of the gross examination, the pathologist next studies the microscopic samples (histology) and performs a chemical analysis of the collected physiological material. When the data from all three phases are complete, the pathologist generates a report that indicates the cause of death. This information, along with the coroner's investigative report, is then forwarded to the local prosecutor's

office for further action. The personal property of the decedent is sent to the respective county/state agencies for distribution to the legimate claimants. If no one claims the property, it is turned over to the state for inclusion in its general fund.

The medical examiner, usually a board-certified forensic pathologist, has his or her own staff to perform the scene investigations, chemical analysis, and other laboratory functions. The medical examiner makes the decision as to whether an autopsy is necessary, and he or she will perform all the procedures and examinations within the office. At the conclusion of the determinations, the generated reports are turned over to the local prosecutor's office. All reports, whether generated by the coroner system or the medical examiner system, are filed with the appropriate local government agency. In most states, there is restricted access to these files, and they are only available to selected government offices/individuals and not the general public.

Regardless of the type of medical-legal death investigation system, a death certificate is signed by either the coroner or medical examiner. This certificate lists all pertinent demographic information, such as age, residence, sex, race, educational level, family history, and disposition of the body. The primary cause of death and any contributing factors are clearly delineated. It is the responsibility of the coroner/medical examiner to determine the manner of death (i.e., natural causes, homicide, suicide, accident, or undetermined), as well as the time and date of death. The completed death certificate allows the funeral director to take possession of the decedent and prepare the body for its final disposition. This certificate is filed with the clerk of the municipality where the death occurred, and a burial/cremation certificate is then issued.

It is the duty of the coroner/medical examiner to advise the appropriate agencies of the nature of the cause of death of an individual and to present documentation that will allow for responsibility to be determined and corrective action taken. Sometimes, this results in a criminal prosecution; other times, a health alert; or even a change in accepted procedures and laws. The overall purpose of both systems is to have someone act as an ombudsman for the decedent.

More specific information on individual states/territories may be obtained from the U.S. Department of Health and Human Services, Centers for Disease Control and Prevention, Atlanta, GA 30347.

General information on death investigation may be obtained from

1. American Academy of Forensic Sciences
P.O. Box 669
Colorado Springs, CO 80901–0669
(719) 636–1100
http://www.aafs.org

2. International Association of Coroners and Medical Examiners
c/o Bibb County Coroner's Office
617 Mulberry Street Room 402 A
Macon, GA 31201
(478) 621–6314
http://www.iacme.info

3. National Association of Medical Examiners
430 Pryor Street
Atlanta, GA 30212
(404) 730–4781
http://www.thename.org

*William J. Stahl*

*See also* Forensic Science

## For Further Reading

Hendrix, R. C. (1972). *Investigation of violent and sudden death: A manual for medical examiners.* Springfield, IL: Charles C Thomas.

Muth, A. (Ed.). (1999). *Forensic medicine source book.* Detroit, MI: Omnigraphics.

# ☙ CORRUPTION/INTEGRITY

By virtue of the fact that policing is a highly discretionary, coercive activity that routinely takes place in private settings, out of the sight of supervisors, and before witnesses who are often regarded as unreliable, it is, as the history of virtually every police agency in the world bears testimony, an occupation that is rife with opportunities for misconduct of many types. One type of misconduct, corruption—the abuse of police authority for gain—has been particularly problematic.

The difficulties of corruption begin with controversy over its very definition. There is a considerable literature which describes complications in the conception of corruption as the abuse of authority for gain. For example, Maurice Punch emphasizes that the gain does not need to be a personal reward but may be for the benefit of a group or the police organization as a whole. In the same vein, John Kleinig makes the point that one may perform a service for which one receives an unauthorized reward but does so without distorting that service or the manner of its delivery. Although such actions, in Kleinig's view, may not be corrupt, the acceptance of them may detract from "the democratic ethos of policing" and should be discouraged.

Despite the complexities and complications of definition, it is probably wise to preserve both the for-gain and the abuse dimensions of the concept. The benefits of doing so are purely administrative. As Herman Goldstein argued persuasively, other forms of police misconduct that do not normally have a for-gain motive for them (e.g., discourtesy, brutality, incompetence) suggest a distinctly different approach to their control. Likewise, the concept of abuse is sufficiently broad to include distortions of the police role or the form in which it is delivered, as well as any undemocratic message it may imply.

The more problematic aspects of police corruption are not its definition but its resistance to measurement and control. Contributing to the difficulties of both measuring and controlling corruption is not only the reluctance of police officers to report corrupt activities of their fellow officers—a phenomenon sometimes identified as the Code or the Code of Silence—and the reluctance of police administrators to admit the existence of corruption, but also the fact that the typical corrupt transaction benefits the parties to it and thus leaves no immediate victim/complainant to report or call attention to it.

Further complicating our understanding of corruption has been a self-serving administrative view of corruption as reflecting the moral defects of individually defective police officers and ignoring those organizational practices that shield and sustain it.

The so-called bad apple theory of police corruption has been discredited in recent years by some experts.

What has come to replace the bad apple, individualistic view of corruption is a view emphasizing the role of the organization. This view of corruption stresses the organization's role in creating, communicating, and enforcing organizational rules; detecting, investigating, and punishing rule violations; circumscribing the code of silence; and managing the pressures that the social and political environment places on police. In this view, it is the police administrators' responsibility to create an organizational environment and culture that is intolerant of corruption.

Complementing the organizational view of corruption has been a rephrasing of the administrative problem from "controlling corruption" to "enhancing integrity." Integrity, defined as the normative inclination to resist temptations to abuse the rights and privileges of the police office, phrases the administrative goal positively; at the same time, it avoids a number of problems that have plagued the issue. By turning the problem of corruption on its head, integrity avoids the reluctance of officers and administrators to discuss corruption openly and measure it quantitatively.

Officers and administrators are quite willing to say how serious they find certain forms of misconduct to be, how severely they believe it should be disciplined, and how willing they would be to report it. In so doing, they reveal how acceptable they find misconduct to be, when it should be excused, and when they should keep silent about it.

It is precisely this strategy that marked the first attempt to measure corruption by measuring its conceptual opposite. An integrity survey was developed in 2000 that asked 3,235 officers from 30 U.S. police agencies to estimate the seriousness of, the expected and appropriate discipline for, and their willingness to report 11 different hypothetical misconduct scenarios. This survey showed enormous differences in the cultures of integrity in U.S. police agencies. In some agencies, activities such as taking free food and other minor tokens of appreciation were strongly condemned, severely disciplined, and

readily reported. In other agencies, offenses as serious as theft from a crime scene or accepting a bribe were tolerated, punished by penalties less than dismissal, and covered by an agency-wide code of silence.

The survey showed that within the same country and the same state under nearly identical laws, environments of integrity within police agencies differed radically. Officers differed in their opinions of how serious they believed different types of corruption to be, how severely it should and would be punished, and their willingness and the willingness of their fellow officers to report it. These differences were not merely the individual opinions of different officers. They were opinions shared by members of different agencies with different cultures of integrity.

In 2003, the same survey was used in the largest quantitative cross-cultural study of police corruption ever conducted to study the police cultures among some 13,000 police officers in 14 different countries. This newer study showed even greater differences in the cultures of integrity between nations.

It should be admitted that although integrity served as the polar opposite of corruption for the purpose of measuring the concept that had been so resistant to measurement otherwise, it is actually a broader concept than simply the opposite of corruption. Integrity is certainly the opposite of corruption, but it is also the opposite of any kind of intentional police misconduct. This suggests that a technique similar to the one used to measure corruption might use the measurement of integrity as a technique to measure police misconduct as diverse as brutality, the planting of evidence, drug or alcohol use by police officers, and discourtesy to citizens.

*Carl B. Klockars*

*See also* Accountability, Ethics, Knapp Commission, Mollen Commission, Rampart Division Scandal

## For Further Reading

Bracey, D. H. (1992). Police corruption and community relations: Community policing. *Police Studies, 15*(4), 179–183.

Carter, D. L. (1990). Drug-related corruption of police officers: A contemporary typology. *Journal of Criminal Justice, 18,* 85–98.

Delattre, E. (2002). *Character and cops: Ethics in policing* (4th ed.). Washington, DC: AEI.

Goldstein, H. (1975). *Police corruption: A perspective on its nature and control.* Washington, DC: Police Foundation.

Goldstein, H. (1990). *Problem-oriented policing.* New York: McGraw-Hill.

Henry, V. (1990) *Patterns of police corruption and reform: Comparing New York City and Queensland* (Research Paper No. 16). Brisbane: Centre for Australian Public Sector Management.

Henry, V. (1994). Police corruption: Tradition and evolution. In K. Bryett & C. Lewis (Eds.), *Un-peeling tradition: Contemporary policing.* South Melbourne, Australia: Macmillan.

Kleinig, J. (1996). *The ethics of policing.* Cambridge, UK: Cambridge University Press.

Klockars, C. B., Kutnjak Ivkovich, S., & Haberfeld, M. (Eds.). (2003). *Contours of police integrity.* Thousand Oaks, CA: Sage.

Klockars, C. B., Kutnjak Ivkovich, S., Haberfeld, M., & Harver, W. E. (2000). *Measuring police integrity.* Washington, DC: National Institute of Justice.

McCormack, R. J. (1996). Police perceptions and the norming of institutional corruption. *Policing and Society, 6,* 239–246.

Morton, J. (1993). *Bent coppers: A survey of police corruption.* London: Little, Brown.

Newburn, T. (1999). *Understanding and preventing police corruption: Lessons from the literature.* London: Home Office.

Punch, M. (1985). *Conduct unbecoming: The social construction of police deviance and control.* London: Tavistock.

Roebuck, J. B., & Barker, T. (1974). A typology of police corruption. *Social Problems, 21,* 423–437.

Sherman, L. W. (1974). Introduction: Toward a sociological theory of police corruption. In Sherman, L. W. (Ed.), *Police corruption: A sociological perspective.* New York: Doubleday.

Stoddard, E. R. (1968). The "informal code" of police deviancy: A group approach to "blue coat crime." *Journal of Criminal Law, Criminology and Police Science, 59,* 201–213.

# ᖇᐧ COUNTERTERRORISM

September 11, 2001, forever changed police operations. Prior to the terrorist attacks of that date, state and local police officers had few responsibilities regarding antiterrorism or intelligence gathering and analysis. Since that time, however, local law enforcement has been asked to accept an ever-expanding role in both intelligence gathering and antiterrorism activities.

Unfortunately, law enforcement, especially at the state and local level, was ill-prepared for these new responsibilities. Homeland security, at first merely a catchphrase, evolved into a government office with rapidly expanding authority. It was widely accepted that state and local law enforcement would play a prominent role in the new high-security environment, but defining that role has become problematic.

The difficulties have revolved around two distinct areas: law enforcement intelligence versus national security, and an almost universal lack of police knowledge about international and domestic terrorist movements. National security intelligence, which is the purview of agencies such as the Central Intelligence Agency, National Security Agency, and military, operates with few legal restraints. Law enforcement, on the other hand, has severe legal restrictions in both the gathering and maintaining of intelligence records. Further complicating the situation is that prior to September 11, 2001, only the largest police agencies had intelligence operations, and many of these had poorly trained staff and were often used improperly.

The reason for the lack of information about terrorist movements is twofold. Historically, local law enforcement has focused internally; agencies were concerned only about conditions within their own jurisdictions. Many agencies paid little attention to events occurring in other jurisdictions, even those that were adjacent. That changed on April 19, 1995, when Timothy McVeigh bombed the federal building in Oklahoma City. Afterward, police agencies looked for conspiracies in their own area, but still remained uninformed regarding events outside the United States.

Local police, with the help of the newly constituted Department of Homeland Security, are now trying to catch up. With funding from the Bureau of Justice Assistance, programs such as the State and Local Antiterrorism Training program are available to police agencies nationwide. Still, there are almost one million police officers in the United States, and with an annual turnover rate of roughly 10%, it is unlikely that every police officer will receive training on this highly complex topic.

A greater problem exists, however, in the absence of intelligence analysts and programs that train them. Unlike training officers about militant political movements, a process that is more education than training, intelligence analysis is a skill that can be developed only through rigorous training and practice. Unfortunately, most contemporary training lies in the arena of national security and military intelligence, and it is of little use for law enforcement. Further complicating local police response to terrorism is that gathering and disseminating information can be legislatively and legally restricted in some jurisdictions. In addition, public concern over privacy can make police reluctant to get involved in intelligence gathering for antiterrorism purposes.

Meeting the new challenges of homeland security will take time, patience, and resources. Since the attacks in 2001, local law enforcement agencies have engaged in a variety of activities depending on the level of threat. For example, some departments have received emergency response training for attacks from biological and chemical weapons. Many are trying to improve their communication systems. A number of localities have conducted disaster drills and instituted hotlines for residents to report suspicious situations. Agencies have formed regional networks, sometimes across state lines, for both response and information gathering. Some have joined federal antiterrorism task forces. The use of canines for explosives detection has greatly increased. A few agencies have officers who have become trained in federal immigration law and procedure and who can be tapped to perform immigration functions at the local level. Residents have formed and increased the number of civilian emergency response teams. When the Department of Homeland Security issues a nationwide color alert, a system still in the process of being refined, it is local law enforcement that decides what action, if any, to take. Although there is federal funding for some of these initiatives, much of the cost has been borne by state and local budgets.

Traditional demands for police service, however, will not decrease simply because there is a new reality facing the nation. Robbery, rape, murder, burglary, domestic disputes, and traffic jams will not go away. Agencies will have to find ways to incorporate existing police roles and duties into the new framework of homeland security.

A number of duties inherent in the homeland security function require closer communication with both the private sector and other police agencies. Local law enforcement is now responsible for conducting threat assessments within its jurisdiction. Because 85% of the nation's critical infrastructure is owned by private industry, police agencies are required to work closely with these industries and their security forces. Moreover, police agencies need help from both the private sector and the federal government to identify what is and is not critical.

Collecting information is meaningless, however, if police agencies are ill-equipped to analyze information and uninformed as to how it should be disseminated. Of the problems besetting the newly created arena of homeland security, the police obsession with secrecy may be the greatest. It is a fundamental truth that police officers and organizations do not like to share information.

The roadblocks to successful implementation of a national internal police intelligence network are threefold. First, the police must learn how to collect intelligence data legally and then create an internal organization capable of maintaining intelligence information. Second, agencies must have intelligence analysts capable of systematically and competently sifting through pages of raw data and information so that projections can be made with some degree of accuracy. Third, agencies must learn to share information. Federal law enforcement agencies are frequently criticized for their unwillingness to share information among themselves and with local law enforcement. This situation was severely criticized in the numerous governmental studies and hearings in the aftermath of the attacks. It should be noted, however, that local police agencies have also been reluctant to share information with each other as well as federal law enforcement organizations. This situation is changing slowly. As evidence of this, the International Association of Chiefs of Police, the U.S. Attorney General, the Director of Homeland Security, and the Director of the Federal Bureau of Investigation (FBI) have all endorsed the National Criminal Intelligence Sharing Plan. The FBI created a new Office of Intelligence, with organizational mechanisms to increase intelligence sharing, and the Department of Homeland Security has been funding Regional Intelligence Centers, once again, to integrate and disseminate critical information. The FBI, as well as other branches of the Department of Justice and Department of Homeland Security, are also making attempts to consolidate their numerous databases for easier access by police.

Additionally, while police develop their intelligence function, they must also become more aware of the many violent political and religious movements throughout the world. Just in the recent past, violent groups once thought to exist only in the Middle East have emerged within the United States. Groups such as Hezbollah and Hamas have established fundraising, recruiting, and indoctrination centers throughout the country. These groups and others have engaged in a variety of criminal activities for the purpose of funding their terrorist activities against Israel.

Moreover, militant groups such as Hezbollah and Hamas have linked to drug traffickers and other criminals both inside and outside the United States to finance their movement. Money from the drug trade, kidnapping, robbery, and extortion all fund political militancy. It is becoming more difficult to separate terrorists from criminal gangs and cults— a fact that every police officer must take into account.

The belief that the United States was immune from violent extremism ended on September 11, 2001. Among the many problems besetting local police, the most egregious could be the naïve belief among many jurisdictions that terrorism could not touch them. Every police agency has the responsibility to work legally with other agencies, the federal government, the private sector, and the citizens of the community to create an environment safe from crime and terror. That is both the role and ultimately the goal of homeland security.

*Richard N. Holden and David L. Carter*

**See also** Chemical and Biological Terrorism, Local Response to; Immigrants (Policy Toward); Terrorist Groups, Domestic; Terrorist Groups, Foreign

## For Further Reading

Carr, C. (2002). *The lessons of terror: A history of warfare against civilians: Why it has always failed and why it will fail again.* New York: Random House.

Emerson, S. (2002). *American jihad: The terrorists living among us.* New York: Simon & Schuster.

Hoffman, B. (1998). *Inside terrorism.* New York: Columbia University Press.

Juergensmeyer, M. (2003). *Terror in the mind of God: The global rise of religious violence* (3rd ed.). Berkeley: University of California Press.

Kinzer, S. (2003). *All the shah's men: An American coup and the roots of Middle East terror.* Hoboken, NJ: Wiley.

Lewis, B. (2003). *The crisis of Islam: Holy war and unholy terror.* New York: Random House.

Rashid, A. (2002). *Jihad: The rise of militant Islam in central Asia.* Middlesex, UK: Penguin.

White, J. R. (2003). *Terrorism: An introduction* (4th ed.). Belmont, CA: Wadsworth.

White, J. R. (2004). *Defending the homeland.* Belmont, CA: Wadsworth.

## CRIME LABORATORIES

A crime laboratory, according to the American Society of Crime Laboratory Directors (ASCLD), is "a laboratory (with at least one full-time scientist) which examines physical evidence in criminal matters and provides opinion testimony with respect to such physical evidence in a court of law" (ASCLD, 1997, p. 1). With the exception of the Federal Bureau of Investigation and some other federal labs, crime labs in the United States developed independently of one another, in a generally haphazard manner, in response to local perceived needs. In the absence of any centralized leadership, the provision of forensic science services to individual police departments evolved in a number of different ways.

During the latter half of the 19th century, there was relatively little reliance on physical evidence in crime solving. Document examination from the 1840s, blood stain analysis from the 1870s, firearm and bullet examination from the 1880s, photography, and microscopy were occasionally, but not routinely, used in criminal investigation. Up until the 1920s, services in these areas were generally supplied by consultants who had acquired their expertise in the course of their nonforensic occupations. One notable consultancy job was carried out by employees of the Springfield Armory in 1907, who provided ballistics evidence in the Brownsville affray. Some private laboratories provided expertise in firearms and document examination, such as those in Seattle, Washington (from 1919); New York City (1923); and Berkeley, California (1919).

The first police crime laboratory was set up in 1924 in Los Angeles, by the LA police chief and noted police reformer August Vollmer. This lab was typical of the early crime labs, being essentially a one-man operation. Unusually, the director had academic training, in biology. A chemist was added in 1929. Vollmer had previously run the Berkeley Police Department, where he had persuaded faculty at the nearby University of California to give classes to officers on the use of physical evidence. In 1916, Vollmer recruited a university microscopist to be the first criminalist at the Berkeley Police Department.

Many labs evolved out of the police identification bureaus. These bureaus generally used the Bertillon systems for identifying people, and from 1904 on, fingerprinting. During the Sacco and Vanzetti case (1920–1927), four firearms experts gave conflicting testimony, dramatically and publicly demonstrating the need for consistent and reliable firearms identification. The responsibility for firearms examinations was generally added to police identification bureaus, and the resulting units renamed as laboratories. These laboratories were usually staffed by self-taught officers with little or no formal training in science.

The firearms testimony of Calvin Goddard during the Sacco and Venzetti case attracted patrons who financed both his tour of European crime labs

in 1929 and his subsequent establishment of a crime lab in 1930. This lab, named the Scientific Crime Detection Laboratory, was affiliated with Northwestern University in Evanston, Illinois. By 1932, it employed 14 full-time staff and provided forensic services to nearby police departments, including Chicago. The lab published a journal, the *American Journal of Police Science,* and gave 4-week courses on physical evidence. Some of the graduates of this course brought it into disrepute when they claimed far greater expertise than such a short, superficial course could possibly have provided. Private funding dried up during the Depression, and a much reduced lab was sold to the Chicago Police Department in 1938.

Prohibition came into effect in 1920, creating a demand for specimen analysis for alcohol. In 1922, the International Association of Chiefs of Police recommended that every police department establish a crime lab. During the 1920s and 1930s, labs were started in municipal police departments across the country. The Philadelphia Police Department used the services of the public health chemist until 1923, when two chemists were hired, initially for alcohol detection, but providing general toxicological testing by 1925. By 1966, the Philadelphia Police Laboratory employed 33 technicians and scientists. Detroit established a police lab in 1927, with the bulk of its work consisting of firearms identification, followed by document examination and a little chemical analysis. Following a number of unsuccessful attempts, the New York Police Department managed to open a lab in 1934 in the police academy, staffed by four officers with "special skills." A joint municipal and county lab was established in 1950 in Pennsylvania, the Pittsburgh and Allegheny County laboratory.

The first labs associated with state police departments were introduced in the 1930s. The first was the California State Division of Criminal Identification and Investigation, in 1931. Michigan state police followed in 1932, West Virginia in 1935, and New York in 1936—the last reportedly better staffed than any other police lab at that time, with two chemists, a photographer, and an artist, among other employees.

Although most crime labs developed within police departments, there were exceptions. The Santa Clara County laboratory opened in 1947 under the administration of the district attorney. Wisconsin established a state lab under statute in 1947, with the duty of providing complete criminalistics services to local law enforcement.

Establishing and improving competent crime labs in the United States was hindered by the dearth of forensic science literature in English and the lack of communication between crime lab scientists. This problem eased when the newly established American Academy of Forensic Sciences commenced publication of the *Journal of Forensic Sciences* in 1950. Educating and training lab staff appropriately was, and to some degree still is, problematic, particularly during the early decades of the 20th century, when no formal academic courses in forensic science were available.

By the late 1970s, there were about 200 publicly funded crime labs in the United States. As crime labs appeared and expanded in agencies across the country, it became apparent that there was a great deal of variation in the methods and procedures followed. The first attempt to assess lab proficiency nationally was a survey carried out in the mid-1970s by the Forensic Sciences Foundation. Only 25% of the labs assessed achieved an acceptable proficiency rating on all of the tests performed. Sixty-five percent of the labs performed acceptably on 80% of the tests they performed. Clearly, improvements in lab practice, quality assurance, and education were needed. The American Society of Crime Laboratory Directors (ASCLD), founded in 1974, attempted to meet these needs with the development of what is now the main crime lab accreditation program within the United States. The first accreditation was awarded in 1982. In 2003, 159 state and 62 local agency crime labs earned ASCLD accreditation. Although crime labs have improved over time, there have been occasions when labs have been found to contain conditions that can lead to the contamination of evidence and personnel who do not interpret evidence correctly.

As crime labs adopted DNA analytical techniques in the late 1980s and early 1990s, the issue of standards became public again. One molecular biologist observed that laboratories use a higher standard to diagnose strep throat than to put someone on death row (Lander, 1989). In 2001, a survey identified approximately 120 publicly operated crime labs that performed DNA analyses for local police and sheriff's offices, with about half also serving state police (Steadman, 2002). Eighteen percent of the labs were not accredited by an official organization, nor had they applied for accreditation. The number of full-time employees varied from 1 to 60, with 6 being the median. These DNA labs also provided other forensic services: About 90% performed analyses in the areas of controlled substances and firearms/toolmarks/footwear/tireprints, and 65% performed crime scene investigation, blood alcohol testing, fire debris analyses, and trace analyses.

Currently, as the field of forensic science has grown in scope and has been popularized by the media, there is a mounting demand for forensic testing, resulting in a need for more crime labs and trained personnel to staff them. To meet this demand, crime labs have been expanded, and numerous programs have popped up in institutions of higher learning throughout the country.

*Ellen Sexton*

**See also** Chain of Custody, Crime Scene Investigation, Forensic Science

## For Further Reading

American Society of Crime Laboratory Directors. (1997, November). ASCLD/Lab newsletter, p. 1.

American Society of Crime Laboratory Directors. (2004). *Laboratory accreditation program.* Retrieved February 20, 2004, from http://www.ascld-lab.org

Dillon, D. J. (1977). *A history of criminalistics in the United States 1850–1950.* Unpublished doctoral dissertation, University of California, Berkeley.

Lander, E. (1989). DNA fingerprinting on trial. *Nature, 339,* 501–505.

Peterson, J. L. (1983). The crime lab. In C. B. Klockars (Ed.), *Thinking about police: Contemporary readings* (pp. 184–198). New York: McGraw-Hill.

Steadman, G. W. (2002, January). *Survey of DNA crime laboratories, 2001* (NCJ 191191). Washington, DC: Bureau of Justice Statistics.

# ✑ CRIME MAPPING

The application of Geographic Information Systems (GIS) to law enforcement problems is called *crime mapping*. The availability of personal desktop computers and GIS software in the 1990s allowed law enforcement agencies to produce digital versions of the pin maps that had been used for decades. The use of maps to visualize and understand the geographic distribution of crime events is a well-established police practice. Although the placement of colored pins on an area map could display a snapshot of a crime problem in a single time period, the digital maps produced with GIS software produced immediate and substantial gains in descriptive and analytic power. As GIS technology became more accessible, it sparked new interest in the analysis of "crime and place" from both academic researchers and police department crime analysts.

GIS software readily allows a user to link crime data files to map files and to display the information jointly. For example, the map of city boundaries and streets may be linked to a database of crime locations, arrest locations, or calls for service through a process of *geocoding*. The mapping software uses a two-dimensional coordinate system to locate data points on a map. All that is required to locate a crime event on a map is one geographic element. If an exact address or intersection is known, the crime event can be placed as a point on the map. Much of the analytic capacity of crime mapping depends on having reliable address data. If only the general location, such as zip code or census tract, is known, the crime events are shown in the aggregate. Mapping crimes in the aggregate is known as *thematic* or *choropleth mapping*.

## DESCRIPTIVE CRIME MAPPING

The new digital crime maps permit users to select layers of information to be shown on a single map. Thus, crime locations can be compared to calls for service; police patrol routes; physical features of the area, such as bars or abandoned buildings; and socioeconomic information. Clusters of crime activity, or "hot spots," can be located by visual inspection. The maps can be viewed at many levels of magnification and can be archived for comparison over time. The information in a map can be limited to the display of specific crime events or to those events occurring in specific time or date intervals. The Compstat meetings that have spread from New York City to police departments across the country use descriptive maps to display crime activity and report plans for reductions. Applications of descriptive mapping by police administrators include (a) resource allocation; (b) identification of persistent trouble spots (e.g., locations that are thought to be crime producers); (c) monitoring of ex-offenders; (d) sharing of crime information with the community by means of an Internet site and collaborative planning; and (d) local and regional data sharing among law enforcement and other public safety agencies. Law enforcement officers in the field now use mobile or hand-held Global Positioning System devices to send data to the department's GIS system. The addition of laptop computers to patrol cars has begun to make the use of information from crime maps a part of police patrol.

## ANALYTIC CRIME MAPPING

The identification of patterns of crime and the evaluation of law enforcement interventions are possible using only descriptive maps, but they are greatly enhanced through the techniques of spatial analysis. Techniques of spatial statistics allow a user to distinguish repetitive or patterned crime activity from more random events. Once a basic understanding of the clustering and dispersion of crime events is achieved, the pattern can be modeled in relation to other factors, and crime prevention interventions can be tried and tested. Subsequent evaluation of the interventions will then inform and improve the continuing efforts at crime suppression.

Techniques of spatial statistics are specific to the types of data that are available for analysis. Data that are continuous, or present in different distribution across a study area, are analyzed using interpolation. The area is divided into sections, or grids, and measurements are taken of several characteristics in selected grids, allowing estimates to be made of their co-occurrence across the study area. Most public safety and crime analysis problems, however, require information about events that occur at specific locations, and the problems are analyzed using a family of techniques that calculates the relationships among these and other points on a map. Proximity and distance analysis, spatial autocorrelation, and Nearest Neighbor Analysis are now in use for the analysis of specific crime problems, for the derivation of hot spots, for geographic profiling, and for the analysis of the efficacy of police interventions.

The process of estimating the distance traveled by an offender to a crime target or location is called "Journey to Crime" analysis and has been applied to the behavior of auto thieves, serial robbers, and juvenile offenders, and also to the acquisition of chemicals by methamphetamine producers. The question of whether consistent suppression of "quality of life" crimes reduces the volume of serious crime in a study area is an active research area that, to date, has yielded inconsistent results. Crime analysis maps are used in various ways to understand the patterns of drug trafficking and the movement of guns. The estimation of the pattern of future crimes in a specific area is called *crime forecasting* and is of crucial importance to police department planners.

Although the efforts of the National Institute of Justice's Crime Mapping Research Center (now renamed Mapping for Analysis and Public Safety) have made police departments the leaders in the use of crime mapping, GIS technologies are also widely used by agents of Border Patrol and Homeland Security forces.

*Margaret Leland Smith*

**See also** Compstat, Hot Spots

*For Further Reading*

National Institute of Justice's Mapping for Analysis and Public Safety (MAPS)
http://www.ojp.usdoj.gov/nij/maps/

The MAPS (formerly Crime Mapping Research Center) Web site is a comprehensive source of information and resources for crime mapping. A general introduction to GIS for law enforcement, *Crime Mapping: Principle and Practice,* is available in PDF format at http://www.ojp.usdoj.gov/nij/maps/pubs.html#p&p

The Seventh Annual Crime Mapping Research Conference was held in Boston from March 31–April 3, 2004. The programs and many of the papers from prior years' conferences are available at http://www.ojp.usdoj.gov/nij/maps/conferences.html

A listing of Internet links to law enforcement agencies using crime maps is provided at http://www.ojp.usdoj.gov/nij/maps/weblinks.html

An Introduction to Spatial Statistics, the outline of a 2001 seminar on spatial analysis and GIS by Michael Goodchild, is available at http://www.csiss.org/learning_resources/content/good_sa/

## ✿ CRIME PREVENTION UNITS

Throughout most of history, preventing crime and responding to criminal behavior was the purview of the victim, his or her family, and community residents. There was no police force (or criminal justice system, for that matter) as we know it today. The earliest responses to crime included retribution and revenge on the part of the victim and his or her family. Indeed, the earliest laws outlined the role of the victim in addressing crimes. The Code of Hammurabi (approximately 1900 BCE), for example, outlined retribution by the victim and/or the family as the accepted response to injurious behavior. *Lex talionis,* the principle of "an eye for an eye," was specifically set forth as a driving principle in the Hammurabic law. Such laws and practices provided legitimacy to individual citizen action.

The existence of formal systems of social control is relatively new. The Norman Conquest of England in 1066 gave rise to an obligatory form of avocational citizen policing where male citizens were required to band together into groups for the purpose of policing each other. If one individual in the group caused harm (to a group or non-group member), the other members were responsible for apprehending and sanctioning the offender. Beyond this obligatory action, a variety of cooperative practices emerged that relied on citizen participation to protect the community and one another. Watch and ward rotated the responsibility for keeping watch over the town or area, particularly at night, among the male citizens. Identified threats would cause the watcher to raise the alarm and call for help (hue and cry). It was then up to the general citizenry to apprehend and (possibly) punish the offender. Those responding to the call for help were not employees of the state. Rather, they were other common citizens. The "watch and ward" and "hue and cry" ideas were codified in 1285 in the Statutes of Winchester. It is apparent throughout these actions that crime prevention was a major responsibility of the citizenry.

Similar citizen responsibility was commonplace in the New World colonies and the early United States. The vigilante movement, which mirrored early ideas of hue and cry, was a major component of enforcing law and order in the growing frontier of the young country. Citizens were required to look out for themselves and band together into posses when an offender needed to be apprehended and punished.

Although most discussions of early social control focus on the apprehension of offenders and the use of retribution and revenge, a great deal of evidence supports the idea that citizens used a variety of other protective actions. Examples of these alternative approaches include the use of walls, moats, drawbridges, and other physical design features around cities that protected the community from external invasion. Yet another early prevention approach was the restriction of weapon ownership as a means of eliminating violent behavior.

The advent of modern policing is typically traced to the establishment of the Metropolitan Police in London in 1829. Interestingly, a key to the Metropolitan Police was the idea of crime prevention. Sir Robert Peel, who was the driving force behind the Metropolitan Police Act, and Charles Rowan, the commissioner of the new organization, both saw crime prevention as the basic principle underlying police work. Even earlier attempts at formal policing, such as that in 17th-century Paris,

emphasized crime prevention through methods such as preventive patrol, increased lighting, and street cleaning. Formal police forces in the United States, mirroring the movement in England, emerged in the mid-1800s and were restricted primarily to the largest cities in the Northeast, leaving most citizens to continue their efforts at self-protection. The advent of the 20th century witnessed a great deal of change in societal response to deviant behavior. Formal police forces became the norm, and crime prevention and responses to crime were taken out of the hands of the general public and placed into the hands of the police.

Although crime prevention is an idea that has been around for as long as there has been crime, the incorporation of formal crime prevention units and activity in policing took hold in the late 1960s. (Some scholars note that crime prevention units were founded in the 1950s, but their function was generally subsumed in community relations units.) The reintroduction of crime prevention to policing can be traced to three primary factors—increasing citizen unrest, increasing crime, and growing research on the causes of crime.

The 1960s saw great increases in both personal and property crime, as well as the growth of citizen action revolving around the Vietnam War, victim's rights, and civil unrest. The police found themselves faced with problems that did not respond to traditional police interventions, and in many instances, the police were considered part of the problems (particularly in relation to civil unrest and police enforcement tactics). One response to these problems was the increased reliance on police–community relations units to connect with the public. Many of these units actively tried to engender citizen participation in crime prevention efforts as a means of bringing the police and the public together to fight crime.

During the same time period, research was emerging that tied crime to a number of different social and environmental factors, including architectural designs, race relations, economics, and other factors. All of these issues pointed to problems that were outside the expertise of the police. As a consequence, the police needed to reach out to other community members in order to address the growing crime problem.

Based on these forces, several commissions and agencies prompted the move to more cooperative approaches to addressing crime. The 1967 President's Commission on Law Enforcement and the Administration of Justice pointed to the inability of the police to solve the crime problem alone and suggested a number of activities, including greater emphasis on crime prevention. The Law Enforcement Assistance Administration, an outgrowth of the President's Commission, offered grants for many police initiatives, including the establishment of community crime prevention. The 1971 National Advisory Commission on Criminal Justice Standards and Goals promoted crime prevention as a cornerstone for criminal justice activity.

All of the above factors led to the establishment of formal crime prevention units in many police departments in the late 1960s and 1970s. These units were instrumental in developing programs such as block watch, citizen patrols, property marking, neighborhood crime prevention meetings, prevention newsletters, and neighborhood improvement projects. The crime prevention units also participated with other professionals in identifying problems and potential solutions, such as working with architects to be sure that building designs were conducive to safety issues.

Unfortunately, crime prevention units do not always enjoy a long life span. Many units are disbanded during times of tight budgets because they are still not viewed as essential to the police function. Although the units may disappear, the crime prevention activities are often assumed by other units, such as community relations or units tasked with addressing specific crime targets.

Since the late 1960s, there has been a growing movement toward bringing the citizenry back as active participants in policing, typically under the rubric of crime prevention. The police recognize that crime prevention must use the wide range of ideas and abilities found throughout society. Community planning, architecture, neighborhood action, juvenile advocacy, security planning, education, and technical training, among many other system and nonsystem activities, all have a potential impact on the levels of crime and fear of crime. Crime prevention units may come and go, but the role of crime prevention has become a staple in modern policing and has influenced the development of a number of policing theories and practices, such as community policing, problem-oriented policing, and attention to quality-of-life crime (i.e., Broken Windows).

*Steven P. Lab*

*See also* "Broken Windows" or Incivilities Thesis, Community Policing, Law Enforcement Assistance Administration, Problem-Oriented Policing, Theories of Policing

### For Further Reading

Holden, R. N. (1992). *Law enforcement: An introduction.* Englewood Cliffs, NJ: Prentice Hall.

Klockars, C. B. (1985). *The idea of police.* Beverly Hills, CA: Sage.

LaGrange, R. L. (1993). *Policing American society.* Chicago: Nelson-Hall.

Stead, P. J. (1983). *The police of France.* New York: Macmillan.

Trojanowicz, R., & Bucqueroux, B. (1990). *Community policing: A contemporary perspective.* Cincinnati, OH: Anderson.

## ◌ CRIME SCENE INVESTIGATION

It would not be an exaggeration to assert that crime scene investigation ranks with the most intellectually challenging and difficult of human activities. It is also one of the most misunderstood. In practice, crime scene investigation is rarely carried out efficiently and effectively. Successful outcomes, when and where they occur, are often fortuitous rather than following from intelligently adaptive plans or designs.

There seems to be an inexplicable disconnect in the public's perceptions of the problem of crime scene investigation. In fictional portrayals dating from the Sherlock Holmes stories of Sir Arthur Conan Doyle to the present, the interpretation of physical clues at a crime scene is seen as the epitome of intellectual prowess. Judging from the allocation of expertise and resources, this is a far cry from the importance accorded this activity in the real world today.

From a philosophical or theoretical viewpoint, the crime scene can be viewed as a recording device and a recording medium. To some degree, the scene provides a continuous and continuing record of events that transpire at the particular location. Events, including those that ultimately may be defined as crimes, involve human-initiated interactions that alter the environment as well as items within it in myriad ways. The alterations may be subtle or profound. It is the creation of these alterations that results in the production of the record. The interactions produce the alterations, and thus the record, according to physical laws. The resulting alterations to the scene and to some subset of the items within it form the physical evidence record. The record is, by its nature, incomplete and, to some extent, transitory. Postevent interactions can complicate the physical evidence record or even overwrite it. It is important to attempt to freeze the record soon after the event of interest, but this is not always possible. Although the concept of a pristine crime scene is a myth, it is important for investigators to act promptly to attempt to preserve the record that remains at the time that law enforcement personnel take control over the scene.

Because the interactions among items and surfaces at the crime scene follow physical laws in producing the physical evidence record, this makes the analysis of the scene itself a scientific problem—a point that is not widely appreciated. Certainly, it has long been recognized that individual items of physical evidence removed from crime scenes require a scientific analysis, but with notable exceptions, this realization has not been extended to crime scenes themselves. In most law enforcement jurisdictions in the United States, scientific expertise is absent from the initial crime scene investigation. This is true for many other parts of the world as well, and it is a situation that needs to be rectified. An argument can be made that scene investigations should be carried out exclusively by forensic scientists, but at the very least, experienced forensic scientists should form part of the crime scene investigation team.

The physical evidence record is produced in varying degrees of detail, but it is axiomatic that it is incomplete, and furthermore, that it is likely to be degraded to some degree following the event. A pristine crime scene is an unrealizable ideal. As noted earlier, it does not exist in the real world. Even in the most favorable circumstances, postevent factors will unavoidably alter the record left by the interactions taking place during the event of interest. The mere discovery of an event, and the steps leading to a conclusion that a crime has taken place and that the scene is worthy of attention, may destroy evidence. This is a reality that must be faced. If there is the possibility of saving the life of an injured person at the scene, the steps necessary to aid the victim take precedence over those directed at documenting and preserving physical evidence. The difficulties increase exponentially with large-scale events involving the injury and death of many people. Of course, this realization is not justification for a cavalier attitude toward scenes and physical evidence.

The term *crime scene processing* is commonly used as a synonym for *crime scene investigation*. This is unfortunate and betrays ignorance about the nature of crime scenes and what is necessary to extract relevant information from them. Crime scene investigation should not be perceived as a mechanical process, carried out in a rote fashion. Too commonly, this is the way it is viewed by law enforcement policymakers; administrators; supervisors; and, perhaps surprisingly, those who actually "process" the crime scene. Change is necessary.

No two cases are ever exactly alike. For this and other reasons, every crime scene is different. Items that are inconsequential in one scene may be of crucial importance in another, and of course, the reverse is also true. Scenes cannot and should not all be treated in the same way and approached in the same manner. We need to expect the unexpected if we are to do the investigation properly. The approach used must be both flexible and thorough. It must be developed de novo in an informed and systematic fashion. The scientific method provides an appropriately flexible and systematic approach. Crime scenes present very challenging and difficult scientific problems.

Crime scene investigation and laboratory analysis are not as effective where the investigators and scientists are operating in an information vacuum. Context is critical in framing questions.

Crime scene investigations are made more difficult by considerations of time. Some evidence can deteriorate with time and must be attended to as quickly as possible. This is especially true at outdoor scenes, where weather may be a factor. Some factors are beyond human control; others are not but can be even more adverse. The complex nature of many crime scenes clearly implies that an appropriate investigation will take a considerable amount of time. Unfortunately, in most jurisdictions, inadequate resource allocation may mean that there are more scenes to be examined than can be handled comfortably by the assigned personnel, and the time available at any given scene is commonly inadequate. Proper crime scene investigation may be seen as being expensive. However, it should be appreciated that improper crime scene investigation can be even more expensive in terms of the consequences that flow from it. There may be substantial monetary costs in terms of lost investigative time, unnecessary court time, and lawsuits, in addition to human costs. Doing it right the first time has many advantages, including economic considerations.

Once a crime scene has been secured, several interrelated stages in crime scene investigation and the handling of physical evidence at the crime scene can be identified. They are the *recognition, documentation, collection, preservation,* and *transportation* of physical evidence. The sequence given is typical and logical, but there is often extensive overlap, and departure from the strict sequence is often necessary. The stages of the crime scene investigation extend beyond the work at the scene. Once the evidence has been *analyzed* in the laboratory, the *scientific interpretation* of the laboratory results may lead to a *reconstruction* of the event.

## RECOGNITION

Informed selection can only take place following *recognition* of the particular significance of given items to the event under investigation. Recognition

of evidence is the key to successful crime scene investigation and reconstruction. It is the central component and is also the most challenging and difficult aspect. It is the process of defining the problem. There is a need to try to anticipate the kinds of questions that are likely to assume importance later. Furthermore, it requires a scientific approach and cannot take place efficiently outside the context of the crime scene.

A crime scene may contain literally thousands of items of potential evidence. Normally, only some small fraction of this large number of items has encoded information about the specific event that is the subject of the investigation and thus is of relevance. Clearly, all of the items at a scene cannot be collected and transported to the laboratory for analysis. Such an approach would overwhelm the laboratory and clog the system. Relatively little would be learned, even if resources were unlimited. Informed selection at the crime scene is necessary. Recognizing significant items among a much larger number that are ultimately irrelevant is a very challenging task. It takes time. Some of the first activities at a scene may be "hands in the pockets," or unhurried observation. There is no need to rush into action. Observation and thought should precede action.

Formal reconstruction will be discussed later in this entry, but it should be noted that an informal, often merely mental, reconstruction will help guide recognition of evidence. Such provisional reconstructions, used to guide recognition, are most useful where the scientific method is employed in developing them. The scientific method will be discussed in more detail in a subsequent section on reconstruction.

## DOCUMENTATION

Proper and effective documentation of crime scenes and physical evidence is essential. Many different media or means of recording information are useful tools at crime scenes. The tools available include handwritten notes, sketches (which would normally include measurements), photography (silver halide emulsion and digital), audio and video recording, and casting. Technology that allows the automated scanning and recording of the coordinates of three-dimensional features at a scene has become available recently and has been used to a limited extent in crime scene investigation. As it becomes more available, it should find wide use in both civil and criminal investigations.

Of the array of documentation tools available, it would not be expected that all would be used at every scene. The particular needs of a given scene must be evaluated on an ad hoc basis. Judgment on the part of the experienced investigator is necessary to decide what combination of tools to employ.

In addition to the choice of media, two general types of documentation are important to distinguish: passive or active. If one is recording the scene and the details of evidence within it, before significance of each such detail is known, the documentation is passive. This is all that may be expected early in an investigation. Passive documentation is often essential, but it is not sufficient. Qualitatively, the documentation must evolve beyond this passive stage during the course of the investigation into an *active documentation* phase. This requires that the significance of certain items of potential evidence be recognized. Thus, it must follow the recognition step. This allows informed selection as to what is thoroughly documented and ultimately collected and preserved for subsequent analysis and interpretation.

## COLLECTION

Once evidence has been recognized and documented, it can be collected. Some items can be picked up and placed in an appropriate container. An important part of the collection process is the choice of the container, which affects the next topic, evidence preservation. If the entire item cannot be collected because of its large size or immobile nature, sampling is necessary. The sampling method chosen will depend on the nature of the evidence and how it will be analyzed in the laboratory. The sample may be cut from the larger object. Although property may be destroyed in the process, this may be the best means of collecting pattern evidence. For example, the best way to preserve the details of

a critical patterned footwear outsole imprint might be to remove a section of flooring. Judgment is necessary. Stains or smears on surfaces may, at times, be collected this way, but more commonly, they are scraped or swabbed from the surface. The type of evidence and laboratory protocol may dictate the choice.

## PRESERVATION

The details of evidence preservation are numerous and complex, and beyond the scope of this entry. For our purposes here, it must be understood that the means of preservation will depend on the nature of the evidence. Evidence that is volatile must be sealed in a suitable container to prevent loss due to evaporation. Biological evidence is subject to degradation from microbial activity. Evidence of this type that is kept in a wet or moist state at room temperature will support microbial growth and will degrade quite rapidly. Such degradation can render the evidence useless. In general, such evidence should be dried or kept at low temperatures, or both. The packaging should not trap moisture. For example, clothing with dried bloodstains should be placed in paper bags rather than plastic ones. The details of biological evidence preservation will depend on the exact nature of the evidence and the proximity of the scene to the laboratory. Fibers, hairs, and particulate trace evidence can often be preserved by placing them in paper folds, often known as "druggist" folds, before they are sealed in labeled envelopes.

## TRANSPORTATION

The major issues with the transportation of physical evidence from the crime scene to the forensic science laboratory are the protection of the physical integrity of the evidence, time, and temperature. The latter two are especially critical with biological evidence, where the possible loss of value due to degradation must be considered and prevented. Where the scene and the laboratory are separated geographically, and where the drying of articles is not possible, practical, or desirable, refrigerated vehicles may be employed for the transportation of the evidence to the laboratory. Particular designs allow for drying to take place at low temperature during transportation. Some evidence may be particularly fragile. Intelligent and informed attention to packaging concerns is usually sufficient to preserve the physical integrity of the evidence during transportation to the laboratory.

## RECONSTRUCTION

Reconstruction is the culmination of the scientific work on the physical evidence in a case. It is at this stage where the information gleaned from the examination of all of the evidence is integrated and interpreted to yield an objective understanding of the event. In most jurisdictions, this activity is given insufficient scientific attention. As indicated above in the discussion of evidence recognition, the scientific method plays a central role in reconstruction.

Our modern understanding of nature dates from a paradigm shift during the Renaissance, when the concept of insisting on "reality checks" of propounded ideas emerged in the form of the requirement of hypothesis testing. The requirement of hypothesis testing replaced "received wisdom" and authority as the arbiters of scientific truth. Scientific advances would have been impossible without this shift.

The core of the scientific method is the rigorous testing of hypotheses. Hypotheses that endeavor to explain the event are put forward, and then an earnest attempt is made to disprove each. A hypothesis that fails this testing is discarded. A modified hypothesis or new alternate hypotheses are developed and tested in turn. Only a hypothesis that survives repeated vigorous testing develops into an explanatory theory of the event. The scientific method and hypothesis testing is a cyclical, iterative process. The key to the process is the vigorousness and rigorousness of the testing. There is a human tendency to identify with a hypothesis that one has developed and to subconsciously overlook observations or data that do not fit the hypothesis. This is antithetical to good science and must be avoided. Scientists must be involved in actively attempting to disprove their own hypotheses.

Advances in digital technology have provided useful tools for crime scene investigation. Some of these have been mentioned above. However, it is important to recognize that some new digital capabilities are not unalloyed blessings. Informed and judicious application is necessary. This is especially true of technologies grouped under the headings of "virtual reality" or computer animation. It is now possible to present what appear to be realistic visual representations of events on a video screen. These animations are distinctly different from computer simulations used in a range of disciplines in science and engineering. In simulations, each pixel in the image is generated from equations linked to physical reality. In animations, realistic-appearing images are generated without such constraints. The animation techniques allow for artistic expression such as that used in recent computer-animated feature films. Thus, legitimate animations in the context of crime scene reconstruction are only a means of illustrating what has been learned by scientific analysis. Unlike simulations, animations are not analytical tools. Despite the possible illusion of computer accuracy, animations may be no more grounded in reality than a hand-drawn cartoon. The least problematic animations for the depiction of the results of a crime scene reconstruction in court are those that illustrate the situation at a single moment in time, and where what is shown is based firmly on the physical evidence record. Legitimate examples include simulated camera pans and fly-bys to give the jury a better appreciation of the geometry at the particular moment in time for which the scientific data can provide a clear picture. Animations purporting to represent a series of crime scene events over time are, in the vast majority of cases, naïve or dishonest. The physical evidence record may allow objective conclusions to be drawn about an event taking place at a scene for a single moment in time, or perhaps even for a series of events at several moments in time. Normally, what it cannot do is provide a smooth, continuous record. With no foundation in fact, the animator must fill in the gaps in the physical evidence record to make a smooth-flowing animation. This is invention, and it is misleading and highly objectionable.

## SUMMARY

Arriving at a crime scene and trying to make sense of the physical evidence record can be a decidedly daunting experience. Initially, it may be necessary to consider literally thousands of items as potential physical evidence. To some degree, the time available to deal with this awesome complexity will always be limited, which only compounds the problem.

Successful crime scene investigation depends on extracting information about the event under investigation from the physical evidence record. It is important to ask meaningful questions of the evidence. Evidence can be interrelated in complex ways, so prioritization may be required. This presents a very challenging problem. Scientific knowledge and a scientific approach are both necessary. Ideally, experienced scientists should be involved in the investigation from the outset.

As noted earlier, there are several interrelated stages in crime scene investigation and the handling of physical evidence. The list included the recognition, active documentation, passive documentation, collection, preservation, and transportation of physical evidence, followed by the analysis in the laboratory; the scientific interpretation of the laboratory results; and, if possible, a reconstruction of the event. The first two and the last two present the greatest scientific challenges. Those in the middle of the series—passive documentation, collection, preservation, and transportation—can be handled algorithmically. Rules, albeit often-complex ones, can be taught and followed to produce successful outcomes. The expertise of an experienced scientist is not necessarily needed for these. However, for recognition, active documentation, interpretation and reconstruction, such expertise is necessary.

Seamless integration of scientific activities with physical evidence from the crime scene, through the laboratory, and to the courtroom is necessary. There is a need for an enhanced role for scientists at each stage. Technicians, no matter how skilled, cannot be relied upon for all functions. A teamwork approach with scientists and technicians is very useful.

Resources allocated to crime scene investigation in most parts of the United States have long been inadequate. This has been true of the dollar amounts allocated and of the backgrounds of those assigned to crime scene investigation. The situation needs to be understood and addressed.

*Peter De Forest*

### For Further Reading

De Forest, P. R. (1999). Recapturing the essence of criminalistics. *Science and Justice, 39*(3), 196–208.

De Forest, P. R. (2001). What is trace evidence? In B. Caddy (Ed.), *Forensic examination of glass and paint* (pp. 1–25). London: Taylor & Francis.

De Forest, P. R., Gaensslen, R. E., & Lee, H. C. (1983). *Forensic science: An introduction to criminalistics.* New York: McGraw-Hill.

# ✌ CRIME STATISTICS AND ANALYSIS

## CRIME

To understand the meaning of crime statistics, one must first define crime. Crime is a very flexible concept, something like a woven carpet, that produces powerful associations from the public and agencies charged with its control. It varies cross-culturally, historically, and spatially, as well as by social morphology and cultural and social differentiation. Since Adolphe Quetelet first advocated that social order could be captured metaphorically by numbers, and the regularity and stability associated with large numbers, commensurability has been sought across measures and numbers have been used to represent social trends. Official crime data, like official statistics generally, are associated with the development of the nation-state and its need to tax and count its citizens. They appear to function differentially in Anglo-American societies and European states. They reflect a belief and trust in numbers and science in fragmented, individualistic, and horizontally differentiated societies, and are less central to policy making in more centralized and integrated societies. Furthermore, the bureaucratically driven capacity of nation-states to monitor, direct, refine, and analyze data is increasing.

## Official Crime

What do crime statistics measure? The public trusts most official data, which they assume are a measure of the distribution, incidence, and prevalence of crime. Some scholars use statistics to measure the difference between an official rate and alternative measures, pursuing the "dark" (or unmeasured) figure of crime; others study crime statistics as indicators of the actions of social control organizations rather than of natural events. *Official crime* is crime recognized and reported, indicated by officially sanctioned and produced reports, and a product of an organizational response to events in the natural world. Official crime is objective, external, real. and constraining to both governments and publics. Black (1970) writes, "[The crime rate is] a social fact, an empirical phenomenon with its own existential integrity" (p. 734). Although official rates such as the Uniform Crime Reports (UCR) have political hegemony, since 1967, other data sources, such as surveys of victims, households, and businesses, have been put in place to tap unrecorded crime; questionnaires have been used; data have been gathered on insurance losses and self-reported crime and victimization; and some ethnographies of policing, neighborhoods, and communities have appeared. In recent years, these sources have been refined and new kinds of data systematically gathered and reported. As Maguire (2002, pp. 325–327) argues, the most significant development in official crime statistics is the explosion of the number and kinds of sources of information on crime, including measuring previously unrecorded crimes and new types of offenses and offenders, exploring the context of offending, and developing more specific classifications.

Many factors shape the official crime rate as presented, including propensity to report, the seriousness of the particular crime, social composition and culture of an area, legal standards and definitions, and the willingness to record and the infrastructure of recording in given agencies. Although crime figures are markers, indicators, or icons of something else, and represent symbolically known or recognized crime, they can also symbolize trust, confidence in the state's devices, fear, marginality and its dramatization, and something of a screen on which diverse emotions can be projected and assessed.

## Crime as Sanctionable Rule Breaking

It is important to understand not only what crime statistics measure, but also how they are produced. Crime is a subcategory of sanctionable rule breaking. Deviance is behavior that is vulnerable to social control. Events that might be sanctioned as deviance are differentially brought to the attention of governmental social control agencies. Thus, there are undetected events; detected events; and detected, sanctioned events. Police agencies detect, recognize, and sanction selectively; they apply governmental social control. For something to be counted, it has to be noticed, marked, set aside, and given a comparable value. Given a dispute, the probability that it will be detected, or responded to, is a function of the social organization of detection and of the event. Whereas informal social control in families, small groups, and kinship networks act as an important filter on reporting, the final decision about what is shown, counted, documented, and recorded is an organizational matter. Once recorded, a number of generic processes occur in any database—attrition, loss, diversion, elimination by virtue of ignorance or error, and how the data are worked on by deciders.

The social organization of detection and recording is central to the discussion of crime and crime statistics. The study of the social organization of response includes questions about the nature of the screening and sensitivity to events in the "natural world"; the resources available to the organization to detect and process such delicts; the databases and recording systems in place; the links between these databases (software and hardware; computers, terminals, mainframes, and servers); the skills, training, and positioning of staff; and the analytic techniques used to disaggregate the mass of incoming data. In the Anglo-American police world, democratic policing is reactive. It aims to scan the environment, react to discovered recognized instances, and record those that require sanctioning. The strategies of these police agencies are premised on detecting rare, randomly occurring events and reducing their risk. Furthermore, and as a corollary, crime statistics are not used to explore crime causation, prevention, restorative needs, or damage to society, nor are they looked at as standing for anything else. They are used, above all and almost exclusively, to present levels of risk to the public and presented as virtually self-explanatory by the police and the media. Whereas criminologists might seek to explain crime or social control patterns, the police, correctly, are concerned with the crime and its recording as a symbolic system sustaining the legitimacy of their mandate. Statistics, as an icon of science, serves to sustain legitimacy in this era and arose as a means of legitimating business in the early period of capitalism. Any efforts at auditing and quality control of police data will have a profound effect as UCR data are merely processed, not checked for validity or reliability. In theory, rates and the reliability of official crime data have been and will be shaped in a most profound fashion by computer-based electronic processing of data, but this has not been systematically studied and is a corollary of the explosion in data noted above.

## NETWORKS AND THE GOVERNANCE OF SECURITY IN THE 21ST CENTURY

Rapid change is underway in the network of control and in policing itself. The present crime control network reflects a history, a set of assumptions about its role and mandate, and a set of processing techniques based on a 19th-century model of law and crime. New forms of crime now exist, such as cybercrime, terrorism, information-based crimes of fraud and malfeasance, and environmental crime, as do recording formats to trace their variations. Consider also the growing globalization of crime, including both new forms and traditional crimes. Although changes in the network of governance; new forms of private policing; professional war makers; gated estates; and corporate police (as well as the loosely linked federal, state, county, and local

public police) are apparent, the implications of these changes for official crime and its sanctioning are being debated. The data needed to find and track crimes on the margins of the traditional criminal law, terrorism across borders, corporate crime, environmental crimes, regulatory crimes, and cyber crimes are not yet known and identified, let alone gathered. These developments will alter radically the screening and response to categories of deviance in the future, and the infrastructure of detection is emergent.

### Information

Police departments are linked into national, local, and state databases, and they maintain their own internal records management system for payroll, budget, and so on. They also maintain calls for service data, and records of arrests, jail populations, fingerprints, and paper files of property. The information considered the core of the policing function is related to the Computer Aided Dispatch data, reported crime, and miscellaneous reports bearing on public order. It is these that have moved to the forefront in crime analysis.

Within the police organization, there are four spheres of processing, with differing levels of facts and information (facts put in a context). The spheres are the uniformed patrol, investigative work, internal affairs and intelligence, and the top command. Within these spheres, there are four types of decisions. The first type are decisions made on the basis of primary data (raw facts becoming information). These are made largely by patrol officers following assignment by the communications center. The second type are those decisions based on once-processed data. These are primarily, but not exclusively, worked on by investigators. The third type are decisions based on twice-processed data, such as those worked on by hate crime units, domestic violence specialized units, internal affairs, and complaints against officers. The fourth type are decisions based on policy-relevant information that arises from outside the organization (from research, consultants, the media) and decisions made primarily by those in top command and research and development. Intelligence units in some departments work with the first three types of information. They gather data by surveillance and informants, process some uniform-originated data, and are given information by other units within the department.

Although the top command may use any or all of these types of data, they are usually dependent on "massaged" data; on the other hand, the patrol officers can use some form of processing to refine the facts with which they are presently working (e.g., the calls for service to a given address, or block, can be pulled up on the screen in the mobile digital terminal in the vehicle and used). These four spheres are linked to some databases and evaluation processes, but for the most part, they involve open-ended decisions; none is reviewed or audited; and the results are sent to independent, nonlinked, cache basins.

The importance of the observations concerning spheres and decision types is that decisions have been made in semiprivacy, and processed and stored, and that information is considered in policing private property of a kind, not a collective good. Furthermore, the core information (named above) is used as and when it is case-related, and also when it goes forward for scrutiny by district attorneys. Until recently, it has not been looked at for pattern, movement, time, and place clustering, or as a means for systematically altering deployment.

## New Forms of Crime Analysis

In the unit beat system put in place in England in the late 1960s, the role of the collator was established. The role was defined as linking the uniformed officers and investigators by providing lists of reported crimes to each sergeant weekly. The implication, not put in practice, was that the collator was to identify, dramatize, and name patterns of crime and disorder, and to alert officers to their existence. Although this system has been refined in recent years, the crime analysts are civilians, under Criminal Investigation Division control, and largely function as pass-through processing clerks, not analysts. The notion of intelligence-led policing, popularized in England by the Kent Constabulary, is a metaphor for sharpening and directing police attention by establishing priorities.

In many respects, the diffusion of crime analysis arose from the concatenation of three discoveries: the temporal and spatial patterning of crime noted by the routine activities perspective; the predictability of repeat victimization and offending; and the phase movement in decentralized, high-memory, capacity servers and parallel computing; and inexpensive software that could map incidents electronically. In many respects, these were made possible by developments and facilitated online, or by just-in-time data. Crime analysis has been rationalized as a model, but in fact is done in widely disparate ways in police departments in North America and the United Kingdom. This model includes

- Data gathering and entering
- Representation of the data (maps, tables, graphs)
- Interpretation of data (pattern, distribution of crime)
- Recommendation for action (what to do and why)
- Evaluation of impact

It is clear that a broad range of analyses is possible—analytical, tactical, and strategic—but research suggests it has been restricted almost entirely to tactical analyses.

The most often cited and lauded example of crime analysis is, in fact, a process of presenting data publicly for discussion, responding to visible clusters, and inducing and rewarding action. In 1994–1996, the New York Police Department, under Commissioner Bratton, developed a process of crime analysis called Compstat. It was composed of several interconnected organizational elements. A series of management papers was drawn up to place emphasis on key missions, values, and practices—guns, misdemeanor offenses, accountability, and so on. Precinct commanders were put on notice that they were responsible for fluctuations in crime. Data were gathered from precincts called to appear (2–4 a week), and semipublic meetings were held in a large conference room. At the front of the room, which all chairs faced, was a podium and a large screen on which facts and figures were projected. In these meetings, a wide variety of data was presented; precinct commanders, detectives, and selected other officers were grilled on the meaning of these data (at first by Deputy Commissioner Jack Maple, and after he retired, by others), and then they were asked to announce in the meeting how they were responding or did respond to crime peaks or outbreaks.

The highly laudatory description of these meetings suggest that short-term peaks in crimes of interest were highlighted and efforts made to decide quickly what to do. The emphasis in Bratton's period was on accountability of senior command to his mission, and Bratton had replaced one third of them in his early days in office. The meetings gained fame in part because of Bratton's and others' efforts, including conservative foundations that trumpet the conventional wisdom about policing and crime control (Heritage Foundation, AEI, and the Manhattan Institute); paid consultants who shaped the process itself; the attribution of crime drop to policing (questioned by Manning, 2003); later academic writing; and the diffusion of the idea to other police departments.

Previous studies of crime analysis meetings have been generally positive, uncritical, and excessively optimistic about the present and future capacity of these meetings to mobilize officers, or, more generally, to control crime. These studies assume a single, logical developmental paradigm (what might be called classic or Weberian rationality) in which problem solving or surfacing uncertainty (a contingency uncertainty), feedback, evaluation, and readjustment of means to ends govern the deciding process. Unfortunately, the logical chain that links the meetings, deployment, and action to crime reduction remains totally unexplicated. Examples given of its workings are either "fictionalized" (Henry, 2002, pp. 269–273); anecdotal (Kelling, 1995); or post hoc, proper hoc (crime dropped so it must have been a result of Compstat and the NYPD; Kelling & Coles, 1996). No published systemic evaluation exists of the impact of the Compstat-focused process meetings on crime; how Compstat affects or shapes crime; or what the environmental consequences are with respect to public trust, justice, attitudes toward the police, or interagency relations, such as the crowding of the courts (given the enormous rise in misdemeanor arrests).

Many explanations, in addition to the managerial aspects of the process, have been advanced in the published versions of Compstat, including incapacitation; a drop in unemployment; economic growth; increased personnel in the NYPD; and a general trend of crime decrease, including international downward trends not specifically associated with actions of the NYPD. No evidence has been provided that shows empirically how and why the information linked to problem solving was the basis for deployment and how that deployment, over time, reduced recorded street crime. The influence of other matters, being unmeasured and unreported, permits the police-based argument that Compstat reduces crime virtually free rein in public discussions. Unless evidence of the connection between crime analysis, the meeting and critiquing process, deployment, and assessment of impact by several kinds of data comes to light, the question of the utility of crime analysis remains an open one.

*Peter K. Manning*

***See also*** "Broken Windows" or Incivilities Thesis, Compstat, Information Technologies, National Crime Victimization Survey, National Incident Based Reporting, Quality-of-Life Enforcement, Uniform Crime Reports

## For Further Reading

Black, D. (1970). The production of crime rates. *American Sociological Review, 35,* 733–748.

Black, D. (1976). *The behaviour of law.* New York: Academic Press.

Bratton, W. (1996). *Turnaround: How America's top cop reversed the crime epidemic.* New York: Random House.

Canadian Law Reform Commission. (2003, November). Working paper on policing. Ottawa: Author.

Carruthers, B., & Espeland, W. (1991). Accounting for rationality: Double-entry bookkeeping and the rhetoric of economic rationality. *American Journal of Sociology, 97*(3), 31–69.

Cope, N. (2003). Crime analysis: Principles and practice. In T. Newburn (Ed.), *Handbook of policing* (pp. 340–362). Devon, UK: Willan.

Henry, V. (2002). *The Compstat paradigm.* New York: Looseleaf.

Kelling, G. (1995). How to run a police department. *City Journal, 5,* 1–12.

Kelling, G., & Coles, C. (1996). *Fixing broken windows.* New York: Free Press.

Maguire, M. (2002). Crime statistics. In M. Maguire, R. Morgan, & R. Reiner (Eds.), *Oxford handbook of criminology* (3rd ed.). Oxford, UK: Oxford University Press.

Manning, P. K. (1997). *Police work: The social organization of policing* (2nd ed.). Prospect Heights, IL: Waveland.

Manning, P. K. (2001). Theorizing policing. *Theoretical Criminology, 5,* 315–344.

Manning, P. K. (2003). *Policing contingencies.* Chicago: University of Chicago Press.

McDonald, P. (2002). *Managing police operations.* Belmont, CA: Wadsworth.

Murphy, C. (2003). The rationalization of Canadian public policing. Available: http://www.policefutures.org/docs/murphy_e.pdf

Porter, T. (1986). *The rise of statistical thinking.* Princeton, NJ: Princeton University Press.

Porter, T. (1995). *Trust in numbers.* Princeton, NJ: Princeton University Press.

Reiss, A. J., Jr. (1974). Discretionary justice. In D. Glaser (Ed.), *Handbook of criminology.* Chicago: Rand-McNally.

Rigakos, G. (2003). *Parapolice.* Toronto: University of Toronto Press.

Shearing, C., & Johnston, L. (2003). *Governing security.* London: Routledge & Kegan Paul.

Silverman, E. (1999). *The NYPD battles crime.* Boston: Northeastern University Press.

Singer, P. (2003). *Corporate warriors.* Ithaca, NY: Cornell University Press.

Tilley, N. (2003). Community policing, problem-solving policing and intelligence-led policing. In T. Newburn (Ed.), *Handbook of policing.* Devon, UK: Willan.

Weisburd, D., Mastrofski, S., McNally, A. M., Greenspan, R., & Willis, J. J. (2003). Reforming to preserve: Compstat and strategic problem-solving in American policing. *Criminology and Public Policy, 2,* 421–456.

Willmer, M. A. P. (1970). *Crime and information theory.* Edinburgh: University Press.

Young, M. (1991). *An inside job.* Oxford, UK: Oxford University Press.

## ✺ CRIME STOPPERS

### HISTORY

The Crime Stoppers organization was founded by Albuquerque, New Mexico, police officer Gregg MacAleese in 1976 as an outgrowth of his efforts to identify and apprehend the perpetrators of a violent homicide. In July 1976, two criminals perpetrating the armed robbery of a gas station shot and killed Michael Carmen, the gas station attendant who was covering the shift of a fellow employee. Michael Carmen was a young college student at the University of New Mexico preparing for his wedding, which was to occur in 2 weeks.

Officer MacAleese, frustrated by the lack of leads in the case, and being no closer to solving the crime 6 weeks after its occurrence, proposed to a local television station manager at KOAT-TV that the station air a reenactment of the crime as part of one of its newscasts. The station manager agreed, and an idea was born. The rationale was simple: Use the local media as a means of reaching a large segment of the local population in the hope of possibly triggering the memory of a witness who might recall seeing something suspicious or out of the ordinary on the night of the murder.

The first reenactment aired in September 1976 on the evening news, and the next morning, the police department received a call from an individual who had seen the reenactment and had information to provide. The caller provided details about suspicious events he had observed the night of the crime, as well as information about a vehicle he had witnessed driving at a high rate of speed near the scene of the crime. The information provided led to the apprehension of the two individuals responsible for Michael Carmen's murder within 72 hours of receiving the original tip.

### CREATION OF CRIME STOPPERS

The positive response to this innovative information-gathering approach led Officer MacAleese to formally create the Crime Stoppers organization. However, Officer MacAleese knew full well that the public is generally reluctant to provide information about criminal events because of fear and apathy. With this in mind, Crime Stoppers would allow callers to remain anonymous when calling a tip line, and cash rewards would be paid for information leading to the solution of crimes.

With Crime Stoppers now an established crime-fighting organization, a board of directors consisting of citizens to provide civilian oversight was selected from the local community. As Crime Stoppers continued to evolve as an organization, community residents became increasingly involved in all facets of the organization, including becoming telephone tip volunteers; making monetary donations to the tip fund; managing daily operations; and, of course, becoming anonymous informants of criminal events leading to the apprehension and successful prosecution of numerous offenders.

As its popularity grew, and as it caught national interest, Crime Stoppers formally organized into Crime Stoppers—USA in 1979 and held its first conference in 1980. Currently, the primary organization is called Crime Stoppers International, having dropped the USA distinction as part of a reorganizing effort to become an international association of national/geographic regions.

## ACCOMPLISHMENTS OF CRIME STOPPERS

Crime Stoppers International has 1,148 known programs worldwide, including programs in such places as South Africa, Australia, Micronesia, the West Indies, Canada, and the United States, as well as numerous other locations worldwide. These worldwide programs have thousands of volunteers aiding and implementing these community-based crime control efforts. Worldwide programs have been responsible for more than 900,000 cases cleared and more than 400,000 arrests made. In addition, the programs have recovered property and narcotics valued at more than $5 billion while paying out more than $60 million in reward money for crime tips.

Just as in the early days of the program, the media continue to play a crucial role in the Crime Stoppers mission. The media are the conduit by which the community is informed about the criminal events that law enforcement is seeking assistance in solving. The local media often participate in televised reenactments, news broadcasts, radio addresses, and newspaper coverage of criminal events. This cooperative venture, facilitated by the media, provides an opportunity for community residents to get involved in crime control initiatives with local law enforcement to reduce crime and improve the neighborhoods and communities in which they reside.

The Crime Stoppers organization and its programs worldwide are widely recognized as a successful approach toward community policing. Despite being a global/international organization, Crime Stoppers effectively brings community members and local law enforcement together to cooperatively fight against crime at the local level. In fact, as part of this effort, a number of national Crime Stoppers programs have worked with the National Association of Town Watch, which sponsors the "National Night Out" campaign. This campaign is designed to promote the partnership between law enforcement and the local community to create a safer country.

Communities and individuals interested in learning more about Crime Stoppers International can read their regularly published bulletin, *The Caller*, which chronicles the events and developments of the organization.

*Jeff Walsh*

**See also** America's Most Wanted

### For Further Reading

MacAleese, G. (n.d.). The Crime Stoppers story. Retrieved from http://www.c-s-i.org/history.htm

Rosenbaum, D. P., & Lurigio, A. J. (1985). *The national evaluation of Crime Stoppers: A synopsis of major findings.* Evanston, IL: Northwestern University, Center for Urban Affairs and Policy Research.

## 🕲 CRISIS INTERVENTION

While organizing the first family crisis intervention program within the New York City Police Department in 1968, psychologist Morton Bard became aware of the dual roles police play while performing their duties. Bard discovered that in addition to the traditional focus on law enforcement, the police worked an array of important human service functions.

This insight on the expanded role of police was not limited to Bard. For years, police agencies throughout the country recognized that both law enforcement and human service functions are combined when police officers deal with people in crisis. Police departments realize that law enforcement officers, serving as first responders to critical events, must have the skills to apply immediate emotional first aid. Whether making death notifications, assisting crime victims, or helping survivors of serious accidents, officers must be ready to provide the emotional support, clarification, and guidance needed to cushion the impact of critical events that can often overwhelm the victim's normal coping skills.

Many large police departments have integrated crisis intervention into recruit and inservice training. As a training topic, crisis intervention is usually limited to a 2- or 3-hour block of instruction in most police academies. Crisis intervention skills, however, are used as integral components when training police officers to respond to such specific traumatic events as domestic violence, sexual assault, or hostage situations. Officers are taught that although time may be limited, brief and purposeful intervention may be vital to the readjustment of people in crisis. Studies have shown that many crime victims vividly recall the few supportive words whispered by a police officer immediately following a crisis.

## DEFINITIONS

Crisis and traumatic stress are overlapping terms used by theorists when defining the condition. Although there are subtle differences in their definitions, there are also certain commonalities. When an individual encounters an obstacle to an important life goal, or has witnessed or been involved in an event that is overwhelming and cannot use his or her usual problem-solving abilities, it is determined that the individual has experienced a crisis or traumatic stress. These incidents, sometimes referred to as *critical events,* are typically unexpected and uncontrollable. They compromise an individual's sense of safety and security and result in feelings of helplessness and vulnerability. Whatever name is used to describe the condition, the impact is the same. Individuals in crisis are left feeling overwhelmed, out of control, and helpless.

## IDENTIFYING THE CRISIS SITUATION

Crisis is not a pathological state; it may occur, under certain conditions, to anyone at any time. Different people faced with the same situation may not necessarily display the same reactions or be similarly affected. An evaluation of individuals involved in a critical incident is the first crucial step law enforcement officers take when making an intervention. Many police departments train their officers to use the evaluative criteria developed by Naomi Golan. The criteria suggest that responding officers answer the following questions:

- Does a crisis exist?
- At what point in the process is the officer entering?
- What should the goals be of the officer's intervention?
- What tasks have to be carried out by the officer, the victim, or others in order to achieve these goals?

To answer the first two questions, officers are trained to examine the circumstances leading to the need for help and to identify appropriate strategies for a resolution.

Most crises that require the intervention of police are situational. A situational crisis is initiated by a hazardous event. This event can be a single catastrophic occurrence or a series of cumulative mishaps. The event disturbs the individual's homeostatic balance and places the person in a vulnerable state. The individual experiencing this uncomfortable dilemma initiates a number of proven problem-solving techniques to regain his or her feelings of normalcy. When these techniques fail, the level of unbalance increases and the person tries new emergency coping methods. When these new processes also fail, tension rises to a peak and a precipitating factor (often some minor event) brings about a turning point where the person becomes disorganized, loses both emotional balance and a sense of control, and is plunged into an active crisis. The actual length of an active crisis state usually lasts between 4 and 6 weeks. During this active crisis period, the person in crisis will take one of three paths. Without any intervention, the person might come out of the crisis with the same level of coping skills he or she had going into the crisis; or, more likely, the person develops other, less effective skills for addressing future crisis situations. With help, however, the person will take the third path and learn more effective ways to cope with the current situation as well as future crisis situations. It is during this time of reintegration that the person is most amenable to outside assistance. A little help, appropriately focused, can prove more effective than more extensive help at a less emotional time. This is the essence of crisis intervention.

## CRISIS INTERVENTION GOALS

*Crisis intervention, emergency mental health,* and *critical incident stress management* are the terms most frequently associated with the process of intervening in crisis situations. It should be noted, however, that no matter what term is applied, police crisis intervention is not a substitute for long-term therapy, nor should the police officers conducting the intervention be considered therapists. Everly (1992) considers crisis intervention to be psychological first aid in that it alleviates the immediate effect of the stressful event. Law enforcement officers use crisis intervention to significantly reduce trauma and increase the coping skills of people in crisis. The goals of crisis intervention by police are limited and related to the immediate crisis situation. The objectives suggested by experts are stabilization of the symptoms (i.e., to prevent symptoms of distress or impairment from worsening), symptom reduction, restoration to precrisis level of functioning, and referral for further assessment and/or higher level of care.

## CRISIS INTERVENTION SKILLS AND TECHNIQUES

Most police crisis intervention training is designed to help officers organize their thoughts and focus their actions in order to defuse emotional upheaval. In this training, officers are taught the following series of human dynamics skills:

> *Engage:* Establish a relationship and promote a dialogue with the person by first introducing

yourself and your interest in helping. Be as open and as honest as the situation permits.

*Establish Calmness:* Create an environment that allows the individual to feel grounded and safe. Communicate confidence and comfort in a slow and purposeful pace. Be aware of heightened levels of stress, and, if necessary, guide the person to breathe more slowly and to take time to collect his or her thoughts. Use silences to allow the person in crisis to process what is being said.

*Empower:* Help the person in crisis to regain control while resisting the temptation to patronize or control. Offer the person interpretations of statements to help him or her gain perspective. Avoid judging or minimizing feelings and experiences. Serve as a referral and information source. Explore options and promote actions the person might take to regain control more quickly.

*Listen:* Actively and compassionately gather and process what is communicated. Acknowledge the person's feelings and allow him or her to vent. Use reflective statements to acknowledge understanding, and use open-ended questions to request elaboration. Summarize the information and reflect it back to the person.

*Question:* Law enforcement officers routinely use questioning techniques to elicit information, reflect experiences, probe feelings, and pursue resolutions. When intervening in a crisis, the officers' vocal tone, pacing, and wording are as important as the content of the questions they ask. Ask questions that are clear, concrete, and specific. Allow time for the person to process the questions. Ask questions one at a time, being aware that questions may trigger emotional reactions. Ask open-ended questions to engage the person and gather information. Use probing questions to get the person to elaborate on a statement or feeling. Use closed-ended questions when a "yes" or "no" answer is sought, or when speaking with a person who is unable to understand abstract or complex thoughts. Use questions concerning "how" and "what" to focus the person on immediate concerns. Limit questions concerning "why" because they may imply that a person must justify or defend his or her statements. Limit questions that probe too heavily into the person's history or that may be more appropriate for long-term therapy.

*Focus:* Help the person in crisis to organize or express thoughts and feelings that may be magnifying the sense of helplessness and chaos. Direct the person to the "here and now," minimizing distractions and extraneous issues, and limit probing to one issue or feeling at a time. Repeat statements and questions to help the person answer or remember. Accept the person's worldview, emotional upset, and level of function.

*Validate:* Acknowledge the individual's attempts to resolve the crisis and seek assistance, as well as the person's courage in talking. Support the person's efforts to understand and resolve the crisis. Give the person involved in a critical incident a sense of hope, and remind him or her that he or she is in control of resolving the crisis.

## HELPING THE HELPER–CRITICAL INCIDENT STRESS MANAGEMENT

Police officers are not immune to the traumatic effects of a critical event. The occupational stress that officers experience when encountering crisis situations can often be overwhelming. Left unattended, this stress can have harmful and lasting consequences. Everly (1992) reports that posttraumatic stress disorder (PTSD) represents the most severe and disabling variation of occupational stress. Critical incident stress management is a multifaceted crisis intervention system designed to help not only the victims of crisis situations, but also members of the public safety organizations who respond to those situations. The Critical Incident Stress Debriefing (CISD) is a component of this comprehensive system. CISD was developed to deal with the damaging results of work-related stress, prevent PTSD, and assist in identifying individual officers in need of professional mental health support. CISD usually takes place 24 to 72 hours after a crisis situation has occurred. The debriefing is 2 to 3 hours of facilitated discussion conducted with officers who have been exposed to a traumatic event. Debriefings help lessen the stress of normal people reacting to abnormal events. During the debriefing, officers have the opportunity to talk about their own feelings and reactions to the event. Debriefings are not used to critique the work of the police, but rather to let the officers talk about their reaction to the work.

*Joyce St. George and Francis P. Canavan*

### For Further Reading

Bard, M., & Ellison, K. (1974). Crisis intervention and the investigation of forcible rape. *Police Chief, 5,* 68–74.

Caplan, G. (1961). *An approach to community mental health.* New York: Grune and Stratton.

Caplan, G. (1964). *Principles of preventive psychiatry.* New York: Basic Books.

Everly, G. S. (1992, November). *The critical incident stress debriefing process (CISD) and the prevention of occupational post-traumatic stress.* Paper presented at the second APA and NIOSH Conference on Occupational Stress, Washington, DC.

Everly, G. S., & Mitchell, J. T. (1999). *Critical incident stress management: A new era and standard of care in crisis intervention* (2nd ed.). Ellicot City, MD: Chevron.

Golan, N. (1978). *Treatment in crisis situations.* New York: Free Press.

Lerner, M. D., & Shelton, R. D. (2001). *Acute traumatic stress management.* Commack, NY: The American Academy of Experts in Traumatic Stress.

Mitchell, J. T. (1983). When disaster strikes . . . The critical incident stress debriefing process. *Journal of Emergency Medical Services, 13,* 43–46.

Rapoport, L. (1970). Crisis intervention as a means of brief treatment. In R. W. Roberts & R. H. Nee (Eds.), *Theories of social casework* (pp. 267–311). Chicago: University of Chicago Press.

## ✑ CROWN HEIGHTS REPORT

In the summer of 1991, New York City suffered the most extensive racial unrest since the 1960s. On August 19, a car in the motorcade carrying Lubavitcher Rebbe Menachem Mendel Schneerson veered out of control and hit a black 7-year-old child, Gavin Cato, and his cousin. The accident set Crown Heights in Brooklyn, a mixed community shared by 20,000 Hasidic Jews and 18,000 blacks, on fire for 4 days. A rumor rambled that a private, Hasidic-run ambulance had removed the car's driver without attending to the injured children. The Cato children were brought to the hospital by the city ambulance, and Gavin was pronounced dead on arrival; his cousin survived his injuries. Anger exploded into outrage, and several hours later, a violent crowd of black youths, one of them Lemrick Nelson, attacked a 19-year-old Australian yeshiva student, Yankel Rosenbaum. Rosenbaum was stabbed four times and died in the hospital that night. Bottles were thrown at police officers and pedestrians, windows were smashed at shops and residences, cars were turned over, and shouting and fighting between blacks and Hasidim continued for several days without the active involvement of the police department or the city's administration. Forty-three civilians and 152 police officers were injured during these disturbances that spread over a 94-block area.

The administration of Mayor David N. Dinkins, New York's first black mayor; his City Hall advisers; and the city's police commissioner, Lee P. Brown, were criticized for not doing enough to stop the violence and allowing it to escalate to a riot. After Lemrick Nelson was acquitted in state court of Yankel Rosenbaum's murder and federal civil charges were brought against him, New York Governor Mario M. Cuomo issued Executive Order No. 160 in 1992, directing New York State Director of Criminal Justice Richard H. Gigenti to review the criminal investigation and prosecution in the murder of Yankel Rosenbaum. In 1993, a state investigative team consisting of attorneys, analysts, researchers, and police experts released a two-volume report titled "Report to the Governor on the Disturbances in Crown Heights: An Assessment of the City's Preparedness and Response to Civil Disorder." Analyzed materials included official documents such as NYPD records and memoranda; logs; duty rosters; administrative guides; 9-1-1 tapes; complaint, arrest, and demographic data; newspaper and magazine articles; videotaped television programs; and interviews with 60 members of the police department, 40 Crown Heights residents, and 15 government officials. Gigenti's report addressed the following questions: How extensive was the violence throughout the riot? How prepared was the NYPD to respond to the civil disturbance? Were the actions of the police department and City Hall adequate? How effective was the 9-1-1 system in serving the public? What recommendations can be made regarding future preparation for responding to civil unrest?

Even though Mayor Dinkins accepted responsibility and blame for the riots at Crown Heights, the report determined that there was no evidence to support the charges that he or Police Commissioner Brown had instructed the police to let the angry black youth "vent" their rage and to not interfere. Still, the Crown Heights affair was a significant factor in Dinkins's failure to win reelection in 1993. Information that the disturbance was not "under control" and that the police were not acting effectively to end the violence should have caused the mayor to look closely at the situation and demand responses from top police officials.

The report found lapses in the NYPD's abilities to handle such a crisis that were due to outdated disorder-planning procedures and lack of practical knowledge among executive-level police officers. It was found that the police department's reaction to the first incidents of violence was too slow and ineffective, and that the police failed to control the criminality associated with roving bands of youth. The report made a recommendation that in such instances, mobile arrest teams and aviation and motorcycle units should be used. The NYPD admitted later that an insufficient number of police had been deployed, and there was no coherent plan to deal with the disturbance. Many 9-1-1 calls were erroneously incident coded instead of being classified as reports of "roving bands." The recommendation was made to review the NYPD's method of handling emergency calls originating from areas that are experiencing a civil disorder.

While the state investigation into the Crown Heights riot was still in process, the NYPD started to work on a new, city-wide civil disorder plan to improve its ability to effectively control future disorders. The department has expanded training in the areas of mobilization, command post operations, conflict resolution, and mediation.

More than a decade later, Crown Heights is still used by candidates seeking public office in New York City as an issue of police protection in racially mixed neighborhoods.

*Maria Kiriakova*

*For Further Reading*

Kifner, J., & Lee, F. R. (2001, August 19). In Crown Heights, a decade of healing after riots, but scars remain. *New York Times*, p. A1.

New York State Division of Criminal Justice Services. (1993). *A report to the governor on the disturbances in Crown Heights: An assessment of the city's preparedness and response to civil disorder.* Albany, NY: Author.

## ∞ CULTURAL COMPETENCY TRAINING/SENSITIVITY TRAINING

### DEMOGRAPHIC SHIFTS CREATE CHALLENGES TO POLICE

Communities within the United States are experiencing dramatic demographic shifts as the birth rates of African Americans and Latinos outnumber those of Caucasians; waves of immigrants, refugees, and undocumented aliens seek new opportunities; and international terrorism concerns increase. The impact of these and other demographic shifts are daunting challenges to training police officers to effectively serve their diverse and multicultural communities.

The U.S. Commerce Department's Census Bureau estimates that the nation's foreign-born population in 2003 numbered 32.5 million, or 11.5% of the total U.S. population. It further reported that many individuals living in the United States are not proficient in speaking, reading, writing, or understanding English. More than 26 million individuals speak Spanish, and nearly 7 million individuals speak an Asian or Pacific Island language at home. Twenty-six percent of all Spanish speakers, 29.9% of all Chinese speakers, and 28.2% of all Vietnamese speakers reported to the Census Bureau that they either could not speak English well or could not speak it at all.

In addition to verbal language, functional literacy on the part of Americans is also a great concern to police. A 1993 national adult literacy survey found that 22% of adult Americans perform at the lowest reading and writing skill levels.

The implications of these demographic changes for policing are extensive. Officers may misread cultural cues if they are unfamiliar with the practices or beliefs of a certain immigrant community. For instance, an officer may assess a person's lack of eye contact during an interaction as an indication of bashfulness or deceit. In the United States, direct eye contact is viewed as a sign of confidence and honesty, but in fact, eye contact is culturally specific, and in certain Asian and Latino cultures, eyes are kept down to show respect to an authority figure. Similarly, an officer reviewing a statement with a crime victim may judge that individual to be non-compliant because he or she refuses to sign a statement, when in fact, illiteracy may be the issue.

Concerns over establishing effective police–community relations with new immigrant groups and communities of color are no longer limited to urban areas within the United States. Different cultural and ethnic groups are settling in small cities and rural sections of the country as well, forcing their police agencies to share the challenge of larger departments of developing relations and serving populations with whom they are unfamiliar.

Compounding the difficulties of bridging linguistic, literacy, and cultural differences is the turbulent history of police relations with communities of color. Incidents scarred this country during the 1990s—such as the riots following the Rodney King verdict in Los Angeles and the waves of civil disorder in New York City following the attack by officers on Abner Louima and the police shooting of Amadou Diallo—and illustrate the tragic chasm in police–community relations. The price tag for these events has been high, with police departments and their municipalities facing scores of lawsuits over racial discrimination, personal injury, and property damage. However, the cost of poor community relations has been recognized to be even greater when examining the damage to public trust and confidence regarding law enforcement.

### TRAINING AS A TOOL TO ADDRESS DEMOGRAPHIC CHANGES

Strategies have been employed by many police departments around the country to address these demographic shifts, including recruiting from within diverse communities, establishing police–community committees, and mandating multiculturalism and related training programs for officers. Police academies have spawned an array of sensitivity and other training programs to enhance their understanding of and skills in cross-cultural encounters. These training programs can be divided into several categories:

1. Multicultural training

2. Sensitivity training

3. Language skills training

3. Targeted cultural population training

5. Equal employment opportunities laws training

## Multicultural Training

Multicultural training, or cultural diversity training as it is called in several police organizations, provides a context around culture and its implications for establishing effective police relations with immigrant and refugee communities. Major police departments, such as New York City, Los Angeles, and Miami, have integrated the study of different cultural groups into recruit, inservice, and supervisory training. Cultural groups to be examined at the training reflect various cultural groups served by the police organization. These courses are usually placed in social sciences departments of police academies and woven throughout the recruit training process. The goal of each course is to increase the awareness of recruits regarding the different beliefs, customs, communication styles, and languages of various cultural groups. To support the training, as well as to build bridges between the police and diverse communities, training academies often invite community members to speak to recruits to provide specific information about their culture and to discuss cultural implications regarding interactions with police.

Police officers also learn about cultural pitfalls, such as concerns over gender-specific mores. For example, interacting with females without a husband or male family member present is considered unacceptable behavior in some cultures. In addition, officers learn how police organizations are viewed by individuals from different cultures, particularly cultures that have traditionally been oppressed by police in their native countries.

## Sensitivity Training

For more than 40 years, police organizations have established sensitivity training programs for experienced officers and recruits in response to incidents involving poor relations with communities of color. The goal of this training is to heighten the sensitivity of officers toward racial oppression in order to reduce police actions that may be viewed by community members as racial profiling, stereotyping, and bias. In contrast to multicultural training, which focuses primarily on providing information about an array of different cultural groups, sensitivity training focuses on exploring assumptions and behaviors of officers toward race. Training programs are therefore intensive, usually lasting from one to several days. The programs are also often highly interactive, with officers engaging in role-plays and other experiential exercises to examine long-held beliefs concerning racism, and to learn ways to improve interactions with communities of color.

## Targeted Cultural Population Training

In response to a specific incident, police agencies may establish training for officers on a targeted cultural population. Following the September 11, 2001, attacks on the World Trade Center and Pentagon, police departments from Minneapolis, Minnesota, to Union City, New Jersey, instituted targeted cultural population training programs for their officers and supervisors on cultural groups representing several Middle Eastern countries. Similar training programs were developed by police organizations prior to the September 11th terrorist attacks as new immigrant groups entered their communities. Targeted cultural population training has also been used to educate officers about nonimmigrant cultural groups seeking improved relations with police. During the 1990s, for example, the San Francisco Police Department implemented targeted training programs to increase officer skills in interacting with people with different sexual orientations as a way to improve relations with the city's growing gay, lesbian, bisexual, and transgendered populations. Because of its focus, targeted cultural population training programs are often limited in time and content, and usually implemented as part of roll call and inservice training for experienced officers.

## Language Skills Training

Language is an important tool for police to establish a cooperative connection with community members. To the extent that police fail to address language barriers and assist communication between police and community members, language mismatches can become fertile sources of misinformation, tension, and violent encounters.

Changing demographics have created dramatic language gaps between police and many communities, prompting police organizations to establish language skills classes for officers. For more than 20 years, police academies in New York City, Phoenix, and other cities with large Latino populations have established "Spanish for Police Officers" language courses. These courses teach officers to speak and comprehend enough Spanish to effectively communicate with Spanish-speaking individuals during routine police encounters. As different immigrant groups enter new communities, other languages have been added to meet the needs of cultural groups, including Russian, Cantonese, and Vietnamese.

Federal mandates provide guidelines for police and other government agencies to provide language access and services to individuals who cannot speak or read English. In 2002, the Department of Justice published guidelines directing government agencies to provide meaningful language access and services to people with limited English proficiency (LEP). People detained by police are mandated to have translation services provided during questioning. Officers often work with translators during interviews and interrogations of foreign language victims, witnesses, and accused.

In view of this, officers may also require training in the proper use of translators. Translation services are available to police both telephonically and in person, but officers require skills in partnering with a translator in order to establish an effective interview or interrogation with an individual lacking English-speaking skills. Specialized courses by translation services and language banks are offered to officers who frequently use these services to increase translation accuracy and reduce miscommunication.

## Equal Employment Opportunities Laws Training

For more than 30 years, affirmative action laws have enabled groups who had traditionally been denied hiring opportunities to join the ranks of police officers. The increase of African Americans, Latinos, Asians, and women in policing has expanded the capacity of police organizations to reflect the communities they serve. It also created new expectations of officer conduct and cooperation. Protected from discrimination and harassment by federal Equal Employment Opportunities laws, women and people of color have brought lawsuits against police agencies for improper hiring and promotional practices, as well as for inappropriate behavior by fellow officers and supervisors.

One outgrowth of these charges has been to provide training in preventing sexual harassment and racial discrimination among officers. These programs cite Equal Employment Opportunities Commission fair employment guidelines based on Title VII of the Civil Rights Act of 1964, and related laws concerning discrimination based on age, disability, equal pay, pregnancy, race, place of national origin, religion, gender, or military status. The sessions also cite state, city, and agency policies related to discrimination, as well as current laws and guidelines to prevent sexual harassment.

Guidelines of appropriate behavior at station houses and in the field are discussed during sessions, and case studies are examined to illustrate appropriate and inappropriate behaviors on the parts of officers toward one another. Therefore, training also includes reporting processes and provides officers with resources and personnel contacts in the event that a complaint must be filed.

Police supervisors receive similar training on discrimination and harassment prevention, and they are advised of their responsibilities to identify and address such inappropriate behaviors among officers.

However, supervisory training goes further than officer training, because supervisors are personally responsible for creating and maintaining a work environment free of harassment and discrimination. Supervisory training also includes protocols for accepting complaints and contacting personnel services to refer the complaint to proper authorities.

## CONCLUSION

The need for police organizations to develop competencies in engaging in cross-cultural encounters will continue to grow as the demographics of this country change rapidly. Training is viewed as a vital strategy to adapt police practices and values to address new or different cultural, ethnic, and other groups entering U.S. communities. Similarly, although recruitment is an essential strategy to meet the needs of a changing society, training also serves as a tool to adapt police cultures and organizational structures to retain new entrants into the police ranks who reflect the communities they serve.

*Joyce St. George*

**See also** Community Relations, Police Training in
the United States, Race Relations

### For Further Reading

Coderoni, G. R. (2002). The relationship between multicultural training for police and effective law enforcement. *FBI Law Enforcement Bulletin, 71*(11), 16–18.

Flores, E. (1993, December). *Leadership training as a tool for confronting racial and ethnic conflicts* (Working paper 93-24). Boulder, CO: Conflict Research Consortium.

Himelfarb, F. (1991, November). A training strategy for policing in a multicultural society. *The Police Chief,* pp. 53–55.

Miller, L. S., & Hess, K. M. (2001). *The police in the community: Strategies for the 21st century.* Upper Saddle River, NJ: Prentice Hall.

Shusta, R. M., Levine, D., Harris, P., & Wong, H. (2001). *Multicultural law enforcement: Strategies for peacekeeping in a diverse society* (2nd ed.). Belmont, CA: Wadsworth.

Speaking in tongues. (2000, October 31). *Law Enforcement News, 26*(542).

http://www.census.gov

http://www.childrensdefense.org

http://www.lep.gov

http://www.usdoj.gov:80/crt/cor/lep

## ⁊ CURFEWS

In general, curfews are regulations that prohibit the presence of people on streets or other public properties during certain hours of the day. For more than a century, curfews have been invoked at various times in the United States in an effort to maintain social order. Curfews enacted in the United States fall into one of two categories: juvenile curfews or riot curfews.

### JUVENILE CURFEWS

America's first juvenile curfew laws emerged in the late 19th century in large urban areas and were intended to eliminate crime among immigrant youth. Curfews were also used by many communities during World War II to prevent children from becoming wayward while their parents were toiling in the war effort. The proliferation of juvenile crime and gang activity during the 1970s created a renewed interest in youth curfews in the United States, and by the early 1990s, many politicians, law enforcement officials, and communities were calling for their establishment. At the present time, most large U.S. cities have enacted some type of juvenile curfew law.

Juvenile curfews in the United States have typically required that minor children be in their places of residence between a certain late-evening hour and a certain mid-morning hour. It is typically articulated, within the statutes themselves, that juvenile curfew laws are intended to protect juveniles from engaging in, or being victimized by, criminal behavior and to strengthen parental control over youths. Some U.S. cities have recently enacted daytime curfews, which require minors to be on school grounds during school hours, in an effort to combat truancy. There are usually exceptions to the imperative: Minors are often allowed in public during curfew hours for emergency reasons, when in the company of a parent or guardian, when immediately outside of their residences, and when exercising their First Amendment rights.

Depending on the municipality, youths identified by law enforcement as being in violation of either nighttime or daytime curfews may be stopped and told to proceed directly home, transported home, arrested and detained at police stations until retrieved by their parents, taken to centers dedicated to housing curfew violators, summoned to court, referred to social or child protective services, or fined. Some municipalities hold the parents of curfew violators to be negligent and have mechanisms by which parents can be fined or punished if their children are found to be in breach of curfew.

As is the case with other types of laws intended to maintain order, such as antiloitering laws, enforcement of juvenile curfew laws in the United States involves the use of much police discretion. Even in the case that a community has a juvenile curfew law on the books, it is usually up to individual officers to decide whether to enforce the law and to determine the course of action that will be taken against the violator. Although juvenile curfews have enjoyed extreme popularity in recent years, they have not been without detractors. Civil liberties advocacy groups and other citizen coalitions have challenged juvenile curfew statutes in court. Such groups argue that curfews infringe upon young Americans' constitutional rights, especially those rights guaranteed by the Fourteenth Amendment's equal protection clause, and that enforcement of curfews inevitably singles out poor and minority children who do not have the option of going home to luxuries such as air conditioning, large-screen televisions, and foosball tables.

Because the constitutional rights of American youths are defined less clearly than those of adults, legal challenges of curfew laws have produced mixed results in the courts. Thus far, the U.S. Supreme Court has not taken a stand on juvenile curfews, and various state and federal courts throughout the country have subjected juvenile curfew laws to differing degrees of scrutiny and issued conflicting opinions regarding their constitutionality.

Many cities throughout the United States have attributed decreases in juvenile crime to the implementation of juvenile curfews. Surprisingly, very few empirical studies of the efficacy of juvenile curfews have been conducted; however, the findings of the handful of studies that do exist suggest that politicians' and citizens' support of juvenile curfews may be fed more by the American public's fear of being terrorized by droves of unruly youths than by curfews' effectiveness in reducing crime—consider that less than one fifth of violent juvenile crime actually takes place during the hours in which most daytime and nighttime youth curfews are in effect (i.e., most juvenile crime takes place between 3 p.m. and 8 p.m., after daytime curfews have ended and before nighttime curfews have begun). Curfew violations are the most common transgression in America for which children are arrested.

## RIOT CURFEWS

Unlike juvenile curfews, which are typically enacted by legislation, apply only to minors, and are designed to be continuous in their enforcement, riot curfews are put into effect by the decree of city executives (typically mayors), apply to citizens of all ages, and are designed to restore order during temporary crises. Riot curfews were used extensively in the United States during the 1960s and 1970s to quell the civil disorder resulting from racial unrest. Prior to the civil rights era, the most notable of riot curfews were those enacted against people of Japanese ancestry during World War II and in response to labor disputes. Recently, riot curfews have been imposed in response to civil disturbances that have erupted in the wake of police shootings and controversial verdicts, such as that of the Rodney King trial in 1992.

A city executive's power to enact a riot curfew generally derives from a state's constitution or legislative delegations of police power, or from a city's ordinances. Typically, the statutes from which the executive's power to institute a riot curfew originates require that the executive must declare a state of emergency in order to exercise the prerogative. The laws tend to give the city executive the authority to enforce emergency curfews in the event of riot or insurrection, or where there is clear and present danger of the preceding, so that life and property may be protected and small incidences of disorder may be quelled before they mushroom into sweeping chaos.

Riot curfews are generally intended to keep citizens off the streets during actual or anticipated incidences of disorder, to prevent pedestrian or vehicular traffic from obstructing law enforcement officers or emergency services personnel, and to reduce the number of calls for police service so that officers can concentrate on eliminating the civil unrest. Riot curfews may be applied to an entire city or to smaller geographic areas within cities. Riot curfew violators are typically punished via fines or imprisonment.

The hours during which a riot curfew is applied depend upon the city executive's assessment of the emergency situation. Sometimes, 24-hour citywide curfews, under which all citizens are confined to their homes, have been imposed. In such cases, citizens are generally allowed only brief daytime reprieves from the curfew to obtain food or supplies. When officials are mainly concerned with prohibiting citizens from congregating in the streets and contributing to social unrest, curfews may be enforced as antiloitering regulations under which people are allowed to pass along the streets for reasons deemed legitimate, and they will be arrested only if they are just hanging around.

Because they are implemented only temporarily and under emergency circumstances, riot curfews are understandably less controversial than juvenile curfews. Although riot curfews restrict citizens' freedom of movement and may therefore impinge upon the rights enumerated in the First Amendment, they generally offer citizens some designated reprieve time during which they may exercise these rights. As is the case with juvenile curfews, police officers possess much discretion when it comes to enforcing riot curfews. Thus, officers must steer clear of violating the Fourteenth Amendment's equal protection clause by discriminating against certain races or classes of people when enforcing riot curfews—uneven enforcement of riot curfews along racial lines not only violates the Constitution, it also has the potential to exacerbate riot conditions.

*Nicole R. Green*

***See also*** Loitering

## For Further Reading

Frese, G. C. (1969). The riot curfew. *California Law Review, 57*(2), 450–490.

Hemmens, C., & Bennet, K. (1999). Juvenile curfews and the courts: Judicial response to a not-so-new crime control strategy. *Crime & Delinquency, 45*(1), 99–121.

Males, M., & Macallair, D. (1999). An analysis of curfew enforcement and juvenile crime in California. *Western Criminology Review, 1*(2). Retrieved February 1, 2003, from http://wcr.sonoma.edu/v1n2/males.html

## DEPOLICING

During the 1990s, police officers in the United States came under attack for the alleged practice of racial profiling. Activists accused law enforcement of singling out African-American men for stops and searches on the basis of race. The term *racial profiling* was used by civil liberties groups to describe this allegation. The decade also witnessed several high-profile police shootings of civilians, primarily minorities, which were blamed on officer bias as well. As a result of the intense criticism that accompanied these incidents, many officers backed off of assertive policing—a phenomenon known as depolicing. In many jurisdictions where the charge of racial profiling was particularly vitriolic, the result was a dramatic decrease in stops and arrests with a corresponding dramatic increase in crime.

The 1990s will be remembered in law enforcement circles as the decade of racial profiling, a term used by the American Civil Liberties Union and others to refer to the alleged police practice of stopping civilians according to race.

For the media, racial profiling became the very hallmark of policing, even though sound statistical evidence for it is nonexistent.

Profiling studies typically compare police enforcement data, such as the number of stops, searches, or arrests, to census data. If the rates of stops or searches for minorities are disproportionate to their share of a population, critics conclude that the police use skin color, not behavior, in deciding whom to stop. For many in the law enforcement community and social sciences, such an analysis is flawed for two reasons: First, it assumes that law breaking is spread evenly across the population, and second, it omits every factor that, unlike race or census data, actually does determine whom the police approach.

The most important benchmark for aggregate enforcement data is crime rates. Police departments target their resources where crime is highest, and that is usually in inner-city minority neighborhoods. In Chicago, for example, homicide rates from 1991 to 2001 were 11 times higher in black beats than in white beats. Such a disparity means that antiviolence initiatives will take place overwhelmingly in black neighborhoods. Once deployed in those areas, police officers look for behavioral cues of criminality—nervousness, furtive gestures, resemblance to a suspect, or hitching up a waistband as if concealing a gun, among other possible factors. Racial profiling would be irrelevant, because the vast majority of residents are of the same race.

As long as crime rates remain racially disproportionate, so will the enforcement data that police critics seize to show racial bias. In 1998, for example, black males between the ages of 14 and

24 committed 30% of all homicides, even though they made up only slightly more than 1% of the population. Only by ignoring law breaking could the police produce enforcement data that would match the nation's demographic profile—the litmus test for avoiding racial profiling accusations.

But although crime rates are the necessary precondition for sound racial profiling analysis, they are not sufficient. Also essential are the demographics of highways and city streets, which change hourly and daily; the distribution of high-profile crimes that would lead to high-intensity policing; age demographics of various populations; and the prevalence of parolees and warrant absconders in different racial groups, to name just a few of the factors that bear on enforcement data. To benchmark highway stops and searches, the analyst needs to know, at a bare minimum, rates of speeding and equipment violations, as well as of drug trafficking.

None of the profiling studies done to date approaches this level of complexity. As a consequence, these studies paint officers as bigots simply for going after crime. Ed Flynn, public safety director of Massachusetts, notes the dilemma facing officers in the era of primitive racial profiling analysis. In "responding to heartfelt demands for increased police presence," he explains, "police departments produc[e] data at the community's behest that can be used against them" (Mac Donald, 2003, p. 24).

When Flynn was chief of the Arlington County, Virginia, police in the late 1990s, the county's black community demanded that the department crack down on local drug dealing. The police did and won plaudits from law-abiding black residents. But, recalls Flynn, the "department had also just generated a lot of data showing 'disproportionate' minority arrests," even though officers had targeted behavior, not race (Mac Donald, 2003, p. 24). Any anticop activist could have used those data to allege racial profiling.

The result of this dilemma has been depolicing. The media, civil rights activists, and politicians have been telling officers that if they have "too many" law enforcement interactions with minorities, it is because they discriminate. Officers are reacting by avoiding all but the most mandatory and cursory interactions with potential minority suspects. An increasing number of states and cities require cops to record their every interaction with civilians on the basis of race. If an officer's stop or search data do not match population ratios, he or she will be red-flagged as a potential bigot. The response of officers in Pittsburgh, Pennsylvania, where a federal monitor has overseen the police department since 1997 as part of a civil rights settlement, is typical: They report arresting by quota. Toward the end of the month, if an officer has searched or arrested "too many" minorities, he will stop making minority arrests and look for whites to apprehend.

The drop-off of enforcement activity following campaigns against the police can be striking. The press routinely portrays New Jersey as the capital of racial profiling; the state police have operated under a federal monitor since 2000. Drug charges filed from the New Jersey Turnpike dropped 94% from 1998—the year the profiling issue reached a boiling point in the state—to 2000. In 1999, New Jersey troopers conducted 440 consent searches on the turnpike; in the 6 months that ended October 31, 2001, they conducted 11. Murder jumped 65% in Newark, a major drug trafficking destination, between 2000 and 2001. The town of Camden has invited the state police back into town to fight its homicidal drug gangs, in a replay of the drug battles of the 1980s.

New Jersey trooper union vice president Dave Jones explains the drop in police activity: "There's a tremendous demoralizing effect of being guilty until proven innocent. Anyone you interact with can claim you've made a race-based stop, and you spend years defending yourself" (Mac Donald, 2003, pp. 30–31).

Other jurisdictions have experienced the same effect from campaigns charging the police with bias. When the mayor of Minneapolis accused the Minneapolis police of profiling and started requiring officers to record their every stop by race, traffic stops fell by as much as 80% in some high-crime neighborhoods in the first 2 weeks of the program. Arrests in Los Angeles fell 25% in the first 9 months of 2000, whereas homicides jumped 25%, during a period of negative scrutiny from the press and Justice Department.

Officers in Prince George County, Maryland, adopted a "no contact, no complaints" approach after repeated negative coverage in the *Washington Post* and investigations by the Justice Department and FBI. In the first 2 months of 2001, felony adult arrests in one of the county's busiest districts dropped 38% compared with the previous year, and misdemeanor adult arrests dropped 28%. Meanwhile, robberies rose 37%, carjackings nearly doubled, and 61 homicides were committed in the first 6 months of 2001, 10 fewer than in all of the preceding year.

Police shootings have also resulted in depolicing. On April 7, 2001, a Cincinnati police officer fatally shot a teenager with 14 outstanding warrants who had just led officers on a chase through the city's most crime-infested neighborhood. Three days of rioting ensued. The national media declared Cincinnati a "model of racial injustice," in the words of *Time* magazine (Ripley, 2001). However, the main piece of evidence for the charge—the deaths of 15 black men at the hands of the police since 1995—was misleading. Nearly all the victims were felons who had used or threatened to use lethal force against the police immediately before their demise. Race was not the motivating factor in their deaths, their own behavior was. Nevertheless, the U.S. Justice Department began investigating the department for racism.

Faced with a firestorm of criticism, the Cincinnati police cut back on discretionary law enforcement. Arrests dropped 50% in the first 3 months after the riots, compared with the same period in 2000; traffic stops fell nearly 55%. Drug dealers operated with near impunity on the streets, and violent crime shot up. There were 60 shootings in the quarter after the riots, compared with 9 the year before.

The trend has continued in Cincinnati for nearly 2 years after the riots. Arrests in 2002 were down 30% compared with 2000, the last full year before the riots. Violent crimes were up 40% in 2002 compared with 2000, and homicide reached a 15-year high. City officials started imploring officers to resume assertive patrol, a demand met with irony by the rank and file. In response to a city councilman's proposal that the police crack down on loiterers who appeared to be selling drugs, the police union president observed that when officers do try to deal with drug dealing, they are labeled as racists—a situation that results in an officer's reluctance to arrest.

An infamous shooting by the New York Police Department produced the same reaction. On February 4, 1999, four undercover officers fired 41 shots at Amadou Diallo, an unarmed illegal immigrant, through a series of faulty tactics and tragic misperceptions. As filtered through the media's accounts, many New Yorkers saw the killing as a racial episode and the very symbol of the New York Police Department, notwithstanding that the use of force by New York City officers was at its lowest point in recent memory. Depicted incessantly as the enemy of black people, the undercover Street Crime Unit, from which the four officers hailed, started ignoring criminal behavior. Arrests dropped 62% in the month after the episode, and shootings and murders jumped 200% in the precincts where the Street Crime Unit worked.

As of early 2003, there was no sign that the movement to address racial profiling was slowing down. In the first 3 months of the year, New Jersey made racial profiling a felony; Maryland required its troopers to hand out instructions for filing profiling complaints to everyone they stop; and California banned its highway officers from conducting consent searches, on the theory that they cannot be trusted to exercise that power fairly. On the horizon, however, are profiling studies in North Carolina, Miami, and New York that try to address the violator benchmark problem. They follow the lead of a pioneering—and assiduously ignored—speeding study from 2002 that found that black drivers on the New Jersey Turnpike were twice as likely to speed as white drivers, a disparity that explains disparate stop rates. As more analyses are attempted of the civilian behavior that triggers police response, the racial profiling movement and consequent depolicing phenomenon may abate.

*Heather Mac Donald*

***See also*** Profiling, Criminal Personality; Profiling, Racial; Race Relations

*For Further Reading*

Chicago Community Policing Evaluation Consortium. (2003). *Community policing in Chicago, years eight and nine* (p. 5). Chicago: Illinois Criminal Justice Information Authority.

Donohue, B., & Mueller, M. (2001, January 31). Drug arrests by troopers plunge. *Newark Star-Ledger,* p. 10.

Fox, J. A. (2000). Demographics and U.S. homicide. In A. Blumstein & J. Wallman (Eds.), *The crime drop in America.* Cambridge, UK: Cambridge University Press.

Herszenhorn, D. (1999, March 29). Arrests drop and shootings rise as the police, Giuliani says, are distracted. *New York Times,* p. B3.

Kersten, K. (2001, February 28). Crackdown on little offenses can help prevent the big ones. *Minneapolis Star-Tribune.*

Kocieniewski, D. (2002, March 9). Officials say figures show that profiling is decreasing. *New York Times,* p. B5.

Lange, J. E., Blackman, K. O., & Johnson, M. B. (2001). *Speed violation survey of the New Jersey Turnpike: Final report.* Submitted to Office of the Attorney General, Trenton, NJ.

Mac Donald, H. (2003). *Are cops racist? How the war against the police harms black Americans.* Chicago: Ivan R. Dee.

Newton, J. (2000, October 15). A glimpse into future of LAPD? *Los Angeles Times,* p. A1.

Rabin, J. L. (2000, November 30). Murder leads increase of violent crime in city. *Los Angeles Times.*

Ripley, A. (2001, April 23). Nights of rage: Another police killing, and Cincinnati explodes. *Time,* p. 44.

Stockwell, J. (2001, August 10). Ward in Pr. George's has drop in arrests. *Washington Post,* p. B5.

Turco, S., & Prendergast, J. (2003, January 30). Officials beginning to discuss slowdown by police: Crime's up and arrests down. *Cincinnati Inquirer.*

Verniero, P., & Zoubek, P. H. (1999). *Interim report of the State Police Review Team regarding allegations of racial profiling.* Available: http://www.state.nj.us/lps/intm_419.pdf

## ᴐᴚᴑ DETECTIVES

Police departments throughout the United States who assign police officers to perform retroactive investigations (investigating past crimes and collecting evidence) are called detectives; investigators; or, less frequently, inspectors. Detectives are also engaged in undercover operations, electronic surveillance, decoys, stings, and stakeouts in order to investigate continuing criminal enterprises. They are usually appointed to this detective designation,

rather than promoted as the result of a competitive civil service exam process, which is the common promotion method for sergeant, lieutenant, and captain. The process for promotion to detective can range from a formal career path, evaluation of arrest activity, training, and education, to an abrupt instant reward for a heroic act or for solving an important or highly publicized case.

The position of detective is the most celebrated, romanticized, and televised activity in the field of policing. Cunning, diligence, intellect, "street smarts," interviewing skills, and the wise handling of informants are but a few of the expected attributes that are called upon to solve every "television crime" within an hour-long show. Unfortunately, this media reality has created an inflated illusion of detectives and what they do. It also has severely skewed the impact that detectives have on the totality of actual crime. The ordinary uniform police are rarely acknowledged for their main importance in solving crimes. Detectives are not line-supervisors of police, but may be tasked with the responsibility of supervising police access and behavior at a crime scene. It is clear that the designation of detective is a most sought-after appointment or assignment, for it awards a police officer with increased status, financial compensation, and discretionary work time. Many police officers strive to work in civilian clothes and avoid wearing a police uniform. In NYPD argot, a detective assignment gets you out of the "bag," or uniform.

A study conducted in 1975 by the RAND Corporation found that only 7% of a detective's work time was occupied with activities in connection with solving a crime and rarely involved scientific evidence collection. Detectives spend most of their time doing administrative or clerical reports and attempting to locate and interview witnesses. The most important factor influencing the solving of a case is the information provided by the victim to the first responding uniform officer. Key information is whether the victim can identify the perpetrator or perpetrators of the crime. Inspection of the *Sourcebook of Criminal Justice Statistics* reveals that only about 21% of all reported crimes are cleared by arrest or exceptional clearance; the vast majority of those arrests were made by the regular uniform patrol force. Serious crimes have clearance rates above the mean. Approximately 90% of the convictions are the result of a plea bargains, not the verdict of a jury at the end of a criminal trial.

Where and how detectives are assigned within a police department depends on the size of the department and the number of crimes referred for investigation. There are management cycles in large departments that go through waves of centralized and decentralized command structures, along with specialization and general practice. Detectives have been under the exclusive command of a Chief of Detectives separate from uniform patrol services, and on other cycles, they have been under the exclusive control of the local uniform precinct commander. Specialty units such as homicide squad, sex crimes squad, hate crimes squad, robbery squad, burglary squad, larceny squad, crime scene squad, and joint federal/state/municipal task forces for terrorism and bank robberies have come in and out of existence depending on the political necessity.

Another emerging area in criminal investigation is criminal profiling, which has been developed and fostered by the Federal Bureau of Investigation, and we now find police/detective criminal profilers in many police agencies. The legitimate use of criminal profiling certainly has its place in professional criminal investigation. A new academic discipline known as forensic psychology has been added in many psychology departments of colleges and universities. Its purpose is to train individuals to be able to identify characteristics and probabilities of the perpetrators of crime by professional forensic analysis of the crime scenes and their patterns of criminal practice.

Unfortunately, most 24-hour cable news networks have popularized criminal profiling because they provide endless "scientific" discussion questions and speculation about high-visibility crimes, and require little accurate information. With this added demand to fill all of the cable television time, a new field of "expert speculators" has emerged; these speculators practice saying little, but in an entertaining manner. In effect, the TV media are pressuring law enforcement to provide speculation

when facts are not yet known. This public practice, which shows little regard for knowing and verifying the facts, can have an influencing effect on public attitudes about the detective investigators and the actual criminal cases they investigate. Real detectives/investigators are being pressured and judged to perform just like the TV detectives on the weekly series. This media attention can actually alter the criminal investigation process. Modern-day detectives have this additional responsibility to handle the media along with solving the case and safeguarding everyone's civil rights.

*William F. McCarthy*

*See also* Profiling, Criminal Personality; Investigation; Television (Police Shows)

*For Further Reading*

Greenwood, P., & Petersilia, J. (1975). The criminal investigation process. In *Sourcebook of criminal justice statistics 1975*. Washington, DC: Bureau of Justice Statistics.

# ❧ DISPATCH

> *"If I had a choice between a two-way radio and a gun, I'd take the radio."*

The above quote is from a former Maryland police officer and reflects the importance of the dispatcher. Although the role of the dispatcher is critical for the survival of law enforcement officers and the citizens who call upon them, administrators, officers, and citizens often misunderstand dispatchers.

## ROLE OF THE DISPATCHER

Dispatchers must process complex information in a matter of seconds to ascertain nonemergency from emergency calls. They must attempt to calm the caller, as some may be in great panic and unintelligible. The dispatcher must determine the nature of the problem and the location of the incident, and inquire if anyone has been injured. This becomes important if the dispatcher needs to contact other emergency personnel, such as fire or rescue. Sometimes, the caller is from another jurisdiction and the dispatcher must determine the appropriate law enforcement agency to contact. Because police personnel are on call 24 hours a day, citizens may contact the police dispatcher when another agency should be notified. For example, a citizen may call the police dispatcher to explain a problem concerning a neighbor's cat, when the most appropriate contact agency is Animal Control.

Once the basic information is received, the dispatcher is required to communicate the necessary facts to road officers. Dispatchers direct the officers to the location and coordinate response activities, including the number of officers needed to respond; contact supervisors and specialty units, such as the Hostage Negotiation Team; and/or notify neighboring law enforcement personnel. Dispatchers must know the location of each officer and record all events/calls. This allows the dispatcher to know which officer is available for a call and the previous location of the officer in the event he or she needs immediate assistance.

Dispatchers must possess basic knowledge of criminal law. For instance, if a store clerk contacts dispatch to state that he or she has just been "robbed," the dispatcher must determine if the caller really means a robbery (a crime against person) or a theft, such as shoplifting (crime against property). The importance of that distinction indicates the number of officers who should be dispatched and the manner of response (lights and siren vs. routine travel).

Dispatchers must be familiar with basic first aid. If the caller notifies the dispatcher that a person has stopped breathing, the dispatcher may actually provide a step-by-step, life-saving procedure (CPR) over the telephone.

Police dispatchers must also be proficient using the computer. Many agencies use Computer Aided Dispatch (CAD), a computer management system designed to aid law enforcement by allowing instant communication between the police dispatcher and field officers. Officers often contact the dispatcher to verify driver license and registration checks during vehicle stops, as well as to see if stopped individuals are wanted by the police on an outstanding warrant.

As revealed, the role of the dispatcher is quite unique and complicated. Because of the multitask

nature and ambiguity surrounding the dispatcher's job function, occupational stress often occurs.

## JOB STRESS

It is important to note that the stressors (those factors that produce job stress) suffered by police dispatchers are similar to those experienced by air traffic controllers (ATCs). The ATC is also required to direct many units in the field; receive, assimilate, and dispatch information from a variety of sources; and be responsible for the lives of others. Both occupations are stressful, and both require making instant decisions that can involve life-or-death situations.

Among the numerous factors that may produce job stress among police dispatchers are a lack of support, shift work, confinement, and a lack of training. A lack of support from officers (and supervisors) may produce job stress. Many police dispatchers are civilians, not sworn police officers. As a result, they are often treated as second-class citizens. There is often a bond between police officers. This rarely extends to police dispatchers. While sworn officers may also be dispatchers, too often, police supervisors use the dispatch center as a dumping ground for injured officers or officers who are disciplinary problems.

Shift work is quite stressful in any job; however, coupled with the many duties assigned to the dispatcher, this becomes a key variable in dispatcher stress. It has been well documented that shift work may cause sleep, eating, and social/family disruptions.

Confinement to one area poses great stress among dispatchers. Whereas street officers are able to leave their patrol vehicle to eat, walk, or socialize, the dispatcher does not have such freedom. He or she must be readily available to answer incoming calls. In fact, in some smaller agencies where the dispatcher is the only person inside the building at a given time, mini-dispatch centers have been set up in the restrooms so citizens may still contact the police agency without delay.

The key to optimal performance in many jobs is intensive training. However, most police dispatchers receive little or no formal training. Most dispatcher training remains "on the job." Police officers must successfully complete a police academy before being allowed to perform their official duties, yet dispatchers do not receive similar treatment, thus reinforcing their status as second-class citizens. In addition to the police academy and inservice training, police administrators often send police officers for specialized training. Specialized training is often not available for dispatchers. The few dispatchers who attend training seminars often do so at their own expense.

Dispatchers are often called upon to perform a variety of roles with great accuracy. Although often overlooked by officers, supervisors, and citizens, dispatchers play a critical role in criminal justice and in the safety of all who call upon them.

*Tod W. Burke*

*See also* Calls for Service, Computer Aided Dispatch

*For Further Reading*

Burke, T. (1991). *The relationship between dispatcher stress and social support, job satisfaction and locus of control.* Unpublished doctoral dissertation, City University of New York.

Burke, T. (1993, February). The correlation between dispatcher stress and occupational dissatisfaction. *APCO Bulletin*, pp. 32, 82.

Burke, T. (1993, March). The correlation between dispatcher stress, burnout and social support. *APCO Bulletin*, pp. 50–54.

Burke, T. (1993, April). The correlation between dispatcher stress and control. *APCO Bulletin*, pp. 39–41.

Burke, T. (1995, October). Dispatcher stress. *FBI Law Enforcement Bulletin*, pp. 1–6.

Burke, T. (1996, Winter). Even dispatchers get the blues. *Minding the Badge* (published quarterly by the *Mental Health Association*), pp. 1–2, 4.

Martindale, D. (1977). Sweaty palms in the control tower. *Psychology Today, 11*(2), 71–75.

Sewell, J. D., & Crew, L. (1984, March). The forgotten victim: Stress and the police dispatcher. *FBI Law Enforcement Bulletin*, pp. 7–11.

## ∾ DNA

Although the discovery of DNA dates back to 1869 with Frederich Miescher's study of a phosphorus-containing substance isolated from the nuclei of cells found in discarded bandages of wounded soldiers, it was not until 1953 that Watson and Crick published its molecular structure. Many studies since then have established that DNA is the material responsible, in part, for the inheritance of virtually all of our traits. Exceptions to this rule include one's fingerprint (ridge) pattern, which is established during the third to fourth month of fetal development. The discovery that DNA is actually an antiparallel double helix helped to explain why this unique molecule, with the assistance of "helper" molecules, is able to replicate within the cell. Molecular biologists and biochemists continue to study DNA to better our understanding of the processes of transcription (transfer of information from DNA to RNA) and translation (the use of RNA in the synthesis of cellular proteins). These activities are essential to cell function and life.

The development of DNA analysis technology for the purpose of human identification in the mid-1980s marked a turning point in the practice of forensic science and has created a revolution in criminal justice. The human genome, coding for approximately 30,000 to 40,000 genes, consists of approximately 3.1 billion nucleotide subunits or building blocks of DNA distributed unevenly on 46 chromosomes that are located in the nucleus of each of our cells. Of the 3.1 billion nucleotide subunits within the human genome, only a small portion (0.1%) makes one person different from another. It is this exceedingly small fraction of DNA that can be used by the forensic scientist to individualize biological samples left behind by perpetrators of violent crimes. Forensic DNA analysis of this evidence is used to obtain identifying information by determining which alleles (genes) are present at a number of specific genetic sites (loci) within the human genome. In each case, a distinct genetic profile is constructed. With this information, a comparison can be made with DNA obtained from the victim and suspect(s). Different profiles indicate that the suspect is *excluded* as the source of the evidence, whereas identical profiles indicate that the suspect *could be* the source. This is analogous to identifying and comparing points of minutiae in a latent fingerprint with an inked print to determine if a match exists. In forensic investigations, exemplar and questioned specimens are compared to determine if there is a relatively high probability or even scientific certainty that there is a common origin.

## POLYMORPHISM AT GENETIC LOCI

Prior to the late 1980s, forensic analysts challenged with the task of associating a suspect with a crime scene or victim analyzed "polymorphic sugars," proteins, and glycoproteins present within biological evidence. Polymorphism refers to the existence of two or more alleles at a particular genetic locus within the population. Because individuals can inherit different alleles from their parents, individuals can be differentiated by studying these polymorphic cellular substances that reflect polymorphic sites within the genome. Barring mutational events or recombination events that occur during sperm and ovum formation, genes are stable, and their study can provide a window into what makes us unique as individuals. For example, each of us can be classified into one of the four major ABO blood groups: A, B, AB, and O. The particular blood group depends on which two of the three most common genes (alleles) are inherited. The more polymorphism there is at a locus, the higher the level of discrimination possible. If there are many frequently occurring alleles at a genetic locus, more distinct types can be formed, and therefore, the more useful the locus will be in human identification. Polymorphic cellular enzymes have been used in conjunction with the ABO system and other genetic markers. However, the level of polymorphism observable for cellular proteins and sugars is relatively low. Furthermore, there is often an insufficient amount of these substances to test, and they tend to be unstable, degrading over relatively short periods of time or when exposed to environmental insult (sunlight, humidity, high temperature, etc.). The use of DNA in human identification has overcome many of these deficiencies because of the high stability, high degree of polymorphism, and our capability of amplifying even moderately degraded specimens to produce more than enough DNA to test. Regardless of the nature of the biochemical studied (sugar, protein, DNA), all loci that are used to establish a genetic profile must be inherited independently of each other if the product rule is to be used

to calculate the rarity of the genetic profile (see below).

## RFLP ANALYSIS

Roy White of the University of Utah described the first polymorphic variable nucleotide tandem repeat (VNTR) marker on chromosome 14 in 1980. In 1985, Dr. Alec Jeffreys, a professor at the University of Leicester in the United Kingdom, developed restriction fragment length polymorphism (RFLP) analysis incorporating the use of VNTR probes to study human identification. VNTRs are sections of DNA that consist of a series of core units generally consisting of 15–700 nucleotide bases that are repetitious and tandemly linked to each other, forming sections that are hundreds or even thousands of bases long. The DNA examined in this procedure is called "junk" DNA because it is noncoding and, at this time, has no known function.

Forensic RFLP analysis methods have been useful for parentage testing, for kidnap and missing persons investigations, in cases of mass disaster such as plane crashes and acts of terrorism, and in the establishment of evidentiary and convicted felon databases. The RFLP method is an extremely powerful way of identifying the source of virtually any biological specimen, including blood, semen, and saliva, which are often found as crime scene evidence. Other physiological fluids or tissues, such as urine, hair, muscle, skin, teeth, and bone, can also be analyzed. The requirement for successful RFLP analysis is that there be a sufficient quantity of high-quality or undegraded DNA for testing. The method employs the following steps: DNA is extracted (using an organic or inorganic isolation technique) from the biological evidence collected at the crime scene; purified DNA is quantitated and its quality determined (at least 50 nanograms are required for successful analysis) it is subjected to repeated molecular cleavage by a well-characterized, bacterial-derived restriction (cutting) enzyme; fragments of DNA are subjected to electrophoresis on a gel to separate them based on size (mass and charge); Southern blotting is performed to transfer the fragments from the gel to a more solid membrane support; fragments are covalently linked to this membrane substrate; a labeled probe is allowed to hybridize with the membrane; the probe becomes hydrogen bonded to the VNTR region present within some of the fragments; the labeled fragment is visualized either on an autoradiogram using x-ray film if the label is a radioisotope, or on a chemilumigram if the label emits light (is chemiluminescent); the banding pattern is analyzed to determine the size in base pairs of the labeled fragments and a comparison is made between fragment sizes for the exemplar and unknown specimens; the probes are stripped off the membrane and a second probe that recognizes a different VNTR locus is allowed to hybridize and the new banding pattern developed and analyzed (this can be repeated a number of times); and a statistical calculation is made to determine the probability of a random match (the rarity of the entire genetic profile). The calculation is based on the use of the product rule and on allele frequencies that have been predetermined and recorded in databases for Caucasians, African Americans, Hispanics, and Asians. Because all genes within and between loci are independently inherited according to Mendel's Laws of Heredity, the frequencies of each allele within the profile can be multiplied to calculate the frequency of the overall genetic profile. It is not unusual for this combined frequency to reach levels of one in hundreds of millions or even billions of individuals. Thus, if a match is found to exist between evidence and suspect and the genetic profile is extremely rare in the relevant population, the likelihood is extremely high that they share a common origin.

## PCR AMPLIFICATION

The same year that Jeffreys published his RFLP work, the first paper on the subject of the polymerase chain reaction (PCR) technique appeared. This method is used to replicate (amplify) exceedingly small amounts of DNA to produce billions of copies of specific DNA segments of forensic interest. The following steps describe the PCR process: DNA is extracted from the biological evidence and quantitated; the isolated DNA is added to a reaction mix containing labeled primers (short, single-stranded

DNA whose base sequence is complementary to a segment on one of the two template strands), a thermally stable DNA polymerase enzyme, magnesium, buffer, and the four nucleotide building blocks, dATP, dTTP, dCTP, and dGTP; the reaction mixture tube is placed in the aluminum block of a "thermal cycler" capable of ramping the temperature up and down rapidly and accurately for short periods of time, and approximately 30 cycles of DNA replication are permitted to take place; samples of the amplified products are then electrophoresed either by gel or capillary electrophoresis to separate them based on size differences; the amplicons (products of repeated replications) are then scanned by a laser and detected and characterized using gene scanning software (a procedure that can also be performed manually); a comparison is made between alleles present in the exemplar and questioned specimens; and a statistical calculation is made using the product rule to determine the rarity of the overall genetic profile.

DNA quantity is seldom a limiting factor when PCR is performed. DNA profiles can be obtained from hair shafts, fingernail clippings, tiny sweat stains, and dried saliva on postage stamps. The PCR technique is so sensitive that there has been a recent report of a successful DNA analysis from the secretions left by a person's fingerprint. In theory, the DNA within a single cell can yield a complete (13 loci) genetic profile. However, in practice, approximately 1 ng of template DNA is required for optimal amplification. Nevertheless, issues of concern about the use of PCR exist, such as contamination of template DNA with other DNA and the existence of PCR inhibitors. In most cases, inhibitors can be chemically or physically removed from the reaction; however, contamination remains one of the major concerns. Contamination can occur at the crime scene, in transit to the lab, or even in the laboratory. Care must be taken to avoid contamination of evidence with product from a previous PCR amplification, because these small molecules can enter the reaction mixture and become preferentially amplified, resulting in failure to amplify the proper template DNA in a significant amount.

In 1989, the FBI came online handling casework using RFLP analysis. More than two thirds of all DNA cases are sexual assault matters. In such cases, there is often a mixture of genetic material, which poses a problem in the interpretation of results. In 1981, the first paper was published dealing with short tandem repeats (STRs). STRs are loci with core repeat units 3–7 bases long. They exhibit fragment length polymorphism as well as sequence polymorphism. Alleles are designated by the number of core repeats they contain. STRs can be successfully amplified when at least 1 ng of DNA can be isolated. They can be detected by silver-staining or by fluorescent fragment analysis after electrophoretic separation.

## Databases

Databasing began in the United Kingdom when the Forensic Science Service started its DNA database. The FBI launched its combined DNA indexing system (CODIS) of databases in 1998, for which it has adopted 13 STR loci. These loci can be simultaneously amplified (multiplexed) in either one or two amplifications and are also found in the database systems in Europe and South America. The 13 STR loci are CSF1PO, TPOX, THO1, vWA, D16S539, D7S820, D13S317, D5S818, FGA, D3S1358, D8S1179, D18S51, and D2S11. The match probability is in the order of 1 in $6 \times 10^{14}$ and typically provides statistics in the range of 1 in billions to trillions. The CODIS databases consist of an evidentiary database, which contains STR genetic profiles of evidence found at crime scenes, and an offender database, which contains genetic profiles of convicted felons. The use of such databases in the past few years has assisted in the investigations of serious violent crimes and has led to the arrest and conviction of many offenders who would have otherwise escaped justice. In the United States, prosecutors order more than 10,000 DNA tests for criminal cases each year. Many of the findings (one third of rape investigations) lead to exonerations prior to trial. The use of DNA analysis has also resulted in the exoneration of more than 140 convicted felons since 1989.

## Y-STR

Recently, an additional method has become available to study sexual assault evidence, where evidence often consists of mixtures of DNA. Most Y-chromosome STR loci are located on the long arm (q) of the Y chromosome, and the remainder are on the short arm (p). These repeat units are highly polymorphic and inherited in a patrilineal manner. The first Y-STR locus was discovered in 1992 (DYS19), and since then, approximately 73 "micro-satellites" have been identified. Unlike autosomal (non-sex chromosome) STR loci (which exist in pairs), there is no homologous (matching) chromosome for the Y chromosome, and therefore, the observed alleles at the various Y-STR sites constitute a pattern known as a haplotype. Some laboratories are developing multiplex kits in which many such loci can be simultaneously amplified and identified. A minimal haplotype set, which requires a single multiplex amplification, contains DYS19, DYS389 I and II, DYS390, DYS391, DYS392, DYS393, and DYS385 I and II. An extended haplotype set consists of all of these plus YCAII a and b. Twenty different loci can now be amplified simultaneously using a new multiplex system (20plex). These loci are DYS19, DYS385 a/b, DYS388, DYS389 I/II, DYS390, DYS391, DYS392, DYS393, YCAII a/b, DYS426, DYS437, DYS438, DYS439, DYS447, DYS448, DYS460, and Y-GATA-H4. Y-STR markers are inherited in a strictly patrilineal manner. Thus, fathers will transmit all Y-chromosome genes to their sons, and sons will pass on these same genes to their male offspring. Molecular anthropologists have studied fathers and sons to determine the geographic origin of mankind and to record population migration patterns throughout our history as a distinct species.

## MITOCHONDRIAL DNA

Mitochondrial DNA is an extranuclear genome consisting of 16,569 nucleotide base pairs. It contains the information for the synthesis of 13 proteins, 22 transfer RNAs, and 2 ribosomal RNAs. The various forms of RNA are used to synthesize proteins within each mitochondrion. Forensic interest has grown in mitochondrial DNA for two reasons. First, each mitochondrial genome contains a region known as the D-loop, or the Control Region, which is highly polymorphic, making it useful for human identification. The high level of polymorphism is due, in part, to errors of mitochondrial DNA replication and mutations that are not repaired. This region contains approximately 1,100 base pairs and is divided into two distinct regions known as hypervariable I (HVI) and hypervariable II (HVII). Second, because there are some 200 or so of these structures within each cell and, on average, each contains 2.2 genomes, then for every nuclear gene, there can be 200 to 400 times as much DNA for each mitochondrial gene. This is helpful when analyzing tissues that have little nuclear DNA, such as hair, especially when there is no root. Although there is little to no usable nuclear DNA within the hair shaft, there is usually ample mitochondrial DNA within a centimeter of hair to successfully develop a profile. The examination of mitochondrial DNA in items such as teeth and bone from unidentified skeletal remains, which are often associated with highly degraded nuclear DNA, can still produce good results because of the high copy number of DNA molecules within these cellular organelles. PCR amplification of the HVI and HVII regions is followed by sequencing of their products, and subsequently comparing these sequences to a reference (Anderson or Cambridge) sequence. Mitochondrial DNA is inherited matrilineally, so that its genes are passed from mother to daughters and sons. However, only daughters continue to pass their mitochondrial DNA along to the next generation.

*Overview*

There is no question that since the introduction of DNA in a criminal case in Orlando, Florida, in 1987, its use has changed the nature of investigation and evidence. It has played an important role in determining both innocence and guilt. In many respects, DNA has been a victim of its own success. The growing reliance on DNA testing of evidence, particularly for rape, has overburdened crime labs throughout the country.

*Lawrence Kobilinsky*

*For Further Reading*

Watson, J., & Berry, A. (2003). *DNA: The secret life.* New York: Knopf.

Watson, J., & Crick, F. (1953). Molecular structure of nucleic acids. *Nature, 171,* 737–738.

http://www.genome.gov/Pages/Education/Kit/main.cfm

Kobilisky, L., Liotti, T. F., & Deser-Sweat, J. (2005). DNA: Forensic and legal applications. New Jersey: Wiley and Sons.

## ൭ DOCUMENT EXAMINERS

Forensic document examination is one of the oldest disciplines in forensic science. There are references to forgery experts in Roman times. The forensic document examiner examines questioned documents to determine how, when, and by whom they were prepared. The questioned document examination can involve determining authorship of documents; identifying forgeries; determining the age of documents; deciphering obliterated, erased, mutilated, or charred documents; or answering any other questions that may be raised about a document.

The forensic document examiner should not be confused with the graphologist or graphoanalyst. The forensic document examiner uses scientific techniques to determine the genuineness of handwriting by comparison of details in the known and the questioned writing. The graphologist tries to determine the character and personality of the writer by the general formation of the letters. Graphology is more of an art form and has not received acceptance in the scientific community or the courts.

No instrument has been used more often in a crime than pen and paper. Documents play a role in every type of crime, from homicide to threatening letters. There does not seem to be any crime or civil dispute in which some kind of document evidence may not play a role. Terrorists and serial killers write letters to the police and press, as in the Son of Sam and Unabomber cases. Bank robbers use notes to rob banks. In today's society, with checks, credit cards, and all types of records, it is almost impossible for anyone not to sign something or use paper in his or her daily activities.

Most of the work of the forensic document examiner involves the identification of handwriting or determining the authorship of a signature. An individual develops a habit in the way that he or she writes or signs his or her name. It is this habit that the examiner tries to determine in the examination of a questioned document. Although general similarities exist in the writing of people who were taught a given handwriting system in school, each person develops his or her own individual characteristics in the way that he or she forms each letter and puts writing on the paper. It is these individual characteristics that the examiner is looking for to make his or her determination.

The results obtained in a handwriting examination are dependent on and directly related to the quality of the questioned document and known writing examples submitted for examination. If available, original documents should be submitted rather than copies.

There are two types of known writing. One is handwriting written in the normal course of business writing, such as letters, checks, reports, records, applications, and so on. A signature alone cannot meet the examiner's needs for comparable material. The forensic document examiner making a comparison must use the same letters and letter combinations to compare the known and questioned writing.

The second class of writing is *request writing,* in which individuals prepare known standards at the request of an investigator. In obtaining these types of standards, the investigator should endeavor to put the individual at ease and tell him or her to write naturally. The circumstances under which the questioned writing was made should be duplicated as nearly as possible. The individual should not be allowed to see the questioned documents. The content of the questioned writing should be dictated word for word. If the individual asks about arrangement, spelling, or punctuation, he or she should be advised to use his or her own judgment. A single piece of paper should be used for each sample. It should be similar to paper of the questioned writing. If the questioned writing is a check, a blank check or a piece of paper the size of the check with lines to match should be used. If the questioned material is on lined paper, then the standards should be submitted on the same kind of lined paper. The same type of writing instrument (ballpoint pen, pencil, fiber tip pen, etc.) should be used. The practice of having the individual write the name a

number of times on the same piece of paper has limited value. It should go without saying that if the questioned material is hand printed, then the standards should be hand printed. If the questioned material is script, then the standards should be written in script. Several standards should be taken, removing the previous ones from the view of the writer. This will prevent the writer from copying the previous ones if he or she is trying to use a disguised rewriting style. It is a good practice to talk to the writer about something else between standards. This makes it harder for him or her to remember what disguise he or she is using. If there are indications that the person may be trying to disguise his or her writing or that a disguise was used in the questioned material, the individual should also be requested to write with his or her other hand. When the questioned writing is a signature, at least 20 separate specimens of the signature should be taken. In letter cases, two or three pages of the specimen, along with specimens of the envelope, should be obtained. In all cases, but particularly in forgery and anonymous letter cases, standards should be obtained from the complainant. In forgery cases, it is necessary to show that the questioned signature is a forgery, and the type of forgery. In letter cases, the complainant is occasionally found to be the author of the anonymous letter.

In other types of document problems, such as paper comparison, ink analysis, erasures, and indented writing, the original document must be submitted. By using infrared photographic techniques, the examiner can show that two different inks were used on a document. Using chemical analysis, it may be possible to identify the make of the pen used and the date that it was first produced. Using a watermark in paper, the examiner may be able to identify the maker of the paper and when it was produced. Impressions in paper can be visualized using oblique light or ESDA (Electrostatic Detection Apparatus). Sometimes, these impressions may be visualized more than 60 years later. With modern analytical and image processing techniques, the examiner can tell much about how and when a document was produced.

*James J. Horan*

*For Further Reading*

Dines, J. (1998). *Document examiner handbook.* New York: Pantex.

Ellen, D. (1997). *The scientific examination of documents: Methods and techniques.* London: Taylor & Francis.

Federal Bureau of Investigation. (1987). *They write their own sentences: The FBI handwriting analysis manual.* Boulder, CO: Paladin.

Hilton, O. (1992). *Scientific examination of questioned documents.* Boca Raton, FL: CRC Press.

Nickell, J. (1996). *Detecting forgery: Forensic investigation of documents.* Lexington: University Press of Kentucky.

Smith, E. (1984). *Principles of forensic handwriting identification and testimony.* Springfield, IL: Charles C Thomas.

http://www.asqde.org/

## ৩৩ DOMESTIC VIOLENCE ENFORCEMENT

Until the early 20th century, what we currently describe as domestic violence was not considered a crime. Before the modern era, women were considered the property of their husbands. Although there are few records of spousal abuse during this time period, the prevailing views on the status of women most likely point not to a lack of abuse, but rather a societal acceptance of the practice, especially by husbands against their wives.

Eventually, all states created criminal or penal codes criminalizing violent crimes, which had previously been enforced by the "common law," handed down by judges. On their face, these statutes neither included nor exempted the cases where the victim of the violent crime was the spouse or intimate partner of the perpetrator. However, although public acquiescence for intimate violence may have declined by the middle of the 20th century, application of these statutes in situations of domestic violence was blocked by official and unofficial policies of nonintervention in "family matters." The result of this hands-off approach manifested itself through low prioritization of domestic calls for police assistance; indifference and even hostility to victims by law enforcement; and encouragement to "work things out" and refusal to arrest spouses or intimate partners, even in cases where serious violence and injury were present.

Law enforcement policy and practice began to change in the 1970s through the efforts of the women's movement and successful lawsuits against the police for failure to protect victims of domestic violence. In perhaps the most widely known of these cases, *Thurman v. City of Torrington* (1984), the plaintiff had requested police assistance on numerous occasions in response to violent battering by her husband. Police refused to arrest him until, finally, he stabbed her numerous times.

Although the general laws prohibiting violent crimes did not include any exception based on the relationship of the parties, the empirical evidence pointed to a lack of enforcement of these laws in domestic situations and highlighted the need for specific legislation to address the problem. Since the 1970s, a wide range of programs has been implemented that affects the police, prosecutors, and the judiciary. In law enforcement, recent developments include the creation of domestic violence as a distinct crime with special requirements upon arrest and conviction; the expansion of arrest powers of police in domestic violence situations; the enactment of mandatory or pro-arrest policies; the establishment of "no-drop" policies by prosecutors; the creation of specialized domestic violence units at all levels of the system; mandatory law enforcement training in domestic violence; and victim assistance, including address confidentiality, counseling, and shelters.

Every state and the District of Columbia have enacted some type of legislation defining domestic violence as a distinct crime. Although these statutes have differences, certain generalizations may be made. First, the conduct is already prohibited by the criminal law. Generally, domestic violence includes the misdemeanor crimes of assault and battery and the felony crimes of aggravated assault, aggravated battery, rape, kidnapping, and homicide. The domestic violence statutes apply when the victim and defendant have a particular relationship. Although domestic violence is commonly understood to apply to a spousal relationship, this is but one of many relationships included in these statutes. The statutes are gender neutral, recognizing the situations where either a male or a female is the batterer (although the overwhelming majority of intimate violence reported is perpetrated by men against their wives or partners). The statutes, although slightly different from state to state, also generally include nonmarried intimates, sometimes limited to cohabiting intimates or those who share a child together. Some statutes also explicitly include former spouses, fiancées, or dating partners. The expansion of the relationship list allows application to same-sex couples who would likely be excluded were the statutes to require a valid marriage or biological children. Many of these statutes cover even broader territory, including violence between brothers and sisters, children and parents, even aunts and uncles, usually with the requirement that the victim and defendant live together as a family. Many domestic violence statutes also provide for mechanisms for the issuance of restraining orders against domestic violence and criminalization of the violation of such orders.

In almost all jurisdictions, absent exigent circumstances, police officers may generally make a warrantless arrest upon probable cause in the belief that a felony has been committed. In the past, they were not able to arrest for a misdemeanor unless it took place in their presence. This limitation caused problems in the domestic violence setting because the overwhelming majority of the crimes occur within the privacy of the home. Recognizing the hidden and often escalating nature of domestic violence, as well as the high rate of recidivism, every state and the District of Columbia now authorize a police officer to make a warrantless arrest upon probable cause that an act of domestic violence has been committed, even if it is a misdemeanor, whether or not it occurred in the officer's presence.

There are specific concerns when it comes to handling misdemeanor offenses. When domestic violence occurs that causes serious bodily harm or death, it is usually taken seriously by police, prosecutors, judges, and juries regardless of the relationship of the parties. However, when the violence does not cause serious injury, even where the law conclusively provides that a crime has occurred, enforcement can be severely hampered by lingering police reluctance to intervene.

To address this problem, many states have expanded their arrest policies by not only permitting warrantless arrests for misdemeanor domestic violence, but explicitly encouraging or even mandating arrests. These policies may be contained in state legislation or local police departments.

Another component of these pro-arrest policies recognizes that, by the time the police arrive, the victim may prefer, or even insist, that the defendant not be arrested. The cyclical nature of domestic violence may be at work whereby the defendant has apologized or the victim has decided or been convinced that he or she deserved it. Victims may also be fearful of retaliation if they support arrest.

The effectiveness of mandatory arrest policies in reducing recidivism has been controversial. Although initially heralded as a deterrent based on the results of a study conducted in the mid-1980s, replication studies failed to produce consistent data that the arrest of the defendant, as compared with mediation on the scene or leaving for the night, decreases the risk of repeat violence. These studies did, however, consistently show that arrest acts as a deterrent for those defendants who have more to lose, such as the employed. It also has clear benefits for the victim, who actually uses the arrest as an opportunity to leave the violent relationship, or who is amenable to support or counseling. Arrest, however, does sometimes lead to an increase in violence. The experiments comparing recidivism rates between defendants arrested for misdemeanor domestic violence and those not arrested have not proven that arrest is either a consistent deterrent or an incitement to future violence.

Domestic violence statutes often explicitly address the situation where both parties have acted violently toward one other. In these situations, dual arrests are often discouraged. Ideally, officers are given guidelines to help determine the primary aggressor. These guidelines often allow the history of violence in the relationship to be used as a determining factor to differentiate between the initial aggressor and the primary aggressor. When the primary aggressor cannot be identified, the officer must choose to arrest both or neither party. If both parties are arrested, both cases are usually dismissed by the prosecutor unless additional evidence shows a clear primary aggressor. Even in those cases, the arrest of the victim by the police generally provides sufficient reasonable doubt to make a conviction of either party unlikely.

When an arrest is made, some jurisdictions provide special guidelines regarding bail and pretrial release to ensure the safety of the victim. These jurisdictions prohibit the defendant from paying a standard bail and getting out of jail before presentment to a judge. They require individualized bail determinations and, in some cases, a mandatory "no contact" or "stay away" order until the case is resolved. This procedure makes contact with the victim a violation of pretrial release, contempt of court, and sometimes a misdemeanor criminal act, unless the victim appears in court and gives good cause, under oath, for the judge to allow nonviolent contact while the case is pending.

When prosecuting domestic violence cases, some victims do not cooperate. Traditionally, if the crime is not serious and the defendant is not dangerous, the victim of a misdemeanor may sign a document requesting nonprosecution of the case, and the prosecutor will dismiss the charges. However, recognizing the particular nature and seriousness of domestic violence, the dynamics of an abusive relationship, the psychological pressures on the victim, and the rate of repeat and escalating violence, many prosecutors have instituted "no drop" policies in domestic violence cases. This does not mean that all domestic violence cases are prosecuted. However, the victim's unwillingness to cooperate, unless it makes the case impossible to prove or calls into question the commission of the crime, will not affect the decision to file and maintain charges. In fact, because of the admissibility of emotional victim statements to emergency personnel under the rules of evidence, and the increasing likelihood that police provide photographs of the victim and the defendant on the scene, a conviction often can be obtained even with no victim participation.

The last stage of domestic violence enforcement involves sentencing. Many jurisdictions require anger management, substance abuse and/or mental health counseling, and minimum probation terms for domestic violence misdemeanor convictions. A conviction for domestic violence may also have adverse effects on a defendant's immigration status; affect sentencing for later crimes under sentencing guidelines that often put heavy weight on domestic violence convictions; and affect other rights, such as the ability to legally purchase a firearm. The federal restriction on firearms is particularly problematic for police, who are required to carry a firearm in the course of their work. Officers who are convicted of domestic violence are often dismissed. Another complication that occurs is that their victims can be reluctant to report the crime to police.

The U.S. Congress has responded to the problem of domestic violence enforcement by passing two major legislative packages, commonly referred to as the Violence Against Women Acts, that, among other things, recognize a federal offense of domestic violence; give full faith and credit to domestic violence restraining orders throughout the country; and provide guidance and funding for law enforcement and community training on both domestic violence and victim support, including funding for shelters and special immigration provisions for domestic violence victims who may face deportation if they report domestic violence to the authorities. With the aid of this federal funding, some police departments, prosecutor's offices, and public defender's offices have established specialized units and novel techniques to handle domestic violence cases. Responding officers may bring trained counselors to domestic disturbances for victim support and follow-up on these cases. Prosecutors also employ counselors to establish and maintain contact with victims and provide services such as financial aid, shelter, and counseling. In addition, some jurisdictions have established separate domestic violence courts.

Although the criminal justice system has improved its handling of domestic violence, it continues to be a significant problem. In 1998, for example, the Department of Justice reported that approximately 900,000 women and 160,000 men were victims of violence at the hands of their spouses or intimate partners.

*Rachel A. Kessler*

*For Further Reading*

Buzawa, E. S., & Buzawa, C. G. (Eds.). (1992). *Domestic violence: The changing criminal justice response.* Westport, CT: Auburn House.

Chestnut, S. (2001). Poverty: A symposium: The practice of dual arrests in domestic violence situations: Does it accomplish anything? *Mississippi Law Journal, 70,* 971.

Developments in the law: Legal responses to domestic violence. (1993). *Harvard Law Review, 106,* 1498–1574.

Jarvis, R. T. (2001). Symposium on integrating responses to domestic violence: A proposal for a model domestic violence protocol. *Loyola Law Review, 47,* 513.

Niemi-Kiesilainen, J. (2001). The deterrent effect of arrest in domestic violence: Differentiating between victim and perpetrator response. *Hasting's Women's Law Journal, 12,* 283.

Rehnson, C. M., & Welchans, S. (Eds.). (2000). Intimate partner violence. *United States Department of Justice, Bureau of Justice Statistics Special Report.* Available: http://www.ojp.usdoj.gov/bjs

Sherman, L., & Berk, R. A. (1984, April). The Minneapolis domestic violence experiment. *Police Foundation Report,* p. 1.

Thurman v. City of Torrington, 595 F.Supp. 1521 (D. Conn. 1984).

Violence Against Women Act of 1994. Pub. L. No. 103-322, 108 Stat. 1796.

Violence Against Women Act of 2000. Pub. L. No.106-386, 114 Stat. 7491.

For examples of legislation covering the policies discussed above, see, for example, Florida Statutes (2002) §741.28 (listing definitions of domestic violence); §741.28-29 and §901.15 [addressing policies for (nonmandatory) arrest and investigation by police]; §741.2901, §941.041, and §741.2902 (addressing pretrial release and policies for judiciary); §741.31 (discussing violations of restraining orders); §790.06 (addressing firearm licensing); and §960.192 (providing for victim assistance). An example of a mandatory arrest statute is D.C. Code §16-1031 (2002).

# ᴇᴏ DRUG ENFORCEMENT IN THE UNITED STATES

The enforcement of drug laws represents one of the major components of American law enforcement. Although drug enforcement has been a function of law enforcement since the early part of the 20th century, it gained considerable momentum in the mid-1970s when drug abuse began to soar and federal money for training, education, and equipment was made available to police agencies to address the problem.

Federal, state, and local law enforcement agencies share responsibility for most of the nation's drug enforcement efforts. When these entities combine their efforts, they primarily deal with the supply side of the nation's drug abuse problem. In 1973, the federal Drug Enforcement Administration (DEA) was formed to restrict the supply of controlled substances through coordination with state and local agencies. Today, the DEA remains the lead federal drug enforcement agency and has nearly 3,000 agents. In 1983, the Controlled Substances Act gave the Federal Bureau of Investigation (FBI) concurrent jurisdiction with the DEA for domestic drug enforcement, although the FBI has decreased its drug enforcement activities in the aftermath of the September 11, 2001, terrorist attacks. Along with the DEA and FBI, numerous other agencies are involved in the drug suppression effort. Many of these agencies are housed within the newly formed Office of Homeland Security and include the Immigration and Naturalization Service, U.S. Customs, U.S. Coast Guard, and U.S. Border Patrol. A number of other federal agencies are also involved in the antidrug effort and attempt to work together in sharing information on known or suspected drug traffickers.

Most arrests for drug law violations, however, take place at the local and state level and often focus on the demand side of the drug problem. In 2002, local law enforcement agencies made more than 1.5 million arrests for drug abuse violations. Many local and most state police organizations have some component dedicated to the suppression of illegal drugs. In general, the goals of local police with regard to illegal drug activity are as follows:

1. Reduce the gang violence associated with the illegal drug trade.

2. Control the street crimes committed by illegal drug users.

3. Improve the quality of life in communities plagued by illegal drug use.

4. Deter users, especially minors, from taking illegal drugs.

In an effort to accomplish these goals, law enforcement tactics such as crackdowns, raids, and surveillance operations are used. In many localities, concerted police activity has had a marked impact on drug abuse. For example, Tampa, Florida, has a Quick Uniformed Action Against Drugs (QUAD) program where police constantly pressure sellers to change their sales venues and pose as buyers in "reverse sting" operations to confiscate illegal drugs. Six months after QUAD was initiated, street-corner drug dealing had been virtually eliminated in the targeted areas.

There is evidence, however, that drug dealers have begun to adjust to aggressive police tactics. In New York City, for example, dealers have responded to reverse sting operations by moving their transactions from street corners into apartment buildings. Within the confines of a closed space, the sellers frisk potential buyers to make sure they are not wearing a bulletproof vest or a hidden transmitter. New York undercover officers have also reported an increase in "forced ingestions," in which the dealers force buyers to sample the drugs before finishing the deal.

Recognizing that local police agencies are often restricted by a lack of resources, the federal government has increased its funding for local supply-side enforcement over the past 20 years. For example, in 1986, Congress established the Edward Byrne Memorial State and Local Law Enforcement Assistance Program, named after a New York City police officer who was shot during a drug arrest. Recipients of Byrne grants must use the funds specifically on programs or technology designed to enforce drug laws. The changing priorities for a number of federal law enforcement funding mechanisms that are now concentrating on antiterrorism activities could diminish support for local antidrug programs. Local law enforcement agencies still routinely team up with federal agencies to form task forces, usually with a specific focus and defined duration. Many police and sheriffs also participate in asset forfeiture programs that help fund local antidrug measures and other related initiatives.

The Office of National Drug Control Policy also supports local law enforcement by funding high-intensity drug trafficking areas (HIDTAs). A HIDTA is an area that has been designated as a primary entry point for illicit drugs into the United States, a primary distribution center for drugs, or a high-density manufacturing site for a specific drug. Within the HIDTA, law enforcement agents from various state, county, and city narcotics units combine their resources to form a multi-jurisdictional drug task force. Twenty HIDTAs are currently operational in nine states, including one that covers Puerto Rico and the U.S. Virgin Islands.

Judging the success of current drug enforcement policies varies depending upon the research. For example, a recent study of homicides in New York offers the following breakdown of drug-related murders: They were overwhelmingly the result of the drug trade (74%), and not of someone acting violently while under the influence of drugs nor of someone killing to get the money to purchase drugs. Such data raise a central question about the nation's current illegal drug policy: Do drug laws cause more harm than illegal drugs?

Critics of American drug policy believe the answer is yes, that the "cure" of drug enforcement is worse than the decrease in drug use it accomplishes. A number of reasons have been cited for this position:

- The drug trade has created opportunities for black markets to flourish, which has greatly benefitted organized crime. By keeping the prices of illegal drugs higher than they would be otherwise, law enforcement has provided a "subsidy" for drug dealers.
- The enormous profits have made corruption of law enforcement officials inevitable.
- Because the quality of illegal drugs is not regulated, consumers face risks of medical complications from poorly manufactured drugs.
- Drugs are expensive not because of their production costs, but because of their illegality. For example, heroin is approximately 100 times more expensive and cocaine 20 times more expensive than they would be if drugs were legal. Consequently, users commit property crimes to obtain the funds necessary to purchase the drugs.

It is very difficult to measure the success of drug enforcement efforts. After all, neither the sellers nor the buyers are eager to report their activities to police agencies. As a result, drug enforcement authorities are not certain of the total amount of drugs being manufactured and sold, and they can only guess as to the overall effect of their efforts. There is, however, one way to gauge these efforts: the price of illegal drugs on the street. This measurement is based on two assumptions:

1. If law enforcement agents are successful in incapacitating those who grow, refine, transport, and sell drugs, the amount of drugs available should drop. When the supply of a resource that many people want—whether it be diamonds, baseball cards, or drugs—decreases, the price should rise.

2. When authorities seize drugs, destroy the means of manufacturing and distribution by arresting those in the drug business, and confiscate equipment, drug lords must then use additional resources to rebuild their operations. If it becomes more expensive to distribute drugs, the dealers will pass on these costs to their customers, and the price should rise.

Overall, the American public is supportive of drug enforcement practices, but many questions remain about the effectiveness of these efforts. The drug enforcement function poses considerable danger to undercover agents, costs a considerable amount of money to fund year after year, and represents a significant drain on available police resources.

*Michael D. Lyman*

*For Further Reading*

Lyman, M. (2001). *Practical drug enforcement.* Boca Raton, FL: CRC Press.

Manski, C. (2003). Credible research practices to inform drug law enforcement. *Criminology & Public Policy, 2*(3), 543–555.

Manski, C., Pepper, V., & Petrie, C. (Eds.). (2001). *Informing America's policy on illegal drugs: What we don't know keeps hurting us.* Washington, DC: National Academies Press.

Nagin, D. (2003). Drug law enforcement. *Criminology & Public Policy, 2*(3), 541–542.

The President's National Drug Control Strategy. (2004). Washington, DC: Office of National Drug Control Policy.

U.S. Drug Enforcement Administration. (n.d.). *Major operations.* Available: http://www.usdoj.gov/dea/major/major.htm

# ᘓᘎ DRUG POLICY AND LEGISLATION

Although much of the public debate surrounding drug policy occurs at the federal level, many important decisions are made at the state and local levels. Local and state narcotics control within the United States emerged in the latter part of the 1800s, originating in those communities directly threatened by drugs such as morphine, opium, and cocaine. A current trend in drug policy involves a growing shift of responsibility from the federal level to the state and local levels. This is plainly seen in the area of enforcement where local police make the preponderance of arrests. Increasingly, states and localities are also assuming larger roles in the funding and implementation of social programs used to combat drug abuse. Both federal and state drug laws typically involve the use of mandatory sentencing. On the state level, laws can vary in severity and change from time to time.

The earliest semblance of local and state narcotics control began during the mid-to late 1800s in those communities directly affected by such substances. In 1860, Pennsylvania, home to leading morphine manufacturers, passed an antimorphine law. Despite early laws prohibiting certain substances, widespread illegalization of drugs did not emerge until the early 1900s. Early antidrug legislation developed to protect the citizenry from "quack" medicines. Although not necessarily hazardous to citizens' health, many of these alleged medications contained high levels of narcotics and alcohol while not possessing the healing properties purported.

In the beginning of the 20th century, physicians developed a clearer understanding of the long-term effects of substances formerly recommended to the general public for common consumption. Although the medical community began to advise against the use of substances such as cocaine, morphine, and heroin, these drugs continued to be peddled by an unregulated patent medicine industry. Between 1901 and 1903, the efforts of the American Pharmaceutical Association prompted states to increase their control of opiates and cocaine.

Local laws met with criticism for disparity regarding their severity. Whereas the complexity and all-inclusiveness of some laws rendered the enforcement of their stipulations nearly futile, others contained loopholes permitting the continued sale of patent medications containing narcotics. By 1905, the Proprietary Association of America, composed of leading manufacturers, condoned strict limitations regarding the amount of narcotics contained in over-the-counter medications. Initially, manufacturers did not divulge the narcotic and alcohol contents contained in their products. In fact, many manufacturers denied the obvious presence of such substances. The 1906 Federal Pure Food and Drug Act mandated that all manufacturers must specify the proportions of alcohol, narcotics, and numerous other substances used in the preparation of the medication. This legislation precipitated the decline of the patent medicine industry.

Today, drug policy encompasses an array of issues more commonly addressed at the state and local levels. States and localities are assuming increasing levels of responsibility in terms of drug policy. Many of the critical decisions concerning drug policy, including enforcement and budgetary decisions, are made beneath the federal level. Increasingly, states and localities are accountable for funding and implementing social programs to combat drug abuse. Funding allocations for law enforcement, drug prevention, drug treatment, job training, health care, mental health programs, and community-based programs are largely determined at the state and local level. One source of funding for drug enforcement and prevention is from asset forfeiture, whereby criminal assets are seized and used by law enforcement and other governmental agencies, such as education, to bolster their efforts in combating drug use.

Drug policy development at state and local levels enables responses that consider distinct local needs and concerns. Community demographics,

such as varying socioeconomic levels and cultural differences, are better addressed when policy emerges from local levels. Policy decided at the state, rather than the federal, level often yields more productive reform because of lessened political and social complexities. At the lower levels, increased opportunities for change and easier political mobilization occur. Perhaps because of grassroots movements, motivation for policy reform appears much stronger at the state level. In addition, policy choices are more immediately evidenced when they occur at the local level.

A growing majority of community members tend to prefer treatment to punishment of drug offenders. Research implicates treatment as being more cost-effective in reducing addictions, drug-related offenses, and health care expenditures. Prevention appears promising in terms of increasing protective factors, such as active involvement in community and religious organizations, while reducing risk factors, including parental substance abuse, that are associated with drug use. Although there is growing popularity in the use of treatment, rather than incarceration, as a means of dealing with drug abuse, both federal- and state-level budgets allocate minimal funds for such services, instead focusing the majority of antidrug funds on police and prisons. For those neighborhoods where drug dealing is associated with high levels of violence and intimidation, residents typically seek a police response.

The focal point of substance abuse prevention tends to be in schools. The primary source of funding for school-based prevention programs is the federal government's Safe and Drug Free Schools and Communities (SDFSC) program. SDFSC revenues far exceed state spending on school-based drug prevention. SDFSC provides $550 million in funding compared to the $80 million disbursed by states. Federal lawmakers have made several attempts to merge SDFSC with other education programs, the goal being the emergence of one large block grant for states. A grant of this caliber would enable states to determine the amount of federal money that would be used on education, including drug and violence prevention programs. Critics argue that the absence of a specific allowance for school-based drug prevention will result in the disappearance of such programs.

Although recent trends in drug policy tend to reflect an increasing community preference for drug treatment, a law enforcement paradigm has dominated state drug control policy for the past two decades. A key term associated with this law-and-order approach is mandatory minimum sentencing. Most states have some form of mandatory minimums. In the 1990s, states increased mandatory minimum penalties when sentencing for drug offenses such as the sale of drugs to minors and drug sales made in close proximity to schools. Proponents of this policy note that mandatory minimum sentences reduce the wide variation in sentences for similar crimes. For example, in the 1970s, sentencing for the possession of a small amount of marijuana could bring almost a life sentence in one state or a 1-year sentence in another. Mandatory minimum sentencing is typically blamed for the dramatic increase in incarceration rates across the country. Legislators are reluctant to repeal such laws for fear of appearing too soft on crime.

New York State's infamous 1973 Rockefeller drug laws have drawn considerable debate over their punitiveness. These laws have provided New York State with its core weapon in the war on drugs for the past 30 years. Based on the premise that severe and certain punishment will deter and lessen drug use and drug-related offending, the New York legislature decided to impose long and typically mandatory sentences for possession and distribution of controlled substances. Under the Rockefeller laws, drug offenses are rated in terms of the dangerousness and quantity of the drug involved. Ascertainment of the drug's dangerousness is based on detailed schedules of controlled substances. Dangerousness is also determined by objective criteria, including the potential for abuse. The greater the quantity of the drug involved, the longer the sentence.

Statutes such as the Rockefeller drug laws invite substantial criticism. The harsh sentences arising from such drug policies are often viewed as too severe for low-level offenders. Mandatory sentencing disables judicial discretion in considering an offender's character and the circumstances of the offense. Such laws are criticized as being ineffective in deterring drug use. The threat of prison appears to be insufficient in changing the drug-using behavior of those whose drug use is an integral part of their lives. Here, the argument for treatment, rather than punishment, appears more valid. The state of New York, however, does not make drug treatment programs readily accessible to those in need. Other criticisms of such laws include the extreme expense of increasing incarceration rates, problems presented by prison overcrowding, and disproportionate effects on minorities. In spite of these marked critiques, reform legislation has not occurred.

It is important to note that sometimes, state laws are in conflict with federal laws that supercede them. For example, it is illegal, as mentioned above, to possess any amount of marijuana anywhere in the United States, yet some localities have enacted medical marijuana laws that permit its use by those who can demonstrate a medical need verified by a physician. Penalties for marijuana can range from a fine, to probation, to life without parole. In 2002, approximately 700,000 people were arrested for violating the marijuana law, more than were arrested for other drugs, such as heroin and cocaine. Those in favor of reforming the country's marijuana policy point to Europe and Canada, where marijuana is moving toward policies that decriminalize this substance. Critics also maintain that law enforcement efforts would be better directed at drugs that are more harmful and dangerous, such as methamphetamine.

The ingredients and process used to manufacture methamphetamine are so toxic and flammable that officers may require hazardous material gear when investigating "meth labs," as they have been called. Labs have been known to explode, and the premises where the drug has been made are often dealt with as toxic waste sites. One of the ways localities have tried to control this drug is to increase penalties for the sale of the drug's ingredients, which are contained in other legal substances, such as cold medicine. Another way is to limit the sale of these otherwise legal substances. For example, in 2004,

Oklahoma stopped the sale of many over-the-counter cold medications in tablet form.

*Christine Ivie Edge*

*See also* Asset Forfeiture, State; Drug Enforcement in the United States; Drug Prevention Education

### For Further Reading

Drug Strategies. (2001). *Critical choices: Making drug policy at the state level.* Chicago: John D. and Catherine T. MacArthur Foundation.

Herman, S. (2000). Measuring culpability by measuring drugs? Three reasons to reevaluate the Rockerfeller Drug Laws. *Albany Law Review, 63,* 777–798.

Inciardi, J. (2002). *The war on drugs III: The continuing saga of the mysteries and miseries of intoxication, addiction, crime, and public policy.* Boston: Allyn & Bacon.

Leven, D. (2000). Our drug laws have failed—so where is the desperately needed meaningful reform? *Fordham Urban Law Journal, 28,* 293–306.

Musto, D. (1999). *The American disease: Origins of narcotic control* (3rd ed.). New York: Oxford University Press.

## ❦ DRUG PREVENTION EDUCATION

Most drug prevention education in America is geared to young people. This is the group most likely to experiment with drugs under the influence of peers. According to *Monitoring the Future,* a national survey that measures drug use among young people each year, 2002 showed the first significant drop in drug use among youth in nearly a decade, with reductions noted among 8th, 10th, and 12th graders. Levels of use for some drugs are now lower than they have been for almost 30 years. Such declines are unusual, and their underlying causes remain unclear. The same survey does show, however, that some drug use among 12th graders, for example, has remained above 40% since 1996, up from 29.4% in 1991. These statistics bring into question whether the comprehensive measures being taken to reduce youth drug use, including drug prevention education programs, are having the desired effect.

Drug prevention education programs are aimed at reducing the risk factors that promote abuse and building protective factors. These programs aim to deliver information, education, and harm-reduction strategies through a variety of media: school-based education programs, television campaigns, billboards, logos, newspaper advertisements, and so forth. Some police departments also disseminate drug prevention information. The government allocates billions of dollars each year to such programs. For example, for 2003, the budget for the Safe and Drug Free Schools program was $694 million; for the Drug-Free Communities Program, $70 million; for the National Youth Anti-Drug Media Campaign, $170 million; and for the Parents Drug Corps Program, $5 million (White House Report, 2003).

There are many national, state, and local drug prevention education initiatives, all aimed at preventing illicit drug use. The following are some of the national-level programs:

- *Boys and Girls Clubs of America:* This program seeks to instill a sense of competence, usefulness, and belonging among young people. The program areas include education, health, arts, careers, leadership development, and athletics. The program includes elements designed to prevent pregnancy, alcohol/drug abuse, and involvement in gangs.

- *Drug Abuse Resistance Education (DARE):* In this school-based program, uniformed police officers teach youth and parents about the dangers of substance abuse. The program derives from the social skills/social influence model of drug education. Although this program was highly popular among police departments when it was first introduced, in recent years a number of law enforcement agencies have dropped the program because its effectiveness still remains in question and because reductions in police budgets have warranted changing priorities.

- *Drug-Free Communities Support Program:* This program assists community-based efforts to reduce youth abuse of alcohol, tobacco, illicit drugs, and inhalants. The program enables community coalitions to strengthen their coordination efforts, encourage citizen participation in substance abuse reduction efforts, and disseminate information about effective programs.

- *Gang Resistance Education and Training (GREAT):* This program provides a wide range of structured, community-based activities and classroom instruction for school-aged children. Certified/sworn, uniformed police officers and federal agents teach youth about the consequences of gang involvement, including violence and drug abuse.

- *Juvenile Mentoring Program (JUMP):* This program supports one-to-one mentoring programs for youth at risk of dropping out of school and becoming involved in delinquency, including gang activity and drug abuse.

- *National Youth Anti-Drug Media Campaign:* This is a multidimensional effort designed to educate and empower youth to reject illicit drugs. The campaign attempts to reach Americans wherever they live, learn, work, play, and pray. It makes use of television, radio, online and print advertising, school-based educational materials, Web sites, and partnerships with civic and faith service organizations.

- *Office of National Drug Control Program's Athletic Initiative:* The Athletic Initiative uses sports as a vehicle to help prevent young people from turning to drugs.

- *Safe and Drug-Free Schools:* This program is designed to prevent violence in and around schools, and to strengthen programs that prevent the illegal use of alcohol, tobacco, and drugs. Program elements involve parents and are coordinated with related federal, state, and community efforts and resources.

- *Strengthening America's Families:* These "best practice" programs are provided by the Office of Juvenile Justice and Delinquency Prevention in collaboration with the Center for Substance Abuse Prevention. The programs aim to strengthen families by working with parents and caregivers, and at least one target child, to reduce risk factors and increase protective factors for problem behavior.

- *Your Time–Their Future:* The Positive Activities Campaign is a national public education campaign developed by the U.S. Department of Health and Human Services. It encourages adults to become involved in volunteering, mentoring, and other efforts that help young people (ages 7–14) participate in positive activities and develop skills that build self-discipline and competence. It is expected that, as a result, the young people will avoid alcohol, tobacco, and illicit drugs.

- *Girl Power:* This is a national public education program sponsored by the U.S. Department of Health and Human Services. It is designed to encourage and motivate 9- to 14-year-old girls to make the most of their lives. It seeks to reinforce and sustain positive values by targeting health messages to the unique needs and interests of girls.

- *Reality Check:* This is a nationwide program designed by the Center for Substance Abuse Prevention to educate the public—particularly parents and teens—about the harms and risks associated with marijuana use, and to reduce its social acceptance.

Despite the recent small decline in drug use among youth, there is little evidence that drug prevention education programs work. Many claims are made for their effectiveness, but several literature reviews and meta-analyses of the programs have concluded that most are ineffective in preventing drug use. For example, a recent review of research studies on DARE, the most popular and visible program that has been adopted by many other countries in the world, concludes that it has been unable to show consistent preventive effects on drug use (Rosenbaum & Hanson, 1998). Whatever effects have been found have been small and short-lived, although the program seems to have more beneficial effects for urban than suburban children.

Although drug prevention education can encourage children and youths to think about the adverse consequences of drugs, some have suggested that these programs can also arouse children's interest in using drugs. Whatever the case, it must be accepted that drug education alone cannot bring an end to drug use among young people. At best, it can only supplement the myriad other efforts made by parents and teachers, communities and neighborhoods, employers and health workers, police and social workers, and society at large to protect young people from drug use.

*Mangai Natarajan*

### For Further Reading

Rosenbaum, P. D., & Hanson, S. G. (1998). Assessing the effects of school based drug education: A six year multilevel analysis of Project D.A.R.E. *Journal of Research in Crime and Delinquency, 35*(4), 381–412.

White House Report. (2003). *National drug control strategy 2003*. Washington, DC: U.S. Government Printing Office.

## ✑ DRUG TESTING OF POLICE

Under the provisions of the Fourth Amendment, a search and seizure can only be made with a warrant, or without a warrant based on probable cause or under certain recognized exceptions. It was left to the courts, however, to determine such issues as whether intrusions beyond the body's surface were reasonable searches and whether individuals could expect to be free from bodily intrusions by government employers. Bodily intrusion, typically in the form of urine testing, is the primary method of drug testing employees. The level of reasonableness in these cases is typically addressed by balancing the employees' expectations of privacy against the agency's needs and interests in testing for the use of drugs. When it comes to law enforcement personnel, the issue of drug testing has an additional ethical dimension because police are generally held to a higher standard. By the middle of the 1980s, partly as an outgrowth of the law enforcement focus on drug use, attention was drawn to drug abuse among American workers. This issue was highlighted in a report by the President's Commission on Organized Crime, published in March 1986. This Commission set forth 71 recommendations, among which was a recommendation that all federal employees and other workers submit to drug tests. The Commission recommended that the president direct all federal agencies to develop employee drug abuse policies that would include guidelines for drug testing.

In September 1986, President Reagan signed an executive order directing the head of each executive agency to develop a plan for achieving a drug-free workplace with due consideration of the rights of the government, the employee, and the public. Specifically, the executive order mandated that these plans include the following: (a) policy statements of the agency's expectations and the actions when drug use is identified; (b) employee assistance programs; (c) training for supervisors in identifying and handling illegal drug use by employees;

(d) provisions for self-referrals and supervisory referrals to treatment with maximum respect for individual confidentiality; and (e) provisions for identifying illegal drug users, including drug testing.

In response to this executive order, the U.S. Customs Service developed a drug-testing program for certain employees. This program was challenged and taken to the U.S. Supreme Court. The Court ruled in *National Treasury Employees Union v. Von Raab* (1989) that the U.S. Customs Service's practice of testing current employees without suspicion but who applied for promotions or transfers into certain positions was constitutional. It is important to note that the Court ruled that this testing was a search under the Fourth Amendment, but the public interest outweighed the privacy concerns. The decision by the Court to uphold drug-testing law enforcement employees, even though limited, resulted in many other law enforcement agencies at all levels beginning to drug test employees.

Urine testing has become the method most commonly used by employers for determining drug use by employees and applicants. In the past decade, in response to the general labor pool and a shortage of law enforcement personnel, many police agencies changed their policies to allow applicants some prior use of drugs, although the types of drugs, the number of times they were used, and the timeframe of their use vary widely in departments throughout the country. However, once an individual is employed by an agency, detection of illegal drug use will usually end his or her career. A growing number of police agencies require officers to submit to urinalysis tests to determine illegal drug usage. These testing programs vary in scope from those based on reasonable suspicion to mandatory random tests of all officers.

Although urinalysis tests can indicate recent drug usage, the results of even the most sophisticated tests cannot prove when a drug was taken or how much was used, nor can they prove intoxication or impairment due to consumption. This being the case, an employer's ability to evaluate or predict job performance is consequently limited, which is why indiscriminate drug testing has been considered by some to be unfair.

The fact that many police departments have modified their drug-testing programs several times attests to the evolving nature of the technical and legal issues surrounding urinalysis tests for drugs. Drug-testing programs must balance the agency's need to ensure a drug-free workplace with employees' right to privacy and due process, and protection from unreasonable searches. Police administrators have compelling needs, ethical considerations, and legal obligations to ensure that officers and other employees are not impaired on the job because of drug use and that officers do not break the laws they swore to uphold.

The future of drug testing will probably focus on specific areas of special interest, such as developing new techniques for detecting drug problems, preventing workplace drug abuse, studying employee testing policies, and measuring the effects of drugs on performance. These and other research efforts may result in significant changes in future drug-testing methods.

*Kim Holland and Jeffry T. Walker*

### For Further Reading

De Cresce, R., Lifshitz, M., Mazura, A., & Tilson, J. (1989) *Drug testing in the workplace.* Washington, DC: Bureau of National Affairs.

Manili, B., Connor, E., III, Stephens, D., & Stedman, J. (1987). *Police drug testing.* Washington, DC: National Institute of Justice.

National Treasury Employees Union v. Von Raab, 489 U.S. 656 (1989).

President's Commission on Organized Crime. (1986). *America's habit: Drug abuse, drug trafficking and organized crime.* Washington, DC: U.S. Government Printing Office.

Skinner v. Railway Labor Executive Association, 489 U.S. 602 (1989).

## ✑ DRUG TRAFFICKING

Drug traffickers are typically depicted in Hollywood movies as larger-than-life people whose elaborate schemes move enormous amounts of drugs across international borders. Despite, and sometimes because of, governmental interventions, these kinds of drug traffickers do exist, but from a law enforcement perspective, drug trafficking can refer to almost any act that facilitates the distribution of an illegal substance, from the biggest drug cartels to the smallest "mule" to the lowliest street-level seller.

Our knowledge about upper-level traffickers has been largely confined to first-person accounts written by retired traffickers and descriptions provided by law enforcement agencies such as the Drug Enforcement Administration (www.usdoj.gov/dea/) or the United Nations Office on Drugs and Crime (www.unodc.org). Because of the difficulty of gaining access to upper-level drug traffickers, there has been little academic research on this topic that does not rely upon "official" data sources. There has been, however, a considerable amount of original research on drug trafficking at the lower end of the chain of distribution.

The crack epidemic of the late 1980s and early 1990s, with its accompanying increase in crime, spurred the government and a generation of social scientists to better understand the economics of illegal drugs, particularly trafficking/distribution and the operation of drug markets. Much of the early work in the field was descriptive in nature and involved minimal analysis. For research to be useful, however, many researchers realized that it was not enough to simply describe drug traffickers; it was necessary to identify distinct types of traffickers, explain the structural and functional differences between them, and understand how they change over time. Following the lead of prominent economists who had written about the underground sector of the economy, and illegal markets in particular, drug researchers began to develop more rigorous approaches to examining drug traffickers and distributors. Two broad areas of inquiry were developed (typically, with input from and funding by law enforcement agencies): research that examined the *social organization* of traffickers/distributors, and research that examined the *technical organization* of trafficking/distribution.

Social organization, in this context, refers to issues of cooperation, differential responsibility, and power and authority among traffickers/distributors.

By comparing and contrasting the growing volume of studies that described drug traffickers and their operations, some researchers have postulated that social organization among drug traffickers reflects a continuum of organizational complexity. At the simplest level are those traffickers who work as independent operators, or freelancers—people who have no obligations at either end of the chain of distribution. The risks and rewards of the business are entirely their own, but because they operate alone, their operations tend to be small and comparatively inconsequential vis-à-vis the overall market for illegal drugs. Freelance distributors typically dominate drug markets that are formed whenever a new product is introduced and a solid consumer base has not yet formed.

At the other end of the trafficking spectrum are large, corporate-style organizations that sometimes employ hundreds or thousands of people to perform a wide variety of jobs, and that operate on many of the same principles as corporations in the legal economy. Corporate-style organizations often feature sharp divisions between ownership, management, and labor over their competing interests, especially around the issues of wages and working conditions, and this has been the source of much of the violence associated with this style of distribution. Competition between rival organizations has also generated a great deal of violence, and it is this feature of drug trafficking that has sparked such interest on the part of government and researchers.

At mid-level along the continuum of traffickers is what might be described as *socially bonded* businesses: People who participate in these types of organizations are usually bound together by some feature (or set of features) beyond simply making money. Family ties, for example, are sometimes the basis of some of the most successful drug-trafficking organizations, but other bonds, such as those of religion, ethnicity, and race, can also be effective in cementing loyalty to the organization. Law enforcement organizations have had some success in addressing corporate-style drug-trafficking organizations because they are comparatively easy to infiltrate, and some employees can be persuaded to cooperate, but organizations that are socially bonded have proven much more difficult to eliminate. Ultimately, knowing about how traffickers are organized has helped law enforcement policymakers and professionals devise better interventions.

Technical organization refers to issues such as the physical location(s) of drug trafficking, and the policies, procedures, technology, and equipment employed by traffickers to advance their business. Traditionally, law enforcement has been more interested in these technical aspects of drug trafficking because knowledge about them is more likely to lead to a quick arrest: For example, trafficking routes that are discovered can be shut down quickly, equipment that is used by traffickers—such as "cigarette boats" (boats that are long, narrow, sleek, and travel at high speeds)—can be neutralized by the adoption of superior technology, and so on. The technical organizations of drug trafficking, however, are constantly in rapid flux. For example, in the space of a few years, street-level drug traffickers evolved from the use of lookouts who shout out warnings of police presence to the use of such sophisticated technology as cell phones and two-way radios for the same purpose. Most researchers do not personally collect data on the technical organization of trafficking; they do not go out and locate trafficking routes or identify new kinds of boats used by smugglers, but advances in information technology (e.g., crime mapping) has enabled them to assist in targeting more effectively those law enforcement resources aimed at drug interdiction.

New distributors enter the market with regularity; some use well-worn methods of selling drugs, whereas others introduce new wrinkles to the drug business. Distributors also learn of new techniques of distribution and evasion of law enforcement from acquaintances or friends in other drug markets. Conventional wisdom asserts that policing is a primary force that shapes drug trafficking, but consumer preferences, capital and labor market flows in the noncriminalized economy, and even such factors as criminal predation upon traffickers can affect patterns of drug trafficking. A major social challenge is to understand how and why changes in the social and technical organization of drug trafficking take place and to respond effectively to them.

*Ric Curtis*

**See also** Asset Forfeiture, State; Drug Enforcement in the United States; Drug Policy and Legislation; Homicide Trends in the United States; Organized Crime Control

## For Further Reading

Adler, P. (1993). *Wheeling & dealing: An ethnography of an upper-level drug dealing and smuggling community.* New York: Columbia University Press.

Dorn, N., Murji, K., & South, N. (1992). *Traffickers: Drug markets and law enforcement.* New York: Routledge.

Reuter, P. (1985). *The organization of illegal markets: An economic analysis.* Washington, DC: National Institute of Justice.

## ᘒᘔ DRUNK DRIVING ENFORCEMENT

Driving while impaired is one of the nation's most frequently committed violent crimes, and Americans rank drunk driving as their number one highway safety concern. Each year, 42,000 people die in motor vehicle crashes, and more than 16,000 of these fatalities are alcohol or drug related. However, fatalities and injuries involving impaired driving, also known as drunk and drugged driving, are largely preventable. Although the definition of impaired driving includes drug-induced impairment, most of the research and arrest data focus on impairment caused by alcohol.

Since 1990, alcohol-related fatalities have been reduced by 25%, from 22,084 in 1990 to 16,653 in 2000. However, in more recent years, the rate of such incidents has been slowly creeping up again. But the overall reduction since 1990 is due largely to concerted efforts by both the public and private sectors, and can be attributed to factors such as the passage of stronger state and federal laws prompted by organizations such as Mothers Against Drunk Driving, tougher enforcement of these laws, the integration of technological tools to identify impaired drivers, stiffer sentences, and the creation

and implementation of educational/promotional campaigns. All of these efforts have contributed to a change in public attitudes and beliefs about the dangers of drinking and drugged driving.

Despite the progress that has been made, in 2000, alcohol-related fatalities accounted for 40% of the total traffic fatalities for the year. These figures represent an average of one alcohol-related crash every 32 minutes. Approximately 1.5 million drivers were arrested in 1999 for driving under the influence of alcohol or narcotics, an arrest rate of one for every 121 licensed drivers in the United States. Recent National Highway Traffic Safety Administration statistics indicate that alcohol-related crashes cost society $40 billion per year. This conservative estimate does not include pain, suffering, or lost quality of life. About 3 in every 10 Americans will be involved in an alcohol-related crash at some point in their lives.

Impaired driving is operating a motor vehicle while under the influence of alcohol. In 34 states, the District of Columbia, and Puerto Rico, it is illegal to drive once the blood alcohol concentration (BAC) level has reached .08. Separately, these activities might be socially acceptable and legal; however, in combination, they can have devastating consequences. An alcohol-related motor vehicle crash occurs when a motor vehicle collides with a nonoccupant (e.g., a pedestrian, a bicyclist) or an object (e.g., another vehicle, a guardrail) and at least one of the drivers or nonoccupants has a positive BAC. Although research clearly documents that drinking alcohol is associated with motor vehicle crashes, it is, of course, true that some motor vehicle crashes involving positive BACs would have occurred even if no alcohol had been consumed because of the presence of other factors such as bad weather, poor road conditions, and so forth. Researchers have estimated the percentage of alcohol-related crashes that are attributable or due to alcohol, that would not have occurred in the absence of alcohol, at various driver BAC levels. The percentages of alcohol-related crashes that are attributable to alcohol are 91% at BACs at or above .10, 44% at BACs .08 through .099, and 24% at BACs less than .08. These data help explain why many states have been reducing their per se limits from

.10 to .08. Eliminating alcohol-related crashes, especially those associated with high BACs, should substantially reduce the numbers of deaths and injuries that occur in motor vehicle-related crashes.

Research indicates that there are many common ties between impaired driving crashes. Crashes, which are not considered accidents because they are preventable, are most likely to occur in the evening hours, on weekends, and during specific holidays, such as Christmas and New Year's, Halloween, St. Patrick's Day, and prom/graduation celebrations. In addition, the offenders who are the most likely to drive under the influence of alcohol or drugs are individuals between 21 and 34 years of age. Repeat offenders or chronic impaired drivers plague the nation's roadways as individuals who drive repeatedly after drinking and often do so with high amounts of alcohol in their blood. And finally, underage drinkers between the ages of 15 and 20 are the most common offenders.

The following laws have created the greatest impact on preventing and deterring impaired driving. Minimum legal drinking age (MLDA) laws make it illegal for individuals who are less than 21 years old to purchase alcoholic beverages. Some states make it illegal to possess or consume alcoholic beverages or for individuals to misrepresent their age to obtain such beverages. MLDA laws are considered to be among the most effective and proven strategies to prevent and deter underage drinking and driving. Zero-tolerance laws established .00 BAC as the legal limit for all drivers under age 21, making it illegal for underage drivers to have any amount of alcohol in their blood. Many states have set the limit a little higher at .01 and .02 BAC to reduce legal challenges that claim mouthwash and cold medication are responsible for high BACs. Illegal per se laws and illegal per se at .08 BAC make it illegal in and of itself to drive with an alcohol concentration at or above the established legal limit. Most states plus the District of Columbia and Puerto Rico currently make it illegal to drive at .08 BAC or above. Administrative license revocation laws give state officials the authority to suspend or revoke the license of any driver who fails or refuses to take a BAC test. Finally, graduated licensing systems allow beginning drivers to obtain experience behind the wheel under low-risk conditions; approaches often vary from state to state.

Highly visible enforcement of drunk driving laws has proven to be instrumental in deterring impaired driving. Local law enforcement agencies can target activities at the general public and those who are under the legal drinking age of 21. Agencies can publicize support of law enforcement's efforts to stop underage drinking and underage purchasing of alcohol. Agencies can promote the use of identification-checking equipment that will aid retailers in identifying underage purchasers, as well as individuals who are using falsified identification. Sanctioning alcohol retailers and minors who violate underage drinking laws is also used to combat the problem.

Local law enforcement agencies sometimes conduct sobriety checkpoints that stop vehicles on a nondiscriminatory basis to identify drivers who may be driving under the influence. Sobriety checkpoints usually incorporate the use of sobriety-testing equipment, including passive alcohol sensors, in-vehicle videotaping equipment, and preliminary evidential breath-testing devices. Many jurisdictions require mandatory BAC testing at the time of the stop whenever an officer has probable cause to believe that a driver has committed an alcohol-related driving offense. These tests usually involve analyzing the breath for alcohol content and observations of other physical impairments. High-visibility enforcement strategies and tactics combined with public awareness and education have proven to be effective in reducing drunk-driving fatalities.

Finally, designated driver programs are a key component of a community-based comprehensive impaired driving prevention effort. Combined with highly visible law enforcement, designated driver programs typically promote the concept of designating a sober driver. Variations may exist depending on the needs of the community. An important part of a community-based designated driver program is the concept of "Safe Ride." These alternative methods of transportation provide people who have consumed alcohol with safe rides home. Some are privately funded, whereas others are run through public–private partnerships.

As in any campaign, it is vital to reach out to the media to promulgate anti-drinking-and-driving messages and publicize events related to the cause. There are a variety of media tools an agency can use to accomplish this task. Press releases, public service announcements, letters to the editor, and opinion editorials are a few of the examples of effective communication with the community.

*Michelle R. Hecht*

*For Further Reading*

http://www.madd.org/home/
http://www.nhtsa.dot.gov/people/injury/alcohol/
http://www.stopimpaireddriving.org/

# ᏬᎧ DUTY BELT

A duty belt, also referred to as a gun belt, is perhaps the most important and conspicuous element of a law enforcement uniform. Generally 1½ to 2¼ inches wide, this belt serves as a portable storage device and displays the tools required for the daily activities of law enforcement. The constant presence of the duty belt and its gear not only serves to equip officers for most daily occurrences, but also is a symbolic show of authority and preparedness, serving as an effective deterrent to would-be criminals.

A multitude of police supply catalogs and Web sites offer a wide variety of duty belts, attachments, pouches, and holsters. Many jurisdictions require officers to purchase their own belts and accompanying accessories, although much of the equipment carried on such belts is department issued. Rules and regulations of individual departments mandate much of what must be carried on a duty belt, but officers may be given considerable latitude in choosing their belts and accessories.

The commonly used term *gun belt* refers to the most important object carried, the firearm, which is held in a holster at the side of the belt. Extra ammunition in the form of bullets, cartridges, or magazines is typically held in pouches affixed to the belt. Traditional items affixed to or stored in pouches on the belt include handcuffs, gloves, keys, a flashlight, a badge, a notebook, and a radio. Changes in law enforcement techniques have added new items to the duty belt, including surgical gloves and masks, chemical sprays such as oleoresin capsicum (commonly known as pepper spray), and even hand-held computers. Since September 11, 2001, New York City police officers have been required to hang a pouch from their belts at all times that contains a gas mask and reflective vest.

Fully loaded with the various accoutrements of daily law enforcement, a duty belt can weigh from 20 to 40 pounds. This burden can cause serious injury to the back, hips, and gastrointestinal tracts of full-time personnel. Innovations in design and materials may significantly lighten the load, reduce injury, and improve agility. Some entire departments, or specific units such as bicycle police, have switched from heavier leather belts and accessories to those made of nylon or other synthetics. These newer materials also offer water-repellent properties, which can be beneficial to the maintenance of firearms and other equipment. Some police departments allow officers to wear suspenders, which redistribute the weight off the back and hips. Items that are traditionally large and heavy, such as batons, flashlights, and guns, have also become smaller and lighter. These innovations to the duty belt and its attached gear have the potential to change the look of today's law enforcement officer from "Mr. Goodwrench" to something sleeker and more tactical.

*Ellen H. Belcher*

*For Further Reading*

Harman, A. (2003). It's a hold-up! RCMP evaluates benefit of suspenders. *Law & Order, 48*(8), 54–58.

Lesce, T. (2000). Consistent evolution in belt gear. *Law & Order, 48*(2), 43–45.

Mandelblit, B. (2001). The latest tools of the trade for your front line security. *Security, 38*(10), 29–31.

# E

## ⳡ EARLY WARNING SYSTEMS

An early warning system (EWS) is a personnel management tool utilized by police command staff to identify individual officer or group performance problems at the earliest possible stage. EWSs collect data on a number of managerially defined police performance indicators (e.g., citizen complaints, use-of-force incidents, arrests, etc.) and compare them to predefined organizational tolerance levels or thresholds. Officers whose levels exceed the threshold for any one given indicator are "flagged" or otherwise noted by the system, and this notice is brought to the attention of supervisory staff, whose duty it is to intervene. EWSs allow police managers to proactively intervene through the use of counseling and retraining, thereby redirecting officers' work performance toward the organization's goals.

EWSs are a police accountability tool. They bolster accountability by establishing quantifiable departmental standards across a broad spectrum of police performance indicators and then capture individual officer or unit performance on each of these indicators. This information can then be easily accessed and utilized by supervisors responsible for evaluating each officer's performance. With one keystroke, supervisors can see all relevant data concerning each officer under their command.

As rank increases, the span of officers reported upon by the system increases up to the point of the chief, who can view the performance profiles of the entire department.

The prevalence of EWS technology is on the rise in the United States. More than 25% of all law enforcement agencies serving populations of 50,000 or more currently have a system in place, and an even greater number are in the early stages of developing a system (Walker, Alpert, & Kenney, 2001). In addition, the advent of police-involved civil litigation and consent decrees has seen the development and use of these systems become judicially mandated reforms in many jurisdictions. Of the five existing consent decrees, all outline and require the use of robust automated early warning systems. In addition, many memoranda of agreements include provisions for early warning systems.

The idea for EWSs grew out of a recommendation by the 1981 U.S. Commission on Civil Rights and its recognition of the problematic officer. The "problem officer" concept, which maintains that a small number of officers account for a disproportionate number of citizen complaints and other troubling behaviors, has been well documented by investigative reporters, journalists, and academics. EWSs attempt to identify these officers by capturing information concerning critical behaviors that are characterized as high risk and therefore could lead to increased agency or individual liability. EWSs alert the command staff to the existence of a problematic officer before the level of his or her transgressions grows beyond control. In addition, EWSs monitor other, more benign behaviors that can often be early signs of an officer in need of intervention. For example, excessive sick leave usage may be an indicator of substance abuse, inability to cope with stress, or a physical impairment, all of which could result in devastating consequences to officer performance and public safety. This information (sick time, overtime, absent without leave, missed court appearances) is also critical to the effective management of a police agency.

EWSs are heavily data driven and data dependent. Accurate and timely information is necessary for the optimum performance of these systems. Early versions of EWSs consisted of simple manual (often paper-driven) systems, but recent years have seen the development of sophisticated automated computerized systems. Automated systems offer greater analytical capacity and increased integrity, thereby allowing for more informative and instantaneous analysis of relevant data. Automated EWSs import data from diverse municipal databases into a centralized system. This allows information about officers and their performance, which is often dispersed throughout multiple divisions and bureaus within the municipal government structure, to be instantly combined into a centralized and relational database allowing for easy access and analysis of key data and patterns. Prior to this, supervisors would often have to comb through reams of paper files in multiple storage rooms throughout a city in order to glean this level of information.

The fundamental analytical operation of EWSs consists of a series of triggers (often referred to as alarms, flags, or thresholds) that is activated when an individual officer or a group of officers exceeds the preestablished acceptability or tolerance level. The standards by which these triggers are established vary substantially. Because there are no hard-and-fast rules, it is up to each agency to decide upon and set its own tolerance levels. Many systems use simple counts, alerting to officers who exceed a certain number of incidents in a specific time frame.

For example, a standard threshold often used concerning citizen complaints is three similar complaints in a year or five dissimilar complaints in that same time frame. Other, more sophisticated systems use more robust analysis, such as the standard deviation calculation, as a threshold. In these systems, officers are compared to their peer officers who work in similarly situated work environments (the same division and shift). If an officer deviates from the mean by one or more standard deviations above or below, that officer is flagged. These analytic schemes have proven their worth, especially for monitoring issues concerning race, such as racial profiling or differential enforcement. Officers who stop only one race or gender will be flagged immediately by the EWS. However, these schemes have their flaws. Such an approach would be unable to discover an entire unit or precinct engaged in inappropriate behavior, such as the Los Angeles Police Department's Rampart Division.

EWSs give the command staff in any police department an instantaneous snapshot of the performance of their entire agency. These systems offer a view of officer performance never before attainable. Commanders can focus in on the performance of individual precincts, units, shifts, or officers. EWSs also allow for the maintenance of a performance history on each officer. These systems make it possible for an officer's performance history to follow him or her through all transfers within the department, alerting the officer's new supervisors to any potential problems or need for intense supervision. Finally, EWSs can reveal the need for revision of training tactics, deployment strategies, and policy revisions.

EWSs have many benefits associated with their use, but there is also a downside. The development or acquisition, implementation, and maintenance of these systems require significant investments of time, money, and personnel. The development of robust automated systems can take years and require the expenditure of millions of dollars. In addition, securing the buy-in of police officers and the union is often difficult. Fear of false alerts and the punitive feel to these systems often cause officer distrust at the early stages, but when used properly in a nonpunitive manner, these systems can often highlight the best performers in a department as well as those in need of intervention. Current research has illustrated this. In the four jurisdictions that have been studied, EWSs have been shown to greatly reduce problematic behavior. In addition, in one of these jurisdictions, the effect of an EWS on officer morale and self-initiated activity was shown to be minimal or nonexistent.

*Christopher W. Ortiz and Karen L. Amendola*

*See also* Accountability, Complaints Against Police, Consent Decrees, Evaluation of Officers

## For Further Reading

Early Warning Systems. (2002). *Model policy.* Alexandria, VA: International Association of Chiefs of Police.

Livingston, D. (1999). Police reform and the Department of Justice: An essay on accountability. *Buffalo Criminal Law Review, 2*(2), 817–859.

Walker, S. (2000). Police accountability: Establishing an early warning system. *International City/County Management Association (ICMA) Inquiry Services Report. Vol. 32*(8).

Walker, S., Alpert, G., & Kenney, D. (2001, July). *Early warning systems: Responding to the problem police officer* (NCJ 188565). Washington, DC: National Institute of Justice.

## ✑ EDUCATION OF POLICE

Improving the education of police has been an enduring feature of reform in America and other Western nations. Although the desirability of a professionally trained police force can be dated at least as far back as Sir Robert Peele (around 1830), the notion received support in America from a variety of police reformers, such as August Vollmer, Theodore Roosevelt, and the Wickersham Commission. Until the mid-20th century, the ambitions of reformers were modest compared to today's standards: first, hiring officers who could read and write, and somewhat later, recruiting officers who had completed a high school education. But after World War II, a high school education became the norm, and college education began to appear in some agencies as an appropriate goal, one that has become increasingly popular as a means of advancement in, if not admission to, the occupation.

Perhaps the real takeoff point in the stimulus for higher education for police came in 1967 with the President's Commission on Law Enforcement and the Administration of Justice, which recommended that all police have baccalaureate degrees (President's Commission, 1967). Numerous other blue-ribbon commissions in the late 1960s and 1970s have promoted higher education for police, and since then, advocacy has been backed by policy. The Law Enforcement Education Program, following on the heels of the President's Commission, provided tremendous financial incentives for officers getting a college education, and it was arguably a significant factor in the profusion of criminal justice programs in academic institutions throughout the United States that occurred in the next decade or so. Today, police professional associations, such as the Police Executive Research Forum and the Police Association for College Education, actively advocate for police officers obtaining baccalaureate degrees.

Formal education of the police occurs in two arenas: institutions of higher learning operated outside the policing industry, and in police institutions themselves, the latter typically distinguished from the former by the term *training*. This entry concerns itself only with formal education obtained outside of police-sponsored institutions. Given contemporary standards (nearly all American police have high school degrees) and ambitions, "education" will be limited to that provided by colleges and universities at the baccalaureate and graduate levels. Comments will focus on police education in the United States.

One thing can be said with confidence of police education: Police officers are getting more of it than ever before. By 2000, 15% of local departments required at least some college, ranging from 10% of departments serving fewer than 2,500 to 33% of departments serving a million or more. In 2000, 32% of local police officers worked in departments requiring at least some college, up substantially from the 10% level in 1990. Only 1% of all departments in 2000 required a minimum of a baccalaureate degree, but a college degree has become a virtual necessity for advancement and pay increases for large numbers of officers. In 2000, 58% of officers were employed by departments offering tuition incentives, and 49% worked in departments that offered incentive pay for education (Hickman & Reaves, 2003, pp. 8–9). A study of Texas peace officers in larger departments showed that higher education reduced the time required for promotion in rank and assignment to specialized positions, and it was associated with appointment to supervisory or administrative positions (Polk & Armstrong, 2001).

Not surprisingly, the number of police officers who have attended college has increased markedly since the 1960s. In 1960, less than 3% of officers had obtained a baccalaureate, but by 1988, the number had grown to nearly 23%, an additional 22% had completed 2–3 years, and another 21% had completed less than 2 years. A national sample survey conducted in the late 1990s showed that 85% of American police officers had attended college, 28% had attained a baccalaureate, and almost 6% had at least some additional graduate or professional education (Weisburd, Greenspan, Hamilton, Bryant, & Williams, 2001, p. 72). More than three fourths of the officers had attended college before becoming sworn, and more than one fourth had obtained a baccalaureate before becoming sworn.

Much less is known about the nature and quality of higher education that police are receiving. Criminology, criminal justice, and police science are by far the most popular majors of officers who have attended college (53%), with business a distant second (12%). Doubts have been raised about the quality of many criminal justice programs that arose in the wake of the federal largesse for supporting a college education for police, but there is little hard evidence on the quality of these programs and their advantages or disadvantages vis-à-vis other academic programs.

Reasons vary for promoting the notion that police should be college educated. An obvious one is that education is considered essential for developing the occupation's professional identity and, not coincidentally, its status and material rewards. However, the ultimate justification of more education is that it will improve the performance of the police and that society will benefit. Promoters

of more education have argued that it improves thinking and communications skills, enhances knowledge of things police can use to be more effective, promotes understanding of people, broadens horizons, makes officers more tolerant, and increases commitment to democratic values. These traits are thought to be especially useful where community policing and problem solving are desired.

Unfortunately, the available body of research does not offer very useful findings that would tell us whether and how higher education of police is producing the results that reformers expect (Committee to Review Research, 2004, p. 140). A great deal of the research focuses on the relationship between more education and officers' attitudes. Early studies were encouraging, suggesting that officers who received a college education were less inclined toward an authoritarian personality, less cynical, less prejudiced, and less punitive (Shernock, 1992). A fundamental problem with these studies is that because they measured officers' attitudes and not their performance, they really provide no insight into whether those attitudes determined the way officers actually behaved while on the job. Because psychologists have established that the linkage between attitudes and behaviors is very weak, little faith can be placed in these studies for the purpose of learning whether higher education is producing tangible results.

A few studies have attempted to link the amount of education police receive to their on-the-job performance (Committee to Review Research, 2004, p. 140). Some studies, based on official records, have found that college-educated officers receive fewer complaints, do more enforcement activities, and have quicker response times (Bowker, 1980; Carter & Sapp, 1990; Cascio, 1977; Finckenauer, 1975; Hudzik, 1978). However, one study found that education was unrelated to the use of lethal force when other characteristics of the officer were taken into account (Sherman & Blumberg, 1981). Studies based on field observations of patrol officers have produced even more mixed results. One study found that officers with 4-year college degrees were more inclined to use reasonable force, but they were about as likely to use force improperly as their peers without a college degree (Worden, 1995). Most of the systematic field studies show that a college degree bears no significant relationship to the way that officers exercise their discretion, and that sometimes, it shows an unexpected, undesirable relationship. For example, the level of education showed no effect on the inclination of officers to be disrespectful toward citizens (Mastrofski, Reisig, & McCluskey, 2002), and college-educated officers were less inclined to provide comfort to citizens than officers who did not have a college education (DeJong, 2000).

There are numerous problems with the existing research on the effects of a college education on the police (Committee to Review Research, 2004, p. 141). Many of the studies do a poor job of measuring those aspects of police performance that most concern the public—whether police are caring, responsive, polite, and thorough. Furthermore, none of the existing studies is able to determine what a college education *adds* to the knowledge and skills a person would have had without getting a college degree. Because college admission and graduation are a screening and winnowing process, it may be that when an association between college education and performance is demonstrated, it is due largely to the traits people possessed *before* attending college. And existing research tells us nothing about the effects of different kinds of college experiences on police performance. Do people who receive their college degree before becoming police officers perform better than those who receive their college degree after they become officers? Do police who major in criminal justice perform better than those who major in English literature or biology? Do police who graduate from prestigious schools do better than those who graduate from lower-ranked schools? Do curricula that focus on theory and science produce students who perform better than curricula that concentrate on practical, hands-on educational experiences?

Because research is so limited and so many important questions remain unanswered, it is not surprising that a National Academy of Sciences panel of experts judged "the available evidence inadequate to make recommendations regarding the desirability of higher education for improving police practice" (Committee to Review Research, 2004, p. 141). It is ironic that a reform trend that has been so successful in its implementation over the past half century has so little scientific evidence available in support of its merits. Researchers should formulate more well-defined studies that will measure the outcomes of higher education on all-around police performance. In general, the value of higher education for the development of a citizen in a democratic society is unquestioned. Researchers, reformers, and educators are thus faced with the challenge in the 21st century to determine what the benefits of college-educated police really are and the means to best realize them.

*Stephen D. Mastrofski*

## For Further Reading

Bowker, L. E. (1980). A theory of the educational needs of law enforcement officers. *Journal of Contemporary Criminal Justice, 1,* 17–24.

Carter, D. L., & Sapp, A. D. (1990). The evolution of higher education in law enforcement: Preliminary findings from a national study. *Journal of Criminal Justice Education, 1,* 59–85.

Cascio, W. (1977). Formal education and police officer performance. *Journal of Police Science and Administration, 5,* 89–96.

Committee to Review Research on Police Policy and Practices. (2004). *Fairness and effectiveness in policing: The evidence.* Washington, DC: National Academies Press.

DeJong, C. (2000). *Gender differences in officer attitude and behavior: Providing comfort to citizens.* Report to the National Institute of Justice. East Lansing: Michigan State University.

Finckenauer, J. O. (1975). Higher education and police discretion. *Journal of Police Science and Administration, 3,* 450–457.

Hickman, M., & Reaves, B. A. (2003). *Local police departments 2000.* Washington, DC: Bureau of Justice Statistics.

Hudzik, J. K. (1978). College education for police: Problems in measuring component and extraneous variables. *Journal of Criminal Justice, 6,* 69–81.

Mastrofski, S. D., Reisig, M. D., & McCluskey, J. D. (2002). Police disrespect toward the public: An encounter-based analysis. *Criminology, 40,* 519–551.

Polk, O. E., & Armstrong, D. A. (2001). Higher education and law enforcement career paths: Is the road to success paved by degree? *Journal of Criminal Justice Education, 12,* 77–99.

President's Commission on Law Enforcement and the Administration of Justice. (1967). *The challenge of crime in a free society.* Washington, DC: U.S. Government Printing Office.

Sherman, L. W., & Blumberg, M. (1981). Higher education and police use of deadly force. *Journal of Criminal Justice, 9,* 317–331.

Shernock, S. K. (1992). The effects of college education on professional attitudes among police. *Journal of Criminal Justice Education, 3,* 71–92.

Weisburd, D., Greenspan, R., Hamilton, E. E., Bryant, K. A., & Williams, H. (2001). *The abuse of police authority: A national study of police officers' attitudes.* Washington, DC: Police Foundation.

Worden, R. E. (1995). The "causes" of police brutality. In W. A. Geller & H. Toch (Eds.), *And justice for all: A national agenda for understanding and controlling police abuse of force.* Washington, DC: Police Executive Research Forum.

# ❧ ELECTRONIC SURVEILLANCE

No area of criminal investigation generates as much controversy as the practice of electronic surveillance. Despite the Fourth Amendment's protections, law enforcement authorities have unsurprisingly and consistently preferred and sought unfettered authority to conduct electronic surveillance. To counter such pressure, the U.S. Congress has obliged law enforcement agents to use electronic surveillance only under strict rules, especially for wiretapping.

The practice of wiretapping in law enforcement was not always so carefully controlled. In 1928, a year before President Hoover had a telephone on his desk, the U.S. Supreme Court allowed (in *Olmstead v. United States,* 1928) that warrantless wiretapping did not violate the Fourth Amendment because there was no actual physical intrusion into the home. This case prompted a well-known dissent from Justice Brandeis that eventually became the basis of a reversal of the Olmstead decision in 1967 (*Katz v. United States*) that firmly placed wiretapping under the domain of the Fourth Amendment. In response to the Court's decision, formal federal regulation of wiretapping began with the passage of Title III of the Omnibus Crime Control and Safe Streets Act in 1968. These rules had the effect of establishing national standards for state and local law enforcement when using electronic surveillance.

The next significant changes in federal law governing electronic surveillance in criminal investigations came in 1986 with the Electronic Communications Privacy Act (ECPA) when Congress made changes in the Title III provisions. ECPA reflected the discomfort over government use of electronic surveillance at the time and required full disclosure of the techniques and results of electronic surveillance in criminal investigations. Thus, both federal and state judges who hear wiretap applications are obliged under ECPA to submit a report on each application to the administrative office of the U.S. Courts.

These reports show that covert wiretaps, those in which neither of the parties to an interception know the line is tapped and to which Title III primarily applied, are rarely used. Over the years, state and local agencies typically reported a combined total of about 800–1,000 wiretap applications each year—a tiny fraction of all criminal cases—compared to a total of about 500–600 per year by federal agencies—a larger but also small fraction of cases. With an average cost in 2003 of about $62,000 per wiretap, the expense of using a wiretap obviously limits how many are attempted. Of the 43 states with laws allowing electronic surveillance, as of 2003, in a given year only a bit more than half report any wiretap applications. The bulk of applications typically are from just four states: California, New York, Pennsylvania, and New Jersey. Some states actually prohibit wiretapping, obliging their agencies to seek cooperation with federal agencies on criminal investigations when they need to do so.

Under ECPA, an application for a wiretap is made to the highest level law enforcement official in the political venue making the application. Designated judges then review the application. In New Jersey, for example, only eight judges in the state are permitted to consider applications for wiretaps. Under ECPA, the duration of a wiretap was strictly limited to 30 days, but applications for extensions were allowed. The USA PATRIOT Act, enacted after the events of September 11, 2001, temporarily allowed for much more leeway in the use of electronic surveillance, to include sidestepping the application procedure in some situations and extending the first period of potential surveillance to 90 days. It remains to be seen whether or not these looser rules will be made permanent. In any case, denials of approval for wiretap applications or their extension, even before the USA PATRIOT Act, were very rare in state courts and unheard of for federal applications. Thus, it is not clear that the USA PATRIOT Act is a harbinger of a sharp increase in wiretapping activity, especially in state and local cases.

Although the classic telephone-based wiretapping techniques of "pen registers" or "trap and trace," which recorded outgoing and incoming telephone numbers, respectively, are still employed in concept, they are now done using software instead of wires as telecommunications first shifted toward digital networks, then to cell phone systems, and most recently to the Internet. Indeed, the networking and data management technologies used for phones and computers are essentially merging. The problem of monitoring the vast amounts of Internet traffic was confronted by the FBI in 1999, when it put into service a controversial and initially unreliable surveillance tool called Carnivore. Despite the mystique that surrounded it when it was first announced, Carnivore turned out to be essentially an ancillary computer that is installed on the router of an Internet service provider and is effectively a "packet sniffer." It is designed to filter all the "packets" of traffic that pass through the router and pick out any items, typically e-mail, that are associated with the subject of a search warrant while ignoring unrelated traffic. It stores the relevant traffic for analysis and as evidence. Eventually, state and local law enforcement agencies that wish to tap Internet traffic will also need Carnivore-like systems for their own use. In general, however, the technological and organizational demands of electronic surveillance in the digital era will require increased cooperation between state and local law enforcement; federal agencies; and the private telecommunications, cable, and Internet service operators. The cooperation of the latter was mandated in 1994 under terms of the Communications Assistance for Law Enforcement Act. Nonetheless, the FBI continues to complain that new networking systems are not being designed to allow a "back door" for ready law enforcement access for surveillance purposes.

If there has been an overall increase in surveillance activity by state and local investigators, if not wiretapping proper, it is more likely because they have begun to try to exploit various other modes of electronic surveillance. For example, surveillance opportunities abound with widening use of ATM cards, automated wireless toll passes used on toll highways and bridges, even digitized fare cards used on buses and subways. These services all offer the potential for real-time or retrospective monitoring of the movement of specific individuals or vehicles. Of course, such surveillance would require a court order or subpoena. As well, however, aerial infrared surveillance has been used to detect indoor raising of marijuana without need of court orders. Another example of real-time surveillance is the common use of GPS ankle bracelets. These are now widely used for supervision of probationers and parolees or those under house arrest. As more mobile telephones are equipped with automatic GPS capability, a feature that will eventually be tied into 9-1-1 systems, that also has obvious surveillance potential. Although state and local agencies have demonstrated a capacity for experimentation in electronic surveillance, as would be expected, not all techniques are effective nor worth the expense. Such proved to be the case with the use of facial recognition technology by the local police department at the Super Bowl in 2001, to look for wanted suspects in the crowd and later in a late-night entertainment district. Not a single suspect was reportedly caught, and the system was abandoned. But fresh approaches at surveillance are inevitable as technology affords, and as state and local police and prosecutors become more familiar and comfortable with, digital technology.

As changes in communications and computer technology yield fresh opportunities for surveillance techniques, they also bring both practical and legal problems. For example, when all telephones were permanently installed within a business or residence, applications for a wiretap had to indicate a specific location for a tap. The problem was that the interception of conversations of parties unassociated with the warrant by government agents would be illegal. This remains a problem; however, wireless mobile phone technology required a change in the law to provide for "roving" warrants that would allow following a suspect from place to place. Likewise, the conversion of analog telephone technology to digital networks and the introduction of a host of new ways for people to communicate have all complicated the once relatively simple task of tapping telephones. These services produce vast amounts of e-mail, instant messaging, text messaging, and Internet-based telephone traffic that are no longer carried over a designated wire. Moreover, the increasing use of encryption with any sort of communication that uses digital technology threatens to limit the effectiveness of surveillance. Federal agencies are likely to lead the way to meeting these challenges with state and local law enforcement left to follow.

Privacy advocates have met every move to enhance law enforcement capacity for electronic surveillance with serious concerns and legal challenges. Some states have enhanced police prerogatives in electronic surveillance in response to security threats, whereas others have been more concerned with protecting privacy. What seems certain is that criminal investigators will face ever-increasing technological challenges and opportunities in using the myriad modes of contemporary telecommunications as sources of evidence and means to monitor criminal behavior. Just as certain is that as they try to do so, the tension between security and privacy surrounding electronic surveillance will yield sharp debate for years to come.

*Richard W. Lovely*

## For Further Reading

*The "Carnivore" controversy: Electronic surveillance and privacy in the digital age: Hearing before the Committee on the Judiciary, United States Senate,* 106th Cong., 2d sess. (2000).

Katz v. United States, 389 U.S. 347 (1967).

Olmstead v. United States, 277 U.S. 438 (1928).

U.S. Congress, Office of Technology Assessment. (1995, July). *Electronic surveillance in a digital age* (OTA-BP-ITC-149). Washington, DC: U.S. Government Printing Office.

U.S. Department of Justice, Criminal Division, Computer Crime and Intellectual Property Section. (2002, July). *Searching and seizing computers and obtaining electronic evidence in criminal investigations.* Available: http://www.cybercrime.gov/s&smanual2002.htm

## ‰ EMERGENCY SERVICES UNITS

An Emergency Services Unit (ESU) is generally described as a unit within a police agency designated for meeting the specialized needs of the agency in terms of providing the ability for special enforcement or investigations, or a specialized or unique response on behalf of the agency most commonly regarding tactical operations, rescues, riots, hostage and rescue operations, and a variety of other high-risk emergency operations requiring a specialized tactical response, specialized training, and specialized equipment.

In defining an ESU within a police department, a foundation must be created in order to place such a definition in its proper context. In the United States, there are more than 17,000 state and local police agencies. The large majority of these are smaller agencies. Approximately 85% of these 17,000 agencies employ fewer than 50 officers. Excluding state agencies and sheriff's departments, there are approximately 12,666 local police agencies as of the year 2000. Each police agency, depending on its size and the community it serves, covers a wide range of tasks and functions.

The main components of modern policing regularly encompass a number of basic, key functions, such as uniformed patrol (including responding to calls for service); criminal investigations; drug enforcement; prevention and outreach programs; administration; internal investigations and inspections; and technical support (e.g., communications, records and property management). Generally, these functions may be divided into four common or basic components: patrol services, special services, technical services, and administration. A special services command or bureau denotes more specialized operational tasks.

Under the special services command, medium- to large-size agencies, generally considered to be those employing more than 125 sworn officers, might commonly operate a number of specialized units. These units may be full-time or part-time, because the officers involved in these functions may be assigned to other functions as well. In smaller departments, officers regularly assigned to patrol duties may manage these functions in addition to their regularly assigned patrol duties. In larger departments, full-time units may accomplish many of these functions. These include, but are not limited to, criminal investigations; gang intelligence; community crime prevention; drug education in schools; drug enforcement; juvenile delinquency enforcement; child abuse investigations; missing children; drunk driving; domestic violence; repeat offenders; bias-related crime; dignitary protection; special events; SWAT; SRT or ERT (special response team, emergency response team, or ESU); directed patrol; traffic enforcement; bicycle and/or motorcycle unit; mounted patrol; sniper unit; negotiation or critical incident team; building collapses; search-and-rescue missions; riot control; and victim assistance.

Agencies often categorize these functions by unit and program. As such, programs that address juvenile delinquency, school-based education programs, police athletic league or police boys and girls clubs, victim assistance, and related prevention programs may be incorporated under a form of community outreach or community services. Missing-person investigations and child abuse investigations, as well as domestic violence investigations, may also be connected to this category, or they may be organized with an investigative unit under criminal investigations, along with investigations involving major crimes such as homicide, rape, robbery, burglary, serious assaults, and major theft and fraud cases. As noted, all of these tasks may be categorized under a special services type of command.

In larger agencies, those with more than 500 sworn personnel, a more defined ESU may also be placed organizationally under the special services command to provide particular aspects of sworn policing duties requiring significant specialized training, specialized equipment, and/or a specialized response. In small- to medium-sized departments, ESU teams may be composed of cross-trained officers who regularly engage in other duties. Larger agencies often employ a separate, full-time unit composed of officers specially trained and equipped to respond to a variety of emergency events. These types of functions often require a tactical response and the development of a preplanned response to a variety of incidents to include such functions as dignitary protection; special events (parades, festivals, races, sports events, demonstrations, concerts, etc.); directed patrol; high-risk arrest and warrant service; bomb and explosive ordnance investigations; barricade situations; canine unit, which may consist of any combination of narcotics dogs, bomb dogs, and bloodhounds; hazardous device team; sniper unit; crisis negotiation or critical incident management; building collapses; search-and-rescue missions; underwater search and recovery team; hostage rescue; riot control; and other types of high-risk tactical operations.

Since September 11, 2001, it is also more common for an ESU to be trained on the basic elements of weapons of mass destruction in order to potentially provide the ability to conduct tasks connected to the response to a weapons of mass destruction event. These units often will be trained on the elements and principles of an incident command system composed of integrated and coordinated communications, and five key functional areas: command, operations, planning, logistics, and finance. In addition, they must be trained and equipped to respond to hazardous materials incidents, to collect evidence, and to assist fire and rescue units. Such a unit would be trained and equipped to collect evidence in hazardous environments, and the training would include hazardous material training, hazardous material operations, and processing weapons of mass destruction crime scenes. Such a team would be capable of detecting and characterizing hazardous materials; biological agents such as bacteria, anthrax, smallpox, plague, botulinum toxin, and ricin; viral hemorrhagic fevers such as Ebola, dengue, and others; staphylococcal enterotoxin B, or other viruses or toxins; chemical agents such as choking agents, blood agents, blister agents, or nerve agents; and radioactive threats such as alpha particles, beta particles, or gamma rays. Many emergency services teams are at least equipped with the most basic of personal protective equipment consisting of Level C suits and respiratory masks. Depending on the size of the agency and its level of funding and expertise, some units also are trained and equipped to use Level B and/or Level A personal protective equipment.

In terms of equipment, ESUs are often equipped with armored vehicles; utility vehicles; trucks; boats; shields; night vision equipment; emergency lighting; road flares; chemical agents; ladders; hydraulic tools; gas saws; gas generators; compressed air chisels; rappel ropes, harnesses, and hardware; animal control tranquilizer pistols and/or rifles; rescue helmets; turnout coats; elevator keys; cold water rescue suits; personal flotation vests; vehicle "slim jim" kits; ballistics helmets; heavy body armor; chemical agent masks; NOMEX® flame retardant gloves and hood; long-range sniper rifles; shotguns; 12-gauge breaching shotguns; submachine guns; and less-than-lethal weapons including, but not limited to, stun guns or tazer-type devices, flash/bang rounds, and beanbag rounds. Emergency response teams may also be supplied with a variety of medical equipment, such as oxygen, bag valve masks, non rebreathers, artificial airways, special immobilization, extrication devices, splints, burn kits, trauma kits, blood pressure cuff and scope, ring cutter, bandages, cervical collars, long boards, personal protective barriers, and various antidotes.

*Kim C. Dine*

*See also* Chemical and Biological Terrorism, Local Response to; National Guard; Task Forces

*For Further Reading*

http://cityofnewhaven.com/police/html/divisions/admin/esu.htm

Dunham, R. G., & Alpert, G. P. (1993). *Critical issues in policing: Contemporary readings*. Prospect Heights, IL: Waveland.

Hickman, M., & Reaves, B. A. (2003). *Local police departments 2000*. Washington, DC: Bureau of Justice Statistics.

*Police Chief* [Entire issue]. (2003, March). Alexandria, VA: International Association of Chiefs of Police.

Vecchi, G. M. (2002, May). Hostage/barricade management: A hidden conflict within law enforcement. *FBI Law Enforcement Bulletin*, pp. 1–7.

Weapons of Mass Destruction and Incident Command Training Material from the Center for Domestic Preparedness, Office of Homeland Security, Anniston, AL.

http://www.ci.nyc.ny.us.html/doc/html/esu.html

http://www.ci.nyc.ny.us/html/nypd/html/pct/esu.html

http://yonkerspd.com/esu.htm

# ✆ ETHICS

Ethical issues infuse all human interactions, especially those in which human interests are at stake. The powers vested in law enforcement personnel, coupled with the complex and exigent circumstances under which they might be employed, make ethical decision making of critical importance, not only to those immediately involved but also to the maintenance of public authority.

## GENERAL

At its most fundamental level, ethics is concerned with how humans should live—that is, how they ought to manage their lives and relate to each other and the world around them. Construed in this way, ethical concerns have a certain normative priority in decision making, functioning as a standard against which other forms of human activity and decision making are to be measured—law, politics, economics, sport, and so forth. Therefore, ethical decision making tends to be universalizable in ways that other forms of decision making are not. Unlike law and politics, its prescriptions are not taken to be jurisdictionally limited or changeable by authoritative fiat; moreover, because of its fundamental character (its concern with the *quality* of relationships), ethical decision making incorporates a regard for intentions and attitudes as well as behavior: a stop and frisk motivated by grounded suspicion of a dangerous weapon has a fundamentally different moral character from one motivated by the racial identity of the person searched.

Because of its centrality to human conduct, much effort has been given to determining the factors that make for good ethical decision making—what makes right acts right and wrong acts wrong, what constitutes the good life and a good character. To answer such questions, a large number of ethical theories have been developed, each claiming to capture what is fundamental to moral acceptability. Some theories focus primarily on the consequences of conduct (broadly speaking, consequentialist theories) in which certain outcomes singly or collectively (pleasure, happiness, knowledge, well-being, and so on) are said to make for ethical acceptability. Other theories focus primarily on internal features of the conduct in question (broadly speaking, deontological theories), looking to the sources of conduct or its structure (divine command, natural law, self-evidence, motivation, and so on) as a basis for claims about ethical acceptability. Yet other theories focus on the social status of principles of conduct (broadly speaking, contractualist or conventionalist theories), seeing ethically acceptable conduct as a socially negotiated phenomenon. These are neither exhaustive nor exclusive accounts, but they track some of the main contours of what remains a highly controversial debate. Given their longevity, it is likely that each cluster of theories captures something that we want to preserve in moral assessment. The difficulty is that the theories sometimes generate incompatible conclusions, thus making the resolution of conflict problematic.

People do not relate to each other exclusively as fellow human beings. Relations are often mediated by specific roles that people have in regard to each other or by virtue of particular relationships in which they exist. So, for example, a person may have the role of parent or child, a person may be a police officer or a citizen, or people may relate as doctor and patient or lawyer and client. Again, people may relate to each other as promisor and promisee, as benefactor and beneficiary, as friends, and so forth. Ethical concerns affect these mediating roles and relationships in two important ways. First of all, the role or relationship itself might be scrutinized ethically. We might wonder, for example, whether the role or relationship of police officer, benefactor, or friend is one that can pass ethical muster—consider some controversial roles, such as soldier, prostitute, prison guard, executioner, or arbitrageur. We may need to consider whether the particular role is to be encouraged and, if so, how it is

to be delimited. And second, having recognized the role's or relationship's acceptability, we need to consider its detailed implications for conduct. There are likely to be things that a person can do as a parent or police officer that cannot be done by those who do not have that role or relationship, and there are likely to be obligations that one has as a result of such a role or relationship that one would not have without it. Some of the most difficult ethical questions arise as a result of some conflict between obligations one has in a particular role and other obligations one has as a human being or by virtue of another role or relationship in which one stands to another. The "blue wall of silence," notorious within police work, often involves a conflict among the obligations one has to fellow officers, the organization, and the larger community or humanity generally.

## CRIMINAL JUSTICE ETHICS

Criminal justice ethics encompasses many interrelated governmental functions associated with securing rights against the wilful encroachments of others. Among its foundational concerns will be issues in legislative ethics, in which policies on criminalization and penalization are established. It will center, though, on law enforcement (or police) ethics—the ethical prerogatives and constraints that should govern the activities of those who execute the legislative will; judicial ethics—the ethical prerogatives and constraints that should govern the activities of those who articulate and apply the legislative will (including prosecutors, judges, juries, witnesses, and defense attorneys); and correctional ethics (including ethical issues in probation and parole)—the ethical prerogatives and constraints that should govern those who execute the judicial will. Along with such central concerns, ethical issues may also arise in such ancillary areas as forensic science.

## LAW ENFORCEMENT ETHICS

Although we generally associate public police officers with law enforcement, that task is nowadays served by a host of private and public officers—customs officers, private security guards, secret service agents, court officers, and so on. For simplicity, we focus here on the traditional public police role, although important ethical questions—particularly of distributive justice and accountability—have been generated by the growth of various forms of private policing.

## Foundations

In civil society, public policing is a governmental function. Civil order is generally grounded in some view of the deficiencies of social life absent some form of governmental organization. John Locke, one of the ideological architects of the modern-day liberal democratic state, argued that a "state of nature"—social life without governmental institutions—would be, if not unmanageable, then very frustrating for rational beings such as ourselves. In his view, for people to go about their lives productively and securely, it would be reasonable, if not essential, for them to institute social structures that would (a) legislate common standards for all, (b) apply and interpret laws so legislated, and (c) ensure that they are executed. This threefold legislative, judicial, and enforcement structure would, Locke believed, provide the social requisites for individuals who wished to enjoy the fundamental rights that are their due as rational beings (rights to life, liberty, and security of possessions).

By means of this "social contract," Locke provided an argument for the ethical legitimacy of the social role that is now occupied by law enforcement. As Locke envisaged it, the role of police was simply to enforce the law. With the expanding role of government into the provision of positive welfare as well as protection, however, the role of contemporary law enforcement officers has expanded to encompass other social tasks of a peacekeeping nature, such as order maintenance, crisis intervention, and some other general forms of public assistance.

Even so, law enforcement has remained a core concern. It also constitutes the source of many of the critical ethical problems in police work. Just because police are vested with authority to use coercive force in the achievement of their social ends, their decisions may have great impact on the well-being of others. Thus, the extent of their discretion is an issue of central ethical concern.

## Law Enforcement Ethics as Professional Ethics

With the increasing differentiation of social roles, attempts have been made to craft ethical understandings appropriate to the specialized and limited natures of those roles. The traditional professions (medicine, law, theology, military) were among the first to formulate such distinctive understandings, often encapsulated in so-called codes of ethics. But over the past century, the formulation of codified ethical frameworks has been extended beyond an expanding group of professions to almost every occupational grouping. Even if professional status is not (yet) their social achievement, an ethic of professionalism is increasingly expected of those who render services, whether private or public. A central expectation of such an ethic is dedication by those who provide services to ensuring that they are delivered with commitment and an eye to their continual improvement. This is encapsulated in a clause added to the 1991 revision to the International Association of Chiefs of Police Law Enforcement Code of Ethics: "I know that I alone am responsible for my own standard of professional performance and will take every reasonable opportunity to enhance and improve my level of knowledge and competence."

The formalization of the modern police role in 1829 brought with it general instructions that sought to delineate in an ethically informed way the tasks of "constables," although it was not until some time later that formal ethical codes for police were developed. As the social demands of police officers have become increasingly sophisticated, ethical codes and guidelines have proliferated. In the United States, with the formation in 1980 of the Commission for Accreditation of Law Enforcement Agencies, it has now become essential for police departments seeking accreditation to develop a formal set of ethical standards.

Although formal standards may have institutional value as limiting considerations for those who provide services and also provide some form of assurance for those who receive them, they do not substitute for individual judgment and are most effective if developed as a collective exercise. A professional ethic, although expressive of a personal commitment, is informed by collective reflection.

## Framing an Ethic of Police Professionalism

An ethic of police professionalism must take into account not only the social role of police but also the various contexts in which police activity takes place. Although we tend to give a certain preeminence to street officer–citizen encounters, there are, in fact, many different contexts in which professionalism may be exhibited (or betrayed). For example, organization–citizen engagements arise when a department, through its chief, decides to focus on speeding or response time or proposes the use of new enforcement strategies. Mediated organization–citizen engagements occur when a community's elected representative proposes a zero-tolerance policy for quality-of-life offenses, or when a department seeks economic support for its programs. Organization–media engagements come about when departments determine and implement policies for reporting and disclosing their activities. Interagency encounters occur when a department determines how it will cooperate with another organization (whether in law enforcement or in some other public service). Organization–research encounters arise when departments decide whether and to what extent to open themselves to the research agendas of academia. Peer encounters occur when officers relate to each other—for example, with respect to gender, race, religion, or sexual orientation. Hierarchical encounters arise as supervisors make decisions regarding deployment, tenure, time off, and so forth. These represent only some of the contexts in which police and their organizations may act professionally or otherwise. A comprehensive ethic of professionalism will engage with all these contexts.

## General Issues for a Professional Law Enforcement Ethic

As part of the social contract that establishes and maintains police authority, several overlapping issues are of central importance to the establishment of a professional ethic.

*An Understanding of Discretion.* Although police manuals often provide a great deal of specific guidance for officers on the street, they cannot encompass all of the circumstances in which officers will find themselves. Thus, officers should exercise discretion as they go about their tasks, particularly in the ways in which they respond to the critical situations to which they are called. Discretionary decision making is a vital yet problematic aspect of police work. It is vital because police cannot avoid making such decisions, often in circumstances that are highly pressured and involve important human interests. It is problematic because, as agents of governmental power, police officers in liberal democratic societies are bound by the rule of law. Whatever else this means, it limits the ways in which police may use their discretion.

Discretion is not simply the capacity to make one's own decisions, but an authority to use one's judgment. An officer who hits a handcuffed prisoner with impunity does not use discretion poorly—he has no discretion to act in that way. Discretion is a limited authority to make certain decisions and, like all forms of social authority, may be withdrawn, curtailed, or even lost if not used wisely. It may have various objects: Discretion can concern the scope of the police role, the interpretation of expectations, the priority that is given to competing tasks, or the strategies to be used to achieve a particular end. Each gives rise to ethically significant questions, although it is probably the last context that generates the greatest public scrutiny.

A professional ethic will acknowledge the need for bounded discretion and seek to ensure that those who have discretionary judgments to make will be prepared to make them well. Departments will have the responsibility of ensuring that officers have sufficient discretion to enable them to decide wisely in the situations in which they find themselves, but not so much discretion that they are left "at sea."

An issue of some controversy concerns the extent to which officers' private lives should be constrained by their public role. Although it may go too far to say that police ought to be communal role models, questions might be raised about the use of discretion on the job or respect for police authority if the private lives of police are too much at variance with what one might expect from their public role.

*Appropriate Accountability.* Police authority is loaned—it is a delegation from those who have entered into the social contract, and therefore must be accounted for to those who have given it. To this end, we recognize a diversity of internal and public strategies—written reports, organizational reporting requirements, media scrutiny, judicial review, and so on—that hold police accountable for what they do. As part of an ethic of professionalism, however, accountability must involve a personal commitment by officers to the wise use of the powers vested in them. These two dimensions of accountability may come into tension: Excessive supervision may erode personal commitment and a sense of personal responsibility; too much reliance on personal accountability can foster sloppiness and opportunistic corruption.

Because the authority given to police is exercised on behalf of the community at large, it is important that police organizations be transparent. This requires emphasis just because there is a tendency for police organizations to operate in a secretive fashion. No doubt certain police work requires secrecy as a condition of its effectiveness. But secretiveness may undermine accountability. The "blue wall of silence" may function at either an individual or organizational level as a strategy whereby individual officers or the department conceal their dirty laundry. Although it is probably important that an association have the option to handle some of its problems internally, there is also a risk that overemphasis on self-regulation will lead to underregulation and a decline in organizational personal integrity.

*Integrity.* The nature of a good deal of police work is such that those with whom police deal have an interest in diverting them through inducements and other means. Added to that, police work offers many situational temptations. Therefore, corruption looms large as a problem for police, and law enforcement ethics is often said to center around the issue of integrity.

Integrity—as a personal virtue, a matter of character—has at least a double meaning. On one hand, it refers to a consistency of character, and to the refusal to be diverted from that to which one is committed as a moral agent by temptations and external pressures of various kinds. More narrowly, it refers to honesty, truthfulness, and transparency. It can be very difficult to maintain integrity in a form of work that often requires deceptiveness as a strategic device, and where pragmatic pressures can foster what has been called "noble cause corruption."

Because of the various pressures on police, police organizations frequently find it difficult to ensure the integrity of their personnel. "Integrity testing," whereby internal investigatory bodies seek through random or targeted means to determine the ethical rectitude of their personnel, may be essential in an organization that has experienced significant lapses, but if used too aggressively, it may undermine professionalism. Ultimately, the best guarantee of integrity is probably an appreciation of the importance of one's role and a pride in fulfilling it.

### Specific Issues for a Professional Law Enforcement Ethic

Law enforcement will, naturally enough, generate specific issues for those who engage in it. The following are among the most important issues.

*The Use of Force.* The contractualist understanding of the police role largely reposes the use of force, and particularly deadly force, in the police: When the use of force might be required to resolve some social conflict, our first recourse is to be the police. But this delegation carries with it a heavy responsibility, both with respect to the occasions on which it is used and the manner of its use when it is called for.

Generally, the use of force is considered to be a last resort, and some police departments encourage adherence to a graduated scale of authoritative engagement. In addition, police agencies have developed or adopted various devices that diminish the long-term impact, although not the effectiveness, of uses of intermediate force—rounded batons, chemical sprays, stun guns, and so on. One potential problem with all such developments is that with increasing noninjuriousness also comes the heightened potential for nondetectable misuse.

The use of deadly force is especially problematic because of its irreversibility. In the United States, the landmark decision of *Tennessee v. Garner* (1985) effectively limited the use of deadly force to those situations in which a person had posed or would pose some grave danger to others, and excluded its use simply to prevent a person from escaping arrest.

*The Use of Deception.* Particularly with the diminished place of confessions (and the third degree that was sometimes used to extract them) and the need for corroborating evidence, the use of deception has greatly increased. Jerome Skolnick (1982) has usefully distinguished three contexts in which law enforcement personnel may employ deception in criminal cases: during the initial investigatory search; as part of interrogation, when a person is in custody; and during sworn testimony.

The greatest latitude for the use of deceptive tactics (such as decoys, informants, and surveillance devices) exists at the initial investigative stage, although clearly, there are ethical constraints arising from rights to privacy as well as general duties of truthfulness. The imbalance of power constituted by custodial interrogation imposes additional constraints on the use of deception. It is generally considered wrong (and sometimes perjurious) to engage in deception when testimony is sworn: The use of deception here subverts the integrity of the adversarial process as well as the legitimate checks that society may wish to impose on the use of deception at the investigative and interrogatory stages.

*John Kleinig*

*See also* Accountability, Corruption/Integrity, Interrogation, Police Discretion, Use of Force

## For Further Reading

Delattre, E. (2002). *Character and cops: Ethics in policing* (4th ed.). Washington, DC: AEI.

Kleinig, J. (1996). *The ethics of policing.* Cambridge, UK: Cambridge University Press.

Kleinig, J., & Zhang, Y. (1993). *Professional law enforcement codes: A documentary collection.* Westport, CT: Greenwood.

Leighton, P., & Reiman, J. (Ed.). (2001). *Criminal justice ethics.* Upper Saddle River, NJ: Prentice Hall.

Locke, J. (1690). *Second treatise of civil government.* Many editions.

Skolnick, J. H. (1982, Summer/Fall). Deception by police. *Criminal Justice Ethics, 1,* 40–53.

Tennessee v. Garner, 471 U.S. 1, 105 S.Ct. 1694, 85 L. Ed. 2d 1 (1985).

## ॐ EVALUATION OF OFFICERS

Evaluation is the process of assessing the quality and/or quantity of an individual's work performance to determine the degree to which it meets an established standard. In many cases, the job description establishes the standard, whereas in others, there may be a specific set of performance standards that may include both quantitative and qualitative measures. Without clearly defined standards of performance, evaluation of officers becomes quite a subjective process, dependent on the person conducting the evaluation. Fundamental to performance evaluation is the definition of the role of the officer; the required knowledge, skills, and abilities; and the means for obtaining objective data on which to base the evaluation.

By nature, performance evaluations require an understanding of what constitutes "good" performance. In some domains, such as manufacturing, performance is simply defined in quantitative terms (e.g., "produced 106 widgets"). However, in law enforcement, the definition of what constitutes good performance has been evolving as the role of the police officer has been expanded to include many qualitative performance dimensions, such as community outreach and problem solving. Because many organizations have adopted a model of community policing, which requires greater service orientation of officers, the domain of performance is expanding and becoming more difficult to define in precise terms.

A law enforcement agency should develop performance standards for the agency during a strategic planning process. These standards should be derived from a clearly articulated mission, vision, and set of values. Once an agency has identified its own performance goals in that process, it can then develop performance standards for its employees.

The first step in developing employee performance standards is to commission a thorough job analysis that delineates the specific tasks required for each position; the frequency and criticality (importance) of those tasks; and the corresponding requisite knowledge, skills, abilities, and other characteristics. The job specifications generated from the job analysis serve as the basis for establishing standards of performance upon which to rate job performance. Individual performance is then gauged against the job description, performance standards, and, ultimately, the organizational goals.

Although traditional indicators of success in law enforcement have included quantitative factors such as number of arrests, citations, case closures, response times, and so on, the majority of experts and practitioners agree that these measures may be poor or insufficient indicators of the law enforcement officer's job, in that they are not always consistent with community expectations and may be seen as "quotas." Some experts have suggested that evaluation of officers should include building a strong relationship with the community, engaging in intergovernmental activities that could improve the quality of life in communities, involving private industry to improve social control, reducing fear of crime, providing greater services to crime victims, developing school-based programs for crime prevention, and promoting civil liberties.

It is important to note that some individuals perform tasks that are outside of the defined role and that contribute to the organizational and social environment. Often referred to as "organizational citizenship behavior," this type of performance includes reducing tensions, organizing social activities, improving relationships, and so on. Similarly, there may be individuals who perform their tasks well, but engage in a range of counterproductive behaviors that limit organizational effectiveness (e.g., promoting negativity, etc.). Indeed, job performance is more than just the completion of individual tasks, but the manner in which tasks are completed and the quality of the services delivered. In fact, psychologists have acknowledged recently that an individual's value to an organization may go beyond his or her behavior to his or her characteristics, such as

integrity or valuing diversity. Any thorough job analysis should take into consideration these community-oriented, organizational, and qualitative dimensions of performance. In fact, many jurisdictions have begun to include community members in the process of identifying the appropriate functions of police and alternative indicators of good performance.

The purpose of regularly evaluating officers is to enhance the ability to make rational and defensible personnel decisions (e.g., promotions, assignments, transfers, etc.); examine deficiencies or improper actions that need to be corrected; identify training or developmental needs; establish new policies or organizational objectives; ensure compliance with organizational policies and standards; and establish accountability within and outside the organization. Therefore, effective performance evaluation requires collecting and analyzing performance data as well as providing feedback to direct an individual's performance toward organizational goals.

Whereas traditional performance appraisals are conducted on a periodic basis (e.g., annually), performance assessment should take place on an ongoing basis in order to avoid biases in ratings. Evaluations can be conducted by comparing performance to absolute performance standards or to others performing the same or similar function. Unfortunately, the information typically used to make these decisions is often based on memory, hearsay, intuition, or haphazard observation. Furthermore, the judgment process itself is inherently subjective, often leading to unfair, biased, or inaccurate ratings. Nevertheless, steps can be taken to make the process more objective. For example, ratings can be behaviorally based, rather than driven by qualities or characteristics like "leadership ability" or "decision-making skills," which are often not defined in behavioral terms. Some international jurisdictions (South Australian Police, New Zealand, and New South Wales) are experimenting with a new method known as "activity measurement" that is being used to determine the extent to which officers devote time or energy to various activities so that these efforts can be linked more closely to outputs.

The primary focus of many performance evaluation systems is the documentation of supervisory assessments of their personnel on performance appraisal forms. There are a variety of types of instruments and methods used in performance evaluation. These include graphic rating scales on which individuals are numerically or categorically (e.g., above average, unacceptable, etc.) rated regarding various dimensions such as quality of work, job knowledge, motivation, and so on. Employee comparison methods involve ranking individuals or placing individuals in a category (e.g., *excellent, poor*) where the categories must be normally distributed. A behavioral checklist is a method for evaluating performance that is designed to be more objective by linking specific behaviors to scores on various work dimensions, such as job knowledge.

Who should evaluate performance? Traditionally, the immediate supervisor is the person who may have the most information about an individual's performance. However, supervisory judgments have been demonstrated to be subject to various individual motivations, biases, lack of knowledge, lack of reliability and validity checks, different frames of reference, hesitancy to criticize officers, or indifference. For these reasons, the objectivity and accuracy of ratings can be highly suspect and have led some law enforcement agencies to reject the performance appraisal process altogether, rather than to work to improve current systems.

Common rating biases include halo, leniency, severity, central tendency, individual bias, recency, primacy, contrast effects, and/or outcome bias. The halo effect occurs when a rater overemphasizes one aspect of an officer's performance to influence his or her ratings on other performance dimensions. Leniency and severity are the tendencies of some raters to rate all individuals too favorably or too harshly. Similarly, central tendency bias occurs when an evaluator focuses on the middle range of the rating scale and tends to rate everyone as average. Individual biases may be based on a variety of things, such as race, age, gender, sexual orientation, religion, friendship, or the degree to which the ratee is similar to the rater. Recency and primacy effects are present when a supervisor tends to rate the individual based on his or her performance during the beginning or ending of the evaluation cycle, rather than during the entire rating period. Contrast effects occur when an individual is compared to the previous person rated. If the previous ratee was particularly exceptional, then one's performance may be rated more poorly than if he or she had been compared to someone who was an average performer. Finally, outcome bias occurs when evaluators use a politically motivated end to influence a person's rating, such as the case when a supervisor wishes to transfer an officer out of his or her unit. Although these biases and errors should be attended to and, where appropriate, remedial action taken, recent research has suggested that these biases do not necessarily result in rating errors and may be relatively trivial. Nevertheless, there are many reasons to be cautious when relying solely on supervisory evaluations.

Given the increasing emphasis on community policing, there may be some relevance to including the recipients of police services in the process. Also, many organizations have included peer, subordinate, and self ratings, a process often referred to as 360° performance evaluations. When relying solely on supervisory judgments, an agency may perpetuate a climate whereby accountability is limited, and ratings are motivated by individual goals rather than organizational ones. It is clear that evaluation of performance does not occur in a vacuum; agencies must consider the broader context within which the performance occurs, the motivations of the evaluators, the individuals selected to conduct the evaluation, and a host of other concerns if they are to encourage organizationally appropriate behavior.

*Karen L. Amendola*

***See also*** Accountability, Arrest, Calls for Service, Community Policing, Quotas, Response Time

## For Further Reading

Alpert, G. P., Flynn, D., & Piquero, A. R. (2001). Effective community policing performance measures. *Justice Research and Policy, 3*(2), 79–94.

Alpert, G. P., & Moore, M. H. (1993). Measuring police performance in the new paradigm of policing. In G. P. Alpert

& A. Piquero (Eds.), *Community policing: Contemporary readings* (pp. 215–232). Prospect Heights, IL: Waveland.

Arvey, R. D., & Murphy, K. R. (1998). Performance evaluation in work settings. *Annual Review of Psychology, 49,* 141–168.

Dadds, V., & Scheide, T. (2000). *Police performance and activity measurement* (Trends and Issues in Crime and Criminal Justice, No. 180). Retrieved from www.aic.gov.au/publications/tandi/ti180.pdf

Marx, G. T. (1976). Alternative measures of police performance. In E. Viano (Ed.), *Criminal justice research.* Lexington, MA: Lexington Books.

## ○○ EVIDENCE

At its most basic level, *evidence* is anything that tends to prove or disprove an alleged fact. Most evidence can be divided into three broad categories: direct evidence, indirect evidence, and physical evidence.

*Direct* evidence establishes an element of a crime through an eyewitness account, confession, or anything observed (including writings and audio, video, or digital recordings of observations). *Indirect* evidence is based on inference and deductive reasoning (e.g., a smoking gun indicates the weapon has been fired and is probably linked to the dead body next to it). *Physical* evidence results from a criminal investigation. It is sought to determine that a crime has been committed or that there is a link between a specific crime and its victim or perpetrator. Many times, these three categories of evidence can overlap: the content of a written confession is direct evidence, the fact that it was offered without coercion on the author's deathbed would be indirect evidence, and the actual note or recording (such as the paper and ink or audiotape) would be considered physical evidence.

Although all categories of evidence are extremely important, recent studies on the unreliability of eyewitness accounts have caused an increased emphasis on physical evidence in the apprehension of suspects and successful prosecution of crimes. Accounts of false or coerced confessions; the existence of wrongful convictions based on mistaken, fabricated, or plea bargain-induced testimony; the inherent fallibility of human judgment; and the reality of offender exonerations based on new scientific technology such as DNA have brought the critical nature of physical—now commonly referred to as *forensic*—evidence to the forefront of police investigation and subsequent legal issues.

## DIRECT EVIDENCE

As the first person called to the crime scene, the police officer is often the most important factor in determining the availability, quantity, and quality of direct evidence. Few officers actually observe the crime in progress, so it is the police's function to gather information and statements from witnesses through a process of interview and interrogation as quickly and thoroughly as possible.

In the late 1990s, research psychologists presented new theories of flawed perception by eyewitnesses, proving that at least 50% of subjects in observational experiments failed to perceive very major things right in front of their eyes. This phenomenon, dubbed "inattentional blindness," brought new understanding to the concept of "change blindness," where people often fail to detect changes in their field of vision during eye movement or other interruptions.

In 1999, Harvard psychologist Daniel Simons updated these phenomena in an experiment where subjects watched a video of two groups of people dressed in black and white passing a basketball between players. Instructed to count the number of passes by the white team, 50% of subjects insisted they never saw the gorilla (a person in a gorilla costume) walk directly into the field of play. Simons's conclusion, called "selective looking," suggested that individualistic variables of both the scene and the observer can raise critical issues about the credibility and accuracy of human eyewitness testimony.

Historically, sketches, diagrams, and photographs were used to record the observations of witnesses and investigators in an effort to minimize the possibility of human error or faulty memory. Still, there are cases where photographic evidence has only contributed to a controversial crime as it is scrutinized by experts with different opinions. The famous Zapruder film of the assassination of

President John F. Kennedy in 1963 has divided experts and spawned numerous theories as to the number of gunmen and shots fired. A photograph of the assumed shooter, Lee Harvey Oswald, bearing a rifle similar to the type used in the assassination, was widely cited as evidence of his culpability as the lone shooter, but it has been rejected by many as a fake composite of several photographs. More than 40 years after the event, forensic experts continue to disagree about the Warren Commission findings of a single "magic" bullet theory, while eyewitnesses—such as Nellie Connolly, who sat in the car with President Kennedy—continue to insist that more than one shot was fired.

The issue of eyewitness accounts of crimes has grown in controversy in recent years, not only because of research on inattentional blindness, but also because of real-life criminal cases that illustrate how human perception is easily influenced by complex variables. In the 1984 case of the "Subway Gunman" Bernard Goetz, multiple eyewitnesses observed Goetz shoot four youths, but their accounts varied greatly in terms of whether the victims were panhandling or robbing, and whether Goetz was provoked into self-defense or just shooting in anger. The videotaped confession of Goetz showed him saying, "I wanted to kill those guys, I wanted to maim those guys. I wanted to make them suffer in every way I could." Whereas some observers considered this statement evidence of a man who shot with vengeance instead of self-defense, others saw the officers' line of questioning as evidence of unethical interrogation tactics, in which positive reinforcement encouraged a highly excitable suspect to exaggerate his motives in an attempt to please his audience. The Goetz case illustrates how law enforcement has an ethical obligation to gather information without undue influence and take statements with objectivity, so that the subsequent legal process can interpret the authenticity and meaning of such evidence.

Audiotape evidence has also entered the gray area between direct, indirect, and physical evidence. An emotional 9-1-1 phone call by Lyle Menendez was recorded by California police in 1989 and initially appeared to corroborate his account of discovering his murdered parents, apparent victims of a botched burglary. After careful analysis of voice inflection and pitch, however, audiolinguistic experts were able to determine that the hysterical crying of Menendez was actually hysterical laughter, rehearsed and presented in an attempt to divert police away from the fact that Menendez and his brother had shot their parents themselves. The phone call became one of the most important pieces of direct evidence in the conviction of the Menendez brothers.

In a different case in 1989, audiotape evidence resulted in a very different outcome. A Kentucky man, Mel Ignatow, was charged with the sadistic rape and murder of his girlfriend. The case was stalled because the most critical physical evidence, the victim's body, was found only after Ignatow's accomplice was wired by the FBI in hopes of eliciting information on the burial site. Based on details from a conversation with Ignatow recorded by the FBI, the body was recovered and the suspect went to trial. Ignatow never directly confessed on the tape, so the case relied completely on the legality and content of the recorded discussion, which led authorities to the body.

The case came down to one muffled word on the tape: Did Ignatow say "site" or "safe" when he said, "It's not shallow that place we dug. . . . Besides, that one area right by where that ("site"? "safe"?) is does not have any trees by it." The jury listened to the tape dozens of times and could not agree on which word he meant, and determined that knowing the word was crucial: Was the suspect referring to a burial site or a buried safe? At least one juror found reasonable doubt, based on the poor quality of the recording and importance of definitively knowing the word spoken, and Ignatow was acquitted. Later, when new direct evidence surfaced (photographs taken of the victim during the rape and murder), the public was stunned to realize that the culprit was protected from further prosecution based on double jeopardy.

Because the nature of observed and recorded evidence is subject to human error, law enforcement now seeks to avoid such pitfalls and maximize admissibility of direct evidence by *videotaping* interviews, interrogations, crime scenes, and forensic evidence collection and processing. Although no video or digital recording is completely tamper-proof, the normalcy of video cameras in our society has brought attention to the increased probability of misconduct by both the public and the police, and has heightened awareness and acceptance of video as a source of evidence comparable to, if not more believable than, audio and eyewitness testimony.

The 1991 videotape of the use of physical force by Los Angeles police officers against a suspect, Rodney King, gained worldwide attention as the officers were brought to trial for the recorded "beating." The case, however, showed that poor-quality video, particularly without an audio recording of the officers' statements at the scene, may raise more questions than answers when pitted against conflicting eyewitness testimony by officers and spectators at the scene. A typed computer record indicating that one involved officer referred to African Americans as "something out of *Gorillas in the Mist*" earlier that day did not convince jurors that the force was unjustified after conflicting police experts dissected the tape frame by frame in an attempt to use it as evidence for both the defense and prosecution.

The acquittal of all four officers accused of using excessive force against King resulted in massive rioting by those who were incredulous that the jury had gone against the "real" evidence of the videotape. Ironically, news cameras videotaped rioters looting, stealing, and assaulting police and innocent bystanders, including an innocent truck driver who was caught in the melee and severely beaten; that videotape evidence was later used by prosecutors to identify and convict dozens of offenders.

## INDIRECT EVIDENCE

Eyewitness and recorded testimony often build the foundation for the level of suspicion of "probable cause" necessary to detain a suspect and gain important evidence, but it is the behavioral science involved in interview and interrogation that most affects the admissibility of a confession. In the 1989 "Central Park Jogger" case, nonmatching physical DNA evidence was not enough to raise reasonable doubt after jurors saw videotape evidence of 10 statements made by "wilding" juveniles (made in the presence of their parents) in which each provided graphic detail of the sexual attack on a young woman.

The young suspects were not so much convicted on the direct evidence of the confession as by the totality of *indirect* evidence linking the suspects to the crime: Police confirmed that the youths in question were seen "wilding" (i.e., randomly terrorizing or attacking others) that night; the suspects confessed on videotape to the rape and beating of the victim, and summarily implicated one another; and the crimes were admitted to in the presence of parents, guardians, and lawyers. The youths spent more than 10 years incarcerated for the crime, but in 2002, they were released from prison after the original DNA evidence was matched to a suspect who confessed to being the sole attacker. The reality of the false confessions focuses attention on police interrogation tactics and the psychological complexity and legal considerations involved with vulnerable suspects.

The practice of using inferential logic based on known facts, particularly empirical evidence of patterns and typologies supported by significant statistical probability, has often been referred to as "profiling." Although founded in tenets of behavioral science, the actual evidentiary variables of known crimes and perpetrators (e.g., murder weapon of choice, location of crime, staging of body) serve as the foundation for constructing the inferential profiles forming indirect evidence.

The validity of profiles and their legitimacy as evidence for investigatory practice and probable cause is highly controversial. The use of known-offender profiles (often referred to as racial profiling) as a basis for probable cause to stop a motorist who fits a typical description of a drug smuggler has pitted due process advocates against crime-fighting law enforcement. Critics argue that variables such as race, physical appearance, vehicle type, state of origin, direction of travel, number of passengers, and so on should not be the basis, even in the face of overwhelming statistical probability, for indirect evidence of a potential crime. Proponents insist that the Boolean logic of inferential statistics can empirically justify such a conclusion.

Although it is empirical in nature, behavioral profiling is less statistically valid and thus a more controversial form of indirect evidence. In 1984, the Green River killer sent a letter to Seattle police, the contents of which indicated direct knowledge of the crime; however, FBI profiler John Douglas conducted an analysis of the letter's message and issued a report determining that there was no behavioral link to substantiate its attribution to the killer. Although the contents provided a direct link to the crimes because the information was highly specific, no further analysis of the physical evidence (the typewriter font, paper, postmark, etc.) was conducted. The failure to find indirect evidence in this case hinged on the fallibility of human judgment, and the killer—Gary Ridgway—continued to murder and eluded police until apprehended in 2003.

In a different serial killing case, FBI profiler Gregg McCrary was able to analyze the physical evidence of crime scenes and locations of body dump sites to construct a behavioral profile of the offender. When the perpetrator returned to the scene of his crime, as predicted by McCrary, law enforcement officers were waiting and arrested the killer—Arthur Shawcross—based on the behavioral and logical link to his presence at the dump site.

Although indirect evidence based on the logic, analysis, and opinions of forensic experts in the social science and business fields remains controversial, police continue to rely on such analyses for investigations, and courts are increasingly accepting such evidence as "scientific." As the number of known facts in real cases continues to rise, with variables being identified, recorded, and statistically analyzed, the validity of indirect evidence will likely rise in consonance.

## PHYSICAL EVIDENCE

With the ongoing controversy over the validity and reliability of direct evidence, courts are more likely to depend on physical evidence. Such *scientific* evidence includes forensic medicine, pathology,

odontology, anthropology, entomology, toxicology, engineering, radiology, botany, metallurgy, and geology. Criminalistics, the scientific examination of trace evidence, involves the study of serums, genetics, hair, fingerprints, fiber, glass, and other physical particles. The stages in physical evidence analysis include (a) recognition and documentation, (b) collection and preservation, (c) examination and identification, (d) comparison and individualization, (e) conclusion and interpretation, (f) reconstruction and reporting, and finally, (g) testimony and court.

DNA science, involving the analysis of genetic markers, has become the most influential development in physical evidence, with new techniques of analysis so profound and probabilities of exclusion so remote that DNA, when present, is the most likely factor in conviction. Likewise, advocates for the wrongfully accused have launched campaigns, such as the Innocence Project, which have used DNA evidence or reanalyzed other physical evidence to overturn convictions—often based on direct evidence prior to the availability of forensic technology—and release innocent prisoners.

For police officers, the proper collection, handling, and storage of physical evidence is paramount to building a case for court and has been a pivotal factor in cases involving contaminated crime scenes, such as the murders of Nicole Brown Simpson and JonBenet Ramsey. Documenting the chain of custody in which evidence moves from crime scene to storage to laboratory has become critical to addressing reasonable doubt issues raised by defense attorneys. Because of the tremendous emphasis placed by law enforcement and prosecutors on the thorough collection of all potential evidence, preservation and storage of evidence has become a challenge from both a scientific and a practical stance.

In the 1998 New York case of serial killer Kendall Francois, police investigators had to collect, document, transport, and store several truckloads of evidence—including 11 mattresses—from the house where the suspect had sexually assaulted, killed, and stored the bodies of eight women. Warehouse units had to be rented in order to safely process, catalog, and store the hundreds of pieces of evidence. In the

City of New York, tens of thousands of pieces of evidence must be stored indefinitely, and the reality of warehousing, tracking, and preserving physical evidence (through careful management of access, security, temperature, humidity, and light) has become a major recordkeeping and financial burden for the police.

## EVIDENCE AND THE LAW

Because of the potential for psychological manipulation or physical coercion when gathering direct evidence, as well as the possibility of unethical recordings of conversations and statements and illegal gathering of physical evidence, the *exclusionary rule* serves to protect suspects from unfounded or aggressive practices that violate a suspect's due process rights by making tainted evidence inadmissible in a prosecutorial case. The rule suppresses any evidence determined by the courts to be illegally obtained, including unexpected evidence of other crimes derived from the illegal police activity called "fruit of the poisonous tree."

The law of search and seizure governs the methods by which police can investigate and collect physical evidence, and the past four decades have witnessed dramatic fluctuations in court decisions governing police practices. Court-mandated exceptions to the exclusionary rule—such as "good faith," "plain view doctrine," and "exigent circumstances," as well as policy issues such as privacy, bodily integrity, public safety, excitable utterances, and inevitable discovery—have extended the circumstances under which police can conduct investigations. The ongoing interpretation of search and seizure law in constantly emerging cases scrutinized under different political circumstances often complicates law enforcement practices.

As courts continue to review and rule on complex evidentiary fact patterns, law enforcement has been forced to include regular and updated training on search and seizure law to ensure that officers do not inadvertently compromise cases. The prevalence of technology in culture as well as science has caused a crossover between direct and physical evidence, in some instances simplifying the challenge of gathering evidence. Security cameras have been the norm in private industry and retail establishments, and some cities—such as Baltimore, Maryland—have actually installed video cameras on the streets of high-crime neighborhoods.

Technology is perhaps the most influential factor for the future of evidence. In 2004, an unmanned security camera recorded the abduction of 11-year-old Carlie Brucia in Florida; in a case without any human witnesses or physical evidence, the videotape offered "eyewitness" testimony of her kidnapping as well as the physical clues (tattoos on the suspect's arms and a nametag on his uniform) that became the physical link between the crime, victim, and perpetrator. With the assistance of NASA's video-image enhancement technology, the identifying marks on the abductor (direct evidence) led police to a tattooed mechanic of the same name embroidered on the suspect's shirt (indirect evidence), who in turn led police to the victim's body (physical evidence).

As the critical front-line players in the criminal justice system, police officers remain the most crucial determiners of which evidence is collected, used, and made admissible in the interest of justice. Because the successful prosecution of crimes ultimately relies on the quality, quantity, and legality of evidence, law enforcement bears the greatest personal responsibility for current, ethical, and accurate knowledge of evidence and its application within the criminal justice system.

*Casey Jordan*

***See also*** Crime Scene Investigation, DNA, Exclusionary Rule, Eyewitness Testimony, Forensic Science, Profiling (Criminal Personality, Drug Courier, Geographic, and Racial/Ethnic)

## *For Further Reading*

Buckles, T. (2003). *Laws of evidence.* Clifton Park, NY: Thompson/West.

Good, P. (2001). *Applying statistics in the courtroom: A new approach for attorneys and expert witnesses.* Boca Raton, FL: CRC.

Hanley, J., Schmidt, W., & Robbins, R. (1999). *Introduction to criminal evidence and court procedure.* Berkeley, CA: McCutchan.

Imwinkelried, E. (1998). *Evidentiary foundations.* Charlottesville, VA: Lexis.

Kiely, T. (2001). *Forensic evidence: Science and the criminal law.* Boca Raton, FL: CRC.

Saferstein, R. (2002). *Criminalistics: An introduction to forensic science.* Upper Saddle River, NJ: Prentice Hall.

# ✐ EXCLUSIONARY RULES

In American courts, exclusionary rules mandate, on motion by an aggrieved criminal defendant, suppression of evidence of the defendant's guilt when that evidence was obtained in violation of the defendant's legal rights. The legal rights at stake are often constitutional; most commonly, they involve the Fourth, Fifth, and Sixth Amendments. However, the rights may be statutory as well, as when evidence is obtained in violation of federal statutes governing electronic surveillance by government officials.

## ORIGINS

The origins of the exclusionary rules are to be found in constitutional decisions rendered by the U.S. Supreme Court in the first half of the 20th century. The most important of these is *Weeks v. United States* (1914), where the Court held that evidence obtained in violation of Weeks's Fourth Amendment rights should have been suppressed at his criminal trial. Subsequent Court decisions expanded on *Weeks* by adding what came to be known as the "fruit of the poisonous tree" rule. This rule mandates suppression, on motion by a defendant, of derivative evidence—that is, evidence obtained through leads provided by the government's initial illegality.

*Weeks* and the many cases that elaborated on it dealt only with evidence acquired in illegal searches and seizures. In *Brown v. Mississippi* (1936), the Court established an exclusionary rule for evidence obtained by means of coercive police interrogations. *Miranda v. Arizona* (1966) modified *Brown* and substantially expanded its scope, holding that the Fifth Amendment requires warnings to a suspect in custody if the suspect's statements to the police are to be admissible.

Two Warren Court decisions of the 1960s established Sixth Amendment exclusionary rules. In *Massiah v. United States* (1964), the Court required suppression of statements by a jailed defendant, who had already been indicted and been accorded counsel, to an inmate acting as a government informant. Three years later, the Court again drew on the Sixth Amendment's right-to-counsel clause in *United States v. Wade* (1967), holding that once a defendant has secured counsel, following indictment, that counsel must be present at the defendant's lineup.

## MODIFICATIONS

The Burger and Rehnquist Courts have shown a marked distaste for the exclusionary rules, but they have pruned them instead of abolishing them altogether. The most important example of pruning is to be found in *United States v. Leon* (1984). There, the Court established an exception for "reasonable good faith mistakes" by officers in the execution of search warrants. Specifically, it permitted the prosecution to use evidence in its case chiefly when that evidence has been obtained in good-faith reliance on a search warrant. The term *good faith* is something of a misnomer. What is critical to *Leon* and the decisions elaborating on it is not an officer's subjective belief that his or her conduct was proper, but rather the objective reliability of an official pronouncement subsequently determined to be invalid—a search warrant (in *Leon*), for example, or a statute authorizing warrantless inspection of business premises. Thus, *Leon*-type exceptions are limited in nature. In particular, it should be noted that the Court has *not* established a general exception for warrantless searches and seizures.

The Court's post-*Miranda* cases have been considerably more complex than its cases dealing with Fourth Amendment violations. At one point, in *Oregon v. Elstad* (1985), the Court explicitly distinguished between coercive custodial interrogation (a full-fledged Fifth Amendment violation) and violations of Miranda that are not coercive in nature. The consequence of a Miranda-only violation, *Elstad* held, is that an incriminating statement obtained without warnings must be suppressed, but the fruits of that statement are admissible. In *Dickerson v. United States* (2000), the Court asserted that *Miranda* is, indeed, a "constitutional decision" (a point cast in doubt by *Elstad*), but it appeared to leave intact *Elstad*'s refusal to apply "fruit of the poisonous tree" rules to derivative evidence obtained through a Miranda violation. The Court has agreed to address this issue in an upcoming session.

## ADMINISTRATION OF THE RULES

Three administrative rules are critical to implementation of exclusion. The most important has to do with "standing"—that is, with the right of a criminal defendant to secure suppression at trial. Although the Court has commented unfavorably on the term "standing," it has steadfastly adhered to the principle that suppression is available only to individuals who can point to government violations of *their* rights. If evidence is obtained through a violation of some other person's rights, a criminal defendant is not entitled to its suppression.

Second, absent unusual circumstances, a motion to suppress must be made *prior* to trial. This rule, which originates in *Weeks*, places the prosecution on notice as to what evidence it can use to sustain its burden of proof. Because most criminal cases are resolved through plea bargaining, the pretrial-motion rule has made it possible for the prosecution and defense to calculate beforehand the likely consequences of a trial.

Finally, American courts have long permitted the admission for impeachment purposes of evidence that is otherwise inadmissible. If a defendant testifies on direct examination to matters that can be impeached by reliable but illegally obtained evidence, that evidence can be employed to challenge the defendant's credibility.

## RATIONALE

What justification can be advanced for the suppression of reliable but illegally acquired evidence of a defendant's guilt? Careful attention should be given to the fact that this is a question only about the suppression of *reliable* evidence of guilt. If *un*reliable

evidence is at issue, the suppression rationale is straightforward: Fact-finders should not be asked to consider unreliable evidence in reaching their verdict. Thus, there is little controversy about confessions obtained through coercive interrogation techniques or lineups conducted in prejudicial ways: These produce unreliable evidence of guilt. Rather, debate centers on illegal procedures that produce reliable evidence of guilt: tangible objects, for example, such as guns or drugs obtained in violation of the Fourth Amendment; statements overheard during the course of judicially unsupervised eavesdropping; or confessions secured in violation of the *Miranda* rules but in the absence of coercion. In these instances, the reliability of evidence of guilt is strong; nonetheless, modern exclusionary rules require the suppression of such evidence.

One rationale commonly advanced for suppressing reliable evidence is grounded in the concept of restorative justice. Given a legal right, it is contended, courts should take steps to restore someone to the position he or she was in prior to the right's violation. A suppression order, it is thus argued, simply reimposes the status quo ante. Unfortunately, this approach is both under- and overinclusive. It is underinclusive because in some instances—think of the conversational privacy lost as a result of illegal eavesdropping—there is nothing that can be done to restore the status quo ante. The rationale is overinclusive in other settings, however. For example, no court has ordered the return of illegally seized weapons or drugs.

An alternative rationale, which is favored by the current Court, relies on deterrence. Whereas the restorative-justice rationale conceives of suppression as a first-party remedy (as a remedy designed to benefit a wronged party), the deterrence rationale treats it as a third-party remedy (as a remedy designed to benefit the public at large and only incidentally generates a benefit for the party seeking it). The *Leon* Court explicitly adopted this rationale for the Fourth Amendment, but a similar approach can be taken for Fifth and Sixth Amendment exclusion. The difficulty with this rationale is that little empirical evidence exists to support it. Given a deterrence justification, exclusion can be defended only if the cost it imposes (lost reliable evidence of guilt) is outweighed by the benefit it generates (foregone acts of illegality attributable to the threat of suppression). It is perhaps unfair to ask defenders of exclusion to provide conclusive evidence that the suppression threat has this effect. It must be noted, though, that the evidence is indeed modest with respect to the exclusionary rule's deterrent power.

*William C. Heffernan*

*See also* Miranda Warnings, Plain View Doctrine, Search and Seizure

## For Further Reading

Amar, A. R. (1997). *The Constitution and criminal procedure: First principles.* New Haven, CT: Yale University Press.

Brown v. Mississippi, 297 U.S. 278 (1936).

Dickerson v. United States, 530 U.S. 428 (2000).

Dripps, D. (2001). The case for the contingent exclusionary rule. *American Criminal Law Review, 38,* 1–46.

Heffernan, W. C. (2000). The Fourth Amendment exclusionary rule as a constitutional remedy. *Georgetown Law Journal, 88,* 799–878.

Massiah v. United States, 377 U.S. 201 (1964).

Miranda v. Arizona, 384 U.S. 436 (1966).

Oregon v. Elstad, 470 U.S. 298 (1985).

Orfield, M. W. (1992). Deterrence, perjury, and the heater factor: An exclusionary rule in the Chicago criminal courts. *University of Colorado Law Review, 63,* 75, 107.

*Miranda* after *Dickerson*: The future of confession law [Symposium]. (2001). *Michigan Law Review, 99*(5).

United States v. Leon, 468 U.S. 897 (1984).

United States v. Wade, 388 U.S. 218 (1967).

Weeks v. United States, 232 U.S. 383 (1914).

## ✑ EYEWITNESSES

The Cardozo Law School Innocence Project Web site regularly reports new cases in which individuals who have been convicted of crimes are exonerated through DNA testing (see www.innocence project .org). The Web site reveals that about two thirds of these cases involve mistaken eyewitness identification. This is no surprise to anyone familiar with research on eyewitness reliability. Studies documenting the role of mistaken identifications in erroneous conviction date back 70 years and have

revealed that mistaken identifications were involved in more than 60% of the hundreds of cases examined by researchers. This rate is especially noteworthy given that eyewitness cases probably constitute a small proportion of all cases.

Although the recent DNA exculpation cases give new emphasis to research on the pitfalls of eyewitness evidence, research on the psychological aspects of eyewitness testimony actually has a long history. Harvard professor Hugo Munsterberg, in his volume *On the Witness Stand* (1908), criticized the legal profession for its ignorance of research in disciplines other than law and particularly noted research on factors that influence eyewitness reliability. Munsterberg's ideas were ridiculed as premature by legal scholars, but other psychologists made further contributions to the study of eyewitness reliability during the first few decades of the century.

Despite this promising beginning, the 1940s and 1950s were unproductive, but the 1960s marked the beginning of new research activity, and by the mid-1970s, scientific eyewitness research was fully rejuvenated. In the past 35 years, the volume of research has mushroomed. This research generally uses experimental methods in which witnesses are exposed to staged or videotaped events and their memory for these events and identification accuracy are tested systematically. This research has identified a wide variety of factors that can influence eyewitness perceptions, the nature of the information that is encoded into memory, the retention of this information, and the later retrieval of this information. Some notable findings are summarized here.

## PERCEPTION AND ESTIMATION PROBLEMS

Although our sensory systems work well—for example, we can detect a candle flame at 30 miles on a dark and clear night—there are clear limitations to our perceptual abilities—for example, reliable identifications of faces seem to require illumination levels higher than those of an urban street with bright street lights at a distance less than 50 feet. Classic and modern studies also demonstrate that people have significant difficulty estimating the ages, heights, and weights of other people; distances; and the duration of events.

## EVENT CHARACTERISTICS

These factors include the frequency and length of exposure to a target person, the seriousness of the event, the presence of a weapon, and event stressfulness.

- *Frequency.* Early research underscored how repetitive exposure to information would improve memory, and modern research has demonstrated that repeated exposure to a target person improves identification accuracy.

- *Exposure Time.* Early researchers noted that witness accuracy should improve as the duration of the target viewing increased—a notion confirmed in more recent research.

- *Seriousness of the Event.* There is evidence that the seriousness of events influences observers at the time of encoding—perhaps because witnesses give more serious events greater attention. Even if the seriousness of an event is not revealed to witnesses until after the fact, it can promote higher identification rates as compared to less serious events.

- *Presence of a Weapon.* Many studies have confirmed the theory that the presence of a weapon attracts the attention of witnesses away from the characteristics of a perpetrator and impairs witness performance.

- *Event Stressfulness.* Events clearly vary in the extent to which they are arousing or stressful, and it has long been speculated that high levels of stress would impair identification accuracy. Recent analyses confirm that heightened levels of stress can undermine witness performance.

## EYEWITNESS CHARACTERISTICS

Eyewitness characteristics can be stable witness characteristics, such as gender and race, or they can be more transient characteristics.

- *Gender.* Females are slightly more likely to make a positive identification, but this tendency is offset by higher levels of false identifications.

- *Race.* An examination of the results of 39 research publications, involving nearly 5,000 participants, found a "mirror effect" pattern in which own-race faces produced a higher proportion of correct identifications and a lower proportion of false identifications compared with other-race faces.

- *Age.* Adult witnesses are much more likely to make correct identifications and less likely to make false identifications than children. Preschoolers are less likely than adults to make correct identifications, but children over the age of 5 do not differ significantly from adults. Children of all ages are less likely than adults to correctly reject a target-absent lineup.

- *Training in Facial Recognition.* A number of studies have found no benefits of training on eyewitness performance.

- *Alcohol Intoxication.* Intoxication does not appear to simply impair eyewitness performance. Some studies have found a hint of impairment in photoarrays and showups that do not contain the target/perpetrator, but there are also indications that high levels of arousal can overcome the debilitating effects of alcohol intoxication.

- *Quality of Descriptions.* A number of studies report very weak relationships between the accuracy and consistency of perpetrator descriptions provided by witnesses and the identification accuracy of those witnesses. There are even indications that memory for peripheral details is inversely correlated with identification accuracy (perhaps because a focus on peripheral information undermines attention to and memory for more central information).

- *Confidence.* Although jurors and the courts give great weight to the confidence a witness expresses in his or her identification, a large number of studies support the notion that there is only a modest correlation between confidence and accuracy. Furthermore, recent studies indicate that events taking place after an identification has been made (e.g., feedback to a witness that he or she has made a correct identification) can substantially (and inappropriately) raise and lower confidence levels. The inflation of confidence is greater for eyewitnesses who have made mistaken identifications than for those who have made accurate identifications—the result is a significant drop in the already weak confidence–accuracy relationship.

## TARGET CHARACTERISTICS

• *Gender.* Target gender is trivially related to identification accuracy.

• *Distinctiveness and Attractiveness.* Target distinctiveness is a strong predictor of identification accuracy. Distinctive targets were more often correctly recognized and less often falsely recognized. Recent research indicates that facial attractiveness is unrelated to accuracy once distinctiveness is taken into account.

• *Changes in Facial Characteristics.* A number of studies have examined the influence on identification accuracy of changes in hairstyle, facial hair, and the addition or removal of glasses. Such changes can produce a dramatic drop in correct identification rates, particularly when hairstyles and/or facial hair are changed.

• *Disguises.* Simply masking a target's hair and hairline with a cap can impair subsequent identification accuracy.

## RETRIEVAL

• *The Length of the Retention Interval.* Early research found that witness reports declined in accuracy over time—a finding replicated many times (e.g., one early study found that voice recognition fell to chance levels after 5 months).

• *Effect of Questions.* Several early eyewitness studies indicated that eyewitness reports could be biased or distorted when the eyewitness was called upon to recall information. Some of this research examines memories elicited by different types of questions—for example, definite articles (*the* vs. *a*) produce higher false reports. Similarly, in 1974, researchers found that they could even manipulate subjects' estimates of the speed of an automobile viewed in accident films. Subjects asked how fast the cars were going when they "smashed" into each other estimated nearly 41 mph. When the word "contacted" was used, the estimate was 32 mph.

• *Mugshot Viewings.* Merely seeing a person's face while viewing mugshots can increase the likelihood that the individual will be mistakenly identified in a later lineup. Research has further shown that if the witness erroneously chooses the mugshot at the initial viewing, the witness is likely to choose the same incorrect face at a later time—even if the correct face is also shown.

• *Facial Composites.* The use of drawings, facial composites, and "photo-kits" to construct "faces" of criminals is a widespread practice in both the United States and Great Britain. Studies that have evaluated the photo-kit system show that performance is quite poor, even when the "witnesses" have photographs available to assist in preparing composites. Constructions from memory are even worse. Similar problems have been reported with computer-based systems for composite production.

*Steven Penrod*

***See also*** Lineups

## For Further Reading

Cutler, B. L., & Penrod, S. D. (1995). *Mistaken identification: The eyewitness, psychology, and the law.* New York: Cambridge University Press.

Loftus, E. F., & Palmer, J. C. (1974). Reconstruction of automobile destruction: An example of the interaction between language and memory. *Journal of Verbal Learning and Verbal Behavior, 13,* 585–589.

Meissner, C. A., & Brigham, J. C. (2001). Thirty years of investigating the own-race bias in memory for faces: A meta-analytic review. *Psychology, Public Policy, & Law, 7,* 3–35.

Munsterberg, H. (1908). *On the witness stand.* New York: Clark-Boardman.

Shapiro, P. N., & Penrod, S. (1986). Meta-analysis of facial identification studies. *Psychological Bulletin, 100,* 139–156.

## FINGERPRINTS

Fingerprints are representations of the papillary, or "friction," ridges on the tips of the fingers. Fingerprint identification is the world's most widely used and widely known method of criminal identification. In law enforcement, it has two primary functions: archival (using the impressions of the complete set of fingerprints, or "ten-prints," to link an individual to his or her criminal record, even if that individual uses an alias, over the course of a lifetime) and forensic (using one or more impressions left at a crime scene to determine that an individual was present at the crime scene). There are also ancillary functions, such as the identification of an unknown corpse.

Although fingerprints have been described and observed since ancient times; were used to authenticate identity in China, Japan, and India; and were studied by 17th-century scientists, the widespread use of fingerprints for law enforcement was not explored until the late 19th century. Albany, New York, detective John Maloy was the first person known to have solved a crime using a bloody fingerprint sometime in the late 1850s. Maloy's accomplishment was forgotten, though, as was U.S. scientist Thomas Taylor's 1877 suggestion that fingerprints left at scenes of crime might identify murderers.

In 1858, William Herschel, a British colonial official stationed in India, began experimenting with using fingerprints to authenticate the signers of contracts and deeds and recipients of pensions. In 1877, he proposed using them to link individuals to their criminal records. In 1880, Scottish physician Henry Faulds published the suggestion that "greasy finger-marks" might be used to identify the perpetrators of crimes.

With the rapid growth of criminal records and law enforcement officials' increasing reliance on them to guide sentencing decisions, demand was high for a method of improving their accuracy, which was vulnerable to evasion by the use of an alias. In the early 1880s, the French police official Alphonse Bertillon devised a method of indexing criminal records according to anthropometry (bodily measurement).

To compete with anthropometry, a method of indexing criminal records according to fingerprint patterns was needed. Drawing on the early 19th-century work of the Czech anatomist Jan Purkyně, the British statistician Francis Galton devised a rudimentary classification system by sorting all fingerprints into three basic pattern types: arches, loops, and whorls, which he published in 1892.

By subdividing Galton's three basic pattern types, the Argentine police official Juan Vucetich and the team of Edward Henry, Chandra Bose, and Azizul Haque, in India, devised working ten-print fingerprint classification systems capable of indexing large numbers of criminal records according to fingerprint patterns almost simultaneously, around 1896. The Argentine police adopted fingerprinting as their primary method of indexing criminal records in 1896, India followed suit in 1897, and Britain in 1901.

Police officials soon began using fingerprints for forensic identification as well; Argentina began in 1892, India in 1897, France in 1902, and England in 1903. After some initial hesitation, courts worldwide accepted fingerprint examiners' claim that they could match latent (crime scene) prints to the finger that made them.

Outside Latin America and the British Empire, fingerprint identification was initially treated as a low-cost alternative to anthropometric systems, which were perceived as more scientific. Misdemeanants were fingerprinted in magistrates' courts and police departments, whereas felons were still subjected to anthropometric identification in prisons. Law enforcement agencies were reluctant to abandon large files of criminal records indexed according to anthropometric measurements. Gradually, fingerprinting won over law enforcement agencies, and by the 1920s, its ascendance was clear.

Fingerprint identification was fast and cheap, allowing criminal identification to shift from the prison (where it would be applied to released convicts) to the police station (where it could be applied to any offender, no matter how petty). Criminal records became even more important in guiding sentencing decisions, and fingerprint files grew rapidly. Law enforcement agencies soon needed to devise extended classification systems to cope with rapidly expanding files. Intricate "single-print" systems were devised to enable the searching of single, latent prints.

Automation would be the solution to the problem of rapidly expanding files, but the process took several decades, beginning with IBM punch-card sorters in the 1920s, holographic systems in the 1960s, and videotape and microfilm systems in the 1970s. By the mid-1980s, the Automated Fingerprint Identification System (AFIS) was robust enough to justify procurements by local and state law enforcement agencies.

AFIS uses optical recognition and automated searching to effect ten-print to ten-print, latent to ten-print, and ten-print to latent searches. It produces a list of candidate matches, which is then reviewed by a human fingerprint examiner, who makes the final determination. As yet, AFIS is not considered accurate enough to replace human examiners.

AFIS has enormously enhanced the capability of fingerprint files by augmenting law enforcement agencies' ability to perform "cold searches" (i.e., searching the entire database when a suspect has not been identified) more often than would have been feasible in the days of manual searching. The internetworking of databases across vendors, localities, states, and countries promises to enhance the scope and utility of databases even more.

Although almost no one would dispute the individualizing potential of complete sets of 10 inked fingerprints, during the 1990s, questions were raised about whether forensic fingerprint examiners could indeed claim to be able to match single, fragmentary, latent prints to a single source finger with absolute certainty. Heated debates have transpired within the forensic community, and legal challenges have been mounted. Although forensic fingerprint identification remains legally admissible, fingerprint matches are now being treated as judgments based on the examiner's experience, rather than scientific determinations.

*Simon A. Cole*

## For Further Reading

Ashbaugh, D. R. (1999). *Quantitative–qualitative friction ridge analysis: An introduction to basic and advanced ridgeology.* Boca Raton, FL: CRC.

Beavan, C. (2001). *Fingerprints: The origins of crime detection and the murder case that launched forensic science.* New York: Hyperion.

Cole, S. A. (2001). *Suspect identities: A history of fingerprinting and criminal identification.* Cambridge, MA: Harvard University Press.

Dilworth, D. C. (Ed.). (1977). *Identification wanted: Development of the American criminal identification system, 1893–1943.* Gaithersburg, MD: International Association of Chiefs of Police.

Lee, H. C., & Gaensslen, R. E. (Eds.). (2001). *Advances in fingerprint technology* (2nd ed.). Boca Raton, FL: CRC.

Ratha, N. K., & Bolle, R. M. (Eds.). (2003). *Advances in automatic fingerprint recognition.* New York: Springer-Verlag.

Sengoopta, C. (2003). *Imprint of the Raj: How fingerprinting was born in colonial India.* London: Macmillan.

Stock, R. M. (1987). An historical overview of automated fingerprint identification systems. In *Proceedings of the International Forensic Symposium on Latent Prints* (pp. 51–60). Washington, DC: U.S. Government Printing Office.

# ✄ FORENSIC ART

Forensic art can be considered a combination of art and science. Art is the subjective element, applying human talent, knowledge, and discretion. The artist uses scientific principles of anatomy and physiology, as well as documented research findings, to create a product that aids the legal process. The information is expressed visually rather than verbally. The forensic artist can turn a victim's description into a picture to be circulated in the media or an unidentified body into an image recognizable by family members. The finished product may be a representation of a victim or an offender. Forensic art is of particular importance in the identification process—missing persons, suspects in crimes against persons, and unknown human remains. The human face is the most frequently depicted focus.

The need for the recording of facial features was recognized by Dr. Alphonse Bertillon in the late 1800s. Bertillon was an anthropologist who worked for the French Sûreté and saw the need for indexing the features of career criminals and to be able to prove their identity. He devised a system of measurements of the face and body that were thought to be individual enough in combination that no two offenders would match. The system was used widely until fingerprint classification took precedence. It provided a strong base for future forensic art development.

The major categories in which forensic art is used today are composite imagery, image modification and identification, demonstrative evidence, and reconstruction.

Composite imagery is most often related to creating a face from the verbal descriptions of individuals witnessing criminal activity. The likeness can then be distributed to law enforcement agencies that may be involved in pursuit of the suspect. It may also be forwarded to the media in an effort to engage the assistance of the public.

In the past, such images were produced by hand. Victims and witnesses would be interviewed by forensic artists, who would then translate the information given into an image of a suspect. Composite imagery now can be accomplished through the use of kits that have been developed specifically for this purpose. These kits allow the witness to mix and match various facial features until a satisfactory likeness is created. Computer programs have also been used successfully to create composites in an efficient manner.

Image modification takes into account the passage of time or life events that can cause a change in appearance. Circulating a 10-year-old photo may be of little or no value. An updated likeness of a known individual is of particular importance when a fugitive has been at large or a child has been missing for a prolonged period of time.

A remarkable example of image modification is the case of John List, a New Jersey man who was responsible for the deaths of his mother, his wife, and their three children in 1971. Starting with a photograph, sculptor Frank Bender of Philadelphia created a three-dimensional bust of List that ultimately resulted in his capture after 18 years at large. Bender incorporated personality traits and medical history as he created the sculpture. He learned that List had surgery that would probably result in a particular area of skin sag on his neck and included this feature. He even gave thought to the type of eyeglass frame that List would prefer. The similarity to the glasses List was wearing when captured was uncanny.

Another of Bender's successes was the facial reconstruction of a young female whose body was discovered in an abandoned lot. Her decomposed body was clothed in a pleated white blouse. This fact caused Bender to sculpt her likeness with an upward tilt to her head, as if she were optimistically looking toward a better future. When the piece was used in an art exhibition, media coverage of the event included a photograph. Someone tossed the newspaper with the article into an office trash can.

The photo of the young woman was discovered by a woman from the cleaning service, and the body was later identified as that of her niece.

The identification of unknown persons has been profoundly affected by the use of forensic art. Decomposition robs the human body of those features that make it recognizable. By using clay to reconstruct lost soft tissue, forensic artists are often able to replace the features that made the victim familiar to friends and family. It is in the triggering of memory that identifications are made. Although a completed work may be technically imperfect, all it has to do is capture some element of the face that made it memorable. Additionally, the forensic artist may also create a viewable likeness of a victim who has been brutalized to such a degree that identification would be difficult.

Demonstrative evidence frequently assists in the judicial process. Visual aids for trial or courtroom use facilitate understanding of complex processes and anatomic structures. Judges as well as jury members benefit from their use.

Crime scene diagrams may also be considered forensic art. They are usually created to be of assistance in an investigation. A bird's-eye view will show relative distances from the victim to other structures and objects in the room. A lateral view will show relative elevations. Each view will give information of potential importance. The officer creating the diagram may choose to use shorthand that will be defined when the initial sketch is in its final form. Measurements and directionality may be of particular importance.

Forensic art has a varied and comprehensive scope. The common thread is the function as an aid in conducting investigations and legal proceedings.

*Diane T. Shkutzko-Penola*

### For Further Reading

Taylor, K. T. (2001). *Forensic art and illustration*. Boca Raton, FL: CRC.

## ⟋⟍ FORENSIC SCIENCE

Forensic science is a unique discipline in which the principles and techniques of the basic sciences (biology, chemistry, and physics) are used to analyze evidence, thereby retrieving information to help solve problems related to civil and criminal law. Forensic scientists may be employed by a public agency, such as a law enforcement department or a medical examiner's office, or they may work for private commercial laboratories. Criminalists are forensic scientists who deal almost exclusively with criminal matters, working cooperatively with law enforcement personnel, pathologists, and other forensic specialists as well as with prosecutors and defense attorneys. They use the scientific method to develop factual information that is presented in a written report and in oral testimony for jurors so that they can make an informed decision as to the guilt or innocence of a defendant. The adversarial criminal justice system uses the Socratic method of question and answer to arrive at the truth; thus, forensic scientists must be cognizant of scientific and legal issues as they perform their function. Some forensic scientists consider themselves generalists, whereas others consider themselves specialists. Generalists have a broad range of knowledge in the field and are skilled in the technical aspects of scientific analysis of many forms of evidence. The latter have good general knowledge of the disciplines of forensic science and advanced skills in a specialized area. Most forensic scientists function as specialists. Because of the exponential growth of the field, owing in part to the recognition of the importance of scientific analysis and testimony in criminal matters, a large body of knowledge and numerous skills must be acquired. Although there have been significant advancements over the past two decades in technology used by forensic scientists, the fundamental nature of the discipline remains the same. Criminalists collect and analyze evidence that can link a suspect to a victim or crime scene. They reconstruct the events of a crime, write a report, and testify about their findings. Unlike any other witness, the expert may render an opinion during his or her testimony.

## HISTORY

Over the past century, forensic science has developed into a large interdisciplinary field consisting of a number of different but related areas such as legal medicine (pathology, odontology, and anthropology); toxicology; forensic chemistry; forensic identification (including fingerprinting and DNA analysis); questioned documents; firearms; and toolmarks. Although forensic medicine is said to date back to the 6th century, forensic science had not often been used by the courts until the mid-1800s. In a highly publicized case, a French court asked M.J.B. Orfila (1787–1853), a Spanish physician, to assist them in determining if a woman had murdered her husband by feeding him food laced with arsenic. Orfila, employing simple analytical chemistry methods, determined that she had, indeed, poisoned him. Another advancement came with the work of Alphonse Bertillon (1853–1914), who attempted to identify individuals (individualization) by recording measurements of a large number of physical characteristics, resulting in a unique profile for every person. In theory, this is possible, but errors of measurement resulted in a lack of reliability of the method and failed to establish absolute identification. Currently, biometric approaches are used to scan large numbers of individuals moving through airports and other high-risk venues to determine if any might be a member of a known group of terrorists. There are still questions about the reliability of this approach.

Bertillon's biometric method of identification was subsequently replaced by fingerprinting. The use of fingerprint analysis by law enforcement to identify people began with the work of William Herschel, Henry Faulds, and Thomas Taylor. These scientists laid the foundation for the comparison of latent prints found at a crime scene with exemplar (known) prints taken from an individual. Subsequently, Edward Henry developed a classification system for fingerprints (Henry system), and in 1910, Edmond Locard (1877–1966) set up the first forensic laboratory in Lyons, France.

## FORENSIC SCIENCE IN THE UNITED STATES

In the United States, forensic science was first used in a court of law in 1907 by August Vollmer, a police chief in Berkeley, California, assisted by a toxicologist from the University of California. After becoming chief of police in Los Angeles in 1923,

and realizing the importance of science in solving criminal cases, Vollmer established the first crime laboratory in the United States. This was followed by the establishment of forensic laboratories under the Los Angeles Sheriff's department (1930) and by the State of California in Sacramento (1931), San Francisco (1932), and San Diego (1936). The FBI "criminological laboratory" was established in August 1932 in Washington, DC. It consisted of a room equipped with a comparison microscope (one head and two stages for bullet comparisons), some ultraviolet light equipment, a large drawing board, a fingerprint "comparator," and not much else. The workload in the laboratory grew from 20 examinations during its first month of operation to the current level of more than half a million analyses per year. In 1943, its name was officially changed to the FBI laboratory.

Most large forensic laboratories are broken into distinct units (divisions or sections), each dealing with a specific area. In a multitask laboratory such as the FBI laboratory, units may include chemistry (drug analysis); toxicology (poisons, drugs, alcohol); ballistics (firearms, ammunition); tool marks; trace evidence (hairs and fibers, soil, glass chips, paint chips, etc.); serology (body fluid identification); DNA; metallurgy; number restoration; spectroscopy; digital evidence; and automobile accident reconstruction, as well as supporting sections such as forensic photography and a section that constructs scale models of crime scenes.

## OFFICE OF THE MEDICAL EXAMINER/CORONER

The individual with the responsibility for determining cause of death is either a medical examiner or a coroner. Although medical examiners are physicians, coroners are elected officials who may or may not be medical doctors. The medical examiner (or coroner) enters an investigation when a person dies and the cause of death is unknown. In addition to determining the cause of death (e.g., homicide, suicide, accident, natural, or inconclusive), he or she is also responsible for determining the manner of death (gun shot, stabbing, strangulation, poisoning, etc.) and the approximate time of death. This is determined by performing an autopsy (a medicolegal procedure in which the body is examined both externally and internally, revealing anatomical information that can aid the legal investigation). Deaths that appear to be the result of accident may, in fact, be due to a disguised homicide. Similarly, apparent suicides may, in reality, be homicides. Bodies may be badly decomposed or reduced to skeletal remains. In such a situation, the medical examiner calls upon the forensic anthropologist to study these remains. If identification is in question, a forensic odontologist may be called upon to examine dental evidence, and a forensic DNA analyst may be called upon to examine biological tissue evidence. The odontologist studies dentition and makes comparisons of unknown, evidentiary specimens to documented x-ray exemplars. The DNA analyst extracts DNA from tissue and bone fragments and performs genetic testing to establish identification. Here, too, comparison must be made between the unidentified specimen and an exemplar. In the absence of an exemplar, genetic profiles of close relatives (mother, father, sisters, brothers, sons, and daughters) can be studied to make the determination. The office also performs toxicology studies on various bodily fluids, tissues, and organs. In some jurisdictions, the medical examiner's office also handles sexual assault cases. Other aspects of the investigation are handled by the police department or sheriff's office crime laboratory. The medical examiner's office is generally separate from the police department crime laboratory, but in some jurisdictions, they are combined.

## CRIME SCENE INVESTIGATION

Crime scene investigators, generally members of law enforcement who are specially trained in recognition and handling of evidence, are called to crime scenes to conduct a search for physical evidence. Evidence that is located must be documented, collected, and transported to the laboratory for analysis. Detection of evidence at the crime scene is generally performed by first establishing the boundaries of the scene and then searching the area methodically and thoroughly. The process begins with a simple walk-through, but prior to collection, the scene is sketched

in the form of a geometric shape so that quadrants or sectors are created within a grid. The scene can be sketched as a rectangle, square, circle, or other geometric shape. The documentation that is done implies more than just note-taking. The scene should be photographed and sketched, with measurements taken of all relevant areas. Videotaping is another useful form of documentation. Searches are then performed in all component sectors of the scene. Collection of evidence is an extremely important function. As each item is located, it must be collected properly; packaged separately; and documented completely, including name of collector, date, time, and precise location within the crime scene. Collection procedures differ depending on the physical nature of the item as well as the substrate upon which the item has been deposited.

Physical evidence is a form of evidence that can help reconstruct the events leading up to and during the commission of a crime. It can be used to associate a suspect with a victim or crime scene, help identify a suspect or verify a witness's testimony, and aid in the investigation so that law enforcement can develop a suspect. Physical evidence is found in many different forms, including biotic (living) and abiotic (nonliving). The former, also known as biological evidence, is a form of physical evidence that originates from a human, animal, or plant (e.g., blood, semen, saliva, hair, nails, fur, leaves of plants, spores, wood). The latter type of physical evidence includes items such as glass, paint, soil, metal, chemicals, poisons, and so on.

Crime scene investigators are also responsible for documenting the chain of evidence and protecting the evidence from contamination or from becoming compromised due to environmental factors. The chain of evidence is maintained through written records describing who has possession of the evidence from the moment it is collected at the crime scene until it appears as evidence in the courtroom. Investigators must be trained to collect any type of specimen (liquid, solid, gas) on any type of substrate (porous or nonporous).

One of the most often quoted principles of forensic science is the Locard Exchange Principle. Essentially, it states that when two objects come into contact, there is a transfer of material between them. The substance transferred may be so small that it may escape detection; however, with the newest techniques and their high sensitivity, even trace amounts of materials can often be detected and analyzed. Latent fingerprints (those not visible to the naked eye) can be chemically or physically enhanced and provide extremely valuable evidence. Sometimes, because it is difficult to remove evidence from a particular object, that entire object (a door, part of a wall, etc.) may end up in a laboratory for examination.

When a number of people have had legitimate access to a crime scene, it becomes necessary to collect their elimination specimens. In this way, they can be excluded as suspects, and the police investigation can focus on those who were likely involved in the crime. In addition to collecting evidentiary and elimination specimens, crime scene investigators must also obtain control samples. Thus, when using a moistened swab to collect a small droplet of dried blood from a floor tile or perhaps a section of a wall or a pane of glass, another swab must be used to sample an area adjacent to the droplet. The second swab is used by the analyst as a substrate control. Examination of evidence in the laboratory always requires the inclusion of positive and negative controls that are handled identically to the evidence. Generally, a number of positive and negative controls of different varieties are included in the testing. Testing should provide the expected result for the positive control and a negative result for all negative controls. In this way, the analyst can judge whether his or her test observations are trustworthy or must be repeated.

## ANALYSIS OF EVIDENCE IN THE LABORATORY

Once the evidence enters the laboratory, it is documented to maintain the chain of custody, and properly stored until a decision is made as to which lab section will analyze the evidence. In some instances, multiple tests must be performed. For example, in the case of a bloody fingerprint, the blood must be analyzed and the print pattern evidence must be documented. Serologists and DNA analysts must share this kind of evidence with fingerprint experts in order to obtain all the information possible that may shed light on the events leading up to and during the crime. This is the process known as *reconstruction*. In order to preserve as much information as possible, nondestructive testing and documenting (sketching, photographing, etc.) is performed prior to destructive testing. Evidence should not be completely expended in testing unless, because of size or quantity constraints, there is no choice. The defense is entitled to have an independent analysis of the same evidence performed by another expert of its choosing. If the evidence consists of two swabs, one must be preserved for the defense. If an item is to be expended, then the defense counsel must be notified and given the opportunity for the defense expert to witness the testing. Regardless of who employs the expert, it is expected that the expert will analyze the evidence in an unbiased fashion and provide the facts as they come to light. However, results can be interpreted differently by different experts, as often happens in the courtroom.

## DIFFERENT KINDS OF EVIDENCE AND METHODS OF ANALYSIS

In virtually all of the following examples, known samples and unknown samples are compared to help identify the source of the unknown or questioned sample.

Soil evidence is usually analyzed using polarizing microscopy to determine mineral content, color, texture, and particle size and density of soil components. Fractured glass evidence analysis includes a determination of chip density and refractive index. Shattered glass can be reassembled like the pieces of a puzzle. The structural characteristics of hair (cortex, cuticle, and medulla) are determined microscopically. Its origin (body part) and stage of growth can be determined. Evidentiary hairs are often sent to the DNA lab for analysis. Polarizing microscopy can be used to determine if a fiber is natural (animal, vegetable, or mineral) or synthetic. Its optical properties (refractive index) and its other physical characteristics (color, cross-sectional shape, melting point, etc.) can be determined.

Illicit drugs can be tested presumptively with crystal tests, but instrumental methods (gas chromatography/mass spectrometry) are used to confirm the identification of the drug and with what it is mixed if it is impure. Visible fingerprints or (chemically or physically) enhanced latent prints are preserved and stored as digital evidence. Chemical enhancement includes ninhydrin, iodine, silver nitrate, or cyanoacrylate fuming. Dusting is performed with high-contrast, magnetic, or fluorescent powders. A high-intensity alternate light source is used alone or in conjunction with these enhancement methods. The Automated Fingerprint Identification System (AFIS) determines if there is a match to the millions of prints maintained within AFIS files. Blood, semen, and saliva are identified by presumptive and confirmatory tests and then analyzed to determine their origin. Firearms, bullets, shell casings, and tool mark evidence are analyzed for class (general) and individual characteristics. Bullets, shell casings, and tool mark evidence are examined with a comparison microscope. Databases that include digital information for bullets and shell casings are now available. When documents become evidence, comparisons are made of paper, handwriting, and inks to determine the age of the document and whether it is a forgery. Biological evidence is individualized in the DNA laboratory. The polymerase chain reaction (PCR) is used to amplify millions of copies of specific regions of the genome known as short tandem repeat (STR) sequences. Thirteen STR regions are analyzed to produce a virtually unique genetic profile for every individual (with the exception of identical twins, who share identical genomes).

## QUALITY CONTROL AND QUALITY ASSURANCE

With the use of forensic DNA analysis becoming more common and more important in a court of law, it has become apparent that a laboratory must have an active quality control and quality assurance program so that judges, jurors, and the public can have confidence that the reports and testimony are considered reliable. The FBI director issued quality assurance standards for forensic DNA testing laboratories in 1998 and subsequently issued quality assurance standards for convicted offender DNA databasing laboratories in 1999. (Both guidelines were updated by the DNA Advisory Board [DAB] in 2000 and are available online.) These standards include educational and training requirements for all personnel involved in the process of analyzing casework DNA. The Scientific Working Group on DNA Analysis Methods (SWGDAM), following up on the work of the DAB, prepared specific guidelines. Standards ensure that the analyst (a) is provided with the formal education and knowledge of the basic sciences used in forensic DNA analysis, (b) is familiar with the general operation and analytical capabilities of the laboratory, (c) understands the scientific and legal aspects of evidence handling, (d) understands each procedure used for the different types of DNA analysis (RFLP and PCR-based methods), and (e) knows how to interpret and report experimental findings following the lab's protocol. At the end of the training period, the analyst is provided with mock casework to test proficiency.

### Quality Control

Quality control includes maintaining records of chemicals, reagents, commercial kits, and other supplies that are purchased by a laboratory for use in testing. Such products are tested to see if they provide reliable results with other reagents. They are stored appropriately, and any expiration date is noted. All equipment in a laboratory that is used to maintain or provide changing temperatures is calibrated and monitored. Such equipment would include refrigerators, freezers, water baths, thermal cyclers (used for DNA work), and so on. All equipment used for weighing must be calibrated on a regular basis and all records maintained. All equipment used for centrifugation must be calibrated and records kept for inspection. Laboratory procedures are maintained in a protocol manual.

### Quality Assurance

Quality assurance covers continuing education, proficiency testing, analyst certification, and laboratory accreditation. Quality assurance is a way of demonstrating that the analyses are valid and that results of testing are reliable.

## PROFICIENCY TESTING

Proficiency testing is an important component of quality control and quality assurance. It is an outgrowth of the DNA revolution in forensic science. Forensic laboratories employ commercial labs that offer mock casework test trials. The casework is assigned to an analyst, who handles it like any other item of evidence. A report is prepared, and the laboratory director can then determine if the results are correct or not. The purpose of proficiency testing is to verify that individual analysts are performing quality work according to the laboratory protocol, reaching the correct conclusion, and reporting it accurately. Failure to do so would result in more training for the analyst. Such proficiency testing can be done in an open or blind fashion. In the former case, the analyst is aware that the casework is not authentic and is being used to test skills and adherence to protocol. In the latter, the analyst is not told the true nature of the casework or that the results will be used as part of a proficiency examination. Blind proficiency testing is not required presently for forensic laboratories.

## CERTIFICATION

Certification is a voluntary process of peer review by which a practitioner is recognized as having attained the professional qualifications necessary to practice in one or more disciplines of criminalistics. Certification is offered by the American Board of Criminalistics (ABC), which is composed of regional and national forensic science organizations. Its purposes are to establish professional levels of knowledge, skills, and abilities; to define a mechanism for achieving these levels; to recognize those who have demonstrated attainment of these levels; and to promote growth within the profession. The ABC offers a certificate in criminalistics (general) and certificates in more specific areas such as forensic biology, drug chemistry, fire debris analysis, and trace evidence.

## LABORATORY ACCREDITATION

In the fall of 1974, crime laboratory directors formed an organization known as the American Society of Crime Laboratory Directors (ASCLD), which is devoted to the improvement of crime laboratory operations through sound management practices. The members promote and encourage high standards of practice by member laboratories. The Crime Laboratory Accreditation Program of the ASCLD/Laboratory Accreditation Board (ASCLD/LAB) is a voluntary program. Any crime lab within or outside the United States may apply for accreditation in order to demonstrate that its management, operations, personnel, procedures, equipment, physical plant, security, and personnel safety procedures meet established standards. Approximately 200 laboratories are now accredited by ASCLD/LAB.

*Lawrence Kobilinsky*

***See also*** Coroners and Medical Examiners, Crime Laboratories, Crime Scene Investigations, DNA, Evidence

## *For Further Reading*

http://criminalistics.com/abc/A.php

DNA Advisory Board. (2000). Quality assurance standards for forensic DNA testing laboratories and for convicted offender DNA databasing laboratories. *Forensic Science Communications, 2*(3). Available: http://www.fbi.gov/hq/lab/fsc/backissu/july2000/codispre.htm

Fisher, B. A. J. (1993). *Techniques of crime scene investigation.* Boca Raton, FL: CRC.

Inman, K., & Rudin, N. (2000). *Principles and practice of criminalistics.* Boca Raton, Florida: CRC.

Lee, H., Palmbach, T. M., & Miller, M. T. (2001). *Henry Lee's crime scene handbook.* New York: Academic Press.

Scientific Working Group on DNA Analysis Methods. (2001, October). Training guidelines. *Forensic Science Communications, 3*(4). Available: http://www.fbi.gov/hq/lab/fsc/backissu/oct2001/kzinski.htm

http://www.ascld.org/accreditation.html

## ⨳ FRATERNAL ORGANIZATIONS

Law enforcement fraternal organizations are social groups consisting of sworn officers who may engage in legislative and work conditions advocacy for themselves and various forms of community service to benefit others. Thus, officers benefit from fraternal organizations by their membership. Often, specific fraternal organizations will require a secondary trait of commonality. For example, Police Officers for Christ is a fraternal organization where the membership has a Christian faith in common, the Gay Officers' Action League is a fraternal organization where the membership is likely to have a homosexual identity in common, and the Policewoman's Endowment Association is one where officers would have a female identity in common. Some fraternal organizations include retired officers and/or honorary non-law enforcement persons in their membership. It is also not uncommon for fraternal organizations to have chapters with memberships that represent professions or occupations related to law enforcement, such as chapters for firefighters, parole officers, or immigration inspectors. Other fraternal organizations may limit their membership largely to retired law enforcement officers, such as the Dinosaur Squad of New York, Retired Sergeants Association, New York 1013, and the Superior Officers' Association.

There are many fraternal organizations. In addition to those mentioned above, other examples include the Anchor Club, Stueben Association, Saint George Association, Saint Paul Society, Honor Legion, Gang Investigators' Association, Narcotic Enforcement Officers' Association, Police Dog Association, Asian Jade Society, Haitian-American Law Enforcement Fraternal Organization, Hispanic Society, Columbia Association, Police Square Club, Fraternal Order of Eagles, Viking Association, Shromrim Society, Police Self-Support Group, County Law Enforcement Officers Association, Regina Coeli, Pulaski Association, Traffic Squad, Patrolmen's Benevolent Association, National Latino Peace Officers' Association, National Organization of Black Law Enforcement Executives, and the New York State Shields, Incorporated. Such groups exist as an important source of peer social support for law enforcement officers. This type of support is very important to many officers, who may perceive that individuals outside of their profession might not understand the rigors of their work.

Fraternal organization chapters are often referred to as "lodges" with a numeral in their chapter name that may or may not hold any particular significance. In some cases, the numbering of lodges once represented the order in which the lodges came into existence and/or the region in which the lodges exist. Nevertheless, with the dormancy or closure of some lodges, many numbering sequences no longer reflect the original numbering intentions. Other terms used for organizational chapters include "aerie" or "parlor." Some fraternal organizations have international chapters, such as the Emerald Society, which has chapters or lodges in the United States and Canada for the support of officers of Irish and/or Gaelic heritage. Another international law enforcement fraternal organization is the International Police Association, which has more than 300,000 members in 58 countries.

However, the oldest law enforcement fraternal organization in the United States is the Fraternal Order of Police. It is a nonprofit group that began in Pittsburgh on May 14, 1915 with two foot patrolmen, Brother Martin Toole and Brother Delbert Nagle, and 21 other officers. It was called Fort Pitt Lodge #1 at its inception, and it had as its focus advocacy for better working conditions for its law enforcement membership. Its motto is "Jus, Fides, Libertatum," which means "Law is a safeguard of freedom." Its emblem is a five-point star symbolizing allegiance to the flag and the authority of law enforcement. A part of the star is blue, symbolizing a duty to protect the community, and the background is white, representing purity. The Fraternal Order of Police now focuses on increasing the pride, professionalism, and brotherhood/sisterhood of law enforcement officers. It often weighs in on legislation, both local and national, that will affect its membership. Presently, it has more than 310,000 members (referred to as "brothers" and "sisters") and about 2,100 lodges in the United States and Canada.

The Fraternal Order of Police also has chapters of affiliate and auxiliary groups. For example, the Fraternal Order of Police Associates membership consists of the relatives and friends of law enforcement officers. They exist to provide various kinds of social and charitable support to their local law enforcement officers. Also, the Fraternal Order of Police Auxiliary was founded in 1920 by a group of wives of law enforcement officers. Today, it has more than 2,000 members in about 140 chapters, and its membership has been extended to include other relatives of law enforcement officers. They exist primarily to encourage the law enforcement officers in their lives. Similar fraternal support groups include Spouses of Troopers on Patrol and PoliceWives.org.

*Camille Gibson*

## For Further Reading

http://ep.com/cops/copscorner.html
http://longmontpolice.com/Fop_Education.htm
http://members.aol.com/eirepages/esgpages.htm
http://www.grandlodgefop.org/lodges/index.html
http://www.ipa-usa.org/right.htm
http://www.maineemeraldsociety.8m.com/about.html
http://www.ncpolice.org/frat.htm
http://www.phoenixmasonry.org/masonicmuseum/fraternalism/
    fraternal_order_of_police.htm

# G

## ⊗ GANGS INVESTIGATION

Aggressive police anti-gang activity in the late 20th century can be dated to the mid-1970s, when the law enforcement campaign against gangs called Total Resources Against Street Hoodlums (TRASH) was initiated in East Los Angeles. This movement toward a robustly proactive approach to street gang crime represented a shift from the social controls traditionally used for dealing with juvenile violence, particularly in urban areas, since the turn of the century. Such a shift in tactics mirrored a hardening in attitudes across local, state, and federal governments toward gang populations in the post-1960s period as gang violence and crime increased dramatically across the country. As a progressive, reformist phase of U.S. history waned, an era of neoconservativism was fully instituted with the first Reagan administration at the beginning of the 1980s. During the decade that followed, the generalized belief that the increasing crime rate, often attributed to the very real signifying elements of gangs, drugs, and violence, was indissolubly linked to the pathological character and cultural deficits of the inner-city poor. This became an ideological mainstay behind calls for more aggressive law enforcement, particularly with regard to urban street gangs.

This change in national politics is the foreground to some of the anti-gang initiatives witnessed in recent years, but it is also important to note the background factors. In the final two decades of the previous century, the United States saw a massive downsizing of its social safety net, including sustained government cuts in welfare, housing, health, and public education. During the same period, the National Youth Gang Center reported that at least 21,500 gangs operated across the country and that more than 731,000 members were active nationwide. To manage the increase in the numbers of criminal activities in the inner city and the suburbs, the areas from which gangs draw the bulk of their recruits, sharp increases in the budgets and resources of law enforcement and correctional institutions have been the rule.

Numerous studies over the past two decades, difficult to overlook, point to the very real crimes of violence perpetrated by gangs in large urban centers all over the country. Also, such gang violence has moved to suburban locations as well. The National Alliance of Gang Investigators Association reported that membership in gangs permeates American society, cutting across all socioeconomic, ethnic, and racial groups.

There is no denying that gang members are responsible for a large number of serious crimes, especially drug-related and violent offenses. In general, gangs account for much more crime than nongang criminals, and that gang-related crime and delinquency are much more violent than nongang delinquency. Criminologists in numerous longitudinal and other studies focusing on such cities as Los Angeles, Chicago, San Diego, St. Louis, and other locales found that gang violence and homicides were more likely to involve minority males and the use of firearms, and that gang members committed more delinquent acts and violent crimes than nongang members. For example, one study found that gang members accounted for 79% of all violent juvenile offenses committed in Denver, and that 35% of the city's homicides were gang related. These studies also found that criminal activity declines when a member leaves a gang. It is in this political and historical context that the need arose for antigang actions among both planners and practitioners of law enforcement.

California has tended to set the trend in the moral and physical war on street gang crime and violence, and by the late 1980s, the strategies of anti-gang law enforcement were the most common tactics in local, state, and federal agencies throughout the United States. While California was dedicating ever more funding and personnel to programs such as the Los Angeles Police Department's renamed Community Resources Against Street Hoodlums (CRASH) and the Los Angeles County Sheriffs' Gang Enforcement Team (GET), Chicago was similarly increasing its specialized gang task force to more than 500 uniformed personnel by 1992. Meanwhile, as anti-gang police units were being formed and expanded throughout the nation, anti-gang legal statutes were being passed, such as California's Street Terrorism Enforcement and Prevention (STEP) Act of 1988 and a string of gang injunctions, such as the City of Chicago's Gang Congregation Ordinance in 1992 (later voided as unconstitutional in 1997), followed by local injunctions against specific street gangs in the California cities of San Jose, Pasadena, and Redondo Beach. Summing up these new levels of anti-gang-related crime strategies, Klein (1995) lists five major approaches as observed in California: (a) prosecution, (b) specialized enforcement, (c) specialized probation, (d) targeting of gang members in juvenile detention centers and prison, and (e) gang injunctions. Klein concludes, however, that gang-oriented services rarely work and, in fact, seemed to lead to the opposite effect, promoting gang cohesion and gang proliferation, and increasing their violent activities.

Recently, the relative ineffectiveness of the anti-gang strategy now in place for more than 20 years is indicated by data provided by the California State Department of Corrections. According to the state's gang identification system for prisons, fully one third of California's 160,000 inmates are now said to be members of a gang. William Bratton, Chief of the Los Angeles Police Department, has publicly stated that there has been no diminution in street gang membership and that the continued growth of this population represents the gravest threat to public order in the United States.

Currently, it is common to see anti-gang violence campaigns organized across a range of law enforcement agencies, such as occurred in New York City in the late 1990s. In May 1998, during what was called Operation Crown, which targeted the Almighty Latin King and Queen Nation, a New York State street gang, agents from the New York Police Department, Federal Bureau of Investigation, Immigration and Naturalization Service, New York State Police, and the Drug Enforcement Agency carried out the biggest police sweep in New York City since the early 20th century. Employing a range of techniques, including systematic harassment of assumed members, phone taps, paid informants, stings, and photographic surveillance, the strategy took on a political character as the administration of Mayor Rudolph Giuliani (1994–2001) repeatedly used the war against gangs to bolster its public image.

It would be an exaggeration, however, to say that political gamesmanship is often behind repressive anti-gang policy, because on most occasions, hard-pressed communities are the first to call for tougher measures against local antisocial elements. The police have also implemented new laws enacted after the terrorist attacks of September 11, 2001, to control gang violence. In May 2004, in response to the notorious killing of a 10-year-old girl, among other violent crimes committed by a gang terrorizing a Bronx, New York, neighborhood, the county prosecutor used the state's new counterterrorist laws to deliver a 70-count indictment against 17 members of the St. James Gang. The prosecutor stated that the gang acted with "the intent to intimidate or coerce a civilian population" (Martinez, 2004, p. 12). This indictment represents the first use of such a law, which would allow more severe sentences against gang members who were also charged with murder, conspiracy, and assault. In addition to drug dealing, auto theft, extortion, property crimes, and home invasion, evidence suggests that gangs have begun trafficking in fake identification papers that very likely could be used by terrorists entering the country illegally. Therefore, law enforcement agencies are taking the lead in responding to these very real local and national needs to protect and stabilize the communities in which gangs are so disruptive.

*David Brotherton*

### For Further Reading

Bennett, W. J., Diliulio, J. J., Jr., & Walters, J. P. (1996). *Body count: Moral poverty . . . and how to win America's war against crime and drugs.* New York: Simon & Schuster.

Brotherton, D. C., & Barrios, L. (2004). *The Almighty Latin King and Queen Nation: Street politics and the transformation of a New York gang.* New York: Columbia University Press.

Curry, G. D., & Decker, S. H. (2003). *Confronting gangs: Crime and community.* Los Angeles: Roxbury.

Esbensen, F., & Huizinga, D. (1993). Gangs, drugs, and delinquency in a survey of urban youth. *Criminology, 31,* 565–587.

Klein, M. (1995). *The American street gang: Its nature, prevalence, and control.* New York: Oxford University Press.

Martinez, J. (2004, May 14). Terror charge for gang that brutalized Bx. nabe. *New York Daily News,* p. 12.

Maxson, C. L., Gordon, M. A., & Klein, M. W. (1985). Differences between gang and nongang homicides. *Criminology, 23,* 209–222.

Spergel, I. (1995). *The youth gang problem: A community approach.* New York: Oxford University Press.

## ⊗ GAYS IN POLICING

Like a number of occupations, policing provides a challenging employment context for the gay population. Some gay officers have experienced not only disapproval and/or discrimination from fellow police officers, but also find that the gay community is hostile toward them as well. This is due, in part, to law enforcement's history of bias toward homosexuals. For example, a number of questions from psychological tests used in the past as part of a police recruit's application process were specifically used to weed out gay men from the field. As a result, gay officers may be closeted at work, and some have even hidden their occupation from peers in the gay community.

The relationship between gay men and women and the policing community has been a tenuous one, with well-documented incidents when police themselves have harassed gays and ignored their victimization. In fact, repeated police brutality toward gay bar patrons ultimately led to the 1969 Stonewall riots in New York City—an event that many consider to have sparked the gay rights movement.

Historically, law enforcement employees have been slow to accept gay men and women into their ranks. Similar to the challenges faced by other minorities in law enforcement—including people of color and women—gay men and women have often been deemed unworthy of their profession by their peers. Traditionally considered to be a macho profession, policing values masculine traits such as brawn, aggression, and toughness. Thus, males perceived to exhibit characteristics that conflict with this stereotype have found themselves the subject of ridicule. Similarly, lesbian officers face harassment and discrimination, along with the additional burden of being placed in the precarious position of being expected to perform job duties "like a man," yet ridiculed if they are too "butch." Beginning in the late 1970s, as the field of policing evolved to incorporate the idea that police personnel should in some way reflect the communities they served, some police chiefs openly began to discuss the active recruitment of gays.

As of 2003, only 13 states prohibited employment discrimination based on sexual orientation, although many cities and counties invoke ordinances, policies, or proclamations prohibiting such bigotry. Despite the lack of state laws to impede such bias, there is some evidence that the policing community is moving forward in its attempts to eradicate institutional bias. Some local law enforcement agencies not only implement their own antidiscrimination policies, but also actively recruit gay men and women. A small number of departments even provide sensitivity training for personnel when dealing with transgendered officers and residents. In many police departments around the country, gay and lesbian officers are fully integrated members of the agency. In the San Diego Police Department, for example, current research indicates that such integration improved the agency's quality and its responsiveness to the community, and did not have any overall adverse impact on performance, morale, or effectiveness. But issues surrounding gay officers are not limited to acceptance. Health care and death benefits are also important, as was demonstrated in the aftermath of the September 11, 2001, attacks, when death benefits to the survivors of gay public safety officers who perished in the line of duty were questioned. On June 25, 2002, President George W. Bush signed the Mychal Judge Police and Fire Chaplains Public Safety Officers' Benefit Act of 2002. This legislation, which affects gay officers and their same-sex partners, requires that death benefits be expanded to beneficiaries other than spouses, parents, and children. In a similar vein, a number of localities in Florida extend health benefits to officers and their unmarried domestic partners, including same-sex couples. But although gay officers are becoming more accepted in the ranks, prejudice lingers.

Unlike their heterosexual counterparts, many gay officers feel compelled to carefully navigate their private and work lives. Although research has demonstrated that sexual orientation has no bearing on job performance in policing, the decision to either reveal their sexual orientation ("come out") or remain "closeted" to fellow officers can bring job-related and personal consequences. Openly gay officers risk abuse from fellow officers, which has ranged from verbal harassment to the failure of their peers to provide backup in a life-threatening situation on the job. Additionally, some gay officers fear that their sexual orientation may impede their chances for career advancement, especially in geographic areas where no legal prohibition against such discrimination exists. To avoid such repercussions, many gay officers keep their sexual orientation private. Although some gay officers come out early in their career, it is more common for them to reveal their sexual orientation to their police partner only after building a trusting, on-the-job relationship. In general, gay officers report that their disclosure is well received as long as they do not fit traditional gay stereotypes and are "good cops," or known by peers as hard-working, reliable, and responsive to other officers when needed.

There is no official estimate of the number of gay police officers in the United States, although there has been an increase in the number of officers serving openly. As this number increases, so, too, has the need for advocacy among gay officers. In response to the lack of workplace support for gay officers, various organizations designed to meet those needs have been developed.

The first such organization, Gay Officers Action League (GOAL), was formed in 1982 by Sergeant Charles Cochrane and Detective Sam Ciccone of the New York Police Department. GOAL serves as a support group with regular meetings, provides a forum for members, and is actively involved in combating discrimination and harassment. The first meeting of GOAL was shrouded in secrecy because of safety concerns and was open only to those who received special permission to attend. Since then, GOAL has expanded to include regional chapters throughout the country. Other groups have also formed to offer support and include the Law Enforcement Gay Alliance, Maryland Gay Law Enforcement Association, Lesbian and Gay Police Association, Arizona Association of Public Safety Professionals, Colorado Public Safety Alliance, Vision, and Golden State Peace Officers Association.

*Nickie Phillips*

## For Further Reading

A study in pink & blue: Integration of gay cops nearly a "non-issue" in SDPD. (2002, February 28). *Law Enforcement News, 28*(572), pp. 1, 8.

Belkin, A., & McNichol, J. (2001). *Pink and blue: Outcomes associated with the integration of open gay and lesbian personnel in the San Diego police department.* Center for the Study of Sexual Minorities in the Military. Retrieved February 12, 2003, from http://www.gaymilitary.ucsb.edu/Publications/SanDiegoPub1.htm

Buhrke, R. (1996). *A matter of justice: Lesbians and gay men in law enforcement.* New York: Routledge.

Canaday, M. (2002). *The effect of sodomy laws on lifting the ban on homosexual personnel: Three case studies.* Center for the Studies of Sexual Minorities in the Military. Retrieved February 12, 2003, from http://www.gaymilitary.ucsb.edu/Publications/canaday2.htm

Folkes, A. (1992, December). They do not belong. *Police: The voice of the service,* p. 26. Retrieved February 12, 2003, from http://www.goalny.org

Koegel, P. (1996). Lessons learned from the experience of domestic police and fire departments. In G. Herek, J. Jobe, & R. Carney (Eds.), *Out in force: Sexual orientation and the military* (pp. 131–153). Chicago: University of Chicago Press.

Leinen, S. (1993). *Gay cops.* New Brunswick, NJ: Rutgers University Press.

Thompson, R., & Nored, L. (2002). Law enforcement employment discrimination based on sexual orientation: A selective review of case law. *American Journal of Criminal Justice, 26*(2), 203–217.

# ഇരു GEOGRAPHIC INFORMATION SYSTEM

At the most basic level, a geographic information system (GIS) is a collection of digital information about physical features and human activities or events that is linked to a spatial coordinate system and available for analysis. The information (or data) is typically stored in a database and referenced, or linked, by means of a geographic coordinate system of measurements. Selected elements are displayed in computer-generated maps as layers of information about a specific area. A geographic information system in use by a police department would include a database of specific information about crimes and arrests that is linked to spatial data for streets, buildings, and other geographic divisions (police beats and/or precincts) and is accessible to department staff through a computer software interface. As needed, various types of crime, or various areas of a community, may be displayed as maps. Geographic information systems are used to create descriptive displays of information, investigate their properties, and analyze their interrelationships.

## ELEMENTS OF A GIS

### Attributes and Features of Physical Space

The information for a GIS database will include the physical elements of a particular space, such as the topography of the area; the locations and names of the rivers, streets, parks, and buildings in a community; social or political boundaries; and attributes of events or incidents, such as crimes or arrests. These map elements, called "features" of a particular space, may be structured as continuous information to be displayed in grids ("image" or "raster" data) or as points, lines, or areas ("vector" data). The relative elevation of terrain in a specific area, as captured through satellite imagery, would be an example of raster, or continuous, data. The exact location, or street address, of a robbery would be shown as a point, an individual street as a line, and a precinct boundary as an area or polygon.

### Coordinate System

The display of information on a map requires a framework to allow location to be fixed, or a coordinate system. The most well-known coordinate system is the measurement of the earth by latitude and longitude in decimal degrees, with the point of origin defined by the equator and the prime meridian. The computer software translates systems of coordinates in pairs, with the east–west location (x) followed by the north–south location (y). The process of producing the location of a feature from a coordinate system is called "geo-coding" the feature.

The development of Global Positioning System (GPS) technology now permits a user to record the exact location of an event with a GPS receiver. The 24 satellites employed in the GPS radio navigation system transmit signals to the computer in the receiver so that its current location can be recorded within a few meters. GPS is sometimes used to keep track of criminals sentenced to house arrest or under mandated supervision, such as some sex offenders.

Although the surface of the earth is curved, maps are flat. This problem is accommodated by means of a map projection, a mathematical system that expresses three dimensions as two. In the United States, many map data use the State Plane Coordinate System. The newest mapping software simplifies the use of data based on different coordinate systems in a single map project.

### Software Interface

Computer software for a GIS system integrates modules for database and display functions. A user can cross-reference the attribute and map data; add, modify, or delete information from the database; and make almost limitless choices about the display of that information in maps. Basic map display functions include a Zoom tool to control the magnification of the map area, a Pan tool to move the map area, an Identify tool to view information about a specific feature from the underlying database, a Measure tool for calculation of distances between features, and a Label tool to add text or graphics to the map. Mapping programs allow a user to build complex mapping projects and to work in multiple windows with a variety of maps and the databases on which they are based. Although many different computer programs have been used to produce maps, three specific software packages are now in common use, ArcGis and ArcView from Environmental Systems Research International, and MapInfo from Statistical Package for the Social Sciences.

*GIS Data.* In the United States, in contrast to many countries in the world, a lot of GIS data are publicly available from agencies in the public sector and from colleges and universities. Although any digital data file that includes at least one geo-referenced piece of information can be geo-coded and added to a GIS project, an increasing amount of social and political information is now available in standard GIS formats.

*GIS for Law Enforcement.* The use of GIS by police departments was spurred by the inauguration of the Crime Mapping Center in 1997 by the U.S. Justice Department's National Institute of Justice.

Now renamed Mapping and Analysis for Public Safety, this project promotes research and evaluation, fosters information sharing, and distributes new GIS software applications.

*Margaret Leland Smith*

**See also** Crime Mapping, Hot Spots

### For Further Reading

Center for International Earth Science Information Network (CIESIN). http://www.ciesin.org/
This NASA-funded demography center's mission is "to provide access to and enhance the use of information worldwide, advancing understanding of human interactions in the environment and serving the needs of science and public and private decision making."
The Web site provides an extensive collection of international demographic data and Web-based data tools, notably *DDViewer*, a Java applet for mapping U.S. Census data (http://plue.sedac.ciesin.columbia.edu/plue/ddviewer/).
Environmental Systems Research International (ESRI). http://www.esri.com
The ESRI Web site is an extensive collection of mapping resources and includes examples of the varied uses of GIS (http://www.esri.com/mapmuseum/index.html) and a distance-learning campus (http://campus.esri.com/). ESRI also sponsors Geography Network (http://www.geography-network.com/), a global network of GIS users providing map, data, and GIS services.

## ✆ GUN CONTROL

Gun control represents legislative, administrative, and enforcement attempts to regulate the manufacture, sale, transfer, possession, and use of firearms. Gun control exists at local levels of government, affecting only individuals within those jurisdictions, and at the national level, affecting individuals across the nation. It is difficult to accurately summarize controls at state and local levels because of their tremendous variation. Gun control policies and proposals also exist on a continuum of very loose regulations to outright prohibitions. The primary gun control approach is to prevent and deter classes of people from possessing and using firearms. Concerns about gun violence, even during periods of decline, focus attention on gun control strategies. Policies that regulate guns are assumed to increase the safety and well-being of people in the United States. At the same time, gun control imposes costs by restricting firearm possession and use among segments of the population. An understanding of gun control allows for assessments of potential and actual outcomes.

Momentum in federal efforts to control firearms grew in the middle 1920s through the 1930s and then faded for nearly 30 years. The National Firearms Act of 1934 and the Federal Firearm Act (FFA) of 1938 represent early legislation that taxed and regulated the manufacture, sale, and transfer of firearms. The FFA of 1938 required firearm importers, manufacturers, and dealers to obtain a federal license. Firearm dealers are still required to obtain federal licenses today. Many provisions of the FFA were repealed and replaced with the Gun Control Act (GCA) of 1968. Significant provisions of the GCA include prohibitions on sales of firearms to classes of people, including felons, drug addicts, and minors; bans on imports of some small caliber handguns; and bans on mail-order sales of firearms and ammunition. The GCA has been criticized for not creating mechanisms that permit actual regulation, such as sales of firearms to felons and private transfers between individuals. The procedures necessary to facilitate enforcement were lacking. The trend toward greater federal restrictions on firearms was reversed somewhat with the 1986 Firearm Owners Protection Act, otherwise known as the McClure-Volkmer Act. The 1986 Act restricted the number of warrantless inspections of federal firearm dealers that Bureau of Alcohol, Tobacco, and Firearms agents could conduct; allowed dealers to conduct business at gun shows; and prevented the federal government from compiling a centralized database of federal firearm dealer records.

A significant and recent piece of federal gun control legislation is the 1993 Brady Handgun Violence Prevention Act. The key component of the Brady Act is a mandated background check on people wanting to purchase handguns. Despite significant legal challenges to the Act in the mid-1990s, most states continued to comply with Brady mandates. In late 1998, the original 5-day waiting period was replaced with a National Instant Criminal Background Check System (NICS) that allowed licensed dealers to verify that a firearm could legally be transferred to a buyer by calling a state point of contact, the FBI, or a combination of both sources. The NICS is not comprehensive in the sense that centralized databases are not available with information on criteria that make some individuals ineligible for firearm purchases, such as drug use, domestic violence, and a history of mental illness. For the most part, background checks are conducted by local law enforcement agencies.

Evidence shows that the Brady Act has resulted in hundreds of thousands of ineligible persons being denied a firearm because of a background check. Felons represent the largest group of ineligible persons who have been denied. This does not mean that some motivated individuals have been completely denied firearms. The secondary market for firearms includes sources that are largely unregulated, such as private transfers between individuals. Surveys of people prohibited from legally purchasing firearms reveal that they rely heavily on unregulated sources. Despite the fact that several states regulate certain private transactions, an important deficiency in gun control is the failure to govern secondary markets.

Federal law does not mandate that individuals obtain permits to possess or purchase firearms. A variety of permit systems exist at the state level. State permit systems vary in terms of several factors, including whether a permit is required to purchase, possess, or both; the types of firearms the permit covers; and the permit's duration. Some permit laws are restrictive and require a citizen to show a need to carry a firearm, whereas other laws are permissive and only require a citizen to meet certain criteria to obtain a permit. Most states also issue permits to citizens that allow them to carry concealed firearms in some locations. State laws that grant carrying permits are either "discretionary" or "shall issue." Under "discretionary" systems, individuals must establish a need to carry, and state authorities have discretion to grant or not grant a carry permit. Individuals who meet established criteria under "shall issue" laws are automatically granted concealed-carry permits. Some states allow local jurisdictions to impose more restrictive gun regulations, whereas other states do not. State and local gun control is a patchwork of laws with considerable variation.

Evidence does not support the idea that gun control measures, in a general sense, reduce levels of violence. This can be the result of failed policy implementation, such as a lack of enforcement mechanisms, or the failure of policy to adequately represent what is known about gun markets and patterns of gun use. Despite simplistic portrayals, explanations for the relationship between firearms and violence are complex. Furthermore, it is a daunting task to regulate the distribution of more than 250 million firearms in the United States. Evidence does suggest that particular strategies hold promise. Despite criticisms of the Brady Act, many experts agree that background checks that rely on improved data systems can be effective. In addition, some research shows that reduced levels of illegal guns and police efforts that target illegal gun possession are associated with lower levels of violent crime. Currently, gun control experts and policy makers have considered a variety of strategies that may increase the likelihood of prosecution and punishment for gun-related offenses, expand control over private transactions, enhance oversight of licensed dealers, increase enforcement of illegal gun possession and carrying, require licenses for all firearm owners and registration of handguns, and facilitate the tracing of firearms used in crimes. Attention to the details of proposed strategies provides the opportunity to assess the potential successes and failures of gun control.

*William M. Wells*

***See also*** Ballistics, Violent Crime Control and Law Enforcement Act of 1994, Weapons

## For Further Reading

DeConde, A. (2001). *Gun violence in America: The struggle for control*. Boston: Northeastern University Press.

Jacobs, J. (2002). *Can gun control work?* Oxford, UK: Oxford University Press.

Kleck, G. (1997). *Targeting guns: Firearms and their control*. New York: Aldine de Gruyter.

Office of Juvenile Justice and Delinquency Prevention. (1999). *Promising strategies to reduce gun violence*. Washington, DC: U.S. Department of Justice.

Stolzenberg, L., & D'Alessio, S. J. (2000). Gun availability and violent crime: New evidence from the National Incident-Based Reporting System. *Social Forces, 78*, 1461–1482.

Vizzard, W. J. (2000). *Shots in the dark: The policy, politics, and symbolism of gun control*. Lanham, MD: Rowman & Littlefield.

# H

## ◊ HATE CRIMES, LAW ENFORCEMENT RESPONSE TO

Crimes motivated by one's hatred toward another's race, ethnicity, national origin, religion, sexual orientation, or other innate characteristics are unilaterally condemned by Western societies as unjustified attacks. Although such crimes have existed for centuries, it was not until the 1980s that they gained recognition as a special type of criminal offense. Today, these crimes are labeled in federal and state statutes, and in local law enforcement policies, as hate- or bias-motivated crimes. James Garofalo and Susan Martin identify three reasons that there is special focus on hate crimes. First, because hate crime offenders target innate characteristics of a group, victims may have greater difficulty in coming to terms with their victimization. Second, some hate crimes appear to have contagious effects on the victim's community. Third, although several racially motivated crimes received national attention, most hate crimes are not serious in terms of penal law and therefore receive only modest police attention. Accordingly, without special law enforcement programs and laws, many believe that these crimes will not receive the resources necessary to adequately sanction offenders, significantly deter future perpetrators, or satisfactorily address community fears and victim needs.

In the early 1980s, many law enforcement agencies began to place greater importance on attaching hate as a motivation for criminal acts. By 1989, the Police Executive Research Forum, the Police Foundation, the National Black Police Association, and the National Association of Blacks in Criminal Justice all supported legislation mandating the collection of information on hate crimes. In turn, these national initiatives gave political impetus for expanding financial resources to local law enforcement agencies. For example, following the several crimes thought to be related to organized hate groups in the late 1970s, several large U.S. police departments, including Boston and New York City, established hate crime investigative units. These units were assigned the responsibility of investigating incidents that responding officers believed were motivated by hate. Often, these units were also given the responsibility of showing that the police gave high priority to these crimes by engaging populations at risk for hate crimes through periodic meetings and community activities. These units were also used to monitor racial tensions to try to address minor problems before they escalated. For instance, the Phoenix Police Department's Bias Related Crime Incident Unit formed a Hate Crimes Advisory Committee to foster better relationships between the police and various religious, racial, and ethnic groups so that victims would be more likely to report potential problems and crimes. Many small U.S. law enforcement agencies also expanded their resources to address hate crimes by training their officers to investigate these incidents, creating agency-wide policies detailing how officers and supervisors should respond to an incident, and creating accounting systems to track the number of hate-motivated crimes. In time, even some smaller departments, such as the New Haven Police Department in Connecticut, followed the lead of large metropolitan police agencies by creating special hate crime investigation units. Similarly, by 1995, 23% of law enforcement agencies on college campuses with 2,500 students had special hate crime programs or units.

Other local and state law enforcement agencies have also expanded their resources to respond to hate crimes. Many prosecutors' offices have established bias crimes units composed of trained investigators who help police or conduct their own investigations. To supplement local law enforcement efforts, states such as New Jersey have created state-level offices dedicated to responding to hate crimes. Placed within the Division of Criminal Justice, New Jersey's agency assists local law enforcement investigations and prosecutions of hate crimes, as well as facilitates police training.

At the federal level, investigation of hate crimes is conducted by the FBI's Civil Rights Division. The FBI's jurisdiction is primarily found in four federal statutes: (a) Title 18, United States Code (U.S.C.), Section 241 (Conspiracy Against Rights); (b) Title 18, U.S.C., Section 245 (Interference with Federally Protected Activities); (c) Title 18, U.S.C., Section 247 (Damage to Religious Property; Obstruction in Free Exercise of Religious Beliefs); and (d) Title 42, U.S.C., Section 3631 (Criminal Interference with Right to Fair Housing).

Despite the many legislative and policy activities initiated since the early 1980s to address hate crimes, definitions of hate crimes remain unclear and vary across jurisdictions. Although there is a national effort to collect comparable statistics, states and the federal government have not reached a consensus on what a hate crime is, who is included among the protected groups, what types of activities constitute "hate incidents," and what conditions are necessary to label a crime as hate motivated. Evaluations of law enforcement efforts at addressing hate crimes are also limited. To date, only one evaluation has tested the effect of enhanced police response to bias crimes. This study, by Garofalo and Martin, compared bias crimes with a matched sample of nonbias crimes from New York City and Baltimore County, Maryland, that occurred during the late 1980s. They found that bias crimes investigated by the police departments' special units received more attention and were more likely cleared, and victims of bias crimes expressed higher rates of satisfaction with the police response. One case study of the Sacramento Police Department response to a 1993 arson series attributed to a hate group has also presented evidence that a multiagency task force might lead to a quicker arrest of hate-crime perpetrators. Thus, there is some evidence that special bias units within law enforcement agencies can facilitate the solving of specific crimes. However, it is not clear whether these case-level outcomes translate into larger positive effects on the targeted communities or a decrease in the prevalence of hate crimes.

*Christopher D. Maxwell*

### For Further Reading

Bureau of Justice Assistance. (1997). *Stopping hate crime: A case history from the Sacramento Police Department* (Fact Sheet No. 161). Washington, DC: U.S. Department of Justice.

Garofalo, J. (1997). Hate crime victimization in the United States. In R. C. Davis, A. J. Lurigio, & W. G. Skogan (Eds.), *Victims of crime* (2nd ed., pp. 134–145). Thousand Oaks, CA: Sage.

Garofalo, J., & Martin, S. E. (1991). The law enforcement response to bias-motivated crimes. In N. Taylor (Ed.), *Bias crimes: The law enforcement response* (pp. 17–34). Chicago: Office of International Criminal Justice.

Garofalo, J., & Martin, S. E. (1993). *Bias-motivated crimes: Their characteristics and the law enforcement response.* Final report submitted to the National Institute of Justice. Carbondale, IL: Center for the Study of Crime, Delinquency, and Corrections.

Jacobs, J. B., & Potter, K. (1998). *Hate crimes: Criminal law & identity politics.* New York: Oxford University Press.

Levin, J., & McDevitt, J. (1993). *Hate crimes: The rising tide of bigotry and bloodshed.* New York: Plenum.

# ❧ HIRING STANDARDS FOR POLICE

Police agencies are governed and influenced by a political and governmental social system operating in interrelated roles with the legislative, executive, and judicial branches of government. Within the system, police hiring practices are influenced by federal, state, and local lawmaking bodies; city managers and mayors; corporation counsels and city planners; community advocates; and federal and state courts. Beneath these exigencies lies a broad and dynamic social system composed of cultural, educational, political, religious, and economic institutions, including the mass media that also shape this process. How police are recruited and hired, trained and retained, must be seen in the context of this vast and complex network of social institutions. The enormous progress during the past two decades in declaring operational efficacy, mission statements, and professional standards by individual police departments represents the most solid evidence for equitable hiring standards of American law enforcement.

In the 1960s–1970s, minorities and women demanded and received equal employment opportunities through the amendments of Title VII of the 1964 Civil Rights Act. As a result, local police agencies are under the mandate to hire a workforce that reflects the racial, ethnic, and gender composition of their communities. Numerous Supreme Court decisions have also substantially affected law enforcement agencies in the past four decades. In response to such rulings, these agencies have placed an increasing emphasis on preserving civil rights in the provision of public safety to the community at large.

Modern police hiring standards are continuously reviewed by a wide variety of federal and state agencies: affirmative action agencies, civil service (merit) systems, and collective bargaining (labor unions); in the case of ongoing litigation, they fall under the purview of a court-appointed special master or compliance monitor.

## STANDARDS AND ACCREDITATION

Standards are promulgated norms for measuring the operative and performance objectives of an agency and its personnel. Compliance with established professional standards is established through voluntary participation and carries no legal authority. Standards serve as guidelines for the accreditation of an agency's adherence to professional, ethical, and legal practices. The key police standards and accrediting body in the United States is the Commission on Accreditation for Law Enforcement Agencies, Inc. Established as an independent accrediting authority in 1979, it includes the four major law enforcement membership associations: the International Association of Chiefs of Police, the National Organization of Black Law Enforcement Executives, the National Sheriffs' Association, and the Police Executive Research Forum. The overall purpose of the Commission's accreditation program is to improve the delivery of law enforcement service by offering a body of standards, developed by law enforcement practitioners, that covers a wide range of police practices.

## POLICE HIRING STANDARDS

Through the guidance of job skills experts, we now have a common ground for defining the skills, knowledge, and abilities needed by police officers in all jurisdictions to perform their duties.

### Entry Exam Processes and Protocol

- Test content, job-related validity
- Integrity of testing and scoring
- Confidentiality of applicant records
- Civil service examination and ranking
- Physical agility test (wide range of requirements)

The principal factors governing hiring procedures include informing candidates of all parts of the selection process at the time of the formal application and ensuring timely notification about their status at all critical points in the process. The agency must comply with all federal, state, and local requirements regarding the privacy, security, and freedom of information of all candidate records and data.

### Candidate Processes and Protocol

Background investigations are generally conducted during the final stages in the selection process. The primary objective is the verification of qualifying credentials, identification of any criminal record, and documentation of letters of recommendation. The candidate is required to submit the following documentation:

- Birth certificate/citizenship
- High school diploma
- Driver's license
- Polygraph, fingerprints/photo

*Medical Standards.* The candidate must meet age and physical standards and provide medical records for the physician to review. (Only licensed physicians may be used to certify the general health of the candidate.)

*Psychological Standards.* A psychological evaluation showing evidence of any behavior patterns or personality characteristics that have been found to be predictive of performance difficulties in law enforcement will result in disqualification. (Only qualified professionals—psychologists and/or psychiatrists—may be used in the assessment of candidates' emotional stability and psychological fitness.)

### NEW-GENERATION TRENDS

A sampling of new-generation trends influencing police officer hiring standards includes the following:

- Higher-education status—some college, 2-year college, 4-year college
- Candidate domestic violence convictions
- Financial standing—bankruptcy, gambling debts
- Driving under influence—alcohol/drugs, disqualification on review

In the post-September 11th era, background investigations in both the private and the public employment sector are evolving into a sophisticated interagency security technology.

### DEVELOPING ISSUES

The dynamic nature of police hiring standards is inextricably linked to emerging case law, statutes, and public policy. For example, the growing consternation surrounding police entrance exams and the use of diagnostic or cognitive skills tests in securing equitable minority hiring standards has led to "anti-test sentiment," reverse discrimination, and negligent hiring (vicarious liability) litigation. As with previous intractable public policy issues, emergent case law and concomitant remediation will ultimately resolve these matters. It is critical that hiring standards for police remain flexible, while also retaining credible, nondiscriminatory access to the ranks of 21st-century law enforcement.

### RESEARCH AND RESOURCES

The primary sources for maintaining active research of police hiring standards include the U.S. Bureau of Justice Statistics—Law Enforcement Management and Administrative Statistics; the *Executive Memorandum on Fairness in Law Enforcement*; the *Sourcebook of Criminal Justice Statistics*; and the Inter-university Consortium for Political and Social Research (ICPSR), consisting of more than 500 member colleges and universities globally. ICPSR maintains and provides access to a vast archive of social science data relevant to the police entry processes and procedures. These resources, coupled with monitoring of case law and related policy development initiatives, offer ideal preventive law resources and strategies for the maintenance of professional law enforcement entry standards.

*Jess Maghan*

### For Further Reading

Maghan, J. (1988). *The 21st century cop: Police recruit perceptions as a function of occupational socialization.*

Unpublished doctoral dissertation 8821104, UMI, Ann Arbor, MI. (800-521-0600).

Maghan, J. (1993). The changing face of the police officer: Occupational socialization of minority police recruits. In R. G. Dunham & G. P. Alpert (Eds.), *Critical issues in policing: Contemporary readings* (2nd ed., pp. 348–360). Prospect Heights, IL: Waveland.

# ෴ HOMICIDE INVESTIGATION

Homicide investigation is a profound duty with awesome responsibilities. The homicide investigator becomes keenly aware of the reality of death and the impact it has on both society and the surviving family. It requires the investigator to develop an understanding of the dynamics of human behavior, as well as the essential details of professional investigation.

The purpose of homicide investigation is to bring justice to the deceased and his or her surviving family, and also to uphold society's interest in apprehending those who commit such acts. This mission is accomplished by conducting a professional and intelligent investigation that results in the identification and apprehension of the killer and a successful prosecution.

In order to conduct an efficient and effective investigation, the investigator must first concentrate on the mechanical aspects of the death, such as motives and methods; wound structures; crime scene reconstruction; the cause, manner, and time of death; as well as other factors that provide clues to the dynamics of the event. The detective then looks for consistencies as well as inconsistencies and must be prepared to change the focus of the investigation as new information develops.

A professional homicide investigator is someone who is a truth seeker; he or she cannot allow opinion, prejudice, or prejudgment to influence the case. There is a need for patience and flexibility in homicide investigation. An integral part of the inquiry is directed toward the elimination of suspects as well as their inclusion. A homicide investigator cannot be an individual with a "lock-and-load" mentality. The true professional must possess a flexible personality that is open to new suggestions, ideas, and concepts that arise in these fluid types of investigations.

In order to be successful, the homicide detective must have an eye for details and the ability to recognize and evaluate evidence. He or she must have above-average intelligence in order to absorb the many details that arise. Most importantly, he or she must be able to effectively interview and interrogate the many different persons with whom he or she will come into contact. The investigation of murder necessitates a certain tenacity and perseverance that transcends the ordinary investigative pursuit.

The investigator must develop the ability to "absorb" the crime scene and must be able to read the uncollectible nuances of the event. These nuances include the psychodynamics, which are the underlying motivations and human emotions, as well as indications of the deliberate staging of the scene in order to mislead or redirect the investigation.

As we enter the 21st century with advanced forensic and technological changes within the law enforcement community, it is important to emphasize the importance of the crime scene. The initial actions taken by the police at the homicide crime scene either will or may eventually determine whether or not the crime is ever solved or the guilty person brought to justice.

In real life, investigators get only one shot at the homicide crime scene and a limited opportunity to question the suspect.

## WHAT IS PRACTICAL HOMICIDE INVESTIGATION?

Practical homicide investigation is simply a reemphasis on the basic time-proven and traditional investigative methodologies that have been used by law enforcement agencies throughout the years, coupled with an appreciation for and an understanding of the advances in forensic science, as well as its application to the investigative process. Investigators should have the following characteristics:

- An in-depth knowledge of the law and legal systems within their own jurisdictional purview
- An awareness of the medicolegal requirements in a death investigation and the importance of forensic evidence

- A working knowledge of the disciplines of psychology and human behavior, and an ability to relate these principles to the real world and the people with whom they come into contact during a murder investigation

The investigation of homicide begins with four basic procedures.

- A careful and intelligent examination of the crime scene and/or the suspect
- The evaluation of the "bits and pieces" of the evidence coupled with any preliminary information, looking for elements of consistency and inconsistency
- Direct eyewitness accounts
- The intelligent interrogation of the suspect

Many times, it is necessary to elicit from the suspect an account of what actually took place and then compare this to the facts and information that have developed and have been discovered during the inquiry.

## THE HOMICIDE CRIME SCENE

The homicide crime scene is the most important crime scene to which a police officer or investigator will respond. Because of the nature of the crime (death by violence or unnatural causes), the answer to "What has occurred?" can be determined only after a careful and intelligent examination of the crime scene and after the professional and medical evaluation of the various bits and pieces of evidence gathered by the criminal investigator.

The three basic principles involved in the initiation of an effective homicide investigation are as follows:

1. Rapid response to the homicide crime scene by patrol officers. This is imperative in order to protect evidentiary materials before they are destroyed, altered, or lost.

2. Anything and everything should be considered as evidence. Whether this evidence is physical or testimonial, it must be preserved, noted, and brought to the attention of the investigators. The *only* evidence collected at this point of the investigation is

eyewitness accounts or spontaneous statements of a suspect at the scene.

3. After the scene is secured, immediate and appropriate notification must be made to the homicide investigators.

## FIRST RESPONDERS

First responders should take five steps upon arrival at a crime scene, and those steps may be remembered by using the acronym ADAPT.

**A** Arrest the perpetrator, if possible

**D** Detain and identify witnesses and/or suspects for the follow-up investigators

**A** Assess the crime scene

**P** Protect the crime scene

**T** Take notes

## THE CRIME SCENE

The investigation of homicide usually starts at the point where the body is originally found. This location is referred to as the *primary crime scene.* However, there might be two or more crime scenes in addition to the location where the body is found. These additional crime scenes may include the following:

- A location from which the body was moved
- The location where the actual assault leading to death took place
- The place where any physical or trace evidence connected with the crime is discovered (this may include parts of the body)
- A vehicle that is used to transport the body to where it is eventually found

## DETECTIVE RESPONSE

1. Upon arrival, ascertain boundaries. Do not move blindly into an area (confer before acting).

2. Decide how to approach the scene. Establish paths of entry and exit. (Confer with first officer or detective.)

3. Conduct an initial survey. Have the first officer escort you through the scene and develop a mental image of the scene.

4. Ascertain whether or not any fragile evidence is present. (Ensure collection of these items as soon as possible before loss or contamination.)

5. Prior to any crime scene process, take Polaroid® or digital pictures. These are "work photos" to limit scene intrusion.

## ESTIMATING THE TIME OF DEATH

The early postmortem interval provides the most effective estimate of time of death for the investigator at the scene. In cases of advanced decomposition, it is utterly impossible to effectively estimate any specific time frame because of the various artifacts and ambient conditions that may have affected autolysis and decomposition. The following postmortem changes are most useful in the early postmortem interval and should be assessed at the death scene and recorded:

Rigor mortis: the stiffening of the body muscles

Livor mortis: the settling of the red blood cells

Algor mortis: the postmortem cooling of the body

Additional factors to consider are the level of potassium in the vitreous humor (eye fluid) and the extent of digestion of the food in the stomach. The stomach normally empties most of a meal within 2 to 3 hours (except under severe stress or because of debilitating injury).

## MECHANISM, CAUSE, AND MANNER OF DEATH (EXAMPLES)

Suppose an individual dies of a massive hemorrhage, and the cause of death is determined to be a gunshot wound to the heart. The investigator must then consider the manner of death:

- Someone shot the individual—homicide
- He shot himself—suicide
- The gun fell and discharged—accident
- The investigator is not sure what occurred—undetermined

## GENERAL TYPES OF EVIDENCE

The four general types of evidence are as follows:

- Physical evidence
- Testimonial evidence
- Documentary evidence
- Behavioral evidence

The recovery and collection of evidence in homicide and death investigations is of paramount importance to the overall investigation. The goal is to establish a link between the various facets of the crime scene, the victim, physical evidence, and the suspect. All of these components must be connected for the successful resolution of the case.

### Collection and Preservation of Physical Evidence

In order to be introduced as physical evidence, an article must

- Be properly identified
- Show a proper chain of custody
- Be material and relevant
- Meet all legal requirements

## SEX-RELATED HOMICIDE INVESTIGATION

Sex-related homicides include interpersonal-oriented disputes and assaults—such as domestic violence homicides involving sexual assault, rape-murders, serial murders, and killings that involve both anal and oral sodomy and other acts of sexual perversion—as well as sexually oriented interpersonal violence cases.

A homicide is classified as sex-related when there is evidence of sexual activity observed at the crime scene or upon the body of the victim. This evidence includes the following:

1. The type of, or lack of, attire on the victim

2. Evidence of seminal fluid on, near, or in the body

3. Evidence of sexual injury and/or sexual mutilation

4. Sexualized positioning of the body

5. Evidence of substitute sexual activity, such as fantasy, ritualism, symbolism, and/or masturbation

6. Multiple stabbings or cuttings to the body. This includes slicing wounds across the abdomen of the victim, throat slashing and over-kill type injuries, which are considered highly suggestive of a sexual motivation.

## LEGAL CONSIDERATIONS

The courts have severely restricted the right of the police to search certain homicide crime scenes without a warrant. The U.S. Supreme Court has rendered three major decisions that require police to obtain a search warrant to search premises where the suspect and the deceased share a proprietary right to the premises: *Mincey v. Arizona* (1978); *Thompson v. Louisiana* (1984); and *Flippo v. West Virginia* (1999). Homicides involving common-law relationships, husbands and wives, or family disputes may necessitate that the detective secure a warrant before premises can be searched.

The courts have recognized certain circumstances that allow for exceptions to the requirement of a search warrant. These exceptions are emergency or exigent circumstances, evidence in plain view, post-arrest search of an individual for weapons and contraband, and consent.

*Vernon J. Geberth*

***See also*** Coroners and Medical Examiners, Crime Scene Investigation, Detectives, DNA, Evidence, Forensic Science, Sex Crimes Investigation

### *For Further Reading*

Flippo v. West Virginia, 98 U.S. 8770 (1999).

Geberth, V. J. (1995). The signature aspect in criminal profiling. *Law and Order Magazine, 43*(11).

Geberth, V. J. (1996a). The classification of sex related homicides. *Law and Order Magazine, 44*(8).

Geberth, V. J. (1996b). *Practical homicide investigation: Tactics, procedures, and forensic techniques* (3rd ed.). Boca Raton, FL: CRC.

Geberth, V. J. (1996c). The staged crime scene. *Law and Order Magazine, 44*(2).

Geberth, V. J. (1996d). The use of videotape in homicide investigations. *Law and Order Magazine, 44*(3).

Geberth, V. J. (1997). The primary crime scene. *Law and Order Magazine, 45*(6).

Geberth, V. J. (1998). Domestic violence homicides. *Law and Order Magazine, 46*(11).

Geberth, V. J. (2003a). Collection and preservation of physical evidence in sex-related death investigations. *Law and Order Magazine, 51*(5).

Geberth, V. J. (2003b). Practical crime scene investigation: Legal considerations. *Law and Order Magazine, 51*(7).

Geberth, V. J. (2003c). *Sex-related homicide and death investigation: Practical and clinical perspectives.* Boca Raton, FL: CRC.

Geberth, V. J., & Turco, R. N. (1997). Antisocial personality disorder, sexual sadism, malignant narcissism, and serial murder. *Journal of Forensic Sciences, 42*(1), 49–60.

Mincey v. Arizona, 437 U.S. 385 (1978).

Thompson v. Louisiana, 469 U.S. 17 (1984).

## ᎒᎒ HOMICIDE TRENDS IN THE UNITED STATES

Homicide rates in the United States had been declining steadily since they reached a peak in 1991–1993. As each report came out, the nation—and particularly the mayors and police chiefs—celebrated the steady decline. By 2000, the rates had reached their lowest level in more than 30 years. For most of that period, U.S. homicide rates oscillated between about 8 and 10 homicides per 100,000 population, a rate that is about five times that of most industrial countries. That rate was 8 in 1985 and climbed about 25% to a value of 10 by 1991, has been declining steadily since 1993, and by 2000 was under 6 per 100,000. These results are shown in Figure 1, along with the graph for robbery (scaled down by a factor

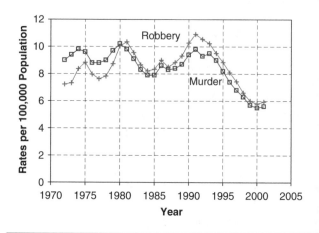

**Figure 1**     Uniform Crime Reports (UCR) Murder and Robbery Rates

of 25), which follows the homicide rate rather closely.

Obviously, that trend cannot continue indefinitely, and we started to see a flattening in the preliminary reports for 2000. The flattening started in the largest cities, the ones that led the upturn in 1985 and the downturn after the 1991 peak. Their rates stopped dropping in 1999, and the entire nation's serious crime rate in 2000 through 2002 is very close to that in 1999.

Whenever crime rates come down, there is usually a rush of both claims of credit ("it's a consequence of my administration's policy of . . .") and of explanation ("demographic shift" is often used—and it was appropriate in the early 1980s when the postwar baby-boom generation was moving out of the high-crime ages, but it happens to be moving in the wrong direction this time). TV news, perhaps with its passion for conserving air time, is always looking for the single explanation and is particularly troubled when more than two mutually supportive factors come together.

Multiple factors together contributed to the crime drop—including, at a minimum, the waning of crack markets; the strong economy; efforts to control guns; intensified policing, particularly in its efforts to control guns in the high-rate communities; and increased incarceration. Different explanations can apply to different population groups.

In this context, it is important to recognize that the aggregate crime rate masks some important differences—across age, for example. Figure 2 examines the trends in homicide arrests for the individual ages of 18, 20, 22, and 24, which were traditionally the peak ages for homicide. Following a period of relative stability from 1970 through 1985, when the peak was fairly flat (as reflected by the closeness of the individual lines), there was a major divergence between the younger and older ages, even in this narrow range. By 1993, the 18-year-olds had more than doubled, and the 24-year-olds showed no growth at all. Juveniles younger than 18 showed even larger growth than the 18-year-olds, and people older than 24 have shown a steady decline since 1975.

It is also the case that the entire increase in the homicides by these young people involved handguns. Between 1985 and 1993, handgun homicides

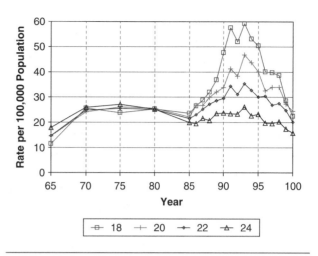

**Figure 2**     Trends in Murder Arrest Rate by Age for Individual Peak Ages 28–24

by juveniles under 18 quadrupled. They doubled for youth 18–24, all with no growth in other kinds of weapons. There was no such shift for 25 and above. We know that young males have never been the world's best dispute resolvers—they have always fought. When the fight is with fists, then a safe resolution is most likely; the loser can withdraw or a third party can intervene and break it up. But the presence of handguns—especially the high firepower, semiautomatic pistols with larger magazines that are now widely available—dramatically changes the dynamics of the conflict. There is no time for withdrawal or intervention. As the guns become more prevalent on the street, that can induce a preemptive strike in order to get a presumed opponent before he gets you. Thus, it is clear that the post-1985 rise in the aggregate homicide rate was all attributable to young people—and to young people with handguns.

The good news from Figure 2 is its right side—the recent years after 1993 when the sharp drop began. The drop has been sharp enough that, by 2002, homicide arrest rates of all ages under 25 dropped below the values that prevailed in 1985, when the rapid rise began.

Handguns available to people who cannot be expected to use them responsibly continues to be a serious problem in the United States. Federal actions initiated in the 1990s to control the underground markets in handguns have been important in reducing the homicides. Perhaps even more important have been actions by local police, with efforts involving stopping individuals suspected of carrying a handgun, along with community efforts that have discouraged the carrying of handguns by gangs and young people.

The widespread carrying of handguns by young people was an outgrowth of the violence associated with the emergence of markets selling crack cocaine in the mid- to late 1980s. Crack first came on the scene in the early 1980s and was marketed predominantly in inner-city areas. Adult arrests for crack started in the early 1980s and kept going up, but juveniles did not show up in those markets until 1985.

These kids were recruited to respond to the increased demand for crack. They were also recruited to replace the large number of adults who were being sent to prison on drug charges. The incarceration rate for drugs grew by a factor of 10 from 1980 to 1996. The nation was trying to solve its drug problem by locking up the adult drug sellers, but no account was taken of the fact that illicit markets like those for drugs are resilient, and they would find ways to serve the demand that appears.

Because they cannot call the police for protection or resort to the courts for dispute resolution, street crack sellers have to defend themselves against a variety of predators, including competitors and robbers, and so they typically carry handguns for that purpose. The mature sellers were typically restrained in their use of the guns, but that restraint was far less evident in the young recruits that were brought in. Also, because young people are much more tightly networked, their friends in the street or in school who were not involved with the drug markets also soon started to carry guns, for some mixture of protection and status. This epidemic of gun carrying by young people led to the dramatic growth in handgun homicides.

Thus, it was not the emergence of a new breed of "superpredators" that some observers had claimed about 10 years ago. Rather, it was the weaponry in the hands of kids who were still in the process of learning the difference between the fantasy of children's gunplay and the reality of live ammunition. They fought much as other boys fight, but the guns made the outcomes much more lethal.

There is an important question of the degree to which the growth of incarceration has been a major contributor to homicide reduction. Some people have argued simplistically by noting that crime has been declining since 1991 and that incarceration was going up over this period, and they then conclude that it must be the incarceration that is driving the crime rate down. That is just too simplistic an analysis; the incarceration rate in the United States has been going up since the mid-1970s, and specifically during the late 1980s, when the crime rate was also going up. There is undoubtedly an important incapacitation effect of the incarceration of the older offenders, the people over age 30, whose crime rates have indeed been coming down rather steadily since the mid-1970s. In fact, two experts, Richard Rosenfeld and William Spelman, both estimated in different ways that about 25% of the crime decline of the 1990s is attributable to the effects of incarceration. That certainly sounds reasonable, because there have undoubtedly been some incapacitation effects at a minimum. Those effects are of decreasing effectiveness because the growth in incarceration has resulted in less serious offenders at the margin as the states dig deeper and deeper into the pool of offenders.

The factors in the decline are more complex than the factors in the rise. They include the efforts by local police and by states and federal agencies to keep guns away from irresponsible people. In 1998, the decline in the number of gun homicides was larger than the decline in the total number of homicides, and that suggests that something right was being done with guns. Efforts to control the guns are particularly difficult because of the strong belief in the United States of individual rights to own and to carry a firearm. As a result, there are strong limits on efforts to control gun sales. The Brady Bill, which went into effect in 1993, requires licensed gun dealers to do a background check of any prospective gun purchaser to discern whether he or she has a felony record before he or she can buy the gun. However, many glaring loopholes exist, such as gun shows, where anyone can buy a gun. The proposals to close the loopholes—background checks at gun shows, cracking down on straw purchasers, limiting gun purchases to one gun per month—all seem reasonable and pose no significant interference with legitimate gun owners and purchasers, but there continues to be considerable political opposition to their implementation.

The decline in crime has also benefited considerably from the decline in the demand for crack by new users. The word from the street gives little credit for that decline to the drug war. Rather, the word has spread—by seeing what it did to parents and older siblings—that crack is bad for you. That message has made a major dent in new users, even though older drug users have generally persisted. That reduction of new users has been important, both in its impact on the drug problem and also in the problems associated with drug markets. It has diminished the role of street markets, which have been a major locus of violence and community disruption. The longer time users can be served much more easily by one-on-one delivery.

Also, the robust economy of the 1990s provided opportunities for the young people who might otherwise have been recruited into the drug markets. There was no longer a need for them in the drug markets, but fortunately, the legitimate economy has been quite able to absorb them. And someone who has a legitimate job also has a strong incentive for conformity more generally.

This experience also highlights the importance of ensuring that vulnerable young people are ready to enter the legitimate economy. It is particularly important that they move into a position where they have the work skills and the job skills to function effectively in the changing economy. It also raises concern over one-dimensional approaches to the admittedly difficult drug problem. There are no simple solutions, and the simplistic ones of get-tough legislation and widespread incarceration have been shown to have profound counterproductive consequences. Pursuing a diversity of approaches—involving treatment, prevention, and enforcement—with careful evaluation of their effects becomes an important and necessary approach.

The recent flattening of the decline in the crime rates raises important questions about the future—whether we will merely see a flattening or whether this is the start of another rise. So far, there are no clear indications of a rise, although a flattening implies that some places will rise and others will continue to decline. A rise could occur if there is a resurgence of violence-involved markets, such as the crack markets, or if there is a serious downturn in the economy that precludes the young people making a normal transition into work. There is widespread hope that these events do not occur, as well as careful monitoring of crime trends to detect the upturn as early as possible to mount whatever response would be appropriate.

*Alfred Blumstein*

## For Further Reading

Blumstein, A., & Wallman, J. (2001). *The crime drop in America.* New York: Cambridge University Press.

Conklin, J. (2002). *Why crime rates fell.* Boston: Allyn & Bacon.

Rosenfeld, R. (2004, February). The case of the unsolved crime decline. *Scientific American,* pp. 82–89.

Travis, J., & Waul, M. (2002). *Reflections on the crime decline: Lessons for the future?* Proceedings from the Urban Institute Crime Decline Forum. Retrieved from http://www.urban.org/url.cfm?ID=410546

## ∽ HOSTAGE NEGOTIATIONS

Hostage taking is an ancient form of criminal activity, and it was even an accepted tool of diplomacy in certain societies. Although such acts have a long history, they are still employed today, as demonstrated in Iraq in 2004, where various factions have seized military and civilian personnel from several countries as hostages in hostilities between those factions and U.S. forces.

Hostage taking is defined by the United Nations as "the seizing or detaining and threatening to kill, injure, or continue to detain another person to compel a third party to do or abstain from doing any act as a condition for the release of the hostage."

Prior to 1973, hostage negotiation did not exist as a function in U.S. police departments until the largest law enforcement agency in the country, the

New York City Police Department (NYPD), reacted to the terrorist hostage holding in Munich, West Germany, by initiating an examination of police operational responses to hostage situations. Terror-related hostage holding, including skyjacking, was not uncommon in parts of Europe and the Middle East during the 1970s.

In the Munich Olympic hostage situation, two members of the Israeli Olympic team were killed in the original takeover. In addition, one West German police officer, five Palestine Liberation Organization terrorists, and eight Israeli hostages died during an attempt to free the hostages by force. The Munich event alerted the NYPD that their jurisdiction could provide a similar opportunity for groups to engage in terroristic diplomacy. The fact that the hostage holding occurred during the upbeat international Olympics; involved American allies, Israel and West Germany; and was broadcast live by the media was enough to prompt an immediate study of the issues. As a result of the NYPD's research, a formal hostage recovery policy was established and hostage negotiators were created. Its primary concerns were with containment of the scene, control of personnel and resources, and communication with the captors. In an NYPD report on police preparedness for terrorist events, the hostage situation guide indicated that it had been designed to focus on functional teamwork, effective communications, and skilled coordination of tactics, under the management of a high-ranking police commander.

The Federal Bureau of Investigation (FBI) initiated research and training in hostage negotiation soon afterward. The FBI has trained approximately 50% of the local police negotiators in the United States. The FBI also maintains a cadre of negotiators and its Hostage Rescue Team for response to incidents under its jurisdiction and as assistance for other agencies.

Subsequently, agencies throughout the country studied the innovation, and the concept was frequently adapted to local requirements. By 1982, hostage negotiation had become an established tactic in American policing, and specifically selected and trained police negotiators are recognized as best suited to carry out this function. Over the past 31 years (1973–2004), countless lives—including hostages, police, and captors—were saved by adhering to procedures that underscored the potential value of coordinated negotiation over potentially premature tactical interventions.

A law enforcement organization designates an individual as the negotiator to engage the hostage holder in a dialogue in an effort to find a peaceful resolution to the instant problem. The hostage holding may be motivated originally by criminal intent, emotional crisis, or politics. The negotiator will attempt to persuade the holder to release the hostage(s) unharmed in return for a pledge that the captor will not be harmed and may even be assisted in resolving perceived problems in a legitimate way. The concept of hostage negotiation is complex because issues of safety, life and death, are always present, and these situations typically involve the response of a large number of law enforcement personnel, a potentially complicated command structure, and observance of special procedures. Media attention is a given at virtually every hostage/crisis negotiation scene.

Negotiation does not automatically presuppose equality between parties, but does recognize the relative strength or power of each side. Implied in the negotiation process is that each side has something that the other wants; that there is no better, mutually acceptable solution immediately available; and that there is a willingness to communicate and to discuss compromise. Hostage negotiation is a police strategy that consists of responding to a situation that involves imminent danger to the life or limb of a person or people being held against their will. There is not necessarily an immediately apparent connection between captor(s) and victim(s).

For situations where negotiation does not appear to be effective, the process will attempt to facilitate the rescue of the victim and apprehension of the perpetrator through close coordination of activities with the tactical (SWAT) officers. The police negotiators and tactical officers generally operate under the command and control of a senior officer, the incident commander. In the NYPD model, the negotiation and the tactical elements each report directly to the incident commander—a format known as the East Coast Model. In the West Coast Model, exemplified by the Los Angeles Police Department, the negotiators report through the tactical element.

Police hostage/crisis negotiation involves bargaining for the life of an innocent person, dealing with a non-hostage-holding barricaded criminal, or dealing with individuals who may be emotionally disturbed or mentally ill. Police generally engage in hostage negotiation in order to save hostage lives, without unnecessarily endangering the lives of the helpers. Captors and other threatening subjects engage in negotiation for these same hostages for a variety of reasons, initially defined by the original motivation for the event, whether criminal, political, or emotional.

A common element in hostage and barricaded subject incidents is defiance by the subject to orders of the authorities to come out peacefully.

Although the methods of hostage negotiation in the United States were initiated as a result of an international terrorist event, early conclusive results, and positive media coverage, convinced administrators to expand negotiator activities to criminal events; to situations involving emotionally disturbed and mentally ill people, including suicidal individuals; and for certain high-risk raid and warrant operations. Because terror-related or siege situations are rare, police jurisdictions in the United States have renamed the process *crisis negotiation* to reflect the reality of their workload.

For three decades, police departments throughout the country have practiced hostage negotiation on a regular basis, largely with positive results. Hostage situations occur in many localities and garner local attention when they do. Most go well. But some cases over the years have received the national spotlight and led to changes and refinements in tactics and policy. These cases include the following incidents:

- The September 1971 Attica prison riot and hostage holding in northwest New York State resulted in death for 28 corrections officers and 10 inmates during a rescue attempt.

- An August 1972 bank robbery hostage situation in Brooklyn, New York, has been perpetuated in a fictionalized account in the popular movie *Dog Day Afternoon.*

- In January 1973, a significant event in the evolution of hostage negotiation took place over a 2-day period in Brooklyn, New York, at a location known as John & Al's Sporting Goods Store.

- An attempt was made to apprehend the kidnappers of Patty Hearst, the Symbionese Liberation Army, in Los Angeles, California in May 1974.

- In 1978, and again in 1985, the interactions between the Philadelphia, Pennsylvania, Police Department and an African-American self-styled separatist revolutionary organization called MOVE resulted in the police bombing of a residential home and the inadvertent burning of numerous homes in the surrounding area. Eleven people were killed and 250 were left homeless.

- During August 1992, the U.S. Marshals Service, and subsequently the FBI, attempted to apprehend white supremacist Randy Weaver at Ruby Ridge, Idaho, killing his wife and son along with a deputy U.S. marshal.

- The Branch Davidian compound near Waco, Texas, was the scene of an incident that began on February 28, 1993, when four ATF agents were killed while attempting to serve search and arrest warrants for federal firearms' violations. It ended 51 days later when a religious cult, the Davidians, resisted a subsequently criticized FBI tactical operation that ended the siege and killed more than 70 adults and children—almost all those in the compound.

*Robert Louden*

***See also*** Crisis Intervention, Police Mediation, SWAT Teams

### For Further Reading

Bolz, F., & Hershey, E. (1979). *Hostage cop.* New York: Rawson Wade.

Louden, R. J. (2001). The development of hostage negotiation by the NYPD. In A. Karmen (Ed.), *Crime and justice in New York City.* New York: McGraw-Hill.

McMains, M. J., & Mullins, W. C. (2001). *Crisis negotiations: Managing critical incidents and hostage situations in law enforcement and corrections.* Cincinnati, OH: Anderson.

## HOT SPOTS

A *hot spot* is a place or geographic location that generates large volumes or high intensities of repeated and predictable crimes or calls for police services. The essence of a hot spot pertains to examining crimes, calls, or problems within a framework defined by their spatial and temporal dimensions. The former reveals that crimes, calls, or problems are distributed randomly, uniformly, or clustered across space, whereas the latter reveals that the timing of such events is random, cyclical (occurring at particular times), or incessant (occurring all the time).

Research during the 1970s seriously questioned the effectiveness and wisdom of the widespread practice of police preventive patrol. Therefore, improving the management and efficacy of the patrol function was sought through the use of novel tactics and programs. Two of these were crime analysis and directed patrol, which involved identifying, describing, and analyzing crimes and problems during particular times at specific places, and, in the case of directed patrol, recommending particular tactics for apprehending offenders or reducing problems. Therefore, paying closer attention to the time and location of events was becoming paramount in police operations.

During the 1980s and early 1990s, two developments met that propelled hot spots into becoming a central focus for policing. First, evolving computer technology for enhancing police communications and records systems interfaced with and became the input for other evolving information systems, such as geographic information systems, for analyzing and visualizing crime and calls-for-service patterns. The second was the sponsorship of two projects by the National Institute of Justice that became showcases for analyzing hot spots. The first, a study in Minneapolis of predatory crimes and calls for service, measured how a few places or addresses generate a majority of the crimes or calls for service.

The second, known as The Drug Market Analysis project, was a series of studies across five cities focusing on identifying, differentiating, analyzing, and evaluating the impact of interdicting drug market hot spots through the use of improved information systems, multiple data sources, spatial analysis, and crime mapping. This project epitomized the benefits of a collaborative partnership between the police operational and academic research communities. Both projects stimulated a widespread diffusion of interest in hot spots as a research concern and a focus for police operations. This diffusion was augmented by the development and distribution of the Spatial Temporal Analysis of Crime (STAC) software by the Illinois Criminal Justice Information Authority. This software was a simple and portable technique for identifying hotspots. The showcase projects demonstrated the rationale and methods for, and the utility of, policing hot spots, whereas STAC gave many practitioners and academics alike the ability to investigate hot spots.

The fundamental advantage gained from identifying and policing places that are hot spots is that the spatial variation and temporal oscillation of activities in places are more predictable than the behavior of an individual. Therefore, identifying and assessing the spatial variation and temporal oscillation of hot spots promotes the implementation and evaluation of customized policies, strategies, tactics, and remedies for minimizing the behavior and/or manipulating the situational context that makes a particular place hot.

There is no single method for defining a hot spot. A hot spot can be a single location that produces a large volume of calls (e.g., a bar); a cluster of locations, such as some residences across several contiguous blocks experiencing burglaries; or an area. This is a geographic space formally delineated by manmade or administratively defined boundaries that exhibits a high rate of crimes or calls for service compared with other areas (e.g., police beats, precincts, or census tracts). The reason for different hot spots is the geographic scale of the crime data (the size of the location[s] being examined) and the appropriate techniques for analyzing and visualizing (mapping) the information for a specific scale. This property—geographic scale—although well known to geographers, has become a major issue of curiosity for hot spot criminologists. Therefore, a hot spot is going to be whatever the criteria are for defining a hot spot.

A benefit of focusing on hot spots is that a police manager is presented with a tangible geographic space in which, during a specific time period, he or she can commit resources for eradicating, reducing, or displacing a particular crime or problem. Therefore, the status of the hot spot before police intervention serves as the baseline from which to measure the effectiveness and efficacy of police intervention.

Research on hot spots has evolved into the development of a hot spot matrix. This matrix cross-classifies the different types of spatial distributions with the different temporal patterns. Hence, tactics or prevention measures are recommended for a particular hot spot exhibiting a specific spatial distribution with a particular temporal pattern.

The police have always known about hot spots, but three events had to occur before hot spots could become a major focus or objective for police operations. First, technological and methodological advances had to make possible the delivery of timely information to police decision makers regarding the description and characteristics of hot spots. Second, there had to be a critical evaluation of past practices by the police, with the conclusion that something different had to be tried. Finally, organizational change had to be conducive to the policing of hot spots.

*James L. LeBeau*

*See also* Crime Mapping, Geographic Information System

*For Further Reading*

Block, R. L. (1995). Space, place and crime: Hot spot areas and hot places of liquor-related crime. In J. E. Eck & D. Weisburd (Eds.), *Crime and place* (pp. 145–183). Monsey, NY: Criminal Justice Press.

Buerger, M. E., Cohn, E. G., & Petrosino, A. J. (1995). Defining the "hot spots of crime": Operationalizing theoretical concepts for field research. In J. E. Eck & D. Weisburd (Eds.), *Crime and place* (pp. 237–257). Monsey, NY: Criminal Justice Press.

Ratcliffe, J. H. (2004). The hotspot matrix: A framework for the spatio-temporal targeting of crime reduction. *Police Practice and Research, 5,* 7–25.

Sherman, L. W., Gartin, P. R., & Buerger, M. E. (1989). Hot spots of predatory crime: Routine activities and the criminology of place. *Criminology, 27,* 27–55.

## ᘓᘒ HOUSING POLICE

Housing police are police hired specifically to provide law enforcement services in public housing developments. The local Housing Authority (HA) that manages the public housing units may establish its own Housing Police Department, or the HA may choose to work with the local police department. The federal Department of Housing and Urban Development (HUD) provides funding and guidance for police services in public housing, but the authorization to establish a police department with full police powers comes from the state legislature. In order to improve the delivery of law enforcement in public housing, HUD commissioned Carroll Buracker and Associates to study policing in six HAs. Their report, *Policing in Public Housing,* provides recommendations for improvement and a model contract for arranging supplemental police coverage from the local police department. Recent changes in housing police departments can be attributed to the Buracker study and subsequent management directives from HUD.

Since 1937, federal funding has been used to build housing for low-income families, the elderly, and disabled individuals. Housing built in recent years tends to be low-rise units; the older projects are huge, high-rise, multifamily units that were built with little attention to the need for "defensible space." These larger projects are located primarily in Chicago, New York, Philadelphia, and Washington, DC. Chicago has nearly 35,000 low-rent units within 171 projects, whereas New York City has more than 160,400 such units within 319 housing projects. The high density of population within the housing projects makes it difficult to provide adequate law enforcement services. Although crime is often not reported separately for public housing, or is underreported because of resistance from tenants and officials, the public impression is that public housing projects are very dangerous places to live. Alex Kotlowitz's nonfiction book, *There Are No Children Here*, brings the horrifying world of the Chicago projects to life by following two boys growing up amid gangs, crime, drug use, violence, and terrible housing conditions.

The first housing police department was created in 1952 as a response to rising crime rates and vandalism in the public housing projects of New York City. After studying the situation, the New York City Police Department recommended that the Housing Authority establish its own housing police department. Over the years, the housing police department expanded by developing their own bureau of investigation and their own training program. But the department ceased to exist in 1995 when the 2,500 housing police, along with the transit police, merged with the New York City Police Department (NYPD). Mayor Rudolph Giuliani promised that the merger would provide better police coverage in the projects and greater efficiencies within the administration of policing services. By 1998, the *New York Times* was reporting a reduction in homicides by one third across the city and an even larger reduction in areas such as the 32nd Precinct in Harlem. The reduction was attributed to the use of computer maps for charting crime and the reassignment of police officers to antidrug campaigns. The housing police now function as the housing bureau within the NYPD.

Similar problems of crime and vandalism led to the creation of the housing police department by the Chicago Housing Authority (CHA). Gang warfare, drug trafficking, and high numbers of murders in the public housing projects of Chicago have been well documented. In 1988, the CHA established Operation Clean Sweep in an effort to reduce violent crime. Teams of Chicago police and housing guards conducted surprise searches of tenants' apartments for needed repairs, drugs, weapons, and illegal aliens. With the Anti-Drug Abuse Act of 1988, HUD funded more police activity focused on drug control programs in local housing authorities. By 1990, CHA had increased police activity in the housing projects and had established their own housing police department.

Police sweeps without prior notification or warrants met with mixed success and led to legal problems. Tenants reported that crime diminished for a short time after the sweep and then resurged a few weeks later. Residents were reticent to assist in crime control efforts for fear of retaliation from gang members. Some tenants supported the sweeps in the hope of making their homes safer, but others questioned the violation of tenants' Fourth Amendment rights. In 1994, the American Civil Liberties Union filed a class action suit against the Chicago Housing Authority. With the settlement of *Pratt v. Chicago Housing Authority*, the CHA was prohibited from performing sweeps without the consent of the particular resident whose apartment would be searched. A HUD proposal in 1995 provided a legal solution by adding a consent-to-search clause in the public housing lease contract that the resident signs.

Despite concerted efforts on the part of housing police and Chicago city police, both living conditions and the crime rate in the housing projects remained intolerable. In 1999, Mayor Richard M. Daley and his team of advisers took control of CHA. The housing police department was abolished, and the housing police who could meet the recruitment standards of the Chicago Police Department were brought in. Many of the huge high-rise and some of the mid-rise buildings were demolished and replaced by townhouses. Former tenants who met stricter qualifications concerning criminal records were housed along with families with moderate incomes.

Today, housing police still work directly for the HAs in 11 cities, including Boston, and Cleveland. In these cities, the number of public housing units range from under 100 to around 14,000, thus making the responsibility manageable. Coordination with local police departments has increased. The Boston Housing Authority prides itself on team efforts with the Boston Police Department. Community policing concepts influence their activities. Some of their activities include floor-by-floor patrols within high-rise buildings, attendance at community meetings, deliberate efforts to be highly visible and available to residents, and organized programs and activities for preteens and those in their early teens. Bicycles are also used for patrols, making the housing police highly visible, approachable, and mobile. Today, the housing police provide a vital enhancement to the policing services provided by the local police departments for residents of public housing.

*Gretchen Gross*

## For Further Reading

Carroll Buracher and Associates, Inc. (1994). *Policing in public housing: Assessment & blueprint.* Harrisonburg, VA: Author.

Cisneros, H. G. (1995). *Defensible space: Deterring crime and building community.* Washington, DC: Department of Housing and Urban Development.

Department of Housing and Urban Development. (2003). *HA profiles.* Retrieved June 11, 2003, from https://pic.hud.gov/pic/haprofiles/haprofilelist.asp

Kotlowitz, A. (1991). *There are no children here: The story of two boys growing up in the other America.* New York: Doubleday.

Popkin, S. J., Gwiasda, V. E., Olson, L. M., Rosenbaum, D. P., & Buron, L. (2000). *The hidden war: Crime and the tragedy of public housing in Chicago.* New Brunswick, NJ: Rutgers University Press.

Roush, C. (1996). Warrantless public housing searches. *American Criminal Law Review, 34,* 261–288.

# I

## ❦ IDENTITY THEFT AND IDENTITY CRIMES

### IDENTITY THEFT DEFINED

*Personal Identity Theft.* Identity theft is the crime of the 21st century, undermining the economy of U.S. businesses and the entire United States. Identity theft is categorized as either "personal" or "business." Personal identity theft is the unauthorized use of another person's personal identifying information to obtain credit, goods, services, money, or property, or to commit a felony or misdemeanor. "Personal identifying information" means a person's name, address, telephone number, driver's license number, social security number, place of employment, employee identification number, demand deposit account number, savings or checking account number, credit card number, or mother's maiden name.

A mother's maiden name is not required to conduct financial or health care transactions, but it is often requested by companies for use as a password. However, a mother's maiden name is also the final piece of information required by perpetrators to obtain one's original birth certificate, which can then be used for a complete "identity takeover." With an original birth certificate, a criminal can easily obtain passports and visas; legal documents; social security; and selective service, armed services, and other government records and documents. A criminal can also gain access to financial holdings.

*Business Identity Theft.* Identity theft has recently taken a new twist and, with it, another definition: business identity theft. Business identity theft is the unauthorized use of a business's identifying information to obtain credit, goods, services, money, or property, or to commit a felony or misdemeanor. "Business identifying information" means a business's name, address, telephone number, corporate credit card numbers, bank account numbers, federal employer identification number (FEIN), Michigan Treasury Number, electronic filing identification number, electronic transmitter identification number (ETIN), e-business Web sites, URL addresses, and e-mail addresses.

Recent increases in corporate credit card frauds suggest that some perpetrators now find business credit card numbers more lucrative than personal credit card numbers. For business credit cards, the monetary limits are often higher than for personal accounts. Also, many business credit accounts are used by more than one employee and therefore contain a relatively large number of monthly transactions in which fraudulent charges are more easily hidden. In addition, the reconciliation of lengthy business credit card statements can take longer, and may be conducted less frequently, compared to personal credit card statements.

In one recent case, a stolen business credit card number was used to purchase and send merchandise to Romania. In another, unrelated case, a business credit card number was used for purchases that were sent via Federal Express to Indonesia. In yet another example, a business's FEIN and ETIN numbers were used to obtain a loan from the Small Business Administration (SBA) in the amount of $480,000. The perpetrator used the business identities to register a subsidiary of the victim's business; the victim discovered the fraud with the receipt of a letter by the SBA informing him that the loan payment was delinquent. A more common example of business identity theft is "Web site cloning," a practice in which criminals create mirror Web sites of legal businesses to obtain names and credit card and social security numbers of unsuspecting customers. In recent months, Web site cloning has been reported frequently in the news media.

*The Overarching Crime.* Identity theft can be further defined as "the overarching crime," because stolen identities are used to commit a preponderance of other crimes, including credit card and bank fraud; wire and telecommunications fraud; computer, Internet, and interstate commerce fraud; auto theft and auto parts fraud; retail account fraud; money laundering; drug trafficking; online stalking and harassment; child pornography; forgery; and terrorism.

In fact, the al Qaeda training manual used in Afghanistan training camps provides terrorists with five sets of different identities along with instructions on how to use them to impersonate others. The attacks by terrorists on the U.S. embassies in Kenya and Tanzania, the bombings of the U.S.S. Cole and the Marine Corps barracks in Lebanon, and the bombings of the World Trade Center in 1993 and on September 11, 2001—all were committed by terrorists who used stolen or fake identities to travel from country to country or from state to state; rent motels and automobiles; and, in other ways, conceal their activities and whereabouts. Therefore, identity theft is distinguished from identity crimes, including the heinous crime of terrorism.

## COSTS OF IDENTITY THEFT

*Costs to Businesses.* The costs due to identity theft are inestimable because the identity theft as well as the crimes committed using a stolen identity can go undetected for weeks, months, and sometimes even years, such as when a criminal takes over an identity to gain employment or to otherwise conceal a criminal record. Also, identity thefts and crimes may go unreported. In addition, some identity theft cases are plea-bargained and the actual financial losses are thus underreported. Furthermore, once stolen, identities are a commodity on the black market of crime, where they are sold and resold, and used and reused, sometimes months or even years later.

Often overlooked is the fact that U.S. businesses, and not just individuals, are victims of identity theft. Business victims absorb the costs much as they do shrinkage (percentage of losses due to shoplifting and employee theft). The costs of fraudulently purchased merchandise are often passed on to consumers as increases in product, service, and transaction fees. One recent estimate is that costs to U.S. businesses are as much as $50 billion annually according to the Federal Trade Commission.

*Costs to People.* The losses to people are financial, emotional, and physical. Research indicates that victims of identity theft can suffer losses as great or greater than do victims of many other crimes. A major difference between identity crimes and other crimes is that with identity theft, the crime can be ongoing for weeks, months, and years, during which time the victim feels helpless and experiences a lack of control over his or her life. The impact and unrelenting "identity rape" creates stress factors that can result in serious psychological and physical illnesses. Currently, there is little understanding of identity rape, and there are also no known federal or state programs designed to assist identity theft victims in their financial, emotional, physical, and personal recoveries.

A compounding problem is the increasing number of e-commerce businesses selling sometimes costly and most often unnecessary legal and other forms of insurance to victims or to others in the event that they become victims. Many identity theft victims are vulnerable and susceptible to easy persuasion, and they become revictimized by start-up businesses that take advantage of these individuals.

An additional problem faced by victims of identity theft is that many police departments still refuse to take a victim's complaint, and most police departments do not yet have policies and procedures for handling identity theft cases. Police officers encounter jurisdictional problems because the identity crimes are most often committed across county, state, and even country borders, impeding apprehension and then prosecution should the perpetrators be caught. Furthermore, in most U.S. police departments today, budgets are being cut, and resources for investigations of identity theft crimes are limited or lacking altogether.

However, victims do have some resources. Large credit card companies are establishing customer call centers in the hope of retaining customers whose credit cards have been fraudulently used, and the Financial Services Roundtable, a Washington, DC-based organization, has established an Identity Theft Assistance Center to assist banking customers who have become victims of identity theft. Also, the Michigan State University—Business Identity Theft Partnerships in Prevention, established in 1999, works with businesses to prevent identity theft; trains law enforcement on how to investigate identity thefts; conducts identity theft research to better understand the victim, the crime, and the criminal; and provides victim advocacy.

## EXPONENTIAL INCREASES ARE PREDICTED

*Ineffective Legislation.* Escalations in identity thefts can be expected in the months and years ahead, for several reasons. Over the past several years and across the United States, widespread legislation has been enacted in attempts to combat identity theft. Yet identity thefts continue to increase according to the U.S. General Accounting Office. Most legislation is reactive rather than proactive in its aims to *prevent* identity thefts, and there are no coordinated efforts to enact a standard set of laws across states. Therefore, criminals can obtain stolen identities in

one state and use them in another, with little chance for apprehension or conviction. Also, criminals are becoming increasingly sophisticated in the use of computer technology to commit crimes, and police officers lack training for online investigations (see below).

*New National Identity Database.* Another reason to anticipate identity theft increases is the enactment of the Health Insurance Portability and Accountability Act (HIPAA, 1996), which provides for perhaps the largest national identity database known in the history of the United States. The HIPAA database contains the names of all U.S. citizens who have health insurance or who have received health care in the past. The database contains social security numbers, addresses, dates of birth, and other forms of personal identifiers on most, if not all, husbands, wives, children, and all single people in the United States. The HIPAA database is accessible to thousands of businesses that are directly and indirectly related to health care, including hospitals; pharmacies; dentists; physicians; medical supply houses; second- and third-party clearinghouses, such as database management companies; and others who need the information. Potentially hundreds of thousands of employees of these businesses now can access the identities of U.S. citizens.

*Identity Theft: A Workplace Crime.* The HIPAA database is highly secured with state-of-the-art Internet and computer technology, but computers do not commit crimes. Contrary to common thought that most identities are stolen by hackers online or by dumpster divers or mailbox thieves, recent research indicates that at least 50% and possibly as much as 70% of identity theft occurs in the workplace and is perpetrated by employees or people impersonating employees. Therefore, identity theft losses to business are far greater than shrinkage ever was. A relatively few dishonest individuals, often contract or temporary workers, are known to steal and fraudulently use the identities of the majority of their hard-working co-workers and customers. Research also indicates that the majority of the identity thefts occur in health care facilities.

*Other Databases.* The HIPAA database is not the only source of identity theft, and, in this information age, many others will be developed. Others in existence for a long time include the databases maintained by each of the four credit reporting agencies—Experian, Equifax, TransUnion, and Innovis. These agencies provide hundreds of thousands of national and international subscriber customers with "credit worthiness" details on U.S. citizens. Credit reports contain names, addresses, dates of birth, social security numbers, credit card and retail account numbers, and other personal information. For purposes of marketing, customers purchase from these agencies lists of names, addresses, and other personal information.

There exist also many state and federal databases, such as those maintained by driver's license bureaus; the Social Security Administration; the U.S. Treasury; and the Selective Service, which maintains a database on all U.S. males. Although purportedly secure, there exist no security standards or statutes for the people who have access to the databases or for the information processes that require the use of personal identities.

*Jurisdictional Problems.* In addition to all of the above, other reasons point to increases in identity thefts. The jurisdictional issue mentioned earlier is one. Even though a state may adopt legislation to resolve or otherwise address jurisdictional problems—investigations, apprehensions, and prosecutions—identity theft rarely is a one-state crime. Identity theft criminals operate in networks across multiple states and countries worldwide. Increasing are reports of international identity theft crimes in which identities are stolen in the United States or from databases abroad and used to send fraudulently purchased merchandise to locations in other countries. In one recent case, a home robbery in Oakland, California, resulted in a fraudulently obtained bank loan for the purchase of a condominium in the United Kingdom. Currently, there is no integrated network of state and federal law enforcement agencies to investigate these identity crimes. Therefore, increases can be expected.

*Identities Are Exported.* Yet other concerns are the outsourcing of U.S. jobs to India, China, Russia, Canada, and Southeast Asia. A majority of the currently exported jobs include benefits, payroll, customer call centers, database management, income tax preparation, and financial accounting—all jobs that, to perform them, require names, addresses, dates of birth, and social security numbers. That is, the job tasks for these types of jobs require the processing of personal identifying information. The outsourcing of U.S. identities together with the threats of terror against the United States and its citizens open wide the crime door of opportunity for the thefts of identities by terrorists.

## THE SOLUTIONS

For the most part, identity theft can be prevented. The solution must begin at the (potential) crime scene: in the workplace where most identities are stolen. The solutions are easy to understand, simple to implement, and inexpensive. However, the overall prevention strategy requires the cooperation of all U.S. businesses working together, which is the challenge.

First, businesses can secure their borders by securing the people—the employees. Second, businesses can secure the information processes inherent in the job positions held by the employees. To secure the people, scientifically developed and highly sophisticated "personnel selection for security instruments" exist. Developed and validated for positions of security, these tests meet the Equal Employment Opportunity Commission and Title VII guidelines for fairness in personnel selection. The instruments exhibit validity and reliability: Validity means a test measures what it purports to measure, and reliability means that it does so consistently. The instruments can be developed for specific job positions, they can be administered to job applicants either individually or in groups, most are relatively easy to score and interpret, and the costs are negligible. This, then, is the first step—to secure the workplace by selecting honest job applicants using 21st-century methods.

The second step is to secure the information processes by which transactions are performed on personal identities. Examples are a bank loan or a paycheck authorization, both of which can involve a series of different job tasks performed by two or more employees holding different job position levels. Wherever personal identifying information is used in the job task, information process risk assessments can be conducted to secure those work processes (Collins, in press). Information process risk assessments are conducted by employee and manager teams to (a) identify the work processes, (b) identify any susceptibilities to theft of identities in those processes, (c) develop mechanisms to secure the processes, and (d) develop both short- and long-term strategic plans for implementing the security mechanisms.

Experience has shown the many benefits of conducting information process risk assessments when managers and employees work together. Employees know the processes best because they are closest to the job tasks, and managers have the information and authority necessary to implement the security mechanisms. Some of those mechanisms may require budgeting, but others can be implemented immediately with little or no cost. Furthermore, employees involved in the risk assessment assume a sense of ownership in the outcome and therefore do whatever is necessary to follow through on the security strategy. In addition, employees feel no threat because they are involved in the process, and, finally, employees gain a sense of security knowing their workplace is now more secure. The final benefit is in the train-the-trainer program in which employees in one department train employees in the next department, and so on, until the information processes in the entire organization are secured, and through which employees gain a sense of "solidarity for security." The internal security of the workplace requires the above people and process solutions together with safeguards for Internet and computer security.

*The Strategy.* The prevention of identity theft in the United States requires that *all* businesses secure their people and processes. An apt analogy is the jurisdictional issue faced by law enforcement. Businesses have boundaries, too, and an inside perpetrator can steal identifying information from one (unsecured) business and use it to defraud a second business, even though the victim's business may have secured internally its people and processes. A coordinated strategy is needed. The plan must involve criminal justice professionals and researchers, state law enforcement and federal agencies, and legislators who can work together to design an interstate uniform plan to combat identity theft and identity crimes.

Finally, there are many ways U.S. citizens can protect the flow of their personal information. Complete step-by-step instructions on how to prevent identity theft, and, for victims, how to recover from identity theft can be found at http://www.cj.msu.edu/~outreach/identity or by contacting the Michigan State University Identity Theft Crime and Research Lab, idtheft@msu.edu or (517) 432-7170, or the Federal Trade Commission at http://www.consumer.gov/idtheft

*Judith M. Collins*

*See also* Computer Crime

## For Further Reading

Collins, J. M. (in press). *Identity theft prevention and control: How to protect your business, customers and employees.* Hoboken, NJ: Wiley.

Collins, J. M., & Hoffman, S. K. (2002). *Identity theft perpetrator profiles.* Manuscript submitted for publication.

Collins, J. M., & Hoffman, S. K. (2003). *Identity theft first responder manual for criminal justice professionals: Police officers, attorneys and judges.* Flushing, NY: Looseleaf.

Equal Employment Opportunity Commission. (2004). *Equal Employment Opportunity Commission guidelines for fairness in hiring.* Available: http://www.eeoc.gov/policy/

General Motors Corporation. (2002). *Final report: Information process risk assessment for four departments, GM Headquarters, Detroit, Michigan.* Conducted by Judith Collins, Michigan State University–Business Identity Theft Partnership in Prevention.

Health Insurance Portability and Accountability Act. (1996). Public Law 104–191. 104th Congress. Retrieved August 8, 2003, from http://www.aspe.hhs.gov/admnsimp/pl104191.htm

Lockyer, W. (2000, April). Statement made by the Attorney General, State of California, at the Opening Ceremony, Annual White Collar Crime Summit, Los Angeles, CA.

McGinley, T. G., & Collins, J. M. (2003, March). *Identity theft: Effect on victimized executives.* Paper presented at the 40th annual meeting of the Academy of Criminal Justice Sciences, Boston, MA.

Powell, E. A. (2004, April 15). *Banks combat identity theft.* Available: www.sanmateocountytimes.com

U.S. Department of Justice. (n.d.). *The al Qaeda training manual.* Retrieved January 13, 2002 from http://www.usdoj.gov/ag/trainingmanual.htm

U.S. General Accounting Office. (2002). *Identity theft: Prevalence and cost appear to be growing.* Washington, DC: U.S. Government Printing Office.

## ❧ IMMIGRANTS (POLICY TOWARD)

Franklin D. Roosevelt once said, "Remember, remember always, that all of us are descended from immigrants and revolutionists" (Roosevelt, 1938, p. 259). America has always prided itself on being a nation of immigrants. Worldwide, people have migrated to the continent since the Norse Vikings explored the North American coast in the 11th century. They continue to come here to this day. Over time, the United States has become known as the "land of opportunity," where anyone who makes a committed effort can prosper—an idea commonly known as The American Dream.

As the nation grew, so did instances of conflict with new arrivals. To restrain the political and social tension resulting from the influx of immigration, laws were passed in 1882 that made it progressively more difficult for people to immigrate to the United States. These restrictions on immigration have resulted in a situation where many more people want to come to the United States than there are visas available. More than 35 million foreigners enter the United States each year (80 IR 1230, August 19, 2002), and hundreds of thousands of them enter illegally, in spite of restrictive immigration laws.

A large portion of the American population is composed of illegal immigrants. This raises genuine concerns regarding the various economic and social aspects of life in America and creates a feeling of uncertainty for the safety and security of its citizens. This reality is well understood by the legislators, who are vested with the difficult responsibility of attempting to balance the vagaries of conflicting political demands. Addressing the concerns surrounding the problem of illegal immigration in this country has historically led to immigration laws that have resulted from political and economic pressure on American lawmakers at all levels of government. All too frequently, the real issues concerning immigrants are misrepresented, and enforcement methods have sometimes been implemented with disparity. Further complicating the issue of immigration is that policy is created at the federal level, and its impact is felt primarily at the local level.

The September 11, 2001, terrorist attacks on the United States not only had a profound impact on the lives of all Americans, but also deeply altered the political discussion over immigration issues. After September 11, 2001, almost everyone on American soil came to realize how vulnerable we are to the surge of anti-American anger worldwide, and most people became sensitized to the concerns surrounding illegal immigration. Although the vast majority of immigrants who violate immigration laws are not terrorists, the perception is that all terrorists are immigrants. Thus, allowing a large undocumented population to remain in the United States creates a sense of unsafety, undermines the foundation of our system of justice, and it "creates a general contempt or disregard for immigration law," as the Executive Director of the Center for Immigration Studies Mark Krikorian stated on the April 10, 2003, House Committee on the Judiciary Subcommittee (80 IR 539, April 14, 2003). In response to ongoing concerns following the September 11, 2001, attack on the United States, President Bush has signed into law several antiterrorism packages, and his administration has initiated new policies and practices to maximize safety and security in this country.

The general consensus has been to optimize the concerted efforts of all parts of the immigration enforcement system to ensure that laws are strictly enforced. Thus, the visa process, inspection and patrol at the borders, the interior enforcement of immigration laws, and the immigration courts' practices were revisited and have undergone major transformation, with many functions now coming under the umbrella of the recently created Department of Homeland Security.

# OFFICE OF HOMELAND SECURITY AND THE HOMELAND SECURITY ACT

On October 8, 2001, President Bush issued an executive order establishing an Office of Homeland Security and the Homeland Security Council to develop and implement a comprehensive domestic antiterrorism strategy. Subsequently the "office" was elevated to cabinet-level status as a "department." The new department combined the functions of multiple agencies in the largest government restructuring since the post-World War II era with the stated goal of preventing further terrorist attacks on the United States and minimizing damage if such attack should occur (79 IR 897, June 10, 2002). On November 25, 2002, President Bush signed into law the Homeland Security Act of 2002.

Interior enforcement systems were reinvigorated with the separation of the Immigration and Naturalization Service's enforcement function from its service function. On March 1, 2003, these functions were transferred to the new Department of Homeland Security (DHS). Under the DHS, border protection, inspection, investigation, and enforcement is handled by the Bureau of Customs and Border Protection (BCBP) and the Bureau on Immigration and Customs Enforcement (BICE), whereas services and benefits are administered by the Bureau of Citizenship and Immigration Services (BCIS) (80 IR 305, March 3, 2003; 80 IR 678, May 12, 2003).

## Bureau of Immigration and Customs Enforcement

BICE's mandate is to "enforc[e] immigration and customs laws within the United States . . . investigat[e] immigration violations, migrant and contraband smuggling, money laundering, trade fraud, and many other criminal activities frequently linked to terrorism," as Under Secretary for Border and Transportation Security Asa Hutchinson outlined on April 10, 2003, when the House Committee on the Judiciary Subcommittee on Immigration, Border Security, and Claims held an oversight hearing to examine this transition (80 IR 537, April 14, 2003).

Hutchinson noted that BICE mandates are "designed to establish a robust continuum of enforcement from the Nation's interiors to its borders and out to the farthest reaches of home countries of illegal aliens . . . and the countries they transit through coming to the United States." He also said that this strategy

> seeks to deter, disrupt and disable terrorist plans, organizations and support networks; identify, apprehend, and remove aliens who threaten the safety and security of the nation; deter and diminish smuggling and trafficking of aliens; protect businesses of national security interests from the vulnerabilities created by the employment of unauthorized alien workers; identify, apprehend, and remove alien criminals; minimize immigration benefit fraud and other document abuse; and respond to community needs related to illegal immigration.

Hutchinson acknowledged that meeting these responsibilities requires "a robust intelligence capability, an air and marine interdiction capability, and an ability to apprehend, detain, and remove illegal aliens" (80 IR 537, April 14, 2003).

## Bureau of Citizenship and Immigration Services

The BCIS administers service and benefits and has assumed all immigration service functions previously performed by the Immigration and Naturalization Service (INS), including the adjudication of immigrant visa petitions, naturalization petitions, asylum and refugee applications, and adjudications performed at INS Service Centers (80 IR 678, May 12, 2003).

# THE USA PATRIOT ACT

On October 25, 2001, without following the usual committee process, the House and Senate approved The United and Strengthening America by Providing Appropriate Tools Required to Intercept and Obstruct Terrorism Act (USA PATRIOT Act), a negotiation between the Senate bill, known as the USA Act, and the House bill, named the PATRIOT Act.

On October 26, 2001, President Bush signed it into law. This is comprehensive

> antiterrorism legislation that gives law enforcement agencies broad new powers to conduct searches, employ electronic surveillance, and detain suspected terrorists. It provides for additional personnel along the northern border, adds new grounds for admissibility for representatives of foreign terrorist organizations and related groups, creates a streamline procedure for the State Department's designation of terrorist organizations, and authorizes the Attorney General to certify and detain any alien he reasonably believes to have terrorist ties. [T]he Act permits the detention of foreign nationals for up to seven years while the government is deciding whether to bring immigration or criminal charges against them. (78 IR 1673, October 29, 2001; also see 78 IR 1703, November 5, 2001)

## AVIATION AND
## TRANSPORTATION SECURITY ACT

On November 19, 2001, the Aviation and Transportation Security Act was signed into law. The Act federalizes airport security screeners for 2 years after a 1-year transition period and requires that qualifications standards for screeners must include U.S. citizenship; an ability to read, speak, and write English at a level sufficient to carry out designated activities; and they must successfully complete a background check (78 IR 1822, December 3, 2001). The law also imposes new restrictions on providing flight training to certain aliens and requires advance notification to the Attorney General before such training can begin (79 IR 1813-14, December 16, 2002).

## ENHANCED BORDER SECURITY
## AND VISA ENTRY REFORM ACT

On May 14, 2002, President Bush signed the Enhanced Border Security and Visa Entry Reform Act. The new law covered a broad range of issues and provided funding authorization for a range of initiatives designed to tighten security at the nation's borders. It provided for interagency information sharing, to ensure that immigration inspectors had access to the information gathered in the visa issuance process contained in the Consolidated Consular database limits on visa issuance and Visa Waiver Program participation, and it provided stricter requirements for foreign students and exchange visitors, mandating closer scrutiny and monitoring of student visa holders.

During the ceremony, the president said that "America is not a fortress; we never want to be a fortress, but . . . we can do a better job of making our borders more secure" (79 IR 769, May 20, 2002).

## THE NATIONAL SECURITY
## ENTRY EXIT REGISTRATION SYSTEM

On August 12, 2002, the INS published The National Security Entry Exit Registration System (67 Fed. Reg. 40581-86, June 13, 2002), which became effective on the date of the 1-year anniversary of the September 11th terrorist attacks. The regulation relates to the special registration and monitoring of certain nonimmigrants who are deemed to be a national security risk and expands the scope of the early registration regulation. Since 1998, citizens and nationals from Iran, Iraq, Sudan, and Libya have been subject to special registration requirements, including fingerprinting, pursuant to 8 CFR & 264.1(f); 63 Fed. Reg. 39109 (July 21, 1998). However, the rule includes additional countries, and the registration requirements are more stringent.

The notice designated nationals and citizens from Afghanistan, Algeria, Bahrain, Eritrea, Iran, Iraq, Lebanon, Libya, Morocco, North Korea, Oman, Pakistan, Qatar, Saudi Arabia, Somalia, Sudan, Syria, Tunisia, United Arab Emirates, and Yemen (67 Fed. Reg. 67766, November 6, 2002). On January 20, 2003, the INS added the following countries to the special registration requirement: Bangladesh, Egypt, Indonesia, Jordan, and Kuwait (80 IR 269, February 24, 2003).

This program was abandoned at the end of 2003 in favor of a system of photographing and fingerprinting foreign travelers who need a visa to enter the United States.

## THE STUDENT AND EXCHANGE VISITOR INFORMATION SYSTEM

The Student and Exchange Visitor Information System (SEVIS) was implemented in April 2003. The system enables the immediate referral of student status violators who might present a heightened security risk to the BICE National Security Unit for appropriate action (80 IR 538, April 14, 2003). The implementation of a foreign student tracking system was first directed by the Illegal Immigration Reform and Immigration Responsibility Act (IIRIRA) of 1996. Then, in 2001, the promulgation of the USA PATRIOT Act required a full implementation of the IIRIRA Act and expanded the foreign student tracking requirements to vocational and other schools by January 1, 2003. It also authorized $36.8 million for this purpose (78 IR 1703, 1705, November 5, 2001). The problem with conventional student tracking initiatives such as IIRIRA and the USA PATRIOT Act is the personnel required and the inability to follow up on individuals who are not in compliance with their status. The newly implemented SEVIS referral program is attempting to overcome this, because all levels of law enforcement—local, state, and federal—are now collaborating in these efforts (80 IR 538, April 14, 2003).

## STATE AND LOCAL IMMIGRATION LAW ENFORCEMENT

Presently, many local law enforcement authorities are not required, nor do they have the authority, to verify the immigration status of civil law violators. Undocumented aliens are referred to the Department of Homeland Security in connection with an arrest pursuant to the commission of a crime. Thus, in the event of traffic infractions, the scope of referral lays with whether the infraction is a crime or a violation in that particular state.

The question of state and local assistance in enforcing federal immigration laws has been a controversial issue for years. The federal government controls policies governing immigration, but it is localities that experience their impact. Local law enforcement agencies have had a mixed response to illegal immigrants. In some localities, illegal immigrants that come to police attention are reported to federal authorities. In these areas, local sheriffs and chiefs have criticized federal authorities for not providing enough immigration personnel to handle the scope of the problem—a problem that involves increased levels of crime. Conversely, in other parts of the country, officers do not report illegal immigrants on a routine basis. Police officials in these areas believe that illegal immigrants are often victims of crime and, for the most part, are law-abiding residents; cooperation with them is essential for good policing. At the time of the September 11, 2001 attacks, there were approximately 1,800 federal immigration agents to deal with 8 million illegal immigrants, and officials sought ways to handle the imbalance.

One method being used to facilitate increased cooperation between federal and local law enforcement and to compensate for federal personnel shortages is that a number of states have engaged in a program to "cross-deputize" local officers—a practice used with other federal law enforcement agencies from time to time. In early 2004, three states—Virginia, Alabama, and Florida—sent a number of officers, usually no more than a few dozen, for training in federal immigration law. These officers can then be stationed throughout the state. In Virginia, officers have been given legal authority to hold suspects for as long as 72 hours without bond until federal agents pick them up. Police officials in these states have emphasized that the vast majority of undocumented aliens are just working people, and it is not their intention to enforce immigration law on a wide-scale basis. Instead, they view this program as a tool that can be used for serious incidents that involve terrorism and violent gang activity. A number of other states are currently considering this program.

As part of the examination that occurred after September 11, federal/local communication and cooperation criticism was leveled at many branches of the country's law enforcement agencies. Local police executives severely criticized federal agencies for not sharing information with them. Yet in the search for terrorist cells within the United States, some police executives refused to cooperate with the Department of Justice by not providing personnel to help interview immigrants from countries associated with the attackers.

Three years after the attack, local enforcement of national immigration laws remains a murky area in many areas around the country. However, to maximize law enforcement efforts in the fight against terrorism, several programs have been undertaken to promote collaboration among various federal, state, and local agencies, and numerous pieces of legislation have been introduced.

### Initiatives

Federal, state, and local law enforcement officers' efforts were brought about by the Alien Absconder Initiative, which aggressively tracks, apprehends, and removes aliens who violated U.S. laws and were ordered deported, but fled before the execution of their deportation order. To facilitate the location of these aliens, their names are entered into the Federal Bureau of Investigation's National Crime Information Center database (78 IR 1899, December 17, 2001; 79 IR 115, January 21, 2002; 79 IR 236, February 11, 2002; 79 IR 261, February 18, 2002).

The Law Enforcement Support Center provides an around-the-clock link between federal, state, and local officers and the immigration database maintained by the BICE to assist these officers in determining whether an individual is an "illegal, criminal, or fugitive alien" (80 IR 1395-1396, September 16, 2002).

The Quick Response Teams established across the United States work directly with state and local enforcement officers to take into custody and remove undocumented aliens who have been arrested on state criminal charges, or who are found to be in the United States without proper documentation (80 IR 538, April 14, 2003).

Operation Southern Focus targets large-scale smuggling organizations specializing in the movement of U.S.-bound aliens from "countries of concern" (80 IR 538, April 14, 2003).

### Newly Introduced Legislation

Senator Charlie Norwood (R-GA) introduced the Clear Law Enforcement for Criminal Alien Removal Act, H.R. 2671, a bill promoting state and local law enforcement of federal immigration laws (AILA Dispatch, April 2004, p. 7). Senators Jeff Session (R-AL) and Zell Miller (D-GA) introduced parallel legislation in the Senate, the Homeland Security Enhancement Act (HSEA), S. 1906. Both bills purport to reaffirm the "inherent authority" of state and local governments to enforce civil immigration laws and would criminalize all immigration status violations for the first time in this country's history. The Clear Act would require state and local police to enforce federal civil immigration laws or lose certain critical funding, whereas the HSEA takes a slightly different tack by denying funding to states or localities that have policies or practices in place that prevent their police from enforcing such laws (AILA Dispatch, April 2004, p. 7).

Representative Dana Rahrabacher (R-CA), on May 11, 2004, introduced The Undocumented Alien Emergency Medical Assistance Amendments of 2004 (H.R. 3722) in the House of Representatives. The legislation proposed to deny hospitals and health care providers reimbursement for uncompensated emergency care to undocumented aliens, unless they report those immigrants to the Department of Homeland Security. This proposed legislation has been a source of great controversy, because it would hold health care providers accountable for verifying the immigration status of all uninsured prospective individuals in need of medical care.

In the absence of voluntary participation, the federal government, by means of this legislation, would find a way to induce localities to act as immigration enforcement agents, while retaining ultimate control over all operations. Immigration officials maintain that federal control over matters regarding aliens and immigration is "plenary and exclusive . . . and that states have no power to interfere. . . . [L]ocalities are not privy to the nature of federal investigations in progress," and situations involving immigrants are governed by federal laws (80 IR 162, February 3, 2003).

## CONCLUSION

The September 11, 2001, terrorist attacks on the United States created a sudden sense of vulnerability that forced America to take a series of necessary antiterrorism measures and changed the direction of federal immigration policies for some time to come. The attacks revealed a country that had little, if any, control over its borders and had almost no idea of who was residing within its borders. Although there is no returning to the practices and policies that prevailed before the attack, the country continues to be a magnet for immigration, legal or otherwise, while immigration policy at all levels of government continues to evolve.

*Isabelle L. Curro*

*See also* Airport Security, Cultural Competency/Sensitivity Training

## For Further Reading

AILA Dispatch. (2004, April). p. 7.

Aviation and Transportation Security Act, Pub. L. No. 1 07-71, 115 Stat. 597 (2001).

Clear Law Enforcement for Criminal Alien Removal Act, H.R. 2671.

Deutsch, H. D. (1992). *Immigration the easy way.* Happauge, NY: Barron's.

8 CFR & 264.1(f).

80 IR 1230 (August 19, 2002).

80 IR 1395-1396 (September 16, 2002).

80 IR 162 (February 3, 2003).

80 IR 269 (February 24, 2003).

80 IR 305 (March 3, 2003).

80 IR 537-539 (April 14, 2003).

80 IR 678 (May 12, 2003).

Enhanced Border Security and Visa Entry Reform Act, H.R. 3525, Pub. L. No. 107-173, 116 Stat. 543 (2002).

Homeland Security Act of 2002, H.R. 2005, Pub. L. No.107-296, 116 Stat. 2135 (2002).

Homeland Security Enhancement Act, S. 1906.

Illegal Immigration Reform and Immigration Responsibility Act of 1996, Pub. L. No. 104-208, 110 Stat. 3009 (1996).

Lazarus, E. (1889). The new colossus. *The Poems of Emma Lazarus, Vol. 1.* Boston: Houghton Mifflin.

PATRIOT Act, H.R. 3162, Pub. L. No.107-56, 115 Stat. 272 (2001).

Roosevelt, F. (1938). Remarks before the Daughters of the American Revolution, Washington, DC, April 21, 1938. *The Public Papers and Addresses of Franklin D. Roosevelt, 1938.* New York: Random House.

78 IR 1673 (October 29, 2001).

78 IR 1703 (November 5, 2001).

78 IR 1899 (December 17, 2001).

79 IR 115 (January 21, 2002).

79 IR 236 (February 11, 2002).

79 IR 261 (February 18, 2002).

79 IR 769 (May 20, 2002).

79 IR 897-899 (June 10, 2002).

79 IR 945 (June 24, 2002).

63 Fed. Reg. 39109 (July 21, 1998).

67 Fed. Reg. 40581-86 (June 13, 2002).

67 Fed. Reg. 67766 (November 6, 2002).

Undocumented Alien Emergency Medical Assistance Amendments of 2004 (H.R. 3722).

## ✑ INFORMANTS

The law enforcement investigative process is a search for relevant and material facts for use in criminal prosecutions, and one of the most effective means of obtaining such information is through the use of an informant. An informant is an individual who has access to information about a past, ongoing, and/or future potential crime; who is motivated to bring this information to the attention of the proper authorities; and who is under the direct control of law enforcement. Informants are either walk-ins or approached by law enforcement, and a thorough background check is done on each to determine his or her potential access to information, motivations, and ability to be controlled. Informants provide information about all types of criminal activity, ranging from petty crimes to crimes that even threaten national and international security. They are a valuable resource and tool for law enforcement because the information they provide would be otherwise unavailable through other investigative means.

Access to information varies from one informant to another. Informants may have either direct personal knowledge of a crime, indirect knowledge through personal association, or outside knowledge through indirect association. The more informants are trusted by their criminal associates, the more access to incriminating information they have, and consequently, the more valuable they are to law enforcement. Active informants are those who provide law enforcement with information while remaining on the inside; they have the most access to information and are consequently the most valued by law enforcement. Other types of informants are eyewitnesses, anonymous tipsters, unwitting informants, and jailhouse informants.

However, the law imposes some limitations and restrictions on whether and how an informant can be developed by law enforcement. Law enforcement must obtain permission before using an individual who is on probation/parole or who is a juvenile. Also, the use of a jailhouse informant presents its own set of unique limitations and restrictions on whether the incriminating information they provide about other inmates will be admissible at trial. Although the determination of admissibility varies on a case-by-case basis, the general rule based on the landmark decision in *Massiah v. United States* (1964) is that a jailhouse informant cannot coerce another inmate by making an affirmative act to question or elicit incriminating information, otherwise Fifth and Sixth Amendment rights, protection against self-incrimination and right to counsel, respectively, will have been deemed to be violated.

Although informants are a valuable resource and tool for law enforcement, there is a negative connotation associated with them, reflected in commonly used terms such as "fink," "rat," "snitch," or "stool pigeon." This negative connotation stems from the fact that informants commit the ultimate betrayal of confidences when they provide incriminating information to law enforcement about their criminal associates. Law enforcement uses less disparaging terminology to name informants, such as "cooperating individual/witness," or "confidential informant/source." Informants are observed with cautious suspicion at best, even in the eyes of the law, because often they may have ulterior motives for providing misleading or even false information to law enforcement in their attempt to milk the system from both ends. The most common informant ulterior motives include the desire to protect themselves from being detected in ongoing criminal activity, to hide a previous lie, or to protect or falsely implicate another. Based on federal and state statutes, false statements made by informants can carry terms of imprisonment depending on the severity of the misrepresentation.

The motivation necessary for an informant to cooperate with law enforcement must be powerful enough to overcome the social and emotional incentives against betraying their criminal associates. The most common motivations for informants are fear (threat of incarceration or threats by associates), revenge, monetary rewards, or repentance or a desire to reform. Most informants have more than one motive for providing law enforcement with information. Knowing an informant's motive is critical in law enforcement's ability to control the informant and reduce those risks associated with their use.

To limit those risks, law enforcement attempts to establish a detached, professional relationship with informants and to institute certain rules and guidelines in their management. Control is the essence of informant management, and at all times, law enforcement, and not the informant, must be in control of the decision-making process. However, law enforcement may consult informants on their unique perspective about situations, problems, solutions, or available alternatives in coming to a decision. Also, the corroboration of information through other investigative techniques supplied by informants (e.g., analysis of physical evidence, interrogation, wiretapping, etc.) is another highly effective and necessary manner of informant control. This is because corroboration is a direct indication of the credibility of informants and the information that they are providing law enforcement.

Not only must law enforcement be able to trust the credibility of its informants, but the opposite is also true, that informants must be able to trust the word, discretion, and competence of law enforcement. Often, informants are risking monetary reward, incarceration, or even their lives to cooperate, so law enforcement has an obligation to protect informants from retaliation by their former criminal associates. Both federal and state witness protection and posttrial relocation programs exist for that specific purpose, by providing informants with new identities, housing at government expense, and personal protection by deputy U.S. marshals.

Law enforcement also prefers to keep an informant's identity a secret at trial not only so the informant can continue to be used as a source of information, but also to protect him or her from retaliation. There are, however, certain legal restrictions on how far law enforcement can go in keeping the informant's identity a complete secret. The filing of criminal charges may require disclosure of the informant, especially if that person will be a witness at trial, because of the landmark decision in *Brady v. Maryland* (1963), the Jencks Act, and the Sixth Amendment, which all basically say that a defendant has the right to be confronted by his or her accusers and the right to be made aware of all exculpatory information. However, in practice, disclosure of an informant's identity is decided on a case-by-case basis, and where guilt or innocence is not directly at stake, courts have been reluctant to disclose the identity of an informant.

Most informants are dropped when their access to information is gone, whereas others are dropped because they had ulterior motives that jeopardized their credibility.

*Enrico DeMaio*

### For Further Reading

Bloom, R. M. (2002). *Ratting: The use and abuse of informants in the American justice system.* Westport, CT: Praeger.

Brady v. Maryland, 272 U.S. 82 (1963).

Levenson, L. L. (2002). Beware of informants. *National Law Journal, 24*(29), B13.

Madinger, J. (2000). *Confidential informant: Law enforcement's most valuable tool.* Boca Raton, FL: CRC.

Massiah v. United States, 377 U.S. 201 (1964).

## ✆ INFORMATION TECHNOLOGIES

The effects of technologies, or the ways that work is done, cannot be understood outside the organizational structures, routines, and tasks in which they are located. Organizations use many different technologies, their workings various, mysterious, and sometimes understood. Although they are often reified, or, on the other hand, ascribed human features, technologies should be seen as *mediating* between actors and extant relationships, norms, rules, and structures. Technologies have a role in shaping organizations but also in configuring them to respond to other, broader socioeconomic challenges. In some sense, the relationship between a technology and an organization is a series of challenges and responses.

Policing is a traditional bureaucratic organization with rigid rules and a conservative purpose and mandate. Its technologies are fitted to these constraints, and even powerful information technologies have yet to alter policing. To discuss information technologies in policing, one must first outline the elements of technology. Technologies display at least four elements:

- *Material Elements.* These include the space occupied and the physical properties of the technology. Imagine the compressed space inside the modern police car resulting from the introduction of laptops or workstations, mobile digital terminals (in-car radio-telephone-computers), and mounted microphones and video cameras. The trunk also contains additional tools, perhaps a video camera and equipment for dealing with traffic accidents. Officers carry weapons, communication devices, notebooks, and miscellaneous equipment. Computers, servers, and terminals take up room in a police organization, as do printers (often, large, map-making size); the clerks or others who enter, retrieve, and analyze data; and storage areas for the maps, paper files, and perhaps computer tapes or disks. Space and time are considerations in materiality. When entire buildings are set aside for computer functions, as in Toronto and Chicago, they are inconveniently located for ease of access by officers.

- *Logical Elements.* These are the underlying (assumed) processes by which work is seen to be accomplished. These processes are only partially visible. The computer screen in the police control room is the epitome of a visible display that masks vast, subtle, and complex invisible processes.

- *Social Elements.* These shape and create social roles and interactions that arise from doing job-related tasks. The social elements of policing technology include answers to questions such as, Who uses what technologies? In what roles? With respect to what routines and situations? To accomplish what "output"? The uniformed patrol officer carrying weapons, driving a car, and carrying out routine patrol and response to calls is a salient, almost iconic example of a social role shaped by technologies.

• *Imaginative Elements*. These make partially visible the processes by which known and recorded outcomes are produced. Police are known for their most *visible* technologies—weapons, talk, training, and means of mobility—on which they expend most of their budgets after personnel costs. However, they also employ less visible technologies. These are transformative technologies used to extend the senses and to present evidence in scientific or quasi-scientific form (laboratory-based or forensic evidence), and analytic technologies, those designed to aggregate, simulate, model, and analyze data that serve crime analysis, crime mapping, and risk analysis in aid of crime prevention.

Information technology, like all technologies, is some-*thing* as well as something thought about. Information technology (IT) encompasses the means by which *data* (raw facts as recorded) are transformed into *information* (data now placed in some context with a purpose) and stored, analyzed, and retrieved. Information technologies convert facts into useful information. They display logical, material, and social elements, and imagination is required to make them work. Ultimately, people work with *and* on technology, and it is the work people do that is the social feature of concern here. IT alters and changes the structures within which it functions, as well as being embedded within them. Information technology is a multisided mirror. It ingests data; shapes and stores it; transforms it in myriad ways; and then produces the texts, screens, files, images, and sounds used to interpret its work and the nature of the external world. It is thus *reflexive*—it is the primary way in which the organization sees itself, speaks to itself, and stores its memories. Its very reflexivity is an enigma because although it is a means by which the organization talks to itself about itself, it is also a conduit of new data and information. Perhaps the fundamental aspect of information technologies is that they receive, process, store, and analyze the data that mark and selectively dramatize the organizational processes they sustain.

## POLICE ORGANIZATIONS

How do information technologies fit into police organizations? Police organizations are typically described as bureaucratically structured, rank-based systems that are rigidly and hierarchically articulated, punishment oriented in their uses of rules, and dominated by the ideology of the lower participants (from 60%–80% of the personnel are in the uniformed patrol division). A great deal of decision-making latitude remains at the bottom. Major resource allocation strategies are responding to calls, deploying random patrol, and making modest effort in crime investigation. In the following sketch, an outline of police work, the dynamics of structure can be characterized and then related to the work of information technologies.

Police organizations are authoritatively coordinated systems of interaction in which the density of interaction is greater within than between members and other organizations, and they typically occupy an identified spatial–ecological niche. They take up space, and this space is invested with significance by the interactions taking place there. The central function of an organization is sense making, or ongoing, social, plausible extraction of cues that order experience retrospectively and serve to enact a responsive environment. The sense making that takes place is *interpersonal*—what is being said and suggested in a meeting? It is also *organizational*—what does this mean for the way the organization works?

Sense-making interactions mean that organizations are echo chambers in which goals are proximal, tacit, and unrecognized; goals are unclear or in conflict; goals are made visible by practices rather than clear statements of mission, purpose, and accomplishment; and organizations, whatever their goals, are characterized by competing rationalities or sanctioned ways of getting things done. The threads that run through an organization are the routines that display its doings. The routines that organize police work are themselves malleable, subject to change and reorganization. The police organization is segmented, with very different notions about the scope of the work, success, promotion, and the utility of given technologies. The particular segments of the police organization, such as top management, middle management, and the lower participants, tend to be loosely connected, one with the other, through occasioned routines.

The rules in police organizations are complex, opaque, and seen as capricious, perhaps because they are designed to reduce temptation and corruption and provide a basis for punishment. Policing is a "mock bureaucracy" designed to provide flexibility in sanctioning from the top, not guidance to lower participants. Rules for organizing are bureaucratic until such matters as exceptions must be handled. Exceptions fall to the top management to define and resolve; thus, what top management does is attempt to define into the modes of action those matters that are, in fact, outside of their control.

Although it displays itself as a militaristic command and control bureau, policing is ecologically dispersed and almost 25% civilian. Officers have great power and authority to shape and use technologies in their own interests. Thus, although any technological innovation may come from the top, its success will lie in the responses of lower participants to the innovation. Directives coming from the top are often subverted, sabotaged, redefined, and redirected by those implementing them.

Work, doing things to produce outputs, may be organized around material objects, but such a view seizes on the superficial because material aspects of technologies are a *foreground* for further imagining. Work practices must be shown, learned, and repeated so that an imagery remains of the work, a sedimentation of how the thing (work) is accomplished here. This demonstrable aspect is particularly powerful in policing because it is a cohort-based, apprentice-like craft learned by watching and emulating, and reinforced by storytelling. The lingering symbolic images of the craft, of good work, or stories that encapsulate what is done and why, are important for sense making. Warnings, cautionary tales, and "cock-ups" (i.e., blunders) mark what is to be avoided, but their generality is always dubious. Tools of the trade shift in and out of importance, and are reified in the oral culture of policing. Cars, weapons, communications equipment, strategies, and tactical lines vary in utility.

## THE SPECIAL CASE OF INFORMATION TECHNOLOGY AND INNOVATION

The present situation with regard to information technologies in policing should be described. Fieldwork in large North American departments

suggests that although departments have acquired new information technologies, and most departments typically possess many of them, they remain unintegrated, scarcely used beyond short-term daily needs, and marginal to the core work as seen by patrol officers. In many respects, the information technologies are not a system, but a collection of databases, software and hardware, clerks and operators, working quasi-independently. Consider these features of current information collections in policing. Large urban departments in North America have the following resources:

• Many nonlinked databases that are locally sourced and electronic, such as computer-assisted dispatch (CAD); the jail and booking system; criminal records; other management data; fingerprints; visual images such as mug shots; a records management system of some sort; and, in most large departments, a geographical information system (GIS) that charts data points spatially. Most computer-assisted systems are linked to incident and arrest data in a records management scheme, but the range of databases linked to the CAD varies, and not all such records systems are online (some are a day or more behind, and others lag much longer). In all departments, the vast majority of records are paper and kept in files, boxes, storage rooms, and vast archival bins. These include the basic records management systems (budgets, personnel, workload, payroll, leaves, and holidays) and various investigative records. Detectives' work—case records, statements, evidence, and court decisions—are kept either in paper files or in separate databases.

• Many nonlinked databases that are maintained by the federal government: The National Crime Information Center keeps records on missing or wanted persons and property, as well as stolen vehicles; the National Incident Check System contains records of persons disqualified from possessing firearms; the Automated Fingerprint Identification System (AFIS); the Criminal History Record Information system contains records of all state offenders; the National DNA Index System contains DNA profiles submitted by states; the National Incident Based Reporting System (NIBRS) includes basic data on offenses and offenders; and the Uniform Crime Reports includes reported criminal incidents and arrests. The number of national accessible databases is large and growing. The still-controversial NIBRS is implemented in only a handful of the largest American departments, even though it is the mandated and preferred system of data collection by the Bureau of Justice Statistics.

• A stated or potential capacity to gather and process data quickly; store it in an accessible and orderly fashion; and develop vast, fact-based files of fingerprints, criminal records, lab reports, arrest documents, and cases, and aggregate them, model them, and do correlations or analyses. This capacity is rarely used, although large departments have hired crime analysts to do some simple aggregation and tabularization of routine data. The growth in storage capacity absent access and use reveals the tendency within policing and perhaps other public agencies to acquire systems without clear standards or stated purposes, and without considering the complexity of creating usable and simple modes of interface, collocation, and analysis. Police swim in a sea of facts. Ironically, the other problem of insufficient capacity exists at times. The burgeoning of tools and databases strains the memory capacity of departments, and computers "crash," or lack functional memory for peak-time operations.

• Incompatible software and hardware that escalates complexity and uncertainty. Numerous software systems exist, such as ArcView, for geocoded material; Pop TRAK, for monitoring problem solving; specialized programs for workload management; and many spreadsheets for accounting and noncriminal records maintenance. Diverse workstations are in place—Macs, IBM clones, desktops and laptops, vehicle-based mobile digital terminals—with several generations of software equipped with many kinds of word processing and other software. Research suggests that even compatible systems are rarely and poorly used, and that data transfer is awkward and flawed.

• Inconsistent user and backside technology interfaces. These include one or more mainframe-based systems (sometimes shared with county or city government), several servers in diverse locations, and links to the Internet from some workstation locations. Perhaps as a result of the ad hoc accretion of these via purchasing, the influence of vendors, trends, and failed innovations, police have disparate information technology clusters that are not additive or cumulative in their effects. Grant-funded programs and software are abandoned when funding vanishes.

• A Web site displaying descriptive materials, some data on calls for service or crime patterns, and hyperlinks to other Web sites. These tend to be taken-as-read texts with no explication or guidance as to their significance.

• Characteristic secrecy and nonlinked access points. Although decentralized terminals allow minimal data access to citizens in neighborhood terminals, as in Hartford, Connecticut, and laptops to be taken home by officers in Charlotte-Mecklenberg, North Carolina, few terminals permit direct access for officers or citizens to detailed maps, selected printouts, or online data. Databases that can be accessed are limited to recent CAD data, and questions of privacy limit access to many databases.

• Multiple and incompatible channels of communication from the public to the police and within the police department. These include, as noted above, Web sites, e-mail, cell and land-based phones, "snail" mail, personal visits to stations, face-to-face encounters, networked communication via fiber optic cables, paper documents, and e-files sent as attachments. None of them is assessed for overlap, inconsistency, validity, or utility.

• A tendency to use mapping information for short-term tactical interventions absent problem solving. These tactical deployments are not assessed as to effect or consequence.

In summary, even the most advanced forms of communicative technologies have been back-fitted to the extant structure and traditional processes of the police organization. In 2004, no police department has refined a systematically integrated collection of technologies to facilitate problem solving, crime prevention, policy analysis, or community interfaces. A 2000 review suggests that the fundamental interfaces between IT and the dimensions of community policing—interface with communities, interorganizational links, workgroup facilitation, environmental scanning, problem orientation, area-based accountability, and strategic management—are nowhere near well-developed.

Technologies have several elements that are combined in organizations to create stimuli or challenges to the status quo ante. The meaning of these challenge–response sets varies over time and in the context of organizational structure. Police organizations, although appearing to be tightly integrated and controlled, are actually loosely coupled, sense-making, organized action. They primarily display weapons and mobility technology, are secondarily concerned with training and transformative technology, and devote the fewest resources to communicative and analytic technologies. In recent years, the police have acquired a variety of communicative devices for sending, receiving, and storing messages from many sources through a variety of devices and channels. The present array of communicative devices, although rich and complex, are underused and seldom applied with skill, and they remain as icons of science.

*Peter K. Manning*

## For Further Reading

Abt Associates. (2000). *Police department Information Systems Technology Enhancement Project (ISTEP).* Washington, DC: U.S. Department of Justice, Community Policing Services Agency.

Barley, S. (1986). Technology as an occasion for structuring. *Administrative Science Quarterly, 31,* 78–108.

Bayley, D., & Bittner, E. (1986). The tactical choices of police patrol officers. *Journal of Criminal Justice, 14,* 329–348.

Bayley, D., & Garofalo, J. (1989). The management of violence by police officers. *Criminology, 27,* 1–25.

Chan, J. (2000). *The technology game.* Final report to the Australian Research Council, University of New South Wales, Australia.

Dunworth, T. (2000). Criminal justice and the information technology revolution. In J. Horney (Ed.), *Criminal justice 2000* (Vol. 3, pp. 371–426). Washington, DC: National Institute of Justice, Office of Justice Programs.

Espeland, W. (1998). *The struggle for water.* Chicago: University of Chicago Press.

Gouldner, A. W. (1960a). *Patterns of industrial bureaucracy.* Glencoe, IL: Free Press.

Gouldner, A. W. (1960b). *Wildcat strike.* Yellow Springs, OH: Antioch.

Greene, J. (2000). Community policing in America. In J. Horney (Ed.), *Criminal justice 2000* (Vol. 3, pp. 299–370).

Washington, DC: National Institute of Justice, Office of Justice Programs.

MacKenzie, D. (1993). *Inventing accuracy.* Cambridge: MIT Press.

Manning, P. K. (1992a). Information technology and the police. In M. Tonry & N. Morris (Eds.), *Modern policing* (pp. 349–398). Chicago: University of Chicago Press.

Manning, P. K. (1992b). Technological dramas and the police. *Criminology, 30,* 327–345.

Manning, P. K. (2001). *The narcs' game* (2nd ed.). Prospect Heights, IL: Waveland.

Manning, P. K. (2003). *Policing contingencies.* Chicago: University of Chicago Press.

Pentland, B., & Feldman, M. (2003). Reconceptualizing organizational routines as a source of flexibility and change. *Administrative Science Quarterly, 48,* 94–118.

Roberts, K., & Grabowski, M. (1996). Organizations, technology and structuring. In S. Clegg, C. Hardy, & W. Nord (Eds.), *Handbook of organization studies* (pp. 409–423). London: Sage.

Roy, D. (1952). Quota restriction and gold bricking in a machine shop. *American Journal of Sociology, 57,* 427–442.

Roy, D. (1954). Efficiency and "the fix": Informal relations in a piecework machine shop. *American Journal of Sociology, 60,* 255–266.

Shearing, C., & Ericson, R. (1991). Culture as figurative action. *British Journal of Sociology, 42,* 481–506.

Weick, K. (1995). *Sensemaking in organizations.* Thousand Oaks, CA: Sage.

Weick, K. (2001). *Making sense of the organization.* Malden, MA: Blackwells.

Weisburd, D., Greenspan, R., & Mastrofski, S. (2001, February). *Compstat and organizational change: Preliminary findings from a national study.* Washington, DC: National Institute of Justice.

## INSPECTORS GENERAL

The first Inspectors General—one for infantry and one for cavalry—were appointed by the French Army in 1668 and had the principal duties of reviewing the troops and reporting to the King. During the American Revolution, George Washington adopted the concept, charging his Inspector General with correcting all abuses and deficiencies within the Continental Army. But it was two centuries later before civilian Inspectors General were established to fight fraud, corruption, and waste in government.

One of the core principles at the foundation of government is that public service is a public trust. An Inspector General is specifically charged with safeguarding that trust and does so by requiring that government is guided by high standards of integrity and honesty. The job of an Inspector General includes identifying, investigating, and deterring misconduct by government officials and employees. In this way, the Inspector General helps ensure that government runs effectively and efficiently, that tax dollars are spent honestly, and that those who work in the government are held accountable to the citizens they serve.

Governments have always tried to fight corruption and monitor integrity, but until the 1970s, this was usually done in the form of a special commission, committee, or task force established in response to a particular scandal. For example, the Watergate Committee, the Knapp Commission, and the Whitewater Independent Counsel were all created in this way and then disbanded once their findings were complete or the threat of the specific crisis passed. Establishing Inspectors General to monitor and oversee government entities showed a commitment to address wrongdoing and improve efficiency proactively. With a combination of legal, law enforcement, and analytical personnel, Inspectors General have institutionalized fraud-fighting efforts and have taken the campaign against government corruption a major step forward.

In 1978, the first U.S. civilian Inspectors General were appointed by Congress in 12 major federal agencies, such as the Department of Commerce and the Department of Education. Concurrently, the idea was reaching state and local government. In 1981, following a scandal involving public construction projects, Massachusetts passed legislation that made it the first state in the country to establish an Inspector General's office with statewide jurisdiction. Other states followed later, such as New York in 1986 and Ohio and Louisiana in 1988. The City of Philadelphia established an Inspector General's office in 1984, and the City of Chicago followed in 1989.

Inspectors General offices are most commonly structured in one of two ways: reporting solely to the executive branch of government or reporting to both the executive branch and the commissioner or head of the agency or agencies the Inspectors General oversee. Those who report only to the executive branch are often viewed as less independent and objective as those with a dual reporting structure. Their dependence on the governor or mayor often brands them as politically motivated. However, those with attention and loyalties divided between the executive branch and agency commissioners are often seen as less effective and less autonomous. Effectiveness is influenced because the Inspector General's staff is often in different physical locations, and therefore, less attention may be paid to cross-agency or multiagency cases and problems. Autonomy may be affected because it may become more difficult to investigate top-level agency officials when working closely with them or reporting to them.

Depending on the law creating his or her authority, an Inspector General may have the power to subpoena and enforce the attendance of witnesses and administer oaths or affirmations. Certain Inspectors General's offices have peace officer or police powers. Most have access to all records maintained by the governmental entities they oversee and the ability to require employees to give testimony concerning any matter related to the performance of their official duties. In addition, many have an affirmative reporting obligation for government employees, asking them to report any improper behavior to the Inspector General. Balancing this requirement is usually some form of "whistle-blower" protection against adverse personnel action for employees who come forward.

The catch-all term used in describing the mission of many Inspectors General offices—corruption—covers a wide range of conduct. Corruption is not a legal term—some corruption is criminal conduct, such as bribery, extortion, theft, perjury, and unlawful gratuities, whereas other corrupt conduct includes violations of codes, regulatory provisions, and internal agency policies and procedures.

In fighting corruption, Inspectors General generally initiate investigations in response to a variety of sources, including complaints from employees, people doing business with the government, and the general public. Potential wrongdoing is also found in areas brought to their attention by audits or other analyses of government programs. Although Inspectors General are concerned with stopping and punishing individual or pockets of misconduct, the larger goal is to improve government by preventing problems from recurring and eliminating opportunities for corruption and abuse. An Inspector General's investigative priorities become those cases that promise the broadest and most significant impact.

If an investigation initiated by an Inspector General's office looks as though it may be criminal, the assistance of local, state, or federal agencies with full police powers is usually sought. Furthermore, because Inspectors General do not have prosecutorial authority depending on the nature of the crime, at some point, the case will be referred to a local district attorney's office, the state attorney general, or a U.S. Attorney's office. Sometimes, the Inspector General will continue in an investigative capacity; sometimes, the prosecutor will completely take over the case.

However, many of an Inspector General's cases are not criminal, but disciplinary or administrative in nature. Often, during the course of an investigation, the major findings are recommendations to a government agency for the reform of policies, procedures, laws, systems, and practices that eliminate opportunities for corruption and improve the effectiveness of government operations. Sometimes, the findings include wide policy recommendations that affect numerous agencies and have a significant impact on public policy.

Once an investigation or proactive policy audit is complete, Inspectors General work with government agencies to design and implement strategies that limit opportunities for misconduct, promote accountability, and ensure effective and efficient programs management. This involves analyzing certain or various aspects of government operations to reduce fraudulent activity and program abuse by streamlining operations, minimizing inefficient procedures, and ensuring that adequate internal controls are in place.

*Anne Ternes*

## For Further Reading

Inspector General Act of 1978 (Pub. L. 95–452, §1, Oct. 12, 1978, 92 Stat. 1101). Available http://www.access.gpo. gov/uscode/title5a/5a_2_.html

http://www.ignet.gov/
http://www.inspectorsgeneral.org/ ·

# ⊘⊘ INTERAGENCY COOPERATION ... OR NOT

Any discussion of interagency cooperation becomes a complex dissection of language, cultural ethos, jurisdictional authority, and political and operational issues. By the year 2000, law enforcement in the United States numbered more than 13,000 local police departments and more than 50 federal agencies with varying and overlapping mandates of intelligence gathering and security (McHugh, 2001). The intent of interagency cooperation is not a new one, with task forces operating as investigative tools since the 1970s and more prominently in the 1980s. Initial reports were mixed regarding task force effectiveness. State and local police agencies usually complained about the one-way nature of relations with federal authorities; more often, the complaints involved the actions of the FBI and the DEA. However, federal authorities did not fair any better in relations with one another. Each exerted control found in statutory mandates or through the control of informants and investigative intelligence.

General Accounting Office (GAO, 1982) and media sources reported divergent outcomes ranging from the disruptive influence of differing philosophies and procedures (both administrative and investigative) to the standard claims of law enforcement success (arrests, warrants, and seizures statistics). Testimonial reports of task force success surfaced as often as those of turf battles. Task forces were designed to combine agency resources and personnel, and to develop cases at the highest level for unprecedented impact. These goals were not fully realized, and the spectre of insufficient shared intelligence and mutual professional respect continued to be expressed. The level of commitment and success on individual task forces seemed tied to creative supervisory leadership and the natural camaraderie of investigators working closely together toward a common goal. It was often agency executives who warned their personnel to "not forget who they worked for" or who gave lip service to the mission. At best, these efforts lacked consistency and genuine acceptance within the fabric of agency cultures and operations.

In the wake of September 11, 2001, the catchphrase has been "seamless coordination." Vows to close the gap in relations among law enforcement entities, as well as the military, the Central Intelligence Agency, and the Department of Homeland Security (DHS) collectively emerged. Law enforcement versus military imperatives are only the most recent layer of discussions dictating the delineation of responsibilities and "turf." Some have suggested DHS's lack of experience would complicate an already crowded task environment where one more entity was out to validate its existence.

Perhaps the most glaring deficiencies are found in the language of cooperation while ignoring the immense influence of human behavior in these outcomes. The need for brutal honesty and enforced accountability is critical if change is to occur. It remains a clash between the oft-reported arrogance of federal officials and the full inclusion of state and local law enforcement. Current Federal Bureau of Investigation (FBI) Director Robert S. Mueller III reported linking the activities of more than 50 joint terrorism task forces with technology and personnel. Director Mueller identified relations with state and local officials as third in the FBI's list of reassessed priorities post-September 11th Director Mueller insisted he is seeking a change to the FBI's long-reported cultural impediments to the one-way relations with state and local colleagues. Changing culture is more than mission reevaluation and resource allocation; changing culture requires reorienting agency groupthink and teaching interagency cooperation as a value held at the highest levels of the agency. In early 2002, Director Mueller appointed a former police chief as head of the FBI's newly established Office of Law Enforcement Coordination. This office is designated to improve communication and relations with state and local officials. A small point, but interesting, is the use of the term *coordination* rather than *cooperation*. Coordination still implies control, whereas cooperation speaks to consensus building. Cooperation is effectively tied to both executive commitment and the socialization of street investigators to the ethics and value of these work groups.

In February 2003 hearings before a Senate subcommittee regarding homeland security and the tangential issues of interagency cooperation, former Congressman Warren Rudman suggested the lack of intelligence sharing and interagency cooperation was about neither obstinacy nor turf. Rudman advised that it was mission and the inability of agencies to share information as a result of policy barriers. He contended that a lack of technology had wholly failed agencies in that regard. Conversely, James S. Gilmore III, Chairman of the Gilmore Commission that was authorized in 1999 to research and advise regarding potential terrorist threat, also testified and reiterated that locals were still groping to have full membership. Gilmore advised that dramatic leadership and accountability was essential for change. He asserted that turf and culture issues have not yet been resolved and suggested the crux was admitting the problem before any changes would realistically occur. Gilmore stated that an inherent feeling of superiority by federal officials existed because of state and local officials' subordinate role in the funding process. The U.S. Congress has contemporaneously demanded that the FBI forge complete and responsible relations with state and local authorities and effect critical changes in its work culture. The 9/11 Commission Report, released July 22, 2004, responded to the acute problems facing information sharing in numerous branches of the government by recommending the creation of "a national intelligence czar, building an overarching counterterrorism center, and reorganizing congressional committees" (Curtius, 2004, p. A14).

## DYNAMICS OF COOPERATION

Interagency cooperation places extraordinary demands on organizations that have defined themselves historically as autonomous and elite. The very secretive nature of police organizations and work complicates the process of cooperation. Outsiders suddenly became insiders and parent agency dependence now shifted to new work groups. Interdependencies challenge both loyalties and the insular work environments of individual organizations. However, terrorism at home demands to be defined as that superordinate goal (Sherif, 1966) with the compelling appeal for all involved that transcends the influence of self-promotion or preservation. Organizational researchers contend that there is a great fear of domination, and equal power and control are important issues affecting cooperative ventures. Most organizations report a preference for liaison without complete integration, thereby maintaining control of their information and the autonomy it represents.

Jurisdiction once defined by geography is now framed and challenged by technology, mobility, and overlapping or concurrent statutory responsibility. It is integral to understanding the rationale of agencies. Self-declared expertise is epitomized through agency image and asserted mastery of the task environment.

Knowledge is power, and investigative intelligence is the currency of primacy and effectiveness. Every police agency has a constituency to whom it presents a public face and through which continued funding and self-preservation is maintained. The control of information is so pivotal because it represents the overall competency of the agency. Research regarding shared information as an element of cooperation identifies it as the basis of human organization, and those with the more recent information have positions of control. This research also asserts that the technology of information requires a collaborative process rather than unilateral control. With the increased mass availability of information, power is diffused; this is a natural consequence of technological progress. Systems of consensus versus command structures get things done. Those who are going to have to make the decision work must be brought into the process; there must be a shared sense of direction among those who form the parade if there is to be a parade. Law enforcement work cultures are notorious for seeking control within joint ventures, and the historical concept of "lead agency" must be replaced by consensus and collegiality. Sociological definitions of "team" report the critical importance of not withholding information from any team member. Research has stated that doing so is

tantamount to withholding a member's ability to exercise the team performance and accomplish the team goal. Withholding information also represents a diminution of the team member. Finally, reduced effectiveness has been measured in cooperative work groups where insular motives and interests of members were prominent.

U.S. Senator Frank Lautenberg provided a succinct statement during the aforementioned February 2003 hearings. Lautenberg indicated his understanding of the issues by remarking, "I like joint ventures too, as long as we own the joint." Former governor of Virginia James S. Gilmore III detailed strongly the need for fusion of personnel in recognition of the power of membership and group cohesion. Gilmore was candid about the reported perceptions of many major city police chiefs and the implied insult relative to "security clearances" for access to federal intelligence and information they should rightly be extended because of their office and responsibilities. Recognition of policies or other legal barriers preventing complete access can be overcome and changed to accommodate the goal.

Conversely, city police chiefs have asserted their control through noncompliance with federal requests. This is best evidenced in the recent post-September 11th initiatives to interview selected individuals identified for watch lists by federal immigration and law enforcement authorities. Several police chiefs across the United States preferred to define the parameters of these contacts and employed it as a forum for continued discussion of partnerships with federal authorities.

## FUTURE PRACTICE AND PROGRESS

Historically, former Governor Gilmore's is not a lone voice. In the aforementioned GAO report, interagency cooperation was in trouble, and agencies classically failed to cooperate fully with GAO access to necessary information. Interagency cooperation has long been a stated goal of federal law enforcement. In 1993, U.S. Attorney General Janet Reno's comments at the International Association of Chiefs of Police won applause for her intent to improve respect and cooperation from federal authorities to state and local colleagues. During his confirmation hearings in 1993 regarding the FBI directorship, Louis J. Freeh personally reported the value of interagency efforts and the need to solidify the commitment of managers. There are and have been numerous successful law enforcement partnerships, as demonstrated by joint task forces involving federal and local law enforcement, that are a mainstay of policing, particularly in the areas of drug enforcement and illegal firearms. Satisfaction and success in these ventures are inextricably tied to collegial respect and unequivocal access to mutually important intelligence. Recent reports of cooperation detail unprecedented cooperative relations, whereas others report reticence. It is clear from these reports that an environment of mutual respect and open communication is an important foundation for continued satisfactory contact.

Law enforcement cooperation in a post-September 11th environment has identified a worthy and important common goal. The goal of cooperation will not be reached if organizations continue to plot courses that ignore the essential component of human behavior; it is not simply a matter of shared resources and personnel. It is intrinsically about human interaction, mutual respect, and open communication. A shift in agency groupthink is also critical. In a perfect world, consensus and full cooperation would result as compelling goals were articulated. However, the entrenchment of organizational image, ethos, and the world of political egos all remain pervasive in law enforcement. These work cultures require dramatic leadership and attitudinal shifts.

*Katherine Newbold*

**See also** Counterterrorism, Task Forces

### For Further Reading

Anderson, W. J. (1982, March 26). *FBI-DEA task forces: An unsuccessful attempt at joint operations* (GGD-82-50). Washington, DC: General Accounting Office.

Curtius, M. (2004, July 24). The 9/11 Commission Report: Lawmakers jolted in midst of campaign: The Commission's urgent tone focuses the minds of politicians, but the drive to enact reforms is competing with the drive to Nov. 2. *Los Angeles Times*, p. A14.

McHugh, A. J. (2001). Coordination within the rings of law enforcement: How local agencies must adapt to a post 9/11 environment. *Johns Hopkins Journal of American Politics.*

National Commission on Terrorist Attacks. (2004). *The 9/11 Commission report: Final report of the National Commission on Terrorist Attacks Upon the United States.* Washington, DC: U.S. Government Printing Office.

Nowicki, E. J. (1990, October). Multi-jurisdictional task force. *Law Enforcement Technology.*

Schein, E. H. (1971). Organizational socialization and the profession of management. *Industrial Management Review, 2,* 37–45.

Schermerhorn, J. R., Jr. (1975). Determinants of interorganizational cooperation. *Academy of Management Journal, 18,* 846–856.

Sherif, M. (1966). *In common predicament: Social psychology of intergroup conflict and cooperation.* Boston: Houghton Mifflin.

## ☙ INTERNAL AFFAIRS

*Internal affairs* is a generic term used in policing and law enforcement to refer to the organizational unit or function devoted to investigating (and often preventing) corruption, criminal behavior, and various forms of misconduct related to the performance of the official duties of sworn and civilian members of the agency. The particular organizational structures, policies, and practices that characterize the internal affairs function vary widely as a reflection of the great diversity found across the landscape of American law enforcement. In some agencies, the internal affairs function focuses narrowly upon serious criminal behavior, whereas in others, it includes investigating a broader range of complaints that may include civilian complaints such as discourtesy, abuse of authority, and excessive force. In some law enforcement entities, it may also include the investigation of internal disciplinary matters and administrative violations. Although larger agencies tend to establish a separate internal affairs unit, a designated supervisor may take on these responsibilities on a part-time basis in medium-sized and smaller departments. Regardless of their size, their mandate, or the specific investigative methods and practices they employ, internal affairs units are an essential management tool and a primary means of ensuring public and organizational accountability by controlling, reducing, and preventing various forms of police misconduct. Because corrupt activities and corruption scandals can easily undermine public confidence in the law enforcement agency, a robust and effective internal affairs capacity facilitates and helps ensure police accountability to the public. Because accountability and discipline are central to the police organization's overall effectiveness and the morale of officers who do not engage in misconduct, most internal affairs units properly operate under the direct authority and supervision of the agency's top executive. Some internal investigative units may operate under the title of "professional standards" or "professional accountability" units.

Although the problems of corruption, misconduct, and criminality by police personnel have been part of American policing since its earliest days, the advent of specialized units charged with the responsibility to investigate and control these behaviors is relatively recent. Organizational strategies and practices to reduce or eliminate corruption were generally weak, ineffective, or absent during the early period of American policing that is often referred to as the Political Era. As a result, such behaviors flourished during that period and severely undermined the legitimacy of the police. Despite reforms that brought about an increased awareness of corruption and its deleterious impact on the police organization, the policies and practices implemented during the Professional Era were unable to achieve the goal of entirely eliminating misconduct and corrupt police activities. Indeed, police corruption has proven over time to be a highly resilient form of criminality. Emerging public and political concerns about real or perceived police misconduct and the control of police behavior during the late 1960s and early 1970s accelerated the creation of separate internal affairs units, and a substantial majority of larger state and local law enforcement agencies have now established such units within their organizational structure.

Although a viable internal affairs function is absolutely essential to the effective control of corruption and misconduct, to gaining and maintaining public trust in the police organization, and to the overall management of the agency, personnel assigned to internal affairs units are often resented and feared or, at best, viewed with ambivalence and some distrust by other officers. This resentment, hostility, and distrust illuminates some of the difficulties involved in staffing the internal investigative function, as well as the compelling need to conduct fair and objective investigations that identify corruption and misconduct effectively without resorting to overzealous disciplinary action for minor administrative transgressions. Police personnel may perceive an excessive focus on misconduct or a draconian approach to internal investigations as persecution or "headhunting" on the part of police executives, rather than as an important and necessary component of police integrity and public accountability. Because the confidential nature of most internal investigations may make them more complex and difficult than other types of investigation, internal investigations often require a great deal of secrecy, and therefore, the units conducting them are often housed in separate offices located away from other police facilities.

One of the controversies surrounding internal affairs investigations is the overall orientation of the investigative practices and strategies employed, and this orientation is generally characterized as taking either a reactive or a proactive approach. Reactive strategies resemble those used in many traditional criminal investigations and involve the retrospective investigation of complaints brought to the agency's attention by members of the public or by members of the department. Proactive investigations reflect a more preventive approach aimed at actively seeking out, identifying, and addressing corruption issues and problems (as well as corrupt officers) before they are formally reported, come to the attention of executives, or result in a full-blown scandal.

The specific proactive strategies that an internal affairs unit might employ include integrity testing, in which officers are purposely placed in potentially compromising situations involving the possibility of corrupt opportunities, with internal investigators carefully monitoring the officers' actions in response to the corruption hazard they encounter. Other proactive strategies include the use of field associates, or officers who have agreed to work as undercover operatives and secretly report corruption and misconduct to the internal affairs unit. Given the highly resilient nature of police corruption over the history of American policing and the tendency for new patterns and practices of corrupt behavior to emerge, these proactive strategies have proven highly effective in controlling, reducing, and preventing corrupt activity. The effectiveness of these and other proactive strategies, however, relies greatly upon the internal affairs unit's capacity to identify new and emerging patterns of corruption and to adapt their strategies and practices accordingly. Furthermore, agency executives must consider the potential adverse consequences of a too-zealous proactive approach on organizational morale.

Continued instances of police corruption and serious misconduct often raise public concerns about the effectiveness of established corruption control policies and practices, and in some cases, these concerns have resulted in the creation of external investigative entities charged with the responsibility to either replace an agency's internal affairs unit or carefully monitor and publicly report on its operations. In some jurisdictions, hybrid investigative bodies are responsible for investigating some forms of misconduct and monitoring the agency's internal investigations of others. This is a controversial public policy issue, and where external investigative entities exist, they can take on a wide variety of roles, mandates, and configurations. Police executives often resist the creation of external review entities, insisting that they interfere with an executive's authority and responsibility to manage the agency, control the disciplinary process, and set performance standards for agency personnel. Police at all levels of the organization may also fear that these external bodies will become politicized, or that the civilian investigators they often employ may lack the knowledge and insight to conduct fair and objective investigations of police officers. Proponents of external review argue that police cannot objectively and fairly investigate corruption and misconduct within their own agency, and that demands for public accountability require that this function be undertaken by an external body.

*Vincent E. Henry*

*See also* Civil Rights Violations by Police, Civilian Complaint Review Boards, Complaints Against Police, Corruption/Integrity, Knapp Commission, Mollen Commission, Police Brutality, Police Misconduct, Rampart Investigation

### For Further Reading

Amir, M., & Einstein, S. (Eds.). (2004). *The uncertainty series: Corruption, police, security and democracy: Volumes I and II.* Huntsville, TX: Office of International Criminal Justice.

Goldstein, H. (1970). *Police corruption: A perspective on its nature and control.* Washington, DC: Police Foundation.

Henry, V. E., & Campisi, C. (2004). Managing police integrity: Applying Compstat principles to control police corruption and misconduct. In R. Muraskin & A. R. Roberts (Eds.), *Visions for change: Crime and justice in the 21st century* (4th ed.). Upper Saddle River, NJ: Prentice Hall.

Los Angeles Police Department Board of Inquiry. (2001, March 1). *Public report of the Board of Inquiry into the Rampart Area corruption incident.* Los Angeles: Los Angeles Police Department.

National Institute of Justice. (1997, January). *Police integrity: Public service with honor* (National Institute of Justice Reports series NCJ#163811). Washington, DC: Author.

New York Knapp Commission. (1973). *The Knapp Commission report on police corruption.* New York: George Braziller.

## ⚬ INTERROGATION

### DEFINING INTERROGATION

Interrogation is a special type of interview. It involves interaction between the interviewer and a suspect for the purpose of obtaining admissions, confessions, or information that can be used later to obtain a conviction. Some experts limit the definition to seeking admissions and confessions, but this is overly narrow. The sophisticated interviewer may strive to entrap the suspect in a damaging lie that may lead to a conviction when that suspect will not admit to a crime. The interrogation, unlike most interviews, involves questioning a hostile or uncooperative interviewee. Just when a conversation becomes an interrogation is not always easy to determine. In a Maryland burglary, the officers took the suspect to the police station for questioning and showed him the tire iron used to pry open the door and told him that they were sending it out for fingerprinting. The defendant's statements made subsequent to this were deemed to have been the products of the equivalent of police interrogation. However, courts have held that it is not interrogation to inform the suspect that three out of four witnesses had identified him in a lineup.

## SETTING

Generally, interrogation takes place with the suspect in custody and in a place where the police or other law enforcement authorities are clearly in control, such as a police station, in the police car, or in a holding cell. This is because the interrogator's success may hinge upon establishing psychological dominance over the suspect. Because this is easier to do away from cues that are comfortable or familiar to the suspect, most interrogations do not take place in the home or office of the suspect.

## METHOD

Fostering the suspect's feelings of trust and dependency on the investigator are common techniques; however, investigators may approach the interrogation from a variety of stances. Most people are familiar with the "good cop–bad cop" method of interviewing, where two officers play the roles of a sympathetic and a hostile investigator. This is only one approach investigators might take. Among other approaches are (a) the direct approach, (b) the emotional approach, (c) the authoritarian approach, and (d) the deceptive approach. The direct approach is simply telling the suspect why the interrogator is there and asking directly for the details about what happened. The emotional approach tries to play upon the suspect's emotions (fear, guilt, sympathy, pride, jealousy, or fear). The authoritarian approach tries to use the power and authority of the interrogator to pressure the suspect into confessing.

Although the interrogator is interested in getting the suspect to tell the truth, many interrogators will use deception to achieve that end. Interrogators may claim to have latent fingerprints that they do not have or statements from co-defendants that they do not have, or they may use other lies in order to get the suspect to confess. One interrogator was able to extract a confession by telling a naive suspect that a copy machine in the corner of the interrogation room was really a voice-activated lie detector that showed the suspect to be lying. Because the courts use a "totality of the circumstances test" in evaluating whether the lies told to the suspect are coercive, the interrogator generally has fairly wide latitude in using deception.

## QUESTION TYPES IN INTERROGATION

Interrogators establish the tone of the interview through their questions. The interviewer may use various types of questions: open or closed, direct or indirect.

Open questions are impossible to answer with a "yes" or a "no." "What can you tell me about Saturday night?" is an open question. These questions draw longer narrative answers from the suspect and force him or her to reveal more information than do closed questions. A closed question either forces the suspect to choose an answer from choices provided in the question, or calls for a yes or no answer. "Did you see the victim from the doorway or from the window?" and "The light was red, wasn't it?" are examples of closed questions. Closed questions are more effective than open questions at channeling or controlling the interrogation, but they elicit less information.

Direct questions are more effective than indirect questions at eliciting specific responses, but they also create more tension and elicit more false responses than do indirect questions. The interrogator may use diversionary questions in order to reduce tension, establish rapport, or misdirect the suspect to make him or her more susceptible to direct questioning. Direct questions let the suspect know exactly what information the interrogator is seeking, whereas indirect questions try to misdirect or trick the suspect into revealing incriminating information. "Weren't you at the store before it was robbed?" is a direct question. "Who did you see at the store before the robbery?" is an indirect question and an attempt to get the suspect to admit that he or she was on the premises before the robbery.

## THE INTERROGATOR'S DILEMMA: EXTRACTING TRUTH OR ENCOURAGING FALSE CONFESSION?

The dilemma for the interrogator is that in order to encourage a reluctant suspect to confess, the interrogator must offer inducements to truth telling and pressure the suspect to tell the truth. However, the stronger the inducement or pressure, the greater the likelihood of a false confession. Over the past several years, U.S. courts have vacated convictions in more than 1% of all cases. False confession is a major contributing factor to the rate of erroneous conviction.

The situation in which the interrogation takes place is inherently coercive. It is generally alien to the suspect, and the police station and the police or prosecutors are intimidating. The isolation from peers, friends, or family adds to suggestibility. The longer the time the suspect is held in isolation or deprived of sleep, the greater the susceptibility will be. The greater the degree of confrontation by the interrogators, the greater the possibility of false confession. Even without this pressure, emotional and psychological factors can lead to false confession. For example, more than 200 people falsely confessed to having kidnapped Charles Lindbergh's baby. More recently, in the case of the Central Park Jogger in New York City, several teenagers were convicted of rape and assault based upon their own statements (which had been videotaped and looked credible). However, DNA evidence showed that the rape had been committed by someone else, and the convictions were overturned.

Pressure from interrogators can create false memories as well. The suspect may remember things that never happened at all, after he or she has been interrogated. These implanted memories may seem as real to the suspect as the memories of actual events.

## INTERROGATION THROUGH TORTURE AND FORCE

Clearly, torture is just the kind of undue pressure that might lead to false confession. However, historically, torture played an important role in interrogation. In ancient Greece and Rome, slaves were routinely tortured to persuade them to tell the truth. In Rome, free men could be tortured during interrogation only in cases of treason, at first, but this rule eventually broadened. In the Middle Ages, interrogators commonly tortured suspects in order to obtain convictions in both religious and secular courts. Interrogators during the Spanish Inquisition favored torture. The French Ordinance of 1670 specifically allowed compulsory self-incrimination. In England under Charles I, the Court of the Star Chamber, which pursued political dissidents, and the Court of High Commission, which pursued religious dissenters, could put suspects under oath before any formal charges had been made and then could beat and imprison suspects who refused to take the oath and answer questions. During the Salem witch trials in Salem, Massachusetts, suspects who stood moot (refused to answer questions) were placed on their backs under a plank that covered their bodies. The plank was then loaded with stones until the suspect either talked or suffocated under the weight. The various types of torture used in the Western world to induce confession were limited only by the dark side of human imagination. These methods ranged from sleep, water, and food deprivation; to simple beatings; to lengthy imprisonment; to the rack, the screw, and the wheel. Under Joseph Stalin in the former Soviet Union, suspects were beaten with clubs. Recently, in the war in Afghanistan between the Taliban and the United States, suspected terrorists who were unfamiliar with Western popular music were made to listen to loud heavy metal music in order to induce them to confess.

## REACTIONS AGAINST COERCED CONFESSION

By the 1600s, torture fell into disfavor because it brought into question the validity of all confessions. Torture was perceived as turning the quest for a confession into an endurance contest rather than a search for truth. England abandoned torture in interrogation in the mid-1600s, and Scottish law abolished it at the beginning of the 1700s. The Fifth Amendment to the U.S. Constitution, which prohibits coerced confession, was a reflection of the thinking of the day.

Both the U.S. Constitution's Fifth Amendment and constitutions or laws in every state prohibit coerced confessions. Courts will not allow coerced confessions to be used in a defendant's trial. In *Miranda v. Arizona* (1964), the U.S. Supreme Court addressed the issue of coerced confessions. The Court was concerned not only with overt torture but also with more subtle coercion that might encourage false confession or violate the suspect's Fifth Amendment rights. The Court expressed concern about the possibility of subtle coercion as well as confessions obtained through brutalizing suspects. Under the Miranda rules, suspects who have been arrested must be read the "Miranda warnings" before an interrogation by any governmental law enforcement official. These warnings inform suspects that they have the right to remain silent; that anything they say may be used against them in a court of law; that they have the right to an attorney; and that if they cannot afford an attorney, one will be provided for them.

## CONCLUSION

Interrogation is an important tool for law enforcement officials. Often, the best witness to events may be the perpetrator, and the best evidence against him or her may be his or her own statements. Interrogators may employ a wide variety of techniques to elicit confessions. The dilemma that the interrogator faces is this: the more powerful the technique employed, the greater the likelihood of getting a confession, but the greater the risk that the confession will be false or contain inaccurate information. Both the U.S. Constitution and state constitutions prohibit the use in court of evidence obtained through coercive interrogation techniques.

*Martin Wallenstein*

*See also* Confessions

### For Further Reading

Chambers v. Florida, 309 U.S. 227 (1940).

Drury v. State, 793 A.2d 567 (Md. Ct. App., 2002).

*Due Process in Criminal Investigation.* (1965) FBI Training Document Number 65.

Fellman, D. (1958). *The defendant's rights.* New York: Rinehart.

Gardner, T. J., & Anderson, T. M. (2004). *Criminal evidence* (5th ed.). Belmont, CA: Wadsworth/Thompson.

Graham, F. P. (1970). *The self-inflicted wound.* New York: Macmillan.

Milne, R., & Bull, R. (1999). *Investigative interviewing: Psychology and practice.* Chichester, UK: Wiley.

Miranda v. Arizona, 384 U.S. 436 (1964).

People v. Allen, 247 F.3d 741 (8th Cir. 2001).

Smith, C. E. (2004). *Constitutional rights: Myths and realities.* Belmont, CA: Wadsworth/Thompson.

Van Meter, C. H. (1973). *Principles of police interrogation.* Springfield, IL: Charles C Thomas.

Walters, S. B. (2003). *Principles of kinesic interview and interrogation* (2nd ed.). Boca Raton, FL: CRC.

Ward, R. H. (1975). *Introduction to criminal investigation.* Reading, MA: Addison Wesley.

Yeschike, C. L. (1993). *Interviewing: A forensic guide to interrogation* (2nd ed.). Springfield, IL: Charles C Thomas.

Zulawski, D. E., & Wicklander, D. E. (1992). *Practical aspects of interview and interrogation.* New York: Elsevier.

## ∞ INVESTIGATIVE TECHNIQUES

Criminal investigation has changed dramatically over the past several decades. with the most important changes relating to advances in science and technology. The development of DNA analysis, firearms identification, single-digit (fingerprint) classification systems, and the application of computer technology to the investigative function bring a new dimension to basic criminal investigation. These have become important tools as a litany of court decisions and other policies have placed greater restrictions on an investigator's use of more traditional methods, such as interviewing, interrogation, and witness identification.

Greater emphasis on human rights and past abuses in conducting investigations has resulted in U.S. Supreme Court decisions that narrow the arbitrary discretion of the investigator. The days of routinely beating suspects and subjecting them to third-degree interrogation methods or lengthy interviews, as well as illegal wiretaps, searches, and detention of suspects for long periods of time without probable cause, are largely practices of the past.

Today's investigator must be familiar with a broad range of social science applications as well as the scientific and technological applications that serve to support his or her mission. Aspects of psychology, sociology, accounting, and statistical probability must be combined with a greater knowledge of the law and criminal procedures to yield effective investigations. Investigators must also be aware of the Supreme Court decisions and legislative changes that affect the investigative function.

To a large degree, the investigation of criminal activity has certainly become more specialized as a result of advances in society, not to mention the emergence of more sophisticated criminals. Traditional types of criminal activity, such as robbery, burglary, rape, and theft, generally involve one to three perpetrators and are usually handled by one investigator. In small- and medium-sized departments, investigators may be charged with handling all types of reported crime. The exception to this rule is more likely to occur with homicides, especially those without an apparent relationship between victim and suspect, and special investigative squads may be formed with investigators from several agencies. In larger departments, the investigative function is frequently separated into violent and property crimes units, whereas the largest departments are able to staff units with greater degrees of specialization, such as robbery-homicide squads, fraud or pickpocket units, vice and drug details, white-collar crime investigators, and bomb and arson units.

Another significant change that has occurred in criminal investigation has been the quality of the investigator and the training available on a broad range of different types of crimes, such as fraud, cybercrime, gang crimes, terrorism, global crime, counterfeiting and forged documents, serial murder, and rape. In medium-sized and larger police departments, most investigators have completed an undergraduate degree, and a large number have completed master's degrees or higher. Although it does not take the place of experience, education has proven to be a way to reduce the time it takes to make an effective and efficient investigator.

The employment of women in all aspects of criminal investigation has also increased significantly from the years prior to 1970, when most women were assigned to juvenile and sex crime investigations. Today, women are involved in all aspects and types of criminal investigation.

## SCIENTIFIC ADVANCES

The utilization of the crime lab has increased over the years, but much still needs to be done in this area. The advent of a single-digit classification system and the rapid advances in the chemical and biological aspects of the crime laboratory improve instrumentation, whereas other advances have made the crime lab a vital part of conducting an investigation. Nonetheless, statistics indicate that the vast majority of cases handled by crime labs relate to drug analysis, which involves ascertaining whether or not a substance is a drug under the criminal law. The lab is used more often in major cases where there is heightened publicity rather than for cases involving more traditional types of offenses. What follows is a brief description of some of the capabilities that can be provided by a good crime laboratory and the instrumentation and other types of equipment used at these labs.

- Fingerprint analyses and Automated Fingerprint Identification Systems (AFIS): enable the use of single-digit fingerprints to be used in searching large databases.
- DNA analysis and CODIS DNA database: perform DNA analysis of biological evidence, such as blood, saliva, seminal stain, perspiration, tissue, and hair to identify suspects (linking them to the crime scene) with a high probability of accuracy. Many states now collect blood samples from convicted felons and enter the DNA characteristics in a database.
- Identification graphics: used to create computerized images of suspects. May also be used to "age" victims or suspects, or to prepare images with different facial configurations, such as mustaches or beards, long or short hair.
- Firearms identification and firearms database: enable scientists to link bullets and shell casings to specific weapons, and to link the use of weapons in different crimes.
- Forensic medicine (autopsies): provide a broad range of information, such as estimated time and

cause of death, types of wounds and instruments used, and physical identification.

- Records management systems: make it possible to analyze various databases, such as criminal records files, correctional institution records, driver's licenses, and court records to narrow the list of suspects. For example, the National Crime Information Center managed by the Federal Bureau of Investigation (FBI) provides a broad range of information on offenders, stolen property, and other demographic information.
- Forensic toxicology and controlled substances analysis: enable the examination of body fluids and organs to determine the presence or absence of drugs and poisons. The controlled substances are identified and analyzed.
- Questioned documents examination: includes comparisons and interpretation of handwriting, mechanically produced material, and photocopied material, as well as the analysis of papers, inks, and other materials used.
- Voiceprint and polygraph analysis: perform an analysis of the voice of a suspect. The sound spectrograph that transforms speech into a visual graphic display could be used. In addition, the polygraph or lie detector is useful for criminal investigation.
- Technological instrumentation: available in a wide range to crime labs and includes the following:
  - Electron microscopes: used to examine minute pieces of evidence
  - Comparison microscope: used to compare questioned and known test firearms evidence
  - Spectroscopy: used for chemical analysis, such as controlled substance, poison, and accelerant identification
  - Genetic analyzer: used for forensic DNA analysis
  - Electrostatic detection apparatus: used for detecting indented writing
  - Sound spectrograph: used to transform speech into a visual graphic display
  - Photography: advanced the use of photographic images through higher resolution and digital technology
  - Alternate light source: used to examine evidence such as latent prints and biological fluid stain
  - Electrostatic dust print lifter: used to lift imprint evidence, such as a shoe print

## SPECIALIZED INVESTIGATIONS

The development of specialized units is increasing throughout the country. Some of these include organized crime units, cyber or computer crime units, terrorism task forces, and cultural objects and art theft units. Combined cooperative units involving several departments are also more common for investigations related to dangerous drugs.

Terrorism task forces, developed by the FBI in the 1970s, have proven to be quite effective from an investigative standpoint, and in some measure represent a different type of investigation, because much of the work of these units involves trying to prevent a terrorist act through investigative methods.

Specialized investigative units have become more common because of the need for greater cooperation and because the geographic mobility of the modern criminal has expanded considerably. The development of task forces and other cooperative arrangements between federal, state, and local officials has proven to be especially effective with respect to narcotics investigations, terrorism investigations, organized crime cases, and in the more recent investigation of large-scale fraud cases against major corporations.

Within the larger police departments, there are also likely to be computer crime specialists, sex crime specialists, cybercrime investigators, crime scene technicians, criminalists, fingerprint technicians, auto crime investigators, undercover investigators, and internal affairs investigators.

## CRIME ANALYSIS

One of the rapidly developing areas of criminal investigation is crime analysis, which brings together several technological advances to assist in the investigation of crime. These advances include geographic information systems, crime mapping, and what are known as relational databases. In essence, the crime analyst is a new kind of detective who sits before a bank of computers, drawing out and bringing together information from a variety of sources, known as databanks, as a means of identifying a perpetrator, or developing patterns that will assist both patrol officers and investigators. The primary theory behind this concept holds that an individual's actions are frequently the same (we are all creatures of habit). This enables the analyst/investigator to combine the individual elements of a crime and the modus operandi (method of operation) to identify or narrow the search for a suspect.

By constructing various models, which may include geographic layouts, the type of victim, the perpetrator's description, the manner in which the crime was carried out, forensic evidence, and other distinctive information, the analyst narrows the search using the computer. Bringing together these disparate pieces of information can be a complex task, made much simpler using advanced technology. Consider the following example of a robbery suspect with the following description:

- Suspect robs only certain types of businesses, such as convenience stores or bars
- Suspect uses stolen cars, which are later located in a particular section of town
- Suspect uses a specific type of weapon, such as a silver-plated automatic
- Suspect uses specific terminology when carrying out the holdup, such as "Put your hands on the counter or I'll kill you."

A relational database, with arrest and incident information for previous investigations, arrests, and reports, could analyze this description to point to a suspect who has been arrested in the past for similar crimes. This model or approach is being increasingly adopted by federal agencies as well as the larger police departments. As databases increase in size and querying technology improves, this will likely have a great impact on the solution of crime.

*Richard H. Ward*

**See also** Detectives, Forensic Science, Informants

## For Further Reading

Baden, M., & Roach, M. (2001). *Dead reckoning: The new science of catching killers.* New York: Simon & Schuster.

Casey, E. (Ed.). (2002). *Handbook of computer crime investigation: Forensic tools and technology.* San Diego, CA: Academic Press.

Dyson, W. E. (2001). *Terrorism: An investigator's handbook.* Cincinnati, OH: Anderson.

Lee, H., & Labriola, J. (2001). *Famous crimes revisited: From Sacco-Vanzetti to O.J. Simpson.* Southington, CT: Strong Books.

Lee, H., Palmbach, T., & Miller, M. (2001). *Henry Lee's crime scene handbook.* San Diego, CA: Academic Press.

Osterburg, J. W., & Ward, R. H. (1999). *Criminal investigation: A method for reconstructing the past* (3rd ed.). Cincinnati, OH: Anderson.

Owen, D. (2000). *Hidden evidence: Forty true crimes and how forensic science helped solve them.* Buffalo, NY: Firefly.

# J

## ✑ JUVENILE CRIMES/PROGRAMS/UNITS

Juvenile crime has occurred for centuries, as has the debate regarding the age of criminal responsibility. Before the 20th century, punishment consisted of severe discipline, and children were seen more as property than as people. In the United States, juveniles have been treated differently from adults in the criminal justice system for only a little over 100 years, but even today, states differ about the age of responsibility for various juvenile crimes. By the early 20th century, all of the states had established separate juvenile courts under the *parens patriae* doctrine. Parens patriae establishes the role of law enforcement and the criminal justice system as a protective entity commissioned to rehabilitate delinquent youth. Juveniles act differently from adults because of a variety of developmental reasons, such as immaturity and inexperience. As a result, juveniles are sometimes held to different legal expectations and punishments. Because of these differences, law enforcement officials face special challenges when responding to juvenile crime.

Over the past 10 years, about 10%–17% of all felony arrestees were juvenile offenders. Although a majority of adolescents will violate the law at one time or another, most do not become serious offenders who move on to criminal careers. Because local law enforcement is typically the first contact a youthful lawbreaker has with the criminal justice system, police are left with the task of discretionary judgment about how to best respond to each individual crime. Traditionally, diversion of juveniles from formal processing in the system has been accepted practice by law enforcement in most localities for minor offenses. Police warnings and release to parents or specific programs such as victim offender mediation, first-offender programs, or counseling has allowed these minor lawbreakers to avoid the stigma associated with criminal processing and the risk of heightened acceptance of criminal roles. More recently, such discretion is becoming less likely as a growing need for retributive justice becomes increasingly popular regardless of age.

Ultimately, local authorities, under their specific state laws, develop regular procedures and practices about handling juvenile offenders. Some jurisdictions have implemented separate juvenile units in their department that focus exclusively on the problem of juvenile crime, which allows the needs of the juvenile offender to be considered more closely and procedural guidelines to be more specialized. Although separate juvenile units may exist in a vast number of local jurisdictions, each jurisdiction may operate very differently.

Historically, juveniles have been treated more informally in the criminal justice system from the first contact at arrest through court proceedings. The Juvenile Justice and Delinquency Prevention Act of 1974 not only mandated deinstitutionalization, but also granted due process to juveniles under the Fourteenth Amendment. Some procedural rights that are granted to juveniles are right of notice of charges, right to counsel, rights of confrontation and cross-examination, and the right to remain silent. Police must also attempt to contact the parent in a timely manner, and one of the best ways to ensure the rights of juveniles is to have a parent present during any questioning. Although constitutionally, juveniles are not granted full protection of rights under the law, many jurisdictions act as though they are. Laws differ from state to state, and most local authorities base their procedures with juveniles on their state laws. As juveniles are granted more equality of rights compared to adults, the treatment of juveniles in the criminal justice system will become less discretionary and more like that of adults. We have seen this trend already in the 1990s with the significant increase in juvenile transfers to adult court, and new state laws allowing this to happen quickly and easily.

Despite predictions about the flood of juvenile "superpredators" slotted to inundate most large cities by the turn of the millennium, violent juvenile crime is on the decrease, particularly with regard to homicide—by 1997, it had reached its lowest level in 25 years. In 1998, only one tenth of 1% of all felony arrests were homicides committed by juveniles, and only 4% of felony arrests were for violent crimes by juveniles. About 73% of juvenile crimes are nonindex crimes. Many state and local law enforcement jurisdictions have placed a significant emphasis on serious habitual offenders in an effort to increase public safety by incapacitating or intensively monitoring the small percentage of juveniles who commit the most serious and numerous incidents of juvenile crime.

Although recognition must be given to the incidents of particularly violent juvenile offenses detailed in news reports, public perception must be put in perspective by law enforcement officers who realistically handle the needs of delinquents in their particular community. Assessment of community needs is vital in risk management of juvenile offenders. In this current era of rapidly advancing technologies and research-based tactics, police departments have been able to use more efficient means of risk management, detection, and investigation. Some states and local jurisdictions have stepped up intelligence efforts, particularly regarding the dissemination of information on gang activity. Some cities have used most of their youth service resources on attempts to regulate street-gang activity, which continues to generate a higher level of violence than that of non-gang members.

Uniform Crime Report (UCR) data have been obtained by law enforcement since the 1930s for reported index crimes and arrests. The age of the offender in these reports gives additional information regarding assessment of commonly reported juvenile crimes in that state and locality. Despite differences in definition, recording, and reporting between law enforcement agencies that can result in inaccurate figures, the UCR can be used as a guide for law enforcement, particularly when other data sources are also taken into consideration. The Monitoring the Future (MTF) survey is another data source that can provide intelligence to law enforcement about where to focus time and resources. Finally, the Office of Juvenile Justice and Delinquency Prevention is a major source of information about national trends in juvenile crime and law enforcement efforts with young offenders.

Rehabilitation has always been met with fierce criticism, some arguing that juvenile offenders are handled too leniently. By the last two decades of the 20th century, a growing visibility of youth gangs; juvenile gun violence; and sensationalized portrayals of predatory youth, such as school shooters, resulted in a departure from early rehabilitative ideals toward a philosophy of just deserts for juvenile offenders. In the 1990s, virtually all of the states adopted laws making it easier for juveniles to be transferred to adult courts, and the informal handling of juveniles on the street and in the courtroom became increasingly less common in law enforcement.

The practice of community policing, or problem-solving policing, has enlisted the cooperation of schools, parents, and community organizations to help curb juvenile crime, mainly focusing on quality-of-life offenses. Also, zero tolerance of minor lawbreaking or disorder can have a profound effect in some localities, with mixed results in other jurisdictions that may have different needs. The Juvenile Justice and Reform Act of 1999 requires that law enforcement work closely with schools, sports organizations, parks, and other community resources to prevent juvenile crime. Law enforcement takes into account appropriate preventive timing by acknowledging that most juvenile crime occurs after school hours and into the early evening. Enforcement of curfew laws are but one example of tactics used by law enforcement to contain the commission of juvenile crime in some communities.

Departments of probation continue to implement juvenile programs in an effort to decrease recidivism and increase public safety, while police departments work with the community to establish effective prevention programs to which they can make appropriate referrals. Even in the earliest periods of U.S. history, the causes of juvenile crime clustered in three areas: poverty, inadequate education, and poor parental discipline. The idea of prevention can be somewhat ambiguous, but generally incorporates community interventions in parenting, socialization, education, and/or increased prosocial opportunities. Also, the goal of prevention can be to decrease the likelihood that a juvenile will break the law, break the law again, or seriously break the law. Instilling a prosocial identity in children and adolescents can take the form of increased awareness of punitive consequences of criminal activity, increased opportunity for legitimate and satisfying activity, adding services to a community, and/or target hardening (e.g., the addition of locks and/or alarms) that makes it difficult to commit a crime.

Different programs focus on different goals and should be based on the needs of the community. Because the role of law enforcement officials is not that of a social worker or therapist, the combined effort of mental health agencies, social service agencies, and other community organizations is required for effective prevention. Preventive interventions typically take the form of counseling, instruction, opportunity enhancement, advocacy, recreation, or police relations. Not all prevention programs are effective, and some can even increase delinquency, so including evaluation components with any programming efforts will ultimately benefit law enforcement. State and local law enforcement officials continue to have a strong investment in the public safety and order of the communities they are serving. Juvenile crime likely will continue to be a matter of debate and challenge for law enforcement, but this continued discussion ensures that problems with juvenile crime on the state and local level will be addressed in the interest of a positive future for our communities.

*Holly Hurban*

***See also*** Curfews, Loitering, Truancy

### For Further Reading

McCord, J., Widom, C. S., & Crowell, N. A. (Eds.). (2001). *Juvenile crime, juvenile justice: Panel on juvenile crime: Prevention, treatment, and control.* Washington, DC: National Academy Press.

Simonsen, C. E. (1991). *Juvenile justice in America.* New York: Macmillan.

Snyder, H. N. (2001, December). *Law enforcement and juvenile crime* (Office of Juvenile Justice and Delinquency Prevention, Juvenile Offenders and Victims National Report Series). Washington, DC: U.S. Department of Justice, Office of Juvenile Programs.

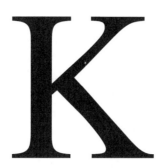

# KNAPP COMMISSION, THE

The Commission to Investigate Alleged Police Corruption in New York City, chaired by Whitman Knapp and known as the Knapp Commission, was created by Mayor John V. Lindsay on May 21, 1971, by Executive Order #11, in response to allegations of widespread corruption in the New York Police Department (NYPD).

The Commission was charged with four tasks: (a) investigating the extent of the alleged corruption and its impact; (b) examining and evaluating the adequacy of existing procedures for investigating, preventing, and responding to corruption; (c) recommending both procedural improvements and additional preventive measures; and (d) gathering evidence and holding public and private hearings necessary to ascertain the facts.

Final Commission membership, both bipartisan and ethnically and racially diverse, consisted of Knapp, a Wall Street lawyer who had served on a number of government commissions, and four highly respected men with extensive public and private sector experience: Cyrus Vance, Franklin A. Thomas, and Joseph Monserrat, with John E. Sprizzo replacing a commissioner who resigned. Four had been prosecutors in either the New York District Attorney's office or the U.S. Attorney's office. Vance had been Deputy Secretary of Defense under President Johnson, Monserrat had been the first Puerto Rican president of the New York City Board of Education, Thomas had been one of the first African American deputy police commissioners in the NYPD, and Sprizzo was a law professor at Fordham University. They were supported by a staff of about 25 investigators and lawyers, a number of them on loan from federal agencies, such as the IRS. The chief counsel, Michael Armstrong, had been a prosecutor in the U.S. Attorney's Office for the Southern District for 5 years.

Behind the scenes, one of the driving forces that led to the creation of the Knapp Commission was the persistence of three people—two NYPD officers, Detective Sergeant David Durk and plainclothes officer Frank Serpico, and investigative journalist David Burnham, whose detailed reports were published in the *New York Times* beginning with a page-1 story on April 25, 1970. Durk and Serpico, after consistently failing over several years to have their allegations of police corruption taken seriously within the department and by city officials, had met first with Burnham on a number of occasions, and then with editors from the *Times*; presented evidence; and persuaded them that this was a story worth investigating.

## THE CHARGES

The corruption charges were dramatic and incendiary. They included claims of widespread payoffs, running into millions of dollars annually, made to officers at virtually all ranks in the department; criminal behavior by police; and further charges that all efforts to have these claims investigated had been ignored or stonewalled for years not only by the department itself, but by the mayor's chief assistant for criminal justice and the city's Department of Investigation. At the same time, the police officers' union attacked the Commission, claiming that the charges were "vicious, unsubstantiated smears of the entire department" and a "Roman circus"; later, the union staged a brief, citywide "sick out" that lasted 6 days.

The Knapp Commission got off to a bumpy start. When Mayor Lindsay first learned privately that the *Times* was planning to publish an exposé of police corruption, he set up an initial commission, headed by the city's corporation counsel, J. Lee Rankin, that also included the Manhattan and Bronx district attorneys, the commissioner of the Department of Investigation, and then-Police Commissioner Howard R. Leary. This commission lasted barely 3 weeks. Its independence and ability to mount a serious investigation were widely challenged, and it was overwhelmed by hundreds of citizen reports of corruption. The members resigned and recommended that the mayor create an independent citizens' commission with a full-time staff; this became the Knapp Commission.

The Knapp Commission began with a number of handicaps. The New York City Council had appropriated a scant $325,000 and set a 6-month deadline for completing the investigation. It lacked subpoena power and could not grant witnesses immunity. However, additional funding was obtained from the federal government, through the Law Enforcement Assistance Administration, and from foundations. At the mayor's request, the city council granted the Commission power to both subpoena witnesses and have them testify under oath or affirmation. The deadline, although still tight, was extended to 1 year. Even with these changes, the work did not proceed smoothly because a number of lawsuits were filed that, for part of the investigation, prevented the Commission from issuing subpoenas.

Police Commissioner Leary resigned and was replaced by Patrick V. Murphy, who had a nononsense reputation for toughness. He supported continuation of the Commission, expressed willingness to work with it, and made eliminating corruption one of his highest priorities. Despite all this and the expertise of the staff assembled, Knapp feared that the Commission would be forced to end its investigation with all charges unsubstantiated. He found that when witnesses were called, "they all lied to us and we couldn't prove anything" (Whitman Knapp, personal communication, July 19, 1999).

## THE INVESTIGATION

The major breakthrough came almost by accident. Two Knapp Commission investigators, conducting surveillance on a police officer, William R. Phillips, caught him in a compromising situation; to the Commission's surprise, he agreed to wear a wire and gather evidence against other corrupt police officers in precincts throughout the city. The events leading to this agreement began with the arrest of a Dutch woman, known as Xaviera Hollander ("the Happy Hooker"), who had run a high-class house of prostitution on Manhattan's Upper East Side, paying police $500 per month to operate unimpeded. After her arrest, by officers unaware of this arrangement, Phillips was one of the officers attempting to negotiate new terms of protection. Phillips's undercover tapes formed the basis for subsequent hearings, with the Commission using only those recorded incidents that could be verified independently.

The Commission examined both illegal activities, from narcotics to loan sharking, and businesses considered susceptible to corruption, such as restaurants and tow trucks. They interviewed complainants, businesspeople, individuals engaged in various illegal activities, and current and former police officers. They used paid informants; conducted electronic surveillance; and, in some cases, went undercover themselves. Targeted groups were surveyed, and corporate records were subpoenaed. They sought to identify patterns of corruption and worked closely with law enforcement agencies that had authority to build criminal cases.

The Commission held 14 days of public hearings between October and December 1971, served more than 620 subpoenas, and heard from 271 witnesses at the public hearings.

## THE FINDINGS

The Commission began by making two sharp points. First, and most important, was that the majority of police officers were not corrupt and hated the corruption that they saw. Second, however, the problem was not one of a few "rotten apples" (or "rogue cops"), as many inside the department, including the police commissioner, tried to claim, but a systemic problem that required rethinking department expectations, culture, and policies.

The Commission found that corruption took a number of forms and was frequently linked to brutality. Two types of payoffs to police were the most common: "the pad" and "the nut." Officers on "the pad" collected regular bi-weekly or monthly payments, that could be as much as $3,500, from gambling establishments in their precincts; divided these payments into equal shares ("the nut"); and distributed the shares through the ranks, with supervisors receiving a share and a half. New members had to demonstrate "reliability" before being included in the system. Monthly shares ranged from $300 to $1,500 depending on location.

Narcotics "scores" were the second broad type of corruption, less organized than gambling pads but dealing with much larger sums of money. Typical shakedowns produced thousands of dollars; the largest amount uncovered by the Commission was $80,000, but this was not considered unique. Payoffs came from protecting drug dealers; selling confidential police files to narcotics suspects; stealing and selling drugs; and, in a few cases, identifying informants, kidnapping witnesses to prevent them from testifying at trial, and participating in their murders.

A third problem, best defined as organizational culture, contributed substantially to the pervasiveness and continuation of corruption. The Commission, drawing on a typology propounded by a former chief of inspectional services (Sydney Cooper), identified three types of officers. "Meat eaters" were "aggressive practitioners of corruption." Larger in number were "grass eaters," those "morally weak" officers who joined corrupt activities mainly as a result of peer pressure. They were an "insidious" problem because they made corruption respectable, labeling as a "traitor" anyone who sought to expose it. Most problematic were the "birds," the large majority of officers who, although not participating in corruption and brutality, failed to report it or take preventive actions.

In addition, Commission hearings identified a variety of other illegal acts, such as planting false evidence ("flaking"); making "accommodation arrests," where someone would agree to be arrested to help an officer meet departmental arrest goals, only to have the arrest thrown out because of deliberately poor paperwork; or police stealing goods and cash when they responded to a store burglary.

## THE COMMISSION'S CONCLUSIONS AND RECOMMENDATIONS

The central conclusion, publicly stated, was that "police corruption cannot be solved merely by focusing on individual acts of wrong doing." Instead, it arose from "an endemic condition" that had to be attacked "on all fronts" (Knapp, 1972, p. 277). Society had "to provide police with every possible support in resisting pressures toward corruption" (Knapp, 1972, p. 278). The most fundamental obstacle to change was "a stubborn refusal at all levels of the Department to acknowledge that a serious problem exists" (Knapp, 1972, p. 6).

### Recommendations

The Commission's recommendations were broad, detailed, and sweeping, addressing both departmental and external changes. One of the strongest proposals was for "command accountability"—the need to hold commanders and supervisors responsible for their subordinates' actions. Among other central recommendations were to reduce opportunities that exposed police to corruption, and provide incentives for "meritorious performance." Changes had to be made starting with upgrading recruit screening and selection methods and standards, and ensuring that recruits were not sworn in as officers until thorough background investigations had been completed.

Personnel files needed to be centralized and updated regularly. Monitoring officer activity had to be improved; officers needed more resources to do their jobs, such as timely reimbursement for expenses; and the department, not individual officers, should pay informants. Monthly reports, summarizing corruption cases and their disposition, should be given to the media. In addition, the police commissioner needed a wider range of administrative disciplinary options, instead of the choice of a 30-day loss of pay or vacation, or dismissal from the force.

Internal investigations needed to be more thorough, completed more quickly, and have substantially increased penalties for corruption. One small, but important, recommendation, swiftly implemented, was a requirement that each officer wear a visible badge identifying him or her by name.

Recommendations for external changes included changing statutes and creating additional external oversight units. Among the proposals were to decriminalize or legalize certain activities, such as gambling and prostitution; repeal hard-to-enforce statutes, such as Sabbath laws; and remove police from enforcement responsibilities for miscellaneous regulations, such as liquor licenses, that could be handled more appropriately by civilian authority. The commissioners recognized that this might not eliminate corruption, but they argued that payoffs to civilians would have "far less impact upon the body politic than corruption among police" (Knapp, 1972, p. 20). Furthermore, those who gave bribes should also be penalized. To address narcotics-related corruption, they urged rethinking criminal sanctions for narcotics use and considering other ways for dealing with addicts.

They also proposed that a special deputy attorney general be appointed by the governor and attorney general for a 5-year term, with authority to investigate and prosecute all crimes involving corruption in the criminal process in all five boroughs. This unit would be completely staffed by "persons wholly unconnected with the Police Department or

any other agency that routinely deals with it" (Knapp, 1972. p. 14). The office would be dissolved some years later.

## RESULTS

One of the clearest changes was elimination of the pad and the nut as part of the organizational culture, and, in general, more than 30 years later, these have not returned. The state legislature repealed the Sabbath laws, but under Governor Rockefeller, criminal sanctions for all narcotics activities were vastly expanded.

The problem of drug corruption remained far more intractable, exploding in a series of newspaper headlines 20 years later, in May 1992, when a number of current and former NYPD officers were arrested as a result of a 5-month undercover investigation by Suffolk County, NY, police that netted 50 suspects. This, in turn, led New York City Mayor David Dinkins to create, by executive order, the Commission to Investigate Allegations of Police Corruption and the Anti-Corruption Procedures of the Police Department (the Mollen Commission) on July 24, 1992.

The Mollen Commission found some of the problems unchanged, defining them once again as systemic. Command accountability remained a problem, as did fundamental inadequacies of the Internal Affairs unit, which regularly ignored or hid reports of corruption, and failed to consistently investigate charges and penalize those found guilty. Numbers of recruits were still being sworn in as officers before their background investigations had been completed, and time allocated to ethics training at the police academy had been reduced from post-Knapp Commission changes. Numbers of police were again involved in using, buying, and selling drugs, and, in a few cases, contributing to the murders of informants or dealers. Officers who sought to report wrongdoing were still considered traitors, a set of values that began at the highest ranks of the department. Like the Knapp investigation, the Mollen Commission was formed as the result of an officer, Sergeant Joseph Trimboli, who went public in order to expose drug corruption within the NYPD.

In the decade after the Mollen Commission report, some improvements could be seen. There was both a steady drop in crime and a decrease in the number of police shootings of civilians.

*Lotte E. Feinberg*

***See also*** Corruption/Integrity, Ethics, Mollen Commission, Whistle-Blowing

## For Further Reading

Dodenhoff, P. (1993). LEN salutes its 1993 Man of the Year, Sgt. Joseph Trimboli of the New York Police Department. *Law Enforcement News, 19*(392), pp. 1, 14–15.

Knapp, W. (1972). *Report of the Commission to investigate alleged police corruption.* New York: George Braziller.

Maas, P. (1973). *Serpico.* New York: Viking Press.

Newburn, T. (1999). *Understanding and preventing police corruption: Lessons from the literature.* London: Her Majesty's Press.

# L

## ❧ LAW ENFORCEMENT ASSISTANCE ADMINISTRATION

Prior to the 1960s, the federal government had no significant involvement in local crime problems. There was technical support from the FBI crime laboratory and central criminal/fingerprint files, along with some technical training of local police and some technical assistance from the Bureau of Alcohol, Tobacco, and Firearms regarding guns and explosives.

President Johnson was elected, and in a special message to Congress on "Law Enforcement and the Administration of Justice" in May 1965, he declared his "war on crime," noting that local crime was now a national concern. He proposed legislation, the Law Enforcement Assistance Act of 1965, which created a small program of federal grants to local governments, funded at $7 million per year and with a small staff of approximately 25.

Subsequently, in 1968, the federal government launched a large funding program of grants to state and local governments out of concern for increasing crime rates. The program titled the Law Enforcement Assistance Administration (LEAA) was ended on April 15, 1982, after national major crime rates had increased from 6,720 in 1968 to 13,408.3 per 100,000 population in 1980, or approximately 200%, while spending $7.7 billion (approximately $1 billion in peak years) in grants to state and local governments (FY 1969–1980). The program had been winding down since 1978, when initial decisions were made to end it. Most of the funds went to police/law enforcement activities.

Internal and external strife continually plagued LEAA until its demise. There was a political struggle of the states versus cities for control of the money. Notwithstanding its failure, LEAA was succeeded by a similar, but much larger ($5.47 billion in FY 2002) program that continues to this day, the Office of Justice Programs.

## BACKGROUND

Notwithstanding the small staff and funding, many present-day programs owe their beginnings to LEAA. These programs benefit all states: police standards and training commissions, data collection and analysis, B.A. degree college programs, police executive training institutes, as well as planning and research units in many police departments.

In July 1965, President Johnson appointed a Presidential Commission on Law Enforcement and the Administration of Justice, which met for 18 months and made many recommendations, some of which were incorporated into his proposed legislation, the Safe Streets and Crime Control Act of 1967, which evolved into the Law Enforcement

Assistance Administration when finally enacted. These recommendations included the following:

- State and local planning
- Education and training
- Surveys and advisory services
- Coordinated national information systems
- Demonstration programs
- Research and development
- Institutes for research and training
- Grants-in-aid for innovations

## LEAA ORGANIZATION, OPERATION, AND EVOLUTION

Initially, LEAA was authorized 225 staff positions with a small budget of $63 million for the balance of the first year. LEAA was organized into central offices; an Office of Regional Programs, which consisted of 10 regional offices for block grants that administered most of the funds to the states; a discretionary office program for direct grants to agencies; and the National Institute of Law Enforcement and Criminal Justice (NILECJ) for research, development, demonstration, training, and publication/dissemination. Other programs were added in reauthorization bills: The National Criminal Justice Reference Service was created as a clearinghouse for the exchange of information; the Office of Criminal Justice Education and Training was established to train criminal justice personnel primarily through grants for college education under the Law Enforcement Education Program; the Public Safety Officers' Benefit program was initiated, which gave grants to families of officers killed in the line of duty; and the Community Anti-Crime Program also saw its beginnings during this time. While the LEAA did serve to champion much of what we now think of as modern policing, it was not without its critics.

In 1978, amid growing reports that found that monies were used for James Bond-type equipment and that there was inadequate oversight of expenditures, President Carter proposed to change LEAA by streamlining the grant process and funneling more money into high-crime areas. In his campaign, he was critical of LEAA and promised a complete overhaul. Major changes included replacing annual grant applications with 3-year applications, changing formula grants to include crime rates as well as population, and the establishment of a Bureau of Criminal Justice Statistics. President Carter's attorney general, Griffin Bell, proposed abolishing LEAA and replacing it with a new National Institute of Justice, to be effective with the 1979 LEAA reauthorization. It would eliminate the state planning process, require a 50% match for administrative costs, create a Bureau of Criminal Justice Statistics headed by a presidential appointee, and grant local government a bigger share of funds.

## DEMISE OF LEAA

In 1977, President Carter, through Bell, started phasing out LEAA by closing the 10 regional offices, which eliminated 200 of 790 positions. A study group was formed to make recommendations for the future. The attorney general's study group recommended the following:

- Refocus the national research and development program into a coherent strategy of basic and applied research, including a demonstration program based on the research.
- Replace the present formula block program with a simpler program of direct assistance to state and local governments, including the use of matching funds to buy into the implementation of national program models developed through research. A committee of the National Academy of Sciences reviewed the issue and recommended a statutory advisory panel, peer review panels for basic research, and research-driven program development.

After further study, the Carter administration decided to eliminate LEAA and began with reductions in funds and staff. The Reagan administration made the final decisions, which became effective on April 15, 1982. Some programs were maintained within the Justice Department: drug abuse treatment, the Public Safety Officers' Benefit program, and a regional organized crime intelligence center.

## POST SCRIPT

In 1984, Congress created and President Reagan signed the Justice Assistance Act of 1984, which was similar to LEAA minus the state planning agencies, but still required biannual plans with most funds funneled through the states. It included the Bureau of Justice Assistance (grants to state and local governments), the Bureau of Justice Statistics, the National Institute of Justice, the Office for Victims of Crime, and the Office of Juvenile Justice and Delinquency Prevention. The FY 2002 budget was $5.47 billion.

Despite the criticisms of LEAA, it did mark the beginning of continued federal assistance for local policing. Many of the data collection systems about the country as a whole are still in use today. It provided the country's first real effort to study and create effective and efficient policing services nationwide. Its college tuition incentives for inservice personnel helped create a generation of police who would later lead law enforcement through decades of innovation and change.

*Lou Mayo*

### For Further Reading

Abuse of U.S. funds disclosed: LEAA case hurts tax sharing. (1971, July 21). *Washington Post,* p. A1.

Anti-crime report. (1972, May 12). *Washington Post,* p. A10.

Bell's LEAA plan would give the states spending leeway. (1977, December 13). *Washington Post,* p. A13.

Carter proposes to streamline LEAA, aid war on crime in public housing. (1978, July 11). *Washington Post,* p. A4.

Commission on Law Enforcement and the Administration of Justice. (1967). *The challenge of crime in a free society.* Washington, DC: U.S. Government Printing Office.

LEAA: Does it have a future? (1978, December 30). *Washington Post,* p. A10.

LEAA, once a big spender, to close its doors April 15. (1981, December 31). *Washington Post,* p. A18.

LEAA's fate weighed at Justice Department. (1977, August 9). *Washington Post,* p. A1.

National League of Cities. (1979). *Ten years of LEAA.* Washington, DC: Author.

Saunders, C. (1970). *Upgrading the American police.* Washington, DC: Brookings Institution.

Statement of the president on approving the crime bills H.R. 9167, H.R. 13551, and H.R. 15766. (1966, November 8). Press release, The White House.

Text of president's message on law enforcement and administration of justice. (1966, March 9). *New York Times,* p. 20L.

##   LAW ENFORCEMENT MEMORIALS

On April 28, 1854, Phil Audax wrote to the *Ohio State Journal* regarding the death of Cyrus Beebe, the first Columbus (Ohio) officer killed in the line of duty:

> Mr. Editor: Mr. Beebe, the murdered policeman . . . fell nobly doing his duty. . . . Is there not therefore an obligation now resting upon his fellow citizens? Such firmness and courage as he displayed, if exhibited on a wider field, warring for his country, would have given his name a place in history. . . . I would suggest therefore that the City Council take measures at once to erect over the remains of the brave executor of the law a suitable monument to commemorate his fidelity and public worth.

Although the Columbus Police Department has him listed on their official memorial at headquarters, a monument to Officer Beebe has not been found.

Mr. Audax alludes to the attention that would have been given had Officer Beebe been a military man who died during wartime. Historically, law enforcement was not given equal and appropriate attention regarding memorials commemorating their death. In fact, law enforcement had incomplete records on officers killed in the line of duty. There was no national memorial honoring slain officers going back to the 1700s, and information from this period is rare. (Finally, in the 1960s, the American Police Hall of Fame opened in Florida and had the names of officers who died in the line of duty from 1960 forward.)

The now much maligned J. Edgar Hoover, Director of the Federal Bureau of Investigation (FBI), probably deserves the credit for compiling national records of slain officers and later publishing details and statistics for purposes of officer survival. In the mid-1930s, Mr. Hoover began keeping data on deaths in agencies serving a population greater than 25,000. Unfortunately, the names, dates, agency names, and details were not retained. In 1961, the FBI began compiling data on felonious deaths, by agency name, date, and officers' names. In 1972, as a result of an order from President Nixon, accidental deaths were included as well. The data included full details on the deaths of these officers.

One of the earliest monuments was in Chicago and was dedicated to the killing of seven officers during the Haymarket riot in 1886. (The monument later had to be moved to the police training academy because protecting it from vandalism had become too expensive.)

Early local memorials included the following:

- On May 30, 1904 (34 years after death), a plaque was placed on a boulder in a Kansas field and dedicated in honor of Abilene and Deputy U.S. Marshal Thomas Smith.
- On May 18, 1927, Kansas City (MO) police planned placement of steel markers on the graves of their slain officers. In 1929, they added a large memorial statue listing the names of slain officers.
- In 1932, Grosse Pointe Park (MI) dedicated a waterfront park.
- In 1958, the National Police Officers Association of America presented posthumous awards in Annapolis (MD) to slain officers.
- In 1962, the 87th Congress authorized the president to proclaim May 15 as Peace Officers Memorial Day, and the week of May 15 as Police Week (Public Law 87-726). President Kennedy later made such a proclamation.
- In 1968, Flowing Wells High School in Tucson (AZ) began holding "Bellamy Days," which honored slain members of the Tucson Police Department. That celebration continues to this day.

In 1982, the Fraternal Order of Police Auxiliary, under the leadership of Suzie Sawyer, began hosting a Memorial Day service in the nation's capital. These services continue annually and include programs from Concerns of Police Survivors, Inc. (COPS). In the June 1982 issue of *The Police Chief*, President Reagan wrote, "It is most fitting that all Americans pay tribute to police officers and that we join with them and the families of their fallen comrades, in honoring the memory of those who have lost their lives while protecting their fellow citizens and communities" (Reagan, 1982, p. 8).

At that time, efforts for law enforcement memorials really began to materialize. The Law Enforcement Memorial Association (LEMA) began researching deaths not only from existing agencies, but also from those that no longer exist, and where the officers had been forgotten. LEMA honors America's Domestic Soldiers, calling them "Forgotten Heroes."

During National Police Week in 1982, retired New York City Police Lieutenant Mario Biaggi, then a U.S. Representative, introduced legislation to establish a national memorial to be built on the grounds of the FBI headquarters, which would not include names. In 1983, he inserted a moving testimonial for slain officers into the Congressional Record, saying, "In simple terms, National Police Week is a time to remember that we need police and they need us."

Subsequently, Mr. Biaggi's efforts resulted in the formation of the National Law Enforcement Officers Memorial Fund and the building of a memorial at Judiciary Square in Washington, where services are conducted annually during National Police Week. Since its dedication in 1991, the names of 16,600 slain officers have been listed on the memorial. The oldest name is that of Darius Quimby, who was an Albany, New York, constable killed in 1791. Names of those officers who have been killed in the line of duty are added each year.

When law enforcement officers die in the line of duty, they are often given public departmental funerals marked with police honors and media coverage, and they are attended by officers from other localities to demonstrate the loss that is felt by all those in the field. The police memorial provides long-term remembrance of their sacrifice.

*Ronald C. Van Raalte*

**See also** Police Museums

### For Further Reference

Reagan, R. (1982). Guest editorial. *Police Chief, 49*(6), p. 8.
http://www.forgottenheroes-lema.org
http://www.nleomf.org

# ∞ LIE DETECTION

Up until the 1900s, unscientific methods dominated the search for detecting liars from truth-tellers. Many methods relied on divine intervention, expressed through ordeals or torture that was rooted primarily in superstition and religious faith. In Europe and colonial America, water ordeals flourished during the witch hunts of the 1600s, when suspects were tied up and thrown into water. If the suspects sank, this meant the water had accepted the purity of truth-tellers; if they floated, it meant the water had rejected the impure liars, who were then executed. Another testing method, the boiling water ordeal, in which the right hand of the accused was plunged into a kettle of boiling water, was used worldwide, whereas fire and hot iron ordeals were commonplace in India and Egypt. Food ordeals involving the chewing and spitting out of dry rice were practiced in ancient China, and during the Spanish Inquisition, a "trial slice" of bread and cheese was used to test the veracity of suspects. The belief underpinning food ordeals was that lying produced reactions of fear and guilt, which caused a decrease in saliva production. If dry-mouth made spitting and swallowing difficult, suspects were declared deceptive. Although ancient techniques for detecting lies were torturous, they had in common with their modern counterparts reliance on the psychophysiological overreactions of suspects. Not until the early 1900s did science intervene with the hope that truth could be uncovered painlessly.

## DEFINITION

Each year, thousands of lie detection tests are carried out in various sectors of U.S. society, primarily among law enforcement agencies. But the term *lie detection* is misleading. No machine can detect lies, only psychophysiological reactions associated with deceit. Accordingly, methods for detecting deception fall into two general categories: psychophysiologically based techniques and paralinguistic techniques.

## PSYCHOPHYSIOLOGICAL METHODS

Techniques that use measures of physiological responses as indicators of deception underpin the various psychophysiological methods of lie detection. Approaches combine aspects of psychology and biology, the belief being that the act of lying creates conscious conflict that induces anxiety or fear, accompanied by physiological changes believed to be measurable and interpretable.

### Polygraph Tests

Commonly called the lie detector, the polygraph is the most well-known method. Polygraph tests include a series of yes/no questions to which suspects respond while connected to sensors that send, by wire to the instrument, the physiological reactions of suspects. Analog or digital technology is used to record changes in suspects' cardiovascular, respiratory, and electrodermal (skin) patterns. Results are then used to determine deception and are based on comparisons made between suspects' physiological responses to relevant questions (those that directly inquire if suspects have committed a crime) and comparison questions (those designed to produce known truthfulness or deceptive responses, such as "Is today Monday?"). Suspects who consistently show more pronounced reactions to relevant questions than to comparison or irrelevant questions are deemed deceptive. Although the polygraph has long been used by law enforcement agencies, its use as a forensic tool continues to be controversial largely because of inaccuracy claims. As of 1988, the federal government has severely restricted businesses from using polygraphs as a screening tool for preemployment and current employment purposes, and polygraphs are still inadmissible in most U.S. courts.

### Validity of the Polygraph

Most of the scientific evidence on polygraph tests stems from specific-event investigations, that is, from criminal cases conducted in laboratory settings. But the instrument's validity has raised criticisms—that laboratory studies cannot be generalized to realistic settings, because consequences for lying are not as serious as in the real world; that physiological responses measured are not uniquely related to deception, because fear of being judged deceptive and anxiety about being tested can also affect responses; that measured responses do not all reflect a single underlying process; and that psychological and physiological changes can be controlled by some suspects, thereby producing false results. Consequently, although polygraphs have some utility in that fear of the machine can elicit admissions and confessions, the relationship among lying, conflict, and emotional and bodily reactions is too vague to support the high (from 80%–98%) accuracy claims of polygraphists.

## ALTERNATIVE PSYCHOPHYSIOLOGICAL METHODS

The polygraph is but one of many tests used to measure psychophysiological reactions to detect lies. Other methods seek to detect dishonesty from measurements of brain activity and other physiological indicators, and from suspects' demeanor. To date, however, none is believed to outperform the polygraph.

### Computerized Voice Stress Analyzer

The computerized voice stress analyzer (CVSA) measures stress that is induced physiologically, but only in the voice itself. Also called Psychological Stress Evaluator (PSE), the CVSA holds much interest because, unlike the polygraph, it requires little training. The CVSA is based on the theory that variations in the voice change when suspects are under psychological stress, and that stress can be detected by analyzing suspects' voice production. While being asked a series of closed questions, a microphone charts suspects' responses on a graph with squiggly lines. Peaks indicate truthfulness, whereas flat tops indicate lies. Involuntary frequency modulations, or "microtremors," in the voice are then measured by the machine and indicate stress, which is itself an indication of deception. Critics, however, say that the CVSA has an accuracy rate much like that of a coin toss.

### Magnetic Resonance Imaging

A relatively new approach being investigated as a substitute to the polygraph is magnetic resonance imaging (MRI), commonly referred to as "brain fingerprinting." This method is based on the theory that a thorough record of a crime is stored in the brain of perpetrators and potentially can be retrieved. Retrieval involves using three different types of stimuli or event-related potentials (ERPs): targets, which are sights, sounds, or other stimuli that suspects know; probes are stimuli that only the guilty would know; and irrelevants are stimuli that suspects are unlikely to recognize. To determine whether a suspect is retaining specific knowledge of a crime, electrodes are attached to the head to measure the brain's electrophysiological reactions to specific words, phrases, or pictures that are flashed on a screen. The brain waves emitted by suspects' reactions are then read and interpreted. MRI has received much attention from the CIA, who has also supported, monetarily, research on MRI. One reason for the CIA's interest is the potential that brain fingerprinting offers investigators of terrorist operations, who could then monitor the brain waves of suspected terrorists. The World Trade Center and Pentagon attacks of September 11, 2001, probably made MRI an attractive alternative. But critics caution that it is premature to conclude that the method is useful in practice because brain fingerprinting has demonstrated only limited external validity. More research is needed before claims can be made that MRI identifies areas of brain activity specific to deception.

### Thermal Imaging

Another recent approach measures radiant energy emitted from the face. It has received some attention because suspects do not have to be hooked up to a machine. Instead, an infrared camera detects temperature changes caused by variations in suspects' facial blood flow during the act of lying. But although this approach is quicker and less invasive than the polygraph, criteria for judging deceptiveness remain unclear. Thermal imaging has not shown enough scientific evidence to support its use as a reliable substitute.

### Detection From Demeanor

Demeanor detection refers to nonmechanical techniques used to interpret the subtle behavioral cues of suspects. Like mechanical methods, responses are related to psychological states induced through questioning; however, unlike mechanical methods, cues are observed through the human senses and include facial expressions, gaze aversion, body movements, posture, voice tone, and content and patterns of speech.

## Facial Action Coding System

The facial action coding system is used to distinguish liars from truth-tellers by interpreting behavioral cues through facial expressions, body movements, and voice. Dr. Paul Ekman, a professor of psychology at the University of California at San Francisco School of Medicine, has identified approximately 35 to 40 nonverbal cues, including a surfacing of guilt, despair, distress, embarrassment, shifts in pitch, pauses in speech, and slow blinks. Ekman notes that flexibility and reliance on a cluster of clues are traits that the best lie detectors have in common. Accordingly, Ekman teaches police what to look for and how to identify justified fear from fear of being caught. However, few associations with deception appear reliably and consistently across large numbers of studies. So, although it might be possible to automate measurements of facial expressions, for example, it is too early to judge accuracy because there is little research on any one cue or combination of cues that might detect deception accurately.

## Neurolinguistic Programming

Neurolinguistic programming (NLP) is also based on reading of behavioral cues, but this approach measures how people normally process information. Based on a complex mathematical theory, NLP focuses on aspects of personality, physiology associated with sense orientation and right- or left-brain dominance, direction of eye movements, and dilation and constriction of pupils. Two elements of NLP are relevant in police work: sense orientation, which refers to the five senses through which human beings access information; and pattern and direction of eye movement, involving remembered experienced events versus events "created" from the imagination. Because the brain is constantly bombarded by the five senses, the conscious mind reduces these sensory inputs into three modes—sight; sound; and kinesthetics (touch, taste, and smell). These three are further reduced to one predominant mode—sight, sound, or feeling. Once a suspect's dominant sense orientation is identified, examiners next determine whether that suspect is right- or left-brain dominant, and it is here that the lie detection aspect of NLP becomes relevant. A right-handed person who is sight-oriented looks up and to the left when remembering a previously observed event; when "creating" a lie, that person looks up and to the right. NLP is said to enhance the ability of police to build rapport with suspects by asking neutral-based questions and by changing interrogation style based on suspects' sensory orientation. Critics doubt the accuracy of this method, but proponents believe the technique is a useful adjunct to police work.

## PARALINGUISTIC TECHNIQUES

The second major category of lie detection methods is not physiologically based, in that it does not use psychophysiological reactions to stimuli to detect liars. Rather, these methods rely on psychological principles believed to be inherent in suspects' language use. Various linguistic techniques are used to indicate deception.

## Linguistic Inquiry and Word Count

Proponents believe there are three differences in how liars use language: They tend to use fewer personal pronouns, they use more words that connote negative emotions, and they tell less complex stories than do truth-tellers. Proponents further believe that counting and categorizing the written or spoken words suspects use to communicate can reveal their underlying emotions, thoughts, and motives. To determine deception, a software program is used to break down the suspects' language, word by word, comparing each word in the sample against a file of more than 2,000 words, which are then separated into 72 different categories. They claim to correctly separate liars 61% overall, but critics say there is not enough empirical evidence to support such claims.

## Graphology

Also known as handwriting analysis, graphologists believe some characteristics of suspects' spontaneous writing offer information about their personality, including honesty and loyalty. But graphology is not concerned with content; instead, specific structural characteristics, such as letter shapes, sizes, and consistency, are examined to make inferences about the veracity of suspects. Opponents say the technique lacks a sound foundation and has not shown evidence of increasing the ability to detect lies.

## Content Analysis

The technique is applied to written statements only and involves analyzing suspects' in-depth accounts of alleged events. Samples of written statements are analyzed in content and form to see how a suspect describes an event and if the writer is withholding damaging information. The methodology is believed to have untapped potential. But although anecdotal accounts claim the technique works, it, too, lacks sound methodology.

## CONCLUSION

Throughout the ages, many different approaches have been used to detect deception. In ancient times, people turned to cruel means; today's techniques have moved away from torture and embraced science. Yet even science has not settled the controversy surrounding the various methods. The polygraph remains the most commonly used, and none of the alternatives has yet surfaced as a definitive substitute for detecting liars from truth-tellers.

*Norma Manatu*

## For Further Reading

Brain fingerprinting gets court OK. (2003, April 30). *Law Enforcement News, 29*(598), 5.

Dale, S. S. (2001, November 26). The brain scientist. *Time, 158,* 81.

Dodenhoff, P. C. (1987, March 10). Steven A. Rhoads: Police chief of East Hazel Crest, Ill., and pioneer in the use of psychological technique for lie detection. *Law Enforcement News, 13*(244) 9–12, 14.

Going beyond pants on fire. (2002, June 30). *Law Enforcement News, 28*(580), 6.

National Research Council. (2003). *The polygraph and lie detection.* Washington, DC: National Academic Press.

Not what they say, but how they say it: DC clears homicides with voice analysis. (1994, September 15). *Law Enforcement News, 20*(407), 6.

Scheck, B., Neufeld, P., & Dwyer, J. (2000). *Actual innocence: Five days to execution, and other dispatches from the wrongly convicted.* New York: Doubleday.

Segrave, K. (2004). *Lie detectors: A social history.* Jefferson, NC: McFarland.

Spotting a liar is no easy task for police. (1999, May 15/31). *Law Enforcement News. 25*(511, 512), 7.

Underwood, R. K. (1995/1996, Spring). Truth verifiers: From the hot iron to the lie detector. *Kentucky Law Journal,* p. 84.

Wilson, J. (2001, October). Truth, lies and polygraphs. *Popular Mechanics, 178,* 42.

## ༀ LINEUPS

Nearly everyone is familiar with the standard American lineup: six individuals (the suspect plus five "foils" or fillers), all of whom are shown (often standing in front of a height chart) to the witness, who views the lineup members from behind a one-way mirror; is given an opportunity to observe each member of the lineup; and is instructed to make an identification, if possible, or reject the lineup. The police officer who assembled the lineup has selected foils who resemble the suspect (often using other police officers or people who are in custody), arranged the presentation (sometimes in consultation with the suspect's defense attorney), and presented the lineup to the witness—sometimes with an admonition that the witness should take his or her time.

The standard lineup has come under intense criticism from the scientific community for two reasons: (a) It is increasingly evident that many erroneous convictions arise from misidentifications of innocent suspects; and (b) many scientific studies have compared the performance of witnesses in the standard lineup versus alternative procedures, and the standard procedures prove inferior in a number of ways. Improved procedures have been recommended by a number of sources, including a set of recommendations compiled in 1999 by the Department of Justice:

*Use larger lineups.* One objective in conducting lineups is to maximize the ratio of correct to incorrect suspect identifications. Incorrect suspect identifications (made by witnesses who guess incorrectly) can, at worst, lead to erroneous convictions and can, at best, waste the time of the police, who may continue to collect evidence against an innocent person while the guilty person remains on the street and the trail of evidence grows cold. Arrays of nine, as used in Britain, would spread identifications by witnesses who are merely guessing across a larger number of known-innocent foils—in fair lineups, the suspect would be guessed in one in nine instances rather than one in six. Experimental and archival studies indicate that witnesses are highly prone to guessing—about 25% of witnesses choose foils even when a perpetrator is present in a lineup or photoarray (and, of course, logic and these numbers dictate that some of the witnesses who identified the suspect/perpetrator merely guessed correctly), and 50% will guess a foil when the perpetrator is not present.

*Use blind presentation.* The person who conducts the lineup or photo spread should not be aware of which member of the lineup or photo spread is the suspect. The rationale is that blind presentation will eliminate the possibility that police officers administering lineups can intentionally or unintentionally communicate information to a witness about which lineup member is the suspect.

*Give strong cautionary instructions.* Eyewitnesses should be told explicitly that the perpetrator might not be in the lineup, and they should not feel that they must make identification. Witnesses should also be told that the person administering the lineup does not know which person is the suspect. Cautionary instructions have been shown to reduce guessing by witnesses.

*Match foils to the description of the perpetrator.* The suspect should not stand out in the lineup or photo spread as being different from the foils, based on the eyewitness's description of the perpetrator or other factors that would draw extra attention to the suspect. Foils generally should not be selected to look like the suspect, but instead should fit the description the eyewitness made of the perpetrator. Such selection strategies can reduce biases against suspects. Description-matched lineups have been shown to produce substantially fairer lineups.

*Collect confidence judgments.* A clear statement of confidence should be taken from the eyewitness at the time of the identification and before any feedback is given as to whether the witness identified the suspect. This ensures that witness confidence levels are preserved at the time the identification is made and that confidence levels are not distorted by events subsequent to the identification.

*Sequential presentations.* In a sequential lineup, an eyewitness views only one lineup member at a time and makes an identification/rejection decision regarding each person before viewing the next lineup member. Sequential procedures reduce witness guessing significantly. When compared to the standard simultaneous procedure, the sequential lineup produces a significantly lower rate of mistaken identifications with little or no loss in the rate of accurate identifications.

*Make more conservative use of lineups.* Another strategy for reducing errors is for the police to use lineups more conservatively—for example, only when there is a reasonably strong likelihood that the suspect is the perpetrator. If a larger proportion of lineups actually contained the perpetrator, this could substantially reduce the number of mistaken identifications of innocent suspects.

*Steven Penrod*

**See also** Eyewitnesses

## For Further Reading

Luus, C. A. E., & Wells, G. L. (1994). The malleability of eyewitness confidence: Co-witness and perseverance effects. *Journal of Applied Psychology, 79,* 714–723.

Penrod, S. (2003). Eyewitness identification evidence: How well are witnesses and police performing? *Criminal Justice, 54,* 36–47.

Steblay, N., Dysart, J., Fulero, S., & Lindsay, R. C. L. (2001). Eyewitness accuracy rates in sequential and simultaneous lineup presentations: A meta-analytic comparison. *Law & Human Behavior, 25,* 459–473.

Technical Working Group for Eyewitness Evidence. (1999). *Eyewitness evidence: A guide for law enforcement* (Report NCJ 178240). Washington, DC: U.S. Department of Justice.

Wells, G. L., Small, M., Penrod, S., Malpass, R. S., Fulero, S. M., & Brimacombe, C. A. E. (1998). Eyewitness identification procedures: Recommendations for lineups and photospreads. *Law and Human Behavior, 22,* 603–647.

# LOITERING

In general, loitering refers to the act of loafing about a specific location. States and localities in the United States have a long history of enforcing laws against loitering in public areas. Early U.S. antiloitering laws were identical to English laws regarding vagrancy. However, over time, these laws were forced to evolve in order to pass constitutional muster. Recently, localities throughout the United States have attempted to use antiloitering laws to thwart gang activities, drug dealing, prostitution, the soliciting of alms, street gambling, and other behaviors that have the potential to affect citizens' quality of life. Although antiloitering ordinances usually apply to people of all ages, they are often used, either in conjunction with or in lieu of youth curfews, to keep youths from congregating in public areas during evening hours—a condition that often elicits fear among community members. Violators of antiloitering laws may be told to "move along," fined, required to appear in court, sentenced to short jail terms, or subjected to a combination of these consequences. Even when localities have antiloitering laws on the books, individual police officers use discretion in deciding whether to enforce the laws or to what extent to enforce the laws (i.e., deciding whether to arrest violators or simply warn them and ask them to move along). U.S. laws against loitering are rooted in the English common law regarding vagrancy. The English laws, which outlawed begging and refusal to work, were initiated as an effort to save feudalism from the increase in wages caused by the decimation of England's labor force by the Black Death. Instead of being repealed or made dormant, vagrancy laws experienced a shift in focus after the 1575 manumission of English serfs. Beginning in the 16th century, English law regarding vagrancy was no longer concerned with controlling the movement of the labor force; rather, it aimed to regulate would-be felons in a newly commercialized and industrialized society so that safe passage could be guaranteed merchants transporting goods. By 1577, first-time offending "loiterers," "ruffians," "vagabonds," "procurators," "jugglers," "pedlars," and "rogues" could be branded on their chests with the letter "V" and enslaved for 2 years. Repeat offenders could be branded on the forehead with the letter "S" and enslaved for life.

In the tradition of the English common law, nearly all U.S. states prohibited vagrancy, begging, and migration of the poor from other states. Although the Privileges and Immunities Clause of the Articles of Confederation denied beggars and vagrants all rights, the Constitution of 1787 left it up to the states to determine vagrancy laws for themselves. By the 1791 ratification of the Bill of Rights, 8 out of 14 states statutorily prohibited begging, and by 1812, four more states and the District of Columbia had implemented statutes that adhered to the English tradition of controlling the so-called dangerous class. By 1956, every state in the nation had statutes prohibiting vagrancy, with the exception of West Virginia, where it was a common-law crime, and the laws were being arbitrarily imposed upon people considered a nuisance. In many cases, state laws were augmented by municipal regulations. In all instances, vagrancy statutes punished individuals for their status (i.e., being poor, idle, or unemployed) rather than for having committed a specific illegal act. U.S. legislation regarding the control of behaviors considered vagrancy under the English common law has passed through several phases toward a rejection of status-based regulations and a requirement that criminal offenses consist of specific behaviors. Around the time of World War II, legal scholars and social welfare advocates spoke out against catch-all vagrancy laws, arguing that these laws had the effect of criminalizing the status of being economically unfortunate and particularly the status of being homeless. The first successful challenge to vagrancy laws was directed at states' attempts to disallow the migration of poor people across their borders. In *Edwards v. California* (1941), the U.S. Supreme Court struck down a California statute that prohibited poor people from entering the state. In *Edwards*, the Court held the statute in violation of the Commerce Clause of the Constitution; however, concurring opinions by two justices, which relied on the Privileges and Immunities Clause of the Fourteenth Amendment, attacked the state's efforts to limit the rights of citizens based on property status and foretold of several Supreme Court decisions of the 1960s that would further undermine status-based vagrancy laws.

Vagrancy laws were slowly replaced by antiloitering laws aimed more specifically at the act of loitering. However, beginning in the late 1950s, courts began to hold both vagrancy laws and antiloitering statutes unconstitutional under the First and Fourteenth Amendments. Vagrancy and antiloitering statutes were considered impermissible restrictions on First Amendment speech-related freedoms because they were overly broad and thus imposed upon First Amendment rights. Similarly, courts found vagrancy laws and antiloitering statutes to violate the Fourteenth Amendment because they were overly vague (i.e., lacking in guidelines regarding lawful behavior that could be understood by reasonable people) and hence provided police officers with too much discretion in determining whether a citizen's behavior was in accordance with the law. In *City of Chicago v. Morales* (1999), the U.S. Supreme Court struck down an Illinois gang-loitering ordinance (i.e., an ordinance that gave police officers the power to disperse any gathering of one or more people when they reasonably believed that at least one of the individuals was a gang member) because it failed to meet constitutional standards for specificity and clarity in that it gave police officers too much discretion.

A series of New York cases that occurred between the late 1950s and early 1970s set the precedent that legislation prohibiting mere loitering was unconstitutional, but that legislation in which "loiter" was used in conjunction with, or to illustrate, another explicitly prohibited behavior was permissible. As a result, laws against "loitering for the purpose of" some specific criminal act (e.g., prostitution, dealing illegal drugs, etc.) sprang up all over the country. However, "loitering for the purpose of" legislation has produced mixed results in the courts. Such legislation has faltered in the courts where the act to which loitering is coupled is a constitutionally protected act. A prime example of this is *Loper v. New York City Police Department* (1993), in which the Second Circuit Court of Appeals upheld a federal district court's finding that New York State's "loitering for the purpose of begging" law was unconstitutional. The court held that begging was expressive conduct, with an act and an expression inextricably intertwined, and was thus deserving of the same First Amendment protections granted charitable solicitation. However, although the court rejected the total ban on begging in New York City because it eliminated all means for beggars to communicate their message, the *Loper* decision did leave open the possibility that more narrowly tailored ordinances that addressed specific behaviors and put forth specific time, place, and manner restrictions (e.g., restrictions on aggressive begging, restrictions on begging at automated teller machines, or restrictions on begging in enclosed areas) would pass constitutional muster. Presently, legal challenges to "loitering for the purpose of" laws have led to the establishment of laws that restrict specific behaviors, such as aggressive begging, obstructing pedestrian traffic, and lying down on sidewalks. Thus far, narrowly tailored laws prohibiting particular behaviors, at specific times, and in precise locations have fared far better in the courts than their more general predecessors.

*Nicole R. Green*

*See also* Curfews

## For Further Reading

Chambliss, W. (1964). A sociological analysis of the law of vagrancy. *Social Problems, 12*(1), 67–77.

City of Chicago v. Morales, 527 U.S. 41, 64 (1999).

Edwards v. California, 314 U.S. 160 (1941).

Foote, C. (1956). Vagrancy type law and its administration. *University of Pennsylvania Law Review, 104*, 615.

Kelling, G., & Coles, K. (1996). *Fixing broken windows: Restoring order and reducing crime in our communities.* New York: Touchstone.

Loper v. New York City Police Department, 999 F.2d 699 (1993), aff'd. 802 F.Supp. 1029 (S.D.N.Y. 1992).

# M

## ⨕ MCCONE COMMISSION, THE

In the late summer of 1965, a predominantly black neighborhood of Los Angeles known as Watts descended into 6 days of massive rioting. California Governor Edmund "Pat" Brown, reeling from the political impact of the unrest, tapped John A. McCone, former director of the CIA and a well-known conservative, to conduct an impartial study of the unrest. McCone proceeded to lead a commission—the McCone Commission, which was made up of six whites and two African Americans, as well as a support staff of 29 assistants, 16 clerks and secretaries, and 26 consultants—through a series of hearings, interviews, and studies. This process was designed to provide descriptive and chronological information about the riots as well as to give recommendations to prevent their recurrence.

After 3 months, and after questioning more than 10,000 people, the McCone Commission released a report, *Violence in the City—An End or a Beginning?* that summarized the riots and provided policy recommendations for preventing future unrest. The immediate cause of the disturbance, according to the report, was the arrest of a drunk driver in Watts, a heavily African American neighborhood, during which police deployed force to subdue the suspect, a young African American male. Bystanders retaliated violently and, over the course of the next 5 days, violence escalated, resulting in the deaths of 34 people and the destruction of more than $40 million worth of property.

According to the report's conclusions, the Watts riots were spearheaded by a small, nonrepresentative sampling of the black community, mainly juvenile delinquents and unemployed "riff raff" elements. The uprising was largely disorganized and, for the most part, unwarranted, stemming from lack of education and an irrational hatred of the police. Most African Americans in Los Angeles, the report asserted, did not participate in the riots, nor did they endorse them.

The report recommended that police–civilian relations in Watts be improved, unemployment reduced, and job training programs established. The report failed to take seriously black grievances regarding systemic police brutality and widespread racial discrimination, shying away from a structural critique of the riots in general. Instead, the report located the nexus of responsibility in the individual failings of marginalized elements within the black community. Reinforcing this nonstructural critique was a second conclusion, namely that Watts differed from urban ghettoes in the Northeast because it was made up of small, one-story houses, rather than tenements, and enjoyed wide, tree-lined streets.

The McCone Commission quickly received criticism for these conclusions. The California Advisory

Committee to the United States Civil Rights Commission challenged the report's findings, as did liberal voices such as civil rights activist Bayard Rustin, Berkeley sociology professor Robert Blauner, and Columbia University professor Robert W. Fogelson. Critics like Fogelson and Blauner argued that a larger segment of the black community participated in and supported the riots than the McCone Commission suggested, and that the riots were structured protests against police brutality and intolerable ghetto conditions. The looting and burning of stores, they argued, was strategic, and only white-owned stores known for overcharging black customers were targeted.

These criticisms, which located the cause of the riots not in the individual failings of the black community but in larger, structural relations of power, gained authority when the University of California at Los Angeles's Institute of Government and Public Affairs produced a study affirming McCone's critics, and Columbia professor Robert Fogelson presented his findings to the President's Commission on Law Enforcement and Administration of Justice.

Undergirding critiques of the Commission's work was the undeniable reality that John A. McCone had been selected by Governor Brown to salvage his own political career. Brown, a known liberal, hoped that John McCone's presence on the Commission would appease white voters in suburban Los Angeles, many of whom viewed the riots as unacceptable and emblematic of a larger black disrespect for law and order. This hope proved futile, and Brown's fears vindicated, when Ronald Reagan, a young conservative and former actor, defeated Brown in the 1966 gubernatorial race on a platform that included a heavy law-and-order component.

The McCone Commission, respected by conservatives and reviled by liberals, remained a point of contention for years in Southern California, yet it possesses a historical relevance that transcends its political life. Its report was the first of its kind to analyze the causes of a riot and would become a blueprint for future reports in the United States.

*Anders Walker*

**See also** Christopher Commission, Crown Heights Report, Rampart Investigation, Riots/Demonstrations (Response to)

*For Further Reading*

Conot, R. (1968). *Rivers of blood, years of darkness: The unforgettable classic account of the Watts riot.* New York: Morrow.

Crump, S. (1966). *Black riot in Los Angeles: The story of the Watts tragedy.* Los Angeles: Trans-Anglo.

Governor's Commission on the Los Angeles Riots. (1966). *Transcripts, depositions, consultants' reports, and selected documents.* Washington, DC: Microcard Editions.

Sears, D. (1973). *The politics of violence: The new urban blacks and the Watts riot.* Boston: Houghton Mifflin.

# ❧ MENTALLY ILL, POLICE RESPONSE TO THE

The nature of police work frequently brings officers into contact with persons with mental illness (PMIs). The police are available around the clock and are often the first responders called to provide a range of social and public services. Unfortunately, most officers have limited knowledge of working with PMIs, and local mental health services may be inadequate to meet the needs of the citizens whom the police encounter. Nonetheless, officers must still attempt to achieve a disposition that benefits the community, the needs of the mentally ill, and the interests of their police department. Throughout its history, the criminal justice system has struggled to develop effective ways to deal with PMIs. At times, such efforts have been clear failures, although recent advances have improved the odds that PMIs will receive the services and treatments they need.

Police officers often find themselves in contact with PMIs for a number of reasons. First, the police are always available to respond to citizen requests for services; the same cannot be said of many other governmental, social, and health care service providers. Because of this general availability, the police must provide a range of functions when service providers are not readily available. Second, as sociologist Egon Bittner noted in a classic essay, the police are empowered with a general right to use coercive force to secure citizen compliance with lawful directives. In other words, the police have broad authority to compel citizens to do things that those citizens would rather not do, such as agreeing to seek mental health services. In limited situations, the police may even have the lawful authority to force someone to seek mental health assistance. More often, their role in dealing with PMIs involves attempting to persuade citizens to voluntarily seek such services. Third, police may find themselves in contact with PMIs when certain behaviors activate a police response. Mental illness may be at the root of calls about disorderly or dangerous conduct, suspicious behavior, public nuisances, or suicidal individuals. Although each of these behaviors may be the result of forces other than mental illness, the latter is, at times, a contributing factor. Thus, in the course of serving a law enforcement or order maintenance function, the police find themselves in contact with PMIs.

Historically, the police have not done an exemplary job dealing with PMIs, although this fact is not entirely the fault of police officers or agencies. The average police officer lacks the education and training to recognize whether an individual's behavior is driven by a mental illness. In addition, a person suffering from a mental crisis may not be thinking and behaving in a rational manner. The training and tactics police normally employ in public encounters provide insufficient insights into the behavior of a PMI, increasing the probability of a situation escalating into violence. Even where a mental illness is recognized, the police often lack adequate ties with local mental health service providers. When such ties exist, finite resources may not allow officers to ensure that PMIs receive treatment. Where resources are present, the police duty to enforce criminal law violations often supersedes other functions. As a result, an officer may opt to arrest a PMI offender, rather than attempting to provide access to the appropriate mental health services.

In recent years, a growing number of American police agencies have recognized the need to improve their interactions with PMIs. Regrettably, many agencies have done so only after an encounter escalated to the point of fatal violence, often with officers shooting citizens. Agencies have come to the realization that officers need specific training to interact effectively with citizens in the midst of a mental health crisis. There has also been a broader shift in the criminal justice system that seeks to avoid using legal sanctions when a person's behavior is largely the

product of a mental illness. For the police, this has translated into the development of "pre-booking" diversion programs. Where appropriate, PMIs are given access to appropriate health services, rather than merely being arrested.

One of the most widely recognized and emulated programs is the Crisis Intervention Team (CIT) model developed in Memphis, Tennessee. The CIT program was initiated following the 1987 police shooting of a mentally ill citizen. In conjunction with local mental health services and advocacy groups, the Memphis Police Department (MPD) developed a plan that provided select officers with additional training and ensured that mental health services would be available to citizens in need. Approximately 10% of MPD officers have been given specialized training (CIT) to help them understand and deal effectively with PMIs. Local mental health services have signed a "no refusal" policy; when officers bring PMIs to these providers, they are obligated to offer appropriate services.

The result of the CIT program is that when the MPD is called upon to deal with a PMI, an officer with CIT training can usually handle the call. These officers attempt to resolve situations by linking the citizen with appropriate mental health services. Traditional police responses of ignoring PMIs or responding with time-honored tactics (i.e., arrests) do little to address the citizen's underlying needs. It is hoped that expanding an officer's options to include providing for a citizen's mental health will better meet the needs of that citizen, as well as the community as a whole. The CIT model has been widely praised for reducing violent conflict between the police and PMIs, providing emergency services to those in need, and reducing the unnecessary incarceration of PMIs. Agencies across the country have begun to emulate the Memphis model in order to develop more humane and less punitive ways of dealing with the mentally ill.

*Joseph A. Schafer and William M. Wells*

## For Further Reading

Bittner, E. (1970). *The functions of police in modern society.* Chevy Chase, MD: National Clearinghouse for Mental Health.

Council of State Government. (2002). *Criminal justice/mental health consensus project.* Lexington, KY: Author.

Klein, M. (2002). Law enforcement's response to people with mental illness. *FBI Law Enforcement Bulletin, 71*(2), 11–14.

Nislow, N. (2000, December 15/31). Psych job: The Memphis PD's Crisis Intervention Team reinvents police response to EDPs. *Law Enforcement News, 26*(545, 546). Retrieved from http://www.lib.jjay.cuny.edu/len/2000/12.31/

Steadman, H. J., Deane, M. W., Borum, R., & Morrissey, J. P. (2000). Comparing outcomes of major models of police responses to mental health emergencies. *Psychiatric Services, 51,* 645–649.

# &oeligtilde; MILITARIZATION OF AMERICAN POLICE

Examining the militarization of civilian police in the United States may seem, at first glance, an odd pursuit in light of the preoccupation in the literature with community policing, a trend that espouses moving away from the traditional paramilitary professional model toward a democratization of police organizations and services. To some police observers, a momentous shift has occurred in the relationship between the police and military: The traditional delineations between the military, police, and criminal justice system are blurring. In breaking with a long-standing tenet of democratic governance and a central feature of the modern nation-state, the traditional roles of the military handling threats to our nation's external security through threatening or actually waging war, and the police targeting internal security problems such as crime and illegal drugs, are becoming increasingly intermingled. This blurring began with the military's heavy involvement in drug law enforcement during the Reagan/Bush drug war and has only broadened and deepened over the past 10 years. It is within this broader sociopolitical context that we can understand the recent and certain trend toward the militarization of a key component of U.S. police.

## DEFINING MILITARISM AND MILITARIZATION

The concepts of *militarism* and *militarization* are at times used in an ideologically charged fashion. This diminishes their power to help us think clearly about the influence the military model has on different aspects of our society.

Militarism, in the most basic terms, is an ideology geared toward solving problems. It is a set of beliefs, values, and assumptions that stresses the use of force and violence as the most appropriate and efficacious means to solve problems. It emphasizes the use of military power, hardware, operations, and technology as its primary problem-solving tools. Similarly, militarization is the implementation of militarism. It is the process of arming, organizing, planning, training for, and sometimes implementing violent conflict. To militarize means adopting and applying the central elements of the military model to an organization or particular situation.

To say that the police are becoming more militarized is simply referring to the process whereby civilian police increasingly draw from, and pattern themselves around, the military model. Four dimensions of the military model provide us with tangible indicators of militarization:

- Culturally—martial language, style (appearance), thinking
- Organizationally—martial arrangements such as "command and control" centers, or elite teams of officers patterned after military special operations squads
- Operationally—patterns of activity modeled after the military, such as in the areas of intelligence, supervision, or handling of high-risk situations
- Materially—martial equipment and technology

Put in this way, it should be clear that since their inception, the civilian police have shared many of these features, at least to some extent, with the military. After all, the foundation of military and police power is the same—the state-sanctioned capacity to use physical violence to accomplish their respective objectives (external and internal security). The police were developed, in fact, as a civilian alternative to the military for the sake of maintaining domestic security.

When discerning police militarization, the real concern is one of degree, or the extent to which a civilian police body is militarized. Militarization must be conceived of on a continuum.

## THE RISE OF POLICE PARAMILITARISM

Two national-level surveys of large and small police departments have yielded data documenting the certain militarization of a significant component of the U.S. police. This militarization is evidenced by a precipitous rise and mainstreaming of police paramilitary units (PPUs). These police units, referred to most often as SWAT teams or special response teams, are tailored after military special operations groups, such as the Navy SEALs. They have been described elsewhere as follows:

> Police paramilitary units can be distinguished from what some experts have called "cop-on-the-beat policing" most simply by their appearance, their weaponry, and their operations. For a more exact identification we must clarify the term "police paramilitary unit." We must distinguish between indications that are necessary in applying the PPU label and those which would only contribute to labeling these units and their activities as paramilitaristic. First among the necessary facts, the unit must train and function as a military special operations team with a strict military command structure and discipline (or the pretense thereof). Second, the unit must have at the forefront of [its] function to threaten or use force collectively, and not always as an option of last resort (e.g., in conducting no-knock or quick-knock drug raid). Operationally, PPUs are deployed to deal with situations that require a team of police officers specifically trained to be use of force specialists. . . . Finally, the unit must operate under legitimate state authority. . . . This criterion would exclude common thuggery, militia organizations, and guerilla groups. Contributing indicators include the hardware they employ and their garb. These teams generally outfit themselves with black or urban camouflage BDUs (battle dress uniforms), lace-up combat boots, full body armor, Kevlar helmets, and ninja-style hoods. PPUs' weapons and hardware include submachine guns (Heckler and Koch brand most popular), tactical shotguns, sniper rifles, percussion grenades, CS and OC gas, surveillance equipment, and armored personnel carriers. (Kraska & Cubellis, 1997, p. 610)

Until recently, these units were only a peripheral part of large police departments' reaction to the rare hostage, barricaded suspect, or civil disturbance incident. As of 1996, 89% of American police departments serving populations of 50,000 people or more had a PPU, almost double what existed in the early 1980s. Their growth in smaller jurisdictions (agencies serving between 25,000 and 50,000 people) has been even more pronounced. There was about a 175% increase in the number of units in these small locales between 1985 and 1997. Currently, about 70% of those small-town agencies have a PPU.

Although formation of teams is an important indicator of growth, these trends would mean little if these teams were relatively inactive. This is not the case. There has been a more than 1000% increase in the total number of police paramilitary deployments, or call-outs, between 1980 and 1997. Today, there are an estimated 40,000 SWAT team deployments a year conducted among those departments surveyed; in the early 1980s, these was an average of about 3,000.

These figures would not be as controversial if this increase in deployments was due to an increase in the PPU's traditional function—a reactive deployment of high-risk specialists for particularly dangerous events already in progress, such as hostage, sniper, or terrorist situations. Instead, more than 80% of these deployments, and hence 80% of the growth of activity, were for proactive drug raids, specifically no-knock and quick-knock dynamic entries into private residences searching for contraband (drugs, guns, and money). This pattern of SWAT teams primarily engaged in surprise contraband raids holds true for the largest as well as the smallest communities. PPUs have changed from being a periphery and strictly reactive component of police departments to a proactive force actively engaged in fighting the drug war. Another important finding sheds additional light on these units' expanding role. Nearly 20% of departments use their unit as least periodically, and some cases routinely, as a patrol force in high-crime areas—or what some of them called "hot spots." One SWAT commander described their approach as such:

> We're into saturation patrols in hot spots. We do a lot of our work with the SWAT unit because we have bigger guns. We send out two, two-to-four men cars, we look for minor violations and do jump-outs, either on people on the street or automobiles. After we jump-out

the second car provides cover with an ostentatious display of weaponry. (Kraska & Kappeler, 1997, p. 10)

## CONCLUSION: DEVELOPMENTS AFTER SEPTEMBER 11TH

Attempting to control the drug problem by conducting tens of thousands of police special operations raids on people's private residences is strong evidence that the U.S. police, and the war on drugs in general, have moved significantly down the militarization continuum. Of course, a militarized response is sometimes necessary and even unavoidable if done in self-defense or to protect lives in immediate danger. The police, military, and nations are undoubtedly put into situations where they are forced to react with violence. The crisis situation at Columbine High School is a solid example of the necessity of having a professional militarized response to a preexisting crisis in need of use-of-force specialists. Quick-knock contraband raids and preventive patrol work, however, are examples of proactive violence where the civilian police, and political officials who encourage this type of policing, are not forced into these deployments. Instead, they are making the proactive choice to manufacture a dangerous event through an extreme, paramilitarized response. The PPU contraband raid phenomenon is a good example of the potential negative consequences of the military model's influence in civilian policing.

The events of September 11, 2001, will no doubt affect the militarization trend. The blurring of the distinction between police and military that occurred during the war on drugs will likely only intensify in the war on terrorism. It is also plausible to assume that our country, and those members of the government in charge of keeping us secure from terrorism, will gravitate more readily toward the ideology of militarism—both for internal and external security threats—when problem solving. What this means for police militarization is unclear. It could be that SWAT teams will find a different purpose in fighting terrorism, will spend the bulk of their energies preparing for their response to it, and will feel less compelled to justify their existence on the drug war.

We might also be left, though, with the problem of the regular police—operating in the context of a society that places a high level of emphasis on militarism—being increasingly seduced by the trappings of paramilitary subculture. Militarism could exert an even stronger influence on what the regular police decide on for uniforms, the weaponry they carry, and the crime control tactics they employ. Whatever happens, keeping track of the movement of civilian police on the militarization continuum will be increasingly important for our field of study.

*Peter B. Kraska*

### For Further Reading

Kraska, P. B. (1994). The police and military in the post-cold war era: Streamlining the state's use of force entities in the drug war. *Police Forum, 4*(1), 1–8.

Kraska, P. B. (1999). Questioning the militarization of U.S. police: Critical versus advocacy scholarship. *Policing and Society, 9*(2), 141–155.

Kraska, P. B. (2001). *Militarizing the American criminal justice system: The changing roles of the armed forces and the police.* Boston: Northeastern University Press.

Kraska, P. B., & Cubellis, L. J. (1997). Militarizing Mayberry and beyond: Making sense of American paramilitary policing. *Justice Quarterly, 14*(4), 607–629.

Kraska, P. B., & Kappeler, V. E. (1997). Militarizing American police: The rise and normalization of paramilitary units. *Social Problems, 44*(1), 1–18.

## &#x2127; MIRANDA WARNINGS

When police take a suspect into custody, they must give the Miranda warnings:

> You have a right to remain silent. Anything you say can and will be used against you in court. You have a right to the presence of an attorney. If you cannot afford an attorney, one will be appointed for you prior to any questioning.

Police officers often carry a Miranda card and read it to a suspect. Without having been "Mirandized," a custodial suspect's confession is usually not admissible evidence in court. If a suspect waives his or her Miranda rights, the waiver must be voluntary, knowing, and intelligent. The waiver may be withdrawn at any point in the interrogation, although suspects usually do not realize this. Miranda warnings do not apply to on-the-scene questioning, only to questioning that takes place after a suspect has been taken into custody.

Miranda warnings were mandated by the famous U.S. Supreme Court case of *Miranda v. Arizona,* decided 5 to 4 with three companion cases in June 1966. Most police officers, district attorneys, and judges have now been accustomed to Miranda warnings for all of their professional lives. The general public knows the Miranda warnings from seeing them on television and in films. In the words of Chief Justice Rehnquist in *Dickerson v. United States* (2000), Miranda warnings have become "routine police practice . . . part of our national culture." In the discussion below, however, we note that some practices and cases have limited Miranda's applicability.

## *MIRANDA V. ARIZONA:* REACTION AND ACCOMMODATION

*Miranda* represented the height of the Warren Court's criminal procedure revolution. It followed the famous cases of *Gideon v. Wainwright* (1963) (right to counsel), *Escobedo v. Illinois* (1964) (right to pretrial counsel), *Mapp v. Ohio* (1961) (states' exclusionary rule), and just preceded *In re Gault* (1967) (juvenile justice). The legal reasoning behind *Miranda* lacked precedent but conformed to the 1960s' demand for social justice. Opponents of the decision thought *Miranda* contributed to a contemporary increase in the crime index. Reflecting that view, both presidential candidates ran in 1968 on a law-and-order platform; Congress passed Section 3501 to the Federal Criminal Code, giving judges the right to decide case by case if confessions were voluntary (later overturned by *Dickerson*); and in 1986, Attorney General Meese issued a report advocating overruling *Miranda* by a newly conservative Supreme Court.

The majority opinion in *Miranda v. Arizona* included seven pages castigating police interrogation manuals, which contributed to its conclusion that custodial interrogation is inherently coercive. The Miranda warnings and waivers were the Court's

attempt to change this relationship between suspects and police. Subsequently, officers learned to accommodate *Miranda* by delivering the warnings in a neutral manner or by reading them from a preprinted form before asking suspects to sign. Sometimes, they could deemphasize the warnings' significance by embedding them in friendly small talk and communicating that this was an unimportant bureaucratic detail. In court, the warnings and voluntary waiver provide the "bright-line" acceptance that incriminating information was not coerced. After *Miranda,* cases were not argued, as they used to be, in due process terms around the "totality of the circumstances" leading to whether the defendant's "will was overborne." By the time of *Withrow v. Williams* in 1993, four national police organizations and 50 former prosecutors joined amicus briefs against overruling *Miranda.* A possible initial decline in the confession and conviction rates, still debated by scholars, gave way to consensus that about three fourths of the accused still confess as they always did.

## CONSTITUTIONAL OR PROPHYLACTIC WARNINGS?

One of the first exceptions to the clarity of the Miranda warnings was *Harris v. New York* (1971), which made non-Mirandized statements admissible for attacking a defendant's credibility on the witness stand. *Michigan v. Tucker* (1974) found the testimony of a witness discovered through a Miranda violation to be admissible to the case-in-chief. *New York v. Quarles* (1984) accepted unwarned questioning if there was a public safety concern. *Oregon v. Elstad* (1985) allowed police to use non-Mirandized statements to develop leads to other tangible evidence of guilt (i.e., the "fruit of the poisonous tree" doctrine does not apply).

While creating these exceptions, the Court more than once characterized Miranda rules as prophylactic, "not themselves rights protected by the Constitution" but only "measures to insure that the right against compulsory self-incrimination was protected" (*Michigan v. Tucker,* p. 444). In *United States v. Verdugo-Urquidez* (1990), Chief Justice

Rehnquist even said in passing that violation of the privilege against self-incrimination "occurs only at trial" (p. 264). Many experts anticipated that *Miranda* would be overruled by *Dickerson* in 2000. Instead, the Court confirmed *Miranda* because of many years of precedent and the difficulty of applying any other standard to confessions. The Court stopped short, however, of emphatically reaffirming the right to remain silent in custodial interrogation as a constitutional right.

## QUESTIONING "OUTSIDE MIRANDA"

The combination of judicial exceptions to *Miranda* and the Court's characterization of the warnings as prophylactic led many police departments, among them Los Angeles, Santa Monica, and Tucson, to train officers in questioning "outside Miranda"— stressing the lack of a constitutional imperative and the results that might come from continual questioning, or questioning before warnings were given. Absent civil liability, there appeared to be little to lose and much to gain by going outside Miranda and gathering discrediting information, physical evidence, and other leads. In *California Attorneys for Criminal Justice v. Butts* (1999) and *Cooper v. Dupnik* (1992), however, the 9th Circuit Court found that questioning outside Miranda did impose civil liability on officers.

## RECENT SUPREME COURT DECISIONS

In May 2003, the Supreme Court, in a 5-to-4 decision, appeared to sanction questioning outside Miranda. Sgt. Chavez continued to question farmworker Martinez in the emergency room after another officer shot Martinez five times, blinding and maiming him, and after Martinez said twice that he did not want to talk and "I am not telling you anything until they treat me." No Miranda warnings were given. The Supreme Court decided that no constitutional issue was raised because Martinez was never prosecuted and his incriminating statements were never used against him at trial. It further found that Officer Chavez was not subject to civil liability for exceeding his official powers.

In June 2004, the Supreme Court decided the case of *Missouri v. Seibert*. This case directly addressed the legality of police questioning outside Miranda. In an amicus brief for Missouri, U.S. Solicitor General Olson claimed that the technique was necessary to win confessions from suspected terrorists. Seibert's defense attorney characterized this type of questioning as the "Missouri two-step." The arresting officer said he had learned the technique during his interrogation training, and it was standard procedure in his police department. An officer woke Seibert at 3 a.m. in her hospital bed. He had been specifically advised not to Mirandize her. He questioned her until she answered "yes" to a police suggestion of guilty of murder. After a 20-minute break, officers gave Seibert the Miranda warnings and asked her to say "yes" again to her guilt. The Court found, 5 to 4, that in most circumstances, the police may not question a suspect outside Miranda and then interrogate again after having given the Miranda warnings.

Another Miranda case was decided on the same day as *Seibert*. In *United States v. Pavane* (2004), the Court found, 5 to 4, an outside-Miranda piece of physical evidence, a gun, to be admissible. The police came to arrest Pavane in a domestic dispute and started to Mirandize him. He said he knew his rights and voluntarily told police where to find his pistol. As a previously convicted felon, Pavane's possession of a Glock was enough to convict him. The Pavane case followed the precedent set by the exception to *Miranda* in *Oregon v. Elstad:* Evidence obtained from an unwarned statement is itself admissible as evidence at trial.

A juvenile status case, *Yarborough v. Alvarado,* also decided 5 to 4 by the Court in June 2004, hinged on whether age and inexperience are factors in defining "in custody" for purposes of Miranda warnings. Alvarado, a 17-year-old, was questioned for 2 hours in the sheriff's office and convicted of second-degree murder and attempted robbery on the basis of the questioning. Alvarado was never told that he was under arrest, he was never Mirandized or offered counsel, and his parents were refused permission to be present. The Court's standard for "in custody" is "if a reasonable person would feel free to leave." The Court found that that standard did apply to Alvarado, despite his age and inexperience with the law.

Juvenile cases pending in the lower courts, addressing "in custody" in the principal's office or applying to younger juveniles, suggest that this may be the next arena of litigation about Miranda warnings.

## CONCLUSION

Forty years after that famous case, the Miranda warnings continue to be debated and interpreted. Detractors of *Miranda*'s constitutional claim note the exceptions created by subsequent cases and stress the warnings' prophylactic nature. Supporters of a firm constitutional basis for *Miranda* point out that practices promoting self-incrimination should be illegal at every step in the criminal justice process. It appears that *Miranda*'s meaning and the balance between competing views will continue to be decided case by case.

*Janice K. Dunham*

*See also* Arrest, Confessions, Evidence, Interrogation

### *For Further Reading*

Brown v. Mississippi, 297 U.S. 278 (1936).

California Attorneys for Criminal Justice v. Butts, 195 F.3d 1039 (9th Cir. 1999).

Chavez v. Martinez, 538 U.S. 760 (2003).

Cooper v. Dupnik, 963 F.2d 1220 (9th Cir. 1992) (en banc).

Dickerson v. United States, 530 U.S. 428 (2000).

Escobedo v. Illinois, 378 U.S. 478 (1964).

In re Gault, 387 U.S. 1 (1967).

Gideon v. Wainwright, 372 U.S. 335 (1963).

Harris v. New York, 401 U.S. 222 (1971).

Klein, S. R. (2003, April). No time for silence. *Texas Law Review, 81*, 1337–1360.

Leo, R. A., & Thomas, G. C., III. (Eds.). (1998). *The Miranda debate: Law, justice and policing.* Boston: Northeastern University Press.

Mapp v. Ohio, 367 U.S. 643 (1961).

Michigan v. Tucker, 417 U.S. 433 (1974).

Miranda v. Arizona, 384 U.S. 436 (1966).

Missouri v. Seibert, 2004 U. S.LEXIS 4578; 124 S. Ct. 2601 (2004).

New York v. Quarles, 467 U.S. 649 (1984).

Oregon v. Elstad, 470 U.S. 298 (1985).

*Questioning: "Outside Miranda."* [Video]. (1990). Anaheim, CA: Greg Gulen Productions.

Thomas, G. C., III, & Leo, R. A. (2002). The effects of Miranda v. Arizona: Embedded in our national culture? In M. Tonry (Ed.), *Crime and justice: A review of research* (Vol. 29, pp. 203–274). Chicago: University of Chicago Press.

United States v. Pavane, 2004 U. S. LEXIS 4577; 124 S. Ct. 2620 (2004).

United States v. Verdugo-Urquidez, 494 U.S. 259 (1990).

White, W. S. (2001). *Miranda's waning protections: Police interrogation practices after Dickerson.* Ann Arbor: University of Michigan Press.

Withrow v. Williams, 507 U.S. 680 (1993).

Yarborough v. Alvarado, 2004 U. S. LEXIS 3843; 124 S.Ct. 2140 (2004).

## ✑ MISDEMEANORS

Historically, under English common law, misdemeanors referred to all offenses except treason and felonies. Felonies were offenses requiring some forfeiture of a person's life and/or property. However, unlike felonies and treason, misdemeanor offenses could be further classified as either mala in se (wrong in themselves) or mala prohibita (wrong according to statute, but not wrong in themselves). Today, in the United States, misdemeanors remain less serious offenses than felonies, which usually require more than a year of incarceration in a prison or death, and more serious offenses than infractions, otherwise called "violations," which are punishable by a small fine and carry no right to a trial or the benefit of counsel.

The differences among all three are largely a matter of the sanctions involved. For misdemeanors, the sanction may include incarceration in a jail for no longer than a year or some combination of the following: probation, suspended sentence, mandatory classes, community service, limitations on the possession of firearms, or a fine (usually not more than $5,000). Examples of misdemeanors include disorderly conduct, prostitution, simple assault, writing bad checks, criminal trespass, driving without a seatbelt, drunk driving, indecent exposure, possessing obscene or indecent materials, vagrancy, destruction of public notices, resisting arrest, and petty theft.

Misdemeanors may be classified as either gross misdemeanors (carrying a jail sentence of 30 days to 1 year) or petty misdemeanors (carrying a sentence of up to 30 days in jail). Additionally, most states further classify misdemeanors in keeping with the following federal classifications:

Class A misdemeanor: up to a year incarcerated

Class B misdemeanor: 30 days to 6 months incarcerated

Class C misdemeanor: 5 days to 30 days incarcerated

For an arrest to occur immediately in a misdemeanor case, there is an in-presence requirement. This means that a law enforcement officer has to observe the offense or otherwise perceive it by any of his or her other four senses (touch, taste, smell, or hearing) before an arrest may be made (*Garske v. United States,* 1924). Otherwise, an arrest warrant would be required to proceed with a misdemeanor arrest. An exception to this would be some cases of domestic violence where state law might mandate arrest if a victim claims to have been victimized (misdemeanor offense) by a family member.

A misdemeanor arrest might also be the result of an officer acting on articulable or reasonable suspicion that an offense had been committed or was about to be committed based on a "totality of the circumstances" involved. Articulable or reasonable suspicion exists when, based on all of the facts of the circumstances, an experienced law enforcement officer would assume that the likelihood that an offense occurred, or was about to occur, was more than 50% or more than a mere "hunch" or slight suspicion, even though probable cause or actual evidence of the offense was not yet apparent. With such a likelihood, the officer is limited to investigating the situation with casual conversation, requesting to search the person or property, following the suspect and observing, or conducting a "stop and frisk." A "stop" is a "seizure" for investigative purposes whereby a "reasonable man" (or person) would not feel free to leave under the circumstances (*Florida v. Bostick,* 1991), and a "frisk" is a search limited to the outer parts of a person's clothing for the purpose of finding deadly weapons (*Terry v. Ohio,* 1968). If such actions on the part of the officer result in evidence of a crime, then probable cause exists, and an arrest may follow.

Unlike felony warrants, which permit officers to make arrests either day or night, misdemeanor warrants may restrict arrests to daylight hours only. The justification for using arrests sparingly in misdemeanor situations was because the threat of harm or destruction of evidence by such offenders has traditionally been considered to be low. In the 2001 *Atwater v. Lago Vista* case, the Supreme Court ruled that "if an officer has probable cause to believe that an individual has committed even a very minor offense in his presence, he may, without violating the Fourth Amendment, arrest the offender," thus reinforcing the in-presence arrest for misdemeanor offenses. In the *Atwater* decision, the Supreme Court also mentioned that even when the in-presence probable cause requirement is met, an arrest is not mandated by the U.S. Constitution, but it merely becomes an option for the law enforcement officer. As necessary for misdemeanor arrests, officers may also use force, but not more than that which is reasonable given the amount of resistance from the suspect. Also, a law enforcement officer may search a person who is about to be arrested for a misdemeanor offense according to the Supreme Court's ruling in *Chimel v. California* (1969). Of course, it is common practice in any arrest for an officer to identify him- or herself, followed by an announcement of the intention to arrest in the hope that this will reduce the likelihood of resistance.

When a person is arrested for a misdemeanor, that individual is often released soon thereafter until the charge must be answered in court. In misdemeanor cases, the charging document is usually called a complaint. It is common practice for the arresting or primary responding officer to write the complaint, which includes a detailed description of the circumstances of the offense and the next legally required action of the suspect. Individuals convicted of misdemeanors are called misdemeanants.

In recent times, many law enforcement agencies have adopted some form of the philosophy of

"Broken Windows." This way of dealing with crime has been said to follow the adage that "if you take care of the little things, the big things will take care of themselves." In that vein, police departments sometimes use their ability to make arrests or issue other sanctions for these less serious violations to improve the quality of life in a given area. Enforcing a misdemeanor offense has sometimes turned up offenders who are wanted for more serious crimes.

*Camille Gibson*

*See also* Arrests, "Broken Windows" or Incivilities Thesis, Police Discretion, Probable Cause

## For Further Reading

Adams, T. F. (2001). *Police field operations* (5th ed.). Upper Saddle River, NJ: Prentice Hall.

Atwater v. Lago Vista 532 U.S. 318 354 (2001).

Chimel v. California, 395 U.S. 752, 762–63 (1969).

Eldefonso, E., & Coffey, A. R. (1981). *Criminal law: History, philosophy, enforcement.* New York: Harper & Row.

Fagin, J. (2003). *Criminal justice.* Boston: Allyn & Bacon.

Florida v. Bostick, 501 U.S. 429 (1991).

Garske v. United States, 1 F.2d 620, 86th Cir. (1924).

Samaha, J. (1997). *Criminal justice.* St. Paul, MN: West.

Schmalleger, F. (2001). *Criminal justice today.* Upper Saddle River, NJ: Prentice Hall.

Senna, J., & Siegel, L. (1993). *Introduction to criminal justice.* St. Paul, MN: West.

Terry v. Ohio, 392 U.S. 1 (1968).

# ळ MISSING PERSONS INVESTIGATIONS

Historically, state criminal law has prohibited non-familial abduction and kidnapping, and the public has expected swift and aggressive investigation into such cases. The kidnapping and murder of the son of Charles A. Lindbergh in 1932 led to a federal statute, the Federal Kidnapping Act, which allowed U.S. Department of Justice intervention and prescribed severe penalties for transporting the victims of kidnapping across state or national boundaries.

According to the FBI, as of 2003, there were 97,297 active missing persons cases in the United States; the majority, 85%–90%, of these missing persons are juveniles. In roughly 725,000 cases, the disappearance of a child or adult was serious enough that it was reported to the police, the police took a report, and entered the report into the FBI's National Crime Information Center (NCIC). The NCIC is a nationwide information system that serves and supports local, state, and federal criminal justice agencies in all 50 states, the District of Columbia, the Commonwealth of Puerto Rico, the U.S. Virgin Islands, and Canada. According to the NCIC, a missing person is defined as (a) a person of any age who is missing and who is under proven physical/mental disability or is senile, thereby subjecting that person or others to personal and immediate danger; (b) a person of any age who is missing under circumstances indicating that the disappearance was not voluntary; (c) a person of any age who is missing under circumstances indicating that that person's physical safety may be in danger; (d) a person of any age who is missing after a catastrophe; or (e) a person who is missing and declared unemancipated as defined by the laws of the person's state of residence and does not meet any of the entry criteria presented in a–d.

The primary NCIC categories in which missing persons reports are entered are either "Juvenile," "Endangered" (adults and juveniles defined as missing and in the company of another person under circumstances indicating that his or her physical safety is in danger), or "Involuntary" (adults and juveniles missing under circumstances indicating that the disappearance was not voluntary). In addition, based on the identity of the perpetrator, there are three distinct types of kidnapping: family (49%), acquaintance (27%), or stranger (24%). Family kidnapping is committed primarily by parents, involves a larger percentage of female perpetrators than other types of kidnapping offenses, equally victimizes juveniles of both sexes, and most often originates in the home. Acquaintance kidnapping involves a comparatively high percentage of juvenile perpetrators, has the largest percentage of female and teenage victims, is more often associated with other crimes, occurs at homes and in residences, and has the highest percentage of injured victims. Stranger kidnapping victimizes more females than males, occurs primarily at outdoor locations, victimizes both teenagers and school-age children, is associated with sexual assaults in the case of girl victims and robberies in the case of boy victims, and is the type of kidnapping most likely to involve the use of a firearm.

In 1975, the FBI created a Missing Persons File within the NCIC database. Missing persons investigators acquired another resource when, 8 years later, NCIC established the Unidentified Person File. The records maintained in this file allowed law enforcement officers to compare information from their missing persons cases against descriptions of unidentified bodies from jurisdictions across the country. An enhancement in that resource was gained in 2000 with the passage of the Child Abuse and Prevention Enforcement Act, which included a provision called Jennifer's Law, a mechanism used in compiling all descriptive information on deceased, unidentified persons throughout the United States whose cases are entered into NCIC. In addition, Jennifer's Law provides incentives for public agencies and nonprofit organizations that develop or improve programs to (a) assist law enforcement and families in locating missing adults; (b) maintain a national, interconnected database for the purpose of tracking missing adults who are determined by law enforcement to be endangered because of age, diminished mental capacity, or the circumstances of disappearance, when foul play is suspected or circumstances are unknown; (c) maintain statistical information of adults reported as missing; (d) provide informational resources and referrals to families of missing adults; (e) assist in public notification and victim advocacy related to missing adults; and (f) establish and maintain a national clearinghouse for missing adults.

In addition to the NCIC, the FBI, in collaboration with the Bureau of Justice Statistics, is replacing its Uniform Crime Reports with a more comprehensive National Incident-Based Reporting System (NIBRS), which collects detailed information on crimes known to the police. One of the improvements introduced by NIBRS is the inclusion of specific data on kidnapping. NIBRS will enable law enforcement and the criminal justice community to learn more about the nature and extent of this crime.

Whereas data storage collection occurs at the national level, investigations of missing persons often falls to local police agencies. Agencies must take into consideration age, mental abilities, the length of time the person has been missing, and other criteria when determining whether or not an investigation is initiated and how intensive that investigation will be. Jurisdictions that have heavy case loads for other criminal activities often do not have the resources to equally address every report of a missing person. Some police observers maintain that more attention to missing persons can turn up serial killers sooner in their criminal careers. In the case of abducted children, the age of which is usually determined by the state, a nationwide Amber Alert system has been implemented that alerts the public of the abduction through television, radio, the Internet, highway signs, and other media.

*Deborah L. Sawers*

*See also* Child Abduction Investigations, Serial Murder Investigations

## For Further Reading

Finkelhor, D., & Ormrod, R. (2000, June). Kidnapping of juveniles: Patterns from NIBRS. *Juvenile Justice Bulletin.* Available: http://www.ncjrs.org/html/ojjdp/2000_6_2/contents.html

42 U.S.C. 14665 (2000).

http://www.fbi.gov/hq/cjisd/ncic.htm

## ✂ MOLLEN COMMISSION, THE

The Mollen Commission was established by then-New York City Mayor David N. Dinkins in 1992 to investigate alleged police corruption in several New York Police Department (NYPD) precincts after an NYPD officer named Michael Dowd, along with five other officers, was arrested in the suburban area where he lived by Suffolk County Police for trafficking illegal narcotics inside and outside of New York City. The Mollen Commission, empowered by a mayoral executive order, was a panel of investigators comprised mainly of attorneys that was independent of the New York City government and the NYPD.

The Mollen Commission was named after the chairperson, Milton Mollen, who was a deputy mayor in New York City and a retired New York State appellate judge. The Mollen Commission held publicly televised hearings in September and October 1993 that detailed corrupt activities related mainly to illegal narcotics, falsifying police testimony, and excessive use of force. (These tapes are now located at the Lloyd George Sealy Library at John Jay College of Criminal Justice.) Most of the police officers involved and arrested as a result of the corrupt activities were front-line patrol officers working in patrol units in one of the city's most troubled areas. After the hearings, the Mollen Commission published a final report in July 1994. The Commission concluded that the corrupt activities were the result of corruption-prone opportunities from the sudden influx of crack cocaine and the decentralized anticorruption units of the NYPD. The Mollen Commission did not find that corruption was systemic in the NYPD, as had previous corruption investigations of the NYPD, such as the Knapp Commission. The Mollen Commission found that corrupt activities were the actions of a "crew" operation; a small group of police officers usually working the same assignment and during the same work hours. The Mollen Commission made 139 recommendations related to police personnel matters such as selection and recruitment; improvement of hiring standards; modification of internal investigation procedures; and creation of a permanent, independent commission to investigate police misconduct.

The enormity of New York City, the size of the NYPD, and New York City's preeminence as the media capital of the world intensified the scrutiny of the NYPD and the NYPD's police officers. The NYPD, as a formal police agency, was chartered and centralized in 1844. Early NYPD "patrolmen," as they were known then, were appointed at the request of local ward politicians and were expected to protect the illegal rackets of the ward politician who appointed the patrolmen, particularly the vice rackets, which, at that time, consisted mainly of selling alcohol illegally and prostitution-related criminal activity. One of the earliest police reformers in New York City,

future president Theodore Roosevelt, was the police commissioner of New York City. Roosevelt, along with a reform-minded clergy official, Charles Henry Parkhurst, initiated the Lexow Committee to investigate police corruption in New York City. According to the Lexow Committee's findings, police corruption in New York City was firmly enmeshed in local government politics. Other commissions that investigated police misconduct in the NYPD followed in 1913, 1930, and 1950.

The Knapp Commission commenced in 1971 to investigate corruption in the NYPD, and reforms recommended during that time perhaps ended systemic police corruption in the NYPD as detailed in the Knapp Commission investigation. One of the principal witnesses in the Knapp Commission investigation was Detective Frank Serpico, whose frustrating endeavors to alert authorities about police misconduct in the NYPD led to drastic changes in the NYPD's internal investigation procedures, including an expansion of internal affairs units and the creation of new field internal affairs units.

At the time, New York City was enduring an illegal street narcotics trade (mainly of heroin) that led to the corrupt activities detailed in the Knapp Commission investigation. The Commission found that corrupt NYPD police officers were collecting "protection money" and being on "the pad," which were terms used to describe bribes from criminals to ensure that their illicit activities could continue without the threat of being investigated or arrested by the police. Many of the criminals involved in bribing police officers prior to the Knapp Commission were involved in vice crime rackets, such as prostitution and gambling. However, the Knapp Commission and subsequent investigations found that the easy flow of currency involved in the illicit narcotics trade afforded new corruption opportunities. The advent of the street crack-cocaine trade in New York City in the 1980s afforded even more opportunities. The corrupt activities consisted of police officers stealing narcotics and cash from narcotics dealers, and in some cases, protecting the illegal narcotic activities. The Mollen Commission found that these corrupt activities were limited to only a few precincts. But it was the level of violence and brutality used in shaking down drug dealers that many found particularly troubling—a phenomenon that had appeared elsewhere in the country (Miami's River Cops in the late 1980s) and would continue to appear (Los Angeles's Rampart Division in the late 1990s). For instance, during the Mollen Commission's hearings, ex-officer Bernard Cawley, known on the street as The Mechanic because he administered tune-ups, was found to have beaten about 300 drug dealers with lead-filled gloves, batons, heavy flashlights, or any other blunt object in order to extort them.

The arrest of Michael Dowd on May 6, 1992, began the initial stages that led to the development of the Mollen Commission. Dowd was working as a patrol officer in New York City. Police investigators from the suburban New York City area of Suffolk County, where Dowd lived, were investigating a narcotics trafficking ring when they monitored Dowd on a wiretap arranging illegal narcotics deals. Dowd had been under investigation by NYPD Internal Affairs investigators for several years prior to his arrest by Suffolk County prosecutors, but Dowd had managed to continually eludes investigators and serious disciplinary actions.

Just as the Knapp Commission had Serpico, the Mollen Commission had Sgt. Joseph Trimboli, who went to the press shortly after Dowd's arrest. Trimboli had been investigating Dowd's corrupt activities for 4 years and had developed a 50,000-word case file—some of which came from anonymous tips made by officers who felt that they could not report elsewhere in the organization. Trimboli, who had been working in Internal Affairs, reported that his investigation was routinely obstructed and stymied by Internal Affairs and that he was ordered to close all his active files on Dowd's investigation, as well as others, in 1990, 2 years before Dowd was arrested as a result of an independent investigation in Suffolk County. Although the arrest received a good deal of news coverage, it was the series of newspaper articles by now-deceased journalist Michael McAlary that detailed the police department's reluctance to deal with reports of corruption and that in turn led to political will for the formation of the Mollen Commission.

After Dowd's arrest, Mayor Dinkins enacted Executive Order Number 42 on July 24, 1992, to create the Mollen Commission. Executive Order Number 42 had three mandates: Evaluate the current Internal Affairs investigating procedures of the NYPD, make recommendations on improving current procedures, and obtain evidence by holding public and private hearings. Executive Order Number 42 also granted the Mollen Commission subpoena power, meaning that it could compel witnesses to appear at the public and private hearings. The Mollen Commission reviewed numerous NYPD personnel and corruption investigation files. One of the Mollen Commission's findings was that excessive force used by police officers is perhaps linked to police corruption involving narcotics because of the evolving violent characteristics of the narcotics trade. One of the Mollen Commission's primary witnesses was Dowd. He agreed to testify as a witness before the Mollen Commission in exchange for possible considerations at his sentencing. Eventually, he was sentenced to 15 years but received a 1-year reduction in his sentence for his crimes. Five other police officers accused of corruption cooperated with Mollen Commission staff to assist them in their investigation.

Among the findings of the Commission were that the department had abandoned its responsibility to ensure integrity and had failed to address aspects of police culture that fostered corruption, command accountability had collapsed, Internal Affairs had abandoned its mission, and integrity training was neglected at both recruit and inservice levels.

The NYPD has instituted many of the recommendations of the Mollen Commission, including raising hiring standards such as increasing the minimum appointment age, requiring at least 2 years of college education or military service, extending probationary periods for new police officers, and other integrity enhancement training procedures. It revamped its Internal Affairs unit, which now acts proactively as well as reactively to corruption and other police wrongdoing and has been used as a model for other police departments around the country. One of the principal recommendations of the

Mollen Commission was to establish a permanent, independent oversight agency to continually investigate police misconduct. This recommendation eventually became the subject of political wrangling, but another former New York City mayor, Rudolf Giuliani, created The Commission to Combat Police Corruption through issuance of an executive order in 1995.

*Joe Pascarella*

## For Further Reading

Baer, H., & Armao, J. P. (1995). The Mollen Commission report: An overview. *New York Law School Law Review, 40*, 73–94.

City of New York. (1994). The City of New York Commission to Investigate Allegations of Police Corruption and the Anti-Corruption Procedures of the Police Department, Milton Mollen, Chair. *Commission Report.* July 4, 1994.

Dodenhoff, P. (1993). LEN salutes its 1993 Man of the Year, Sgt. Joseph Trimboli of the New York Police Department. *Law Enforcement News, 19*(392).

Jeffers, H. P. (1994). *Commissioner Roosevelt: The story of Theodore Roosevelt and the New York City police, 1895–1897.* New York: Wiley.

Knapp, W. (1973). *Report of the New York City Commission to investigate allegations of police corruption and the city's anti-corruption procedures.* New York: George Braziller.

Mayor's Office of New York City. (2003). *Commission to Combat Police Corruption.* Retrieved February 25, 2003, from http://nyc.gov/html/ccpc/html/about.html

McAlary, M. (1994). *Good cop, bad cop: Detective Joe Trimboli's heroic pursuit of NYPD Officer Michael Dowd.* New York: Pocket.

New York Legislature, Senate Committee on the Police Department of the City of New York. (1895). *Report and Proceedings of the Senate Committee appointed to investigate the Police Department of the City of New York.* Albany: New York State Printer.

Parkhurst, Charles Henry. (2003). In *Columbia encyclopedia.* Retrieved February 19, 2003, from http://encyclopedia.com/html/p/parkhurs.asp

## ᗷ MORALE

Morale is the sum total of an individual's feelings or attitudes with regard to his or her work or membership in a group or organization. The two primary components of morale are job satisfaction and organizational commitment. An individual's satisfaction with his or her job is task oriented and an important part of morale. Organizational commitment is reflected in allegiance to and belief in a group or collective above the individual. Research on morale in law enforcement has generally focused on the causes and consequences of low morale. Low morale has been linked to high staff turnover, low organizational commitment, poor job performance, low job satisfaction, and unethical decision making.

The susceptibility of police officers to low morale and its consequences has been a focus of study within law enforcement since the early 1960s. Early research attributed the prevalence of low morale to the very nature of policing. Police work was seen as placing the officer in an inherently antagonistic relationship with the public. Low morale was the product of negative feedback from hostile citizens and the perception that the public did not support the police. This led to an officer's alienation from society and the police management, which was, in turn, beholden to that larger society. Police administrators were viewed as having little power to influence the incompatible goals that society sets or to alleviate the inevitable hostility that comes with police interaction with the public. As a result, management was seen as having a very limited ability to affect officer morale.

The effect of perceived public hostility on morale outweighs the effects of organizational factors. Low morale was seen by some as the root cause of many police problems, such as corruption and brutality. An individual officer's low morale increased his or her alienation from society and contributed to the creation of a police subculture, a subculture based on an insular police fraternity that viewed the public as hostile. However, many of these studies were conducted 30 to 35 years ago, and the deep enmity between police and citizens they described has not been found in more recent research.

More recent research has reached different conclusions as to the main source of poor officer morale. Low police morale emerges as a symptom of particular management problems in the organization and not as endemic to police work in general. Surveys of officers found a link between low morale and the organizational context of policing, rather than general public hostility. In particular, the perceived lack of organizational support was an issue repeatedly raised in the various studies of police morale. Officers viewed police administration, not the public, in an adversarial light. The police organization, and not perceptions of a lack of public support, emerged as the key factor in the creation and maintenance of morale.

This was a very important distinction, because the ability to improve police officer morale was dependent on the causes of low morale. If the primary source of low morale was organizational issues, then police management could have an immediate effect on officer morale levels through administrative reforms. However, if the chief cause of low police morale were an adversarial relationship between the public and the police, something almost inherent in police work, then organizational changes would have little impact on morale levels. A fundamental transformation of the nature of police work would be needed, something beyond the ability of police management.

Although the potential consequences of low morale within police departments have been difficult to quantify, a number of problems confronting police organizations have been linked to demoralization. Low morale linked to dissatisfaction with the bureaucratic system, such as administrative policies, procedures, and management, was the primary motivator in officers' decision to resign from departments in both Australia and the United States. Also, ample anecdotal evidence exists in officers' personal accounts of the effects of low morale. Demoralization led to the failure to look for crime or the adoption of a deliberate strategy of crime avoidance and intentional inefficiency. Moreover, a number of police departments, following morale-damaging incidents, experienced significant declines in enforcement efforts and an increase in the crime rate. However, an exact correlation between officer morale and crime-fighting performance has not been proven. In addition, departments with a demoralized rank and file have historically been plagued with corruption scandals. Police integrity depends heavily on the organizational culture and the degree of commitment an officer has to his or her department.

There are divergent opinions regarding the effect of personal attributes on morale. Various researchers have reported evidence that shows an officer's race and gender have both influenced morale and had little effect on it. Tenure in a police force consistently has been found to have a strong and inverse relationship to morale: As an officer's years of service increased and his or her career progressed, his or her morale and commitment to the organization underwent steady erosion. This developmental pattern has been found to be unique to police organizations and consistent across different countries.

*John Brendan McAndrew*

## For Further Reading

Golembiewki, R., & Byong-Seob, K. (1990). Burnout in police work: Stressors, strain, and the phase model. *Police Studies, 13*(2), 74–80.

Gould, L. (2000). A longitudinal approach to the study of the police personality: Race/gender differences. *Journal of Police and Criminal Psychology, 15*(2), 41.

Kohan, A., & Mazmanian, D. (2003). Police work, burnout, and pro-organizational behavior: A consideration of daily work experiences. *Criminal Justice and Behavior, 30*(5), 559–583.

Paoline, E., III. (2001). *Rethinking police culture: Officers' occupational attitudes*. New York: LFB.

Zhang, S., & Benson, T. (1997). Cost-effectiveness and officer morale of a personally assigned patrol vehicle program: A comparative analysis. Policing, 20(4), 749–765.

## ∽ MUNICIPAL POLICING

The concept of municipal policing is the backbone of public safety and order maintenance in Western democracies. Local control of government services is a core value in free societies. Conversely, in nondemocratic countries, policing generally falls to the military. Military systems support the prevailing order of the day, whereas municipal policing upholds laws, justice, and the social values of communities. Municipalities are primarily urban political units having corporate status and, usually, powers of self-government. Police forces are made up of trained officers entrusted by a government with maintenance of public peace and order, enforcement of laws, and prevention and detection of crime. Contemporary municipal police departments operating in democratic societies are, for the most part, publicly financed, publicly accountable, paramilitary in structure and appearance, bureaucratic, and on duty 24 hours a day. Most police agencies are organized functionally into line (patrol and investigative operations), staff, and support functions. Departments are led by a police chief or police commissioner with subordinate positions designated by military-style rank, such as major, captain, lieutenant, sergeant, and corporal.

Municipal policing in the United States dates from colonial times. In 1636, the city of Boston established a Night Watch. All males over the age of 18 were required to serve when called upon. In 1651, New York City took a similar approach with its Shout and Rattle Watch. The rattle was an actual rattle, used to sound the alarm by a rattle watcher. By the turn of the 18th century, large cities like Philadelphia found it necessary to divide the city into 10 nighttime patrol areas in order to maintain order. Each patrol area was manned by a constable, who recruited citizen volunteers to keep watch with him.

Early in the 19th century, the developing British system of policing became a major influence on the fledgling American policing system. In 1829, British Home Secretary Sir Robert Peel launched a public civil police force in England with the introduction of the Metropolitan Police Act. The act established a Police Office, administered by commissioners in charge of planning and creating the Metropolitan Police District, staffed by paid constables. Peel believed that "the police are the people and the people are the police." His model of a police department providing police service integrated into the daily life of communities spread to the United States. By 1833, Philadelphia had organized an independent, 24-hour-a-day police force. By 1844, New York City had two police forces, daytime duty and the night watch. During this period, known as the Spoils Period, police departments were headed by police chiefs who were appointed and accountable to political bosses. Officers were hired to pay off political debts, and corruption was commonplace.

In the almost 100 years between the Revolutionary and Civil Wars, the rapid growth of population and industrialization in America mandated the further development of municipal police departments. Municipal policing evolved from the Spoils Period into the Political Era (1833–1928). This era saw control of the police by political bosses who wanted to maintain the political status quo, control crime and disorder, and give broad social services to those in political favor. The Traditional Era (1929–1970s) was marked by the advent of hierarchical, bureaucratic, centralized command. This traditional or professional era saw the development of municipal police responding to calls channeled through a central dispatch. The 9-1-1 system was implemented and the practice of patrolling beats in cars expanded. The 1980s ushered in the current Community Policing era. This policing philosophy emerged out of the civil rights movement of the 1950s and 1960s and in response to a rising tide of crime in the 1970s and 1980s. Connected to the issue of civil rights was the ongoing mistrust between a significant number of minority citizens and their local police. The widespread perception that the police are routinely guilty of bias in how they treat racial minorities and a concurrent rise in drug crimes and related violence presented municipal police forces with challenges to the delivery of police services. Community and police leadership responded by bringing together the elements of community partnerships, collaborative problem solving, and police organizational change to improve the quality of municipal police service. The result has been an emphasis on a more proactive police response to crime, a focus on reducing racially biased policing, and an increase in the number of racial minorities and women in police service. During this period, and as part of this movement, problem-oriented policing was also developed whereby police would focus on specific problems and develop, sometimes in concert with the community and other service providers, a plan for mitigating or eliminating the problem.

Community policing is a collaborative effort between the police and the community that identifies problems of crime and disorder and involves all elements of the community in the search for solutions to these problems. It is founded on close, mutually beneficial ties between police and community members. Two thirds of all local police departments have full-time sworn personnel engaged in community policing activities. These local police departments have an estimated 102,598 full-time sworn personnel serving as community police officers or otherwise regularly engaged in community policing activities.

Today, municipalities manage 13,353 police agencies employing 441,000 sworn officers and 293,823 civilians. A majority of these agencies (72%) serve communities with populations of 50,000 or less. During the year 2000, these local governments spent more than $50 billion on employment contracts to provide police services.

Contemporary police leaders of municipal police agencies are able to point to a number of positive changes in the administration and delivery of police services. These changes—the advent of community and problem-oriented policing, integration of new technology, improvement in education and training of officers, and creation and implementation of higher professional standards—all spring from municipalities that are committed to the provision of public safety by local government.

*Drew Diamond*

***See also*** Community Policing, Problem-Oriented Policing

## For Further Reading

Diamond, D., Fridell, L., Lunney, R., & Kubu, B. (2001). *Racially biased policing: A principled response.* Washington, DC: Police Executive Research Forum

Geller, W., & Stephens, D. (Eds.). (2003). *Local government police management* (4th ed.). Washington, DC: International City/County Management Association

Trojanowicz, R., & Bucqueroux, B. (1990). *Community policing: A contemporary perspective.* Cincinnati, OH: Anderson.

# N

## NATIONAL CRIME VICTIMIZATION SURVEY

Victimization surveys yield estimates of how many individuals and households are touched by crimes of violence and theft each year, and of the extent and seriousness of the financial losses and physical injuries these people experience. An International Crime Victims Survey has been translated into many languages and is being administered in countries across the globe. In the United States in 1966, the President's Commission on Law Enforcement and the Administration of Justice commissioned the first large-scale survey about criminal victimization because of scientific skepticism about the accuracy of crime statistics maintained by law enforcement agencies and forwarded to the Federal Bureau of Investigation (FBI) for compilation in its annual nationwide Uniform Crime Report (UCR). As anticipated, a sizable percentage of the individuals from all walks of life in the sample who told interviewers that they had been harmed by offenders acknowledged that they had not reported the incident to the police. The reporting rate varied substantially by the characteristics of the victim, the type of crime, and the degree of seriousness of their injuries and losses. This confirmation of the existence of a "dark figure" of unreported crimes underscored the importance of routinizing this alternative method of measuring patterns and trends in crime rates. Ever since 1973, the U.S. Census Bureau, on behalf of the U.S. Department of Justice, has been interviewing members of the general public about their misfortunes. Until 1992, the undertaking was known as the National Crime Survey (NCS). It was renamed the National Crime Victimization Survey (NCVS) in 1992 after some questions and procedures were revised.

NCVS interviewers administer to respondents a questionnaire that can run more than 20 pages long. The questioning begins with a series of screening items such as, "During the last 6 months, did anyone steal or attempt to steal your vehicle?" If the respondent answers "yes," follow-up questions are asked to collect details about the incident. The questionnaire focuses on three types of interpersonal violence (forcible rapes and other sexual assaults, armed and unarmed robberies, and simple and aggravated assaults). Interviewers also inquire about two kinds of theft against people (personal larceny with and without contact) and three types of stealing directed at a household's possessions (burglary, larceny by nonintruders, and motor vehicle theft). Because the survey is geared toward uncovering the suffering of individuals 12 years old or older and the losses experienced by entire households, criminal acts committed against children (e.g., molestations and physical abuse) and against businesses (e.g., commercial robberies and burglaries) are not probed. The list of offenses analyzed in the NCVS is not exhaustive and excludes kidnapping, property damage due to vandalism or arson, and identity theft and other swindles.

The completed survey provides a great deal of data about attempted as well as completed crimes of violence and theft. Interviewers record details about the location and time of the incidents; the extent of any physical injuries or financial losses; descriptions of the perpetrators; and the weapons that were used (firearms, knives, and other types), if any. Victims willing to disclose their misfortunes are asked whether their attackers were complete strangers or nonstrangers (acquaintances, friends, family members, even intimates), and to cite the reasons why they filed a complaint or chose not to report the incident to the police. Interviewers note the age, sex, race (white, black, other), and ethnicity (Hispanic, Asian, other) of all respondents; their marital status, educational attainment, and income level; and whether they own or rent their home. The survey yields victimization rates per 1,000 individuals or households per year. Geographically, rates are projected for four regions of the country (Northeast, Midwest, West, and South) and three residential settings (urban, suburban, or rural areas), but the size of the sample does not permit estimates of victimization rates to be derived for specific cities, counties, or states.

The NCVS has been revised over the years. Questions were added about how the victim behaved while under attack (self-protective measures), what the victim was doing when trouble struck, whether the offender seemed high on drugs or alcohol at the time of the crime, and what contacts victims had with criminal justice system officials. Some questions were reworded to provide cues that could help jog victims' memories about events and details, especially about sexual assaults and domestic violence. Although not on an ongoing basis, questions have also been added to ascertain the level of interaction with police and whether force was involved. However, in order to cut costs, the size of the sample has been trimmed down over the decades to roughly 42,000 housing units with about 76,000 respondents in 2002 (out of roughly 232 million Americans over the age of 11). Phone interviews assisted by computerized prompts increasingly substitute for expensive, time-consuming, face-to-face home visits. The response rate (proportion of people contacted who were willing to participate) was about 87%.

Victimization surveys have several limitations and suffer from certain sources of inaccuracies. Estimates and projections derived from samples must be interpreted as having a margin of error and are reliable only to the extent that the national sample is unbiased and truly representative of the population of the whole country. Because the NCVS is household-based, it might fail to fully capture the experiences of transients or people who wish to keep a low profile. Underestimates persist if respondents remain reluctant to disclose incidents to interviewers that they also refused to bring to the attention of the police. Forgetfulness ("memory decay") also results in information losses, especially about minor offenses that did not inflict serious injuries or major expenses. But overestimates of actual rates can occur as well because of forward telescoping, or the tendency to believe that an incident took place more recently than it really did. Also, NCVS interviewers tend to accept at face value accounts of incidents that seem unlikely or exaggerated and that experienced detectives could exclude from police recordkeeping as "unfounded."

Each year, the overwhelming majority of respondents answer that they have not been victims of street crimes during the time period in question. For example, the estimated U.S. robbery rate in 2002 was 2 victims for every 1,000 individuals. However, certain groupings (based on age, gender, race, class, and geographical location) face dramatically different risks of being harmed than do others. Over the past decade, the nationwide trend generally has been downward across the board. By the early years of the 21st century, the rates of interpersonal violence and property crime victimization were the lowest recorded by NCVS interviewers since the survey's inception in 1973.

*Andrew Karmen*

*See also* Crime Statistics and Analysis; Homicide Trends in the United States; National Incident-Based Reporting System (NIBRS); Uniform Crime Reports; Victims, Police Response to

*For Further Reading*

Karmen, A. (2004). *Crime victims: An introduction to victimology* (5th ed.). Belmont, CA: Wadsworth/Thomson.

O'Brien, R. (2000). Crime facts: Victim and offender data. In J. Sheley (Ed.), *Criminology: A contemporary handbook* (3rd ed., pp. 59–83). Belmont, CA: Wadsworth/Thomson.

Rennison, C., & Rand, M. (2003). *Criminal victimization, 2002.* Washington, DC: Bureau of Justice Statistics.

## NATIONAL GUARD

The National Guard is a military organization staffed by part-time members who are trained to supplement the active military. On occasion, the National Guard has been called to active service to assist the civil authorities in cases of natural disasters or riot situations. The United States has a long history of not using the military to enforce the law or to police the civilian community. This tradition was codified with the passage of the Posse Comitatus Act of 1878 (18 U.S.C. 1385), which ended the use of the military in policing southern states during the Reconstruction Era. However, the Act allows for the military to assist civil authorities in the case of emergency situations in which local or state governments are unable to deal with a problem. The National Guard is the military unit most often called to assist in these emergency situations.

The National Guard represents one of the branches of the U.S. military and is the oldest established military organization in the country. Organized on a state level and under the control of the state governors in peacetime, National Guard units are affiliated with the Army and Air Force. Some states also have a naval militia. A New York militia unit adopted the term "National Guard" in 1824 during the visit of the Revolutionary War hero the Marquis de Lafayette, who had commanded a Paris militia unit, *Guarde Nationale*. The term became popular and was used to describe state-sponsored militia units. The U.S. military also has

reserve components of the various branches of the armed forces that are not under the control of state governments and can be called to active duty only by the federal government.

The National Guard is a continuation of the citizen militia, which was first formed in colonial America. In 1620, the Massachusetts Bay Colony organized an armed citizen militia under the leadership of Captain Miles Standish to defend against attacks by Native Americans. Other colonies organized militia units for local area defense, and these units were called to active duty in the various wars against Native Americans and in the French and Indian War of 1754–1763. The Revolutionary War also was heavily dependent on militia units. After the Revolutionary War, the temporary nature of militia service forced the U.S. Congress to establish a regular Army on September 29, 1789. The small regular Army, however, still depended on the support of the more numerous militia units. In 1792, Congress enacted legislation to require states to establish militia companies organized into regiments, brigades, and divisions under the civilian leadership from within the military districts. The militia was to be supported by state funds when not on federal service. Many militia units often existed only on paper, with members reporting once a year for a muster. The militia served as more of a possible manpower pool rather than a prepared military force. However, some units organized themselves into voluntary units known as the Organized Militia. These units were equipped with uniforms, weapons, and military equipment, which was financed by the state government or purchased by the militia members.

During the last quarter of the 19th century, some elements of the establishment began to view with alarm the wave of new immigrants from southern and eastern Europe. The increasing militancy of labor resulted in a feeling that labor and the new immigrants were anti-American and were a threat to the American way of life.

Support for the National Guard came from industrialists, who could not always depend on the support or ability of small local police agencies. Some critics of the National Guard viewed it as becoming a constabulary or industrial army to control the labor movement. Between 1879 and 1900, industrialists funded the Pennsylvania National Guard. Armories, weapons, and equipment were often paid for by private funds. The Pennsylvania Railroad transported the entire National Guard division to the inauguration of James A. Garfield and financed the first summer training session of the Guard in 1880.

In 1877, the National Guard began to be used in labor disputes to suppress striking workers. A nationwide railroad strike caused the mobilization of 45,000 National Guard troops in 11 states and led to a period of industrial warfare. The entire Pennsylvania National Guard, augmented by private armies organized by the railroads, steel mills, and mine operators, was called to put down the strike. During the railroad strike of 1877, 100 strikers lost their lives in battles with the National Guard and private industrial armies. Between the end of the Civil War and 1906, National Guard units were used in 156 instances to suppress strikes, often with fatal consequences. The use of National Guard units resulted in civilian deaths in Milwaukee strikes in 1886, the Homestead strike of Carnegie Steel in 1892, and the Pullman Sleeping Car strike in 1894. Perhaps the worst disaster occurred in April 1914, when 20 men, women, and children were killed during the Ludlow, Colorado, mining strike. The National Guard unit on the scene fired into a tent encampment of miners striking against the Colorado Fuel and Iron Corporation, owned by the Rockefeller family.

Labor criticism of the National Guard and recruiting difficulties forced states to attempt to replace the policing duties of the Guard with a state police. Pennsylvania established a state police department in 1905, and most industrialized states began state police departments after World War I.

However, the National Guard is still called to support local police during social disorder. In August 1965, the governor of California called up the Guard when the local police could not control racial rioting in Watts. In 1966, racial riots in Chicago, Cleveland, Dayton, and Milwaukee required the use of the National Guard to support the local police. During the turbulent years of the Vietnam War, protests led to situations that could not be controlled by local police, and the Guard was called to assist. In a tragic incident in 1970 at Kent State University in Ohio, the Guard fired at rioters and killed four students. Critics of the use of the National Guard to assist in policing the civilian population stress the lack of training of Guard personnel in riot control and the use of inappropriate weapons that are more suited to the battlefield than policing. In a more recent example, the Guard was called up in California to help local authorities deal with riots that occurred in the 1992 acquittals of four white officers accused of beating Rodney King. But perhaps the most extensive use of the National Guard was during the aftermath of the September 11, 2001, terrorist attacks, when the Guard assisted law enforcement in guarding sensitive areas.

*Hugh E. O'Rourke*

**See also** State Police

*For Further Reading*

Collins, R. F. (1989). *America at its best: Opportunities in the National Guard.* New York: Rosen.

Cooper, J. (1997). *The rise of the National Guard: The evolution of the American militia, 1865–1920.* Lincoln: University of Nebraska Press.

Dupry, R. E. (1971). *The National Guard: A compact history.* New York: Hawthorne.

Hill, J. D. (1964). *The minute man in peace and war: A history of the National Guard.* Harrisburg, PA: Stackpole.

Mahon, J. K. (1983). *History of the militia and the National Guard.* New York: Macmillan.

## ❧ NATIONAL INCIDENT-BASED REPORTING SYSTEM (NIBRS)

There is a prevailing belief that the advancement of efficient and effective criminal justice policy requires an accurate picture of crime. The primary tool for assessing crime in America has been the FBI's Uniform Crime Reports (UCR) since its inception during the 1930s. Criticism of the UCR began almost as soon as the program began. One of the most frequent concerns was how crimes were counted. The original purpose of the UCR was to provide a basis for comparison. This led to a measure of crime that, although it provided an easily comparable set of indexes, failed to provide in-depth information about specific incidents of crime that would be extremely useful to theorists, researchers, and the police themselves.

In an effort to bridge some of the gaps in the crime data, the FBI has attempted to broaden the utility of America's crime data with the implementation of the National Incident-Based Reporting System (NIBRS). The thrust of NIBRS is to replace the UCR summary system with an incident-based system, which will provide detail about the circumstances surrounding crimes. Whereas the UCR provided little more than frequency counts, the NIBRS system provides many details on each criminal incident. The ability to accurately identify when and where crime takes place and the characteristics of its victims and perpetrators is seen by many as an invaluable weapon in the war on crime. NIBRS data can be summarized easily to produce the types of indexes available with the UCR, but allow for much more detailed analyses. Of special interest to social scientists and policymakers is the ability to conduct detailed crime analyses within and across law enforcement jurisdictions. Regional law enforcement agencies can share information more easily, and strategic and tactical crime analyses can be made at the local and regional levels. Such data are essential to understanding the root causes of crime and to allocating resources to address crime problems. NIBRS data, because it contains information about the location of offenses, can be used with innovative crime-mapping technologies. Such maps are useful for identifying hot spots of crime, evaluating the effectiveness of strategic decision making, and looking for interactions between crime and other variables that have a known spatial component.

The transition from summary data collection to incident-based data is not complete at the national level. The FBI began accepting crime data in the NIBRS format in 1989, expecting national compliance by 1999. As of 2004, only 22 state-reporting programs were compliant. Although participation in the NIBRS program grows steadily, data are still not pervasive enough to make broad generalizations about crime in the United States. Poor coverage remains the biggest problem with NIBRS. However, several studies have demonstrated the value of NIBRS data. This growing number of research reports provides support for the argument that NIBRS is worth the effort and expense involved in its full implementation.

## INFORMATION COLLECTED IN NIBRS

Incident-based reporting systems involve comprehensive data collection at the incident level on various aspects of reported criminal incidents: location, offenses, offenders, victims, and arrestees. An important advantage of NIBRS over the UCR is that NIBRS records and counts all offenses, not just the most serious offense, as with the hierarchy rule used with the UCR.

NIBRS provides more categories of offenses than does the UCR. Crimes reported in NIBRS are divided into two categories: Group A offenses, which consist of 22 serious offenses, and Group B offenses, which consist of 11 lesser offenses. Group A offenses are arson, assault offenses, bribery, burglary/breaking and entering, counterfeiting/forgery, destruction/damage/vandalism of property, drug offenses, embezzlement, extortion/blackmail, fraud offenses, gambling offenses, homicide offenses, kidnapping/abduction, larceny/theft offenses, motor vehicle theft, pornography, prostitution, robbery, forcible sex offenses, nonforcible sex offenses, stolen property offenses, and weapons law violations. Group B offenses, those for which only arrest data are reported, are bad checks, curfew/loitering/vagrancy violations, disorderly conduct, driving under the influence, drunkenness, nonviolent family offenses, liquor law violations, Peeping Tom offenses, runaways, trespassing, and a generic "all other offenses" category. (One of the early criticisms of NIBRS is that it lacks specific classifications for domestic violence.)

## PROBLEMS IN IMPLEMENTING NIBRS

Because the data for NIBRS are more detailed than those in the traditional UCR system, local agencies must do more data entry and processing. State and local agencies must use their own incident-based reporting systems and translate their data into the NIBRS format before submitting it to the FBI.

As with the UCR, the quality of the data provided to the FBI is uneven. Insofar as the FBI is concerned, participation in both the UCR and NIBRS is voluntary. Some states have enacted legislation that requires agencies to report data to the FBI or to a state agency that reports aggregate data for that state to the FBI. These measures, however, are often not well enforced. Other problems are technical in nature. Software and other problems have prevented some agencies from sending NIBRS data to the FBI.

Another critical concern is the lack of human and technical resources within many departments. Translation of paper-based incident reports into computer code is a tedious and time-consuming process that is prone to error. A more efficient method has been to ensure that local law enforcement agencies have the necessary technology and training to use incident-based systems on the departmental level. This has proven to be impossible for many small agencies that cannot spare the funds or the personnel to develop and maintain such a program. Many small agency administrators report that they do not have the human resources to participate in the UCR program, which requires much less time than does NIBRS. A solution to this dilemma has been to allocate funding on the state and federal level to provide local agencies with hardware, software, and training to implement NIBRS-compatible data collection systems. Such a partnership helped South Carolina become NIBRS compliant earlier than the vast majority of states.

*Adam J. McKee*

**See also** National Crime Victimization Survey, Uniform Crime Reports

### For Further Reading

Bibel, D. (2002). *Crime mapping using IBR data*. Retrieved from http://www.jrsa.org/ibrrc/mapping/mapping_ibr.pdf

Dodenhoff, P. (1990). 1989's People of the Year: The study and redesign team behind the new uniform crime reporting system. *Law Enforcement News, 14*(307), p. 1.

Federal Bureau of Investigation. (various dates). *Uniform crime reports*. Available: http://www.fbi.gov/ucr/ucr.htm

Mississippi Statistical Analysis Center. (2002). *Information and technology capabilities of Mississippi law enforcement agencies*. Available: http://www.usm.edu/mssac/publications/information.7.31.2002.pdf

http://www.jrsa.org/ibrrc

## ✑ NEWS MEDIA AND POLICE

Only a very small portion of the public has any direct contact with the criminal justice system. Although citizens have more opportunities to interact with the police than they do with other public servants or government employees, they still get most of their information regarding police activity from the media. From the perspective of both the police and the media, police–media relations, although often contentious, are vitally important. The news media are always looking for stories that will capture audience attention and inform residents of events that occur in their locality. Reports of crime often fit that bill. Because the police make good official sources, local crime reporters often develop working relationships with local law enforcement and turn to the police for information on a daily basis. Police departments, for their part, recognize the power of the media and, where possible, use it to their advantage. In the immediate aftermath of a crime, media coverage can advance the investigation of a crime significantly through generating leads that might not have otherwise materialized. A good example of this relationship is the posting of descriptions, sketches, and even photographs of those wanted in connection with serial rape and other types of violent crime.

In 1966, the news media actively and successfully lobbied for passage of the Freedom of Information Act (FOIA), which provides greater public access to government documents and records. Although the FOIA allows the media no special right of access to the information, the fees to access documents are usually waived for media representatives. The U.S. Supreme Court has also ruled that the First Amendment grants members of the press no greater rights than those granted to any other person. Despite the lack of a legal or constitutional basis for greater access, law enforcement often accommodates the news media to a greater extent than they would the general public. Until recently, law enforcement even allowed the news media to ride along as they served arrest and search warrants. In 1999, the Supreme Court ruled that these media ride-alongs violate the suspect's Fourth Amendment rights. "Perp walks" were conducted largely to accommodate photojournalists.

The relationship between the police and the news media is not always so symbiotic, however. Police can withhold information and impede the media's ability to cover a story. Journalists sometime face bureaucratic hurdles that also hinder the news process. The press also serves as an oversight mechanism, as it does with other governmental entities. Investigative journalists trying to uncover or document police misconduct have come up against the "blue wall of silence"—the unwritten rule that police officers refuse to talk when other officers are under investigation. Coverage of a topic can often lead to law enforcement policy changes, as has been the case with issues such as the registration of sex offenders, how a department deals with missing persons, and use-of-force policy.

The police have a vested interest in enforcing the law, ensuring that evidence is not compromised, and managing their public image. The news media have, at times, interfered with law enforcement in each of these respects. Police officials often complain that the press is not treating them fairly or accurately. Early in 2000, these concerns were borne out when reporters from some of the country's major news organizations were found to have fabricated stories, many of which included criminal justice content.

The print, television, and radio news media have a duty to keep the public informed by providing timely, accurate, and objective information. Despite this duty, and much to the chagrin of criminal justice professionals, including the police, the media tend to emphasize sensational events over routine activities. It has long been recognized that through emphasizing particularly violent, though relatively infrequent, crimes, the news media actively contribute to the public's misperception of the problem of crime. Just as they are more likely to cover exceptional crimes, the media are also more likely to cover exceptional police incidents.

Rarely does a hostage incident, standoff, police chase, or shooting go unnoticed by the media. Representatives of the news media who track police activity by monitoring police frequencies on scanners often arrive at crime scenes at the same time as, or shortly after, the police. Such incidents have all the characteristics of a good news story: They tend to be visually stimulating and filled with action, and they hold the audience's interest. Seldom do the media focus on the non-law enforcement duties of the police or on the mundane nature of the vast amount of police work. Simply put, routine police activity lacks the excitement of exceptional incidents and therefore is less newsworthy. Because of the selective nature of media reporting regarding law enforcement, much of the public has a distorted view of the police.

Police departments are well aware of the impact the news media can have on their public image and recognize the importance of good police–media relations. In 1991, the International Association of Chiefs of Police (IACP) developed a model policy that included a number of guidelines for police–media relations. The IACP's model policy encourages cooperative police–media relations, suggesting that departments provide the media with reasonable access to the police and be forthcoming with all facts relevant to a case as long as the disclosure of those facts does not violate any laws, compromise individual rights, or jeopardize the investigation and eventual prosecution of the case. According to the guidelines, material facts such as the type of crime, the location of the crime, and a general description of the incident usually can be provided to members of the news media by ranking officers at the scene. In addition, the guidelines recommend that police furnish reporters with names of officers on the scene and victim characteristics and identities (except in the case of sex crimes). Details about the identity of potential suspects, eyewitnesses, critically injured or deceased victims, and juveniles are more sensitive and should be released to the media only at the discretion of the department chief. The IACP model policy provides guidelines for the furnishing of information to the media at each stage of the criminal justice process, from the initial report through the final adjudication.

Police departments' policies regarding media vary depending upon the size of the department and the amount of media exposure the department experiences. Whereas smaller departments will often allow their officers to talk with the media fairly freely, larger departments have either a dedicated public relations department or specific officers appointed as public information officers. They can be sworn officers or civilians.

It is important to recognize that, regardless of any official department policies in effect, and despite good faith efforts on the part of the police to protect the rights of individuals and the integrity of investigations, there will always be individuals within police departments willing to leak information to the news media. Whereas more reputable news media outlets will often respect the sensitivity of the information being leaked and not report it, others quite willingly push aside professional ethics to be the first to run a particularly provocative story.

The police often condemn the news media for prematurely releasing the details of an investigation or inadvertently destroying evidence at a crime scene, but they also use their established relationships with the media to their advantage. In the 2002 search for the Washington, DC-area sniper, Montgomery County Police Chief Charles A. Moose used press conferences to keep the public informed, chastise media coverage, and communicate with the suspects. In several nationally covered press conferences, Chief Moose appealed to the suspects to contact the police (they had allegedly made several unanswered calls to the police hotline and communicated to the police in writing). At the same time, Chief Moose criticized the news media for jeopardizing the search for the suspects by publicizing a vital piece of evidence that had been leaked from within the department.

The media coverage most damaging to police, however, is that of police misconduct, corruption, and brutality. Although media coverage of such incidents has tarnished the reputation of the police and, in many cases, strained police–community and police–media relations, it has also led to greater police accountability and organizational change. Following media exposure of some particularly egregious police misconduct, blue ribbon panels, or commissions, have been charged with investigating the nature and extent of the misconduct, corruption, or brutality and putting forth recommendations for reform.

In 1970, the *New York Times* broke one of New York City's biggest police corruption scandals. After police department channels proved futile, police officer Frank Serpico turned to the media to expose the vast corruption within the NYPD. Serpico's allegations of widespread bribery and payoffs led to the development of the Knapp Commission. Serpico's story reached even wider audiences when it became the subject of Peter Maas's bestselling book *Serpico* and a film of the same name starring Al Pacino. Just 20 years later, when several officers were arrested on narcotics charges, a second commission, the Mollen Commission, was created to investigate further allegations of corruption after Sergeant Joseph Trimboli turned to the press when he could not convince his superiors to take seriously the corrupt activities of the same officers.

In March 1991, an amateur photographer captured on film the beating of Rodney King by members of the Los Angeles Police Department (LAPD). The media covered this story relentlessly, airing the footage of the beating literally hundreds of times in the weeks that followed. Following intense media coverage of the LAPD's use of force in the King incident, the Christopher Commission, headed by former Secretary of State Warren Christopher, was established to investigate the LAPD's use of force. The Christopher Commission report documented the pervasive problems within the LAPD, recommended more than 100 reforms, and led to the retirement of then-police chief Daryl F. Gates.

Although investigative reports that focus on police misconduct can strain police–media relations, daily crime reporters generally are not the investigative reporters who uncover and report on these scandals. Police departments, particularly those that have dedicated public relations departments, develop fairly close relationships with their local crime reporters and willingly share information that might be useful or important to the public.

*Natasha A. Frost*

***See also*** Knapp Commission, Perp Walk

*For Further Reading*

Crawford, K. A. (1994). News media participation in law enforcement activities. *FBI Law Enforcement Bulletin, 63*(8), 28–33.

Hanlon v. Berger, 119 S.Ct. 1706 (1999).

Houchins v. KQED, Inc., 438 U.S. 1 (1978).

International Association of Chiefs of Police. (1991). *Model policy on police–media relations.* Alexandria, VA: Author.

Perlmutter, D. D. (2000). *Policing the media: Street cops and public perceptions of law enforcement.* Thousand Oaks, CA: Sage.

Surette, R. (1992). *Media, crime & criminal justice: Images and realities.* Pacific Grove, CA: Brooks/Cole.

Wilson v. Layne, 119 S.Ct. 1692 (1999)

# ❧ NONLETHAL WEAPONS

Today, police officers are being called upon more often to resolve dangerous situations outside of their conventional training and technology. The incidents that challenge traditional problem-solving capabilities vary, and include such things as

- People who call for police "assistance" when attempting suicide
- Noncompliant armed subjects who do not create a *direct* threat

Historically, officers facing such tactical dilemmas had few options between verbal challenges and deadly force. As a result, police agencies have begun adopting a variety of tools to assist in such endeavors, and three of the more common are pepper spray, impact projectiles, and electromuscular disruption systems.

## HISTORICAL OVERVIEW

### Pepper Spray

Since 1923 and the creation of the first civilian chemical munitions company, law enforcement has sought out methods, tools, tactics, and techniques to assist with subduing violent individuals through "less than deadly" force. During the turbulent 1960s, President Lyndon Johnson created a Blue Ribbon Commission to study crime and violence. One of the committee recommendations called for the development of nonlethal weapons, which resulted in a number of technological advancements including CN-based Chemical Mace®. The product was designed to be a safer alternative to hands-on tactics and gave officers immediate access to a weapon that allowed them to engage suspects from beyond the fist/foot range. Safe and arguably effective, the product's demise was ultimately two-fold:

1. Chemical Mace® did not stop a significant percentage of those who were sprayed—especially those who were drunk, drugged, or mentally deranged.

2. Chemical Mace® earned a well-deserved reputation for secondary contamination. More than a few officers "cleared the jail," or drove to headquarters with their heads out the window because the suspect was contaminating them from the back seat of the car.

The product definitely reduced injuries to officers and suspects alike, but the failure rate and secondary contamination caused most agencies to stop issuing it by 1980. In 1988, oleoresin capsicum or pepper-based sprays (extracted from the essential oil of the cayenne pepper plant) caught the eye of progressive police trainers. Similar agents had been tested by the military in the 1930s, used by mail carriers on dogs since the 1960s, and introduced to law enforcement as an alternative to Mace® in 1971. The pepper products ultimately proved much more effective than CN and are on practically every duty belt in America today. Pepper spray is considered by many to be the most significant injury-reduction tool in law enforcement history.

### Impact Projectiles

In the Bible, the First Book of Samuel documents the slaying of Goliath by the shepherd boy David. The Philistine was armed with proximity weapons, including a bronze javelin, iron spear, and sword. These were heavy weapons, and even the giant had to get close to use them. David was well aware of this, *and* his vulnerability should he end up within their range. So he kept his distance, reached into his bag, and lifted out five smooth stones.

The use of extended-range impact energy is nothing new. From Biblical times to the present day, people have recognized the safety that comes with distance. This is especially true when facing an adversary armed with a weapon that requires direct access to be effective. Significant events in the chronology of impact rounds are outlined as follows:

- In the late 1880s, police officers in the East launched sawed-off sections of broom handles at rioters. They used black powder ten-gauge shotguns to deliver stick-like energy from afar.
- In the late 1960s, West Coast police officers used 12-gauge and 37 mm lead shot-filled "bean bags" to quell Vietnam antiwar protests.
- In 1971, New Mexico officers recorded the first known fatality from a "nonlethal" 12-gauge bean bag round. The incident involved a 14-year-old boy who was struck in the chest. This caused the collective abandonment of bean bag ammunition by American police agencies for the next 17 years.
- In 1985, the British ARWEN 37 mm (*A*nti-*R*iot-*W*eapon-*EN*field) plastic baton launcher was purchased by a number of U.S. police agencies. The weapons were intended to provide assistance when facing mentally deranged and suicidal subjects.
- In 1989, bean bag ammunition began creeping back into the American police arsenal. The previous round was a 2 × 2-inch square cloth bag filled with #9 lead shot, which traveled at 400 feet per second. The new version had the same physical characteristics, but was reduced to 300 feet per second.
- In 1992, the SL6 37 mm launcher became the "American ARWEN" and was ultimately procured by a large number of police agencies.
- Between 1989 and 1997, "bean bags" and "less lethal" became buzzwords in law enforcement. Agencies clambered for anything that was thought to be less likely to kill than conventional weapons. As a result, distributors began offering a variety of impact projectiles to police agencies. This influx of technology dramatically increased the number of operational deployments. Not surprisingly, the deployments increased more rapidly than contemporary training. As a result, there was also an increase in the number of deaths and serious injuries of suspects.

- In 1998, the square bag paradigm was broken with the introduction of a bean bag shaped like a baby sock. The new design redefined the concept of potential accuracy, energy density, and consistent angle of presentation for this popular class of weapon.
- In 2003, Police Ordnance begins manufacturing the ARWEN in Canada.

Generally, impact rounds have been proven safe and effective when properly used by trained personnel. Likewise, the potential for death or serious injury with impact rounds is a reality. As of 2003, a beanbag or 37 mm plastic bullet has been involved in at least 12 deaths in the United States and Canada, and countless other serious injuries. The single most important way to prevent such negative outcomes is shot placement.

## Electromuscular Devices

In the 1960s, NASA scientist Jack Cover responded to President Johnson's Blue Ribbon call by experimenting with electricity. He discovered that when short-duration, high-energy DC electric pulses were applied to humans, immediate incapacitation without negative side effects almost always occurred. This led to a delivery system he named the TASER, after the 1920s fictional book, *Thomas A. Swift's Electric Rifle*. Cover spent several years perfecting the futuristic device and introduced it to the public in the 1976 Clint Eastwood film *The Enforcer*. The Los Angeles Police Department and Los Angeles County Sheriff's Office adopted the TASER and used it more than 5,000 times between 1981 and 1991—including during the infamous traffic stop of Rodney King. This very public failure raised questions about TASER technology and caused a number of agencies to discontinue its use. Likewise, the need for alternative tools did not diminish, and the early 1990s saw a resurgence of impact projectile technology, specifically 12-gauge bean bags, 37 mm plastic bullets, and pepper spray. Unfortunately, pepper spray and impact projectiles rely on pain to overcome a suspect's resistance to police commands. In addition, a significant number of suspects today use mind-altering drugs, abuse alcoholic beverages, or are mentally deranged. Each of these factors increases their tolerance for pain, which correspondingly decreases the effectiveness of "pain compliance" tools. In such cases, officers attempt to use minimal force options and routinely find that they have little or no effect. Should the problem continue, the escalation of force needed to stop the threat often results in serious or even fatal injury.

Problems such as this generated renewed interest in TASER technology, which does not rely on pain compliance to be effective. The original TASER was a 50,000-volt/7-watt system. As previously noted, a number of agencies did not find this system sufficiently effective in actual encounters. Additional testing and research was conducted, and the advanced TASER M26 was introduced in 1999, followed by the X26 in 2003. The new devices are in the 50,000-volt/26-watt range and are designed to override the central nervous system and dramatically increase effectiveness over earlier systems.

The new devices have been tested on more than 40,000 volunteers and used operationally more than 30,000 times since 1999. It is important to note that 41 suspects have died after a TASER deployment, but the device itself reportedly has not been the direct cause of any of the deaths. There has been cardiac and pacemaker safety testing done on the devices, and the totality of information at this time suggests that they do not create an increased risk of pacemaker malfunction or heart fibrillation, nor do the devices create a risk of death or serious injury beyond the legitimate concern of secondary injuries from falling. As a result, TASERs are being used by police officers with surprising frequency, and at an early enough point in the confrontation to prevent escalation to where greater levels of force would likely be needed.

## CONCLUSION

The devices outlined above are a long way from perfect, but they have greatly assisted police officers as they face some of law enforcement's most challenging events. The goal with such use is to reduce the probability of injury to everyone involved, and to that end, they have been very effective. Deaths and injuries continue to occur when officers and suspects clash, but the hope is that with additional technology and training, the numbers on both sides of the badge can be reduced in the future.

*Steve Ijames*

***See also*** Use of Force, Weapons

## *For Further Reading*

Ijames, S. (1995). Less lethal force: Concepts and considerations in the de-escalation philosophy. *Tactical Edge, 13*(3), 51–55.

Ijames, S. (1996). Less lethal projectiles: Seeking a balance. *Tactical Edge, 14*(4), 76–84.

Ijames, S. (1997). Testing and evaluating less lethal projectiles (Part 1). *Tactical Edge, 15*(2), 12–15.

Ijames, S. (1998). Less lethal force options: Tactics, training and technology for unconventional encounters. *Police Chief Magazine, 65*(3), 31–37.

Ijames, S. (1999). Force options and legal challenges. *Tactical Edge, 18*(3), 102–104.

Ijames, S. (2000). Less lethal projectile tests. *Tactical Edge, 18*(3).

Ijames, S. (2001, November). Zeroing in on accuracy: Managing the potential for impact projectile deaths and serious injuries. *Police and Security News.*

Ijames, S. (2002, November/December). Chemical munitions deployment: Thoughts and considerations for use in public disorder. *Police and Security News.*

Ijames, S. (2003a). Impact projectiles: Lessons learned thus far. *Tactical Edge, 21*(4).

Ijames, S. (2003b). Patterns of injury, recognition, and treatment for less lethal law enforcement techniques. *Emergency Medicine*, pp. 316–325.

## ✑ ORGANIZED CRIME CONTROL

There is no consensus on the definition of the term *organized crime,* but it is generally thought of as either a business that primarily engages in an ongoing pattern of illicit activity, or a syndicate that regulates the operations of such businesses. Frequently, the notion of structure and the ability and willingness to use force and corruption to attain economic advantage are seen as indispensable attributes of such businesses or groups.

Today, the term *Mafia,* which properly refers to a specific group indigenous to Sicily (and that is also known as "the Mob"), is often used generically to refer to any group engaged in organized crime or, indeed, other conspiratorial behavior. Although there were, and currently are, numerous other criminal syndicates, U.S. law enforcement tended historically to focus on Italian American groups and developed its approach to combating organized crime from its experiences in doing so.

During the first few decades of the 20th century, crime in the Little Italys of America received little attention from law enforcement. Indeed, for a long time, the FBI denied the Mob's very existence. Whatever enforcement existed was at the local level, where, in the 1930s, Tom Dewey and Frank Hogan became known as the Rackets Busters, using electronic surveillance; pioneering legislative reform; and convicting major underworld leaders, corrupt public officials, and labor racketeers.

By the beginning of the 1950s, changes were beginning to occur. The Kefauver Committee hearings in 1950 and 1951 awakened the public to the scope of the problem. In 1957, after several well-publicized shootings and a national meeting in Appalachin, New York, the FBI began to use non-evidentiary intelligence bugs and wiretaps to gather information. In 1963, underworld figure Joseph Valachi testified before a Senate committee and explained the inner workings and structure of Italian American organized crime. He was asked the name of the organization.

    A.  Cosa Nostra.

    Q.  That is in Italian?

    A.  That is "Our Thing" and "Our Family" in English.

Significantly, Cosa Nostra is not a subsidiary or subdivision of the Sicilian Mafia. Instead, it is a distinctly American organization that, although drawing on Mafiosa traditions, developed in response to the unique social forces and culture of the New World. Nonetheless, those who comprised Cosa Nostra at its inception were the possessors of 19th-century old world values. Like the Mafia, Cosa Nostra was an "honored society." The ties that bound its members together were originally those of kinship and respect, as well as the duty of *omerta,* the traditional code of silence, which was first broken publicly by Valachi.

Valachi's testimony occurred just as Attorney General Robert Kennedy had revitalized the Organized Crime and Racketeering Section (OCRS) of the Justice Department, modeling it on the Hogan Rackets Bureau. When he left that position following the assassination of his brother, President John F. Kennedy, the program was allowed to wither.

Shortly afterwards, however, G. Robert Blakey, a former member of Kennedy's OCRS, became chief counsel to John McClellan, Chair of the Senate Judiciary Committee. Blakey understood that with layers of insulation protecting the Mob higher-ups from direct involvement in criminal activity, there were logically only three ways of developing evidence of their incriminating conversations—be a participant, have a participant cooperate, or overhear the conversation. Legislation designed to achieve those objectives followed.

In 1968, Blakey drafted the Omnibus Crime Control and Safe Streets Act, which authorized court-ordered electronic surveillance at the federal and state level. Two years later, in 1970, Congress passed the Organized Crime Control Act (OCCA). This Act, of which Blakey was again principal draftsman, would revolutionize federal law enforcement's approach to organized crime. OCCA provided for, among other things, testimonial immunity; increased jurisdiction for the federal government in gambling enforcement; enhanced sentencing in organized crime cases; grand jury reports; the Witness Protection Program; and, most significantly, the Racketeer Influenced and Corrupt Organizations Act (RICO), a radically new legal approach to the investigation and prosecution of organized crime. RICO provided the means by which members of a criminal syndicate conducting multiple conspiracies could be tried together and a variety of remedies and sanctions not traditionally associated with prosecution could be used.

With RICO, prosecutors had a tool specifically designed to deal with illicit enterprises. The target became the criminal syndicate (instead of individuals, against whom the war of attrition had seemed endless). Civil remedies were made available to criminal division attorneys in their efforts. Strike forces had recently been established to bring together federal investigative agencies and Justice Department attorneys. (Strike forces have since been merged into the U.S. Attorneys' offices.) With the death of FBI Director J. Edgar Hoover and the tragedy of Watergate, first Clarence Kelly and then William Webster changed the direction and focus of the FBI. In the area of organized crime, they became aggressive and proactive, and they began to work more effectively with local law enforcement. Perhaps most significantly, individuals at policy-making levels within the FBI came to understand RICO as an investigative tool, and attorneys understood it as a means of achieving successful prosecutions of groups of criminals and employment of remedial action.

States now followed the federal example, with many passing their own versions of the RICO statute, authorizing the use of electronic surveillance and creating their own organized crime units. The Law Enforcement Assistance Administration provided funds to create and maintain an Organized Crime Institute at Cornell Law School to undertake scholarly and empirical research in organized crime and train mostly state and local law enforcement in the use of the newer procedural and substantive laws relating to syndicated criminal activity.

These changes in the sophistication of law enforcement coincided with sociological changes in the Mob. Honor, kinship, and respect, which characterized at least the ethos of the original Mob members, were replaced by money and power in the second- and third-generation Americans, who were unwilling to take the time to develop the skills and undertake the responsibilities of their predecessors. By the 1980s, for many family members, traditional values had been replaced by simple cost–benefit analysis. When faced with prosecution, forfeiture, and incarceration, they chose instead to cooperate with law enforcement. They testified not only before Senate committees, as Valachi had done, but at trials as well. Some were even willing to wear concealable recorders to gather evidence against their colleagues. Ironically, instead of retreating from the limelight, several "elder statesmen" and their progeny reacted to the changes in the Mob by becoming media stars.

The synergistic effect of the sociological and law enforcement changes became apparent. Increased aggressiveness of law enforcement, using modern substantive and procedural law in a sophisticated way, created new leverage against potential witnesses. And Mob figures, disenchanted with the organizations of which they were a part, chose to cooperate more and more frequently. The result has been that entire crews and the upper echelons of families have been indicted and convicted. Indeed, the Commission itself, the mafia "ruling body", made up of the heads of the five New York families, was treated as a racketeering enterprise and its members convicted under the RICO statute. With the structures collapsing, Cosa Nostra families are unable to fulfill their primary purpose—providing "governmental services" for its members, setting and enforcing rules, allocating resources and territories, settling disputes, and dealing with competitive syndicates.

Nevertheless, organized crime remains a significant problem and poses significant challenges to law enforcement. A wide variety of organized crime syndicates remain and are developing. Each developed in its own way, is structured differently, and presents different challenges to law enforcement. Organized crime is not a monolith subject to one set of enforcement techniques nor one ethnic group. The location of the group's leaders, the language spoken by its members, the activities in which it engages, its association with terrorism, its ability to launder the profits of illicit businesses, and its sophistication and internal discipline all affect what means of investigation and prosecution will prove most effective. The approaches taken to deal with Soviet émigré organized crime will, of necessity, be different from that for Colombian drug cartels, Southeast Asian groups, or even inner-city gangs. Some of the organizations will be the focus of federal agencies, whereas others will tend to be targeted by local law enforcement.

Today's syndicates are involved in a large number of enterprises, some of which are wholly illicit, such as gambling and narcotics trafficking, and others of which exist within the framework of otherwise licit industries, such as construction, waste hauling, and the commercial waterfront. These industries, and often the unions that operate within them, each have their own unique racketeering susceptibility (measured by the ability of an organized crime group to gain influence or control) and potential (measured by the amount of obtainable illicit gain).

Thus, the current challenges to law enforcement include the ability to analyze the nontraditional organized crime groups and understand the racketeering susceptibility and potential associated with the criminal activities in which they engage. Without the formulation and execution of a coherent strategy based upon such analyses, the impact of criminal prosecutions is haphazard at best, and counterproductive at worst.

A variety of remedies must be considered and employed in developing and executing whatever strategy is chosen. Criminal prosecution leading to incarceration and fines is only one remedy, and often has substantial limitations. RICO envisions the use of civil remedies, including forfeiture, injunctions, and suits for monetary damages. The restoration of democratic and legitimate practices in institutions and industries that have been corrupted, dominated, or infiltrated by organized crime may require the use of trusteeships and the employment of independent, private sector Inspectors General.

The design and implementation of truly effective strategies require the skills and disciplines of both police and prosecutors, investigative accountants, tactical and strategic analysts, technologists, industry specialists, and academics.

Finally, a set of principled policies needs to be developed to deal with tensions arising from the numerous agencies at different levels of government with overlapping jurisdictions active in organized crime investigation and prosecution. In such cases, conflicts and jealousies are virtually inevitable; they often breed confusion and mistrust, and may result in turf wars that prevent the flow of information from one agency to another. On the other hand, the multiplicity of agencies—even if unplanned and resulting from historical anomaly—has certain benefits. Monopolies in law enforcement may produce short-term efficiencies, but, as in the marketplace, the long-term result of a lack of competition is likely to be complacency; lack of innovation; decreased responsiveness; and, ultimately, corruption. Constructive, as opposed to destructive, competition often provides incentives to agencies to work harder and smarter, and to be more inventive. There is little question that federal successes in organized crime prosecutions often resulted from the need to be more capable than the competition, and that the best ideas, approaches, and personnel often originated in local law enforcement.

*Ronald Goldstsock*

## For Further Reading

Blakey, G. R., Goldstock, R., & Rogovin, C. H. (1978). *Rackets bureaus: Investigation and prosecution of organized crime.* Washington, DC: National Institute of Law Enforcement and Criminal Justice.

Cressey, D. R. (1969). *Theft of the nation.* New York: Harper & Row.

Jacobs, J. B. (1999). *Gotham unbound: How New York City was liberated from the grip of organized crime.* New York: New York University Press.

Landesco, J. (1929). *Organized crime in Chicago.* Chicago: University of Chicago Press.

Nelli, H. S. (1976). *The business of crime.* New York: Oxford University Press.

New York State Organized Crime Task Force. (1990). *Corruption and racketeering in the New York construction industry.* New York: New York University Press.

Sondern, F., Jr. (1959). *Brotherhood of evil: The Mafia.* New York: Farrar, Straus and Cudahy.

Thrasher, F. M. (1927). *The gang.* Chicago: University of Chicago Press.

Whyte, W. F. (1943). *Street corner society.* Chicago: University of Chicago Press.

# P

## PAROLE OFFICERS

Like probation officers, parole officers must balance two roles: cop and social worker. These roles, often in conflict with each other, are at the heart of what constitutes the job of a parole officer. More so than probation officers, parole agents have a greater law enforcement orientation. Everyone they supervise has already been to prison, and many have been convicted of violent offenses. In 1999, one fourth of everyone on parole supervision had been sentenced to prison for a violent crime, another 33% were drug offenders, and 31% were property offenders (Bureau of Justice Statistics, n.d.). By the end of 2002, there were more than 750,000 people under parole supervision in the United States. During that same year, about 470,000 people were released from prison and placed on parole (Glaze, 2003).

In many states, parole supervision is part of the state's Department of Corrections, and in others, it is a separate state agency. Many parole officers carry guns, and because those under parole supervision are still technically considered state prisoners, parole officers have broad powers to make unannounced searches of parolees themselves as well as of their living areas.

Parole officers are expected to assist parolees' adjustment to the community once they have been released from prison, monitor their progress, and make sure they adhere to the conditions of parole. The conditions of parole are fairly standard in every state and include remaining drug free, having a job or being actively engaged in looking for employment, not consorting with other felons, regularly reporting to parole officers, and attending all required treatment programs.

Parole officers have a tremendous amount of discretion in how they do their jobs. Some officers take a primarily punitive approach to their jobs and, after making clear to parolees what they are expected to do, simply wait for them to violate their conditions and arrest them for a technical parole violation. Because parole officers have the ability to take a parolee back to jail or prison immediately for a violation hearing if they believe a violation has occurred, they wield a significant amount of power. In fact, their ability to search and question a parolee at will, along with their ability to incarcerate a parolee immediately based on an alleged technical violation, gives them powers that not even police have.

Other parole officers can take a more social or welfare worker approach to their jobs and deemphasize the enforcement side of the job in order to concentrate on assisting the parolee with his or her transition back into the community. This can include everything from finding appropriate treatment and employment programs to working with the parolee and his or her family to deal with issues such as drug use, family reunification, and parenting skills.

Between these two extremes of parole officer emphasis on control versus assistance are gradations that combine both perspectives.

Just examining some of the characteristics of those who are leaving prisons can illustrate the difficulty of a parole officer's job. In 1999, 84% of those leaving prison had used drugs or alcohol at the time of the offense, more than 14% were diagnosed with a serious mental illness, and more than 12% were homeless at the time of the arrest (Hughes, Wilson, & Beck, 2001). Combine these characteristics with a criminal history that includes at least one felony conviction, low educational levels, and poor employment histories, and it becomes clear that the barriers to successful reentry for these parolees are extraordinarily difficult. Just how difficult is borne out by statistics that show that almost 70% of parolees were rearrested within 3 years of their release from prison (Bureau of Justice Statistics, n.d.).

The pressures felt by parole officers during the course of their jobs are substantial. They have growing caseloads (60 to 70 cases per officer is not unusual) of a very difficult population. It is clear, given the problems faced by parolees, that substantial numbers of them will not be able to adhere to the basic conditions of parole. Not using drugs is extraordinarily difficult for someone who might have been using drugs for years prior to prison. Having or even actively looking for employment is likewise difficult given the poor skills and work histories of many parolees, coupled with a job market that is very difficult for anyone who has a felony conviction. Regular reporting and having a permanent address is also challenging for those parolees who are homeless or who cannot afford permanent housing. Thus, parole officers have caseloads where parole violations are common, and the decision about how to react to those violations is both difficult and stressful.

For instance, the choice between filing a parole violation for a parolee who has tested positive for drugs or allowing him to continue on parole is not an easy one. On one hand, the drug use is a violation of parole, and sending the parolee back to prison makes clear that behavior will not be tolerated. It also serves the function of at least temporarily lowering the parole officer's caseload and ensures that there will be no political fallout if that parolee was to go on to commit a serious crime. On the other hand, the process of getting off drugs will usually include some drug use, and the decision to send someone back to prison for this can ruin the chances of someone who might have made a successful transition back to the community. This latter decision is accompanied by the risk that, after allowing the parolee to continue on parole, he or she might commit a serious or high-profile crime. This is a concern that is never far from any parole officer's mind. The public usually reacts with outrage when people on parole commit violent crimes. Although people's anger might be directed more at the mere existence of the parole function than at a particular parole officer, it is certainly not unusual for parole officers to lose their jobs or be subject to severe disciplinary action if this occurs. This risk can permeate all aspects of a parole officer's job and play a role in almost every important decision that an officer makes.

Some parole officers have caseloads composed of only very dangerous violent or sex offenders. These caseloads tend to be lower than average, involve a high level of monitoring and control, and demonstrate little tolerance for any violation of the conditions of parole. A parole officer who has a caseload of sex offenders usually will not hesitate to file a technical violation if parole conditions are not met. Giving these offenders a second chance is a risk that few parole officers want to take.

The trend over the past 20 years has been for parole officers to be enforcement oriented and risk averse. Partnerships between police officers and parole officers are becoming more common because many jurisdictions have found that by working together, these agencies can increase the monitoring and control of parolees. Sending people back to prison for committing technical violations has also become far more common as parole officers take more of a "risk management" rather than social work approach to their jobs.

Parole officers, like probation officers, usually have to have a bachelor's degree as a minimum educational requirement, which is more than that required of almost all police and corrections officers. Substantial skills are required to diagnose the needs and problems faced by parolees, match up those needs with appropriate services, and be able to maintain control and surveillance of large caseloads.

*Michael Jacobson*

*See also* Probation Officers, Repeat Offenders

## For Further Reading

American Probation and Parole Association. Available: http://www.appa-net.org

Bureau of Justice Statistics. (2003). *Probation and parole in the United States, 2002.* Washington, DC: Author.

Bureau of Justice Statistics. (n.d.). *Reentry trends in the United States.* Retrieved from http://www.ojp.usdoj.gov/bjs/reentry/reentry.htm

Burke, P. (2003). *APAI handbook for new parole board members.* Retrieved from http://www.apaintl.org/ Handbook.html

Glaze, L. E. (2003). *Probation and parole in the United States, 2002.* Washington, DC: Bureau of Justice Statistics.

Hughes, T. A., Wilson, D. J., & Beck, A. J. (2001). *Trends in state parole, 1990–2000.* Washington, DC: Bureau of Justice Statistics.

New York City Office of Operations. (2004). *The mayor's management report, fiscal 2004 preliminary.* Retrieved from http://www.nyc.gov/html/ops/downloads/pdf/2004_mmr/0104_indicators.pdf

Petersilia, J. (2003). *When prisoners come home: Parole and prisoner reentry.* New York: Oxford University Press.

# ∾ PATROL METHODS, TACTICS, AND STRATEGIES

Patrol has long been considered the backbone of police service. The London Metropolitan Police manual, written in 1829, required constables to patrol their assigned beats on foot and in uniform. All police departments based on the London model have followed this requirement. Patrol members are the visible manifestation of public security through the uniformed police presence in the community. The mere presence of the uniformed police officer on foot or in a marked vehicle is considered a deterrent to criminal activity because the criminal is never sure when the police officer will turn the corner.

The patrol force is always the largest component of any police department and is staffed by police personnel who are considered generalists. Patrol members are trained and prepared to handle a wide variety of assignments ranging from criminal matters to calls for assistance from citizens. The major role of the patrol officer is best described as order maintenance or peacemaking.

## PATROL METHODS

### Foot Patrol

Foot patrol is the original and most basic form of police patrol. Prior to the introduction of the 9-1-1 emergency number and increased communications, citizens usually communicated with a police officer in person. People with problems would find the local police officer on his or her beat and communicate their concerns. With the introduction of 9-1-1, most citizens contacted the police by telephone, and motorized patrol cars were required to respond to the calls. Personnel to fill the motorized units came from the ranks of the foot police officers. Modern police administrators have criticized foot patrol for its expense. Police officers on foot patrol can cover only a small area and cannot be expected to respond to calls except within their beat. Officers on foot are hampered by the inability to carry extra equipment or additional administrative forms. Inclement weather also has a large impact on the performance of officers on foot patrol.

Despite the drawbacks, modern police administrators now recognize the advantages of foot patrol in the community. Foot patrol helps cement a positive relationship between the department and the community. Police officers on foot traditionally interact well with the citizens and are most knowledgeable on community concerns and problems. In areas with high street traffic or dense urban populations, foot patrols justify their costs in creating good will in the community and in the higher quality and more personalized police service. In the 1980s, interest in foot patrol was renewed as a result of the Newark foot patrol experiment. The experiment found that although foot patrol did not reduce crime significantly, it had a positive effect on citizens' attitudes toward the police. Foot police officers were also found to have increased concern for helping the people in their areas. The Newark experiment in foot patrol led to research on the interactive police–citizen connection. Community policing or problem-oriented policing requires the police officer and the community to work together on issues to solve underlying problems. Therefore, the police are expected to be proactive rather than reactive in dealing with problems.

## Motorized Patrol

Motorized patrol is the most popular method of modern policing. It is cost-effective because a police officer can respond rapidly to numerous calls throughout a tour. Motorized patrol beats can be large areas, and a single officer can be expected to patrol the entire area in the police vehicle, in which the police officer is shielded from the weather. Unfortunately, the increased efficiency has resulted in a decrease in the quality of the relationship between the police and the community. The unknown police officer in the radio car who too often reacted indifferently to the community has replaced the friendly and well-known foot officer.

Others forms of motorized patrol involve the use of motor scooters for summons duty and motor-cycles for highway patrol. However, the use of two-wheeled vehicles increases the possibility of injury to the police officers assigned. Several police departments, including Boston and Atlanta, are now experimenting with the Segway two-wheeled computerized scooter to assist the foot patrol officer.

## Bicycle Patrol

The establishment of community policing and the renewed interest in foot patrol has caused interest in the advantages of bicycle patrol. Bicycle patrol has many of the advantages of foot patrol with the closer interaction of the police officer and the community. Bicycles also give the police officer greater mobility and speed to chase suspects or to answer calls for service over a wider area. Many police officers also enjoy the increased physical fitness possibilities offered in bicycle patrol.

## Horse or Mounted Patrol

Many large urban police departments still use mounted horse units to patrol downtown areas or parklands. Horses are very effective in dealing with crowds and riot situations. The extra height also gives the mounted officer a clear view of activities in crowds.

## Nonuniformed Patrol

Although the presence of the uniformed police officer is believed to deter criminal activity, many police departments augment the uniformed patrol with police officers in civilian clothes. The New York City Police Department assigns 5% of the patrol strength to anticrime duties within the patrol precincts. The nonuniformed police officers focus on arresting criminals in the commission of street crimes such as robbery and auto larceny.

## Helicopter Patrol

Many police departments have an aviation division to assist the motorized and foot patrol units. Helicopters can check roofs, follow fleeing vehicles, conduct surveillance, observe traffic problems, and search rugged terrain much easier than motorized units. Critical to the use of helicopters in patrol is the coordination of the efforts of the ground units and the helicopters. Communications between the ground and air units must be perfected to gain the advantage of the air units.

## Directed and "Hot Spot" Patrol

Recently, police managers have questioned the effectiveness of patrol officers in handling problematic conditions in their beats. When patrolling all areas within a beat, specific locations with drug dealing, public disorder, and other problems are sometimes ignored. Directed patrol methods use crime analysis to examine areas within patrol beats that require additional attention. Police officers are directed to be at these locations at certain times during the tour. The "hot spot" approach locates addresses within a precinct that generate an exceptionally high number of calls for service. Police units not responding to radio calls are required to park in the vicinity of the address to reduce criminal activity. Some critics of these programs suggest that the criminal activity just gets moved to another location.

## Questions Concerning the Effectiveness of Patrol

An investigation into the effectiveness of having police officers patrol a geographic area in an irregular manner to deter criminal activity resulted in some surprising results. The Kansas City Preventive Patrol Experiment (1972–1973) divided an area into three possible patrol styles: (a) Reactive beats received no preventive patrol, and police officers responded only when citizens called; (b) proactive beats received two or three times the normal patrol activity; and (c) control beats received the normal patrol activity. The results indicated that crime remained the same in all three areas. Furthermore, citizens did not notice any differences in police strength in the three areas.

*Hugh E. O'Rourke*

## For Further Reading

Goldstein, H. (1977). *Policing a free society.* Cambridge, MA: Ballinger.

Goldstein, H. (1990). *Problem oriented policing.* New York: McGraw-Hill.

Kelling, G. L., Pate, T., Dieckman, D., & Brown, C. (1974). *Kansas City preventive patrol experiment.* Washington, DC: Police Foundation.

Police Foundation. (1981). *The Newark foot patrol experiment.* Washington, DC: Author.

Sherman, L. W., Gartin, P. R., & Buerger, M. (1989). Hot spots of predatory crime: Routine activities and the criminology of place. *Criminology, 27*(2), 27–55.

Walker, S. (1992). *The police in America* (2nd ed.). New York: McGraw-Hill.

Wilson, J. Q. (1973). *Varieties of police behavior.* New York: Atheneum.

# ❧ PATROL SHIFTS

## THE PROS AND CONS OF SHIFT WORK

Because most law enforcement agencies operate 24 hours a day, they schedule officers so that there is some coverage around the clock. Officers at the state and local level, at one time or another in their careers, deal with working a shift. It is a fundamental component of police work and is often arbitrated during contract negotiations. More than 20 million Americans currently work irregular schedules, night shifts, or extended hours. What may seem, on the surface, a rather insignificant issue can cause good officers to quit or even lose their jobs. Shift work is a constant source of contention within the law enforcement community. No shift pleases everyone, and generally, there is no one specific shift that is better than the other. It is up to the officers and the administration to decide which shift is the best to embrace. Officer morale, community concerns, calls for service, crime patterns, and availability are just a few of the factors that must be taken into account when deciding what type of shift schedule the agency should utilize. All shifts have their benefits and weaknesses.

When agencies make decisions regarding shifts, typically the first decision to be made is whether to have rotating or permanent shifts.

## Permanent Shift

A permanent shift is just that. Officers typically bid for it, or it can be assigned by the administration. The officer is assigned one shift and only one shift.

The advantages of this type of shift consist of being able to familiarize yourself with the problem areas and become acquainted with troublemakers and/or police-friendly citizens. The citizens are more at ease when dealing with the same officer every day. Not having to explain their issues to different officers each time there is a problem enables citizens to feel as though their problems/concerns are being addressed.

Another advantage is that the officer is able to make accommodations in advance for issues such as vacation time. Knowing that he or she will be on the same shift a year from now enables the officer to schedule appointments, vacations, educational/training activities, and so on ahead of time. For those officers who have enough seniority, a permanent shift is desired if the shift is chosen in a bid process. The senior officer is able to choose the shift that is most conducive to his or her likes or schedule.

One disadvantage to the permanent shift could be a stagnant or bored feeling for the officer. Some officers desire change, and those who do often see permanent shifts as holding them back. The rookie officer who may desire a midnight shift or evening shift in a high-crime area may end up on a day shift in a low-crime residential area. This can cause a new officer, who desires high-priority or in-progress calls, to become disillusioned because of the high amount of service-related calls that the day shift can produce.

### Rotating Shift

A rotating shift is typically a shift that places the officer on a day shift for a certain amount of time, then an evening shift, and then a midnight shift, before starting over again. It can range from rotating every week, to every month, bimonthly, and so on. This can be an especially difficult type of shift to endure.

The advantages of this type of shift work can include a frequent change that does not allow the officer to become stagnant. In rotating from days to evenings to midnights, the officer acquires a taste of every facet of police work. Every shift produces different types of calls, some exclusive to that specific shift. The rotation of shifts does not overwhelm the officer with service calls and/or high-priority calls on a regular basis.

One of the disadvantages is being unfamiliar with the area that is worked. By changing shifts every so often, the officer is unable to become acquainted with the citizens and crime patterns in the area in which he or she is working. Just when an officer begins to understand the patterns, it becomes time to change to another shift.

Another disadvantage is an interruption in the body's circadian rhythm. Once the body becomes used to a certain shift and sleep pattern, it suddenly has to change and must start all over again in adjusting to the new schedule. Shift work has also been shown to increase the risk of abnormal heart rhythms, according to research in the area of occupational and environmental medicine. Like law enforcement officers, nurses also are required to work shift, and according to the *Australian Nursing Journal,* studies have shown that people who work shift have a much greater risk of heart disease over the long term than do people who do not work shift (Harulow, 2000).

Lack of normalcy is another factor. With the rotating shift, it can be extremely difficult to schedule vacations, classes, and so on. Typically, college semesters last approximately 3 or 4 months. With a rotating shift that changes every week or month, attending school is virtually impossible.

Once the agency makes a decision on whether to have permanent, temporary, or rotating shifts, the next choice is the duration of a shift. Shifts can range from 24 hours down to 8 hours, with some room to adjust in between.

### 24-Hour Shift

Although rare, a 24-hour shift might be used by some agencies, specifically small agencies with low populations. Although acting more as a reactive police force as opposed to a proactive police force, this shift has its advantages and disadvantages.

One of the advantages is that it is a cost-effective tool for the agency. Because it is a reactionary type of approach, it can lead to fewer officers on the street and more time spent waiting for something to happen. Money is saved by less wear and tear on vehicles and less manpower. Another advantage for the individual officer is that it gives the officer plenty of time off to relax, spend time with the family, pick up a second job, or work extra duty jobs.

Although the reactive approach can be a cost-saving feature for the agency, it is typically that—reactive. There is little room for the proactive approach. Officers wait for incidents to occur before responding. Administrators cannot expect their officers to work a 24-hour cycle and remain proactive; the burnout with this type of shift can be extreme.

Another concern is that fatigue can affect officer safety. When officers work 24 hours straight, their bodies naturally will begin to shut down and become sluggish. This can cause changes in perception, slowed reaction times, eyesight distortions, decreased metabolism, and so on.

### 10-, 11-, or 12-Hour Shifts

Today, many agencies are switching over to a modified shift that consists of 10, 11, or 12 hours straight. Although some agencies continue to use the 8 hours a day, 5 days a week cycle, many agencies are beginning to understand that the modified shift can have plenty of advantages. It is not a panacea, though, because this shift also has drawbacks.

The advantages of this type of shift are shared by all. With the modified shift, time off can consist of either 3 or 4 days per week. This allows the individual officer to take the recovery time he or she requires to return to work. It allows the officer to spend time with the family, work extra duty jobs, and attend court without feeling fatigued. Because of the hours, rotating days off enables the officer to occasionally have weekends off to spend relaxing, and will occasionally give the officer weekdays off to spend time running errands, and so on.

Some of the disadvantages can be child care issues and school attendance. Because of the long days, scheduling drop-off or pick-up times for the children can be difficult. School can also be an issue because of the length of shift. If an officer wants to attend school, it can be a difficult task to schedule classes around this type of shift.

## 8-Hour Shift

Years ago, it was virtually unheard of for agencies to use anything but the 8-hour shift. Today, numerous agencies have deviated from this and switched to modified shifts, yet there are still agencies that continue with the 8-hour shift. Like other schedules, it has both benefits and disadvantages.

The advantages are that it gives the individual more of a "normal" life. By working 8-hour days with 2 days off, the officer can put in a "typical" day's work and return to his or her life. The 8-hour shift can also reduce the amount of fatigue the officer experiences because there are no extended hours.

One of the disadvantages is little recovery time. With only 2 days off, the officer can still feel fatigued because of working 5 days and then having only 2 days off to recover. Extra duty work can be cut short because of having only 2 days off. Officers who are required to work overtime or who elect to work extra hours can suffer from fatigue because the 8-hour shift is then extended to 12 or 16 hours a day, still leaving only 2 days of recovery time.

## Power/Relief Shift

Some agencies will use a power shift or a relief shift. This type of shift is atypical and can consist of odd times or odd hours. The power shift can be either a desired or an undesired shift.

Because these shifts are typically at peak times, the aggressive officer usually desires them. The volume of calls is generally higher during these times, and some officers find this shift suitable. Also, this shift can be an advantage for the officer who has a difficult time with the shift or rotation that his or her agency has chosen.

The disadvantages are that the shift is typically used during peak times, which can produce a large amount of work, and that can be a negative factor to the stagnant officer. Also, during these shifts, most of the department is working at different times; therefore, most of the officer's colleagues are working other assignments, making it difficult for the officer to socialize with other police officers in his or her department.

*Dennis Rodriguez*

## For Further Reading

*Guide to scheduling the 24-hour operation* (2nd ed.). (1998). Circadian Technologies.

Harulow, S. (2000). Are you losing sleep over shift work? *Australian Nursing Journal, 8*(1), 26–28.

Heart disease: Shift workers experience increases in abnormal heart rhythms. (2001, October). *Heart Disease Weekly*, p. 5.

Morgan, D. (1996). *Sleep secrets for shift workers & people with off-beat schedules.* Duluth, MN: Whole Person Associates.

Shift work takes its toll on families. (2003, February). *Industrial Safety and Hygiene News, 37*(2), 10.

Vila, B. (2000). *Tired cops: The importance of managing police fatigue.* Washington, DC: Police Executive Research Forum.

## ❧ PATROL WORK

Patrol work is the job of those officers who are least specialized in a general-purpose police department. Patrol officers are the point of first response for most of the work done by the agency, and as such, they are key decision makers about what the agency knows about matters of interest to the police. They also exert tremendous influence, if they do not outright determine, what the police are likely to do about matters brought to the agency's attention. Often called the backbone of the police department, the patrol division is invariably the largest unit in local agencies. A 2000 census of local police departments showed that 68% of all police were assigned to answer calls for service from the public, which is one of the central responsibilities of patrol officers. In departments serving communities of 50,000 or more residents, typically 6 out of 10 officers served this function; in departments serving less than 2,500 residents, more than 9 out of 10 officers were assigned this duty.

Egon Bittner's (1974) characterization of patrol work is apt: tending to "something-that-ought-not-to-be-happening-and-about-which-someone-had-better-do-something-now!" (p. 30). The core patrol task in these situations is restoring order or preventing disorder that might arise from the immediate circumstances of the situation. This is, and has long been, the defining feature about which the policies, procedures, and practices of patrol work have been structured. The police department's specialists have narrowly constructed missions. Detectives investigate cases where a crime has been alleged or seems possible; vice and narcotics units focus on detecting and repressing specific types of crime; juvenile officers focus on the problems that young people create; gang units attempt to develop intelligence on gang membership and activities; and tactics units, bomb squads, and other special operations units focus on how to respond to particular kinds of crises. Much of the work of these specialist units is structured around "cases" or crisis events, the character of which has already been well-defined before the specialist receives the assignment. On the other hand, patrol officers are expected to detect or respond to reports of things that are or might be awry, but the police do not know for sure that something is wrong or what is amiss. From an organizational workload perspective, patrol officers' primary task as first responders is to figure out (a) whether it is police business, and if so, (b) whether it can be handled solely by the officer or whether it will be referred to another part of the organization, and if it is not police business, (c) whether and to whom

the problem will be referred outside the police organization. Often, then, the first order of the patrol officer's business when he or she encounters a potentially troublesome situation is to determine whether it is a problem and the nature of that problem.

Patrol officers' work has traditionally been divided into two parts: (a) watching and waiting for something that deserves their intervention, and (b) the interventions themselves. Police organizations structure patrol both geographically and temporally, assigning officers to patrol specific beats during specific work shifts. Police departments vary considerably in the ratio of their patrol staffing to their workloads, but a large body of research suggests that patrol officers typically spend much more time watching and waiting than intervening in the affairs of citizens. A 1996–1997 study of Indianapolis and St. Petersburg found that only one fourth of the typical patrol work shift was given to encounters with the general public, and the remainder was spent on watching and waiting (general patrol), driving en route to a specific destination, conducting some activity targeted at a particular problem (e.g., traffic surveillance), gathering information, administrative activities, and personal activities. This is not necessarily a recent phenomenon; a series of studies in the 1970s and 1980s also showed that the considerable majority of patrol officers' time is typically spent uncommitted to doing specific assigned work from dispatchers and supervisors.

Since the earliest days when police began performing patrol work as a full-time occupation, the lowly patrol officer has enjoyed considerable discretion in determining what occupies his or her time. Before the advent of the two-way radio, it was challenging for a patrol sergeant to determine where and how his subordinates were spending their time—often goofing off in saloons and pool halls. Technological changes in transportation, communications, and information processing have increased the capacity of the department hierarchy to track and control the activities of patrol officers. Indeed, harnessing police mobilizations to calls for service and the 9-1-1 emergency response system is widely thought to have virtually determined where and when police officers will be mobilized to intervene—enmeshing them in reactive policing that makes them helpless to exercise discretion in deciding what problems need the most attention. However, systematic empirical research indicates that these impressions have no basis in fact. Since at least the 1970s, the majority of patrol officers' work time is not dedicated to activities directed by the dispatcher or the organization's hierarchy, but remain at the officer's discretion, ranging from about two thirds to more than three fourths of the typical work shift. This pattern holds regardless of the type of neighborhood to which the officer is assigned, including those that have relatively high workloads as well as those with relatively low ones. Furthermore, for a large portion of the typical work shift (regardless of type of neighborhood), officers enjoy time free of specific work assignments in blocks of at least 60 uninterrupted minutes for about 47%–59% of their work time. Plus, police supervisors are seldom present to tell patrol officers what to do, they seldom offer advice or commands by radio or at the scene, and they rely upon those patrol officers' own reports to determine what occurred after the fact. All this is to say that patrol officers are not nearly as "handcuffed" by 9-1-1 and calls for service as some researchers and reformers claim, nor are they heavily directed by their supervisors. Rather, when, where, and how they choose to engage in their work is loosely constrained, but still largely a matter of the rank-and-file officer's choosing.

Police supervisors, police chiefs, and the public care most about what the police do in the limited amount of time that they engage the public in face-to-face interactions, called "encounters." What do officers do during these encounters? No one has conducted a study with a stop watch, but it is probably safe to assume that most of the time committed to those encounters is spent trying to determine the nature of the problem, whether it is a traffic stop or a domestic dispute. What Bittner and others have made clear, however, is that many of the activities that are popularly attributed to the police (making arrests, using physical force, using forensic methods to solve crimes) are relatively infrequent occurrences. One study found that on an average 8-hour shift, patrol officers sought information on about

six possible "wrongdoers," and they provided direct service to about 4.5 citizens. On average, they arrested, cited, or used physical force on fewer than one citizen per shift. Not uncommonly, patrol officers ask the public to help them deal with the situation, which may include asking a citizen to stop misbehaving, control other citizens who are or might be misbehaving, provide information, or seek assistance elsewhere. These encounters are also the occasion for citizens to ask the police to do things: to make or persuade other citizens to alter their behavior or to provide a direct service (information, physical assistance, filing a report, intervention on their behalf). Research has shown that more often than not, patrol officers will either grant the citizen's request or take a positive step in that direction. However, officers are much less likely to fulfill a citizen's request to coerce another citizen (either by a warning or an arrest) than to advise, persuade, or banish another citizen from the scene. Thus, it is clear that patrol officers take their public servant role seriously, but they are far less inclined to exercise the more extreme forms of their authority simply because someone at the scene asks them to do so.

Since the advent of community policing and problem-oriented policing, police departments have placed increasing pressure on patrol officers to engage in other types of activity. This includes spending less time dealing with specific incidents, complaints, and suspicious situations, and more time on establishing a collaborative relationship with members of the community and identifying, analyzing, and solving long-term problems that tend to manifest themselves in repeated events. Has this pressure produced a substantial change in the nature of patrol work? At this time, the answer appears to be that the change, if any, is quite modest. The general patrol officer's work appears largely unaffected by these changes for two reasons. First, police departments are inclined to assign much of the responsibility for community and problem-oriented policing to specialist patrol officers who are relieved of the obligation to respond to routine calls for service so that they can engage in concerted community policing and problem solving. These officers constitute only a small portion of the entire uniformed division, with the vast majority still assigned to watching/waiting and responding to calls for service. Second, neither the general patrol officers nor the community policing specialists appear to spend large portions of their time engaged in these new activities. For example, a study of Indianapolis and St. Petersburg found that, on average, community policing patrol specialists spent 7–19 minutes per 8-hour shift on attending community meetings, and they averaged only 51–81 minutes on problem solving. Patrol generalists spent substantially less time than that (1–4 minutes on community meetings and 30–36 minutes on problem solving). This study was undertaken in departments widely regarded as committed to community and problem-oriented policing. Why the impact of these changes should be so small is not entirely clear, but it may be related to the newness of these practices to most officers, inadequate training and supervision to support these practices, and the pressure of demands from the public and dispatchers for officers to engage in traditional patrol activities. What seems most likely is that the departments had not yet figured out how best to manage and supervise community and problem-oriented policing, and that the members of the organization, perhaps subconsciously, remained committed to the notion that the core activities of police patrol remain those of watching/waiting and intervening when any of a host of problems might arise.

An alternative perspective on patrol work has recently emerged and deserves some consideration. Some have argued that in the late 20th century, the core function of patrol shifted from intervening in situations that might need police attention to gathering, processing, and disseminating a wide range of information on risks facing neighborhoods, communities, and societies. The risks on which police gather information are often quite tangential to what police and society generally consider at the core of the police mission. For example, the police concern with traffic accidents is primarily to facilitate emergency assistance to the injured, determine who is at fault for purposes of the administration of justice, and minimize disruption to traffic flow, yet the vast majority of the time they spend on traffic accidents is given to investigating and writing reports that

serve the needs of state motor vehicle departments, insurance companies, and automobile manufacturers. Even the immense care patrol officers give in reporting crime incidents generates information that has nothing to do with the arrest and prosecution of offenders, but rather serves the needs of other organizations and institutions in society that are concerned with the quality of life in the community (e.g., realtors, investment bankers, neighborhood groups, school administrators, employers). This perspective perceives much of community policing as the practice of "risk communications," where the prime function of the police is to provide various segments of the community with information about the risk of crime and disorder of different sorts. This perspective emphasizes the key activities of police as "knowledge workers," which illuminates a very different set of patrol officer activities and choices than has been raised in previous research. Here the concern is what, where, and how police gather information; how they process it; and how they disseminate it. However, not much is known about the sorts of decisions patrol officers make on such matters as surveillance and communicating the information from that surveillance to others, an especially important concern in light of a traditional occupational culture that encourages officers not to share information about crime and suspicious situations widely within the organization. To what extent are these priorities influenced by management and supervision? These questions seem particularly important to answer in a time when local patrol officers are expected to play an important role in the production of useful intelligence on terrorist activity.

*Stephen D. Mastrofski*

***See also*** Task Forces

## For Further Reading

Bayley, D. H., & Bittner, E. (1984). Learning the skills of policing. *Law and Contemporary Problems, 47*, 35–59.

Bittner, E. (1974). Florence Nightingale in pursuit of Willie Sutton: A theory of the police. In H. Jacob (Ed.), *The potential for reform of criminal justice.* Beverly Hills, CA: Sage.

Ericson, R. V., & Haggerty, K. D. (1997). *Policing the risk society.* Toronto: University of Toronto Press.

Hickman, M., & Reaves, B. A. (2003). *Local police departments 2000*. Washington, DC: Bureau of Justice Statistics.

Mastrofski, S. D., & Parks, R. B. (2002, November). *Beyond 911 and the myth of reactive policing*. Paper delivered at the annual meeting of the American Society of Criminology, Chicago.

Mastrofski, S. D., Snipes, J. B., Parks, R. B., & Maxwell, C. D. (2000). The helping hand of the law: Police control of citizens on request. *Criminology, 38*, 307–342.

Parks, R. B., Mastrofski, S. D., DeJong, C., & Gray, M. K. (1999). How officers spend their time with the community. *Justice Quarterly, 16*, 483-518.

Parks, R. B., Mastrofski, S. D., Reiss, A. J., Jr., Worden, R. E., Terrill, W. C., DeJong, C., Stroshine, M., & Shepard, R. (1998). *St. Petersburg project on policing neighborhoods: A study of the police and the community*. Bloomington: Indiana University Press.

Rubinstein, J. (1974). *City police*. New York: Ballantine.

Snipes, J. B. (2001). *Police response to citizen requests for assistance: An assessment of deservedness, workload, social status, and officer predisposition perspectives*. Unpublished doctoral dissertation, State University of New York at Albany.

Sparrow, M. K., Moore, M. H., & Kennedy, D. M. (1990). *Beyond 911: A new era for policing*. New York: Basic Books.

Walker, S. (1984). "Broken windows" and fractured history: The use and misuse of history in recent police patrol analysis. *Justice Quarterly, 1*, 75–90.

## ⊘ PEACE OFFICERS

At first glance, the terms *police officer* and *peace officer* do not appear distinct. But an examination of the history and responsibilities of the peace officer prove otherwise. Like the police officer, the peace officer has arrest powers (per respective jurisdiction); like the civilian, there is no existing administrative or review board to which the peace officer must answer. In truth, the peace officer has a blended identity: part civilian, part law enforcement officer.

Although legislation such as the United Peace Officer Bill, as passed in New York State in 1980, serves to delineate the differences between police and peace officers, the powers and responsibilities of peace officers vary by region and/or state. In general, peace officers are officials who can arrest citizens and carry firearms. They can be hired by private persons for work, including providing security, serving warrants, serving subpoenas, and transporting prisoners. Although primarily employed to handle civil matters, peace officers are also allowed to direct traffic and take mentally unstable people into custody.

Just as their responsibilities differ, so do the means by which one becomes a peace officer. Whether appointed or elected, peace officers must complete training as required per geographic region. Although training requirements vary, possible curricular offerings include appropriate terrorism response, CPR, weapons training, mental preparedness, and physical fitness. Just as training programs differ, so does the intensity of such programs. The state of Nevada, for example, requires its peace-officers-in-training to live in an academic dormitory for the duration of their training.

In a move toward accountability and professionalism, numerous organizations seek to improve the public image and private operations of peace officers. For example, the Alaska Peace Officers Association, California Peace Officers' Association, Peace Officers Research Association of California, Peace Officers Research Association of Nevada, and the Women Peace Officers Association of California all host Web sites listing training requirements, membership benefits, and support services for peace officers. In additional to those groups, the National Constable Association, National Peace Officers Association, National Latino Peace Officers Association, and Texas Peace Officers Association—the first organization for black peace officers in America—also provide professional status. And the State of Nevada Commission on Peace Officers' Standards and Training has produced a lengthy description of the Commission's activities and missions, including detailed reports on departmental audits, training and education of prospective peace officers, and the organization's chain of command. Common aims of affiliation in such organizations are adequate compensation and health, disability, and accident benefits, not to mention the ongoing support of members' professional and economic lives.

Despite such attempts to professionalize their station, once peace officer status has been achieved, there is no formal means of disciplinary action against problem officers and no formal chain of command. One trade-off for such an arrangement is that peace officers receive no taxpayer funding—they are hired by private individuals and must purchase their own work-related equipment, including uniforms, firearms, and ammunition. So, although peace officers are charged with protecting the public, they are responsible for any expenses relative to their training or other equipment. In accordance with these contradictions, the position of the American peace officer is not without controversy or confusion, as evidenced by the history of the peace officer in America.

Based on the European model of the constable, the peace officer remains a fixture of American history in general, and the western United States in particular. In contrast to popular notions, the "wild" of the storied Wild West was composed of the activities of police officers and gamblers—civilians and peace officers rarely were involved in violence. In short, the Wild West was more western than wild. Thanks to the work of numerous authors, including historians such as Harold J. Weiss and Robert M. Utley, the colorful histories of characters such as Wild Bill Hickok, Lone Wolf Gonzaullas, and Wyatt Earp are tempered with the less-noted heroism of peace officers such as James Gillett, George Scarborough, Frank Canton, and "Bear River" Thomas Smith. But the work of contemporary peace officers is not without criticism. Like their law enforcement counterparts, a small number of peace officers have been accused of inappropriate behavior, excessive use of force, assault, and other offenses. However, because of lack of administrative powers, such individuals are rarely sanctioned.

And although peace officers receive some monetary reward for their job-related activities (e.g., in Texas's Williamson County, peace officers collect $40 per citation issued, $40 per summons issued, and $100 per temporary restraining order), negative by-products of their profession are numerous. As is generally true for police officers, numerous sources report that the life expectancy of peace officers is approximately 10 years shorter than that of a civilian. Peace officer divorce rates far exceed those

of civilians (ranging up to 75%), as do rates for substance abuse and suicide. Ironically, although the peace officer is a civilian, he or she has a lifestyle more similar to that of a police officer.

Despite a lack of uniform standards concerning peace officers' authority, powers, and history, peace officers remain an essential component of American history and contemporary American life. Their sacrifices are beyond doubt.

*Marsha Clowers*

## For Further Reading

Allen, F. (2001). Montana vigilantes and the origins of 3-7-77. *Montana, 51,* 2–19.

DeArment, R. K. (1995). A look at two professional frontier lawmen: George A. Scarborough and Frank M. Canton. *Journal of the West, 34,* 8–12.

Egloff, F. R. (1995). Lawmen and gunmen: A contrasting view of Old West peace officers in Kansas and Texas. *Journal of the West, 34,* 19–26.

Secrest, W. B. (1994). *Lawmen and desperadoes: A compendium of noted, early California peace officers, badmen, and outlaws.* Spokane, WA: Arthur H. Clark.

## ✑ PERFORMANCE EVALUATION OF POLICE DEPARTMENTS

Among other things, police departments can be seen as producing organizations: They take resources from their environment, and they use those resources to produce results. In general, citizens give police departments two key resources they need to operate: money and the authority of the state. Using their professional expertise, the police deploy these resources through a particular set of activities, such as patrol, criminal investigation, and traffic enforcement. These activities, in turn, produce an immediate set of results: surveillance of public spaces, rapid response to calls for service, arrests, and citations. These immediate results are, in turn, thought to be related to socially desirable results such as reduced crime, reduced traffic fatalities, and the kind of justice we associate with calling offenders to account.

When we think of police departments as organizations that spend valuable resources to produce results, it is natural to wonder about the value produced by the organization relative to the costs of providing it. This requires us to think about what we should recognize and count as the valuable results produced by a police organization.

For the most part, police leaders, citizens, and academics have had to content themselves with a small number of routinely created and traditionally recognized performance measures: (a) crimes reported to the police, and (b) arrests made (and cases cleared) by the police. With the advent of computer-aided dispatch systems to manage patrol forces, police departments have also been able to report regularly on their response times to calls for service.

In recent years, the various stakeholders interested in evaluating the performance of the police have become less content with these traditional measures. First, reported crime is imperfectly correlated with the actual level of victimization and not well connected with citizen fear. Second, the police produce more products and services than simply reducing crime and calling offenders to account; they engage in a wide range of activities that includes providing important kinds of emergency medical and social services and engaging young people in athletic activity. Third, existing measures do not capture whether the police are being economical with scarce taxpayer monies and, most importantly, whether the citizens who are served by the police felt that they were being well and justly served—that those who called the police felt that they got an acceptable response from these public servants, and that those who were cited or arrested by the police at least had their rights protected in the encounter.

Many of these new understandings about the effects that the police produced on communities, and the methods they used to produce these effects, were captured in a changed understanding of what the mission and strategy of the police should be. This new conception of the overall ends and means of the police has been variously called *community policing, problem-oriented policing,* or *community problem-solving policing.* As the conception of the important ends and means of policing changed, so

did the ideas about how to measure the performance of the police.

At present, the best means of evaluating the performance of the police is not a settled matter; it is a contested issue. The debate is not simply about the technical issues of what is feasible to measure, and what the best ways are to measure the effects that interest us; it is also about the political and philosophical question of what we would like a police department to be, what we would like it to produce, and what we think are the best methods of producing the desired results. Some key strategic issues in evaluating the performance of police departments are presented below.

## THE UNIT OF ANALYSIS: ORGANIZATION AS A WHOLE, SPECIFIC POLICIES AND PROGRAMS, OR SUBORDINATE UNITS

When thinking about measuring and evaluating the performance of police departments, one should distinguish among (a) performance measures for the organization as a whole, (b) evaluation of specific tactics or programs used by the police department to achieve different purposes or to deal with different problems, and (c) performance measures for subordinate units in the department. Indeed, these differences turn out to be very important depending on the function one wants performance measurement and evaluation to serve.

If one is primarily interested in using performance measurement to achieve the managerial tasks of increasing both the external accountability of a police department to its community and the internal accountability of subordinate units to the leader of the department, then one is primarily interested in measures of performance that are closely tied to both the ultimate objectives and the operational procedures of particular organizational units. The reason is simply that in order for accountability to do its work of motivating performance in an organization, the measures used have to be tied to a particular person who can be held accountable for performance. That usually means someone who is in a structural position in the organization where he or she has accepted responsibility for accomplishing a specified purpose with a specified set of resources.

On the other hand, if one is interested in generating reliable scientific knowledge about the effectiveness of a particular policy or program on which an organization is relying, then one might be more interested in the evaluation of specific policies and procedures. This is often the goal of program evaluation. It assumes that the particular policies and procedures being evaluated are merely examples of fixed, robust "technologies" that could be used to achieve particular results in any department in which they were tried. To develop reliable knowledge about whether the programs work or not, one has to not only see the effects that such efforts seem to be producing, but also develop reliable methods for ensuring that the effects that are apparently being produced by the program are, in fact, being produced by the program and not by some other factor.

Sometimes, these two different ideas of performance evaluation—the managerial and the scientific—can be combined in the aspiration to help all police departments become "learning organizations"—organizations that are reflective and thoughtful about the measures they are using to deal with different categories of crimes and problems, that are curious about the real impact that their programs are having, that eagerly seek out information about both the means and the impact, and that create discussion opportunities within the police department to think about what they are now doing, and what they might do better.

## THE STAGE OF PRODUCTION: INPUTS, ACTIVITIES, OUTPUTS, OR OUTCOMES

The second big question to be addressed in developing performance measures for policing is where along the production process one should try to measure performance. Generally speaking, a police department takes in *inputs* in the form of tax dollars and state authority. The dollars and authority are used (in part) to sustain a patrol force and a detective unit. Those organizational units, in turn, use the resources to sustain *activities* that could be described as patrol operations, rapid response to calls for service, and

criminal investigation. These activities, in turn, produce *outputs* in the form of threatened and actual arrests of criminal offenders. These outputs, in turn, produce *outcomes* in the form of reduced criminal victimization, enhanced security, and the kind of justice we associate with holding criminal offenders accountable for their crimes. This could be described as the "value chain" that leads from inputs to outcomes, and presumably increases the value of the resources at each step along the way. An important question in measuring police performance has been exactly where along this value chain police performance should, ideally, be measured.

Much of the contemporary discussion of this subject emphasizes the importance of going beyond the measurement of "process" and focusing more attention on the measurement of "outcomes." The reason for this is not hard to understand. Ultimately, the outcomes are the valuable results of the organization—the effects that would justify the expenditure of resources. Unless outcomes are measured, stakeholders cannot be sure that they are getting what they wanted or expected from an organization. Nor can police departments effectively learn about whether the policies and procedures on which they are relying can produce the desired results.

However, although it is important to get the police focused more on measuring outcomes, it is also important that the police stay focused on processes as well. Citizens who call for help or services are obvious clients of police departments, and there is a growing concern about capturing their "customer satisfaction." Individuals who are the objects of police enforcement activities are less obvious clients. The goal of these encounters involves the delivery of obligations—issuing citations, making arrests, and so on—in a way that maintains the legitimacy of the police. Although these encounters do not need to result in happy clients, clients do need to feel like they have been treated fairly and respectfully. Society as a whole also has an interest in the details of these encounters beyond the reaction of the individual. Society wants to be sure that the authority and force of the state that were used by the police in making stops and arrests were used both economically and fairly.

Police managers should not restrict themselves to simply one outcome measure to assess the value created by policing. It probably makes sense for them to develop a battery of measurements that includes (a) outcome measures, both as ultimate measures of value created and as ways of testing whether innovative programs work; (b) activity and output measures to focus managerial attention on the way authority and money are being used to achieve results; and (c) expenditure and investment measures to help organizations manage effectively the transition from traditional styles of policing to the new style.

## DIMENSIONS OF PERFORMANCE

This brings us directly to the third important question raised by the issue of performance evaluation: namely, what particular dimensions of performance should we try to measure? Moore (2002) suggested that the police should monitor their performance on at least seven dimensions: (a) reduce crime; (b) call offenders to account; (c) reduce fear and enhance personal security; (d) guarantee safety in public spaces; (e) use financial resources fairly, efficiently, and effectively; (f) use force and authority fairly, efficiently, and effectively; and (g) satisfy customer demands/achieve legitimacy with those policed. It is worth noting that the measures include three different *outcome* dimensions: reduced crime, enhanced personal security, and reduced fear in public spaces. The measures also include two different measures of the *inputs* used by the police: public money, and force and authority. And they include two important *outputs* of policing: "offenders held accountable for crimes" and "customer satisfaction." These measures all seem to work fairly well in terms of a utilitarian view of the police department as an organization that spends money and authority to produce responses to calls for assistance, and seeks to reduce crime and fear by calling offenders to account for their crimes. They work a bit less well when we think about evaluating the performance of police departments as organizations that are trying to produce justice and fairness as well as a set of practical results such as reduced

fear and reduced crime. To measure the extent to which the police produce justice and fairness, and a sense of legitimacy among those who are policed, one has to develop measures that allow one to determine the fairness with which police use their authority, and the legitimacy that both citizens in general and those who are arrested confer on the police as a consequence of their operations.

## METHODS OF MEASURING PERFORMANCE

Virtually all police departments have some basic systems for measuring their performance. That baseline system typically consists of (a) a financial accounting system that recognizes the financial costs of running the department, (b) some output measures (e.g., arrests and response time), and (c) some outcome measures (e.g., levels of reported crime). However, as mentioned above, these systems are limited in assessing the value provided to citizens by police departments.

Clearly, additional data need to be collected and analyzed. Some of these data already exist within the administrative records in police departments. Police departments have access to information on proactive misdemeanor and traffic arrests, shootings, civilian complaints, and civil suits against the department. To make greater use of this information, it simply needs to be collated, analyzed, and reported.

Some of the data needed to assess the value of police departments, however, must be developed through investments in new measurement systems. Information must be gathered by asking those outside the department what their experiences with the department have been. This is essentially survey information. At least three different groups could be surveyed: the general population, those who call the police or ask for help, and those who are cited or arrested by the police. Information also needs to be collected to understand the effects of particular problem-solving initiatives. This could take the form of relatively sophisticated program evaluations of new programmatic ideas, or it could take the form of much less formal "after-action assessments."

## CONCLUSION: THE DYNAMIC PROCESS OF DEVELOPING MEASUREMENT SYSTEMS

To improve current systems of police performance measurement, three conceptual steps must be taken. First, we must recognize the wide variety of valuable contributions that police departments make to their communities and treat all of these valuable effects as important, interlocking components of the police mission. Second, we must recognize that we are interested in economizing on the use of force and authority, as well as money, and that the police must be evaluated in terms of the quality of the justice they produce, as well as the amount of safety and security. We have to develop measures that allow us to see how fairly the police operate and how much legitimacy they enjoy, as well as how efficient and effective they are. Third, we must recognize our interest in helping police departments strengthen their capabilities for the future. Once these conceptual steps are taken, we have to be prepared to make a sustained investment in improving our ability to measure how the police are performing in these new terms.

*Mark H. Moore and Anthony A. Braga*

### For Further Reading

Moore, M. H. (2002). *Recognizing value in policing: The challenge of measuring police performance.* Washington, DC: Police Executive Research Forum.

## ✂ PERP WALK

It was a cool, crisp, sunny Friday afternoon in downtown Manhattan, like many other spring days before or since. But this particular day, March 30, 1984, was special, unlike any other in the annals of law enforcement.

A team of city, state, and federal investigators left FBI headquarters at 26 Federal Plaza along with Mafia boss Paul Castellano and began walking slowly toward the U.S. District Courthouse at Foley Square a few short blocks away as newspaper photographers and television cameras recorded every step.

Castellano, whose name would become a well-known example of mob violence the following year as the victim of a spectacular midtown Manhattan assassination orchestrated by John Gotti, was an important organized crime figure in his own right. He had been arrested that morning as the lead defendant in a racketeering indictment that accused him of heading an enterprise that had killed 25 people during a 10-year period.

And although the racketeering indictment contained more murders as predicate acts than any other, the truly unique law enforcement aspect of the case was a 9-minute perp walk that he took down Duane Street and across Lafayette and Center streets to the U.S. District Courthouse, where he would be arraigned on the charges.

Unlike most defendants, Castellano was not handcuffed or otherwise restrained. More astounding, Castellano—not the investigators who accompanied him—suggested, and then insisted, that he walk to the courthouse rather than wait for an FBI car to take him.

"I can't stand being here," said Castellano, referring to the FBI building. "Let's walk."

"The Perp Walk," opined the Second Circuit Court of Appeals in Manhattan, "is a widespread police practice in New York City (and many others) in which the suspected perpetrator of a crime, after being arrested, is walked in front of the press so that he can be photographed or filmed."

Perp walks have been around for decades and come in several varieties. In most cases, suspects are transported to or from a police precinct as part of the arrest and booking process, as the press, through its own diligence or advance notice, takes photos or footage of the "perp," or perpetrator. The exercise is lauded by police as a deterrent to similar crimes, and it is justified by the media as an aid in informing the public of important news about crime. The defense bar scorns perp walks as offensive, self-aggrandizing efforts by police that humiliate suspects and prejudice their rights to a fair trial even before they get to court.

No matter the justifications or legal ramifications, perp walks are often great theater, producing memorable images and/or remarks by the suspects.

Without question, the most dramatic episode to emanate from a perp walk was witnessed by a national television audience on November 24, 1963, when Lee Harvey Oswald was paraded through a crowd of reporters and others in the basement of

Dallas police headquarters and shot dead by bar owner Jack Ruby.

In 1952, legendary bank robber Willie Sutton, when asked by a New York reporter why he robbed banks, said, "Because that's where the money is."

Seven years later, again in New York, during the perp walk of Salvador Agron, a 16-year-old gang leader dubbed The Capeman because he wore a black cape with a flaming red lining during a double homicide, TV newsman Gabe Pressman hurled evocative questions to Agron about his motives and any possible remorse he may have felt.

"I don't care if I burn," Agron said as the cameras rolled. "My mother could watch me."

The courts have consistently held that perp walks that result from the transportation of suspects from one place to another are legally permissible, even if cops notify the press in advance. Staged events, however, in which police walk a suspect out of a station house for no reason other than a photo shoot are another matter, according to a landmark decision in July 2000 by the Second Circuit Court of Appeals in Manhattan.

The case involved the arrest of John Lauro, a doorman at an Upper East Side apartment building in 1995. Lauro was arrested on minor burglary charges—they were ultimately dismissed—taken out of a police station in handcuffs, placed into a car at the request of a television news station, driven around the block, and brought back to the station house minutes later.

Lauro's arrest had been triggered by a tenant at the Upper East Side apartment building. The tenant, Matthew Eberhart, had given Lauro keys to his apartment and asked him to water his plants while he was on vacation. He rigged a wireless camera that videotaped Lauro several times as he entered the bedroom, went through his drawers, without taking anything. Eberhart also determined that nothing had been stolen from his apartment.

Eberhart sold the videotape to a local TV station for $200, then contacted the police, who arrested Lauro. Two hours later, the office of the Deputy Commissioner of Public Information contacted the arresting officer and told him to take Lauro on a perp walk, during which the TV station obtained footage of Lauro that was subsequently broadcasted.

Deciding that Lauro's perp walk was "a staged recreation" that was "an inherently fictional dramatization of an event that transpired hours earlier," the Appeals Court ruled that the "perp walk . . . not only intruded upon the privacy protected by the Fourth Amendment, but also lacked any legitimate law enforcement purpose, and was hence unreasonable."

New York City later settled out of court with Lauro for $250,000.

*Jerry Capeci*

*See also* News Media and Police

# ✐ PHYSICAL FITNESS AND TRAINING

Police officers who are unfit put their own lives, the lives of their partners, and the lives of the public at risk. Today, American police academies lasting 12 weeks or more graduate fit recruits. The unsolved problem for many police departments is the rapid and severe physical deterioration of too many of those academy graduates.

The general definition of physical fitness as the ability to perform everyday activities without injury or undue fatigue applies to police but is incomplete. Police physical fitness refers also to the officer's ability to perform all job-related tasks successfully.

The earliest police system in America began as a night watchman function in New York City without physical training standards of any kind, and it continued that way for the rest of the 19th century. In the first two decades of the 20th century, scholars began to study all aspects of police training. August Vollmer, who was also Chief of Police for Berkeley, California, stated that successful fulfillment of police responsibilities would be best accomplished by college-educated officers, and physical education classes would be part of that preparation. However, such adjustments in the physical training of police did not occur until 50 years later as a result of three factors. In the 1960s, there was a significant rise in crime in the United States; in the 1970s, there was an increase in awareness of the department's role in attending to the health of its officers; and in the 1980s, there were several relevant court decisions. These three developments led gradually to changes in three aspects of police physical training: selection process, recruit training, and the department's contributions to postacademy fitness programs.

Postacademy fitness programs included department subsidies for fitness center memberships; department sponsorship of sports, races, and competitions; return of unspent sick leave monies; provision of exercise equipment in the precinct; promotional exam points based on fitness test scores; and special fitness bars for uniform display.

Vollmer's vision of college physical education classes did eventually prove to be useful to some police officers, but his plan for recruit preparation was not nearly sufficient to meet police needs. By 1913 in New York City, a Special Committee to Investigate the Police Department suggested that unfit men admitted by civil service tests should be dropped as a result of unsatisfactory showing in the school. By 1927, there was a law in New York State requiring physical tests for the state police based on standards set by the superintendent.

When compared with departments across the nation, the New York State law was the exception, and there were few advances in police physical training in the United States from 1916 to 1963. Many recruits during that period had been introduced to physical training and combat techniques in one of the U.S. military's boot camps.

With the dramatic rise in crime in the 1960s came a realization by American society that the police needed to set higher training standards for themselves.

In 1968, the U.S. Department of Justice described tasks required by an officer, including exhibiting a number of complex psychomotor skills, such as firing a weapon under extremely varied conditions; maintaining agility, endurance, and strength; and showing facility in self-defense and apprehension, as in taking a person into custody with a minimum of force.

By the 1970s, many police agencies required some form of medical screening by a physician prior to hire. Some departments also required candidates to pass physical fitness or job-related tests. Passing scores on the physical fitness tests were often determined with the use of percentile rankings taken from fitness normative data charts developed at the Cooper Institute in Dallas, Texas. A passing score on the job-related tests was determined by the candidate's ability to complete a series of activities within a given time frame.

The physical fitness tests most often conducted were the following:

Aerobic Power: How long will it take the recruit to run 1.5 miles? Or, how far can the recruit run in 12 minutes?

Body Composition: Based on skinfold measurements taken with a specially designed instrument such as a Lange skinfold caliper, an estimate could be made as to what percentage of the recruit's weight was body fat. (Many recruit training sites did not conduct this test because it required specialized training, which the average academy instructor did not possess.)

Flexibility: In the Sit & Reach Test, the flexibility of the recruit's lower back and hamstring muscle group is measured in inches.

Muscular Endurance: How many pushups can be completed in 1 minute? How many full sit-ups can be completed in 1 (or 2) minutes?

Strength: What is the maximum weight in pounds the recruit can lift for a single repetition on a bench press machine?

The second approach to evaluating a recruit's readiness to begin working in the field involved testing for tasks conducted during an officer's work shift.

Climbing: Did recruit have the ability to climb over a wall or fence 4 to 5 feet high?

Dragging: Did the recruit have the ability to drag a mannequin weighing between 120 and 175 pounds a distance of 50 feet?

Grip Strength: Did the recruit have the grip strength needed to meet or exceed the department's minimum standard when tested with a dynamometer?

Pursuit: Did the recruit have the foot speed to complete either the 400-meter dash or the shuttle run test within the department's specified time?

The physical demands of policing can be different depending on whether the officer is working in a large city, a suburban setting, or in rural America. As a result of these differences, the choice of job-related tests and the scores/times needed to pass the tests vary from department to department.

Upon passing the physical tests, it was common practice for the new hires to be sent to a training center or academy for 6 to 22 weeks. Three to five times per week, recruits participated in military-style calisthenics classes, ran one or more miles, stretched major muscle groups, learned basic self-defense techniques, and practiced firearms proficiency (shown to be dependent partly on hand and forearm strength).

In 1976, the first nationwide examination of police fitness took place when a survey sponsored by the National Institute of Law Enforcement and Criminal Justice showed that 90% of responding officers favored a department-sponsored physical fitness program. But such programs were in place in only 14% of the responding agencies. This percentage began to increase in response to three legal decisions that occurred in the 1980s.

In 1985, in *Tennessee v. Garner*, the U.S. Supreme Court restricted the use of deadly force to apprehend a fleeing, nondangerous felon.

In 1988, in *United States v. City of Wichita Falls*, a federal district court held that the city could conduct physical assessment tests for people seeking employment with the police department, and physical agility testing for recruits after they had entered the academy.

In another 1988 decision, *Parker v. District of Columbia*, a Washington, DC, circuit court upheld a $425,000 jury verdict for a man who was shot by a Washington, DC, police officer in the course of an arrest. The court noted that the officer had received no physical fitness training in 4 years and was incapable of subduing the plaintiff, thereby forcing him to resort to the use of a gun. In recent times, a small but growing number of law enforcement agencies have instituted policies that require police to undergo physical fitness tests periodically.

An important court decision upholding police fitness performance occurred in 2000 when the District Court of Pennsylvania ruled that the Southeastern Pennsylvania Transportation Authority (SEPTA) standard—that male and female applicants be able to run 1.5 miles in 12 minutes or less—does measure a minimum characteristic (the specific aerobic capacity) necessary to perform the duties of a SEPTA police officer.

Some departments have taken SEPTA's approach and mandated one performance standard for both men and women, whereas other departments, in an effort to increase numbers of women in their ranks, have conducted fitness testing using gender-based norms.

While legal decisions were shaping police fitness policies, the private sector was documenting the favorable cost-benefits of employee wellness programs. Because studies had shown that police officers were generally less healthy and less fit than inmates, some police departments initiated similar wellness programs in an effort to reduce costs of premature medical conditions while simultaneously avoiding expensive lawsuits due to poor field performance of physically unfit officers.

Since the advent of the 21st century, the majority of physical programs for recruits now include all the training developed since the 1970s, as well as a certain amount of focus specifically on health and wellness for the officer after the academy training has been completed. Recruits learn how to achieve proper nutrition even while on patrol, how to cope with police stress and shift work, and how to maintain balanced physical fitness throughout their careers.

*R. G. "Nick" McNickle*

## For Further Reading

Brooks, J. D. (2001, May). Law enforcement physical fitness standards and Title VII. *FBI Law Enforcement Bulletin*, pp. 26–32.

Collingwood, T., Hoffman, R., & Smith, J. (2003). The need for physical fitness. *Law & Order, 51*(6), 44–50.

Cooper Institute of Aerobic Research. (2002). *Physical fitness norms for law enforcement*. Available: http://www.cooperinst.org/shopping/lawstand3.pdf

McNickle, R. G. (1996, October). Police fitness: Is there life after the academy? *Law Enforcement News*, pp. 10, 11.

Parker v. District of Columbia, 850 F.2d 708 (D.C. Cir. 1988).

Tennessee v. Garner, 471 U.S. 1 (1985).

United States v. City of Wichita Falls, 704 F. Supp. 709 (N.D. Tex, 1988).

http://www.cophealth.com

## &#x0298;&#x0298; PLAIN VIEW DOCTRINE

The plain view doctrine states that an item within the sight of a police officer who is legally in a position to see the item may be seized without a warrant, as long as the item is immediately recognizable as contraband or evidence subject to seizure. Plain view is a recognized exception to the warrant requirement of the Fourth Amendment, although a plain view observation technically does not constitute a search, as there is no reasonable expectation of privacy regarding items left out in the open.

### THE "VALID PRIOR INTRUSION" REQUIREMENT

For the plain view doctrine to apply, the police must be lawfully present. This means the police must have a legal right to be where they are when they observe an item in plain view. This is sometimes referred to as a "valid prior intrusion" (*Harris v. United States,* 1968). Some examples of situations in which a law enforcement officer is lawfully present include executing a warrant, conducting a stop and frisk, pursuing a fleeing suspect, and responding to an emergency.

Hot pursuit was the justification for the seizure in *Warden v. Hayden* (1967). Police chased an armed robbery suspect into a house. While searching for the suspect and the weapons that he had used in the robbery, an officer looked in a washing machine and found clothing of the type that the suspect was said to have worn. The Court held that the seizure of the clothing was lawful because the officer was looking in a place where the suspect's weapons could be hidden. Thus, the observation of the clothing occurred within the scope of the hot pursuit search.

### THE "IMMEDIATELY APPARENT" REQUIREMENT

Under the plain view doctrine, police may seize an item only if it is "immediately apparent" that the item is subject to seizure (*Coolidge v. New Hampshire,* 1971). This means that before an item may be seized, the police must have probable cause that the item is subject to seizure without conducting any further examination of the object. In other words, the officer must be able to tell, by just looking at an item that is out in the open, that the item is seizable. A law enforcement officer cannot move or otherwise manipulate an item to determine if it is seizable.

How much an officer could handle an item under the plain view doctrine was at issue in *Arizona v. Hicks* (1987). In this case, police, investigating a shooting, entered Hicks's apartment to search for the shooter, other victims, and weapons. One officer noticed expensive stereo components that seemed out of place in the ramshackle apartment and, suspecting they were stolen, moved the equipment in order to obtain a view of their obscured serial numbers, then read and recorded the serial numbers. After checking with headquarters and learning that the stereo equipment was stolen, the officer seized it. The Court held that the officer's moving of the stereo equipment constituted a search, beyond the scope permissible under the plain view doctrine.

Although the plain view doctrine does not allow a law enforcement officer to conduct a further search of an object to determine its incriminating nature, it is well settled that an officer may use mechanical aids to assist in observing items of evidence and may alter his or her position to gain a better view. In *Texas v. Brown* (1983), a police officer changed his position and bent down in order to see into a suspect's car. He also shined his flashlight into the car. This allowed him to observe drugs inside the car. The Supreme Court held that the police officer's changing of position to get a better vantage point to look inside the vehicle and the use of the flashlight were both permitted under the plain view doctrine.

### The Inadvertence Requirement

Justice Stewart's opinion in *Coolidge* suggested that the discovery of evidence in plain view must be "inadvertent" to satisfy the "immediately apparent" requirement. Lower courts in many states have focused on this language, but the Court has since made clear that inadvertence is not necessary. In *Horton v. California* (1990), a police officer sought a search warrant for stolen property and weapons used in an armed robbery. The search warrant issued by the judge, however, authorized a search only for the stolen property. In executing the warrant, the officer did not find the stolen property but did find (and seize) the weapons. The officer testified that while he was searching for the stolen property, he also hoped to find the weapons. Thus, he did not discover the weapons "inadvertently." The Court upheld the seizure of the weapons, noting that there is no reason to exclude items in plain view just because a police officer has reason to believe he will see them before he actually observes them.

## PLAIN SMELL AND TOUCH

Some courts have expanded the plain view doctrine to the other senses of smell and touch. These courts frequently cite *United States v. Johns* (1985), in which the Court suggested that it was "debatable" whether there is a privacy interest in a package "reeking of marijuana."

In *Minnesota v. Dickerson* (1993), the Supreme Court applied the principles of the plain view doctrine to a situation in which a police officer discovered contraband through the sense of touch. In *Dickerson*, a police officer conducting a lawful Terry stop—an investigatory stop that requires only reasonable suspicion that criminal activity is afoot—felt a small lump in Dickerson's jacket. The officer squeezed the lump with his fingers and determined it to be a lump of crack cocaine. The officer then reached into Dickerson's pocket and retrieved a small bag of crack cocaine. The Court stated that the plain view doctrine "has an obvious application by analogy" to instances involving the discovery of contraband through the sense of touch. This is because, just as there is no reasonable expectation of privacy in an item left in plain view and observed by an officer with a right to be where he or she sees the item, there is no reasonable expectation of privacy in an item that an officer determines is contraband during a lawful frisk. In this case, however, the Court held the seizure of the package of cocaine to be illegal, because even though the officer was lawfully in a position to feel the lump in Dickerson's jacket, the incriminating nature of the pocket's contents was not immediately apparent. It was only after the officer manipulated the pocket's contents that he determined that it was cocaine. This manipulation was beyond the scope of the search permitted during a stop and frisk, because it was clear that the lump could not possibly be a weapon.

*Craig Hemmens*

**See also** Evidence, Exclusionary Rules, Probable Cause, Search and Seizure, Stop and Frisk

## For Further Reading

Arizona v. Hicks, 480 U.S. 321 (1987).
Coolidge v. New Hampshire, 403 U.S. 443 (1971).
Ferdico, J. N. (2002). *Criminal procedure for the criminal justice professional*. Belmont, CA: Wadsworth.
Harris v. United States, 390 U.S. 234 (1968).
Hemmens, C., Worrall, J., & Thompson, A. (2003). *Criminal justice case briefs: Significant cases in criminal procedure*. Los Angeles: Roxbury.
Horton v. California, 496 U.S. 128 (1990).
LaFave, W. R., & Israel, J. H. (1998). *Criminal procedure*. St. Paul, MN: West.
Minnesota v. Dickerson, 508 U.S. 366 (1993).
Texas v. Brown, 460 U.S. 730 (1983).
United States v. Johns, 469 U.S. 478 (1985).
Warden v. Hayden, 387 U.S. 294 (1967).

## ❧ POLICE BRUTALITY

Police brutality, which can be loosely defined as the excessive, illegitimate, and/or illegal use of force by a police officer or a group of police officers upon one or more civilians, is a complex, difficult, and enduring social problem that has attracted significant attention from the public, the political sphere, the media, and the criminal justice community. The complexity and subjective nature of the issues involved and the circumstances in which force is often used can frustrate attempts to define police brutality more precisely and to distinguish reasonable force from unreasonable force.

The central issue distinguishing brutality from the legitimate use of force is the appropriateness and reasonableness of the quality and degree of force police use in light of the specific circumstances involved. Police are legally empowered to use various degrees of nonnegotiable coercive force upon civilians in order to ensure compliance with laws and social norms, and these degrees of force occur across a continuum where appropriateness is defined by the specific situation, the nature of the crime, and the type of violence or resistance used against the officer. This continuum ranges from the coercive power of the officer's mere presence and the persuasive or threatening language he or she uses (which might be deemed appropriate to persuade a disorderly person to quiet down) through the use of physical force (including the use of punches, kicks, or chemical sprays that might reasonably be used to subdue a suspect violently resisting arrest) and ultimately to the kind of deadly physical force that often involves the use of a firearm (which might be deemed appropriate only if used in defense of the officer's life or the life of another person). A significant deviation from this standard of reasonableness constitutes an excessive and unreasonable use of force and can be considered brutality.

Statutes, case law, and police department regulations recognize the tremendous variety of situations an officer may encounter and the tremendous range of factors that can influence the decision to use force, and therefore, they rarely provide police with the guidance of a "bright-line" rule that narrowly defines the type and quality of force appropriate to a given situation. Rather, laws and policies generally adopt a standard of reasonableness (Was the degree and type of force used reasonable in light of the force used against the officer?) and generally require that the degree of force employed is the least force necessary to accomplish the enforcement goal.

Several recent high-profile cases of police brutality, including the videotaped 1991 beating of black motorist Rodney King by LAPD officers and the 1997 incident in which a white NYPD officer sodomized Haitian immigrant Abner Louima with a broomstick in a police station, may illuminate the perception that racial or ethnic bias often motivates police brutality. Although racial bias may be a contributing factor in some instances of police brutality, racial or ethnic animus is not a necessary condition for brutality to occur.

*Vincent E. Henry*

*See also* Use of Force

### For Further Reading

Alpert, G., & Dunham, R. (1997). *The force factor: Measuring police use of force relative to suspect resistance.* Washington, DC: Police Executive Research Forum.

Garner, J., Buchanan, J., Schade, T., & Hepburn, J. (1996). *Understanding the use of force by and against the police* (NCJ 158614). Washington, DC: U.S. Department of Justice.

Roleff, T. (1999). *Police brutality: Current controversies.* San Diego, CA: Greenhaven.

Skolnick, J. (1994). *Justice without trial: Law enforcement in democratic society* (3rd ed.). Englewood Cliffs, NJ: Macmillan.

Skolnick, J., & Fyfe, J. (1993). *Above the law: Police and the excessive use of force.* New York: Free Press.

## ◌ POLICE CODE OF SILENCE

Variously referred to as "The Blue Wall, "The Blue Wall of Silence," "The Blue Curtain," "The Code of Silence," or simply "The Code," the concept refers to the informal prohibition in the occupational culture of policing that discourages the reporting of misconduct by fellow police officers. Exactly what behavior is covered by the Code varies enormously among police agencies. In some agencies, it may cover only relatively low-level misconduct; in others, it may cover corruption of even the most serious degree. Moreover, the Code differs not only in the type of behavior it covers but also with respect to the people to whom the benefits of its coverage are extended. In some agencies, the Code is largely limited to police partners who enjoy, vis-à-vis one another, a testimonial immunity that police liken to traditionally privileged relationships between husband and wife, physician and patient, or attorney and client. In other departments, the benefits of the Code may be extended to all police officers, even those employed by other agencies. Finally, both who and what the Code covers can vary substantially, not only between but also within police agencies. Particularly in large police agencies, the occupational culture of integrity can vary substantially between precincts, task forces, and work groups. Drug enforcement units can, for example, share a very different code from that of traffic, juvenile, or patrol units.

Some form of code of silence develops in virtually every group that finds itself vulnerable to discipline (e.g., criminals, students, soldiers, slaves, prisoners). The Code develops in every police agency at least in part as a response to the punitive orientation of the quasi-military police adminis-trative system. Quasi-military police administration works, to the extent that it works, by creating hundreds and sometimes thousands of rules, and punishing deviations from those rules severely. It is a sociological inevitability that under such adminis-trative and organizational conditions, some form of the Code will evolve as a mechanism of worker self-protection.

Because most police officers believe the Code protects them and serves as a basis of trust among them, most officers support it and regard obedience to it as a matter of professional honor and loyalty to one's colleagues. The officer who does not respect the provisions of the Code may earn a reputation as a "rat," "snitch," "informer," "cheese eater," or other name of disdain. At the same time, many police administrators realize that because the Code shields officer misconduct, permits it to flourish unre-ported, and allows offending officers to go unpun-ished, they are obliged to limit its influence.

The administrative technology of controlling the Code is composed of five steps. First, it must be a matter of policy that all officers have an affirmative obligation to come forward to report the miscon-duct of fellow police officers whenever they know about it. Many departments punish a failure to report as seriously as or more seriously than the offense itself. The second step is to reward officers who come forward to report misconduct. This may be a secret or public reward, as the situation requires. Third, the department must encourage anonymous and confidential reporting, making it possible for officers who wish to report misconduct to avoid the animosity that may be directed toward those who violate the Code. Fourth, the department must make lying in the course of an integrity inves-tigation an offense that, if discovered, carries auto-matic dismissal. In departments in which this provision prevails, it severely limits officers' will-ingness to conceal the misconduct of their fellow officers. It does so in two ways: (a) It gives enor-mous power to integrity investigators to extend the scope of an investigation, and (b) it also creates

another powerful norm that can be juxtaposed to the norm that urges officers to protect their fellow offi-cers' welfare. That norm removes the right of any officer to demand that other officers risk their careers and livelihood by lying to cover the mis-conduct of a fellow officer.

Finally, departments may weaken the Code of Silence by undermining the norms of collegial solidarity on which the Code is based through administrative encouragement of diversity, transfer, promotion, occupational distance, and term limits. The thought that an organization should intention-ally undermine collegial solidarity is offensive to many police officers, both line officers and admin-istrators. Many officers embrace the idea that a career in policing involves becoming part of a police fraternity. They cherish the common bonds of solidarity that mark the relations between "broth-ers and sisters" in blue uniforms. It may well be that this solidarity is at the foundation of the Code, and that one cannot be minimized without the other.

Although descriptions of the Code are common in both police fiction and ethnographies, and there has been theoretical speculation on its causes and consequences, quantitative empirical evidence that seeks to measure the strength of the Code is limited to a survey of 3,235 officers by Klockars, Kutnjak Ivkovich, Harver, and Haberfeld (2000) and an inquiry by Trautman (2001) based on the survey responses of 3,714 officers. Klockars's measure-ment instrument, however, has recently been employed in 14 countries, allowing the inter-national comparison of the contours of the Code in those countries (Klockars, Kutnjak Ivkovich, & Haberfeld, 2003).

*Carl B. Klockars*

***See also*** Corruption/Integrity, Ethics, Police Misconduct

## For Further Reading

Klockars, C. B., Kutnjak Ivkovich, S., & Haberfeld, M. (2003). *The contours of police integrity.* Thousand Oaks, CA: Sage.

Klockars, C. B., Kutnjak Ivkovich, S., Harver, W., & Haberfeld, M. (2000, May). *The measurement of police integrity.* Available: http://www.ncjrs.org/pdffiles1/nij/181465.pdf

Trautman, N. R. (2001). *Identifying what factors influence the law enforcement code of silence.* Unpublished doctoral dissertation, St. John's University, Springfield, LA.

## ✆ POLICE CORPS

The Police Corps and the federal Office of the Police Corps and Law Enforcement Education (Office of the Police Corps) were established by the Violent Crime Control and Law Enforcement Act of 1994 (P.L. 103-322). To participate in the program, a state "lead agency" designated by the governor must submit a state plan for approval. Individuals apply to the state where they are willing to serve. The overall goal of the program is to address violent crime by helping local and state law enforcement agencies increase the number of officers with advanced education and training who serve on community patrol. Students accepted into the Police Corps receive up to $3,750 a year (up to a total of $15,000) to cover the expenses of study toward a baccalaureate or graduate degree. (Until February 1, 2004, participants received up to $7,500 per year, up to a total of $30,000.) Allowable educational expenses for full-time students include reasonable room and board. To be eligible for the program, a student must attend (or be about to attend) an accredited public or nonprofit 4-year college or university. Undergraduate participants must attend school full time. Participants may choose to study criminal justice and law enforcement or may pursue degrees in other fields. Men and women of all races and ethnic backgrounds are eligible, regardless of family income or resources. All Police Corps participants must possess the necessary mental and physical capabilities and moral characteristics to be an effective officer, meet the admission standards of the state Police Corps, meet the hiring standards of the law enforcement agency with which they will serve, and demonstrate sincere motivation and dedication to law enforcement and public service. Students who attend community college are eligible once they are accepted to a 4-year institution. Upon graduation, the participants must serve at least 4 years as a sworn law enforcement officer. (Until November 2002, law enforcement agencies hiring program graduates received $10,000 per year for each of the graduate's first 4 years of service.)

Students interested in the Police Corps apply to the lead agency of the participating state in which they wish to serve. (As of 2004, 27 states were involved.) Applications are then evaluated on a fully competitive basis according to defined admission criteria. No exceptions to the competitive standards are permitted. States with Police Corps programs are expected to advertise the availability of scholarships to the full range of prospective participants and to make special efforts to encourage applications from members of all racial, ethnic, and gender groups.

The Police Corps Act provides funding for basic law enforcement training that is to go well beyond the "minimum standards" training available to police officers in many states. This training is intended to teach the knowledge, skills, and attitudes essential to serve effectively on community patrol; to develop the physical, moral, and analytical capabilities of the participants; and to teach self-discipline and organizational loyalty. Police Corps training places special emphasis on leadership, integrity, effective communication, understanding of social context, problem solving in multicultural settings, and commitment to the principles embodied in the U.S. Constitution, including respect for the dignity of all people. All trainees must satisfy high performance standards for physical, mental, and emotional fitness. The 16 to 24 weeks of training may take place at a state or regional facility approved to offer Police Corps training. Although not specifically required by statute, the Guidelines for Training issued by the Office of the Police Corps require participating states to provide training in a residential, live-in facility. The Police Corps Act does, however, specifically authorize the Director of the Office of the Police Corps to authorize expenditures for "subsistence, quarters, and medical care" to participants at training centers (42 U.S.C. 14097 (a) (4)). The law enforcement agencies with which individual participants serve provide additional training as appropriate.

Police Corps participants become members of police departments or sheriffs' offices in geographic areas that have a great need for additional officers and are expected to be deployed to challenging beats where they can be most effective. Each participant is tentatively assigned to an eligible law enforcement agency at the time he or she is accepted into the Police Corps. Except with the permission of the Director, no more than 25% of a state's participants may be assigned to state police agencies.

Police Corps officers have all of the rights and responsibilities of—and are subject to all rules and regulations that apply to—other members of the law enforcement agencies in which they serve. Participants must meet all agency hiring standards. They must be compensated at the same rate of pay and receive the same benefits as other officers of the same rank and tenure.

If a Police Corps participant fails to complete his or her bachelor's degree, Police Corps training, and 4 years of required service with the assigned agency, he or she must repay all scholarships and reimbursements received through the program, plus 10% interest.

The program has not been without critics, however. In the late 1990s and early 2000s, some police departments refused to participate because the program's intensive, military-style training was incompatible with community policing. Other criticisms that arose concerned the program costs and popularity, when, in 1997, $54 million had been spent on the program to put just 246 officers on the streets.

*Anthony Pate*

**See also** *Education of Police*

## For Further Reading

Corps values: Navy SEAL type training for Police Corps recruits questioned. (2000). *Law Enforcement News, 26*(540), pp. 1, 7.

# ❧ POLICE DISCRETION

Police officers exercise a tremendous amount of discretion in carrying out their functions. That is, they make many choices from a range of possible actions or inactions available to them that are not specifically prescribed by law. This simple notion, that seems self-evident to some and controversial to others, lies at the heart of many issues of policing in democratic societies.

That police do exercise discretion was only openly acknowledged beginning in the 1960s. The conventional views prior to that time, and persisting among some long thereafter, was that the police function was entirely a ministerial one, that police took only those actions specifically authorized or mandated by legislative bodies. Under this view, policing was understood to be simply a matter of enforcing the laws on the books. But a number of research studies of policing in action found that the law was silent on many important matters involving police action, and ambiguous on others; also, police officers did not always adhere to what the law prescribed, even where the law was clear and specific.

The exercise of discretion is nearly inevitable in policing. Some laws are practically unenforceable—some are outdated and widely unpopular, some are unconstitutional, and some lack enforceable sanctions. Legislatures pass laws, and fail to abolish others, for a variety of purposes, only one of which is to establish clear expectations and guidelines for police action. Moreover, police seek to achieve various objectives in carrying out their duties, and, at times, those objectives conflict with one another. In such instances, police must decide which objectives take precedence over others. For example, during a public demonstration held in the streets, police may find that the objective of keeping traffic avenues clear conflicts with the objective of safeguarding citizens' rights to peaceful protest.

Even absent conflicting objectives, police and other criminal justice resources are far too limited to allow police to enforce all laws aggressively. Most communities would not tolerate full enforcement of the law, even if resources would allow it, preferring a degree of police tolerance, especially for minor legal transgressions. The very capacity of the criminal justice system to continue functioning in many communities depends to a great extent on the police not fully enforcing the law. Sudden increases in police arrest activity can seriously challenge the capacity of the system to process the resultant cases.

Discretion is exercised in policing at all levels of the police hierarchy. In contrast with other occupations and professions, the greatest amount of discretion in policing is exercised at the line level by patrol officers and detectives, but supervisors and policymakers also exercise large amounts of discretion.

## TYPES OF DISCRETIONARY DECISIONS MADE BY POLICE

Perhaps the most profound types of discretionary decisions made in policing are the decisions to use force and to arrest. Police make many other types of discretionary decisions, including decisions about which laws to invoke when an arrest or other form of detention is made; whether to refer matters to other agencies; what tactics to adopt in mounting proactive operations; what conduct to investigate, what investigative techniques to apply, and how intrusive those techniques are; what level of resources to commit to various activities, places, and problems; whether to secure prior authorization for certain actions (e.g., whether to apply for search warrants or other court orders); what level of urgency to give to various duties; whether to authorize others for certain activities (e.g., where police are responsible for issuing certain licenses and permits); and so forth.

## GUIDING AND CONTROLLING POLICE DISCRETION

Although police discretion may be inevitable, it is widely accepted that it should not be unfettered, that it needs to be guided and controlled. Statutes and local laws can and do guide police discretion to a certain degree. Some legislatures have sought to restrict police discretion in certain types of cases, notably in the realm of domestic violence through laws mandating arrest of offenders. Court rulings, and the possibility of holding police officials civilly liable for their discretionary judgments, also influence the exercise of police discretion at the margins. But by themselves, laws are inadequate for guiding and controlling police discretion.

Written policies and procedures are increasingly used by police agencies to set out the parameters of officers' discretion in certain types of cases, and to provide contextual guidance for the proper exercise of it. Police accreditation standards, although not typically dictating the substance of most discretionary judgments, can help create an organizational structure that supports administrative rule making. Police training programs are essential for improving officers' decision-making skills in the application of policies and procedures. The development of a body of knowledge, grounded in research and practice, about how police can address public safety problems effectively and fairly also holds promise for shaping important discretionary decisions. Many police agencies are increasingly looking to citizens to provide them with guidance on a range of discretionary matters, from what public safety problems to focus on to what means to use in addressing them. Citizen input can be provided at the policy-making level as well as through systematic input to line officers.

How police officers exercise their discretion also turns on the informal norms of each policy agency—norms that are shaped by community values, police leaders, supervisors, and peer officers. "The way things are done around here" is not exclusively a matter of what the rules say.

## THE CONTRARY VIEW

There remain principled arguments against acknowledging and sanctioning police discretion. Some see discretionary application of the law as inherently discriminatory and as a violation of the principle of equal treatment under the law. Indeed, the phrase "professional discretion" is sometimes used in policing to refer to the practice of not enforcing the law against fellow police officers. Others object from a balance of government powers perspective, believing that all significant rule making is best left to legislative bodies and not to executive bodies like the police.

*Michael S. Scott*

***See also*** Accountability, Arrest, Community Policing, Problem-Oriented Policing, Use of Force, Zero Tolerance

## For Further Reading

Brown, M. K. (1981). *Working the street: Police discretion and the dilemmas of reform.* New York: Russell Sage.

Davis, K. C. (1969). *Discretionary justice.* Westport, CT: Greenwood.

Goldstein, H. (1963). Police discretion: The ideal versus the real. *Public Administration Review, 23,* 140–148.

Goldstein, H. (1977). *Policing a free society.* Madison: Board of Regents of the University of Wisconsin.

Goldstein, J. (1960). Police discretion not to invoke the criminal process: Low-visibility decisions in the administration of justice. *Yale Law Journal, 69,* 543–589.

LaFave, W. (1965). *Arrest: The decision to take a suspect into custody.* Boston: Little Brown.

## ❧ POLICE EXPLORERS

Police Explorers is a career educational program for teenagers that is organized through local police departments or law enforcement agencies. Because the original programs were initiated in the 1930s under the umbrella of the Explorer program of the Boy Scouts of America (BSA), many of the programs carry the name Police Explorer Post. Today, the programs provide opportunities for boys and girls, ages 14 through 20, to learn about police work through classroom instruction and special activities such as gun training and patrol car ride-along programs. Participants are also encouraged to develop leadership abilities, strong character, and a commitment to community service. A system of state and national conferences and competitions for the Explorers and their advisors provides additional educational opportunities.

Litigation about the antigay policy of the BSA in the past two decades has forced police departments with Explorer programs to rethink their association with BSA. With the Supreme Court case *Boy Scouts of America v. Dale* in 2000, the Court's majority opinion held that as a private organization, the BSA had the right to set its own membership policy. But the BSA exclusion of gays violated the civil rights ordinance of certain cities. In reaction to the BSA policy, the Police Explorer program in Portland, Oregon, disassociated from the BSA and changed its name to Police Cadet Program. Insurance was arranged through the National Association of Police Athletic Leagues. Other Police Explorer programs in other areas chose to keep the Explorer name, but established independent sources for funding and insurance.

In the midst of the litigation period, BSA made some changes to the Explorer program. The name for their teen program was changed from Explorer to Venture. And in 1998, BSA transferred the career and vocational training part of the former Explorer program to a relatively new subsidiary called Learning for Life. The new subsidiary does not have the BSA requirement that homosexuals must be excluded. Although the relationship between Learning for Life and BSA is not widely publicized, it also is not hidden. Learning for Life reports that currently there are more than 3,000 active Police Explorer Posts and Law Enforcement Posts under its umbrella. Numerous similar Explorer programs are now run as independent units by local law enforcement agencies or as programs under the National Association of Police Athletic Leagues.

The Police Explorer programs vary at the local level, but the programs are encouraged to follow the same general guidelines. Teens must obtain parental approval in order to join. Each program is encouraged to have a written policy about the restrictions in force to ensure that the Explorers are not exposed to potentially dangerous situations. Strict guidelines are given for the involvement of teens in ride-along programs. Police Explorers may not drive a marked police car. They are not permitted to be used in undercover operations, or police actions such as arrests, breath analyzer tests, frisks, impounds, interrogations, issuance of citations, pursuits, searches, seizures, stops for investigative purposes, surveillances, or any use of force. Explorers are generally restricted to carrying only a notebook, pen, flashlight, and whistle. They are not allowed to carry firearms, batons, or chemical Mace®.

Recent media coverage has drawn attention to the problem of police sexual abuse of teenagers involved in the Explorer program. In 2003, Walker and Irlbeck reported that half of the 66 teenager cases involing police that were reported in the media involved Explorers. Most cases involved teenage girls, but five cases involved teenage boys. Guidelines have been rewritten by Learning for Life in an attempt to preclude future problems. Ride-along programs in patrol cars should be allowed only with police of the same gender. Outings for Explorers should include two adults. Walker recommends that police chiefs must carefully select the particular police officers that supervise the Explorer program.

A gun marksmanship program is one of the big attractions of some Explorer programs. The instructors must be certified by the National Rifle Association or by the law enforcement agency. Training starts with a class in basic pistol safety and marksmanship. Then, participants start using a shooting range, where they shoot at a distance of 25 yards using bull's eye targets. Shooting is done slowly until the participant is skilled enough to try timed-fire or rapid-fire shooting. Competitions are held on a state and national level. Skill is rewarded with awards for the top performance by individuals and Explorer Post teams.

The Police Explorer programs provide a valuable training opportunity for young men and women while also providing a recruitment channel for police and law enforcement agencies across the country. Many of today's police officers developed an interest in police work when they were teenagers in a Police Explorer Post, so they are eager to perpetuate the program. The programs will continue to evolve as the leaders try to solve problems that arise.

*Gretchen Gross*

### For Further Reading

Boy Scouts of America v. Dale 530 U.S. 640 (2000).

Mechling, J. (2001). *On my honor: Boy Scouts and the making of American youth.* Chicago: University of Chicago Press.

Walker, S., & Irlbeck, D. (2003, June). *Police sexual abuse of teenage girls: A 2003 update on "driving while female."* Available: http://www.policeaccountability.org/PPIfirstyearrept.pdf

http://www.learning-for-life.org/exploring/lawenforcement

## ᏬᎧ POLICE FICTION

The evolution of crime/detective fiction culminates in the 20th century with the police procedural novel. However, the roots of modern police fiction can be traced to the 19th century. Police fiction developed in conjunction with and parallel to developments in law enforcement in Europe and later in the United States. The real-life exploits of criminal investigators and the methods used by police detectives influenced the works of writers of fiction.

In 1829, Eugéne François Vidocq, the former criminal who became chief of the Sûreté, published his *Memoires de Vidocq*. Vidocq's account of his career inspired a number of writers, including Edgar Allan Poe, "the father of the mystery short story" and creator of the brilliant armchair detective, Monsieur C. Auguste Dupin (Richardson, 1999, p. 479). In England, Charles Dickens and Wilkie Collins offered the early British police detective in the context of a fictional investigation. Inspector Bucket appears in Dickens's *Bleak House* (1853), and Sergeant Cuff is the officer on the case in Collins's *The Moonstone* (1868).

In the Sherlock Holmes series by Sir Arthur Conan Doyle, police officers have recurring roles. However, as in Poe's three short stories ("The Murders in the Rue Morgue," "The Mystery of Marie Roget," and "The Purloined Letter"), the law enforcement officers play second fiddle to the brilliant protagonist. Anna Katherine Green, often identified as "the mother of the detective novel," gives a more significant role to Ebenezer Gryce, the New York lawyer and police officer who makes his debut in *The Leavenworth Case: A Lawyer's Story* (1878).

In his study of the police procedural novel, Dove (1982) notes that the police officers in early classic detective fiction and in private eye (or tough guy) crime fiction share several characteristics in common. Perhaps the most important characteristic is that these representatives of official law enforcement either seek the help of the amateur detective or private investigator, or they resent and obstruct the investigation by the non-law enforcement hero. Sometimes, they do both. In these early works, police officers are sometimes portrayed as bumbling, brutal, and/or corrupt. However, after his analysis of the works in which they appear, Dove (1982) argues that these fictional police officers are a "mixed bag." There are negative images of police officers in early crime/detective fiction, but there are also depictions of competent law enforcement officers. There is the suggestion in some works that police officers are capable of handling the ordinary run of cases, but are not up to the challenge of the more complex puzzles that the brilliant amateur and the private investigator (PI) are called on to solve (Dove, 1982).

However, by the 20th century, police officers had become more visible in popular culture. The

Pinkerton agent—hero of the volumes published by agency founder, Allen Pinkerton, and model for the fictional PI created by Dashiell Hammett—was supplanted in popular culture by the "G-Men," or government agents. The production code introduced by Hollywood in the 1930s to avoid external censorship offered a list of do's and don'ts to which moviemakers were required to adhere in order to receive the Hays Office seal of approval. Prominent on this list was the mandate that "crime must not pay." Crime movies that had featured gangsters as heroes now offered G-Men as the protagonists. At the same time, radio offered programs such as "Gangbusters," "Policewoman," "Treasury Agent," "Dick Tracy," and "Dragnet." Created by Chester Gould, the "Dick Tracy" comic strip debuted in 1931. Created by Jack Webb, "Dragnet" began as a radio show in 1949 and moved to television in 1951. Scholars point to the important contributions made by Dick Tracy, the comic strip cop who also became a star of radio, television, and feature films, and Joe Friday, the taciturn, deadpan LAPD detective portrayed by Jack Webb, to the development of the police procedural (Collins & Javna, 1988; Dove, 1982; Roberts, 1993).

But the appearance of the police procedural novel as a subgenre of crime/detective novels is generally dated from the publication of Lawrence Treat's *V as in Victim* (1945). Prior to Treat, other authors had created police protagonists who functioned as solitary and brilliant crime solvers. Treat portrayed police officers within the setting of the station house, engaged in the investigation of multiple crimes, and following procedures and using techniques that were realistic (i.e., those used by real-life police officers). During this same era, Hillary Waugh (*Last Seen Wearing*, 1952) and John Creasey (*Gideon's Day*, 1955) also introduced important series featuring police detectives. Ed McBain's 87th Precinct debuted in 1956 with *Cop Hater* and remains one of the most popular police procedural series.

The police procedural novel has proved adaptable. It has been used as a vehicle to depict police systems all over the world. It has also evolved to reflect the changes occurring in society; thus, female detectives, gay and lesbian detectives, and detectives of color are now to be found among the ranks of fictional protagonists (Dove, 1982). In modern police procedurals, events such as the riot in Los Angeles following the decision in the Rodney King police beating case have been incorporated into plots. In fact, these novels often depict the grittiness of urban life. However, other settings, such as small towns and Native American reservations, also appear in police fiction.

Whether in books or in television dramas such as *NYPD Blue* and *Law and Order* (heirs to the groundbreaking *Hill Street Blues*), police procedurals deal with issues of crime and justice. The authors and creators of this fiction attempt to depict the stresses inherent in police works, such as poor police–community relations, job burnout, administrative pressures, and family problems. One of the issues for scholars is how well police fiction portrays the realities of police work. A second issue is how fictional images of police officers and their work affect the responses of a diverse public to the police.

*Frankie Y. Bailey*

**See also** News Media and Police, Public Perceptions/Attitudes of Police, Television (Police Shows), Vidocq Society

### For Further Reading

Collins, M. A., & Javna, J. (1988). *The best of crime & detective TV*. New York: Harmony.

Dove, G. N. (1982). *The police procedural*. Bowling Green, OH: Bowling Green University Popular Press.

Richardson, B. (1999). Vidocq, Eugene Francois. In R. Herbert (Ed.), *The Oxford companion to crime and mystery writing*. New York: Oxford University Press.

Roberts, G. G. (1993). *Dick Tracy and American culture: Morality and mythology, text and context*. Jefferson, NC: McFarland.

## ❧ POLICE MANAGEMENT

Because policing is government's primary instrument in achieving social control, its management is of particular importance. Management theory attempts to identify and predict the behavior of organizations and their members. Police management refers to the administrative functions associated with managing a law enforcement agency, including identifying and training qualified candidates, directing and coordinating personnel, monitoring the performance of personnel in areas such as regulatory enforcement and their ability to provide the public with access to existing services, and practicing crime prevention and reduction. For modern police managers to apply theory with street reality in an effort to develop innovative strategies, it is essential that they possess an understanding of the historical foundations of management (or organizational) theory. Employing the appropriate theory or combining aspects of several different theories can enable the police manager to consistently select the optimal daily response to the challenges associated with the planning, organizing, leading, and controlling of personnel and resources, which in turn positively influence the productivity and/or outputs of the organization and the individual. Law enforcement agencies—particularly the larger ones—have turned to the private sector for models.

Several theories are classified as classical approaches to management. In 1911, Frederick Taylor published *The Principles of Scientific Management*. This publication became the foundation of the scientific management approach in its contention that the primary objective of management lay within the development of a system, based upon the identification of casual relationships in an attempt to predict potential outcomes based upon existing conditions, that ensures the employer maximum prosperity while also ensuring that the employee enjoys a comparable level of prosperity. Management systematically addresses the challenges and obstacles to prosperity and verbalizes said challenges, following extensive analysis and discussion, so that all within the organization successfully comprehend and respond to said challenges. To ensure that the organization and the employee prosper, management develops and defines the skill sets required to accomplish the task, meticulously screens and selects the most appropriate and qualified candidates for the selected mission, provides the appropriate levels of training and incentives to ensure success, and controls the work environment by reducing or removing the distractions associated with the operation. In 1916, Henri Fayol furthered the theory

of scientific management with the publication of *Administration Industrielle et Generale,* identifying the five critical "rules" of management: foresight, organization, command, coordination, and control. The judicious application of discipline and sanctions, unity of command and direction, clearly delineated lines of authority, and the subjugation of individual interests to the general interests of the organization are several of his more critical principles. In 1937, Luther Gulick refined the concept of functional management with the publication of *Papers on the Science of Administration*, which introduced the acronym POSDCORB, which declared that planning, organizing, staffing, directing, coordination, reporting, and budgeting were the critical functions of management.

Police managers embraced the theories associated with the classical approach to management and the resultant rational and efficient form of bureaucratic organization. The daily operations associated with command and exigencies of the service preclude many police managers from formally pursuing the study of management theory. Thus, the appeal of the concise renditions of the essential elements associated with the managerial process offered by the scientific approach—as well as the logic and order that accompany the division of labor and authority, clearly delineated and defined duties and responsibilities, standardized rules and procedures, and a hierarchical line of authority—is obvious.

Shifts in social consciousness and attitudes in the 1960s compelled police managers to reevaluate the application of solely scientific approaches to management. Rigidity, resistance to change, and employee malaise—several of the flaws associated with bureaucratic systems—prompted internal challenges during the decade from officers and agents who contended that longevity, tenure, rank, and/or formal education were not flawless indicators of eventual managerial success. These officers and agents observed that repressive bureaucracies afforded rank-and-file employees with rarified opportunities for input, which fostered a mistrust and apprehension of the organization on the part of the employee that manifested itself in reduced morale and diminished productivity. As a result, police managers revisited several theories referred to as behavioral approaches to management, each based upon the presumption that individuals are social and self-actualizing, perpetually seeking satisfying social relationships and personal fulfillment and possessing an inherent desire for acceptance that makes them responsive to peer/group pressures.

In 1924, the Western Electric Company initiated a series of studies related to employee productivity in the company's Hawthorne Works plant in Chicago. Research related to lighting conditions and varied lengths of the workday or break periods demonstrated that the productivity of those employees studied increased. Initially, researchers were unable to isolate the variable responsible for the change, but ultimately concluded that enhanced organizational attention toward the employee and an inclusion in the decision-making process, and the resultant increase in employee morale and self-esteem, were more critical than the environmental changes and variations implemented in an attempt to increase productivity. In 1943, Abraham Maslow forwarded his behavioral theory of management by articulating that individuals have physiological and psychological needs, and that these needs, when not met, result in tensions that adversely affect an individual's attitudes, performance, and behaviors. This "hierarchy of needs," a pyramidal construct erected upon a foundation consisting of biological maintenance (food, shelter, water, etc.) and achieving a pinnacle with self-actualization, illustrates that people act to satisfy a perceived deprivation of a need, and that needs must be met at each level to enable the individual to achieve self-actualization. Maslow contended that effective management hinged on the ability of the manager to remove the obstacles that prevent personal satisfaction by providing an employee with avenues for need fulfillment while enabling the employee to continue supporting the organization's goals. In 1960, Douglas McGregor published *The Human Side of Enterprise*, which was heavily influenced by both the Hawthorne studies and the observations of Maslow. McGregor advocated a realignment of managerial perspective from the Theory X model, which held that subordinates by nature abhorred work, were irresponsible, lacked ambition, and preferred to remain subordinate, to the Theory Y model, which recognized that subordinates were naturally willing to work and accept responsibility, and were capable of self-direction, self-control, creativity, imagination, and ingenuity.

Ideological shifts in social consciousness and attitudes in the 1960s also prompted external challenges to law enforcement organizations, compelling effective police managers to evaluate modern approaches to management. The modern approach to management attempts to meld the rationality and economy of the classical approach to management with the social and self-actualization concerns articulated within the behavioral approach to management. Police managers also realized that the perception, both internal and external, of the law enforcement agency as a closed system with no input from the community and limited input from the other suborganizations of the criminal justice system had evolved. Societal demands of greater accountability and an expectation of the police to perform duties and furnish services once considered outside the realm of law enforcement illustrated that law enforcement agencies function within an open system, wherein a collection of interrelated parts function together to achieve a common purpose or obtain a mutual goal. Community reaction, in the form of feedback, reflects the effectiveness of an organization, enabling the police manager to abandon, adjust, or maintain policies and initiatives in order to improve organizational productivity.

The applications of modern approaches to management have resulted in the development of two effective police management responses: community policing and the Compstat process. Community policing is a reflection of an operational philosophy wherein the community has significant input in the creation of the agency's values system and actively participates in problem solving and the decision-making process. This application of the contingency theory of management compels the manager to respond to each situation independently, creating an organizational response, based upon personnel, resources, and technology, that meets the community's demands. Police administrators and managers decentralize authority, create specialized units, and determine staffing and organizational placement within the agency based upon specific conditions, with a focus on crime prevention through education, intervention, and conflict resolution. The Compstat process incorporates aspects of the quantitative approach to management, in particular the use of computers to systematically analyze crime in an attempt to forecast or predict crime and suggest the most optimal solution, with aspects of the total quality approach to management that focus specifically on managerial accountability based upon organizational structure, operational response, and the manner in which the consumer receives the services provided.

*Angelo Pisani and John Rowland*

*See also* Community Policing, Compstat, Morale, Patrol Work, Performance Evaluation of Police Departments, Unions

*For Further Reading*

Alsabrook, C., Aryani, G., & Garrett, T. (2001). The five principles of leadership. *Law & Order, 49*(5), 112–115.

Hoover, L. (Ed.). (1992). *Police management: Issues & perspectives*. Washington, DC: Police Executive Research Forum.

Moore, M. (2003). Sizing up Compstat: An important administrative innovation in policing. *Criminology & Public Policy, 2*(3), 469–471.

Walsh, W. (2001). Compstat: An analysis of an emerging police managerial paradigm. *Policing: An International Journal of Police Strategies and Management, 24*(3), 347–362.

## ❧ POLICE MEDIATION

Police mediation refers to police officers assisting disputing parties in airing their differences, including feelings and perceptions; listening to each other; and helping the parties resolve the situation that triggered the police response. For police officers, their role as mediators is both old and new. In its simplest form, police mediation has existed as long as there have been disputing parties who have called upon police officers to intervene. Typically, police mediation was done without formal training in mediation.

With the increasing popularity, acceptance, and institutionalization of mediation in a wide range of settings since the 1970s, the rich, long history of informal and intuitive police mediation associated with traditional police work has come under increasing scrutiny. Not only are police officers now receiving more formal training in mediation skills, they are also working more closely with mediation practitioners, usually those connected with community-based mediation centers. The nexus between the community mediation programs and local police departments has increased police mediation capabilities. In those instances where police mediation cannot or does not work, the community mediation programs have provided police officers with an invaluable referral resource. Police can refer people in conflict to mediation practitioners who can take the time to assist the parties in working through their differences, particularly where the issues are complicated and deeply rooted.

### MEDIATION: WHAT IS IT?

Understanding how mediation interfaces with police work requires an understanding of the nature of the mediation process itself. Although there are many stylistic and philosophical differences about what mediation is and how it should be practiced, it is generally understood to be a process where parties are assisted in working through their differences with the assistance of a third party known as the mediator. The mediator usually guides the process by establishing guidelines for interaction between the parties, helping them to share how they see the situation, brainstorming options, negotiating possible arrangements, and crafting an understanding for the future. Although mediation usually occurs in face-to-face sessions with both parties, separate sessions with each side are common.

Central to mediation is self-determination by the parties. What this means is that, unlike other contexts where judges and arbitrators have the power and authority to make decisions for the parties, mediators do not. Mediators rely on persuasion and a variety of skills and techniques to move the disputing parties toward consideration of common ground.

In mediation, the disputing parties themselves are expected to work through their differences and come up with a mutually agreeable outcome to resolve the situation they are experiencing. Underlying the mediation process is the notion that the parties will engage openly, listen to each other, generate options, and design their own solutions. Because the parties need to give and take creatively and flexibly, all should be able to walk away with something, rather than one party winning and one losing, as is common in more traditional adversarial proceedings. As a result, mediation is widely referred to as a win–win process.

Of paramount concern for mediators is confidentiality. In order to provide an opportunity for parties to open up and have genuine discussions, mediators assure the parties that information that is communicated in connection with the mediation efforts will not be shared with others. Usually, the only public output of a mediation session is the agreement that is signed by the parties.

## POLICE MEDIATION: TWO APPROACHES

In the police context, there are two basic ways that police can use mediation. They can serve as mediators themselves in response to conflict situations on the scene, or they can refer cases to mediators in their respective communities.

When serving as mediators themselves, police officers can be creative and resourceful problem solvers. Rather than responding as decision makers, police as mediators provide citizens with an opportunity to sort through their concerns, facts, and feelings. Control of outcomes remains with members of the community. This mode of intervening resonates with community and problem-oriented policing, where police officers are expected to work with the community.

The proliferation of mediation throughout the United States has provided police with a vast set of additional resources. At the local level, countless community-based mediation programs have been established to accept referrals from a wide range of sources, including the police. Police referrals include cases that could have resulted in arrests and been processed subsequently by the criminal courts. Usually, they are the less serious criminal matters, although felony cases are also referred. For the most part, the cases involve parties who have ongoing

relationships and have agreed to work through their differences voluntarily with the assistance of a trained mediator.

## THE POTENTIAL OF POLICE MEDIATION

Mediation holds many promises for police whether they mediate cases themselves or refer them to mediation practitioners, who are usually situated at local community-based mediation programs. Regardless of approach, similar benefits result. Mediation has been found to reduce the escalation of conflicts, strengthen police–community relations, diminish the number of repeat calls, and decrease the amount of time that the police have to devote to handling a variety of situations. In situations where police are not able to mediate or choose to refer the more intractable cases to local mediation centers, the community mediators pick up where the police left off and assist the parties in having a difficult conversation that may take many hours and require multiple sessions in order to settle.

## THE CHALLENGES OF POLICE MEDIATION

Because mediation requires a major paradigm shift about what is valued as police work, it poses numerous challenges for the police. To conduct mediation in accordance with principles guiding the emerging field of mediation, at a minimum, police will have to undergo additional training, and police departments will have to consider innovative reward structures. Although police officers are taught some mediation skills and techniques during recruit and inservice training, they are not commonly trained in the entire mediation process. Moreover, the way in which their intervention work is evaluated will also require some rethinking.

In those instances where police mediate themselves, the traditional police model can be severely challenged. Police mediation can be time-consuming and trigger even more resistance from parties. If the parties' differences are deeply rooted and police try to mediate, the challenges are even greater. Moreover, unlike other contexts where parties go to the mediators, police usually encounter the parties when they are immersed in the heat of their conflict and on the parties' turf, with potential bystanders and others often ready to play a role. Of particular significance, police are not able to grant the parties confidentiality, a major ingredient of mediation in other contexts. Because mediators do not make decisions, the fact that police can make a variety of decisions, which may include using coercive force and making arrests if necessary, causes a clash with the core values of good mediation practice. Finally, because mediation interventions may not be easily quantifiable, like an arrest or summons is, there may not be an easy way to reward officers.

In those instances where cases are referred to a mediation center, attention needs to be paid to referral arrangements and what feedback, if any, is provided to the police. Because mediators usually maintain confidences, little or no information is usually shared with others. For police who may have subsequent interactions with the parties, this may mean loss of vital information or control over the case. Moreover, referral of a case may have budgetary implications because it may not count as a police intervention.

## RESEARCH TO DATE

Early police research that addressed police mediation often did so in the context of domestic situations. Although there is a growing body of literature focusing on police mediation, with few exceptions, the literature is impressionistic and sorely lacking in empirical data, or else it defines police mediation inaccurately to broadly include decision-making processes such as arbitration.

The emerging empirical studies to date indicate that police mediation is promising. Most of the recent studies focus on the police use of mediation whereby police refer cases to community mediation centers. Generally, data indicate that mediation has reduced costs for police departments and decreased the request for repeat calls. In an exploratory study on police use of mediation as understood by community mediation programs in New York State, findings indicate that the use of mediation by police is widely recognizable.

*Maria R. Volpe*

## For Further Reading

Bard, M. (1970). *Training police as specialists in family crisis intervention.* Washington, DC: U.S. Department of Justice.

Buerger, M., Petrosino, A., & Petrosino, C. (1999). Extending the police role: Implications of police mediation as a problem-solving tool. *Police Quarterly, 2*(2), 125–149.

Charkoudian, L. (2001). *Economic analysis of inter-personal conflict and community mediation.* Unpublished doctoral dissertation, Johns Hopkins University, Baltimore, MD.

Cooper, C. (1999). *Mediation & arbitration by patrol police officers.* Lanham, MD: University Press of America.

Cooper, C. (2000a). Police mediators: Training hones skills. *Dispute Resolution Magazine 7*(1), 17.

Cooper, C. (2000b). Training patrol officers to mediate disputes. *FBI Law Enforcement Bulletin, 69*(2), 7.

Hedeen, T. (2002). Does the journey change the destination? The influence of referral source on mediation participation and outcomes. *New York Mediator, 20,* 4.

Palenski, J. (1984). The use of mediation by police. *Mediation Quarterly, 5,* 31–38.

Shepherd, R. (1995). Neighborhood dispute settlement center's program with City of Harrisburg Bureau of Police. *Executive Summary for Board of Directors, Neighborhood Dispute Settlement of Dauphin County.* Harrisburg, PA.

Volpe, M. (1989). The police role. In M. Wright & B. A. Galaway (Eds.), *Mediation and criminal justice: Victims, offenders, and community.* Newbury Park, CA: Sage.

Volpe, M., & Christian, T. (1989). Mediation: New addition to cop's toolbox. *Law Enforcement News, 15*(294), 8–13.

Volpe, M., & Phillips, N. (2002, November). *Understanding police mediation: Promises and challenges.* Paper presented at the annual meeting of the American Society of Criminology, Chicago.

Williams, P. (1997, Fall). Police and mediation: Win-win partnership. *Oregon Police Chief,* pp. 24–26.

## ‧ POLICE MISCONDUCT

Although "police misconduct" is a rather sweeping and somewhat amorphous concept, it is generally used in reference to illegitimate police behaviors or activities that are related to the performance of an officer's official duties and violate state or federal criminal laws, department policies, professional ethics, or administrative rules and procedures. Police misconduct is an important public policy issue as well as a recurring problem that is widely discussed and debated by police officers, police administrators and executives, lawmakers and public officials, and members of the public. The diverse definitions of misconduct are, like the behaviors, motivations, and contexts involved, highly complex and multifaceted. Even a cursory review of the history of American policing reveals that misconduct has been a perennial and enduring problem in policing, and that repeated police misconduct scandals have been a powerful (if not entirely effective) impetus for the reform of police organizations as well as the institution of policing as a whole.

The study or discussion of misconduct is hampered by a need for greater definitional precision as well as by the multiple contexts in which the various behavioral patterns and practices falling under the expansive rubric of misconduct can take place. Although some might improperly equate police misconduct with police corruption, for example, the two are distinguishable insofar as some actual violation of state or federal law is generally a necessary definitional feature of corruption. This is not the case with the more broadly defined concept of police misconduct, and therefore, corruption can be considered a subset of misconduct.

The competing definitions or conceptions of precisely what constitutes police misconduct vary widely according to the particular context in which specific behaviors are considered: public definitions and discussions of misconduct, for example, are generally more inclusive and embrace a greater range of illegitimate activities than do legal conceptions, which tend to narrowly specify the particular activities and necessary motivations involved. Because organizational and public notions of misconduct generally include activities that violate an agency's administrative procedures, these definitions can also vary among and between agencies and communities. A police department that unequivocally forbids officers from accepting free meals under any circumstances, for example, would label this behavior as misconduct, whereas an agency with no such formal proscription would probably not. Some members of the public might view the acceptance of free meals under any circumstances as de facto misconduct, whereas others are likely to have a more tolerant view regardless of the agency's policy. Finally, an individual officer may encounter exigent situations where the acceptance of a free meal does not compromise his or her professional ethics or personal integrity, and that officer would likely not subjectively define the behavior as misconduct. The legitimacy or illegitimacy of a particular police behavior (or misbehavior) must therefore be considered in terms of the social, organizational, legal, and ethical contexts in which it occurs. Discussions of police misconduct must also recognize the nature and quality of misbehavior involved and the fact that these behaviors reflect a continuum of severity: Some instances of misconduct (e.g., administrative rule violations) are intrinsically less injurious or harmful than others (e.g., serious criminal offenses engaged in under color of law).

The various behaviors that constitute police misconduct can involve a single individual, a group of officers, or an entire police organization. Instances of misconduct by individual officers are frequently explained in terms of the "rotten apple in a clean barrel" theory—that the offense was an isolated deviant incident that is not representative of (nor tolerated by) the organization or other officers. The media and many academicians often attribute widespread instances or patterns of misconduct by groups of officers or by entire police organizations to the emergence of a deviant occupational culture, but this attribution is often simplistic and ultimately misleading. In fact, widespread instances or patterns of misbehavior are almost always symptomatic of an absence of adequate management control systems designed to ensure organizational and public accountability, a substantial breakdown in those systems, or the tacit or direct encouragement of the behavior(s) by managers and executives. Public revelations of multiple instances or patterns of misconduct often lead to a sequence of media-driven scandals followed by some official reaction (i.e., an official public or organizational inquiry into the nature and causes of the misconduct) followed by various organizational reforms or policy revisions. In many cases, public and/or organizational attention to the issues of misconduct abates over time, a period characterized by apathy or inattention to the issues and problems ensues, and new forms or patterns of misconduct emerge to again initiate the sequence. This sequence is illustrated in the history of the New York Police Department, where a series of six major corruption scandals have emerged at approximate 20-year intervals since 1894.

A number of typologies of misconduct can be found in the academic literature of policing, and these typologies reflect the way definitions and concepts of police misconduct have expanded and evolved over the course of American police history. Although definitions of misconduct historically focused on police graft, bribery, and other forms of corruption involving personal gain, concerns about police brutality and civil rights resulting from the urban riots of the 1960s led to dramatically increased public, legal, and organizational attention. Brutality and civil rights violations ultimately entered public discourse about misconduct during that era. Similarly, the notion of racial profiling entered the lexicon of police misconduct when that pattern of behavior was recognized. The notion of "noble cause corruption"—such activities as perjury, falsifying or planting evidence on suspects, and other illegal or illegitimate behaviors that can be rationalized as serving a legitimate criminal justice goal and do not involve an implicit material gain for the officer involved—has recently received media and academic attention and has been subsumed within definitions of police misconduct.

The resilience and recurring nature of police misconduct illuminates the need for effective police accountability, both to the organization and to the public. Given the ever-increasing complexity of contemporary police work, the necessarily broad range of discretion afforded to officers, and the intrinsic difficulty of adequately and continually supervising their activities, some degree or quantity of police misconduct is always to be expected. This is particularly true in regard to the lesser offenses of administrative rule violations that comprise the vast majority of police misbehavior. It is virtually impossible for any police agency to create and enforce supervision and accountability structures or practices that will be entirely effective in eliminating all forms of misconduct. The most effective way to limit misconduct is through enhanced public accountability and organizational transparency, achieved through a sustained and multifaceted process of ongoing policy review and adaptation.

*Vincent E. Henry*

*See also* Accountability, Civil Rights Violations by Police, Civilian Complaint Review Boards, Consent Decrees, Corruption/Integrity, Ethics, Internal Affairs, Knapp Commission, Mollen Commission, Police Brutality, Rampart Investigation

## For Further Reading

Barker, T., & Roebuck, J. B. (1974). An empirical typology of police corruption: A study in organizational deviance. Springfield, IL: Charles C Thomas.

Lersch, K. M. (Ed.). (2002). *Policing and misconduct*. Upper Saddle River, NJ: Prentice Hall.

Palmiotto, M. J. (Ed.). (2001). *Police misconduct: A reader for the 21st century*. Upper Saddle River, NJ: Prentice Hall.

## ◎ POLICE MUSEUMS

Police museums preserve the rich history of law enforcement and educate the public about the role of police in the society. It is not known how many exist in the world. Fire museums, for comparison, are organized into the Fire Museum Network and number slightly more than 200 in the United States and Canada, but there is no equivalent organization for police museums. Police museums differ in size as well as scope: Some occupy just a room in a police department, some are housed in designated buildings on several floors, but all of them grew out of personal collections of police memorabilia.

The oldest known police museum is The Crime Museum at Scotland Yard. In 1874, Inspector Neame came up with the idea to use items seized at crime scenes for practical training on how to detect and prevent burglary. Officially opened in 1875 as a private institution, The Crime Museum is still closed to the general public and is used to lecture and train police professionals in subjects of investigative techniques, law, forensic science, and pathology.

The New York City Police Museum (NYCPM) dates back to the 1880s when Inspector Byrnes, the first Chief of Detectives, started an exhibit in a corner of police headquarters. The official establishment of the museum occurred in 1929. For many years, it was housed in the police academy and served as a teaching tool for the cadets. In 2001, a building at 100 Old Slip in downtown Manhattan, the site of the old First Precinct stationhouse, was dedicated by Mayor Rudolph W. Giuliani as the home of the New York City Police Museum. The NYCPM exhibits focus on the history of the police department and policing as well as crime in New York. The museum is open to the public and attracts visitors of all ages and professions. The exhibits combine historical information presented in the form of photographs, old police equipment, uniforms, badges, the whole arsenal of weaponry used by gangsters, with sensational elements of interactive computer technology providing visitors with a first-hand experience of a police officer's or forensic scientist's work. The NYCPM maintains a Web site where one can read curious facts about the history of the department and view photographs of current exhibits.

The first national police museum was the American Police Hall of Fame and Museum (APHF) in Titusville, Florida. Along with 11,000 exhibits and artifacts, it houses two American law enforcement associations—the National Association of Chiefs of Police and the American Federation of Police and Concerned Citizens. The museum includes a canine memorial devoted to the dogs that have either died in the line of duty or been retired from law enforcement after many years of faithful service. The museum also functions as a memorial dedicated to law enforcement officers killed in the line of duty. Each year, the APHF holds a memorial service during Police Week (May 15th of every year) for the survivors of the killed law enforcement officers. When the APHF opened in 1960 in North Port, Florida, it had only 57 names inscribed on the wall of the memorial; today, there are more than 7,000 names, and new names are added weekly.

In 2000, Congress authorized the building of the National Law Enforcement Museum (NLEM) (P.L. 106-492). The privately funded construction will be built on federal property in Washington, DC. The museum will be owned and operated by the National Law Enforcement Officers Memorial Fund, the nonprofit organization that, in 1991, built and now oversees the National Law Enforcement Officers Memorial honoring more than 16,600 federal, state, and local law officers killed in the line of duty, dating back to the first known death in 1792. The new museum will be located underground, across the street from the memorial, and is scheduled to receive its first visitors in 2009. The mission of the NLEM is "to generate a better understanding and appreciation of the vital contributions our law officers made to the nation" as well as educate professionals about how to better protect police on the job. The NLEM will be the largest and most comprehensive law enforcement museum and research facility found anywhere in the world.

The biggest police museum existing today is the World Police Museum at the Central Police University in Taoyuan, Taiwan. The museum has seven floors and includes exhibits on police history in Taiwan and around the world, plus collections of police uniforms, equipment, and literature from Europe, Asia, Africa, and America. The central part of the museum is devoted to the history of Chinese police dating back to 1000 B.C.

*Maria Kiriakova*

*For Further Reading*

http://www.aphf.org
http://www.nleomf.com
http://www.nycpolicemuseum.org

# ∞ POLICE OFFICER STANDARDS AND TRAINING COMMISSIONS (POST COMMISSIONS)

Police officer standards and training commissions, often referred to simply as POST commissions, are state organizations that set standards for police officer minimum selection criteria, basic and inservice training requirements, licensure or certification, and suspension or decertification. Forty-nine states and the District of Columbia have POST commissions, or organizations that have the same administrative and functional mandates, which involve critical issues of police officer standards for their respective states. Hawaii does not have a POST commission or similar agency. These state-level commissions provide law enforcement agencies with guidelines, established by administrative regulations or law, and require compliance by all municipal, county, and state law enforcement agencies, to maintain a baseline for police officer standards and training.

Although referred to by the common acronym POST, not every state has an agency using that name. The acronym POST owes its origin to the California POST, which was established in 1959 to provide selection and training standards for California law enforcement. That same year, New York State passed legislation, the New York Training Act, that created an advisory council to make recommendations to the governor on issues related to police training programs in New York. Although a variety of names are used, when discussing state standards for police officer selection and training, the acronym POST is universally understood to include all of these organizations regardless of their actual title. In 2004, only 15 state organizations used the title POST, whereas other states used names such as the Kentucky Law Enforcement Council, the Massachusetts Municipal Police Training Council, the Indiana Law Enforcement Training Board, the Maryland Police & Corrections Training Commissions, the Alaska Police Standards Council, and the Michigan Commission on Law Enforcement Standards, to just name a few. Some POST commissions are embedded within the organizational structure of a centralized state-level police training academy.

## HISTORY

Policing in the United States is composed of an overlapping, fragmented web of law enforcement agencies providing the historical foundation for local public safety responsibility. Within this historical context, it is not difficult to understand why state standards for police officer selection and training were not adopted until the second half of the 20th century.

The emphasis on police training standards owes its heritage to several police reformers and presidential commissions that studied the needs for law enforcement reform and professionalism. Most noteworthy were August Vollmer of the Berkeley (CA) Police Department and O. W. Wilson of the Chicago Police Department, who were early advocates of increased police professionalism.

Vollmer established the first formal basic training programs for police officers in the United States and was one of the first to establish strict entry requirements for police officers. Wilson, who literally wrote the textbook on police administration in the United States, supported strict officer selection standards and effective police training programs.

The Wickersham Commission, established by President Herbert Hoover to study crime and criminal justice, made recommendations for establishing training and entry standards, including testing for entry-level police officers, minimal physical standards, and preservice/inservice police training. In 1967, the President's Commission on Law Enforcement and the Administration of Justice issued a report, "The Police," which included recommendations that all states establish a POST commission to create minimum statewide standards for police officer selection, training curricula, police officer certification, and adequacy of training facilities. These goals were reaffirmed by the 1973 National Advisory Commission on Criminal Justice Standards and Goals.

## POST COMMISSION ADMINISTRATION

Today, state POST commissions provide a variety of services and maintain state standards related to police standards and training. Although there is no uniformity in selection and training standards, state POST commissions, through cooperative participation in the International Association of Directors of Law Enforcement Standards and Training (IADLEST), receive assistance and guidance in "establishing effective and defensible standards for employment and training of peace officers." The primary membership of IADLEST is made up of the directors of state POST commissions, other members of POST commissions, and those involved in police training activities. Most state POST commissions have established minimum standards for entry-level selection of police officers; basic police training standards; inservice training requirements; discipline, certification, and decertification; and curricula for police training. IADLEST has published a model for minimum state standards in an effort to provide state POST commissions with guidelines for selection, retention, and training of police officers (IADLEST, 2004). The *IADLEST Model Minimum State Standards* provides recommendations for state standards in the following areas: POST administration, to include the authority to establish and regulate standards for police officers, commission membership, and director qualifications; police officer selection standards; recruit officer basic training; police officer inservice training; certification of police officer training instructors; police officer training curriculum standards; police officer professional conduct, to include certification, decertification, and recertification standards; and compliance enforcement.

Despite the efforts of IADLEST to establish a minimum standard for POST administration, many differences in state POST commission operations and standards remain. For example, in 2000, a study of POST-mandated curricula indicated that the minimum number of required hours for basic police officer training varied from 320 to 800 hours, and the basic training mandated curriculum topics varied widely. A recent IADLEST publication indicated that only 44 states currently have procedures for decertification of police officers, and only 13 states participate in an IADLEST national decertification database. These differences in the state standards for police officer certification and decertification vary enough that IADLEST publishes the *Reciprocity Handbook* as a reference source to assist POST commissions with certification decisions for police officers seeking employment in a state other than where the officers' basic training was taken.

## CONCLUSION

State POST commissions, despite their varied names, missions, scopes of operations, and diverse standards, provide a valuable service to policing in the United States. The effort to raise the level of standards of selection and of training of police officers is a worthy goal. State POST commissions, although not achieving uniformity, do strive to attain the goal of providing standards that seek to advance the level of police professionalism through improved police officer selection and training.

*Jeffrey S. Magers*

**See also** Physical Fitness and Training, Police Training in the United States

### For Further Reading

Carte, G. E., & Carte, E. H. (1975). *Police reform in the United States: The era of August Vollmer, 1905–1932.* Berkeley: University of California Press.

Dantzker, M. L. (2003). *Understanding today's police* (3rd ed.). Upper Saddle River, NJ: Prentice Hall.

Franklin, R. A. (2003). *The IADLEST national decertification database.* Available: http://www.iadlest.org/nddreport.pdf

Haberfeld, M. R. (2002). *Critical issues in police training.* Upper Saddle River, NJ: Prentice Hall.

IADLEST. (2004). *International Association of Directors of Law Enforcement Standards and Training Model Minimum State Standards.* Available: http://www.iadlest .org/ modelmin.htm

Magers, J. S. (2002). Police basic training: A comparative study of state standards in the United States. *Illinois Law Enforcement Executive Institute Forum, 2*(2), 103–113.

Magers, J. S. (2003). IADLEST: Shaping the future of law enforcement training and standards. *Police Chief, 46*(1), 31–33.

Palmiotto, M. J. (2003). *Policing & training issues.* Upper Saddle River, NJ: Prentice Hall.

http://www.iadlest.org

## ✿ POLICE OFFICERS' BILL OF RIGHTS

After several decades of reform, a consensus has emerged about the need to balance our efforts to hold police accountable while simultaneously ensuring that individual officers' rights are not violated. Failure to achieve this balance, police observers claim, will place officers at constant professional risk—a condition that will impede honest police efforts while reducing the ability of citizens to hold officers accountable when transgressions do occur. One result of this consensus has been the creation and adoption of protective Bills of Rights for police.

Although many versions of the Officers' Bill of Rights exist, nearly all are focused on a few similar provisions. For example, most specify that officers under investigation retain a fundamental right to be informed of the nature of any investigations against them before an interrogation can occur. In addition, officers under investigation have a right to representation by the person of their own choice, and, at the discretion of the officer, that representative may be present at all times during any interrogation of the officer. Evidence obtained otherwise is generally held to be inadmissible in any subsequent disciplinary proceedings. Finally, many provisions go further to protect officers' rights to engage in political activity as long as those activities do not occur while on duty or while the officer is acting in an official capacity. Although individual jurisdictions are free to expand or enlarge officers' legal rights, where an officers' Bill of Rights has been implemented, agency heads and community leaders are generally prohibited from diminishing or abridging the rights granted either administratively or through collective bargaining.

*Dennis Kenney*

## ✂ POLICE PURSUITS

After observing a traffic violation or being alerted to a person or vehicle, a police officer can signal a driver to stop. In a vast majority of the cases, the driver will pull over and the situation will end without further concern. However, on rare occasions, the driver will refuse to stop or will take evasive action and flee. In these situations, a routine traffic stop turns into a dangerous pursuit. When that occurs, the police officer must decide whether or not to continue a chase, recognizing that if a person refuses to stop, the agency's pursuit policy attaches, and the officer must therefore take into account both policy and training before reaching a decision. Accordingly, the officer must balance both the risks and the potential benefits when deciding whether or not a pursuit is necessary.

A pursuit is initiated when a suspect refuses to obey an officer's order to stop. The fleeing suspect is likely to become erratic and a danger to anyone in the area. Unfortunately, the risks of a chase not only include the police officer and the suspect, but also the public in an interactive triangle.

This interactive triangle is made up of (a) the officer, who is trying to apprehend a suspect; (b) the police vehicle; and (c) the environment, which includes the fleeing suspect, traffic, and pedestrians, all of which are forces brought into play in this interaction. The suspect's goal is to remain free and avoid arrest, and unless he or she has a death wish, the suspect will often run until he or she feels safe or crashes. The suspect, who has refused to heed the commands of the officer, has the primary responsibility to stop the chase by pulling over. The suspect is also directing the pursuit by selecting the course, speed, and recklessness of the driving. However, any increased recklessness on the part of the suspect may be affected by the officer's attempt to apprehend him. The officer's natural desire to apprehend the suspect must be tempered by concerns for public safety. Because of the nature of pursuits, the suspect is necessarily influenced psychologically by the officer's actions.

The goal of the officer is to apprehend the suspect and make the arrest. Accordingly, it is the officer who must become aware of personal capabilities and take into account environmental conditions that may affect his or her ability to accomplish the mission of police, which is to protect lives. The police officer must factor into the decision-making process the risk created by the suspect's driving; the potential actions of innocent bystanders, passengers, and others who may become involved; and the influence of his or her actions on the suspect's driving. In addition, the likelihood of apprehension must be factored into the decision to continue or not continue a chase.

A pursuit is an exciting event and involves one person running to escape and another chasing to catch. If it continues, it resembles a drag race until one party terminates it or there is a crash. The problems include the inability to force a fleeing suspect to stop without applying deadly force. In addition, it is necessary for officers to place a priority on the coexisting and meritorious goals of law enforcement and public safety.

Unfortunately, to achieve one goal, the other may have to be sacrificed. On one hand, if the enforcement of a particular law were treated to the exclusion of public safety, then any cost of pursuit driving would be justified. On the other hand, if public safety were considered paramount and laws were to be enforced only when there was no risk to the public, no pursuit would ever be justified. Obviously, neither of these two extremes is acceptable. Proper police conduct must balance the two goals. Although no one has seriously advocated taking firearms away from the police, the trend has been to restrict their use to defense or preservation of life situations. Similarly, it would not be in society's best interest to remove the ability to pursue criminals from the police, but as with the use of firearms, there is a marked trend to restrict its use. There exists a need to balance these two critical social demands: the need to immediately apprehend a suspect and the risk to the public created by a pursuit.

## BALANCING LAW ENFORCEMENT WITH PUBLIC SAFETY

The purpose of pursuit is to apprehend a suspect within the mission of police, which is to protect lives. Tactics and activities undertaken must consider apprehension secondary to public safety. One way to help officers understand this balance is to have them apply the same standards used in weighing the alternatives to firing a weapon in a situation where innocent bystanders may be endangered. Whenever an officer fires a weapon, he or she must be concerned that the bullet may accidentally hit an unintended target. By comparison, in pursuit, the officer not only has his or her vehicle to worry about, but also must consider the pursued vehicle creating dangerous situations as well as other vehicles creating danger by attempting to get out of the way.

Historically, pursuit driving has been available to the police in the fight against crime. Unfortunately, the inherent nature of pursuit creates a significant danger to the officers, law violators, and general public. Whether or not this danger and the resulting property damage, injuries, and deaths are worth the benefits is the question police administrators and policymakers have been examining for years. One appropriate response has been to limit pursuits to situations in which a fleeing suspect is suspected of a violent felony. By limiting pursuits to these serious felonies, the police are able to use their skills to attempt to apprehend the most serious criminals

while protecting the public from risk created by chases for traffic and property offenses.

*Geoffrey P. Alpert*

### For Further Reading

Alpert, G. (1997). *Police pursuit: Policies and training* (Research in Brief). Washington, DC: National Institute of Justice.

Alpert, G. P., & Fridell, L. (1992). *Police vehicles and firearms: Instruments of deadly force*. Prospect Heights, IL: Waveland.

Alpert, G., Kenney, D., Dunham, R., & Smith, W. (2000). *Police pursuits: What we know*. Washington, DC: Police Executive Research Forum.

## ✪ POLICE RESIDENCY REQUIREMENTS

Police residency requirements, which mandate that officers live within a specified geographic area, may be found in state statutes, state and local civil service rules, or departmental regulations. According to the 1991 International City Management Association Survey of Police Personnel Practices, 29% of American cities with populations over 10,000 have some form of residency policy. Eight percent had residency requirements for new appointees, 13% had such requirements for all officers, 5% required residency of officers hired after a specified date, and 10% required the police chief to reside locally. Among America's six largest police departments, polled in 2003, Philadelphia and Chicago require in-city residency, and New York, Detroit, Houston, and Los Angeles do not.

Residency requirements generally fall into two categories. *Durational* residency entails a job aspirant's living in an area for a given length of time as a prerequisite for being hired. *Continuous* residency involves an employee's living in a prescribed area as a condition for keeping his or her position. This latter type may have substantial long-term effects on police officers' lives and has long been a source of labor–management conflict.

Police residency rules were a natural outgrowth of the political patronage system that developed in the early 19th century, when local political leaders rewarded their immigrant supporters with jobs in the police department and other city agencies. Police reformers, drawn from more upper-class society, sought to break the ward leaders' hold over hiring and broaden the pool of police applicants by eliminating residency requirements. As "professional" police became the gospel of progressive departments throughout the first half of the 20th century, residency requirements fell out of favor.

The racial unrest in many cities in the 1960s revived interest in residency laws, as critics of police conduct argued that the high proportion of white officers from outlying suburban residences were insensitive and antagonistic toward minority communities. Over the next two decades, primarily in the northeastern and north central areas of the United States, municipalities began reinstating residency rules, both to address racial tensions and provide job opportunities to urban minorities. The trend was most pronounced in cities experiencing economic difficulties, where the hiring of resident officers was intended to both ease unemployment and encourage officers to spend their paychecks within city borders.

A comparison of police residency requirements surveyed in 1982 and 1990 found a 1% net decrease in such policies, with more central cities and suburbs dropping residency requirements and more independent communities adopting them. Research suggests that municipalities that embraced residency rules over this period were more likely to have been experiencing economic decline. In these instances, the residency restrictions were associated with a reduced pool of applicants, decreased applicant screening and selection efforts, and lowered wages, which in turn reduced the cost of police services and ultimately may have contributed to improved fiscal health. Police agencies with residency rules were also associated with the use of numeric goals to achieve racial diversity, suggesting that the rules served to deter nontargeted groups from applying. Finally, those with residency policies tended to have more extensive inservice training, as well as officer skills and professionalism that were comparable to agencies without residency requirements.

The 1976 Supreme Court decision in *McCarthy v. Philadelphia Civil Service Commission* upheld the constitutionality of continuous residency requirements, ruling that they were neither "irrational" within the due process or equal protection clause, nor violative of the constitutional right to travel. Subsequent court battles over residency have often concerned the definition of residency when officers maintain both in-city and out-of-city addresses, and the reasonableness of mandatory residency in jurisdictions where housing is unavailable or prohibitively expensive. In several suburban communities, the U.S. Justice Department has challenged residency laws whose preferential treatment of community residents has effectively excluded minorities from municipal jobs.

Beyond professionalism, police–community relations, fiscal policy, equal opportunity, and case-specific legal questions, the residency controversy invokes still other issues. Advocates of regulation argue that resident officers are more familiar with the geography, languages, and customs of their work areas, making them better service providers and crime fighters; that resident officers have a greater personal commitment to their communities; and that they evoke greater respect from the public. However, empirical evidence fails to support these claims. For instance, one study of 24 midsized cities found that regardless of residency, the officers most familiar with the community and its organizations were simply the ones who were most busy interacting with citizens. Another study, of Washington, DC, officers, found that those who lived out of town made more arrests leading to convictions than those who were city residents. A 1992 summary of civilian complaints filed against New York City officers reported that nonresident officers received slightly *fewer* complaints than city-dwellers.

Those favoring residency requirements also maintain that resident officers enhance public safety because they can enforce the law while off-duty and be mobilized more quickly during emergencies. Opponents counter that individual off-duty police actions are infrequent and often mishandled; that prompt emergency response mostly depends on planning and coordination; and that forcing officers to live in close proximity to their work area is not only stressful but possibly dangerous to them and their families. The many unproven assertions and conflicting priorities that confound this debate assure us that police residency rules will remain in flux for many more years.

*Edith Linn*

## For Further Reading

Chase, A. (1977). Residency laws: Should police be free to live where they choose? *Police, 2*, 62–65.

Fyfe, J. J. (1987). Police personnel practices, 1986. *Municipal Yearbook 1987.* Washington, DC: International City Management Association.

International City/County Management Association. (1991). *Police personnel recruitment and special training programs.* Washington, DC: Author.

Mastrofski, S. (1983). Police knowledge of the patrol beat: A performance measure. In R. R. Bennett (Ed.), *Police at work: Police issues and analysis.* Beverly Hills, CA: Sage.

McCarthy v. Philadelphia Civil Service Commission, 424 U.S. 465 (1976).

Schall, D. J. (1996). *An investigation into the relationship between municipal police residency requirement, professionalism, economic conditions and equal employment goals.* Unpublished doctoral dissertation, University of Wisconsin—Milwaukee.

## ❧ POLICE SHOOTINGS

Recent years have seen a good deal of research on the use of deadly force by police officers. Law enforcement professionals, for example, regularly examine shootings in order to develop a more complete understanding of such events to thereby reduce their frequency and increase the odds that officers will act appropriately in those events that do occur. Largely overlooked in this research effort, however, is the matter of how officers experience events in which they discharge their weapons. This entry discusses what we do know about the reactions that officers can experience during shootings and discusses some implications for a broader understanding of these incidents. Following a brief discussion of the research on officers' reactions during

shootings, what we know about the reactions that officers who shoot can experience is presented in two categories: thoughts and feelings, and perceptual distortions.

## SHOOTING RESEARCH

Systematic information on officers' reactions during shootings comes from a handful of studies that asked officers who have been in shootings about how they experienced these events. Most of these studies simply reported whether officers who had fired their weapons experienced a small number of specific thoughts, feelings, or perceptual distortions during shootings. More recently, however, one study (Klinger, 2001) took a more detailed look at reactions during shootings by asking officers who shot suspects in the line of duty about several specific thoughts, feelings, and perceptual anomalies they may have experienced during two distinct phases of these events—prior to firing and when they pulled the trigger. The information reported below is drawn from this study.

### Thoughts and Feelings

Officers almost always (96% of the time) experienced at least one of the following thoughts or feelings at some point during shootings:

- Disbelief about what was happening, which officers experienced prior to firing (32%) and as they fired (34%)
- A sense of fear for their own safety, which officers experienced prior to firing (35%) and as they fired (30%)
- A sense of fear for someone else's safety (i.e., fellow officer or citizen), which officers experienced prior to firing (54%) and as they fired (49%)
- A need to survive, which officers experienced prior to firing (27%) and as they fired (23%)
- A rush of strength or adrenalin, which officers experienced prior to firing (44%) and as they fired (46%)
- Intrusive thoughts about irrelevant matters (e.g., friends or family members), which officers experienced prior to firing (10%) and as they fired (9%)

- Officers also often experienced a variety of miscellaneous reactions during shootings, 29% of the time prior to pulling the trigger, 30% as they fired. Counted among these other thoughts and feelings are concerns about the tactical situation that the officers faced (e.g., being in a cross-fire with other officers), apprehension about the placement of shots officers were about to fire, a sense of calm, and anger at the suspect for trying to harm the officer or some innocent third party (e.g., hostages).

## Perceptual Distortions

As is the case with thoughts and feelings, officers almost always (95% of the time) experienced some sort of perceptual anomalies during shootings. In terms of specific distortions, officers experienced some sort of visual anomaly in 82% of shootings, auditory distortion in 85%, time distortion in 66%, and some other sort of perceptual distortion in 13%. More specifically,

- Prior to firing, officers experienced tunnel vision (i.e., a narrowing of the visual field) in 31% of the cases, a sense of heightened visual detail in 37%, and both visual distortions in another 10%.
- Upon firing, officers experienced tunnel vision in 27% of the cases, heightened visual acuity in 35%, and both visual distortions in 11%. Prior to firing, officers experienced a diminution of sound in 42% of the cases and amplified sound in 10%.
- Upon firing, officers experienced diminished sound in 70% of the cases, intensified sound in 5%, and both auditory aberrations in 8%.
- Prior to firing, officers experienced time passing more slowly than usual (i.e., slow motion) in 43% of the cases and time passing more quickly than usual (i.e., fast motion) in 12%.
- Upon firing, officers experienced slow motion in 40% of the cases, fast motion in 12%, and both time distortions in 2%.
- Officers experienced some other sort of distortion prior to firing in 6% of the cases and as they fired in 9%. Of particular interest here is that some officers reported their sense of distance was distorted so that the actual distances between themselves, suspects, other officers, citizen bystanders, and inanimate objects (e.g., vehicles) were either far greater or substantially less than they had perceived at the time of the shooting.

## IMPLICATIONS

Why officers act as they do during shootings is a critical question. Knowledge of the sorts of thoughts, feelings, and perceptions that officers can experience during shootings provides valuable insight into this issue. Decisions to initiate gunfire, to continue firing, and to cease firing are all predicated upon officers' understanding of what is transpiring before them. Officers' perceptions of what is taking place, and the thoughts and feelings that flow from these perceptions, are the key link between what is occurring during shooting incidents and officers' actions regarding the application of deadly force. Awareness that officers often feel fearful; that they frequently think they must shoot in order to survive; and that they regularly experience perceptual anomalies such as tunnel vision, for example, helps us understand the ways in which officers define situations in which they come to discharge their weapons and why they decided to take the actions they took.

*David A. Klinger*

*See also* Assaults on the Police, Suicide by Cop, Use of Force

## For Further Reading

Adams, R. J., McTernan, T. M., & Remsberg, C. (1980). *Street survival: Tactics for armed encounters.* Evanston, IL: Calibre.

Artwohl, A., & Christensen, L. W. (1997). *Deadly force encounters: What cops need to know to mentally and physically prepare for and survive a gunfight.* Boulder, CO: Paladin.

Campbell, J. H. (1992). *A comparative analysis of the effects of post-shooting trauma on the special agents of the Federal Bureau of Investigation.* Unpublished doctoral dissertation, Michigan State University.

Fyfe, J. J. (1996). Training to reduce police–citizen violence. In W. A. Geller & H. Toch (Eds.), *Police violence: Understanding and controlling police abuse of force.* New Haven, CT: Yale University Press.

Klinger, D. A. (2001). *Police responses to officer-involved shootings: Final report* (NCJ-192286). Washington, DC: U.S. Department of Justice.

Nielson, E. (1981). *Salt Lake City Police Department deadly force policy shooting and post shooting reactions.* Mimeograph.

Solomon, R. M., & Horn, J. H. (1986). Post-shooting traumatic reactions: A pilot study. In J. T. Reese & H. A. Goldstein (Eds.), *Psychological services for law enforcement officers.* Washington, DC: U.S. Government Printing Office.

## ෩ POLICE STRIKES/"BLUE FLU"

The first recorded police strike in the United States occurred in Ithaca, New York, on April 3, 1889. As a result of a pay cut from $12 to $9 a week, the entire force, all appointed by a prior Republican administration, protested and were removed. A new force of loyal Democrats was quickly appointed to fill these vacancies. Several days later, the old pay rate was reinstituted. Salaries would continue to be the cause of unrest among police officers. In 1918, following the social unrest and skyrocketing inflation caused by World War I, several police agencies were being affected by moves toward unionization and strike.

In early September 1918, some officers in the Cincinnati Police Department met clandestinely to discuss forming a union; word spread, and the police chief suspended all those involved. Quickly, all the officers of the department refused duty. The National Guard was mobilized, and traffic duties were taken over by the Boy Scouts. The mayor stepped in, and a settlement was quickly reached—the officers would forget their plans for a union, and the strikers were welcomed back. Several weeks later, in Boston, the situation and outcome would be much different.

For quite some time, the police officers of the Boston Police Department had been discussing the formation of a union and affiliation with the American Federation of Labor (AFL). On September 9, the newly formed Boston Policemen's Union voted for a strike, and at 5:45 p.m., 1,117 patrolmen, more than 80% of the force, walked off their jobs. The commissioner quickly suspended all of those officers. The state militia was mobilized, and volunteers were recruited from all over Boston, including Harvard's football team. Federal troops and naval forces in the Boston area were ordered to full alert.

Unlike the situation in Cincinnati, rioting quickly broke out in Boston. Over the course of the next few days, Guard units opened fire on the rioters. Calvary units, with drawn sabers, charged the mob in Scollay Square. The city was under marshal law, and the state governor, Calvin Coolidge, who assumed command, did not believe that police had a right to strike. The end result of this strike was seven people killed, including one striking officer, 22 seriously wounded, and millions of dollars in damages. All 1,117 striking officers were fired, losing all benefits and pensions, and an entirely new force was recruited.

Throughout the next 50 years, the Boston Strike continued to have an effect on policing in the United States. After the disaster in Boston, many jurisdictions, including the federal government, passed legislation forbidding the formation of or membership in a union by police officers. In 1944, and again in 1958, the International Association of Chiefs of Police (IACP) issued bulletins that condemned this police strike and the chaos it created.

Much of this was to change with the militancy of the 1960s. A new breed of officers was rising to leadership roles and was looking to explore other avenues to press their negotiating position.

The use of the "Blue Flu," or sick-out, by these officers was a new approach to labor negotiations. Other new ideas were the "work to rule," to slow down the general workings of the department; failing to "see" violations or write tickets for them; and declining overtime assignments. These ideas were all taken from other labor organizations that had a more traditional labor–management relationship.

The officers of both the Boston and New York Police Departments were to use a combination of these tactics in the early 1960s to achieve a variety of goals. Through these tactics, the Boston Police, over an extended period of concentrated "sick" calls and other maneuvers, were able to achieve government recognition of their Patrolmen's Benevolent Association (PBA) as a contract-negotiating "union," something their predecessors had failed to do. Likewise, the New York City PBA was able to increase its negotiating position with the city authorities without resorting to a strike. Today, the rule book slowdown is a greater threat to the bottom line of a city than ever before. In New York City, for example, the amount of money going into the general fund from all traffic ticketing is in the millions of dollars every week. The effects of a failure to "see" these violations or to opt out of a ticketing blitz by some 30,000 members of the NYC PBA are obvious.

Today, the realities of labor management have caused fundamental changes in the relationship of officers to the department. Clearly, the question of a complete strike or refusal to report for duty is almost gone, thanks to the "Ghost of 1919." But it is not totally forgotten. In the 1970s, the San Francisco, Memphis, and New Orleans police all went out on strikes, usually for a limited duration. The alternate strategy of the "Blue Flu" and the disruption of the workings of police departments to enhance or achieve negotiating positions is more the reality of policing today.

*Joseph F. King*

*See also* Unions

*For Further Reading*

King, J. (1999). *Police strikes of 1918 and 1919 in the United Kingdom and Boston: Their effects.* Unpublished doctoral dissertation, City University of New York.

Koss, F. (1966). *The Boston police strike of 1919.* Unpublished doctoral dissertation, Boston University.

Meyers, J. (1975). Police strikes: A model to study underlying factors. *Australia & New Zealand Journal of Criminology, 8,* 190–206.

# ෨෩ POLICE TRAINING IN THE UNITED STATES

Police training in the United States can be divided into four distinct categories: basic academy training (the basic police academy training), the field training officer (FTO) program, specialized and developmental training, and supervisory and management training.

## BASIC ACADEMY TRAINING

The term *police academy* usually refers to three main types of police academies in the United States: agency, regional, and college-sponsored. Agency schools are generally found in large municipal areas or are established for the state police or highway patrol. Regional academies handle the training functions for both large and small departments located in a designated geographical area. The college-sponsored training academies operate on the premises of postsecondary institutions, particularly community colleges. These college-sponsored academies allow a person to take police training and earn college credit.

Modern police training has come a long way since the times when the training was so inadequate, or even nonexistent, that officers were ignorant of their own duties. Despite such drawbacks, it was still possible to have a "successful" career as a policeman.

Historically, the Berkeley Police School in Berkeley, California, was the model for modern police training. It owed its ambitious program to its police chief, August Vollmer. Appointed to the position in 1909, he held that office continuously until his retirement in 1932. In 1914, he set up the Berkeley Junior Police, and shortly thereafter, he reorganized the Berkeley Police School curriculum, a training program that, over the next several decades, was copied in whole or in large part not only by police agencies in many American states, but also by a number of police departments abroad. However, despite the efforts to define policing as a profession in most cities, the process of reform was painfully slow. Some cities did not offer any meaningful training until the 1950s. The situation in smaller jurisdictions was even more discouraging. In New Jersey, for example, in 1961, the Sussex County Police School offered a basic training of 2 hours per night "as long as needed," the Union County Police School offered 1 week of school, Burlington County Bridge Commission Police School offered a 10-hour course, and Morris and Essex Counties offered 2 hours per night for 8 weeks.

It was in California in 1959 that a training council first established police officer standards and training guidelines. Although this was a state and not federal initiative, within approximately 4 years, many states throughout the country had developed their own standards for training.

In 1967, the President's Commission on Law Enforcement and Administration of Justice recommended that a Peace Officer Standards and Training (POST) commission be established in every state. These POST Commissions or boards were empowered to set mandatory minimum requirements and were appropriately funded so that they might provide financial aid to governmental units for the implementation of established standards. The two important charges of the POST commissions were the following:

- Establish mandatory minimum training standards (at both the recruit and inservice levels), with the authority to determine and approve curricula, identify required preparation for instructors, and approve facilities acceptable for police training
- Certify police officers who have acquired various levels of education, training, and experience necessary to adequately perform the duties of the police service

In 1993, the Bureau of Justice Statistics surveyed more than 12,000 municipal and county law enforcement agencies. They found that, on average, departments required 640 training hours of their new officer recruits: 425 classroom training hours and 215 field training hours. By 2000, the Bureau reported that officers in large jurisdictions with 100,000 or more residents received an average of 1,600 hours compared to 800 hours for smaller jurisdictions. Despite the findings, caution must be used as to the nature of academy training at the beginning of the 21st century. The key word "average" does not take into consideration the implications of the less-than-average number of hours, after which a given recruit is sent to perform as a police officer.

Nationally, most training programs can be divided according to the following areas:

1. Administrative procedures: This covers quizzes, graduation, and instruction on note taking.

2. Administration of justice: This covers history of law enforcement, police organization, probation, parole, and social services.

3. Basic law: This covers constitutional law, offenses, criminal procedure, vehicle and traffic law, juvenile law and procedures, and civil liability.

4. Police procedures: This covers patrol observation; crimes in progress; field notes; intoxication; mental illness; disorderly conduct; domestic violence; police communication; alcoholic beverage control; civil disorder; crowd and riot control; normal duties related to traffic enforcement, including accidents and emergency vehicle operations; and criminal investigations, including interviews and interrogations, control of evidence, and various kinds of cases, such as burglary, robbery, injury, sex crime, drugs, organized crime, arson, and gambling.

5. Police proficiency: This covers normal firearm training, arrest techniques, emergency aid, courtroom testimony and demeanor, and bomb threats and bombs.

6. Community relations: This covers psychology for police, minority groups, news media relationships, telephone courtesy, identification of community resources, victim/witness services, crime prevention, officer stress awareness, law enforcement family, and police ethics.

7. The newest addition to the police training curriculum around the country is assorted counterterrorism modules that have been added during both the basic academy and the inservice training.

After graduating from the basic police academy, recruits are exposed to the field training officer programs that are offered primarily at the various police departments and, less frequently, in the in-house academies.

## THE FIELD TRAINING OFFICER PROGRAM

Not until the early 1970s was a credible FTO model developed and implemented with the degree of success that allowed other agencies to emulate it. That model was the San Jose, California, Police Department's "Field Training and Evaluation Officer (FTO) Program."

### The San Jose FTO Model

Begun in 1972, the San Jose Model FTO program is the most widely recognized program of its kind. It is emulated by law enforcement agencies throughout the country that are seeking to achieve several key organizational objectives, primarily the improvement of recruit officer training.

The San Jose program was developed in response to an incident that occurred in the early spring of 1970. A recruit police officer was involved in a serious traffic accident while negligently operating a police vehicle on duty. A passenger in the other vehicle was killed, and the officer was seriously injured. The officer was dismissed by the city. A review of his personnel record revealed serious inadequacies in the department's recruit training and evaluation procedures. The incident led San Jose Police Department managers to conclude that the process by which rookie officers acquired practical, on-the-job knowledge and skills needed to be formalized. What emerged from San Jose's experience was the concept of the FTO program.

The original San Jose FTO model is a mentoring-type model, designed to provide a practical "information bridge" from the training academy to the job. San Jose's model is 14 weeks long: three 4-week periods of training, followed by a 2-week evaluation period. Upon graduation from the training academy, a recruit is immediately assigned to the FTO program. Training occurs on each of the three workday shifts and is concentrated in two districts. The FTO team working with the recruit-trainee plans days off and study time well in advance. The recruit-trainee is assigned to a different FTO for each training period. This enables the trainee to be exposed to various styles of police work and ensures that he or she will not be penalized because of a personality clash with a single FTO. Each FTO provides specific training consistent with a curriculum developed for the program; each FTO evaluates the trainee's abilities and developing skills and knowledge.

FTO programs have been implemented by hundreds of law enforcement agencies across America. The original San Jose program has been modified by many agencies to suit their own needs and objectives; many other agencies have developed their own unique programs.

Following the completion of the FTO program, police officers are exposed, depending on the agency, to specialized and developmental inservice training.

## SPECIALIZED AND DEVELOPMENTAL TRAINING

The major drive for police agencies to send their officers for specialized and advanced training appears to be related to law enforcement standards mandated by each state's POST Commission. Usually, each Commission mandates a number of annual hours of certified inservice training, in addition to firearms recertification or requalification.

For example, every person employed as a full-time law enforcement officer in Virginia must attend 40 hours of certified inservice training within 2 years of completion of a basic school. Absences from inservice training prevent recertification with the Department of Criminal Justice Services. Every hour missed must be made up. However, this training will differ in each and every state. Compulsory inservice standards have the following training modules:

- Mandatory legal training: 4 hours
- Career development: 16 hours
- Elective: 20 hours. No more than 8 hours of firearms are permitted as elective subject. Firearms recertification standards require that every officer who carries a firearm in performance of his or her duty shall qualify annually, attaining a minimum qualifying score of 70%. This qualification must occur on one of the following courses:
- the Virginia Modified Double Action Course for Revolvers
- the Virginia Modified Double Action Course for Semi-Automatic Pistols
- the Virginia 50-Round Tactical Qualification Course for Revolvers and Semi-Automatic Pistols
- a Special Weapons Course using shotguns and/or similar weapons

The specialized and advanced course offered to and by police agencies can be divided into a number of categories offered by in-house municipal police academies; federal, state, and regional law enforcement agencies; private individuals; and private organizations.

Some of the newer topics that have been covered recently in police training are

- Stress training
- Dealing with terrorist activity
- Domestic crisis intervention
- AIDS awareness

- Domestic violence training
- Stalking
- Tactical operations
- Diversity
- Bias crimes
- Americans with Disabilities Act
- Computer/video simulation
- Interactive teleconferencing/cable TV

The training is offered externally, either on the premises of the offering agency or in a designated location. Some of the training is customized to the needs of the clients and brought directly to the department, either through distance learning techniques or television networks, or in person.

Some of the training modules are offered exclusively to public law enforcement officers, some are open to both private and public law enforcement, and still others are open to the general public. This mix of publics, in itself, appears to contribute in a significant manner to the problems associated with the effectiveness of any given instructional module.

Historically, a number of attempts have been made to mandate or at least recommend some changes in the advanced/supervisory training approach. In 1973, the National Advisory Commission on Criminal Justice Standards and Goals published a volume of recommendations titled *Police*. "Training before promotion" as a policy in any given department was advocated, as well as management programs for middle management. The Commission advocated for the programs for middle management to be integrated with college and business programs.

The final and most advanced level of training is geared toward and offered to the executive/supervisory level within police agencies.

## SUPERVISORY AND MANAGEMENT TRAINING

The executive level of police training is composed of numerous programs offered around the country by various providers representing both government and private agencies. Following is a sample of such training opportunities.

### The National Police Academy

The National Academy, located in Quantico, Virginia, is sponsored by the Federal Bureau of Investigation and offers advanced-level courses for police executives. The goal of the FBI National Academy is to enhance the ability of experienced law enforcement personnel to fulfill their responsibilities within a constitutionally structured free society.

The philosophy of the National Academy is a holistic one in that a healthy lifestyle and physical fitness are stressed, along with academic achievement. A typical session lasts for about 11 weeks. To qualify for the training, one must apply to the FBI and be sponsored by the employing agency.

There are no charges for tuition, books, or equipment used. Meals, lodging, dry cleaning, and laundry services are also provided without cost. The individual officers or their agency must assume the travel cost and the assessment fee.

Officers who successfully complete the National Academy Program earn college credit through the University of Virginia. Credits earned are identical to those earned on the main campus at the university. All students who complete 13 semester hours of coursework with an average grade of C or better, and who do not fail a course, are awarded a certificate by the Division of Continuing Education at the University of Virginia.

### The Northwestern University Traffic Institute

The Traffic Institute was established at Northwestern University in 1936. The Institute is a national nonprofit organization that serves public agencies responsible for law enforcement, criminal justice, public safety, traffic management, and highway transportation systems. Local, county, state, and federal government agencies, as well as agencies from foreign countries, are served through programs of specialized training, continuing education, research and development, publications, and direct assistance.

The staff can develop programs designed for the instructional requirements of a given agency. The courses are based on an agreement between the agency and the director of the Police Operations and Administration Training Division. If the agency is large enough, with a group of managers/executives that needs to be trained on site, the Institute can present a customized seminar at the agency's site. The courses are directed and taught by Traffic Institute professional staff members.

### The Federal Law Enforcement Training Center and the FLETC Management Institute

The Federal Law Enforcement Training Center is located in Glynco, Georgia. With a clearly defined mission to be a provider of world-class law enforcement training in a cost-effective manner, it provides training to more than 25,000 students annually. The fee for attending the program is paid by the individual agency, and it varies every year. Learning methodologies include lectures, small-group discussions, case studies, problem-solving exercises, simulations, role-plays, individual and group presentations, and computer-generated management style inventories.

The FLETC Management Institute designs, develops, coordinates, and administers training programs for federal law enforcement supervisors and managers. Additional, executive-level training is developed by in-house academies and through college-based initiatives that provide primarily executive-level supervisory/leadership training.

*Maria (Maki) Haberfeld*

**See also** Cultural Competency/Sensitivity Training, Physical Fitness and Training, Police Officer Standards and Training Commissions (POST Commissions)

### For Further Reading

Bennett, W. B., & Hess, K. M. (1996). *Management and supervision in law enforcement* (2nd ed.). St. Paul, MN: West.

Haberfeld, M. R. (2002). *Critical issues in police training.* Upper Saddle River, NJ: Prentice Hall.

Kaminsky, G. F. (2002). *The field training concept in criminal justice agencies.* Upper Saddle River, NJ: Prentice Hall.

http://www.jjay.cuny.edu/PoliceStudies/

## ✑ PRIVATE POLICING

We tend to think of policing as a public sector institution, but there are, in fact, more private security personnel than sworn police officers. This entry describes this other, more pervasive side of policing. It describes the forces that produced the growth in this industry and the effects on public safety. It concludes with a look to the future of privatization, with an identification of critical issues related to current trends and an examination of directions that have been identified as offering promise for improving service in both the public and private domains of policing.

### PRIVATIZATION AND PRIVATE SECURITY

Privatization typically means the absence of government in the provision of protective services. Private citizens and institutions often buy services to protect life and property and to reduce fear, and they determine how these services will be allocated. This includes a myriad of self-help approaches to protecting private property and personal safety, including the following:

- Hiring of security guards and private investigators
- Installation of surveillance, lighting, locks, secure doors and windows, and alarm systems
- Use of citizen foot patrols and block watches, and escort services for senior citizens and university women
- Citizens-band radio automobile patrols and radio-alert networks for taxis, busses, and commercial vehicles
- Carrying of concealed weapons by private citizens

Privatization occurs within the government, too, as when federal, state, or local governments contract with private sources for specific services. The federal government is, in fact, the largest employer of private security guards. Examples of the activities for which private agents are hired by governments can include the following:

- Security of government buildings
- Court security
- Prisoner custody

- Computer and communications system maintenance
- Training
- Laboratory services
- Radio dispatching
- Video surveillance
- Traffic and parking control

Private security, as opposed to public law enforcement, focuses more on crime prevention than response, typically including the work of security guards; corporate security and loss prevention personnel; alarm and surveillance specialists; private investigators; armored vehicle personnel; manufacturers of security equipment; locksmiths; security consultants and engineers; and people involved in a variety of related roles, from private forensic laboratory scientists to guard dog trainers and drug-testing specialists.

## TRENDS IN PRIVATIZATION

The shift toward privatization that occurred toward the end of the 20th century was both sudden and sharp, especially when viewed over the almost 200 years since the creation of the first metropolitan police department in London. Table 1 displays more precisely the dimensions of the shift, in terms of the ratios of private security industry personnel to sworn officers over the period 1965 to 1995.

The number of people employed in private security jobs began to surpass the number in sworn officer positions in the 1960s, and this numerical advantage has continued to grow in the years since. There were about 2 million members of private security organizations in 1990; the Bureau of Justice Statistics estimates fewer than one third as many police officers for the same year, some 600,000. By the mid-1990s, Sears employed 6,000 security guards, more than the total number of sworn officers in the Los Angeles Police Department.

The numbers of sworn officers and private security personnel have varied, and so too have the respective costs associated with each category. Total private sector spending on protection against crime has been estimated at $300 billion annually, about three times the amount spent on the entire public criminal justice system.

**Table 1**  Sworn Officers and Security Officers: 1965–1995

|  | 1965 | 1975 | 1985 | 1995 |
| --- | --- | --- | --- | --- |
| Security Officers per Sworn | 0.9 | 1.9 | 2.4 | 3.7 |

Sources: Cunningham, Strauchs, and Van Meter (1991), p. 3; LEMAS, selected years

As the police demonstrated that their powers to deal with crime were, in fact, quite limited, and as pressures to control public spending increased, private sector responses materialized in their place. Private expenditures for security equipment, personnel, and services soared—in office buildings, subways and other public transportation systems, shopping centers and warehouses, universities and schools, hospitals, and large apartment complexes and condominiums. The proportion of homes with alarm systems increased from 1% in 1975 to 10% in 1985. Although the number of sworn officers has increased in the new terrorist era of policing, the number of private security personnel appears to have increased as well.

Privatization has occurred also in the areas of investigative services, perimeter safeguards, surveillance systems, risk management, and armed courier and armored car services. Private investigation alone now encompasses services that range from the investigation of disability claims and marital infidelity to the delivery of legal papers ("process serving"), criminal investigations aimed at undermining the prosecutor's evidence, and the investigation and resolution of sophisticated computer crimes.

Citizens and organizations, both public and private, came to recognize that their municipal police departments have limited capacities, with a focus on response rather than prevention, and they took matters into their own hands. In addition to hiring private agents for specific security services, laws permitting the carrying of concealed weapons by private citizens became increasingly popular in the 1990s, especially in the South. Today, even police departments now contract out many functions previously done internally.

Some communities, aware of the inefficiencies in providing conventional police services, have bypassed their police departments altogether and contracted out portions of public protective services to private agencies. State and local government spending on private services mushroomed from $27 billion in 1975 to some $100 billion in 1987, with another $197 billion of federal expenditures for private security services by 1987. Municipalities throughout the country have expanded contracts for guard services and experimented with all-private police forces, often finding them to deliver services at lower costs and with no decline in quality of service.

Whereas most police departments have grown modestly since 1975, the private security industry has exploded. No single factor can be identified as the primary cause of the shift to privatization over the past 40 years, but a few factors stand out as leading candidates: the 1960s crime explosion that overwhelmed public resources, growth of specialization throughout the economy, an increased ability of the middle class to turn to private alternatives, and a decline in the popularity of public sector solutions to domestic problems generally.

These developments have not been unique to the United States. A 1988 survey in the United Kingdom found 239 patrols operated by private firms on behalf of local authorities. Britain and Canada had twice as many private security agents as public police by 1990. Similar trends have been reported in Australia, Switzerland, Bavaria, and elsewhere.

## Critical Issues

Questions such as whether privatization is good or bad and whether we need more or less privatization of policing are too simplistic and sweeping to warrant serious answers. These issues can be approached more effectively by focusing more precisely on how various forms of privatization and use of sworn officers in a variety of roles can better serve the public.

This much is clear: The notion that either our corps of sworn police officers or the expanding array of private security agents is uniquely equipped to protect society and maintain order without the other has no credible support. Neither the public nor the private sector is endowed with attributes to ensure that policing in either domain will be automatically superior in

every respect to the alternative. Neither has revealed the capacity to respond effectively to the variety of social trends that characterize our contemporary landscape, trends that suggest the inevitability of more crime and disorder in many segments of society—changing demographics, increased use of guns by adolescents, the decline of family, expanded exposure of youth to violence, and vast disparities in education and wealth. The public and private sectors alike have demonstrated extraordinary accomplishments as well as more than ample capacities for ineffectiveness, waste, preferential treatment, and corruption.

Acceptable solutions to satisfying the public's needs for security are bound to consist of a widely varied mix of public and private alternatives: sworn officers serving in a variety of roles; civilians working as specialists in police departments; private firms hired under contract by police departments and municipal governments to serve well-defined security and support needs; subsidies for poor people to have access to resources that make their environments safer; security guards and specialists hired to protect commercial interests; citizens serving voluntarily to protect their communities, typically in coordination with the police; and citizens augmenting and substituting public protection with a range of goods and services to protect private property and provide personal protection. Such a panoply of options working simultaneously is virtually certain to serve to fill gaps in service that more limited alternatives cannot accomplish.

Debate over the appropriate mix of options—a mix that adequately satisfies the extraordinary variety of the public's security needs—has been too often contaminated by deep faith in either governmental or market solutions, combined with equally deep suspicion of the other sector. A more coherent and effective resolution is likely to result from thoughtful consideration of the extent to which each option contributes to each aspect of our need for security—in terms of its effectiveness, equitability, economy, and legitimacy, and the extent to which it permits freedom of choice.

*Brian Forst*

## For Further Reading

Benson, B. L. (1998). *To serve and protect: Privatization and community in criminal justice.* New York: New York University Press.

Bittner, E. (1980). *The functions of the police in modern society: A review of background factors, current practices, and possible role models.* Cambridge, MA: Oelgeschlager, Gunn and Hain.

Cunningham, W. C., Strauchs, J., & Van Meter, C. (1991). *Private security: Patterns and trends.* Washington, DC: National Institute of Justice.

Davis, M., Lundman, R., & Martinez, R., Jr. (1991). Private corporate justice: Store police, shoplifters, and civil recovery. *Social Problems, 38,* 395–408.

Forst, B., & Manning, P. K. (1999). *The privatization of policing: Two views.* Washington, DC: Georgetown University Press.

Jacobs, J. B. (1983). Police: Private police and security forces. In S. H. Kadish (Ed.), *Encyclopedia of crime and justice* (Vol. 3). New York: Macmillan and Free Press.

Johnston, L. (1992). *The rebirth of private policing.* London: Routledge.

Klockars, C. (1985). *The idea of police.* Beverly Hills, CA: Sage.

Office of International Criminal Justice. (1995, March). *Readings.* Ninth Annual Futures Conference on Privatization in Criminal Justice: Public and Private Partnerships, University of Illinois at Chicago.

Poole, R. W., Jr. (1978). *Cutting back City Hall.* New York: Free Press.

Private firms take over public functions: Germany, Switzerland. (1980, September). *Urban Innovation Abroad, 4,* 1.

Private probes for public jobs. (1996, July 7). *Washington Post,* p. C6.

Rau, C. (1989, October 16). Security industry faces a control crisis. *The Age.*

Shearing, C. D. (1992). The relation between public and private policing. In N Morris & M. Tonry (Eds.), *Crime and justice: An annual review of research* (Vol. 15). Chicago: University of Chicago Press.

Skolnick, J., & Fyfe, J. (1993). *Above the law: Police and the excessive use of force.* New York: Free Press.

Sparrow, M. K., Moore, M. H., & Kennedy, D. M. (1990). *Beyond 911: A new era for policing.* New York: Basic Books.

Stewart, J. K. (1985). Public safety and private police. *Public Administration Review, 45,* 758–765.

Walsh, W. F., & Donovan, E. J. (1989). Private security and community policing: Evaluation and comment. *Journal of Criminal Justice, 17,* 187–197.

## PROBABLE CAUSE

In common with other Bill of Rights provisions, the Fourth Amendment to the U.S. Constitution safeguards fundamental individual liberties against unjustified encroachment by the government. Privacy interests—"the right of the people to be secure in their persons, houses, papers, and effects"—lie at the heart of the Fourth Amendment. The Amendment's first clause forbids unreasonable searches and seizures, and the second provides that "no Warrants shall issue, but upon probable cause, supported by Oath or affirmation, and particularly describing the place to be searched, and the persons or things to be seized." *Probable cause* is integral to the warrant clause, and its presence or absence often (although not inevitably) helps answer whether searches and seizures conducted without the prior authorization of a warrant are unreasonable. Understanding the origins, essential function, and definition of probable cause, as well as how probable cause is established in the search and seizure context, is indispensable to appreciating the design and operation of the Fourth Amendment.

### ORIGINS AND FUNCTION

Antecedents of the concept of probable cause date at least as far back as 14th-century England. By the 16th century, justices of the peace in false imprisonment suits and habeas corpus actions were called on to assess whether "the cause of suspicion be good" to support citizens' arrests. Sir Matthew Hale's influential treatise on the criminal law of England, *The History of the Pleas of the Crown,* which was written in the 17th century but first published in 1736, affirmed that a warrant for arrest could issue on a showing of "probable cause of suspicion" that a named individual had committed a felony, even if the accuser "cannot positively swear [that the suspect] be guilty" (p. 579). The Sugar Act of 1764 protected British customs officers from lawsuits arising from their seizure of ships suspected of engaging in smuggling activities if a judge later determined that "probable cause" justified the seizure, even if no evidence of smuggling was found. Drawing on these and other precedents, James Madison's original draft of the Fourth Amendment, which was revised in significant respects before its adoption by the House of Representatives and its eventual ratification, included a prohibition against "warrants issued without probable cause."

American colonists deeply resented British customs officers entering their private dwellings and business establishments in search of smuggled goods, acting under the authority of writs of assistance. Although issued by judges, these notorious writs were not grounded on sworn information, did not specify the place to be searched, were of indefinite duration, and consequently functioned as open-ended warrants to be executed as the officers' own whims or suspicions dictated. Responding to such unjustifiable incursions on privacy, the warrant clause of the Fourth Amendment requires that information supporting an application be provided under oath or by affirmation, that the desired place or object of a search or seizure be particularly described, and that a warrant be based on probable cause. Because a judicial official must determine that these requirements are satisfied before a warrant is issued, and hence in advance of a search or seizure, the warrant clause helps guard against law enforcement officers' engaging in general exploratory searches or making indiscriminate seizures with the hope that something incriminating will surface.

The probable cause standard establishes the threshold measure of suspicion that must be satisfied before a warrant is issued to authorize a search, the seizure of a person (i.e., an arrest), or the seizure of property. The threshold is designed to work a compromise between legitimate law enforcement needs and individuals' privacy rights. The Supreme Court explained this essential function of probable cause as follows:

> These long-prevailing standards seek to safeguard citizens from rash and unreasonable interferences with privacy and from unfounded charges of crime. They also seek to give fair leeway for enforcing the law in the community's protection. . . . The rule of probable cause is a practical, nontechnical conception affording the best compromise that has been found for accommodating these often opposing interests. Requiring more would unduly hamper law enforcement. To allow less would be to leave law-abiding citizens at the mercy of the officers' whim or caprice. (*Brinegar v. United States,* 1949, p. 176)

Although probable cause is explicitly required to support an arrest or search warrant, its role outside of the warrant context is considerably more equivocal. Although warrantless searches are presumptively considered to be unreasonable, the Supreme Court has recognized many exceptions to this general rule and has expressly endorsed the reasonableness of warrantless arrests. Some searches that are considered lawful even though not authorized by a warrant must at least be supported by probable cause, such as automobile searches. Other warrantless searches may be permissible without probable cause, such as a pat-down frisk for weapons, which is justifiable on a lower threshold showing of individualized suspicion. Still others may be constitutionally reasonable absent any grounds for suspicion, such as a search incident to a lawful arrest or the drug testing (which is considered a search) of high school athletes. Similarly, some warrantless seizures of persons must be supported by probable cause (e.g., arrests), others may be allowed on reasonable suspicion short of probable cause (e.g., a brief investigative stop), and others require no individualized suspicion whatsoever (e.g., detaining motorists at a sobriety checkpoint).

## DEFINITION

Probable cause may be required to justify a search, the seizure of a person (i.e., an arrest), or the seizure of property (e.g., when authorized by a warrant or when a police officer discovers contraband or evidence of a crime in plain view that has not been named in a warrant). In the context of searches, the question is whether probable cause exists to believe that the item or items sought will be found in the place to be searched. For arrests, the focus is on whether there is probable cause to believe that a particular individual has committed or is committing a crime. With respect to seizures of property, there must be probable cause to believe that the item in question is properly seizable because, for example, it is contraband or the fruit or evidence of a crime. These questions must be considered separately. For example, the existence of probable cause to arrest an individual does not automatically justify a search of the arrestee's home, automobile, or personal effects. Similarly, there may be probable cause to search a business or home for evidence, yet no basis to suspect the individual occupants of having committed a crime.

Probable cause does not lend itself to precise definition. It is clear that far less must be shown than is required to prove guilt in a courtroom (proof beyond a reasonable doubt) or even to win a civil lawsuit (proof by a preponderance of the evidence). The Supreme Court has said that "probable cause is a fluid concept—turning on the assessment of probabilities in particular factual contexts—not readily, or even usefully, reduced to a neat set of legal rules" (*Illinois v. Gates,* 1983, p. 232). In the arrest context, "probable cause exists where 'the facts and circumstances within their [the arresting officers'] knowledge and of which they had reasonably trustworthy information [are] sufficient in themselves to warrant a man of reasonable caution in the belief that an offense has been or is being committed" by the suspect (*Draper v. United States,* 1959, p. 313). In deciding whether there is probable cause to support a search warrant,

> the task of the issuing magistrate is simply to make a practical, common-sense decision whether, given all the circumstances set forth in the affidavit . . . there is a fair probability that contraband or evidence of a crime will be found in a particular place. (*Illinois v. Gates,* 1983, p. 238)

Although defying specific definition, probable cause is located somewhere on a continuum between the lower threshold showing of "reasonable suspicion" that justifies stop-and-frisk activity, and the more demanding standard of proof by a "preponderance of the evidence" that is commonly used in civil litigation. There is some debate about whether probable cause represents a fixed point on this continuum of proof or whether its meaning varies depending on such factors as the seriousness of a suspected crime. For example, it is not clear whether the same showing must be made to support the arrest of a suspected terrorist or the search of a car's trunk for a kidnapped child, versus the arrest of a suspected shoplifter or the search of a car for moonshine whiskey.

## ESTABLISHING PROBABLE CAUSE

By design, probable cause is an objective standard. Determining probable cause is not ultimately entrusted to the discretion or good faith judgment of a police officer. The existence of probable cause, in the final analysis, is a judicial question. When a warrant is issued, a magistrate or a judge has decided that probable cause exists, and such a decision will be respected by reviewing courts as long as there was a "substantial basis" for it. When a law enforcement officer makes a warrantless arrest or search, the officer's judgment that probable cause existed is later subject to review in court. Although courts will give some deference to the officer's training and experience, they must independently determine whether the facts known to the officer and reasonable accompanying inferences supplied probable cause. It is axiomatic that probable cause must exist at the time that an arrest or a search takes place. Information discovered after an arrest or as a result of a search cannot be used to help establish probable cause.

In keeping with the premise that the probable cause decision is properly entrusted to the judiciary, rather than to law enforcement officers, it is imperative that the police detail the underlying facts relevant to probable cause when they apply for an arrest warrant or a search warrant. Although hearsay evidence is properly considered, police officers may not summarily set forth their own conclusions and expect a magistrate or a judge simply to ratify them and issue a warrant. For example, the Supreme Court invalidated a search warrant that had been issued on the basis of a "bare bones" application that read, in relevant part,

> Affiants [i.e., the police officers] have received reliable information from a credible person and do believe that heroin, marijuana, barbiturates and other narcotics and narcotic paraphernalia are being kept at the above described premises for the purpose of sale and use contrary to the provisions of the law. (*Aguilar v. Texas,* 1964, p. 109)

The deficiencies in this application are apparent. Most conspicuously, the conclusory nature of the allegations deprived the magistrate of the ability to make an independent assessment of the officers' information, and whether that information was "reliable" and the source was "credible." The absence of supporting facts and details caused the magistrate to defer entirely to the police officers' judgment about these crucial matters.

The police can obtain the facts supporting a probable cause determination either through their own firsthand observation or by relying on information supplied by others, about which they have no direct, personal knowledge. These methods also can be combined, such as when the police receive a tip from an informant and then learn additional or corroborating information based on their own follow-up investigation. Establishing probable cause is relatively straightforward when law enforcement officers witness a suspected crime or personally observe events that may justify a search. The observed facts are simply itemized, and accompanying inferences are drawn and then measured against the corresponding objective standards governing probable cause to arrest or search. Probable cause determinations are somewhat more complicated when reliance is placed on information supplied by third-party informants.

Two essential questions must be answered to help evaluate an informant's tip. The first concerns the informant's basis of knowledge. Did the informant see or overhear incriminating information as opposed to relying on speculation, rumor, or guesswork? Even if the informant reports having firsthand knowledge of the supplied facts, a second question involves the basic trustworthiness of the information. Commonly referred to as the *veracity* prong of the inquiry, the focus turns to the informant's credibility or the reliability of the provided information. An informant's basis of knowledge and veracity are both relevant because it is conceivable, for instance, that an informant who reports having seen a drug transaction (the "basis of knowledge") is a pathological liar or is totally unfamiliar with illegal substances. Conversely, an honest citizen or a generally dependable underworld informant (i.e., a credible source or one who has supplied reliable information in the past) might be relying on wild assumptions or speculation (a dubious basis of knowledge) when supplying information on a particular occasion.

For many years, it was thought that these questions had to be answered separately before an informant's tip could be used to establish probable cause. The police remained at liberty to try to confirm or independently corroborate the details of a tip, which would be useful to bolster the reliability of the information or help support an inference that the informant had inside information (i.e., a good basis of knowledge) about the activity in question. Still, the informant's basis of knowledge and veracity were considered to require independent substantiation before the information could be credited properly. The Supreme Court ruled otherwise, however, in *Illinois v. Gates* (1983):

> The "two-pronged test" directs analysis into two largely independent channels—the informant's "veracity" or "reliability" and his "basis of knowledge." There are persuasive arguments against according these two elements such independent status. Instead, they are better understood as relevant considerations in the totality of circumstances analysis that traditionally has guided probable cause determinations: a deficiency in one may be compensated for, in determining the overall reliability of a tip, by a strong showing as to the other, or by some other indicia of reliability. (p. 233)

The Supreme Court's definition of probable cause, including its adoption of the more flexible "totality of the circumstances" test announced in *Illinois v. Gates* in lieu of an approach requiring an independent assessment of an informant's basis of knowledge and veracity, sets the federal constitutional standard. State courts have the authority to interpret state constitutions to afford citizens within their jurisdictions protections that go beyond those provided under the U.S. Constitution. Several state courts have declined to follow the Supreme Court's approach to defining probable cause articulated in *Illinois v. Gates*. The states are not free to define probable cause in a way that restricts individuals' privacy rights, but some have interpreted their state constitutions as imposing a somewhat more demanding, and thus more protective, test than the U.S. Supreme Court requires under the Fourth Amendment.

*James R. Acker*

*See also* Informants, Search and Seizure,
Search Warrants, Stop and Frisk

## For Further Reading

Aguilar v. Texas, 378 U.S. 108 (1964).

Brinegar v. United States, 338 U.S. 160 (1949).

Draper v. United States, 358 U.S. 307 (1959).

Hale, M. (1736). *The history of the pleas of the Crown* (Vol. 1). London: S. Emlyn.

Hall, J. W. (2000). *Search and seizure* (Vol. 1, 3rd ed.). Charlottesville, VA: Lexis Law.

Illinois v. Gates, 462 U.S. 213 (1983).

LaFave, W. R. (1996). *Search and seizure: A treatise on the Fourth Amendment* (Vol. 2, 3rd ed.). St. Paul, MN: West.

Lerner, C. S. (2003). The reasonableness of probable cause. *Texas Law Review, 81,* 951–1029.

Maclin, T. (1997). The complexity of the Fourth Amendment: A historical review. *Boston University Law Review, 77,* 925–974.

Maclin, T. (1993). The central meaning of the Fourth Amendment. *William and Mary Law Review, 35,* 197–249.

Shapiro, B. J. (1991). *"Beyond reasonable doubt" and "probable cause": Historical perspectives on the Anglo-American law of evidence.* Berkeley: University of California Press.

# ෧ PROBATION OFFICERS

In 1841, John Augustus, a Boston bootmaker, convinced Judge Peter Oxenbridge Thatcher of Boston Police Court to release into his custody a man charged with being a common drunkard. After a 3-week probationary period, the man convinced the judge that he had changed his ways and, instead of jail, received only a nominal fine. Thus was born the first probation officer and the beginnings of probation in the United States.

More than 160 years later, Augustus would probably be dumbfounded at the sheer size and scope of the U.S. probation system. As of 2002, more than 3.9 million people were under a sentence of probation in the United States, almost twice as many people as in U.S. jails and prisons (Glaze, 2003). Not only is probation the largest alternative to incarceration, it is also by far the largest segment of the U.S. correction system in terms of the number of people under supervision. Unlike the common drunkard who was the first probationer, half of everyone on probation in the United States has been convicted of

a felony offense (Glaze, 2003). In some cities, such as New York, the percentage of probationers who have been convicted of felonies reaches more than 60% (New York City Office of Operations, 2004).

Probation officers perform two primary functions: investigation of those found guilty of misdemeanors or felonies and supervision of those sentenced to probation. Those under probation supervision include both adults sentenced to probation by criminal courts and juveniles placed on probation by family or juvenile courts.

## THE INVESTIGATION FUNCTION

Probation officers who perform investigations are responsible for researching and writing Pre-Sentence Investigation (PSI) reports to the court. PSIs contain information about the crime as well as the offender's background; an evaluation of the offender; and, often, a sentence recommendation to the judge. The probation officers who perform this function will interview the convicted offender and then seek to verify and expand on much of the information gleaned from the interview by consulting police reports, court records, and victim statements. In addition, depending on the officer's caseload, he or she might also examine other documents, such as school and employment records, and also interview relevant social service providers, teachers, and family members in an attempt to capture as much information as possible for the sentencing judge about the offender and the crime.

Probation officers who work as investigators spend the bulk of their time interviewing, and then researching and writing their reports. Although they do not have a caseload per se, they are usually expected to complete a certain number of PSIs every month. Most large probation departments now have specialized probation officers who either perform investigations or supervise probationers. Probation officers who perform investigations produce a very tangible product (a PSI). They spend a significant amount of their time with other human service professionals and have close working relationships with judges who value their work; thus, they probably suffer less stress and have a higher degree of self-esteem than their colleagues in supervision.

## THE SUPERVISION FUNCTION

The role of the supervising probation officer is quite different from that of an investigations officer. The number of probationers whom a probation officer must supervise varies greatly throughout the United States. Some large probation departments, such as New York City and Los Angeles County, have caseloads of more than 200 cases per officer. Others, such as the Maricopa County (Phoenix) probation department, have supervision caseloads closer to 50 per officer. Most supervising probation officers have caseloads of more than 100. The huge caseloads, as well as the seriousness of the crimes for which many are on probation, make the job of supervising probationers both difficult and stressful. In addition, probationers have high levels of drug use, poor job histories, and low education levels.

All supervising probation officers must first establish a relationship with the probationer and explain the terms and conditions of probation. These might include attendance in a drug program, regularly scheduled reporting, and employment. It is the officer's job to enforce these conditions through monitoring, supervision, and helping the probationer deal with the significant problems he or she faces in his or her life. This can take the form of the probation officer meeting regularly with the probationer (this is considered a direct contact) or with the probationer's employer, teachers, or treatment providers (this is considered a collateral contact). In addition, the probation officer should assist probationers in dealing with any of the innumerable social and psychological issues faced by those on probation. This can include locating and placing the probationer in drug treatment and job training programs, finding temporary or permanent housing, and dealing with a variety of mental health and counseling providers.

If the probationer is not reporting regularly or is otherwise not meeting the conditions of probation, and if a probation officer has done all he or she can to ensure compliance, then the officer must file a probation violation with the sentencing judge.

Probation officers can have a variety of other jobs, including making arrests of probationers who have absconded, working as liaisons to court, collecting fines and restitution, and developing community service programs. The majority of those who are probation officers, however, work in either investigations or supervision.

## ROLE CONFLICT AND STRESS

Over the past three decades, the job of the supervision probation officer has become more complex and stressful. Larger caseloads of increasingly higher-risk probationers have stretched the resources of probation agencies and officers. Many probation officers have role conflict about whether they are primarily social workers or law enforcers. As it becomes more difficult to address the complicated needs faced by so many probationers, greater numbers of officers are adopting an approach to their job that weighs heavily toward law enforcement. Many officers use drug testing and curfew checks as a way to monitor the growing number of probationers and catch them violating the conditions of probation in order to request that judges terminate probation and sentence the probationers to prison. This mirrors the recent trend for probation officers to team up with police officers as a way to increase the law enforcement oversight of probationers.

Some worry that the "helping" function of probation is slowly being lost as officers adopt more traditional enforcement roles. More probation officers are starting to carry guns on duty, and many probation departments have armed warrant units that perform the home visits that supervising probation officers once did as well as make arrests of probationers who have absconded or are suspected of committing a crime. Given large caseloads, limited resources, and the fact that the public holds probation officers responsible for crimes committed by those they are supervising, this trend toward more enforcement is understandable but also can conflict with the original purpose of probation, which was purely rehabilitative.

The best probation officers are those who can combine these two different aspects of the job in a way that assists the probationer while also making him or her understand the consequences of not abiding by the rules.

One of the reasons that almost every large probation department in the United States requires probation officers to have a bachelor's degree is that it is one of the most complicated and difficult jobs in the criminal justice system. Balancing the dual role of helper and enforcer; dealing with people who have high levels of drug addiction, homelessness, low education, and who lack job skills; managing high caseloads with dwindling resources; and worrying whether someone on your caseload will commit a heinous crime requires intelligence, creativity, and dedication.

*Michael Jacobson*

*See also* Parole Officers

## For Further Reading

Bureau of Justice Statistics. (n.d.). *Reentry trends in the United States.* Available: http://www.ojp.usdoj.gov/bjs/reentry/reentry.htm

Glaze, L. E. (2003). *Probation and parole in the United States, 2002.* Washington, DC: Bureau of Justice Statistics.

Hughes, T. A., Wilson, D. J., & Beck, A. J. (2001). *Trends in state parole, 1990–2000.* Washington, DC: Bureau of Justice Statistics.

Morris, N., & Tonry, M. (1990). *Between prison and probation: Intermediate punishments in a rational sentencing system.* New York: Oxford University Press.

New York City Office of Operations. (2004). *The mayor's management report, fiscal 2004 preliminary, supplementary indicator tables, New York City.* Available: www.nyc.gov/html/ops/downloads/pdf/2004_mmr/0104_indicators.pdf

Petersilia, J. (1998). *Community corrections: Probation, parole and intermediate sanctions.* New York: Oxford University Press.

Petersilia, J. (2002). *Reforming probation and parole in the 21st century.* Lanham, MD: American Correctional Association.

## ✧ PROBLEM-ORIENTED POLICING

Problem-oriented policing is a comprehensive framework for improving police service that was first articulated by law professor Herman Goldstein in 1979. Since then, many police agencies and police research institutions have sought to incorporate its principles and methods into the routine business of policing.

Goldstein (2001) summarized the basic elements of problem-oriented policing as follows:

Problem-oriented policing is an approach to policing in which discrete pieces of police business (each consisting of a cluster of similar incidents, whether crimes or acts of disorder, that the police are expected to handle) are subject to microscopic examination (drawing on the especially honed skills of crime analysts and the accumulated experience of operating field personnel) in hopes that what is freshly learned about each problem will lead to discovering a new and more effective strategy for dealing with it. Problem-oriented policing places a high value on new responses that are preventive in nature, that are not dependent on the use of the criminal justice system, and that engage other public agencies, the community and the private sector when their involvement has the potential for significantly contributing to the reduction of the problem. Problem-oriented policing carries a commitment to implementing the new strategy, rigorously evaluating its effectiveness, and, subsequently, reporting the results in ways that will benefit other police agencies and that will ultimately contribute to building a body of knowledge that supports the further professionalization of the police.

## THE BASIC PREMISES UNDERLYING PROBLEM-ORIENTED POLICING

Problem-oriented policing builds upon some basic lessons learned about policing over the past several decades. Among the most critical of those lessons are the following:

- The function of the police is, and always has been, much broader than merely enforcing criminal laws. Police are expected to address a wide range of community problems that threaten public safety and order. Enforcement of the criminal law, often thought to be the basic purpose of the police, is better understood as but one means to achieving the ends of public safety and order.

- The police exercise a tremendous amount of discretion, at all levels of their hierarchy, in carrying out their function. Problem-oriented policing represents a significant effort to harness and guide that discretion toward more effective and fair policing.

- The police, as an institution, operate not merely as the front end of the criminal justice system, but as a key institution in a web of social institutions that share responsibility for providing for public safety and order. Problem-oriented policing encourages police to collaborate both within and outside the criminal justice system to address public safety problems.

- For various reasons, the police have been compelled to rely excessively on the criminal justice system as a means for addressing crime and disorder. The overuse and misuse of the criminal law has contributed to major problems in policing. Problem-oriented policing promotes the use of alternatives to arrest as a means of addressing problems.

- Police have long used formal and informal alternatives to criminal arrest to address problems, but the use of those alternatives has not always been officially sanctioned or even acknowledged. Police officers have long been left to improvise in situations where the use of criminal law is inadequate. Problem-oriented policing stresses the importance of giving formal sanction to legitimate alternative methods of dealing with problems.

- The main strategies employed by the police—rapid response to citizen calls for service, criminal investigation, and random preventive patrol—have proven far more limited in their capacity to provide for the public's safety than commonly believed. Consequently, although these strategies remain important aspects of police service, they are insufficient for achieving the entire police mission. Problem-oriented policing acknowledges the practical limitations of these main strategies while capitalizing on their benefits. It urges police to explore a much wider range of responses to problems beyond the conventional strategies.

- Police managers and others who shape police policy and practice have become preoccupied with the administration of police organizations to the exclusion of focusing on how police organizations can best deliver services to address public safety problems and meet community needs. Problem-oriented policing serves as a corrective to this means-over-ends syndrome.

- Line-level police officers, as well as community members, have a reservoir of knowledge, talent, and resources that can be better tapped by police managers for understanding and responding to public safety problems. Problem-oriented policing promotes new styles of working relationships between the police and the public, and between police management and line officers—relationships that can make better use of line officers and community members than have conventional police management approaches.

These and other conclusions helped form a much more realistic understanding of the police institution, with all its flaws and limitations, than existed before. It was upon this foundation of knowledge that problem-oriented policing was built.

## THE ELEMENTS OF PROBLEM-ORIENTED POLICING

Problem-oriented policing introduces a new basic unit to police work: the problem. In conventional policing, a call for police service, or a case, is the basic unit of police work. Each call and each case is handled separately. Once handled, each call or case is considered closed, and attention is turned to the next call or case. Problem-oriented policing looks for patterns among individual calls and cases—patterns that may be formed by a common set of offenders, victims, locations, times, or behaviors. It clusters calls and cases into new basic units known as problems. The enterprise of policing is thereby transformed from one of merely handling individual calls and cases to one of addressing problems.

Some examples of problems commonly faced by police are assaults in and around bars, retail theft in shopping malls, cruising along commercial strips, traffic control during large public gatherings and demonstrations, street prostitution, disorder at budget motels, speeding in residential areas, homicide among intimate partners, sexual abuse of children, drug dealing on street corners, illicit sexual activity in public parks, loud parties, and street robbery, to name but a few.

These sorts of problems constitute the business of policing. These problems can be experienced and addressed at various levels of aggregation. That is, problems may be experienced at particular locations or at multiple locations throughout a jurisdiction.

In order to address problems, police must first understand the conditions that contribute to these problems. Developing this understanding requires that police carefully and completely examine and analyze the factors that are contributing to or causing the problems. Doing so requires the police to go well beyond merely proving the elements of a crime or filling in the boxes on a standard police incident report. It calls for blending social science research principles with practical police experience to explore such questions as

- How big and how serious is the problem? Who is harmed by the problem, and how? How concerned is the community about the problem?
- What conditions and factors contribute to the problem? Where does the problem exist, and, conversely, where does it not exist? What explains the difference?
- How do police currently handle the problem, and with what effect? Is the current police response helpful or ineffectual, or does it perhaps create more serious problems?
- What other groups, organizations, and individuals share responsibility for addressing the problem, and how are they currently addressing the problem? What is the police interest in seeing this problem addressed, and what is the proper role for police in addressing it?
- How are similar problems handled elsewhere? What alternatives are there to handling the problem that might improve upon the current response? Are those alternatives currently feasible, and if not, what needs to be done to make them so?

With new insights into the problems gained from careful problem analysis, police are encouraged to develop new responses to problems, responses that are tailored to the problem and to the particular conditions of the local setting in which it occurs. Police are encouraged to develop responses, or more typically, combinations of responses, beyond the conventional. They are especially encouraged to consider responses that minimize the need for police to use force, that have community support and engagement, and that have the potential to prevent future incidents or to minimize the harm caused by them. Alternatives to the conventional responses of arrest and preventive patrol might include pressuring others who control the conditions that give rise to problems to alter those

conditions; mediating conflicts; physically redesigning buildings, streets, and other structures; mobilizing the community; conveying information; or using civil laws to regulate problematic conduct or conditions.

Previously, analyzing problems in this fashion has not been routine for police. To the extent police have analyzed crime problems, it has typically been with an eye toward predicting the next crime in a series and trying to interrupt it and apprehend the offenders. The sort of problem analysis prescribed by problem-oriented policing goes well beyond conventional crime analysis. Thus, the concept will require police to develop a much greater capacity to analyze the problems that constitute their business, and a capacity to use that analysis to inform their policies and practices.

A problem-oriented approach to police work requires that police adopt an open posture with respect to their work—that they be willing to critique their own actions, actively search for ways to improve their responses, and rigorously assess their efforts to inform further improvements. It requires a new level of openness and candor with the public and other government officials about what is realistic to expect of the police with respect to various problems. It calls for a new level of engagement by various sectors of the community and the government to assist the police in addressing difficult public safety problems.

The overarching objective of problem-oriented policing is to make police more effective in addressing the wide range of public safety problems that they routinely confront. Merely making police more efficient, and even better liked and supported by the public, are secondary objectives to the ultimate set of objectives related to keeping society safe and orderly, consistent with the principles of a constitutional democracy.

## PROBLEM-SOLVING PROCESSES

Problem-oriented policing makes use of any of a number of problem-solving methodologies, all rooted in the social scientific method of inquiry. Perhaps the best known problem-solving methodology associated with problem-oriented policing is the one known as the SARA model. SARA is an acronym that stands for Scanning, Analysis, Response, and Assessment. It was developed by researchers in an early experiment applying problem-oriented policing in Newport News, Virginia, in the 1980s. The SARA model, like other similar problem-solving models, is commonly portrayed as a linear or sequential model—that is, it flows neatly from beginning to end. In fact, it is an iterative or cyclical model—inquiries lead to some answers and to more inquiries, and all the while that the inquiry is under way, police and others may be taking interim action to address the problem. Assessment or evaluation of the effort may well lead to the development or refinement of responses or to new lines of inquiry.

Each stage of the SARA model calls for the following specific steps to be taken.

### Scanning

The scanning phase involves identifying recurring problems of concern to the public and the police, identifying the consequences of the problem for the community and the police, prioritizing those problems, developing broad goals, confirming that the problems exist, determining how frequently the problem occurs and how long it has been going on, and selecting problems for closer examination.

### Analysis

The analysis phase involves identifying and understanding the events and conditions that precede and accompany the problem, identifying relevant data to be collected, researching what is known about the problem type, taking inventory of how the problem is currently addressed and the strengths and limitations of the current response, narrowing the scope of the problem as specifically as possible, identifying a variety of resources that may be of assistance in developing a deeper understanding of the problem, and developing a working hypothesis about why the problem is occurring.

### Response

The response phase involves brainstorming for new interventions, searching for what other communities with similar problems have done, choosing among the alternative interventions, outlining a response plan and identifying responsible parties, stating the specific objectives for the response plan, and carrying out the planned activities.

### Assessment

The assessment phase involves determining whether the plan was implemented (a process evaluation), collecting pre- and postresponse qualitative and quantitative data, determining whether broad goals and specific objectives were attained, identifying any new strategies needed to augment the original plan, and conducting an ongoing assessment to ensure continued effectiveness.

## RELATIONSHIP OF PROBLEM-ORIENTED POLICING TO OTHER POLICE REFORM IDEAS

Problem-oriented policing shares common features with several other movements in police reform and crime prevention, among them community policing, team policing, and situational crime prevention. It also draws upon other conceptual frameworks for analyzing and responding to crime problems, including crime prevention through environmental design, crime analysis, the Compstat method, hot spot policing, and crime mapping. Problem-oriented policing rejects, however, the premises underlying such concepts as zero-tolerance policing because those concepts imply that police discretion will be suspended and that the widespread use of criminal arrest will be used as a viable solution to many public safety problems.

Certain innovations in prosecution and court management run parallel to problem-oriented policing. They recognize that the roles of prosecutors and courts, too, are broader than merely processing cases through the legal system, and that public safety problems require changes in the conditions that cause them and a more preventive perspective in addressing them. Concepts such as community prosecution and restorative justice are generally considered compatible with problem-oriented policing.

## IMPLICATIONS FOR THE MANAGEMENT OF POLICE ORGANIZATIONS

Full incorporation of the basic elements of problem-oriented policing into the mainstream of policing requires substantial changes in the ways that police organizations are managed and supported. The most profound changes necessary for problem-oriented policing to exploit its full potential are described below.

### Developing a New Capacity for Analyzing Police Business

Police organizations, either with internal resources or with assistance from outside research institutions, will need to improve their capacity to organize and analyze information about the demands made upon them, in order to be able to improve their responses to public safety problems.

### Building a Body of Knowledge About Policing

In contrast to most other professions and trades, police lack an organized, accessible, well-researched body of knowledge about how they ought to respond to the many public safety problems they confront. Problem-oriented policing represents a commitment to learning what works, under what conditions, for what kinds of problems. Building this body of knowledge will require contributions from police agencies, research institutions, and government funding agencies. The *Problem-Oriented Guides for Police,* funded by the U.S. Department of Justice's Office of Community Oriented Policing Services, represents one effort to build this sort of body of knowledge.

### Training and Educating Police

The shift away from an incident-driven style of policing—in which police merely respond to emergencies, handle calls for service, and investigate crimes—to a problem-oriented style of policing will require that police officials at all levels of the hierarchy learn new knowledge and new skills. They will need to learn more about the dynamics that give rise to many public safety problems, as well as the skills necessary to identify and analyze problems and to manage problem-oriented police operations. New educational and training methodologies will be in order as well. Problem-based learning methodologies will need to replace conventional police training methodologies.

### Supporting Police

For police organizations to become more effective in controlling public safety problems, they will require a level of support that is different from simple funding for police officers and police equipment. The respective governments under which police organizations exist, as well as the public at large, must come to view public safety in broader terms—to see public safety not as the sole province of police, but as the joint responsibility of police, other government agencies, nongovernmental organizations, and the various sectors of the community. It will require greater recognition of the interrelationship of crime and other realms, such as land use planning, architecture, urban design, civil code regulation, mental health and substance abuse treatment, youth services, product design, and business policies and practices. It will require that the ownership of various public safety problems be negotiated among the various sectors of society, police included, that have stakes and interests in those problems.

Problem-oriented policing implicates nearly every aspect of police management. In addition to the changes described above, it calls for rethinking how police officers are recruited and selected, how police officers' and police agencies' performance is measured, how police agencies are organized and staffed, and how public expectations for police service are managed.

*Michael S. Scott*

***See also*** Community Policing; Compstat; Crime Mapping; Education of Police; Hot Spots; Patrol Methods, Tactics, and Strategies; Police Discretion; Police Training in the United States; Prosecutors; Quality-of-Life Enforcement; Response Time; Restorative Justice; Theories of Policing; Zero Tolerance

### For Further Reading

Eck, J., & Spelman, W. (1987). *Problem-solving: Problem-oriented policing in Newport News.* Washington, DC: Police Executive Research Forum.

Goldstein, H. (1977). *Policing a free society.* Madison: Board of Regents of the University of Wisconsin.

Goldstein, H. (1979). Improving policing: A problem-oriented approach. *Crime & Delinquency, 25,* 236–258.

Goldstein, H. (1990). *Problem-oriented policing.* Philadelphia: Temple University Press.

Goldstein, H. (2001, October). *Problem-oriented policing in a nutshell.* Unpublished document prepared for the International Problem-Oriented Policing Conference, San Diego.

Office of Community Oriented Policing Services. (2000). *Problem-oriented guides for police.* Available: http://www.cops.usdoj.gov

Sampson, R., & Scott, M. (2000). *Tackling crime and other public-safety problems: Case studies in problem-solving.* Available: http://www.cops.usdoj.gov

Scott, M. (2000). *Problem-oriented policing: Reflections on the first 20 years.* Available: http://www.cops.usdoj.gov

# ᘒ PROFILING, CRIMINAL PERSONALITY

Despite being used as an investigative tool as far back as World War II, criminal personality profiling (also referred to as criminal investigative analysis or offender profiling) can still be best classified as an art rather than a scientific pursuit. Although clearly growing out of the behavioral sciences, as well as the practical experiences of law enforcement practitioners, profiling continues to be considered with a high degree of suspicion by psychologists and has begun only recently to receive the needed empirical attention.

## USES OF THE CRIMINAL PROFILE

The psychological profile as an investigative tool helps to focus investigators on individuals with similar personality traits that parallel the traits of others who have committed similar offenses in the past. As an investigative strategy, a criminal profile allows investigators to narrow the field of options and generate educated guesses about the perpetrator. Criminal personality profiling has been practiced with offenses as diverse as sexual homicide, arson, stalking, and terrorism.

The profile is generated based upon what can be termed a psychological assessment of the crime scene. The profiler identifies and interprets evidence at the crime scene that might be indicative of the personality type of the individual(s) committing the crime. Depending on the type and amount of available evidence, the elements of a profile may include

- Perpetrator's race
- Sex
- Age range
- Marital status
- General employment
- Reaction to questioning by police
- Degree of sexual maturity
- Whether the individual might strike again
- The possibility that he or she has committed a similar offense in the past
- Possible police records

These items make up the core social and psychological variables of the offender's personality. A carefully prepared profile may also be able to help connect past unsolved crimes to the current offender and provide an indication as to whether or not future attacks are likely. The profile can also suggest possible items to add to a search warrant, such as souvenirs, pornography, and photos. Finally, the profile should suggest possible interrogation strategies designed to elicit information from the suspect.

## CLASSIFICATION AND PROFILING

Recognizing the constraints of traditional methods of offender classification in providing leads to investigators, an interdisciplinary team from the Federal Bureau of Investigation's (FBI) Behavioral Science Unit set out to examine the correlation between offender characteristics and offense characteristics in one of the first efforts to advance profiling theory and methods. By the mid-1980s, the Violent Criminal Apprehension Program was developed.

Based upon these and later findings highlighting the correlation between crime scene indicators and offender characteristics, profilers develop a classification of the likely offender rather than classifying according to the psychological symptoms that may be the basis for the official diagnosis under which an offender might fall. Just as the various symptoms or behaviors of his or her client are of principal importance to the psychologist or physician conducting an evaluation, the profiler sees the crime scene, particularly a bizarre one, as a reflection of the behavior or symptoms of the perpetrator.

In producing the profile, each profiler will likely have his or her own process; however, the following elements are generally assumed to be necessary:

1. Appraisal of the crime and crime scene

2. Complete evaluation of the crime scene(s)

3. Thorough analysis of the victim(s)

4. Evaluation of preliminary police reports

5. Assessment of the medical examiner's autopsy

6. Development of a profile with critical offender characteristics

7. Investigative suggestions derived from the profile

8. Possible suspect apprehension strategies

The major classification used by the FBI for sexual homicide cases identifies whether or not a crime scene is organized or disorganized, from which certain profile elements are then assumed. For example, the organized crime scene suggests a more sociable, psychopathic offender who likely did not know the victim, whereas the disorganized offender is more asocial and unkempt, and may have even known the victim on at least a passing basis.

Experts claim that because the violence inherent in the types of crimes profiled is extremely difficult to comprehend, it is thought to reflect an underlying pathological personality condition. A clinician expects the pathologies of variously classified disorders to be apparent in the day-to-day lives and homes of the individual; the profiler similarly expects the crime scene to be reflective of the symptoms of such pathology.

Given these central assumptions, it is clear that profiling will not offer any added value to the investigation of crimes that lack some underlying pathology. Examples of offenses useful for profiling are sadistic torture in sexual assaults, evisceration, postmortem slashing and cutting, motiveless fire setting, lust and mutilation murder, rape, satanic and

ritualistic crimes, stalking, some forms of terrorism, and pedophilia.

Using the criminal investigative analysis techniques of profiling as a base, a *Crime Classification Manual* has been developed (Douglas, Burgess, Burgess, & Ressler, 1992) that serves as the investigator's own version of the *Diagnostic and Statistical Manual of Mental Disorders* documenting psychological conditions for the clinician. Empirical validity and reliability will be established as social scientists heed the call for much-needed research in this area.

## TRAIT THEORY AND THE MO/SIGNATURE DISTINCTION

The main underlying assumptions of profiling rely heavily on elements of the trait theory discussed pervasively in the psychological literature. It is argued that the "person variable" shows a greater consistency and weight as one starts to deal with the pathology apparent in bizarre and repetitive crimes.

A distinction is made in profiling between the traditional methods of operation (MOs) discussed in the investigation of any crime, and the signature left behind at the crime scene of a pathological offender. The MO involves any action or behavior that is necessary for the offender to commit the crime. In contrast, the signature goes beyond simply those actions necessary to commit the offense because it includes elements of the violent, repetitive offender's behavior that are necessary in order to express his or her violent fantasies. It is this paraphilic fantasy element that allows us to assume that the offender will likely repeat these crimes in a very similar fashion.

## PRELIMINARY EMPIRICAL WORK ON PROFILING: A CHALLENGE TO RESEARCHERS

Some preliminary studies have been conducted on the reliability and validity of profiling and its central assumptions, but few of the findings have been replicated in any systematic way. Some studies of the profiling process have found that although profilers did not differ significantly from detectives in terms of how they processed evidence, they were more accurate in answering specific questions in sex-related cases, suggesting the importance of an underlying psychopathology to make profiling useful. A study of the interrater reliability of profilers found that for the classification of crime type, profilers agreed on 77% to 100% of the cases. Current empirical testing is focusing on documenting correlations between offender and offense characteristics, an essential ingredient to the development of sound profiling theory and practice. Positive results are beginning to be evidenced in this area.

## THE DISTINCTION BETWEEN CRIMINAL PERSONALITY PROFILING AND RACIAL PROFILING

Although race may be one element contained within an offender profile, it is based on a critical analysis of a particular crime *after* it has been committed, and related to what is known about similar offenders in the past. For example, within the crime of sexual homicide, offenders are almost always the same race as the victim. Although this may not always be the case, the profile may suggest the same racial background as the victim for the offender.

*Heath B. Grant*

*See also* Profiling, Drug Courier; Profiling, Racial; Serial Murder Investigation

### For Further Reading

Ault, R., & Reese, J. (1980). A psychological assessment of crime profiling. *FBI Law Enforcement Bulletin, 49*(3), 22–25.

Browdy, J. (1985, January 7). LEN's 1984 Man of the Year: Pierce R. Brooks, homicide investigator extraordinaire and creator of the VI-CAP system. *Law Enforcement News*, pp. 8–10.

Douglas, J., Burgess, A., Burgess, A., & Ressler, R. (1992). *Crime classification manual.* San Francisco: Jossey-Bass.

Douglas, J., Ressler, R., Burgess, A., & Hartman, C. (1986). Criminal profiling from crime scene analysis. *Behavioral Sciences and the Law, 4*, 401–421.

Geberth, V. (1995, November). The signature aspect in criminal investigation. *Law and Order*, pp. 45–49.

Holmes, R., & Holmes, S. (1996). *Profiling violent crimes: An investigative tool.* Thousand Oaks, CA: Sage.

McCann, J. (1992). Criminal personality profiling in the investigation of violent crime: Recent advances and future direction. *Behavioral Sciences and the Law, 10*, 474–481.

Pinnizzotto, A., & Finkel, N. (1990). Criminal personality profiling: Outcome and process. *Law and Human Behavior, 14*(3), 215–233.

Ressler, R., Burgess, A., & Douglas, J. (1988). *Sexual homicide: Patterns and motives.* New York: Lexington Books.

Rossi, D. (1982). Crime scene behavioral analysis: Another tool for the law enforcement investigator. *Police Chief, 49*(1), 152–155.

## ⚮ PROFILING, DRUG COURIER

In the early 1970s, the drug courier profile emerged as a law enforcement tool used to combat the influx of drugs into the United States. A drug courier profile consists of a list of characteristics assumed typical of individuals carrying illicit drugs. Commonly used by law enforcement officials to distinguish drug traffickers from regular citizens, an individual's exhibition of multiple profile traits triggers the suspicion of expert narcotics officers. Such profiles have been used extensively by the Drug Enforcement Agency (DEA) at airports to counter the trafficking of illegal drugs into source cities, such as Miami, Fort Lauderdale, Los Angeles, and New York. Successful DEA use of the profiles in identifying drug couriers at airports prompted state and local law enforcement to use similar profiles. Drug trafficking on the country's highways has been a significant method of drug distribution. Because jurisdiction for the nation's roads falls to local law enforcement agencies, many of these agencies adopted drug courier profiling as part of the country's overall antidrug strategy. Despite its considerable utility in detection of drug couriers, use of these profiles has been the subject of considerable legal debate, particularly on the state and local level, where expanded use of drug courier profiles primarily includes their application during automobile stops. In the 1990s, the use of drug courier profiles by local law enforcement, who had adapted it from the federal government for use on the nation's highways, led to charges of racial profiling in numerous jurisdictions around the country. It is a controversy that still continues.

DEA Special Agent Paul Markonni is credited as the developer of the original drug courier profile in 1974. Before the profile's inception, the absence of a comprehensive profile made narcotics officers dependent upon the tips provided by other law enforcement agencies and airline personnel in the identification of drug traffickers. Without the profile, many couriers evaded DEA detection. Over time, the DEA noted a pattern of characteristics exhibited by drug couriers, enabling agents to decipher them from other passengers.

Although no single national drug courier profile exists, the profiles consulted by each law enforcement office are quite similar. All drug courier profiles include a set of characteristics routinely associated with narcotics traffickers. Although the characteristics are seemingly irrelevant to the typical civilian, specially trained law enforcement officers recognize them as indicative of drug trafficking. Despite various commonalities shared by existent profiles, profiles do differ from airport to airport.

In *United States v. Elmore* (1979), the Court of Appeals for the Fifth Circuit outlined seven primary characteristics central to the drug courier profile established by Agent Markonni: arrival from (or departure to) a recognized source city (e.g., Miami or Los Angeles); carrying little or no luggage (or numerous empty suitcases); suspicious itinerary (including rapid turnaround time preceding lengthy airplane travel); use of an alias; presence of unusually large amounts of currency in thousands of dollars on their person, in briefcases, or in bags; purchasing airline tickets with a large amount of small-denomination currency; and unusual nervousness beyond that which is typical of average passengers. Furthermore, the court in *Elmore* specified four secondary characteristics of the drug courier profile: a near-exclusive use of public transportation (particularly taxicabs) when leaving the airport, immediate phone calls following deplaning, providing the airline used with a false or fictitious telephone number, and excessively frequent travel to source/ distribution cities.

The contemporary DEA drug courier profile includes numerous characteristics not outlined in *Elmore*. These additional signifiers are physical and behavioral characteristics of the suspected courier. Physical traits involve unusual attire, age between 25 and 35 years old, and paleness typically associated with intense anxiety. In terms of behavioral characteristics, drug couriers often opt to carry their bags onto the plane rather than checking them. In an effort to distance themselves from their narcotics-filled baggage, traffickers do not typically use luggage identification tags. When couriers do use such tags, they often provide false information. Drug couriers may purchase their ticket the same day as departure (frequently less than an hour before their flight). Upon arrival, drug traffickers often attempt to exit the plane first or last in an effort to evade detection. They may immediately discard their airline tickets upon arrival or insist that they do not have their tickets, and they often use forged identification or claim that they do not have identification on them.

Although drug courier profiles assist law enforcement in the detection and apprehension of drug traffickers, the use of these profiles incites numerous legal debates. Much of the conflict over use of this profiling involves protections afforded by the Fourth Amendment. Drug courier stops evoke the Fourth Amendment in that they have been deemed "seizures." The Fourth Amendment ensures protection of all citizens from unreasonable searches and seizures, and is applied to each state through the Fourteenth Amendment. Per the U.S. Supreme Court, all evidence gained through an illegal search and seizure must be excluded from trial. However, if a court determines that the government's interest supercedes the relative intrusiveness of the search and seizure, the search and seizure are typically deemed reasonable and in accordance with the Fourth Amendment.

In addition to their application at airports, drug courier profiles were adapted for use by local law enforcement on the roads as a basis for automobile stops. Drug courier profiles lessen the standard of automobile stops from probable cause to a standard commonly referred to as "articulable suspicion." In current practice, profile stops provide a basis for an additional search. The expanding use of drug courier profiling suggests that officer suspicion (a component of police work thought to enhance officer safety) transcends traditional legal bases for search and seizure.

*Christine Ivie Edge*

*See also* Profiling, Criminal Personality; Profiling, Racial; Race Relations

### For Further Reading

Crank, J. (1998). *Understanding police culture.* Cincinnati, OH: Anderson.

Dey, I. (1998). Drug courier profiles: An infringement on Fourth Amendment rights. *University of Baltimore Law Forum, 28,* 3–11.

Mahoney, K. (1981). Drug trafficking at airports: The judicial response. *University of Miami Law Review, 36,* 91–113.

United States v. Elmore, 595 F.2d (5th Cir., 1979).

Wilson, B. (1996). The war on drugs: Evening the odds through use of the airport drug courier profile. *Boston Public Interest Law Journal, 6,* 203–242.

# ∽ PROFILING, GEOGRAPHIC

Geographic profiling is a methodology for delineating the probable area containing the residence of an unknown offender ostensibly responsible for a series of crimes. The probable area of the offender's residence stems from an analysis of the locations of a series of crimes. Therefore, geographic profiling can be used for a series of crimes or a single crime that contains multiple locations or scenes. Geographic profiling has been used mostly for serial homicides, rapes, and arsons, but its most vivid or notable application was with the DC Beltway Sniper cases during October 2002.

The idea of geographic profiling has been around since the mid-1980s, but it was not until the mid-1990s that the idea was converted into operational software for development and testing. The method incorporates theories and concepts from a variety of disciplines and fields, such as cartography, computer science, environmental criminology, environmental psychology, geography, information science, mathematics, statistics, and transportation planning. There are several geographic profiling systems, but they all tend to model or imitate three specific or major systems. Each of these systems incorporates varying amounts of the theories and concepts from previously mentioned fields and disciplines.

All the geographic profiling systems share the same basic logic that is fairly straightforward, but the mathematics can be very involved. The locations for a series of crimes believed to have been committed by the same offender are plotted on a computer or digital map. A grid is placed over the entire area of the offenses. A series of mathematical functions known as distance decay functions are applied to the crime locations and to each cell of the grid. The distance decay functions approximate or model the travel behavior of the offender from his or her residence to the crime scenes. The resulting calculations create a probability value for each cell. When the cells are mapped with their varying probabilities, it is possible to delineate areas that have a greater likelihood of containing the offender's residence.

The premier geographic profiling system is Rigel, developed by Dr. D. K. Rossmo, then in Vancouver, British Columbia. This system incorporates and models important concepts and theories in environmental criminology pertaining to crime pattern theory, the routine activity space of offenders, and offender travel behavior. This system appears to be very popular with the law enforcement community because it was the first available and its creator was a former police officer. Moreover, this system has received considerable publicity.

Dragnet is another system that was created by Dr. David Canter in the United Kingdom. This system does not incorporate the exact theoretical base seen in Rigel and uses a restricted number of distance decay functions, but its major asset is that it is supposed to aid investigators in developing a practical search strategy for an offender. Finally, a third model, The Journey to Crime Routine, is part of the Crimestat suite of techniques authored by Dr. Ned Levine. This model provides a purely statistical solution to the problem of defining the possible area of an offender's origin. Moreover, this model gives the user the option of using a range of different distance decay functions.

Geographic profiling is beset by three major controversies or debates. The first debate pertains to access to the technique or software. One system requires users to purchase the software and extensive training; therefore, access is very restricted. At the other extreme, the software is open access or free. Therefore, it is assumed the user has the appropriate training to use the software or that the science behind profiling is so understandable that the user can acquire the skills to perform geographic profiling. The second controversy is the fact that geographic profiling is a very exotic technique that has the potential of bringing considerable acclaim and status to its practitioners. Therefore, instead of debating the science of geographic profiling, a few of its practitioners have refrained from this discussion citing proprietary reasons. The third controversy, which results from the second, is that exhaustive evaluations and comparisons of the different geographic profiling systems are difficult to implement. Moreover, geographic profiling has yet to be subjected to the acid test of evaluating its role and utility in criminal investigation.

*James L. LeBeau*

## For Further Reading

Brantingham, P. L., & Brantingham, P. J. (1993). Environment, routine, and situation: Toward a pattern theory of crime. In R. V. Clarke & M. Felson (Eds.), *Routine activity and rational choice* (pp. 259–294). New Brunswick, NJ: Transaction Books.

Canter, D., Coffey, T., Huntley, M., & Missen, C. (2000). Predicting serial killers' home base using a decision support system. *Journal of Quantitative Criminology, 16,* 457–478.

LeBeau, J. L. (1992). Four case studies illustrating the spatial-temporal analysis of serial rapists. *Police Studies, 15,* 124–145.

Levine, N. (2002). Journey to crime estimation. In *Crime Stat II: A spatial statistics program for the analysis of crime incident locations* (pp. 341–416). Washington, DC: National Institute of Justice.

Rossmo, D. K. (2000). *Geographic profiling.* Boca Raton, FL: CRC.

## ∾ PROFILING, RACIAL

Starting in the 1990s, law enforcement agencies nationwide faced accusations of "racial profiling." Generally, the citizens complained that police were targeting racial and ethnic minorities for vehicle stops because of a heightened suspicion that they were disproportionately involved in criminal activity. Indicative of the breadth of national concern was the December 1999 Gallup poll that showed a majority of both whites and blacks surveyed believed that racial profiling was prevalent. That is, 56% of the whites and 77% of the blacks believed the following practice was widespread: "police officers stopping motorists of certain racial and ethnic groups because the officers believe that these groups are more likely than others to commit certain types of crimes." (Data were not provided for other races/ethnicities.) A 2001 Gallup poll indicated that 44% of blacks surveyed believed that "police have stopped them at some point in their life because of their race or ethnic background." Only 7% of the white respondents and 29% of the Hispanic respondents felt this way. The phenomenon became known, particularly among racial/ethnic minorities and civil rights groups, as "Driving While Black" or "Driving While Brown."

Two lawsuits helped bring this issue to national attention—one in New Jersey (*New Jersey v. Soto,* 1996) and one in Maryland (*Wilkins v. Maryland State Police,* 1993). In the former, brought in 1990, public defenders representing Pedro Soto and others sought to suppress evidence obtained during searches conducted by New Jersey troopers, alleging that the searches were the result of racial profiling practices. These public defenders had detected an alarming number of cases involving black people who were stopped by troopers on the turnpike. The defendants obtained data on New Jersey State Police traffic stops in various areas from 1988 through 1991 and hired a social scientist, John Lamberth, to analyze the data. The court relied heavily on the results of his analysis—indicating overrepresentation of blacks among people stopped—in deciding to suppress the evidence. The 1992 Maryland lawsuit arose out of an encounter by Maryland State Police with a Harvard-educated public defender, Robert Wilkins. Maryland State troopers detained him and members of his extended family by the side of an interstate highway. Refusing the troopers' request to search, the family was then required to stand in the rain while a drug-sniffing dog checked the car, finding nothing. The American Civil Liberties Union filed a suit on behalf of Wilkins and his family, alleging that the police detention was the result of racial profiling. The case was eventually settled. The settlement included a mandate for the Maryland State Police to collect data on traffic stops. The results from these stop data—again analyzed by John Lamberth—"strongly support the assertion that the state police targeted the community of black motorists for stop, detention and investigation within the Interstate 95 corridor" (Lamberth, 1996, p. 10). These cases sparked additional stories and lawsuits alleging that police were engaging in racial profiling, and the issue became one of the most critical issues facing law enforcement in the late 1990s.

In tracing the origin of racial profiling, some law enforcement practitioners and other experts point to the use of drug courier profiles developed during the war on drugs and, in particular, in training conducted by the Drug Enforcement Administration (DEA) during the 1980s. Although DEA officials claim that race was never part of the training on profiles, other observers and some local and state law enforcement practitioners report that local and state police came to link blacks and Hispanics with criminal drug activity as a result of exposure to this training.

In the early 2000s, the national discussion of racial profiling broadened. There was increased recognition—promoted by various law enforcement associations—that racial profiling was really a new label for one aspect of the long-standing allegation that law enforcement officers in the United States treat racial and ethnic minorities in a biased fashion. Terms such as *racially biased policing* and *bias-based policing* emerged that were intended to define the issue more broadly. These terms were adopted to advance the discussion beyond the narrow concern about the potential for police bias based on perceptions of group criminality during traffic stops to the broader concern that there may be many other possible manifestations and motivations (both conscious or unconscious) for biased policing. Accordingly, the search for the origins of potential bias focused beyond DEA training in the 1980s to the long-standing history in this country of tense, sometimes even volatile, relations between the police and minority communities and the concomitant accusations against police of bias.

During this national discussion, police agencies came under significant pressure from concerned residents, local policymakers, and state and federal legislators to respond to this concern. National policing organizations and civil rights groups produced reports that provided guidance to help law enforcement agencies respond to racial profiling and the perceptions of its practice. An interesting aspect of reform efforts was that the major response measure—promoted by civil rights groups and other stakeholders—was the collection of police-citizen contact data to gauge whether racial profiling was occurring. That is, the major emphasis of reform efforts was not on policy, training, hiring, officer discipline, or other, more traditional police reform measures, but rather on measuring the phenomenon of concern. (This may reflect the impact of the two lawsuits mentioned above, both of which had data collection as part of either the evidence or the settlement.) Many agencies—either voluntarily or as a result of political pressure or legal mandates—began to have their officers record information regarding each of their citizen stops. In many agencies, these data are collected for all vehicle traffic stops or all vehicle stops, both traffic and investigatory. A few agencies are collecting these data for pedestrian stops as well. The data collected are the race and/or ethnicity of the driver; other demographic information (e.g., age, gender) on the driver; the reason for the stop; the location of the stop; what occurred during the stop (e.g., searches); and the outcome of the stop (e.g., arrest, citation, warning, "no disposition").

Preliminary discussions among law enforcement executives, other policymakers, and social scientists focused on what data to collect and how. A few years later, the discussion turned to the question of how to analyze and interpret the data. Researchers and others raised issues related to "benchmarking"— efforts to make meaning of the data that are collected. For example, if an agency determines through its data collection efforts that 25% of the vehicle stops by police are of racial/ethnic minorities, the question at the core of benchmarking is, "To what should this be compared?" Analysis efforts reflect a quest to develop a demographic profile of the people who are at risk of being stopped by police if they had no bias based on race or ethnicity. Most jurisdictions to date have used "census benchmarking" to understand their data. That is, they have compared the race/ethnicity breakdown of the people stopped by police to the race/ethnicity breakdown of the jurisdiction's residents as measured by the U.S. Census. The people who live in a jurisdiction, however, do not represent the same people who are at legitimate risk of being stopped by police in their vehicles. Recognizing the great limitations of census benchmarking for drawing conclusions regarding the nature and extent of racially biased policing, some agency researchers and other social scientists around the nation are developing and using alternative methods that involve developing more appropriate comparison groups. For example, some social scientists are using observation methodology to determine the demographic profile of people who are driving within specific geographic areas of the jurisdiction or to determine the demographics of the drivers who are violating various, specific traffic laws. Other social scientists or agency analysts are comparing the stop data of "similarly situated" officers within an agency; comparing the driver demographics for those stopped by police on patrol to the driver demographics for those caught by various blind technologies, such as cameras used to detect red-light running or speeding; and developing other methods for benchmarking the police–citizen contact data.

By early 2003, about half of the states had adopted legislation related to racial profiling. Most of these laws included data collection requirements, and a minority of these statutes included provisions related to other areas of reform, such as

- Antibiased policing policy
- Training and education
- Recruitment and hiring
- Supervision and accountability
- Outreach to diverse communities (Fridell, Lunney, Diamond, & Kubu, 2001)

Policy reforms are linked to attempts to define racial profiling or, more specifically, to identify when it is and is not appropriate for police to use race/ethnicity to make law enforcement decisions. At minimum, law enforcement's use of race and ethnicity for making decisions must be consistent with the equal protection provision of the Fourteenth Amendment. The Fourth Amendment provisions related to search and seizure further dictate law enforcement behaviors. The U.S. Supreme Court provides little guidance because it has not yet directly addressed the various nuances of this issue involving circumstances away from national borders. Some key aspects of this multifaceted issue are being addressed within the lower courts, sometimes inconsistently.

The policies adopted by agencies in the late 1990s—setting parameters on how race/ethnicity could be used to make decisions—were not very restrictive. Reflecting an early, very narrow definition of "racial profiling," these policies declare that officers cannot stop someone *solely* on the basis of race or ethnicity. This definition does not even encompass biased two-factor decisions—such as when an officer makes a decision to stop someone because the person is black and male. Some agencies have adopted "suspect-specific policies" that define much more narrowly the circumstances in which race/ethnicity can be used to make decisions. The suspect-specific policies generally read as follows: *Officers may not consider the race or ethnicity of a person in the course of any law enforcement action unless the officer is seeking to detain, apprehend, or otherwise be on the lookout for a specific suspect sought in connection with a specific crime who has been identified or described in part by race or ethnicity.* Other policies adopted by agencies reflect restrictions that fall between suspect-description policies and those that permit consideration of race/ethnicity, so long as it is not the sole reason for making a stop.

The terrorist attacks on September 11, 2001, had several impacts related to racial profiling. First, the national discussion about racial profiling—previously focused on police treatment of blacks and Hispanics—was broadened to include people of Arab descent and Muslims. Second, the issue of what constituted inappropriate use of race/ethnicity to make law enforcement decisions reemerged in the context of a national crisis and citizens' associated fear. A Gallup poll conducted soon after the terrorist attacks indicated that 71% of black respondents favored intense scrutiny of Arabs boarding airplanes. Finally, law enforcement's new sensitivities to the issue of racial profiling became apparent. This was reflected, for instance, in some law enforcement executives' refusal to assist the FBI in questioning Middle Eastern immigrants as part of the investigation into the September 11, 2001, attacks.

Although September 11th raised public awareness about the need to consider all races/ethnicities when assessing and evaluating bias in our country—whether in law enforcement or in other realms—and highlighted the increased sensitivity to bias on the part of many law enforcement agencies, the basic issues remain and will require continued efforts for years, maybe decades, to come. Homeland security and sensational cases ultimately cannot guide the reforms that are required to ensure impartial policing and trust between police and minority citizens.

*Lorie Fridell*

*For Further Reading*

Fridell, L., Lunney, R., Diamond, D., & Kubu, B. (2001). *Racially biased policing: A principled response.* Washington, DC: Police Executive Research Forum. Available: www.policeforum.org

Harris, D. A. (1999). *Driving while black: Racial profiling on our nation's highways. An American Civil Liberties Union Special Report.* New York: American Civil Liberties Union. Available: http://archive.aclu.org/profiling/report/index.html

Harris, D. A. (2002). *Profiles in injustice: Why racial profiling cannot work.* New York: New Press.

Lamberth, J. (1996). *Revised statistical analysis of the incidence of police stops and arrests of black drivers/travelers on the New Jersey Turnpike between interchanges 1 and 3 from the years 1988 through 1991.* Unpublished report submitted by the defendant's expert in New Jersey v. Soto, 734 A. 2d 350 (N.J. Super. Ct. Law. Div., 1996).

National Organization of Black Law Enforcement Executives (NOBLE). (2001). *A NOBLE perspective—Racial profiling: A symptom of biased-based policing.* Landover, MD: Author.

New Jersey v. Soto, 734 A.2d 350 (N.J. Super. Ct. Law. Div. 1996).

Ramirez, D., McDevitt, J., & Farrell, A. (2000). *A resource guide on racial profiling data collection systems: Promising practices and lessons learned.* Washington, DC: U.S. Department of Justice.

Wilkins v. Maryland State Police, Civil Action No. CCB-93-483 (D. Md. 1993).

# ᢙᢧ PROSECUTORS

Prosecutors are often called America's "chief law enforcement officers." That term, however, is not sufficiently descriptive and leads to a lack of appreciation of the role of the prosecutor as an officer of the court. Prosecutors are public figures and can establish the tone and public perception of the fairness of law enforcement and justice administration. By whatever name, the prosecutors, without a doubt, are the dominant actors in American criminal justice. As the Supreme Court commented in *Young v. United States* (1987), "Between the private life of the citizen and the public glare of criminal accusations stands the prosecutor. [The prosecutor has] the power to employ the full machinery of the state in scrutinizing any given individual." The prosecutors' dominance comes from their deciding which charges to bring, whom to charge, whether to proceed to trial, and what punishment to recommend for those found guilty.

The prosecution of crime in the United States differs strikingly from prosecution in other Western democracies and even markedly from other English-speaking countries. First, in the United States, there is no central government authority for prosecution, no office that even remotely resembles such an office as the Home Office's Crown Prosecution Service in England. Although the prosecution for violations of federal law rests with the U.S. Department of Justice, the overwhelming volume of the criminal prosecutions are handled at the state and local level and have no connection with the Justice Department. And even the federal prosecutions are divided among 94 somewhat independent U.S. attorneys.

At the local level, each state defines its system for prosecution. This results in a variety of state governmental styles. In some states, the prosecutorial power is either divided or shared with different independent officials. For instance, in Kentucky, the county attorney handles less serious crimes, such as misdemeanors and traffic offenses, and determines at the first instance whether to lodge charges of a more serious nature for the Commonwealth Attorney to try later. On the other hand, in New Jersey, the appointed attorney general has complete jurisdiction and selects the local prosecuting attorneys in each county to handle all criminal cases. In California, the locally elected district attorneys share power with the attorney general, who, on rare occasions, can supercede the district attorneys in individual cases and take over the prosecution. The state attorneys general usually have tightly circumscribed criminal jurisdiction at the trial level, although as a rule, they are responsible for handling criminal appeals. Almost all of the states provide for prosecution on a county level with an office for the prosecutor in or near the county courthouse.

Prosecutors go by a variety of names: district attorney (as in New York); state's attorney (as in Illinois); county attorney (as in Minnesota); prosecuting attorney (as in Ohio); or district attorney general (as in Tennessee). By whatever name, even within states, the various prosecutors' offices may differ dramatically. Some, such as the district attorney in Los Angeles County, have hundreds of deputies who handle cases in many locations throughout the city, whereas Alpine County, in the same state, has one office with only one lawyer, the elected district attorney. Most of the more than 1,800 state prosecutors in the nation are in very small offices, many of which are part-time.

Perhaps the salient characteristic of American prosecution is its political nature. In all but a handful of states, the prosecutors are elected. No other country in the world elects its prosecutors. Even in those states in which the prosecutors are appointed, their appointments are often connected to the political process. The election of prosecutors is designed in theory to make prosecutors independent of other government officials and thereby responsible only to the electorate. As a consequence, although the prosecutors exercise executive powers, they are not a formal part of the state government and stand apart from the other elected executives, such as the governors, mayors, or county executives. Prosecutors run for office in elections, usually every 4 years, or in the case of Arkansas and Wisconsin, every 2 years, and in Tennessee, every 8 years.

The principal duties of prosecutors involve the preparing and trying of criminal cases in court. This usually consists of reviewing police investigations and citizen complaints and making the important decisions as to which charges to use in accusing alleged wrongdoers. As a consequence, the prosecutors' law enforcement roles connect with the police, and even may overlap, but institutionally, the police and prosecutors are separate agencies of government.

Although they are not police, prosecutors do have some investigative functions. Certain crimes, by their nature, require lawyer participation in gathering evidence, using the subpoena power of the grand jury, or both. In those cases, investigators who are either directly employed by or assigned by a police agency to the prosecutor's office often prepare investigations together with prosecutors.

Even though considered a part of the executive function of government and a part of law enforcement, the various prosecutors, when lodging charges or appearing in court, are viewed as exercising a judicial function and are consequently "officers of the court." For example, police enjoy only limited tort immunity and can be sued by citizens, whereas prosecutors, like members of the judiciary, when exercising their court functions as opposed to investigative roles, possess absolute immunity and are not subject to suit. On the other hand, police accused of wrongdoing have the protections of the Law Enforcement Officers' Bill of Rights, whereas prosecutors who are similarly accused have no equivalent rights and must answer to state lawyer disciplinary boards. Although prosecutors' decisions and actions are often the subject of controversy, unlike the police, their activities are rarely checked in any formal way.

Next to the political nature of the prosecutor's office, the chief characteristic is its power to exercise unbounded discretion. The power to charge and investigate is not subject to review by any other official(s). Likewise, the refusal to charge or investigate is equally not reviewable. Prosecutors who have to run for reelection do submit themselves to the political process, which can subject their records for public approval or disapproval, but in practice, seldom are the discretionary decisions the issues in those elections.

Prosecutors often are publicly called upon to defend a universal practice peculiar to American justice called "plea bargaining." In exchange for guilty pleas, prosecutors settle or dispose of pending criminal cases by either reducing the seriousness of lodged charges or agreeing to limit defendants' exposure to criminal penalties. The necessity for the practice, some commentators say, comes from the overwhelming caseloads that, in some jurisdictions, make it impossible to try most cases. Others comment that the practice is grounded in the prosecutors' responsibility to do justice and recommend and bring about fair outcomes.

Recent years have seen the development of a strong victims' rights movement that has influenced, both formally and informally, some plea bargaining and the exercising of other prosecutorial discretion. By passing statutes, court rules, or constitutional amendments, some states have required victim consultation in negotiating pleas and given victims the right to address the court or comment upon prosecutors' exercising of discretion, particularly at sentencings.

Recently, some prosecutors' offices have expanded their missions and have gone beyond the charging of defendants and trying of criminal cases. They have branched out to provide services to victims or witnesses, even in situations in which there are no pending criminal cases. Some offices also provide mediation services to settle disputes or programs for the diversion of cases into community service or drug abuse treatment. Some have followed the police example of community policing and involved their offices in problem solving to prevent crime and eliminate conditions that cause crime. However, the core function for prosecutors remains acting as the voice of the citizens of the jurisdiction in charging and taking to court those accused of violations of the law.

*Andrew Sonner*

## For Further Reading

Cox, S. (1976). Prosecutorial discretion: An overview. *American Criminal Law Review: A Symposium, Prosecutorial Discretion, 13,* 383–434.

DeFrances, C. (2002). *Prosecutors in state courts, 2001* (NCJ 193441). Washington, DC: U.S. Department of Justice.

Goldkamp, J., Irons-Guynn, C., & Weiland, D. (2002). *Community prosecution strategies: Measuring impact.* Washington, DC: Crime and Justice Research Center.

McDonald, W. (1979). *The prosecutor.* Beverly Hills, CA: Sage.

Melilli, K. (1992). Prosecutorial discretion in an adversary system. *Brigham Young University Law Review, 3,* 669–705.

Miller, F. (1969). *Prosecution: The decision to charge a suspect with a crime.* Boston: Little Brown.

Miller, F. (1986). *Cases and materials on criminal justice administration.* Minneola, NY: Foundation Press.

Nissman, D., & Hagen, E. (1982). *The prosecution function.* Lexington, MA: Lexington Books.

Young v. United States, 481 U.S. 787, 814 (1987).

# ∂∞ PSYCHOLOGISTS/ PSYCHOLOGICAL SERVICES

Psychologists working with law enforcement agencies deliver a range of direct psychological services to officers and the departments they serve. Relatively unheard of until the 1960s, the practice of using psychological services evolved as law enforcement executives recognized that repeated exposure to a difficult environment takes a toll on the human being. Acknowledging the unique culture of police work, they sought proactive approaches to optimize the psychological functioning and personal adjustment of officers and to reduce occupational stress. Over time, a core set of technologies evolved that is generally accepted as the basic framework of psychological services. However, not all who provide mental health services to law enforcement are psychologists.

## CORE TECHNOLOGIES

The new sets of skills that psychologists brought to law enforcement agencies defined the core technologies. Federal discretionary funds from the Law Enforcement Assistance Administration (LEAA) encouraged law enforcement to use psychological tests to screen police officers and sheriff's deputies and created a psychological screening specialization. To a lesser extent, LEAA funds also were instrumental in psychologists becoming involved in operational areas such as assisting in criminal investigations and developing a hostage negotiation capacity in police departments. Success of those efforts provided support for developing counseling programs for officers, particularly following line-of-duty critical incidents, and training programs on psychological issues also emerged. With this evolution came the recognition that law enforcement personnel were subject to unique stressors, leading psychologists to develop stress management programs. Currently, there is a growing emphasis on wellness and disease prevention approaches to respond to police stress.

## GAINING ACCEPTANCE

Initially, the tradition-clad departments were not fully accepting of psychological services. Psychologists had to work to gain credibility and to solve professional practice issues. Questions emerged, such as, "Who is the client—the applicant or the organization; or, for counseling programs, the officer or the organization?" The latter affected confidentiality of communications, generally identified as the cornerstone of psychological services, but not fully understood in nonhealth organizations that have operated as closed systems. Many of these issues were resolved by state laws that govern the practice and licensure of psychologists. Yet these issues can still emerge in the specialization involving psychological examinations that assess officer fitness for duty.

## PREVALENCE

Psychologists have made significant inroads into improving psychological functioning in the highly traditional occupations that are responsible for public safety and law enforcement in this country. Three national surveys (1988, 1994, 2002) present confirming evidence that the use of psychologists by police and sheriffs continues to increase. Findings show that psychology has made a strong impact on policing since first introduced in the 1960s,

and that psychological services are becoming institutionalized in law enforcement. These events signify a major cultural shift.

## KEY EVENTS THAT STRENGTHENED CULTURE SHIFT

The broad acceptance of psychologists reflects a major cultural shift in policing across the country. A series of key events supported this shift.

1. FBI Symposia—A series of week-long police psychology conferences hosted by the Federal Bureau of Investigation (1984–1994) brought psychologists together to discuss issues relative to providing services in law enforcement agencies.

2. Police psychology presence achieved in professional organizations—Two examples are the Psychological Services Committee of the International Association of Chiefs of Police (IACP) and the Police & Public Safety Psychology Section (Division 18) of the American Psychological Association (APA).

3. APA Police Chiefs Roundtable Series—Fifteen years after affiliating with APA, police chiefs met with an APA governance committee and sought input on managing problems that affect the quality of American policing.

4. *APA Monitor on Psychology*—This publication has included articles (2000–2002) about psychologists working with law enforcement showing the breadth of their activities.

## MODELS OF SERVICE DELIVERY

How services are actually delivered in law enforcement agencies varies, but some models have become more prevalent. Many departments use consultants to provide services, which is the most common model; others link to Employee Assistance Programs. A model that is more prevalent in large departments provides a full range of psychological services to officers and the organization through in-house psychological service units. In 1995, 61 service activities were identified that are now provided by police psychologists. They were categorized into three general areas: Individual Service Activities;

Program/Technical Support, and Organizational Support. These data are another measure of the growth of psychology in law enforcement.

## CURRENT TRENDS

As the use of psychology continues to expand, some departments are using psychologists to assist them in addressing significant national policing issues, such as the interactions between law enforcement officers and citizens. In a series of Police Chief Roundtables conducted in conjunction with the annual meetings of the American Psychological Association (1998–2000), police chiefs met with psychologists and identified needs for assistance in ending racial profiling, intervening in police brutality, strengthening police integrity, and developing greater understanding of police officer fear. They also examined alternatives to arrest of the homeless, the prevalence of hate crime, and skill development for officers in the areas of mediation and anger management. The Roundtables generated ideas for research on psychological issues, such as studying how observing violence affects police officers, particularly in relationship to police officer domestic violence, and how the research on self-fulfilling prophecies and stereotype change processes could intervene in ethnic profiling. These events demonstrate current trends in the activities of psychologists in law enforcement agencies and suggest a level of growth and impact that would have been unbelievable 40 years ago. As the events and aftermath of September 11, 2001, place new demands on officers and their organizations, law enforcement will face additional stressors. With psychological services better institutionalized, departments now have a capacity to meet the changing psychological needs of officers.

*Ellen Scrivner*

### For Further Reading

Delprino, R. P., & Bahn, C. (1988). National survey of the extent and nature of psychological services in police departments. *Professional Psychology: Research and Practice, 19*(4), 421–425.

Harpold, J. A., & Feemster, S. L. (2002). Negative influences of police stress. *Law Enforcement Bulletin, 71*(9), 1–6.

Kurke, M. I., & Scrivner, E. M. (1995). *Police psychology into the 21st century.* Hillsdale, NJ: Lawrence Erlbaum.

Scrivner, E. M. (1994). *The role of police psychology in controlling excessive force* (National Institute of Justice Research Report). Washington, DC: U.S. Department of Justice.

## ❧ PUBLIC PERCEPTIONS/ ATTITUDES TOWARD POLICE

The idea that the police should concern themselves with their public image would seem to be common sense. Only in recent decades, however, has this ideal truly entrenched itself within America. Largely driven by the civil unrest and discontent with the government that emerged in the 1960s, public perceptions of the police have become a legitimate police concern, as well as a growing area of social science inquiry. Despite what many police officers may believe, the majority of citizens hold favorable impressions of their local police. Factors shaping individual impressions include citizen demographics, contact with the police, and community context.

A founding principle of modern policing is that the efficacy of the police depends upon the trust and support of the general public. This notion emerged in England with the 1829 establishment of the London Metropolitan Police Service (MPS) and its "Peelian Principles" (named after Home Secretary Sir Robert Peel, who championed the creation of the MPS). According to the Peelian Principles, the MPS would be able to achieve its goals and objectives only when it had the consent, support, and confidence of the London citizenry (an ideal termed "policing by consent"). The public's consent was earned, in part, by caring about public perceptions of the police. To this day, police officers throughout England are conditioned to remember this principle and keep it in mind as they perform their daily duties.

In America, the extent to which the police have concerned themselves with their public image has varied across place and time. Most American communities did not adopt the ideal of policing by consent when modern police forces were instituted in the mid-19th century. The civil unrest of the 1960s generated numerous violent clashes between the police and the public. Police leaders, politicians, community advocates, scholars, journalists, and average citizens began to question the public's view of the police, as well as other branches of the government. In response, a new form of public opinion research emerged, focusing on citizen perceptions of the police and policing services.

Early efforts aimed at understanding public perceptions of the police tended to be simplistic and narrowly focused. Researchers and pollsters asked citizens about their attitudes toward the police, perceptions of police officers, and opinions about policing services in their community. Surprisingly, these early surveys found that despite the turbulent relationship between the police and some segments of the population, most citizens expressed positive views of the police. Although ratings tended to be lower among groups of citizens who had strained relations with the police, the average minority or youth citizen still expressed positive views.

Early studies tended to consider only the relationship between perceptions of the police and independent citizen basic demographics (age, race, gender, and income). In the intervening decades, social scientific inquiry into public perceptions of the police has become increasingly sophisticated. Using more powerful statistical techniques, scholars are better able to understand how a range of variables influences citizen attitudes about the police. This information is meaningful for more than just academic reasons. Since the 1960s, police leaders and organizations have become more concerned with how they are viewed by the public. Although agencies may not use the term "policing by consent," they recognize that their ability to serve their community effectively is contingent upon maintaining positive and supportive relations with the public.

In general, three categories of variables have been found to influence citizens' perceptions of the police: demographics, neighborhood context, and contact with the police. Surprisingly, research examining the effect of demographic factors on public perceptions of the police has not yielded consistent results. Variables such as age and gender have not been found to be reliable in predicting a citizen's attitude toward the police. The only two demographic variables related with perceptions of the police are race and income (which tend to be linked in American society). As a general rule, African American and Hispanic citizens

have less favorable impressions of the police when contrasted with Caucasian citizens. In addition, citizens in lower income brackets are less positive in their views of the police. Neither generalization is always true; within all race and income groupings, there is variation in how people view the police.

The neighborhood where a citizen lives has also been found to influence perceptions of the police. Most citizens do not have regular contact with the police, so they form their opinions and perceptions based upon experiences they hear about from family, friends, and neighbors. The nature of social relations within a neighborhood can also influence how people view the police. Residents of neighborhoods exhibiting more commitment to cooperating with the police and improving quality of life tend to report more positive perceptions. Also, citizens who think that their neighborhood is a good place to live express more favorable views. These findings are not particularly surprising. Because we tend to view the police as being partially responsible for community conditions, citizens who are less satisfied with their neighborhood might be expected to express less satisfaction with the police.

Contact with the police has been found to be a powerful force shaping what citizens think about the police. Citizens who are dissatisfied with recent contact they had with the police report more negative views of the police than do citizens who were satisfied with recent contact and those who have had no recent contact. In other words, when citizens are dissatisfied with their contact with the police, they tend to develop a negative general attitude toward the police; citizens who have satisfactory contact are no more or less likely to view the police in a positive fashion. In many ways, this finding is very good news for the police and illustrates how social science research can enhance the practice of policing. A citizen's race, income, and neighborhood context are largely beyond the control of the police. Satisfaction with police contact, however, is something the police can influence (within reason). Although officers may not be able to satisfy citizens in every public encounter, striving to maximize satisfaction can ensure that officers do not generate broader ill will toward their profession.

*Joseph A. Schafer*

## For Further Reading

Cao, L., Frank, J., & Cullen, F. T. (1996). Race, community context and confidence in the police. *American Journal of Police, 15*(1), 3–22.

Huang, W., & Vaughn, M. S. (1996). Support and confidence: Public attitudes toward the police. In T. J. Flanagan & D. R. Longmire (Eds.), *Americans view crime and justice: A national public opinion survey* (pp. 31–45). Thousand Oaks, CA: Sage.

Reisig, M. D., & Parks, R. B. (2000). Experience, quality of life, and neighborhood context: A hierarchical analysis of satisfaction with police. *Justice Quarterly, 17,* 607–629.

Schafer, J. A., Huebner, B. M., & Bynum, T. S. (in press). Citizen perceptions of police services: Race, neighborhood context, and community policing. *Police Quarterly.*

## QUALITY-OF-LIFE ENFORCEMENT

*Quality of life*, *quality-of-life offenses*, and *quality-of-life enforcement* entered the criminal justice lexicon in a major way during the late 1970s. This was at a time when American policing was in a crisis. Crime was increasing, and research suggested that the dominant tactics of the time—preventive patrol and rapid response to calls for service—were of limited effectiveness. Starting during the 1920s and continuing through the 1970s, police saw their "business" as responding to serious "index" crimes: Murder, rape, assault, robbery, and burglary topped their priorities. The police put forward several values to justify their strategic emphasis: Index crimes *were* serious and demanded police attention; limited resources required that police establish priorities; and focusing on serious crime with reactive tactics—preventive patrol, rapid response to service, and criminal investigation—limited how intrusive police were into community life.

This strategy was largely endorsed by President Johnson's Commission on Law Enforcement and the Administration of Justice—a point of view that shaped professional police and academic criminal justice thinking for decades. Minor offenses, ranging from drunkenness to prostitution, were either virtually or actually decriminalized and given scant attention by police, prosecutors, and the courts.

Nonetheless, disorderly conditions and behaviors bother citizens. Even surveys conducted for the President's Commission documented the close links between disorder and citizen fear of crime—a finding confirmed again and again in surveys and focus groups, and by community groups. Citizens also act on those fears: Many barricade their homes, abandon cities, and/or withdraw from public spaces as a result of disorder and minor crimes. Compounding the problem, the deinstitutionalization of the mentally ill without adequate community services flooded public spaces, especially in inner cities, with an often obstreperous and unpredictable population, many of whom were soon considered to be the homeless.

"Broken Windows," published in 1982 by James Q. Wilson and this author, is perhaps the most well-known articulation of the links between disorder and fear. A metaphor, broken windows argues that just as a broken window left untended shows that nobody cares and leads to more broken windows, disorder, left untended, indicates that nobody cares and leads to citizen fear of crime. "Broken Windows," however, is controversial, especially in academia, for at least two reasons. First, it challenged reigning views of the time regarding decriminalization; deinstitutionalization; and the narrow focus of police, prosecutors, and courts on serious crime. Second, "Broken Windows" put forward a hypothesis: Not only does disorder create citizen fear, but it is also a precursor of serious crime. Both issues remain contentious, especially in academia.

Nonetheless, a broad consensus has developed that maintaining, developing, and restoring order is an end in itself. Neighborhood problems ranging from litter, graffiti, and abandoned cars to public drunkenness in parks, prostitution, and drug dealing severely diminish the quality of life in communities. Children cannot play in parks or on the sidewalk, the elderly cannot walk to neighborhood shopping centers, and families cannot sit on the stoops of their homes or apartments. Quality-of-life offenses, then, are minor crimes: aggressive panhandling, prostitution, drug dealing in public spaces, illegal vending, and other such crimes.

Quality-of-life enforcement is an integral part of community policing and the incipient movement toward community prosecution and community courts. In each case, as practitioners reached out to neighborhood and community residents and institutions, they discovered the high priority put on quality-of-life offenses. Indeed, the reigning model of community courts—New York City's Midtown Community Court—is built around issues of maintaining the quality of neighborhood life.

Prosecutors, too, have recognized the importance of quality of life for neighborhoods and have become active partners with police in quality-of-life enforcement, using not only the criminal code but the civil code as well to maintain or restore order. The City Attorney's Office in Los Angeles, for example, has a community prosecution unit and assigns an assistant city attorney to each of the Los Angeles Police Department's districts. It regularly enforces ordinances against quality-of-life offenses using the housing code or other forms of civil authority as well as the criminal code.

Finally, measurements of the quality of neighborhood life are now used regularly to evaluate police and, in some cases, other criminal justice agencies. New York's Midtown Community Court, for example, is an agency that has been carefully evaluated on the basis of its contribution to its neighborhood's quality of life.

*George Kelling*

**See also** "Broken Windows" or Incivility Thesis, Compstat, Community Policing, Problem-Oriented Policing, Zero Tolerance

## For Further Reading

Jacobs, J. (1961). *The death and life of great American cities.* New York: Random House.

Skogan, W. G. (1990). *Disorder and decline: Crime and the spiral of decay in American neighborhoods.* New York: Free Press.

Wilson, J. Q., & Kelling, G. L. (1982, March). Broken windows: The police and neighborhood safety. *Atlantic Monthly*, pp. 29–38.

# ✑ QUOTAS (TICKETS, ARRESTS)

Law enforcement quotas for the issuance of traffic tickets (citations) are illegal. According to many police union representatives, however, they do exist in practice under other names like "performance expectations," "performance standards," "performance criteria," "quantitative expectations," "statistical targets," and "traffic goals." According to police ethics, quotas requiring a certain number of tickets over a certain time period would be unethical, because this could be seen as coercing law enforcement officers to issue tickets when they might not otherwise do so in order to avoid administrative reprisal or a negative work evaluation. State laws might also specify that quotas for traffic stops and traffic warnings are illegal. For instance, at least 12 states have passed laws to prohibit any law enforcement agency from requiring traffic officers to meet quotas for numbers of traffic stops or arrests. In general, rank and file police usually support such legislation, as do agencies. In addition, there is a public perception that government bureaucrats responsible for city or state budgets will require quotas "to fill city coffers" or to make up for governmental budgetary shortfalls. In such cases, issuing traffic tickets to improve traffic flow and public safety would be displaced by the goal of raising funds. Importantly, the use of quotas, if set too high, could create the perception that law enforcement was not acting in the public interest and would negatively affect public cooperation with the police. Nevertheless, it remains common practice to include as a part of some field officer's performance evaluation a requirement that a certain number of traffic tickets are written in a month or per day. In some instances, federal transportation funds that are awarded to the states are based, in part, on a state's enforcement of traffic regulations as demonstrated by the number of tickets its enforcement agencies have meted out.

Traffic ticket quotas or "performance expectations" may also be the result of the average performance of an officer's peers. When such is the case, an officer might not be informed of how many traffic tickets he or she is expected to write over a certain time period. However, the officer's supervisor, who is aware of the average peer performance, may find an officer who falls below the average in ticket production to be underperforming, or to be overperforming if the officer writes more tickets than the peer average. Depending on the perceived traffic needs in a jurisdiction, an officer's performance expectations may include a certain number of specific types of traffic tickets—for example, 60 speeding tickets, 10 driving under the influence tickets, and 50 tickets of commercial vehicles in a month. Although traffic quotas are generally considered to be illegal, in some jurisdictions, a certain number of tickets for traffic infractions may be used. In some jurisdictions, law enforcement officers may be expected to demonstrate that they have had a certain number of public contacts when it comes to traffic enforcement of speeding, reckless driving, driving under the influence of alcohol, seatbelt violations, and commercial vehicle violations in order to analyze problems; gauge agency effectiveness;

or satisfy a municipal, state, or federal reporting requirement.

The number of arrests also may be considered a measure of law enforcement productivity for individual officers as well as for the agency itself. Like traffic citations, under- or overperformance in making arrests may be a matter of comparisons to the peer average. The possible consequences of having arrest quotas include false arrests, or predatory arrest practices where some of the most vulnerable (e.g., homeless people) might be easy targets. However, it is illegal in most cases to make decisions about benefits, dismissals, promotions, or demotions based on quotas or "quota-like" expectations. If included in an officer's evaluation, a quota-like measure should be, and often is, only one of a series of other points considered.

Although having a written or verbal policy that a certain number of tickets or arrests be made within a certain time period is illegal, the law generally permits the use of statistics for the purpose of advising officers about enforcement areas in need of greater attention. One such area where quota-like procedures are followed is vice enforcement. If a department receives increasing complaints for offenses such as street prostitution or drug dealing, the agency might then consider using a numeric goal.

*Camille Gibson*

***See also*** Arrest, Police Discretion, Traffic Enforcement

Adams, T. F. (2001). *Police field operations* (5th ed.). Upper Saddle River, NJ: Prentice Hall.

Miller, M. (2000). *Police patrol operations* (2nd ed.). Incline Village, NV: Copperhouse.

# R

## ❧ RACE RELATIONS

In 1967, the President's Commission on Law Enforcement and the Administration of Justice found that, in general, the public holds favorable attitudes toward the police. Despite this general finding, when attitudes are examined across race, most contemporary studies of race and attitudes toward the police reveal that blacks are far less favorable than their white counterparts. This pattern has held for the past 30 years. In the 1970s, only one fifth of blacks polled thought that local police officers applied the law equally (Feagin & Hahn, 1973). A majority (between 62% and 72%) believed that

1. Cops were "against" blacks.

2. Local law enforcement agents were dishonest.

3. Police officers were more concerned with injuring African Americans than with preventing crime.

Nearly 19 years later, a 1989 Gallup poll revealed that 50% of all blacks interviewed believed that most police officers view all blacks as suspects, and that in cases involving black suspects, the police are likely to arrest the wrong person. Survey results from the early 1990s found that 25% of the black men polled reported that they had been harassed by the police while driving through predominantly white neighborhoods.

In the search for the answer to why negative relations exist between black communities and police agents, researchers have found that the explanations include both historical and contemporary factors. Among these factors are the police role in enforcing slavery, the police role in enforcing racially discriminatory laws and social practices, and contemporary police practices such as targeted enforcement and racial profiling.

### SLAVE PATROLS AS THE PRECURSOR TO MODERN POLICING

With the introduction of the African slave to the American colonies in 1619 came the responsibility of keeping those slaves under control. Slave owners and others to whom service was owed wanted to protect their investments. Hence, whereas many historians credit northern cities with beginning "modern policing" in the 1800s, other policing scholars make the argument that the first American modern-style policing occurred in the South during the 1700s, with the creation of "slave patrols." Slave patrols were developed by white slave owners as a means of recovering runaway slaves and as a means of protecting themselves against potential slave uprisings. In a land where the underlying legal philosophy was freedom and equality, as outlined in such documents as the Declaration of Independence and the U.S. Constitution, men, women, and children were held captive by others, with race being the primary determining factor of who was free and who was not.

South Carolina is noted as having established slave patrol legislation during the 1740s. Documenting the point that American policing began with slave patrols, J. F. Richardson (1974) notes in his book, *Urban Police in the United States*, that

> [many other cities with] elaborate police arrangements were those with large slave populations where white masters lived in dread of possible black uprisings. Charleston, Savannah, and Richmond provided for combined foot and mounted patrols to prevent slaves from congregating and to repress any attacks upon the racial and social status quo. In Charleston . . . police costs constituted the largest item in the municipal budget. (p. 19)

Similarly, in 1757, the neighboring colony, Georgia, included the following language in the preamble to its law establishing and regulating slave patrols:

> It is absolutely necessary for the Security of his Majesty's Subjects in this Province, that Patrols should be established under proper Regulations in the settled parts thereof, for the better keeping of Negroes and other Slaves in Order and prevention of any Cabals, Insurrections or other Irregularities amongst them. (Chandler, 1910, p. 225)

Under such legislation, slave patrols, which consisted almost exclusively of white male "officers," were given the power and authority to go onto any plantation; to forcefully enter "Negro houses when slaves were suspected of keeping arms" (Peak & Glensor, 1996, pp. 20–21); to punish and recapture any person accused of being a runaway slave; and to punish any slave suspected of stealing or other crimes.

## SLAVES, FREE BLACKS, AND THE LAW

Even prior to the enactment of legislation establishing slave patrols, Slave Codes were established in

the southern states. These codes, established in 1690, severely restricted the legal rights and protections afforded slaves. Among other restrictions, they prevented slaves from carrying weapons, owning property, and traveling without an appropriate pass. In many locations, the Codes forbade anyone to teach slaves to read and/or write. The Slave Codes also outlined various barbaric forms of punishment for those found in violation of the restrictions: whipping, branding, hanging, castration, or other heinous forms of torture or death. To be effective, these Codes required enforcement. Although often enforced by private vigilantism, government agents such as local sheriffs, constables, deputies, posses, and so on were empowered and expected to enforce the Codes.

The Slave Codes proved difficult to enforce because there were free blacks living in the colonies before, during, and after the importation of African slaves. Consequently, it became difficult for the authorities to distinguish between free blacks and slaves. That being the case, the legislators in several provinces (later, colonies, and ultimately, states) enacted statutes that equated blackness with slavery or placed the same restrictions on free blacks as those imposed on slaves under the Slave Codes. By legislative enactment, several colonies denied free blacks the opportunity to live there. As early as 1663, Maryland considered all "negroes" within its borders to be slaves. Other states allowed free blacks to remain within their borders only temporarily, or run the risk of being fined. Failure to pay the fine could result in enslavement as punishment. Again, these laws required enforcement by some official body, thus pitting law enforcement agents against blacks, both free and slave.

## POLICING AND JIM CROW

With the end of slavery, blacks still found themselves in a subordinate position vis-à-vis the law. "Black Codes" were enacted in many southern states. These codes limited the rights of blacks to own or rent property, allowed for imprisonment for breach of employment contracts, prevented blacks from holding certain types of jobs, and denied them the right to bring charges or testify against whites in court. So complete was the control of blacks under the Black Codes that in some towns, they were not permitted to be on the public streets after dark.

Although the Fourteenth Amendment was enacted in 1868, with words that guaranteed "equal protection of the law" to all residents, the 1896 U.S. Supreme Court decision in *Plessy v. Ferguson* allowed the states to continue to enact laws that restricted the liberty of blacks. These laws, often referred to as "Jim Crow" laws, were zealously enforced by state and local law enforcement officers, sometimes resulting in the lynching of blacks who had only been *accused* of committing some crime.

Although overt racism through formal law is most often associated with legislative and law enforcement functions in the South, as early as 1830, when Alexis de Tocqueville toured the United States, he was surprised to discover that "there was more overt hostility and hatred towards Blacks in the North, where slavery did not exist, than in the South, where it did" (Williams & Murphy, 1990, p. 4). In fact, the subordinate position of blacks in the North was reflected as early as 1638 in a New Amsterdam (now New York City) ordinance. The ordinance made it a crime to engage in "adulterous intercourse with heathens, blacks, or other persons" (Burrows & Wallace, 1999, p. 35). The *Plessy* decision allowed all states to segregate their populations by race. State and local law enforcement officers were called on to maintain the separations. Even in 1954, when the Supreme Court decided that segregation in public schools was unconstitutional, it took federal law enforcement efforts to secure black childrens' rights to attend schools that had previously been all white.

Similarly, during the 1960s and 1970s, when blacks began to push for their right of "equal protection of the law" via the sit-ins, marches, and boycotts of the civil rights era, state and local law enforcement officials worked to maintain the racial status quo. Images of police dogs and water hoses being used against men, women, and children attempting to obtain civil rights are recorded on video documentaries such as *Eyes on the Prize.* Some police chiefs became (in)famous for the zeal with which they went after civil rights organizers and marchers. The long history of enforcing unequal laws seemed to be something that they were unwilling to give up.

## RACE RIOTS

Upheld by judicial interpretations, the early legislators established an unequal legal order that law enforcement officials were charged with maintaining. Over the years, race riots broke out in large cities (e.g., New York; Chicago; Detroit; Newark, New Jersey; and Los Angeles). These riots were often spurred by police action associated with the unequal enforcement of the law. As early as 1834, there were so many public disturbances in New York City that the period became known as "The Year of the Riots." During the late 1950s and into the 1960s, protest riots by blacks in major U.S. cities led to a large-scale federal investigation that culminated in a classic comprehensive report by the President's Commission on the "Causes and Prevention of Violence." Twenty-five years later, the acquittal of four white police officers for the videotaped beating of a black motorist in Los Angeles led to a riot that cost the city millions of dollars. Similar riots occurred after similar incidents in cities such as Philadelphia; Miami; Cincinnati; and Long Beach, California. Ironically, during the late 1800s, it was racial tensions of this nature that had led to the hiring of black police officers by some jurisdictions. In several locations, however, the powers of arrest for black officers extended only to arresting black suspects. They were not authorized to detain or arrest whites.

## CONTEMPORARY POLICE PRACTICES

Today, police agencies still tend to be manned mostly by white males. During the late 1990s, racial profiling—the use of race by police as the sole or primary factor in decisions to stop, question, search, or frisk a "suspect"—became the most contentious aspect of police–community relations.

Many of those stopped contended that their race was the sole basis for the police suspicion. Statistics gathered across the country confirmed that minority residents (particularly blacks and Latinos) were being stopped by police in disproportionate numbers. These stops included both pedestrians and motorists.

So significant were the complaints of unequal treatment by police that they prompted one jurisdiction (New Jersey) to make racial profiling a crime of the third degree if engaged in by its officers. Several other states and the federal government proposed legislation to monitor and curtail the practice. Because the U.S. Constitution and numerous state statutes forbid race discrimination, numerous civil judgments, amounting to millions of dollars, were awarded against state and local police departments across the country (e.g., California, Colorado, Florida, Illinois, Maryland, New Jersey, and Pennsylvania).

During the 1980s and 1990s, many drug "sweeps" failed to distinguish innocent blacks and Latinos from those actually involved in the drug trade. Heavy levels of police surveillance concentrated in predominantly poor and minority communities gave the impression, right or wrong, that a primary function of the police was to control these populations. But given the high crime rates and gang-related terrorism in many of these same neighborhoods, numerous communities themselves requested a heavy police presence to quell the violence on their streets.

In "Fixing Broken Windows or Fracturing Fragile Relationships," O'Donnell (2004) discusses how New York City's 1990s zero-tolerance policing strategy reduced crime at the expense of alienating the black and Latino community. In Los Angeles, a policing strategy designed to reduce gang activity degenerated into murders, assaults, and cover-ups by the police, with blacks and Latinos as the main victims. Investigative reports by the Department of Justice, civil rights organizations, and state attorney general offices continue to find that blacks and other minorities are disproportionately the victims of excessive force or brutality at the hands of the police.

Given this history, it is not surprising that relations between blacks and other minorities and police agencies have been poor. Through the use of community policing, police–community partnerships, and other techniques dependent more on cooperation than coercion, many police agencies are attempting to bridge the apparent gap in their connection to diverse communities. Initial assessments of some of these efforts show promise for improved relations.

*Delores D. Jones-Brown*

**See also** Affirmative Action in Policing; Depolicing; Gangs Investigation; Profiling, Racial

## For Further Reading

Adamson, C. R. (1983). Punishment after slavery: Southern state penal systems, 1865–1890. *Social Problems, 30*(5), 555–569.

Browning, S., Cullen, F., Cao, L., Kopache, R., & Stevenson, T. (1994). Race and getting hassled by the police: A research note. *Police Studies, 17*(1), 1–11.

Burrows, E., & Wallace, M. (1999). *Gotham: A history of New York City to 1898.* New York: Oxford University Press.

Chandler, A. (Ed.). (1910). *The colonial records of the state of Georgia* (Vol. 18). Atlanta: Charles P. Byrd, State Printer.

Crockett, G. W. (1972). Racism in the law. In L. E. Reasons & J. L. Kuykendall (Eds.), *Race, crime and justice.* Pacific Palisades, CA: Goodyear.

Davis, J. (1974, Fall). Justification for no obligation: Views of black males toward crime and the criminal law. *Issues in Criminology, 9,* 69–87.

Feagin, J., & Hahn, H. (1973). *Ghetto revolts: The politics of violence in American cities.* New York: Macmillan.

Ginzburg, R. (1962). *One hundred years of lynchings.* Baltimore, MD: Black Classic Press.

Hagan, J., & Albonetti, C. (1982). Race, class and the perception of criminal injustice in America. *American Journal of Sociology, 88*(2), 329–355.

Higginbotham, A. L., Jr. (1996). *Shades of freedom.* New York: Oxford University Press.

Jones-Brown, D. D. (2000a). *Race, crime and punishment.* Philadelphia: Chelsea House.

Jones-Brown, D. D. (2000b). Race as a legal construct: The implications for America justice. In M. Markowitz & D. Jones-Brown (Eds.), *The system in black and white* (pp. 137–152). Westport, CT: Praeger.

Mann, C. (1993). *Unequal justice: A question of color.* Bloomington: Indiana University Press.

McIntyre, C. (1993). *Criminalizing a race: Free blacks during slavery*. Queens, NY: Kayode.

Miller, R. R. (1957). *Slavery and Catholicism*. Durham, NC: North State Publishers.

O'Donnell, E. (2004). Fixing broken windows or fracturing fragile relationships? In D. Jones-Brown & K. Terry (Eds.), *Policing and minority communities: Bridging the gap*. Upper Saddle River, NJ: Pearson/Prentice Hall.

Owens, C. E., & Bell, J. (1977). *Blacks and criminal justice*. Lexington, MA: D.C. Heath.

Peak, K., & Glensor, R. (1996). *Community policing and problem solving: Strategies and practices*. Upper Saddle River, NJ: Prentice Hall.

President's Commission on Law Enforcement and Administration of Justice. (1967). *Task force report: The police*. Washington, DC: U.S. Government Printing Office.

Richardson, J. F. (1974). *Urban police in the United States*. Port Washington, NY: National University Publications.

Russell, K. K. (1998). *The color of crime*. New York: New York University Press.

Stevens, D. (2002). *Policing and community partnerships*. Upper Saddle River, NJ: Prentice Hall.

Williams, H., & Murphy, P. (1990). *Evolving strategy of the police: A minority view*. Washington, DC: National Institute of Justice.

## ✸ RADAR

Traffic enforcement officers are responsible for enforcing and citing various violations of the traffic code. Their primary focus is often on the most common violation, speeding. There are numerous benefits to speed enforcement, including the ability to lower crime rates; the ability to increase safety on the roadways; monetary savings in lower insurance, health care, and tax costs; revenue generation; and gains from asset forfeitures. Speed limits are determined scientifically through the use of traffic engineering and are enforced by way of scientific equipment; speeding convictions are validated by technical testimony about the scientific principles underlying detection by radar and other speed detection devices. Posted speed limits are generally designed for 70% of all drivers, with a standard deviation of approximately 15%. Drivers who operate outside of this range can be considered unsafe drivers. The most effective devices are radio detection and ranging (RADAR), visual average speed computer

and record (VASCAR), and light amplification by simulated emission of radiation (LASER; sometimes called LIDAR).

Radar in law enforcement was a military technology developed during World War II to alert of approaching enemy aircraft. Law enforcement radar is distinguished because it is a pulse-type radar. It sends a cone-shaped stream of radio wave crests that is reflected or bounced back. The echo is returned by the object detected. The number of wave crests is the frequency. When the object is stationary, the frequency of the echo is the same as the frequency of the transmission. However, when an object is moving, the echo will have a different frequency, which can be calibrated by a voltmeter on an mph scale. This change in echo frequency for moving objects, known as the Doppler Effect, was first established in 1842 by Christian Doppler.

Traffic radar units are manufactured by at least six different companies and come in a variety of shapes and sizes. They are all alike in that they produce low-level microwave radiation and a low-power electromagnetic field. In thousands of research experiments, it has been shown repeatedly that long-term exposure to microwave radiation and electromagnetic fields can have detrimental biological effects on the exposed individual. Studies cite the U.S. Environmental Protection Agency as having stated that exposure to microwave radiation and radio-frequency radiation is potentially cancerous. The Office of Health and Environmental Assessment (OHEA) and the EPA staff recommended that radio-frequency and microwave radiation be labeled as a Class C carcinogen. Class C comprises those substances that are possible human carcinogens, such as methyl chloride, trichlorethane, and saccharine.

Traffic radar can provide a technological deterrent to slow down motorists, making the roadways safer. However, many safety questions have yet to be answered. The organization primarily responsible for setting exposure limits is the American National Standards Institute (ANSI). The current exposure limit allowed by ANSI for traffic radar frequencies is about the exposure limit in some European countries. Many of the radar units produced today, used by American police departments, would be banned overseas. As a result, throughout the early 1990s, as a result of research and articles presenting the inherent danger of long-term exposure to radiation, many departments began searching for alternatives for speed detection and enforcement. Currently, radar and microwave sources are recommended to be operated, if at all, with great care, and ideally, external to the vehicles in which radar is operated. All operators should be apprised of the potential hazards involved.

Prior to the use of radar, a number of jurisdictions in some 30 states built into patrol cars a stopwatch-type device called VASCAR. When a speeding vehicle passed a first checkpoint, the mechanism was started, and when the vehicle passed a second checkpoint, the mechanism was stopped. The device then used the time and distance between the two points to calculate speed. Although some departments still use VASCAR in aerial patrol, its popularity in patrol cars waned with the introduction of radar, which was easier to use and less sensitive to temperature variations and jostling, which sometimes hindered VASCAR performance.

The latest technology on the nation's roads is based on the use of lasers. The most common versions project a tighly focused beam of invisible light that is reflected upon contact and read by calibrated speedometer. Although its effectiveness can be limited by weather conditions, many law enforcement practitioners prefer laser to radar because there are fewer available countermeasures and because there have, as yet, been no claims concerning the health risk to officers.

By far, the most popular technology to be used to enhance road safety is photo-radar. These stationary units, usually mounted on traffic lights or lampposts, can photograph the license plate of the car and/or the face of the driver. The license plate number is extracted from the picture, and a ticket is sent to the registered owner of the vehicle. When this technology was first introduced, there were some concerns regarding privacy. These fears have abated for the most part, and the use of this technology continues to spread. Photo-radar is well-liked by law enforcement officials because it frees officer time, which can be used for other purposes,

and acts as an ongoing deterrent to speeding. Also, the tickets generated are rarely challenged.

*Michelle R. Hecht*

### For Further Reading

Clark, J. (1991). Can traffic radar lead to cancer? *Law Enforcement News, 17*(332).

Daly, N., & Proffitt, W. (1991). The radar dilemma: One agency's response. *Law Enforcement News, 17*(348).

Goodson, M. (1985). Technical shortcomings of Doppler traffic radar. *Journal of Forensic Science, 30,* 1186.

Hand, B., Sherman, A., & Cavanagh, M. (1980). *Traffic investigation and control.* New York: Macmillan.

Moenssens, A., Starrs, J., Henderson, C., & Inbau, F. (1995). *Scientific evidence in civil and criminal cases.* Westbury, NY: Foundation Press.

O'Connor, T. R. (2004). *Scientific speed detection.* Retrieved March 16, 2004, from http://faculty.ncwc.edu/toconnor/425/425lect04.htm

Poynter, G. (1990a). Experimentation without informed consent: Casualties of traffic radar use. *Law Enforcement News, 16*(325).

Poynter, G. (1990b, November 15). The hidden hazard of traffic safety. *Law Enforcement News, 16*(324).

Poynter, G. (1995, November 15). The last piece in radar's unsolved puzzle. *Law Enforcement News, 21*(433).

Zaret, M. (1991). An electronic smog is threatening our police. *Law Enforcement News, 17*(331).

Zaret, M. (1992). The smoking gun in the radar-cancer controversy. *Law Enforcement News, 18*(365).

## &#9758; RAMPART INVESTIGATION, THE

The Los Angeles Police Department (LAPD) Rampart Division scandal of the late 1990s involved a cabal of tightly knit cops within Los Angeles's Rampart police station who behaved like the gangs they were supposed to police. Giving currency to the phrase "gangster cop," the officers robbed, stole drugs and sold them on the street, committed murder, and planted evidence to cover up crimes.

The Rampart scandal was significant for many reasons. First, the LAPD had not seen such systemic, blatantly criminal conduct since the 1930s, when Mayor Frank Shaw presided over what was known as the "Shaw spoils system." Under that system, municipal officers ranging from district attorneys to the LAPD Central Vice Squad took bribes from madams, bootleggers, and gamblers. Political scandals and kickbacks involving the police were legion.

Second, the Rampart scandal was significant because it combined murder and drugs on a scale and level of lawlessness rarely found in police departments in the rest of the nation. The first time in recent history that America saw a major police scandal where cops killed and sold drugs was in Florida's Miami "River Cops" scandal of 1989. That case involved a similarly tightly bound group of officers from the narcotics division of the Miami Police Department who broke into dealers' boats, cars, and homes; stole their drugs; plotted to kill witnesses; and sold the drugs for millions of dollars. In one incident, officers chased six smugglers whose drugs they had stolen into the Miami River, where three of the smugglers drowned, thus giving rise to their eponyms.

Although drug-related corruption occurred in a number of police departments during that period, the only other major case since the Miami River Cops of police officers selling drugs and committing murder was in the New Orleans Police Department. More than 50 officers were arrested, indicted, or convicted between 1993 and 1995 on charges that included drug trafficking and murder.

The Rampart scandal centered on the LAPD's Rampart Division, a police station in one of Los Angeles's poorest, toughest neighborhoods near downtown Los Angeles. When the Rampart station opened in 1966, few street gangs roamed the area. But by the mid-1980s and 1990s, the 7.9-square-mile area, the most densely populated in Los Angeles, with many Latino immigrants and Korean shopkeepers, was prey to at least 30 different gangs that boasted thousands of members among them. By the early 1990s, the area routinely led the city in homicides, narcotics activity, and violent crime arrests.

To deal with gangs, the LAPD established specialized units in police stations around the city called Community Resources Against Street Hoodlums (CRASH). CRASH units were funded by a grant in the early 1970s. The Rampart CRASH unit was staffed with one to two sergeants and up to 24 officers.

CRASH units were armed with special powers. Injunctions to curb gang violence, such as a law prohibiting gangs from blocking sidewalks and carrying pagers, gave officers broad discretion to disperse and arrest suspected gang members. CRASH officers also easily obtained injunctions placing gang members under curfew.

In the Rampart CRASH, these sweeping powers and a confrontational, high-stakes policing style led to extensive abuses that were unveiled in September 1999, when Rafael Perez, a Rampart CRASH officer, agreed to testify about wrongdoing in exchange for a lighter sentence for stealing cocaine.

Hints that something was profoundly amiss in the Rampart CRASH, however, had come several years before Perez started talking. The first hint came in the fall of 1997, when a former Rampart CRASH policeman was charged with robbing hundreds of thousands of dollars from a bank in the Rampart area. It surfaced that the officer was close friends with a number of Rampart cops and had gone to Las Vegas shortly after the robbery with CRASH unit officer Perez. This officer was eventually convicted in March 1999 of federal bank robbery and sentenced to 14 years and 3 months in prison. The second red flag went up in February 1998, when another CRASH unit officer was charged with the false imprisonment and beating of a handcuffed arrestee.

The third incident—the one that would eventually blow the lid off the case—occurred in March 1998, when officers in the LAPD Property Division discovered that Perez had checked out a number of kilograms of cocaine for a court appearance that he never returned. Perez was tried for possessing cocaine to sell, grand theft, and forgery. He received a hung jury.

As prosecutors, with the help of Chief of Police Bernard C. Parks, who had assembled an internal task force in May 1998 to investigate, prepared to try Perez a second time, additional evidence against him began to mount. Perez agreed to cooperate with police investigators in return for a reduced sentence on a cocaine-theft conviction and immunity from further prosecution.

In about 2,000 pages of testimony delivered over 5 months, Perez revealed an underworld in the Rampart CRASH where officers would frame suspects by planting drugs and guns on them, intimidate witnesses, assault people on the streets for fun, steal drugs, and perjure themselves to get convictions. Although Perez's allegations must be viewed with caution in that he had incentives to implicate others to satisfy his plea agreement, the picture he paints is internally consistent. Moreover, investigators have corroborated a number of his allegations.

Among his more lurid allegations, Perez told of an officer who raped a woman while on duty, others who beat a handcuffed man during an interrogation until he vomited blood, still others who checked the immigration status of suspected gang members and threatened to turn over any illegal aliens who had witnessed their misconduct to the Immigration and Naturalization Service (a violation of Los Angeles policy), and a list of inmates who were allegedly convicted based on fabricated evidence.

The Rampart CRASH unit, according to Perez, behaved somewhat like a gang itself. New recruits often underwent brutal initiation rituals not dissimilar to gang hazings. Officers would celebrate after any of them successfully raided a gang. Their use of violence intimidation resembled gang brutality. Perez told of one officer who tracked down a gang member suspected of slashing his car tires. The cop and his partner allegedly left him naked in a rival gang's neighborhood. Another officer allegedly shot a suspect repeatedly with a beanbag shotgun, normally used to knock suspects to the ground, for the fun of it.

To cover up their crimes, Perez said that crooked Rampart CRASH officers would routinely plant evidence. He said that he had filed off the serial number from a gang member's gun so that he could use it to frame people, and he described three incidents where CRASH officers planted guns next to people they had shot. In one case, Perez said that he and his partner, during a raid on a violent gang in 1996, had shot one of its members, Javier Francisco Ovando, after handcuffing him. Perez said he and

his partner planted a gun on the paralyzed victim to make it look as if he had assaulted the police first. Ovando was sentenced to 23 years in prison. He was released in September 1999 in the wake of Perez's testimony.

Unlike the Rodney King case of the early 1990s, where a formal external commission unconnected to the LAPD—the Christopher Commission, headed by former secretary of state Warren Christopher—was convened to examine the case, the only official report dealing directly with the Rampart allegations per se was an internal one. That report, released on March 1, 2000, was the work of an LAPD Board of Inquiry (BOI) assembled by Chief Parks in September 1999. (An independent panel, the Rampart Independent Review Panel, was also subsequently convened. But that Panel's report focused not on explaining CRASH abuses, but on addressing the broader issues the scandal raised, such as civilian oversight, police culture, and community policing.)

The BOI's 362-page report blamed corruption primarily on lack of supervision and a subversive subculture in the Rampart CRASH. The BOI concluded that Rampart CRASH officers saw themselves as operating in an "us versus them" world, "engaged in a life and death struggle" against savage gangs, that enabled them to rationalize rule breaking. The unit deliberately set out to walk the fine line between aggressive policing and illegal "warfare." Sweeping antigang injunctions and the breathy rhetoric of government officials to "take the streets back" encouraged highly aggressive policing tactics and sent a message that led many officers to believe they should do whatever it took to win.

The real dangers that Rampart CRASH officers faced at the hands of gangs further encouraged aggression and led them to band together like a tightly knit fraternity. Gangs often knew which officers would be working on given nights and what time they would go home. Officers were sometimes outgunned by gangs four to one. As they struggled to overcome such threats, Rampart CRASH officers started wearing logos and patches and eventually giving plaques to colleagues who shot gang members.

The BOI report additionally blamed lax LAPD supervision for permitting a renegade culture to flourish at the Rampart CRASH. In 1995, overcrowding in the main Rampart station house prompted the CRASH unit to be relocated to a substation nearly two miles away from the oversight of watch commanders and other patrol supervisors. Without meaningful oversight, the CRASH unit was able to make up its own rules. CRASH officers reinforced their independence by rekeying the entrance locks to their substation, making it different from all other police stations in Los Angeles and thus less accessible to officers from other station houses.

The Rampart Division scandal has had many implications for the LAPD and, more broadly, the city of Los Angeles. By calling into question the credibility of LAPD officers, the scandal led to the overturning of more than 100 convictions. Additionally, more than 80 officers were arrested, and nearly 90 were implicated, for Rampart-related offenses occurring between 1995 and 1998. Although the district attorney's office rejected dozens of the arrests that the LAPD submitted to it for review, as of February 2003, eight officers had been convicted, including Perez and his partners. Moreover, about 10 police officers resigned from the LAPD to avoid facing administrative investigations and disciplinary charges. Additional convictions and charges are likely because other officers are awaiting trial, and investigations by the district attorney and FBI are ongoing.

The Rampart scandal has also resulted in numerous significant internal reforms of the LAPD—unlike the aftermath of the Rodney King case, when many of the Christopher Commission's recommendations were not implemented. Among the more significant reforms, the FBI launched a civil rights probe in March 2000, joining the Police Commission, district attorney's office, LAPD Internal Affairs unit, and the BOI in probing allegations against officers. The civil rights case resulted in a federal consent decree that put the LAPD under federal supervision for the first time in its history. The consent decree, administered by a federal judge and monitored by a private security firm, lasts a minimum of 5 years,

during which the LAPD must demonstrate substantial compliance with its provisions.

The consent decree requires that the LAPD establish a computerized "early warning system" to spot and track problem cops, and create a unit to investigate LAPD shootings. The department is also to monitor arrests to ensure that officers do not use racial profiling, and expand the public's access to information about its operations.

Although it is too soon to judge these various reforms, as is the case with many reforms that are instituted in response to such scandals, the Rampart investigation—with its consent decree and the changes in protocols used to report and investigate misconduct by sworn personnel—will have an effect not only on the Los Angeles Police Department, but on other jurisdictions as well.

*Lydia Segal*

**See also** Corruption/Integrity, Ethics, Knapp
      Commission, Mollen Commission

*For Further Reading*

Board of Inquiry. (2000, March 1). *Rampart area corruption incident.* Los Angeles: Los Angeles Police Department.

Cannon, L. (2000, October 1). One bad cop. *New York Times Magazine,* p. 6.

Cohen, A. (2000, March 6). Gangsta cops. *Time,* pp. 30–34.

Los Angeles agrees to federal proposals to reform police. (2000, September 22). *Crime Control Digest, 34*(38), 2.

Report of the Rampart Independent Review Panel. (2000, November 16). Available: www.lacity.org/oig/rirprpt.pdf

Reppetto, T. (1978). *The blue parade.* New York: Free Press.

# RANK STRUCTURE

Since the origins of modern American municipal policing, police departments have followed an organizational rank structure often referred to as the "military model." Given the fact that both police and military organizations are characterized by similar operational demands involving issues of chain of command, unity of command, internal discipline, strict accountability, training, the use of force, and the need for effective supervision and leadership, the military model is generally considered an appropriate and viable organizational structure for police agencies.

Although some variation can be found among American police agencies depending upon their relative size and the complexity of their mandate and functions, the hierarchical police rank structure typically involves at least five (but often more) separate ranks or positions. These ranks generally equate with the ranks used by the American military, and police insignia of rank typically correspond to those of their easily recognizable military (specifically, Army) counterparts. Similarly, the rank arrangement resembles a kind of pyramid, with the number of personnel in each rank decreasing as one ascends through the chain of command.

Entry-level police personnel are usually appointed through some sort of civil service examination process and typically hold the rank of police officer; their insignia may be a single stripe worn on the sleeve that is similar to the insignia worn by an Army private. Police officers are superceded in rank by sergeants, who again are typically promoted through a civil service examination process and wear the three-stripe chevron as their sleeve insignia. Lieutenants, who typically wear the single collar bar of an Army lieutenant, supervise and supercede sergeants, and they, in turn, are supervised and superceded by captains. Police captains, who again generally wear the double-bar collar insignia of an Army captain, may earn their rank through civil service examination, or they may be appointed by the chief of police or by municipal officials. The chief of police, who typically wears the star insignia of an Army general officer, holds the highest rank or position in the agency. He or she may earn this rank through a civil service process, but more commonly, the chief is appointed by the municipal officials to whom he or she reports. In a handful of localities, such as areas of Louisiana, they are elected.

Although some agencies may designate a cadre of officers assigned to investigative duties as detectives, this designation is generally an appointive position with no civil service tenure rather than a formal rank with supervisory responsibilities.

It must again be emphasized that the number of ranks within a given agency generally varies according to its size and complexity; smaller agencies with a flatter command structure necessarily require fewer separate ranks, and larger and more complex police organizations may require additional ranks. The New York Police Department, for example, is the nation's largest and arguably most complex police agency, and its rank structure prescribes 10 separate ranks for sworn personnel as well as superceding civilian positions of assistant commissioners, deputy commissioners, and the police commissioner.

*Vincent E. Henry*

**See also** Militarization of American Police

## ✑ REPEAT OFFENDERS

Researchers agree that a significant percentage of crime is committed by a relatively small number of offenders who violate the law again and again, not necessarily getting caught each time but rather eventually and repeatedly. This well-substantiated finding informs criminal justice policy and practice in a variety of ways, particularly affecting law enforcement officers, who are on the front lines when it comes to preventing, investigating, and solving crime. The study of recidivism—the tendency to return to criminal behavior—is growing more nuanced and moving beyond the question of *whether* someone reoffends into *how soon* after initial or prior offense, and has begun to document specific behavior trends. Inquiry of this sort has been further expanded to include the issue of repeat victimization, a phenomenon in which the same target is repeatedly violated, as well as crime pattern analysis. As this knowledge base grows, so, too, does the sophistication with which law enforcement responds to and incorporates such data, thus greatly influencing how funds are distributed, where resources are focused, training tactics, and what types of strategies police forces employ to get the job done.

Recidivism data actually measure an offender's return to the criminal justice system via any one or a combination of the following: a rearrest, a reconviction, and possibly a new term of punishment. This does not necessarily mean a person has repeated the proscribed act for which he or she was *originally* judged guilty. He or she may have committed an entirely different offense and, in numerous cases, is not, in fact, responsible for a criminal act but rather has violated the mandates of his or her freedom. At the end of 2001, 4.7 million adult men and women were on either probation or parole. These are people under some form of federal, state, or local guardianship as either a punitive sentence (probation) or an early provisional release from incarceration (parole). Such status is conditional, and if probationers or parolees do not adhere to the terms of their liberty, they are subject to rearrest, revocation of freedom, and additional punitive measures. A significant number of repeat offenders fall into this category. The response to technical violations, as these transgressions are commonly known, is in the hands of law enforcement, which has a great deal of discretion in these cases. The decision as to whether to bring someone in on the basis of refractory behavior is usually left up to the parole, probation, or police officers at hand.

In a 1994 study, 272,111 offenders discharged that same year accounted for 4,877,000 arrest charges over their recorded careers. Although these are not "careers" in the popular sense, some criminals do "specialize" in a particular class of offense, such as drug dealing, fraud, and auto theft. Violent crimes such as assault, murder, and rape tend to be impulsive behaviors, but that does not prevent their repetition. However, less serious offenders—those arrested for prostitution, the purchasing of drugs, and public drunkenness, for example—are considered more likely to repeat offend at higher rates. By concentrating on the career criminal population, and decreasing their numbers on the streets, officers can greatly abate or prevent crime. Multiple tactics help achieve this goal.

One important and developing strategy used to target repeat offenders is tracking. Police departments compile lists of foremost career criminals and then shadow their movements and whereabouts. By keeping an attentive eye, officers are right there in the hope of deterring criminal behavior and, if or when these people reoffend, pick them up immediately. In this vein, emerging laws at the federal, state, and local levels, focused particularly on sex offenders, mandate that upon release, such convicts register with local authorities, and in many jurisdictions, the public is also notified. Such measures arouse disquiet on many levels, from worries about vigilantism, which have been repeatedly sustained, to significant civil liberty concerns. Other legislative tools aimed at helping law enforcement keep the repeat offender population off the streets, such as three-strikes laws and the Career Criminals Amendment Act of 1986, are equally controversial and raise similar constitutional questions. Many critics argue that these types of policies, because they address *possible* future criminal behavior, challenge the national edict of innocent until proven guilty, advocate unwarranted invasions of privacy, and fall well within the territory of cruel and unusual punishment. Nevertheless, repeat offender databases serve as critical investigative resources and heighten law enforcement's capabilities. As technology advances and departments commit to working together and sharing information, tracking becomes increasingly effective.

The concept of repeat victimization, that certain targets—people, businesses, neighborhoods, vehicles—are consistently victimized, emerged during the last quarter of the 20th century and has been gaining currency and growing more complex ever since. By recognizing offense patterns, law enforcement can concentrate resources with more precision, generating focused interventions to improve prevention and detection. Education campaigns to teach and inform the public are popular and produce results. Efforts include warning subway riders to keep their wallets in a front pocket or encouraging women to walk in groups rather than alone when out at night. Police can increase their presence in a crime-prone location, often referred to as a "hot spot," or work with the community to reduce target vulnerability or attractiveness by introducing bright street lights, rerouting traffic, or developing self-defense classes.

Analyzing crime according to location, or crime mapping, is a relatively new and increasingly vital strategy. Computers and assorted software have significantly enhanced capabilities in this arena. But whether it is pushpins on a map, or advanced statistics organizing data street by street, knowing exactly where, when, and how often offenses occur in a given location is indispensable. Not only does this approach earmark patterns and enable law enforcement to better direct interventions, but it also serves as a highly effective way of holding management accountable for what is, and is not, happening in their locale. Charting criminal events can help to determine if specific policing tactics have been successful by reporting a reduction or eradication of offending. Many police departments have regularly scheduled meetings, referred to as Compstat, to review such data, and in 1996, the National Institute of Justice established the Crime Mapping Research Center. The field is expanding, and mapping is becoming increasingly important.

A task force is a group of individuals and resources organized, directed, and dedicated to accomplishing a specific objective. This often-deployed tactical approach is a specialized and decentralized way to address repeat offenders and crime patterns. Departments create exceptionally trained groups that are particularly equipped to center on specific targets or goals. Examples include task forces aimed at parole violators, auto theft, or terrorism.

Whether departments are able to tailor their operations depends on the fiscal and logistical resources available in that jurisdiction. This varies greatly, from the big city to the small locality to the federal government. Public support, another critical variable, relies on the nature of past public–police relations as well as the political climate. It is important to note that not all populations are policed in the same manner; some forces and individual officers use characteristics illegitimately associated with crime, such as race, to inform their behavior or policies. This is a troubling issue plaguing every corner of today's criminal justice landscape. Those who are more heavily supervised and investigated are more likely to be found committing proscribed acts, not because they are necessarily offending at a

higher rate but because they are watched more intensely. This acute problem notwithstanding, practices continue to adapt to and incorporate the expanding scholarship and theoretical developments in strategic policing. Tactics grow ever more focused and training more fine-tuned, and as technology matures, data will be easier to access, evaluate, and share.

*Dana Greene*

***See also*** Compstat, Crime Mapping, Hot Spots, Parole Officers, Probation Officers, Task Forces

## For Further Reading

Blumstein, A., Cohen, J., Roth, J. A., & Visher, C. A. (Eds.). (1986). *Criminal careers and "career criminals."* Washington, DC: National Academy Press.

Farrell, G., & Pease, K. (Eds.). (2001). *Repeat victimization.* Monsey, NY: Criminal Justice Press.

Harries, K. (1999). *Mapping crime: Principles and practice* (NCJ 178919). Washington, DC: U.S. Department of Justice.

Palmiotto, M. J. (1997). *Policing: Concepts, strategies, and current issues in American police forces.* Durham, NC: Academic Press.

##   RESPONSE TIME

Response time is a commonly used indicator of police effectiveness and efficiency often measured as the length of time between a citizen call for service and an on-scene response by police. A faster response is considered more desirable, increasing the likelihood of an on-scene or near-scene apprehension of an offender and preventing citizen dissatisfaction with police. Rapid response is strongly tied to the idea of random preventive patrol, because patrol cars randomly dispersed throughout any geographic area are in a better position to respond quickly to calls wherever they may occur. It is true that rapid response matters in some cases, particularly those in which the police are notified while the crime is in progress. However, research has shown that rapid response does not itself influence citizen satisfaction or increase the probability of arrest in most cases.

One of the underlying assumptions of rapid response is that a faster response time increases the likelihood of an on-scene or near-scene arrest. If the police arrive quickly at the scene of a crime, the criminal might be thwarted in his or her efforts to complete the crime and/or will have little time to flee the scene. Consequently, a rapid response enhances police effectiveness by increasing the probability of apprehension. Although a rapid response certainly leads to an on-scene or near-scene arrest in some cases, particularly when the time between the offense and the citizen call to the police is minimized, research conducted since the 1970s has shown that a quick response is unrelated to apprehension in the vast majority of cases. Why is rapid response largely unrelated to apprehension probability? In many cases, the crime is discovered when the victim awakens, returns home from school or work, or some other similar situation. In these cases—often property crimes such as burglaries, larcenies, or automobile thefts—it is very unlikely that a response, however fast, will lead to an on-scene or near-scene arrest because the offense was likely committed some time before and the offender has long since fled the scene.

In other cases, the victim may indeed witness the criminal act in progress or be personally involved (e.g., as the victim of an attack). But for any number of reasons, including injury, disorientation, or lack of access to a telephone, there is often a delay in reporting the crime to law enforcement authorities. As a result, the response time, generally only several minutes or less if the police are notified while the crime is in progress, is much greater when the time lag between the time of crime commission and the time of crime reporting is taken into account. In these cases, the offender has likely fled the scene, negating any influence rapid response might have on the probability of apprehension. Response time can vary from place to place and can even vary within a specific jurisdiction. Numerous factors can contribute to the time it takes from the initial call for service to the time an officer arrives. Weather; traffic conditions; the caseload; staffing levels; available patrol cars; and the distance from the responding officer to the scene—which, in some cases, such

as Indian reservations, can be substantial—all contribute to response time.

Even if rapid response is unlikely to lead to an arrest in most cases, intuitively, response time should be inversely related to citizen satisfaction with the police; the greater the length of time before the police arrive on scene, the less favorable the citizen's view of the police. Although appealing, this widely held view has not generally withstood empirical scrutiny. Citizen satisfaction is influenced less by the actual response time (e.g., number of minutes between call for service and on-scene arrival) and more by the police department's ability to meet citizen expectations of response time. Citizens prefer a response time that meets their own expectations of how long it should take the police to respond. Dissatisfaction is produced when the actual response time exceeds the citizen's expectations. Conversely, citizens are likely to be satisfied with the police when there is congruence between actual police response time and the citizen's expected response time, or when the actual response time is faster than the expected response time. These findings suggest that police agencies should provide citizens with estimates of response time and work to meet those expectations.

Again, it should be emphasized that, despite the empirical findings discussed above, rapid response is still important for several classes of calls for service, such as those related to violent crimes and those involving crimes in progress. The recognition of this distinction between calls where rapid response might matter and those where a rapid response would not likely matter has led to several law enforcement innovations related to response time. Some agencies have experimented with or have implemented differential response practices where calls for service are screened and sorted. Those calls requiring a rapid response are dispatched accordingly, whereas others are dealt with using a variety of alternative techniques, such as taking reports over the phone or scheduling appointments with the victim. Other agencies have adopted nonemergency numbers (e.g., 3-1-1) to be used as alternatives to the traditional 9-1-1 emergency number. These innovations reflect knowledge that has been generated since the 1970s and attempt to satisfy the needs of citizens who require a rapid police response and those who do not.

*Matthew J. Giblin*

*See also* Calls for Service; Patrol Methods, Tactics, and Strategies

## For Further Reading

Brandl, S. G., & Horvath, F. (1991). Crime-victim evaluation of police investigative performance. *Journal of Criminal Justice, 19*(3), 109–121.

Cordner, G. W., Greene, J. R., & Bynum, T. S. (1983). The sooner the better: Some effects of police response time. In R. R. Bennett (Ed.), *Police at work: Policy issues and analysis* (pp. 145–164). Beverly Hills, CA: Sage.

Hirschel, D., Lumb, R., & Johnson, R. (1998). Victim assessment of the police response to burglary: The relative effects of incident, police action, outcome, and demographic variables on citizen satisfaction. *Police Quarterly, 1*(4), 1–20.

Larson, R. C., & Cahn, M. F. (1981). *Synthesizing and extending the results of police patrol studies.* Cambridge, MA: Public Systems Evaluation.

Pate, T., Ferrara, A., Bowers, R. A., & Lorence, J. (1976). *Police response time: Its determinants and effects.* Washington, DC: Police Foundation.

Percy, S. L. (1980). Response time and citizen evaluation of police. *Journal of Police Science and Administration, 8*(1), 75–86.

Spelman, W., & Brown, D. K. (1984). *Calling the police: Citizen reporting of serious crime.* Washington, DC: National Institute of Justice.

# ⟨⟩ RESTORATIVE JUSTICE

Restorative justice is an alternative paradigm for justice that contrasts with the traditional values and procedures of the criminal justice system. An immense variety of programs operate under the restorative mantle, and characterizing them with across-the-board language is insufficient. But for the most part, these programs differ from the traditional criminal justice system in many assumptions and practices, and they can best be defined by reference to those differences.

## Definitions of Crime

Traditional criminal justice represents crime as a violation of the laws of the state. Criminal accusations are claims made by the state (through its prosecutors) that the criminal is guilty of a violation of the law, and thus is subject to penalties imposed by the state. Restorative justice sees crimes as problems or conflicts between people, one of whom is a wrongdoer and the other a victim. The purpose of the restorative justice process is to identify the sources and consequences of the problem or conflict, and to rectify them.

## Definitions of Justice

Traditional criminal justice holds that justice is served when those who are guilty of crimes are punished for them fairly, according to the law. Restorative justice holds that justice prevails when the wrongdoer accepts the wrongfulness of the conduct, recognizes its harmful consequences for the victim, and undertakes to restore the victim's losses so that the harmful consequences can be undone.

## Participants in the Justice Process

Under traditional criminal justice, the state is the accuser and the defendant is the adversary. The two engage in a trial in which the state is forced to prove the accusation. The role of the victim arises only after the case has been proven in trial, and the role of the community is to determine the laws under which the accusation will be pressed by the state. In restorative justice, the accused and the victim have active roles, in which they are expected to describe the antecedents and consequences of the criminal event, and provide a "human" view of the facts of the crime. The community also has a role to present to the accused the community-level costs of criminal conduct, and to present to the victim a commitment to restore the losses the victim has experienced. The state is responsible for managing the process by which each participant's views and values are presented and received by the others.

## Practices Used to Adjudicate Accusations

Traditional criminal justice resolves criminal accusation through a trial, in which carefully restrictive rules of evidence and testimony are used to structure a serial interrogation that results in a verdict of guilt or innocence. In practice, trials are rare in most jurisdictions, and instead, a series of inducements is offered to the defendant to waive the right to an evidentiary trial by pleading guilty and accepting the state's right to impose a punishment. By contrast, there are several different types of restorative justice processes, varying in degree of formality and procedural regularity. But all restorative justice processes have three aspects that set them apart from traditional criminal justice approaches. First, what people are allowed to say is less formally restricted in style and content than a traditional trial. People are expected to speak from personal experience rather than "give testimony," and the rules that apply to what may be said are considerably relaxed. Second, there is no jury to determine guilt, for restorative process begins with an assumption that the defendant accepts responsibility for the criminal act itself. Third, the process is conversational and informal, not legalistic and adversarial.

## Priorities for Programs and Strategies and Results

The programmatic priority for traditional criminal justice is the imposition of a just penalty on the guilty. There is also a secondary concern for crime control, especially the direct control of the convicted criminal. Restorative justice seeks to find strategies that will restore the victim's losses from the crime and, ultimately, enable the offender to be restored to full citizenship. Most programs emphasize amelioration of problems instead of control of the convicted.

Restorative justice programs have been offered on a very limited basis for decades. Early restorative justice programs were developed by religious organizations (such as the Mennonites and Amish in New York State and the Quakers of Pennsylvania), but there has also been a long-standing tradition of the restorative philosophy among native peoples in former colonies, such as the United States, Canada, New Zealand, South Africa, and Australia. The growing harshness of the traditional criminal justice system in the last quarter of the 20th century led reformers who were troubled by this increasingly

draconian system of justice to turn to new models for inspiration. The restorative programs of religious groups and native peoples came to symbolize a completely different way of thinking about crime and justice, and among critics of the justice system, this alternative began to grow in importance.

Restorative justice remained a fringe idea with little serious interest among the criminal justice community for most of the 1970s and 1980s. But in the 1990s, mainstream thinkers began to contemplate restorative justice with new enthusiasm, and the idea has since become an accepted alternative strategy, or at least an idea, although restorative justice programs still are not considered mainstream.

For the most part, existing restorative justice programs are limited to low-level crimes and nonserious criminals. They operate as options that victims and offenders may choose, although the traditional criminal justice system remains the backup for restorative justice strategies that do not succeed.

The infrequent application of restorative justice strategies for serious crime and criminals has led some to believe that it has limited value. Some reformers, however, have begun to experiment with restorative justice for serious crimes, including murder, and a growing body of evaluations has provided positive results, including greater satisfaction for all parties to the criminal event—victims, offenders, and community representatives—and has led to a lower rate of repeat crime. With such results, experimentation with restorative justice as an alternative to traditional criminal justice is sure to continue.

*Todd R. Clear*

## For Further Reading

Braithwaite, J. (1989). *Crime, shame and reintegration.* New York: Cambridge University Press.

Clear, T., & Cadora, E. (2003). *Community justice.* Belmont, CA: Wadsworth.

Daly, K. (2002). Restorative justice: The real story. *Punishment & Society, 4*(1), 55–79.

Karp, D., & Clear, T. (2002). *What is community justice? Case studies of restorative and community justice.* Thousand Oaks, CA: Sage.

Umbreit, M., Vos, B., & Coates, R. (2002). *Victims of severe violence meet offenders: Restorative justice through dialogue.* Monsey, NY: Criminal Justice Press.

Wright, M., & Galaway, B. (Eds.). (1989). *Mediation and criminal justice: Victims, offenders and community.* London: Sage.

## ✌ RIOTS/DEMONSTRATIONS (RESPONSE TO)

Riots and demonstrations, although sporadic, have been a constant throughout American history. Not surprisingly, local and state authorities, and even the federal government, have struggled repeatedly to suppress these forms of popular unrest. Perhaps the earliest response to riots and demonstrations involved the military.

In 1794, George Washington mobilized an army of approximately 13,000—as large as the one that had defeated the British—to suppress violent demonstrations by Pennsylvania farmers angered at heightened federal excise taxes on whiskey. When confronted with this overwhelming military force, dissent dwindled, thereby establishing the military as an effective riot-suppression tool, one that would be used again and again throughout American history.

Although the use of the military to quell riots continued into the 20th century, the general burden of responding to riots and demonstrations shifted gradually to local police departments. The first police training in riot control occurred in the aftermath of the Astor Place Riot in New York City in 1849. During this riot, which was caused by the scheduled performance of an unpopular British actor in New York, a mob overwhelmed 250 police, resulting in the deployment of the military. Two divisions of soldiers fired into the crowd of more than 10,000, resulting in 23 deaths and calls for more humane forms of suppressing demonstrations in the United States, among them the use of clubs rather than firearms to subdue crowds.

Professional training of police in riot control proved its worth during the Civil War, when massive riots broke out, again in New York, over the conscription of men into the Union Army. Drilled in military tactics but refraining from the use of deadly force, a contingent of 200 New York metropolitan police officers routed a mob of more than 2,000. Although federal troops eventually had to be called to quell the violence, the success of the New York police set the stage for using local law enforcement as the primary tool for quelling popular unrest in the United States.

To facilitate this role, police departments began to develop specific technologies for crowd control. In the 1870s and 1880s, mounted police became a popular modality of dispersing crowds. In the aftermath of World War I, tear gas became widespread. In 1926, the New York City Police Department founded its Emergency Service Division, one of the country's first riot squads.

Interest in riot technology surged during the 1960s, when city after city succumbed to widespread rioting, most of it in heavily African American neighborhoods. These riots, beginning with a 6-day riot in the Watts neighborhood of Los Angeles, forced municipalities to reevaluate crowd control techniques, basic police procedure, and even structural problems that exacerbated race- and class-related tensions, among them lack of educational opportunity and jobs. Several ground-breaking studies of riots emerged, first among them the McCone Commission report on the rioting in Watts. Second, and perhaps even more important, the Kerner Commission Report on urban unrest in general, published in 1968. Although both reports drew criticism, they elevated the riot as a topic of serious policy interest.

They also sought to create a general theory of riot control. The Kerner Commission report, for example, stressed the importance of mounting a rapid, overwhelming response, noting that "sufficient manpower is a prerequisite for controlling potentially dangerous crowds; the speed with which it arrives may well determine whether the situation can be controlled." The Kerner report also stressed the use of nonlethal force, particularly gas.

The use of gas as a means of crowd control has continued and has been augmented by more sophisticated techniques, including marking dyes, sticky tapes, adhesive blobs, and liquid foam, all designed to immobilize rioters. Riots in Los Angeles and in a number of other cities in 1992, triggered by the acquittal of police officers for the beating of

Rodney King, an African American male, led to a resurgence of interest in rioting, particularly after the publication of a study on the causes of the riots known as the Webster Report. The Webster Report stressed a constant police presence and the establishment of a command and control center in the field. It also recommended containing areas of unrest by limiting access, and then pacifying smaller segments of each area.

These conclusions were reinforced nearly a decade later when, in 2001, massive rioting erupted in Cincinnati, again over police procedure in heavily black neighborhoods. To address this, Cincinnati police sought not only new methods of riot control, but proactive measures aimed at improving the image of the police in the community, high-profile walking patrols among them. Although many of the riots that have occurred involve race, there are other examples in recent years, such as Seattle in 1999, that center on public policy concerning trade, the environment, and other issues. Conflicts with police in these situations often involve issues of crowd control and the tactics employed by the police and the demonstrating group, both of which continue to evolve.

*Anders Walker*

*See also* Christopher Commission, Crown Heights
    Report, McCone Commission, Race Relations

### For Further Reading

Federal Bureau of Investigation. (1992). *Prevention and control of civil disturbance: Time for review.* Quantico, VA: FBI Academy.

## ᘿᘀ RURAL POLICE

Police agencies in nonmetropolitan counties, counties with fewer than 50,000 people and that are not immediately adjacent to and economically dependent upon larger metropolitan areas, include sheriffs' offices with countywide jurisdiction and relatively small municipal police departments. In the United States, these nonmetropolitan departments outnumber departments in metropolitan counties by about 1,700 agencies.

It is difficult to provide a simple description of rural police while also recognizing that rural areas vary tremendously from one part of the country to the next. For example, some sections of Appalachia have extreme levels of violent crime, whereas other rural areas have relatively little. Many nonmetropolitan counties are steeped in poverty, and others are relatively wealthy. Parsimony demands that the current discussion focus on the typical or average rural agency, recognizing that not all rural areas are alike.

There is a public perception that rural areas have little crime and that rural policing is not "real" police work, that it is easy and safe compared with the dangers of urban policing. Although the overall crime rate is lower, rural crime is still a problem. Drug use and domestic violence rates are similar to those in cities, and methamphetamine and marijuana production occurs more often than in cities. At the same time, rural police work may be substantially more demanding and more dangerous than urban policing, and will often be performed with relatively fewer resources. On average, per-officer annual expenditures for rural police are about one half those of urban police, and in some jurisdictions, rural police work without benefit packages. It is not unusual for rural police to pay for their own weapons and uniforms, and job applicants who have already paid for state-mandated training often have an edge in hiring.

Rural police are poorly positioned to demand better pay and resources because they often work in economically weak areas with small tax bases, and only about a quarter of rural police agencies are unionized. In many jurisdictions, rural police must also contend with the issue of geography, in that they are often responsible for large areas. The average county in Arizona, for example, is about the size of New Jersey. This can mean long response times and long waits for backup.

Rural departments tend to be small. The typical nonmetropolitan municipal department has three officers, and about 80% of rural municipal departments have fewer than 10 officers. Small budgets, small numbers of officers, and large geographic areas mean that rural police often patrol alone and without nearby backup. One national survey found that in rural agencies, an average of 60% of domestic violence calls were responded to with only one officer—something few urban departments would even consider. To compound the problem, in-service training for rural police is often limited, both by budget constraints and by the reality that sending an officer away for 1 or 2 weeks of training can cause hardships for those officers who remain in a three-person department in which citizens still expect the department to fully respond to their needs.

Small departments mean that rural police are more likely to be generalists. Rural chiefs, for example, often spend a substantial portion of their time on patrol, and rural agencies may not have the luxury of having officers who specialize in juvenile cases, traffic, or investigation. There are small-town chiefs whose duties include putting up Christmas lights on city streets and checking on chemicals in the water treatment plant. In many rural areas, the police are the only social service agency available 24 hours a day, 7 days a week.

Rural policing is not only demanding but also more dangerous. The rate at which rural officers are killed in the line of duty is about double that of the largest cities.

Despite these handicaps, rural police do a better job of solving crime. For every major index offense, clearance rates (the percentage of crimes solved through an arrest) are higher in rural agencies than in urban agencies. For example, in rural areas, about 78% of murders are solved through an arrest, whereas in the largest cities, only about 57% are solved. Despite substantial advances in technology and in the science of criminal investigation, homicide clearance rates in the largest cities have dropped substantially over the past 40 years, but have dropped only slightly in rural areas.

Part of the success of rural police may be attributed to their familiarity with the citizens. It is common for rural police to live in the community they police and to interact with citizens outside of their formal police role, such as in churches, grocery stores, and civic organizations. In addition, rural police work is highly public and visible. The citizen stopped for speeding may well ask, "Why am I getting a ticket when you didn't give one to Fred last week?" Familiarity and visibility may make rural police agencies more accountable to their public. Accountability is enhanced by the fact that sheriffs may be voted out of office and municipal chiefs can be dismissed by the city council, often at will and with little notice. All of this may help explain why rural citizens have a more positive view of their police than do urban residents. For example, urban citizens are three times more likely than rural citizens to believe their police engage in brutality and corruption. Given their superiority in crime fighting and in their relationship with the public, it might be argued that a better understanding of rural police agencies may be useful for improving policing in general.

*Ralph A. Weisheit*

## For Further Reading

Thurman, Q. C., & McGarrell, E. F. (Eds.). (2003). *Community policing in a rural setting* (2nd ed.). Cincinnati, OH: Anderson.

Websdale, N. (1998). *Rural woman battering and the justice system.* Thousand Oaks, CA: Sage.

Weisheit, R. A., Falcone, D. N., & Wells, L. E. (1999). *Crime and policing in rural and small-town America.* (2nd ed.). Prospect Heights, IL: Waveland.

# S

## ❧ SCHOOL CRIME/ SECURITY/RESPONSE

Crime in the schools first became evident to law enforcement and school personnel as early as the 1950s. By the 1960s, state and local authorities viewed school safety as an important goal, but eventually, this goal became secondary in light of budget constraints and other salient police agendas. Schools were faced with a choice as to whether they would incorporate a police presence into the educational environment or leave discipline up to existing staff by expanding their duties. Before the mid-1970s, police were contacted mostly in response to specific incidents at local schools. Since then, preventive efforts combining police and educators became necessary in the face of a growing crime rate in schools. In the final decades of the 20th century, the heightened visibility of youth gangs, juvenile gun violence, and school shootings saturating the media prompted state and local law enforcement to permanently partner with schools and communities to address school crime in more innovative and collaborative ways.

Although media coverage of school crime may lead to a perception that schools are dangerous places, school crime, particularly that involving serious violence, is currently on the decrease in most states and localities. Violent victimization has never been considered common in most school settings, although even minor threats and bullying can admittedly have a profound effect on students' perceptions of crime. Fear of crime at school can also affect a student's ability to succeed academically, despite low incidence of actual crime. The true extent of victimization is unknown, because many crimes go unreported by students. Theft remains the most steady and frequent crime committed on school grounds across the states, with drug possession often found as well. Even when crime in certain schools is high, the school may simply mirror the community in many of these localities, with the home and the neighborhood remaining places much more likely to experience violence.

Recognizing that a few schools in districts across the nation do have a serious problem with crime and violence, the majority of schools deal with problems more commonly associated with disorder, such as vandalism, horseplay, rule violation, disruptive behavior, bullying, and truant teenagers loitering in or near the school. The necessity of evaluating the extent of intervention in each particular state and locality is important in maintaining the least invasive police presence in the educational setting while also minimizing delinquent activity that could prompt fear, create a disorderly climate that promotes higher levels of crime, or damage the learning environment.

The use of technology, such as metal detectors and security cameras, as well as the restructuring of the physical environment in the school, such as allowing only one entry point, have become popular in some states and local schools. This target-hardening approach may be a deterrent for weapons and prevent some crime, but it does have drawbacks. In some schools, it can take up to 45 minutes for the students to enter school in the morning, with a resulting consequence of tardiness, missed instruction, and failing grades. Studies find that low academic success may contribute to delinquent behavior and criminal careers, so one should keep in mind that some target-hardening approaches may counteract the initial goal. Although some of the larger urban schools may require target hardening, the right to privacy is compromised with this type of intervention when used in districts that have low levels of weapon-related crime. There remain, however, schools in which students are contending with fear on a daily basis. Although they are rare, mass shootings like that of Columbine High School in Littleton, Colorado, in 1999 have caused police to rethink their strategies and tactics when dealing with an attack that is occurring. School resource officers (SROs)—police in the school setting— were introduced in the 1950s. Although their popularity faded somewhat during the 1980s and most of the 1990s, the Department of Justice introduced the COPS in Schools program as part of its Office of Community Oriented Policing Services in 2000. Part of this initiative consisted of hiring almost 600 SROs in communities throughout the states. The roles, duties, and training of SROs differ in each state and local jurisdiction, but having law enforcement within the school continues to offer a workable solution to improving and maintaining safety and reducing fear in the learning environment. SROs bring the concept of community policing into the school. This concept considers the community and draws on collaborative efforts with parents, school administrators, educators, and social services. President Clinton introduced the Safe Schools/ Healthy Students Initiative in 1999, administered by the U.S. Departments of Education and Health and Human Services, and the criminal justice system, calling for an integrated approach to combating school crime and promoting healthy students. On the tail of the Safe and Drug-Free Schools and Communities Act of 1994, 54 local communities devised a new plan to help ensure a safe school environment and provide prevention programs focused on drug and alcohol abuse, violence, strengthening of families, and mental health. In addition, early intervention programs were addressed, as was educational reform and policies for safe schools.

This public health approach had its third evaluation component completed in 2003. Most successful school safety programs are comprehensive and include the particular needs of that locality and state. Intensive planning and assessment are necessary, as are considerations of the physical, social, and cultural aspects of the school and the community. Law enforcement must collaborate with school officials not only in response to juvenile crime, but also in prevention. Students should have active involvement in promoting a safe school. The schools are the top source for police in identification of juveniles at risk, although profiling violence-prone students remains controversial. The Family Educational Rights and Privacy Act depicts what information the school can legally share with law enforcement about particular students. Successful programs have a problem-solving component as well. Some of the many programs that have shown success are The School Safety Program, sponsored by the Police Executive Forum; I Can Problem Solve; Positive Alternative Thinking Strategies; and Positive Action Through Holistic Education.

Finally, in the current retributive climate, many local schools have now adopted zero-tolerance policies, consistently expelling students for weapons on school grounds and violent assaults. Law enforcement and the criminal justice system have followed with harsher punishment for juveniles. States and communities show wide differences in alternative school programs and detention settings for these students with varying success. Although "just deserts" may be an acceptable justification for zero tolerance, effective deterrence has not been demonstrated with that goal, and public safety could be compromised with expelled students now on the street. Collaborative preventive and rehabilitative measures do show success with juvenile offenders in a well-structured school setting, and law enforcement continues to benefit from these measures.

*Holly Hurban*

*See also* Campus Policing, Juvenile Crime/Programs/
Units, Truancy

## For Further Reading

Elliot, D. S., Hamburg, B. A., & Williams, K. R. (1998). *Violence in American schools.* New York: Cambridge University Press.

Kaufman, P., Chen, X., Choy, S. P., Chandler, K. A., Chapman, C. D., Rand, M. R., & Ringel, C. (1998). *Indicators of school crime and safety, 1999.* Washington, DC: U.S. Departments of Education and Justice.

Kenney, D. J., & Watson, T. S. (1998). *Crime in the schools.* Washington, DC: Police Executive Research Forum.

http://ojjdp.ncjrs.org

## ᘇ SEARCH AND SEIZURE

The words "search and seizure" are associated with the Fourth Amendment to the U.S. Constitution, which prohibits "unreasonable searches and seizures." These words presuppose state action; that is, the Fourth Amendment is applicable only if a law enforcement agent or a private citizen acting at the behest of the police conducted the search or seizure.

The U.S. Supreme Court currently defines the Fourth Amendment term *search* as a police intrusion upon a legitimate or reasonable expectation of privacy. A mere subjective belief that an activity or object is private is insufficient to trigger Fourth Amendment protection. The expectation of privacy must be one that, in the view of the courts, society acknowledges. Thus, police rummaging through trash placed at curbside in closed opaque containers is not considered a search in the Fourth Amendment sense, because the Supreme Court has concluded that there is no reasonable expectation of privacy in discarded trash (*California v. Greenwood*, 1988). By contrast, the courts afford the interior of a home maximal protection from police intrusion, and in the absence of exigent circumstances, demand advance judicial approval for home entries.

The definition of *seizure* depends on whether it is a person or property being seized. Property is seized when there is meaningful interference with an individual's possessory interest in the item. This could include removing the object from an individual's possession, destroying it, or securing premises (such as a residence) by restricting access to it. Merely moving an object to examine it is ordinarily not a seizure.

A person is seized if he or she is rendered physically incapable of leaving the scene, or when, in view of all of the circumstances, a reasonable person would believe that he or she is not free to leave. Whereas an arrest is a seizure, not every seizure is an arrest. A person could be briefly detained (seized) by the police and be released rather than arrested. Furthermore, not all confrontations between private citizens and police are seizures. A mere nonforcible approach to a person, along with the asking of questions, is not a seizure. On the other hand, if the police make a show of authority, such as an order to stop or the display of a weapon, and if the individual submits to that authority, he or she will be considered seized.

Whether or not someone or something is searched or seized is significant in determining the applicability of the Fourth Amendment and the limitations it imposes on law enforcement agents. In the absence of a search or seizure, the police are not required to secure a warrant or to respect Fourth Amendment law governing warrantless searches and seizures. Evidence obtained by the police in such circumstances is not subject to the exclusionary rule, which is the remedy for Fourth Amendment violations.

By contrast, where the police conduct is deemed a search or seizure, the Fourth Amendment is triggered, and evidence secured in violation of its mandates (i.e., secured without a warrant or without observing the rules of warrantless searching and seizing) may be deemed inadmissible against the defendant whose person or property was searched or seized. In short, Fourth Amendment rules apply only to Fourth Amendment events, and intrusions by private citizens, or police intrusions that do not implicate legitimate privacy expectations, are nonevents insofar as the Fourth Amendment is concerned.

## ORIGINS OF THE FOURTH AMENDMENT

An examination of the history of search and seizure, which is really a history of the Fourth Amendment, reveals that the use of the judiciary to restrict law enforcement agents has ancient origins, but the effective use of the courts through the imposition of an evidentiary exclusion rule is a relatively recent development. The Fourth Amendment to the U.S. Constitution reads as follows:

The right of the people to be secure in their persons, houses, papers, and effects, against unreasonable searches and seizures, shall not be violated, and no Warrants shall issue, but upon probable cause, supported by Oath or affirmation, and particularly describing the place to be searched, and the persons or things to be seized.

In the middle of the 18th century, the English colonies of North America, which later became the United States, were subjected to various trade restrictions by England. To enforce these laws, search warrants were issued. The colonists objected strenuously to these general warrants on the grounds that they were nonspecific as to the subjects of the search, a return (to the court) on the warrant was not required, and any British subject could execute them. The authority of any person to assist in the search—the warrants were called writs of assistance—was particularly galling to the colonists and became the focus of the famous argument of James Otis, Jr. (1725–1783), a Massachusetts attorney, against the writs. Otis, who represented outraged Boston merchants, lost the case (in 1761), but was so stirring in his defense of privacy that John Adams, writing years later, asserted that "American independence was then and there born."

Precedent more favorable to privacy, or at least to private property, was issued in England, where *Entick v. Carrington* (1765) held, in a case of seditious libel, that a general warrant to seize and carry away personal papers was illegal and void. *Entick* greatly influenced American thinking about search and seizure law, and was relied upon by the U.S. Supreme Court in *Boyd v. United States* (1886), discussed below.

After they declared their independence (1776), the American states adopted for their constitutions the immediate forerunners of the Fourth Amendment. The first to use the phrase "unreasonable searches and seizures" was the Massachusetts Declaration of Rights (1780), the 14th Article of which said the following:

Every subject has a right to be secure from all unreasonable searches, and seizures, of his person, his houses, his papers, and all his possessions. All warrants, therefore, are contrary to this right, if the cause or foundation of them be not previously supported by oath or affirmation, and if the order in the warrant to a civil officer, to make search in suspected places, or to arrest one or more suspected persons, or to seize their property, be not accompanied with a special designation of the persons or objects of search, arrest, or seizure; and no warrant ought to be issued but in cases, and with the formalities prescribed by the laws.

Note that the text of the Massachusetts provision, as of the Fourth Amendment, has two clauses. There is a general right against unreasonable searches and seizures, primarily intended to protect a person and his or her property from trespass by the authorities. In the Fourth Amendment, this clause was largely hortatory because the Amendment was not applicable to state or local governmental agents in the 18th century, and there was no exclusionary rule to enforce it.

The second clause establishes restrictions on warrants, reflecting the colonists' unhappy experiences with general warrants. Today, the Supreme Court prefers that the police obtain warrants, while recognizing that much police conduct (e.g., searches of an arrested person) will not or cannot be authorized in advance by a court.

There was little court activity respecting the Fourth Amendment throughout most of the 19th century. This was a reflection of the lack of any fully developed concept that the judiciary should restrain the police. It also reflected the fact that policing in the United States was, and still is, primarily a matter of local responsibility, and the Bill of Rights, including the Fourth Amendment, had no applicability to state or local governments. The most significant 19th-century Supreme Court case concerning the Fourth Amendment was *Boyd v. United States* (1886), which stressed the notion that the Amendment was intended to protect property, a perspective that came to be rejected in the 20th century. *Boyd* held that a court order to produce private papers was tantamount to a search and seizure, and that because the papers were not themselves contraband, the order violated the Fourth Amendment.

Four 20th-century developments radically altered the law of search and seizure. First was the imposition of the exclusionary remedy. Second was the application of the Amendment and its exclusionary remedy to the states through a process known as "incorporation." The third major event was the establishment of the expectation of privacy doctrine. The final event was the creation by the Supreme Court of Fourth Amendment rules covering warrantless searches and seizures.

## THE EXCLUSIONARY RULE AND INCORPORATION

In *Weeks v. United States* (1914), the Supreme Court held for the first time that the Fourth Amendment requires that evidence seized in violation of its strictures may not be used to convict the person whose rights had been violated. Thus was launched a controversy that lasted for most of the century and lingers still. Proponents of the exclusionary rule (or suppression doctrine) rely primarily on the lack of equally effective alternative enforcement mechanisms, the principal one being civil suits against the offending police. Opponents of the rule are skeptical that it actually restrains the police, but whether or not it does, they see it as a hindrance to the administration of justice because of its benefits for the factually guilty defendant.

The *Weeks* decision had little practical impact, since in 1914, the Fourth Amendment and the suppression rule still had no application to local police officers. Only state constitutions and ordinary state laws could restrict municipal police, who constitute the overwhelming majority of law enforcement personnel in the United States. By the 1940s, however, approximately one third of the states had adopted state constitutional exclusionary rules to enforce state law versions of the Fourth Amendment.

In *Wolf v. Colorado* (1949), the Supreme Court held that the privacy that is at the core of the Fourth

Amendment was enforceable against the states, including municipal police, through the due process clause of the Fourteenth Amendment. This foreshadowed Supreme Court decisions in the 1960s, which held that selected rights established by the Bill of Rights were incorporated into due process. (The Fourteenth Amendment expressly limits state and, by implication, local government: "nor shall any State deprive any person of life, liberty, or property, without due process of law.") Significantly, however, *Wolf* did not consider the exclusionary remedy to be a part of the Fourth Amendment core, and it was not incorporated.

The Supreme Court's incorporation decisions were momentous for American constitutional law because they compelled the states to honor rights that had previously been imposed by the Bill of Rights only upon the federal government. Incorporation was controversial, however, because, apparently contrary to principles of federalism, it reduced the authority of the states to determine their own criminal procedures. It also markedly expanded the power of the U.S. Supreme Court, which, through its authority to interpret the Constitution, could effectively determine rights and procedures for the entire nation.

In the 1960s, the Supreme Court, under the leadership of Chief Justice Earl Warren, embarked on a course of major reform of the American legal system. Among a series of decisions expanding civil rights and liberties was *Mapp v. Ohio* (1961), which, reversing in part *Wolf v. Colorado*, incorporated the Fourth Amendment exclusionary rule. As a consequence, every criminal court in the United States was compelled to enforce Fourth Amendment requirements by suppressing illegally obtained evidence. Pretrial "Mapp hearings," conducted before judges without juries, were needed to determine whether or not the police acted properly. If the Fourth Amendment was violated, the unlawfully seized evidence would have to be suppressed, even if the defendant obtained, through a reduction of the evidence against him, an acquittal or a better plea-bargaining position.

After 1970, when the judges who served on the Warren Court had retired or died, a more conservative Supreme Court under Chief Justices Warren Burger (1969–1986) and William Rehnquist (1986– ), became increasingly disenchanted with the Fourth Amendment exclusionary rule. In *United States v. Leon* (1984), the Court held that the rule is inapplicable when police act in good-faith reliance on a search warrant subsequently found to be defective. This "good faith exception" to the exclusionary rule does not apply to warrantless searches, however, which constitute the vast preponderance of searches by police.

## EXPECTATION OF PRIVACY

In addition to making the Fourth Amendment and its exclusionary rule applicable to the states, the Warren Court broadened the scope of the Amendment itself. Originally, and up to the middle of the 20th century, the Fourth Amendment was considered to be primarily protection of property. This was vividly illustrated by *Olmstead v. United States* (1928). In *Olmstead*, federal officers used wiretaps to intercept conversations, but never entered the homes or offices of the targets. The Supreme Court held that the wiretaps were not subject to Fourth Amendment limitations because the officers never trespassed into protected areas. This triggered a famous dissent from Justice Louis Brandeis, who argued that the Amendment protects intrusions upon the "right to be let alone," regardless of the means used to conduct the intrusion.

In 1967, in *Katz v. United States,* the Warren Court repudiated the trespass doctrine in favor of the "reasonable expectation of privacy" approach. The *Katz* case involved the recording of conversations made from a public telephone booth. The government argued that, as the recording device was placed outside the phone booth, there was no trespass into a constitutionally protected area. The Supreme Court held that the occurrence or not of a trespass was irrelevant; it was the privacy of the conversation that was protected. Justice John Marshall Harlan, concurring, provided the phrase that has since served as the standard for the application of the Fourth Amendment. Harlan discerned a "twofold requirement, first that a person have exhibited an actual (subjective) expectation of privacy and, second, that the expectation be one that society is prepared to recognize as 'reasonable.'"

Subsequently, the Supreme Court rendered a number of decisions in which it determined that the Fourth Amendment was or was not applicable, depending on whether or not the Justices recognized the expectation of privacy to be "reasonable." The *Katz* approach enabled the courts to apply the Amendment to situations, such as technologically sophisticated interceptions of conversations, which previously had been insulated from constitutional limitation by the trespass doctrine.

However, the expectation of privacy test also proved to be rather elastic. The Supreme Court under Chief Justices Burger and Rehnquist frequently held that there could be no reasonable expectation of privacy for activities exposed to members of the public. Thus, for example, bank transactions exposed to third-party bank personnel were denied Fourth Amendment protection (*United States v. Miller,* 1976).

## LAW OF WARRANTLESS SEARCHES

In addition to incorporating the Fourth Amendment and the exclusionary rule, and extending the scope of the Amendment to activities society (as understood by the Justices) deems private, the Supreme Court developed a series of protocols for the police to engage in warrantless searches and seizures. These activities cover a wide range of standardized police activities, including searches with the consent of the subject; searches incident to a lawful arrest; stationhouse inventory searches of an arrested person's possessions; inventories of lawfully seized vehicles; the so-called automobile exception to the warrant requirement; vehicle searches incident to the arrest of an occupant; protective stops and frisks; and administrative and regulatory inspections, including drug tests of certain categories of persons. This is not a complete list, but it gives a good idea of the breadth of the law's development.

As an illustration, consider the Court's ruling in *Chimel v. California* (1969), a leading case on searches incident to a lawful arrest. The Court recognized that it would have been wholly impractical to demand a warrant before police could search the person and area around an arrestee. On the other hand, it was clear that permitting wide-ranging postarrest searches in a home or office could subvert the warrant requirement normally applicable to investigations in such locations. As a result, the Court developed a rule for police conduct without a search warrant—a rule enforced by the threat of suppression of the evidence. The *Chimel* rule states that upon a lawful arrest, police may search the arrestee and the area under his or her immediate control, "construing that phrase to mean the area from within which he might gain possession of a weapon or destructible evidence." Thus was born the "grab area" rule for searches incident to arrest.

As already noted, there are a considerable number of such warrantless search protocols, generally designed for standardized law enforcement activities. Unfortunately, these rules may be difficult to apply with certainty because of the factually diverse circumstances faced by real-life police. So, for example, where is the grab area for an arrested motorist? Does it include the entire front seat of the vehicle? The rear seat? The glove compartment? And what if the occupant was removed from the vehicle and restrained so that he or she had no access to it? The confusion that arose from lower court attempts to answer these questions led the Supreme Court to create a special rule for vehicle arrests. *New York v. Belton* (1981) deemed the entire passenger compartment a grab area.

A second problem with warrantless search and seizure law is that the police must familiarize themselves with these rules (or rely on guidance from prosecutors), because they will not have the benefit of advance judicial approval. This leads not infrequently to miscalculations and suppressed evidence or pressures on police to offer perjured testimony at suppression hearings.

## RECENT DEVELOPMENTS

By the 1990s, the major principles of Fourth Amendment law had been established to the satisfaction of the Supreme Court. Consequently, it reviewed fewer and fewer Fourth Amendment cases each year. Application of these principles was left to the state courts, which had always had the lion's

share of responsibility for determining the lawfulness of police activity.

Perhaps ironically, some of the state supreme courts, believing that their counterpart in the federal system had not gone far enough in protecting defendants' rights, began relying once again on their state constitutions, in some cases construing them more broadly than the Fourth Amendment. For example, several states have repudiated the good faith exception to the exclusionary rule established in *United States v. Leon* (1984). The effect of these decisions is to apply state constitutional exclusionary rules to police conduct that is permissible under the U.S. Constitution. (Under well-established interpretation of the supremacy clause of the U.S. Constitution, the states may create broader rights based on state law, but they may not enforce narrower state rights, because to do so is to effectively veto federal rights.)

The massive increase in Fourth Amendment law and its application to local police from the 1960s to the 1980s has sometimes been described as part of a criminal justice revolution in the United States. In response, police departments throughout the country have established training components in the complex law of search and seizure, so as to prevent bungled investigations and their concomitant suppression of evidence. Defenders of the "revolution" claim that improved police training and fewer rights abuses are the great by-products of the Supreme Court's efforts. Critics believe that the cost in "breaks" for factually guilty criminals has been too high, and indeed, that the crime wave that began in the 1960s was in part attributable to the Court's permissive doctrines.

*Barry Latzer*

***See also*** Exclusionary Rules, Plain View Doctrine, Probable Cause, Search Warrants

## For Further Reading

Amar, A. R. (1994). Fourth Amendment first principles. *Harvard Law Review, 107,* 757–819.

Amsterdam, A. G. (1974). Perspectives on the Fourth Amendment. *Minnesota Law Review, 58,* 349–403.

Boyd v. United States, 116 U.S. 616 (1886).

Bradley, C. M. (1985). Two models of the Fourth Amendment. *Michigan Law Review, 83,* 1468–1501.

California v. Greenwood, 486 U.S. 35 (1988).

Chimel v. California, 395 U.S. 752 (1969).

Dressler, J. (2002). *Understanding criminal procedure* (3rd ed.). New York: LexisNexis.

Entick v. Carrington, 19 How.St.Tr. 1029 (1765).

Katz v. United States, 389 U.S. 347 (1967).

LaFave, W. (1996). *Search and seizure* (3rd ed.). St. Paul, MN: West.

Landynski, J. W. (1966). *Search and seizure and the Supreme Court: A study in constitutional interpretation.* Baltimore, MD: Johns Hopkins University Press.

Mapp v. Ohio, 367 U.S. 643 (1961).

New York v. Belton, 453 U.S. 454 (1981).

Olmstead v. United States, 277 U.S. 438 (1928).

Stewart, P. (1983). The road to Mapp v. Ohio and beyond: The origins, development and future of the exclusionary rule in search-and-seizure cases. *Columbia Law Review, 83,* 1365–1404.

United States v. Leon, 468 U.S. 897 (1984).

United States v. Miller, 425 U.S. 435 (1976).

Weeks v. United States, 232 U.S. 383 (1914).

Weinreb, L. W. (1974). Generalities of the Fourth Amendment. *University of Chicago Law Review, 42,* 47–85.

Wolf v. Colorado, 338 U.S. 25 (1949).

## ᴗᴗ SEARCH WARRANTS

A search warrant is a judicial order authorizing agents of the government to search a home or other place. A law enforcement officer seeking a warrant must generally file an application with a competent court. Among the warrant application materials submitted is an affidavit detailing the information known to the police that supports the allegation that a crime has been committed. A search warrant is issued at an ex parte hearing, meaning that the defendant does not have a right to attend or even know the hearing has taken place.

The Fourth Amendment of the U.S. Constitution provides most of the controlling principles regarding search warrants. The Amendment provides that

> the right of the people to be secure in their persons, houses, papers and effects, against unreasonable searches and seizures, shall not be violated; and no warrants shall issue, but upon probable cause, supported by oath or affirmation, and particularly describing the place to be searched, and the person or things to be seized.

The Supreme Court of the United States, having the power of interpreting the Constitution, has decided many cases regarding the Fourth Amendment. Those cases have spelled out exactly what is required for the issuance of a constitutionally valid search warrant.

## MAGISTRATE CHARACTERISTICS

A neutral and detached judicial officer must issue search warrants. The rationale is that the magistrate provides a buffer between the citizen and the police. Police officers, because of their duty to apprehend criminals, may become overzealous and reach incorrect conclusions about the existence of probable cause. Neutrality refers to the idea that the issuing magistrate can have no interest in the resolution of the case, or profit from the issuance of the warrant. For example, in *Connally v. Georgia* (1977), the Court said that a magistrate who was paid when he issued a warrant, and not paid when he failed to issue a warrant, was not a neutral magistrate. Similarly, the Supreme Court ruled in *Coolidge v. New Hampshire* (1971) that a state attorney general cannot issue warrants because, as the highest law enforcement official in the state, he or she is not neutral. In *Lo-Ji Sales, Inc. v. New York* (1979), the Court concluded that a magistrate who accompanied officers on the execution of the warrant and instructed them on which items could properly be seized compromised his neutrality, thus invalidating the warrant.

Although a magistrate must be neutral and detached, there is no requirement that the magistrate be an attorney or have any special legal training. In *Shadwick v. City of Tampa* (1972), the Court considered whether a municipal court clerk could issue search warrants. The critical question before the Court was the issue of whether a clerk was a magistrate for Fourth Amendment purposes. The Court ruled that the clerks, although not lawyers, worked within the judicial branch under supervision of municipal court judges and were qualified to make the determination of whether there is probable cause.

## DETERMINATION OF PROBABLE CAUSE

Because the police are considered biased in their ability to determine the existence of probable cause, the duty falls on the magistrate. Generally, officers seeking a warrant will submit an affidavit to the court containing all of the pertinent facts about a case known to the police. It is this information that the magistrate uses to determine if the evidence meets the probable cause standard.

If the police provide the magistrate with false information in the affidavit filed with the court in support of the warrant application, the defendant is not without remedy. If the defendant can make a showing that a false statement knowingly and intentionally, or with reckless disregard for the truth, was included by the police in the affidavit, and if the allegedly false statement is necessary to the finding of probable cause, the Fourth Amendment requires that a hearing be held at the defendant's request. This procedure, developed by the court in *Franks v. Delaware* (1978), is known as a Franks hearing. If the affidavit still contains sufficient information to establish probable cause when the false information is not considered, then the warrant is still valid. If that is not the case and the warrant is found to be invalid, then any evidence resulting from a search based on the invalid warrant cannot be used at trial.

One of the most difficult requirements of a search warrant to define is that it must describe the place to be searched with particularity. If the place to be searched is not specifically described, then the warrant is not valid. The reason for the difficulty in defining particularity is that it depends on the characteristics of the place to be searched. As a general rule, a warrant will be valid if there is sufficient information contained in the warrant to guide the police to the correct address. The things to be seized must also be described with particularity. Some law enforcement officers, in an effort to comply with the particularity requirement, list every conceivable thing that might, however remote the possibility, be uncovered during the search. This, too, is inappropriate. The use of catch-all descriptions in warrants is problematic.

## EXECUTION OF WARRANTS

The Fourth Amendment is silent regarding the actual execution of a search warrant. Most states, however, regulate the execution of search warrants by law enforcement with statutory provisions. The Court has ruled on some specific issues that arise during the execution of warrants, usually based on some established constitutional protection. For example, individuals generally cannot be searched just because they happen to be on the premises where a search is being executed. If however, there is some reason to believe that the individuals may be armed, then they can be frisked under the provisions outlined by the court in *Terry v. Ohio* (1968). Although those present generally cannot be searched unless the search of particular people is specified in the warrant, they can be detained while the search is conducted. The Court considered the matter of detaining residents during a search in *Michigan v. Summers* (1981). In this case, the Court determined that such detentions served three compelling government interests: They facilitate the orderly completion of the search, prevent flights in the event that incriminating evidence is discovered, and minimize the risk of harm to the officers executing the warrant.

## KNOCK AND ANNOUNCE

As a general rule, officers must give notice before entering private premises. This rule originated in common law and has been added to American constitutional law via the reasonableness requirement of the Fourth Amendment. In *Wilson v. Arkansas* (1995), the Court determined that the entry of a private home without giving notice was unreasonable, even though the officers had a valid warrant. There are exceptions to the knock and announce rule. In *Richards v. Wisconsin* (1997), the Supreme Court determined that if there was a reasonable suspicion that knocking and announcing their presence, under the particular circumstances, would be dangerous or futile, or would inhibit the effective investigation of the crime (such as destroying evidence), then the knock and announce rule could be legally ignored.

The Court has established that the decision not to knock and announce must be made on a case-by-case basis.

## SCOPE OF SEARCHES

Generally, a warrant that authorizes the search of a premises authorizes the search of any area in that premises that may contain the item described in the warrant. It is generally not permissible to search containers that could not possibly contain the listed item. In the case of homes, the scope of the search generally extends to the area around the house (curtilage), including yards and outbuildings. Automobiles within the curtilage are also subject to search, as long as the items specified in the warrant could reasonably be contained in them.

Under certain circumstances, items not specifically listed in a warrant may be seized. In *Coolidge v. New Hampshire* (1971), the Court stated that once a lawful search had begun, it would be inconvenient and dangerous to require the police to ignore some items while a warrant was obtained. The Court later specified that such a seizure was legal only if probable cause exists to believe that the objects to be seized constituted the fruits, instrumentalities, or evidence of a crime. Mere reasonable suspicion is not sufficient to extend a search beyond its scope. If officers do not regard the scope of the warrant when conducting a search pursuant to a warrant, then any evidence discovered as a result of the search may be excluded at trial.

## TECHNOLOGY AND REASONABLENESS

Early cases regarding the use of wiretaps and other technologies to gather evidence generally did not constitute a search for Fourth Amendment purposes. The Court decided these early cases on the basis that the police never actually trespassed on the defendant's premises, and only intangible things like conversations were seized. More recent decisions have been made on the reasonable expectation of privacy. It is difficult to predict whether the use of a new police technology that helps in gathering information will constitute a search until the Court actually rules on the issue. As a general rule, if the technology provides evidence that could

not have otherwise been obtained without physical intrusion into a constitutionally protected area, then a warrant is required.

*Adam J. McKee*

***See also*** Exclusionary Rules, Plain View Doctrine, Probable Cause, Search and Seizure

### For Further Reading

Connally v. Georgia, 429 U.S. 245 (1977).
Coolidge v. New Hampshire, 403 U.S. 443 (1971).
Franks v. Delaware, 438 U.S. 154 (1978).
Lo-Ji Sales, Inc. v. New York, 442 U.S. 319 (1979).
Michigan v. Summers, 452 U.S. 692 (1981).
Richards v. Wisconsin, 520 U.S. 385 (1997).
Shadwick v. City of Tampa, 407 U.S. 345 (1972).
Terry v. Ohio, 392 U.S. 1 (1968).
Wilson v. Arkansas, 515 U.S. 927 (1995).

# &#x2767; SERIAL MURDER INVESTIGATION

A serial murder investigation is generally initiated by an agency or group of agencies following the identification of a series or probable series of related homicides. This occurs in four different situations:

1. One or more unsolved murders are connected to the original case by victims, crime scenes, attacks, geography, or any actions or situations that convince investigators that they are dealing with a series. This was certainly the case when people were shot in and around Washington, DC, in the fall of 2002. That series of murders quickly became known as the "DC Sniper case."

2. A non-law enforcement source places enough pressure on an agency or group of agencies for a formal serial murder investigation. In the case of Baton Rouge, Louisiana, relatives of homicide victims convinced the police to check for similarities of DNA among the victims, which resulted in the arrest of Derek Todd Lee, who has been linked to seven homicide victims.

3. Through happenstance or a fluke, a serial murderer is revealed through routine police work in response to a seemingly unrelated criminal event. Ted Bundy was pursued in a stolen car and arrested

in Pensacola, Florida. Also, two Milwaukee police officers, on the evening of July 22, 1991, checked out a reported assault and handcuffing of a man, and had no idea what they would find in Jeffery Dahmer's apartment.

4. The event under investigation is considered unique, singular, and nonsequential until the suspect alerts the police to multiple acts by confessing to a number of homicides. When Henry Lee Lucas was arrested in Montague County, Texas, for violation of parole and suspicion of killing an 84-year-old woman, he began confessing to the killing of scores of people across the country and was subsequently convicted of 10 homicides.

Regardless of how a serial murder is identified, the undertaking of such an investigation poses numerous problems for the investigating agency.

## SEVEN MAJOR PROBLEMS OF A SERIAL MURDER INVESTIGATION

A review of serial murder investigations conducted in the United States, Canada, and England over the past decade, as well as recent investigations of serial murder in Australia, South Africa, Sweden, Poland, Russia, and Austria, reveals seven major problems common to such investigations:

1. Contending with and attempting to reduce linkage blindness

2. Making a commitment to a serial murder investigation

3. Coordinating investigative functions and actions

4. Managing large amounts of investigative information

5. Dealing with public pressure and limiting the adversarial nature of relations with the news media

6. Dealing with missing persons reports that result in homicides

7. Being aware of the "less-dead" as likely victims of serial killers

### Linkage Blindness

Often, law enforcement investigators do not see, are prevented from seeing, or make little attempt to see beyond their own jurisdictional responsibilities. The law enforcement officer's responsibility stops at the boundary of his or her jurisdiction except for hot pursuit. The very nature of local law enforcement in this country, and a police department's accountability and responsiveness to *its* jurisdictional clients—which isolate the department from the outside world—results in an agency not sharing information on unsolved murders with other agencies. The term, sometimes called *linkage blindness,* denotes this major problem of intergovernmental cooperation between law enforcement agencies and is unfortunately a somewhat common occurrence. The reasons for this lack of sharing are as varied and as numerous as the agencies; however, there seems to be a common basis for most of this conflict. The basis is a real or perceived violation of an agency's boundaries or geographical jurisdiction, or of the specific responsibilities of an agency to enforce specific laws over a wide geographical area. Agencies continually practice boundary maintenance in order to protect their jurisdiction from intruders—other police agencies moving onto their turf. There are also legal boundaries when it comes to sharing information. Serial killers can and do take advantage of these situations and, in many instances, continue to kill until cooperative agreements or arrangements are made among the opposing agencies. When such agreements or arrangements are made, resources can then be combined and information can be shared in order to investigate killings that cross jurisdictional boundaries.

Linkage blindness exemplifies the major weakness of our structural defenses against crime and our ability to control it. Simply stated, the exchange of investigative information among police departments in this country is very poor. Linkage blindness is the nearly total lack of sharing or coordinating of investigative information and the lack of adequate networking prevalent among today's law enforcement officers and their agencies. As a result, linkages between similar crime patterns through modi operandi or signatures are rarely established across geographic areas of the country. Although law enforcement agencies operate on information, they can fail to seek it out or share it with their counterparts in other agencies. As a result, the traveling killer becomes immune because of his or her mobility.

## Lack of Commitment

Given the public fear that can ensue, law enforcement administrators are sometimes reluctant in making a public commitment to initiate a serial murder investigation. They can be slow to admit that there is a serial killer running loose throughout their jurisdictions killing strangers at will. Serial killers make the police look bad. To commit to trying to catch one can make the police look inept in the public's eye.

Commitment not only brings police abilities, however misperceived by the public, under close scrutiny, but also means that one agency may have to work with at least one other, and frequently more than one other agency—and police agencies do not work well together. They are not trained to work together.

## Coordinating Investigative Functions and Actions

Because police agencies do not train together nor often work together on homicide investigations, when they are forced to work together because a criminal offender is committing crimes in a number of jurisdictions, the first question to arise invariably is "Who is in charge?" or "Who will get the credit for the arrest?" Unless this has been specifically worked out beforehand, determining who will lead the investigation takes a great deal of time. Mutual aid pacts are allowed in most states, as specified by state legislation. However, police agencies generally fail to take advantage of these laws in a timely manner.

An agency's commitment to a serial murder investigation means that an inordinate number of investigatory personnel will have to be reassigned to the effort. In addition, equipment will have to be dedicated, including vehicles, radios, and computers. Few agencies have the necessary contingency budgets to allow for such extra expenditures without seeking additional funds from the policymakers of their respective jurisdictions. An additional consideration is that the mass media will undoubtedly cause a great deal of chaos for the investigatory personnel assigned to the case. In some cases, the media become almost frenzied in their search for information on the investigation.

A serial murder investigation is a major and complicated effort that requires a tremendous amount of coordination. Police commanders must know the status of assigned personnel and be able to monitor their activities at all times. In other words, the left hand needs to know what the right hand is doing so that no mistakes are made and important pieces of information are acted on and not lost in the confusion of multiple tasks and different assignments.

## Managing Large Amounts of Investigative Information

In a serial murder investigation, the amount of information and data that is generated is almost always unmanageable without the aid of the computer. However, the problem is that most police departments use their computing machines simply as fast-retrieval file cabinets, not realizing the great potential of the computer in the 21st century. A fast electronic file drawer alone will almost certainly fail to provide timely and accurate information with the necessary speed for such an investigation.

In order to exploit the computer's ability to process information, the team of investigators must be able to cross-reference and retrieve aggregate data very rapidly. Command-level personnel who understand the need for such a capability may not be available to the agencies involved. Outside consultants may be required, but this has not always worked very smoothly in these sensitive and stress-filled investigations.

In addition, agencies may wish to use regional or state databases designed to assist them in a serial murder investigation. One such system is the Homicide Investigation and Tracking System (HITS) operated by the state of Washington. HITS provides three major services to law enforcement. First, it supplies information related to murder and predatory sexual assault cases, including incidents with similar characteristics, evidence, victimology, offender characteristics, modus operandi, associates, geography, and vehicles. It also provides identification of known murderers and sex offenders living in a particular community. Second, HITS permits analysis of murder cases to identify solvability factors, linkages, and statement verification.

Third, HITS provides investigators with advice and the names of experts who could possibly assist in their investigation.

## Public Pressure and Mass Media Pressure for Information

Most law enforcement agencies, although adequately prepared to withstand a great deal of public pressure to capture criminals and prevent crimes, are ill prepared to deal effectively with the mass media. The fact that serial murder investigations frequently involve more than one police jurisdiction only complicates the task of media relations. In some recent serial murder investigations, reporters have gone from one public source to another, seeking information about the investigation. Coordination with the detectives counterparts in the other agencies involved is a topic that is almost always neglected in training courses in police–media relations.

The result of intense mass media pressure added to public pressure is that the press comes to be viewed as an adversarial and intolerant critic of the investigatory effort and all personnel assigned. Therefore, a great deal of antagonism is generated between investigators and journalists, resulting in poor and sometimes slanted reporting of the progress and effectiveness of the investigatory efforts. However, it must be remembered that, whereas the media sometimes seem to get in the way of an investigation, in the final analysis, they are much more likely to have a positive effect than a negative one and are likely to bring witnesses forward who are useful to the investigation.

## Dealing With Missing Persons Reports That Result in Homicide

The problem any agency faces when a person goes missing is when to act. Recently, the Amber Alert system went into effect, eliminating one population from this question facing authorities. Another group, the "less-dead" (marginalized groups of society such as prostitutes or the homeless), should be acted upon immediately because statistically, individuals falling into this class are more likely to have disappeared because of foul play.

## Being Aware of the Less-Dead as Likely Victims of Serial Killers

When a victim of a homicide comes from a powerless and marginalized sector of our population, there is little pressure to solve the case and apprehend the killer. As other cases are assigned, the less-dead victims (the throwaways of our society) receive less and less priority. Without public or mass media pressure, these less-dead victims become less and less important. If the less-dead constitute most of the serial killer's victims, law enforcement agencies are inadvertently placing a low priority on solving a homicide that has a fairly high probability of being part of a serial killer's pattern, allowing the serial killer to kill and kill again.

## CONCLUSION

Because of the rarity of serial murder cases, most police agencies have little knowledge about serial murder, know little about the serial killer victim profiles, and have only limited knowledge of how police agencies have responded to serial murder investigations in the past. All agencies, regardless of their size, should have at least one person who is aware and keeps current on developments of serial murder.

*Steven A. Egger*

***See also*** Homicide Investigation; Interagency Cooperation . . . or Not; Missing Persons Investigations; Profiling, Criminal Personality; Profiling, Geographic

## For Further Reading

Egger, S. (2002). *The killers among us: An examination of serial murder and its investigation.* Upper Saddle River, NJ: Prentice Hall.

Hickey, E. (1997). *Serial murderers and their victims.* Belmont, CA: Wadsworth.

Holmes, R., & Holmes, S. (1998). *Serial murder.* Thousand Oaks, CA: Sage.

Lester, D. (1995). *Serial killers: The insatiable passion.* Philadelphia: Charles Press.

Levin, J., & Fox, J. (1994). *Overkill: Mass murder and serial killing exposed.* New York: Plenum.

Ressler, R. K., Burgess, A. W., & Douglas, J. E. (1988). *Sexual homicide: Patterns and motives.* Lexington, MA: Lexington Books.

# ✑ SEX CRIME INVESTIGATION

Sexual offenses differ from other criminal offenses in many ways, particularly in that they are private offenses that often take place in the home of the perpetrator and/or the victim. They are crimes of secrecy, rather than public crimes, and as such, sexual offenses are difficult to prevent. The police response is almost always one of control after the crime has been committed. There are some public attacks committed by strangers, yet these are not nearly as common as offenses committed by acquaintances or intimates. Because of the high level of secrecy involved in this type of offense, sex crimes are difficult to investigate.

## THE POLICE

There are two primary roles in the investigation of sex crimes: that of the police and that of the hospital collecting evidence. The police must conduct investigations and determine if there is probable cause to believe that a sexual offense did occur, and if so, who the perpetrator of the crime is. They must collect evidence and liaise with the prosecution to determine whether the evidence is sufficient to continue with a prosecution on the case.

Evidence in a sex crime comes from three main sources: the victim, the suspect, and the crime scene. Many police departments have formed Sex Crimes Units (alternatively called Special Victims Units) that are specially trained to investigate these offenses, because sex crimes are unique and often require specialized investigative skills. In most cases of sexual assault, whether the victims are children or adults, there are no witnesses to the offense. As such, it is pertinent for the police to interview the victim who is likely the only witness to the crime. Adult victims are often reluctant to speak to the police, because sexual assault is such an intrusive and personal offense. Therefore, it is helpful if the police are trained in interviewing victims of sexual assault sensitively, with an awareness of the victim's desire for privacy. In order to get the most accurate and thorough statement, the police may come across as interrogating the victim. The victim may interpret this as a lack of sensitivity, or that the police do not believe his or her story. Additionally, when relaying the account of the offense, the victim might forget details of the crime. The police should not consider this, or any emotional outbursts, the result of a false allegation but rather the effect of a severe trauma.

Child victims present a different set of difficulties. The police interviewer must be trained in interviewing children and have special skills in order to elicit truthful information from the child. The National Institute of Justice describes three main techniques used in questioning. First, the interviewer may use anatomically correct dolls, an approach that is beneficial in reducing stress, reducing vocabulary differences between children and adults, and reducing embarrassment for the child. However, the dolls may have an adverse effect by provoking negative emotions related to the abuse or contaminating the child's memories at the sight of the genitalia. A second way in which children can be questioned is through normal interview techniques but with leading questions, although this is a risky approach and may lead to inaccurate or false information. A third method of questioning is to use videotapes, which are beneficial because they reduce the number of interviews, show the child's body language in response to questions, and can be used as evidence in court cases. Whatever the interview technique used, the interviewer must establish the level of maturity and competency of the child.

The victim is the most important source of information in a sex crime, but is often not a sufficient source. The information collected from the victim includes the identity of the offender (if known) and details about the offense. If the victim does not know the offender or does not offer a sufficient description, the police must depend upon other sources for their information; namely, they must collect evidence such as hair and semen samples from the crime scene. Ultimately, many cases of sexual assault on adults depend upon the testimony of the accused and the victim rather than evidence if the suspect says the sexual act was consensual. Nonetheless, all evidence collected and the manner in which it is collected is important and can have an effect on the outcome of the case, which is why specialized training is necessary. The police report is particularly important because it will be used in court, in the development of the presentence investigation (PSI), and in treatment for the offender. Once the offender is arrested and the case is passed on to the prosecution, the police work at the investigative stage is essentially complete.

## THE HOSPITAL

The hospital is a key institution in rape investigation because it is often the first place that victims go after a sexual assault. It is the goal of the hospital to examine the victim and take evidence relating to the offense. Because the medical exam must be thorough, it is generally quite intrusive, and victims spend several hours at the hospital while the staff treats them both medically and psychologically.

The role of the hospital is to examine victims of sexual abuse. This examination includes a physical exam, a pelvic exam, and a collection of laboratory samples, as well as questions about the offense and perpetrator. The main purpose of the examination is to determine if there are physical indications that a crime was committed and, if so, to preserve the evidence. However, there are many difficulties in doing this. In cases of both rape and child molestation, many victims do not go to the hospital immediately after the offense occurs. Even some who do go to the hospital shortly after the assault shower or bathe first, thereby eradicating any forensic evidence from their bodies. In cases where forensic evidence is available, the perpetrator may claim that sexual intercourse took place but was consensual. This is particularly prevalent in cases where an acquaintance, date, or spouse assaults the victim.

Cases of child abuse present another set of difficulties in obtaining forensic evidence, beginning with the fact that many doctors will not do vaginal examinations on children. When an examination is done, the purpose is to check for evidence of sexual abuse, usually penetration, and this is done through examination of the hymen. Unfortunately, this evidence is often inconclusive because the hymen can be stretched or broken in several ways, and the medical examination does not necessarily prove penetration. Because the sexual abuse of children does not usually take the form of intercourse,

however, there is rarely any forensic evidence collected from children during the examination.

All hospitals should have rape-designated facilities in order to ensure proper collection of evidence and medical and psychological treatment for the victims. Some states have such facilities available in designated hospitals, whereas others have gone further and have established hospital-based Sexual Assault Nurse Examiners (SANEs). SANEs are forensically trained nurses who are specifically taught how to conduct evidentiary exams on sexual assault victims. They are involved in cases from the initial collection of evidence through the prosecution and can testify as experts in court as to the meaning of evidence. This is true even in cases where the victim has no physical injuries or there is no sperm (and therefore no forensic evidence) available. In many communities, they create a link between the evidence collection in a hospital and the criminal justice process, thereby increasing the likelihood of conviction for the sexual offender. The victim is never required to report the assault to the police, but when he or she does, the police face the task of responding sensitively to the complainant while collecting evidence and finding the perpetrator of the crime.

*Karen J. Terry*

***See also*** Megan's Law, Sexual Offender Civil Commitment, Special Victim Units

## *For Further Reading*

Littel, K. (2001). *Sexual Assault Nurse Examiner (SANE) programs: Improving the community response to sexual assault victims.* Washington, DC: U.S. Department of Justice, Office for Victims of Crime.

National Institute of Justice. (1992). *When the victim is a child* (2nd ed.). Washington, DC: U.S. Department of Justice, Office of Justice Programs.

New York City Alliance Against Sexual Assault. (2001). *Comprehensive sexual assault treatment programs: A hospital-based model.* New York: Author.

Prior, V. (2001). Invited comments to: Children's response to the medical visit for allegations of sexual abuse: Maternal perceptions and predicting variables. *Child Abuse Review, 10,* 223–225.

Ward, C., & Inserto, F. (1990). *Victims of sexual violence: A handbook for helpers.* Kent Ridge: Singapore University Press.

# ❧ SEXUAL OFFENDER CIVIL COMMITMENT

Several states have passed legislation requiring that sexual offenders be committed to a mental institution if they are assessed as having a mental abnormality or personality disorder and are dangerous. Labeled a "sexually violent predator" (SVP), the purpose of this legislation is to incapacitate recidivist sexual offenders until they are rehabilitated. This legislation assumes a relationship between mental disorder, risk, and sexual violence, and is based largely upon the ability of clinicians to accurately predict the risk an offender may present to the public in the future. Risk assessments are controversial, though, and most experts agree that they produce high rates of false positives for sex offenders except in extreme circumstances (e.g., with psychopathic, violent sex offenders who have at least two previous offenses). Although the Supreme Court has declared SVP legislation constitutional, legal challenges against it are continuing.

The concept of civilly committing sexual offenders is not new. In the 1930s, a number of states passed sexual psychopathy statutes based on the idea that sexually deviant behavior is caused by a diagnosable disorder and is treatable. Individuals who were diagnosed sexual psychopaths were civilly committed to a mental institution until rehabilitated. These statutes were enacted after emotionally charged sex crimes occurred, like those of Albert Fish. Fish committed numerous assaults, sexual offenses, and murders against children, culminating in the mutilation and cannibalism of a 12-year-old boy. Because such offenders are rare, however, the statutes fell into disuse and were repealed in most states by the 1980s.

Like the sexual psychopathy laws, SVP legislation was passed after emotionally charged sex crimes in the late 1980s. At this time, criminal legislation was ineffective at incapacitating dangerous sexual predators if they had a finite criminal sentence. Washington was the first state to enact SVP legislation, in 1990, and this was largely a response to cases like that of Earl Shriner. Shriner had a history of sexual violence and murder, and he had been in and out of institutions since the age of 15. During his time in prison, he bragged to inmates and staff, and confided in a journal, that he fantasized about killing again. He explained that when he was released, he would buy a van, kidnap boys, take them into the woods, and torture them. There was nothing the state could do to keep him incapacitated, and, once released, he kidnapped a 7-year-old boy, cut off his penis, and left him for dead. Shortly after Earl Shriner's crime of sexual mutilation, Washington passed the Community Protection Act of 1990, which contained 14 separate provisions for ensuring community safety against such predators. Sixteen states have since implemented similar statutes.

An SVP is generally defined as a person who has been convicted of a sexually violent offense and who suffers from a mental abnormality or personality disorder that makes the person likely to engage in predatory acts of sexual violence. SVP statutes were enacted specifically to target "a small but extremely dangerous group of SVPs who do not have a mental disease or defect that renders them appropriate for involuntary treatment" (Kansas SVPA § 59-29a). The statute requires proof of past sexually violent behavior and a present mental condition that is likely to cause similar violent behavior in the future.

The general format of a commitment process follows six steps. First, the correctional agency refers the sex offender to the court shortly before his or her release from prison. Second, the prosecuting attorney files a petition to incapacitate the offender as an SVP. Third, there is a hearing, during which the prosecutor must show probable cause that the offender is an SVP. The offender has due process rights at this hearing that are similar to those in a criminal trial, including the right to notice of the hearing, an opportunity to be heard, the right to counsel, the right to present evidence, the right to cross-examine witnesses, and the right to view and copy all petitions and documents in his or her file. Fourth, if the court determines that probable cause does exist, the sex offender is transferred to a psychiatric facility for evaluation. If the psychiatrist then determines that the sex offender poses a high risk and does have a mental or personality disorder, the fifth step is a trial. During the trial, the offender has a right to counsel, a jury trial, and an examination by an expert of his or her choice. If the offender chooses to have a jury trial, the verdict must be unanimous. If a judge decides or the jury unanimously decides that the offender is an SVP, he or she is then transferred to a special containment facility (e.g., mental hospital, special secure unit) until rehabilitated.

The most crucial step of this process is the risk assessment. This is a subjective evaluation that aims to determine a person's future behavior. Although each state differs in its method of evaluation, most combine clinical assessments and actuarial-based assessments. Actuarial-based instruments, such as the commonly used STATIC-99, measure the offender's past offenses and personal characteristics. By measuring the base rate of reoffense for a particular cohort of sexual offenders, it is supposedly possible to determine whether an individual will reoffend.

Although based on the same concept and procedures, SVP statutes differ in each state in seven primary ways. The first difference is with the definition of a sexually violent predator. Most states use the three-pronged criteria of mental abnormality, dangerousness, and no availability of less restrictive alternatives to declaring an individual an SVP; other states replace mental abnormality with personality or mental disorder, thereby increasing the chance that an individual will be determined an SVP. A second difference is with the standard of dangerousness for commitment. These standards include "highly likely" to recidivate, an "extremely high" rating of dangerousness, if they are "most likely to reoffend," or are "distinctively dangerous." Similarly, the standard of proof for commitment differs. Whereas most states require the same standard for commitment as with a criminal trial—proof beyond a reasonable doubt—other states (e.g., Florida) require the lesser standard of "clear and convincing evidence" that is generally required in civil trials. A fourth difference between states is the length of commitment. Whereas most states require that the civilly committed sex offender remain incapacitated until rehabilitated, other states (e.g., California) require that the offender be reevaluated

every 2 years. The facilities for containment are a fifth difference, and they range from prisons to hospitals to special secure facilities. Cost is a sixth difference, and this is largely dependent upon the facility, the trial procedure, and type of treatment provided. Taking into consideration the cost of housing, treatment, and legal fees, the facilities range in cost from approximately $130,000 per offender per year (in Washington) to $238,000 per offender per year (in Iowa). A final difference between states is method of assessment. Although most states use clinical and actuarial risk assessments, not all do, and the actuarial assessment scales vary by state. Because of all these differences, the number of incapacitated sex offenders varies in each state. California has committed the most sex offenders of all states—370—with many others awaiting various stages of the commitment process. In total, nearly 5,000 offenders have been referred for commitment in that state. Alternatively, only about 50 sex offenders have been referred for commitment in Iowa.

Almost immediately after its inception, claimants challenged the SVPA in the courts on several grounds, including ex post facto application, double jeopardy, due process, equal application, vagueness of the statute, and definition of an SVP. Although several cases went through state courts in Washington, Minnesota, and New Jersey, for instance, the U.S. Supreme Court first examined the Kansas statute. In 1997, the Court upheld the commitment of Leroy Hendricks, a recidivist pedophile, in *Kansas v. Hendricks*. Leroy Hendricks had a long history of sexual deviancy, with convictions of sexually abusing children beginning in 1955. He explained to psychologists that he harbored strong sexual desires for young children and was diagnosed a pedophile. The state assessed him as a sexually violent predator and incapacitated him, but Hendricks challenged his civil commitment on substantive due process grounds. The Court upheld Hendricks's civil commitment and declared the Kansas SVP statute constitutional on all grounds, stating that it is a civil rather than criminal statute and therefore does not constitute punishment. Therefore, it does not violate double jeopardy or ex post facto application of the law. In addition, the

Court dismissed the idea that the term *mental abnormality* was a vague standard for commitment and claimed that the statute does not violate due process rights.

*Karen J. Terry*

*See also* Megan's Law, Sex Crime Investigation

### For Further Reading

Alexander, R. (1993). The civil commitment of sex offenders in light of Foucha v. Louisiana. *Criminal Justice & Behavior, 20,* 371–387.

Hanson, R. K., & Thornton, D. M. (1999) *STATIC 99: Improving actuarial risk assessments for sex offenders.* Ottawa: Public Works and Government Services.

Hoberman, H. M. (2001). Dangerousness and sex offenders: Assessing risk for future sex offenses. In A. Schlank (Ed.), *The sexual predator: Legal issues, clinical issues, special populations* (Vol. 2). Kingston, NJ: Civic Research Institute.

Jenkins, P. (1998). *Moral panic: Changing concepts of the child molester in modern America.* New Haven, CT: Yale University Press.

Kansas v. Hendricks, 521 U.S. 346 (1997).

Kansas Sexually Violent Predator Statute § 59-29a.

## ☙ SHERIFFS

The office of sheriff has developed into what it is today over a long period of history. The office began in medieval England when the country was divided into tribal areas known as shires, the equivalent of a modern county. In antiquity, the King's justice was administered by "shire-reeves," who presided over the shire courts. The sheriff, then, is the modern counterpart of the shire-reeve. After William the Conqueror claimed the English crown in 1066, there was no uniform criminal law in England. The many individual shire courts were dominated by sheriffs, who enforced the village rules as they saw fit. Formal law enforcement agencies emerged in England in the 13th century, evolving to meet the needs of the day.

The first colonists in America established law enforcement institutions as the first communities were established. These colonists brought with them the forms of law enforcement they had known in England: the sheriff, the constable, and the watch. Over time, these English institutions evolved and took on decidedly American features. The sheriff, who was generally appointed by the colonial governor, was the head of the local government. The sheriff was empowered to make arrests and to raise the *posse comitatus* to pursue fleeing felons. In addition to law enforcement, the sheriff was responsible for collecting taxes, conducting elections, maintaining roads and bridges, and numerous other duties. This system of political appointment soon gave way to local elections because of citizens' fear of lodging such great authority in the state. This system was thought to increase the sheriff's accountability to the public and remains in place in most jurisdictions today. This led to a highly decentralized system of law enforcement in the United States that remains largely autonomous today. Advocates of community policing have criticized modern law enforcement agencies as reactive rather than proactive, largely because calls for service take up most of an officer's time. The early sheriffs were truly reactive; they only responded to complaints brought to them and had no systematic preventive patrol strategy.

It has been estimated that there are nearly 3,100 sheriffs' offices operating nationwide with an estimated 290,707 full-time employees, including about 186,000 sworn personnel. Most sheriffs serve small, sparsely populated jurisdictions, and a few very large agencies employ a majority of officers. Although only a sixth of sheriffs' offices serve a jurisdiction with 100,000 or more residents, such agencies employ about two thirds of all sworn personnel. About a fifth of sworn personnel are employed in jurisdictions with 1 million or more residents. In contrast, about half of all sheriffs' departments serve populations under 25,000.

Modern sheriffs are rather unique in law enforcement in that they are elected by the people of the county, usually for a period of 4 years. (In Louisiana, many police chiefs are elected, as are some in Texas and New Hampshire.) This means that a new sheriff can come from outside a department or even outside of law enforcement in general. Usually, however, sheriffs will have some background in law enforcement, such as within a sheriff's department, a police department, or the state police. As were their historical counterparts, modern sheriffs are the chief law enforcement officers of their counties. The office of sheriff is constitutionally based in most states.

## MODERN FUNCTIONS

The primary function of the modern sheriff's department is law enforcement and the attendant preventive patrol operations. Sheriff's deputies perform basic law enforcement functions outside of incorporated areas where city police do not have jurisdiction. Nearly all sheriffs' departments use automobiles to provide routine patrol services in their jurisdictions. Many jurisdictions use other types of patrols, such as foot patrols, horse patrols, bicycle patrols, motorcycle patrols, and marine patrols. The vast majority of sheriffs' offices also respond to citizen calls for service. Most sheriffs' departments are part of the 9-1-1 system and can be dispatched as the result of a call to 9-1-1. More than two thirds of sheriffs' offices have access to enhanced 9-1-1 systems, which are capable of automatically displaying a caller's phone number and address.

The vast majority (93%) of sheriffs' offices routinely investigate crimes. The larger the jurisdiction a department serves, the more likely it is that another agency will investigate certain types of crimes that can be handled more easily by those with special expertise. For example, whereas 76% of sheriffs' officers investigate arsons, less than half of the sheriffs' officers serving 1 million or more residents handle arson investigations. On the other hand, specialized units that require special and often expensive training and equipment are more likely to be found in larger departments. For example, 29% of sheriffs' departments have special drug enforcement units. More than half of the offices serving 100,000 or more residents have a full-time drug enforcement unit. This involvement in drug enforcement can be an important source of revenue. More than half of all sheriffs' offices receive money, property, or goods from drug asset forfeiture programs.

Almost all sheriffs' offices serve in some capacity as officers of the court. The most common activities are executing arrest warrants, serving civil process, and providing court security. In many small sheriffs' offices, generalist patrol deputies find that a large amount of their time is taken up with the processing of court writs, both criminal and civil. Because most of these writs are of a civil nature, deputies often cannot find the time for proactive law enforcement activities, as can their problem-oriented municipal counterparts.

The majority of sheriffs operate jails. Most of the prisoners are being detained pending a trial, but a growing number are convicted felons serving their sentence in the county jail rather than a state prison. Generally, only those offices that serve very small populations do not operate jails. More than 90% of all sheriffs' officers work for an agency that operates at least one jail. About one fifth of sheriffs' offices operate at least one temporary adult holding facility that is separate from the primary jail. A much smaller proportion (7%) of sheriffs' offices have a lockup facility for juveniles. Many community corrections efforts, such as work release programs, are administered by sheriffs' departments.

Many sheriffs' departments perform functions outside routine patrol activities. Many times, this is because there is simply no one else to perform those functions. A majority of sheriffs' offices perform search and rescue functions, tactical operations (SWAT), and a host of other public services.

## PROFESSIONALISM AND LIABILITY

Recent trends in the administration of sheriffs' offices have included a move toward professionalism. This has been due in large part to civil liability concerns. One of the most common results of these concerns is the development or adoption of official departmental policies governing professional behaviors that are attended by high risk of damage to property and injury to people. Almost all (98%) sworn personnel in the United States must work within the framework of a written use-of-force policy. Most officers (94%) must also follow written policies when using less than lethal force, such as pepper spray, batons, and rubber bullets. A growing number of departments have also instituted pursuit-driving policies, severely limiting the circumstances in which officers may engage in high-speed chases. Most jail operations are guided by written policy.

## COMMUNITY POLICING

Community policing promotes organizational strategies to address causes of crime and reduce citizens' fear of victimization. The fundamental shift from traditional policing to community policing requires an emphasis on problem solving and community partnership. In some respects, most county sheriffs have been practicing elements of community policing for decades. Successful management of a patrol area as large as a county requires strong bonds with the community. Such large jurisdictions are impossible to monitor with routine patrol; citizen involvement in monitoring what goes on in the county is critical. The trust and respect of these citizens is a prerequisite of that vital information being shared with the sheriff's office. This, coupled with the nature of an elected office, suggests that most sheriffs desire a strong bond with their community despite their opinions regarding community policing as a policing philosophy.

Many sheriffs' offices do officially subscribe to the community policing philosophy. Almost three fourths of sworn personnel work for an agency with some type of community policing plan in place. The majority of sheriff's office personnel undergo some type of community policing and problem-solving training, both as recruits and as inservice officers. The majority of departments (71%) assign patrol officers to patrol specific geographic areas; this is to increase familiarity with citizens, improving the vital bond between the sheriff's office and citizens. Many departments contribute to community projects, such as meeting with school groups, neighborhood associations, senior citizens' groups, neighborhood watch organizations, and business groups.

The rural nature of most sheriffs' departments makes these agencies largely different from municipal police departments. In many rural areas, the sheriff often is the central organization of policing rather than a tangential or support agency, as in municipal settings. The most general definition of rural encompasses the jurisdiction of the sheriff: the unincorporated areas of the county where there are no municipal police departments. In addition, sheriffs' departments are called upon to provide police services for municipalities that are not large enough to afford around-the-clock police services of their own. Sheriffs may also serve as a central coordinating agency for several small local departments.

With the exception of Rhode Island and Hawaii, sheriffs hold elective offices. This serves to subject the sheriff to the power of the community and public opinion. The employees of the sheriff's office "serve at the will and pleasure" of the sheriff in many jurisdictions. This means that deputies tend to be loyal to a particular sheriff rather than the department in general. For these reasons, sheriffs' offices tend to operate in a personal, informal manner.

The rural nature of most sheriffs' departments provides investigators with an advantage. Often, investigators will know by sight and by name many of the citizens in their jurisdiction. Witnesses are much more likely to recognize suspects they observed. This may help explain why rural agencies have better resolution rates than their urban counterparts for almost every type of crime. Along with these advantages come some personal disadvantages for sheriffs and deputies in these rural areas. The sheriff's office is often called upon to render services for a wide variety of irregular occurrences, only a very few of which are law enforcement activities. There tends to be more social work than law enforcement work much of the time. Personnel often complain that the job takes away their personal lives. Everywhere rural sheriffs go, they are sheriffs and are expected by citizens to act in their official capacity at all times.

In essence, the nature of a well-run sheriff's department is community policing. Some commentators have observed that rural sheriffs often do not practice community policing, largely because they do not have written policies and programs formalizing the philosophy. In many ways, the community policing efforts of large urban departments are efforts to formalize what sheriffs in many rural jurisdictions have been doing for a long time. By being a part of the community, they have accountability to the community. They are also connected intimately with the members of the community, with a keen awareness of their concerns. Generally, officers will strive to address those concerns because they are shared concerns. Rural sheriffs are natural problem solvers because rural citizens expect sheriffs to handle problems long before they become criminal matters.

The small size and small budgets of rural sheriffs' departments do not mean that they are ineffective. To the contrary, sheriffs in rural areas typically have higher clearance rates than urban departments. In addition, rural offices tend to garner more positive regard from citizens. Regardless of whether rural agencies are evaluated from the vantage point of the crime fighter paradigm or the community paradigm, it seems that rural sheriffs do a better job than their urban counterparts do. The stereotype of bumbling crooks as sheriffs portrayed by Hollywood simply is not the norm. This stereotype is unfortunate and may explain why most of the evaluations of community policing have been done in large urban areas rather than in the rural areas where the practice is long-standing.

*Adam J. McKee*

*See also* Asset Forfeiture, State; Community Policing; Rural Policing

## For Further Reading

Hickman, M. J., & Reaves, B. A. (2003). *Sheriffs' offices 2000.* Washington, DC: Bureau of Justice Statistics.

Walker, S., & Katz, C. M. (2002). *The police in America* (4th ed.). New York: McGraw-Hill.

Weisheit, R. A., Wells, L. E., & Falcone, D. N. (1995). *Crime and policing in rural and small-town America: An overview of the issues.* Washington, DC: National Institute of Justice.

# ඓ SPECIAL JURISDICTION LAW ENFORCEMENT AGENCIES

Police protection is the function of enforcing the law, preserving order, and apprehending those who violate the law, whether these activities are performed by a city police department, a county sheriff's department, or a state police or federal law enforcement agency. In the United States, both federalism and tradition have resulted in a fragmented police structure at three levels of government: federal, state, and local. This fragmentation is compounded by the separation of local government into two levels: municipal and county. Discounting federal law enforcement agencies, the most recent, comprehensive census of state and local law enforcement agencies identified 17,784 full-time police agencies as of June 2000. The Bureau of Justice Statistics (BJS), which conducted this study, identified those agencies employing at least one full-time sworn officer with general police arrest powers. Of the nearly 18,000 state and local police agencies, 1,376 were classified as "special jurisdiction agencies."

## DEFINITION AND ROLES

In the literature on policing, these special jurisdiction agencies have been given myriad labels over the years, such as specialized agencies, special police agencies, special-purpose police agencies, limited-purpose law enforcement agencies, special function police, and special district police. The title used here will be special jurisdiction law enforcement agencies (SJLEAs). Just as there has been a great deal of ambiguity about what to call these agencies, there also has been much uncertainty regarding how to define them and their role. In essence, these SJLEAs have special geographic jurisdictions and/or special enforcement responsibilities. These agencies may be administered by municipal, county, or state levels of government. Because the United States does not have a national, general-purpose police force, all of the federal law enforcement agencies are, by definition, special-purpose law enforcement agencies. Most federal law enforcement agencies exercise very wide territorial authority, although their specific functions are limited. But the SJLEAs in this discussion and in the aforementioned BJS census are *not* administered by the federal government, but by state and local levels of government.

These special-purpose law enforcement agencies are charged with serving a broad range of specific organizations/entities. These local and state agencies serve our nation's transportation systems, parks and forests, colleges and universities, hospital complexes, public school districts, bridges and tunnels, and similar entities. These special jurisdiction agencies are separate and distinct, and should not be confused with specialized units belonging to a single department (e.g., bomb squad, detective, motorcycle, K-9, forensics, SWAT, etc.), although, of course, some of the SJLEAs do have their own specialized units. From a legal standpoint, it is also interesting to note that the majority of these agencies have concurrent jurisdiction with local and/or state general-purpose police departments. So, it is quite important that these SJLEAs communicate, coordinate, and cooperate with the appropriate departments.

Of the nearly 70,000 full-time state and local law enforcement employees working for these agencies, 43,413 (70%) are full-time sworn personnel who have met certified training standards and possess police arrest powers. About two thirds (68%) of sworn personnel primarily handle patrol duties, whereas 17% are criminal investigators. Although most officers who work in SJLEAs wear uniforms and carry sidearms, some officers are deployed in plain clothes and may or may not carry firearms.

## TYPOLOGY

For the first time in the 2000 census of SJLEAs (Reaves & Hickman, 2002), a typology of the various categories of special function police agencies was created. The BJS identified five different types of SJLEAs. The largest single subcategory was classified as "Government buildings/facilities," which accounted for more than two thirds (68%, or 934) of all the agencies as well as 41% (17,584) of all the sworn personnel working in SJLEAs. This subdivision includes police agencies responsible for safety and security at state capitols (e.g., Arizona, Florida, Iowa, Pennsylvania, Virginia, and 12 other states as well) and other government buildings, medical school/hospital complexes, public housing projects, public school districts, and college and university campus police at both the 2-year and 4-year level. Fifty percent (689) of all SJLEAs provide policing at the nation's public colleges, and 26% (11,319) of all special jurisdiction law officers are campus cops who are certified by the state and have general arrest powers. Many of the smaller colleges and private ones also use private security on campus

or their own nonsworn security officers. Although campus police are discussed elsewhere in this volume, it is important to be cognizant of the growing number and importance of public school district police departments, which represent 12% (162 agencies) of all SJLEAs (the largest single subcategory after campus police). The Los Angeles Unified School District (LAUSD) Police Department started off as a security section in 1948 and gradually grew into a police department. It is the largest public school district police force in the nation, with slightly more than 300 officers. This police force serves a school district composed of almost 66,000 teachers and staff and 880,000 students, and it covers 910 schools and centers spread out over 708 square miles. Although all officers are armed and most are in uniform, some officers work undercover on investigations into drug and gang activities.

The second largest subdivision of SJLEAs is "Conservation laws/parks and recreation," and it is composed of 174 law enforcement agencies (13% of the total). Many of these agencies have statewide or county-wide jurisdictions in protecting fish and wildlife, safeguarding parks and recreational areas, enforcing environmental laws, protecting forestry resources, and enforcing boating regulations. New York City and several other entities even have a police force to protect their water resources. New York City's Bureau of Water Supply police force was formed in 1905 to protect the 21 reservoirs that supply water to the nation's most populous city. About 50 police officers protect these reservoirs, which are scattered over New York's sprawling 2,000-square-mile watershed. Currently, this police force is part of New York City's Department of Environmental Protection, and it cooperates with local and sheriffs' departments as well as the New York State Police on law enforcement concerns throughout the watershed. The Missouri State Water Patrol does not protect the water supply, but it is a statewide police agency responsible for law enforcement and boating safety on Missouri's rivers and lakes. Almost 90 highly trained officers are responsible for everything from administration of boat safety education programs to enforcement of state boating laws to rescue and recovery assistance during floods.

The third group of SJLEAs is classified as "Transportation systems/facilities." Ten percent (138) of the total number of SJLEAs fall into this group, and they use 8,400 sworn officers (19% of the total personnel). Most of these agencies come under the oversight of the relatively new federal Transportation Security Administration. Some 87 airports have police departments to provide for protection of both passengers and property. They range in size from the Dallas-Fort Worth International Airport Police Department, with just over 300 officers, to the Monterey Peninsula (CA) Airport Police Department, with five officers. Mass transit systems and railways are in this class of SJLEAs also. The railroad police are the nation's earliest special purpose forces, with some of them going back to the late 19th century. Railroad police have a unique responsibility. The Norfolk Southern Railway, the Union Pacific Railroad, and nine others have police officers who investigate crimes against the railroad, including theft, vandalism, burglary, and arson. They are responsible for protecting the interests of their railroad and protecting the passengers and cargo traveling upon that company's rails. Railroad police officers are commissioned peace officers within the states where they work. Collectively, the railroad police make up the largest *private* police force in the country. Mass transit police departments, such as the Washington (DC) Metropolitan Area Transit Authority, the Southeastern Pennsylvania Transit Authority, the Metropolitan Atlanta Rapid Transit Authority, New Jersey Transit, and others are primarily concerned with the safe and secure passage of hundreds of thousands of commuters to and from major metropolitan areas each and every day.

SJLEAs also included in the subdivision "Transportation systems/facilities" are police agencies charged with protecting port facilities; others assigned to safeguard specific roadways, bridges, and tunnels; and still others designated to police multiple types of transportation modes as well as the infrastructures that sustain them. One of 17 such agencies charged with port protection is the San Diego Harbor Police Department. Its jurisdiction is the San Diego Unified Port District. It safeguards oceangoing ships entering and leaving the harbor and provides assistance to numerous recreational boaters. The 138 sworn police officers provide both law enforcement and marine fire fighting services throughout San Diego Bay. They also have the responsibility of policing the San Diego International Airport.

Two of the five police departments that provide police protection to critical roadways and bridges are the Delaware River and Bay Authority (DRBA) Police and the Chesapeake Bay-Bridge Tunnel (CBBT) Police Department. In the DRBA police, some 60 officers patrol the twin spans of the Delaware Memorial Bridge, which is a critical link in the I-95, East Coast highway corridor. Since the mid-1980s, they also provide a police presence on the ferries that run between Cape May, New Jersey, and Lewes, Delaware. In addition, the force provides policing to five small airports in Delaware and New Jersey. The CBBT Police Department patrols the 17-mile-long link that spans the Chesapeake Bay and connects the Virginia Beach/Norfolk metropolitan area with the Delmarva Peninsula. More than 40 police officers ensure safe and efficient traffic flow across the facility.

The largest police agency serving multiple types of transportation facilities and the largest of *all* the SJLEAs is the Port Authority of New York and New Jersey Police Department. Currently, close to 1,700 officers have full enforcement powers in both states. The PAPD has a multitude of responsibilities quite varied in scope. The department is responsible for policing the facilities owned and operated by the Port Authority: three international airports (JFK, LaGuardia, Newark Liberty); four interstate bridges (George Washington, Goethals, Bayonne, Outerbridge Crossing); two interstate tunnels (Holland, Lincoln); two passenger terminals (Bus Terminal and Passenger Ship Terminal); three marine terminals (Port Newark, Port Elizabeth, Brooklyn Piers); and an interstate rail transit system (Port Authority Trans-Hudson). Police officers assigned to work at the airports are also trained in firefighting and aircraft rescue and are assigned those tasks as well as patrol. At the time of the terrorist attacks on America on September 11, 2001, the World Trade Center was still under the jurisdiction of the PAPD. In that attack, 37 Port Authority police officers died in the line of duty. No police department in this country's history lost as many officers in a single incident, or in a single year for that matter, as did the PAPD on that day.

The fourth of the five SJLEA subdivisions is labeled "Criminal investigations." The 101 agencies in this subdivision (just 7% of the total number) employ just over 3,000 sworn personnel (also just 7% of the total). Agencies in this category include state and municipal arson investigation units, with the New York City Fire Department's Bureau of Fire Investigation being the nation's largest with approximately 170 sworn personnel. Fire marshals in such agencies are cross-trained in fire and criminal investigation; they are armed and have police arrest powers.

A number of states have state bureaus of criminal investigations. These agencies are commonly found in states that have highway patrols (with limited investigative authority) and therefore have a need for statewide units to investigate criminal activities. The Georgia Bureau of Investigation, the North Carolina State Bureau of Investigation, the Ohio Bureau of Criminal Identification and Investigation, and the Oklahoma State Bureau of Investigation are four such agencies. The remainder of agencies in this subcategory are criminal investigation units that are found at the municipal or county level, and they are independent from local police agencies. All 21 county prosecutors' offices in New Jersey fall into this category as well. The chief law enforcement official in New Jersey's counties is the county prosecutor, and as such he or she wields much discretionary legal power. Local police departments and their detective staffs (where they exist) perform much of the original investigative work and arrest of criminal suspects. County prosecutors and their staff of detectives, however, have overall responsibility. Although much of the county detective investigative work is reactive in nature, some of the investigations are proactive, particularly in the areas of drug distribution, gambling, organized crime, or government corruption.

The smallest of the SJLEA subdivisions is classified as "Special enforcement" agencies. Only 29 agencies (just 2% of the total) employing 1,832 sworn personnel (4% of the total) fall into this group. The agencies in this category have varied

responsibilities over such areas as drug enforcement, regulation of the gambling and racing industry, enforcement of agricultural laws, and—the most common of all—regulation and control of the alcohol industry. Many states have Alcoholic Beverage Control (ABC) Commissions (or similarly named organizations) that are responsible for enforcing laws regulating the manufacture, distribution, and sale of alcoholic beverages. Seventeen states have given ABC investigators law enforcement authority to conduct investigations and enforce compliance with state laws and regulations at hearings or in court. The California Department of ABC is the largest such agency.

The following table summarizes the preceding discussion of the newly created BJS typology of SJLEAs.

*Type of Full-Time Sworn*
*Special Jurisdiction Agencies Personnel*

1. Government buildings/facilities 934 (68%) 17,584 (41%)
2. Conservation laws/parks and recreation 174 (13%) 12,577 (29%)
3. Transportation systems/facilities 138 (10%) 8,400 (19%)
4. Criminal investigations 101 (7%) 3,020 (7%)
5. Special enforcement 29 (2%) 1,832 (4%)

TOTAL 1,376 (100%) 43,413 (100%)

*Note:* From Reaves and Hickman (2002), p. 12. Adapted with permission.

## THE FUTURE

It should be obvious that special jurisdiction law enforcement agencies are a small but vital part of the nation's law enforcement sector. Too often, the general public, police officials, and even academics do not consider SJLEAs when discussing or analyzing policing. Yet according to Reaves and Hickman (2002), special jurisdiction police agencies account for 8% of the total number (17,784) of state and local law enforcement agencies, and the sworn personnel working in these agencies are 6% of the total number (708,022) of state and local police officers. The numbers of SJLEAs and the numbers of sworn officers working in them are *not* insubstantial, and these agencies fill an important niche in American policing.

The officers in these agencies have critical roles to play in terms of law enforcement and public safety and security. Prospective police officers should not overlook these agencies when pursuing careers. There are many well-established professional SJLEAs that offer training, equipment, promotional opportunities, salaries, and benefits that are on a par with, if not better than, state and local police departments. Also, it would not be surprising to see the number of such agencies and the number of sworn personnel working in them increase in the future. Already, there are clear indications that this is happening. Since the Columbine (CO) High School shootings in April 1999, and in the aftermath of September 11, 2001, many SJLEAs have hired more officers and increased the size of their agency. Some new special jurisdiction agencies are on the drawing board as well. For example, the Delaware River Joint Toll Bridge Commission plans to spend more than $2.5 million a year on its proposed armed police force of 30 officers and supervisors to protect its 20 bridges that span the Delaware River from Trenton, New Jersey, northward. These officers will have to undergo police training from either New Jersey or Pennsylvania. The creation of this new public safety department was in direct response to September 11th.

Something that underscores the growing significance of SJLEAs is that, for the first time ever, the FBI created a new table to identify such agencies and their personnel in its 2001 edition of *Crime in the United States*. Table 82, titled "Law Enforcement Employees as of October 31, 2001, by Other Agencies by State," supplies employee data for law enforcement agencies charged with serving a broad range of specific organizations/entities. Although only 171 such agencies were identified in this initial survey, it is expected that, in the future, this table will become more comprehensive and accurate. The creation of this new table by the FBI gives emphasis to the fact that in our changing world, SJLEAs will most likely have an increasingly critical role to play.

*Peter Horne*

*See also* Airport Security, Campus Policing, Housing Police, Private Policing, School Crime/Security/Response, Transit Police

## For Further Reading

Delaware River and Bay Authority Police. (n.d.). *Department history*. Retrieved March 9, 2003, from http://drba.net/police/history.html

Federal Bureau of Investigation. (2002). *Crime in the United States, Uniform Crime Reports 2001*. Washington, DC: U.S. Government Printing Office.

James, G. (1999, May 9). Policing the Port Authority's domain. *New York Times*, p. NJ 7.

Larson, R. (1998, Nov/Dec). On track. *9-1-1 Magazine*. Retrieved April 2, 2003, from http://www.9-1-1magazine.com/magazine/1998/1198/feas/32Larson/index.html

Missouri State Water Patrol. (n.d.). *History*. Retrieved March 18, 2003, from http://www.mswp.state.mo.us/wphist.htm

Reaves, B., & Hickman, M. (2002, October). *Census of state and local law enforcement agencies, 2000* (NCJ 194066). Washington, DC: U.S. Department of Justice.

Water, water everywhere (and hardly a cop in sight). (1999, March 15). *Law Enforcement News*, 25(507), p. 7.

http://www.laspd.com/home

http://www.portofsandiego.org/sandiego_sdhp

## ✂ SPECIAL VICTIMS UNITS

### DEFINING SPECIAL VICTIMS UNITS

Law enforcement agencies across the country have started organizing Special Victims Units in an effort to centralize the investigation and prosecution of sensitive cases that include, but are not limited to, sex crimes, child abuse, domestic violence, missing persons, stalking, and the exploitation and abuse of the elderly. In addition to investigating both adult and child sex crimes, some Special Victims Units are also responsible for investigating crimes in which sex offenders have failed to comply with registration and/or community notification statutes. For example, in Polk County, Florida, a Special Victims Response Team (SVRT) has been organized and is responsible for locating and arresting those offenders who have failed to comply with requirements set forth in sex offender statutes. In New York City, a similar unit called the Sex Offender Monitoring Unit, a division of the Special Victims Unit, is the designated department for tracking sex offenders.

## THE MISSION OF SPECIAL VICTIMS UNITS

The mission of Special Victims Units is to conduct a thorough and efficient investigation while protecting the physical and emotional needs of the victim. These units employ a multidisciplinary, multijurisdictional approach to investigating and prosecuting these cases to help limit the possibility of revictimization. Partners in this endeavor often include specialized forensic hospital personnel, such as Sexual Assault Nurse Examiners (SANEs) or Sexual Assault Forensic Examiners (SAFEs), mental health professionals, Children's Services, and victim advocate agencies. This collaborative approach minimizes additional trauma to the victim while enhancing investigative procedures.

The minimization of additional trauma is achieved through joint interviews, where a detective, assistant district attorney, social worker, and/or psychologist may be present while the interview is conducted. In these cases, while one person is doing the interview, the other parties are observing through a one-way mirror. These procedures not only minimize the revictimization produced when the individual has to recount the traumatic experience, but also help to limit problems, such as confusion and inconsistent testimony associated with having to repeatedly recount a painful experience. In addition, incorporating specialized forensic examiners, such as SANEs or SAFEs, significantly improves the collection of physical evidence, ultimately leading to improved prosecutions.

## WHERE ARE SPECIAL VICTIMS UNITS LOCATED?

Special Victims Units are usually located within larger police departments, especially in major cities where there is a need for specialized units in direct relation to crime rates. These units investigate cases that result from citizen complaints, as well as referrals from county and state law enforcement departments, child protective services, and social service agencies. There are many benefits to having these centralized and specialized units, including improved and more efficient communication between investigators, better tracking and speedier recognition when similar or serial crimes are occurring, standardization of procedures, and fewer jurisdictional issues.

## WHO WORKS IN SPECIAL VICTIMS UNITS?

These units are often composed of detectives in partnership with prosecutors, social workers, psychologists, and advocates who have and continue to receive specialized training in investigating and working with victims of violent crime. Although the training varies by police department and victim typology, examples of specialized training include interviewing and interrogation techniques, procedural requirements, and evidence collection. Interviewing techniques vary according to whether the investigator is working with the victim, witnesses, hospital personnel, responding officers, or the suspect. The interviewing process also varies greatly depending on victim type; for example, children and elderly individuals should be interviewed in very different manners. In all cases, victims need to feel safe and comfortable during the investigative process. Victims comprise the most important evidence in these types of cases, and therefore, establishing good rapport is essential. Additional training can assist in this endeavor.

In addition, many of the crimes that Special Victims Units investigate, such as sex crimes, are highly sensitive, and many receive media attention, which make these cases particularly difficult to investigate and prosecute. Thus, law enforcement needs to be particularly careful to follow all procedures, collect all available evidence, and document carefully all phases of the process.

*Lisa A. Williams and Jessica Saunders*

**See also** Child Molestation; Child Welfare; Megan's Law; Serial Murder Investigation; Sex Crime Investigation; Victims, Police Response to

## For Further Reading

Changing its stripes: New look, and attitude, for Philly SVU. (2003). *Law Enforcement News, 29*(604), 5.

Donofrio, D. (2002). Establishing specialty units in small agencies. *Law Enforcement Technology, 29*(9), 114–119.

U.S. Department of Justice. (2002, January). *Terrorism and International Victims Unit*. Washington, DC: Office for Victims of Crime. Available: http://www.ojp.usdoj.gov/ovc/publications/factshts/tivu/fs000276.pdf

Whitcomb, D. (1982). *Assisting child victims of sexual abuse: The Sexual Assault Center, Seattle, Washington and The Child Protection Center–Special Unit, Washington, DC* (NCJ number 84606). Washington, DC: National Institute of Justice.

http://www.ci.ftlaud.fl.us/police/crim_inv.html#sv

http://www.rcdaoffice.org/overview.htm#SecCrimesSpecial VictimsBureau

http://www.vbgov.com/dept/police/division/invest/detective/0,1701,10619,00.html

# ❧ STATE POLICE

Traditionally, law enforcement in the United States has been organized on a local level. Until the beginning of the 20th century, police departments were organized on a village, town, city, or county basis. If emergency conditions called for more manpower, the militia or National Guard could be called to assist. However, in some industrial states, the frequent mobilizations and subsequent reluctance of the National Guard to deal with labor disputes at the turn of the 20th century resulted in the creation of a large police department under the control of the governor. The popularity of the automobile also created a need for a police agency that had jurisdiction within the entire state and could pursue violators anywhere in the state. The state police could also serve as an agency to patrol in rural areas that were without local police departments. In some states, the existence of corruption in local police agencies was another factor in establishing a police agency under state control. The creation of state police departments also strengthened the power of state governors, who now had an enforcement agency with statewide powers.

Currently, every state has a state police agency except Hawaii. In 2000, state police agencies employed more than 98,000 personnel. State police agencies, which are also known as public safety departments or state highway patrols, usually have patrol and investigative components. Michigan, Kentucky, Texas, Louisiana, New Mexico, Pennsylvania, New York, Rhode Island, and Oregon are full-service police departments with statewide jurisdiction. Highway patrols, which are usually found in the South, have more limited authority. The state police agencies in Florida, North Carolina, Nevada, and Ohio are limited to traffic activities. Investigations in these states are conducted by other state agencies with investigative powers or sheriffs' departments. In addition to state police and highway patrol agencies, 35 states have investigative agencies that are independent of the state police. These investigative agencies are most common in states with state highway patrol agencies.

Some states also have specialized enforcement units to handle issues involving wildlife control, parks management and safety, fire marshals' offices, attorneys general investigators, and revenue or tax enforcement units. Some state police agencies centralize these enforcement responsibilities within the state police department, whereas other states spread the enforcement duties among several state agencies, such as the parks or tax departments.

Most state police agencies provide a blend of the following services.

1. *Patrol.* All states contain modern highway systems that require patrol for the safety of the motorists. Traffic laws on the highways must be enforced, and many local jurisdictions refuse to provide for patrol on these roads. Most state police departments use the largest amount of manpower on highway patrol. State police agencies also provide for patrol operations in sparsely populated areas that do not have adequate local police agencies.

2. *Investigations.* State police agencies provide an investigative function for local departments without investigative units and for the investigation of crimes committed in areas under the jurisdiction of the state police, such as highways, state parks, state buildings, and so on.

3. *Record Keeping and Computer Services.* Local police agencies use the databases of the state police in investigating criminal backgrounds. Fingerprint records, wanted persons lists, criminal histories, and other record-keeping functions are maintained by state police agencies.

4. *State Crime Laboratory.* Most state police agencies provide a forensic laboratory to support

local police departments that lack the resources or expertise to support their own laboratory.

5. *Police Academy.* Many states maintain a central police academy for the training of state and local police officers. Some states do not train local police officers but mandate curriculum or minimum levels of training for local police.

## HISTORY OF STATE POLICE AGENCIES

Texas established the first state police agency in 1835. However, the Texas Rangers were more of a semimilitia unit than a police agency. Their services were required in a state without adequate local government. The first true state police department was founded in Pennsylvania in 1905. The agency was organized after 28 years of labor strife that required the frequent mobilization of the National Guard (NG). The involvement of the NG in labor conflicts resulted in resentment of the NG by the labor movement, which also adversely affected recruitment and morale. Because local police agencies could not be depended upon to handle strikes, the leadership of the NG urged the governor to establish a police agency under his control to deal with these problems. The industrialists also supported the concept of a state police in Pennsylvania. The use of the Pennsylvania state police in labor unrest caused the labor movement to oppose the creation of state police agencies nationwide. The New York State police was organized in 1917 only after the state government assured labor that the state police was not being created to put down strikes. By 1925, most states recognized the need for a statewide agency and established a state police.

*Hugh E. O'Rourke*

*See also* National Guard

*For Further Reading*

Bureau of Justice Statistics. (2003). *Sourcebook of criminal justice statistics, 2001.* Available: http://www.albany.edu/sourcebook/

Gaines, L. K., Kappeler, V. E., & Vaughn, J. B. (1994). *Policing in America.* Cincinnati, OH: Anderson.

Lyman, M. A. (1999) *The police: An introduction.* Upper Saddle River, NJ: Prentice Hall.

Torres, D. A. (1987). *Handbook of state police, highway patrols, and investigative agencies.* New York: Greenwood.

Walker, S. (1992). *The police in America* (2nd ed.). New York: McGraw-Hill.

## ✑ STATE WITNESS PROTECTION PROGRAMS

With witness intimidation on the rise, the need for states to adopt a formal witness protection program (WPP) has become increasingly important. However, only a handful of states have done so. Some states have tried to model their program after the Federal Witness Security (WITSEC) Program but have been unable to replicate it because of financial deficits. Whereas WITSEC has the U.S. Marshals at its disposal for safeguarding protected witnesses, most states must rely on local law enforcement for protection. Moreover, whereas WITSEC received an estimated $61.8 million in 1997 from the government, most states are struggling to find money to implement and/or maintain this costly endeavor. States lacking formalized programming may have some counties that have been able to implement small-scale WPPs. Unfortunately, these programs are not under guidelines set forth by the state. They are managed and under the discretion of local law enforcement. Therefore, neighboring counties may have entirely different policies and procedures for guarding protected witnesses, and some counties within the same state will lack policies and procedures entirely. Until there are formalized programs in place, many witnesses may be too afraid to cooperate with law enforcement. Consequently, many criminals have the opportunity to evade justice under our legal system.

## THE IMPORTANCE OF HAVING STATEWIDE WPPS

Only witnesses involved in federal cases are eligible to apply to WITSEC. Under WITSEC, witnesses are relocated; receive entirely new identities; stay under the supervision of the U.S Marshals; and receive assistance with housing, medical care, job training, and employment. These federal witnesses are also provided with monthly stipends. However, most witnesses are not involved in federal cases. Therefore, they fall under the jurisdiction of the prosecuting state, and most states cannot afford to provide the same services offered to witnesses in WITSEC.

Many cases involving witness intimidation are gang- or drug-related, and witnesses are afraid to testify because they know that local law enforcement cannot guarantee their safety. Unlike WITSEC, where 97% of witnesses have prior criminal histories, most state witnesses are innocent community members who happened to witness or fall victim to a criminal act.

When witnesses are threatened, they may decide to remain quiet when questioned by authorities, they may decide not to report a crime, they may refuse to testify, or they may perjure themselves on the stand. Furthermore, the penalties for threatening witnesses are typically far less than the penalty for the crime of which the suspect is accused. A suspect has nothing to lose and everything to gain if he or she can prevent a witness from coming forward. Witness intimidation can also weaken the public's faith in the police's ability to protect them. This problem is found mostly in large cities with serious street-gang problems, but it is not limited to these areas. Threats may be verbal or physical and made against the witnesses themselves and/or their families. When witnesses refuse to cooperate, prosecutors may not have enough evidence to secure a conviction, and they may be forced to dismiss the case. In New York State, witness intimidation is a growing problem and believed to be responsible for the dismissal of one fourth of all prosecutions in Manhattan.

## PROBLEMS FACING STATE WPPS

Financial limitations are the biggest reason why most states have not been able to adopt a formalized program. Those states that have implemented programming have found that dwindling budgets negatively affect the effectiveness of their program. In New York City, most of the program's funds are generated through the prosecutor's office. Prosecutors have found it difficult to support the city's growing number of witnesses and their family members requiring protection. Threatened witnesses can place an application with the NYC Housing Authority Program, which is supposed to move threatened families to a different housing project. When the program was implemented in 1988, it was hailed as the most creative program in the country for protecting individuals living in crime-ridden housing projects. Since its inception, the program has been overwhelmed with applications. Housing Authority officials have also been plagued with bogus claims from people who are only seeking to move into better apartments. Consequently, approval can take several months, and there is a waiting list of approximately 3,000 people.

Many localities are fearful of liabilities and lawsuits, and budget restraints allow them to offer only limited services. California is the only state with a major statewide program, and to minimize liability, state workers have immunity from lawsuits. They are not liable for denying protection to a particular witness or for terminating a witness from the program. This program was implemented in 1998, and it provides protected witnesses with new identities, stipends for moving expenses, and covers health care costs. WITSEC provides protection indefinitely, but California can guarantee protection for only 6 months, which is still better than most other states are able to offer. California's budget is much less than WITSEC; it spends approximately $2,500 to $10,000 per witness compared to WITSEC's $160,000. A new California Supreme Court ruling, which states that prosecutors are not allowed to withhold the name of a threatened witness without violating the defendant's Sixth Amendment right to confront all witnesses, may also hinder the progress of the state's program.

Cases involving murdered witnesses, which have been sensationalized by the media, may also result in fewer witnesses coming forward. In 1999, Connecticut was the first state to adopt a WPP that encompasses provisions specifically for child witnesses after an 8-year-old witness and his mother were murdered. The program provides family relocation, police protection, and a 24-hour hotline. The law makes it illegal to intimidate or threaten witnesses (subject to 10 years' imprisonment), and child witnesses can be taken into custody if parents cannot or have not been able to adequately protect them. Also, judges can decide whether or not to release a child witness's name to the defense.

Most witnesses who enter WPP become lonely and bored and may place themselves in areas or in contact with individuals that prove to be deadly. Furthermore, because most witnesses to gang-related crimes are teenagers, teenagers are more reluctant than adults to relocate and maintain participation. Parents are also less likely to allow their children to testify, especially if they believe that the police cannot guarantee their safety. There is no state program that can provide the same services offered by WITSEC. Until states can offer these services and find the money to implement a formalized program (which appears unlikely), it is believed that many witnesses will be unwilling to assist law enforcement.

*Kimberly Collica*

*See also* Victims, Police Response to

### For Further Reading

Comparet-Cassani, J. (2002). Balancing the autonomy of threatened witnesses versus a defendant's right of confrontation: The waiver doctrine after Alvarado. *San Diego Law Review, 39*, 1165–1244.

Kennedy, R. (1996, January 19). He spoke up for the law and died for it. *New York Times*, p. B1.

Musante, F. (1999, June 27). Boy is murdered, and state passes a tough witness law. *New York Times*, p. CT1.

Wood, D. (1998). Refuge for endangered witnesses. *Christian Science Monitor, 90*, 1.

## ✆ STOP AND FRISK

The Fourth Amendment provides that "the right of the people to be secure in their persons, houses, papers, and effects, against unreasonable searches and seizures, shall not be violated." The precise text of the Amendment can be misleading. In *Katz v. United States* (1967), the U.S. Supreme Court determined that the right protected people, not property. The practical implication of this ruling was that the Court would no longer consider whether the violation was against "houses, papers, and effects," but rather whether an individual's reasonable expectation of privacy was violated. Thus, the Court shifted from a property analysis to a privacy analysis when considering the constitutionality of a search. The *Katz* Court handed down its decision during a period of rapid change in the law of police procedure under then-Chief Justice Earl Warren; legal scholars often refer to this period as the *procedural revolution*. During this revolution, the bright line between what was a search and what was not a search blurred.

In the landmark *Terry v. Ohio* (1968) case, the state argued that the police should be allowed to stop a person and detain him or her briefly for questioning upon suspicion that he or she may be connected with criminal activity. In addition, it argued that upon suspicion that the person may be armed, the police should have the power to frisk the person for weapons. The state also urged the Court to recognize a distinction between a *stop* and an *arrest* (which, for Fourth Amendment purposes, is a *seizure* of a person), and between a *frisk* and a *search*. At the time, this approach was novel. Generally, there were no degrees of intrusion into a citizen's privacy by the police—either it was a search under the Fourth Amendment, or it was not.

The other side of the argument was that the authority of the police must be strictly defined by the law of arrest and search as it had already developed in the traditional jurisprudence of the Fourth Amendment. The basic contention was that there was not—and should not be—a type of police activity that simultaneously did not depend solely upon the voluntary cooperation of the citizen and stopped short of an arrest based upon probable cause. The opponents of the proposed stop-and-frisk exception argued that the core of the Fourth Amendment is a severe requirement of specific justification for any intrusion upon protected personal security, coupled with a highly developed system of judicial controls (the exclusionary rule and the fruit of the poisonous tree doctrine) to force law enforcement to abide by the Fourth Amendment. Agreement by the courts in the compulsion in the field interrogation practices at issue in *Terry*, it was argued, would constitute an abandonment of judicial control over, and even an encouragement of, substantial interference with liberty by police officers whose judgment is necessarily biased because of their duty of apprehending criminals.

The question before the *Terry* Court came down to whether the exclusionary rule applied to evidence obtained from a stop and frisk. The Court stated that the issue was not the "abstract propriety of the police conduct, but the admissibility against petitioner of the evidence uncovered by the search and seizure." If the exclusionary rule, which is designed to punish police for illegal searches, did apply, then it was tantamount to a prohibition against the practice. On the other hand, a ruling admitting evidence so obtained in a criminal trial would have the effect of legitimizing the stop-and-frisk practice by the police.

The Court emphatically rejected the notion that a mere frisk was not a search. The Fourth Amendment governs seizures of the person that do not result "in a trip to the station house and prosecution for crime—'arrests' in traditional terminology." The Court established that whenever a police officer confronts an individual and restrains his or her freedom to walk away, the officer has seized that person. The Court colorfully refutes the state's argument in this regard as follows:

> And it is nothing less than sheer torture of the English language to suggest that a careful exploration of the outer surfaces of a person's clothing all over his or her body in an attempt to find weapons is not a "search." Moreover, it is simply fantastic to urge that such a procedure performed in public by a policeman while the citizen stands helpless, perhaps facing a wall with his hands raised, is a "petty indignity." It is a serious intrusion upon the sanctity of the person, which may inflict great indignity and arouse strong resentment, and it is not to be undertaken lightly.

By merely establishing that a stop and frisk was, indeed, a search and seizure, the Court did not necessarily prohibit it. It must be remembered that the U.S. Constitution does not prohibit searches and seizures, only unreasonable ones. With this in mind, the concern of the Court shifted to the governmental interest that allegedly justified police intrusion upon the constitutionally protected privacy interests

of a private citizen. Of critical concern was the interest of the police officer in taking steps to ascertain whether the suspect was armed with a weapon that could be used unexpectedly. The Court stated that it would be unreasonable to require that police officers take unnecessary risks in the performance of their duties. Accordingly, the Court determined that when an officer is justified in believing that the individual whose suspicious behavior is being investigated is armed and presently dangerous to the officer or to others, it would be unreasonable to deny the officer the power to take measures to determine whether the person is, in fact, carrying a weapon, and to neutralize the threat. The officer need not be certain that the individual is armed. The test to determine the constitutionality of the stop and frisk established by the Court is one of objective reasonableness: "The issue is whether a reasonably prudent man in the circumstances would be warranted in the belief that his safety or that of others was in danger." Because the justification for the search is essentially officer safety, it is inappropriate for the scope of the search to exceed its purpose, which is to look for weapons that could be used to harm a police officer.

*Adam J. McKee*

**See also** Probable Cause, Search and Seizure

### For Further Reading

*Katz v. United States,* 389 U.S. 347 (1967).
*Terry v. Ohio,* 392 U.S. 1 (1968).

## ❦ STRESS

Police officers encounter work-related stressors unknown to most other professionals. Street-level police work often places the officer in imminent risk of physical injury or death. Even when their own personal safety is not at risk, officers are often witness to others who have been brutalized or killed, and are suffering. Coupled with this often-unpredictable work environment, many officers also experience stress as a result of their exposure to the bureaucratic structure of the police department itself. Officers experience both acute and chronic stressors that, over time, can affect job performance, personal relationships, and long-term psychological adjustment and physical health. At their most severe, the effects of stress may manifest in posttraumatic stress disorder (PTSD), substance abuse, divorce, or suicide. Law enforcement agencies, recognizing the impact stress can have on officers and their families, are implementing prevention and reduction strategies.

Police routinely interact with the most antisocial elements of society. They face unusual and disturbing events, such as child victims and violent death. Frequent encounters with habitual rule breakers, capable of great manipulation and violence, begin to distort the officer's perception of human character. The job is often reactive, not proactive, and split-second decisions are required. Responsibility for the safety of self and others is paramount, and officers are expected to counter these highly emotional circumstances with restraint and calm.

The stress of physical danger is often secondary to the stress inherent in the bureaucratic nature of most police organizations. When officers enter the academy, they are instructed on the hazards they may face in the community, but they are often unprepared for the hierarchy of internal departmental organization. Like the military, the police institution often requires sacrifice of the individual for the good of the police fraternity and the community. Because it is a public entity, officers often are under great public scrutiny and are discouraged by the sometimes-adverse publicity.

The paramilitary nature of police organizations requires line officers to exercise considerable discretion under the watchful eye of often-rigid management. Managers themselves experience stress from a perceived lack of support from the department and the strain of having to discipline subordinates. In many instances, leadership remains predominantly white and male, and opportunities for advancement are limited. Emphasis on organizational efficiency and tight control of standards and procedures causes stress, because officers must adhere to inflexible, impersonal administrative policies, as well as strict chains of command and rules for paperwork. Line officers seldom have a say in the management decisions that directly affect their

work environment. In particular, mandatory, rotating shift work is very arduous on an officer's life, both at work and at home. An officer doing shift work rarely gets a chance to establish normal patterns for eating, sleeping, and time with family.

Stress can be acute or chronic. Officers experience a different kind of stress called *burst stress;* they transition from low arousal to high activity and pressure in a burst. This acute kind of stress is usually the result of a critical incident, a sudden and unexpected event that officers may encounter on the front line of police work. Death or serious injury to another officer, responsibility for wounding or killing a suspect or bystander, mass disaster casualties, and being wounded or in extreme danger themselves are all events that may overwhelm officers' ability to cope. The critical incident is an event experienced outside the realm of normal human experience, and it disrupts an officer's sense of control. Developing PTSD is a resulting concern in these types of encounters. PTSD is experienced as a cluster of symptoms that includes persistent reexperiencing of the event in flashbacks or nightmares; avoidance or numbing to the event; detachment from normal life; and extreme arousal and agitation manifesting in sleep disruption, an inability to concentrate, and/or overreaction and hypervigilance.

Over time, the inability to cope effectively with stressful events can lead to chronic stress, reduced efficiency, burnout, low morale, excessive aggressiveness, absenteeism, and early retirement. Markedly inhibiting the immune system, chronic stress can lead to heart attacks, ulcers, and weight gain. The use of alcohol and other substances to cope, and marital or family discord (extramarital affairs, divorce, or domestic violence), are also severe reactions to stress. The most troublesome effect of stress is suicide. Divorce, the use of alcohol, depression, and the failure to get help are all contributing factors in many police suicides. Whereas police suicide is often considered more directly related to relationship problems, relationship problems are conversely related to job stress. Officers who get in serious trouble on the job, are suspended, or face termination are also more likely to commit suicide.

The cost of employee turnover because of stress-related early retirement or disability is great. Each officer trained at the academy is an investment, and agencies recognize the need to protect that investment. The impact of stress on the law enforcement profession was recognized in the 1994 Omnibus Crime Act, which mandated a response from the federal government. The National Institute of Justice (NIJ), responsible for carrying out the mandate, commissioned research and evaluations of existing stress reduction programs in state and local agencies. Through the Corrections and Law Enforcement Family Support (CLEFS) program, the NIJ established research and demonstration grants to sites piloting innovative ways to combat stress. There are costs in establishing and operating any new program, but stress reduction programs may mean cost savings in the long term.

Police departments established psychological services in the agency through the police union, chaplain, and employee assistance programs. However, psychological services provided by the department are often not used by officers out of the fear of being stigmatized and disciplined. Some department-run psychological services cannot guarantee confidentiality, if stressors are seen to be affecting an officer's fitness to perform his or her duties. As a result, peer support programs were implemented. Alarmed by the high rate of NYPD officer suicide during the mid-1990s, the New York City Patrolmen's Benevolent Association and the Members Assistance Program (MAP) trained working officers to be volunteer peer supporters. MAP was developed as an independent entity, not bound to answer to the larger police department, thereby ensuring confidentiality. The most common method for combating stress remains training officers to recognize its symptoms and sources, and to develop individual coping strategies. Continued training and peer support programs seek to stamp out the stigma once attached to seeking assistance.

*Karyn Hadfield*

*See also* Morale, Psychologists/Psychological Services

## For Further Reading

Goldfarb, D. A., & Aumiller, G. S. (2004). *The heavy badge.* Available: http://www.heavybadge.com

Hans, T. (2002). *Stress in policing.* Washington, DC: American Psychological Association.

Kates, A. R. (1999). *Cop shock: Surviving posttraumatic stress disorder (PTSD).* Tucson, AZ: Holbrook Street Press.

National Institute of Justice. (2000). *On-the-job stress in policing: Reducing it, preventing it.* Washington, DC: Author.

Zhao, J., He, N., & Lovrich, N. (2002). Predicting five dimensions of police officer stress: Looking more deeply into organizational settings for sources of police stress. *Police Quarterly, 5,* 43–62.

## ☙ SUICIDE BY COP

The term *suicide by cop* (SbC), as used in law enforcement and the media, is a form of occupational shorthand describing a phenomenon wherein a subject intentionally provokes an officer into using deadly force with the purpose of causing the subject's death. These types of incidents can be pre-planned by the subject or, in some cases, may be a spontaneous act of a desperate person.

As a generalization, an SbC incident involves a subject who uses the anticipated response of a law enforcement officer as a mechanism, vis-à-vis the use of deadly force, to commit suicide. Similar terminology used to categorize an SbC incident includes *suicide by police, police-assisted suicide,* and *victim-precipitated homicide.* However, the use of these terms interchangeably is problematic in that they may be misleading. The term *suicide by police* may be mistaken for an incident involving an officer who commits suicide. Use of the term *police-assisted suicide* is not intended to infer that the police are willing participants considering the provocation involved in an SbC incident. Finally, *victim-precipitated homicide* is intended to categorize incidents of homicide wherein the victim is believed to have contributed to the circumstances leading up to and causing his or her death. An SbC incident would fit these criteria to some extent. However, not all incidents of homicide precipitated by the victim would fit the criteria of SbC.

The mechanics of an SbC incident would most likely involve a subject using an instrument of some sort—a firearm, an edged weapon, imitation or nonfunctioning weapons, or other device—in such a way that threatens an officer or a third party in the presence of an officer, and the officer resorts to the use of deadly force to neutralize the threat. The threat of force by the subject is intentional and provoking in the majority of cases. The object of the subject is to have the officer cause a desired outcome—death—which the subject is not willing to complete.

Studies that have analyzed a vast number of SbC incidents in the United States and Canada have identified some common variables among the subjects who precipitate the violence. Many of the SbC incidents are preceded by domestic violence incidents; substance and alcohol abuse by subjects are common; and subjects may suffer from some form of mental or physical illness. The vast majority of subjects are male, ranging in age from their late teens to middle age, and firearms and edged weapons are the primary choices of instrument by the subjects. Many of these studies have also revealed that the officer involved in an SbC incident may manifest symptoms of posttraumatic stress that can be intensified by the fact that the officer was provoked by the subject, the weapon was not real, and/or that the officer was not in control of the incident.

An SbC incident is very complex, often precipitated by a series of events involving the suicidal subject. Not all subjects will broadcast their intentions, and an officer may be confronted with an SbC subject and forced to react without consideration of less-lethal options. Although an SbC subject may let his or her feelings about death be known, it may well be done in such a way as to leave an officer no option but to resort to the use of lethal force based on the threat from the subject. The threat may be as overt as firing or pointing a firearm at the officer, or as subtle as slowly raising a hand holding a firearm. Either way, the officer may be forced to make a split-second decision to use deadly force.

To further complicate the understanding of this term is that from a legal standpoint, a culmination of an SbC incident would fit the criteria of a homicide, not a suicide. The killing of the subject by the officer would be a homicide. The question of justification of the use of deadly force in an SbC incident would be left to an investigative or judicial body to determine if the actions of the officer were lawful and appropriate. An SbC incident would be considered justifiable when it can be shown that the officer used lethal force as a last resort in self-protection or protection of a third party, and that the officer did not exacerbate the situation by pressing the subject to act.

Other significant factors to weigh in examining SbC are the legal and mental health issues associated with suicidal individuals, specifically those who opt to use SbC. Questions of sanity can be raised in attempting to determine the cognitive ability of the subject who resorts to an SbC course of action. Legal questions arise as to the state of mind of a subject who has provoked an officer to use deadly force for the sole purpose of ending his or her life. The appropriate professionals must examine carefully the fine line between sanity and insanity in SbC cases. Assumptions that all people who resort to SbC are mentally ill or deranged are erroneous. Case studies of SbC incidents in North America have uncovered incidents wherein a subject has intentionally provoked an officer into using deadly force as a means to an end. However, without direct evidence, in some cases left by the subject choosing SbC, a clear-cut classification of SbC is difficult and often speculative. It is suggested that this can be accomplished best by conducting a psychological autopsy of the subject by an objective source, a person detached from the investigation and/or litigation.

*James J. Drylie*

## For Further Reading

Kennedy, D. B., Homant, R. J., & Hupp, R. T. (1998). Suicide by cop. *FBI Law Enforcement Bulletin, 67*(8), 21–27.

Klinger, D. A. (2001). Suicidal intent in victim-precipitated homicide: Insights from the study of suicide by cop. *Homicide Studies, 5*(3), 206–226.

Lord, V. B. (2001). Law enforcement-assisted suicide: Characteristics of subjects and law enforcement intervention techniques. In D. C. Sheehan & J. I Warren (Eds.), *Suicide and Law Enforcement* (pp. 607–625). Washington, DC: U.S. Department of Justice.

Wolfgang, M. E. (1958). *Patterns in criminal homicide.* Oxford, UK: Oxford University Press.

# ⟰ SWAT TEAMS

The social tumult of the 1960s presented many challenges to American law enforcement. Protests, riots, rising levels of violence, and other sorts of social problems caught the police off guard and led to many reforms that have helped shape the landscape of policing today. One of the more visible police innovations that emerged from the watershed decade of the 1960s was the advent of Special Weapons and Tactics (SWAT) teams, specially trained and equipped groups of officers that deal with situations that present an elevated degree of danger. The need for such teams was demonstrated most dramatically in 1966, when a young man named Charles Whitman shot almost four dozen people from a perch he took atop a tower on the campus of the University of Texas before an ad hoc group of officers was able to shoot him. Believing that incidents of this kind, as well as other sorts of special threat situations such as hostage takings, could be handled better by squads of officers who were equipped and trained to deal with them, a few large agencies developed SWAT teams by the end of the decade.

Since then, many police departments of all sizes have developed some sort of special unit to deal with incidents that have an increased potential for violence. SWAT is the generic term for these units, but many agencies call their tactical unit something else, such as Special Response Team, Tactical Action Group, or Emergency Response Team. Just as the names for SWAT teams have multiplied, so, too, have the sorts of incidents they are called upon to handle. Today, SWAT teams are asked to handle a wide variety of situations, such as protecting dignitaries, tailing criminal suspects, conducting stakeouts, dealing with suicidal individuals, and serving search-and-arrest warrants that pose a higher-than-normal risk of injury to officers.

Whatever the name, and whatever their assignments, the structure of these units is generally related to community demand and the resources of the agency in which they exist. Large agencies that regularly confront special threat situations will often have officers assigned to a SWAT team on a full-time basis. Other agencies assign officers to these units on a part-time basis, as an ancillary duty to their primary assignment (e.g., patrol or investigations). A structural form that has become increasingly popular in recent years is the multi-jurisdictional SWAT team, which is composed of officers from some number of agencies that are in close geographical proximity. This approach allows smaller agencies access to a SWAT team without incurring all of the costs that would come from maintaining a complete team.

Early SWAT units relied on the teamwork and tactics of officers and a limited inventory of equipment in order to resolve special threat situations. Subsequent years have seen continuing improvements in these attributes, including an upgrade in firearms and training as well as the incorporation of new technologies. Among the most visible technological improvements are less lethal weapons, which can deploy munitions such as beanbags, or rubber batons that can allow officers to take armed individuals into custody without injuring them seriously. Other notable improvements include thermal imaging equipment and ambient light devices (e.g., night vision goggles), which greatly enhance SWAT officers' ability to gather information that can help them resolve many sorts of high-risk missions.

The ability of SWAT teams to manage special threat situations has also been improved by the parallel development of hostage and crisis negotiators. Since the early 1970s, there has been an evolution in law enforcement in the employment of verbal communication tactics that are intended to deescalate crisis situations by negotiating the surrender of confrontational individuals. Early approaches in this area focused on hostage situations and were directed at developing techniques that would help secure the safe release of individuals being held against their will. Negotiations proved to be valuable when dealing with hostage incidents, and over time, they were adapted for use in other crisis situations, such as suicidal individuals and barricaded gunmen.

As the value of negotiations became increasingly apparent, formalized negotiation procedures were developed and integrated into the ways that SWAT teams dealt with many sorts of incidents. Over time, two basic approaches to the structure of the negotiation component of managing crisis situations developed. In one approach, negotiators are members of the SWAT team who have special training for this particular duty. In the other, negotiators are not SWAT officers, but respond to incidents along with the SWAT team to conduct any negotiations that might be necessary. However they are structured, negotiations play a critical role in current SWAT response to special threat situations.

The goal of SWAT is to resolve dangerous events peacefully, but sometimes, they are not able to do so. And this has led to some notable criticism, especially when SWAT officers use deadly force in questionable circumstances. High-profile incidents involving the Federal Bureau of Investigation's Hostage Rescue Team—namely, the mistaken shooting of a fugitive's wife in Ruby Ridge, Idaho, in 1992, and the death of individuals when a religious compound burned down at the end of a standoff in Waco, Texas, in 1993—exemplify this issue. Furthermore, some observers have been critical of the increased use of SWAT teams to serve drug search warrants, arguing that this approach represents the militarization of policing and pointing to mishaps during search warrants as evidence that using SWAT teams for such work is misguided. In one prominent instance, for example, the accidental shooting of a 12-year-old during a drug raid in California led the state's attorney general to convene a fact-finding commission to review SWAT teams and operations. Although the commission recognized the contributions that SWAT has made to law enforcement by deescalating violent situations, it asserted that there was ample room for improvement, particularly in the areas of organization and training, which would likely reduce the incidence of SWAT error. Such critiques illustrate the constant balancing act that all elements of law enforcement must conduct in order to carry out their duties while responding to public demands for accountability.

*Jeff Rojek and David A. Klinger*

**See also** Crisis Intervention, Emergency Services Units, Hostage Negotiations, Militarization of American Police, Use of Force

## For Further Reading

California Attorney General's Office. (2002). *Commission on Special Weapons and Tactics (S.W.A.T): Final report.* Sacramento, CA: Author.

McManis, M. J., & Mullins, W. C. (2001). *Crisis negotiations: Managing critical incidents and hostage situations in law enforcement and corrections* (2nd ed.). Cincinnati, OH: Anderson.

Mijares, T. C., McCarthy, R. M., & Perkins, D. B. (2000). *The management of police specialized tactical units.* Springfield, IL: Charles C Thomas.

# T

## ⊘⊘ TASK FORCES

The law enforcement multijurisdictional task force can be a very effective tool in investigation, arresting and prosecuting individuals involved in certain kinds of criminal activity. The task force configuration varies depending on the nature and the scope of the crime that it is created to investigate. Task forces fall into two broad categories: local and federal.

Typically, the local task force consists of, but is not limited to, representation from local law enforcement agencies, which may include municipal, county, city, and state police departments. It may also consist of local prosecuting attorneys' offices, probation and parole offices, and sheriffs' departments. The federal task force typically includes the above-referenced entities but may also include federal law enforcement agencies such as the U.S. Attorney's Office; the Federal Bureau of Investigation; the Drug Enforcement Agency; the Bureau of Alcohol, Tobacco, and Firearms; the Secret Service; the Internal Revenue Service; and the Office of Homeland Security.

### DECISION MATRIX

Some of the more common purposes for the establishment of a task force are as follows:

- The nature of the crime or the ongoing criminal investigation is linked to terrorist activities and groups.
- The nature of the crime or the ongoing criminal investigation crosses local, state, and/or federal law enforcement jurisdictional boundaries (e.g., narcotics trafficking, street gangs, identity theft rings, human trafficking).
- An ongoing criminal investigation has such vastness and scope that one agency could not possibly provide all of the needed resources to accomplish its investigative mission (e.g., the RICO investigation or the CCE investigation).
- A single event or a string of events is of such magnitude that its investigation requires resources and/or expertise from many different law enforcement agencies (e.g., the "DC Sniper" investigation).

### POTENTIAL OUTCOMES

When a task force is established, the following benefits may be recognized immediately:

- Enhanced authority to investigate crimes outside of one's jurisdiction
- Enhanced financial resources to target a specific criminal activity
- Increased staffing resources with access to subject matter experts on a specific crime trend
- Shared intelligence across agencies

- Enhanced communication across agencies
- Increased access to a state/federal grand jury and greater subpoena power for records, documents, and testimony by coconspirators
- Greater access to state/federal prosecuting attorneys for the purpose of pre- and post-case preparations and trial
- Greater potential for the seizure of and sharing of criminal assets via the state and federal assets forfeiture process

Task forces are particularly helpful to smaller law enforcement agencies, which have limited resources. For example, a small agency plagued by a specific criminal activity that crosses jurisdictional boundaries may have only one detective dedicated to the investigation of that criminal activity. By joining a task force, that agency can use the task force concept as a force multiplier to attack a regional problem.

## ORGANIZATIONAL CHALLENGES

The organizational challenges that a task force faces are rooted in the various organizational cultures, priorities, and agendas that are represented. Each member of the task force brings his or her own ego, agenda, organizational value system, customs, and practice to the task force arena. The task force configuration must be structured in such a manner that the ultimate goals of public safety, preservation of peace, and the prosecution of the criminal enterprise override the human tendency to promote one's self, one's agency, or the agency's value system.

Task force members have to learn to work in an organizational environment that is different from the one to which they are accustomed. This environment may require them to work with different levels of supervision, in a team structure to which they are not accustomed. Task force members have to learn new rules, report-writing criteria, policies, procedures, and paperwork that may be associated with different local, state, and federal prosecutorial systems.

## SELECTION OF PERSONNEL

The common denominators associated with the failure of a task force are the lack of a mission, poor leadership, poor personnel selection, and failure to recognize each contributing agency.

To this end, simply stating, "Go get 'em!" is a recipe for disaster. The leadership for a task force is critical. It must clearly establish a mission and define who is accountable. At times, federal authorities should be the lead agency; however, there are times when the local agency is the lead agency. The mission—its scope and objectives—will dictate the ultimate authority.

The success of the task force starts with the person selected to lead the group. If the selection process is flawed, the task force will struggle. The task force leader has to be a person of considerable experience. He or she must be a person who commands tremendous respect. His or her organizational rank or title from his or her agency will not help in a task force environment. The leader must be able to lead individuals from various backgrounds, training, and expertise. His or her leadership style must be vested in the individual and not in rank or title. He or she must understand the dynamics, egos, and special needs of small, specialized units.

After selecting a leader, the task force staff must be selected. Typically, most agencies will farm out their "problem child" or rookie detective to a task force environment. This approach is selfish and short-sighted. Task forces are usually formed because there is a significant problem or issue that needs to be addressed. Only the best and brightest should be detailed to a task force. The task force leadership should have input as to who will be assigned. At the very least, the leader should have the ability to immediately remove anyone who does not meet the task force's mission or standards.

## SUMMARY

The task force is not a panacea. It must have a defined mission and clear objectives. It must be properly led and structured to build team cohesion toward the mission and objective. Finally, its success and failures must be shared equally among the contributing agencies. Sometimes, the local agency will know the targets of an investigation best, but it will need the help of state/federal officials to gain the most leverage over the targets in criminal proceedings. This process can be reversed for the federal system.

The decision to establish a task force allows the law enforcement community to have the greatest amount of flexibility to deal effectively with a crime issue that faces its communities. It gives the task force members the ability to operate anywhere at any time for the preservation of peace. It also strengthens the members' nexus to the prosecuting attorney's office by its mere structure, thus reducing the problematic legal issues that are normally present during criminal investigations. In conclusion, if a federal task force is established, it will allow task force members greater access to the enhanced penalties that are associated with federal RICO or CCE convictions.

*Tyrone Russell Morrow*

*See also* Interagency Cooperation . . . or Not, Organized Crime Control, Serial Murder Investigation

### For Further Reading

Birbeck, C., Hussong, M., Lafree, G., & Wilson, N. (1995). *An evaluation of multijursidictional task forces.* Albuquerque: New Mexico Statistical Analysis Center.

Bureau of Justice Assistance. (1997). *Multijurisdictional task forces: Ten years of research and evaluation: A report to the attorney general.* Washington, DC: Author.

Hayeslip, D., & Russell-Einhorn, M. (2002). *Evaluation of multi-jurisdictional task forces project: Phase I final report.* Washington, DC: National Institute of Justice.

## ❧ TELEVISION (POLICE SHOWS)

The television police show is a crucial, or even sole, source of information about policing for large numbers of citizens. Many citizens have limited contact with the police and thus develop their ideas about police work and crime from television.

Police work, as represented in television drama, has consistently differed from the views in film, books, and television crime news. Film noir and detective novels from the 1930s onward depicted a morally corrupt world in which police officers operated. This is a contrast to *Dragnet* (1951–1959 and 1967–1970), the first series developed in the "police procedural" format. The procedural has served as a basic model for the police series up through the present. Generally, police drama through the decades has had a strong theme of social restoration: First, a dramatic or violent breach of the moral order takes place in the form of a crime; second, police seek to interrupt the ambitions and activities of the transgressors; and finally, police mete out justice. The comeuppance for the criminal serves to restore the victims to wholeness, or to restore the public's faith in the role of police in maintaining the social contract.

The above describes the major theme of police shows; there have been, however, some notable shifts in the way that police are shown to accomplish their larger task. Each new generation of police drama claims to represent greater "realism" than the past, suggesting that previous programs were fraught with naive views of the subject. Three significant trends may be seen as interrelated.

First, there has been an increasing emphasis on violent crime; on crimes that are, from a strictly empirical viewpoint, aberrant or atypical; and on crimes committed by strangers to the victim. Often, the perpetrator is portrayed as powerful, intelligent, and ruthless, and thus a "worthy opponent" for the officers. The need for officers to use force is overemphasized. The most common crime in police drama is murder—a crime that most police officers will encounter rarely.

This increasing "seriousness" focus also shifts viewer attention away from what J.Q. Wilson has termed the "order maintenance" function of policing, which is generally constabulary and preventive—and also more typical of an officer's experiences—and toward specialized policing. Thus, there has been an increasing centrality of detective work over beat or patrol policing. Increasing emphasis on serious or aberrant crimes may reflect increased social concern about them, or it may also contribute to an inflated perception of that threat. Another explanation of this shift is that advertisers wish to purchase access to more affluent audiences, and thus networks may favor shows with more middle-class officers and quasi-officers, such as college-educated detectives and supervisors, hand-picked task force officers, crime scene analysts, and forensic psychologists.

Second, police dramas have responded to the diversification of police forces along the lines of race, ethnicity, and gender by featuring women and minority police officers. Beginning in the late 1960s and early 1970s with *The Mod Squad* (1968–1973) and *The Rookies* (1972-1976), for instance, it became more common to feature African American police officers, first as brothers-in-arms (and much later, sisters-in-arms on street patrols and then in positions of leadership. On one hand, this can be seen simply to reflect real-world changes in the police force. On the other hand, it may be said that police dramas reflect the desire to reaffirm the allegiance of black communities to the legitimacy of the police and to an ideology of law and order after a period of civil unrest, politicization, and rebellion against brutal and discriminatory treatment.

Finally, the individual personalities of police officers in crime drama have been transformed. In early shows, officers were loyal to the law in the abstract, to their policing organizations, and to the team of other agents of justice. Thus, the outward personality of the police officer was one that was harmonious with his assigned role: competent, respectful, highly focused, but never excessive or openly emotional. Joe Friday of *Dragnet*, then, could be interested in "just the facts" without seeming cold or boorish.

In the intervening years, however, officers have been shown as mavericks who were emotionally overwrought about the moral transgressions that accompany serious crime. It was especially the case in dramas of the 1970s, such as *Baretta* (1975–1978) and *Starsky and Hutch* (1975–1979), that the reserved personality of the previous era was seen as inadequate to modern policing. Officers were now depicted as having personal lives, having emotional attachments to victims, and as somewhat contemptuous of the law-and-order establishment (which might variously include complacent or corrupt top brass or perceived "hand-tying" by constitutional limitations).

By the 1980s and 1990s, personality flaws and personal struggles in police officers' lives became more central. *Hill Street Blues* (1981–1987), *NYPD Blue* (debut 1993), and *Law and Order* (debut 1990) featured officers who were active or recovering alcoholics, had hair-trigger tempers or womanizing tendencies, or whose personal entanglements made them particularly vulnerable to projections of excessive zeal upon new cases. All of these "imperfections," far from disqualifying the officer as a symbolic agent of justice, only enhanced his or her dedication and skill in this respect.

A countervailing trend can be seen in the emergence of "reality" crime television shows such as *COPS* (debut 1989). Produced in cooperation with police agencies, they concern real activities of officers and cases. Here, the image of the officer has reverted to a reserved and unconflicted one. The officer is a tour guide: He or she stands in as the viewer's representative of respectability, who is at the same time privy to a world of pain, predation, and hopelessness. Being focused on patrol activities, however, means that some reality shows do feature more typical calls, such as domestic violence, than one might see in dramas.

Crime and police shows have been a staple of popular programming since the beginning of the television age. As television has become a global phenomenon, so has the police show. Although the United States is an exporter of its shows, police shows made in other countries nearly always appear that match or exceed the popularity of American versions. This suggests that there is something fundamental about the relationship between television, modernization, and the appeal of the crime or police show worldwide.

*Pamela Donovan*

### For Further Reading

D'Acci, J. (1994). *Defining women: Television and the case of Cagney and Lacey*. Chapel Hill: University of North Carolina Press.

Dominick, J. R. (1973). Crime and law enforcement on prime-time television. *Public Opinion Quarterly, 37*(2), 241–250.

Fishman, M., & Cavender, G. (1998). *Entertaining crime: Television reality programs*. Hawthorne, NY: Aldine de Gruyter.

Sparks, R. (1992). *Television and the drama of crime: Moral tales and the place of crime in public life*. Buckingham, UK: Open University Press.

# ∽ TERRORIST GROUPS, DOMESTIC

Public concern about international terrorism changed dramatically after al Qaeda successfully attacked the World Trade Center and the Pentagon. Although it was the most significant mass casualty terror attack in the history of the United States, it was not the first. As recently as 9 years ago, Timothy McVeigh, a right-wing extremist who has been called the American Terrorist (Michel & Herbeck, 2001), destroyed the Alfred P. Murrah federal building in Oklahoma City, Oklahoma, killing 168 people and injuring many more. This attack, like the September 11, 2001, attacks, shocked the public and changed people's concerns about terrorism. In order to understand terrorism and the threat of terror, it is important to consider both international and domestic threats. This entry focuses on the latter.

This discussion serves as an overview of domestic terrorism in America. We focus on four issues: (a) We establish a working definition of domestic terrorism; (b) we compare domestic terrorist groups by their ideology, economic views, base of operations, tactics, and targets; (c) we discuss the extent of domestic terrorism in America; and (d) we briefly examine the relationship between media coverage, public concern, and the government's response to domestic terrorism.

## THE DEFINITION OF DOMESTIC TERRORISM

Although distinguishing terrorist acts from routine criminal acts is difficult, a working definition is necessary to begin our discussion of domestic terrorism. White (2002) argues that acts of domestic terrorism are often labeled routine crimes. Official statistics are misleading because local law enforcement often labels domestic terrorism under nonterrorist headings in the Uniform Crime Report (UCR).

Most definitions of terrorism do not discriminate between international and domestic terrorism, and focus on three distinct elements: method, target,

and purpose of violence (Kushner, 1998). Two definitions are provided below:

> The use of force (or violence) committed by individuals or groups against governments or civilian populations to create fear in order to bring about political (or social) change. (Kushner, 1998, p. 10)

> The unlawful use of force or violence against persons or property to intimidate or coerce a government, the civilian population, or any segment thereof, in furtherance of political or social goals. (FBI Terrorist Research and Analytical Center, 1991, p. 25)

These definitions are helpful, but we focus here on terrorist acts committed by Americans against Americans within the United States.

## TYPOLOGIES OF DOMESTIC TERRORISTS: RIGHT-WING VERSUS LEFT-WING EXTREMISTS

Terrorist researchers have also differed in their classifications of domestic terrorist groups. White (2002) points out that researchers have classified terrorist groups by how governments respond to them, as guides to investigation (Cooper, 1979), and for criminological analysis (Smith, 1994). Smith's (1994) classification system covers right-wing extremists, left-wing extremists, and international terrorists. He argues that left-wing groups vary considerably in terms of tactics, strategies, and ideology, but right-wing groups are more consistent. Drawing from Smith's analysis, we will compare the ideologies, economic views, base of operations, tactics, and targets of both the right- and left-wing terrorist groups.

### Ideologies

The ideologies of left-wing and right-wing groups are significantly different. Left-wing groups are driven by a Marxist ideology. The well-known Marxist-Leninist group Students for a Democratic Society (SDS) began in the 1960s as a basis for student action against racism, militarism, nationalism, and capitalist exploitation of third-world countries. Two well-known terrorist organizations evolved from SDS, the United Freedom Front (UFF) and May 19th Communist Nation (M19CO), named after Ho Chi Minh's birthday. These groups were responsible for most of the left-wing domestic terrorist acts committed during the 1980s.

Whereas most left-wing groups ignore religion, right-wing ideology focuses primarily on religion. One such example is the bombing of abortion clinics. Smith (1994) argues that the racist Christian Identity Movement is the thread that ties American right-wing groups together. Members of the movement, such as the Aryan Nation, believe that Aryans, not Jews, are God's chosen people; view America as the promised land; and view violence against non-Aryans and the "corrupt" American government as justified. Christian Identity doctrine follows that man has evolved from two "seed lines": one from Adam and Eve, and one from Satan and Eve. Whites, or Aryans, are descendents of Adam and thus are the real children of Israel. Blacks and other races are considered soulless "pre-Adamic" races and are commonly referred to as Jews, or "mud people," by believers (see Neiwert, 1999).

## Economic Views

Terrorists' views on human nature and motivation determine how they view the world, the American government, and the use of tax dollars. Right-wing groups believe that people should be rewarded according to their labor value and look unfavorably on programs oriented toward aiding the unemployed and minority groups. The Sheriff's Posse Comitatus (SPC), for example, believes that the federal government is a corrupt organization controlled by Jews, and therefore, there is no authority higher than the county government. Consequently, members of the SPC have been known to refuse to pay federal taxes (see Chermak, Bailey, & Brown, 2003; Dees, 1996; Smith, 1994).

Whereas right-wing extremists focus on the value of labor in capitalist societies, left-wing groups focus on the tendency for capitalism to "unleash and encourage a manipulative greed in humans" (Smith, 1994, p. 39). Left-wing groups, such as the M19CO and UFF, believe that capitalist societies exploit minorities and the working class. Whereas right-wing groups strongly oppose economic programs for the disadvantaged, Marxist, left-wing groups feel that current affirmative action programs are inadequate.

## Base of Operations

Left-wing groups are commonly located in urban settings, whereas right-wing extremists settle in rural areas. For example, the M19CO are located in New York; New Jersey; and Washington, DC, and the Aryan Nation and SPC are nestled in the forests of Idaho and Oregon, respectively. Smith points out that the areas in which extremist groups have settled were not chosen arbitrarily, but rather because of ideological and tactical differences. Left-wing groups prefer urban settings to strike more easily at capitalist systems and to facilitate escape into the anonymity of the crowd. Right-wing groups choose rural settings to escape ethnic minorities and liberal lifestyles, and to prepare for Armageddon.

## Tactics

Terrorist groups face a tactical dilemma. The right- and left-wing extremist groups need publicity to grow and accomplish goals, but also secrecy to carry out acts of terror. In the past, extremist groups have depended on safe houses and "mail drops" as a means for anonymous communication (Smith, 1994). With the onset of electronic media, left- and right-wing groups are now able to communicate by distributing information on Web sites and by replacing conventional letters with electronic mail. Left-wing extremists usually adopt a cellular structure for their organizations, allowing small groups, or cells, of terrorists to operate without a centralized leadership. The advantage to using the cell structure is that if one cell is discovered, other cells remain active. Although the cell structure, also known as leaderless resistance, of left-wing groups allows them to successfully evade arrest, it severely limits recruiting.

For the most part, right-wing extremist groups have rejected the use of cell structures and opted for more centralized rural compounds in which entire families can devote themselves to the cause. There are, of course, exceptions, as the militia movement was organized by a cell structure during the 1990s. Right-wing groups, such as Aryan Nation, have an easier time recruiting members, but their centralized compounds are easily observed by authorities (Smith, 1994).

*Targets*

Smith (1994, p. 43) argues that domestic terrorists attack for two reasons: to prove a political/social point, or to obtain funds used to support future terrorist acts. He argues that because terrorism is a staged media event, the symbolic nature of chosen targets is important. For example, right-wing terrorists usually target Jewish individuals or organizations awarding special benefits or equal treatment to sexual or ethnic minorities. In contrast, left-wing terrorists have focused primarily on symbols of capitalism and governmental representatives.

## THE EXTENT OF DOMESTIC TERRORISM

The difficulty in measuring the extent of left-wing domestic terrorism has been credited to ambiguous reporting techniques of law enforcement and leaderless resistance tactics adopted by modern left-wing organizations. Smith (1994) points out that the only reported left-wing terrorist acts were committed by the M19CO and UFF during the early 1980s. During this time, the UFF committed 25 reported acts of terror in addition to the bank robberies committed to fund their operations (Smith, 1994). By 1985, most of the UFF and M19CO leaders had been arrested, and no reported terrorist acts have been committed by this type of communist, left-wing group since the mid-1980s. During the second half of the 1980s, the environmental terrorists caught the attention of law enforcement, particularly the Earth Liberation Front (ELF) and Animal Liberation Front (ALF). ELF and ALF groups accounted for all seven of the reported environmental terrorist acts committed by 1990, and they remained active throughout the 1990s.

Because the Federal Bureau of Investigation (FBI) increased its expenditures for counterterrorism at the same time that right-wing extremists became violent, few planned right-wing terrorist acts were actually committed during the 1980s. By 1985, federal agents had arrested the majority of right-wing terrorists as they prepared to wage war on selected targets. Although right-wing extremist groups lost momentum in the late 1980s, right-wing ideology did not. Three incidents involving the federal government and citizens served as a catalyst to the rejuvenation of right-wing reorganization in the early 1990s. First, the Brady Bill was introduced in 1991, allowing right-wing extremists to play on fears of an intrusive federal government out to destroy gun ownership (White, 2002). Second, in 1992, was the Ruby Ridge standoff, in which FBI snipers shot and killed extremist Randy Weaver's pregnant wife and young son. Weaver was being sought for tax evasion and for selling illegal firearms to undercover Bureau of Alcohol, Tobacco, and Firearms agents. Finally, in 1993, a federal siege of the Branch Davidian compound in Waco, Texas, that killed more than 70 people became another symbol of federal tyranny for the extreme right. As a result, the number of right-wing extremist groups increased, peaking in 1996, and has consistently declined every year since. Some attribute the decline in participation of right-wing extremism to the movement's association with the Oklahoma City bombing. The unwanted publicity may have deterred some from joining right-wing organizations and caused others to leave for fear of being associated with the actions of Timothy McVeigh. Still other organizations may have opted to organize under the leaderless resistance theory of collective action to avoid unwanted attention. The Anti-Defamation League reported 858 organized right-wing extremist groups in 1996, and only 194 right-wing groups in 2000. Nevertheless, it is reasonable to suspect that future "tyrannous" acts by the federal authorities could ignite another reorganization of right-wing extremists.

The severity of a terrorist act is usually measured in terms of how many lives are lost. Interestingly, researchers have found that even large acts of terror, such as the Oklahoma City bombing, have little effect on Americans. Lewis (2000) found that most Americans saw terrorism as an abstract problem instead of a personal threat. Although more Americans did identify terrorism as an important problem directly after the 1995 Oklahoma City bombing, their concern had largely subsided by the summer of 1996. Lewis concluded that despite the significant amount of media attention given to acts of terror, people are likely to think that terrorism is something that happens to other people. It is reasonable to suspect that this may have changed since September 11th.

## U.S. RESPONSE TO DOMESTIC TERRORISM

During the past 30 years, most political activity responding to terrorism has followed a major act of terrorism. The laws enacted typically create new offenses that give criminal justice authorities more power (Hewitt, 2003). For example, in response to the Oklahoma City bombing, the federal government enacted a new antiterrorism bill, allowing the United States to deny suspected terrorists entry into the country, permitting the deportation and prosecution of people with terrorist ties, and designating significant services to respond to terror. Similarly, after the attack on September 11th, U.S. government and FBI powers were extended further under the USA PATRIOT Act. This allows federal authorities to tap any telephone a suspected terrorist may be using and grants new powers to monitor Internet and e-mail communications. These new powers gave way to the creation of the Office of Homeland Security, mandated by an executive order from President George W. Bush. Although the new branch of U.S. government was welcomed by most after the September 11, 2001, attack, the extent to which the USA PATRIOT Act gave federal authorities new antiterrorist powers continues to raise concerns about violations of individual rights.

## CONCLUSION

This discussion is a brief overview of the scholarly contributions made to the study of domestic terrorism.

In this overview, we chose to consider domestic terrorism as terrorist acts committed by Americans on American soil. We employed Smith's analysis of terrorism groups to classify extremists as either right-wing or left-wing, with the left-wing classification covering all single-issue groups. Within these classifications, the ideologies, economic views, operational bases, tactics, and targets of American extremists were compared. We concluded that right-wing groups are commonly racist and are ideologically based in religion and the value of capitalistic labor, whereas left-wing groups shun religion and are more concerned with countering the exploitative consequences of capitalism. The most destructive single-issue groups, ELF and ALF, focus primarily on capitalism's exploitation of the land and animals, respectively. Right-wing extremists commonly move to the countryside to escape the pollutants of liberal lifestyles, whereas left-wing groups settle in urban areas under the anonymity of the crowd to be closer to potential capitalist targets. Right-wing groups have had little success in carrying out acts of terror and have experienced more arrests due to the increasing counter-terrorist measures of the late 1980s. Because left-wing terrorist cells became violent before the upgrade in counterterrorism, they have successfully committed more reported terrorist acts than right-wing groups without being arrested. In response to large terrorist attacks on America, such as Oklahoma City or September 11th, the U.S. government has extended federal authority to investigate suspected terrorists, causing concern for the protection of civil liberties for both liberal and conservative politicians. However, it is likely that future acts of domestic terrorism will cause the U.S. government to further extend its powers to identify terrorists.

*Steven Chermak and Jeff Gruenewald*

## *For Further Reading*

Chermak, S., Bailey, F., & Brown, M. (2003). *Media representations of 9/11.* Westport, CT: Praeger.

Cooper, B. (1979). *Merleau-Ponty and Marxism: From terror to reform.* Toronto: University of Toronto Press.

Dees, M. (1996). *Gathering storm: America's militia threat*. New York: HarperCollins.

FBI Terrorist Research and Analytical Center. (1991). *Terrorism in the United States: 1990*. Washington, DC: U.S. Department of Justice.

Hewitt, C. (2003). *Understanding terrorism in America: From the Klan to al Qaeda*. New York: Routledge.

Kushner, H. (1998). *Terrorism in America*. Springfield, IL: Charles C Thomas.

Lewis, C. (2000). The terror that failed: Public opinion in the aftermath of the bombing in Oklahoma City. *Public Administration Review, 60,* 201–210.

Michel, L., & Herbeck, D. (2001). *American terrorist: Timothy McVeigh and the Oklahoma City bombing*. New York: ReganBooks.

Neiwert, D. A. (1999). *In God's country: The patriot movement and the Pacific Northwest*. Pullman: Washington State University Press.

Smith, B. L. (1994). *Terrorism in America: Pipe bombs and pipe dreams*. Albany: State University of New York Press.

White, J. R. (2002). *Terrorism: An introduction*. Belmont, CA: Wadsworth.

# ⟡ TERRORIST GROUPS, FOREIGN

The term *terrorism* is rooted in the French Revolution during Maximilien Robespierre's reign of terror, a period when potential enemies of the government were ruthlessly exterminated. Terrorism itself is much older than the origins of the term. For example, the Assassins, a group related to mainstream Shiite Muslims in Iran, committed acts of terrorism more than 1,000 years ago. Likewise, the Thugs of India terrorized travelers in ritualistic fashion for more than three centuries.

There is no single accepted definition of what constitutes terrorism. More than 100 definitions have been offered by academe and law enforcement agencies through decades of research. The pejorative nature of the term, as well as the politics involved in designating an act of violence as terrorism, contribute to the difficulty in developing a single definition. The Federal Bureau of Investigation (FBI) defines terrorism as the unlawful use of force or violence against persons or property to intimidate or coerce a government, a population, or any segment thereof in furtherance of political or social

objectives. International terrorism is further delineated by the FBI as acts of violence that fit the definition of terrorism and occur outside the United States or transcend national boundaries in terms of the means by which they are accomplished. Under the FBI's definition, a bombing committed by foreigners in the United States in furtherance of a political or social objective, such as in protest of economic policy or the deployment of troops, can constitute international terrorism.

Terrorist groups have enjoyed a number of safe havens over the past few decades; these havens have not only sheltered terrorists from interdiction and prosecution, but also served as bases for recruitment; training; fund raising; and acquisition of travel documents, such as passports and visas. A notable example is Sudan, where al Qaeda was able to train, recruit, and establish a number of businesses to aid in financing. Hizballah members also took refuge in Sudan and came into contact with other international terrorist groups. Lebanon, Syria, Libya, and a host of other countries have also supported terrorist groups both overtly and covertly.

However, the ever-changing face of terrorism presents new threats in the way terrorists operate and seek sanctuary. The United States may provide a perfect haven for terrorists to travel freely throughout the world. Indeed, the United States presents an appealing scene for terrorists who wish to take advantage of civil liberties, gun ranges, and citizens sympathetic to the cause.

Foreign terrorists have operated in the United States for decades. In the 1970s and 1980s, Armenian terrorist groups carried out terrorist attacks against Turkish officials and facilities in American cities. In 1982, the Justice Commandos for the Armenian Genocide (JCAG) claimed responsibility for the murder of the Turkish Consul General in Los Angeles and the Honorary Turkish Consul General in Boston.

Another notorious terrorist group, the Irish Republican Army (IRA), has used the United States for many years to fund its terror campaign against the British government. In 1969, Michael Flannery established the Irish Northern Aid Committee (NORAID) in the United States to provide relief for families of Republican guerrillas. In 1977, the U.S. Department of Justice mandated that NORAID register as an agent of the Provisional IRA. The IRA and its splinter factions are also suspected of purchasing weapons in the United States. On July 26, 1999, FBI agents in southern Florida arrested three Irish nationals who allegedly had been buying handguns and mailing them to accomplices in Ireland.

Latin American terrorist groups, such as the Armed Forces of National Liberation (FALN) in Puerto Rico and the United Self-Defense Forces (AUC) in Colombia, have also either committed attacks on U.S. soil or have used the United States for fund-raising purposes. In the 1970s and 1980s, FALN committed an estimated 72 bombings and 40 incendiary attacks in the United States, causing more than $3 million in property damage. The AUC, designated as a foreign terrorist group in 2001, was connected to a drugs-for-arms plot in November 2002. A Houston, Texas, resident was arrested for allegedly planning to supply the AUC with $25 million worth of weaponry in exchange for drugs.

With the exception of the FALN, the majority of terrorist groups mentioned above used the United States for funding and resource allocation or to target foreign elements on U.S. soil. This is illustrated once again by Armenian terrorists, who have taken advantage of Armenian Americans' willingness to participate in terrorist activities, and the IRA, which can count on at least minimal support from a portion of 40 million Americans who claim Irish ancestry. The network of Middle Eastern extremists operating in the United States is similar in many ways to what has already been experienced with the groups previously mentioned. Islamic terrorist groups have used the United States for training, fund raising, education, and refuge. However, the key difference between the traditional nationalist and left-wing groups that have operated in the United States and the Islamic brand of terrorism is perhaps the most important and startling. As illustrated by the attacks on September 11, 2001, these Islamic groups, driven by religious imperative, can attack the United States with fewer constraints, and they have operated freely inside the United States for many years.

Harakat al-Muqawamah al-Islamiyya, a Palestinian terrorist group popularly known as Hamas (Arabic for "zeal"), is one such terrorist group with an extensive presence in the United States dating back to the 1980s. Hamas has used the United States to raise funds for terror operations in Israel and the Palestinian territories. One charity used by Hamas was the Occupied Land Fund (later renamed the Holy Land Foundation for Relief and Development). Terrorists have recognized that operating under the guise of a charitable organization offers easy entrance into the United States and provides a plausible explanation for global travel to regions that could otherwise arouse suspicion from government officials.

An example of how Hamas has furthered terrorist activities abroad by working within the United States occurred at the Bridgeview Mosque in Chicago, Illinois. Jamal Said, the imam of the mosque, was implicated in terrorist activities. In 1993, two members of the mosque were arrested in Israel for transferring money from the United States to terrorists in the West Bank. Mohammad Jarad, arrested in connection with the activities, told the Israelis that none other than Jamal Said sent him on the mission.

Another Palestinian terrorist group that has operated in the United States is the Palestinian Islamic Jihad (PIJ). In the late 1980s, the Islamic Committee for Palestine (ICP), with a post office box in Tampa, Florida, published *Inquiry*, a magazine that carried many articles about the PIJ. The ICP also published two Arabic-language magazines. One such publication, *Al-Mujahid*, had the PIJ logo on each issue. The ICP also organized a number of Islamic conferences in the United States in the early 1990s in which PIJ members were present, often as keynote speakers. One such guest was the PIJ's spiritual leader, Sheikh Abdel Aziz Odeh. Sheikh Odeh remains an unindicted coconspirator in the first World Trade Center bombing in 1993. Further illustrative of the PIJ's presence in the United States was the group's change of leadership in October 1995. After the assassination of PIJ secretary-general Fathi Shikaki, Ramadan Abdullah Shallah filled the empty position. Prior to becoming secretary-general, Shallah was an adjunct professor of Middle

Eastern Studies at the University of Southern Florida.

Other Middle Eastern terrorist groups that have operated in the United States include the Egyptian Islamic Jihad and the Lebanese group Hizballah. The latter was responsible for the most American casualties in a terrorist attack prior to September 11, 2001. In July 2000, federal agents uncovered Hizballah operatives in the United States using a cigarette scam to funnel money back to Lebanon, where the group is headquartered. The investigation, code-named Operation Smoke Screen, began in 1996 when an off-duty deputy sheriff in Iredell County, North Carolina, reported seeing people loading large quantities of cigarettes into cars with out-of-state license plates. The individuals involved in the scam obtained cigarettes at a much lower tax rate in North Carolina and smuggled them to Michigan, where they were sold in the Arab community for a large profit. An FBI informant who penetrated the group reported seeing illegal weapons at many of the group's weekly meetings.

Sheikh Omar Abdel Rahman, leader of the Egyptian Islamic Jihad, came to the United States in 1990 to coordinate and provide assistance to terrorists. Rahman served as a spiritual guide for U.S.-based Islamists in the early 1990s. In June 1993, Rahman and nine of his followers were arrested in connection with the infamous Day of Terror plot in New York. The terror plot, which was never carried out, involved multiple bombings of the United Nations Head-quarters, the Lincoln and Holland Tunnels, the George Washington Bridge, and a federal office building.

The al Qaeda organization, headed by Osama bin Laden, grew out of the Alkhifa Services Office for the Mujahideen in Afghanistan. Abdullah Azzam, a man who inspired bin Laden, started the Services Office. This organization would later morph into the al Qaeda organization, taking advantage of a large global network of Islamists who fought in Afghanistan against the Soviets. The Services Office had locations worldwide, including Brooklyn, New York; Jersey City, New Jersey; and Tucson, Arizona. The Brooklyn office was also home of the Al-Farooq Mosque, where FBI informants reported seeing a cache of weapons in 1987.

The arrest of Khalid Sheikh Mohammed on March 1, 2003, has shed more light on al Qaeda and the Jihad network operating on American soil. According to Mohammed, al Qaeda is attempting to make inroads among America's Black Muslims, as well as Muslims who are legally in the United States. In fact, this appears to have already happened. One example is the case of Clement Hampton-El, known as Dr. Rashid. Born in the United States, Rashid is a Black Muslim who fought in Afghanistan; he was implicated in the Day of Terror plot. Al-Fuqra, a Black Muslim funda-mentalist group in the United States, has also been tied to Middle Eastern terrorist groups. Members of al-Fuqra were indicted in the World Trade Center bombing, and the group is believed to have acquired weapons and recruited volunteers for the Afghan jihad as early as 1988.

Khalid Sheikh Mohammed has revealed an over-haul of al Qaeda's approach to targeting America. To foil the security after September 11th, al Qaeda began to rely on operatives who would be harder to detect, including U.S. citizens and people with legitimate documentation. According to Justice Department documentation describing Mohammed's interrogation, the al Qaeda operative asked a former resident of Baltimore, Majid Kahn, to proceed with a plan to destroy several U.S. gas stations by simulta-neously detonating explosives in the stations' under-ground storage tanks. One of Khan's relatives, a truck driver and longtime resident of Columbus, Ohio, named Iyman Faris, reportedly colluded with Mohammed to execute an attack on the Brooklyn Bridge by severing the bridge's support cables. On June 20, 2003, Faris pleaded guilty to two counts of aiding a terrorist organization.

Although these incidents are prominent examples, they are by no means the only ones of foreign terrorists groups that have operated, and continue to operate, on American soil. The attack on September 11, 2001, however, served as a wake-up call for state and local law enforcement agencies in a way that has been unprecedented. The destruction of the World Trade Center and the Pentagon by Islamic extremists that killed nearly 3,000 people remains the most lethal attack that

America has experienced so far at the hands of foreign terrorists.

*Adam Dulin*

*See also* Counterterrorism; Terrorist Groups, Domestic

### For Further Reading

Emerson, S. (2002). *American jihad: The terrorists living among us*. New York: Free Press.

Gold, D. (2003). *Hatred's kingdom: How Saudi Arabia supports the new global terrorism*. Washington, DC: Regnery.

Hill, S. (2002). *Extremist groups: An international compilation of terrorist organizations, violent political groups, and issue-oriented militant movements* (2nd ed.). Huntsville, TX: Office of International Criminal Justice.

*Terrorist hunter: The extraordinary story of a woman who went undercover to infiltrate the radical Islamic groups operating in America*. (2003). New York: Ecco.

## ॐ THEORIES OF POLICING

A discussion of theories of policing must first define police and policing, then distinguish types of policing, and then theorize about them. There are five types of policing, one of which is Anglo-American democratic policing, and this latter has some notable features. Theories of policing do not exist. There are, however, some metaphoric sketches of policing that make salient certain of their features and therefore can be used to describe police practice.

### REQUIREMENTS FOR A DEFINITION

There are at least five international or global types of policing: Islamic-traditional, authoritarian, democratic, Asian, and continental (Bayley, 1996). The Anglo-American democratic police are the focus of this entry. Although all nation-states have security police that are linked to the protection of sacred people, places, and buildings, and these police have, in theory, rather wide powers, democratic societies have sought, except in times of extreme crisis, to limit police powers.

A definition of democratic policing should place the features of the police, their violence, their constraint, their ordering and self-serving functions, as well as their "natural" dramatic potential and actuality in the context of the politics of the modern democratic state. The drama of policing, it seems, requires both opposition and negation. A useful listing of what is needed (*desiderata*) is provided by Liang (1992, p. 2). He argues that democratic policing should be legalistically guided; focus on individuals, not groups and their politics; eschew terrorism, counterterrorism, and torture; and strive to ensure minimal damage to civilians. In addition, he argues that marginal types of policing highlight and sustain what is wanted from democratic policing. These are at the *fringe* of his definition and include high or political police who focus on state security in various facets (Brodeur, 1983), self- or voluntary policing, and counter- and parallel policing (such as private security and regulatory agencies). Liang argues persuasively, based on historical evidence, that it is through the resistance of parallel and counterpolice forces that the need for a democratic police is sustained. These fringe forms sustain the tension that permits the general strategies of democratic (at least European) police, potential violence, divide and conquer, threat of force, violence and deceit, and sustaining myths to work over long periods of time (Liang, 1992, pp. 14–17).

Consider this definition of police:

> The police in Anglo-American societies, constituted of many diverse agencies, are authoritatively coordinated legitimate organizations that stand ready to apply force, up to and including fatal force, in a legitimate territory to sustain political ordering.

Having advanced this definition, it is also true that it raises issues.

- Many agencies act as police, but few are authoritatively coordinated, that is, bureaucratically structured to ensure compliance with command.
- Police legitimacy, or the mandate, is a negotiated acceptance of the scope of the occupation's claim, not an absolute or unchanging matter.
- "Standing ready" echoes sociologist Max Weber's terms, meaning that the threat of violence awaits and is there to be imposed if proffered solutions of the police are not embraced by the citizen.

- The specification of political territory is itself a problematic issue in practice, but in theory, it is used to define the domain of police forces. The trends to transnational policing—in the form of agreements, task forces, and ad hoc "policing actions" as in Kosovo, Bolivia, Colombia, and Haiti—are with us (Scheptycki, 2000).

- "Ordering" is a political matter at root. By narrowing the scope of analysis to isolated items of performance such as arrests, interactions, or complaints, social scientists obscure the broader questions of authoritative ordering, for whom collectively and by whom, and certainly obviates the central question of organizational loyalty and its sources. "Political ordering" has no fundamental, acontextual, ahistorical definition. As Bittner (1972) correctly points out, any action or group from which resistance might be imagined can be the target of policing.

- The police, even democratic police, are not neutral, nonpolitical forces absent their own motivations, interests, ideological readings of events, and self-serving actions. When the occasional police scandal emerges, police become defensive, and media tend to elaborate and embellish the "official line" or narrative voice of the police. Thus, the broader question of police interests is obscured or enveloped in allegations, individual corruption, or malfeasance.

- The police are loyal, but to what and to whom? To whom do the police owe their loyalty in a democratic society? Although the answer is perhaps clearest in the United Kingdom, with loyalty to the Crown well understood, it is not so clear elsewhere in the Anglo-American world. Various notions such as "the law," sloganeering such as "to serve and protect" (what?), local icons, seals and symbols on the car, uniforms, and buildings all suggest clarity of purpose while obscuring the locus of obligation and accountability. This is, of course, increased by the local funding of the some 50,000 police agencies in the United States.

## POLICE AND POLICING

Police organizations do policing, but a theory of police connotes an organizational and sociolegal analysis, whereas an analysis of policing suggests a concern for the patterns of recognition, sanctioning, and processing that exist and are associated with police organizations. As Loader and Mulchay (2003) argue very persuasively, the most comprehensive study of policing would examine the degree of fit between policing as a practice and organization with the sociocultural milieu in which it is embedded. In a useful turn of phrase, they call this the study of policing cultures. As this suggests, it is virtually impossible to isolate an explanation of what police do from what they are meant to do—the moral and political context in which they operate.

## CRIMINOLOGICAL THEORIES

It is not possible to use a review of standard criminological theories (Rock, 2002) as a basis for fashioning a theory of policing. Whereas most criminological theories focus on the offender and the victim, and on explanations for crime and deviance, and others focus on explaining the actions of social control agencies more generally, the mandate of policing is always clouded by its unique capacity to routinely apply fatal force in the interests of political ordering and, through this, a constant dialectical relationship with national security and internal and external threats.

## METAPHORS OF POLICING

Traditionally, in social science, theory tends to be defined as a set of interrelated axioms and propositions designed to explain an empirical phenomenon. Few examples of deductive theorizing exist, and most instances of theory are more like mini-theories designed to explain a facet of social life—organizational behavior, suicide, homicide, crime rates, or gang behavior. Most empirical work in criminology leans heavily on a few borrowed concepts—deterrence, frustration-aggression, rational choice—rather than adoption of the entire panoply of a given theory. Grand schemes of theorizing, such as the brilliant and creative work of Jack Gibbs, often come to no satisfactory conclusions because the conceptual and/or measurement problems are so acute and irresolvable. Thus, we will call the work on theories of policing *theorizing* as a working term.

In some sense, one could call such attempts to theorize policing analogical work, or metaphoric exercises—seeing something in terms of something else. There are four types of metaphoric exercises (using metaphor very widely in this case). Some of these attempts are metaphoric in the sense that they use a scheme to generalize about policing (here, I include sociocultural theories—Bittner, Loader and Mulcahy, Manning, Shearing and Ericson, Malcolm Young, Holdaway). Some use synecdoche in that they take a part for a whole, but see policing as a whole (J. Q. Wilson, Skolnick, Brown, Sheingold, basic administrative theories, and Chan) and elevate it to centrality in their theorizing. Others use grand theory to make police an example of it (Marxist theory as rendered by Hall, Critcher, Jefferson, Clarke, and Roberts; Jefferson and Grimshaw; and Chambliss). Some theories are metonymical in that they adopt a part of a list of features as representing the most important part of policing (Reiss; Mastrofski and Ritti; Clark and Sykes; Banton; Rubinstein; Cain; and Chan).

The metaphoric, sociocultural theories of policing are totalistic, influenced by Durkheim and symbolic interactionism, and focus on the ways in which the culture of policing influences the practice of policing both internally and externally and shapes its goals as a political organization. They are not, strictly speaking, subcultural theories, even though as such they are falsely characterized by Reiner and Crank, although the culture of the lower participants is a font for rationales within the organization. The focus of this writing is the role of the organization in the political-customary moral and symbolic world and the way the mandate and structure shape meanings.

Synecdocheal theories take a part of the policing apparatus as determinant, its administrative, quasi-legal structure including latitude at the bottom; situational application of resource problems; ecological dispersal of personnel and loose supervision; and, in some cases, an emphasis of efficiency or at least production (traffic, arrests, stops, whatever counts). Chan's earlier work combines this administrative-organizational theme with a strong version of socialization as a source of the fundamental character of policing.

Studies using grand theories have never found a strong place in influencing research in policing, with the exception of the work of Stuart Hall on mugging and the arguments about the constraint of the law on chief constables and the link of the law to state control. Lesser Marxist versions of policing are found in Harring and Gerda (1999) and Chambliss (1994). The Marxist tradition has had more influence in sociolegal studies (e.g., Taylor, Walton, & Young, 1973) than in studies of the police per se.

The metonymical studies are the most difficult to characterize because by a certain reductionism of method, they convert a focus on citizen–police interaction into a picture of policing full stop. Although they sketch the police organization and its culture, they primarily elevate to centrality the interactive face of policing—its maintenance of boundaries with citizens. The master of this approach is Albert J. Reiss, Jr., and his student, Donald Black, but their influence is shown in the major works of Stephen Mastrofski. Much more behavioristic is the Sykes and Clark (1975) study, whereas Banton and Cain focus on the role (expectations of self and others) of the police. Rubinstein, trained as an historian, has written a detailed ethnography of the urban world as seen from the driver's seat of a police car in a big city; it is both partial and rich in nuance.

This is a somewhat truncated picture, and many important articles contribute to our understandings of policing (Westley, Waddington, Klockars, Van Maanen, Fyfe, Kelling), but several important points should be taken from this analytic scheme. First, theorizing policing cannot be reduced to describing police culture (Crank & Langworthy, 1998; Reiner, 2000). This is a caricature, and it confounds and confuses verbalizations with actions (Waddington, 1999). Second, policing is clearly embedded in a cultural and institutional structure that cannot be ignored. This point is put in sharp relief when considering questions of democratic policing and its practices after the attacks of September 11, 2001. Third, although the law is not the source of the legitimacy of the police, the connections made between police crime control and politics generally have been explored by common-sense "theories" of policing, such as the "broken windows" thesis. Ideas in a mass readership magazine are caricatures of what police believe rather than theories in the sense defined earlier (see Harcourt, 2001; Taylor, 2001). Fourth, as a result of the Home Office, the National Institute of Justice, and COPS Office funding, we are in the midst of a rich and significant third wave of policing studies after a long drought (e.g., Chan, 1997, 2002; Innes, 2002; Mastrofski & Ritti, 2000; Newburn, 2003; Newburn & Jones, 1996). Fifth, a systematic theory of policing does not exist, but theorizing policing as a specific exercise seems to be emerging in the writings of Loader and Mulchay (2003), Johnston and Shearing (2003), and Manning (2003). Sixth, the emerging issues in theorizing are a result of broadening the ambit of concern and refining new paradigms such as "security governance" (Johnston & Shearing, 2003); "police studies" (including public and private, and examining the blurred boundaries); "governmentality" (Cohen, 1985; Garland, 2001); and widening concern to networks of social control in which police play a partial role and in which policing rather than the police is the focus (Canadian Law Reform Commission Report, 2003).

*Peter K. Manning*

## For Further Reading

Banton, M. (1964). *The policeman in the community*. New York: Basic Books.

Bayley, D. (1996). Policing: The world stage. *Journal of Criminal Justice Education, 7,* 241–251.

Black, D. (1980). *The manners and customs of the police*. New York: Academic Books.

Bittner, E. (1972). *Function of the police in modern society*. Washington, DC: National Institute of Mental Health.

Brodeur, J. (1983). High policing and low policing: Remarks about the policing of political activities. *Social Problems, 30,* 507–520.

Brown, R. (1991). Vigilante policing. In C. Klockars & S. Mastrofski (Eds.), *Thinking about police: Contemporary readings* (2nd ed.). New York: McGraw-Hill.

Cain, M. (1996). Policing there and here: Reflections on an international comparison. *International Journal of the Sociology of Law, 24,* 399–425.

Canadian Law Reform Commission. (2003). *Law reform in Canada*. Ottawa: Author.

Chambliss, W. (1994). Policing the ghetto underclass. *Social Problems, 41,* 177–194.

Chan, J. (1997). *Changing police culture*. Cambridge, UK: Cambridge University Press.

Chan, J. (2002). *Fair cop*. Toronto: University of Toronto Press.

Cohen, S. (1985). *Visions of social control: Crime, punishment and classification*. Cambridge, UK: Polity.

Crank, J., & Langworthy, R. (1998). An institutional perspective of policing. In L. Gaines & G. Cordner (Eds.), *Policing perspectives: An anthology*. Los Angeles: Roxbury.

Fyfe, J. (1981). Observations on police deadly force. *Crime & Deliquency, 18,* 376–389.

Gaines, L., & Cordner, G. (Eds.). (1998). *Policing perspectives: An anthology*. Los Angeles: Roxbury.

Garland, D. (2001). *The culture of control: Crime and social order in contemporary society*. Chicago: University of Chicago Press.

Hall, S., Critcher, C., Jefferson, T., Clarke, J., & Roberts, B. (1978). *Policing the crisis: Mugging, the state and law and order*. London: Macmillan.

Harcourt, B. (2001). *Illusion of order: The false promise of broken windows policing*. Cambridge, MA: Harvard University Press.

Harring, S., & Gerda, R. (1999). Policing a class society: New York City in the 1990s. *Social Justice, 26,* 263–281.

Innes, M. (2002). The "process structures" of police homicide investigations. *British Journal of Criminology, 42,* 669–688.

Jefferson, T., & Grimshaw, R. (1987). *Interpreting policework*. London: Unwin.

Johnston, L., & Shearing, C. (2003). *Governing security: Explorations in policing and justice*. London: Routledge.

Kelling, G., & Coles, C. (1996). *Fixing broken windows: Restoring order in American cities*. New York: Free Press.

Klockars, C. (1985). *The idea of police*. Beverly Hills, CA: Sage.

Liang, H.-H. (1992). *The rise of the European state system from Metternich to the end of the Second World War*. Cambridge, UK: Cambridge University Press.

Loader, I., & Mulchay, A. (2003). *Policing and the condition of England*. Oxford, UK: Oxford University Press.

Manning, P. (2003). *Policing contingencies*. Chicago: University of Chicago Press.

Manning, P., & Van Maanen, J. (Eds.). (1978). *Policing*. Santa Monica, CA: Goodyear.

Mastrofski, S., & Ritti, R. (2000). Making sense of community policing: A theory-based analysis. *Police Practice and Research, 1*(2), 183–210.

Newburn, T. (Ed.). (2003). *A handbook of policing*. Cullompton, UK: Willan.

Newburn, T., & Jones, T. (1996). Policing and the idea of democracy. *British Journal of Criminology, 36*(2), 182–198.

Reiner, R. (2000). *The politics of the police* (3rd ed.). Oxford, UK: Oxford University Press.

Reiss, A. (1971). *The police and the public*. New Haven, CT: Yale University Press.

Reiss, A. (1992). Police organization in the twentieth century. In M. Tonry & N. Morris (Eds.), *Modern policing* (pp. 51–97). Chicago: University of Chicago Press.

Rock, P. (2002). Criminological theories. In M. Maguire, R. Morgan, & R. Reiner (Eds.), *The handbook of criminology* (3rd ed.). Oxford, UK: Oxford University Press.

Rubenstein, J. (1973). *City police*. New York: Ballantine.

Scheptycki, J. (2000). *Issues in transnational policing*. London: Routledge.

Shearing, C., & Ericson, R. (1991). Culture as figurative action. *British Journal of Sociology, 42,* 481–506.

Skolnick, J., & Bayley, D. (1987). Theme and variation in community policing. In M. Tonry & N. Morris (Eds.), *Crime and justice* (pp. 1–37). Chicago: University of Chicago Press.

Sykes, R. E., & Clark, J. P. (1975). A theory of deference exchange in police–civilian encounters. *American Journal of Sociology, 81*(3), 584–600.

Taylor, I., Walton, P., & Young, J. (1973). *The new criminology: For a social theory of deviance*. London: Routledge.

Taylor, R. (2001). *Breaking away from broken windows: Baltimore neighborhoods and the nationwide fight against crime, grime, fear and decline*. New York: Westview.

Waddington, P. (1999). Police [canteen] sub-culture: An appreciation. *British Journal of Criminology, 39*(2), 287–309.

Westley, W. (1970). Secrecy and the police. In N. Johnston, L. Savitz, & M. E. Wolfgang (Eds.), *The sociology of punishment and correction* (2nd ed.). New York: Wiley.

Wilson, J., & Kelling, G. (1982, March). Broken windows: The police and neighborhood safety. *Atlantic Monthly,* pp. 29–38.

# &#x24D0;&#x24CE; TRAFFIC ENFORCEMENT

There are three primary purposes for every traffic stop: to stop a violation of the law for public safety, to serve as a general deterrent to other drivers, and to change the driver's future driving behavior. There are numerous benefits of traffic safety units, such as the ability to lower crime rates; increased safety on the roadways; monetary savings in lower insurance, health care, and tax costs; revenue generation; and gains from asset forfeitures. Additionally, traffic law enforcement is a time-proven method of increasing pedestrian safety; increasing seat belt, child safety seat, and helmet use; reducing incidences of impaired and aggressive driving; and increasing the apprehension of dangerous criminals.

Law enforcement officers are trained in every aspect of their jobs, for which agencies have developed standard policies and procedures. Conducting professional traffic stops is no different from any other aspect of the law enforcement profession. Practices should be discussed with law enforcement supervisors and used to form guidelines for improved professionalism and courtesy at traffic stops. This entry is not intended or designed to countermand officer discretion or an agency's policies or procedures. The problematic concerns and uses of radar, quotas, and racial profiling in the act of traffic enforcement are covered in other entries in this encyclopedia.

Officers should be trained to handle typical stops, special conditions, confrontational drivers, and suspicious and felonious stops. Law enforcement officers can improve typical traffic stop experiences by using a few techniques. Law enforcement officers are encouraged to invoke the Golden Rule and treat motorists the way they or their family members would like to be treated in a similar situation. Law enforcement officers should always state their name and law enforcement agency at the commencement of the stop, immediately explain the reason for the traffic stop, and state the action that will be taken. Officers should always be prepared to answer motorists' questions about the stop. If an officer is not in uniform, or is traveling in an unmarked vehicle, it is imperative to present identification to the stopped motorist. Officers should always consider the traffic stop environment. Many motorists can be uncomfortable stopping in a deserted or poorly lit area. These motorists may be put at ease by allowing them to proceed to a more populated or better illuminated location.

Officers' interaction with drivers during the stop will be a major determining factor in their attitude toward law enforcement in the future. The goal is to achieve voluntary compliance with traffic regulations, but also acceptance of the laws and enforcement. Professionalism is essential at the traffic stop. Because most citizens come into contact with law enforcement officers at traffic stops, this becomes a critical moment for law enforcement agencies in a public relations effort. Traffic stops can be a frightening experience for a motorist, and fear can bring out a person's worst side. It is imperative for law enforcement officers to always consider officer and motorist safety. Traffic stops have many positives;

they are an opportunity to inform and educate the public.

Traffic stops requiring special conditions can require the consideration of calming children and other occupants who may be frightened by the presence of an officer. Officers can be well served by carrying cards written in Spanish and in other appropriate languages that indicate the officer's request for the driver's license, registration, or proof of insurance. Officers should never base the stop or poststop actions on race, gender, religion, people with disabilities, national or ethnic origin, sexual orientation, or socioeconomic status. Traffic enforcement must be conducted in full compliance with the constitutional and statutory safeguards established to preserve the rights of all citizens. Traffic enforcement that is discriminatory or inconsistent with the democratic ideals, values, and principles of American policing is not a legitimate or defensible public protection strategy. In fact, officers should place a special emphasis on enhancing communication and understanding between law enforcement agencies and the diverse communities they serve.

Traffic stop encounters can enhance the public relations and image of the law enforcement agency. Officers need to help maintain the credibility of the law enforcement agency and to minimize the number of complaints. At many agencies, more complaints may generate from traffic stops than from any other form of citizen contact. Adequate training will also prepare officers to deal with confrontational motorists. When the driver or occupants are hostile, minimize the potential for escalation by ignoring their attitudes, concentrating on the driving behavior, and getting the violator to respond to your requests. Also, the officer should continually reinforce that he or she is taking this action to correct the driving behavior and not because of other, personal reasons. One should remain polite and professional at these times, even if the incident escalates to an arrest. If questioned about a specific procedure or action, officers can say that it is a state law or an agency policy. This indicates that the officer's action has a legal or procedural basis, and that the action is not being taken for some personal reason.

Finally, traffic enforcement can play an important role as a crime-solving tool. Because a great

majority of criminals use motor vehicles for transportation to and from crime scenes, not to mention general, everyday transportation, it is clear that active traffic officers can play a significant role in preventing and solving crimes. Traffic stops may detect possible evidence of a more serious offense, such as the most common one of driving under the influence of alcohol and/or drugs. In most cases, this can be done by casual observation and questioning, without causing offense. Well-trained, alert, and motivated officers often prevent or solve crimes by intercepting criminals during simple traffic violations. Alertness and perseverance of traffic officers who discover evidence, stolen property, or tools of a crime can reduce crime in the community. In essence, the community's fear of crime is a major influence in the attempt to reduce criminal activity. With these proven concepts, the battle against crime to reduce these feelings of fear and improve the quality of life must include aggressive traffic enforcement programs.

*Michelle R. Hecht*

*See also* Community Relations; Immigrants (Policy Toward); Profiling, Racial; Quotas, Radar

### For Further Reading

National Highway Traffic Safety Administration. (1996). *Traffic safety & crime: Keeping pace.* Washington, DC: Author.

National Highway Traffic Safety Administration. (2001). *The traffic stop and you: Improving communication between citizens and law enforcement* [Brochure]. Washington, DC: Author.

http://www.nhtsa.dot.gov/people/injury/enforce/professionalism/during.html

## ✑ TRANSIT POLICE

Transit police are specialized police officers who protect transit systems and transit customers (passengers) from crime, threats, and disorder. Transit systems include urban metros or subways, light-rail (trams and trolleys), buses, rail, passenger ferries, and terminals. These facilities, like the rest of the urban environment, can become the setting for crime, threats (including terrorism), disorder, and emergencies. Transit policing is not a separate discipline from policing, but it addresses many aspects that require specialized training and familiarization in order to be effective.

## TRANSIT POLICE AGENCIES

Transit police may include officers of a separate agency or members of a specialized unit within a general service police or sheriff's department. The first transit police agency in the United States was the New York City Independent Subway Special Police, formed in 1933 with six members. This agency evolved into the New York City Transit Police Department (now merged into the New York Police Department as the Transit Bureau), one of the largest police entities in the nation. Several large transit systems employ special units of their jurisdictional police provider. The New York Police Department patrols the New York City subway, the Los Angeles Sheriff's Department's Transit Services Bureau patrols bus and rail systems throughout the Los Angeles region, and the Chicago Police Public Transportation Section patrols Chicago's transit system.

A number of independent police agencies also police transit systems. These include the Port Authority of New York and New Jersey Police, who patrol the PATH system. The Metro Transit Police are responsible for the Washington Metro and buses in the District of Columbia, Virginia, and Maryland; the BART Police protect the Bay Area Rapid Transit system in the San Francisco Bay area; and the MBTA Police work in metropolitan Boston. In New York, the Metropolitan Transportation Authority Police patrol the Long Island Rail Road and Metro-North Commuter railways. Cities with newer public transit systems, such as Dallas and Houston, also have dedicated transit system police officers. In addition, Amtrak Police are responsible for patrolling the national Amtrak rail system. In Great Britain, the national British Transport Police provide police services to the London Underground and other railways. A number of other countries in Europe and Asia also assign designated officers to their transit systems.

## EARLY TRANSIT CRIME FIGHTING

Transit crime is as old as transit systems. Well before the creation in 1933 of New York City's subway special police, members of the public were concerned about transit-related crime and safety. As early as 1859, Philadelphia street car operators were forced to eject intoxicated passengers and to worry about the dangers of children playing on or near tracks. Fare evasion, smoking, victimization by pickpockets, and assaults were common complaints as early as the 1860s and 1870s, when theft of revenue by employees also plagued transit agencies. Early crime complaints often came from women who were forced to endure sexual comments and gestures from male riders. Responding to these complaints, for a short time in 1909, the Hudson and Manhattan Railroad, which ran under the Hudson River from New York City to Jersey City, New Jersey (the current PATH, or the Port Authority Trans-Hudson line operated by the Port Authority of New York and New Jersey), operated a ladies' car, as did many long-distance railroads.

Although transit systems rarely faced the dramatic train robberies that occurred in the western portions of the United States and Canada, such cases were not unknown. Generally, though, these types of crimes could occur because of the remote nature of rail travel, whereas transit agencies, usually in urban, highly developed parts of the country, faced crime problems more commonly associated with crowding and with the forced intermingling of people of different sexes, races, and social statuses. Added to this was the fear that many felt in traveling through unknown parts of the communities and, for those in cities with underground systems, primarily New York, New Jersey, Boston, Philadelphia, and Chicago, the fear of being trapped in a dark and unfamiliar environment. These concerns by passengers continue to influence the policing strategies of transit agencies and the officers assigned to transit facilities.

## MODERN TRANSIT CRIME FIGHTING

Because of passenger concerns for their own safety, maintaining an environment free from crime and disorder is as essential in the transit setting as it is in the community at large. Security and order, or the lack of either, affect the lives of people who use or work in the transit system, as well as those who live and work in surrounding communities. Transit police and their general service counterparts need to understand the dynamics of transit crime and order issues and their relationship with the community in general.

Transit systems possess unique environmental aspects that influence crime and public perception of crime and disorder. First, transit systems often carry large numbers of people in a compressed space. This concentration of people within a specific place during predesignated times can contribute to vulnerability, in that a crime can be planned to exploit the terrain and demographic patterns. At peak travel times, the presence of large numbers of people may facilitate some types of crime, such as pickpocketing, and limit others, such as robbery, armed assault, and sex crimes. At other times, low ridership contributes to isolation, which enhances vulnerability to victimization. Another component of the transit terrain is the physical setting. Transit systems are separated from other elements of the community. They can be underground, frequently in older, narrow spaces. They can be subject to noise that can contribute to perceptions of fear, confinement, or claustrophobia among users. In addition, they contain unique hazards, such as high voltage power lines (e.g., third rails); fast-moving, hard-to-stop trains; tunnels; and the right-of-way itself with automated switches, and so on, that pose hazards to patrol officers and emergency responders.

Transit systems inhabit a unique environment that is narrow in scope, lacking some of the complexity of the city at large. Thus, transit crime, although varied in intensity from city to city and influenced by system-specific attributes, is generally defined by a narrow range of issues: robbery, assault, vandalism, graffiti, and fare evasion. Sex crimes, right-of-way (or route) crime such as trespassing, placing obstructions on the tracks, auto theft at parking facilities, counterfeit fare media, and disorderly conduct are also concerns. Quality-of-life issues, such as graffiti and disorder, are particularly acute in the transit setting because they can enhance perceptions of vulnerability, which influence passenger choice of whether or not to use the system.

Although not specifically crime issues, response to transit incidents such as crowd conditions; accidents (grade-crossing accidents, derailments, train collisions, and people struck by trains); and threats (such as bomb threats and terrorist potentials) also influence perceptions of safety and security. Transit systems, like the rest of the urban built environment, are vulnerable to terrorism. The transit environment and its systemic nature (i.e., an attack at one point can affect remote sections of the system) make prevention and response to terrorism an important element of transit policing. Sabotage; direct assault; bombings; and use of chemical, biological, and radiological weapons are contemporary issues of concern. Transit police play a key role in supporting transit operators by providing passenger assistance and crowd management, and preventing or resolving threats and emergencies.

## TRANSIT CRIME PREVENTION AND PATROL STRATEGIES

Transit crime and disorder can be addressed through operational measures (patrol and enforcement); environmental factors (Crime Prevention Through Environmental Design, or CPTED); and situational prevention (disruption of crime by limiting opportunities to commit crime). Key strategies include police operations (uniformed or plainclothes patrol). Patrol may use fixed posts; riding (train or bus) patrol; mobile random foot (or vehicle) patrol; saturation patrols; and specialized tactics such as decoy, undercover, or canine patrols. Coordination with system personnel (such as station managers, train crews, fare inspectors); surveillance (e.g., video monitors or CCTV); and regular maintenance or "good housekeeping" are other elements. CPTED measures such as clear sight lines and adequate lighting, combined with situational measures such as limiting operations, consolidation of passenger use areas, and the introduction of legitimate use, should be integrated with enforcement measures. All transit policing strategies need to be closely integrated with transit operations and off-system police to maximize effectiveness.

As more cities and regional centers expand their public transit options to encourage citizens and visitors to forsake their cars as their primary means of travel, transit policing will become more visible and will need to address the concerns of new generations of riders. Patrol strategies that were formulated primarily for rail systems will have to integrate the differing needs of bus transit systems while also responding to new fears of terrorist-related incidents for which public transit is an attractive target.

*John P. Sullivan and Dorothy Moses Schulz*

## For Further Reading

DeGeneste, H. I., & Sullivan, J. P. (1994). *Policing transportation facilities.* Springfield, IL: Charles C Thomas.

Schulz, D. M. (1996). Strategies for combining community crime prevention with crime prevention through environmental design: The transit experience. *Security Journal, 7,* 253–257.

Schulz, D. M., & Gilbert, S. (1995, July), Developing strategies to fight crime and fear. *Police Chief,* pp. 20–27.

Sullivan, J. P., & Kozlow, C. (2000). *Jane's facility security handbook.* Alexandria, VA: Jane's Information Group.

# ✆ TRIBAL POLICING

Responsibility for policing Indian country has belonged to the federal government since the early 1800s. The agency carrying out that responsibility is the Bureau of Indian Affairs (BIA) Law Enforcement Services, located in the Department of the Interior, with officers who are federally trained and certified. In some circumstances, however, either state or tribal authorities police Indian lands.

## JURISDICTION

Regardless of who does the actual policing, questions of jurisdiction bedevil law enforcement in Indian country. Congressional actions and Supreme Court decisions made over many years have created complex arrangements that tend to expand federal power and diminish Native American sovereignty. The first of these is the Major Crimes Act (1885), which, with supporting legislation, gives federal authorities jurisdiction over almost all felonies. This means that the small number of FBI agents near Indian lands have investigatory responsibility for all major crimes. Also, tribes have no jurisdiction over crimes outside of Indian lands, even if the victim or perpetrator is Indian. Finally, tribes have jurisdiction on Indian land only if the alleged offender is Indian; there is even some question as to whether they have jurisdiction over nonmember Indians. An increasingly common way of dealing with some of these difficulties is cross-deputization of tribal officers on one side and state or local officers on the other.

## TRIBAL DEPARTMENTS

Many Indian tribes have taken advantage of Public Law 638, the Indian Self-Determination and Education Act of 1975. This law allows tribes to contract with the BIA to provide certain services that had previously been provided directly by the BIA. One of these services is policing.

Contracts with the BIA Division of Law Enforcement spell out the organization of the new tribal police department, its budget, and a list of performance standards. The federal government must approve the contract; it then funds the budgeted items, although many tribes provide additional monies. Both police officers and civilians are employees of the tribe. The police agency resembles most of American law enforcement in being answerable to local government—in this case, tribal government—for order and crime control in the community.

Amendments to Public Law 638 passed in 2000 provide even greater autonomy to tribal police forces that prefer not to be subject to federal approval of their organizations. The Self-Governance Amendments provide for compacts rather than contracts. The difference is that compacts are funded as block grants rather than as line items. Some tribes have chosen to go even further in bypassing federal control by refusing federal monies and funding their own police departments entirely. Given the shortage of resources on most reservations, only a very small number of tribes have chosen this option. By the year 2000, tribes operated a combined total of 171 law enforcement agencies, whereas the BIA administered approximately 40, according to the Bureau of Justice Statistics.

Not all tribal police departments provide the full range of police services. Although most tribal departments patrol and answer calls for service, only about 75% serve civil processes and 25% operate jails. Some tribal departments provide patrol services but contract with the BIA to provide criminal investigation.

Another model results from the Department of Justice's Community Oriented Policing Service (COPS). The program funds new local community-policing officers, but these cannot be federal employees. Therefore, tribes with BIA law enforcement must hire COPS-funded officers as tribal employees. Friction may result from the better pay and benefits available to the federal police.

## STATE CRIMINAL JURISDICTION

Indian lands in California, Nebraska, Wisconsin, and most of Oregon and Minnesota display yet another model of law enforcement. As part of an effort to "terminate" Indian tribes as sovereign entities, Congress in 1953 enacted Public Law 88-280 (P.L. 280), which eliminated tribal criminal jurisdiction in these states and gave it to state governments. State and local police departments have responsibility for law enforcement on Indian lands in these states, and cases are tried in state courts.

Tribal police departments are not always staffed by members of their own tribes. A study conducted in 2000 found that two thirds of the officers in the surveyed departments were Native American, and only 56% were members of the tribes they served. Although this raises problems of language and culture, the close-knit relationships in many tribal populations often makes it easier for nontribal members to enforce the law. For this reason, the Oneida Nation of New York State explicitly excluded Native Americans from serving on its police force.

## TRAINING

Tribal officers receive training at local, regional, and state police academies. Tribal departments may hire officers who have had training and experience in other police agencies. The Federal Law Enforcement Training Center (FLETC) has a branch in Artesia, New Mexico, that houses the Indian Police Academy (IPA). The IPA provides a 16-week Integrated Police Training Program designed for both BIA and tribal law enforcement officers. In addition to the training provided by most police academies, the IPA includes a special unit on Indian country law. Many tribal officers are actually triple certified, first as tribal officers empowered to enforce tribal codes, then as state peace officers enforcing state law, and finally as federal officers with limited jurisdiction in cases of federal offenses.

## RESOURCES

Indian country law enforcement agencies are underfunded when compared to rural non-Indian jurisdictions, the national average, and communities with similar crime rates. In each case, Indian country has fewer officers per 1,000 residents, fewer dollars spent per capita of population, and fewer dollars spent per employee. Other problems result from the large size and widespread populations of many reservations, necessitating extensive travel time on patrol and in answering calls for service. Tribal departments often have little or no capital budgets, relying entirely on operating budgets. This results in shabby facilities, inadequate vehicles, and outdated technology. The situation is no better in P.L. 280 states, where Congress gave states responsibility for policing Indian lands without giving them the funds with which to do it.

Lack of resources combine with high crime rates and dysfunctional laws of jurisdiction to make policing Indian country one of America's greater challenges.

*Dorothy H. Bracey*

## For Further Reading

Bureau of Justice Statistics. (2003). *Census of state and local law enforcement agencies, 2000.* Washington, DC: Author.

Clark, J. (1996, April 15). Complex job in changing times: Law enforcement in Indian country is anything but easy. *Law Enforcement News, 22*(443), 1.

Marker, M. (1998). *Policing in Indian country.* Guilderland, NY: Harrow and Heston.

Wakeling, S., Jorgensen, M., Michaelson, S., & Begay, M. (2001). *Policing on American Indian reservations.* Washington, DC: U.S. Department of Justice.

# ❧ TRUANCY

Truancy, or unexcused absence from school, is a major problem among American youth. Many cities report daily truancies numbering in the thousands, and some report absence rates as high as 30%. No national data on truancy rates are available, in part because no uniform definition of truancy exists, but in a 1998 report, public school principals nationwide identified student absenteeism, cutting class, and tardiness as their primary disciplinary problems. Truants are more prone to teen pregnancy; drug abuse; gang membership; and crimes committed during school hours, such as burglary, auto theft, and vandalism. Truants frequently drop out of school, and in adulthood, they have greater difficulty earning an adequate income, raising children, and keeping within the bounds of the law. Society pays other costs as well, such as the loss of attendance-based federal and state funds, and the expense to businesses of training an undereducated, unprepared workforce.

School attendance has not consistently received the attention it deserves. Although the majority of states had passed compulsory education laws by 1890, legislators created few mechanisms for their enforcement. Not until the early 20th century were numerous rules enacted defining the duties of truant officers, establishing truant schools, delegating jurisdictional power, and changing child labor laws to encourage school attendance. As state aid became tied to average daily attendance during this period, school attendance departments sought impressive statistics of parents and children prosecuted, parents convicted, and children committed to correctional institutions for truancy. The era from 1890 to 1930 also marked the first time that youth over age 14 were directed en masse into high schools, spurred by the perceived need to acculturate millions of immigrant children before they entered the job market. Eventually, most states required school attendance up to age 16.

The 1960s brought a relaxing of attitudes toward school attendance, accompanied by a questioning of educational "strictures," increased drug use among youth, skyrocketing educational costs, and cutbacks to attendance programs. The National Commission on Secondary Education reported in 1973 that coercing students into attending school was no longer working. Average daily attendance in urban schools was running as low as 45% and was also dropping in suburban schools; tardiness and cutting class were common as well. However, by the 1980s, increases in serious juvenile crime, particularly among youth under age 15, led to renewed concern over school attendance and to greater involvement of law enforcement in fighting truancy.

In recent decades, the juvenile justice system has increasingly served as a mechanism for intervening with chronic truants and as the final stop for truants. A 1998 report indicated that truancy cases had increased 85% since 1989. These cases were about equally divided between boys and girls, with the typical truant being age 15, although some were as young as 10.

The growing caseload points to the need for schools and communities to establish ongoing truancy prevention programs that address truancy's underlying causes. These include family issues, such as lack of adult supervision, ignorance or indifference toward education, and interpersonal problems within the home; school variables, such as poor attendance monitoring, peer encouragement, and fear of violence; economic influences, such as single-parent homes or student employment; and student variables, such as learning difficulties or substance abuse.

According to the Justice Department's Office of Juvenile Justice and Delinquency Prevention (OJJDP), the most successful approach to truancy is implementing a comprehensive strategy that (a) involves parents in all truancy prevention activities; (b) ensures that students face firm sanctions for truancy;

(c) creates meaningful incentives for parental responsibility; (d) establishes ongoing truancy prevention programs in school; and (e) involves community resources, such as local law enforcement, in truancy prevention efforts. A variety of OJJDP-sponsored programs are employing these principles. In Milwaukee, parents are called at home at night automatically if their child did not attend school that day. In Tacoma, Washington, police can drop youth off at a truancy center for assessment. In Philadelphia, parents are trained and hired as truant officers, making home visits to explain possible legal consequences of truancy and available social services. In New Haven, Connecticut, truancy courts composed of high school students question truants, identify solutions, assign mentors, create a written contract, and conduct follow-up. In Pima County, Arizona, parents are informed after three unexcused absences that they are subject to criminal prosecution and their child subject to a truancy petition in juvenile court unless they participate in a diversion program involving a written agreement to participate in counseling, parenting skills classes, and other services. In Yaphank, New York, probation officers monitor attendance in collaboration with school personnel, and they facilitate access to school- and community-based services. Houston's community police officers visit the homes of chronic truants, assess family functioning, explain the truancy laws, and issue summons to court for truancy petitions.

*Edith Linn*

## For Further Reading

Baker, M. L., Sigmon, J. N., & Nugent, M. E. (2001, September). Truancy reduction: Keeping students in school. *Juvenile Justice Bulletin*. Washington, DC: Office of Juvenile Justice and Delinquency Prevention.

Garry, E. M. (1996, October). Truancy: First step to a lifetime of problems. *Juvenile Justice Bulletin*. Washington, DC: Office of Juvenile Justice and Delinquency Prevention.

Heaviside, S., Rowland, C., Williams, C., & Farris, E. (1998). *Violence and discipline problems in U.S. public schools 1996–97*. Washington, DC: National Center for Educational Statistics.

Katz, M. S. (1976). *A history of compulsory education laws*. Bloomington, IN: Phi Delta Kappan Educational Foundation.

National Commission on the Reform of Secondary Education. (1973). *The reform of secondary education: A report to the public and the profession*. New York: McGraw-Hill.

Puzzanchera, C., Stahl, A. L., Finnegan, T. A., Tierney, N., & Snyder, H. N. (2003). *Juvenile court statistics 1998*. Washington, DC: Office of Juvenile Justice and Delinquency Prevention.

U.S. Department of Education & U.S. Department of Justice. (1996). *Manual to combat truancy*. Available: http://www.ed.gov/pubs/Truancy/

# U

## ✂ UNDERCOVER OPERATIONS

Both traditionally and historically, police under-cover operations are one of the best ways for police to learn what is happening in any given criminal environment. Simply put, the undercover officer's job is to watch, listen, and collect evidence of criminal wrongdoing. Doing so will help him or her to obtain, firsthand, the essential information for prosecuting criminal offenders. Undercover work can be used in virtually any criminal enterprise but is typically used in drug investigations. Although generally effective, police officers working in an undercover capacity are undertaking one of the most dangerous police activities. These officers, who typically work under minimal supervision, must be aware, alert, and ready for the unexpected.

For decades, armies, governments, and the police have long used undercover agents and informants as tools for criminal investigation. Often referred to as "spies" or "secret agents," their necessity in criminal investigation is clear.

The public's perception of a police undercover officer is one of disguise: The police officer pretending to be a taxi driver to combat robberies of cabdrivers, a female undercover officer dressed as a prostitute or a male undercover officer dressed as a homeless person in order to deter muggings, rapes, and robberies, and sometimes even serial killers.

In virtually all crimes, investigative techniques range from the traditional to the unconventional. The technique of using undercover agents to infiltrate criminal groups has been an investigative staple for decades and one of the most effective methods for obtaining credible, firsthand criminal intelligence. In spite of this, the activities and the role of the undercover agent are probably the least understood of any criminal investigation procedure—even within the law enforcement community.

The use of undercover agents poses critical problems for police managers and prosecutors with regard to manpower, training, funding, specialized equipment, and other unique resources. In some agencies, procedures for undercover work may be clearly and explicitly documented, but in others, procedures may be unique to each case, creative, and untried. In either case, undercover investigations must be carried out in strict compliance with agency policy and established procedural and legal restraints.

In addition to the benefits reaped by undercover agents, the technique has both pros and cons. It is the one investigative technique in which the officer can see firsthand the inner workings of criminal organizations. Undercover officers can also converse and strategize with their criminal targets and learn the ways in which criminal minds think. The downside, however, is that constant and close interaction with the criminal element may place the officer in jeopardy by inadvertently revealing something inconsistent with his or her cover story. Furthermore, exposure to criminal elements in a close undercover capacity for extended periods might reflect poorly on the officer's credibility and professionalism.

In spite of these concerns, undercover work today is a recognized and accepted law enforcement practice. Many of the agencies that employ undercover agents provide them with specialized training. In some cases, undercover agents are chosen directly from graduating police academy classes because their identity as law enforcement officers has not become known to the general public yet. Police administrators must be careful in the selection of candidates for undercover work. It is important for police managers to look for traits such as a friendly and approachable personality, special skills in given areas, or just an aptitude for dangerous and challenging work.

Not every police officer can function properly and professionally in an undercover capacity. Typically, the undercover officers work with minimal direct supervision. Doing so requires the officer to be more reliant on his or her personal integrity when opportunities for illegal or immoral activities present themselves, as they will. One of the greatest challenges to undercover officers is the development of skills that maximize their effort to match wits with some of the most intelligent and artful criminals on the street.

Undercover assignments can be either short-term or long-term ("deep cover"). Short-term undercover operations are normally considerably safer for the officer than those that are deep cover. The short-term operation permits the help of surveillance officers and affords protections that undercover agents working in a deep-cover capacity do not have. However, the benefits of working in a deep-cover undercover operation allow a criminal suspect time to gain total trust of the undercover agent to the point of openly discussing criminal operations. This is a greater advantage to an undercover agent because as a rule, criminals are very suspicious of potential buyers of illegal drugs or stolen merchandise after being introduced by a third-party who could potentially be (and sometimes is) a police informer.

Although no two cases are exactly alike, certain common elements are observable: (a) the introduction, (b) the acceptance, (c) the buy, (d) the arrest, (e) coverage of the informant, and (f) the "after action."

The informant typically makes the introduction of the undercover operative to the suspect, which initiates the case. The undercover agent is then accepted or not. When the suspect does not accept the agent, it might be necessary for the informant to meet the suspect at a later time without the undercover agent to determine why the agent was not accepted at the time of the introduction. It may be necessary for the informant to bring in another agent with a different cover story to try to overcome the difficulties of the previous encounter.

After the introduction of the undercover agent to the suspect, there is a short period of "bobbing, weaving, and circling," where the suspect gets to know or feel if he can trust the prospective buyer (the undercover agent). If a feeling of trust is established, conversation will quickly turn to the contraband that is to be purchased by the agent. Such conversation will generally result in the undercover agent asking for or obtaining samples, and the suspect will quote the purchase price. After the samples have been delivered and the undercover agent has had an opportunity to examine them, the agent informs the suspect of how large a purchase he is willing to make. The purchase may or may not go through. In other words, a decision must be made whether or not to arrest a suspect when he delivers the contraband (also known as a "buy-bust") or to take that action after subsequent deliveries (known as a "buy-walk").

The first buy is usually a small one. In an agency that does not mind losing "seed" money, undercover officers can make bigger purchases at a later time. As a rule, the second purchase or, if necessary, several subsequent purchases are usually large enough to warrant not only the appearance of a suspect but also some of the people connected with him. These individuals could be present in several capacities—countersurveillance, protection, main participants, equal partners, perhaps even "higher-ups." Sometimes, however, it becomes necessary because of the development of circumstances surrounding the case to arrest a suspect when an initial delivery is made.

In summary, undercover operations are one of a number of investigative choices available to police agencies. They require a commitment of training and financial expenditures that may make this choice unfeasible for many law enforcement agencies. However, undercover operations can make powerful inroads into criminal organizations that are not available through other, more traditional investigative methods.

*Michael D. Lyman*

*See also* Drug Enforcement in the United States, Investigative Techniques, Informants

## For Further Reading

Barefoot, K. (1995). *Undercover investigation.* Newton, MA: Butterworth-Heinemann.

Buckwalter, A. (1983). *Surveillance and undercover investigation.* Newton, MA: Butterworth-Heinemann.

Bureau of Justice Assistance. (1990). *Informants and undercover investigations.* Washington, DC: U.S. Government Printing Office.

Fijnaut, C., & Marx, G. (1995). *Undercover: Police surveillance in comparative perspective.* The Hague: Kluwer.

Lyman, M. (2002). *Practical drug enforcement.* Boca Raton, FL: CRC.

Marx, G. (1988). *Undercover: Police surveillance in America.* Berkeley: University of California Press.

Marx, G. (1992). When the guards guard themselves: Undercover tactics turned inward. *Policing and Society, 2*(3), 151–172.

## ⨕ UNIFORM CRIME REPORTS

The Uniform Crime Report (UCR) program, administered by the Federal Bureau of Investigation (FBI) since its inception in 1930, is a nationwide system for the collection, analysis, and public reporting of data concerning crimes and arrests reported to police. The UCR program has grown tremendously since 1930, when approximately 400 police agencies in 43 states participated; today, more than 18,000 law enforcement agencies representing jurisdictions in all 50 states participate voluntarily in the UCR program. The program has also undergone a series of enhancements and improvements in its data collection, definition, analysis, and reporting techniques over the years, and in 1989, a dramatically improved National Incident-Based Reporting System was implemented to correct various deficiencies and generally improve the usefulness of UCR as a measure of crime and police activity.

The creation of the UCR system can be traced to the activities of the International Association of Chiefs of Police (IACP) and that organization's recognition of the need to quantify and publicly report on various standardized measures of police performance. The IACP's leadership, which included August Vollmer and O. W. Wilson, was also influenced by the basic principles of scientific management as espoused by Frederick Winslow Taylor, and they campaigned for a standardized system to measure and compare interagency performance. In this regard, the UCR can be seen as one of policing's earliest attempts at comparative performance management. Prior to the UCR, there existed no systematic process with which to gauge the performance of different police agencies, particularly in the area of crime control. Various agencies prepared annual reports or other statistical reports on crime and other measures of police performance, but these reports varied greatly in terms of the type and quality of crime-related data they presented, making interagency comparisons difficult at best. Further compounding the problem of standardized measurement was the fact that various state penal laws classified offenses according to different criteria: The penal code definition of grand larceny in one state, for example, might differ significantly from the definition in other states. This necessitated the creation of an entirely new set of offense definitions, based on an internal FBI classification system, that could be applied across all states and all jurisdictions.

The UCR uses two primary categories or indexes for crime and arrest data. The Part I Index is the best known and most frequently cited statistic, and it consists of the seven major offenses of murder and non-negligent manslaughter, forcible rape, robbery, aggravated assault, burglary, larceny-theft, and motor vehicle theft. Although arson was added to the list of Part I offenses in 1979 as an eighth offense category, it is not included in many or most discussions of serious Part I Index crimes. Part II offenses cover simple assault, curfew offenses, loitering, fraud, forgery and counterfeiting, disorderly conduct, embezzlement, driving under the influence, drug offenses, gambling, liquor offenses, offenses against the family, prostitution, public drunkenness, sex offenses, stolen property, vandalism, vagrancy, and weapons offenses. The UCR data for Part II offenses are derived from reports of arrests made (rather than crimes reported), because many of these offenses are not reported to the police as crimes. The FBI further categorizes Part I Index crimes in the Violent Crime Index, comprising the sum of all reported offenses in the murder and non-negligent manslaughter, forcible rape, robbery, and aggravated assault categories, and the Property Crime Index, comprising all reported burglary, larceny-theft, and motor vehicle theft offenses.

The FBI makes UCR data available to the public in its annual and semiannual *Crime in the United States* statistical reports, as well as in special analytic reports on such selected offenses as hate crimes, murders, and assaults committed against law enforcement officers. The *Crime in the United States* reports provide fairly detailed analyses of reported Part I offenses, including the overall number of crimes reported, crime trends for various offense categories, and crime victimization rates (the number of crimes per 100,000 population) for specific cities or metropolitan statistical areas as well as for specific regions and demographic categories (i.e., age, gender, and race). The report also provides similar statistical analyses for arrests. Finally, the *Crime in the United States* report provides data on "offenses cleared"—the percentage of reported Part I Index offenses cleared or solved, most typically through the arrest of the offender responsible. An "exceptional clearance" can be granted without an arrest when the offender is identified and sufficient evidence exists to charge him or her, but some reason outside of law enforcement precludes making an arrest (e.g., the offender is dead, the victim refuses to prosecute, or the offender is incarcerated in another jurisdiction and cannot be extradited).

Although the UCR program provides a fairly useful measure of reported crimes and arrests and permits some comparison across jurisdictions and agencies, the program has several important limitations. Because its data are derived entirely from offenses and arrests reported to police, the UCR cannot measure unreported crime and therefore cannot reveal the actual scope and dimension of crime. The UCR offense definitions, along with some of the methods used to collect and process the raw data, also impose several significant limitations on the data's utility. The forcible rape offense definition, for example, does not include sexual assaults committed against men. Furthermore, in a multiple-offense situation (where several related offenses are committed at the same time and place, regardless of the number of victims), the "hierarchy rule" requires that only the highest ranking offense is recorded: In the case of a robbery and forcible rape that leads to murder, for example, only the murder would be reflected in the Crime Index. Thus, a fairly substantial but undetermined number of crimes are never captured by the UCR program or reflected in UCR reports.

Given the importance of accurately determining the true or actual number and rates of crime, the U.S. Department of Justice established the National Crime Victimization Survey (NCVS) program in 1973 in order to complement the UCR data by estimating the number of unreported crimes nationwide. Based on a methodology that obtains data by surveying a representative sample of approximately 42,000 households across the nation, the NCVS program provides an accurate estimate of unreported crime and victimization rates.

*Vincent E. Henry*

***See also*** Crime Statistics and Analysis, National Crime Victimization Survey, National Incident Based Reporting System (NIBRS)

## *For Further Reading*

Federal Bureau of Investigation. (2002). *Crime in the United States, 2001.* Washington, DC: U.S. Department of Justice.

Federal Bureau of Investigation. (2003). *Age-specific arrest rates and race-specific arrest rates for selected offenses, 1991–2001.* Washington, DC: U.S. Department of Justice.

## ✣ UNIONS

Trade unions are defined by *Webster's Dictionary* as an "association of wage earners to further or maintain their rights and interests through collective bargaining with their employer." Various attempts have been made at organizing police officers into such an association (i.e., welfare or benevolent associations) since the latter part of the 19th century. In the United States, these attempts have been restricted to the thousands of local jurisdictions and usually regard matters of employment, salary, or discipline.

One of the basic problems for police officers in their attempts to combine their voices to improve their condition has been their position as "guardians of the peace" and "protectors of society." In the 20th century, police officers have seen their fellow workers improve their lot by bettering their working conditions and salaries through unionization. One of the first attempts to organize a union in a police department, in Cincinnati in 1918, evoked statements from the mayor, who made it clear that unions had no place in police departments because such a relationship was inherently incompatable with the discipline and work of the department.

Also during this time, a nationwide attack on any form of police unionization began, ranging from the Mayor of Jersey City, who questioned how police could serve two masters—organized labor and the people—to U.S. Senator Myers, who proposed denial of pay to any police officer who joined a union. The course of police unionization was inevitably altered by these events and the Boston Police Strike of 1919.

The events of this strike and its aftermath were to have a lasting effect on police unionization. Indeed, the principal legacy of this strike was described as the death of police unionization in the United States. Whereas other countries, especially the United Kingdom, moved toward some type of national union or federation for all of its police officers, trade unionism in U.S. policing was dead. In a 1944 report, the IACP saw fit to remind its members that police unionization would bring sweeping public resentment against the police because of this concept of divided allegiance. Again in 1958, the IACP felt it necessary to restate its position on the destructive nature of police unionization. Needless to say, the IACP, an association of police chiefs and upper management, saw, and still see, unionization as a threat to their supremacy in the policing pyramid.

Whereas the early history of police unionization was a series of repressive laws and policies by their "political masters," the economic downturn in the 1960s was to be an unexpected boost to police unionization. The New York City Patrolman's Benevolent Association (PBA) was to be in the forefront of pushing its agenda for salaries and work rules. The PBA was one of the first unions to use political clout, campaign endorsements, and contributions to gain power in the mayoral and gubernatorial elections of 1964 and 1968. Their policies of confrontation and politicization of negotiations were to be copied by other associations, such as the Los Angeles Protective League and the Boston PBA.

These methods allowed the Boston PBA to receive legal recognition in 1964 by the Massachusetts legislature, over the objections of Boston city authorities. Indeed, the Boston PBA, with the memories of the disastrous strike of 1919, was not a proponent of striking. It was, however, in the vanguard of the development of rule book slowdowns and political demonstrations by off-duty officers, their wives, and their families.

In more recent times, police unions have, through national organizations such as the Fraternal Order of Police (FOP) or the International Union of Police Associations, or through affiliation with the AFL-CIO, such as the U.S. Capitol Police, sought to bolster their political influence on the national scale. Endorsements from police organizations are usually sought by politicians. These efforts have been aimed at funding and other work-related issues, and also to secure a "place at the table" for local police officers in the new Homeland Security environment.

In some cases, the unions have been more aggressive and effective in the political and legal arenas than the employing political unit. Recently, the local chapter of the FOP in Columbus, Ohio, was able to defeat the U.S. Justice Department's efforts to secure a consent decree from the City of Columbus. This decree, a common practice of the Justice Department, would have allowed the Justice Department to "oversee" certain practices, such as hiring, assignments, and arrest practices, in the Columbus Police Department. The local FOP, with support from the national organization, was able to pay for additional legal work, through union dues and special assessments on the member, to block the Justice Department's efforts to gain authority over the police department. This situation also served to bolster the union's position with its members and remind the local political parties of the clout that the FOP can bring to the table, whether in court, at the bargaining table, or at the ballot box.

Although these various matters have an overall effect on policing, the primary goals of the union have been to better the members' lot and to give them a voice in the department. Over the years, various unions, under several titles, associations, lodges, or protective leagues, have been able to become the recognized bargaining agent for the rank and file with the employing police department. Through the power of collective bargaining and contracts, some of these unions have been able to secure a variety of benefits and counterbalance the authority of the individual police chiefs in the internal discipline of the force. In certain cities, such as Boston and Philadelphia, the police commissioners have complained publicly about their inability to manage the workforce effectively because of the existing contracts and the political influence of the unions.

One recent tool that police unions have added to their arsenal is the "no confidence vote." Although this vote has no legal weight, it does act as a counterbalance to the authority of the chief, who does have to survive in a political world. It is usually employed over a contract issue. It should also be noted that, at present, 19 states have legislation forbidding all government employees from forming or joining a union.

*Joseph F. King*

**See also** Police Strikes/"Blue Flu"

### For Further Reading

*History of police unions in the United States.* (1984). Huntsville, TX: Justex Systems.

Heustis, C. (1958). Police unions. *Journal of Criminal Law, Criminology & Political Science, 64,* 644.

International Association of Chiefs of Police. (1958). Police unions. *Bulletins on Police Problems.* Alexandria, VA: Author.

King, J. (1999). *Police strikes of 1918 and 1919 in the United Kingdom and Boston and their effects.* Unpublished doctoral dissertation, City University of New York.

# ᙂᙇ  USE OF FORCE

In the United States, police authority to use force is defined by criminal statutes. These statutes typically define *deadly physical force* as force capable of killing or likely to cause death or serious (e.g., crippling or permanently maiming) injury. *Physical force* is defined as force capable of causing lesser types of injury. In practice, deadly force most often occurs when officers fire their weapons at other people, although, in a few instances, police have killed or maimed people by allowing dogs to attack them or by striking them in sensitive areas of the body. Nonlethal police physical force usually involves restraining grips and holds; striking with hands and clubs, or "batons"; and applying a variety of technological devices, such as chemical sprays and electronic shocking devices, or "stun guns."

## AUTHORIZATION FOR POLICE USE OF FORCE

State criminal law statutes distinguish criminal acts (e.g., assault, manslaughter, murder) from justifiable force by police and citizens. These provisions grant police greater authority than citizens to use force

**Table 1**     New York City Police Scale of Escalating Force

| Provocation or Condition | Appropriate Force Response |
| --- | --- |
| Imminent threat of death or *serious* physical injury | Deadly force: usually the firearm |
| Threatened or potential lethal assault | Drawn and/or displayed firearm |
| Physical assault likely to cause physical injury | Impact techniques: batons, fists, and feet |
| Threatened or potential physical assault likely to cause physical injury | Pepper spray |
| Minor physical resistance: grappling, going limp, pulling or pushing away, etc. | Compliance techniques: wrestling holds and grips designed to physically overpower subjects and/or to inflict physical pain that ends when the technique is stopped and that causes no lasting injury |
| Verbal resistance: failure to comply with directions, etc. | Firm grips on arms, shoulders, etc., that cause no pain, but that are meant to guide people (e.g., away from a fight; toward a police car) |
| Refusal to comply with requests or attempts at persuasion (see below) | Command voice: Firmly given directions (e.g., "I asked for your license, registration, and proof of insurance, Sir. Now I am telling you that if you don't give them to me, I will have to arrest you." |
| Minor violations or disorderly conditions involving no apparent threats to officers or others | Verbal persuasion: Requests for compliance (e.g., "May I see your license, registration, and proof of insurance, Sir?") |
| Orderly public places | Professional presence: The officer on post deters crime and disorder; the Highway Unit deters speeding. |

Source: New York City Police Department, *Police student's guide*, Chapter 30, p. 7 (2003).

justifiably. Typically, they authorize police to use deadly force in order to protect themselves or others against life-threatening attacks and/or to apprehend people suspected of such violent offenses as murder, rape, assault, and armed robbery. Officers generally are authorized by law to use nonlethal grades of physical force in order to defend themselves or others against physical assault or to take into custody suspects who do not otherwise submit to police authority.

Criminal statutes have two great weaknesses as controls on police officers' discretion in use of force. First, they are extremely broad, and they give very little detailed guidance to officers, who must make quick decisions under stressful conditions. Second, absent unambiguous evidence that a police officer has used force in unauthorized ways (e.g., as in the videotape of the Los Angeles police assault on Rodney King or the bathroom assault on Abner Louima, whose injuries verified his claim that New York police had sodomized him with a stick), these laws are virtually unenforceable. To prove in a criminal proceeding that an officer has unjustifiably shot somebody, for example, a prosecutor usually must convince jurors beyond a reasonable doubt

that the officer was *not* in reasonable fear for his or her safety at the instant of the shooting. Except in clear instances of brutality like the King and Louima cases, proof of this negative proposition rarely exists.

## INTERNAL CONTROLS ON POLICE USE OF FORCE

Because of the vagueness of criminal statutes and the difficulty of enforcing them, most U.S. police departments have adopted rules and policies that define more clearly the circumstances in which officers may use various levels of force. These are enforced in internal administrative proceedings in which evidentiary standards are less rigorous than those of the criminal courts. Such policies typically instruct officers that they are obliged to use no more force than is reasonably necessary to resolve a particular situation. This general direction is given substance by reference to *escalating scales of force,* such as in the New York City Police Department scale illustrated in Table 1. Here, clearly defined levels of force are matched with the situations that may authorize them. Thus, officers should use no

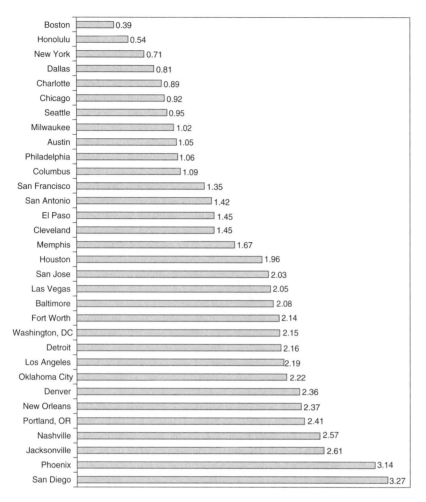

**Figure 1**    Annual Fatal Shooting Rates per 1,000 Officers in Municipal
             Police Departments, 1990–2000

Source: Derived from the *Washington Post,* July 1, 2001.

more than the described compliance techniques to overcome such minor physical resistance as grappling or attempting to pull away from officers. The degree of force matched to each situation defines the maximum appropriate level of force for such cases, so that anything exceeding it can be classified as excessive force. The scale does not require officers to begin at the bottom and work their way up until they find a successful level of force.

This scale's lowest levels describe police activities—mere presence, verbal persuasion, command voice—that involve no physical contact and that most people do not regard as forcible conduct. Police are taught, however, that the general purpose of using force is to put an end to objectionable conduct (e.g., disorderly

or criminal activity) and, where no such conduct exists, to ensure that it does not occur. Therefore, whether on foot patrol at a public event or in a patrol car on an interstate highway, the mere visible presence of a police officer is considered by police to be a method of deterring misconduct and compelling citizens to behave appropriately by reminding them of the force available to the state.

## FREQUENCY OF POLICE USE OF FORCE

In the United States, there is no systematic method of measuring the frequency with which police officers use any level of force. The U.S. Department of Justice estimated in 1997, however, that about one fifth of 1% (0.2%) of the U.S. population had been subjected to some degree of police force during 1996 (Greenfield, Langan, & Smith, 1997). Similarly, efforts to measure the frequency of police use of deadly force have been sporadic. No national system reports on the number of incidents in which police fire their weapons at others, so that there exists no measure of the police use of deadly force. Both the FBI's Uniform Crime Report program and the National Vital Statistics System collect data on deaths inflicted by police, but independent studies of these systems indicate that both greatly underreport the data (Fyfe, 2002; Lofton, Wiersema, McDowell, & Dobrin, 2003; Sherman & Langworthy, 1979).

The most extensive and accurate data on deadly force originated with the *Washington Post,* which, as part of a series on the subject, activated U.S. freedom of information laws to obtain data about fatal police shootings during 1990–2000 directly from several municipal police agencies. The results are illustrated in Figure 1, presented as annual rates of fatal shooting per 1,000 officers. The figure is

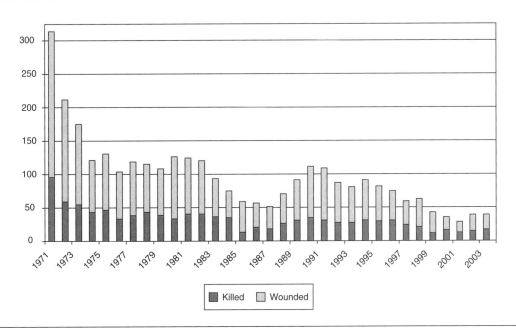

**Figure 2**    Persons Shot by New York City Police, 1971–2003

Source: New York City Police Department Training Bureau (2004).

remarkable for two reasons. First, it shows that there is great variation in the rate of police shootings across U.S. jurisdictions: From 1990–2000, police officers in San Diego were more than eight times as likely as Boston officers to have shot and killed citizens (3.27 annual fatal shootings per 1,000 officers vs. 0.39 annual fatal shootings per 1,000 officers). Second, the figure shows that fatal shootings are a rare event for police officers anywhere. The San Diego rate translates to one fatal police shooting for about every 300 years of police service; the Boston rate reflects one fatal police shooting for every 2,500 years of police service.

The best available data also indicate that police use of deadly force has declined over the past generation as police policies and training have grown more sophisticated. The New York City Police Department records summarized in Figure 2 show that its officers shot 314 people in 1971 (killing 93 and wounding 221), and that these figures have decreased

considerably since then. In 2003, the last year shown on the figure, New York City officers shot 38 people (wounding 24 and killing 14). Data on lesser degrees of force are not available but are presumed by responsible officials to have decreased similarly.

*James J. Fyfe*

## For Further Reading

Fyfe, J. J. (2002). Too many missing cases: Holes in our knowledge about police use of force. *Justice Research and Policy, 4,* 87–102.

Greenfield, L. A., Langan, P. A., & Smith, S. K. (1997). *Police use of force: Collection of national data.* Washington, DC: Bureau of Justice Statistics.

Loftin, C., Wiersema, B., McDowell, D., & Dobrin, A (2003). Underreporting of justifiable homicides committed by police officers in the United States, 1976–1998. *American Journal of Public Health, 93,* 1117–1121.

Sherman, L. W., & Langworthy, R. (1979). Measuring homicide by police officers. *Journal of Criminal Law and Criminology, 70,* 546–560.

## ∞ VEHICLE SEARCHES

The Fourth Amendment of the U.S. Constitution provides most of the controlling principles regarding searches. The Amendment provides that

> the right of the people to be secure in their persons, houses, papers and effects, against unreasonable searches and seizures, shall not be violated; and no warrants shall issue, but upon probable cause, supported by oath or affirmation, and particularly describing the place to be searched, and the person or things to be seized.

The U.S. Supreme Court, which is responsible for interpreting the Constitution, has decided many cases that have spelled out exactly when a search warrant is required and when a warrant is not required. Vehicles are generally considered an exception to the Fourth Amendment's search warrant requirement. This exception is also known as the Carroll doctrine because it was in *Carroll v. United States* (1925) that the Supreme Court ruled that automobiles were unique. The most important characteristic of an automobile cited by the Court in formulating the automobile exception is its mobility. As the court stated in *Chambers v. Maroney* (1970), "The car is movable, the occupants are alerted, and the car's contents may never be found again if a warrant must be obtained." Because automobiles travel

on public roadways in the public view, there is a lesser expectation of privacy than elsewhere.

The controlling factor in the search of an automobile without a search warrant is probable cause to believe that the vehicle contains items that are connected with criminal activity. Such items are subject to seizure. Probable cause depends on the circumstances of the particular case. The degree of evidence suggesting criminal activity must be objective and such that a warrant could have been issued by a magistrate based on it. Evidence seized from a vehicle will not be admissible in court if the seizure is not based on probable cause.

Delays in the warrantless search of a vehicle can be problematic for law enforcement. Warrantless searches should be conducted immediately at the scene where the vehicle is stopped. The only exception to this expediency requirement is when the search would be unsafe or impractical. Where safety is an issue, the vehicle can be moved to a safe location before the search is conducted. The Supreme Court has ruled that a vehicle may be searched even after it has been impounded and in police custody. In *United States v. Johns* (1985), the Court suggested that such a search would be impermissible after 3 days have elapsed.

The language used by the court in *Chambers v. Maroney* (1970) suggested that exigent circumstances must be present to justify a warrantless search of a vehicle. This has been interpreted by some to mean that the police must demonstrate some emergency situation to justify the search in addition to the probable cause requirement. This analysis is incorrect. The very fact that an automobile is readily movable provides the necessary exigency. If the vehicle is not readily movable, then exigent circumstances must be articulated by the police. For example, in *California v. Carney* (1985), the Court stated that a motor home connected to utilities and elevated on blocks would not be considered readily movable, and thus a search warrant would be required.

Suspects moving an automobile onto private property do not invalidate the Carroll doctrine. In *Scher v. United States* (1938), a tip from an informant and subsequent surveillance gave police officers probable cause to believe that a particular automobile contained contraband. Officers followed the car until the suspect parked in his garage. The Court ruled that the warrantless search that followed was valid.

In general, the legality of a search is determined in part by the scope of the search. In the case of vehicle searches, there is a distinction between a search of the vehicle and a search of a container found in the vehicle. The controlling factor in the scope of vehicle searches is the nature of the contraband that the police have probable cause to believe exists. Generally, officers may search any part of the vehicle or any container in the vehicle in which they have probable cause to believe contraband will be found. If officers have probable cause to believe that the contraband will be found in a specific container, then the scope is limited to that container. For example, probable cause to believe that a container placed in the trunk of a taxi contains contraband or evidence does not justify a search of the entire cab.

Police often impound vehicles for a variety of reasons, such as when a vehicle endangers public safety or when the driver has been arrested. This allows for a different type of search from that under the Carroll doctrine, and thus involves a different set of legal issues. The police may lawfully inventory the contents of an impounded vehicle according to a standardized set of procedures in order to protect the owner's property and to protect the police from civil liability and potential danger. The primary consideration in determining the legality of an inventory search is the departmental procedures for conducting such inventories. Because of the nature of such searches, an officer may not directly look for evidence of a crime. If, however, an officer finds contraband while conducting a bona fide inventory, then the contraband or other items subject to seizure may be seized lawfully under the plain view doctrine.

The Supreme Court has yet to rule on the legal implications of using drug-detecting dogs in vehicle searches. All of the cases dealing with this issue to date have come from the lower federal and state courts. Although the preponderance of guidance from these courts has been that a dog detecting the smell of drugs in a vehicle does not violate the owner's rights, the issue is not settled. One legal scholar suggests that the safest procedure for law enforcement officers is to make sure that drug-detecting dogs are reliable and to obtain a warrant before conducting a search based on a dog's reactions to potential contraband.

*Adam J. McKee*

***See also*** Probable Cause, Search and Seizure, Search Warrants

## For Further Reading

California v. Carney, 471 U.S. 386 (1985).

Carroll v. United States, 267 U.S. 132 (1925).

Chambers v. Maroney, 399 U.S. 42 (1970).

Ferdico, J. N. (1999). *Criminal procedure for the criminal justice professional* (7th ed.). Belmont, CA: West/ Wadsworth.

Scher v. United States, 305 U.S. 251 (1938).

United States v. Johns, 469 U.S. 478 (1985).

## ❧ VICTIMS, POLICE RESPONSE TO

More than 25 million people in the United States become victims of crime every year. The experience can destroy victims' sense of safety and trust in other human beings, and become emotionally and financially devastating. In the aftermath of crime, victims rely on the police—the first responders to crime scenes—for support, information, and guidance through the criminal justice and social service systems. When police are effective gateways to such support, victims are more likely not only to recover from their experience, but also to help police solve crimes and prevent revictimization.

## EXPERIENCE OF VICTIMIZATION

Although crime affects individuals in different ways, victims often have similar emotional responses in the hours or days immediately after a crime. Many victims experience a crisis reaction, often with shock and numbness during the initial phase, when most first responders interact with victims. Fight-or-flight responses (impulses to fight back or flee the crime scene), shock, and disorientation occur frequently. Some victims experience emotional or physical paralysis that prevents them from making rational decisions, such as seeking medical attention or reporting an incident to the police. Many victims feel helpless, vulnerable, and frightened.

The long-term impact of crime can also be profound. Although some victims recover quickly, others suffer continuing trauma. Lowered academic performance, decreased work productivity, and severe loss of confidence are not unusual. Mental illness, suicide, and drug and alcohol abuse are more common among crime victims than the general public.

## POLICE RESPONSE

To be effective and productive in their interaction with victims, police should understand victims' basic needs in the aftermath of crime: to feel safe, to express their emotions, and to know what to expect from the criminal justice process. Police should

- Express regret that the incident has occurred
- Stress that the crime was not the victim's fault
- Ensure that the victim's injuries are treated
- Offer to contact family members, friends, or crisis counselors

- Interview victims in a place where they feel secure
- Inquire about the victim's special concerns or needs
- Allow victims to tell their stories without interruption or judgment
- Urge victims to relate all details, even those that might not seem important
- Allow victims to air their emotions about the trauma of the crime

Setting expectations helps victims feel safe and regain their sense of control over their lives. Police officers should

- Tell victims what to expect from police on the scene
- Explain what officers will do after the initial interview
- Explain how victims can minimize their own risk, how others can help, and what to expect during the first few weeks after the crime
- Explain law enforcement procedures such as filing the report, investigating the crime, and arresting and arraigning the suspect
- Describe the types of interviews to expect, the nature of medical forensic examinations the victim may be asked to undergo, and what specific information will be available to news organizations
- Advise victims that lapses of concentration, memory losses, depression, and physical ailments are normal reactions for crime victims
- Give victims, in writing, contact information and encourage them to call police with further questions, information, or requests for help
- Provide information about what services are available for victims in the community and how to access them

## SAFETY PLANNING

A key responsibility of first responders is to help victims prepare a safety plan—a comprehensive, detailed set of strategies to protect victims from further harm. Safety planning is crucial because once someone has been a crime victim, the likelihood that he or she will be victimized again increases significantly (Pease, 1998). Police can convey the important message that although the perpetrator is responsible for the crime, victims have the power, by taking certain steps, to reduce the likelihood that the crime will happen again. Police can help victims secure the premises, identify advocates and other support services, plan daily activities, select travel routes, enlist neighbors as supporters, and conduct a standard list of preparations that increase victim safety. Working with victims on safety plans also helps police investigate the incident and identify patterns that may help prevent future crimes.

## VICTIMS' RIGHTS

Another key police responsibility is to notify victims of their legal rights to participate in the criminal justice system. All 50 states have enacted statutory rights for crime victims, and many have adopted constitutional amendments protecting victims' rights. Among the most commonly legislated rights are the rights to be notified of proceedings and the status of the defendant, to be present at certain proceedings, to make a statement at sentencing or other times, and to seek restitution from a convicted offender. Many states provide victims the right to be consulted before a case is dismissed or a plea agreement entered, the right to a speedy trial, and the victims' right to keep their contact information confidential. Contact with the police is often the first and only way victims learn about many of these rights.

Police also notify victims about their states' victim compensation programs. All 50 states, the District of Columbia, the U.S. Virgin Islands, Guam, and Puerto Rico have crime victim compensation programs. Although these programs differ from state to state, victim compensation programs usually offer reimbursement for medical costs, mental health counseling, funeral and burial costs, and lost wages or loss of support. Some programs offer crime scene cleanup, the cost of travel to receive treatment, moving and relocation expenses, and the cost of housekeeping and child care. To be eligible for compensation, victims must comply with state statutes and rules, which generally require victims to cooperate with reasonable requests from law enforcement and to submit a timely application to the compensation program.

## GATEWAY TO SERVICES

As first responders, police serve as the primary gateway to the more than 10,000 victim service providers and advocates throughout the United States. Police often distribute information cards that provide hot line numbers, alert victims about their rights, and list agencies they may contact for help. Police can refer victims to victim/witness advocates; victim compensation offices; domestic violence and rape crisis centers; support groups; and specialized counseling and support centers for special populations, such as immigrants or specific ethnic groups. These services often pick up where the police response leaves off in helping victims to rebuild their lives.

## PARTNERS WITH VICTIMS AND VICTIMS' ORGANIZATIONS

Police departments are increasingly aware that victims and victim service organizations can serve as problem-solving partners and invaluable resources to police. In a recent survey conducted by the National Center for Victims of Crime and the Police Foundation, more than 95% of police executives reported that crime victims have something special, beyond what other witnesses offer, to add to police efforts to solve crimes (Ready & Weisburd, 2002). Victims can serve as partners to police in solving crime and preventing more crime in their communities.

Some police departments promote police–victim partnerships by establishing victim assistance programs. In 1999, roughly 209 police and sheriffs' departments—out of 18,000 law enforcement agencies nationwide—received federal grants to establish such programs (Herman, 2002). Victim service providers can also be found in prosecutors' offices and corrections and juvenile justice departments, as well as community-based settings such as domestic violence shelters and rape crisis centers. These professionals offer a range of services, including individual and group counseling, crisis intervention, safety planning, emergency financial assistance, advocacy with criminal justice and social service agencies, and court accompaniments. They also serve as an effective liaison between victims and law enforcement.

In working with victim service organizations, victims often give different kinds of crime-related information to counselors than they would to police officers. While respecting the confidentiality of their clients, these agencies can still identify patterns of crime as well as gaps and deficiencies in police services that police may not be aware of, participate in problem-solving activities, and help prevent repeat victimization. Through their work with victims, victim service organizations can play an important part in community policing, which unites police and the community in solving crimes and crime-related problems.

As the community policing philosophy takes hold throughout the country, police are establishing problem-solving partnerships with victims and victim service organizations. For instance, one sheriff's department set up "victim-assisted" investigations that have dramatically increased the office's ability to solve crimes. Officers explain to victims the type of information they need to make an arrest and guide them on the role they can play in the department's investigation. In addition, several victim assistance programs are working with police to ensure comprehensive services for intimidated victims of such crimes as gang violence or sexual assault. Such partnerships help police solve crimes, support victims, and reduce reliance on resource-intensive crime-solving tools (e.g., data collection, crime map analysis, and police officer surveys).

## CUSTOMER SATISFACTION

To maintain and enhance the effectiveness of their response to victims, police organizations can regularly seek victim feedback, report the results, and ensure that their departments respond to the feedback. For example, in 2001 in the District of Columbia, the Metropolitan Police Department published a survey of 401 people who had been victims of crime during November and December 2000. The surveyors selected victims on the basis of police reports of five crime types. The survey found that despite an overall satisfaction with the department, less than one half of victims had received information about their rights, and most had not received referral information about agencies that could assist them. The department response included launching the *Call on Us* public awareness campaign, which publicized the helpline of the National Center for Victims of Crime, 1-800-FYI-CALL. This helpline links victims to an extensive array of services.

*Susan Herman*

*See also* Crisis Intervention, National Crime Victimization Survey

### For Further Reading

Herman, S. (2002). Law enforcement and victim services: Rebuilding lives, together. *Police Chief, 69*(5), 34–37.

Kilpatrick, D., Beatty, D., & Howley, S. (1998). *The rights of crime victims—Does legal protection make a difference?* National Institute of Justice Research in Brief (NCJ Publication No. 173839). Washington, DC: U.S. Department of Justice.

Mayhew, P., & Van Dijk, J. (1997). *Criminal victimization in eleven industrialized countries: Key findings from the 1996 International Crime Victims Survey.* The Hague: Ministry of Justice.

National Association of Crime Victim Compensation Boards. (2002). *Crime victim compensation directory 2002.* Alexandria, VA: Author.

Pease, K. (1998). *Repeat victimisation: Taking stock.* Crime Detection and Prevention Series Paper 90. London: Home Office Police Research Group. Retrieved June, 3, 2003, from http://www.homeoffice.gov.uk/rds/prgpdfs/fcdps 90.pdf

Ready, J., & Weisburd, D. (2002). Victims and victim service organizations in American policing: Selected findings from a national survey. *Networks, 17,* 3–4, 16–20.

U.S. Department of Justice, Office of Community Oriented Policing Services. (2002). *Bringing victims into community policing.* Washington, DC: Author.

U.S. Department of Justice, Office of Justice Programs, Office for Victims of Crime. (1998). *New directions from the field: Victims' rights and services for the 21st century.* Washington, DC: Author.

U.S. Department of Justice, Office of Justice Programs, Office for Victims of Crime. (2001). *First response to victims of crime 2001.* Washington, DC: Author.

## VIDEO IN PATROL CARS

Perhaps no issue has been debated more hotly by both the public and law enforcement than the validity of police stops. The issue has touched nearly every large-city police department in the United States. Much of this debate focuses on how traffic and pedestrian stops transpire between the police and ethnic/racial minorities. Since the 1980s, for example, the policy of profiling has been used as a campaign against drug trafficking throughout various states. Media coverage of the 1998 allegations that the New Jersey State Police used race as a criterion to combat such trafficking, as well as the 1991 Rodney King incident in Los Angeles, catapulted the issue of biased enforcement onto the national stage, fueling the debate. Distrust of the police led various citizens' groups to begin videotaping police activity during stops in order to ensure that the stops were not being made on the basis of ethnicity or race. And in a counter-response, several state legislatures mandated that in-car video cameras be installed as a means of documenting police handling of events during stops.

## HISTORY

Whereas concern over biased policing has been long-standing in U.S. law enforcement, video cameras in cruisers are a fairly new phenomenon. However, some departments have had a long time in which to evaluate their use. The Virginia State Police have used cameras since 1991; Montana, since 1993; Alabama and Tennessee, since 1994; and Iowa since 2002. Although most police cruisers do not yet have in-car cameras, the number is growing. New York State Police have cameras in 335 of their 900 cruisers. All 224 of Seattle's cruisers now have cameras, and the California Highway Patrol has cameras in 72 of its 2,400 cars.

## CAMERAS AS "EYES"

Traditionally, determining the accuracy of a stop by police proved difficult because such situations generally involved one person's word against another: Minority groups allege routine stops involving harassment and abuse; the police assert that deployment patterns affect the ethnic/racial proportion of stops, because resources are deployed to those areas where crime occurs most. The numbers vary

substantially, but data suggest that ethnic/racial minorities are stopped twice as frequently as their numbers in the population. In-car videos document the actuality of stops, providing dramatic evidence of their validity or lack thereof.

## POLICE OPINION OF VIDEOS

In a recent poll among selected law enforcement agencies, 92% of respondents said cameras are beneficial. Viewed by some as enforcement and investigative tools, in-car cameras provide irrefutable evidence of events. Cameras streamline traffic investigations, provide easy suspect identification, reduce the number of Internal Affairs investigations, serve as training tools for new officers, and are methods of self-critique of officer performance. They have exonerated officers from false accusations and have provided evidence when officers are assaulted by those they stop. It has also decreased police brutality and racial profiling claims. Some believe in-car cameras improve police accountability, resulting in fewer costly litigations and forced settlements for municipalities. But complaints regarding the need for cameras and use of the equipment itself have surfaced on several fronts.

The number one concern is cost. Cameras can range from $1,500-$10,000 per car—costs that most departments and states cannot afford. Another concern is storage for tapes, although with digital recording, space concerns become moot. Other complaints include training time, maintenance costs, and lack of officer acceptance. Despite these concerns, some law enforcement agencies agree that the advantages outweigh the disadvantages.

## CAMERA OPERATION

Cameras vary depending on their technology. The palm-held camera mounts against the windshield and connects to a video recorder in the cruiser's trunk. The camera swings 360 degrees, and a remote microphone adds sound to the video. Tapes can be started and stopped by remote control, and a small television allows replay of the tape. Another widely used high-resolution camera is the Eyewitness

In-Car Video System, which mounts above the rear-view mirror next to a small video monitor. Its recorder is locked in a stainless steel case in the trunk, allowing for preservation of tapes in the event of fire or other disasters. Activity is captured in front of the cruiser; wide angle and zoom lenses allow for manual adjustment inside the car, and its audio aids the camera's visuals. Ninety-five percent of polled respondents said that with improved technology, cameras are becoming easier to use.

## FUTURE CONSIDERATIONS

Video cameras are valuable tools for police in their arsenal of crime prevention, but only 52% of departments polled use them. Concerns point to the need for policies that foster officer acceptance of and familiarity with the cameras. Presently, some officers fear that videos indicate distrust by top brass, and policies to use videos in patrol cars should make clear that in-car cameras protect both police and the public. Policies should also dictate the recording, storing, and cataloguing of tapes. Many departments still leave open those incidents that officers can record; each is expected to use his or her judgment as to when to activate the video. But not all officers are trained in proper use of the cameras. Currently, only 45% of polled departments train all officers to use the videos, but officers who are unfamiliar with the equipment can cause problems.

Where cost is concerned, both departments and states have conflict between the desire for in-car cameras and the availability of funds, and many localities have turned to the federal government for assistance. Once clear policies and expectations are adopted and in-car cameras become commonplace, behavioral change can result that will reduce claims of police misconduct.

*Norma Manatu*

*See also* Profiling, Racial

### For Further Reading

Carter, D. L., Katz-Bannister, A. J., & Schafer, J. (2001). Lansing Police Department MATS data: Six month analysis. Available: http://www.lansingpolice.com

McMahon, P. (2002, July 18). Increased clamor for cameras in cop cars. Available: http://www.usatoday.com/news/nation/2002/07/19/copcameras.htm

Patrol car's camera films problem officer. (2002, December 20). *Crime Control Digest,* p. 7.

Sharp, A. G. (2000, October). On the wrong side of the law and the lens. *Law and Order, 98,* 97–102.

Smith, M. R., & Petrocelli, M. (2001). Racial profiling? A multivariate analysis of police traffic stop data. *Police Quarterly, 4*(1), 4–27.

## ◦◦ VIDOCQ SOCIETY

A number of former and present law enforcement professionals founded the Vidocq Society in 1990 to solve cold cases. The society was aptly named after Eugène-François Vidocq (1775–1857), a master criminal who was active in France in the early 19th century. Vidocq was so clever at his trade that the city of Paris made him its Chief of Detectives (1809–27, 1832). He became legendary in the annals of crime and punishment, and a number of novelists modeled characters after him, including Emile Gaboriau's police officer M. Lecoq. Most famously, Honoré de Balzac supposedly based his master criminal, Vautrin, who appears throughout *Le Comédie Humaine,* on Vidocq's life. Vidocq was not only a successful thief and detective, but also an author of books on crime and criminals, such as his work on criminals' customs and slang, *Les Voleurs, Physiologie de Leure Moeurs et Leur Langage . . .* (1837), and his popular autobiography, *Mémoires de Vidocq, chef de la police de Sûreté jusqu'en 1827* (1828).

Vidocq was creative in solving mysterious crimes, and in 1811, he founded the elite undercover unit of the Paris police, the Sûreté. Vidocq used ingenious disguises and a variety of unconventional and innovative methods to solve crime. He is credited with such crime-fighting techniques as indexed recordkeeping, criminalistics and ballistics studies, and plaster casts of foot and shoe impressions. After his tenure as chief of police, he founded his own very successful private detective agency. He also held patents on indelible ink and unalterable bond paper. Therefore, when William Fleisher, a former FBI agent; Frank Bender, a forensic psychologist; and William Richard Walter, another forensic psychologist and profiler, founded their society to help with unsolved crimes, they considered it appropriate to name the society after Vidocq because of his reputation for investigating crimes.

The club is limited to 82 members, one for each year of Vidocq's life. The Society also has approximately 150 associate members from around the world. The membership includes attorneys, judges, profilers, coroners, psychologists, police detectives, forensic scientists, and others. Only regular members can vote on taking a case. They devote each monthly meeting in Philadelphia to an unsolved homicide or death. The members examine whatever evidence exists and attempt to revive the investigation among offices. Originally, the group met at lunch to talk about old cases. The discussion became so lively that the members began an organization to see if they could actually solve old crimes. The members, many former law enforcement officers, decided early on that they would not interfere with official agencies, and that the latter would have to approve of the Society's involvement.

The Society has solved a number of homicides. Most prominent from the Philadelphia area were the murders of Terry Brooks and Deborah Lynn Wilson. Brooks, an assistant manager at a Roy Rogers restaurant, was murdered during a hold-up in 1986. The members recommended a new investigation and an examination of the DNA evidence, which was not checked at the time of the murder. They found a former boyfriend of the victim and matched his DNA with that found at the crime scene. He eventually confessed to the crime in 1999.

In 1984, a Drexel University student, Deborah Lynn Wilson, was beaten and strangled to death, and left without her shoes or socks in a basement hallway. In 1992, the Vidocq Society took up the case and suggested that Philadelphia police look for known foot fetishists and cross-reference them with possible suspects. They came up with a campus security guard who had been court-martialed for stealing women's sneakers and socks. The police arrested the guard, and he was convicted of murder in 1995.

Recent cases include a 1996 stabbing death of a 33-year-old divorced mother from Tennessee, the 1991 killing of a Kentucky farmer, and the 1990 brutal killing of an 11-year-old girl and 32-year-old woman in Florida. The Society's 2003 meeting concentrated on the 1974 murder of an Oklahoma woman.

In 1957, the naked body of a battered child was found inside a cardboard box in Philadelphia. Clues led nowhere, and in 1998, the Society adopted this case and rechristened the "boy in the box" as America's Unknown Child. Although the Society continues work on the case, it remains unsolved.

The Society also serves as an educational body for law enforcement. Members of the Vidocq Society hold annual conferences and seminars on uncovering leads and in the use of new crime-fighting techniques. In 2002, they held a 2-day seminar sponsored by the Delaware Office of the Chief Medical Examiner that covered such topics as serial murder (ritualistic, child murder, sexual deviants, and others); statement analysis; media relations; exhumations; forensic odontology; and interviews and interrogations. In 2004, Alabama's third annual governor's conference for law enforcement training, sponsored by the state's crime victims' organization, invited Vidocq Society members to address the meeting. Richard Walter, a member of the Society, summarized for the conference attendees the Society's basic principles of cold-case investigations: "The key to solving crime often is found in the initial examination of the crime scene and in using good investigative techniques instead of relying solely on DNA and other scientific analysis." He went on to say how the crime scene should be examined for the presence or absence of evidence, recognition of evidence, patterns of the crime, and known criminal behavior, among other things.

The Vidocq Society's techniques present a good illustration of combining tried-and-true investigative methods with the latest scientific advances in solving crimes. The Society has the advantage, however, of not being an official organization tied to bureaucratic timetables and productivity measures that limit investigations; therefore, members have the luxury of devoting their full attention to whichever crime they choose to focus on.

*Larry E. Sullivan*

**See also** Cold Case Investigations

## For Further Reading

*Area law enforcement personnel to attend "cold-case" seminar.* (2002, September 16). Delaware Health and Social Services press release.

Group's luncheon menu includes cold cases. (2002, July/August). *Law Enforcement News,* p. 6.

Officers hope to turn cold cases hot: Training will cover DNA evidence, probe techniques. (2004, February 28). *Birmingham News.*

Profilers warm to killer's trail. (2002, July 19). *St. Petersburg Times.*

*Top scientists meeting on Oklahoma murder case.* (2003, July 16). Retrieved April 24, 2004, from www.Vidocq.org.

## ෨෬ VIGILANTES

Vigilante activity in the United States dates as far back as the mid-1700s. Waves of vigilantism spread across the country in order to deal with rising crime rates on the expanding frontier and in gold rush and mining communities around the time of the Civil War. Vigilance committees were usually formed by local men as an attempt at restoring law and order whenever there was an absence of a well-established legal institution or an inadequate law enforcement system. These committees were usually composed of prominent men who banded together to capture, try, and punish those who were perceived as engaging in unlawful activities. Many of their practices included beating, flogging, forced labor, or lynching, depending on the severity of the crime. Vigilantism is often characterized by moblike violence, but it is markedly different because vigilance committees use careful organization, planning, and structure, even if the committee exists only briefly. Although the exact date of the first vigilance organization is unclear, there is evidence of vigilante activity in South Carolina backcountry as early as 1767. Vigilante movements in San Francisco in the mid-1850s and Virginia City, Montana, in 1864 were among some of the largest. However, after the Civil War, the popularity of vigilance committees began to subside as strong legal institutions or police forces were established.

The identity of most vigilantes was private. Members often tried their victims in secret and rarely spoke of their participation. The vigilante justice system often consisted of a trial whereby everyone on the committee had to agree on the ruling and the punishment. However, in many instances, this practice was abandoned in favor of hunting down those that members were convinced were guilty, often administering punishment before a trial took place. Lynching was the most extreme of the punishments administered. Lynching consisted of hanging a person and leaving the body for public display. Most often associated with racist violence in the South, lynching derives its name from Colonel Charles Lynch of Virginia, a planter and vigilante who used this method to punish looters and loyalists during the Revolutionary War. Lynching was frequently used by the frontier men. The accused was usually exiled for minor crimes such as petty theft, but for crimes such as rape or horse and cattle stealing, the accused was lynched.

Prior to the 1856 San Francisco committee, the terms *vigilance* and *regulator committees* were used interchangeably. Regulator was the more popular term and was used in reference to the South Carolina Regulators of 1767–1769, thought to be among the first of such committees. However, the San Francisco committee used the term *vigilante* because an outlaw group in the area was already using the name Regulators. Because of the widespread knowledge of the San Francisco committee, vigilance became the more commonly used term across the country.

The 1767 South Carolina Regulator movement was largely composed of wealthy men committed to restoring order by fighting off bands of outlaws and capturing runaway slaves. Without an official court system for punishing criminals, backcountry planters and farmers created an association to regulate any activity deemed unlawful. For 2 years, the South Carolina Regulators fought criminals, tracked runaway slaves, and established their own court system to resolve disputes. By 1769, an official court system was created in the backcountry, and the Regulators disbanded.

By the mid-1800s, the population increase in gold rush areas such as San Francisco provided for waves of looting, murders, and other unlawful activities. Gangs overwhelmed the relatively small and unorganized police force, even after the establishment of a volunteer force in 1849. By 1851, the San Francisco Committee of Vigilance was formed for the purpose of arresting and trying many of the people deemed to be guilty. The trials resulted in several public hangings. Within 2 months, the crimes subsided and the vigilance committee disbanded. However, by 1856, the crime rate was on the rise again, and the San Francisco Committee of Vigilance resumed, this time consisting of several thousand members who either exiled or hanged criminals. This time, their efforts were focused on repressing crime and the development of a more military-like police force.

Bannack and Virginia City, Montana, a large mining community, was another active vigilante area during the Civil War. From 1863 to 1865, committees assembled to repress the activities of an organized band of criminals known as road agents, who were responsible for more than 100 killings and robberies. Modeled after San Francisco, the 1863 Montana Vigilance Committee lynched 22 men between January and February 1864, including William Henry Plummer, the sheriff of the Bannack mining district, whom the Vigilance Committee claimed was the leader of the road agents. There is no evidence indicating that Plummer or any of the other men were guilty of the crimes for which they were hanged. By 1864, vigilantism in northern Montana had claimed more than 65 lives.

Large vigilante movements steadily declined in frontier and mining communities after the establishment of a proper police force or structured legal system. However, smaller groups of vigilantes sometimes continued their extrajudicial activities, punishing those they deemed guilty even if they were found innocent under the law. Although exercising the right to protect and instill law remained the justification, many other people, such as Mormons, Chinese, African Americans, and abolitionists, were persecuted. For example, some vigilance committees in San Francisco and Montana disapproved of the influx of minorities and often targeted them as a means of discouraging their settlement in the community.

Although considered outside of the traditional definition of vigilantism, modern organizations using extrajudicial approaches emerge periodically in response to the perceived absence of adequate law enforcement. One such example is The Guardian Angels, a group established in 1987 to provide safe travel on the New York City subway system at a time when there was a rise in violent crimes. The group has established a few chapters in a number of cities across the United States.

*Dara N. Byrne*

### For Further Reading

Ethington, P. J. (1987). Vigilantes and the police: The creation of a professional police bureaucracy in San Francisco, 1847–1900. *Journal of Social History, 21*(2), 197–227.

Hine, K. D. (1998). Vigilantism revisited: An economic analysis of the law of extrajudicial self-help or why can't Dick shoot Henry for stealing Jane's truck? *American University Law Review, 47,* 1221–1255.

Mather, R. E., Boswell, F. E., & Smith, J. J. (1999). *Hanging the sheriff: A biography of Henry Plummer* (2nd ed.). Historic Montana Publishing.

Nolan, P. B. (1987). *Vigilantes on the middle border: A study of self-appointed law enforcement in the states of the Upper Mississippi from 1840–1880.* New York: Garland.

## ❧ VIOLENT CRIME CONTROL AND LAW ENFORCEMENT ACT OF 1994

### WHAT IS THE VIOLENT CRIME CONTROL AND LAW ENFORCEMENT ACT OF 1994?

The Violent Crime Control and Law Enforcement Act was first referred to the House Committee on the Judiciary on October 26, 1993, and was eventually signed by President Clinton on September 13, 1994. It became the largest crime-fighting bill passed by Congress, with provisions for spending almost $30.2 billion from 1995 through 2000.

The Violent Crime Control and Law Enforcement Act of 1994 (Crime Control Bill) (P.L. 103-322) amended the Omnibus Crime Control and Safe Streets Act of 1968, the first federal program deliberately designed as a block grant to assist state and local law enforcement agencies in crime reduction. The Crime Control Bill was a comprehensive bill that affected a variety of crime-fighting legislation. There was grant funding to be dispersed across governments and agencies, in addition to many substantive provisions.

## GRANT FUNDING

It provided more than $30 billion to state, local, and Indian tribal governments, both public and private agencies, and other multijurisdictional associations to enhance public safety and combat crime. This included $3 billion in immigration initiatives, and the remaining funding was spent on a multitude of grants.

The immigration funding was spent on various aspects of immigration control, such as border control, deportations, and the tracking and monitoring of the influx of aliens, and it provided $1.8 billion for reimbursement to states that comprehensively criminalized illegal immigration, also known as the State Criminal Alien Assistance Program.

The remaining grant initiatives totaled around $27.2 billion and encompassed an array of programs and initiatives. These include, but are not limited to, crime prevention block grants, the Brady Act, Byrne grants, Violence Against Women Act, DNA analysis, education and prevention programs to help reduce sexual assaults, National Domestic Violence Hotline, battered women's shelters, delinquent and at-risk youth, drug courts, drug treatment, crime prevention, community and family endeavor schools, crime prevention in public parks, police corps, rural law enforcement, community policing, and correctional facilities and boot camps.

The greatest contribution was provided to the competitive grant program (COPS Program), a community policing program. This program was to receive a total of $8.8 billion between 1995 and 2000 to increase police presence by 100,000 officers and to improve communication and collaboration between law enforcement agencies and community members. This initiative was also known as "cops on the beat." The next largest contribution of almost $8 billion was to go to correctional facilities,

boot camps, and alternative correctional facilities in an attempt to increase prison space for the more violent criminals.

## SUBSTANTIVE PROVISIONS

The Crime Control Bill also had substantive criminal provisions. This law greatly affected the way in which states prosecuted their criminal populations. It called for harsher punishments for a variety of crimes, as well as enacted new legislation to control certain crimes.

### The Federal Death Penalty Act of 1994

This Act expanded death penalty sentencing to an additional 60 offenses. These additional crimes included some acts of espionage, terrorist acts, homicide, and the murder of federal law enforcement officers. It also covered certain crimes, such as hostage situations, kidnapping, genocide, and carjacking, if death occurred during their commission.

### Violent Offender Sentencing

The Crime Control Bill required states to mandate that their violent prisoners complete at least 85% of their sentences, or else the states would be ineligible to receive incarceration funding. This was part of the truth-in-sentencing initiative. In addition, federal repeat offenders who were convicted of violent crimes or drug trafficking were subject to "three strikes" mandatory life imprisonment sentencing.

### Sex Offender Legislation

Sex offender legislation was amended so that offenders would be punished more harshly and could be supervised more effectively. For repeat sex offenders convicted of federal sex crimes, the new legislation doubled the maximum term of imprisonment. The Crime Control Bill also required states to enact legislation that would require sexually violent predators and those convicted of violent sexual offenses to register with law enforcement for 10 years after their release from prison. This legislation has also become known as the Jacob Wetterling

Crimes Against Children and Sexually Violent Offender Registration Act. Furthermore, the bill required community notification. It also provided the stipulation that states that did not execute these registration and notification systems would lose 10% of their allotted share of federal crime-fighting funds.

### Punishment for Young Offenders

The Crime Control Bill also required that juveniles receive more severe punishments. For example, it allowed for individuals age 13 and older who were charged with possessing a firearm during an offense to be prosecuted as adults.

### Public Safety and Recreational Firearms Use Protection Act

The Crime Control Bill also called for greater gun control. It banned for 10 years the manufacture, transfer, and/or possession of 19 styles of semiautomatic assault weapons and certain firearms with ammunition magazines that held more than 10 rounds. (Despite public support the ban expired on September 13, 2004 because Congress failed to introduce legislation that would have extended it.) It also made it illegal to sell assault weapons and firearms to, and for those weapons to be possessed by, domestic abusers and juveniles. The Crime Bill also strengthened federal licensing requirements for gun dealers, requiring that they obtain both a photograph and fingerprints with the applicant's license request. Finally, it enhanced penalties involving possession and use of firearms, especially crimes involving drug trafficking and violence.

### Violence Against Women Act

According to President Clinton, the Crime Control Bill also became the first comprehensive federal effort to focus on violence against women. It accomplished this by prosecuting offenders more harshly and providing victim assistance programs. The Violence Against Women Act called for various measures, such as mandatory restitution to victims of sex crimes; the employment of victim/witness counselors for the prosecution of sex crimes and domestic violence crimes; and the revision of Rule 412 of the federal rules of evidence, which made certain evidence inadmissible, such as the alleged victim's past sexual behavior.

*Lisa A. Williams*

***See also*** Law Enforcement Assistance Administration

### For Further Reading

Dodenhoff, P. (1994, December 31). LEN's 1994 People of the Year: The makers of the Violent Crime Control Act. *Law Enforcement News, 20*(414), 1, 14.
National Criminal Justice Reference Service. (1994). *Violent Crime Control and Law Enforcement Act of 1994 fact sheet.* Available: http://www.ncjrs.org/txtfiles/billfs.txt

## ∽ VOLUNTEERS

According to some experts, volunteerism is the most effective, democratic, and humane anticrime strategy currently available to Americans. Volunteers participated in America's law enforcement scene prior to and after the arrival of the first white European settlers. Some of the first European volunteers consisted of the militia forces organized by Captain Myles Standish, the military leader of the Pilgrims who landed in America and founded the colony of New Plymouth in 1620. Significantly, prior to the arrival of the Europeans, some Native American nations had also developed their own style of policing that relied heavily on voluntary participation. For example, the Plains nations established honorary military societies to police their annual reunion ceremonies, gatherings, and buffalo hunts.

The use of militias and town watches in America can be traced to 13th-century England and the reign of Henry III, who mandated that all his male subjects (between 15 and 50) own a weapon other than a knife so that they could stand guard to preserve the peace. During the colonial period in America's seaport towns, a constable was elected for each ward, and a nighttime patrol called "the watch" was instituted. The earliest watch organizations relied on local citizen participation or the use of paid substitutes. In addition, prior to the end of the Civil War in 1865, militia units were widely used to contend with domestic threats to the safety of European settlers. In the South, slaves were controlled through a system of slave patrols that relied on the militia model to preserve the slave system. Even after the Civil War, such organizations as the Ku Klux Klan and the White Caps fostered a sense of fear and dread among minority groups.

During the 19th century, several other types of volunteer law enforcement organizations appeared in America. For example, throughout the 19th century, a variety of separately authorized anti-horse thief and detective societies were chartered to protect private property. In addition, a number of aid societies were established to oversee the selection and distribution of private welfare. The New York Charity Organization Society was the largest. These groups worked parallel with or in place of local police for the accomplishment of their specific objectives, such as liquor law enforcement.

The American Protective League (APL) was active during America's involvement in World War I. Created by a Chicago advertising executive, it was authorized by the U.S. Department of Justice to carry out the following duties: protection of property, reporting of disloyal or suspicious people and activities, locating of draft violators, assistance in the arrest of deserters, and the enforcement of vice and liquor law regulations in areas around naval and army bases. More than 200,000 citizens were recruited for this organization, and historians have acknowledged that the APL was the largest spy network ever authorized by the U.S. government.

During World War I, many cities established citizen home defense leagues as well as state and home guard organizations to provide homeland security. The latter groups were organized to fill the vacuum left when the National Guard was called upon for active military service. The former organizations were instituted by some large-city police chiefs concerned about both natural and manmade disasters. For example, in New York City, nearly 21,000 citizens were recruited in 1916 out of concern that the war in Europe would deplete police ranks or require their services for guarding vital resources (e.g., reservoirs, bridges, transportation

lines, etc.). The volunteers were asked to perform routine patrol duties and to participate in training programs. In 1918, New York City's home defense league was reorganized into a police reserve organization.

World War I also witnessed the birth of a variety of police- and school-sponsored systems involving youth activities. Initially, junior police programs were established in California, Iowa, Ohio, and New York. Programs for youth continue to this day. Since the 1970s, thousands of young men and women between the ages of 14 and 20 have joined Law Enforcement Explorer Posts jointly sponsored by police agencies and the Boy Scouts of America. Their activities have included traffic control and community crime prevention projects.

Although some reserve and auxiliary police units were established during the 1930s, they became numerous during World War II. Most auxiliary units were recruited as emergency forces under the guidelines of the U.S. Office of Civilian Defense. Similarly, during the Korean War and the cold war, additional units were established, and many of these have become permanent. Three specific federal security-related organizations were also created at the time of World War II: the Auxiliary Military Police (to guard industrial war plants), the Civil Air Patrol (to assist with search and rescue), and the Coast Guard Auxiliary. The Auxiliary Military Police was created in 1942 when plant guard forces were so designated by the Secretary of War. The Auxiliary Military Police was composed of conscripts and was disbanded at the end of the war.

The Civil Air Patrol (CAP) was founded in 1941, one week prior to the attack on Pearl Harbor. Its initial purpose was to patrol harbors for enemy ships, but it shifted its mission to assisting in search and rescue work after World War II. It became permanently established in 1946 and became the Air Force's official auxiliary in 1948. Currently, it has 34,000 adult volunteer members and 26,000 cadets. Cadet members may be as young as 12. Today, CAP flies 85% of the nation's federal inland search and rescue mission hours. The Coast Guard (CG) Auxiliary was established in 1939 in response to an increase in the number of recreational boating accidents. Currently, the CG Auxiliary has about 28,000 members.

Since the terrorist attacks on America on September 11, 2001, the roles of CAP and the CG Auxiliary have been expanded to include some security functions. If terrorists strike again, CAP would provide aerial reconnaissance, operate emergency communication systems, and transport disaster workers. CG Auxiliary flotillas in the New York metropolitan area currently look for anything suspicious—boats moored beneath bridges, vessels straying close to tunnel vents, mariners heading toward power plants. The assignment is known as "marine domain awareness," and the U.S. Coast Guard has been made a part of the U.S. Department of Homeland Security.

In 2002, President Bush created the Citizen Corps to help enlist volunteers in order to cope with disasters of all kinds and, generally, to promote safer communities. It is coordinated by the Federal Emergency Management Agency, another new division of the U.S. Department of Homeland Security. Since the attacks of September 11th, the Corps has become the president's main program to involve citizens in homeland security. The Citizen Corps includes four major components: Community Emergency Response Teams (CERTs), a Medical Reserve Corps, the Neighborhood Watch, and Volunteers in Police Service. Under the Corps, local Neighborhood Watch groups are incorporating terrorism awareness education into their existing crime prevention missions, and the Medical Reserve Corps is seeking to coordinate volunteer health professionals to provide ongoing support for community health needs and resources during large-scale emergencies.

CERTs were initially organized in 1993 by the Los Angeles City Fire Department in order to train citizens to take care of themselves and others in the aftermath of a disaster. Today, many communities have organized CERTs to respond to any emergency in neighborhoods, workplaces, and schools. The responsibilities vary from place to place. They can include taking stolen property reports, monitoring unattended vehicles, conducting home security surveys, assisting in traffic control, checking homes for residents on vacation, and writing parking tickets. CERTs can consist of rescue workers; reception

clerks at community substations; technicians and aides for special investigation units; volunteer police chaplains; actors for disaster training exercises; recruiters and trainers for Neighborhood Watch groups; computer crime-mapping aides; Citizen's Band (CB) radio patrollers; amateur radio operators, of which there are an estimated 700,000; and communication specialists.

The Neighborhood Watch is the most well-known and the largest police program involving volunteers. It is sometimes called Crime Watch, Block Watch, or Town Watch. Typically, a Neighborhood Watch program begins through a combination of citizen and police effort. Neighbors hold meetings, select a watch leader, exchange telephone numbers, and agree to keep an eye on each other's property. Some communities also organize neighborhood patrols in order to help guard residential areas or any other locations. Police personnel provide classes on community crime prevention and safety precautions. They will also help to post signs and decals to advertise a community's participation in the program. The watch concept is flexible, and there can be watches established for apartment houses, schools, utilities, parks, or businesses. The expansion of Neighborhood Watch is one of the goals of President Bush's Citizen Corps initiative for the specific purpose of enhancing homeland security.

One of the latest trends in volunteers is the development of Citizen Police Academies (CPAs). CPAs have become one of the most effective ways to inform community members about police work and volunteer opportunities. The typical CPA presents a highly condensed version of a police academy curriculum and affords a unique experience for average citizens to learn about the nature of policing and how they can directly assist in community policing activities.

*Martin Alan Greenberg*

***See also*** Auxiliary/Reserve/Part-Time Police, Citizen Police Academies

## For Further Reading

Bonsall, D. M. (1993). *Volunteers in law enforcement: The coproduction of police services in the community.* Unpublished master's thesis, University of South Florida.

Conley, J. (2003, January 22). New Bedford program to help the elderly. *Roanoke Times & World News*, p. B5.

Friedman, W. (1998). Volunteerism and the decline of violent crime. *Journal of Law and Criminology, 88*(4), 1453–1474.

Greenberg, M. A. (2001). *The evolution of volunteer police in America.* Unpublished doctoral dissertation, City University of New York.

Jordan, W. T. (1998). *Citizens' police academies.* Unpublished doctoral dissertation, Florida State University.

Maller, P. (2003, February 17). Civil Air Patrol taking on terror. *Milwaukee Journal-Sentinel*, p. 1B.

Shepnick, P. (2002, March 18). T.O.'s VIPs give police break from the routine. *Ventura County Star*, p. B1.

## ✍ WEAPONS

There is a peculiar axiom that has driven the development of weapons and the tactics of war, and it is that each advance will far exceed its predecessor in size, complexity, or ruthlessness. Thus is weapons development an asymmetrical activity, invariably going far beyond what one imagines will be the next incarnation, and appearing to break all of the written and unwritten rules of engagement. This has been true throughout human history, as stone weapons gave way to metal, and metal ceded the field to firearms, which laid the foundation for the nuclear bomb.

### IN THE BEGINNING

Weapons development began even before the beginning of civilization, when humans had yet to appear and animals were either born with or developed the ability to attack and defend themselves. Humankind was no different—creating and refining the ability to survive through the development of weapons and the means to defend against those that were developed.

Weapons have been intimately connected with humankind's propensity to war, which appears to have been sparked more than 20,000 years ago when nomadic tribes began to settle in relatively permanent communities. Societies began to accumulate possessions. They stored food and collected objects valuable to their own sensibilities, use, and culture. Thus was the concept of ownership born, and with it, the need to protect one's belongings and community, and, if possible, increase one's power through the accumulation of additional property or objects.

By 3500 B.C.E., stone weapons had given way to metal. Middle Eastern groups learned to produce bronze, which allowed for the creation of the sword, spear, axe, and metal-tipped arrows. This sparked the reciprocal development of helmets, primitive types of body armor, and shields to protect against these deadly new weapons.

Like all phases of weapons development, the discovery of gunpowder in the 1300s and the subsequent creation of the firearm went far beyond any previous level of technology, thereby catapulting the business of war to an entirely new level. It could conveniently kill quickly, from a distance, and with deadly accuracy.

### KEEPING THE PEACE

As powerful as the handgun was, early law enforcement eschewed its use. The "schout fiscal" or sheriff attorney of New Amsterdam (the southern end of Manhattan Island) in the 1620s was unarmed, escorting arrestees not to jail but to a whipping post. The "burgher guard" of the 1640s patrolled unarmed and only at night. It evolved into the "rattle wacht" or rattle watch, a contingent of night patrols armed only with a rattle to summon the aid of fellow officers. By the 1800s, these contingents of volunteer night watchmen segued into a paid municipal police force that patrolled around the clock. They wore civilian clothes, hid their badges, and were armed with a 33-inch wooden club.

The introduction in the 1830s of the Colt multi-shot pistol transformed the nature of policing. But it did not happen quickly. At first, few officers carried a weapon. If they did, it was in a coat or pants pocket, and the gun was often looked upon as unfit for the job. The handgun's acceptance in law enforcement was facilitated primarily by the Texas Rangers, who used it to chase down and engage their enemy on horseback and with multiple shots, rather than the traditional method of dismounting and felling the foe with long-range rifle fire.

In the end, the unpredictable nature of police–citizen encounters, the increasing number of arrests, and the fact that criminals regularly carried weapons and had no qualms about using them, forced the handgun to be placed under the rubric of standard police equipment.

The Colt revolver was an early result of mass production technology. It was cheap and easy to get. It also paved the way for a succession of similar products. By the late 1800s, police departments around the country were officially armed, some with the Colt revolver, and others, like Boston, with the Smith & Wesson .38-caliber revolver. The handgun had officially arrived.

Firearms developers continued to look to the future, creating powerful weapons that offered more shots, greater penetrating power, and increased range and effectiveness. Semiautomatic pistols, such as the Colt .45-caliber ACP, were adopted by some agencies, with the eventual widespread adoption of the double-action semiautomatic pistol, a self-loading gun that uses part of the energy generated by burning gunpowder to cycle the next shot.

This kind of widespread acceptance and technological sophistication did not foment an increase in the handgun's use, however. Instead, modern law enforcement is scrutinized more closely than ever with regard to firearms training, proficiency testing, and routine inspection of the weapon itself.

Officers today still carry clubs, or as they are now known, batons. They may carry either chemical Mace® or pepper spray to incapacitate a subject. They may also have access to a stun device, a technology that reemerged in popularity in the early 2000s. Weapons that use nonlethal ammunition, such as rubber bullets or beanbag rounds, are also employed. These are all considered nonlethal weapons whose real function is to prevent physical harm to a suspect while allowing the officer to control a situation without the use of deadly force. In the end, however, the use of any kind of weapon—lethal or nonlethal—is governed entirely by a use-of-force continuum that requires the officer to respond to a subject's level of aggression with a commensurate and reasonable level of force. If pepper spray will incapacitate the subject safely and sufficiently, then there is no immediate need to fire a lethal weapon. It is only when an officer's or a citizen's life is threatened that the use of deadly force is sanctioned by either the department or society.

## FUTURE WEAPONS TECHNOLOGIES

Weapons, particularly guns, are inextricably bound up in the use-of-force continuum and the decision to use deadly force. Yet many still hope for the ultimate weapon, one that would be affordable and easy to carry, and that would always hit and incapacitate the target without permanent damage. As the military finds itself in an increasing number of peacekeeping missions, and as police find themselves under ever-increasing scrutiny of their actions, the need for an effective nonlethal device grows. Scientists, engineers, and researchers have spent years trying to come up with such a thing. They have experimented with the use of chemical incapacitants, with lasers that can distract or disorient, with thermal guns that can heat up an entire room to such a degree that a barricaded subject is completely disoriented, and with an electromagnetic pulse that can knock a suspect senseless. They have even studied the viability of acoustic weapons, which use energy as the bullet.

Thus far, however, none has the reliability, accuracy, or power of the simplest technology in the world—the handgun.

*Lois Pilant Grossman*

**See also** Nonlethal Weapons, Use of Force

### For Further Reading

Alexander, J. B. (1999, October). Nonlethal weapons: When deadly force is not enough. *The Futurist*, p. 34.

Bailey, W. G. (Ed.). (1995). *The encyclopedia of police science* (2nd ed.). New York: Garland.

Berger, M. L. (1979). *Firearms in American history.* New York: Watts.

Fyfe, J. J., Greene, J. R., Walsh, W. F., Wilson, O. W., & McLaren, R. (1997). *Police administration* (5th ed.). New York: McGraw-Hill.

O'Connell, R. L. (1990). *Of arms and men: A history of war, weapons, and aggression.* New York: Oxford University Press.

Tennenbaum, A. N., & Moore, A. M. (1993, September/October). Non-lethal weapons: Alternatives to deadly force. *The Futurist*, pp. 20–23.

Vila, B., & Morris, C. (Eds.). (1999). *The role of police in American society: A documentary history.* Westport, CT: Greenwood.

Zimring, F. E., & Hawkins, G. (1999). *Crime is not the problem: Lethal violence in America.* New York: Oxford University Press.

## ∞ WHISTLE-BLOWING

The origin of the term *whistle-blower* is unclear. Some have argued that the word is derived from an English police officer's use of a whistle while trying to apprehend a criminal. Others have analogized the word with a referee who blows a whistle to announce an illegal action during a game. Although the word's origin is in dispute, its definition is not. A whistle-blower is an individual who reports the illegal or unethical behavior of his or her employer, coworkers, or some other business or government entity to the appropriate authorities. Whistle-blowers provide an important public service by reporting abuse, fraud, dangerous working conditions, a hostile work environment, or numerous other forms of misconduct.

Law enforcement officers have a heightened ethical duty to report the wrongdoings of their colleagues in order to secure the trust of the public whom they serve. The duty to blow the whistle on unethical behavior traditionally has been juxtaposed against an officer's moral obligation to support and defend the other officers and support personnel working in his or her organization. This support and defense has been termed "the Blue Wall of Silence," a pejorative expression used to describe the refusal of police officers to engage in whistle-blowing.

In the late 1960s, this blue wall came crashing down when a New York City police officer named Frank Serpico blew the whistle on fellow officers who were engaging in illegal activities, including taking bribes from drug dealers and members of organized crime. Initially, Officer Serpico was unsuccessful in his reported attempts to convince his superiors to take action against the corrupt officers. Eventually, he went to the press. This led the mayor of New York to form a commission to investigate the claims of corruption in the New York City Police Department.

In the early 1990s, another officer, New York City Sergeant Joseph Trimboli, would also blow the whistle on a department that had failed to take seriously allegations of brutal and corrupt behavior on the part of a number of corrupt cops who operated in some of the city's toughest neighborhoods. As was the case some 20 years before, a commission was set up to investigate. The Mollen Commission recommended changes in the department's methods of handling reports of police wrongdoing.

These cases illustrate that police reforms, which have been adopted across the country, can be the result of a law enforcement officer who reports wrongdoing. Today, law enforcement officers are trained in their ethical obligation to report wrongdoing by fellow officers. Although the training differs in the various departments and agencies nationwide, the following elements should be common to all in the organization:

- A clear exposition of ethical standards should be codified and communicated to all members.
- Those who break this ethical standard must be dealt with swiftly, fairly, and uniformly.

- Would-be whistle-blowers must be able to report concerns to superiors without fear of reprisal.
- Independent agents should be charged with investigating allegations of wrongdoing.
- Police should be reviewed and reformed as necessary.

Although police have a higher ethical standard to report wrongdoing among their own, the decision to become a whistle-blower is never taken lightly. It requires a careful review of the pertinent facts and the exercise of good judgment. Would-be whistle-blowers may expose themselves to risks for reporting wrongful behavior. The most significant risk is retaliation—being persecuted by the organization accused of wrongdoing. Before making the decision to become a whistle-blower, individuals should consider how confident they are regarding the suspected wrongful behavior. Important questions one should consider are, How certain am I that wrongful behavior has occurred? What is my true motivation for alleging misconduct? Does the alleged misconduct justify publicly reporting this behavior? Am I exposing myself to personal liability if a report is made?

After answering questions of this sort, a whistle-blower is then charged with reporting any allegations to the correct authorities. Depending on the severity of the alleged misconduct, a whistle-blower may choose to seek the advice of legal counsel. However, this is not mandatory. In recognition of the value whistle-blowers have in our society, a number of federal and state laws have been enacted that protect whistle-blowers in the United States. Often, these laws do not use the actual word "whistle-blower," but the majority of these statutes are directed at employers by prohibiting them from retaliating against an employee who reports wrongdoing. Actions that are typically considered to be retaliatory against a whistle-blower include firing the employee, subjecting him or her to a layoff or forced retirement, altering the employee's compensation, or transferring the employee to a new position or geographic location.

The main federal law that protects employees against employer retaliation is Title VII, the Civil Rights Act of 1964, which was amended in 1991. Section 2003a of this law provides that an employer may not discriminate against an employee or applicant who charged the employer with certain wrongful behavior. The Civil Rights Act of 1964 also established the U.S. Equal Employment Opportunity Commission (EEOC). The EEOC's primary responsibility is to ensure that all employers in the United States comply with governing federal equal employment opportunity laws.

Other federal laws coordinated by the EEOC include the Equal Pay Act of 1963, the Age Discrimination in Employment Act of 1967, and portions of the Americans with Disabilities Act of 1990. Other federal laws that prohibit retaliation against whistle-blowers, not specifically coordinated by the EEOC, include the Occupational Safety and Health Act, the Notification and Federal Employee Antidiscrimination and Retaliation Act of 2002, the Whistleblower Protection Act, and the False Claims Act, which is perhaps the most significant. The False Claims Act was passed during the Civil War and significantly amended in 1986. This law sets forth criminal and civil penalties against any person or organization that knowingly submits a false bill to the federal government. The Act provides specific protections to private citizens who blow the whistle on companies that are defrauding the federal government.

In addition to the many federal statutes and regulations that prohibit retaliation against whistle-blowers, various states have either enacted similar statutes or generated relevant common laws. These laws often provide protections, at the state level, that are equal to or superior to those granted by the federal laws. Specifically, state whistle-blower laws are often directed at protecting state government employees and whistle-blowers who report fraud perpetrated against a state government; in some states, laws are crafted for the benefit of whistle-blowers working in the private sector who report misconduct that adversely affects the state's citizenry.

A number of public and private organizations also have been established to assist whistle-blowers. As mentioned above, the EEOC is a major federal resource for whistle-blowers. Three of the most prominent nongovernmental organizations dedicated to assisting whistle-blowers are The Government Accountability Project, The National Whistleblower Center, and Taxpayers Against Fraud. These and other organizations provide resources and support at the state, national, and even international levels.

Although, arguably, the United States has the strongest laws prohibiting retaliation, other countries, including Israel, Australia, and Great Britain, have similar protections. There are still a number of countries without any such safeguards. Consequently, whistle-blower advocacy groups have recognized the difficulty in enforcing consistent standards on all multinational organizations. In the event an organization is engaged in wrongdoing in a country that has no laws prohibiting retaliation, bad publicity and public pressure often serve as replacements for missing legal remedies. Numerous advocacy groups monitor the business practices of large multinational organizations in order to exert such pressures.

*Daniel Agatino*

*See also* Corruption/Integrity, Knapp Commission, Mollen Commission

## For Further Reading

Johnson, R. A. (2003). *Whistleblowing: When it works and why.* Boulder, CO: Lynne Rienner.

Kohn, S. M. (2001). *Concepts and procedures in whistleblower law.* Westport, CT: Quorum.

# WOMEN IN POLICING, STATE AND LOCAL

The official recognition of women in policing in the United States is usually associated with the appointment of Alice Stebbins Wells to the Los Angeles Police Department in 1910 as the first woman to be called a "policewoman." Wells's employment set in motion a movement for policewomen that, despite setbacks, culminated in the late 1960s and early 1970s with women winning the right to equal employment in policing. However, women had served both officially and unofficially as matrons in prisons and jails, and as sheriffs' deputies, since the late 1880s.

What made Wells different was not just that she was actually called a policewoman; her appointment was not only for the convenience of women caring for women, but was also part of a larger movement in the late 19th and early 20th centuries both to reform policing and to increase the roles of women in public events and local government. The first policewomen were very similar to their supporters; they were mostly upper-middle-class women, many of whom had been educated and had worked as social workers, and who were concerned with what they saw as increasing immorality in society, juvenile delinquency, and alcohol consumption. Based on these issues, the strongest support for policewomen came not from within the police organization, but from women's groups such as the Women's Christian Temperance Union and the General Federation of Women's Clubs. They were joined by Progressive Era reformers, feminists, and others who sought to reform policing.

Although many of the early women's corrections leaders came from the same groups, matrons and women who worked in jails did not. The municipal jail and police station matrons were primarily poor police widows who were given the jobs as a form of pension, or they were non-police widows who were advocated for the job by community leaders—generally women—because it often came with a place to live. The women who worked as matrons in rural jails were most often the wives of the elected sheriffs. In addition to caring for inmates, particularly any women, they were also responsible for preparing meals. In most cases, their labor was considered part of their wifely roles, but in some cases, they were paid a small stipend for their efforts.

The role of women working in the jails along with their sheriff husbands was so well established that many actually were appointed or elected as sheriff when their husbands died. Beginning in 1916, Texas appointed more than 100 widows to fill their husbands' terms of office. In a slightly different pattern, Wisconsin voters between 1924 and 1966 elected almost 50 women as sheriffs as a way to evade term limits that would have forced their husbands out of office. In these cases, the women were elected with the understanding that their husbands would continue to act as the county's chief law enforcement officer.

Despite these developments in sheriffs' departments, the tendency in the past, similar to today, is to focus primarily on municipal policing, and this is where much of the focus on women has been and remains. In 1915, Alice Wells again broke new ground with the creation of the International Association of Policewomen, a group that would discontinue in 1932 but reemerge in 1956 as the current International Association of Women Police. By 1917, primarily because of concern over female immorality, 30 U.S. cities employed policewomen. The women enforced a large number of morality laws, including those pertaining to prostitution; searched for missing persons; and provided social service information to women. Their roles defined women's jobs in police departments in the 1970s and continued well into the 1980s.

Concern with women's sexual encounters during wartime led to women's tentative entry into state policing in Connecticut during World War I and in Massachusetts in 1930. In Connecticut, six women were employed as the State Women's Police Corps. The women were paid with temporary, war-related funds; attempts to add them permanently to the state police were defeated, and the unit was disbanded on March 1, 1919. Because of the funding arrangements, even though the women made many cases, and records of their activities existed in state police archives, the women were never officially recognized as members of the force—a distinct difference from World War II-era women, who did identical jobs but received recognition. Massachusetts hired two policewomen in 1930 to assist in investigations involving female juveniles and to assist undercover male troopers as undercover operatives. By 1968, the department employed five women, each assigned to a specific area of the state.

With a few less-documented exceptions, women did not serve in the state police until the 1970s, when they were reluctantly accepted to work patrol and other positions that had previously been open only to men. The Pennsylvania State Police began accepting applications from women in September 1971; the first coeducational class of cadets included 15 women, 14 of whom graduated in July 1972. In 1980, the New Jersey State Police experimented with an all-female cadet class. Despite a high dropout rate, a number of women graduated, and in 2004, a few were among the highest-ranking women in the NJSP. Many felt, though, that they were forced to spend too much time convincing men that their training had really been equal, and the unisex academies fell from favor as quickly as they had begun. The representation of women in state policing is lower than in municipal departments or in sheriffs' departments. Fewer than 6% of state police officers in all ranks in 2004 were women, and only two state police agencies, the Washington State Patrol and the Minnesota State Patrol, have been led by women.

The roles of women in all types of police agencies began to change in 1968. Prior to that time, women were not on uniformed patrol answering routine calls for service, often had not attended a recognized police academy, and frequently did not own uniforms. Those who did have uniforms wore them solely for ceremonial events. Their duties, with the exception of undercover assignments, and usually at the specific request of male managers, had not changed radically from the early days of their entry into policing. The changes that came in the late 1960s and 1970s were brought about by a combination of individual lawsuits by policewomen and sheriffs' jail officers, but the largest impact was created by changes in federal laws. In 1972, Title VII of the 1964 Civil Rights Act extended to police agencies the earlier prohibitions against employment discrimination on the basis of sex. A year later, the Crime Control Act specified that agencies that were guilty of discrimination would not receive federal funds, and a number of agencies began to take seriously the requirement that they hire women. Within the decade, the titles of policewoman and policeman (or patrolman) were replaced with the unisex title of police officer.

By the 1990s, women constituted just over 13% of all police officers; by the early years of the 21st century, the percentages had increased slightly to more than 14%. The percentages, though, are not equally distributed across types of agencies. Large, municipal police departments have tended to have higher representation of women, sometimes more than 25%. Small agencies have lower percentages, sheriffs' departments vary considerably, and state police agencies average fewer than 6% women.

Women have also begun to emerge in greater numbers as chiefs. By 2004, about 200 women were chiefs of police, including those in 4 of the 16 largest departments in the nation (Detroit, San Francisco, Boston, and Milwaukee). About 30 women served as elected sheriffs, including those in such large jurisdictions as Santa Clara County, California; Travis County, Texas; and Fulton County, Georgia. Although the percentages of women in policing have not been increasing overall, it remains to be seen whether increasing numbers of women in high-profile leadership positions will result in greater numbers of women viewing policing as a viable career opportunity despite obstacles that have persisted in their acceptance by some male peers and societal issues that make it difficult for women with families to succeed in professions that require frequent transfers or weekend and night work.

*Dorothy Moses Schulz*

## For Further Reading

Lyon, T. (1973, May). The trooper was a lady. *Law & Order*, pp. 70–71, 81.

Martin, S. E., & Jurik, N. C. (1996). *Doing justice, doing gender*. Thousand Oaks, CA: Sage.

Patterson, M. J. (1980, September). Training tailored for women. *Police Magazine*, pp. 23–29.

Powers, W. F. (1968, March). State policewomen in Massachusetts. *Law & Order*, pp. 82–85, 96.

Schulz, D. M. (1989). The police matron movement: Paving the way for policewomen. *Police Studies, 12*(3), 115–124.

Schulz, D. M. (1995). *From social worker to crimefighter: Women in United States municipal policing*. Westport, CT: Praeger.

Schulz, D. M. (2004). *Breaking the brass ceiling: Women police chiefs and their paths to the top*. Westport, CT: Praeger.

# Z

## ∽ ZERO TOLERANCE

The term *zero tolerance* was first used during the 1980s, with special reference to drug usage and dealing near schools. During the 1980s and 1990s, the term's usage in schools broadened to include bullying, violence, and weapons. Zero tolerance first began to be used in reference to policing and other criminal justice agency policies and practices during the 1990s, especially regarding order maintenance policies practiced by the New York City Police Department.

The order maintenance policies in the New York City Police Department during the mid-1990s were explicitly based on the broken windows hypothesis that James Q. Wilson and George L. Kelling put forward in their 1982 article in the *Atlantic Monthly*. Both Rudy Guiliani, then mayor of New York City, and William Bratton, Guiliani's first police commissioner, were outspoken advocates of the broken windows hypothesis. In fact, during Bratton's tenure as chief of the New York City Transit Authority Police during the early 1990s, Bratton first advocated and used the broken windows philosophy to restore order and reduce crime in New York City's subways. When these ideas were applied in the city itself, it was within the context of a range of crime control strategies that specifically predicted double-digit drops in specific crimes,

as well as crime in general. Nonetheless, order maintenance was an integral aspect of New York City's crime control efforts.

As is well known, crime did decline dramatically throughout the latter part of the 1990s and into the 21st century in New York City. This decline sparked a debate that continues today: Was the decline in crime the result of police and other community action, or was it the result of broad social factors, such as changing drug use patterns, changes in the economy, or changes in the demographic makeup of New York City? This debate was exacerbated by charges from a variety of interest groups that claimed that the practices of the New York City Police Department might be effective, but only at an unacceptable cost of brutality and harassment.

The purpose of this entry is not to become involved in the debate as to whether the policies and practices of the New York City Police Department significantly contributed to the drop in crime or whether the decline was at an unacceptable cost. Suffice it to say that during this period, zero tolerance became equated with the broken windows hypothesis for many authors and many publications. Clearly, many of them used the concept of zero tolerance derogatorily, implying police zealotry; antagonism to cultural pluralism; and heavy-handed rote, nondiscretionary use of citation and arrest (as against warnings, education, persuasion, etc.).

Complicating the picture, zero tolerance became broadly accepted as a synonym for broken windows in Europe and in South and Central America. In many of these countries, this term was adopted but without the critical innuendo of the phrase as used in the United States. In cities such as Mexico City, Buenos Aires, Rio de Janeiro, and others, many officials are perplexed when objections are raised to the use of the term zero tolerance.

Again, however, the arena in which zero-tolerance policy has been most formalized is in education, where schools have adopted policies and practices that permit no discretion in the handling of children involved with drugs, weapons, or violence in school. The resultant controversy within educational circles has been even more heated than in policing and criminal justice. On one hand, advocates argue that drugs, weapons, and violence in school are so threatening to the safety of children that absolutely no discretion should be given to the school administrators as to whether or not to take drastic action in the presence of such commodities or behaviors. On the other hand, critics of zero tolerance have argued that the enforcement of these policies has resulted in inappropriate disciplines for children in the conduct of relatively innocent activities by young, unknowing adolescents.

In policing, those who object to the use of the term zero tolerance as a synonym for broken windows or order maintenance (even by those who intend it to be positive) argue that zero tolerance of minor offenses and disorderly conditions and behaviors is simply not feasible: Context, rather than specific behaviors, always determines the seriousness of minor offenses, and police must and will take it into account when determining the wisest way to handle such offenses. One can, however, think of something like zero tolerance for limited time periods or geographical areas. For example, Greenwich Village has vibrant night street life and entertainment. It attracts many visitors from nearby areas in and around New York City. It is also an area where many gays live and/or frequent. "Gay-bashing" became a serious problem. Youths from outside the area, rather than drinking in bars and restaurants in the area, brought six-packs of beer with them and, after much drinking, thought that gay-bashing would be part of their night's fun. The ultimate police response was to aggressively enforce New York City's public drinking ordinance: As soon as the first can of beer was opened, the perpetrator was cited or arrested, as was anyone else who drank illegally in the area. Gay-bashing was stopped in the area. Is this a form of zero tolerance? In a way, but not in the mindless sense that the phrase often is used to connote.

In sum, zero tolerance is a controversial term in policing and criminal justice (not to mention education). For some, zero tolerance—like broken windows—is a metaphor that signifies a commitment to deal with minor offenses, both as an end in itself and as a way to prevent crime; for others, zero tolerance implies mindless, harsh, and brutal policing that criminalizes reasonably innocuous behaviors, especially in poor communities, and harasses racial and ethnic minorities.

*George Kelling*

***See also*** "Broken Windows" or Incivilities Thesis, Compstat, Theories of Policing

## For Further Reading

Eck, J. E., & Maguire, E. R. (2000). Have changes in policing reduced violent crime? An assessment of the evidence. In A. Blumstein & J. Wallman (Eds.), *The crime drop in America*. Cambridge, UK: Cambridge University Press.

Kelling, G. L., & Sousa, W. H. (2001). *Do police matter? An analysis of the impact of New York City's police reforms* (Civic Report No. 22). New York: Manhattan Institute.

Wilson, J. Q., & Kelling, G. L. (1982, March). Broken windows: The police and neighborhood safety. *Atlantic Monthly*, pp. 29–38.

# Master Bibliography

Abt Associates. (2000). *Police department Information Systems Technology Enhancement Project (ISTEP)*. Washington, DC: U.S. Department of Justice, Community Policing Services Agency.

Abuse of U.S. funds disclosed: LEAA case hurts tax sharing. (1971, July 21). *Washington Post*, p. A1.

Adams, L. (1974). *Art cop Robert Volpe: Art crime detective*. New York: Dodd, Mead.

Adams, R. J., McTernan, T. M., & Remsberg, C. (1980). *Street survival: Tactics for armed encounters*. Evanston, IL: Calibre.

Adams, T. F. (2001). *Police field operations* (5th ed.). Upper Saddle River, NJ: Prentice Hall.

Adamson, C. R. (1983). Punishment after slavery: Southern state penal systems, 1865-1890. *Social Problems, 30*(5), 555-569.

Adler, P. (1993). *Wheeling & dealing: An ethnography of an upper-level drug dealing and smuggling community*. New York: Columbia University Press.

Aguilar v. Texas, 378 U.S. 108 (1964).

AILA Dispatch. (2004, April). p. 7.

Alexander, J. B. (1999, October). Nonlethal weapons: When deadly force is not enough. *The Futurist*, p. 34.

Alexander, R. (1993). The civil commitment of sex offenders in light of Foucha v. Louisiana. *Criminal Justice & Behavior, 20*, 371-387.

Allen, F. (2001). Montana vigilantes and the origins of 3-7-77. *Montana, 51*, 2-19.

Alpert, G. (1997). *Police pursuit: Policies and training* (Research in Brief). Washington, DC: National Institute of Justice.

Alpert, G., & Dunham, R. (1997). *The force factor: Measuring police use of force relative to suspect resistance*. Washington, DC: Police Executive Research Forum.

Alpert, G., Kenney, D., Dunham, R., & Smith, W. (2000). *Police pursuits: What we know*. Washington, DC: Police Executive Research Forum.

Alpert, G., & Piquero, A. (2000). *Community policing: Contemporary readings* (2nd ed.). Prospect Heights, IL: Waveland.

Alpert, G. P., Flynn, D., & Piquero, A. R. (2001). Effective community policing performance measures. *Justice Research and Policy, 3*(2), 79-94.

Alpert, G. P., & Fridell, L. (1992). *Police vehicles and firearms: Instruments of deadly force*. Prospect Heights, IL: Waveland.

Alpert, G. P., & Moore, M. H. (1993). Measuring police performance in the new paradigm of policing. In G. P. Alpert & A. Piquero (Eds.), *Community policing: Contemporary readings* (pp. 215-232). Prospect Heights, IL: Waveland.

Alsabrook, C., Aryani, G., & Garrett, T. (2001). The five principles of leadership. *Law & Order, 49*(5), 112-115.

Amar, A. R. (1994). Fourth Amendment first principles. *Harvard Law Review, 107*, 757-819.

Amar, A. R. (1997). *The Constitution and criminal procedure: First principles*. New Haven, CT: Yale University Press.

*Amber Alert success*. (2003, March). *Law & Order, 51*(3), 6.

Amber Alert sweeps the nation. (2002, December 15/31). *Law Enforcement News, 28*(589-590), p. 6.

American Probation and Parole Association. Available: http://www.appa-net.org/

American Society of Crime Laboratory Directors. (1997, November). ASCLD/Lab newsletter, p. 1.

American Society of Crime Laboratory Directors. (2004). *Laboratory accreditation program*. Retrieved February 20, 2004, from http://www.ascld-lab.org

Amir, M., & Einstein, S. (Eds.). (2004). *The uncertainty series: Corruption, police, security and democracy: Volumes I and II*. Huntsville, TX: Office of International Criminal Justice.

Amsterdam, A. G. (1974). Perspectives on the Fourth Amendment. *Minnesota Law Review, 58*, 349-403.

Anderson v. Creighton, 483 U.S. 635 (1987).

Anderson, B. C. (2001, July/August). The illusion of order [Book review]. *Commentary, 112*, 69-70.

Anderson, W. J. (1982, March 26). *FBI-DEA task forces: An unsuccessful attempt at joint operations* (GGD-82-50). Washington, DC: General Accounting Office.

Anti-crime report. (1972, May 12). *Washington Post*, p. A10.

Area law enforcement personnel to attend "cold-case" seminar. (2002, September 16). Delaware Health and Social Services press release.

Arizona v. Hicks, 480 U.S. 321 (1987).

Arnaldo, C. A. (Ed.). (2001). *Child abuse on the Internet: Ending the silence*. New York: Berghahn.

Arnold, A. (2002). *Final activities report for the National Communications Interoperability Assessment Project*. Washington, DC: U.S. Department of Justice.

Artwohl, A., & Christensen, L. W. (1997). *Deadly force encounters: What cops need to know to mentally and physically prepare for and survive a gunfight*. Boulder, CO: Paladin.

Arvey, R. D., & Murphy, K. R. (1998). Performance evaluation in work settings. *Annual Review of Psychology, 49*, 141-168.

Ashbaugh, D. R. (1999). *Quantitative-qualitative friction ridge analysis: An introduction to basic and advanced ridgeology*. Boca Raton, FL: CRC.

Ashbaugh, R. L. (2000, August). *State and local equitable sharing program: Memorandum audit report* (Office of the Inspector General Report No. 00-18). Available: http://www.usdoj.gov/oig/au0018.

Atwater v. Lago Vista 532 U.S. 318 354 (2001).

Ault, R., & Reese, J. (1980). A psychological assessment of crime profiling. *FBI Law Enforcement Bulletin, 49*(3), 22-25.

Aviation and Transportation Security Act, Pub. L. No. 1 07-71,115 Stat. 597 (2001).

Baden, M., & Roach, M. (2001). *Dead reckoning: The new science of catching killers*. New York: Simon and Schuster.

Baer, H., & Armao, J. P. (1995). The Mollen Commission report: An overview. *New York Law School Law Review, 40*, 73-94.

Bailey, W. G. (Ed.). (1995). *The encyclopedia of police science* (2nd ed.). New York: Garland.

Baker, M. L., Sigmon, J. N., & Nugent, M. E. (2001, September). Truancy reduction: Keeping students in school. *Juvenile Justice*

509

*Bulletin.* Washington, DC: Office of Juvenile Justice and Delinquency Prevention.

Banton, M. (1964). *The policeman in the community.* New York: Basic Books.

Bard, M. (1970). *Training police as specialists in family crisis intervention.* Washington, DC: U.S. Department of Justice.

Bard, M., & Ellison, K. (1974). Crisis intervention and the investigation of forcible rape. *Police Chief, 5,* 68-74.

Barefoot, K. (1995). *Undercover investigation.* Newton, MA: Butterworth-Heinemann.

Barker, T., & Roebuck, J. B. (1974). An empirical typology of police corruption: A study in orgaizational deviance. Springfield, IL: Charles C Thomas.

Barley, S. (1986). Technology as an occasion for structuring. *Administrative Science Quarterly, 31,* 78-108.

Bassiouni, M. C. (1977). *Citizen's arrest: The law of arrest, search and seizure for private citizens and private police.* Springfield, IL: Charles C Thomas.

Bayley, D. (1996). Policing: The world stage. *Journal of Criminal Justice Education, 7,* 241-251.

Bayley, D., & Bittner, E. (1986). The tactical choices of police patrol officers. *Journal of Criminal Justice, 14,* 329-348.

Bayley, D., & Garofalo, J. (1989). The management of violence by police officers. *Criminology, 27,* 1-25.

Bayley, D. H., & Bittner, E. (1984). Learning the skills of policing. *Law and Contemporary Problems, 47,* 35-59.

Beavan, C. (2001). *Fingerprints: The origins of crime detection and the murder case that launched forensic science.* New York: Hyperion.

Beeler, K. J., Bellandese, S. D., & Wiggins, C. A. (1991). *Campus safety: A survey of administrative perceptions and strategies.* Washington, DC: National Association of Student Personnel Administrators.

Belkin, A., & McNichol, J. (2001). *Pink and blue: Outcomes associated with the integration of open gay and lesbian personnel in the San Diego police department.* Center for the Study of Sexual Minorities in the Military. Retrieved February 12, 2003, from http://www.gaymilitary.ucsb.edu/Publications/SanDiegoPub1.htm

Bell's LEAA plan would give the states spending leeway. (1977, December 13). *Washington Post,* p. A13.

BellSouth announces partnership with AMBER Alert programs to support search efforts in child abduction cases across Southeast. (2003). Retrieved July 15, 2003, from http://web.lexis-nexis.com/universe/document?_m=0d640bf2e1150

Bennett, W. B., & Hess, K. M. (1996). *Management and supervision in law enforcement* (2nd ed.). St. Paul, MN: West.

Bennett, W. J., DiIulio, J. J., Jr., & Walters, J. P. (1996). *Body count: Moral poverty . . . and how to win America's war against crime and drugs.* New York: Simon and Schuster.

Benson, B. L. (1993). Community policing works at Michigan State University. *Journal of Security Administration, 16*(1), 43-52.

Benson, B. L. (1998). *To serve and protect: Privatization and community in criminal justice.* New York: New York University Press.

Berger, M. L. (1979). *Firearms in American history.* New York: Watts.

Bibel, D. (2002). *Crime mapping using IBR data.* Retrieved from http://www.jrsa.org/ibrrc/mapping/mapping_ibr.pdf

Birbeck, C., Hussong, M., Lafree, G., & Wilson, N. (1995). *An evaluation of multijursidictional task forces.* Albuquerque: New Mexico Statistical Analysis Center.

Bittner, E. (1970). *The functions of police in modern society.* Chevy Chase, MD: National Clearinghouse for Mental Health.

Bittner, E. (1972). *Function of the police in modern society.* Washington, DC: National Institute of Mental Health.

Bittner, E. (1974). Florence Nightingale in pursuit of Willie Sutton: A theory of the police. In H. Jacob (Ed.), *The potential for reform of criminal justice.* Beverly Hills, CA: Sage.

Bittner, E. (1975). *The functions of the police in modern society: A review of background factors, current practices, and possible role models.* New York: Jason Aronson.

Bittner, E. (1980). *The functions of the police in modern society: A review of background factors, current practices, and possible role models.* Cambridge, MA: Oelgeschlager, Gunn and Hain.

Bivens v. Six Unknown Named Agents of Federal Bureau of Narcotics, 403 U.S. 388 (1971).

Black, D. (1970). The production of crime rates. *American Sociological Review, 35,* 733–748.

Black, D. (1976). *The behaviour of law.* New York: Academic Press.

Black, D. (1980). *The manners and customs of the police.* New York: Academic Books.

Blackstone, W. (1979). *Commentaries on the laws of England* (Vol. 3). Chicago: University of Chicago Press.

Blakey, G. R., Goldstock, R., & Rogovin, C. H. (1978). *Rackets bureaus: Investigation and prosecution of organized crime.* Washington, DC: National Institute of Law Enforcement and Criminal Justice.

Block, R. L. (1995). Space, place and crime: Hot spot areas and hot places of liquor-related crime. In J. E. Eck & D. Weisburd (Eds.), *Crime and place* (pp. 145-183). Monsey, NY: Criminal Justice Press.

Bloom, R. M. (2002). *Ratting: The use and abuse of informants in the American justice system.* Westport, CT: Praeger.

Blumstein, A., Cohen, J., Roth, J. A., & Visher, C. A. (Eds.). (1986). *Criminal careers and "career criminals."* Washington, DC: National Academy Press.

Blumstein, A., & Wallman, J. (2001). *The crime drop in America.* New York: Cambridge University Press.

Board of Inquiry. (2000, March 1). *Rampart area corruption incident.* Los Angeles: Los Angeles Police Department.

Bobb, M. J., Epstein, M. H., Miller, N. H., & Abascal, M. A. (1996). *Five years later: A report to the Los Angeles Police Commission on the Los Angeles Police Department's implementation of Independent Commission recommendations.* Los Angeles: Special Counsel, Los Angeles Police Commission.

Bolz, F., Dudonis, K., & Schulz, D. (2002). *The counterterrorism handbook: Tactics, procedures and techniques.* Boca Raton, FL: CRC.

Bolz, F., & Hershey, E. (1979). *Hostage cop.* New York: Rawson Wade.

Bonsall, D. M. (1993). *Volunteers in law enforcement: The coproduction of police services in the community.* Unpublished master's thesis, University of South Florida.

Bowker, L. E. (1980). A theory of the educational needs of law enforcement officers. *Journal of Contemporary Criminal Justice, 1,* 17-24.

Boy Scouts of America v. Dalem 530 U.S. 640 (2000).

Boyd v. United States, 116 U.S. 616 (1886).

Bracey, D. H. (1992). Police corruption and community relations: Community policing. *Police Studies, 15*(4), 179–183.

Bradley, C. M. (1985). Two models of the Fourth Amendment. *Michigan Law Review, 83,* 1468-1501.

Brady v. Maryland, 272 U.S. 82 (1963).

Brain fingerprinting gets court OK. (2003, April 30). *Law Enforcement News, 29*(598), 5.

Braithwaite, J. (1989). *Crime, shame and reintegration.* New York: Cambridge University Press.

Brandl, S. G., & Horvath, F. (1991). Crime-victim evaluation of police investigative performance. *Journal of Criminal Justice, 19*(3), 109-121.

Brandl, S. G., Stroshine, M. S., & Frank, J. (2001). Who are the complaint-prone officers? An examination of the relationship between police officers' attributes, arrest activity, assignment, and citizens' complaints about excessive force. *Journal of Criminal Justice, 29,* 521-529.

Brantingham, P. L., & Brantingham, P. J. (1993). Environment, routine, and situation: Toward a pattern theory of crime. In R. V. Clarke & M. Felson (Eds.), *Routine activity and rational choice* (pp. 259-294). New Brunswick, NJ: Transaction Books.

Bratton, W. (1996). *Turnaround: How America's top cop reversed the crime epidemic.* New York: Random House.

Bratton, W. J. (1998). *Turnaround: How America's top cop reversed the crime epidemic.* New York: Random House.

Brinegar v. United States, 338 U.S. 160 (1949).

Brodeur, J. (1983). High policing and low policing: Remarks about the policing of political activities. *Social Problems, 30,* 507-520.

Brooks, C. M., Perry, N. W., Starr, S. D., & Teply, L. L. (1994). Child abuse and neglect reporting laws: Understanding interests, understanding policy. *Behavioral Sciences and the Law, 12,* 49-64.

Brooks, J. D. (2001, May). Law enforcement physical fitness standards and Title VII. *FBI Law Enforcement Bulletin,* pp. 26-32.

Brotherton, D. C., & Barrios, L. (2004). *The Almighty Latin King and Queen Nation: Street politics and the transformation of a New York gang.* New York: Columbia University Press.

Browdy, J. (1985, January 7). LEN's 1984 Man of the Year: Pierce R. Brooks, homicide investigator extraordinaire and creator of the VI-CAP system. *Law Enforcement News,* pp. 8-10.

Brown v. Mississippi, 297 U.S. 278 (1936).

Brown, M. K. (1981). *Working the street: Police discretion and the dilemmas of reform.* New York: Russell Sage.

Brown, R. (1991). Vigilante policing. In C. Klockars & S. Mastrofski (Eds.), *Thinking about police: Contemporary readings* (2nd ed.). New York: McGraw-Hill.

Brown, W. F., Jr. (1993). Technical reserve program: Community volunteers in action. *FBI Law Enforcement Bulletin, 62*(3), 10–11.

Browning, S., Cullen, F., Cao, L., Kopache, R., & Stevenson, T. (1994). Race and getting hassled by the police: A research note. *Police Studies, 17*(1), 1-11.

Buckles, T. (2003). *Laws of evidence.* Clifton Park, NY: Thompson/West.

Buckwalter, A. (1983). *Surveillance and undercover investigation.* Newton, MA: Butterworth-Heinemann.

Buerger, M. E., Cohn, E. G., & Petrosino, A. J. (1995). Defining the "hot spots of crime": Operationalizing theoretical concepts for field research. In J. E. Eck & D. Weisburd (Eds.), *Crime and place* (pp. 237-257). Monsey, NY: Criminal Justice Press.

Buerger, M., Petrosino, A., & Petrosino, C. (1999). Extending the police role: Implications of police mediation as a problem-solving tool. *Police Quarterly, 2*(2), 125-149.

Buhrke, R. (1996). *A matter of justice: Lesbians and gay men in law enforcement.* New York: Routledge.

Bumphus, V. W., Gaines, L. K., & Blakely, C. R. (1999). Citizen police academies: Observing goals, objectives, and recent trends. *American Journal of Criminal Justice, 24*(1), 67-79.

Bureau of Justice Assistance. (1990). *Informants and undercover investigations.* Washington, DC: U.S. Government Printing Office.

Bureau of Justice Assistance. (1997). *Multijurisdictional task forces: Ten years of research and evaluation: A report to the attorney general.* Washington, DC: Author.

Bureau of Justice Assistance. (1997). *Stopping hate crime: A case history from the Sacramento Police Department* (Fact Sheet No. 161). Washington, DC: U.S. Department of Justice.

Bureau of Justice Statistics. (2003). *Census of state and local law enforcement agencies, 2000.* Washington, DC: Author.

Bureau of Justice Statistics. (2003). *Local police departments 2000.* Washington, DC: Author.

Bureau of Justice Statistics. (2003). *Probation and parole in the United States, 2002.* Washington, DC: Author.

Bureau of Justice Statistics. (2003). *Sourcebook of criminal justice statistics, 2001.* Available: http://www.albany.edu/sourcebook/

Bureau of Justice Statistics. (n.d.). *Reentry trends in the United States.* Available: http://www.ojp.usdoj.gov/bjs/reentry/reentry.htm

Burke, P. (2003). *APAI handbook for new parole board members.* Retrieved from http://www.apaintl.org/ Handbook.html

Burke, R. (2000). *Counter-terrorism for emergency responders.* New York: Lewis.

Burke, T. (1991). *The relationship between dispatcher stress and social support, job satisfaction and locus of control.* Unpublished doctoral dissertation, City University of New York.

Burke, T. (1993, April). The correlation between dispatcher stress and control. *APCO Bulletin,* pp. 39-41.

Burke, T. (1993, February). The correlation between dispatcher stress and occupational dissatisfaction. *APCO Bulletin,* pp. 32, 82.

Burke, T. (1993, March). The correlation between dispatcher stress, burnout and social support. *APCO Bulletin,* pp. 50-54.

Burke, T. (1995, October). Dispatcher stress. *FBI Law Enforcement Bulletin,* pp. 1-6.

Burke, T. (1996, Winter). Even dispatchers get the blues. *Minding the Badge* (published quarterly by the *Mental Health Association*), pp. 1-2, 4.

Burrows, E., & Wallace, M. (1999). *Gotham: A history of New York City to 1898.* New York: Oxford University Press.

Burton, B. (1984). *Bounty hunter.* Boulder, CO: Paladin.

Burton, B. (1990). *Bail enforcer: The advanced bounty hunter.* Boulder, CO: Paladin.

Buzawa, E. S., & Buzawa, C. G. (Eds.). (1992). *Domestic violence: The changing criminal justice response.* Westport, CT: Auburn House.

Cain, M. (1996). Policing there and here: Reflections on an international comparison. *International Journal of the Sociology of Law, 24,* 399-425.

California Attorney General's Office. (2002). *Commission on Special Weapons and Tactics (S.W.A.T): Final report.* Sacramento: Author.

California Attorneys for Criminal Justice v. Butts, 195 F.3d 1039 (9th Cir. 1999).

California v. Carney, 471 U.S. 386 (1985).

California v. Greenwood, 486 U.S. 35 (1988).

Campbell, J. H. (1992). *A comparative analysis of the effects of post-shooting trauma on the special agents of the Federal Bureau of Investigation.* Unpublished doctoral dissertation, Michigan State University.

Canaday, M. (2002). *The effect of sodomy laws on lifting the ban on homosexual personnel: Three case studies.* Center for the Studies of Sexual Minorities in the Military. Retrieved February 12, 2003, from http://www gaymilitary.ucsbedu/ Publications/canaday2.htm

Canadian Law Reform Commission. (2003). *Law reform in Canada.* Ottawa: Author.

Canadian Law Reform Commission. (2003, November). Working paper on policing. Ottawa: Author.

Cannon, L. (2000, October 1). One bad cop. *New York Times Magazine,* p. 6.

Canter, D., Coffey, T., Huntley, M., & Missen, C. (2000). Predicting serial killers' home base using a decision support system. *Journal of Quantitative Criminology, 16,* 457-478.

Cao, L., Frank, J., & Cullen, F. T. (1996). Race, community context and confidence in the police. *American Journal of Police, 15*(1), 3-22.

Caplan, G. (1961). *An approach to community mental health.* New York: Grune and Stratton.

Caplan, G. (1964). *Principles of preventive psychiatry.* New York: Basic Books.

*The "Carnivore" controversy: Electronic surveillance and privacy in the digital age: Hearing before the Committee on the Judiciary, United States Senate,* 106th Cong., 2d sess. (2000).

Carr, C. (2002). *The lessons of terror: A history of warfare against civilians: Why it has always failed and why it will fail again.* New York: Random House.

Carroll Buracher and Associates, Inc. (1994). *Policing in public housing: Assessment & blueprint.* Harrisonburg, VA: Author.

Carroll v. United States, 267 U.S. 132 (1925).

Carruthers, B., & Espeland, W. (1991). Accounting for rationality: Double-entry bookkeeping and the rhetoric of economic rationality. *American Journal of Sociology, 97*(3), 31–69.

Carte, G. E., & Carte, E. H. (1975). *Police reform in the United States: The era of August Vollmer, 1905-1932.* Berkeley: University of California Press.

Carter proposes to streamline LEAA, aid war on crime in public housing. (1978, July 11). *Washington Post,* p. A4.

Carter, D. L. (1990). Drug-related corruption of police officers: A contemporary typology. *Journal of Criminal Justice, 18,* 85–98.

Carter, D. L., Katz-Bannister, A. J., & Schafer, J. (2001). Lansing Police Department MATS data: Six month analysis. Available: http://www.lansingpolice.com

Carter, D. L., & Sapp, A. D. (1990). The evolution of higher education in law enforcement: Preliminary findings from a national study. *Journal of Criminal Justice Education, 1,* 59-85.

Cascio, W. (1977). Formal education and police officer performance. *Journal of Police Science and Administration, 5,* 89-96.

Casey, E. (Ed.). (2002). *Handbook of computer crime investigation: Forensic tools and technology.* San Diego, CA: Academic Press.

Cavender, G., & Fishman, M. (Eds.). (1998). *Entertaining crime: Television reality programs.* New York: Aldine de Gruyter.

Center for International Earth Science Information Network (CIESIN). http://www.ciesin.org/

Chambers v. Florida, 309 U.S. 227 (1940).

Chambers v. Maroney, 399 U.S. 42 (1970).

Chambliss, W. (1964). A sociological analysis of the law of vagrancy. *Social Problems, 12*(1), 67-77.

Chambliss, W. (1994). Policing the ghetto underclass. *Social Problems, 41,* 177-194.

Chan, C. (2004). *Aviation legislation: 2003 state legislative summary.* Available: http://www.ncsl.org/programs/esnr/03aviationleg.htm

Chan, J. (1997). *Changing police culture.* Cambridge, UK: Cambridge University Press.

Chan, J. (2000). *The technology game.* Final report to the Australian Research Council, University of New South Wales, Australia.

Chan, J. (2002). *Fair cop.* Toronto: University of Toronto Press.

Chandler, A. (Ed.). (1910). *The colonial records of the state of Georgia* (Vol. 18). Atlanta: Charles P. Byrd, State Printer.

Changing its stripes: New look, and attitude, for Philly SVU. (2003). *Law Enforcement News, 29*(604), 5.

Chapman, R., Baker, S., Bezdikian, V., Cammarata, P., Cohen, D., Leach, N., Schapiro, A., Scheider, M., Varano, R., & Boba, R. (2002). *Local law enforcement responds to terrorism: Lessons in prevention and preparedness.* Washington, DC: U.S. Department of Justice, Office of Community Oriented Policing Services.

Chapman, S. G. (1990). *Police dogs in North America.* Springfield, IL: Charles C Thomas.

Charkoudian, L. (2001). *Economic analysis of inter-personal conflict and community mediation.* Unpublished doctoral dissertation, Johns Hopkins University, Baltimore, MD.

Charney, S. (1994). Computer crime: Law enforcement's shift from a corporeal environment to the intangible, electronic world of cyberspace. *Federal Bar News and Journal, 41*(7), 489–494.

Chase, A. (1977). Residency laws: Should police be free to live where they chose? *Police, 2,* 62-65.

Chavez v. Martinez, 538 U.S. 760 (2003).

Chermak, S., Bailey, F., & Brown, M. (2003). *Media representations of 9/11.* Westport, CT: Praeger.

Chestnut, S. (2001). Poverty: A symposium: The practice of dual arrests in domestic violence situations: Does it accomplish anything? *Mississippi Law Journal, 70,* 971.

Chevigny, P. (2002). Conflict of rights and keeping order. *Criminology & Public Policy, 2*(1), 155-160.

Chicago Community Policing Evaluation Consortium. (2003). *Community policing in Chicago, Years Eight and Nine* (p. 5). Chicago: Illinois Criminal Justice Information Authority.

Child-snatchings are news, but a problem? (2002, December 15/31). *Law Enforcement News, 28*(589-590), p. 6.

Chimel v. California, 395 U.S. 752 (1969).

Christopher Commission. (1991). *Report of the Independent Commission on the Los Angeles Police Department.* Los Angeles: Author.

Cisneros, H. G. (1995). *Defensible space: Deterring crime and building community.* Washington, DC: Department of Housing and Urban Development.

City of Chicago v. Morales, 527 U.S. 41, 64 (1999).

http://cityofnewhaven.com/police/html/divisions/admin/esu.htm

City of New York. (1994). The City of New York Commission to Investigate Allegations of Police Corruption and the Anti-Corruption Procedures of the Police Department, Milton Mollen, Chair. *Commission Report.* July 4, 1994.

Civil Rights Division's Activities and Programs Brochure. (2002). United States Department of Justice. Retrieved October 31, 2003, from http://www.usdoj.gov/crt/activity.html

Clark, J. (1991). Can traffic radar lead to cancer? *Law Enforcement News, 17*(332).

Clark, J. (1996, April 15). Complex job in changing times: Law enforcement in Indian country is anything but easy. *Law Enforcement News, 22*(443), 1.

Clear Law Enforcement for Criminal Alien Removal Act, H.R. 2671.

Clear, T., & Cadora, E. (2003). *Community justice.* Belmont, CA: Wadsworth.

Coderoni, G. R. (2002). The relationship between multicultural training for police and effective law enforcement. *FBI Law Enforcement Bulletin, 71*(11), 16-18.

Cohen, A. (2000, March 6). Gangsta cops. *Time,* pp. 30-34.

Cohen, S. (1985). *Visions of social control: Crime, punishment and classification.* Cambridge, UK: Polity.

Cohn, E. (1996). The citizen police academy: A recipe for improving police-community relations. *Journal of Criminal Justice, 24*(3), 265-271.

Cole, S. A. (2001). *Suspect identities: A history of fingerprinting and criminal identification.* Cambridge, MA: Harvard University Press.

Collingwood, T., Hoffman, R., & Smith, J. (2003). The need for physical fitness. *Law & Order, 51*(6), 44-50.

Collins, J. M. (in press). *Identity theft prevention and control: How to protect your business, customers and employees.* Hoboken, NJ: Wiley.

Collins, J. M., & Hoffman, S. K. (2002). *Identity theft perpetrator profiles.* Manuscript submitted for publication.

Collins, J. M., & Hoffman, S. K. (2003). *Identity theft first responder manual for criminal justice professionals: Police officers, attorneys and judges.* Flushing, NY: Looseleaf.

Collins, M. A., & Javna, J. (1988). *The best of crime & detective TV.* New York: Harmony.

Collins, R. F. (1989). *America at its best: Opportunities in the National Guard.* New York: Rosen.

Commission on Accreditation for Law Enforcement Agencies. (1999). *Standards for law enforcement agencies* (4th ed.). Fairfax, VA: Author.

Commission on Law Enforcement and the Administration of Justice. (1967). *The challenge of crime in a free society.* Washington, DC: U.S. Government Printing Office.

Community Research Associates. (2004). *Developing multi-agency interoperability communications systems: User's handbook.* Washington, DC: U.S. Department of Justice.

Committee to Review Research on Police Policy and Practices. (2004). *Fairness and effectiveness in policing: The evidence.* Washington, DC: National Academies Press.

Comparet-Cassani, J. (2002). Balancing the autonomy of threatened witnesses versus a defendant's right of confrontation: The waiver doctrine after Alvarado. *San Diego Law Review, 39,* 1165-1244.

Conklin, J. (2002). *Why crime rates fell.* Boston: Allyn & Bacon.

Conley, J. (2003, January 22). New Bedford program to help the elderly. *Roanoke Times & World News,* p. B5.

Connally v. Georgia, 429 U.S. 245 (1977).

Conot, R. (1968). *Rivers of blood, years of darkness: The unforgettable classic account of the Watts riot.* New York: Morrow.

Coolidge v. New Hampshire, 403 U.S. 443 (1971).

Cooper Institute of Aerobic Research. (2002). *Physical fitness norms for law enforcement.* Available: http://www.cooperinst.org/shopping/lawstand3.pdf

Cooper v. Dupnik, 963 F.2d 1220 (9th Cir. 1992) (en banc).

Cooper, B. (1979). *Merleau-Ponty and Marxism: From terror to reform.* Toronto: University of Toronto Press.

Cooper, C. (1999). *Mediation & arbitration by patrol police officers.* Lanham, MD: University Press of America.

Cooper, C. (2000a). Police mediators: Training hones skills. *Dispute Resolution Magazine* 7(1), 17.

Cooper, C. (2000b). Training patrol officers to mediate disputes. *FBI Law Enforcement Bulletin,* 69(2), 7.

Cooper, J. (1997). *The rise of the National Guard: The evolution of the American militia, 1865-1920.* Lincoln: University of Nebraska Press.

Cope, N. (2003). Crime analysis: Principles and practice. In T. Newburn (Ed.), *Handbook of policing* (pp. 340–362). Devon, UK: Willan.

Cordner, G. W., Greene, J. R., & Bynum, T. S. (1983). The sooner the better: Some effects of police response time. In R. R. Bennett (Ed.), *Police at work: Policy issues and analysis* (pp. 145-164). Beverly Hills, CA: Sage.

Corps values: Navy SEAL type training for Police Corps recruits questioned. (2000). *Law Enforcement News,* 26(540), pp. 1, 7.

Cote, A., & Bugbee, P. (1988). *Principles of fire protection.* Quincy, MA: National Fire Protection Association.

Council of State Government. (2002). *Criminal justice/mental health consensus project.* Lexington, KY: Author.

Cox, S. (1976). Prosecutorial discretion: An overview. *American Criminal Law Review: A Symposium, Prosecutorial Discretion, 13,* 383-434.

Crank, J. (1998). *Understanding police culture.* Cincinnati, OH: Anderson.

Crank, J., & Langworthy, R. (1998). An institutional perspective of policing. In L. Gaines & G. Cordner (Eds.), *Policing perspectives: An anthology.* Los Angeles: Roxbury.

Crawford, K. A. (1994). News media participation in law enforcement activities. *FBI Law Enforcement Bulletin,* 63(8), 28-33.

Cressey, D. R. (1969). *Theft of the nation.* New York: Harper & Row.

Crime Awareness and Campus Security Act of 1990, 20 U.S.C. 1092 (1990).

http://criminalistics.com/abc/A.php

Crockett, G. W. (1972). Racism in the law. In L. E. Reasons & J. L. Kuykendall (Eds.), *Race, crime and justice.* Pacific Palisades, CA: Goodyear.

Crump, S. (1966). *Black riot in Los Angeles: The story of the Watts tragedy.* Los Angeles: Trans-Anglo.

Cunningham, W. C., Strauchs, J., & Van Meter, C. (1991). *Private security: Patterns and trends.* Washington, DC: National Institute of Justice.

Curry, G. D., & Decker, S. H. (2003). *Confronting gangs: Crime and community.* Los Angeles: Roxbury.

Curtius, M. (2004, July 24). The 9/11 Commission Report: Lawmakers jolted in midst of campaign: The Commission's urgent tone focuses the minds of politicians, but the drive to enact reforms is competing with the drive to Nov. 2. *Los Angeles Times,* p. A14.

Cutler, B. L., & Penrod, S. D. (1995). *Mistaken identification: The eyewitness, psychology, and the law.* New York: Cambridge University Press.

D'Acci, J. (1994). *Defining women: Television and the case of Cagney and Lacey.* Chapel Hill: University of North Carolina Press.

Dadds, V., & Scheide, T. (2000). *Police performance and activity measurement* (Trends and Issues in Crime and Criminal Justice, No. 180). Retrieved from www.aic.gov.au/publications/tandi/ti180.pdf

Dale, S. S. (2001, November 26). The brain scientist. *Time, 158,* 81.

Daly, K. (2002). Restorative justice: The real story. *Punishment & Society,* 4(1), 55-79.

Daly, N., & Proffitt, W. (1991). The radar dilemma: One agency's response. *Law Enforcement News,* 17(348).

Dantzker, M. L. (2003). *Understanding today's police* (3rd ed.). Upper Saddle River, NJ: Prentice Hall.

Davis, J. (1974, Fall). Justification for no obligation: Views of black males toward crime and the criminal law. *Issues in Criminology, 9,* 69-87.

Davis, K. C. (1969). *Discretionary justice.* Westport, CT: Greenwood.

Davis, M., Lundman, R., & Martinez, R., Jr. (1991). Private corporate justice: Store police, shoplifters, and civil recovery. *Social Problems, 38,* 395-408.

Davis, R., Ortiz, C., Henderson, N., Miller, J., & Massie, M. K. (2002). *Turning necessity into virtue: Pittsburgh's experience with a federal consent decree.* New York: Vera Institute of Justice.

DeArment, R. K. (1995). A look at two professional frontier lawmen: George A. Scarborough and Frank M. Canton. *Journal of the West, 34,* 8-12.

DeConde, A. (2001). *Gun violence in America: The struggle for control.* Boston: Northeastern University Press.

De Cresce, R., Lifshitz, M., Mazura, A., & Tilson, J. (1989) *Drug testing in the workplace.* Washington, DC: Bureau of National Affairs.

Dees, M. (1996). *Gathering storm: America's militia threat.* New York: HarperCollins.

De Forest, P. R. (1999). Recapturing the essence of criminalistics. *Science and Justice, 39* (3), 196–208.

De Forest, P. R. (2001). What is trace evidence? In B. Caddy (Ed.), *Forensic examination of glass and paint* (pp. 1-25). London: Taylor & Francis.

De Forest, P. R., Gaensslen, R. E., & Lee, H. C. (1983). *Forensic science: An introduction to criminalistics.* New York: McGraw-Hill.

DeFrances, C. (2002). *Prosecutors in state courts, 2001* (NCJ 193441). Washington, DC: U.S. Department of Justice.

DeGeneste, H. I., & Sullivan, J. P. (1994). *Policing transportation facilities.* Springfield, IL: Charles C Thomas.

DeHaan, J. D. (1991). *Kirk's fire investigation.* Englewood Cliffs, NJ: Prentice Hall.

DeJong, C. (2000). *Gender differences in officer attitude and behavior: Providing comfort to citizens.* Report to the National Institute of Justice. East Lansing: Michigan State University.

Delattre, E. (2002). *Character and cops: Ethics in policing* (4th ed.). Washington, DC: AEI.

Delattre, E. (2002). *Character and cops: Ethics in policing* (4th ed.). Washington, DC: AEI.

Delaware River and Bay Authority Police. (n.d.). *Department history.* Retrieved March 9, 2003, from http://drba.net/police/history.html

Del Carmen, R., & Smith, M. (1997). Police, civil liability, and the law. In R. Dunham & G. Alpert (Eds.), *Critical issues in policing: Contemporary readings* (3rd ed.). Prospect Heights, IL: Waveland.

Delprino, R. P., & Bahn, C. (1988). National survey of the extent and nature of psychological services in police departments. *Professional Psychology: Research and Practice, 19*(4), 421-425.

Dempsey, J. S. (1999). *An introduction to policing* (2nd ed.). Belmont, CA: Wadsworth.

Denning, D. E., & Baugh, W. (1997). *Encryption and evolving technologies: Tools of organized crime and terrorism.* Washington, DC: U.S. Working Group on Organized Crime, National Strategy Information Center.

Department of Housing and Urban Development. (2003). *HA profiles.* Retrieved June 11, 2003, from https://pic.hud.gov/pic/haprofiles/haprofilelist.asp

Deprivation of Rights Under Color of Law, 18 U.S.C. § 242.

Deutsch, H. D. (1992). *Immigration the easy way.* Happauge, NY: Barron's.

Developments in the law: Legal responses to domestic violence. (1993). *Harvard Law Review, 106,* 1498-1574.

Dey, I. (1998). Drug courier profiles: An infringement on Fourth Amendment rights. *University of Baltimore Law Forum, 28,* 3-11.

Diamond, D., Fridell, L., Lunney, R., & Kubu, B. (2001). *Racially biased policing: A principled response.* Washington, DC: Police Executive Research Forum

Dickerson v. United States, 530 U.S. 428 (2000).

Dillon, D. J. (1977). *A history of criminalistics in the United States 1850–1950.* Unpublished doctoral dissertation, University of California, Berkeley.

Dilworth, D. C. (Ed.). (1977). *Identification wanted: Development of the American criminal identification system, 1893-1943.* Gaithersburg, MD: International Association of Chiefs of Police.

Dines, J. (1998). *Document examiner handbook.* New York: Pantex.

DNA Advisory Board. (2000). Quality assurance standards for forensic DNA testing laboratories and for convicted offender DNA databasing laboratories. *Forensic Science Communications, 2*(3). Available: http://www.fbi.gov/hq/lab/fsc/backissu/july2000/codispre.htm

Dodenhoff, D. (1990). 1989's People of the Year: The study and redesign team behind the new uniform crime reporting system. *Law Enforcement News, 14*(307), p. l.

Dodenhoff, P. (1993). LEN salutes its 1993 Man of the Year, Sgt. Joseph Trimboli of the New York Police Department. *Law Enforcement News, 19*(392), pp. 1, 14-15.

Dodenhoff, P. (1994, December 31). LEN's 1994 People of the Year: The makers of the Violent Crime Control Act. *Law Enforcement News, 20*(414), 1, 14.

Dodenhoff, P. C. (1987, March 10). Steven A. Rhoads: Police chief of East Hazel Crest, Ill., and pioneer in the use of psychological technique for lie detection. *Law Enforcement News, 13*(244) 9-12, 14.

Dominick, J. R. (1973). Crime and law enforcement on prime-time television. *Public Opinion Quarterly, 37*(2), 241-250.

Donofrio, D. (2002). Establishing specialty units in small agencies. *Law Enforcement Technology, 29*(9), 114-119.

Donohue, B., & Mueller, M. (2001, January 31). Drug arrests by troopers plunge. *Newark Star-Ledger,* p. 10.

Dorn, N., Murji, K., & South, N. (1992). *Traffickers: Drug markets and law enforcement.* New York: Routledge.

Douglas, J., Burgess, A., Burgess, A., & Ressler, R. (1992). *Crime classification manual.* San Francisco: Jossey-Bass.

Douglas, J., Ressler, R., Burgess, A., & Hartman, C. (1986). Criminal profiling from crime scene analysis. *Behavioral Sciences and the Law, 4,* 401-421.

Dove, G. N. (1982). *The police procedural.* Bowling Green, OH: Bowling Green University Popular Press.

D'Ovidio, R., & Doyle, J. R. (2003). Cyberstalking: Understanding the investigative hurdles. *FBI Law Enforcement Bulletin, 72*(3), 10–17.

Draper v. United States, 358 U.S. 307 (1959).

Dressler, J. (2002). *Understanding criminal procedure* (3rd ed.). New York: LexisNexis.

Dripps, D. (2001). The case for the contingent exclusionary rule. *American Criminal Law Review, 38,* 1-46.

Drug Strategies. (2001). *Critical choices: Making drug policy at the state level.* Chicago: John D. and Catherine MacArthur Foundation.

Drury v. State, 793 A.2d 567 (Md. Ct. App., 2002).

DuBow, F., McCabe, F., & Kaplan, G. (1979). *Reactions to crime: A critical review of the literature.* Washington, DC: U.S. Government Printing Office.

*Due process in criminal investigation.* (1965) FBI Training Document Number 65.

Dunham, R. G., & Alpert, G. P. (1993). *Critical issues in policing: Contemporary readings.* Prospect Heights, IL: Waveland.

Dunworth, T. (2000). Criminal justice and the information technology revolution. In J. Horney (Ed.), *Criminal justice 2000* (Vol. 3, pp. 371-426). Washington, DC: National Institute of Justice, Office of Justice Programs.

Dupry, R. E. (1971). *The National Guard: A compact history.* New York: Hawthorne.

Dyson, W. E. (2001). *Terrorism: An investigator's handbook.* Cincinnati, OH: Anderson.

Early Warning Systems. (2002). *Model policy.* Alexandria, VA: International Association of Chiefs of Police.

Eck, J., & Spelman, W. (1987). *Problem-solving: Problem-oriented policing in Newport News.* Washington, DC: Police Executive Research Forum.

Eck, J. E., & Maguire, E. R. (2000). Have changes in policing reduced violent crime? An assessment of the evidence. In A. Blumstein & J. Wallman (Eds.), *The crime drop in America.* Cambridge, UK: Cambridge University Press.

Edwards v. California, 314 U.S. 160 (1941).

Egger, S. (2002). *The killers among us: An examination of serial murder and its investigation.* Upper Saddle River, NJ: Prentice Hall.

Egloff, F. R. (1995). Lawmen and gunmen: A contrasting view of Old West peace officers in Kansas and Texas. *Journal of the West, 34,* 19-26.

8 CFR & 264.1(f).

80 IR 1230 (August 19, 2002).

80 IR 1395-1396 (September 16, 2002).

80 IR 162 (February 3, 2003).

80 IR 269 (February 24, 2003).

80 IR 305 (March 3, 2003).

80 IR 537-539 (April 14, 2003).

80 IR 678 (May 12, 2003).

Eldefonso, E., & Coffey, A. R. (1981). *Criminal law: History, philosophy, enforcement.* New York: Harper & Row.

Ellen, D. (1997). *The scientific examination of documents: Methods and techniques.* London: Taylor & Francis.

Elliot, D. S., Hamburg, B. A., & Williams, K. R. (1998). *Violence in American schools*. New York: Cambridge University Press.

Emerson, S. (2002). *American jihad: The terrorists living among us*. New York: Simon & Schuster.

Enhanced Border Security and Visa Entry Reform Act, H.R. 3525, Pub. L. No. 107-173, 116 Stat. 543 (2002).

Entick v. Carrington, 19 How.St.Tr. 1029 (1765).

Environmental Systems Research International (ESRI). http://www.esri.com

http://ep.com/cops/copscorner.html

Equal Employment Opportunity Commission. (2004). *Equal Employment Opportunity Commission guidelines for fairness in hiring*. Available: http://www.eeoc.gov/policy/

Ericson, R. V., & Haggerty, K. D. (1997). *Policing the risk society*. Toronto: University of Toronto Press.

Esbensen, F., & Huizinga, D. (1993). Gangs, drugs, and delinquency in a survey of urban youth. *Criminology, 31,* 565–587.

Escobedo v. Illinois, 378 U.S. 478 (1964).

Espeland, W. (1998). *The struggle for water*. Chicago: University of Chicago Press.

Ethington, P. J. (1987). Vigilantes and the police: The creation of a professional police bureaucracy in San Francisco, 1847-1900. *Journal of Social History, 21*(2), 197-227.

Everly, G. S. (1992, November). *The critical incident stress debriefing process (CISD) and the prevention of occupational post-traumatic stress*. Paper presented at the second APA and NIOSH Conference on Occupational Stress, Washington, DC.

Everly, G. S., & Mitchell, J. T. (1999). *Critical incident stress management: A new era and standard of care in crisis intervention* (2nd ed.). Ellicot City, MD: Chevron.

Executive Office for Asset Forfeiture. (1994). *Guide to equitable sharing of federally forfeited property for state and local law enforcement agencies*. Washington, DC: U.S. Department of Justice.

Fagin, J. (2003). *Criminal justice*. Boston: Allyn & Bacon.

Farrell, G., & Pease, K. (Eds.). (2001). *Repeat victimization*. Monsey, NY: Criminal Justice Press.

FBI Terrorist Research and Analytical Center. (1991). *Terrorism in the United States: 1990*. Washington, DC: U.S. Department of Justice

Feagin, J., & Hahn, H. (1973). *Ghetto revolts: The politics of violence in American cities*. New York: Macmillan.

Federal Bureau of Investigation. (1987). *They write their own sentences: The FBI handwriting analysis manual*. Boulder, CO: Paladin.

Federal Bureau of Investigation. (1992). *Prevention and control of civil disturbance: Time for review*. Quantico, VA: FBI Academy.

Federal Bureau of Investigation. (2001). *Crime in the United States, 2000*. Washington, DC: U.S. Government Printing Office.

Federal Bureau of Investigation. (2002). *Crime in the United States, 2001*. Washington, DC: Government Printing Office.

Federal Bureau of Investigation. (2003). *Age-specific arrest rates and race-specific arrest rates for selected offenses, 1991-2001*. Washington, DC: U.S. Department of Justice.

Federal Bureau of Investigation. (various dates). *Uniform crime reports*. Available: http://www.fbi.gov/ucr/ucr.htm

Federal Bureau of Investigation. (various years). *Law enforcement officers killed and assaulted*. Washington, DC: Author.

Federal Communications Commission. (2003). *The AMBER plan*. Retrieved July 15, 2003, from http://ww.fcc.gov/cgb/consumer facts/AMBERPlan.html

Fellman, D. (1958). *The defendant's rights*. New York: Rinehart.

Ferdico, J. N. (1999). *Criminal procedure for the criminal justice professional* (7th ed.). Belmont, CA: West/Wadsworth.

Ferdico, J. N. (2002). *Criminal procedure for the criminal justice professional*. Belmont, CA: Wadsworth.

Fijnaut, C., & Marx, G. (1995). *Undercover: Police surveillance in comparative perspective*. The Hague: Kluwer.

Finckenauer, J. O. (1975). Higher education and police discretion. *Journal of Police Science and Administration, 3,* 450-457.

Finkelhor, D., & Ormrod, R. (2000, June). Kidnapping of juveniles: Patterns from NIBRS. *Juvenile Justice Bulletin*. Available: http://www.ncjrs.org/html/ojjdp/2000_6_2/contents.html

Finn, P. (2001). *Citizen review of police: Approaches and implementation*. Washington, DC: U.S. Department of Justice.

Fisher, B. A. J. (1993). *Techniques of crime scene investigation*. Boca Raton, FL: CRC.

Fisher, B. S., Sloan, J. J., Cullen, F. T., & Lu, C. (1997). The on-campus victimization patterns of students: Implications for crime prevention by students in post-secondary institutions. In S. P. Lab (Ed.), *Crime prevention at a crossroads*. Cincinnati, OH: Anderson.

Fishman, M., & Cavender, G. (1998). *Entertaining crime: Television reality programs*. Hawthorne, NY: Aldine de Gruyter.

Flango, V. (2001, April). Measuring progress in improving court processing of child abuse and neglect cases. *Family Court Review*. Retrieved February 1, 2003 from http://web.lexis-nexis.com/universe

Flippo v. West Virginia, 98 U.S. 8770 (1999).

Flores, E. (1993, December). *Leadership training as a tool for confronting racial and ethnic conflicts* (Working paper 93-24). Boulder, CO: Conflict Research Consortium.

Florida v. Bostick, 501 U.S. 429 (1991).

Folkes, A. (1992, December). They do not belong. *Police: The Voice of the Service*, p. 26. Retrieved February 12, 2003, from http://www.goalny.org

Foote, C. (1956). Vagrancy type law and its administration. *University of Pennsylvania Law Review, 104,* 615.

Forst, B., & Manning, P. K. (1999). *The privatization of policing: Two views*. Washington, DC: Georgetown University Press.

42 U.S.C. 14665 (2000).

42 U.S.C. Section 14141.

Fox, J. A. (2000). Demographics and U.S. homicide. In A. Blumstein & J. Wallman (Eds.), *The crime drop in America*. Cambridge, UK: Cambridge University Press.

Franklin, R. A. (2003). *The IADLEST national decertification database*. Available: http://www.iadlest.org/nddreport.pdf

Franks v. Delaware, 438 U.S. 154 (1978).

Frese, G. C. (1969). The riot curfew. *California Law Review, 57*(2), 450-490.

Fridell, L., Lunney, R., Diamond, D., & Kubu, B. (2001). *Racially biased policing: A principled response*. Washington, DC: Police Executive Research Forum. Available: www.policeforum.org

Friedman, W. (1998). Volunteerism and the decline of violent crime. *Journal of Law and Criminology, 88*(4), 1453-1474.

Frost, G. A. (1993). Law enforcement responds to campus crime. *Journal of Security Administration, 16*(1), 21-29.

Fyfe, J. (1981). Observations on police deadly force. *Crime & Deliquency, 18,* 376-389.

Fyfe, J. J. (1987). Police personnel practices, 1986. *Municipal Yearbook 1987*. Washington, DC: International City Management Association.

Fyfe, J. J. (1996). Training to reduce police-citizen violence. In W. A. Geller & H. Toch (Eds.), *Police violence: Understanding and controlling police abuse of force*. New Haven, CT: Yale University Press.

Fyfe, J. J. (2002). Too many missing cases: Holes in our knowledge about police use of force. *Justice Research and Policy, 4,* 87-102.

Fyfe, J. J., Greene, J. R., Walsh, W. F., Wilson, O. W., & McLaren, R. (1997). *Police administration* (5th ed.). New York: McGraw-Hill.

Gadson, L., Michael, M., & Walsh, N. (2003). *FBI Bomb Data Center: 1999 bombing incidents general information bulletin 99-1.* Quantico, VA: Federal Bureau of Investigation.

Gaines, L., & Cordner, G. (Eds.). (1998). *Policing perspectives: An anthology.* Los Angeles: Roxbury.

Gaines, L. K., Kappeler, V. E., & Vaughn, J. B. (1994). *Policing in America.* Cincinnati, OH: Anderson.

Gans, H. J. (1967). *The Levittowners.* New York: Pantheon.

Gardner, T. J., & Anderson, T. M. (2004). *Criminal evidence* (5th ed.). Belmont, CA: Wadsworth/Thompson.

Garland, D. (2001). *The culture of control: Crime and social order in contemporary society.* Chicago: University of Chicago Press.

Garner, J., Buchanan, J., Schade, T., & Hepburn, J. (1996). *Understanding the use of force by and against the police* (NCJ 158614). Washington, DC: U.S. Department of Justice.

Garofalo, J. (1997). Hate crime victimization in the United States. In R. C. Davis, A. J. Lurigio, & W. G. Skogan (Eds.), *Victims of crime* (2nd ed., pp. 134-145). Thousand Oaks, CA: Sage.

Garofalo, J., & Laub, J. (1978). The fear of crime: Broadening our perspective. *Victimology, 3,* 242–253.

Garofalo, J., & Martin, S. E. (1991). The law enforcement response to bias-motivated crimes. In N. Taylor (Ed.), *Bias crimes: The law enforcement response* (pp. 17-34). Chicago: Office of International Criminal Justice.

Garofalo, J., & Martin, S. E. (1993). *Bias-motivated crimes: Their characteristics and the law enforcement response.* Final report submitted to the National Institute of Justice. Carbondale, IL: Center for the Study of Crime, Delinquency, and Corrections.

Garry, E. M. (1996, October). Truancy: First step to a lifetime of problems. *Juvenile Justice Bulletin.* Washington, DC: Office of Juvenile Justice and Delinquency Prevention.

Garske v. United States, 1 F.2d 620, 86th Cir. (1924).

Geberth, V. (1995, November). The signature aspect in criminal investigation. *Law and Order,* pp. 45-49.

Geberth, V. J. (1995). The signature aspect in criminal profiling. *Law and Order Magazine, 43*(11).

Geberth, V. J. (1996a). The classification of sex related homicides. *Law and Order Magazine, 44*(8).

Geberth, V. J. (1996b). *Practical homicide investigation: Tactics, procedures, and forensic techniques* (3rd ed.). Boca Raton, FL: CRC.

Geberth, V. J. (1996c). The staged crime scene. *Law and Order Magazine, 44*(2).

Geberth, V. J. (1996d). The use of videotape in homicide investigations. *Law and Order Magazine, 44*(3).

Geberth, V. J. (1997). The primary crime scene. *Law and Order Magazine, 45*(6).

Geberth, V. J. (1998). Domestic violence homicides. *Law and Order Magazine, 46*(11).

Geberth, V. J. (2003a). Collection and preservation of physical evidence in sex-related death investigations. *Law and Order Magazine, 51*(5).

Geberth, V. J. (2003b). Practical crime scene investigation: Legal considerations. *Law and Order Magazine, 51*(7).

Geberth, V. J. (2003c). *Sex-related homicide and death investigation: Practical and clinical perspectives.* Boca Raton, FL: CRC.

Geberth, V. J., & Turco, R. N. (1997). Antisocial personality disorder, sexual sadism, malignant narcissism, and serial murder. *Journal of Forensic Sciences, 42*(1), 49-60.

Geller, W., & Stephens, D. (Eds.). (2003). *Local government police management* (4th ed.). Washington, DC: International City/County Management Association

General Motors Corporation. (2002). *Final report: Information process risk assessment for four departments, GM Headquarters, Detroit, Michigan.* Conducted by Judith Collins, Michigan State University–Business Identity Theft Partnership in Prevention.

Genge, N. E. (2002). *The forensic casebook: The science of crime scene investigation.* New York: Random House.

Gideon v. Wainwright, 372 U.S. 335 (1963).

Ginger, J. (1997). *Pittsburgh monitor's first quarterly report.* Pittsburgh, PA: Author.

Ginzburg, R. (1962). *One hundred years of lynchings.* Baltimore, MD: Black Classic Press.

Glaze, L. E. (2003). *Probation and parole in the United States, 2002.* Washington, DC: Bureau of Justice Statistics.

Going beyond pants on fire. (2002, June 30). *Law Enforcement News, 28*(580), 6.

Golan, N. (1978). *Treatment in crisis situations.* New York: Free Press.

Gold, D. (2003). *Hatred's kingdom: How Saudi Arabia supports the new global terrorism.* Washington, DC: Regnery.

Goldfarb, D. A., & Aumiller, G. S. (2004). *The heavy badge.* Available: http://www.heavybadge.com

Goldkamp, J., Irons-Guynn, C., & Weiland, D. (2002). *Community prosecution strategies: Measuring impact.* Washington, DC: Crime and Justice Research Center.

Goldsmith, A. J. (Ed.). (1991). *Complaints against the police: The trend to external review.* Oxford, UK: Clarendon.

Goldstein, H. (1963). Police discretion: The ideal versus the real. *Public Administration Review, 23,* 140-148.

Goldstein, H. (1975). *Police corruption: A perspective on its nature and control.* Washington, DC: Police Foundation.

Goldstein, H. (1977). *Policing a free society.* Cambridge, MA: Ballinger.

Goldstein, H. (1979). Improving policing: A problem-oriented approach. *Crime & Delinquency, 25,* 236-258.

Goldstein, H. (1990). *Problem oriented policing.* New York: McGraw-Hill.

Goldstein, H. (2001, October). *Problem-oriented policing in a nutshell.* Unpublished document prepared for the International Problem-Oriented Policing Conference, San Diego.

Goldstein, J. (1960). Police discretion not to invoke the criminal process: Low-visibility decisions in the administration of justice. *Yale Law Journal, 69,* 543-589.

Goldstein, S. (1999). *The sexual exploitation of children: A practical guide to assessment, investigation, and intervention* (2nd ed.). Boca Raton, FL: CRC.

Goldstein, S. L. (1999). *The sexual exploitation of children: A practical guide to assessment, investigation, and intervention* (2nd ed.). Boca Raton, FL: CRC.

Golembiewki, R., & Byong-Seob, K. (1990). Burnout in police work: Stressors, strain, and the phase model. *Police Studies, 13*(2), 74-80.

Good, P. (2001). *Applying statistics in the courtroom: A new approach for attorneys and expert witnesses.* Boca Raton, FL: CRC.

Goodson, M. (1985). Technical shortcomings of Doppler traffic radar. *Journal of Forensic Science, 30,* 1186.

Gottfredson, L. (1996). Racially gerrymandering the content of police tests to satisfy the U.S. Justice Department: A case study. *Psychology, Public Policy, and Law, 2*(3/4), 418-446.

Gould, L. (2000). A longitudinal approach to the study of the police personality: Race/gender differences. *Journal of Police and Criminal Psychology, 15*(2), 41.

Gouldner, A. W. (1960a). *Patterns of industrial bureaucracy.* Glencoe, IL: Free Press.

Gouldner, A. W. (1960b). *Wildcat strike.* Yellow Springs, OH: Antioch.

Governor's Commission on the Los Angeles Riots. (1966). *Transcripts, depositions, consultants' reports, and selected documents.* Washington, DC: Microcard Editions.

Grabosky, P., Smith, R. G., & Dempsey, G. (2001). *Electronic theft: Unlawful acquisition in cyberspace.* Cambridge, UK: Cambridge University Press.

Graham, F. P. (1970). *The self-inflicted wound.* New York: Macmillan.

Green, L. (1995). Cleaning up drug hot spots in Oakland, California: The displacement and diffusion effects. *Justice Quarterly, 12,* 737–754.

Green, L. (1996). *Policing places with drug problems.* Thousand Oaks, CA: Sage.

Greenberg, M. A. (1984). *Auxiliary police: The citizen's approach to public safety.* Westport, CT: Greenwood.

Greenberg, M. A. (1991). Citizen police academies. *FBI Law Enforcement Bulletin, 60*(8), 10-13.

Greenberg, M. A. (2001). *The evolution of volunteer police in America.* Unpublished doctoral dissertation, City University of New York.

Greene, J. (2000). Community policing in America. In J. Horney (Ed.), *Criminal justice 2000* (Vol. 3, pp. 299-370). Washington, DC: National Institute of Justice, Office of Justice Programs.

Greene, J. R., & Taylor, R. B. (1988). Community-based policing and foot patrol: Issues of theory and evaluation. In J. R. Greene & S. D. Mastrofski (Eds.), *Community policing: Rhetoric or reality?* (pp. 195–224). New York: Praeger.

Greenfeld, L. A., Langan, P. A., & Smith, S. K. (1997). *Police use of force: Collection of national data.* Washington, DC: Bureau of Justice Statistics.

Greenwood, P., & Petersilia, J. (1975). The criminal investigation process. In *Sourcebook of criminal justice statistics 1975.* Washington, DC: Bureau of Justice Statistics.

Grieco, E. M., & Cassidy, R. C. (2001). *Census 2000: Overview of race and Hispanic origin.* Washington, DC: U.S. Census Bureau.

Griffaton, M. C. (1993). Forewarned is forearmed: The Crime Awareness and Campus Security Act. *Case Western Law Review, 43,* 525-590.

Group's luncheon menu includes cold cases. (2002, July/August). *Law Enforcement News,* p. 6.

*Guide to scheduling the 24-hour operation* (2nd ed.). (1998). Circadian Technologies.

Haberfeld, M. R. (2002). *Critical issues in police training.* Upper Saddle River, NJ: Prentice Hall.

Hagan, J., & Albonetti, C. (1982). Race, class and the perception of criminal injustice in America. *American Journal of Sociology, 88*(2), 329-355.

Hale, M. (1736). *The history of the pleas of the Crown* (Vol. 1). London: S. Emlyn.

Hall, J. W. (2000). *Search and seizure* (Vol. 1, 3rd ed.). Charlottesville, VA: Lexis Law.

Hall, S., Critcher, C., Jefferson, T., Clarke, J., & Roberts, B. (1978). *Policing the crisis: Mugging, the state and law and order.* London: Macmillan.

Hand, B., Sherman, A., & Cavanagh, M. (1980). *Traffic investigation and control.* New York: Macmillan.

Hanley, J., Schmidt, W., & Robbins, R. (1999). *Introduction to criminal evidence and court procedure.* Berkeley, CA: McCutchan.

Hanlon v. Berger, 119 S.Ct. 1706 (1999).

Hans, T. (2002). *Stress in policing.* Washington, DC: American Psychological Association.

Hanson, R. K., & Thornton, D. M. (1999) *STATIC 99: Improving actuarial risk assessments for sex offenders.* Ottawa: Public Works and Government Services.

Harcourt, B. E. (1998). Reflecting on the subject: A critique of the social influence conception of deterrence, the broken windows theory, and order-maintenance policing New York style. *Michigan Law Review, 97,* 291–389.

Harcourt, B. E. (2001). *Illusion of order: The false promise of broken windows policing.* Cambridge, MA: Harvard University Press.

Harlow v. Fitzgerald, 457 U.S. 800 (1982).

Harman, A. (2003). It's a hold-up! RCMP evaluates benefit of suspenders. *Law & Order, 48*(8), 54-58.

Harpold, J. A., & Feemster, S. L. (2002). Negative influences of police stress. *Law Enforcement Bulletin, 71*(9), 1-6.

Harries, K. (1999). *Mapping crime: Principles and practice* (NCJ 178919). Washington, DC: U.S. Department of Justice.

Harring, S., & Gerda, R. (1999). Policing a class society: New York City in the 1990s. *Social Justice, 26,* 263-281.

Harris v. New York, 401 U.S. 222 (1971).

Harris v. United States, 390 U.S. 234 (1968).

Harris, D. A. (1999). *Driving while black: Racial profiling on our nation's highways. An American Civil Liberties Union Special Report.* New York: American Civil Liberties Union. Available: http://archive.aclu.org/profiling/report/index.html

Harris, D. A. (2002). *Profiles in injustice: Why racial profiling cannot work.* New York: New Press.

Hartman, V. E. (2001). Implementing an asset forfeiture program. *FBI Law Enforcement Bulletin, 70*(1), 1-7.

Harulow, S. (2000). Are you losing sleep over shift work? *Australian Nursing Journal, 8*(1), 26-28.

Hawley, D. L. (1997, February). K-9 bite liability is a growing concern. *Police,* p. 16.

Hayeslip, D., & Russell-Einhorn, M. (2002). *Evaluation of multi-jurisdictional task forces project: Phase I final report.* Washington, DC: National Institute of Justice.

Health Insurance Portability and Accountability Act. (1996). Public Law 104-191. 104th Congress. Retrieved August 8, 2003, from http://www.aspe.hhs.gov/admnsimp/ pl104191.htm

Heart disease: Shift workers experience increases in abnormal heart rhythms. (2001, October). *Heart Disease Weekly,* p. 5.

Heaviside, S., Rowland, C., Williams, C., & Farris, E. (1998). *Violence and discipline problems in U.S. public schools 1996-97.* Washington, DC: National Center for Educational Statistics.

Hedeen, T. (2002). Does the journey change the destination? The influence of referral source on mediation participation and outcomes. *New York Mediator, 20,* 4.

Heffernan, W. C. (2000). The Fourth Amendment exclusionary rule as a constitutional remedy. *Georgetown Law Journal, 88,* 799-878.

Hemmens, C., & Bennet, K. (1999). Juvenile curfews and the courts: Judicial response to a not-so-new crime control strategy. *Crime & Delinquency, 45*(1), 99-121.

Hemmens, C., Worrall, J., & Thompson, A. (2003). *Criminal justice case briefs: Significant cases in criminal procedure.* Los Angeles: Roxbury.

Hendrix, R. C. (1972). *Investigation of violent and sudden death: A manual for medical examiners.* Springfield, IL: Charles C Thomas.

Henry, V. (1990) *Patterns of police corruption and reform: Comparing New York City and Queensland* (Research Paper No. 16). Brisbane: Centre for Australian Public Sector Management.

Henry, V. (1994). Police corruption: Tradition and evolution. In K. Bryett & C. Lewis (Eds.), Un-peeling tradition: Contemporary policing. South Melbourne, Australia: Macmillan.

Henry, V. (2002). *The Compstat paradigm: Management accountability in policing, business, and the public sector.* Flushing, NY: Looseleaf.

Henry, V. E., & Campisi, C. (2004). Managing police integrity: Applying Compstat principles to control police corruption and misconduct. In R. Muraskin & A. R. Roberts (Eds.), *Visions for change: Crime and justice in the 21st century* (4th ed.). Upper Saddle River, NJ: Prentice Hall.

Heramb, R. B., & McCord, B. R. (2002). The manufacture of smokeless powders and their forensic analysis: A brief review. *Forensic Science Communications, 4*(2). Available: http://www.fbi.gov/hq/lab/fsc/current/mccord.htm

Herman, S. (2000). Measuring culpability by measuring drugs? Three reasons to reevaluate the Rockerfeller Drug Laws. *Albany Law Review, 63,* 777-798.

Herman, S. (2002). Law enforcement and victim services: Rebuilding lives, together. *Police Chief, 69*(5), 34-37.

Herszenhorn, D. (1999, March 29). Arrests drop and shootings rise as the police, Giuliani says, are distracted. *New York Times,* p. B3.

Heustis, C. (1958). Police unions. *Journal of Criminal Law, Criminology & Political Science, 64,* 644.

Hewitt, C. (2003). *Understanding terrorism in America: From the Klan to al Qaeda.* New York: Routledge.

Hickey, E. (1997). *Serial murderers and their victims.* Belmont, CA: Wadsworth.

Hickman, M., & Reaves, B. A. (2003). *Local police departments 2000.* Washington, DC: Bureau of Justice Statistics.

Hickman, M. J., & Reaves, B. A. (2003). *Sheriffs' offices 2000.* Washington, DC: Bureau of Justice Statistics.

Higginbotham, A. L., Jr. (1996). *Shades of freedom.* New York: Oxford University Press.

Hill, J. D. (1964). *The minute man in peace and war: A history of the National Guard.* Harrisburg, PA: Stackpole.

Hill, S. (2002). *Extremist groups: An international compilation of terrorist organizations, violent political groups, and issue-oriented militant movements* (2nd ed.). Huntsville, TX: Office of International Criminal Justice.

Hilton, O. (1992). *Scientific examination of questioned documents.* Boca Raton, FL: CRC Press.

Himelfarb, F. (1991, November). A training strategy for policing in a multicultural society. *The Police Chief,* pp. 53-55.

Hine, K. D. (1998). Vigilantism revisited: An economic analysis of the law of extrajudicial self-help or why can't Dick shoot Henry for stealing Jane's truck? *American University Law Review, 47,* 1221-1255.

Hirschel, D., Lumb, R., & Johnson, R. (1998). Victim assessment of the police response to burglary: The relative effects of incident, police action, outcome, and demographic variables on citizen satisfaction. *Police Quarterly, 1*(4), 1-20.

*History of police unions in the United States.* (1984). Huntsville, TX: Justex Systems.

Hoberman, H. M. (2001). Dangerousness and sex offenders: Assessing risk for future sex offenses. In A. Schlank (Ed.), *The sexual predator: Legal issues, clinical issues, special populations* (Vol. 2). NJ: Civic Research Institute.

Hoffman, B. (1998). *Inside terrorism.* New York: Columbia University Press.

Holden, R. N. (1992). *Law enforcement: An introduction.* Englewood Cliffs, NJ: Prentice Hall.

Holmes, R., & Holmes, S. (1996). *Profiling violent crimes: An investigative tool.* Thousand Oaks, CA: Sage.

Holmes, R., & Holmes, S. (1998). *Serial murder.* Thousand Oaks, CA: Sage.

Homeland Security Act of 2002, H.R. 2005, Pub. L. No.107-296, 116 Stat. 2135 (2002).

Homeland Security Enhancement Act, S. 1906.

Hoover, L. (Ed.). (1992). *Police management: Issues & perspectives.* Washington, DC: Police Executive Research Forum.

Horton v. California, 496 U.S. 128 (1990).

Houchins v. KQED, Inc., 438 U.S. 1 (1978).

Huang, W., & Vaughn, M. S. (1996). Support and confidence: Public attitudes toward the police. In T. J. Flanagan & D. R. Longmire (Eds.), *Americans view crime and justice: A national public opinion survey* (pp. 31-45). Thousand Oaks, CA: Sage.

Hudzik, J. K. (1978). College education for police: Problems in measuring component and extraneous variables. *Journal of Criminal Justice, 6,* 69-81.

Hughes, T. A., Wilson, D. J., & Beck, A. J. (2001). *Trends in state parole, 1990-2000.* Washington, DC: Bureau of Justice Statistics.

Hunter, A. (1978). *Symbols of incivility.* Paper presented at the annual meeting of the American Society of Criminology, Dallas, Texas.

Hurewitz, B. J., & Lo, A. M. (1993). Computer-related crimes. *American Criminal Law Review, 30,* 495–521.

IADLEST. (2004). *International Association of Directors of Law Enforcement Standards and Training Model Minimum State Standards.* Available: http://www.iadlest.org/modelmin.htm

Ijames, S. (1995). Less lethal force: Concepts and considerations in the de-escalation philosophy. *Tactical Edge, 13*(3), 51-55.

Ijames, S. (1996). Less lethal projectiles: Seeking a balance. *Tactical Edge, 14*(4), 76-84.

Ijames, S. (1997). Testing and evaluating less lethal projectiles (Part 1). *Tactical Edge, 15*(2), 12-15.

Ijames, S. (1998). Less lethal force options: Tactics, training and technology for unconventional encounters. *Police Chief Magazine, 65*(3), 31-37.

Ijames, S. (1999). Force options and legal challenges. *Tactical Edge, 18*(3), 102-104.

Ijames, S. (2000). Less lethal projectile tests. *Tactical Edge, 18*(3).

Ijames, S. (2001, November). Zeroing in on accuracy: Managing the potential for impact projectile deaths and serious injuries. *Police and Security News.*

Ijames, S. (2002, November/December). Chemical munitions deployment: Thoughts and considerations for use in public disorder. *Police and Security News.*

Ijames, S. (2003a). Impact projectiles: Lessons learned thus far. *Tactical Edge, 21*(4).

Ijames, S. (2003b). Patterns of injury, recognition, and treatment for less lethal law enforcement techniques. *Emergency Medicine,* pp. 316-325.

Illegal Immigration Reform and Immigration Responsibility Act of 1996, Pub. L. No. 104-208, 110 Stat. 3009 (1996).

Illinois v. Gates, 462 U.S. 213 (1983).

Imwinkelried, E. (1998). *Evidentiary foundations.* Charlottesville, VA: Lexis.

Inbau, F. E., Reid, J. E., & Buckley, J. P. (1986). *Criminal interrogation and confessions* (3rd ed.). Baltimore: Williams and Wilkins.

Inciardi, J. (2002). *The war on drugs III: The continuing saga of the mysteries and miseries of intoxication, addiction, crime, and public policy.* Boston: Allyn & Bacon.

Inman, K., & Rudin, N. (2000). *Principles and practice of criminalistics.* Boca Raton, Florida: CRC.

Innes, M. (2002). The "process structures" of police homicide investigations. *British Journal of Criminology, 42,* 669-688.

In re Gault, 387 U.S. 1 (1967).

Inspector General Act of 1978 (Pub. L. 95-452, §1, Oct. 12, 1978, 92 Stat. 1101). Available http:// www.access.gpo.gov/uscode/title5a/5a_2_.html

International Association of Chiefs of Police. (1958). Police unions. *Bulletins on Police Problems.* Alexandria, VA: Author.

International Association of Chiefs of Police. (1991). *Model policy on police-media relations.* Alexandria, VA: Author.

International Association of Chiefs of Police. (2002). *2002 state legislative report.* Retrieved April 1, 2004, from http:// www.theiacp.org/leg_policy/Legupdate/2002/2002statereport.htm

International Association of Chiefs of Police. (2003). *2003 state legislative report.* Retrieved April 1, 2004, from http://www.theiacp.org/documents/pdfs/WhatsNew/2003%20State%%20Report.pdf

International City/County Management Association. (1991). *Police personnel recruitment and special training programs.* Washington, DC: Author.

Jacobs, J. (1961). *The death and life of great American cities.* New York: Random House.

Jacobs, J. (1968). Community on the city streets. In E. D. Baltzell (Ed.), *The search for community in modern America* (pp. 74–93). New York: Harper & Row.

Jacobs, J. (2002). *Can gun control work?* Oxford, UK: Oxford University Press.

Jacobs, J. B. (1983). Police: Private police and security forces. In S. H. Kadish (Ed.), *Encyclopedia of crime and justice* (Vol. 3). New York: Macmillan and Free Press.

Jacobs, J. B. (1999). *Gotham unbound: How New York City was liberated from the grip of organized crime.* New York: New York University Press.

Jacobs, J. B., & Potter, K. (1998). *Hate crimes: Criminal law & identity politics.* New York: Oxford University Press.

James, G. (1999, May 9). Policing the Port Authority's domain. *New York Times,* p. NJ 7.

Jarvis, R. T. (2001). Symposium on integrating responses to domestic violence: A proposal for a model domestic violence protocol. *Loyola Law Review, 47,* 513.

Jeffers, H. P. (1994). *Commissioner Roosevelt: The story of Theodore Roosevelt and the New York City police, 1895-1897.* New York: Wiley.

Jefferson, T., & Grimshaw, R. (1987). *Interpreting policework.* London: Unwin.

Jenkins, P. (1998). *Moral panic: Changing concepts of the child molester in modern America.* New Haven, CT: Yale University Press.

Jernigan, D., & LaBrusciano, M. (1994). Bomb squads: Developing mutual aid agreements. *FBI Law Enforcement Bulletin, 63*(10), 18-21.

Johnson, R. A. (2003). *Whistleblowing: When it works and why.* Boulder, CO: Lynne Rienner.

Johnson, R. P. (1994). Implementing community policing in a university environment. *Campus Law Enforcement Journal, 24*(3), 17-21, 34-35.

Johnston, L. (1992). *The rebirth of private policing.* London: Routledge.

Johnston, L., & Shearing, C. (2003). *Governing security: Explorations in policing and justice.* London: Routledge.

Jones-Brown, D. D. (2000a). *Race, crime and punishment.* Philadelphia: Chelsea House.

Jones-Brown, D. D. (2000b). Race as a legal construct: The implications for America justice. In M. Markowitz & D. Jones-Brown (Eds.), *The system in black and white* (pp. 137-152). Westport, CT: Praeger.

Jordan, W. T. (1998). *Citizens' police academies.* Unpublished doctoral dissertation, Florida State University.

Juergensmeyer, M. (2003). *Terror in the mind of God: The global rise of religious violence* (3rd ed.). Berkeley: University of California Press.

Kaminski, R. J., Jefferis, E. S., & Chanhatasilpa, C. (2000). A spatial analysis of American police killed in the line of duty. In R. L. Turnbull, H. E. Hendrix, & B. D. Dent (Eds.), *Atlas of crime: Mapping the criminal landscape* (pp. 212–220). Phoenix, AZ: Oryx.

Kaminsky, G. F. (2002). *The field training concept in criminal justice agencies.* Upper Saddle River, NJ: Prentice Hall.

Kansas v. Hendricks, 521 U.S. 346 (1997).

Kansas Sexually Violent Predator Statute § 59-29a.

Kappeler, V. E., Sluder, R. D., & Alpert, G. P. (1998). *Forces of deviance* (2nd ed.). Prospect Heights, IL: Waveland.

Karmen, A. (2004). *Crime victims: An introduction to victimology* (5th ed.). Belmont, CA: Wadsworth/Thomson.

Karp, D., & Clear, T. (2002). *What is community justice? Case studies of restorative and community justice.* Thousand Oaks, CA: Sage.

Kassin, S. M. (1997). The psychology of confession evidence. *American Psychologist, 52*(3), 221–233.

Kates, A. R. (1999). *Cop shock: Surviving posttraumatic stress disorder (PTSD).* Tucson, AZ: Holbrook Street Press.

Katz, M. S. (1976). *A history of compulsory education laws.* Bloomington, Indiana: Phi Delta Kappan Educational Foundation.

Katz v. United States, 389 U.S. 347 (1967).

Kaufman, P., Chen, X., Choy, S. P., Chandler, K. A., Chapman, C. D., Rand, M. R., & Ringel, C. (1998). *Indicators of school crime and safety, 1999.* Washington, DC: U.S. Departments of Education and Justice.

Kelling, G. (1995). How to run a police department. *City Journal, 5,* 1–12.

Kelling, G. L., & Coles, C. (1996). *Fixing broken windows: Restoring order and reducing crime in our communities.* New York: Martin Kessler.

Kelling, G. L., Pate, T., Dieckman, D., & Brown, C. (1974). *Kansas City preventive patrol experiment.* Washington, DC: Police Foundation.

Kelling, G. L., & Sousa, W. H. (2001). *Do police matter? An analysis of the impact of New York City's police reforms* (Civic Report No. 22). New York: Manhattan Institute.

Kennedy, D. B., Homant, R. J., & Hupp, R. T. (1998). Suicide by cop. *FBI Law Enforcement Bulletin, 67*(8), 21-27.

Kennedy, R. (1996, January 19). He spoke up for the law and died for it. *New York Times,* p. B1.

Kenney, D. J., & Watson, T. S. (1998). *Crime in the schools.* Washington, DC: Police Executive Research Forum.

Kerner, O. (1968). *Report of the National Advisory Commission on Civil Disorders.* New York: Bantam.

Kersten, K. (2001, February 28). Crackdown on little offenses can help prevent the big ones. *Minneapolis Star-Tribune.*

Kiely, T. (2001). *Forensic evidence: Science and the criminal law.* Boca Raton, FL: CRC.

Kifner, J., & Lee, F. R. (2001, August 19). In Crown Heights, a decade of healing after riots, but scars remain. *New York Times,* p. A1.

Kilpatrick, D., Beatty, D., & Howley, S. (1998). *The rights of crime victims—Does legal protection make a difference?* National Institute of Justice Research in Brief (NCJ Publication No. 173839). Washington, DC: U.S. Department of Justice.

King, J. (1999). *Police strikes of 1918 and 1919 in the United Kingdom and Boston: Their effects.* Unpublished doctoral dissertation, City University of New York, New York.

Kinzer, S. (2003). *All the shah's men: An American coup and the roots of Middle East terror.* Hoboken, NJ: Wiley.

Kirchner, R. W. (1992). Looking for a challenge? Try being a cop. *Medical Economics, 69*(9), 197–201.

Klain, E. J., Davies, H. J., & Hicks, M. A. (2001). *Child pornography and the criminal justice response.* Washington, DC: American Bar Association Center on Children and the Law.

Kleck, G. (1997). *Targeting guns: Firearms and their control.* New York: Aldine de Gruyter.

Klein, H., & Vorst, M. (2001). *Containment devices for small terrorist bombs for law enforcement* (Final report). Washington, DC: National Institute of Justice.

Klein, M. (1995). *The American street gang: Its nature, prevalence, and control.* New York: Oxford University Press.

Klein, M. (2002). Law enforcement's response to people with mental illness. *FBI Law Enforcement Bulletin, 71*(2), 11-14.

Klein, S. R. (2003, April). No time for silence. *Texas Law Review, 81,* 1337-1360.

Kleinig, J. (1996). *The ethics of policing.* Cambridge, UK: Cambridge University Press.

Kleinig, J., & Zhang, Y. (1993). *Professional law enforcement codes: A documentary collection.* Westport, CT: Greenwood.

Klinger, D. A. (2001). Suicidal intent in victim-precipitated homicide: Insights from the study of suicide by cop. *Homicide Studies, 5*(3), 206-226.

Klinger, D. A. (2001). *Police responses to officer-involved shootings: Final report* (NCJ-192286). Washington, DC: U.S. Department of Justice.

Klockars, C. (1985). *The idea of police.* Beverly Hills, CA: Sage.

Klockars, C. B., Kutnjak Ivkovich, S., & Haberfeld, M. (Eds.). (2003). *Contours of police integrity.* Thousand Oaks, CA: Sage.

Klockars, C. B., Kutnjak Ivkovich, S., Harver, W., & Haberfeld, M. (2000, May). *The measurement of police integrity.* Available: http://www.ncjrs.org/pdffiles1/nij/181465.pdf

Klockars, C. B., Kutnjak Ivkovich, S.,Haberfeld, M., & Harver, W. E. (2000). *Measuring police integrity.* Washington, DC: National Institute of Justice.

Knapp, W. (1972). *Report of the Commission to investigate alleged police corruption.* New York: George Braziller.

Knapp, W. (1973). *Report of the New York City Commission to investigate allegations of police corruption and the city's anti-corruption procedures.* New York: George Braziller.

Kocieniewski, D. (2002, March 9). Officials say figures show that profiling is decreasing. *New York Times,* p. B5.

Koegel, P. (1996). Lessons learned from the experience of domestic police and fire departments. In G. Herek, J. Jobe, & R. Carney (Eds.), *Out in force: Sexual orientation and the military* (pp. 131-153). Chicago: University of Chicago Press.

Kohan, A., & Mazmanian, D. (2003). Police work, burnout, and pro-organizational behavior: A consideration of daily work experiences. *Criminal Justice and Behavior, 30*(5), 559-583.

Kohn, S. M. (2001). *Concepts and procedures in whistleblower law.* Westport, CT: Quorum.

Koss, F. (1966). *The Boston police strike of 1919.* Unpublished doctoral dissertation, Boston University, Boston.

Kotlowitz, A. (1991). *There are no children here: The story of two boys growing up in the other America.* New York: Doubleday.

Kraska, P. B. (1994). The police and military in the post-cold war era: Streamlining the state's use of force entities in the drug war. *Police Forum, 4*(1), 1-8.

Kraska, P. B. (1999). Questioning the militarization of U.S. police: Critical versus advocacy scholarship. *Policing and Society, 9*(2), 141-155.

Kraska, P. B. (2001). *Militarizing the American criminal justice system: The changing roles of the armed forces and the police.* Boston: Northeastern University Press.

Kraska, P. B., & Cubellis, L. J. (1997). Militarizing Mayberry and beyond: Making sense of American paramilitary policing. *Justice Quarterly, 14*(4), 607-629.

Kraska, P. B., & Kappeler, V. E. (1997). Militarizing American police: The rise and normalization of paramilitary units. *Social Problems, 44*(1), 1-18.

Kurke, M. I., & Scrivner, E. M. (1995). *Police psychology into the 21st century.* Hillsdale, NJ: Lawrence Erlbaum.

Kushner, H. (1998). *Terrorism in America.* Springfield, IL: Charles C Thomas.

LaFave, W. (1965). *Arrest: The decision to take a suspect into custody.* Boston: Little Brown.

LaFave, W. R. (1996). *Search and seizure: A treatise on the Fourth Amendment* (Vol. 2, 3rd ed.). St. Paul, MN: West.

LaFave, W. R., & Israel, J. H. (1998). *Criminal procedure.* St. Paul, MN: West.

LaGrange, R. L. (1993). *Policing American society.* Chicago: Nelson-Hall.

Lamberth, J. (1996). *Revised statistical analysis of the incidence of police stops and arrests of black drivers/travelers on the New Jersey Turnpike between interchanges 1 and 3 from the years 1988 through 1991.* Unpublished report submitted by the defendant's expert in New Jersey v. Soto, 734 A. 2d 350 (N.J. Super. Ct. Law. Div., 1996).

Lander, E. (1989). DNA fingerprinting on trial. *Nature, 339,* 501–505.

Landesco, J. (1929). *Organized crime in Chicago.* Chicago: University of Chicago Press.

Landynski, J. W. (1966). *Search and seizure and the Supreme Court: A study in constitutional interpretation.* Baltimore, MD: Johns Hopkins University Press.

Langan, P., Greenfeld, L., Smith, S., Durose, M., & Levin, D. (2001). *Contacts between police and the public: Findings from the 1999 national survey.* Washington, DC: U.S. Department of Justice.

Lange, J. E., Blackman, K. O., & Johnson, M. B. (2001). *Speed violation survey of the New Jersey Turnpike: Final report.* Submitted to Office of the Attorney General, Trenton, NJ.

Larson, R. (1998, Nov/Dec). On track. *9-1-1 Magazine.* Retrieved April 2, 2003, from http://www.9-1-1magazine.com/magazine/1998/1198/feas/32Larson/index.html

Larson, R. C., & Cahn, M. F. (1981). *Synthesizing and extending the results of police patrol studies.* Cambridge, MA: Public Systems Evaluation.

Lasley, J., & Hooper, M. (1998). On racism and the LAPD: Was the Christopher Commission wrong? *Social Science Quarterly, 79*(2), 378-389.

The law of citizen's arrest. (1965). *Columbia Law Review, 65,* 502-513.

Lazarus, E. (1889). The new colossus. *The Poems of Emma Lazarus, Vol. 1.* Boston: Houghton Mifflin.

LEAA: Does it have a future? (1978, December 30). *Washington Post,* p. A10.

LEAA, once a big spender, to close its doors April 15. (1981, December 31). *Washington Post,* p. A18.

LEAA's fate weighed at Justice Department. (1977, August 9). *Washington Post,* p. A1.

LeBeau, J. L. (1992). Four case studies illustrating the spatial-temporal analysis of serial rapists. *Police Studies, 15,* 124-145.

Lee, H. C., & Gaensslen, R. E. (Eds.). (2001). *Advances in fingerprint technology* (2nd ed.). Boca Raton, FL: CRC.

Lee, H., & Labriola, J. (2001). *Famous crimes revisited: From Sacco-Vanzetti to O.J. Simpson.* Southington, CT: Strong Books.

Lee, H., Palmbach, T. M., & Miller, M. T. (2001). *Henry Lee's crime scene handbook.* New York: Academic Press.

Lehrer, E. (2002, Summer). Broken windows reconsidered. *Public Interest, 148,* 146–151.

Leifer, A., Avissar, Y., Berger, S., Wax, H., Donchin, Y., & Almog, J. (2001). Detection of firearm imprints on the hands of suspects: Effectiveness of PDT reaction. *Journal of Forensic Science 46*(6), 1442–1446.

Leighton, P., & Reiman, J. (Ed.). (2001). *Criminal justice ethics.* Upper Saddle River, NJ: Prentice Hall.

Leinen, S. (1993). *Gay cops.* New Brunswick, NJ: Rutgers University Press.

Leo, R. A., & Thomas, G. C., III. (Eds.). (1998). *The Miranda debate: Law, justice and policing.* Boston: Northeastern University Press.

Lerner, C. S. (2003). The reasonableness of probable cause. *Texas Law Review, 81,* 951-1029.

Lerner, M. D., & Shelton, R. D. (2001). *Acute traumatic stress management.* Commack, NY: The American Academy of Experts in Traumatic Stress.

Lersch, K. M. (Ed.). (2002). *Policing and misconduct.* Upper Saddle River, NJ: Prentice Hall.

Lesce, T. (2000). Consistent evolution in belt gear. *Law & Order, 48*(2), 43-45.

Lester, D. (1995). *Serial killers: The insatiable passion.* Philadelphia: Charles Press.

Leven, D. (2000). Our drug laws have failed—so where is the desperately needed meaningful reform? *Fordham Urban Law Journal, 28,* 293-306.

Levenson, L. L. (2002). Beware of informants. *National Law Journal, 24*(29), B13.

Levin, J., & Fox, J. (1994). *Overkill: Mass murder and serial killing exposed.* New York: Plenum.

Levin, J., & McDevitt, J. (1993). *Hate crimes: The rising tide of bigotry and bloodshed.* New York: Plenum.

Levine, J., Musheno, M., & Palumbo, D. (1986). *Criminal justice in America: Law in action.* New York: Wiley.

Levine, N. (2002). Journey to crime estimation. In *Crime Stat II: A spatial statistics program for the analysis of crime incident locations* (pp. 341-416). Washington, DC: National Institute of Justice.

Lewis, B. (2003). *The crisis of Islam: Holy war and unholy terror.* New York: Random House.

Lewis, C. (2000). The terror that failed: Public opinion in the aftermath of the bombing in Oklahoma City. *Public Administration Review, 60,* 201-210.

Lewis, S. (1922). *Babbitt.* New York: Harcourt Brace.

Liang, H.-H. (1992). *The rise of the European state system from Metternich to the end of the Second World War.* Cambridge, UK: Cambridge University Press.

Lilly, R. J., & Puckett, M. B. (1997). Social control and dogs: A sociohistorical analysis. *Crime & Delinquency, 43*(2), 123-147.

Lipsky, M. (1980). *Street-level bureaucracy: Dilemmas of the individual in public services.* New York: Russell Sage.

Lite, Greenberg, DePalma, Rivas, and Public Management Resources. (2001). New Jersey monitors' fourth quarterly report (2001). Available: www.state.nj.us/lps/monitors_ report_4.pdf

Lite, Greenberg, DePalma, Rivas, and Public Management Resources. (2003). New Jersey monitors' seventh quarterly report (2003). Available: http://www.njpublicsafety.com/monitors_report_7.pdf

Littel, K. (2001). *Sexual Assault Nurse Examiner (SANE) programs: Improving the community response to sexual assault victims.* Washington, DC: U.S. Department of Justice, Office for Victims of Crime.

Livingston, D. (1999). Police reform and the Department of Justice: An essay on accountability. *Buffalo Criminal Law Review, 2*(2), 817-859.

Loader, I., & Mulchay, A. (2003). *Policing and the condition of England.* Oxford, UK: Oxford University Press.

Locke, J. (1690). *Second treatise of civil government.* Many editions.

Lockyer, W. (2000, April). Statement made by the Attorney General, State of California, at the Opening Ceremony, Annual White Collar Crime Summit, Los Angeles, CA.

Loftin, C., Wiersema, B., McDowell, D., & Dobrin, A (2003). Underreporting of justifiable homicides committed by police officers in the United States,1976-1998. *American Journal of Public Health, 93,* 1117-1121.

Loftus, E. F., & Palmer, J. C. (1974). Reconstruction of automobile destruction: An example of the interaction between language and memory. *Journal of Verbal Learning and Verbal Behavior, 13,* 585-589.

Lo-Ji Sales, Inc. v. New York, 442 U.S. 319 (1979). http://longmontpolice.com/Fop_Education.htm

Lonsway, K. (2000). *Hiring & retaining more women: The advantages to law enforcement agencies.* Available: http://www. womenandpolicing.org

Loper v. New York City Police Department, 999 F.2d 699 (1993), aff'd. 802 F.Supp. 1029 (S.D.N.Y. 1992).

Lord, V. B. (2001). Law enforcement-assisted suicide: Characteristics of subjects and law enforcement intervention techniques. In D. C. Sheehan & J. I Warren (Eds.), *Suicide and Law Enforcement* (pp. 607-625). Washington, DC: U.S. Department of Justice.

Los Angeles agrees to federal proposals to reform police. (2000, September 22). *Crime Control Digest, 34*(38), 2.

Los Angeles Board of Police Commissioners. (1996). *In the course of change: The Los Angeles Police Department five years after the Christopher Commission.* Los Angeles: Los Angeles Police Department.

Los Angeles Police Department Board of Inquiry. (2001, March 1). *Public report of the Board of Inquiry into the Rampart Area corruption incident.* Los Angeles: Los Angeles Police Department.

Louden, R. J. (2001). The development of hostage negotiation by the NYPD. In A. Karmen (Ed.), *Crime and justice in New York City.* New York: McGraw-Hill.

Luus, C. A. E., & Wells, G. L. (1994). The malleability of eyewitness confidence: Co-witness and perseverance effects. *Journal of Applied Psychology, 79,* 714-723.

Lyman, M. (2002). *Practical drug enforcement.* Boca Raton, FL: CRC.

Lyman, M. A. (1999). *The police: An introduction.* Upper Saddle River, NJ: Prentice Hall.

Lyon, T. (1973, May). The trooper was a lady. *Law & Order,* pp. 70-71, 81.

Maas, P. (1973). *Serpico.* New York: Viking.

MacAleese, G. (n.d.). The Crime Stoppers story. Retrieved from http://www.c-s-i.org/history.htm

Mac Donald, H. (2003). *Are cops racist? How the war against the police harms black Americans.* Chicago: Ivan R. Dee.

MacKenzie, D. (1993). *Inventing accuracy.* Cambridge: MIT Press.

Maclin, T. (1993). The central meaning of the Fourth Amendment. *William and Mary Law Review, 35,* 197-249.

Maclin, T. (1997). The complexity of the Fourth Amendment: A historical review. *Boston University Law Review, 77,* 925-974.

Madinger, J. (2000). *Confidential informant: Law enforcement's most valuable tool.* Boca Raton, FL: CRC.

Magers, J. S. (2002). Police basic training: A comparative study of state standards in the United States. *Illinois Law Enforcement Executive Institute Forum, 2*(2), 103-113.

Magers, J. S. (2003). IADLEST: Shaping the future of law enforcement training and standards. *Police Chief, 46*(1), 31-33.

Maghan, J. (1988). *The 21st century cop: Police recruit perceptions as a function of occupational socialization.* Unpublished doctoral dissertation-8821104, UMI, Ann Arbor, MI. (800-521-0600).

Maghan, J. (1993). The changing face of the police officer: Occupational socialization of minority police recruits. In R. G. Dunham & G. P. Alpert (Eds.), *Critical issues in policing: Contemporary readings* (2nd ed., pp. 348-360). Prospect Heights, IL: Waveland.

Maguire, K., & Pastore, A.L. (Eds.). (1997). *Sourcebook of criminal justice statistics 1996.* Washington, DC: Bureau of Justice Statistics.

Maguire, M. (2002). Crime statistics. In M. Maguire, R. Morgan, & R. Reiner (Eds.), *Oxford handbook of criminology* (3rd ed.). Oxford, UK: Oxford University Press.

Mahon, J. K. (1983). *History of the militia and the National Guard.* New York: Macmillan.

Mahoney, J. (1981). Drug trafficking at airports: The judicial response. *University of Miami Law Review, 36,* 91-113.

Males, M., & Macallair, D. (1999). An analysis of curfew enforcement and juvenile crime in California. *Western Criminology Review, 1*(2). Retrieved February 1, 2003, from http://wcr.sonoma.edu/v1n2/males.html

Maller, P. (2003, February 17). Civil Air Patrol taking on terror. *Milwaukee Journal-Sentinel,* p. 1B.

Mandelblit, B. (2001). The latest tools of the trade for your front line security. *Security, 38*(10), 29-31.

Manili, B., Connor, E., III, Stephens, D., & Stedman, J. (1987). *Police drug testing.* Washington, DC: National Institute of Justice.

Mann, C. (1993). *Unequal justice: A question of color.* Bloomington: Indiana University Press.

Manning, P. (2003). *Policing contingencies.* Chicago: University of Chicago Press.

Manning, P., & Van Maanen, J. (Eds.). (1978). *Policing.* Santa Monica, CA: Goodyear.

Manning, P. K. (1992a). Information technology and the police. In M. Tonry & N. Morris (Eds.), *Modern policing* (pp. 349-398). Chicago: University of Chicago Press.

Manning, P. K. (1992b). Technological dramas and the police. *Criminology, 30,* 327-345.

Manning, P. K. (1997). *Police work: The social organization of policing* (2nd ed.). Prospect Heights, IL: Waveland.

Manning, P. K. (2001). *The narcs' game* (2nd ed.). Prospect Heights, IL: Waveland.

Manning, P. K. (2001). Theorizing policing. *Theoretical Criminology, 5,* 315–344.

Manning, P. K. (2003). *Policing contingencies.* Chicago: University of Chicago Press.

Manski, C. (2003). Credible research practices to inform drug law enforcement. *Criminology & Public Policy, 2*(3), 543-555.

Manski, C., Pepper, V., & Petrie, C. (Eds.). (2001). *Informing America's policy on illegal drugs: What we don't know keeps hurting us.* Washington, DC: National Academies Press.

Maple, J. (1999). *The crime fighter: Putting the bad guys out of business.* New York: Doubleday.

Mapp v. Ohio, 367 U.S. 643 (1961).

Marker, M. (1998). *Policing in Indian country.* Guilderland, NY: Harrow and Heston.

Martin, S. E., & Jurik, N. C. (1996). *Doing justice, doing gender.* Thousand Oaks, CA: Sage.

Martindale, D. (1977). Sweaty palms in the control tower. *Psychology Today, 11*(2), 71-75.

Martinez, J. (2004, May 14). Terror charge for gang that brutalized Bx. nabe. *New York Daily News,* p. 12.

Marx, G. (1988). *Undercover: Police surveillance in America.* Berkeley: University of California Press.

Marx, G. (1992). When the guards guard themselves: Undercover tactics turned inward. *Policing and Society, 2*(3), 151-172.

Marx, G. T. (1976). Alternative measures of police performance. In E. Viano (Ed.), *Criminal justice research.* Lexington, MA: Lexington Books.

Massiah v. United States, 377 U.S. 201 (1964).

Mastrofski, S. (1983). Police knowledge of the patrol beat: A performance measure. In R. R. Bennett (Ed.), *Police at work: Police issues and analysis.* Beverly Hills, CA: Sage.

Mastrofski, S., & Ritti, R. (2000). Making sense of community policing: A theory-based analysis. *Police Practice and Research, 1*(2), 183-210.

Mastrofski, S. D., & Parks, R. B. (2002, November). *Beyond 911 and the myth of reactive policing.* Paper delivered at the annual meeting of the American Society of Criminology, Chicago.

Mastrofski, S. D., Reisig, M. D., & McCluskey, J. D. (2002). Police disrespect toward the public: An encounter-based analysis. *Criminology, 40,* 519-551.

Mastrofski, S. D., Snipes, J. B., Parks, R. B., & Maxwell, C. D. (2000). The helping hand of the law: Police control of citizens on request. *Criminology, 38,* 307-342.

Mather, R. E., Boswell, F. E., & Smith, J. J. (1999). *Hanging the sheriff: A biography of Henry Plummer* (2nd ed.). Missoula: Historic Montana Publishing.

Maxson, C. L., Gordon, M. A., & Klein, M. W. (1985). Differences between gang and nongang homicides. *Criminology, 23,* 209-222.

Mayhew, P., & Van Dijk, J. (1997). *Criminal victimization in eleven industrialized countries: Key findings from the 1996 International Crime Victims Survey.* The Hague: Ministry of Justice.

Mayor's Office of New York City. (2003). *Commission to Combat Police Corruption.* Retrieved February 25, 2003, from http://nyc.gov/html/ccpc/html/about.html

Mazerolle, L. G., Kadleck, C., & Roehl, J. (1997). Controlling drug and disorder problems: The role of place managers. *Criminology, 36*(2), 371–404.

McAlary, M. (1994). *Good cop, bad cop: Detective Joe Trimboli's heroic pursuit of NYPD Officer Michael Dowd.* New York: Pocket.

McBride, D. (Ed.). (2003). *Bioterrorism: The history of a crisis in American society.* New York: Routledge.

McCann, J. (1992). Criminal personality profiling in the investigation of violent crime: Recent advances and future direction. *Behavioral Sciences and the Law, 10,* 474-481.

McCarthy v. Philadelphia Civil Service Commission, 424 U.S. 465 (1976).

McCord, J., Widom, C. S., & Crowell, N. A. (Eds.). (2001). *Juvenile crime, juvenile justice: Panel on juvenile crime: Prevention, treatment, and control.* Washington, DC: National Academy Press.

McCormack, R. J. (1996). Police perceptions and the norming of institutional corruption. *Policing and Society, 6,* 239–246.

McDonald, M. G. (2003). *Judicial changes that have impacted police operations.* Unpublished manuscript.

McDonald, P. (2002). *Managing police operations: Implementing the New York crime control model: Compstat.* Belmont, CA: Wadsworth.

McDonald, W. (1979). *The prosecutor.* Beverly Hills, CA: Sage.

McGinley, T. G., & Collins, J. M. (2003, March). *Identity theft: Effect on victimized executives.* Paper presented at the 40th annual meeting of the Academy of Criminal Justice Sciences, Boston, MA.

McHugh, A. J. (2001). Coordination within the rings of law enforcement: How local agencies must adapt to a post 9/11 environment. *Johns Hopkins Journal of American Politics.*

McIntyre, C. (1993). *Criminalizing a race: Free blacks during slavery.* Queens, NY: Kayode.

McMahon, P. (2002, July 18). Increased clamor for cameras in cop cars. Available: http://www.usatoday.com/news/nation/2002/07/19/copcameras.htm

McManis, M. J., & Mullins, W. C. (2001). *Crisis negotiations: Managing critical incidents and hostage situations in law enforcement and corrections* (2nd ed.). Cincinnati, OH: Anderson.

McNickle, R. G. (1996, October). Police fitness: Is there life after the academy? *Law Enforcement News,* pp. 10, 11.

Mechling, J. (2001). *On my honor: Boy Scouts and the making of American youth.* Chicago: University of Chicago Press.

Meier, E. (2000, July/August). Current legislative issues related to children. *Pediatric Nursing, 26.* Retrieved February 1, 2003 from http://web12.epnet.com/delivery

Meissner, C. A., & Brigham, J. C. (2001). Thirty years of investigating the own-race bias in memory for faces: A meta-analytic review. *Psychology, Public Policy, & Law, 7,* 3-35.

Melilli, K. (1992). Prosecutorial discretion in an adversary system. *Brigham Young University Law Review, 3,* 669-705.

http://members.aol.com/eirepages/esgpages.htm

http://members.aye.net/~bspen/ballistics.html

Meyers, J. (1975). Police strikes: A model to study underlying factors. *Australia & New Zealand Journal of Criminology, 8,* 190-206.

Michel, L., & Herbeck, D. (2001). *American terrorist: Timothy McVeigh and the Oklahoma City bombing.* New York: ReganBooks.

Michigan v. Summers, 452 U.S. 692 (1981).

Michigan v. Tucker, 417 U.S. 433 (1974).

Mijares, T. C., McCarthy, R. M., & Perkins, D. B. (2000). *The management of police specialized tactical units.* Springfield, IL: Charles C Thomas.

Miller, F. (1969). *Prosecution: The decision to charge a suspect with a crime.* Boston: Little Brown.

Miller, F. (1986). *Cases and materials on criminal justice administration.* Minneola, NY: Foundation Press.

Miller, L. S., & Hess, K. M. (2001). *The police in the community: Strategies for the 21st century.* Upper Saddle River, NJ: Prentice Hall.

Miller, M. (2000). *Police patrol operations* (2nd ed.). Incline Village, NV: Copperhouse.

Miller, R. R. (1957). *Slavery and Catholicism.* Durham, NC: North State Publishers.

Milne, R., & Bull, R. (1999). *Investigative interviewing: Psychology and practice.* Chichester, UK: Wiley.

Mincey v. Arizona, 437 U.S. 385 (1978).

Minnesota v. Dickerson, 508 U.S. 366 (1993).

*Miranda* after *Dickerson*: The future of confession law [Symposium]. (2001). *Michigan Law Review, 99*(5).

Miranda v. Arizona, 384 U.S. 436 (1966).

Mississippi Statistical Analysis Center. (2002). *Information and technology capabilities of Mississippi law enforcement agencies.* Available: http://www.usm.edu/mssac/publications/information.7.31.2002.pdf

Missouri v. Seibert, 2004 U. S.LEXIS 4578; 124 S. Ct. 2601 (2004).

Missouri State Water Patrol. (n.d.). *History.* Retrieved March 18, 2003, from http://www.mswp.state.mo.us/wphist.htm

Mitchell, J. T. (1983). When disaster strikes . . . The critical incident stress debriefing process. *Journal of Emergency Medical Services, 13,* 43-46.

Moenssens, A., Starrs, J., Henderson, C., & Inbau, F. (1995). *Scientific evidence in civil and criminal cases.* Westbury, NY: Foundation Press.

Monroe v. Pape, 365 U.S. 167 (1961).

Moore, M. (2003). Sizing up Compstat: An important administrative innovation in policing. *Criminology & Public Policy, 2*(3), 469-471.

Moore, M. H. (2002). *Recognizing value in policing: The challenge of measuring police performance.* Washington, DC: Police Executive Research Forum.

Morgan, D. (1996). *Sleep secrets for shift workers & people with off-beat schedules.* Duluth, MN: Whole Person Associates.

Morial, M. H. (2001). *A national action plan for safety and security in America's cities.* Washington, DC: United States Conference of Mayors.

Morris, N., & Tonry, M. (1990). *Between prison and probation: Intermediate punishments in a rational sentencing system.* New York: Oxford University Press.

Morris, R. (2002). *Aviation security state legislation in 2002: Transportation review.* Retrieved April 1, 2004, from http://www.ncsl.org/programs/esnr/aviationrev02.htm

Morton, J. (1993). *Bent coppers: A survey of police corruption.* London: Little, Brown.

Munsterberg, H. (1908). *On the witness stand.* New York: Clark-Boardman.

Murphy, C. (2003). The rationalization of Canadian public policing. Available: http://www.policefutures.org/docs/murphy_e.pdf

Murphy, P., & Plate, T. (1977). *Commissioner: A view from the top of American law enforcement.* New York: Simon & Schuster.

Musante, F. (1999, June 27). Boy is murdered, and state passes a tough witness law. *New York Times,* p. CT1.

Musto, D. (1999). *The American disease: Origins of narcotic control* (3rd ed.). New York: Oxford University Press.

Muth, A. (Ed.). (1999). *Forensic medicine source book.* Detroit, MI: Omnigraphics.

Nagin, D. (2003). Drug law enforcement. *Criminology & Public Policy, 2*(3), 541-542.

National Association of Crime Victim Compensation Boards. (2002). *Crime victim compensation directory 2002.* Alexandria, VA: Author.

*National body armor survey.* (1991). New York: City University of New York, John Jay College of Criminal Justice and Strategic Polling Corporation.

National Commission on the Reform of Secondary Education. (1973). *The reform of secondary education: A report to the public and the profession.* New York: McGraw-Hill.

National Commission on Terrorist Attacks. (2004). *The 9/11 Commission report: Final report of the National Commission on Terrorist Attacks Upon the United States.* Washington, DC: U.S. Government Printing Office.

National Crime Prevention Council. (1995). *Lengthening the stride: Employing peace officers from newly arrived ethnic groups.* Washington, DC: Author.

National Criminal Justice Reference Service. (1994). *Violent Crime Control and Law Enforcement Act of 1994 fact sheet.* Available: http://www.ncjrs.org/txtfiles/billfs.txt

National Fire Protection Association. (2001). *NFPA 921: Guide to fire and explosion investigations.* Quincy, MA: Author.

National Highway Traffic Safety Administration. (1996). *Traffic safety & crime: Keeping pace.* Washington, DC: Author.

National Highway Traffic Safety Administration. (2001). *The traffic stop and you: Improving communication between citizens and law enforcement* [Brochure]. Washington, DC: Author.

National Institute of Justice. (1992). *When the victim is a child* (2nd ed.). Washington, DC: U.S. Department of Justice, Office of Justice Programs.

National Institute of Justice. (1997, January). *Police integrity: Public service with honor* (National Institute of Justice Reports series NCJ#163811). Washington, DC: Author.

National Institute of Justice. (2000). *On-the-job stress in policing: Reducing it, preventing it.* Washington, DC: Author.

National Institute of Justice. (2002). *NIJ special report: Using DNA to solve cold cases.* Washington, DC: Author.

National Institute of Justice. (2002a). *Ballistic resistance of personal body armor.* Washington, DC: Author.

National Institute of Justice. (2002b). *Stab resistance of personal body armor.* Washington, DC: Author.

National Law Enforcement and Corrections Technology Center. (2001). *Selection and application guide to personal body armor.* Rockville, MD: Author.

National League of Cities. (1979). *Ten years of LEAA.* Washington, DC: Author.

National Organization of Black Law Enforcement Executives (NOBLE). (2001). *A NOBLE perspective—Racial profiling: A symptom of biased-based policing.* Landover, MD: Author.

National Research Council. (2003). *The polygraph and lie detection.* Washington, DC: National Academic Press.

National Treasury Employees Union v. Von Raab, 489 U.S. 656 (1989).

Neiwert, D. A. (1999). *In God's country: The patriot movement and the Pacific Northwest.* Pullman: Washington State University Press.

Nelli, H. S. (1976). *The business of crime.* New York: Oxford University Press.

New Jersey v. Michaels, 136 N.J. 299 (1994).

New Jersey v. Soto, 734 A.2d 350 (N.J. Super. Ct. Law. Div. 1996).

New York City Alliance Against Sexual Assault. (2001). *Comprehensive sexual assault treatment programs: A hospital-based model.* New York: Author.

New York City Office of Operations. (2004). *The mayor's management report, fiscal 2004 preliminary.* Retrieved from http://www.nyc.gov/html/ops/downloads/pdf/2004_mmr/0104_indicators.pdf

New York Knapp Commission. (1973). *The Knapp Commission report on police corruption.* New York: George Braziller.

New York Legislature, Senate Committee on Police Department of the City of New York. (1895). *Report and Proceedings of the Senate Committee appointed to investigate the Police Department of the City of New York.* Albany: New York State Printer.

New York State Division of Criminal Justice Services. (1993). *A report to the governor on the disturbances in Crown Heights: An assessment of the city's preparedness and response to civil disorder.* Albany: Author.

New York State Division of Criminal Justice Services. (2002). *Missing and Exploited Children Clearinghouse: The AMBER Alert plan.* Retrieved July 15, 2003, from http://criminaljustice.state.ny.us/missing/aware/amber.htm

New York State Organized Crime Task Force. (1990). *Corruption and racketeering in the New York construction industry.* New York: New York University Press.

New York v. Belton, 453 U.S. 454 (1981).

New York v. Munn, 688 N.Y., S.2d 384 (1999).

New York v. Quarles, 467 U.S. 649 (1984).

Newburn, T. (1999). *Understanding and preventing police corruption: Lessons from the literature.* London: Home Office.

Newburn, T. (Ed.). (2003). *A handbook of policing.* Cullompton, UK: Willan.

Newburn, T., & Jones, T. (1996). Policing and the idea of democracy. *British Journal of Criminology, 36*(2), 182-198.

Newton, J. (2000, October 15). A glimpse into future of LAPD? *Los Angeles Times,* p. A1.

Nickell, J. (1996). *Detecting forgery: Forensic investigation of documents.* Lexington: University Press of Kentucky.

Nicolls v. Ingersoll, 7 Johns. 145, 154 (N.Y. 1810).

Nielson, E. (1981). *Salt Lake City Police Department deadly force policy: Shooting and post shooting reactions.* Mimeograph.

Niemi-Kiesilainan, J. (2001). The deterrent effect of arrest in domestic violence: Differentiating between victim and perpetrator response. *Hasting's Women's Law Journal, 12,* 283.

*9-1-1 fast facts.* Retrieved from http://www.nena.org/911_facts/911fastfacts.htm

Nislow, N. (2000, December 15/31). Psych job: The Memphis PD's Crisis Intervention Team reinvents police response to EDPs. *Law Enforcement News, 26*(545, 546). Retrieved from http://www.lib.jjay.cuny.edu/len/2000/12.31/

Nissman, D., & Hagen, E. (1982). *The prosecution function.* Lexington, MA: Lexington Books.

Nolan, P. B. (1987). *Vigilantes on the middle border: A study of self-appointed law enforcement in the states of the Upper Mississippi from 1840-1880.* New York: Garland.

Not what they say, but how they say it: DC clears homicides with voice analysis. (1994, September 15). *Law Enforcement News, 20*(407), 6.

Nowicki, E. J. (1990, October). Multi-jurisdictional task force. *Law Enforcement Technology.*

O'boye, S. (2004, April 2). Broward sheriff's office begins review of "cleared" cases. *South Florida Sun-Sentinel.* Available: http://forum.parklandvote.com/viewtopic.php? t=88

O'Brien, R. (2000). Crime facts: Victim and offender data. In J. Sheley (Ed.), *Criminology: A contemporary handbook* (3rd ed., pp. 59-83). Belmont, CA: Wadsworth/Thomson.

O'Connell, P. (2001). *Using performance data for accountability: The New York City Police Department's CompStat model of police management.* Arlington, VA: PricewaterhouseCoopers.

O'Connell, R. L. (1990). *Of arms and men: A history of war, weapons, and aggression.* New York: Oxford University Press.

O'Connor, T. R. (2004). *Scientific speed detection.* Retrieved March 16, 2004, from http://faculty.ncwc.edu/toconnor/425/425lect04.htm

O'Donnell, E. (2004). Fixing broken windows or fracturing fragile relationships? In D. Jones-Brown & K. Terry (Eds.), *Policing and minority communities: Bridging the gap.* Upper Saddle River, NJ: Pearson/Prentice Hall.

Office of Community Oriented Policing Services. (2000). *Problem-oriented guides for police.* Available: http://www.cops.usdoj.gov

Office of International Criminal Justice. (1995, March). *Readings.* Ninth Annual Futures Conference on Privatization in Criminal Justice: Public and Private Partnerships, University of Illinois at Chicago.

Office of Juvenile Justice and Delinquency Prevention. (1999). *Promising strategies to reduce gun violence.* Washington, DC: U.S. Department of Justice.

Office of the United States Attorney Middle District of Florida. (2003). Press release. Retrieved October 31, 2003, from http://www.usdoj.gov/usao/flm/pr/012703waldon.pdf

Officers hope to turn cold cases hot: Training will cover DNA evidence, probe techniques. (2004, February 28). *Birmingham News.*

http://ojjdp.ncjrs.org

Olmstead v. United States, 277 U.S. 438 (1928).

Oregon v. Elstad, 470 U.S. 298 (1985).

Orfield, M. W. (1992). Deterrence, perjury, and the heater factor: An exclusionary rule in the Chicago criminal courts. *University of Colorado Law Review, 63,* 75, 107.

Osborn, D., & Gaebler, T. (1993). *Re-inventing government: How the entrepreneurial spirit is transforming the public sector.* New York: Plume.

Osterburg, J. W., & Ward, R. H. (1999). *Criminal investigation: A method for reconstructing the past* (3rd ed.). Cincinnati, OH: Anderson.

Owen, D. (2000). *Hidden evidence: Forty true crimes and how forensic science helped solve them.* Buffalo, NY: Firefly.

Owens, C. E., & Bell, J. (1977). *Blacks and criminal justice.* Lexington, MA: D.C. Heath.

Ozanich, B. (1996). *E 9-1-1 data base guide.* Coshocton, OH: National Emergency Number Association.

Pagon, M. (1995). Policing the university community: Police discretion and officer-student relations. *Campus Law Enforcement Journal, 25*(1), 3-8, 35.

Palenski, J. (1984). The use of mediation by police. *Mediation Quarterly, 5,* 31-38.

Palmer, N. (Ed.). (1998). *The recovery of stolen art: A collection of essays.* London: Kluwer.

Palmiotto, M. J. (1997). *Policing: Concepts, strategies, and current issues in American police forces.* Durham, NC: Academic Press.

Palmiotto, M. J. (Ed.). (2001). *Police misconduct: A reader for the 21st century.* Upper Saddle River, NJ: Prentice Hall.

Palmiotto, M. J. (2003). *Policing & training issues.* Upper Saddle River, NJ: Prentice Hall.

Paoline, E., III. (2001). *Rethinking police culture: Officers' occupational attitudes.* New York: LFB.

Park, R. C., & Waltz, J. R. (1999). *Cases and materials on evidence* (9th ed.). New York: Foundation Press.

Parker, D. B. (1976). *Crime by computer.* New York: Scribner.

Parker v. District of Columbia, 850 F.2d 708 (D.C. Cir. 1988).

Parkhurst, Charles Henry. (2003). In *Columbia encyclopedia.* Retrieved February 19, 2003, from http://encyclopedia.com/html/p/parkhurs.asp

Parks, R. B., Mastrofski, S. D., DeJong, C., & Gray, M. K. (1999). How officers spend their time with the community. *Justice Quarterly, 16,* 483-518.

Parks, R. B., Mastrofski, S. D., Reiss, A. J., Jr., Worden, R. E., Terrill, W. C., DeJong, C., Stroshine, M., & Shepard, R. (1998). *St. Petersburg project on policing neighborhoods: A study of the police and the community.* Bloomington: Indiana University Press.

Parrilla, L. (2002, December 12). Ranks of reserves dwindle. *Ventura County Star,* p. A1.

Pate, T., Ferrara, A., Bowers, R. A., & Lorence, J. (1976). *Police response time: Its determinants and effects.* Washington, DC: Police Foundation.

PATRIOT Act, H.R.3162, Pub. L. No.107-56, 115 Stat. 272 (2001).

Patrol car's camera films problem officer. (2002, December 20). *Crime Control Digest,* p. 7.

Patterson, M. J. (1980, September). Training tailored for women. *Police Magazine,* pp. 23-29.

Payton v. New York, 445 U.S. 573 (1980).

Peak, K., & Glensor, R. (1996). *Community policing and problem solving: Strategies and practices.* Upper Saddle River, NJ: Prentice Hall.

Pease, K. (1998). *Repeat victimisation: Taking stock.* Crime Detection and Prevention Series Paper 90. London: Home Office Police Research Group. Retrieved June, 3, 2003, from http://www.homeoffice.gov.uk/rds/prgpdfs/fcdps90. pdf

Penrod, S. (2003). Eyewitness identification evidence: How well are witnesses and police performing? *Criminal Justice, 54,* 36-47.

Pentland, B., & Feldman, M. (2003). Reconceptualizing organizational routines as a source of flexibility and change. *Administrative Science Quarterly, 48,* 94-118.

People v. Allen, 247 F.3d 741 (8th Cir. 2001).

Percy, S. L. (1980). Response time and citizen evaluation of police. *Journal of Police Science and Administration, 8*(1), 75-86.

Perkins, D., & Taylor, R. B. (1996). Ecological assessments of disorder: Their relationship to fear of crime and theoretical implications. *American Journal of Community Psychology, 24,* 63–107.

Perkins, D. D., Meeks, J. W., & Taylor, R. B. (1992). The physical environment of street blocks and resident perceptions of crime and disorder: Implications for theory and measurement. *Journal of Environmental Psychology, 12,* 21–34.

Perkins, D. D., Wandersman, A., Rich, R., & Taylor, R. B. (1993). Physical environment of street crime: Defensible space, territoriality and incivilities. *Journal of Environmental Psychology, 13,* 29–49.

Perlmutter, D. D. (2000). *Policing the media: Street cops and public perceptions of law enforcement.* Thousand Oaks, CA: Sage.

Petersilia, J. (1998). *Community corrections: Probation, parole and intermediate sanctions.* New York: Oxford University Press.

Petersilia, J. (2002). *Reforming probation and parole in the 21st century.* Lanham, MD: American Correctional Association.

Petersilia, J. (2003). *When prisoners come home: Parole and prisoner reentry.* New York: Oxford University Press.

Peterson, J. L. (1983). The crime lab. In C. B. Klockars (Ed.), *Thinking about police: Contemporary readings* (pp. 184-198). New York: McGraw-Hill.

Phillips, P. W. (1993). Campus law enforcement as community policing and problem-oriented policing. *Campus Law Enforcement Journal, 23*(6), 19-22.

Pierson v. Ray, 386 U.S. 547 (1967).

Pinnizzotto, A., & Finkel, N. (1990). Criminal personality profiling: Outcome and process. *Law and Human Behavior, 14*(3), 215-233.

*Police Chief* [Entire issue]. (2003, March). Alexandria, VA: International Association of Chiefs of Police.

Police Foundation. (1981). *The Newark foot patrol experiment.* Washington, DC: Author.

Polk, O. E., & Armstrong, D. A. (2001). Higher education and law enforcement career paths: Is the road to success paved by degree? *Journal of Criminal Justice Education, 12,* 77-99.

Pollard, J. W., & Whitaker, L. C. (1991). Cures for campus violence, if we want them. In L. C. Whitaker & J. W. Pollard (Eds.), *Campus violence: Kinds, causes, and cures.* New York: Haworth.

Poole, R. W., Jr. (1978). *Cutting back City Hall.* New York: Free Press.

Popkin, S. J., Gwiasda, V. E., Olson, L. M., Rosenbaum, D. P., & Buron, L. (2000). *The hidden war: Crime and the tragedy of public housing in Chicago.* New Brunswick, NJ: Rutgers University Press.

Porter, T. (1986). *The rise of statistical thinking.* Princeton, NJ: Princeton University Press.

Porter, T. (1995). *Trust in numbers.* Princeton, NJ: Princeton University Press.

Portwood, S., Grady, M. T., & Dutton, S. (2000, February). Enhancing law enforcement identification and investigation of child maltreatment. *Child Abuse & Neglect, 24,* 195-207.

Powell, E. A. (2004, April 15). *Banks combat identity theft.* Available: www.sanmateocountytimes.com.

Powers, W. F. (1968, March). State policewomen in Massachusetts. *Law & Order,* pp. 82-85, 96.

Poynter, G. (1990a). Experimentation without informed consent: Casualties of traffic radar use. *Law Enforcement News, 16*(325).

Poynter, G. (1990b, November 15). The hidden hazard of traffic safety. *Law Enforcement News, 16*(324).

Poynter, G. (1995, November 15). The last piece in radar's unsolved puzzle. *Law Enforcement News, 21*(433).

President's Commission on Law Enforcement and the Administration of Justice. (1967). *The challenge of crime in a free society.* Washington, DC: U.S. Government Printing Office.

President's Commission on Law Enforcement and the Administration of Justice. (1967). *Task force report: The police.* Washington, DC: U.S. Government Printing Office.

President's Commission on Organized Crime. (1986). *America's habit: Drug abuse, drug trafficking and organized crime.* Washington, DC: U.S. Government Printing Office.

The President's National Drug Control Strategy. (2004). Washington, DC: Office of National Drug Control Policy.

Prior, V. (2001). Invited comments to: Children's response to the medical visit for allegations of sexual abuse: Maternal perceptions and predicting variables. *Child Abuse Review, 10,* 223-225.

Private firms take over public functions: Germany, Switzerland. (1980, September). *Urban Innovation Abroad, 4,* 1.

Private probes for public jobs. (1996, July 7). *Washington Post,* p. C6.

Profilers warm to killer's trail. (2002, July 19). *St. Petersburg Times.*

Punch, M. (1985). *Conduct unbecoming: The social construction of police deviance and control.* London: Tavistock.

Puzzanchera, C., Stahl, A. L., Finnegan, T. A., Tierney, N., & Snyder, H. N. (2003). *Juvenile court statistics 1998.* Washington, DC: Office of Juvenile Justice and Delinquency Prevention.

*Questioning: "Outside Miranda."* [Video]. (1990). Anaheim, CA: Greg Gulen Productions.

Rabin, J. L. (2000, November 30). Murder leads increase of violent crime in city. *Los Angeles Times.*

Ramirez, D., McDevitt, J., & Farrell, A. (2000). *A resource guide on racial profiling data collection systems: Promising practices and lessons learned.* Washington, DC: U.S. Department of Justice.

Rapoport, L. (1970). Crisis intervention as a means of brief treatment. In R. W. Roberts & R. H. Nee (Eds.), *Theories of social casework* (pp. 267-311). Chicago: University of Chicago Press.

Rashid, A. (2002). *Jihad: The rise of militant Islam in central Asia.* Middlesex, UK: Penguin.

Ratcliffe, J. H. (2004). The hotspot matrix: A framework for the spatio-temporal targeting of crime reduction. *Police Practice and Research, 5,* 7-25.

Ratha, N. K., & Bolle, R. M. (Eds.). (2003). *Advances in automatic fingerprint recognition.* New York: Springer-Verlag.

Rau, C. (1989, October 16). Security industry faces a control crisis. *The Age.*

Ready, J., & Weisburd, D. (2002). Victims and victim service organizations in American policing: Selected findings from a national survey. *Networks, 17,* 3-4, 16-20.

Reagan, R. (1982). Guest editorial. *Police Chief, 49*(6), p. 8.

Reaves, B., & Hickman, M. (2002, October). *Census of state and local law enforcement agencies, 2000* (NCJ 194066). Washington, DC: U.S. Department of Justice.

Regini, C. L. (1997). The cold case concept. *FBI Law Enforcement Bulletin, 66,* 1-6.

Rehnson, C. M., & Welchans, S. (Eds.). (2000). Intimate partner violence. *United States Department of Justice, Bureau of Justice Statistics Special Report.* Available: http://www.ojp.usdoj.gov/bjs

Reiner, R. (2000). *The politics of the police* (3rd ed.). Oxford, UK: Oxford University Press.

Reisig, M. D., & Parks, R. B. (2000). Experience, quality of life, and neighborhood context: A hierarchical analysis of satisfaction with police. *Justice Quarterly, 17,* 607-629.

Reiss, A. (1971). *The police and the public.* New Haven, CT: Yale University Press.

Reiss, A. (1992). Police organization in the twentieth century. In M. Tonry & N. Morris (Eds.), *Modern policing* (pp. 51-97). Chicago: University of Chicago Press.

Reiss, A. J., Jr. (1974). Discretionary justice. In D. Glaser (Ed.), *Handbook of criminology.* Chicago: Rand-McNally.

Render unto seizure: Colorado cops get short shrift in forfeiture debate. (2002, June 30). *Law Enforcement News, 28*(580), pp. 1, 10.

Rennison, C., & Rand, M. (2003). *Criminal victimization, 2002.* Washington, DC: Bureau of Justice Statistics.

Report of the Rampart Independent Review Panel. (2000, November 16). Available: http://www.lacity.org/oig/rirprpt.pdf

Reppetto, T. (1978). *The blue parade.* New York: Free Press.

Resch, R. C. (1997, February). K-9s in law enforcement: They're worth the effort. *Police,* p. 5.

Ressler, R. K., Burgess, A. W., & Douglas, J. E. (1988). *Sexual homicide: Patterns and motives.* Lexington, MA: Lexington Books.

Reuter, P. (1985). *The organization of illegal markets: An economic analysis.* Washington, DC: National Institute of Justice.

Richards, E. (2002, October). Collaboration between public health and law enforcement: The constitutional challenge. *Emerging Infectious Diseases, 8*(10), 1157-1159.

Richards v. Wisconsin, 520 U.S. 385 (1997).

Richardson, B. (1999). Vidocq, Eugene Francois. In R. Herbert (Ed.), *The Oxford companion to crime and mystery writing.* New York: Oxford University Press.

Richardson, J. F. (1974). *Urban police in the United States.* Port Washington, NY: National University Publications.

Rigakos, G. (2003). *Parapolice.* Toronto: University of Toronto Press.

Ripley, A. (2001, April 23). Nights of rage: Another police killing, and Cincinnati explodes. *Time,* p. 44.

Roberg, R., Kuykendall, J., & Novak, K. (2002). *Police management.* Los Angeles: Roxbury.

Roberts, G. G. (1993). *Dick Tracy and American culture: Morality and mythology, text and context.* Jefferson, NC: McFarland.

Roberts, K., & Grabowski, M. (1996). Organizations, technology and structuring. In S. Clegg, C. Hardy, & W. Nord (Eds.), *Handbook of organization studies* (pp. 409-423). London: Sage.

Robinson, J., Lawton, B., Taylor, R. B., & Perkins, D. P. (in press). Multilevel longitudinal impacts of incivilities: Fear of crime, expected safety, and block satisfaction. *Journal of Quantitative Criminology.*

Rock, P. (2002). Criminological theories. In M. Maguire, R. Morgan, & R. Reiner (Eds.), *The handbook of criminology* (3rd ed.). Oxford, UK: Oxford University Press.

Roebuck, J. B., & Barker, T. (1974). A typology of police corruption. *Social Problems, 21,* 423–437.

Roleff, T. (1999). *Police brutality: Current controversies.* San Diego, CA: Greenhaven.

Roosevelt, F. (1938). Remarks before the Daughters of the American Revolution, Washington, DC, April 21, 1938. *The Public Papers and Addresses of Franklin D. Roosevelt, 1938.* New York: Random House.

Rosen, M. (1999, May 15–31). If it's broken, fix it! An interview with Professor George Kelling. *Law Enforcement News, 25,* 511–512.

Rosenbaum, D. P., & Lurigio, A. J. (1985). *The national evaluation of Crime Stoppers: A synopsis of major findings.* Evanston, IL: Northwestern University, Centre for Urban Affairs and Policy Research.

Rosenbaum, P. D., & Hanson, S. G. (1998). Assessing the effects of school based drug education: A six year multilevel analysis of Project D.A.R.E. *Journal of Research in Crime and Delinquency, 35*(4), 381-412.

Rosenfeld, R. (2004, February). The case of the unsolved crime decline. *Scientific American,* pp. 82-89.

Rossi, D. (1982). Crime scene behavioral analysis: Another tool for the law enforcement investigator. *Police Chief, 49*(1), 152-155.

Rossmo, D. K. (2000). *Geographic profiling.* Boca Raton, FL: CRC Press.

Roush, C. (1996). Warrantless public housing searches. *American Criminal Law Review, 34,* 261-288.

Roy, D. (1952). Quota restriction and gold bricking in a machine shop. *American Journal of Sociology, 57,* 427-442.

Roy, D. (1954). Efficiency and "the fix": Informal relations in a piecework machine shop. *American Journal of Sociology, 60,* 255-266.

Rubenstein, J. (1973). *City police.* New York: Ballantine.

Russell, K. K. (1998). *The color of crime.* New York: New York University Press.

Saferstein, R. (2002). *Criminalistics: An introduction to forensic science.* Upper Saddle River, NJ: Prentice Hall.

Samaha, J. (1997). *Criminal justice.* St. Paul, MN: West.

Sampson, R., & Scott, M. (2000). *Tackling crime and other public-safety problems: Case studies in problem-solving.* Available: http://www.cops.usdoj.gov

Saunders, C. (1970). *Upgrading the American police.* Washington, DC: Brookings Institution.

Savage, D. (1996, February 29). Necessary weapon, or excessive force? *Los Angeles Times,* p. A-1.

Schafer, J. A., & Bonello, E. M. (2001). The citizen police academy: Measuring outcomes. *Police Quarterly, 4,* 434-448.

Schafer, J. A., Huebner, B. M., & Bynum, T. S. (in press). Citizen perceptions of police services: Race, neighborhood context, and community policing. *Police Quarterly.*

Schall, D. J. (1996). *An investigation into the relationship between municipal police residency requirement, professionalism, economic conditions and equal employment goals.* Unpublished doctoral dissertation, University of Wisconsin–Milwaukee.

Scheck, B., Neufeld, P., & Dwyer, J. (2000). *Actual innocence: Five days to execution, and other dispatches from the wrongly convicted.* New York: Doubleday.

Schein, E. H. (1971). Organizational socialization and the profession of management. *Industrial Management Review, 2,* 37-45.

Scheptycki, J. (2000). *Issues in transnational policing.* London: Routledge.

Scher v. United States, 305 U.S. 251 (1938).

Schermerhorn, J. R., Jr. (1975). Determinants of interorganizational cooperation. *Academy of Management Journal, 18,* 846-856.

Schlanger, E. (2002, June). *Baltimore CitiStat presentation.* Paper presented at the Columbus, Ohio 3-1-1 Summit, Columbus, OH.

Schmalleger, F. (2001). *Criminal justice today.* Upper Saddle River, NJ: Prentice Hall.

Schulz, D. M. (1989). The police matron movement: Paving the way for policewomen. *Police Studies, 12*(3), 115-124.

Schulz, D. M. (1995). *From social worker to crimefighter: Women in United States municipal policing.* Westport, CT: Praeger.

Schulz, D. M. (1996). Strategies for combining community crime prevention with crime prevention through environmental design: The transit experience. *Security Journal, 7,* 253-257.

Schulz, D. M. (2004). *Breaking the brass ceiling: Women police chiefs and their paths to the top.* Westport, CT: Praeger.

Schulz, D. M., & Gilbert, S. (1995, July). Developing strategies to fight crime and fear. *Police Chief,* pp. 20-27.

Scientific Working Group on DNA Analysis Methods. (2001, October). Training guidelines. *Forensic Science Communications, 3*(4). Available: http://www.fbi.gov/hq/lab/fsc/backissu/oct2001/kzinski.htm

Scott, M. (2000). *Problem-oriented policing: Reflections on the first 20 years.* Available: http://www.cops.usdoj.gov

Scrivner, E. M. (1994). *The role of police psychology in controlling excessive force* (National Institute of Justice Research Report). Washington, DC: U.S. Department of Justice.

Sears, D. (1973). *The politics of violence: The new urban blacks and the Watts riot.* Boston: Houghton Mifflin.

Secrest, W. B. (1994). *Lawmen and desperadoes: A compendium of noted, early California peace officers, badmen, and outlaws.* Spokane, WA: Arthur H. Clark.

Segrave, K. (2004). *Lie detectors: A social history.* Jefferson, NC: McFarland.

Sengoopta, C. (2003). *Imprint of the Raj: How fingerprinting was born in colonial India.* London: Macmillan.

Senna, J., & Siegel, L. (1993). *Introduction to criminal justice.* St. Paul, MN: West.

78 IR 1673 (October 29, 2001).

78 IR 1703 (November 5, 2001).

78 IR 1899 (December 17, 2001).

79 IR 115 (January 21, 2002).

79 IR 236 (February 11, 2002).

79 IR 261 (February 18, 2002).

79 IR 769 (May 20, 2002).

79 IR 897-899 (June 10, 2002).

79 IR 945 (June 24, 2002).

Sewell, J. D., & Crew, L. (1984, March). The forgotten victim: Stress and the police dispatcher. *FBI Law Enforcement Bulletin,* pp. 7-11.

Shadwick v. City of Tampa, 407 U.S. 345 (1972).

Shapiro, B. J. (1991). *"Beyond reasonable doubt" and "probable cause": Historical perspectives on the Anglo-American law of evidence.* Berkeley: University of California Press.

Shapiro, P. N., & Penrod, S. (1986). Meta-analysis of facial identification studies. *Psychological Bulletin, 100,* 139-156.

Sharp, A. G. (2000, October). On the wrong side of the law and the lens. *Law and Order, 98,* 97-102.

Shearing, C. D. (1992). The relation between public and private policing. In N Morris & M. Tonry (Eds.), *Crime and justice: An annual review of research* (Vol. 15). Chicago: University of Chicago Press.

Shearing, C., & Ericson, R. (1991). Culture as figurative action. *British Journal of Sociology, 42,* 481-506.

Shearing, C., & Johnston, L. (2003). *Governing security.* London: Routledge & Kegan Paul.

Sheehan, R., & Cordner, G. (1995). *Police administration.* Cincinnati, OH: Anderson.

Shepherd, R. (1995). Neighborhood dispute settlement center's program with City of Harrisburg Bureau of Police. *Executive Summary for Board of Directors, Neighborhood Dispute Settlement of Dauphin County.*

Shepnick, P. (2002, March 18). T.O.'s VIPs give police break from the routine. *Ventura County Star,* p. B1.

Sherif, M. (1966). *In common predicament: Social psychology of intergroup conflict and cooperation.* Boston: Houghton Mifflin.

Sherman, L., & Berk, R. A. (1984, April). The Minneapolis domestic violence experiment. *Police Foundation Report,* p. 1.

Sherman, L. W. (1974). Introduction: Toward a sociological theory of police corruption. In Sherman, L. W. (Ed.), *Police corruption: A sociological perspective.* New York: Doubleday.

Sherman, L. W., & Blumberg, M. (1981). Higher education and police use of deadly force. *Journal of Criminal Justice, 9,* 317-331.

Sherman, L. W., Gartin, P. R., & Buerger, M. (1989). Hot spots of predatory crime: Routine activities and the criminology of place. *Criminology, 27*(2), 27-55.

Sherman, L. W., & Glick, B. D. (1984). *The quality of police arrest statistics.* Washington, DC: The Police Foundation.

Sherman, L. W., & Langworthy, R. (1979). Measuring homicide by police officers. *Journal of Criminal Law and Criminology, 70,* 546-560.

Shernock, S. K. (1992). The effects of college education on professional attitudes among police. *Journal of Criminal Justice Education, 3,* 71-92.

Shift work takes its toll on families. (2003, February). *Industrial Safety and Hygiene News, 37*(2), 10.

Shusta, R. M., Levine, D., Harris, P., & Wong, H. (2001). *Multicultural law enforcement: Strategies for peacekeeping in a diverse society* (2nd ed.). Belmont, CA: Wadsworth.

Silverman, E. (1999). *NYPD battles crime: Innovative strategies in policing.* Boston: Northeastern University Press.

Silverman, E. B., & O'Connell, P. (1999). Organizational change and decision making in the New York City Police Department. *International Journal of Public Administration, 22*(2), 217-259.

Simonsen, C. E. (1991). *Juvenile justice in America.* New York: Macmillan.

Singer, P. (2003). *Corporate warriors.* Ithaca, NY: Cornell University Press.

67 Fed. Reg. 40581-86 (June 13, 2002).

67 Fed. Reg. 67766 (November 6, 2002).

63 Fed. Reg. 39109 (July 21, 1998).

Skinner v. Railway Labor Executive Association, 489 U.S. 602 (1989).

Skogan, W. (1986). Fear of crime and neighborhood change. In A. J. Reiss, Jr., & M. Tonry (Eds.), *Communities and crime* (Vol. 8, pp. 203–230). Chicago: University of Chicago Press.

Skogan, W. G. (1990). *Disorder and decline: Crime and the spiral of decay in American neighborhoods.* New York: Free Press.

Skogan, W. G., & Hartnett, S. (1997). *Community policing, Chicago style.* New York: Oxford University Press.

Skolnick, J. (1966). *Justice without trial.* New York: Wiley.

Skolnick, J. (1994). *Justice without trial: Law enforcement in democratic society* (3rd ed.). Englewood Cliffs, NJ: Macmillan.

Skolnick, J., & Bayley, D. (1986). *The new blue line: Police innovations in six American cities.* New York: Free Press.

Skolnick, J., & Bayley, D. (1987). Theme and variation in community policing. In M. Tonry & N. Morris (Eds.), *Crime and justice* (pp. 1-37). Chicago: University of Chicago Press.

Skolnick, J., & Bayley, D. (1988). *Community policing: Issues and practice around the world.* Washington, DC: National Institute of Justice.

Skolnick, J., & Fyfe, J. (1993). *Above the law: Police and the excessive use of force.* New York: Free Press.

Skolnick, J. H. (1982, Summer/Fall). Deception by police. *Criminal Justice Ethics, 1,* 40-53.

Sloan, J. J., Fisher, B. S., & Cullen, F. T. (1997). Assessing the Student Right-to-Know and Campus Security Act of 1990: An analysis of the victim reporting practices of college and university students. *Crime & Delinquency, 43*(2), 148-168.

Smith, B., & Tolman, T. (2000, April). Public safety and the interoperability challenge. *National Institute of Justice Journal.* Washington, DC: National Institute of Justice.

Smith, B. L. (1994). *Terrorism in America: Pipe bombs and pipe dreams.* Albany: State University of New York Press.

Smith, C. E. (2004). *Constitutional rights: Myths and realities.* Belmont, CA: Wadsworth/Thompson.

Smith, E. (1984). *Principles of forensic handwriting identification and testimony.* Springfield, IL: Charles C Thomas.

Smith, M. R., & Petrocelli, M. (2001). Racial profiling? A multivariate analysis of police traffic stop data. *Police Quarterly, 4*(1), 4-27.

Snipes, J. B. (2001). *Police response to citizen requests for assistance: An assessment of deservedness, workload, social status, and officer predisposition perspectives.* Unpublished doctoral dissertation, State University of New York at Albany.

Snyder, H. N. (2000). *Sexual assault of young children as reported to law enforcement: Victim, incident, and offender characteristics* (NCJ 182990). Washington, DC: National Center for Juvenile Justice.

Snyder, H. N. (2001, December). *Law enforcement and juvenile crime* (Office of Juvenile Justice and Delinquency Prevention, Juvenile Offenders and Victims National Report Series). Washington, DC: U.S. Department of Justice, Office of Juvenile Programs.

Snyder, H. N., & Sickmund, M. (1999, September). *Juvenile offenders and victims: 1999 national report.* Washington, DC: National Center for Juvenile Justice.

Sobieraj, S. (2002, January 31). Bush asks Americans to volunteer. *The Daily Gazette,* p. A4.

Solomon, R. M., & Horn, J. H. (1986). Post-shooting traumatic reactions: A pilot study. In J. T. Reese & H. A. Goldstein (Eds.), *Psychological services for law enforcement officers.* Washington, DC: U.S. Government Printing Office.

Sondern, F., Jr. (1959). *Brotherhood of evil: The Mafia.* New York: Farrar, Straus and Cudahy.

Sparks, R. (1992). *Television and the drama of crime: Moral tales and the place of crime in public life.* Buckingham, UK: Open University Press.

Sparrow, M. K., Moore, M. H., & Kennedy, D. M. (1990). *Beyond 911: A new era for policing.* New York: Basic Books.

Speaking in tongues. (2000, October 31). *Law Enforcement News, 26*(542).

Spelman, W., & Brown, D. K. (1984). *Calling the police: Citizen reporting of serious crime.* Washington, DC: National Institute of Justice.

Spergel, I. (1995). *The youth gang problem: A community approach.* New York: Oxford University Press.

Spiel, R. E., Jr. (2000). *Art theft and forgery investigation: The complete field manual.* Springfield, IL: Charles C Thomas.

Spotting a liar is no easy task for police. (1999, May 15/31). *Law Enforcement News. 25*(511, 512), 7.

State v. Johnson, 90 N.J.Super. 105, 216 A.2d 397 (App.Div.1965), aff'd 46 N.J. 289, 216 A.2d 392 (1966).

State v. Roszkowski, 129 N.J. Super. 315, 323 A2d 531 (App.Div. 1974).

Statement of the president on approving the crime bills H.R. 9167, H.R. 13551, and H.R. 15766. (1966, November 8). Press release, The White House.

Stead, P. J. (1983). *The police of France.* New York: Macmillan.

Steadman, G. W. (2002, January). *Survey of DNA crime laboratories, 2001* (NCJ 191191). Washington, DC: Bureau of Justice Statistics.

Steadman, H. J., Deane, M. W., Borum, R., & Morrissey, J. P. (2000). Comparing outcomes of major models of police responses to mental health emergencies. *Psychiatric Services, 51,* 645-649.

Steblay, N., Dysart, J., Fulero, S., & Lindsay, R. C. L. (2001). Eyewitness accuracy rates in sequential and simultaneous line-up presentations: A meta-analytic comparison. *Law & Human Behavior, 25,* 459-473.

Stevens, D. (2002). *Policing and community partnerships.* Upper Saddle River, NJ: Prentice Hall.

Stewart, J. K. (1985). Public safety and private police. *Public Administration Review, 45,* 758-765.

Stewart, P. (1983). The road to Mapp v. Ohio and beyond: The origins, development and future of the exclusionary rule in search-and-seizure cases. *Columbia Law Review, 83,* 1365-1404.

Stock, R. M. (1987). An historical overview of automated fingerprint identification systems. In *Proceedings of the International Forensic Symposium on Latent Prints* (pp. 51-60). Washington, DC: U.S. Government Printing Office.

Stockwell, J. (2001, August 10). Ward in Pr. George's has drop in arrests. *Washington Post,* p. B5.

Stoddard, E. R. (1968). The "informal code" of police deviancy: A group approach to "blue coat crime." *Journal of Criminal Law, Criminology and Police Science, 59,* 201–213.

Stogner v. Superior Court, 93 Cal. App. 4th 1229 (2001).

Stolzenberg, L., & D'Alessio, S. J. (2000). Gun availability and violent crime: New evidence from the National Incident-Based Reporting System. *Social Forces, 78,* 1461-1482.

Strandberg, K. (1998). Bomb squads. *Law Enforcement Technology, 25*(6), 42-44.

A study in pink & blue: Integration of gay cops nearly a "non-issue" in SDPD. (2002, February 28). *Law Enforcement News, 28*(572), pp. 1, 8.

Sullivan, J. P., & Kozlow, C. (2000). *Jane's facility security handbook.* Alexandria, VA: Jane's Information Group.

Sullivan, P. (1987). Attitude structures of different ethnic and age groups concerning police. *Journal of Criminal Law and Criminology, 78,* 177-196.

Surette, R. (1992). *Media, crime & criminal justice: Images and realities.* Pacific Grove, CA: Brooks/Cole.

Swanson, C. R., Territo, L., & Taylor, R. W. (1993). *Police administration: Structures, processes, and behavior* (3rd ed.). New York: Macmillan.

Sykes, R. E., & Clark, J. P. (1975). A theory of deference exchange in police-civilian encounters. *American Journal of Sociology, 81*(3), 584-600.

Taylor, I., Walton, P., & Young, J. (1973). *The new criminology: For a social theory of deviance.* London: Routledge.

Taylor, K. T. (2001). *Forensic art and illustration.* Boca Raton, FL: CRC.

Taylor, R. (2001). *Breaking away from broken windows: Baltimore neighborhoods and the nationwide fight against crime, grime, fear and decline.* New York: Westview.

Taylor, R. B. (1987). Toward an environmental psychology of disorder. In D. Stokols & I. Altman (Eds.), *Handbook of environmental psychology* (pp. 951–986). New York: Wiley.

Taylor, R. B. (1988). *Human territorial functioning.* Cambridge, UK: Cambridge University Press.

Taylor, R. B. (1999). The incivilities thesis: Theory, measurement and policy. In R. L. Langworthy (Ed.), *Measuring what matters* (pp. 65–88). Washington, DC: National Institute of Justice/ Office of Community Oriented Policing Services.

Taylor, R. B. (2001). *Breaking away from broken windows: Evidence from Baltimore neighborhoods and the nationwide fight against crime, grime, fear and decline.* New York: Westview.

Taylor v. Taintor, 83 U.S. (16 Wall.) 366, 21 L. Ed. 287 (1872).

Technical Working Group for Eyewitness Evidence. (1999). *Eyewitness evidence: A guide for law enforcement* (Report NCJ 178240). Washington, DC: U.S. Department of Justice.

Tennenbaum, A. N., & Moore, A. M. (1993, September/October). Non-lethal weapons: Alternatives to deadly force. *The Futurist,* pp. 20-23.

Tennessee v. Garner, 471 U.S. 1 (1985).

*Terrorist hunter: The extraordinary story of a woman who went undercover to infiltrate the radical Islamic groups operating in America.* (2003). New York: Ecco.

Terry v. Ohio, 392 U.S. 1 (1968).

Texas v. Brown, 460 U.S. 730 (1983).

Text of president's message on law enforcement and administration of justice. (1966, March 9). *New York Times,* p. 20L.

Thomas, G. C. (2000). The end of the road for Miranda v. Arizona? On the history and future of rules for police interrogation. *American Criminal Law Review, 37*(1), 1-40.

Thomas, G. C., III, & Leo, R. A. (2002). The effects of Miranda v. Arizona: Embedded in our national culture? In M. Tonry (Ed.), *Crime and justice: A review of research* (Vol. 29, pp. 203-274). Chicago: University of Chicago Press.

Thompson v. Louisiana, 469 U.S. 17 (1984).

Thompson, R., & Nored, L. (2002). Law enforcement employment discrimination based on sexual orientation: A selective review of case law. *American Journal of Criminal Justice, 26*(2), 203-217.

Thrasher, F. M. (1927). *The gang.* Chicago: University of Chicago Press.

Thurman v. City of Torrington, 595 F.Supp. 1521 (D. Conn. 1984).

Thurman, Q. C., & McGarrell, E. F. (Eds.). (2003). *Community policing in a rural setting* (2nd ed.). Cincinnati, OH: Anderson.

Tilley, N. (2003). Community policing, problem-solving policing and intelligence-led policing. In T. Newburn (Ed.), *Handbook of policing.* Devon, UK: Willan.

Top scientists meeting on Oklahoma murder case. (2003, July 16). Retrieved April 24, 2004, from www.Vidocq.org.

Torres, D. A. (1987). *Handbook of state police, highway patrols, and investigative agencies.* New York: Greenwood.

Transportation Security Administration. (2004, April 22). *TSA releases performance report on contract screeners at five U.S. airports.* Retrieved May 12, 2004, from http://www.tsa.gov/public/display?content=090005198009d340

Trautman, N. R. (2001). *Identifying what factors influence the law enforcement code of silence.* Unpublished doctoral dissertation, St. John's University, Springfield, LA.

Travis, J., & Waul, M. (2002). *Reflections on the crime decline: Lessons for the future?* Proceedings from the Urban Institute Crime Decline Forum. Retrieved from http://www.urban.org/url.cfm?ID=410546

Trojanowicz, R., & Bucqueroux, B. (1990). *Community policing: A contemporary perspective.* Cincinnati, OH: Anderson.

Turco, S., & Prendergast, J. (2003, January 30). Officials beginning to discuss slowdown by police: Crime's up and arrests down. *Cincinnati Inquirer.*

Turner, R., & Kosa, R. (2003). *Cold case squads: Leaving no stone unturned* (BJA Bulletin). Washington, DC: Bureau of Justice Assistance.

Umbreit, M., Vos, B., & Coates, R. (2002). *Victims of severe violence meet offenders: Restorative justice through dialogue.* Monsey, NY: Criminal Justice Press.

Underwood, R. K. (1995/1996, Spring). Truth verifiers: From the hot iron to the lie detector. *Kentucky Law Journal,* p. 84.

Undocumented Alien Emergency Medical Assistance Amendments of 2004 (H.R. 3722).

United States v. City of Wichita Falls, 704 F. Supp. 709 (N.D. Tex, 1988).

United States v. Dickerson, 166 F.3rd 667 (4th Circuit, 1999).

United States v. Elmore, 595 F.2d (5th Cir., 1979).

United States v. Johns, 469 U.S. 478 (1985).

United States v. Leon, 468 U.S. 897 (1984).

United States v. Mendenhail, 446 U.S. 544 (1980).

United States v. Miller, 425 U.S. 435 (1976).

United States v. Pavane, 2004 U. S. LEXIS 4577; 124 S. Ct. 2620 (2004).

United States v. Verdugo-Urquidez, 494 U.S. 259 (1990).

United States v. Wade, 388 U.S. 218 (1967).

U.S. Bureau of Justice Statistics. (1994, November). *Pretrial release of felony defendants, 1992* (NCJ-148818). Washington, DC: Author.

U.S. Congress, Office of Technology Assessment. (1995, July). *Electronic surveillance in a digital age* (OTA-BP-ITC-149). Washington, DC: U.S. Government Printing Office.

U.S. Department of Education & U.S. Department of Justice. (1996). *Manual to combat truancy.* Available: http://www.ed.gov/pubs/Truancy/

U.S. Department of Health and Human Services. (1993). *The third national incidence study of child abuse and neglect.* Washington, DC: National Clearinghouse on Child Abuse and Neglect Information.

U.S. Department of Health and Human Services, Administration on Children, Youth and Families. (2003). *Child maltreatment 2001.* Washington, DC: U.S. Government Printing Office.

U.S. Department of Justice. (2002, January). *Terrorism and International Victims Unit.* Washington, DC: Office for Victims of Crime. Available: http://www.ojp.usdoj.gov/ovc/publications/factshts/tivu/fs000276.pdf

U.S. Department of Justice. (n.d.). *The al Qaeda training manual.* Retrieved January 13, 2002 from http://www.usdoj.gov/ag/trainingmanual.htm

U.S. Department of Justice, Criminal Division, Computer Crime and Intellectual Property Section. (2002, July). *Searching and seizing computers and obtaining electronic evidence in criminal investigations.* Available: http://www.cybercrime.gov/s&smanual2002.htm

U.S. Department of Justice, Office of Community Oriented Policing Services. (2002). *Bringing victims into community policing.* Washington, DC: Author.

U.S. Department of Justice, Office of Justice Programs, Office for Victims of Crime. (1998). *New directions from the field: Victims' rights and services for the 21st century.* Washington, DC: Author.

U.S. Department of Justice, Office of Justice Programs, Office for Victims of Crime. (2001). *First response to victims of crime 2001.* Washington, DC: Author.

U.S. Drug Enforcement Administration. (n.d.). *Major operations.* Available: http://www.usdoj.gov/dea/major/major.htm

U.S. General Accounting Office. (2002). *Identity theft: Prevalence and cost appear to be growing.* Washington, DC: U.S. Government Printing Office.

Van Meter, C. H. (1973). *Principles of police interrogation.* Springfield, IL: Charles C Thomas.

Vecchi, G. M. (2002, May). Hostage/barricade management: A hidden conflict within law enforcement. *FBI Law Enforcement Bulletin,* pp. 1-7.

Verniero, P., & Zoubek, P. H. (1999). *Interim report of the State Police Review Team regarding allegations of racial profiling.* Available: http://www.state.nj.us/lps/intm_419.pdf

Vila, B. (2000). *Tired cops: The importance of managing police fatigue.* Washington, DC: Police Executive Research Forum.

Vila, B., & Morris, C. (Eds.). (1999). *The role of police in American society: A documentary history.* Westport, CT: Greenwood.

Violence Against Women Act of 1994. Pub. L. No. 103-322, 108 Stat. 1796.

Violence Against Women Act of 2000. Pub. L. No.106-386, 114 Stat. 7491.

Violent Crime Control and Law Enforcement Act, 42 U.S.C. § 14141 (1994).

Vizzard, W. J. (2000). *Shots in the dark: The policy, politics, and symbolism of gun control.* Lanham, MD: Rowman & Littlefield.

Volpe, M. (1989). The police role. In M. Wright & B. A. Galaway (Eds.), *Mediation and criminal justice: Victims, offenders, and community.* Newbury Park, CA: Sage.

Volpe, M., & Christian, T. (1989). Mediation: New addition to cop's toolbox. *Law Enforcement News, 15*(294), 8-13.

Volpe, M., & Phillips, N. (2002, November). *Understanding police mediation: Promises and challenges.* Paper presented at the annual meeting of the American Society of Criminology, Chicago.

Waddington, P. (1999). Police [canteen] sub-culture: An appreciation. *British Journal of Criminology, 39*(2), 287-309.

Wakeling, S., Jorgensen, M., Michaelson, S., & Begay, M. (2001). *Policing on American Indian reservations.* Washington, DC: U.S. Department of Justice.

Walker, S. (1984). "Broken windows" and fractured history: The use and misuse of history in recent police patrol analysis. *Justice Quarterly, 1,* 75-90.

Walker, S. (1992). *The police in America* (2nd ed.). New York: McGraw-Hill.

Walker, S. (2000). Police accountability: Establishing an early warning system. *International City/County Management Association (ICMA) Inquiry Services Report. Vol. 32*(8).

Walker, S. (2001). *Police accountability: The role of citizen oversight.* Belmont, CA: Wadsworth.

Walker, S. (2003, February). *Best practices in police accountability* [Online]. Available: http://www.policeaccountability.org

Walker, S., Alpert, G., & Kenney, D. (2001, July). *Early warning systems: Responding to the problem police officer* (NCJ 188565). Washington, DC: National Institute of Justice.

Walker, S., Archbold, C., & Herbst, L. (2002). *Mediating citizen complaints against police officers: A guide for police and community leaders.* Washington, DC: Office of Community Oriented Policing Services.

Walker, S., & Irlbeck, D. (2003, June). *Police sexual abuse of teenage girls: A 2003 update on "driving while female."* Available: http://www.policeaccountability.org/ PPIfirstyearrept.pdf

Walker, S., & Katz, C. M. (2002). *The police in America* (4th ed.). New York: McGraw Hill.

Walsh, J. (1997). *Tears of rage: From grieving father to crusader for justice.* New York: Pocket.

Walsh, J. (2001). *Public enemies: The host of* America's Most Wanted *targets the nation's most notorious criminals.* New York: Pocket.

Walsh, W. (2001). Compstat: An analysis of an emerging police managerial paradigm. *Policing: An International Journal of Police Strategies and Management, 24*(3), 347-362.

Walsh, W. F., & Donovan, E. J. (1989). Private security and community policing: Evaluation and comment. *Journal of Criminal Justice, 17,* 187-197.

Walters, S. B. (2003). *Principles of kinesic interview and interrogation* (2nd ed.). Boca Raton: CRC.

Ward, C., & Inserto, F. (1990). *Victims of sexual violence: A handbook for helpers.* Kent Ridge: Singapore University Press.

Ward, R. H. (1975). *Introduction to criminal investigation.* Reading, MA: Addison Wesley.

Warden v. Hayden, 387 U.S. 294 (1967).

Water, water everywhere (and hardly a cop in sight). (1999, March 15). *Law Enforcement News, 25*(507), p. 7.

Watson, J., & Berry, A. (2003). *DNA: The secret life.* New York: Knopf.

Watson, J., & Crick, F. (1953). Molecular structure of nucleic acids. *Nature, 171,* 737-738.

Watson, J. W., & Labe, L. J. (2001). Bail bonds. In American Bar Association (Ed.), *The law of miscellaneous and commercial surety bonds* (pp. 127-142). Chicago: American Bar Association.

Weapons of Mass Destruction and Incident Command Training Material from the Center for Domestic Preparedness, Office of Homeland Security, Anniston, AL.

Websdale, N. (1998). *Rural woman battering and the justice system.* Thousand Oaks, CA: Sage.

Weeks v. United States, 232 U.S. 383 (1914).

Weick, K. (1995). *Sensemaking in organizations.* Thousand Oaks, CA: Sage.

Weick, K. (2001). *Making sense of the organization.* Malden, MA: Blackwells.

Weinblatt, R. (2001). Reserves aid rural counties. *Law and Order, 49*(1), 30–32.

Weinreb, L. W. (1974). Generalities of the Fourth Amendment. *University of Chicago Law Review, 42,* 47-85.

Weisburd, D., Greenspan, R., Hamilton, E. E., Bryant, K. A., & Williams, H. (2001). *The abuse of police authority: A national study of police officers' attitudes.* Washington, DC: Police Foundation.

Weisburd, D., Greenspan, R., Hamilton, E. E., Williams, H., & Bryant, K. A. (2000). *Police attitudes toward abuse of authority: Findings from a national survey.* Washington, DC: U.S. Department of Justice.

Weisburd, D., Greenspan, R., & Mastrofski, S. (2001, February). *Compstat and organizational change: Preliminary findings from a national study.* Washington, DC: National Institute of Justice.

Weisburd, D., Mastrofski, S., McNally, A. M., Greenspan, R., & Willis, J. J. (2003). Reforming to preserve: Compstat and strategic problem-solving in American policing. *Criminology and Public Policy, 2,* 421–456.

Weisheit, R. A., Falcone, D. N., & Wells, L. E. (1999). *Crime and policing in rural and small-town America.* (2nd ed.). Prospect Heights, IL: Waveland.

Weisheit, R. A., Wells, L. E., & Falcone, D. N. (1995). *Crime and policing in rural and small-town America: An overview of the issues.* Washington, DC: National Institute of Justice.

Wells, G. L., Small, M., Penrod, S., Malpass, R. S., Fulero, S. M., & Brimacombe, C. A. E. (1998). Eyewitness identification procedures: Recommendations for lineups and photospreads. *Law and Human Behavior, 22,* 603-647.

Westley, W. (1970). Secrecy and the police. In N. Johnston, L. Savitz, & M. E. Wolfgang (Eds.), *The sociology of punishment and correction* (2nd ed.). New York: Wiley.

Westrick, A. J. (1998). Surviving "fatal" encounters: An analysis of violence involving police officers wearing body armor, their situational definitions, interactional experience and symptoms of post traumatic stress disorder (Doctoral dissertation, Wayne State University, 1998). *Dissertation Abstracts International,* 9915750.

Whitcomb, D. (1982). *Assisting child victims of sexual abuse: The Sexual Assault Center, Seattle, Washington and The Child Protection Center–Special Unit, Washington, DC* (NCJ number 84606). Washington, DC: National Institute of Justice.

White House Report. (2003). *National drug control strategy 2003.* Washington, DC: U.S. Government Printing Office.

White, J. R. (2002). *Terrorism: An introduction* (4th ed.). Belmont, CA: Wadsworth.

White, J. R. (2004). *Defending the homeland.* Belmont, CA: Wadsworth.

White, W. S. (2001). *Miranda's waning protections: Police interrogation practices after Dickerson.* Ann Arbor: University of Michigan Press.

Whyte, W. F. (1943). *Street corner society.* Chicago: University of Chicago Press.

Wilkins v. Maryland State Police, Civil Action No. CCB-93-483 (D. Md. 1993).

Williams, H., & Murphy, P. (1990). *Evolving strategy of the police: A minority view*. Washington, DC: National Institute of Justice.

Williams, H. E. (2001). *Asset forfeiture: A law enforcement perspective*. Springfield, IL: Charles C Thomas.

Williams, P. (1997, Fall). Police and mediation: Win-win partnership. *Oregon Police Chief*, pp. 24-26.

Willis, C. L., & Wells, R. H. (1988). The police and child abuse: An analysis of police decisions to report illegal behavior. *Criminology, 26*, 695-714.

Willmer, M. A. P. (1970). *Crime and information theory*. Edinburgh: University Press.

Wilson v. Arkansas, 515 U.S. 927 (1995).

Wilson, B. (1996). The war on drugs: Evening the odds through use of the airport drug courier profile. *Boston Public Interest Law Journal, 6*, 203-242.

Wilson, J. (2001, October). Truth, lies and polygraphs. *Popular Mechanics, 178*, 42.

Wilson, J. Q. (1973). *Varieties of police behavior*. New York: Atheneum.

Wilson, J. Q. (1975). *Thinking about crime*. New York: Basic Books.

Wilson, J. Q., & Kelling, G. L. (1982, March). Broken windows: The police and neighborhood safety. *Atlantic Monthly*, pp. 29-38.

Wilson v. Layne, 119 S.Ct. 1692 (1999).

Withrow v. Williams, 507 U.S. 680 (1993).

Wolf v. Colorado, 338 U.S. 25 (1949).

Wolfgang, M. E. (1958). *Patterns in criminal homicide*. Oxford, UK: Oxford University Press.

Wood, D. (1998). Refuge for endangered witnesses. *Christian Science Monitor, 90*, 1.

Wood, J., & Garven, S. (2000). How sexual abuse interviews go astray: Implications for prosecutors, police, and child protection services. *Child Maltreatment, 5*(2), 109-118.

Worden, R. E. (1995). The "causes" of police brutality. In W. A. Geller & H. Toch (Eds.), *And justice for all: A national agenda for understanding and controlling police abuse of force*. Washington, DC: Police Executive Research Forum.

Wright, M., & Galaway, B. (Eds.). (1989). Mediation and criminal justice: Victims, offenders and community. London: Sage.

http://www.americanbailcoalition.com
http://www.aphf.org
http://www.ascld.org/accreditation.html
http://www.asqde.org/
http://www.bounty-hunter.net/home.htm
http://www.census.gov
http://www.childrensdefense.org
http://www.ci.ftlaud.fl.us/police/crim_inv.html#sv
http://www.ci.nyc.ny.us.html/doc/html/esu.html
http://www.ci.nyc.ny.us/html/nypd/html/pct/esu.html
http://www.cophealth.com/
http://www.csiss.org/learning_resources/content/good_sa/
http://www.eskimo.com/~jbm/ballistics/cdkd.html
http://www.fbi.gov/hq/cjisd/ncic.htm
http://www.firearmsid.com/A_distanceExams.htm
http://www.forgottenheroes-lema.org

http://www.genome.gov/Pages/Education/Kit/main.cfm
http://www.grandlodgefop.org/lodges/index.html
http://www.iadlest.org
http://www.icpc4cops.org
http://www.ignet.gov/
http://www.inspectorsgeneral.org/
http://www.ipa-usa.org/right.htm
http://www.jjay.cuny.edu/PoliceStudies/
http://www.jrsa.org/ibrrc
http://www.laspd.com/home
http://www.learning-for-life.org/exploring/lawenforcement
http://www.lep.gov
http://www.madd.org/home/
http://www.maineemeraldsociety.8m.com/about.html
http://www.ncpolice.org/frat.htm
http://www.nena.org
http://www.nhtsa.dot.gov/people/injury/alcohol/
http://www.nhtsa.dot.gov/people/injury/enforce/professionalism/during.html
http://www.nleomf.com
http://www.nycpolicemuseum.org
http://www.ojp.usdoj.gov/nij/maps/
http://www.phoenixmasonry.org/masonicmuseum/fraternalism/fraternal_order_of_police.htm
http://www.portofsandiego.org/sandiego_sdhp
http://www.rcdaoffice.org/overview.htm#SecCrimesSpecialVictims Bureau
http://www.stopimpaireddriving.org/
http://www.usdoj.gov:80/crt/cor/lep
http://www.vbgov.com/dept/police/division/invest/detective/0,1701,10619,00.html

Yarborough v. Alvarado, 2004 U. S. LEXIS 3843; 124 S.Ct. 2140 (2004).

Yeschike, C. L. (1993). *Interviewing: A forensic guide to interrogation* (2nd ed.). Springfield, IL: Charles C Thomas.

http://yonkerspd.com/esu.htm

Young, M. (1991). *An inside job*. Oxford, UK: Oxford University Press.

Young v. United States, 481 U.S. 787, 814 (1987).

Zaret, M. (1991). An electronic smog is threatening our police. *Law Enforcement News, 17*(331).

Zaret, M. (1992). The smoking gun in the radar-cancer controversy. *Law Enforcement News, 18*(365).

Zhang, S., & Benson, T. (1997). Cost-effectiveness and officer morale of a personally assigned patrol vehicle program: A comparative analysis. *Policing, 20*(4), 749-765.

Zhao, J. (1996). *Why police organizations change: A study of community-oriented policing*. Washington, DC: PERF.

Zhao, J., He, N., & Lovrich, N. (2002). Predicting five dimensions of police officer stress: Looking more deeply into organizational settings for sources of police stress. *Police Quarterly, 5*, 43-62.

Zimring, F. E., & Hawkins, G. (1999). *Crime is not the problem: Lethal violence in America*. New York: Oxford University Press.

Zulawski, D. E., & Wicklander, D. E. (1992). *Practical aspects of interview and interrogation*. New York: Elsevier.

# Appendix

*Law Enforcement News*

15 Years in Review (1989–2003)

*Marie Simonetti Rosen*

# 1989 IN REVIEW

# New Players in the Safety Game, New Challenges for Police

With its record-breaking levels of violence and a commensurate increase of concern on the part of the public, the media and government at all levels—in short, on the part of just about every American—1989 can stand on its own in the catalog of years, yet it is impossible to set aside the fact that the year ends a decade of dramatic change for law enforcement and begins a decade of dramatic challenges. Whether viewed as a year in isolation or as the culmination of a decade, 1989 bore witness to portentous changes in the role of the police in the overall production of public safety.

Ten years ago, the police were seen as the authority on crime. They were the experts. In many respects the profession thought of itself as having a monopoly on safety and public order. Over the past ten years, however, the field has gradually acknowledged that it cannot shoulder this responsibility alone, and other segments of society have started to participate in crime prevention and protection. Perhaps the single most significant manifestation of this change in 1989 came with the official entry of the military into the drug war.

## THE IRONY OF MILITARY INVOLVEMENT

There is a certain irony to the notion that, at a time when police departments are increasingly moving away from the military model of management, branches of the military have joined with local, state and Federal law enforcement officers, who to date have been the only line of defense on the nation's streets and borders. In at least 48 states and the District of Columbia, the National Guard was called upon to provide radar and air surveillance, eradicate domestic marijuana crops, and assist the Customs Service with cargo checks at border crossings and airports. Whether helping Washington, D.C., police with searches or getting involved with police efforts against gangs and illegal drugs, as was

reported in Portland, Ore., thus far Guard units have worked under the direction of local and Federal law enforcement agencies. As the year progressed, however, the temptation to change that picture appeared to be growing. The Miami chapter of the NAACP had requested the involvement of the Guard in patrol duties, citing unsubstantiated fears of a "look-the-other-way" response from police protesting the conviction of a fellow officer for the shooting of a civilian. In New York and Detroit, local elected officials called for deployment of the Guard to address street-level drug dealing in their high-crime neighborhoods. San Francisco considered calling in the Guard to free police for patrol duties as a result of increasing gang violence. Army doctors in Los Angeles received their training by working in inner-city hospitals on gunshot wounds incurred in gang wars. As the year ended, the contingent of 50 Marines assigned to assist the Border Patrol exchanged fire with drug smugglers for the first time.

With lobbying efforts already underway in Washington to allocate the so-called "peace dividend"—as much as $10 billion by some reports—the military's entry into the war on drugs comes at an opportune time for the armed forces to justify retaining certain resources—including high tech, big-ticket items—by redeploying.

Congressional officials are already on record when it comes to the drug war and the military. Said one committee chairman, "With all the billions spent on the military, if they can't help us, then we don't need them." Policing in America has traditionally been decentralized—fragmented, some would say—and while the debate on consolidation of small departments ebbs and flows on the waves of demographics and politics, local police authority has remained part of the American bedrock. Could the use of the National Guard be seen as a dent in the armor of local law enforcement control? Regardless of the answer, the future holds increased interaction between the military and law enforcement.

## FEAR, VIOLENCE STALK THE STREETS

For local communities, the battlegrounds of the drug war, the year was fearful at best and violent at worse. One poll published in October indicated that more than 70 percent of Americans feared becoming a victim of drug-related violence. Media reports in five U.S. cities compared sections of those cities to Beirut on the basis of having reached a stage of "civil insurrection." With increasing frequency in 1989, the community took matters into hand. In Berkeley tenants found a way to evict drug dealers through legal proceedings in small claims courts. In some of the nation's public housing developments, the U.S. Department of Housing and Urban Development stepped in with streamlined eviction procedures and help from the U.S. Marshals Service to eject drug dealers. Communities formed patrols, they engaged in activities ranging from prayer vigils to burning down crack houses. Nor was extreme action limited to residential properties; it was also to be found in the schools. The increase in handguns carried by adolescents prompted six of the ten largest school districts in the country to make use of metal detectors. Drug-free zones were created around schools to permit higher penalties for drug offenses. And, to be sure, it took the murder of five schoolchildren and the wounding of numerous others in Stockton, Calif., to rivet public attention on the issue of assault rifles.

But whether or not one lived in a high-crime area, the media brought the crime issue, particularly drug-related crime, into almost every household on a daily basis, dramatically increasing the regular coverage of criminal justice issues. Print and broadcast media alike not only expanded their news coverage, but added expanded feature stories on the problems of drugs and crime. For television, law enforcement issues also ranked high on the list of prime-time entertainment formats. From controversial "fact-based" dramas of particularly heinous crimes, to "realistic" police shows, television has moved to capitalize on Americans' growing fear of crime. Syndicated shows like "America's Most Wanted" and "Unsolved Mysteries" have joined local Crime Stopper shows in providing a forum for community involvement in apprehending offenders, while at the same time proving a profitable cog in the entertainment machinery.

## FOR SOME, CRIME IS GOOD FOR BUSINESS

Private-sector endeavors against crime are increasing as well, with evidence of dramatic growth in the number of persons employed in private security. By some estimates, more than 1.2 million Americans were employed in the private security field in 1989—1.6 percent of the workforce. (Sworn officers and civilians in state and local police agencies are estimated to number about 758,000.) While labor experts express concern over the productivity lag that such employees create—by adding to the cost of products without aiding in their production—police experts fear that an unequal ability to purchase protection creates unequal protection. Civil libertarians, for their part, point to some small

private companies whose marketing pitches boast that they do not operate under the same legal restraints as the police. With the 1989 Supreme Court decision, drug-testing companies are quickly becoming a growth industry. Prison construction industries are booming. From proliferating locks and alarms, to high-fashion bulletproof clothing, to the more than 4 million firearms produced in 1989 alone, private industries are growing up and prospering on public fear and high crime rates.

[Even public-sector employment has prospered. Helped by increases in correctional jobs, more Americans are said to be employed by government than at any other time in the nation's history. Over the past six years, the Justice Department experienced the highest level of staff increases of any Federal agency—some 30 percent. (The Department of Education, meanwhile, experienced a 30-percent decrease in manpower.)]

The economic dimensions of crime and criminal justice received more attention in 1989. Surpluses in several branches of the Federal Reserve Bank were attributed to drug-related proceeds. Compared to 1988, public safety costs rose by an average of nearly 33 percent in the country's 50 largest cities and by 14 percent for the states. For police departments nationwide, new sources of funding were found in the assets seized from record-breaking drug busts. The forfeited assets were applied to the luxury items that police departments, particularly those in tight financial straits, cannot readily afford, from four-color slick departmental magazines to helicopters. All of these forfeited assets, and the means by which they are obtained, are making some police officials uneasy. Although taking the property and money away from criminals is widely regarded as a worthwhile endeavor that has the added benefit of promoting interagency cooperation, local law enforcement initiatives are being influenced more and more by revenue-raising rather than by community needs like foot patrol. Some fear that police agencies are in danger of having a monkey on their backs: an addiction to drug money.

While the Federal Government concerns itself with the economic dependency of Latin American countries on illegal drugs, it is ignoring the economic dependencies that are emerging under its own doorstep. The combination of a redeployed military, the volume of resources devoted to public and private security, regional economies bolstered by laundered drug money and the growing reliance of law enforcement on forfeited assets to supplement dwindling budgets risks creating a vicious cycle of social and economic dependency on crime. A paraphrasing of President Eisenhower's one-time admonition regarding the military may be apt: Beware the growing public safety-industrial complex.

## THE 24-HOUR-A-DAY PUBLIC OPINION POLL

Now that law enforcement has been joined by the community, the private sector and the military, why aren't things getting better? Some experts are of the opinion that more coordination is needed, but at what level and under whose direction are questions that remain unanswered. A more immediate issue for law enforcement, however, is the overall allocation of resources now that these other segments of society are engaging in public safety work, because despite the growing number of participants in public safety and the recognition that law enforcement alone cannot solve the crime problem, the public still wants a greater police presence. To that end, 1989 was a year of enormous pressure to put more police on the street. In recognition of this increased pressure, departments continually grappled with juggling calls for service versus high-pressure anti-crime tactics versus foot patrol. For that matter 1989 found law enforcement executives re-examining the question of what really constitutes essential services.

There is probably no escaping the issue of 911 when essential services are mentioned. In the past, police experts have thought of calls for service as "the tail wagging the dog," and yet the information that can be gleaned from these calls can provide a deep perspective into the demographics and needs of a neighborhood. To be sure, analyses of 911 calls placed in the hands of community members and problem-oriented police officers could serve as valuable tools for ascertaining the needs of those in the community who do not participate in civic activities. In essence, calls for service are an ongoing opinion poll of what the community wants and needs. Irrespective of police feelings about calls for service, the fact remains that the public likes 911. And why shouldn't they? It provides 24-hour access to local government that the public cannot get through other means. While the 1980's saw police departments assessing, ranking and redirecting their calls for service, the future will demand the speedy analysis and dissemination of information from the calls as a priority in itself.

In the face of escalating crime, however, many departments had to redirect personnel in order to handle the increased load of calls for service and to staff the high-pressure approaches that became popular around 1987 and 1988. These tactics were successful insofar as providing relief, if only temporarily, for crime-ridden neighborhoods, but they resulted in paralyzed local courts and prisons. The revolving door speeded up. While some experts argued that tough punishment for first offenders was a deterrent, others argued that the system cannot even hold all the violent repeat offenders. And clearly, the police were being asked to deal with increasingly violent criminals whose fear of the legal system was questionable at best. To enhance visibility, police departments used a variety of means, some traditional, some innovative.

Efforts were made in Dallas and Cleveland to implement one-officer patrols. Mandatory overtime was tried in Washington, D.C. The nation's capital also tried putting supervisory or desk-bound personnel back on the streets, as did Philadelphia. In Houston, a police shooting was attributed to the reassignment of an officer from desk duty to street patrol. Video arraignment proved successful in helping Port Authority of New York police officers get back to patrol more quickly. Philadelphia started a mobile precinct. In Fort Myers, Fla., forfeited assets were used to hire retired officers for school-based anti-drug programs, thus freeing full-time officers for patrol work.

## POLICE RECRUITMENT IN THE NEW AGE

When it comes to increasing police visibility, however, hiring new officers remained the most straightforward approach. Such an approach will no doubt be a temptation for many departments in the immediate future, notwithstanding the pitfalls of hasty recruitment, as has been demonstrated by Miami in recent years. The need to recruit will be exacerbated by the retirement of baby-boom police officers who were hired in the middle to late 1960's and will soon have put in their 20 or 25 years. For those departments with the fiscal luxury to hire, the recruitment pool will require careful scrutiny.

The labor market will contain a significant portion of the population who cannot read. It has been reported that 1 of 5 adults are functionally illiterate (although many of them have high school diplomas). Thirty-eight percent of the 118 companies examined in one private-sector survey asserted that high school graduates were not prepared for the world of work. In the face of increasingly complex police work, and spurred perhaps by low levels of literacy even among high school graduates, more and more departments are adopting college requirements either for entry or as part of promotion. With 1989 seeing the lowest jobless rate in 15 years, employment analysts predict that the current low unemployment rate is a sign of labor shortages in the future.

At a time when police recruitment efforts will be more complicated than ever, the changing role of the armed forces will have its effect. With military bases closing down both here and abroad, the troops will be coming home. Reports issued last spring estimated that as many as 1.5 million G.I.'s will be discharged in the next 10 years. They will be armed with higher educational benefits and they will need jobs. Not since what some police chiefs have called the good old days of military disciplined recruits in the early 1970's has the law enforcement profession had access to such an employment pool. It is rather ironic that, at a time when the military model of policing is more diluted than ever, the profession will likely be drawing its future recruits from military trained personnel. Yet for many law enforcement administrators this will be a blessing, since departments that took cuts in the mid-to-late 70's and rehired in the late 80's have reported declining levels of maturity and a resulting increase in officer misconduct.

For the profession, the last 10 years have been nothing less than a metamorphosis. The beginning of the decade saw most of the country's police departments viewing themselves purely as law enforcers—as separate from the community. They reacted to crime. By the end of the decade, earlier experiments in team policing turned into proactive community-oriented policing. What began as crime prevention has turned into problem-oriented policing. Victims' rights advocates emerged as a political force. Science and technology reshaped evidence-gathering, identification and communication. Computerization allowed departments to gather and analyze information as never before. National broad-based research efforts became more focused and localized. Along the way, the profession saw the growing acceptance of national accreditation, a changing workforce with the increased representation of minorities and women and growing higher levels of education. The decade witnessed declining acceptability of the use of force, but a growing public outcry for police intervention. While drugs have always influenced the crime rate, the types of drugs that grew in popularity in the mid-to-late 80's—those like crack and crank—had the additional disadvantage of producing staggering amounts of illegal profits and accelerated levels of violence, a phenomenon that has contributed to the crisis that is engulfing the criminal justice system. Yet for all the professional changes that have occurred over the decade, public safety continues to decline and the decade ended as it began, with record-breaking levels of crime. Literally and figuratively, the 80's went out with a bang.

## MAINTAINING POLICING'S LEADERSHIP ROLE

The decade ahead, meanwhile, will no doubt see changes in the field of law enforcement, particularly in the role it will play. Whether or not police will maintain a position of leadership in the area of public safety will very much depend on the decisions made in the immediate future to handle the demographic changes that are largely outside the realm of police control. The United States is going through a spreading-out process. Since 1986 the rural and suburban populations are growing more rapidly than the urban population. The urban village is taking hold from Los Angeles to New York as the economy moves from manufacturing to service-based industries. As this trend continues, the public safety needs of these evolving and growing communities could overwhelm existing levels of police resources. With crime going up in small communities, interagency task forces are springing up at the state, county and local levels. At present 80 percent of America's police departments have less than 10 sworn officers. In the future, police observers predict somewhat larger departments and a mix of county policing with local enforcement.

Another immediate socioeconomic problem police will have to contend with is the effect of a widening income gap. Although 1989 saw some of the lowest levels of unemployment in recent memory, the income disparity is greater now than at any time in the past 42 years, with 32 million people living below the poverty level. In addition, immigration policies will influence the communities police will serve, particularly in California, New York, Florida, Massachusetts and Texas. Ethnic and racial population shifts will occur, with minorities becoming majorities in some localities and the likelihood increasing for interethnic competition for a piece of the American dream. Police futurists and marketing experts alike predict an age of activism, anger and urban decay. For the law enforcement field, that translates to a decade of turbulence. In the face of growing social problems and static or shrinking budgets, the police profession will have to muster all available resolve and apply the lessons learned amid civic turmoil from the 1960's onward if it is to withstand a challenge to its leadership role in the production of public safety.

Source: From *Law Enforcement News*, January 31, 1990, Vol. XV, No. 307.

# 1990 IN REVIEW

# Amid Gloom, Hunkering Down

War is not only hell—it can also be frightfully costly. Consider one recent conflict: At least 20,000 civilians killed, with many thousands more wounded; more than 600,000 people confronted by guns in enemy hands; hundreds of front-line troops killed or wounded; more than $60 billion spent.

This is not the war in the Persian Gulf; it was the war being waged against crime on the streets of America in 1990. The damage assessments coming in from the front clearly show that, unlike the war in the Gulf, America is losing the war on crime.

By the summer of 1990, the year was already proving to be one of the deadliest in recent memory. Homicide records were being broken in cities, suburbs and rural communities. Even the nation's park and wilderness lands witnessed dramatic increases in criminal activity. Despite reports—frequently challenged—that drug use was declining, crime soared. One explanation is a criminological convergence—the deadly synergism of the "baby boomerang" generation committing crimes at earlier ages, a declining economy characterized by an increase in joblessness, depressed public spirits, increased racial tensions, and an abundance of easily obtained firearms.

In a nutshell, said one observer, 1990 saw an America that was "gloomy, less rich, less safe, and less certain of the future."

## HUNKERING DOWN

To make matters worse for law enforcement, the historically severe crime wave was compounded by unprecedented budget cuts. The profession's reaction to these conditions can best be described as "hunkering down," as budget cuts and increased workloads became the two preoccupations of the year. While the nation's economy was spinning into decline, the ranks of law enforcement underwent a general shrinkage: Attrition increased as "baby-boom" officers retired in growing numbers, and departments found themselves generally unable to get the funds to maintain personnel levels. To a great extent, small counties lost proportionately larger numbers of officers, but cities also felt the decline. The Chicago Police Department, for one, fell to its lowest sworn strength in 20 years as a result of attrition, hiring freezes, and budget cuts. The attrition-versus-hiring standoff in many jurisdictions is not likely to improve significantly into the early 90's.

Law enforcement agencies of all sizes struggled to accommodate budget reductions by cutting services, and the ways in which police and sheriffs' departments responded were as different as the localities they served. Some police agencies stopped having officers testify in court on minor traffic tickets; sold off unaffordable equipment such as aircraft; ordered officers to gas up and maintain their own patrol cars; or transferred large numbers of sworn personnel from desk or plainclothes jobs back to the streets. Illegal aliens arrested in one Kansas county were routinely dropped off across the border in the next county because of a lack of prosecutorial resources. Police in San Diego "unarrested" indigents who needed medical attention and left them in hospitals to relieve the city from picking up the tab for medical expenses. And, to be sure, more than a few police departments shifted certain responsibilities to other public agencies.

## SPEND LESS OR MAKE MORE

In balancing a budget, of course, the alternative to cutting expenses is to bring in more money, and again the approaches were many and diverse. In one particularly drastic move, California police departments were told that they will be charged as much as $200 per prisoner when booking arrestees into county correctional facilities. As a result, some departments in that state have refused to book all but the most serious felons. Police in Chicago began charging lawyers a fee for responding to subpoenas. Where fines or fees were increased, many law enforcement agencies found themselves in the precarious position of having to emphasize activities that raise funds—often to the dismay of communities that desperately wanted more foot patrol.

Significantly, in cities ranging in size from Jackson City, Mo., to New York City, tax increases were proposed that were specifically earmarked for crime-fighting purposes, and law enforcement officials in some cases found themselves in the delicate role of political lobbyist. Deputy sheriffs in Mohave County, Ariz., for example, went door to door to rally public support for a budget override that would permit new hiring for the department. The catch, however, is that when taxpayers are told to go deeper into their pockets with the promise of increased public safety, they will expect something for their money. In areas where increased taxes are set aside exclusively for law enforcement agencies, police administrators would do well to give some thought to how to demonstrate to the public that their money has been well spent. The expanding use of public safety-specific taxes will no doubt require an accounting in years ahead.

## WHITHER COMMUNITY-
## ORIENTED POLICING?

Citizens paying more for increased public safety are as likely as not to expect increased police presence in their neighborhoods. For a growing number of police departments, this translates into community-oriented policing. For as popular as COP is, however, it also has a small but vocal cadre of critics and skeptics. There are those who claim that although it is a laudable philosophy, it is difficult to implement in definable and measurable practices, especially on a large scale. Others feel that there are definitional problems. Who is the community and who represents it? In New York, where community-oriented policing is now the official guiding principle, the city's layered and diverse neighborhoods almost defy community definition. There is also a growing professional concern that community leaders could be misled into believing that they alone will determine the agenda for the police. More importantly to some, the public is being led to believe that crime will go down as a result of community-oriented policing programs. Another, more tangible criticism is that the approach is expensive, and at a time of recession such talk invites intensified scrutiny—and certainly community-oriented policing is too new, in relative terms, to have demonstrated that it can bring about meaningful reductions in violent crime.

Within the context of community-oriented policing, and in light of increased budget scrutiny, officer productivity measures will become ever more critical in the near future.

Traditionally, police departments have been centralized organizations with strict pyramidal structures. Employee advancement has been a vertical ladder climbed by a combination of testing, number of arrests and personal contacts. Eventually the ladder leads to a desk. Just how the field adapts to accommodate a community-oriented approach, with its need for decentralization, without changing its productivity measures will be an important challenge. As importantly, how can patrol work be made more desirable for the officer, many of whom aspire to a desk assignment within their first weeks on the job? As one researcher put it: "We need to set up a system for police departments whereby officers can grow in income, status and perhaps even authority while they are actually doing police work."

## PRESSING THEIR SUITS

But measuring productivity isn't the only personnel issue of topical concern to the profession. Affirmative action practices, in some departments now 20 years old, continued to be challenged by all sides. A decade ago, most of the lawsuits were brought by minority officers; now white officers are claiming reverse discrimination in promotional matters. There is probably no more highly competitive aspect of the job than promotional testing, where police careers can be made or broken on the basis of one point. For many departments, the method used to achieve departmental affirmative-action goals is to put less emphasis on strict numerical scores and, in effect, create two separate lists. To many officers, these departmental "goals" are nothing more than semantically disguised "quotas," and a trail of court cases attests to their discontent. In Dallas, for the fourth time since 1988, white lieutenants filed a suit claiming that they were passed over for promotion in favor of black and Hispanic candidates who were lower on the list. White sergeants in Grand Rapids, Mich., filed a $7.5-million lawsuit for discrimination in promotions. In Dayton, Ohio, the FOP brought a reverse-discrimination case on behalf of two white officers who were denied promotion to sergeant. In St. Paul, Minn., the Chief made a videotaped roll-call message for his officers to reassure them that promotions were not rigged in favor of minorities.

## TACTICS AND SANCTIONS

On the front lines, police continue to use high-pressure tactics and a variety of problem-oriented techniques to control crime while responding to the never-ending calls for service. The year saw increased attention placed on the nation's highways and housing projects. Numerous jurisdictions increased DWI penalties and enforcement efforts. Thirteen states are testing a new device to measure alcohol levels. Video cameras are becoming popular additions to patrol cars (in some cases provided to economically strapped departments by insurance companies). In jurisdiction after jurisdiction, drivers licenses are being seized or revoked for those who refuse to take or who fail a breath-alcohol test. The cars of repeat offenders are being confiscated or emblazoned with special license plates. And the U.S. Supreme Court gave its official blessing to sobriety checkpoints, a practice that had become popular in the late 1980's.

In the area of criminal sanctions, 1990 saw a resurgence in the age-old practices of public humilation, ostracism and banishment. The names and offenses of wrongdoers in some localities are now published in newspapers—often becoming popular reading material. In Miami Beach, employers may be notified of an employee's arrest on drug charges. Landlords and tenant groups in some areas have been granted access to criminal records in an effort to reduce crime in housing projects by keeping out undesirables. Pilot programs have begun to deny Federal benefits to drug offenders. Proponents of such practices hope they will provide punishment without consuming valuable jail space. For civil libertarians, it is a nightmare.

And what of 1991? At least in part, the forecast would seem to be bad news, good news and then more bad news. The bad news: Unemployment may grow to 7 percent, bringing with it a host of social ills that affect police work. The good news: Increasing unemployment, coupled with the new Police Recruitment and Education Program, will enable law enforcement agencies to be more competitive and selective when recruiting. [See story, Page 1.] The second dose of bad news: Most localities will not have the money in their budgets to hire.

## POLICING A CHANGING LANDSCAPE

The landscape that police face will change. For starters, the median age of the population continues to rise. The continuing population shift away from the country's older cities, particularly in the Northeast, to the Sun Belt and to suburbs in general, will have many departments recalculating their officer/population ratios. Immigration patterns will change from Asian and Latin American countries to European countries. And, in light of reports that the income gap is growing, with the total income of the top 1 percent of the population equaling that of the bottom 40 percent, it appears law enforcement will find itself policing a poorer population as well.

From January until August of last year, the public's attention was directed toward crime and the economy—and thence will it return when the war in the Persian Gulf is over. In fact, it may be argued that the onset of trouble in the Middle East turned around the sense of gloom that pervaded the public's mood for much of last year, by focusing attention away from weighty social and economic ills at home. It remains to be seen whether the zeal and sense of purpose accompanying U.S. actions in the Gulf will ultimately be translatable to domestic issues, and whether America will discover a way to police itself with the kind of success that characterizes recent efforts at playing "global policeman."

Source: From *Law Enforcement News,* Jan. 15/31, 1991, Vol. XVII, No. 329.

# 1991 IN REVIEW

## Graphic Images Paint a None-Too-Pretty Picture

More than most years, 1991 lent itself to graphic video images. It began with the pictures of the Persian Gulf war in scenes that bore a striking if artificially benign resemblance to fireworks and video games. As gripping as those images were, though, the pictures from America's streets were far more terrifying. There was an officer shot and killed during a traffic stop in Nacogdoches, Tex., as his dashboard-mounted camera recorded the event. In Detroit, a mob engaged in a bias-motivated beating. In New York City, a gang of teenagers videotaped themselves as they beat a man with a hammer, In Chattanooga, Tenn., a hidden video camera recorded a baby-sitter beating a child.

While these pictures visually demonstrate growing levels of violence in this country, the video that had the greatest influence on law enforcement in 1991 was that of the beating of Rodney King by Los Angeles police officers. The amateur videotape, played over and over on TV news programs, sent a shock wave through law enforcement that touched all levels. Police departments from Hawaii to Maine reviewed use-of-force policies and modified or expanded training. Officers were made to watch the tape as an example of what not to do. Many localities considered— or reconsidered—civilian review. Some departments devised computerized systems to keep closer track of complaints against officers. After March 3, the use of force was scrutinized in a way unlike anything one has seen in more than a decade. Even the Justice Department got caught up in the furor and promised to conduct a national study of police brutality.

More than simply contributing to growing levels of public anxiety about crime, these home videos of gratuitous violence also demonstrated the evolving nature of surveillance. No longer is it dominated by the criminal justice system and private investigators. As one legal scholar put it, "Big Brother is now your neighbor." Such a development does not come problem-free, however. Among lawyers there is palpable concern about such videos and their impact on individual privacy rights and pretrial publicity. Worried public-policy analysts, for their part, question whether local officials are responding to the get-tough wishes of constituents by relying more and more on surveillance as a cheaper alternative to increasing police and other criminal justice services. In Newark, N.J., for example, 24-hour camera surveillance was installed in a two-square-mile section of the city—an action that just a few years ago would have seemed more at home in an Iron Curtain country. But as the public mood becomes increasingly fearful and frustrated, some observers see signs of an attitude of resigned acceptance with respect to such surveillance efforts.

## CRIME AND POLITICS

While the national agenda turned from the war to domestic economic woes in 1991, on the local level the spotlight continued to focus on crime. Many political careers across the country were made or broken on the basis of public safety issues. In cities such as San Francisco, Houston, Indianapolis, Philadelphia, Columbus, Ohio, and Savannah, Ga., citizens cast their vote on the basis of real or perceived levels of danger. Strikingly, in comparison to previous election years that had an emphasis on crime, a number of winning candidates emerged from the criminal justice ranks. Newly elected mayors and county managers came from such backgrounds as that of police chief in San Francisco, a county prosecutor in Indianapolis, a former district attorney in Philadelphia, a police sergeant in Brockton, Mass., and a former FBI agent in Suffolk County, N.Y. As public concern about crime continues to mount, there would seem to be a growing role in politics for criminal justice professionals.

Voters spoke their minds in other ways as well, as referendums capped a year that brought numerous pieces of local and state legislation concerning criminal justice issues. Voters cast their ballots in favor of increased victims rights in New Jersey, bonds for new jails and drug centers in Texas, taxes for 911 in Washington, and holding gun makers and dealers in Washington, D.C., liable for damages and injuries that firearms cause. In the meantime, and much to law enforcement's dismay, 1991 was a year without national crime legislation, as Congress failed to pass its omnibus crime bill. In an eleventh-hour vote, senators and representatives found themselves unable to reconcile differences about the life-and-death provisions of the legislative package, notably gun control and habeas corpus.

## COMMUNITY-ORIENTED POLICING AND POLITICAL CORRECTNESS

At one time, community-oriented policing came into a department at the instigation of a progressive police chief. Aided by a handful of researchers, the department would conduct a pilot test, usually, but not always, tied to a specific geographic area. If the community and the police were satisfied, and if budget considerations allowed, community-oriented policing would be expanded to include a larger segment of the department and the city. Inevitably, as community-oriented policing grew in popularity and use, questions arose: Just who is "the community," and who represents it? Can COP and its decentralized, "bottoms-up" style, fit into policing's tradition-bound, heavily hierarchical structure? What is the happy medium between officer discretion and accountability? How does one balance COP with calls for service? Will it create a potentially dangerous division within a department, where one group of officers answers calls for service while another makes acquaintances? Such questions were openly discussed throughout the law enforcement and academic communities, with believers, skeptics and non-believers alike all engaged in the debate. That is how it used to be.

COP has now entered the political arena. These days, one frequently finds community-oriented policing recommended by management consultants hired by a mayor. In the past year, outside consultants hired to analyze police departments in such cities as Milwaukee, Chicago, Los Angeles and Boston urged implementation of a community-oriented policing approach. Just how COP will fare with the vagaries of electoral politics remains to be seen. Bridled by political influence, some observers fear, COP will be used to create unrealistic public expectations. One researcher, a long-time believer in COP, observed, "Pretty soon they'll be saying it cures the common cold." There are also concerns that COP will become primarily a lip-service approach for the sake of public relations, and its longevity

(if not impact) will be limited to the term of office of a mayor or police chief.

The evolution of COP is characterized by more than simply the way in which it is introduced into a community; the nature of debate about the concept has also changed. The issues that are raised now concern primarily cost and evaluation. Community-oriented policing still has its believers, skeptics and non-believers, but observers say with increasing frequency that it is becoming politically incorrect to question the viability or implementation of COP in some jurisdictions.

## YOUTHFUL OFFENDERS

A 14-year-old shot a cop. A 12-year-old shot a taxi driver. A 15-year-old tried to poison another child. A 10-year-old was arrested for a second-offense armed robbery (this time for putting a .38 to an 8-year-old's head while demanding a yo-yo). Five teenagers (two of them 14) gang-raped and shot a woman in the presence of her four children. An 18- and a 15-year-old were charged with killing a sheriff's deputy while he was writing out a report on their alleged shoplifting. While these cases are just a handful of the 2.3 million arrests for serious crime, they and many more like them demonstrate the growing concern over juvenile crime. Law enforcement officials in some jurisdictions estimate that as many as 40 percent of those arrested for serious crime are juveniles. Twenty percent of high school students regularly carry weapons, according to the Federal Centers for Disease Control. (One can only wonder at how high the number would be if the estimate included dropouts.) Figures such as these have given rise to a reexamination of juvenile justice in many areas around the country. Of particular focus was the tracking of criminal records and the circumstances under which juveniles should be prosecuted as adults. The method most used in 1991 for controlling youth crime, however, was the imposition of a curfew. In numerous localities large and small, curfews were adopted in response to public fear. While some local officials felt that curfews complemented and reinforced parental initiatives, civil libertarians, along with some law enforcement officials, criticized such action for diminishing civil rights with little impact on safety.

The bottom line, in the opinion of one researcher, is that as long as youthful offenders perceive there to be little or no risk of punishment, the crime rate in the United States will continue to go up. His research indicates that this perception differs among groups and is influenced by a young person's friends, peers and family. When it is observed that criminal behavior goes unpunished, young people expect that they too can get away with crime. The frightening conclusion of this research is that not only is the overburdened, "revolving-door" criminal justice system not helping to reduce crime, it is actually contributing to an increase in crime.

## CRIMES, CLEARANCES AND CUTS

Law enforcement practitioners did not need to wait for national crime statistics to be released in order to know that violence was increasing. Local reports, whether from both urban or rural areas, showed that 1991 was yet another year of matching or breaking murder records, with an end-of-year estimate of 24,000 nationwide. But as the number of homicides continued to mount, the clearance rate has dropped significantly, from 86 percent in 1970 to 68 percent in 1989. Experts offer a smorgasbord of reasons to explain the decline: an overall increase in the number of homicides with a growing level of stranger-to-stranger violence; the mobility of career criminals; few and/or fearful witnesses; increased availability of high-powered weapons; skeptical, increasingly hard-to-convince juries, and a shortage of investigative personnel (the latter a problem that will not be alleviated any time soon).

In 1990, police departments cut muscle; in 1991 they cut bone. Few departments went unscathed by the budget ax. Budgetary coping methods used in 1990, such as redeployment of personnel and imposition of user fees, gave way in 1991 to layoffs, furloughs, givebacks, deferred hiring, consolidations and mergers. A growing number of one-person departments simply disappeared. In departments large and small, the ranks of sworn officers dwindled. Nearly every part of the country was hit in some way. Some departments turned to the ranks of reserves and auxiliaries; sometimes the slack was picked up by private security. More often than not, services simply diminished. While the recession continues, these cuts will come at a time when demand for police service is dramatically increasing.

## SUPPLY AND DEMAND

In the last national election, the Willie Horton gambit enabled the Republicans to make the crime issue—or, more accurately, fear of crime—a key campaign theme. The 1992 campaign, at least on a national level, will be dominated by economic issues. At best, crime will be relegated to a back seat. Recent opinion polls suggest that crime and drugs are no better than halfway up the list of leading public concerns. That's not to say that the economic situation, and policies adopted to deal with it, won't affect law enforcement. Rising unemployment will have a two-pronged impact on policing. It will require that more services be directed to hard-hit areas, and at the same time it will diminish the tax base, the source of police funding. (The only positive effect one may see in the continuing recession is that it may lead to lower attrition rates due to retirement.) High unemployment will also exacerbate the problem of homelessness in America, which reportedly rose by 7 percent in major cities last year. Tighter public-sector budgets have also taken a toll on the mental-health care system, and some officials are saying that as many as one-third of the homeless are mentally ill.

Police will find themselves responding to significantly greater numbers of emergency calls in 1992. Diminished resources, increased societal violence, and a spillover effect from unabated social problems will force law enforcement to make tough choices in setting priorities. These problems, individually or in combination, are by no means new to policing. What is different is that the current demand for police services far outstrips the ability of police to supply such services. This dire imbalance, coupled with gloom about the economy and continued fears for one's safety, have given rise to a trend already spotted and labeled by marketing forecasters: the "Armored Cocoon." It is marked by an increased in gun ownership among women and growth opportunities in so-called "paranoia industries."

Growth opportunities in the private sector are of little benefit to the police in this instance. While such growth opportunities point out the importance that the public attaches to crime and safety concerns, they also demonstrate a disturbing propensity to find solutions that do not involved public-sector law enforcement. Cocoons, armored or otherwise, may provide security to those on the inside. The police, however, risk being caught on the outside looking in—in more ways than one.

Source: From *Law Enforcement News*, Jan. 31, 1992, Vol. XVIII, No. 351.

# 1992 IN REVIEW

## Eruptions, Aftershocks and a Shifting Landscape

On April 29 at 3:30 P.M. Pacific time, the law enforcement community went into red alert as riots erupted in response to the acquittal of four Los Angeles police officers accused in the beating of Rodney King. At the epicenter of this man-made disaster, South Central Los Angeles, some 1,000 fires burned out of control, 52 people were killed, 2,383 were injured, more than 16,000 were arrested, and damages were estimated to be as much as $1 billion. With local law enforcement personnel unable to control the upheaval, the National Guard and the U.S. military were called in to handle what appeared to be a complete breakdown of law and order. The rioting was called the nation's worst civil disorder in this century. Indeed, the nation had not experienced anything even remotely close in the area of civil unrest in more than 20 years.

While Los Angeles clearly suffered the worst of the riotous upheaval, the controversial verdict triggered a shock wave of disturbances in many other cities as well, and police departments often found themselves less than ideally prepared for the surges of violence that ensued. Thus, just as 1991 saw a re-examination of police policies and practices on the use of force, 1992 saw the law enforcement profession hastily reviewing, revising or making up policies for handling civil unrest.

For those cities that experienced violent unrest firsthand, evaluations of police response to such disturbances were very often sharply critical of the lack of communication and coordination—internally as well as with other agencies—political indecision, and a lack of preparedness on the part of line officers. The situation was exacerbated by the fact that most officers serving today have an average of about seven years experience and, therefore, have no experience with civil disturbances.

In October, the F.B.I. released a handbook titled "Prevention and Control of Civil Disturbance: Time for Review," which was based on concerns voiced by a number of major city chiefs. In the document, the contributors cite such problems as out-of-date equipment, a lack of officer training, the failure to develop new tactics to deal with the increased use of firearms by rioters, threats to innocent people, and the role of arson in urban riots. The question police chiefs and other public officials had to grapple with was whether it was better to deal swiftly and agressively with disturbances or take a slower, more measured approach. For a number of police officials the consensus was that it was better "to take quick and decisive action rather than to let the situation defuse itself." The F.B.I. handbook notes that recent experience with civil disorders tends to suggest that slow or ineffective first response by the police contributes to a significant increase in property damage, additional loss of life, and an increase in the number of neighborhoods involved in civil disorder. In some cities, of course, mass violence seemed inevitable but never occurred, due in part to the police use of various mechanisms for letting off steam—hot lines, open dialogue with constituents, and access to information to dispel rumors. Generous doses of luck didn't hurt, either.

### CONSEQUENCES OF UNREST

The riots of 1992 were not limited to those that occurred in reaction to the Los Angeles verdict. In Chicago a riot was triggered by fans celebrating a basketball championship. In Belmar, N.J., violence grew out of a pop music concert. Police shootings sparked riots in Mobile, Ala., and in New York. Whatever the cause, for many cities the cost of rioting included a scarred political landscape. In Los Angeles both the mayor and the police chief paid the price. The political response to a police shooting in New York caused what some say is the deepest schism in 20 years between the mayor and the rank and file. The mayor displayed what some perceived as undue sympathy to the family of the man who had been shot—an armed drug dealer—thereby leaving many with the impression that the officer had acted improperly, even criminally. The officer was later exonerated by a grand jury, and the prosecution witnesses—relatives of the drug dealer—were said to have committed perjury. In light of the rioting that accompanied the original shooting, the department did plan for the worse when the grand jury's decision was announced. Snippets of the testimony and evidence were released over a period of time, and the timing of the actual announcement even took into consideration the phase of the moon. The city remained calm, but the repercussions didn't end there. The demoralization of many officers over the mayor's response to the situation was a significant undercurrent to a raucous police demonstration later in the year.

Even as civil unrest was a constant underlying concern for law enforcement in 1992, the use of force continued to dominate many agendas. The Justice Department's review of police brutality, ordered in 1991 in the aftermath of the Rodney King beating, was met with sharp Congressional criticism for its failure to take a critical, discerning look at police misconduct. That shortcoming, however, was said to stem largely from the irregular nature of record-keeping for such incidents. Issues of civilian oversight of police, which resurfaced on the local agenda in 1991, came under the spotlight once again in 1992. At least 10 cities considered civilian-review proposals as police chiefs and others argued that civilian review boards would not help to reduce police wrongdoing. The general public, however, had its own views on the subject. In a national poll conducted by Louis Harris and Associates Inc., and John Jay College of Criminal Justice, 8 of 10 Americans said they favored a board with a mixed composition of both police and civilians. Seen against the backdrop of the times, this surprising result—one that cut across demographic and racial lines—should prompt localities to look closely at public attitudes when the issue of civilian review comes to the fore.

## BACK TO THE COMMUNITY

Just what impact these spasmodic events have had on community policing—whether a mild temblor or a major tectonic shift—is difficult to determine. With many aspects of community policing, there are simply no generally accepted measuring methods. As important, now that scores of the country's largest cities have begun to adopt the philosophy, there is still no consensus definition of community policing. How does one know if the policing style of a particular city is indeed community-oriented? Assuming that it is, how can one assess the impact? In the biggest cities, there is growing concern that the adoption of the community-oriented approach is more difficult than may have been believed at the outset. The cynicism of officers at all levels, the amorphous nature of community policing, the media consciousness of political officials—all have helped to slow the process. In some instances, these factors and others lead to little more than a community-policing charade.

In some localities, community policing is being credited with declines in crime. In other areas, where crime has gone up, community policing is being offered as an explanation because increased interaction between officers and the community has fostered increased reporting of crime. One police researcher put it simply: "The question is how do we disentangle the crime stats." Others say crime rates cannot be used at all to measure community policing. Different measures will have to be used, but such measures are as yet unformulated.

Yet notwithstanding the lack of measurements and a simmering sub-surface skepticism, community policing did receive an endorsement last year from the Law Enforcement Steering Committee, a coalition of 11 major law enforcement organizations. The community-based approach was also incorporated into the "seed" portion of the Justice Department's Weed & Seed program for reducing local violence. Although community policing continues to reshape law enforcement to varying degrees, the most dramatic transformation of the profession—at least over the short term, and possibly for many years to come—is occurring because of unprecedented changes in the ranks of police executives.

## A CHANGING OF THE GUARD

"All is change; all yields its place and goes." This ancient saying was amply applicable to law enforcement in 1992. Not in the 17-year history of Law Enforcement News has there been a year with such movement at the top. More than one-third of nation's 50 largest cities experienced changes in police leadership: New York, Los Angeles, Chicago, Houston, Philadelphia, Detroit, San Diego, San Francisco, Washington, Denver, Austin, Long Beach, Pittsburgh, Tulsa, Cincinnati, Tucson and Oakland. The wave of departures and new appointments washed ashore in many other cities as well: Salt Lake City, Portsmouth, Va., Elizabeth, N.J., Tampa, St. Petersburg, and Birmingham. Such change was almost epidemic in the New York metropolitan area, affecting the NYPD along with the New York Transit Police and the Nassau and Suffolk County police forces. As a result, nearly 40,000 officers in a radius of less of than 50 miles are now working under new leadership.

Political differences between police executives and elected officials underscored many of the departures, while others left because it was simply their time. In some instances, new chiefs lasted just a matter of weeks. Suffolk County, N.Y., and San Francisco each went through four top cops in one year. The gain will be new people with fresh ideas; the loss is a wealth of experience and talent. The extent to which this dramatic change in leadership will influence the public safety agenda remains to be seen. There will be no small number of chiefs who will need to get in touch quickly with the needs of their constituencies. The large number of new chiefs on the block, combined with numerous new Federal appointees, will necessitate the forging of new professional relationships—what usually would be called an "old boy network." But the network will be neither old nor solely male.

1992 proved to be a good one for women in law enforcement. Four women were appointed as police chiefs in major cities—in Tucson, Austin, Elizabeth, N.J. and Portsmouth, Va. Two came up through the ranks of the departments they now head. Two others were career officers who relocated from other departments. Even the FBI got into the act, appointing its first female as head of a field office. These appointments, while statistically insignificant among the more than 16,000 police departments nationwide, mark the first time that more than one woman at a time has occupied the chief's office in major cities. While their numbers are few, they are the first generation.

Regardless of gender, new police executives will find themselves facing officers who feel overly scrutinized and who are trying to contend with community-oriented policing. These chiefs will be dealing with elected officials who want more say on issues of public safety than they have had in the past. They will face budgets that continue to be inadequate. They will face a public that is frustrated, frightened and criminally victimized at the rate of more than 1 out of every 4 households. And, if some reports are correct, it is a public that is increasingly arming itself in response to such events as the Los Angeles riots and the election of Bill Clinton (who favors a Federal waiting period on the purchase of handguns).

## WHEN IS AN ISSUE NOT AN ISSUE?

As law enforcement prepared for the possibility of civil unrest last year, the country prepared for a Presidential election. Yet despite the heightened tensions on the streets, and even though the country's domestic agenda had center stage during the campaign, law and order issues were not high on the list of public priorities. With the nation's attention focused on the economy, President Bush and Governor Clinton offered only occasional passing remarks on criminal justices issues. As the country's second largest city was partially destroyed by rioters, a collective amnesia seemed to set in, as if the scene were too disturbing to contemplate for very long. To an extent, the election served as an almost welcome diversion from the sight of U.S. troops patrolling the streets of a devastated American city.

The resources and energies of the country are being focused, for the moment, on major economic issues. That should please the police officials and criminal justice theorists who believe that improvements in the areas of poverty, joblessness, and education will help reduce crime. Of course, many experts are just as hopeful that the new Administration will provide greater support for local law enforcement, with less bureaucracy to get in the way. They want gun-control legislation, assistance with community policing efforts, and increased funding for research, technical assistance, officer education and training enhancements. Before any of these things can be accomplished, however, law enforcement must first get the ear of the new Administration. On the score, the line forms to the left.

Will the Administration eventually turn its attention to issues of public safety? Obviously time will tell.

Source: From *Law Enforcement News*, Jan. 15/31, 1993, Vol. XIX, No. 373.

# 1993 IN REVIEW

# Mega-Events and the Fears of Everyday Life

By all reasonable measures, 1993 marked an about-face for law enforcement when compared to the previous year. Issues of public safety, which struggled for attention during the 1992 Presidential campaign, had moved foursquare into the spotlight by the end of 1993. The Federal attitude toward local law enforcement, only recently marked by a hands-off posture, took a hands-on turn that in some cases bordered on outright intervention (as witness Congress's federalization of certain crimes). Police departments, which were frequently scrutinized in 1992 for the excessive use of force, found themselves under the microscope for corruption in 1993. Federal law enforcement agencies went from being praised for their actions to being criticized for their failures.

At last, it appeared, 1993 saw a nation whose attention was galvanized on issues of public safety and seemed poised to do something about them. In citizen-generated actions, in legislation, in elections, in opinion surveys and in numerous other ways, the public gave voice to its growing fear and frustration over violence. The convergence of this increased public attention with a new Administration in Washington provided the critical mass necessary to get a Federal gun law enacted, and may yet lead to passage of the first significant crime legislation in years.

## THE BIG-BANG SCENARIO

It was a year highlighted by mega-events: a titanic bomb blast; a prolonged and deadly siege; the worst floods in hundreds of years; wind-driven wildfires aided by the hands of arsonists. The magnitude of these events stunned and mobilized the law enforcement community in ways that heretofore were only contemplated. And it all started, both figuratively and literally, with a bang that symbolized the type of year it would turn out to be.

Of the thousands of bombing incidents that occurred in 1993, one stood above all others. At lunchtime on a snowy Feb. 26, a terrorist bomb rocked New York's World Trade Center, one of the largest office-building complexes in the country. More than 1,000 people were injured. Six people were killed, and it was generally agreed that it was miraculous that the number of fatalities was not far greater. Thousands of uniformed personnel—Federal, state, local, even private security officers—sprang into action, joining forces for both the rescue and the ensuing investigation. The blast created a 200-foot-wide, five-story-deep crater, which in weeks to come would be visited by police personnel from around the country who sought some insight from a first-hand look at a crime scene that defied description. What differentiated this bombing from others in 1993 was not simply the size of the blast, but the fact that those who allegedly planted the explosives were not homegrown extremists. With this incident, international terrorism on American soil, which had long been predicted, had come to pass.

Had the bombing of the World Trade Center been 1993's only shocking act of extremist religious fundamentalism, it would have been more than enough. But just two days after the bombing, yet another horrific situation unfolded, this time in Waco, Texas. On Feb. 28, agents of the Bureau of Alcohol, Tobacco and Firearms, attempting to serve a warrant for weapons violations, stormed the compound that was home to the Branch Davidians, until then a little known religious cult. It proved to be the darkest day in ATF's history, as four agents were killed in the raid.

Yet even this deadly episode was but a prelude. The FBI took command of the scene, and for nearly two months waffled between negotiating and applying tactical pressure on the cultists to leave the compound. At length, tactical measures won out as the bureau's patience wore thin. On

April 19, the tanks rolled in, punching holes in the compound's flimsy walls and pumping in canisters of CS gas. Abruptly, the compound exploded into flames, apparently set by the cult members inside. In short order, the fire—fed by the compound's wooden construction, the kerosene and ammunition stored within, and a brisk wind—reduced the compound and its occupants to ashes. While public opinion felt it manifestly clear that David Koresh and his followers brought this frenzy of lethal violence upon themselves, police experts were privately critical of how the siege was handled. In the space of only two months, the praise that had been heaped on the ATF and the FBI for their response to the World Trade Center bombing turned into harsh criticism of the Waco debacle.

## THE SMOKING GUN

As riveting as these mega-events were, on a day-to-day basis the country was bombarded with reports of violence, making gun-control legislation increasingly popular. A once-unthinkable stream of politicians reexamined their relationships with the National Rifle Association, with many concluding that continued support for the NRA could mean a loss of voters. Although polls indicate that public support for gun regulation has been growing for years, it was not until this past year that gun control finally found a friend in the White House. The Clinton Administration's support of gun control—a radical policy shift from the past—helped to bring about the eleventh-hour passage of the Brady Bill, which has been lingering in Congress for years. With it, it would seem, a corner has been turned on gun control. By the end of the year, talk turned to regulating or taxing ammunition and enacting other controls on firearms, those who sell them, and those who use them.

The new Federal agenda is more than just gun control, however. The appointment of an Attorney General who had been a local prosecutor and thus had worked closely with police was viewed as a indication that violent crime would be an overriding concern of the Department of Justice— much to the delight and relief of law enforcement personnel. Attorney General Janet Reno's agenda is nothing less than comprehensive. She has stated that she wants to: take the politics out of policing; provide "truth in sentencing"; build more prisons; come to grips with mandatory sentencing that has non-violent offenders serving longer sentences than violent criminals; deport illegal aliens who are taking up space in American prisons; crack down on juvenile crime; create a shared, comprehensive information base; stop interagency turf wars; have Federal law enforcement agencies share more information with their local counterparts, and create partnerships with other social-service providers. Still, the new Federal agenda doesn't stop there.

## THE CORPS OF AN IDEA

For years, local law enforcement has asked the Federal Government to provide additional front-line resources to fight crime, and the Clinton Administration appears ready to do just that. Of course, along with those funds will come no shortage of attached strings as to how the dollars are to be used. The two most obvious examples of this are the proposed creation of a national Police Corps and providing funds for the local hiring of community police officers. Both of these initiatives will have direct implications for local policing in the years ahead. No doubt many departments will benefit from these programs, but there is a growing feeling on the part of police chiefs that local autonomy is being eroded.

Not since the so-called "good old days" of the late 1960's and 70's has policing benefited directly from an infusion of funds to encourage higher education. Through the Law Enforcement Education Program—known far and wide simply as LEEP—those funds primarily went to those who were already sworn officers, and the beneficiaries of that program have gone on to lead police departments throughout the country. LEEP funds also spurred a growth in criminal justice education programs—an effect that the new initiatives are likely to repeat. Like the LEEP program, the Police Corps will also affect a generation of officers— future officers. Therein lies the difficulty.

Unlike LEEP, the Police Corps concept raises questions of whom to hire and when to hire—issues that have traditionally been within the purview of local authorities. The fear on the part of many police chiefs is that the Police Corps will infringe on that self-determination. Over the course of more than 10 years, the Police Corps has been debated, even tried in a handful of jurisdictions, and it has consistently run into the same obstacles. Whether the national Police Corps is modified to address local concerns remains to be seen. What is clear, however, is that another hopeful step will be taken toward the 1967 goal of a college-educated police service.

## COMMUNITY-MINDEDNESS

The latest step in the evolution of community policing is occurring on the Federal level. In the late 1970's and early 1980's, community policing was typically brought in by a chief; by the late 1980's it was often the result of a mayor's will or other political mandate. We are now witnessing the direct infusion of resources through the Justice Department, to the tune of $150 million that will be used to pay for officers' salaries and benefits for three years in cities over 150,000 population. The appeal of such funding is undeniable, as witness the traffic jam of Federal Express trucks at the Justice Department on the day grant applications were due. Nonetheless, there remain a number of concerns on the part of many police executives. What criteria were used to judge the grant applications? After three years, how will cities pay to keep these newly appointed officers on the job (particularly when 53 percent of all cities are running deficits)? If these officers incur job-related injuries, who will foot the bill for potentially lifelong disability benefits? Despite these and other serious reservations, some chiefs felt pressured by their local government to apply for these additional officers. Even state police agencies have applied for community-police funds.

Adding a sprinkling of more police officers around the country is not the only Federal measure to incorporate community policing. The Justice Department is underwriting five to nine community policing experiments in larger cities that will seek to integrate the concept, evaluate outcomes and disseminate the information. Community policing continues to thrive in some jurisdictions, while in others it remains maddeningly elusive. Police supervisors complain that officers are talking with community members and writing reports about how they spend their time, but nothing in the way of better policing is being produced. In the estimation of some scholars, there is no validity to the idea that more cops equals less crime. As one observer put it, "To prevent crime, the police must become inventive, not simply more numerous."

## CRACKS IN THE BADGE

In the face of deadly serious crime problems, police found themselves dealing with communities that felt increasingly unsafe—and all too frequently, the sense of unease was intensified by reports of drug-related police corruption.

In 1991 and 1992, police departments found themselves taking a hard look at excessive force and riot control. This year, the emergence of several major-city scandals prompted departments to reassess their vulnerability to corruption. It is not the type of corruption that rocked policing in the 1960's, which emphasized payoffs for looking the other way to cover illegal vice activities. Contemporary corruption is far more aggressive, far more vicious, with rogue police officers stealing and reselling drugs, indiscriminately beating people, even participating in drug-related murders.

Police observers attribute the current wave of corruption, at least in part, to lowered entry standards, accelerated hiring that led to inadequate background and psychological checks, and institutional environments that do not actively weed out corruption. Many departments around the country will attach a paramount importance to integrity issues in 1994. As local finances improve to permit renewed hiring, and with the Federal Government standing by to infuse tens of thousands of additional local officers, agencies will have to summon the will not to skimp on background checks and psychological screens. More than ever, it seems, organizational environments are needed that promote integrity, and seek out and combat corruption—however unpleasant a task that may be.

## THE ONLY THING WE HAVE TO FEAR?

In 1993, Americans 'fessed up: They were scared. In the course of one year, public priorities appeared to shift. At the end of 1992 the nation was riding out a Presidential election in which one campaign mantra was "It's the economy, stupid." This year, public and, at last, political attention focused on public safety—or the lack of it. Official statistics suggested that crime was declining slightly, but Americans just didn't feel safe. (And, to be sure, their fears were borne out by end-of-year data showing new homicide records in nearly two dozen major cities.)

More and more communities found themselves facing increasingly violent, increasingly visible gang activity. Some localities tried gang summits, others enacted get-tough legislation. The extent of the problem was underscored by an edict issued by a prison gang in California, warning local gang members to stop drive-by shootings because they were proving bad for business. Violent crime by the young increased, and by some estimates it has doubled in the last five years. Many experts note that young people value life less than they had in previous generations when a car, not a handgun, was the dominant status symbol.

Another catch phrase was added to the lexicon of fear: sexual predator. With evidence increasingly indicating that many sex offenders cannot be rehabilitated, the year saw a crackdown on them and their crimes. Many communities required convicted child molesters and other sex offenders to register with police. In some areas, released offenders were run out of town, sometimes before they could even settle in. Anti-stalker laws became a fact of life for many localities. In some states, prison terms were lengthened—to the point of indefinite confinement—for incorrigible offenders deemed likely to commit more sex crimes upon release.

Where possible, Americans took action to deal with their fears. They voiced their fear in the voting booth during numerous local elections where crime was a major issue. There were increased calls for curbs on the pervasive violence in TV programs and movies. In the main, though, people changed their habits and tried to put themselves out of harm's way—a phenomenon that is not accounted for in crime statistics. If possible, they moved to safer areas. Stores were encouraged to close early. Vacation plans were changed or canceled. Christmas Eve midnight masses were canceled or moved up to earlier starting times to cut the risk to parishioners. Some communities sacrificed a measure of their privacy in order to use surveillance cameras; others blockaded themselves from outsiders. City residents in particular altered their daily habits or, at a minimum, lived in a state of constant alert. The cocooning of America, a trend that began in the past few years, has in some neighborhoods turned into self-imposed imprisonment.

More and more, the American habitat is threatened by violence. The simple truth is that, in setting after setting, people do not feel safe. They do not feel safe in the workplace; on the highways; in the post office; in schools; in shopping malls; in parking lots; in taxis; at convenience stores; in fast-food restaurants; on the streets; on commuter trains. And, for too many people, they do not feel safe in their own homes.

Could it be that the country is finally fed up with violence?

Source: From *Law Enforcement News,* Dec. 31, 1993, Vol. XIX, No. 392.

# 1994 IN REVIEW

# Frustrated, Angry & Ready to Get Tough

## Americans Roll Up Their
## Sleeves & Say 'Enough is Enough'

There weren't urban riots as in 1992. There wasn't a foreign terrorist bombing or cult-related fiery inferno of the kind that galvanized 1993. Still, 1994 will be remembered as a watershed year in criminal justice, as a public that was becoming angrier and more frustrated about crime insisted that something be done. The increasing levels of fear that have dominated the 1990's turned into action in 1994 as America rolled up its sleeves and got tough.

Nowhere was this toughness more evident than in the legislative arena. There was, of course, the passage of the Federal crime bill, the most comprehensive crime legislation in a generation. But there was also an avalanche of criminal justice lawmaking on the local and state levels. Scarcely a week went by without some legislative body considering laws aimed at improving community quality of life and getting violent offenders out of society for as long as possible. The phrase "three strikes and you're out" may have been missing from ball parks after August, but it was a year-long battle cry that reverberated nationwide among those who had had their fill of violence.

## THROWING AWAY THE KEY

In part, the public's ire was an outgrowth of the perceived growing disparity between court-imposed sentences and actual time served—what has come to be known in the criminal justice lexicon as "truth in sentencing." By late February, 30 states were considering three-strikes laws. This approach is not without its critics, with some criminal justice experts pointing to enormous costs that in California alone could run as high as $5.5 billion a year.

Such expenditures, it is argued, could seriously undermine government funding of other essential services like education. The three-strikes approach might also turn prisons into old-age homes for those violent offenders who grow out of crime, as well as intensify the pressure to plead down the charges for first or second violent offenses.

For other critics, three strikes is not tough enough. (In Georgia, the law allows only two strikes.) Three strikes would leave no prison space for misdemeanor offenders. Thieves and drug dealers would no longer be dealt with harshly enough, they say. These criticisms notwithstanding, proponents say that with as few as 7 percent of violent offenders committing 70 percent of the crimes, three-strikes legislation and its focus on repeat offenders will reduce the human and economic costs of crime.

In the move to get tough, states also increased prison time by curtailing or abandoning parole and good time, and by moving prisoners from halfway houses back to secure cells. In some jurisdictions, violent offenders will now have to serve up to 85 percent of their sentence. And while offenders spend more time behind bars, the quality of that time has been diminished as well, as legislators took away such prison perks as cable television, entertainment equipment, and physical fitness gear—over the objections of prison officials who fear an escalation of prison violence.

One specific crime category demonstrated the get-tough mood more than any other—sex offenses. Coupled with, and fueled by, several nationally publicized cases, a growing public awareness that rehabilitation is often impossible led to an onslaught of legislation aimed at serial sex offenders—criminals who by some estimates commit 30 offenses for every time they are caught. Taking the lead from the state of Washington, many jurisdictions opted to keep sexual predators incarcerated for longer periods by mandating indefinite prison terms, parole denials or civil commitments.

Authorities are keeping tabs on such offenders as never before. More states joined the ranks of those requiring DNA samples from offenders, and 1994 also saw the growing popularity of requirements that sex offenders register with local police upon release, and that the public be notified of their whereabouts. (One released sex offender in Nevada asked to be returned to jail because his presence sparked protests by neighborhood residents.) Soon Californians will even have the ability to call a state-run telephone hotline to get information on the whereabouts of paroled child molesters. Local school officials, for their part, are demanding to know about juvenile sex offenders who sit in their classrooms. Law enforcement agencies are sharing more information with each other and with the public in the investigation of serial rapists and killers, and some departments even use the information superhighway in their efforts.

## MAKING A FEDERAL CASE OUT OF DOMESTIC VIOLENCE

Domestic violence, like sex crimes, deals primarily with female victims, and like sex crimes, was a major focus of increased public attention, with much of the activity again taking place in the legislative arena. Under Title IV of the 1994 crime control act, gender-based violence is now a Federal civil rights violation, and under certain circumstances violating a court order of protection is a Federal offense. (The law also imposes a ban on gun possession by domestic abusers.) Some states are already convicting batterers under bias-crime statutes, thereby allowing for added sanctions. Police policies requiring mandatory or preferred arrest were initiated by legislation in numerous jurisdictions, while in other areas police departments zeroed in on repeat domestic offenders, forming a coordinated front with prosecutors, courts and social service agencies to deal with such cases. One major Midwestern department even launched a program to address domestic violence within its own ranks. It appears that law enforcement will continue its decade-long increased focus on domestic violence.

Early in the year Federal officials reported that two-thirds of the 2.5 million women who were victims of violent crime were attacked by friends, family or acquaintances. As happens so often, however, there was one highly publicized incident that drove the issue into the spotlight—the O.J. Simpson case. Reports of domestic violence surged almost everywhere at once. Yet while the legal proceedings against Simpson continue to captivate the public and the news media, there always seems to be room in the headlines for a particularly heinous crime committed by a child.

## NEVER TOO YOUNG TO BEGIN A LIFE OF CRIME

A 7-year-old selling crack. . . . Two 9-year-old boys charged with sexually assaulting a 4-year-old girl. . . . Two 12-year-old boys accused of murdering a transient. . . . From one coast to another, in cities, suburbs and rural hamlets, no region of the country was spared the tide of juvenile violence that seemed to involve ever-younger criminals and increasingly vicious crimes. In some areas the number of youths charged with murder has doubled in the past 10 years. Confronting this disheartening increase in violent crime committed by children is a juvenile justice system that is largely the product of another era and was not designed to handle this kind of shock wave—a wave that researchers say will get worse. Consequently, more and more localities are opting to put violent juvenile offenders in the hands of the adult criminal justice system. Prosecutors sought and usually got legislative changes aimed at getting tough on violent juveniles.

A number of experts see dysfunctional families and the easy access to firearms as the primary causes of rising juvenile violence. There is no question that one of the most frightening elements of youth crime is the arsenal of firearms at their disposal. For law enforcement personnel everywhere, concern about gun-related violence among the young is paramount. In one major-city, a survey found that one in five high school students carries a weapon. The arming of juveniles, it seems, has gone beyond those who deal drugs or belong to gangs. It now permeates the youth culture itself.

## HEEDING THE PUBLIC'S CALL TO CURB WEAPONS

More so than in recent years, 1994 brought an uncompromising focus on getting illegal weapons off the street. Backed by surveys indicating that a significant percentage of the population favors restrictions on weapons, legislators called for curbs on gun possession and increased penalties for firearms misuse, while police in many localities stepped up enforcement of existing laws.

In the main, local law enforcement's response to the proliferation of guns came in the form of stepped-up efforts against violators. (Of course, one cannot overlook the handful of challenges filed by county sheriffs against the 1993 Brady Law, questioning whether the Federal Government could mandate local compliance in conducting background checks of handgun purchasers.) Nationwide, search-and-seizure practices were bolstered in a variety of ways. In a crime-ridden Chicago housing project, the community applauded the city's housing police for going into apartments to conduct warrantless searches for weapons—a practice civil libertarians were quick to stop. St. Louis police tried a different tack, with consensual searches at the homes of suspected youth gang members. In Kansas City and Indianapolis, officers assigned to patrol "hot spots" are using "reasonable belief" as a basis for stopping cars for weapons searches—an experimental initiative that so far is proving successful in cracking down on illegal weapons and their owners. Rhode Island set up what was described as the nation's first gun court to fast-track offenders into prison In New York City, police were ordered to aggressively pursue the origin of a weapon when making an arrest.

But the battle against illegal weapons is far from joined. Many police agencies have no idea how many firearms their officers seize annually because they don't keep records on the subject. Just how far there is to go in tracking illegal guns was demonstrated on Oct. 29 when a Colorado man fired a semiautomatic rifle at the White House. He had lied on his gun-purchase form about a prison record and his dishonorable discharge, but there is currently no mechanism for checking the truth or accuracy of the information at the point of purchase. Still, while there remains a long way to go in getting illegal weapons out of circulation, it is clear that the public has made weapons violations a priority.

## ANYBODY REMEMBER THE DRUG WAR?

Even as the country was taking aim at violent offenders, domestic abusers, weapons violators and sexual predators, the get-tough mood did not extend to drugs. That's not say that there weren't hundreds of thousands of drug busts, increasingly huge drug seizures, and hundreds of acres of crops burned, but drug issues were booted from the front pages by the bloody appeal of violent crime.

Among the headlines that did crop up were the likes of: "The War on Drugs is Over (Drugs Won)"; "The Phony War/The Real Crisis"; "End War on Drugs/Too Many Casualties"; and "Forget the War on Drugs." And if donations to pet causes are any indication, consider the following: In July the Partnership for a Drug Free America reported that contributions have fallen 20 percent in the last two years. That same month, the Drug Policy Foundation, an organization which promotes alternatives to current drug policies, announced it had received a $6-million philanthropic donation. To be sure, a small but growing number of people in the legal profession are voicing objections to the war on drugs. In California, a judge refused to sentence a man to a 6-year mandatory term for a drug offense. The current president of the American Bar Association supports decriminalization, and a special committee of the Association of the Bar of the City of New York has came out in favor of dropping current prohibitions. What critics of U.S. drug policy have in common is the view that existing enforcement-based strategies have not worked. In their view, drug use is primarily a public health issue and should be treated as such.

It has been reported that more than 300,000 Americans are behind bars for drug offenses, and that one out of every five Federal prisoners is a first-time nonviolent drug offender. Although most Americans oppose decriminalization—and clearly do not want drug dealing on their streets—they are vexed and perplexed when mandatory sentencing policies mean that drug offenders serve longer terms than do violent criminals. Now, with the recent crackdown on violent crime, prison space has become an even more valuable commodity. To accommodate get-tough policies like "three strikes," the criminal justice system will have to make room. Even with the building of additional prisons, many states have had to diminish sentences for some non-violent offenses—like drug possession. In Texas, for example, a plan was adopted which requires, among other things, that all violent and sexual offenders serve at least half of their sentences. In order to accomplish that, state legislators decided to significantly reduce the sentences for certain drug offenses.

## CHARGING AHEAD
## WITH COMMUNITY POLICING

One undeniable feature of 1994 has less to do with getting tough than with getting smart—the continued popularity of community policing. Just about every police department in the country, if asked, would likely say it had some variety of community policing in effect, yet some pioneers of the concept fear that it has become little more than an overused catchphrase—where officials do nothing more than talk about it.

Law enforcement practitioners and researchers, having had little success in resolving the definitional dilemma of community policing, have moved on to the issue of measurement. But evaluating community policing is proving just as elusive as defining it. Some feel that measurements ought to be taken of things like fear, crime reduction, problem solving, officer effectiveness, customer satisfaction and police/community civility indicators. So far, though, there are no standardized yardsticks. And as one scholar noted, the Federal Government is "putting 100,000 more cops out there to do [community policing] . . . without a clue to its effectiveness." Community policing is moving full speed ahead.

Even before the passage of the crime bill, the Justice Department pipeline for applying for more officers was jammed, and the department realized early on that properly evaluating the applications from potentially thousands of police departments would prove nearly impossible and politically unwise. It's been said that some applications didn't even include the phrase "community policing." Whether or not police chiefs really wanted more officers or were politically pressured into applying for the extra personnel, they couldn't queue up fast enough. To expedite matters, the Justice Department achieved a minor bureaucratic breakthrough with the streamlined "COPS Fast" application kit for small departments that is one of the simplest forms ever created by the Federal Government.

Locally, community policing continues to evolve. For those departments that have been at it awhile, a decentralization and flattening of the command structure has occurred. The San Diego Police Department, one of the leaders in community policing, announced in April that the city would be divided into 21 communities to be served by mini-police departments. In Tempe, Ariz., the Police Department went citywide with an approach known as "geographic deployment," where each of the city's 15 beats, under the direction of a sergeant, controls its own scheduling and deployment. In departments where community policing is still in its embryonic stages, such as in Los Angeles and Chicago, academic experts and institutions have been brought on board to help steer the initiative from the outset and evaluate outcomes.

The kind of community policing a locality gets is in large part determined by the officers it has—their level of enthusiasm, the nature and extent of middle management involvement in the process, their training and education, and last but certainly not least, their level of experience. In New York, the average age of officers is 23; in Chicago, it's 42. The type of community policing that evolves in these two cities will be greatly determined by officer age.

The "community," however defined, is supposed to be a partner in the production of public safety. And variations in communities are part and parcel of American society. Communities want and need different things, amid day-to-day problems that can range from shootings, robberies and drug dealing to drag racing, panhandling and quarreling neighbors. If departments know nothing else about community policing, they know that residents want quality-of-life improvements.

But what happens to community policing when a community wants something that is unenforceable, even unconstitutional? One New Jersey borough passed an ordinance outlawing cursing in public, but the police chief has refused to enforce the law. Beyond that, what happens when one segment of the community wants to be rid of another? Consider the recent passage of Proposition 187 in California. Many police chiefs in the Southwest and elsewhere have worked long and hard to establish good relationships with all residents—legal and otherwise—of their communities and have had tenuous relations with immigration officials. If police are required to report illegal aliens, cooperation from witnesses and victims would certainly become problematic, as would community involvement in improving the quality of life. Some believe bias crime will increase and the overall level of civility may drop. Community policing has had its share of police organizational and resource problems that threaten its existence. But what happens to community policing when a community tries to pull itself apart?

## THE FORECAST: KEEPING BUSY, WITH PARTNERS

Among the commitments made by Attorney General Janet Reno after she took office in 1993 was to have Federal law enforcement agencies share more information with their local counterparts, and to create partnerships with other social service providers. Reno has made significant headway thus far; there is hardly a group that she has yet to reach out to. In this respect, one of the hallmarks of 1994 was the improved working relationships among different agencies, within the Justice Department itself, within the law enforcement profession generally, and between policing and other government entities.

Seven Cabinet-level agencies have joined forces in a sweeping initiative to address youth violence. And, in another interagency milestone, the departments of Justice and Defense have linked up in a research and development-sharing venture that could open the doors to new technologies for law enforcement. (Of course, even as high-tech military technologies slowly make their way into the police market, there are still police agencies operating with rudimentary, even primitive equipment. One department in the Northeast only recently made the step up to copying machines from manual typewriters and carbon paper.)

The partnership approach to tackling crime will likely result (with the help, no doubt, of crime-bill funding) in a flurry of activity in law enforcement and in allied research and academic institutions. They'll have their hands full with hiring, training, educating, upgrading, implementing, analyzing, researching, evaluating, disseminating, assessing and reporting. 1995 will be a busy year.

Source: From *Law Enforcement News*, Dec. 31, 1994, Vol. XX, No. 414.

# 1995 IN REVIEW

# The Sweet Smell of Success, the Sour Taste of Bad Apples

Charles Dickens was referring to the late 18th century when he wrote, "It was the best of times, it was the worst of times." He might as well have been talking about American law enforcement at the close of the 20th century. Few would argue that the times have rarely been as good as they were in 1995, in light of policing's overriding success story of the year—the dramatic, almost unimaginable reductions in serious crime. At the same time, one would be hard-pressed to recall another time filled with such frequent reports of police wrongdoing, enough to cast a yearlong shadow over law enforcement's image and its otherwise remarkable record of accomplishment.

This was more than a tale of just two cities. In one locality after another, the bottom fell out of the crime rate, and especially so in the case of homicide. This was apparently no blip, no product of creative number-crunching; it was a genuine and major drop. Preliminary figures for the first half of the year showed murder rates dropping by more than 25 percent in San Diego, Miami, Las Vegas, and Long Beach, among other cities; by more than 30 percent in Hartford, Houston, New York, Tampa, Kansas City, Mo., and Seattle, and by an astounding 40 percent or more in Bridgeport, Louisville, Buffalo, and Fresno.

Confronted with these numbers, the first question many people tended to ask was "How did this happen?" The answer depended largely on whom one asked. Success, it seemed, had many potential parents.

Politicians, predictably, wanted their due for the sharp reduction in crime. Officials from the President of the United States to local council members, aldermen and free-holders all claimed credit, citing the enactment of "get-tough" legislation such as the Crime Bill, three-strikes, registration of sex offenders, adult treatment for juvenile offenders, and the implementation of curfews. Some officials said increased sentences made the difference by keeping would-be recidivists off the streets longer. Others thought it had to do with toughening the kinds of sentences served, such as the re-emergence of chain gangs.

Community residents, for their part, say it is their increased participation in public safety issues that has made the difference in the crime rate. Others, more sanguine, say they simply have learned to adapt to hostile environments.

## DOING THE UNTHINKABLE

It was no surprise that politicians would take some credit for a decrease in crime. The shocker was that some police chiefs actually did the unthinkable—they publicly ascribed credit for the decrease to good police work. Conventional wisdom has always held that you don't take credit for a drop in crime if you're not prepared to take the heat for an increase—crime happens, for whatever the reason, and police react to it. They have little or nothing to do with how much occurred. As one police planner put it, "We leave [that] to the social scientists and psychologists." But with the proactive stance that has taken hold in recent years, it seems more and more police executives believe that crime prevention through policing is possible. (Some chiefs have gone so far as to put a statement atop their résumés proclaiming that crime reduction is their top priority.)

In assessing the sharp drop in crime, police executives have pointed to increased community policing efforts and/or improved problem-solving techniques. Yet whether or not police departments are actually "doing" community policing—and most departments claim that they are—there is an enhanced, almost palpable "can do" feeling taking hold throughout law enforcement. In the not-too-distant past, many police were of the view that they can't prevent crime, don't do a very effective job of solving crime, and have little or no responsibility for allaying public fear. There was a general sense of ineffectiveness and resignation in the face of rising crime and victimization. But that was then, and police now are assuming increasingly active—and thoughtful—roles in dealing with problems like domestic violence, school safety, child abuse, truancy, street-level drug dealing, gun crimes and gang activity.

Consider, for example, the nation's largest police department. New York City police officials credit the crime decreases there to increased precinct-level command accountability, backed up by the use of enhanced crime information and mapping systems, quick dissemination of the information, an increased emphasis on quality-of-life crimes, and strategies that focus on specific crime hot spots. Weekly early-morning meetings of borough-based commanders with top brass are becoming the stuff of legend. (The sessions in the headquarters "war room" are an amorphous mix of statistics, strategy, and stress.) The Police Department is spurred by a mayor who is an ex-Federal prosecutor and for whom crime-fighting is a top priority. It also doesn't hurt to have had many thousands of officers appointed in the last five years. One veteran police manager concedes: "I don't know why it [crime] is going down; I just know that we're paying more attention to it."

## CRIME-TREND CASSANDRAS?

Taking credit for crime decreases is laudable, even brave. But will the police be as willing to bear some of the responsibility when crime goes up, as crime forecasters predict it will in 10 years with an explosion in the juvenile population?

Those forecasters—social scientists, demographers and others—were hard pressed to offer a definitive explanation for the crime decrease, but that didn't stop many from trying. Some cited a drop in the population of 18-year-old males (although that doesn't hold true for all cities.) Other criminologists speculate that crime dropped in major cities due to maturing drug rings engaging in fewer turf battles.

For the most part, however, criminologists did not see this decline coming. When crime rates in some major cities began to slowly decline a few years ago, analysts dismissed the reductions as being too low to have any significance. Curiously, though, now that the decreases in crime are great enough to command attention, there is still little in the way of definitive analysis—despite a crying need. For example, when it comes to homicide, we don't know who didn't die, or why. Were there fewer innocent bystanders caught in crossfires? Fewer drug dealers or gang members settling disputes with lethal consequences? Fewer victims of domestic violence? Could improved medical and paramedic response be responsible for vicious assaults not turning into murders? (Heaven knows it's not a lack of availability of lethal weapons.) With robbery down by 10 percent nationwide in the first half of 1995, could it be that one-time victims of murder-robberies are the ones who aren't dying because would-be robbers are turning instead to larceny—the only offense that showed an increase, one of 7 percent. Are criminals, cowed by increased penalties, opting for less serious, less violent offenses? Have classifications and reporting criteria changed? Could the drop in homicide be a result of more aggressive policing, like SWAT teams on patrol in Fresno?

The picture would be a whole lot clearer if the National Incident-Based Reporting System—a perfect adjunct to problem-oriented policing—were in wider use. It's not that police departments cannot generate incident-based information; for the most part, it simply cannot be gotten expeditiously. It's said that a deep-seated lack of enthusiasm for NIBRS within some high-level law enforcement circles is hampering the project. NIBRS, and the study of declining crime, do not seem to be a high priority in the Justice Department's research agenda. While there is always an abundance of information about crime increases, there is typically much less available as to why crime goes down. Still, a small but growing number of departments are dropping out of the Uniform Crime Reporting program and turning, agency by agency, to the NIBRS format because it provides them with valuable "hot spot" information that allows them to tailor policing efforts to community needs. Had there been more departments participating—especially the larger ones—for the past several years, a clearer picture would have emerged by now as to why crime is down so dramatically.

## FROM HUBCAP THEFT TO MURDER

In a nutshell, then, many residents of large cities felt safer in 1995 than in the recent past. Sadly, though, law enforcement found itself unable to capitalize more fully on the diminishing fear of crime. For the reasons why, one must turn to the year's failures, a variety of events that tarnished law enforcement's image in the eyes of the general public.

Even as hundreds of thousands of officers carry on bravely, professionally and, sadly, in anonymity, one—Mark Fuhrman—became a household name, if for all the wrong reasons. Yet with that, Fuhrman was but one manifestation of police misconduct in 1995, as scandals great and small erupted on a seemingly recurring basis. In New York, Philadelphia, Atlanta, New Orleans and numerous other jurisdictions, incidents were reported that involved a virtual laundry list of offenses by police: stealing hubcaps, child abuse, domestic violence, sexual assault, robbery, fraud, bribery, drug dealing, even murder. Granted, police are generally held to higher standards of conduct and tend to be the most scrutinized of all occupational groups. As such, incidents of wrongdoing tend to make the headlines when they occur, and easily overshadow all the good that is done. To the profession's credit, some of the year's wrongdoing was uncovered by the departments on their own, providing hopeful signs that police can police themselves.

(Of course, even with increasing reports of wrongdoing, it is hard to know for certain if the incidence of misconduct has in fact risen, or merely the reporting of such acts. One police veteran points out that in the relatively recent past, corruption and misconduct was often overlooked or covered up, for fear that even the smallest eruption could kill a commander's career. Thus, while police misconduct may indeed be rising, it seems just as likely that police departments and individual officers are edging ever closer toward zero-tolerance of such acts.)

One aspect of police wrongdoing that continues to haunt the profession, but is the subject of increased attention, is the use of excessive force. Acting on a mandate built into the 1994 Crime Control Act, the Bureau of Justice Statistics has said it will begin collecting national data on the use of force by police (once issues pertaining to definitions of terms and uses of the data are settled). The likelihood is that the information will derive at least in part from the addition of questions to the annual victimization survey. In conjunction with this, the IACP has announced plans to create a comprehensive national data base modeled on one used by the Virginia chiefs' association.

## FOCUS ON THE FEDS

Over the years, tens of millions of dollars have been awarded in damages to the victims of police abuse, and it has typically been local law enforcement authorities who were in the hot seat for questionable uses of force. What made 1995 different by anyone's measure was that the glare of official and media scrutiny was focused, for a change, on Federal law enforcement, most notably in the form of televised Congressional hearings on Waco and Ruby Ridge. In a rare admission of error, the Justice Department agreed to pay $3.1 million to white separatist Randy Weaver, members of whose family were shot and killed at the Ruby Ridge siege. And through the entire episode, Federal law enforcement officials got a no-nonsense reminder of the consequences of cavalierly disregarding policies governing the use of deadly force. In some cases, officials paid for the errors with their careers.

The scrutiny of Federal law enforcement agencies for their handling of right-wing extremists was not without its irony, however, coming as it did in the wake of the literal explosion of such fringe groups onto the scene. In the blink of an eye, the right-wing movement was linked to the most lethal terrorist incident in American history, the bombing of the Alfred P. Murrah Federal Building in Oklahoma City.

As horrifying as the April 19 bombing was, with its 169 victims, what made it all the more troubling—shocking, even—to the American public was that those suspected of committing the crime were not some international terrorists, but a cadre of home-grown extremists. In this instance, not only was the terrorist incident committed on American soil, but the alleged perpetrators were themselves American. In truth, heavily armed right-wing extremists are nothing new to law enforcement, as witness the showdowns in the 1980s with such groups as the CSA, the Order and the Posse Comitatus. Still, Federal agents and local authorities alike are now feeling the threat of such groups more frequently. There have been bomb threats and attacks on Federal personnel, outright confrontation with police and sheriff's deputies in Montana, and numerous other threats against the lives of law enforcers.

Such extremists, whether anti-abortionist, white supremacist or constitutionalist, tend toward local and regional organizations, and some have fragmented further in the aftermath of the Oklahoma City bombing. Nonetheless, through optimal use of the means of mass communication, such as faxes, e-mail and the Internet, even the smallest group can engage in far-reaching networking. (More than one teen-ager has been reported to have cooked up a homemade bomb using instructions found on the Internet.) The hard-to-take realization that the enemy is within has changed things. There are even reports that a group called Police Against the New World Order is actively trying to recruit members from the ranks of law enforcement. The changing order of things is clearly seen in the FBI's process of conducting background checks on potential personnel. The question once asked regarding applicants was, "Is he now or has he ever been a member of the Communist Party." That question now ends with ". . . a member of a militia."

## THE ROAD AHEAD

The successes and failures of the past year almost set the tone for what lies ahead in 1996. Certainly community policing, which continues to thrive and is given partial credit for the recent reductions in crime, remains a high priority for the Clinton Administration as well as for local jurisdictions. The Justice Department's Office of Community Oriented Policing Services—the COPS Shop—went full throttle in putting officers on the streets. To date, more than 30,000 community policing officers have been hired with Federal funds under the 1994 Crime Act. But the program, which also provides funding for technology that would free officers' time for community policing efforts, has been in political danger from the start, with the Republican majority in Congress attempting to scrap the COPS program in favor of no-strings block grants to the states. As the year ended, legislation that would have done just that was vetoed by President Clinton.

The National Institute of Justice awarded a $2.5-million grant to the Urban Institute for a thorough evaluation of community policing, while the COPS office took over the funding of the Community Policing Consortium, to the tune of $4 million. This consortium, which comprises the Police Foundation, the National Organization of Black Law Enforcement Executives, the National Sheriff's Association, the Police Executive Research Forum and the International Association of Chiefs of Police, is intended to provide training and technical assistance to departments that have received community police funding through the COPS office. The NIJ also funded nearly $5 million in community policing projects and evaluation efforts. If for no other reason than the substantial amount of money now available in this area, it is no great surprise that most police chiefs are indicating that community policing is the mainstay of their departments.

## BUILDING A BETTER POLICE FORCE

One can also expect in the coming year that police misconduct and the use of excessive force—or, more accurately, how to prevent them—will remain high-priority items. The BJS effort to collect national statistics on use of force, which doubtless will receive its share of media attention, will require police chiefs to become acquainted with the reporting system—that is, if they wish to have meaningful input into the process.

There also appears to be increased attention being given to "conduct unbecoming," and to this end departments are becoming more sophisticated in keeping an eye on officers—tracking civilian complaints, monitoring off-duty behavior, and more. The police image took a battering in the course of the O.J. Simpson trial, and the public will be expecting police personnel to do a significantly better job when it comes to gathering and protecting evidence and testifying. ("Testilying" became part of the police vernacular in 1995.) Many departments are already training and retraining in these areas.

Policing has learned from past scandals that selection, screening, training and supervision are among the keys to preventing police wrongdoing. Departments can't be too careful, too rigorous. To that end, many departments are taking a long, hard look at entry standards, whether it's requiring college (as the NYPD finally said it would, beginning in 1997) or raising the minimum age. What departments hope to gain is a more mature individual who is less prone to wrongdoing and more inclined toward personal accountability. One would hope that policing has also learned from past scandals that, in the midst of expanded or accelerated hiring, the selection process is not something that can be short-changed in a rush to meet deadlines. As is now well documented, all too often the seeds of corruption scandals are found to have been sown in selection.

## DO IT AGAIN

As to the No. 1 police success of 1995, the crime-rate reductions, an inescapable truth is that one is usually expected to repeat the success. For those departments that have enjoyed significant crime-rate decreases, the pressure will be on to continue the trend. 1996 will no doubt bring increased efforts to bring the crime rate down even further, but given some of the large declines in homicide, it may be difficult to maintain such dramatic results. For some, it would even seem likely that some leveling off may occur.

Repeating the successes may be made more difficult by the lack of an absolute, definitive explanation as to why crime went down so dramatically in the first place. (In the long run, the answer will probably be found in a combination of good police work, get-tough legislation, community involvement and demographic variables.) Sadly, though, law enforcement, politicians, researchers and governmental agencies continue to be more concerned with what's going wrong than with what's going right. Wherever the answer may lie, one can say without fear of challenge that the recent crime-rate successes have tasted sweet, and law enforcement is not likely to be eager to return to the way things were. That fact alone—coupled with the emerging "can do" attitude of the 1990s-era problem-solving cop—may provide all the impetus that's needed.

Source: From *Law Enforcement News,* Dec. 31, 1995, Vol. XXI, No. 437.

# 1996 IN REVIEW

## Forget Events in the Spotlight—Local PD's are Where the Action Is

### Working Harder & Smarter Pays Off In Continuing Crime Declines

It was a year punctuated by events that captured the national spotlight: the Freeman standoff in Montana; the capture of the alleged Unabomber; the crash of TWA flight 800, and the terrorist bombing at the Olympic games. It was also an election year with all the usual prerequisite law and-order campaigning.

But while public attention focused in one direction, on these and other events, the real action was elsewhere, as local police departments, usually with little notice, were busy—very busy.

Police departments drew increasingly upon past research—especially in the area of problem solving. They incorporated new technologies, and shared information about what works. They looked to other jurisdictions where successful strategies had been implemented and duplicated them. Day-to-day operations were reformulated with a view to reducing crime. In growing numbers, police executives are convinced that effective policing can decrease crime, and even a growing cohort of criminologists is conceding that police work is responsible for the recent notable decline in crime. Nationwide, there are clear signs of departments reorganizing, refocusing and implementing anti-crime strategies, targeting problems and attacking them with verve. And from all indications it appears that their efforts are paying off, as 1996, like the years immediately preceding it, witnessed significant drops in the crime rate.

### HOT SPOTS AND COLD CASES

Police went after drug-dealing hot-spots and public housing crime. They tracked down guns, mounted camera surveillance devices and notified the community of burglars working in the area. They went after stolen goods and set up telephone hot lines that residents could call for crime information. Fugitive and warrant units and cold-case squads were set up or reinvigorated. (In Houston, for example, warrant enforcement has reportedly generated 8,860 arrests and cleared 38,126 cases. The New York City Police Department, with help from the U.S. Marshals Service and the FBI, will be going after as many 87,000 fugitive felons and 403,000 misdemeanor offenders.) Many departments redirected resources to high-crime areas and peak activity periods. Some departments, such as those in Bridgeport, Conn., Gary, Ind., Camden, N.J., and Minneapolis, got temporary reinforcement from state police units.

Clearly, 1996 was the year of the crackdown, but perhaps the most common approach was a crackdown on quality-of-life crime. In city after city, quality-of-life enforcement became a priority, in part because such a focus was desired by the community, but as important, because evidence increasingly points to the fact that going after minor violators contributes directly to reductions in major crime.

### IN WITH THE NEW

When it comes to reducing crime, increased innovation and accountability rule, with many large and mid-sized departments continuing to undergo significant organizational transformations. LEN's People-of-the-Year award is testimony to the kinds of structural changes that are going on around the country. The San Diego Police Department has brought all of its divisions on-line and given its lieutenants

24-hour responsibility and commensurate increases in accountability. Boston officials attribute the city's recent drop in crime to increased accountability throughout the ranks and the reorganization of the city into two-block-square reporting areas, so that emergency calls can be routed to the line officer responsible for a given neighborhood. In Montgomery County, Md., police district boundaries have been redrawn to provide a fairer, more realistic distribution of police workloads and greater success in preventing crime. And supplementing local efforts in organization change, the National Institute of Justice has provided Federal funds to export the NYPD's ground-breaking Compstat process to Indianapolis and Prince George's County, Md.

As internal changes sweep the nation's police departments, the role of supervisory personnel, notably lieutenants and captains, is coming under renewed scrutiny. Since the advent of community policing, the focus has been on the beat cop, on how well he knew and interacted with his neighborhood, and on foot patrol, substations and mini-precincts, community meetings and the like. In 1996, the focus has been on the supervisory ranks, with redefinition of their roles and increases in their responsibilities and accountability. No longer are they mere conduits that filter information upward and commands, directives and influence downward. Supervision and middle management are now bound more closely than ever to their geographic areas and what goes on there. Specifically, supervisors and managers have been charged with problem identification, tactical and strategic planning, and problem-solving that directly lead to crime reduction.

The impact of these changes on crime is clear. But what about the impact on the middle management ranks themselves?

While many departments credit "re-engineering" for crime reduction and enhanced community policing, such changes have not come without a price, in the form of organizational tension. In Austin, for example, lieutenants became the "power rank," when sectors were put under their control. This change has become a linchpin of community policing efforts in the Texas capital, and is considered a success, but one of the negatives is that the captains are miffed because they feel they are no longer in the loop.

In New York, the focus of community policing—the "power rank"—is the captain. But with power comes pressure—lots of it. Scores of captains and other precinct commanders have been reassigned for failing to meet their basic responsibility for bringing neighborhood crime rates down. Even those who do deliver are subjected to high-stress debriefings at the regular Compstat meetings. At least one possible result of these changes is that fewer lieutenants than usual are applying to take the recently announced captains' exam, and that even many of those who are taking it are ambivalent about wanting the rank. Captain's bars may no longer be as desirable as they once were for many NYPD lieutenants (although one could also surmise that a kind of "Darwinian policing"—survival of the fittest—is

taking hold, with new, more intense demands on captains helping to screen out candidates).

Austin's police chief, Betsy Watson, summed up the ambiguities that are taking hold in middle management: "What is it that a captain can do that a lieutenant should not or cannot do? What is it that a deputy chief can do that a captain should not or cannot do . . .? We haven't defined roles and responsibilities that are commensurate with each rank in the organization and then we bemoan our inability to hold folks accountable. Accountable for what? For a job that was never defined, never clearly explained and for which people have never been formally prepared. It is not a problem of our people. It is a problem of structure."

Once again, the military-based structure of departments, while good for some things, doesn't often accommodate community policing, department restructuring or teamwork.

## THEN AND NOW

Nearly 30 years ago, the Federal Government stepped in to foster police professionalism through the Law Enforcement Assistance Administration. The enactment of the Crime Control Act of 1994, with the resources it has provided and the role it is playing in police work, is very much akin to the golden days of LEAA. There is a great deal of Federal assistance for police departments, for new technology, for research, for finding out what works, for training, and more.

The striking difference between the LEAA days and today is that the Federal Government is now putting far greater emphasis on putting more officers on the street. To date, the Office of Community Oriented Policing Services—the COPS shop—has made commitments for 50,000 new officers. In the LEAA days, on the other hand, the Federal Government invested in the officers we already had by providing educational benefits for in-service personnel through the LEEP program, and many of today's police leaders point to that educational incentive as a key stepping stone for their careers. According to a Bureau of Justice Statistics survey released this year, the number of police departments that require recruits to have some level of higher education doubled from 6 percent in 1990 to 12 percent in 1993—still a far cry from the recommendation of the 1967 President's Commission report, which said "the ultimate aim of all police departments should be that all personnel with general enforcement powers have baccalaureate degrees." Granted, more officers today than ever before have college educations, but it remains regrettable that the 1994 crime act's provisions regarding educational benefits for in-service personnel are underemphasized, underutilized and, to be sure, parsimonious.

As the COPS shop continues to fulfill its goal of putting 100,000 community policing officers on the nation's streets, there is no doubt that the public safety field has grown. This is especially true if one includes private security forces under the heading of public safety. Forbes magazine reported that as of 1995 the number of police and security guards had grown to 1.8 million, ranking 11th among the country's top 30 job classifications. In 1960 it ranked number 22, with 500,000. According to BJS, approximately 374,000 sworn, full-time officers are currently at work in more than 12,000 county and municipal police departments.

## GROWING PAINS

While expanding in size, the field has also grown philosophically. It has been struggling with the concepts and the practice of community policing, which has helped to change how police do what they do. Consider the late 1980's, when many big-city departments unveiled operations known by catchy names like TNT, Clean Sweep and SNIP to crack down on drug hot-spots. Even the Feds got into the act with the "Weed" component of the Weed and Seed program. But eventually, these and other crackdowns were back-burnered because they cost too much, they generated huge numbers of arrests that strangled the courts, and they often angered the very communities they were meant to help. What's different this time? For one thing, the 1996 crackdowns have been better coordinated with the court system, there is far more jail space now than in the late 1980s, and alternatives to incarceration are getting a renewed look. As important, police point to greater input from the community in developing aggressive anti-crime tactics. Through community policing, the police and the public have gained a greater mutual familiarity—and, arguably, trust—thus making today's crackdowns different from those of the past.

Still, there are those who fear for the future of community policing, concerned that high-pressure police tactics signal the concept's abandonment. There is also concern that community policing's intent has become too convoluted, making evaluation and research projects now underway all the more difficult to measure.

That's not to say impossible to measure. One recent study offered a dose of good news, finding that community police officers in Richmond, Va., while less likely to make an arrest, had a much higher probability of having people do what the officers told them to do. The study's author observed: "The pro-community policing officers were much more likely to engage and stop suspects on the street, to be a little more active. While they had a lower batting average, they got to bat a lot more." In view of the problems of excessive force that so often plague law enforcement—often as a result of individuals not responding to officers' commands—the Richmond finding is all the more significant.

## ALL HANDS ON DECK

There is no longer much doubt among practitioners that police strategies and tactics can reduce crime; there is also a growing confidence that community activism can play a major role in crime reduction. Such activism comes in a variety of forms: loud protest marches in front of known drug locations; midnight barbecues on street corners known for drug dealing; watchdog groups, sometimes armed with cellular phones donated by departments; increased volunteerism; more information being provided to police.

But it's not just neighborhood residents who are taking on a greater role in public safety. In the broadest sense, society is taking action with policies aimed at deterrence, collectively telling criminals, "We know who you are and we know where you live."

More than ever, communities have access to information concerning the status and location of offenders. Computerized telephone systems in numerous localities can now inform residents as to where ex-offenders live. In Northern Virginia, communities for the first time made public a list of the names and addresses of about 9,500 people on parole for crimes such as burglary, drunken driving, drug dealing, sexual assault and murder. Registries for released sex offenders have grown in popularity, despite court challenges. In California, a molester hot line has received thousands of calls since its inception in July 1995. More newspapers routinely publish photos of wanted fugitives. (That's not to say that the approach is without problems, as was seen in Minnesota when a privately published anti-crime newspaper had to print a retraction after it mistakenly identified a number of St. Paul residents as child molesters.) And, of course, perhaps the most visible sign of the "we know who you are" trend was the rescue of the TV show "America's Most Wanted" through an appeal from the public and the law enforcement community.

A better-informed public was not the only example of community involvement in crime reduction. The concept of penalty has broadened as well. In addition to imprisonment, an offender now risks losing housing, welfare and educational benefits. Criminal background checks are being conducted with increasing frequency, and are being used to bar ex-offenders from a growing list of occupations. A number of states are expanding the definitions of criminal behavior, such as Florida, which added deadbeat parents into its state crime computers. In response to the growing national concern over underage single-family households, many jurisdictions are once again enforcing statutory rape charges that for years had been collecting dust.

## IMPACT STATEMENT

The increased crime-fighting capability of police, better coordination with other criminal justice and social agencies, community action, improved economic conditions and the linkage of criminal deterrents and entitlement programs are now starting to coalesce. And just what impact has this energetic, synergistic trend had? For many, it is the combination of factors that has led to a decreasing crime rate.

The latest Uniform Crime Reports and BJS victimization study show nationwide declines in the violent-crime rate of 3 percent and 9 percent, respectively. Adult crime is down. Domestic crime is down. The number of burglaries is at its lowest level in the past two decades. Even juvenile crime dipped slightly for the first time in a decade.

Granted, throughout most of the year, criminologists continued their warnings regarding a coming surge in juvenile crime. As the year ended, however, several experts changed their tune and now say that the future with respect to juvenile criminality is not as dire as they had previously predicted.

But despite the good news, there are still concerns that juvenile crime remains at particularly high levels, and police departments around the country—perhaps acting on the earlier gloomy forecast—focused their attention on young offenders. Many departments worked more closely with schools, and developed strategies for dealing with truancy. The Los Angeles Police Department, for example, developed a program that fines parents $135 for a child's first truancy offense, with subsequent violations carrying fines up to $675. The police also give parenting "how-to" classes. They report that within 180 days of launching the program, burglary dropped 6 percent, car theft, 12 percent, and shoplifting, 18 percent.

The International Association of Chiefs of Police, for its part, issued a report on youth violence that recommends, among other things, the development of closer relationships between law enforcement and schools. The issue of education was enough of a hot button to prompt a number of police officials and organizations to publicly voice their opposition to a bill in Congress that would deny public schooling to the children of illegal immigrants. And one survey found that most police chiefs believe that for the crime problem to experience a permanent downward shift, more resources have to be put into addressing the needs of children.

The focus on juveniles is not limited to the police. In the past two years, at least 44 states have changed their juvenile laws or are considering statutory changes—usually with an eye toward making proceedings and penalties tougher. Teen courts, designed for first-time minor offenses, have grown in popularity, with 280 of them now in operation in 31 states and the District of Columbia. Although the year ended with some criminologists retreating from their earlier dire predictions, educators are becoming more worried about the teen-agers of tomorrow. It was recently reported that there is a wider gap in the skills of children entering kindergarten this year than 20 years ago. One facet of this disadvantage, experts say, is that such children develop little ability to tolerate frustrations—a phenomenon with troubling implications for educators and the police alike.

## THE HOME FRONT

Domestic violence, long considered a crime about which police could do little or nothing, has seen its share of increased police attention of late. Police departments, spurred in part by Federal resources made available under the Violence Against Women Act, are actively developing a variety of domestic violence programs: computerized offender histories, specialized units and officer training programs, relationships with social agencies, and streamlined protocols for dealing with prosecutors and the courts. The police have been giving out cellular phones and alarm pendants to victims. Specialized courts have sprung up in numerous areas with simplified processes for obtaining orders of protection. Hot lines have been set up to notify victims when attackers are released from jail.

One development on the domestic front that carries the potential for significant impact was the enactment in 1996 of Federal legislation that prohibits the possession of a gun by anyone convicted of a misdemeanor domestic violence offense. With no exception built in for law enforcement or military personnel, the new law has forced police agencies to take a hard look at their internal policies and practices. In mid-December, for example, the NYPD changed its selection process to exclude those with a history of domestic violence. But what about officers already on the job who have domestic violence convictions? Colorado has begun exploring whether any State Patrol or state Bureau of Investigation officers must turn in their guns because of the law. The Denver Police Department reportedly has placed some officers on desk duty until the department figures out how to comply with the Federal law—a scenario likely to play out in many departments around the country. Local police unions and national police organizations have signaled their discomfort with the new law, and a number of them are considering challenging it. But it bears keeping in mind that with all the efforts police departments are making to deal with domestic violence, it would be politically, legally and ethically tricky for police to enforce a law from which they were exempted.

## PUTTING TECHNOLOGY TO WORK

Clearly, many of the achievements of the year were made possible through technology—specifically, information technology. The mapping software now being used by a number of departments has given crime maps the look of fine art. In Baltimore County, Md., for example, police warned residents about a series of burglaries through a calling network connected to the department's mapping system. Many departments have set up home pages on the World Wide Web to provide information to citizens. In Florida, at least 52 police and sheriffs departments have home pages that can be accessed through the Citizen Safety Center of the Attorney General's office.

The FBI is in the throes of a massive overhaul of its crime files—entailing some 40 million records in 17 data bases. The vaunted NCIC 2000 project got off to a rocky start, with delays and cost overruns, but officials now say things are back on track. As planned, NCIC 2000 will have an increased capacity, allow for greater integration and cross-referencing (e.g., mug shots with fingerprints), integrate state systems that don't talk to each other, and reduce from minutes to mere seconds the time it takes for information transactions. (At present, NCIC handles over 1.7 million transactions per day, an average of 1,183 per minute, compared to roughly 158 transactions per minute 20 years ago.)

For its part, the Bureau of Justice Statistics announced that $33 million would go to 48 states and Washington, D.C., to improve criminal history records, with a view toward keeping felons from purchasing handguns, preventing sex offenders from working with children and the elderly, and identifying repeat offenders who may be subject to three-strikes laws.

Scientific and technological advances have not occurred without a price. Forensic labs cannot meet demands currently being placed on them. The level of refinement for evidence analysis has never been greater, yet such increased precision remains underutilized largely because crime labs are overwhelmed. A survey reported last August found that eight out of 10 lab directors believe their caseload has grown faster than their budgets, their staffs or both. Delays in evidence analysis, according to some observers, have created a major bottleneck in the system. For the FBI, the wait is nine months to a year. Some hope looms. Plans are in the works for a new $150-million lab at the FBI Academy in Quantico, Va. In addition, the National Institute of Justice announced that it would provide funds to develop ways of bringing down the price of DNA testing from several hundred dollars to $20.

## KEEP IT UP

In 1996, the police community benefited in no small way from the resources of the Crime Act of 1994, enhanced technology and a renewed sense of determination to bring down the crime rate. While there is a growing belief that policing can have a significant impact on crime, there remain a number of specific reasons that were credited for crime reductions in various localities (see sidebar, above). The common denominator in many of the explanations, however, was the vigorous way police have targeted specific problems and focused creative energy and resources on them. The police are working harder and working smarter, and their efforts, at least for now, are paying off.

Source: From *Law Enforcement News,* Dec. 31, 1996, Vol. XXII, No. 458.

# 1997 IN REVIEW

# Policing Moves Along Parallel Tracks of Introspection & Outreach

## *Community Policing Comes of Age in '97, Although Critics Still Abound*

Generally speaking, 1997 was a relatively quiet year on the national scene for policing. It lacked the large-scale terrorist bombings, raging crime rates, major riots and other galvanizing events that have seemed the cornerstones of recent past years. That's not to say that the year didn't have its moments for law enforcement, as many local agencies will quickly attest. For the most part, though, it was a time for introspection and outreach— assessing where the field of policing is going as the millennium approaches, and then building the road that will get it there.

Moving along the first of these parallel tracks, law enforcement, with the help of the research community, paused to visit some of the more sensitive and nagging issues that have long dogged policing: the use of force; civilian complaints; corruption and integrity. Crime trends remained under the microscope as well, with particular attention being paid to what's driving crime down.

Along the adjacent track, community policing has continued to evolve, arguably coming of age in 1997. As it has, two schools of thought appear to be emerging. On the one hand are those who see community policing as "adrift," seriously threatened by the variety of methods being applied under its rubric. Others believe just as passionately that it is the nebulous and open-ended nature of community policing that is responsible for its growth. Its diversity is an essential piece of the philosophy, a source of its strength, and allows for local tailoring, increased creativity and, ultimately, expansion.

## GROWTH CHART

Community policing has come a long way since it first began to emerge from the primordial ooze of law enforcement thinking more than 20 years ago. Just about every police agency in the country has been exposed to it in some way, and many have tapped into the recent abundance of Federal resources to implement it. But just how far departments have come along the development continuum of community policing depends on who they are, when and how they got started, how they define the concept, and the level of resources they've committed. For some departments, community policing means more officers and equipment; for others it's a brand new way of doing business—a philosophical underpinning that permeates nearly all aspects of policing. Some departments continue to vest community-policing responsibilities in specialized units, while others are satisfied with nothing less than a department-wide embrace.

Problem-solving—which many view as a key element of, or adjunct to, community policing—can be anything from implementing a bicycle patrol to the sophisticated use of the S.A.R.A. model. Take the Glendale, Calif., Police Department, which won the 1997 Herman Goldstein Award from the Police Executive Research Forum for its insightful and effective problem-solving approach to chronic nuisance problems brought about by day laborers. The Police Department's solution was to spearhead a vigorous effort that involved partnerships with the community, local businesses and other government agencies. To be sure, the growing tendency of criminal justice agencies in general to form problem-solving partnerships was a development of particular importance in 1997. Certainly task forces are nothing new to police departments, which have usually formed them with other law enforcement agencies for limited periods of time and specific purposes. The partnerships that are now emerging, however, involve a closer relationship with other branches of the system.

## SYSTEMATIC GAINS

For years, the phrase "criminal justice system" has been derided as a misnomer, a kind of cruel irony. It's not a system, critics say, but rather an assortment of agencies with an on-again, off-again mutual dependence that, more often than not, translates into working in isolation from each other and at cross-purposes. In the context of community policing, more than a few observers have pondered how police would ever succeed in getting other governmental agencies and the community to work with them when it was so problematic to form productive relationships with prosecutors, courts, prisons, probation and parole and other branches of "the system." However, the Law Enforcement News People of the Year Award for 1997 is testimony to what can be achieved when the various components of the criminal justice system work together toward a common goal, namely stopping juvenile gun violence. The Boston Gun Project—now known to some as "the Boston Miracle"—has been responsible for driving juvenile firearms deaths to near zero over a period of more than two years.

But juvenile crime is not the only issue that is being tackled successfully through the collaborative efforts of criminal justice agencies. A growing variety of crime problems are being addressed by closely networked components of the system focusing on a common purpose. Domestic violence offers a particularly telling example, with police, prosecutors, courts, probation and social work agencies in some areas working together with such a degree of refinement that they are able to deal with different types of batterers in different ways. Other localities are moving successfully to establish community prosecution and community court programs. The financial encouragement of the National Institute of Justice and the Office of Community Oriented Policing Services is also helping to promote partnerships, with 39 grants currently supporting joint police-university research efforts. No doubt that when it comes to building partnerships, a key ingredient of community policing, 1997 was a good year.

## BUMPS IN THE ROAD

Despite the successes of community policing, and the application of some of its precepts by other branches of the

criminal justice system, there are still those—including some of the staunchest advocates of community policing—who are concerned that it is adrift and in danger of being watered down. One criminologist, a former practitioner, went so far as to warn that community policing is threatened by "trivialization, perversion and replacement." Moreover, some fear, because problem-solving was often introduced at the bottom of the organizations as a first stage in community policing, the ability of either concept to permeate all ranks is limited.

A particular sore spot to many community-policing advocates is the term "zero tolerance." They point to the increasing use of crackdowns, particularly on quality-of-life offenses, as reverting to a law enforcement-dominated kind of problem-solving with no attempt to identify and analyze the underlying conditions. No less a figure than Herman Goldstein, the pioneer of problem-oriented policing, says of zero-tolerance: "It's not surgical and creates more dependence on the criminal justice system. It implies less discretion and is unrefined." Such criticisms may have taken hold. There are signs that those who favor an emphasis on quality-of-life crime are backing away from the term "zero-tolerance," claiming that such an emphasis does not necessarily mean a heavy-handed approach.

For all of its recent gains, community policing is still having a tough time fitting into the typical organizational structure of law enforcement. The quasi-military framework of policing has not changed in any fundamental way since the inception of community policing. For that matter, to some observers it hasn't changed all that much since Sir Robert Peel created the London police nearly 170 years ago. The police culture itself is seen as a barrier to organizational modification, and for policing to fundamentally change it first needs to determine its core values and then modify or rebuild its structure to suit. But for all the discussion in recent years about organizational structure and its relationship with community policing, most practitioners agree that with the exception of some flattening of ranks, the quasi-military structure of policing will not change any time soon.

Another example of the troublesome fit between community policing and police organizations concerns performance evaluations—which are difficult enough in most cases, and all the more so when done in the context of a loosely and varyingly defined concept like community policing. Different evaluation methods are under consideration throughout the country, with departments developing core competencies for each rank and assessing an officer's ability to acquire knowledge, skills and attitudes. Once this is established, an officer is required to do a problem-solving project, to be judged by the community result. For the most part, though, departments are trying to supplement long-standing evaluation criteria by simply grafting on a community-policing component. Reports indicate that officers are skeptical about all such approaches because they believe the criteria to be subjective. Their skepticism may be warranted. After all, training in community policing is fairly new and it would seem unfair, if not impossible, to test officers on that which they haven't learned.

## LEARNING CURVES

A recent NIJ-sponsored study found that departments are in need of training that deals with the general concepts of community policing, problem-solving, cultural diversity and conflict resolution. Even departments that have already offered such training identified such a need—an indication that such training should be enhanced and periodically reinforced. Most police academies put community policing precepts into existing training modules—or, at best, have added new modules while leaving much of the curriculum intact. A handful of agencies have tried approaches that are more radical in concept and design, and there are those police chiefs who feel radical change is just what police academies need. As one chief put it: "Academies should not be run like boot camps. They should be more like officer candidate schools used by the military."

The quality of recruits has improved in recent years, according to some chiefs. Most recruits now have at least some college background, and a growing number of police departments now require at least a two-year degree for entry. Yet while many departments require a bachelor's degree to advance in rank, there are still only a relative few where it is needed for employment. This past year the Portland, Ore., and Tulsa, Okla., police departments joined the small cadre of such departments, and Tulsa Police Chief Ron Palmer summed up the prevailing thinking on the subject when he observed that officers with four-year degrees "come to you a little bit more mature, they're a little more aware of diversity issues, and they're more prone to use their minds to problem-solve than those who don't have that type of background."

## IN THE KNOW

But a larger issue has also begun to surface in this respect, with a growing number of practitioners and researchers asking the same fundamental question: What is it police should know?

Some criminologists believe that police, particularly those involved in problem-solving, should become familiar with such concepts as environmental criminology, situational crime prevention, repeat victimization and routine-activity theory—all concepts that would aid practitioners in hot-spot analysis, crime mapping and reducing opportunities for crime. In growing numbers, researchers are looking at crime in the context in which it occurs rather than focusing on the offenders. Such an emphasis cannot help but make their research more valuable to law enforcement policy-makers. Even under the auspices of community policing, after all, there is little that police do about influencing an individual's criminal behavior. The study of criminal offenders, while valuable in itself, has only a limited benefit for the cop on the street or behind a desk. But with the popularity of mapping and hot-spot analysis, police can do something about the context in which crime happens.

## GOING DOWN

There is no shortage of crime-reduction strategies and programs being implemented and replicated throughout the country, and the continuing sharp drop in crime rates makes every successful program that much more appealing to those scanning the landscape for new ideas. There has been virtually no let-up, for example, in the number of departments adapting and adopting Compstat, the system that figures so prominently in New York City's dramatic crime downturn of recent years. Many departments increased their attention to quality-of-life crime and truancy. Cities installed surveillance cameras, roadblocks and gates. They launched resident officer programs (and the Federal Government is now aboard that bandwagon). Police sub-stations have sprouted up in a seemingly endless array of unlikely places, including convenience stores and fast-food restaurants.

Police departments went after problems where they existed, and when they had to improvise, they did so. Such was the case with sex-offender registries and community-notification laws, which departments had to figure out how to implement, sometimes with very little guidance. How they did it ranged from hosting good old-fashioned town meetings to creating CD-ROMs and Internet sites.

Explanations abound as to why crime continues to drop, yet one group that has remained strangely silent in the discussion has been those criminologists who believe there to be a significant, inextricable link between poverty and crime. One might have thought that such criminologists would be crowing "I told you so" during the past year. After all, the economy is booming, and crime is down. Some suggest that the poverty-and-crime proponents have held back because they attribute the economic boom to low-paying jobs that do not lead to the mainstream.

## CAUSAL FACTORS

More significant, perhaps, was an analysis released this year by the National Institute of Justice that deals a sharp blow to the notion of a significant connection between crime and poverty. The NIJ research, which looked at homicide trends in eight cities between 1985 and 1994, shows there to be a weak link at best between overall homicide trends and poverty and employment levels.

The research also found a clear link between juveniles, crack cocaine and guns that caused the sharp spike in crime from the late 1980s to the mid-1990s. In addition, intra-group homicide was found to be the norm, with black-on-black crime the most dominant. Inmate flows in and out of prison did have some effect on homicide rates, with prison detentions linked to declines and prison releases linked to increases (although the research data was admittedly limited).

Another study analyzed police policy and practice and found that what made a difference in the localities studied was aggressive law enforcement (often targeted deployment), particularly when it comes to its emphasis on misdemeanor offenses. Such enforcement usually comes with the blessing of the community, whose tolerance for heavier-handed approaches is higher during times of rising crime. (Of course, when crime goes down, as it has been doing, such tolerance might wear thin.)

There are still other views on the decline in homicide, with some suggesting that it's the result of the end of drug-trafficking turf wars, and because crack is a single-generation drug whose users are aging out of the crime-prone years. Others say that there are fewer domestic homicides due to a decline in domesticity. (Indeed, some go so far as to suggest that the divorce level and the decrease in marriage have helped to reduce domestic violence.)

Opinions differ on whether or not a wave of juvenile crime is looming on the horizon, but a study released in 1997 by the Child Welfare League found a strong correlation between having an incarcerated parent and the likelihood that a child will later be arrested for a crime. (This finding would seem to bode ominously for the future, given the 1.5 million parents currently incarcerated and the 1.6 million children they have.) The study also found that abused or neglected children are 67 times more likely to be arrested between the ages of 9 and 12 than those who aren't—thus giving statistical muscle to the long-held belief that family violence is transmittable through generations. Such information was not lost on a growing number of police executives, who continue to beseech Congress to "invest in kids" by allocating more for early-childhood programs.

## WARNING SIGNALS

As policing and police agencies turn some of their attentions inward, meanwhile, one of the year's most notable trends was the increased emphasis on monitoring personnel. More than a few departments put in computerized "flagging" systems to identify potential problem officers. Most such systems were sold to the rank and file as early-warning systems aimed at permitting prompt intervention as needed. To the extent that an early-warning system is used to that end, of course, it would be of considerable value to both the officer and the department. Following the "stitch in time" adage, such systems could prevent an officer from destroying his career, embarrassing himself and the department, incurring enormous liability and damning public faith in the police.

But just how these systems will be used is still, for the most part, unknown. A number of issues remain to be ironed out. Just what information goes into this system? How is it acquired? How does it get into the system? What is the threshold for intervention? What form will intervention take? Who is responsible for it? Who has access to the information and under what circumstances? At what point do the civil rights of an officer come into conflict with the department's standards and managerial prerogatives?

A hint of an answer to these questions was provided as the year ended when the New York Police Department announced that 500 officers who were the subject of domestic-violence complaints, whether substantiated or not, would be made to undergo two eight-hour training sessions. Even the New York Civil Liberties Union, not usually known for pro-police stances, is troubled by the possible impact that an unsubstantiated and possibly false report could have on an officer's career. (The NYPD is also taking monitoring efforts to another level by looking into any officer who has fired his weapon on three or more occasions. The action was prompted by an end-of-year police shooting of an unarmed man by an officer who had been involved in eight prior shootings during his 14-year career.)

Beyond local efforts, computerized monitoring systems are also being supplemented by NIJ's Office of Science and Technology, which is working to identify and develop early-warning systems for identifying officers with potential problems. Other NIJ efforts include a five-department study of the use-of-force and a longitudinal study of New York officers who were dismissed, resigned or forced to resign because of corruption or brutality. An organizational integrity study is also underway in three cities. Perhaps tellingly, it seems the field no longer studies "corruption"; it studies "integrity."

## UNPRECEDENTED INTROSPECTION

While incidents of corruption and brutality litter policing's past, rarely, if ever, has the profession undergone the level of introspection in these areas that is now underway. In November, the Bureau of Justice Statistics released an unprecedented study that showed that about 1 percent of those who had contact with police alleged that force was threatened or used during the contact. The survey estimated that 45 million adults had face-to-face contact with police, and of those 500,000 reported that force was threatened or used during the contact. (The finding begs the question, of course, as to which is the more consequential statistic: that 500,000 Americans experienced some level of police use of force, or that force was a factor in only 1 percent of all contacts.)

Those involved in the area of police use of force welcomed the study, which was required by the 1994 Crime Control Act, and expressed hope that there would be future studies in order to ascertain trends. At present, however, BJS has not been funded to do another survey and observers are concerned that what might be a useful tool for determining levels of use of force will be abandoned.

Within the next few months, statistics should be available from IACP's newly developed national data base on police use of force. In addition, over the next few years research results will become available from the 17 police departments nationwide that are currently involved in NIJ-sponsored corruption and use-of-force studies. That so many departments are involved in these efforts (a record number, according to NIJ Director Jeremy Travis) speaks loudly to the sea change that policing has undergone. Receptiveness to such study would have been unheard of just 10 years ago.

## AVERTING A "BIG ONE"

Will 1998 be a year that allows for the kind of self-analysis that occurred in 1997? Who can say? As most practitioners agree, you never know when a "big one" can go off on your doorstep, bringing it with the kind of high-level scrutiny that can divert attention from more useful analyses that can make policing better. Still, as many departments are realizing, the risks of a "big one"—especially one that results from police action—can be minimized by the kind of research and self-monitoring that is now underway.

In sum, it was a good year for law enforcement. Police demonstrated that they can make a difference in reducing crime by focusing on specific problems and dealing with them. Police continued to make partnerships with the community, business and with other public agencies, most notably other branches of the criminal justice system. Community policing will continue to flourish, with the economy good and crime down. Federal resources continue to be abundant, in terms of funding for new officers and equipment as well as for research. Call it a golden age, a renaissance, of police development. Not since the days of the Law Enforcement Assistance Administration has the field been given this kind of boost.

Just how long it will last is unclear, of course. But with any luck crime rates will continue to drop, the economy will continue to prosper, and Federal resources will continue to flow. At least for now, then, let the good times roll.

Source: From *Law Enforcement News,* Dec. 31, 1997, Vol. XXIII, No. 480.

# 1998 IN REVIEW

# Getting Nice & Comfy? Don't.

## *From Manpower Levels to Crime Stats, Numbers That Look Good Now May Yet Haunt Law Enforcement*

You can't get too comfortable.

On its surface, 1998 seemed like a good year. The economic picture remains favorable, as does the crime rate, which continues to drop. Crime slipped from the spotlight as the nation's attention focused on pocketbook issues and, almost unavoidably, sordid intimacies in government. There were more Americans at work than ever before, according to the Labor Department, and the poverty rate is falling, especially among blacks and Hispanics. Generally speaking, as a nation we appear to be richer and safer.

Still, the very attributes that made 1998 a good year for police and the communities they serve have given rise to some specters that very well may haunt law enforcement in the years ahead. Rising prosperity and increased public safety are contributing to a labor shortage the likes of which the field has not experienced since the late 1970s, and its impact is already being felt in a growing number of departments from coast to coast. If the past is prologue, then today's labor shortage will likely affect policing for years to come. Despite hiring efforts catalyzed by the Office of Community Oriented Policing Services, which so far has added a reported 88,000 officers to 12,000 communities, and reports that the number of sworn officers in state and local departments rose by 10 percent between 1992 and 1996, to more than 660,000, many police agencies find themselves shrinking.

## THE MORE THINGS CHANGE...

Twenty-five years ago, the officers and recruits were there but the resources needed to hire them were not. The country was in recession, officers were being laid off and hiring came to a virtual standstill. As the economy gradually improved and police hiring resumed, departments rushed to increase their ranks, in some cases skimping on the recruit screening process—often with dire results. Some of the officers recruited at the time proved especially vulnerable to the influence of the violence and drug money that abounded in the mid-80s. To make matters worse, the bubble in hiring also led to corresponding gaps in the supervisory ranks—a situation that would eventually play a role in numerous major police scandals.

Now, however, the resources are there but the recruits are not. Exacerbating the problem is the growing wave of retirements of the baby-boomer cops who now have more than 20 years of service. In Washington, D.C., for example, more than 25 percent of the department is expected to retire in the next two years. In Washington state, the Seattle Police Department, which is already operating at 10 percent below authorized strength, is bracing for a wave of retirements that could mean the loss of 150 veteran officers by the end of 1999. In Atlanta, the department's vacancy rate, which is estimated to be 19 percent, became a legal issue when the Mayor's office refused to release the number of sworn officers to a major newspaper. And the manpower problem is not just limited to large departments. In Washington Township, N.J., for example, police officials are concerned about filling five positions, which represents almost 18 percent of the department.

Departments attribute the problem to an nationwide unemployment rate that is currently at a 25-year low and the increased competition from the private sector as well as

# 1999 IN REVIEW

# The High Price of Success

## *Despite Gains for Police, Troubles Still Abound*

It was not all that long ago that the term "profiling" had a certain cachet within law enforcement, as investigative luminaries such as Robert Ressler, John Douglas and Pierce Brooks popularized the practice of getting inside the heads of serial killers, rapists and arsonists to create psychological pictures of unidentified offenders.

But, as they say, that was then, and this is now. In 1999, "profiling" was once again a term that cast a huge shadow over law enforcement, with a spillover into many other segments of society. But the connotation this time, unlike the mid to late 1980s, was dramatically different. Just ask most black or Hispanic males—or, for that matter, almost any sworn member of the New Jersey State Police and several other police departments.

The great irony of 1999 is that, at a time of diminishing crime rates and a vigorous economy, police departments across the country found themselves unable to enjoy any complacency or self-satisfaction. There was the need to prepare for and respond to large-scale criminal acts: school shootings, terrorism and, of course, bigger-than-ever New Year's Eve celebrations. Agencies and personnel responded to natural disasters and geared up for the frightening possibility of man-made computer disasters. These and other preparations were frequently made in the midst of growing, often painfully intense scrutiny from Federal authorities, state and local prosecutors and civilian oversight boards. And through it all was the nagging, unsettling issue of racial profiling—an issue that had been percolating for at least a year and would not go away easily.

For policing, it appeared, the price of recent successes was going to be high. The abundance of riches that should have come with sharp and continuing decreases in crime would translate instead to an uneasy affluence at best.

## PROFILE—A ONE-SIDED PICTURE?

The year was barely underway when the racial profiling issue managed to find a new high-water mark, with the firing of Supt. Carl Williams of the New Jersey State Police for published remarks on profiling and criminality that were deemed racially insensitive. His firing on Feb. 28 came just a few weeks after the state reluctantly released information showing that blacks represented a hugely disproportionate share of those motorists searched and arrested by troopers.

In short order profiling would take center stage not only in New Jersey but nationwide. Attorney General Janet Reno announced in April that she planned to add questions about police behavior to the annual National Crime Victimization Survey. And in a development that made most of the law enforcement community sit up and take notice, a bill was introduced in Congress that would require

police to collect racial data on motorists stopped for traffic violations, with the data then to be analyzed by the Justice Department. Numerous line organizations voiced their concern about the bill. The International Association of Chiefs of Police found little support among its members for federally mandated data-collection but called for the funding of state and local data bases. The Police Executive Research Forum, for its part, is looking at the development of a national standard. Even the National Organization of Black Law Enforcement Executives, while supporting the legislation, did not feel it necessary for officers to ask drivers their race or ethnicity, but instead suggested that they rely on observation. This notion cut to the heart of one of the central issues of the data-collection debate. Police, who know all too well that there is no such thing as a "routine traffic stop," strongly felt that asking drivers for the desired information would inevitably and unnecessarily intensify an already tense situation, possibly to the point of violence.

Despite the concerns, numerous jurisdictions went ahead on their own to undertake the task—and not without some cost. The Florida Highway Patrol, for example, estimated that its efforts on data collection would cost between $1.1 million and $4.7 million, depending upon the method selected to record and analyze the information.

Profiling has long been a practice of businesses ranging from insurance to banking to marketing. It has been used by law enforcement to intercept airplane hijackers, hassle hippies and thwart drug couriers. But recent developments are now showing law enforcement what portrait artists have long known—a profile presents just one side of a picture, not the full face, and the other side of the picture can be strikingly different from the one that is presented. Some police policy-makers have lamented the looseness or complete absence of any generally accepted definition of the profiling problem. One chief went so far as to suggest that racial profiling "has come to mean all things which inconvenience people of color involving the police." Until a definition of the problem can be reached, a solution will remain elusive.

Police agencies are forced to grapple with the question of whether crime-suppression efforts are worth a distrustful, even hostile relationship with the minority community. Granted, many of the recent high-profile examples of improper racial profiling have come from agencies that patrol the nation's highways, where there are striking differences from patrolling the neighborhood streets of a city or town. For highway patrol agencies, the "community," as it were, tends to be just passing through on the way to somewhere else. Municipal policing, however, is generally less anonymous, and police stops in the age of computerized crime-mapping are often based on detailed information about a neighborhood and its hot spots. As important, said one lieutenant, "Profiling is just another fancy word for experience." Still, there is always the risk that this could fall into the category of unacceptable police practice.

The racial-profiling debate was not without its political overtones. One chief observed that for some people "there is much mileage to be gained by marginalizing the police and using [them] to mobilize their constituencies." Others refer to a kind of "modern-day McCarthyism," and note that one cannot ignore the fact that in some areas drug buyers are white and sellers are black. Still, police departments today know that community perceptions count—whether real, imagined or stirred up—and so many police officials have undertaken an examination of the problem, as have other outside entities. Not least of these is the Justice Department, which in December reached agreement with the State of New Jersey on a consent decree that includes the appointment of a monitor for the State Police, who will report directly to a Federal judge on just about any police function.

A lingering question that emerged from the year's focus on racial profiling and other controversial police practices is just what impact heightened public scrutiny of police will have on the level of drug interdiction on interstate routes. Although a final answer has yet to be arrived at, anecdotal evidence suggests cause for concern. As the year ended, reports from various jurisdictions indicated that arrests were dropping. For example, through September arrests by the New Jersey State Police had decreased by 42 percent compared to the same period in 1998. Certainly one explanation was that the attention to profiling was forcing some officers to change their racially driven ways. Some police union officials, however, contend that the decline is due to troopers' fear of being falsely accused of racial profiling. Officers with good intentions and honorable records, it would seem, are not taking any chances.

## LOOKING OVER COPS' SHOULDERS

In all likelihood, at any given time there is always an investigation of a police department going on somewhere in the country. If 1999 seemed to bring an inordinate number of such investigations—Chicago, Los Angeles, Detroit, Cincinnati, Seattle and Hartford, to name several—it may be a reflection of the prevailing philosophy of the Justice Department, a penchant for more thorough self-examination by police and, to be sure, politics.

The New York City Police Department began the year still reeling from the August 1998 torture of Abner Louima by police, and on Feb. 4, the proverbial "other shoe" dropped. An unarmed peddler named Amadou Diallo was killed in a hail of police bullets, and in short order there were no fewer than five outside agencies investigating the incident. The four officers involved in the shooting were indicted for murder. Despite statistics showing that police shootings were declining, a poll conducted just weeks after the Diallo shooting indicated that 72 percent of blacks, 62 percent of Hispanics and 33 percent of whites believed that most officers used excessive force. (On the other hand, a survey commissioned by the NYPD found that most residents, including a majority of blacks and Hispanics, respect the police.)

The notoriety surrounding the Diallo shooting focused not only on the particulars of the incident itself, but on the whole notion of quality-of-life crime enforcement, with its critics saying such efforts are excessive and tend to violate civil rights. Defenders focused on what they saw as the opportunistic and political nature of the criticism, calling it "an ideological attack on a successful philosophy of policing." Quality-of-life enforcement, they argued, did indeed prevent crime and they had the stats to prove it.

In recent years the Justice Department and its agencies have been very generous to law enforcement, but they have also been tough, as demonstrated by the sharp increase in the number of police officers serving prison terms—from 107 in 1994 to 655 in June 1999. While some chiefs welcome and even invite Federal authorities, and have used their investigations to advantage, many chiefs have complained that Federal probes have been initiated without their knowledge, thus leaving them to operate in a vacuum. It undermines the responsibility of the chief and the municipality, they say. Some even question whether direct intervention is a proper role for the Federal Government to play. Federal authorities have not done the best job investigating themselves, some critics point out, as shown by the reopening of the Waco investigation. The Columbus, Ohio, Police Division is one agency that has told the Feds, in effect, to buzz off, refusing to enter into a consent decree with the Justice Department. Columbus officials told Federal prosecutors that they will have to prove in court their allegations that police engaged in a pattern of abuses ranging from excessive force to improper search and seizure.

The irony of these investigations and the attention they received, of course, is that in general police around the country use very little force. Through the efforts of the Justice Department and various professional organizations, a national picture is starting to emerge, highlighted by a first-of-its-kind report released in October, which found that only 1 percent of people who had face-to-face encounters with police said that officers used or threatened force, and that firearms are used in just 0.2 percent of arrests. While emphasizing that more study is needed, the report also states with "modest confidence" that use of force is more likely to occur when they are dealing with persons under the influence of alcohol or drugs or with the mentally ill, and that only a small percentage of officers are involved disproportionately in use-of-force incidents. Not even addressed was the question of whether or not the use of force was wrongful—a statistical shading that would seem likely to make the report even more favorable to law enforcement.

## THE NUMBER CRUNCH

A personnel drought has begun to spread its withering heat across the field of policing, confronting agencies with the prospect of operating short-handed in the years ahead. Overtime will be a fact of life. Labor-intensive initiatives may have to be cut back. Supervisory skills will go begging. Pressure will increase in some quarters to reduce standards.

The truth is, America's booming economy is not good for policing. Competition for recruits has been fiercely competitive, with some departments gaining at the expense of others. The Seattle Police Department, for example, visited some 10 cities to recruit; one of them, Atlanta, was chosen because it has well trained officers with low morale. The NYPD spent $9 million on a recruiting campaign that yielded a smaller applicant pool than officials had hoped for. Departments went overseas to scour military bases for recruits.

Nationwide, seasoned officers are leaving, including a growing number in the upper ranks. With police salaries growing more slowly than those in the private sector, many sworn personnel take a moment to calculate pensions and other benefits and find they can make almost as much money by not working. Weighed against a backdrop of increased pressure from superiors, the public and the press, retirement has a distinct appeal. Departments will find themselves getting younger and less experienced. Officers make an average of roughly $33,000. Should localities consider increasing salaries to make staying on the job more lucrative? Do they have the ability and the will to do so? Should they consider the potential adverse consequences of having an unusually young and inexperienced work force?

## STILL MAKING A DIFFERENCE

Through it all, police have continued to drive down crime rates, and that drop in crime in some areas has given police free time that allows them to focus more attention on things like investigating computer crime and backlogged warrants. They've developed after-school programs; they've trained landlords to spot drug labs. They've worked with residents to make a difference. And despite publicity that was often harshly critical, appreciation of police by their "clients" is strong. In a landmark Justice Department study of 12 cities, roughly 85 percent of residents reported that they were well served by their police, notwithstanding higher than average victimization. There were differences in the approval ratings given by white and nonwhite residents—roughly 14 percentage points on average. There's room for improvement, but it's certainly not bad.

Source: From *Law Enforcement News,* Dec. 15/31, 1999, Vol. XXV, Nos. 523, 524.

# 2000 IN REVIEW

# 2000: A Year in Profile

## *Sometimes Bad Things Happen to Good Professions*

Despite the best efforts of well-intentioned people, some problems just seem to get worse. Consider two recent examples: In February, the Riverside, Calif., Police Department added civilian support staff to free up officers for enhanced recruitment efforts. That same month, half a continent away, the St. Louis County Police Board revised its police manual, adding a provision forbidding racial profiling.

By year's end, police departments from one end of the country to another found themselves grappling with the issues of personnel and racial profiling simultaneously and with increasing urgency. By no means are these problems new to law enforcement; in 2000 they simply took center stage. In terms of racial profiling, the overriding issue was data collection: whether to do it, how to do it, what forces are driving it, and what the results mean. The major concerns with respect to personnel, on the other hand, were the simultaneous problems of declining recruitment and increasing attrition. When it came to people, departments had to figure out how to get them and how to keep them.

## THE PEOPLE PUZZLE

We all know the reasons why there is a labor shortage in American policing: the primary culprits appear to be high employment rates, competition from both the private sector and other law enforcement agencies, and the demonization of the police in the public eye. Reciting this litany became a ritual repeated time and again throughout the country and throughout the year. While there have been recruiting success stories, for the most part the efforts of police departments have fallen short of expectations. It has not been for

lack of trying. Departments took up the challenge with zest. They gave recruitment a higher priority within the organization. They jazzed up their promotional materials. They sent their representatives far and wide, sometimes to explore previously untapped manpower pools. They implemented or enhanced lateral mobility provisions. Some jurisdictions even bit the bullet and increased starting salaries for officers.

Despite a host of such efforts, though, the problem remains and it many areas it is worsening. The serious implications of such a labor shortage beg the question of whether it is time to deal with the problem on a national level. Police organizations should consider forming partnerships with leading marketing firms to put together a generic advertising campaign that would have the net result of assisting the field as a whole. That's not to say that departments would or should reduce their own efforts as a result, but a nationwide campaign would provide policing with a necessary boost at this critical point in time. Such an effort, carefully done, might also have the added result of improving the overall public image of police.

In any profession, a labor shortage puts a squeeze on qualifications and standards. Although some professions can get away with cutting corners and trying to make due, many feel that when it comes to law enforcement, there's simply too much at stake. Of course, that didn't stop a number of jurisdictions from rethinking college requirements out of concern for being able to fill positions. But before departments reduce their standards in this area, they should consider the recent experience of one Northeast jurisdiction that requires just a high school diploma. More than 100 high school graduates could not pass the police test with its 10th-grade reading level.

The shortage of personnel has also put a damper on the issue of residency requirements, at least for now. In an ideal world, the police recruit comes from the community and stays in it. But with departments searching far and wide for candidates, such an ideal applicant may not be possible these days. Casting a wider net for recruits has added a whole new dimension to conducting background checks. Interviewing family, friends and neighbors is a more time-consuming, complicated and costly affair when candidates come from hundreds, if not thousands of miles away. (That is, if it's done correctly—and recent history is replete with examples of jurisdictions willing to cut corners on back-ground checks, and then later paying dearly for their short-sightedness.)

Even the role of municipal civil service was widely called into question, particularly on the issue of who has the final say on a candidate—the department or the municipal-ity, through its civil service commission. Like any employer, police departments want to have the final say on who works for them, since the actions of individual officers are ultimately the responsibility of the agencies they serve. Attendant questions abound: Should police have access to the sealed criminal records of juveniles? Should police applicants be required to waive the confidentiality of such records? Do departments have the means to deal with the specifics of individual cases?

Hand in hand with the knotty issue of recruitment has been an escalation in attrition, a trend that shows every indi-cation of continuing, if not worsening. There are short- and long-term consequences to a dwindling number of experi-enced supervisors and officers. With authority and respon-sibility having become more localized at the lower ranks than in the past for many departments, supervisory inexpe-rience may have the reverse effect of moving levels of accountability higher up the chain of command. If time in rank is reduced when filling supervisory positions, will inexperienced officers be able to handle the pressure of an environment that increasingly stresses officer monitoring?

Communities will have to ask themselves how much experience is worth? Are there incentives that could be used to keep experienced officers from leaving? How much would such incentives cost? Are they affordable? What is the price in human terms if such incentives are not applied? In addition to finding ways to keep experienced officers on the job, departments should consider whether they are unwittingly contributing to their own attrition problems. One veteran observer has noted that overtime-based high-intensity operations can lead to a substantial increase in retirements, since many police pensions are based on the final year's salary. Since high-intensity tactics like New York's Operation Condor are employed throughout the country, particularly when it comes to purging neigh-borhoods of quality-of-life crime, departments may find themselves achieving productivity gains in the present by mortgaging their future.

## STOP SIGNS

A look at the centerfold of this issue will show just how the issue of racial profiling landed on the doorsteps of law enforcement agencies throughout the country, where it was handled in a variety of ways. Police chiefs in some places signed agreements to voluntarily collect information on motorists they stopped, while others had the task mandated for them. In some localities, such data were analyzed by the departments themselves or with the help of outside researchers, while in other areas the local news media analyzed police stops, sometimes aided by civil liberties groups. Legislators scurried to draft and pass relevant laws, while the courts took on a growing volume of lawsuits spawned by racial profiling. Taken together, such events gave greater dimension and urgency to the issue of race relations in 2000.

Some police chiefs look back to the 1980's when profil-ing first hit drug enforcement. Aided and encouraged by federal law enforcement, notably the Drug Enforcement Administration, state and local police used race-based information to improve interdiction efforts, particularly on the interstate highways. When 91,000 pages of information on racial profiling were released this fall in New Jersey, many of the documents were found to call attention to the role of federal law enforcement agencies that used racial profiling as a weapon in the war on drugs. But in any arse-nal used to defeat an enemy, there are some arms that are just too lethal to be deployed in most combat situations. It begs the question of whether the perception—or the reality—of civil-liberties infringement is simply too much firepower to use in this war.

A recent survey by the Police Executive Research Forum, presented at a forum on racial profiling in the fall, indicated that over 15 percent of departments are involved in some way with collecting data on race. A number of departments reported having been advised by legal experts not to count. The reason is that counting traffic stops by race gives a number that is without context. Social science researchers contend that without "contextuality," as they like to call it, results are questionable, if not utterly invalid. For example, since the total number of traffic violators broken down by race is not known, researchers rely on "proxy" data like residential information, census data, access to autos by race, racial breakdowns of traffic accidents, and visual observations of driving patterns in order to measure the number of stops made by police. Yet getting even the best information in these categories can be misleading.

Experts feel that departments collecting traffic-stop data would do well to arrange with a research entity to analyze and interpret the results. And, since counting seemed to have been central to the year 2000 in politics and well as in policing, much depends on who is doing the arithmetic. For a number of jurisdictions, particularly in states with expan-sive sunshine laws, the counting was done by the press and/or civil liberties groups. Often in these situations, news coverage leaves out information as to what level of analysis and what "proxy" data is being used, thereby giving the public a picture that is as unclear as it is potentially inflammatory.

At the PERF forum, legal advocates who believe police should collect racial data pointed to the necessity of building and maintaining community trust, without which police undermine their essential mission. As evidence, they point to juries and judges declining to give police the benefit of the doubt—thereby eroding what has been a fundamental, if unstated pillar of the criminal justice system. Whether racial profiling is real or merely perceptual, police should tackle the issue head-on. Arrest and incarceration rates may be higher for African Americans and Latinos, but they are not an accurate reflection of overall offending behavior. These groups are arrested more often for consensual crimes where there is no individual victim, when police have not been called, and when police are exercising a high degree of discretion. It therefore proceeds, the analysts say, that arrest rates are about police activity rather than offending behavior. Statistically, blacks are stopped more often than whites although they represent a smaller portion of the population and although their level of drug use is less than that of whites. In addition, the "hit" rate—when contraband is actually found—is the same for both blacks and whites. Therefore, these experts maintain, disproportionate stops demonstrate racial profiling.

Police officials retort that a discussion of racial profiling must address the issue of the substantially disproportionate racial breakdowns in victimization and in those identified as perpetrators. Officers and are sent "where crime is," police officials maintain—particularly since the advent of community policing, problem solving and the focus on quality of life. Such factors as where the calls for service come from, how vocal the community is about wanting police presence, and where crime analysis determines a criminal pattern exists will determine police activity in any given locality. Looking for a match between demographics and stops is basically flawed. Simply comparing the number of stops to the racial demographics of a locality, as is usually done, does not necessarily mean a department is engaged in racist activity. As one African American police official put it, "Sixty-one percent of my city's population is black, homicide victims are 92 percent black, and 98 percent of the suspects are black. So what am I supposed to do, look for an Asian?"

For some police executives, any discussion about data collection is really political. Officers in one department came up with a values statement and brought it to the community—a community that was more interested in greater enforcement of quality-of-life crime connected to drug activity. Some months later, after the department had accommodated the community and had received numerous accolades for its efforts, a call came for the collection of data. As the chief of this department put it, "In the same week the department received a letter of praise for its efforts from the community, the NAACP called for the collection of numbers, and I realized that I had just spent the summer generating statistics that would be held against the department."

Others see the issue of racial profiling as being about weeding out racist cops and requiring greater civility on the part of officers when stops are made. Increasingly, departments require officers to articulate, sometimes in writing, the reason for making a stop. The personal dynamics of the traffic and street stops have become critical to the perception of fairness. There is some information, researchers say, that shows well meaning officers can also act with inadvertent insensitivity. To address this, departments implemented or enhanced training on making a stop—or at least they tried to. The paucity of training available in this area—training that balances caution and command with courtesy—remains a matter of concern for many police administrators.

Data collection has been shown to have more chilling consequences, as one city experienced when traffic accidents increased after data collection began—largely because officers became "gun shy" about making even legitimate traffic stops. In a rush to make good public policy in the sensitive area of racial profiling, legislators may have failed to realized, or willfully ignored, the impact in these very human terms. Will more people be hurt on the nation's roads? While there is no really trustworthy information on bad driving habits, sorted by race, there are indications that fewer African Americans wear seat belts. Should efforts to crack down on lack of seat-belt use be curtailed? If such efforts are minimized, will more people be injured, or worse? The current state of affairs puts police in the difficult predicament of collecting data by race to "do the right thing," as it were, a decision that may ultimately lead to an erosion in public safety.

## POLITICAL WINDS

For the last eight years, the Department of Justice has been sensitive to the needs of policing on the local level. Through its various branches, it gave to the field copious resources in terms of personnel, research, information, technology and equipment. Just as importantly, it provided a voice to police. Having an Attorney General with recent practical experience working with local police certainly helps to explain the emphasis that the Justice Department put on the community level. Some see it as a golden age of policing—a time that will influence events in the future. That's not to say that the field has always been approving of Janet Reno's actions. As one police chief put it, referring to the issue of federal monitoring, "I don't know whether I'm dealing with 'Justice-the-Good' or 'Justice-the-Bad.'" For the most part, however, the Justice Department under Reno tried and often succeeded in delivering a coordinated approach to problems. It promised to deliver increased interagency cooperation, and for the most part it did. It was uncommonly active in supporting some measure of gun control. It dealt directly with local law enforcement agencies, particularly in the area of funding. Such local interest did not come without a good deal of local scrutiny, of course. It was also a Justice Department that emphasized police monitoring, some would say to a fault.

At the juncture between two administrations, particularly with a change in the party in power, it is hard to say what the future will bring for law enforcement. In the 2000 presidential campaign, crime was simply not on the agenda. Will the new administration continue the activist role of the federal government in scrutinizing local police departments, or will it back off? Some departments, notably those in New York and Columbus, Ohio, have a significant vested interest in the answer. Will police departments continue to receive federal resources directly, or will they once again engage in a statewide competition through a resurgence in block grants—a situation that had led to interagency competitiveness rather than cooperation? Will the new government maintain the same degree of emphasis on keeping track of the country's firearms? Will local law enforcement maintain the same level of access to the feds? Will the resources be there?

Given the close and contentious nature of the last election, it is difficult to predict what the future might hold for law enforcement at the federal level. Locally, though, police will still be dealing with the everyday realities of crime, which is bound to begin creeping up again soon, with keeping their ranks filled, and trying to get a grip on the slippery issue of race relations.

Source: From *Law Enforcement News,* Dec. 15/31, 2000, Vol. XXVI, Nos. 545, 546.

# 2001 IN REVIEW

# 2001: A Year in Profile

## *Life in Law Enforcement, Before and After 9/11*

It took only 78 minutes on the morning of Sept. 11 to alter the very nature of law enforcement in this country. At 8:48 A.M. on a beautiful, late-summer morning, an act of war occurred on American soil. It was unthinkable, shocking, horrific.

Foreign invaders—Islamic militants who apparently had been in this country for some time—had hijacked commercial jetliners and turned them into guided missiles to strike the World Trade New York City and the Pentagon. A third target was avoided only by the courageous acts of American civilians. The death toll was unimaginable, the repercussions both enormous and ongoing. These attackers made good on past threats—threats that, in retrospect, had not been taken seriously.

In the hours after the attacks, the country, caught napping, began preparing for war at home and abroad. Nearly everything stopped. Transportation ground to a halt. Businesses shut down. The borders were sealed. Even crime dropped in the immediate aftermath of the attack. The country was in a self-imposed lockdown. The military began to mobilize and appear en masse. And as if that weren't enough, just one week later a chain of events began at a New Jersey post office that would ultimately point to a new threat—biological weapons. The threat, in the form of letters that were later found to contain anthrax spores, seemed to be aimed primarily against Congress and the news media, and would eventually leave five people dead, 18 others infected and thousands obtaining antibiotics for protection.

America became a country transformed in 2001. A confident nation had been made painfully aware of its vulnerabilities, of which there were many. While just about every segment of society was touched in some way by the attack on Sept. 11, the country's law enforcement community was changed almost overnight. Its mission was fundamentally recast.

## A CHANGE IN EMPHASIS

"To protect and serve" is a catch phrase at the heart of American policing. The words are found in mottoes, mission statements, painted on patrol cars, sewn into insignias, and would seem to embody the feelings of most police personnel. In retrospect, though, it appears that police have long had the luxury of being able to concentrate on the "serve" portion of that motto. That's not to say that police haven't had their dealings with truly bad people—organized crime figures, street gangs, serial killers, child killers, mass murderers, even terrorists. Nevertheless, with the advent of community policing more than two decades ago, police over time have been able to improve service for their communities by solving problems. They have been able to deal with quality-of-life crime and have had a significant impact on bringing down the crime rate. Agencies have even had the time to go into cold cases.

On Sept. 11, however, the emphasis in the phrase "to protect and serve" suddenly switched to the word "protect." Things change when the battlefield is your own backyard or mail box and the enemy is somewhere in your midst. Information gleaned about the attackers clearly demonstrated to law enforcement just how invisible the enemy can be—hiding within plain sight, as it were, in many sections of the country.

## STRETCHED TO THE MAX

Police worked long hours protecting airports and other transportation hubs, buildings, bridges, reservoirs, crops, nuclear power plants, government buildings and other facilities, often working closely with the National Guard and military reservists. Already facing an ambitious if not overwhelming national investigation, an additional and unnecessary burden came with the dramatic increases in the occurrence of hoaxes, both for bombs and anthrax. (In New York City in just one day, police dealt with more than 90 reports of suspicious packages and bomb threats.) Almost immediately, jurisdictions imposed harsher penalties on the hoaxers. When biological weapons were introduced into the mix, the nature of the hoaxes became even more complicated, requiring both a public health and a law enforcement response—a response that was not always well coordinated.

Overtime reached record-breaking levels in the course of an effort never before undertaken by the country's law enforcement agencies—an effort that cannot be maintained indefinitely at such high levels of intensity. As the year ended, police found themselves stretched to the max. Increases in responsibilities of this magnitude do not come without a price. Just as the declining crime rate is beginning to plateau and even go up in some places, police are finding themselves faced with lots to do amid changing priorities.

To make matters worse, recruitment is still down and attrition is mounting in many departments, sometimes as a direct result of the overtime produced by the terrorist attacks. As the nation ratcheted up its military defenses, law enforcement agencies were hit by the call-up of military reservists thereby further depleting police ranks. Even before Sept. 11, policing wrestled with the serious problem of dwindling ranks, forcing departments to cast an ever-widening net for recruits. The temptation to lower standards, always a recipe for trouble, continued. A number of departments dropped or modified college requirements. Residency requirements received a second look and were often dropped.

While personnel shortages were bad and getting worse prior to Sept. 11, the almost overnight growth of jobs in federal law enforcement and private security also took their toll on local policing. More entry level and management positions became available in both fields, drawing growing numbers of seasoned personnel from local police ranks. As luck would have it, though, increased joblessness in other sectors of the economy may ultimately help to increase the ranks of the many police departments. Yet even if applications go up, it will have little immediate impact on the loss of supervisory personnel, a precarious situation sure to unfold in the near future.

Despite new and expanded responsibilities for police, there remains the job of handling routine crime-fighting activities and investigation. No one wants a return to the early 1990s, when crime in the United States peaked with more than 20,000 homicides. With some localities already seeing signs of crime-rate creep, there is the danger that the current set of overshadowing priorities will take time and personnel away from effective crime-reduction strategies and quality-of-life crime initiatives. Compounding the problem, the economic slowdown that occurred early in 2001 was already necessitating cuts in many departments well before Sept. 11. It is clear the future will not be easy.

But "help is on the way," insists Tom Ridge, the former governor of Pennsylvania who heads the new White House Office of Homeland Defense. The alerts announced by his office, while sensible, have yet to be translated into practical deployment issues on the ground and in the pocketbook. So far, the Sept. 11 attacks have cost $700 million in added public safety costs. Making war is costly and it became all too clear to many cities that federal money is urgently needed for the law enforcement effort at home. While Ridge has conceded that it could take months, even years, to build a truly viable homeland defense program, policing's more immediate needs include help in protecting vulnerable targets, training, equipment and enhanced border control. Data bases need to be integrated, coordinated and, in some cases, built from scratch. But one of the most important elements of warfare, whether foreign or at home, is good and timely intelligence. The events of Sept. 11 magnified the urgent need for information on the local level and the need for enhanced coordination at the federal level. Law enforcement agencies nationwide desperately needed information. They didn't always get it.

## LEARNING TO SHARE

Law enforcement's "dirty little secret"—that intelligence is not often shared—became household news and a matter of vital importance to the country's homeland security. To be sure, the FBI had been having a bad year even before Sept. 11: Congressional oversight hearings; a pending reorganization; a document foul-up that forced a delay in the execution of Oklahoma City bomber Timothy McVeigh, and the discovery of an agent who had been spying for the Russians.

Many in New York law enforcement will recall the FBI's attempt to discredit the ATF agent who had found the vehicle identification number—a crucial piece of evidence—from the truck involved in the 1993 bombing of the World Trade Center, as a telling example of the bureau's steamrolling over a major investigations. It certainly did not help the bureau's image when it was learned in the aftermath of the Sept. 11 attacks that FBI officials refused to approve a wiretap on the computer of Zacarias Moussaoui, the alleged 20th hijacker. After the attacks, numerous police officials bitterly complained that they were kept in the dark and not provided with enough information to adequately protect the public. At year's end, relations between the bureau and local law enforcement had improved in some areas, but for the most part signs of strain were never far from the surface.

## A DIFFERENT PERSPECTIVE ON PROFILING

Although the tensions between local and federal law enforcement often ran high, it still came as a shock to many in policing when the Portland, Ore., Police Bureau and a handful of other departments announced that they would not assist in the efforts of federal agents to interview thousands of Middle Eastern subjects. Some viewed this action as nothing less than a dereliction of duty—a case of political correctness gone too far. After all, some maintain, while two cities were attacked, the operatives lived, trained and conspired in many regions of the country. Nationwide criminal investigations have always been part of police work and, despite rivalries, a fair amount of cooperation takes place regularly in law enforcement. Given the current threat level, inattention in one place can lead to devastation in another.

Still, it is not surprising that racial profiling, which has dominated policing in the last few years, remains a sensitive topic even through this period of emergency. Prior to the attacks, departments across the country continued to be obsessed with counting stops by race and issuing policy directives. But just how valuable the numbers will be remains to be seen [see Page 11]. What did become clear during the year was that in the aftermath of a racially charged incident or some kind of accusation of racism, police engage in what is now known as "depolicing." Arrests go down and crime goes up largely because officers simply do not want to put themselves in harm's way. While it is easy for some to say that police should continue to do their work without regard for the media blitz that can envelop them, that would appear to be unrealistic.

The issue of racial profiling was transformed on Sept. 11. In the aftermath of the attacks, pollsters repeatedly asked the public about the issue of profiling—specifically as it applies to Middle Eastern men. Those queried have consistently responded that law enforcement should not ignore the obvious similarities among those who have been already identified in connection with the recent threats and attacks against this country. Solid majorities of respondents to two polls said they want Arab-looking travelers singled out for extra scrutiny at airports. Even in Detroit, which is home to a large Arab-American population, a local newspaper reported that 61 percent felt "extra questioning or inspections are justified." One cannot ignore the fact that the Sept. 11 attacks, as well as other attacks against Americans here and abroad, were all committed by male Islamic militants of Middle Eastern descent. It would be foolish and potentially fatal to minimize the realities of this threat. As then-Supreme Court Justice Arthur Goldberg stated in 1963, echoing the view of former Justice Robert Jackson, "while the Constitution protects against invasions of individual rights, it is not a suicide pact."

## MAY I SEE YOUR PAPERS, PLEASE?

The issue of identifying wrongdoers, now taking on new definition and urgency, was on the police agenda even before the attack. When Tampa used sophisticated facial-recognition surveillance during the Super Bowl, public opinion was accepting but cautious. In today's environment, such systems have gained in popularity and are a welcome asset to a security system.

The year also brought a surge in the popularity of hand-held wireless devices that allow officers to quickly and unobtrusively check criminal data bases. Yet of all the issues of identification that arose in 2001, primary concern focused on the rapid identification of spores and microbes, and the growing problem of identity theft and fake IDs. Given the prevalence of fake identification throughout the country, a number of states began to improve the quality of their driver's licenses in hopes of making them more difficult to counterfeit. One idea being given serious consideration in the aftermath of Sept. 11 is a high-tech national identification card for all American citizens. A variation of this theme is already being practiced at the Mexican border. A new "laser visa," which among its features includes fingerprints and data encrypted in magnetic strips, is required of Mexicans who cross the 1,952-mile border.

The thorny issue of immigration and border control, long a concern to federal and local jurisdictions alike, also took on added dimensions after Sept. 11, as it became eminently clear that the government is clueless when it comes to accurate and up-to-date knowledge of non-citizens in the United States. Inadequate State Department and INS policies and procedures, a lack of enforcement and, to be sure, a lack of will gave the United States a border more porous than the mountains of Afghanistan.

Cooperation with the INS has been a mixed bag for local police. For some departments, illegal immigrants are often victims of crimes and in an effort to keep crime down, departments have refused to report illegal aliens to federal authorities. In some other localities, complaints to federal authorities about illegal aliens have tended to fall on deaf ears, so the locals think, "Why bother?" To address current concerns, the Justice Department has elected to split INS into two parts: one to provide service to immigrants and the other to patrol the nation's borders to block the entry of terrorists. The attack on the homeland will no doubt influence future relations between local law enforcement and federal Immigration and State Department officials, particularly in terms of countries that overtly or covertly support violence against America.

In the post-9/11 era, though, reinforced borders and revised immigration policies might seem superfluous without an accompanying beef-up in air safety and security. The long-dormant Sky Marshal program was quickly revived. A new law enforcement entity was created with the federalization of airport passenger- and baggage-screening personnel, who have been the focus of increasing public outcry over repeated (and sometimes egregious) lapses of security. Planes large and small were scrutinized, as even low-flying crop dusters became a source of concern amid the growing specter of bioterrorism. AWACS surveillance planes, used overseas and in the Caribbean, now fly missions over sensitive targets in the U.S., and the rules of engagement have been changed for fighter pilots who might have to deal with another commercial jetliner being used in a terrorist attack.

A well known adage warns that those who fail to learn from history are condemned to repeat it. In that context, consider that in 1993, when the World Trade Center was bombed the first time, the Immigration and Naturalization Service was ordered by Congress to track more than half a million foreign students attending colleges in the United States. At the time, civil libertarians successfully opposed this initiative, along with other measures intended to keep America safe. Since then, Palestinian terrorists have been arrested in Brooklyn for conspiring to set off a bomb in the New York City subway system. Plots were thwarted to bomb the Los Angeles airport and the Space Needle in Seattle on the eve of the millennium. Then came Sept. 11 and, predictably, civil libertarians once again rose up in righteous indignation. Their arguments revolve around the idea that it is inappropriate to closely look at the many in order to catch the few. Should they prevail again, the consequences could be mean death and injury to thousands. After all, it took only 19 hijackers to kill more than 3,000.

It is unfathomable what 500 or 1,000 terrorists on American soil could do.

## WHAT A DIFFERENCE A YEAR MAKES

It's hard to believe that just 12 months ago crime was down, public safety was not atop the public agenda, the economy was relatively good and the country was at peace. How things change. The police role as first responders, for instance, now means dealing with the terrifying possibility of biological and nuclear weapons. Law enforcement enters 2002 facing a new world with a new and unconventional enemy posing threats that must be anticipated and prevented. By some estimates, more than 50,000 people have passed through the Al Qaeda terrorist training camps. The terrorist network reportedly operates in 60 countries, and no doubt some of its operatives are still living here. Many experts believe a wave of terrorist acts is likely in the near future. In the months ahead, routine will reassert itself in many parts of the country, and law enforcement's daily tasks will dominate the day. But as time goes by, it will be important to bear in mind that—for police as well as for the military—the war on terrorism can be won through good intelligence and vigilance, just as it can be lost through complacency and naiveté

Source: From *Law Enforcement News,* December 15/31, 2001, Vol. XXVII, Nos. 567, 568.

# 2002 IN REVIEW

# 2002: A Year in Retrospect

## *What a Difference 12 Months Can Make for Law Enforcement*

What a difference a year makes. 2002 began with a sense of resolve and clarity of mission born of the Sept. 11, 2001, terrorist attacks, coupled with classically American optimism and "can-do" spirit. The year proceeded amid flurries of activity as law enforcement agencies on all levels scrambled to incorporate homeland security and anti-terrorism measures into their agendas, despite problems of understaffing and underfunding. Departments sought equipment and training—both commodities in short supply—and did their best to implement or improve internal and external communications networks.

As the year ended, however, the grim reality of dwindling resources seemed more dire than ever, with states and localities facing what some describe as the gravest fiscal crisis in the past half-century. Moreover, the promise of federal funding has gone unfulfilled. The once-clear mission has become muddied, and the sense of urgency has in many places turned into little more than heightened consciousness.

Certainly, some departments have done more to prepare than others—or have done so more visibly. New York City, notably and for obvious reasons, has probably done the most. As Police Commissioner Raymond W. Kelly noted, "We're all on the front lines here, so to speak"—and he wasn't being metaphorical. To defend this front line, the department created new positions and filled them with former high-ranking officials from the Central Intelligence Agency and the Marine Corps. Like other departments, it sent officers to Israel to learn more about suicide bombers, and planned to have some officers work in concert with intelligence agencies throughout the world. New equipment, such as radiation-detection gear and bio-hazard suits,

is on hand or on order. While continuing its emphasis on quality-of-life offenses and dousing the periodic crime hot-spot, the department appears to be spending its crime "peace dividend," generated by its declining crime rates, on actively protecting the city from another terrorist attack.

For many localities, however, prevention and preparedness efforts fell short, in many cases because the promise of federal funding had failed to fully materialize by year's end. The Bush administration bottled up $1.5 billion in law enforcement and antiterrorism assistance, citing Congress's inability to pass appropriations bills (although some surmise that it may have more to do with the White House's desire to have more control over the fate and fortunes of the Office of Community Oriented Policing Services).

Even with lean resources, however, police departments managed to get in some training, frequently in the form of joint haz-mat response exercises with other emergency personnel. New joint anti-terrorist task forces emerged from improved communications between the FBI and state and local departments. Statewide communication systems were enhanced; public terrorist tip lines were established. A number of states are now putting visa expiration dates on driver's licenses. Although not widely publicized, plans were developed by some local governments for evacuation and quarantine scenarios. For personnel in some larger departments, training in intelligence analysis took priority—only to be met with a glaring lack of expertise in this critical area. But for all the initiatives that were undertaken, and all the practitioners for whom anti-terrorism activities have become a full-time job, law enforcement preparedness is not what it could or should be, some experts contend.

Amid improved communications between local and federal law enforcement agencies, there remain thorny issues concerning the extent to which police should go in interacting with illegal immigrants. To a large extent, the debate centered on whether or not local law enforcement should shoulder some of the enforcement duties that have long been the province of the beleaguered Immigration and Naturalization Service. The Florida Department of Law Enforcement entered into a partnership with INS to train 35 municipal officers, sheriff's deputies and FDLE agents, who would be assigned to regional anti-terrorism task forces and authorized to stop, question and detain illegal aliens. Other jurisdictions flirted with the idea. Still, there were clear divisions among law enforcement officials on the issue, with some placing local priorities over the national interest. Many departments, such as Houston and Tulsa, pointed to the help illegal immigrants give them with investigations and how difficult the job would become if officers had to aggressively target those in this country illegally. Some, such as Pasadena, Calif., have taken a more moderate approach, allowing officers under certain conditions to arrest and detain illegal immigrants for a prescribed period, pending notification of the INS. By June, the Justice Department had backed away from its plan to have police enforce general immigration laws. Not lost on some police observers was the irony that local police, who are often quick to accuse the FBI of not sharing information and other resources in the aftermath of the terrorist attacks, are now themselves unwilling to share information with the bureau.

One protocol that has been worked out, which does not require changes to existing local law enforcement practices, would focus on those who enter from specially designated countries, linking their admission documents to a National Security Entry-Exit Registration System. Failure to complete the required registration within 30 days would be considered a federal misdemeanor, and the names of those aliens will be entered into the NCIC as "Wanted," to be handled by local officers as a "hit." Such hits require that local INS offices respond in a timely manner. Given the track record of INS and its chronic shortage of personnel, with some 1,800 agents to handle 8 million illegal immigrants, it is not surprising that this protocol allows federal authorities to ask local law enforcement agencies to detain the individual, for which they would be reimbursed. Whether locals respond affirmatively when asked remains to be seen, but given the number of federal agents assigned to the task, without local cooperation on some level, it would appear that INS, no matter how it is reconstituted, will continue to have its hands full, if not tied.

As Congressional scrutiny bore down on the nation's intelligence community and its pre-9/11 lapses and shortcomings, the phrase "connect-the-dots" became a part of regular news copy. Inquiries revealed an intelligence community whose components don't communicate with each other and, as importantly, don't communicate within their own agencies. Political correctness and legal restraints are said to have hampered the FBI's ability to go forward with investigations or share information with other intelligence agencies. The hearings also showed the FBI to lack focus when it came to terrorism, compounded by insufficient personnel and inadequate technology (with agents using 386-level computers with no external e-mail).

There were a number of agents who uncovered evidence of potential terrorist threats and issued warnings to their superiors—warnings that went unheeded. As one FBI field agent recently put it, "Headquarters is like a black hole. Information goes in but nothing comes out." Just what happened to their warnings remains unclear, with some members of Congress asserting that the bureau and the CIA were still covering up those who had impeded pre-9/11 investigations. To be sure, the inquiries did not go far enough, having failed to look into lapses by such agencies as INS, the State Department, motor vehicle offices and the Federal Aviation Administration, all of which made critical mistakes. Yet another investigation began as the year ended, and the FBI found itself in the embarrassing position of having to remind some field offices that their top priority should be terrorism, while at the same time fending off suggestions that another agency similar to England's MI-5 be created to deal with domestic intelligence-gathering. With almost two dozen federal entities already collecting intelligence of various kinds, it is clear that channeling relevant information to one place—a so-called "fusion room"—is still far from reality.

The year did witness the creation of a new super-agency, a Cabinet-level department whose work force of 170,000 would come from the ranks of 22 agencies and take years to fully implement. The Department of Homeland Security, which represents the largest government overhaul in decades, would not include the FBI, CIA or National Security Agency, which many criticized as a serious omission. Although most agree that the integration of federal agencies was necessary to speed and streamline the dissemination of information and services, significant questions and concerns remain. Just how will this new department interact with the multitude of intelligence agencies, and with local law enforcement? Will pre-existing agency loyalties and priorities affect the interaction of the workforce? As important, will the diminution of collective bargaining rights for workers—an issue that delayed legislation to create the new agency—lead to deflated employee morale? Can an agency with so much responsibility in such a critical area afford to have employees that are unhappy?

Things remain murky on the legal front, although some pragmatic clarity was provided when Justice Department guidelines were amended in May to allow the FBI to use commercial databases in investigations. Prior to the change, agents could not even use a common search engine like Google to look for terrorist activity. In November a decision by a special appellate panel of the Foreign Intelligence Court of Review validated the broad surveillance powers under anti-terrorism laws passed in 2001. For federal law enforcement officials, this decision razed what some called an "artificial barrier" between investigation and intelligence that had deterred the sharing of information. Even prior to the ruling, the CIA had begun increasing its presence at FBI field offices.

At the local level, however, such barriers still exist, as demonstrated in New York, where the NYPD asked a federal district court judge in September to lift 17-year-old restrictions that curtail police monitoring of political activity. These restrictions require investigators to have specific information that a crime will be committed or is being planned before they can monitor such political activities. Such restrictions exist elsewhere, as in Seattle, but even when these fetters are loosened, as was the case in Chicago last year, police remain reluctant to use the authority.

If police needed any reminders, a number of arrests, accomplished with varying degrees of local input, served notice that terrorist threats can take root and grow in one's own backyard. Suspects with links to the al Qaeda terrorist network were rounded up in Portland, Seattle, Detroit and Lackawanna, N.Y., while the arrest of one-time Chicago gang-banger Jose Padilla helped assure that the words "dirty bomb" would be added to the law enforcement lexicon for the foreseeable future.

Terror of a different, more conventional kind seized the nation's attention in October, beginning with a seemingly random sniper shooting in a Maryland suburb of Washington, D.C. Over the next three weeks, a total of 10 people would die and 3 more would be wounded, all while engaging in patterns and practices of everyday life. As the sprawling, complex investigation would later reveal, the spree began in effect in Washington state, spanning thousands of miles and going on to claim lives in Louisiana and Alabama as well as Maryland and Virginia. The investigation that led to the arrests of John Allen Muhammad, 41, and John Lee Malvo, 17, inevitably focused attention on the ability of law enforcement agencies at a variety of levels to work cooperatively, a task that was accomplished for the most part. It also focused attention on the difficulties police confront when sifting through thousands of tips, some of which, in hindsight, would have proven to be valuable, while others turned out to be red herrings. Law enforcement used the three-week reign of terror as a test of local preparedness for handling emergencies, demonstrating yet again that locals will be the first to respond when the public faces imminent danger. The killings also rekindled debate about the usefulness of ballistic fingerprinting and the importance of maintaining and sending information to the nation's crime databases.

The Beltway sniper shootings left a number of criminal profilers sporting egg on their faces, as some predictions proved to be wildly off the mark. There were two suspects, not one; they were black, not white; they drove a dark sedan, not a white van; they were out-of-state drifters, not local residents with mundane jobs.

Distinct from criminal profiling and its role in such crimes as the Beltway shootings, racial profiling still crept into the year's news in some jurisdictions, often with the first issuance and analysis of traffic-stop data. New Jersey reluctantly made such data public in March, only to leave officials rattled when researchers found that black drivers tended to speed more than whites on a certain stretches of highway. Officials tried unsuccessfully to blame the researchers for a flawed methodology, which included using teams to determine the race of motorists from more than 26,000 photos taken of speeders and non-speeders alike. Even with many other localities releasing the first analyses of traffic-stop data, the once-heated rhetoric surrounding racial profiling was more muted in 2002 than it had been in years—perhaps an outgrowth of 9/11.

It would be an understatement to say that law enforcement faces a challenge in the year ahead. Declining budgets, severe labor shortages, continuing terrorist threats and, for some, resurgent Part I crime all combine to equal hard times. With local governments experiencing their worst financial straits in decades, the resources are simply not there to get up to speed. Personnel shortages remain a source of concern as officers continue to be called up for National Guard and military reserve duty. And, to the consternation of some officials, local departments will also have to pick up the slack as the FBI divests itself of some former responsibilities.

Law enforcement continues to be frustrated by local and regional computer systems, many representing large investments of time and money, that fail to live up to expectations and are difficult to use and maintain. Many major federal databases are antiquated and still cannot communicate with each other in any meaningful way. While this is not a new problem for law enforcement, it does take on a higher priority in the aftermath of Sept. 11. This hodgepodge network of information creates an acute vulnerability that will be difficult to correct. Nor is the problem limited to computer systems; emergency radio communications in many areas are dire need of integration and improvements to their interoperability, as a number of post-9/11 studies concluded.

That's not to say that law enforcement isn't better off now than it was 15 months ago. Agencies were able to put in improvements with whatever meager resources were available. Just as dangerous as a lack of resources, however, is a lack of will. An attitude that "it can't happen in our town" may be a luxury in which civilians naively indulge, but one that the government and, by extension, the police cannot afford. A basic premise for the existence and legitimacy of government is its ability to protect its citizens. Has American law enforcement improved its level of prevention and preparedness? Yes. Is it enough to keep America safe? Not yet.

Source: From *Law Enforcement News*, December 15/31, 2002, Vol. XXVIII, Nos. 589, 590.

# 2003 IN REVIEW

## 2003: A Year in Retrospect

### *Can Criminal Justice Tame the "Monster" That's Eating It?*

"Terrorism," in the estimation of Massachusetts Public Safety Secretary Edward Flynn, "is the monster that ate criminal justice." Combating this Hydra-like creature has commandeered much of the national agenda in law enforcement, as local and federal agencies expend increasing amounts of time and money on detecting it, preventing it and responding to it.

All that attention notwithstanding, however, local law enforcement in this country is still trying to define its role in the larger scheme of things, particularly when it comes to intelligence gathering and sharing and sorting out inter-agency relationships. Add to this the changes that have been occurring at the federal level and, clearly, the whole field is in motion. Yet for all the activity, numerous reports issued this year have pointed to the fact that more than two years after the Sept. 11 terrorist attacks, law enforcement and intelligence gathering agencies are still not sharing information to a degree that would prevent another attack.

Numerous examples underscored the nation's vulnerability: weapons smuggled onto airplanes; an undetected radiation device in a ship's cargo container; undercover agents carrying false identification who were able to get circumvent all manner of security checks, to name just a few. While no level of preparedness offers an airtight guarantee of complete safety, it seems apparent that the country's level of preparedness still leaves a lot to be desired.

Despite the voracious appetite of this shape-shifting giant, the funds that are being devoted to addressing the terrorist threat remain unequal to the task at hand, particularly since the added demand comes at a time when local budgets are woefully stretched. Federal dollars have been slow to reach local agencies, but it is also the method of funding that is troubling to many police executives. As in the late 1980s and early '90s, federal dollars are being funneled through the states. It is a method favored by Republican administrations—less bureaucracy at the top, more bureaucracy at the bottom. This process, however, can turn local departments into competitors just when they should be working together. To mitigate the problem, Massachusetts officials implemented a policy requiring police departments to develop their plans and present them to the state as a region. While this approach may not solve the problem of regions that transcend state lines, it does require just the kind of cooperation that would be necessary in a disaster situation.

## THE POLITICS OF FUNDING

To many officials, the issue of funding is bigger than simply one of how much money there is, what it is being used for and how it is doled out. It is a question of fairness. In one of the numerous reports issued this year on the nation's preparedness—or lack of it—for a terrorist attack, a panel led by former Senator Warren Rudman, whose previous report on terrorism foreshadowed the 9/11 attack, warned that funding allocations for homeland security that were not based on vulnerability, as opposed to political considerations, would undermine public safety. His fears were borne out as federal allocations were finally made, with New York City receiving a $5-per-capita share of federal first-responder funds while Wyoming received $35 and North Dakota received $29. New York City Police

Commissioner Raymond W. Kelly called the federal formula "blind to the threats this country faces and blind to the consequences of an attack." One can scarcely blame him.

The federal funding that did get through the pipeline to local departments continues to be spent, for the most part, on emergency equipment, protective gear, voice communications systems and data-sharing technology. The interoperability of voice communications remains a problem. A "report card" issued in April by the Public Safety Wireless Network indicated that there is still a long way to go in this area despite improvements in some jurisdictions. One of the major stumbling blocks is the lack of sufficient radio frequencies to accommodate public safety needs. With too few to go around, agencies often find themselves competing for a place on the radio band. The other stumbling block, of course, is money; communications upgrades are a very costly proposition. One agency, the Chesterfield County, Va., Police Department spent approximately $70 million to put in a state-of-the-art system. Outdated equipment, the lack of redundant systems, new systems that are unable to communicate with old ones, and decades of localized implementation and purchasing have made a patchwork of systems that desperately need to be integrated.

## SEARCHING FOR THE GRAIL

Interoperability failings also plague public safety data-sharing. An enormous amount of information currently exists (as imperfect as it may be) that law enforcement agencies have a legal right to, but the process of retrieving the information from myriad non-networked systems of varying ages is simply too slow and painstaking. Law enforcement has always known that criminals and terrorists are often able to exploit the boundaries of geography and jurisdiction. Finding the solution to this incompatibility problem—which can exist among agencies within an individual locality, among neighboring localities, and among state and federal agencies—has been a virtual search for the Holy Grail. Some law enforcement officials in Louisiana felt they had found the grail in a database-linking system developed by a software entrepreneur who practically donated it to a number of sheriff departments. Florida and more than a dozen other states hoped to find the grail in the Matrix, a system whose parent company was able to identify five of the Sept. 11 hijackers before the federal authorities had done so. The program has been in use for more than a year in Florida where law enforcement officials sing its praise. As the year ended, however, a number of states have dropped out, with most citing the cost, but some worried about privacy issues highlighted by other corporate rivals and civil libertarians.

(The concerns of civil libertarians were also directed toward the USA Patriot Act, the sweeping anti-terrorism legislation that is due for reauthorization next year. To address some of this concern, Attorney General John

Ashcroft took to the road in a series of appearances aimed at defending the expanded powers that the act gives law enforcement. The country still appears to strongly support the act, with a poll taken in September indicating that 71 percent think the government has either struck the right balance or has not gone far enough to fight terrorism. Nonetheless, the poll also found a slow, steady increase in those who believe the legislation has gone too far—their concern fueled by fears that the powers of the Patriot Act will be used on routine types of criminal activity rather than just terrorism.)

Early in the year a Terrorist Threat Integration Center was announced that would provide federal anti-terrorist screeners with "one-stop shopping." As of August, however, 12 separate terrorist watch lists maintained by at least nine federal agencies had not yet been consolidated. As the year wound down, and after much public criticism, officials subsequently announced that the center would be operational by December 1.

## WHO'S WHO

Spotting potential terrorists has become an increasingly thorny problem as law enforcement practitioners wrestle with the growing phenomenon of identity theft. With cases of identity theft already at alarming levels and continuing to skyrocket, the situation bodes ill for the cop on patrol as well as for society at large. To the average officer, checking identity usually means scrutinizing a driver's license. This ritual, carried out thousands of times each day, remains fraught with tension and peril. Since 9/11, driver's licenses have assumed added importance and many states are still trying to make their licenses more foolproof, and in some cases have also adopted measures to link licenses with information on the holder's immigration status. In many areas of the country, notably California, debate continues to swirl around the acceptance of Mexican ID cards—the matricula consular—as valid proof of identification for obtaining a driver's license.

This form of ID is currently accepted in at least 13 states. Some law enforcement officials support the policy as a practical matter, noting that illegal Mexican immigrants in this country are already driving illegally anyway, that some identification is better than none, and that the use of the ID card will increase the number of insured drivers on the road. Others criticize what they see as the security risks inherent in acceptance of the cards. According to the FBI, the matricula consular IDs have become "a major item on the product list" of fraudulent documents around the world. They are easy to forge and there is some indication that the consulates that issue them are not taking even cursory steps to assure their validity. They are subject to corruption and Mexican authorities do not keep track of those to whom the identity cards are issued. Critics of their use also point to the fact that the driver's license is in essence a pass-key into other forms of identification fraud.

Disagreement over the acceptance of Mexican ID cards is no less a factor among federal agencies as it is within local and state law enforcement. While the Justice Department remains firmly opposed to the practice on security grounds, the Treasury Department supports it as a way of making it easier for illegal immigrants to put their money in American banks. The controversy over the ID cards is symptomatic of the schizophrenic attitude the country feels towards illegal aliens. Federal officials estimate that there are 8 million to 9 million undocumented immigrants currently living in the US, a stunning increase of between 1 million and 2 million from the number estimated in 2000. The increase comes despite figures indicating that new arrivals in this country are dropping. What may be at work is a change in deportation policy, as the emphasis shifts away from Mexicans. Federal officials reported that in 2002, 75 percent more undocumented immigrants from Arabic and Muslim nations were deported than the year before—this despite a 16-percent decrease in the overall number of deportations of illegal immigrants.

In the first eight months of the year alone, the Department of Homeland Security raised the nation's terrorism alert level to "orange" on four occasions. Initially, editorial cartoonists and late-night comics had a field day making jokes about duct tape and plastic window sheeting, but to local police it was no laughing matter, as they complained that the alerts were overly vague and put added pressure on local overtime budgets that were already under enormous strain. The Department of Homeland Security promised to rethink the issue and by November it reported that the system had been fine-tuned, with a more refined stream of information furnished to local agencies. Not all problems were addressed or eliminated. Local officials in Las Vegas were furious when they were not informed about photos of the city that turned up in a federal terrorist investigation. And amid the clamor over the type of information supplied to local law enforcement, left unanswered was the question of how the information will get to the public.

## MEANWHILE, LIFE GOES ON

With all the re-sorting and redefinition of local and federal anti-terrorism roles, and the local resources that have had to be devoted to anti-terrorism efforts, the day-to-day business of law enforcement goes on undiminished: answering calls for service, trying to prevent crime, and responding to and investigating those crimes already committed. Beyond the added burden of counterterrorism responsibilities, many local and state agencies find themselves stretching budgets even further as they pick up the slack in areas that the feds have backed away from, especially drug enforcement and bank robbery investigations. While many FBI agents were reassigned to anti-terrorism activities, the Drug Enforcement Administration has yet to get additional resources, and the burden has been passed along to localities. In

June, the General Accounting Office reported that the number of FBI assigned to drugs had fallen by more than half and that new investigations fell to only 310 by midyear. The White House drug policy office released data showing that the 25 largest cities are the sites of 40 percent of all drug-induced deaths and drug-related arrests. In drug enforcement as well as bank-robbery investigation, the feds are offering "cooperation," but what localities really need are resources, and little of that appears to be forthcoming. Bank robbery has soared in many localities, frequently committed by perpetrators who defy conventional profiling. In the absence of federal assistance, localities were left to appeal to the banking industry to play a more vigorous and vigilant role in its protection.

## DOING MORE WITH LESS

The monster was also on the prowl as local spending was seriously curtailed amid historic budget deficits. Some small departments all but disappeared. Community policing efforts were scaled back and officers who had been dedicated to the purpose were redeployed to answer calls for service. Officers were laid off, retirements continued to accelerate, and recruit classes were rescheduled. In some localities, station houses were closed at night. To cope with dwindling resources, some departments, like Richmond, Va., gave volunteers more responsibility for such things as taking reports for nonviolent crime. New York City assigned rookies fresh from the academy to work in high-crime areas. While crime rates have not returned to the level of the early 1990s, there is a nagging and uneasy sensation in the police community that things are not going as well as they had been. Quality-of-life crime is on the rise in some areas, while other areas are experiencing significant and disturbing increases in homicides. One leading police expert described it as "watching 'broken windows' in reverse." All in all, it's not a good sign.

With budgets stretched to the limit, a number of departments have tried to recapture control of the personnel time lost to answering false alarms. The Salt Lake City Police Department implemented a policy in 2000—over vigorous opposition from private security companies—that mandates verified response to alarms. The policy change resulted almost immediately in a 90-percent reduction in police dispatches to alarms. It replicates an approach—and the results—previously achieved by the Las Vegas Metropolitan Police Department in the early '90s. Yet taking on the private security industry and its burglar-alarm clientele can be a dicey proposition, as was demonstrated in Los Angeles when the police tried to tinker with the response policy and the City Council stepped in to assert jurisdiction over the issue. Help in dealing with false alarms is available from the Justice Department's COPS Office, which has produced a continuing series of guides on this and other issues, including the benefits and consequences of police crackdowns, financial crimes against the elderly, and check and credit-card fraud. The problem-oriented guides currently cover more than 20 topics, with more on the way.

During the course of 2003, public safety personnel have been confronted with blizzards and hurricanes, fires and floods, computer network hackers, a major power blackout that blanketed the Northeast and Midwest, heightened anti-terrorism alerts, patrol cars that explode and body armor that doesn't stop bullets—and all the while dealing with the day-to-day business of policing.

Law enforcement personnel must be prepared to handle disasters of all types, both natural and man-made. That includes a terrorist attack, for, as Shakespeare's Hamlet observed: "If it be not now, yet it will come. The readiness is all."

We are still not ready.

Source: From *Law Enforcement News,* December 15/31, 2003, Vol. XXIX, Nos. 611, 612.

# Master Index

Investigative techniques, 253–256
    *See also* Detectives; Forensic science;
        Informants; Undercover operations
Investment Act of 1940, 905
Investment Advisors Act of 1940, 905
Investor's Overseas Services (IOS), 639–640
Iran, 1124–1125
Iraq, 1125–1127
Ireland, 1127–1130
Irey, E. L., 719
Irlbeck, D., 339
*Irvine v. California* (1954), 650
Israel, 1130–1134
Italy, 13, 1134–1140
Ivkovich, S. K., 1032
Ivory Coast (Côte D'Ivoire), 1028–1030

Jacob Wetterling Crimes Against Children and
    Sexually Violent Offender Registration Act,
    493, 896
Jacobs, J., 31
Jacobson, M., 315, 371
Jaffe, J., 807
Jamaica, 1141–1144
James Guelff & Chris McCurley Body Armor Act
    of 2002, 25
Japan, 1022, 1144–1147, 1263
Jardini, N. J., 720
Javna, J., 341
Jeanne Clery Disclosure of Campus Security
    Police and Campus Crime Statistics Act of
    1998, 573, 574, 723
Jeffreys, A., 140
Jenckes, T. A., 617
Jencks Act, 239
Jennifer's Law, 290
Jim Crow laws, 396–397
Johnson, A., 861
Johnson, L. B., 687, 735, 761, 812, 823, 868
Johnston, L., 463
Johnston, R., 801
Joint task forces, 731–733
Jones, A. S., 794
Jones, G. W., 860
Jones, T., 463
Jones-Brown, D. D., 398

Jordan, 1148–1149
Jordan, C., 182
Journalists. *See* News media and police
Judiciary Act of 1789, 590, 616, 870
Julie Y. Cross Memorial Award, 911
Junior police programs, 339–340, 495
Justice Commandos for the Armenian Genocide
    (JCAG), 457
*Justice definitions,* 408
Justice Prisoner and Alien Transportation Service
    (JPATS), 873
Justice System Improvement Act of 1979, 736
Juvenile crimes/programs/units, 257–259
    *See also* Curfews; Loitering; Truancy
Juvenile Justice and Delinquency Prevention Act
    of 1974, 258
Juvenile Justice and Reform Act of 1999, 259
Juvenile Mentoring Program (JUMP), 154

Kaczynski, T., 884
Kadleck, C., 34
Kansas, 32, 428
Kansas City Preventive Patrol Experiment,
    736, 780
*Kansas v. Hendricks* (1997), 429
Kantor, M., 56
Kaplan, R. S., 1064
Karmen, A., 298
*Katz v. United States* (1967), 166, 418, 442, 641
Katzenbach, N., 813
Kavanaugh, D., 1130
Kayode, A. C., 1214
Kazakhstan, 1151–1153
Kefauver Committee, 309
Kelley, C. M., 659
Kelling, G., 31, 32, 120, 392, 462, 507, 508
Kelling, G. L., 1020, 1092
Kellogg, E., 832
Kelly, C., 310
Kennedy, R., 310
Kennedy, R. F., 620, 694, 813, 841
Kenney, D., 6, 161, 352
Kentucky, 385, 439
Kenya, 1153–1156
Kerner, O., 761
Kerner Commission, 30, 65, 410, 761–763